ENGLISH PRONUNCIATION
1500–1700

ENGLISH PRONUNCIATION
1500–1700

BY

E. J. DOBSON

VOLUME II
PHONOLOGY

SECOND EDITION

OXFORD
AT THE CLARENDON PRESS
1968

Oxford University Press, Ely House, London W. 1
GLASGOW NEW YORK TORONTO MELBOURNE WELLINGTON
CAPE TOWN SALISBURY IBADAN NAIROBI LUSAKA ADDIS ABABA
BOMBAY CALCUTTA MADRAS KARACHI LAHORE DACCA
KUALA LUMPUR HONG KONG TOKYO

© OXFORD UNIVERSITY PRESS 1968

FIRST EDITION 1957
SECOND EDITION 1968

PRINTED IN GREAT BRITAIN

CONTENTS

V. STRESS AND SENTENCE PHONETICS	445
PART 1. STRESS	445
PART 2. SENTENCE PHONETICS—STRONG AND WEAK FORMS	450
VI. THE QUANTITY OF STRESSED VOWELS	465
PART 1. QUANTITY VARIATIONS DESCENDED FROM ME	465
PART 2. LATE ME AND MOdE SHORTENING	497
PART 3. LENGTHENING	517
Lengthening before *r*	517
Lengthening before voiceless spirants	525
Other cases of lengthening of ME *ă* and *ŏ*	529
The phonetic process whereby lengthening occurs	535
Dialectal lengthening of ME *ĭ* and ME *ĕ*	544
VII. THE FREE DEVELOPMENT OF THE STRESSED VOWELS	545
PART 1. THE SHORT VOWELS	545
ME *ă*	545
ME *ĕ*	565
ME *ĭ*	569
ME *ŏ*	576
ME *ŭ*	585
PART 2. THE LONG VOWELS	594
ME *ā*	594
ME *ę̄*	606
ME *ẹ̄*	651
ME *ī*	659
ME *ǭ*	671
ME *ọ̄*	681
ME *ū*	683
ME [y:], ME *iu*, and ME *ęu*	699
VIII. THE INFLUENCE OF CONSONANTS ON THE DEVELOPMENT OF THE STRESSED VOWELS	714
PART 1. RAISING INFLUENCES	714
PART 2. THE ROUNDING INFLUENCE OF LABIALS	716
PART 3. THE INFLUENCE OF *r* ON THE DEVELOPMENT OF VOWELS	724
The rounding influence of *r*	725
The lowering influence of *r*	726
The development of a glide [ə] between a vowel or diphthong and *r*	760
PART 4. VARIOUS OTHER CONSONANTAL INFLUENCES	763

CONTENTS

IX. THE DEVELOPMENT OF THE STRESSED DIPHTHONGS — 765
   ME *ai* and ME *ẹi* — 765
   ME *au* — 782
   ME *ẹu* — 798
   ME *ẹu* and ME *iu* — 804
   ME *ou* — 804
   ME *oi* and ME *ui* — 810

X. THE VOWELS OF SYLLABLES NOT BEARING THE MAIN STRESS — 827
   Introduction — 827
   General considerations — 830
   Variations in pronunciation caused by secondary stress in post-tonic syllables — 838
   Quantity variations in pretonic syllables — 855
   Other variations in pronunciation in unstressed syllables — 859
   Changes of quality of unstressed vowels in ME — 860
   Syncope — 874
   Loss of ME unstressed *ĕ* — 879
   Syllabic consonants and related developments — 887
   Later changes in the quality of unstressed vowels — 915
   Later changes in quantity — 921
   Glide-vowels — 925

XI. CONSONANTS — 927
   Voicing and Unvoicing — 927
      Variations between voiced and voiceless consonants — 927
      Voicing — 936
      Unvoicing — 942
   Other Changes of Articulation — 945
      Isolative changes — 945
      Combinative changes — 949
   Loss of Consonants — 960
      Simplification of consonant-groups — 960
      Vocalization of consonants — 979
   Glide Consonants — 993
      Glide [j] and [w] — 993
      Glide and 'excrescent' stops after nasals — 1001
      Glide and 'excrescent' stops after other consonants — 1003
      'Intrusive' [n] and [ŋ] — 1004
   Miscellaneous Notes on the Consonants — 1005

BIBLIOGRAPHY (INCLUDING ABBREVIATIONS USED IN CITATION OF WORKS) — 1011
APPENDIX I: CHRONOLOGICAL LIST OF ORTHOEPISTS — 1020
APPENDIX II: THE HART GENEALOGIES — 1023
INDEX OF WORDS — 1033
SUBJECT-INDEX TO VOLUME II — 1077

stressing on the second; in recent adoptions the foreign stressing is apt to prevail. There is a general hesitancy in words beginning with a prefix in applying the English principle of initial stressing, obviously because certain native prefixes are unstressed. In words of Latin origin, or thought to be of Latin origin, there is conflict between the stressing of the Latin 'strong' forms (the nominative singular of nouns and the 1 sing. pres. indic. of verbs) and that of the 'weak' forms (the acc. sing. of nouns and the infin. or p.p. of verbs); the former is apt to replace the latter (as in *horizon*). There is also the influence of etymologically related words on each other, and the effects of 'terminational accentuation', i.e. the tendency of certain suffixes to become associated with one particular type of stressing, which is then applied in all words ending in that suffix; this last factor is not much in evidence before 1700. In general there seems to be a tendency, as secondary stress becomes rarer, to prefer, in words of three syllables or more, stressings however originated in which the unstressed syllables are more evenly balanced around the stressed syllable. No attempt is made, in what follows, to distinguish in detail the effects of these various influences; a brief sketch only is given of some of the variations in stressing explicitly recorded by the orthoepists in words of two, three, and more syllables. In some cases the stressings given seem erroneous, either because a secondary stress is mistakenly taken for the main stress because it coincides with the Latin stress (cf. the accent-marking *adversáry* condemned by Lane), or because of purely Latinistic stressing (cf. the case of *orator* discussed below), or because of what looks like the arbitrary application of general rules, for example, that compound verbs are stressed on the second element.

In words of two syllables, Levins shows variation in participles adopted from Latin, having *legáte*, *renáte* 'renatus', and *solúte* against *prélate*, *quádrate*, *póllute*, &c.; the latter is the commoner type. Levins and Coles accent *July* on the first syllable; Coles and the 'homophone' lists (see Vol. I, p. 406) similarly have *áustere*. Young's 'homophone' list shows *entire* and *inter* vb. stressed on the first (see Vol. I, p. 412). Cooper (followed by Aickin) gives *pedánt*, *backbíte* vb., and *back-slíde* vb. He also says that *gállant* and *gázet* (marked thus) vary in stress. In many words the difference in stressing marks a difference of meaning or grammatical category, as in *mínute* and *minúte*, *a cónvert* and *to convért*. This difference is one of the commonplaces in the works of the orthoepists. Most words show the same differences as in PresE; two interesting cases are Cooper's distinctions of *to cónjure in witchcraft* and *to conjúre* 'to entreat' and *tóward* adj. and *towárd(s)* prep. But some of the distinctions recorded have since been lost. Butler contrasts *énvy* and *to envý*, *rélapse* and *to relápse*, *récompense* and *to recompénse*. Wharton and Hunt have *ábuse* and *to abúse*, *éxcuse* and *to excúse*. WSC-RS has *cément* sb. against *to cemént* vb., and *húmane* used attributively (as in *humane learning*) against *humáne* used predicatively (as in *Christ had two natures, the one divine, the other humane*); this is different from (and in the instance given runs counter to) the present distinction.

Of words of three syllables, *horizon* varies between *horíson* and *horisón* in J. Smith; stressing on the second syllable is shown by Gil's transcription *horjzon* (in which *j* represents ME *ī*) and by Cooper and *WSC*. J. Smith similarly has *orátor* (which Lane describes as a Latin and not an English accentuation) beside *orător*, and also *Cæsárea* beside *Cæsaréa*. Coles has *Aríel, barbárous,* and *belcóny*; he is followed, as regards the last word, by Cooper and Aickin. Strong and Young, in their 'phonetically spelt' lists, give *mischeevus* 'mischievous'; the second syllable would seem to be stressed. Cooper stresses the final syllable of *complaisánce*, and *WSC-RS* has *frontiér*. There is special uncertainty where to place the stress in words beginning with a prefix; some allowance has perhaps to be made for the artificial stressings used by schoolmasters in teaching prefixes. Levins stresses the prefix in *dístribute, énrolment, óbservance,* and *préferment,* Coles against his usual custom has *rémedy*, and *WSC-RS* has *cóncordance*. But the second syllable is stressed in *divúlgate, adúmbrate, incúlcate, pertúrbate,* and similar words in Levins, and such stressing seems to be not less common in the seventeenth century. Coles has *retínue, revénue, confíscate, contémplate, enérvate, exórcist, promúlgate,* and *remónstrate*; he seems regularly to keep the stress off the prefix. Cooper seems also to prefer to put the stress on the second syllable, as in *illústrate, obdúrat, recúsant, disrégard,* and *disréspect*. But variation is said to occur in *ádjacent, conféssor,* and *succéssor* by Cooper, and in *cóntribute* and *dístribute* by J. Smith (the markings presumably indicate the pronunciations which they themselves preferred).

In words of more than three syllables the stress is as a rule marked on the first syllable, if not a prefix, in the sixteenth and seventeenth centuries. Thus Levins gives *bárbarity, própriety, húmidity, prósperity* (after *barbarous, proprius,* &c.?), *Máhumetry,* and *hóspitable*. Cooper gives *ácademy* (< Lat. *ácadémia* against *acádemy* < OF). But the stress, following that of Latin, falls on the second syllable in Levins's *calámity* and *capácity*; Coles similarly marks *casúalty*, but perhaps merely to show that the *u* is 'long'.

If the first syllable is a prefix, variation in stressing is more frequent. Sometimes the accent is placed on the prefix. Levins has *própitiatory, défensory, áccessary, cónvenient, délectable, éxcusable, éxplicable, dívisible,* and *précipitate*. Butler has *réceptacle, cónventicle,* and *péremptori,* Hodges *dērivātive* (in which the long vowels may show where the accents fall), and Cooper *áccessóry, ámbulatóry,* and *réfractóry*. But the stress falls on the second syllable in Levins's *infírmity*. Coles regularly keeps the stress off the prefix; thus he has *restórative* and *remédiless* (against *rémedy*). J. Smith shows that the stress varies in *commendable, acceptable, combustible,* and *corruptible*; in the last two words his marking shows only the stressing on the second syllable, this being probably what he preferred, but the existence of the alternative stressing may be inferred from the context. Cooper says that *corrúptible* and *accéptable* vary in stress, though his own marking shows only stress on the first syllable, with a secondary stress on the third. When the negative *in-* is prefixed to any of these words, it is unstressed if the simplex is stressed on its first syllable (itself a prefix) but receives a (secondary?) stress if the simplex is stressed on the second syllable. Thus J. Smith gives *inéxorable* and *incórruptible* as variants beside *inexórable* and *incorrúptible*; the latter method of stressing is shown by *inconvénient* (against *cónvenient*) in Levins, and *inexórable* in Coles.

It will be observed that whereas Levins and Butler show a preference for placing the stress on the first syllable, even if it is a prefix, Coles prefers to place it on the second syllable, while J. Smith and to a lesser extent Cooper show variation between stress on the first syllable and stress on the second. The change is doubtless to be attributed to the loss (or weakening) of the secondary stress and the desire for more balanced forms.

Note 1: For an elaborate and painstaking account of the history of the stressing of certain classes of words see B. Danielsson, *Studies on the Accentuation of Polysyllabic Latin, Greek, and Romance Loanwords in English* (Stockholm Studies in English, iii, 1948). Danielsson naturally makes much use of Levins's detailed evidence, of which a mere sketch is given here; but he is not always happy in his interpretation of the evidence.

Note 2: PresE usually has the stress on the first syllable in disyllabic words, but far from regularly; cf. *pollute, July, austere, gazette, relapse,* and *cement,* of those cited above.

Some of Levins's stressings of such words seem to be unreliable; see Vol. I, p. 29. If they were accepted, they would show nouns with the stress on the second syllable (*a contráct*, &c.) and verbs with it on the first (*to ábsent*); this is contrary not only to PresE stressing, but also to the evidence of other sixteenth- and seventeenth-century orthoepists. Levins's Northern origin may perhaps be the explanation, but error seems more likely.

§ 3. The interesting ModE development of 'fluctuating' stress (as in *inside* or *upstairs*), which is itself a by-product of 'level stress' (in, for example, *a bláck bírd, a stóne wáll, a séa-wáll*), is remarked on by Gil, who says that whereas some compounds are stressed on the first and others on the second syllable, some are stressed on either; his examples are *church-yard* (a genuine case of 'fluctuating' stress) and *outrage* and *outrun* (to which in fact different explanations apply; see Note).

Note: Outrage (< OF) varies between French end-stress and English initial stress; *outrun* between the initial stressing of an old 'separable' compound verb (meaning 'to run out') and the stem-stressing of an 'inseparable' compound (meaning 'to surpass in running').

Part 2: Sentence Phonetics—Strong and Weak Forms

§ 4. The only serious attempt to discuss sentence phonetics, and the assimilations that occur when words are joined together in sentences, is that of Hart; see Vol. I, pp. 76–78. Robinson may also have considered such assimilations, though there is doubt whether his forms like *du(w)* 'to' are really intentional. There is some evidence concerning the reduced forms which lightly stressed words assume in rapid speech, but hardly as much as can be found in contemporary spellings; the most interesting sources are Salesbury (Vol. I, p. 18), Tonkis (Vol. I, p. 316), Hodges in his 'homophone' list (Vol. I, p. 397), Howell (Vol I, p. 378), and Ridpath (Vol. I, p. 394). The reduced forms most often shown are [ə] for *he*, [t] for *it* after a vowel, forms of *her* and *his* with no vowel, [t] for *to* before a vowel, and [ð] for *the* either before a vowel or where the [ð] may be linked with the preceding word—in general, where the preceding word ends with a vowel. Similar to these reduced colloquial forms are the variant 'strong' and 'weak' forms of certain words which may be either stressed or unstressed in the sentence and therefore develop both as stressed and unstressed syllables. The orthoepistical evidence on the whole shows that the variation between these strong and weak forms in the sixteenth and seventeenth centuries no longer strictly depended on whether the word was stressed or unstressed; the weak form may be used in stressed and the strong form in unstressed position. But Hart, Robinson, and Gil make some attempt to discriminate; Robinson and Gil undoubtedly try to use certain forms in accordance with their stress, and show an understanding of the reason for the differences of form—though they use other variants indiscriminately. It may be pointed out that some of the variants which Hart tried to explain as due to assimilation to the following word (see Vol. I, pp. 76–77) seem rather to be due to variation, often not according to any clear rule, between strong and weak forms. A list follows of the chief words which have strong and weak variants.

A: the indefinite article is developed from the ME weak form of OE *ān*. Robinson has twice *ā* against usual *a*, and Newton also has [ɛ:] < ME *ā*; this represents a new strong form developed from ME *ă*.

And: The variant (unstressed) form *an* is recorded by the *Welsh Hymn*, Hart (as a colloquial form; see Vol. I, pp. 77–78), Robinson (twice only), Wallis (as a colloquialism), and in Strong's 'homophone' list.

Are: the weak form *ăr* is the only one used by Robinson, Butler, Daines, Newton, and the shorthand-writer Everardt. Bullokar, Gil, Hodges, and Poole vary between *ăr* and *ār*, and Hodges seems to use the former in unstressed and the latter in stressed position. The 'homophone' lists show the strong form by equating *are* with *air* and *heir*, and Cooper says that *are* and

§ 4]   PART 2: SENTENCE PHONETICS   451

air are identical in pronunciation. But the weak form seems to have been much more common, as might be expected for this word; Gil uses it seven times more often than the strong form. *Art* occurs only with *ă*.

As: the word is recorded with [z], developed in unstressed position, by all orthoepists except Hart, who says that it has [s] or [z] according, as he thinks, to the following sound (cf. Jespersen, *Hart*, § 42); P. G., who seems to give [s]; Gil, who has *as* four times against regular *az*; and T. Willis. The strong form was clearly rare in the sixteenth, and died out in the seventeenth, century.

Be: Robinson is careful to distinguish *bī*, used in stressed position twenty-two times, from *bĭ*, used in unstressed position thirty-one times; but he uses *bī* in unstressed position thrice. Gil remarks on the same distinction, and Hart gives transcriptions with both *ĭ* and *ī*. Hart also has *ĕ* (four times in *be*, twice in *being*), which may represent a ME weak form.

Been p.p.: the orthoepists are almost unanimous in recording the weak form *bĭn*. Wallis, it is true, says that *bin* for *been* is a spelling error comparable to *hee's* for *his*, and Cooper prefers the spelling *been*, but it would appear from this that they used the pronunciation *bin*. The only evidence for the strong form [biːn] comes in Newton and in the 'homophone' lists; Wharton puts *been* with both *bin* and *been* 'bees', and Coles puts it with *bean* in the *Eng.–Lat. Dict.*, but with *bin* in the more careful *Schoolmaster*. (The *Welsh Hymn* records *ĭ* in the ME present tense plural *been*.)

By: Smith and Bullokar show a weak form with ME *ĭ*; otherwise [əi] is regular.

Could: the orthoepists record four main pronunciations, [kʌuld], [kuːld], [kʊd], and [kʌd]. The *l* of the written form is due to the analogy of *would* and *should*, and it is clear that pronunciation was similarly affected. The transcriptions of Smith, Hart, Bullokar, Gil, and Robinson show only forms with [l], and Hodges gives a form with [l] beside one without it. Tonkis says that *could* is 'contracted' to *cou'd*, from which it would appear that the [l] was pronounced in more formal speech. Brown in his 'phonetically spelt' list writes *coold* (beside *cud*) for *could*, and the 'homophone' lists from Hodges onwards put *could* by *cool'd*. Poole's rhymes show that he pronounced [l]. Tonkis gives the first evidence of the form without [l]; he is followed by Hodges, Wallis, Hunt, Cooper, and Brown. The evidence of other orthoepists is of uncertain significance. As for the vowel, [ʌu], the normally developed strong form, is shown by Smith, Hart (beside ME *ŭ*), Bullokar, Poole, Price, who in his homophone list puts *could* with *cold* (which has [ʌu] in his speech) as well as with *cool'd*, and Wallis, as a (rare?) variant (see Vol. I, p. 246, footnote). The equivalent of ME *ŭ*, the normally developed weak form, is shown by Hart's *kuld*, Tonkis's *cou'd*, and Brown's 'phonetic' spelling *cud* and his equation of *could* and *cud* in his 'homophone' list. Newton seems to have known [ou] < ME *ou*, which is due to the analogy of *should* and *would*. The vowel most frequently recorded is [uː], which seems to be due to relengthening of ME *ŭ* in the open syllable of ME *cŭde*; as this is a new strong form, [l] is usually combined with the long vowel, as in Laneham, Hart (once), Robinson, Gil, Hodges (beside [ʊ]), and the 'homophone' lists, which put *could* beside *cool'd*. It does not appear whether or not the *l* is pronounced from the evidence of Sherwood, Butler, Wharton, Lye, Coles, and Richardson, who teach [uː] as the vowel. Finally there is a form with [ʊ], recorded by Hodges; this seems to be a new weak form with shortening from the strong form with [uː], after the unrounding of ME *ŭ*. With this vowel Hodges shows no [l]. (This is, of course, the form of PresE.) The evidence of Wallis, Hunt, Wilkins, and Cooper is ambiguous, and may show either [ʊ] or [uː]; the former seems more likely for Wallis (see Vol. I, pp. 239–40), and the latter for Cooper. Wallis and Cooper show no [l], but Wilkins, if his transcription is fully accurate, shows the [l] pronounced.

Do: the PresE [duː] is normally developed from the ME strong form, and is shown by the evidence of the *ABC for chyldren* and many subsequent orthoepists; it was clearly the normal sixteenth- and seventeenth-century form. From it develops a new weak form *dŭ*, which is recorded by Hart as his normal form (sixty-four times, against eleven for *dū*), Mulcaster (see Vol. I, p. 124), Gil (about twenty-five times, more often than [duː]), and Robinson (once only, but there can be no error). But there is also evidence for a seventeenth-century pronunciation [doː], which would appear to be due to restressing and lengthening of a ME *dŏ* (after ME *ǭ* had become [uː]?). This is recorded by the 'homophone' lists from Wharton on, which put *do* beside *doe* and *dough*, by Wallis, who thinks that *do* is 'rectius' pronounced with [oː] than [uː], and by Cooper (followed by Brown), who puts *do* with *so*, *no*, &c., as examples of final [oː] not spelt *ow* as in *bowe* 'arcus', &c. (Cf. rhymes, such as Marvell's *do : know* in the *Horatian Ode*.)

Done: a strong form with [uː] seems to be recorded by Cheke's *doon*, and is certainly shown by Hart's *dūn*. Hodges has [dʊn], which seems to be a new weak form developed from this [uː] after the unrounding of ME *ŭ*. But Gil says that the long vowel is dialectal, either in Lincolnshire or more probably the North generally (his meaning, as regards the place where it is used, is not clear). Levins has [uː], perhaps because he is a Yorkshireman. There is also a weak form with ME *ŭ*, from which the present pronunciation develops; it is recorded by Hart (twice, against usual [uː]), Robinson, Gil, Poole, Wilkins, Lodwick, and the 'homophone' lists, among others; it was clearly the normal form. Wharton's *doon* is ambiguous; *oo* represents ME *ŭ* as well as [uː] in the list in which the word occurs.

§ 4] PART 2: SENTENCE PHONETICS 453

Dost, doth: these words show similar forms to those of *done*. [u:] is recorded by Hart (twice), Bullokar, Robinson (who has only [u:]), Gil (rarely), and Butler; Hodges has [ʊ] by later shortening from [u:]. But ME *ŭ*, becoming [ʌ], is shown by Hart, Gil, Hodges (once only), and by the spelling-books and their 'homophone' lists. The rhymes of Poole and Coles show [o:] in *doth*, which is clearly due to the analogy of the form of the infinitive with [o:], discussed above.

Down has normally [ʌu], but Young in his 'homophone' list indicates a form with ME *ŭ* (see Vol. I, p. 412).

Either and *neither* have a variety of forms in early ModE (see § 129 (*a*)). Of these, ME *ai, ẹ̄*, and *ī* are certainly strong forms; ME *ĕ* (and ME *ĭ* developed from it) may be regarded as developing under weak stress in the conjunctions, but analogous shortening of ME *ẹ̄* to ME *ĕ* occurs in similar words (though less often) in which no question of stress is involved (see § 8, under (*c*) (i)).

Have, hast, hath: the strong forms of these words have ME *ā* (developed in the infinitive), the weak forms ME *ă*. In the sixteenth and seventeenth centuries the two forms are mostly used indiscriminately in either stressed or unstressed position; but Gil and Hodges show more discrimination in their use. Gil states explicitly that the strong form of *have* is used when the word is stressed and the weak form when it is unstressed; he uses the strong form about thirty times and the weak form about seventy times. Hodges restricts the use of the strong form to his transcriptions of Biblical passages, except for a single case in rhyme, so that it would appear to be characteristic of formal speech; the weak form, however, occurs in both the Biblical and non-Biblical passages, and would then seem to be capable of unrestricted use. The other evidence is as follows. Levins and Coles rhyme *have* on ME *ā*, but Coles knew *ă* also. Cheke, Smith, and Newton show the strong form only, as does Hart, except for two cases of *ă* in *having*. Robinson uses *hāv* in Ashmole 1153, except for a single case of *hăv*, and *hăv* in Ashmole 826, except for a single case of *hāv*. *Hast* and *hath* have normally ME *ă*, as in Hart and Gil; but Cheke has *haast* and *haath*, Robinson in Ashmole 1153 has *hāst* and *hāþ*, and Hodges has *hāst* once against *hăst* eight times, and *hāþ* twenty times against one possible case of *hăþ* (p. 96, l. 3); Kauter in his edition seems inclined to take this isolated instance as *hāþ* with the diaeresis, the sign of length, accidentally omitted through bad printing (see his footnote), though in his monograph (§ 17) he had regarded it as an intended form. In the 'homophone' lists Hodges and Strong equate *hast* and *haste*; this probably depends on the strong form of *hast*, but may possibly show *ă* in *haste*, as once (out of three occurrences) in Gil. At the end of the seventeenth century Brown equates *hath* and *heath*; this must show ME *ā* in the former. Poole rhymes *hath* with *faith*, &c., and

Coles with *bathe*; the *ā* is that of the strong form, but Coles's [ð] must be developed under weak stress.

He: the normal form, developed from the ME strong form, is [hi:]; it is recorded by Cheke, Hart, Robinson, Gil, and later orthoepists. Cooper says that the word would be better spelt *hee* (as final *e* normally represents ME *ẹ̄*); compare Milton's (and other poets') spelling. From this pronunciation a new weak form *hĭ* develops; it is recorded by Hart, Robinson (once only), and Gil (twice only, out of many cases). In addition there seems to have been in the sixteenth century a pronunciation [hɛ:], with the equivalent of ME *ẹ̄*; Cheke seems to say that though the ordinary pronunciation of *he* (and *me*) was [hi:] (and [mi:]), it was possible to say [hɛ:] (and [mɛ:]) without incurring blame. But the isolated *hē* in Hart 1570 is apparently a printer's error and is corrected by hand in the Folger Library copy. Such a pronunciation would be due to restressing and lengthening of a weak ME *hĕ*, perhaps after the change of ME *ẹ̄* to [i:]; cf. *the*.

Her: ME *ẹ̄* is recorded in the 'homophone' lists of Young (see Vol. I, p. 413) and Cocker, and is by lengthening under stress of ME *ĕ* in the form *hĕre*; Laneham's spelling *heer* probably shows [i:] < ME *ẹ̄* by lengthening under stress of ME *ĭ* in the form *hĭre* (though it might show *ĭ*). ME *ĭ* is recorded beside *ĕ* by Hart, Bullokar, and Gil; it also is a stressed development of *hĭre* (with the common failure of lengthening of ME *ĭ*), since unstressed ME *ĭ* before *r* is not distinguished from unstressed ME *ĕ*. Otherwise *ĕ* is recorded; it represents a weak form from ME *hĕr(e)* (since lengthening of ME *ĕ* would not fail under stress in such a word as *hĕre*) or (if the *e* stand for [ə], as it often must) from ME *hĭr(e)*.

His: the normal pronunciation is with [z], which develops in the weak form. But Higgins, in his revision of Huloet's dictionary, seems to teach [s], and Hart says that the word has either [s] or [z], according, he believes, to the following sound; he uses [s] in *his servant*, &c., and when *his* is final in the sentence (i.e. attributive, and therefore stressed; cf. Jespersen, Hart, § 42). Gil has *his* nine times against *hiz* about 100 times. T. Willis rhymes *his* on [ɪs]; Coles seems to know both [s] and [z]. Fox and Hookes, in their 'homophone' list, equate *his* and *hiss*, but we cannot be sure that they are not ignoring the difference between a voiced and a voiceless consonant. Cheke twice uses the spelling *hijs*, which should show ME *ī*; there is no confirmation for such a pronunciation, and it seems impossible to explain.

If: Mulcaster says that *f* is pronounced as [v] in this word, and Hart twice transcribes it *iv* before a vowel, while Robinson has once *iv* (but this could easily be an error due to the omission of the 'aspirate' mark). The pronunciation with [v] would be developed in a weak form; cf. *of*.

Is: all the orthoepists record [z], developed in the weak form, except Smith (who gives [s] twice), Hart (who says that the word has [s] or [z] according to the following sound, though his own transcriptions—in which *s* occurs in about one-quarter of the cases—do not bear this out), and T. Willis.

Me: Smith and all later orthoepists give [iː], but a weak form with *ĭ* is also recorded by Smith, Hart, Robinson, and Gil. Cheke seems to have known a possible variant [mɛː] (see under *he* above), and Hart has *ĕ* once; these forms could represent a ME weak form with *ĕ*.

Mought: this form of *might*, described by Cooper as a barbarism, is recorded by Hart as *mŭht* and by Laneham as *moought*, i.e. with [ʌu] from ME *ū*; both are strong forms (see § 177).

My: the normal form has [əi] < ME *ī*, but a weak form *mĭ* is recorded by Bullokar (in *my* and *myself*), Robinson (twice; but normally he has [məi] even in unstressed position), and Gil (four times, beside [məi] many times).

Neither: see under *either* above. The form with *ĕ* was common.

No: the normal form has ME *ǭ*, but a form with *ŏ* is alone recorded by Smith, Hart, Bullokar, and Gil; this *ŏ* may develop under weak stress, but see § 40, Note 3.

Not: Lodwick records a pronunciation [nət]; see Vol. I, p. 279.

Of, off: the latter is in origin the strong form of the former, and so has regularly [f], as in Mulcaster, Gil, Jonson, Cooper (who says that *off* has lengthened [ɒː], whereas *of* has short [ɒ]), and *WSC*, which follows Cooper. The strong form also remains, beside the weak, for *of*; thus the *Welsh Hymn* has *off* 'of'; Hart has *of* beside *ov* (on his use of these forms, see Jespersen, *Hart*, pp. 16–17); Tonkis gives [ɒf] as the formal, and [ɒv] or *o'* as the colloquial form (see Vol. I, p. 316); Gil writes regularly *of*, in accordance with the pronunciation of the 'docti', though 'frequentius dicamus *ov*'; Hodges has thrice *of* (regarded by Kauter as errors, but unnecessarily) beside regular *ov*; Merriott does not distinguish *of* and *off*; the 'homophone' lists pair the two words; and Wilkins transcribes *of* as [ɒf]. The rhymes of Levins and T. Willis show [f]. But Mulcaster, Robinson, Jonson, Coles in his 'phonetically spelt' list, Cooper, and *WSC* give only [ɒv] for *of*, and so distinguish it from *off*. Gil and Hodges, as is shown above, regard *ov* as the more common form. Reduction to *o'* is recorded by Tonkis and Wallis, and to *a* (for [ə]) by Hunt and Cooper. The words *hereof, thereof, whereof*, in which *of* receives stress, regularly have [f]; so in Hart, Robinson, Gil, and Hodges.

Other: the normal strong form has [uː]; it is recorded by Smith and Hart. From it develops one with shortening to the equivalent of ME *ŭ* before unrounding took place; it is recorded by Smith, Hart (normally), Tonkis Robinson, Gil (who says it is the common form, though he follows the 'docti', who say *oðer*, in his transcriptions), Hodges, and Cooper. This is hardly to be regarded as a weak form; analogous shortening occurs in *mother*. There is also a form with *ŏ*, probably developed in OE under weak stress; it is implied by Hart 1551 for *other* 'or' and recorded in his *nŏðer* 'neither' 1569, and is the basis of Gil's transcriptions (see above), presumably because it conforms with the spelling. On Hodges see § 15 below. Gil's isolated *ōðer* (1621, for *oðer* 1619), where Campion's quantitative verse requires a trochee, seems an imperfect correction for an intended *ūðer*, since ME *ǭ* < restressed *ŏ*, though possible, is unlikely.

Out has normally ME *ū*, but Bullokar once rhymes on *ŭ* (see Vol. I, p. 112).

Shall, shalt: the strong forms have the equivalent of ME *au*, the weak of ME *ă*. Both forms of *shall* are recorded by Smith, Hart (ME *ă* twice only), Bullokar, Gil (who says the word varies, but in the 1621 edition has ME *au* once only, though more often in the 1619 edition), and Jonson. The strong form alone is recorded by the *Welsh Hymn*, Robinson, Butler, Hodges, Wharton (followed by J. Smith), Poole, Coles, Wilkins, *The Compendious School-Master*, Hawkins, Ray, and *RS*. The weak form alone is recorded by Mulcaster and Brooksbank. The strong form of *shalt* is well evidenced, being recorded by Hart, Bullokar, Hodges, Wallis (with loss of *l*), Hunt, Poole, Coles, and Hawkins. The weak form is recorded by Mulcaster and Gil (who has also, in the 1619 edition only, ME *au* once); perhaps also by Wallis's *sha't'ou* 'shalt thou' in his representation of colloquial pronunciation. It would seem that the strong forms were the more common, in careful speech, in the sixteenth and seventeenth centuries. There is no attempt to distinguish the use of strong and weak forms according to whether they are stressed or unstressed in the sentence.

She: beside the regular strong form with [i:] there is recorded a weak form with *ĭ* by Smith, Hart, Robinson (once only), and Gil (once only).

Should: there are two questions to be considered with this word, the pronunciation or not of the *l* and the nature of the vowel. The *l* is certainly shown to be pronounced by the transcriptions of Cheke, Hart, Bullokar, Robinson, Gil, and Hodges (beside a form without *l*), and the rhymes of Poole; its pronunciation in careful speech is implied by the evidence of Tonkis and Jonson (followed by Evelyn). Its loss is shown by Tonkis, who says that the word is 'contracted' to *shu'd*, Jonson, who says that it is often shortened to *shoud*, Evelyn (after Jonson), Hodges (who says that it is pronounced *šud*, with [ʊ] not [ʌ], as well as *šūld*, the form he uses otherwise), Wallis, and Hunt; this loss of [l] occurs in the weak form. Other orthoepists do not say whether or not the *l* is pronounced. Various vowels occur in the word. Bullokar's transcriptions show [ʌu] < ME *ū*; Wallis also seems to have known this pronunciation, presumably as a (rare?) variant (see Vol. I, p. 246, footnote), and Poole's rhymes depend on it. It may be explained as a strong form developed from Anglian *scŭlde* with the change of *ŭ* to *ū* before *ld* recorded by *WSC-RS* and in *shoulder* by Laneham and Bullokar himself (see § 174 below); but there is also evidence of a process whereby ME *ou* before *ld* became late ME *ū* (see § 169 below), so that it could also develop from *scŏlde*. The analogy of ME *ū* in *could* doubtless supported it. Newton seems to have known [ou] < ME *ou* (see Vol. I, p. 251). The normal weak form is with ME *ŭ*, and represents OE (Anglian) *sculde*, ME *shŭlde*, in which the vowel is due to the analogy of the stem of the present tense indicative plural and subjunctive; it is shown possibly by Cheke's *schold*, by Hart's *šuld*, Tonkis's *shu'd*, possibly by Jonson's and Evelyn's *shoud*, and by Newton (beside other forms). The most common vowel is [u:], which probably descends from the late OE *scōlde* (with lengthening before *ld*). This, a strong form, is shown by Cheke, Robinson, Gil, Sherwood, Daines, Hodges (as his normal form), Wharton (followed by J. Smith), Lloyd, Lye, Coles, and Brown. The present vowel [ʊ] is by shortening, after the unrounding of ME *ŭ*, of this [u:]; it is thus a new weak form. It is shown by Hodges's *šud* [ʃʊd], which he says may be used as well as his normal *šūld*, and by Newton (beside other forms). Wallis (see Vol. I, pp. 239–40) may mean either that [ʊ] (as seems more probable) or that [u:] is used; Hunt's 'phonetic' spelling is similarly ambiguous. Price in the introductory discussion of phonetics (taken from Wallis) in *VO* seems to give [ʊ] for *should*, but there is no evidence elsewhere in his writings that he recognized the sound [ʊ] as distinct from [ʌ]. Cooper, followed by *WSC-RS*, is also ambiguous; it seems more probable that he means [u:] than [ʊ].

So: the normal form has ME *ǭ*, but a form with *ŏ* is alone recorded by Smith, Hart, and Bullokar, and Gil has *ŏ* many times beside *ǭ* but once. This *ŏ* may develop under weak stress; but see § 40, Note 3.

The: the normal strong form, with [i:] < ME *ē̜*, seems not to have been very common in the sixteenth and seventeenth centuries; it is recorded only by Daines (who says that *the* and *thee* ought to have a distinction but 'we seldom give it', and elsewhere seems not to distinguish the value of *e* in *the* from that in *be*, &c.), apparently by Howell, and by *RS* (which, however, does not distinguish ME *ē̜* and *ẹ̄* in any words). A weak form, from ME *ĕ*, is recorded by Hart (regularly), Robinson (*ðe* is the normal form in Ashmole 1153), Gil, and Hodges (again as the normal form). Wallis also teaches short *e* (see Lehnert, § 89). A new strong form, with relengthening of this *ĕ* to the equivalent of ME *ē̜*, is recorded by Mulcaster, Sanford, Robinson (fairly frequently; it is the only form in Ashmole 826), Gil (four times only), Colson, Sherwood, Jonson, T. Willis, perhaps Wallis, Newton, Coles, the *Welsh Breviary*, Lodwick, Cooper (followed by Aickin), and Brown. Finally, there is a form *ðĭ* recorded by Smith and twice by Robinson; it must be a new weak form developed from that with [i:]. Whatever the vowel, the consonant is regularly [ð], which develops from OE *þ* owing to the word's being unstressed; but the *Welsh Hymn*, l. 63, has a form with [þ].

Thee: this word also has regularly [ð], but the *Welsh Hymn*, l. 77, has [þ] and Robinson has it once, in stressed position; Robinson's transcription might be an error, but the faulty inclusion of his 'aspirate' sign is less likely than its omission, and there is probably a real survival of [þ] from the old strong form. The word usually has [iː], but ĭ is recorded by Smith (four times), Robinson (twice), and Gil (once); this is a new weak form, used in unstressed position. Robinson has also once ŏe, which if not an error is an older weak form from ME ŏĕ.

Their: some orthoepists, such as Bullokar, Gil, and Butler, show no special development of ME *ai* in this word (i.e. they have a strong form). But others show monophthongization to identity with ME ẹ̄ (which is proved to have occurred in ME itself by the fourteenth-century form *þer(e)*), even when they do not show this development for ME *air* in other words: so Robinson and Hodges (who use the transcription ŏēr; contrast Robinson's ŏār 'they're'), Daines and Johnson, who say it is identical with *there*, and the 'homophone' lists, which pair it with *there*; in Coles's list in the *Schoolmaster* this pairing is shown by the arrangement to depend on [ɛː] (i.e. the reflex of ME ā and ME ẹ̄ before *r*), but is the only pairing in that list to show monophthongization of ME *ai*. Lye says that in *their* the *ei* is pronounced as '*a* long', and Strong gives the 'phonetic spelling' *thare*; this Cooper describes as a 'barbarism' (of spelling rather than of pronunciation?); *WSC*, though following Cooper, admits that the word is so pronounced. The form *thare* could develop either from the strong form (with monophthongization of ME *ai* to identity with ME ā) or from the weak form with ME ẹ̄ (since by the later seventeenth century ME ẹ̄ and ME ā were identical before *r*). The shorthand-writer Everardt and Hunt say that the *i* is silent. Hart has ĕ nine times in *their(s)*, beside normally-developed ē some 80 times; and Poole rhymes *theirs* on ĕ. The form with ĕ develops from ME ẹ̄ as a further weakening; it gives rise to seventeenth-century [ðər], which Milton's spelling *thir* obviously represents.

There: only [ð], developed in the weak form, is recorded. The vowel is normally long (ME ẹ̄), but Hart has ĕ more often than ẹ̄ in the simplex and always in compounds (*thereby*, &c.) and Gil has ĕ twice (beside ẹ̄ thirteen times) in the simplex and ĕ five times (beside ẹ̄ thrice) in compounds; the shortening occurs under weak stress.

These: only [ð], developed in the weak form, is recorded. The vowel is normally either ME ẹ̄ or ME ẹ̆, developed by lengthening in the open syllable of ME ĕ or ME ĭ respectively (see § 120 below); this lengthening must have been characteristic of stressed forms in ME. But Hart has ĕ six times beside ẹ̄ seven times, Gil ĕ twice beside ẹ̄ nine times.

They: Tonkis and Richardson, who normally show ME *ai* as a diphthong, nevertheless give it in this word as a monophthong (identified with ME ẹ̄ by the former and with ME *ā* by the latter); the special development is due to weak stress.

This: the word is regularly recorded with [ð], developed in the weak form; the only exceptions are the *Welsh Hymn*, l. 11 (where the alliteration is on [þ]) and a single transliteration *þis* in Robinson (which might be an error, but the wrong inclusion of his 'aspirate' mark, as here, is less likely than its omission). Hart and Laneham record forms with [z] beside [s]; Hart would explain the variation according to the following sound, and himself uses *ðiz* chiefly before voiced sounds (Jespersen, *Hart*, § 42). Mulcaster, in an unclear passage, seems to mean that *s* is pronounced as [z] in *this*, and Robinson has a single case of *ðiz*, which may be an error due to the omission of his 'aspirate' mark.

Those: the word is normally recorded with [ð], developed in the weak form, but Robinson has once *þoz* (which might possibly be due to the faulty inclusion of his 'aspirate' mark).

Thou: Bullokar has *ðŭ* (the only form recorded in Zachrisson's word-list), which is an unstressed development of ME *ðū*.

Though: the only possible record of a strong form with voiceless [þ] is Robinson's *þâw̧* (in which [þ] might possibly be an error). The ME weak form *ðŏh* gives Hart and Gil's *ðoh* and (with restressing) T. Willis's pronunciation (in which [χ] is probably retained; see Vol. I, p. 417). Robinson's *ðâw̧* is related to this form, being from ME **ðăh* < *ðŏh*. Smith's *ðōu*, in its retention of ME *ou* developed under stress from *ŏ* before [χ], and Laneham and Robinson's *ðow* with [ʌu] (a variant development of *ŏ* before [χ]; see § 170 below, and compare Hodges's pairing of *though* and *thou* as 'near alike') are as respects the vowel a stressed development; but the early loss of the [χ] is due to the weak form. Newton retains [χ], with [o:] < ME *ou*. Similarly Price says that the *gh* is pronounced as *h*, which shows the survival of some form of the [χ], and gives [o:] for the vowel; as ME *ou* is generally monophthongized in his speech, his form probably descends from late ME [ðouχ]. A new weak form, with early monophthongization of *ou* and loss of [χ], is [ðo(:)], which is recorded by Smith (beside [ðou]) and Robinson (but only when his exemplar has *tho*). The same pronunciation when recorded by Hodges, Wallis, the *Welsh Breviary*, Cooper, and the spelling- and shorthand-books, might develop from the strong form (since these authors show general loss of [χ] and monophthongization of *ou*) but is as likely to represent the weak form. If only the strong form had survived, we might expect to find *thof* (as in modern Northern and South-western dialects), with the change of [χ] to [f] in final position as in *cough* and *trough*; Fielding in *Tom Jones* records this pronunciation in vulgar speech, perhaps as a Somerset dialectal feature (cf. Wright, *EDG*, Index).

Through: the pronunciations [þrʌuχ], recorded by Bullokar (repeatedly) and Gil (four times), beside other forms, and [þrʌu], recorded by Daines, are strong forms; on their development see § 177. Gil also gives [þruχ] (seven times), as does Hart (once); this may be a weak form, but can be explained as another possible strong form of ME *þrŭh* (see § 177). Under weak stress the [χ] is lost early, giving ME *þrŭ*, which Hart has in *prulei*; with re-stressing and lengthening after ME *ŭ* had become [ʌu] there arises the pronunciation [þru:] shown by Hart's *þrū*, Robinson's *pruw*, Hodges's *þrū*, and the spellings *thrue* in Strong's and *threw* in Brown's 'phonetically spelt' lists (which seem to be inverted spellings depending on the reduction of earlier [iu] to [u:] after *r*). This pronunciation may also be shown by the spelling *throogh* used by Laneham and Butler, if we regard the *gh* as being merely graphic and retained because of the influence of the conventional spelling; but other explanations are possible. In Laneham's case at least the *oo* may well stand for ME *ŭ*, as it often does, and so the spelling *throogh* may represent the pronunciation [þruχ] recorded by Hart and Gil; or it may represent a pronunciation [þru:χ], which would be a blend of the new form with [u:] and the old strong form with [χ]. Bullokar records [þurouχ], which (if he is correct in showing retention of the final spirant) is a strong development of ME *þŭrŭh*. But he also gives [þurou], a weak development of the same ME form; Gil similarly records (once) the form *þuro*, and Butler has the spelling *thoorrow*. Finally, as a special development of early ME *ŭ* before [χ] (see § 175), there arises a pronunciation [þro:(χ)], which is recorded by Willis (see Vol. I, p. 427) and is shown (with loss of the [χ], perhaps under weak stress) by the spelling *thro* of the shorthand-writers T. Shelton, Bridges, Heath, Hopkins, Mason, and Ridpath, by the *thro* of the *Treatise of Stops*, and by Cocker's 'phonetic' spelling *thro'*. The homophone lists from Butler onwards put *through* by *thorow*, but their purpose in doing so is not apparent; they may mean to show that though there is no difference in pronunciation, the spelling is to be differentiated according to the differing uses of the word, but they are not at all consistent in the distinctions of use which they draw. Ellis and Cocker equate both forms with *throw*, and Fox and Hookes, Coles, and Young equate the form *through* with *throw*. Coote appears to teach [ð] for *through*; on this, see Vol. I, p. 36.

Thy: the normal form has [əi] < ME *ī*, but a weak form *ðĭ* is recorded by Bullokar and by Gil (six times, beside [ðəi] many times); Gil also has once [ði:] in the 1621 edition, but this is an error for the [ðəi] of the 1619 edition.

To, together, too: *to* has several different forms. The strong form with [u:] is recorded by the *Welsh Hymn*, Salesbury, Hart (twice only), Coote, Robinson (nineteen times in stressed and ten times in unstressed position), Gil (once only), Sherwood, Daines, Hodges, Wilkins, the *Welsh Breviary*,

Lye, and Brown. A weak form developed from this is *tŭ*, recorded by Hart (regularly), Mulcaster, Robinson (about 100 times in unstressed and twenty-six times in stressed position), and Gil (regularly), and in Daines's *tut* 'to it', which he says is an improper pronunciation. There is also a form with [oː] developed, with restressing and lengthening, from a ME weak form *tŏ*; it is recorded by Newton, Cooper (who is followed by Brown), and the 'homophone' lists from Wharton on, which put *to* with *toe* and *tow* as well as *too*. The ME weak form *tŏ* occurs nine times in Hart, four times in Gil; Hodges also has once *to*, which should mean short [ɔ] and would then represent the ME weak form, but which may well be an error due to the omission of a diacritic. The same forms are found in *together*, for which [uː] is recorded by Bullokar and Hodges, [ʊ] by Hart, Robinson, and Gil (once only) and its descendant [ʌ] by Hodges (once only), [oː] by Butler (twice), and *ŏ* by Gil (thrice). *Too* is in origin the strong form of *to*, and the recorded forms are in accordance with its origin. Smith has *tū*, Robinson *tuw*, and Gil *tū* (ten times). But a new reduction from [uː] is shown by Smith's *tu tu* 'too too', Gil's *tu* (twice), and his *tū tu* 'too too'. Because of its identity with the strong form of *to*, it is not distinguished from it by Butler, Merriott, *RS*, and the 'homophone' lists. Robinson in five instances has [d]; in one at least this seems to be an error, but in the others he may mean to show assimilation to a preceding voiced consonant.

Was: [z], developed in the weak form, is shown by most orthoepists from Laneham on as the only pronunciation. But Smith has [s]; Hart has [s] nine times, beside more frequent [z], and not only before voiceless consonants; Mulcaster says that [s] is as frequent as [z]; and Gil has [s] five times against [z] about thirty-eight times. Robinson shows early rounding of the vowel to [ɒ] owing to the lack of stress (as also in *what*, but in no other word), and Coles (see Vol. I, p. 443) and *WSC-RS* (see Vol. I, p. 301) give [ɒː], which shows not only rounding but also lengthening.

We: beside the regular strong form with [iː] there is recorded a weak form with *ĭ* by Hart (normally) and by Gil (twice only); others (e.g. Robinson) have [iː] even in unstressed position.

Well: Brown records [iː], probably a Northernism; *ĕ* is normal.

Were, wert: *were* is normally recorded in the strong form with ME *ē̜*, but Laneham has *wer* beside *were* and Gil has *wĕr* thrice against *wēr* thirteen times. Poole has [iː] < ME *ē̜* < Anglian *ē*. Robinson gives *ĕ* in *wert*, though he has ME *ē̜* in *were*; but Tonkis spells the word *weart* (which shows ME *ē̜*) and Cooper in his English edition says that it is pronounced *wârt*, which also shows ME *ē̜* (become identical before *r* with ME *ā*, for which his symbol is *â*).

Who: either [oː] or [uː], the normal and the abnormal variants descended from ME ǭ, are regularly shown by the orthoepists, except Hart (who regularly gives short [ɔ]; cf. Jespersen, *Hart*, § 39) and Gil (who has [ʊ] twice beside [uː] often); Hart's is a weak form developed from ME ǭ itself, and Gil's is developed from late ME ǭ by raising of ME ǭ. *Whom* has ŏ in Smith, Hart, Gil (once), and probably in Poole, and ŭ in Price; *whose* has ŏ in Hart. These also may represent weak forms; but see § 33 below.

With, &c.: the strong form with [þ] is the more frequently recorded. It is shown by the *Welsh Hymn*, Smith, Levins, Hart (chiefly before voiceless consonants), Bullokar, Robinson (chiefly when stressed; also unstressed before a consonant), Gil (who though he uses this form in his transcriptions admits that [ð] is more usual in speech, and yet attacks Hart's transcription with [ð]), Butler, Daines, Hodges, T. Willis, Wallis, Coles, and Cooper. The weak form with [ð] is twice required by the alliteration in the *Welsh Hymn* and is used by Hart (beside [wɪþ]), Bullokar (beside [wɪþ]), and Robinson (unstressed, and twice stressed); it is admitted to be the more common by Gil, and described as the only pronunciation by Price. In compounds like *wherewith* the strong form is to be expected; Levins and Hodges have [þ], but Hart [ð] beside [þ]. In *withal, within, without*, &c., the weak form is to be expected, and is used by Hart and Robinson; but Bullokar has [þ] beside less frequent [ð], and Gil, Butler, Hodges, and Wallis record only [þ]. In *withdraw*, &c., the weak form is similarly to be expected, and is found in Bullokar; but Robinson, Gil, and Hodges have [þ]. Robinson's evidence is the most interesting; it shows that though there was still some distinction, according to the presence or absence of stress, between the forms, they were not sharply distinguished; Hart's evidence shows the same. There was clearly a tendency to use the strong form in unstressed position before consonants, and even before vowels; the use of the weak form is less well evidenced.

Would: the forms are exactly parallel to those of *should* (see above). The pronunciation of [l] is shown by the *Welsh Hymn*, Smith, Hart, Bullokar, Robinson, Gil, Hodges, Poole, the 'phonetically spelt' lists of Strong and Young, and by implication by Tonkis and Jonson. The loss of [l] is shown once in the *Welsh Hymn*, by Tonkis and Jonson (as a colloquial contraction), and by Hodges (beside the form with [l]), Wallis, Hunt, and Cooper. In other cases the transcriptions may show [l] pronounced, but it is uncertain how far they are phonetic. The vowels in use were the same as in *should*. The *Welsh Hymn*, Laneham, and Bullokar show [ʌu] < ME ū, beside other forms; Wallis seems to give it as a (rare?) variant (see Vol. I, p. 246 footnote), and Poole's rhymes depend on it. The most likely explanation of this form is that it develops from ME *wŭlde* (itself an analogical formation on the ME present tense *wŭll(e)*), with the change of eME ŭ to late ME ū before *ld* (recorded in *shoulder* by Laneham and Bullokar themselves; see

§ 174 below); but it could develop from *wŏlde* by the process whereby ME *ou* became late ME *ū* before *ld* (see § 169 below). In either case it would be supported by the analogy of *could*. The vowel most frequently recorded is [u:], which must represent late OE *ō* by lengthening of *ŏ* before *ld*; it is given by the *Welsh Hymn* (if we may assume that [wu:ld] is the value of its spelling *wld*, used once), Smith, Laneham, Tonkis (beside ME *ŭ*), Robinson, Gil, Sherwood, Daines, Hodges (beside [ʊ]), Wharton (followed by J. Smith), Strong and Young, Lye, Coles, Richardson, and Brown. By shortening from this after the unrounding of ME *ŭ* arises Hodges's *wud* [wʊd], which he says is a possible alternative to *wūld* and himself uses once otherwise (against three other occurrences of *wūld*); Newton also has [ʊ]. It is uncertain whether [ʊ] or [u:] is intended by Hart, Wallis ([ʊ] seems more likely; see Vol. I, pp. 239–40), Hunt, Price (who seems to mean [ʊ], but is only following Wallis without understanding), Wilkins, and Cooper (followed by *WSC-RS*), who seems more likely to mean [u:]. Some evidence shows the equivalent of ME *ŭ* in *would*; this may represent a shortening from [u:] in unstressed position which occurred earlier than the unrounding of ME *ŭ*, or may be a survival in unstressed position of ME *wŭlde*. Cheke's *wold* may represent this form; Bullokar has *wuldst* once (against *wouldst* with [ʌu]); Gil has once *wvld*, where *v* is an error for *u* (or perhaps for *ū*, which he uses otherwise); Tonkis gives *wu'd* beside *woo'd*, and *wu'dst*; Jonson's *wou'd* may show ME *ŭ*, as in *bloud* 'blood'; Cooper includes *wudst* (apparently this means [wʌdst]) in his list of barbarisms. Hart uses, in addition to *ūld* = [wuld] or [wu:ld], an unstressed form *uld* = [ʊld] in which the initial [w] is lost; see Vol. I, p. 87, note 1.

Ye: the most common pronunciation is with [i:]; this is recorded probably by Hart's *ī* (with graphic omission of *i* for [j] before [i:]), by Gil's *yī*, and by Jonson, Hodges, Wharton (followed by J. Smith and Lye), Poole, Price, Wilkins, Richardson, and *RS*. A weak form with [ɪ] (by late ME or eModE shortening of ME *ē̦*) is recorded by Robinson and by Gil in unstressed position. But there was also a ME weak form *yĕ*, with [e] by early (OE?) shortening; it is recorded by Gil for the Western dialect (so 1619 edition; 1621 *yi*). From it, by restressing and consequent lengthening of the vowel (either in later ME or in eModE, i.e. after short *ĕ* had become an open sound), there develops a form with ME *ę̄*, which is recorded by Mulcaster and Robinson (once). The evidence of the 'homophone' lists, which pair *ye* with *yea*, is ambiguous; Hodges certainly meant the pairing to depend on [i:] (ME *ē̦*) in both words, but Coles equally certainly meant it to depend on [e:] (ME *ę̄*); the intention of the other writers cannot be determined.

You: a strong form with [ʌu] is recorded by Smith, Bullokar, Coote, and Gil (as a variant used by some, though according to him most say, and he usually writes, *yū*; but he has *you* [jʌu] nine times); Daines does not distinguish the value of *ou* in *you* from that in *thou*, and Poole and Aickin rhyme *you* with *vow*, &c. But Hunt says that '*yow* for *you*' is 'too broad ... the countryman's fault'; Price in his 'homophone' list warns his readers against pronouncing *you* as *yowe*; and Cooper includes among his 'barbarisms' *yau* (Latin text erroneously *yαu*), which is best explained as a phonetic spelling, in accordance with his system, for [jau]. Newton gives *yaw* as a variant spelling of *you*; his pronunciation was [au] < ME *ū*. It is clear that this old strong form was rare in the sixteenth century, and came to survive only as a vulgarism in the later seventeenth. A still rarer form is the *Welsh Hymn*'s [jo:] (< *ēow* as *trow* < *trēowian*). A third strong form is [jiu], which shows palatal influence acting on ME *ū* to change it into ME [y:]; for the detailed evidence see § 178 below. A weak form [jʊ] (from ME *yŭ*) is recorded by Hart (see Vol. I, pp. 80–81) and perhaps by Newton (see Vol. I, p. 251). Finally there is the pronunciation [ju:], which in orthoepists who do not show the development of ME [y:] to [ju:] is to be explained by restressing and lengthening of the ME weak form *yŭ*; it is recorded by the *Welsh Hymn*, Hart (see Vol. I, p. 81, note 2), Laneham, Gil (normally), Hodges, Newton (normally), Wilkins, the shorthand writers J. Willis, Everardt, and Hopkins, and by the 'homophone' lists, which follow Hodges in equating *you* with the name of the letter *u*, *yew*, and *ewe* (but see under *your* below).

Your: the forms are the same as for *you*. The α-MSS of the *Welsh Hymn*, Bullokar, Gil (thrice, against usual [ju:r]), Daines, Brooksbank, and Poole give [ʌu]; so possibly (as a variant only) *RS*. A number of orthoepists give the equivalent of ME [y:]; see § 178 below. A form [ju:r] (either by analogy with [u:] in *you*, or because of the influence of the following *r* on ME *ū*) is recorded by the *Welsh Hymn*, Levins, Laneham, Gil (his normal form), Hodges, Newton, and Lye; so too the shorthand writer Hopkins. The 'homophone' lists from Hodges on equate *your* and *ure*, which certainly shows a pronunciation [ju:r]; but as it also proves that ME [y:], at least initially, has become [ju:], it is possible that [ju:r] for *your* may be developed from ME [jy:r] and not from ME *yūr*. The same comment applies, though less certainly, to the 'homophone' lists' equation of *you* and *yew*, &c. (see above).

VI

THE QUANTITY OF STRESSED VOWELS

PART 1: QUANTITY VARIATIONS DESCENDED
FROM MIDDLE ENGLISH

§ 5. In many words there occurred in the sixteenth and seventeenth centuries variations of the quantity of the stressed vowels which were the same as and had descended from those of late ME (themselves often the result of OE or early ME changes in quantity). It is with these that the present part deals; variations in quantity resulting from late ME or early ModE processes of shortening, especially in closed syllables, are dealt with in Part 2, and those resulting from ModE lengthening in Part 3. The variations that descend from ME have mostly been lost from PresE owing to one or other of the forms having in individual words ousted the other, though there remains much inconsistency in the vowel-quantities of analogous words; in the period with which we deal, and particularly in the seventeenth century, there is a marked tendency for the form which PresE has generalized to predominate. But there is much evidence to show that there was considerably less uniformity, even within educated pronunciation, in the sixteenth and seventeenth centuries than there is now. The rhymes of the poets provide perhaps even fuller evidence, to the same effect as that of the orthoepists; for the most part it is not cited in corroboration in this part, but those familiar with it will realize that the orthoepists' evidence is amply supported—and itself vindicates the rhymes.

Note: In words from OF, quantity-variation may not result from an absence of distinctions of quantity in OF, as is commonly assumed, but on OF and AN developments in quantity as modified by ME shortening and lengthening; see A. J. Bliss's excellent articles in *Archivum Linguisticum*, iv. 121–47 and v. 22–47.

VARIATION BETWEEN ME ă AND ā

§ 6. As ME ā in native words results only from the lengthening of ME ă in open syllables (except in Northern dialects), variation between ME ă and ME ā in such words is almost invariably associated with this process. In some words it results because lengthening fails in a monosyllabic nominative singular, but occurs in disyllabic oblique forms. Thus although ME ă is normal in *path*, Cheke writes the plural (ME *pāðes*) as *paaths*, which shows ME ā. Fox and Hookes show variation between ă (from the nom. sing.) and ā (from oblique forms) in *fat* 'vat' (see Vol. I, p. 408). *Waist*

(ME *wast*) has ME ă in Fox and Hookes and Coles, *Eng. Dict.* (who pair it with *wast*), as is to be expected from the nom. sing.; PresE [ei] < ME ā must develop in oblique forms, and is shown by Coles's *Schm.*, which pairs the word only with *waste* in the section appropriate to ME ā (see Vol. I, p. 409). Similarly the adjective *bare* (OE *bǣr*) would normally have ModE ă; ME ā, recorded by Bullokar and Gil (but Gil gives the normal spelling, not a proper phonetic transcription), develops in oblique forms. The adverb *barely* (OE *bǣrlīce*) retained ă in the seventeenth century, but apparently only in vulgar speech; it is recorded in the 'homophone' lists of Hodges ('near alike' only), Fox and Hookes, Coles (only in the careless *Eng.–Lat. Dict.*), and Strong ('near alike', following Hodges), which pair the word with *barley*. In *shamefast* Hart gives ME ă, developed in the nom. sing., but Hodges has ME ā (whence the sixteenth-century corruption *shamefaced*); Hodges also has ā in *mast*, and Butler in *wasp*. In *staff* Daines had ME ā from oblique forms (Vol. I, p. 333); contrariwise Coles knew ă beside ā in *stave*. *Shape* has ă (representing the OE sb. *gescĕap*) in Levins and Poole (in whom it is a Northernism); ME ā develops in the verb (which owes its ModE form to the OE p.p. *sceāpen*). Smith gives *bāð* beside *bāð* for the verb *bathe*; Hodges pairs *bath* and *bathe* in his 'near alike' list, Hunt seems not to distinguish them, and Poole rhymes *bath* with *faith*. In Smith's case the sb. has by analogy given ME ă to the verb, in Poole's the reverse has occurred; Hodges's pairing may depend on either process. Bullokar has ă (which is due to the analogy of the sb.) in *graze* vb. *Wrath* is a complex case owing to the existence of variant forms (*wrǣþu* and *wrǣþ*, *wrǣþþu* and *wrǣþþ*) in OE. *Wrǣþþu*, with shortening before the geminated consonant, gives ME *wrăþþe*; this is represented by Gil's *wraþ*, *wraþful* and the 'phonetic' spelling *rath* given by Strong, and by the rhymes of Willis and Coles. But blending with OE *wrǣþu* produces an eME *wrăþe*, in which lengthening to ME ā and the change of [þ] to [ð] would regularly occur; this is shown by Levins's rhyme of *wrath* (spelt *wrathe*) with *scathe* and *swathe* and by Hodges's pairing of *wrath* and *rathe* as homophones. Further blending gives a form with ME ā but with [þ]; this is shown by Butler's *wrāþ*, Hodges's *rāþ* (in *EP*; contrast the 'homophone' list of *SH-PD*), and probably by Poole's rhyme (which is certainly on ME ā and probably on [þ]). Poole also seems to have ME ā in *lath* (for which ME apparently had *lāþe* beside *lăþþe*; see *OED*), but Bullokar, Hodges, and Coles have ă. Gil transcribes *scathe* sb. as *skăþ*, following Spenser's spelling *scath* (in rhyme with *wrath*); but the rhyme is more likely to be on ā (cf. ON *skaðe*). In *drake* ME ă (shown by Hodges's 'near alike' list, followed by Strong) is due to WGmc *drakko- beside *drako-.

In the cases so far discussed lengthening in open syllables occurs in one form of the word but not in another; but there are others in which in one and the same form the lengthening sometimes occurs and sometimes fails.

A syllabic consonant in the second syllable often has the effect of preventing lengthening. Thus *father* has ME *ă* in Levins, Smith, and Bullokar (five times), but ME *ā* in Robinson, Hodges, Wilkins, and the 'homophone' lists of Hunt and Fox and Hookes; it varies in Hart (*ă* twice and *ā* six times) and Gil (*ă* twice and *ā* four times). *Rather* has *ă* in Hart and Bullokar but *ā* in Robinson; it varies in Gil (*ă* twice and *ā* thrice; the 1619 edition prints all cases as short but has the sign of length added in ink) and in Hodges (*ă* five times and *ā* once). *Master* (partly from OE, partly from OF) has both *ă* and *ā* in Hart (once each); otherwise it is recorded with *ă*, as in Gil and Robinson (who so transcribes it despite its rhyme with *plaster*, which has the *a* marked long). *Plaster* itself (from OE, in part reinforced by OF) has *ā* in Bullokar as well as in Robinson. *Water* has *ă* beside *ā* in Levins, *ă* thrice and *ā* six times in Gil, and *ā* thrice in Hodges; the PresE pronunciation is developed from the *ă* form. *Haven* and *brazen* have *ă* in Bullokar (but in the latter case perhaps only to show its derivation from *brass*). *Maple* and *staple* have *ă* in Levins; these are doubtless Northern dialectal forms. *Babble* (ME *babel*) has *ā* (in the sb.) beside *ă* (in the verb) in Gil. The suffix *-ī* also inhibited lengthening (cf. Jordan, § 25, Anm. 3), but not regularly. *Many* has *ă* in Hart, Gil, and Hodges, but *ā* regularly in Robinson; Cooper (Part II, Ch. 2, Rule 2) gives [ɛ:] < ME *ā*. *Any* (ME *ăni* beside *ęni* &c.) has *ă* in Hart and Gil but *ā* five times beside *ă* twice in Robinson. *Wary* and *unwary* have *ă* in *RS*; this suggests that though the two words are first certainly recorded in the sixteenth century, they are in fact ME formations (cf. *OED*, s.v. *unwary*).

Analogous variation occurs in words adopted from French. *Ace* (OF *as*) and *lace* (OF *las*) are shown with ME *ă* by Brown's 'homophone' list pairings with *ass* and *lass*. *Taste* (OF *tast*) has ME *ă* in Hart, Bullokar, Hunt, and Poole; the variant in ME *ā*, now generalized, is appropriate to ME oblique forms or more particularly to the verb (ME *tasten*, a disyllable). Similarly *waste* (AN *wast*) has commonly ME *ă*, which is recorded by Gil (once in the adj., beside *ā*) and Hunt and is the basis of the 'homophone' list pairing (from Hodges onwards) with *wast*; but ME *ā* is recorded by Levins, Smith, Bullokar, Gil (once in the adj. and once in the noun), other 'homophone' lists (including Coles's reliable list in the *Schm.*), and Cooper (who gives *waste* and *wast* as words that differ in pronunciation). The long vowel is usually held to develop in a ME blend-form *waste* produced by contact between AN *wast* and OE *wēste*, but the analogy of *taste* shows that this hypothesis, though not certainly wrong, is unnecessary; ME *ā* would be natural in the verb (ME *wasten*). Other words from OF, in which ME *ā* is to be expected, show also ME *ă*, probably in part because of the analogy of the variation in *taste* and *waste* (but see below on ME *ă* in open syllables in words from French). *Haste* (an OF feminine, therefore disyllabic in OF and ME) has *ă* once beside *ā* twice in Gil (cf. the spelling *hast*) and *ă* in

Hunt; the 'homophone' lists pair it with *hast*, but the latter may have *ā* as well as *ă*. *Hasty* has *ă* (twice) in Gil. *Paste* is paired with *past* by 'homophone' lists from that of Hodges onwards. *Chaste* has *ă* in Hart, in Gil (once in the superlative, beside *ā* four times in the positive), and in Poole. Bullokar gives *ă* in *chasten* but *ā* in *chastised* and *chastity*; in derivatives, however, his quantity-marking is often theoretical and can be relied on only to show the quantity of the vowel he used in the simplex—in this case, that he varied between *ă* and *ā* in *chaste*.

Failure of lengthening before syllabic [l] occurs in *fable*, which has *ă* in Smith, and in *able*, which has *ă* beside *ā* in Hart and in Gil (the latter has *ă* once, *ā* twelve times). *Vary* (cf. *wary*) has *ā* in Levins, Hart, and Bullokar; so *variance* in Bullokar. *Contrarily* also has *ă* in Bullokar. Lengthening fails sometimes before consonant-groups; *sacred* and *matron* have *ă* in Bullokar (cf. *sacrilege*). Before [dʒ] (treated as if < OE *cg*), *ă* occurs in *page* 'servant' in Smith, and in *page* 'leaf' in Hart (beside *ā*); Bullokar has *ă* in *courageous* and Gil in *aged* and in *raging* (twice, beside *ā* four times in *rage*), and Poole seems to have *ă* in such words as *cage* and *gage*. Lengthening normally fails in trisyllabic words, especially those with marked secondary stress (cf. Jordan, § 25); but *challenge* (in which the *l* was originally single) has *ā* in Gil against *ă* in Robinson, *majesty* has *ā* beside *ă* in Gil, and *raven* vb. (OF *raviner*) has *ā* in Robinson.

In all these cases there are analogues in native words for the variation in the words from French. But the latter also show variation in circumstances in which it would not occur in native words. Thus ME *ă* occurs beside ME *ā* in open syllables before a single consonant, in which only ME *ā* would be possible in native words; sometimes the occurrence of ME *ă* may be associated with the shift of stress in English (cf. the variation between short and long vowels in Latin words when the stress is shifted in English; see § 23 below), but it also occurs in words in which the stress remains unchanged. (*a*) *With shifted stress*. *Ague* has *ă* in Bullokar and *ă* twice against *ā* once in Gil. *Favour(ed)* has *ā* once against *ă* twice in Hart and *ă* in Bullokar and Gil; *savour(y)* and *labour* have *ă* in Bullokar. Gil has *ă* in *famouser* beside *ā* in *famous*. *Nature* has *ă* in Hart, Bullokar, and Gil (once, beside *ā* twice), but only *ā* in Robinson and Hodges. *Compare* is transcribed by Bullokar with *ā* (three times; so *comparative* twice, *comparatively* once, and *comparison* five times), but he may rhyme the p.t. *compared* on ME *ă* (see Vol. I, p. 110). In all these words, of course, ME *ā* is normal in the orthoepists as in PresE. (*b*) *With unchanged stress*. Bullokar transcribes *blame* with *ā* (twice) but may rhyme it on *ă* (see Vol. I, p. 110), and Gil has *ă* once beside *ā* twice. *Dame* has *ă* once beside *ā* once in Bullokar and is paired in 'homophone' lists with *dam*; but it is perhaps subject to special development under weak stress. Before *s*, where rhymes (as in Spenser) often suggest ME *ă*, *mace* and *grace* vary between *ă* and *ā* in Bullokar and

§ 6] PART 1: QUANTITY VARIATIONS FROM ME 469

grace is paired with *grass* by the 'homophone' lists of Fox and Hookes and Young. Bullokar also gives *ă* in *gracious(ly)*. *Misplacing* has *ă* in Hart. On *ă* in *haste, paste*, and *chaste* see above. *James* has *ă* beside *ā* in Bullokar. But normally such words are recorded with *ā*. It will be observed that, apart from the 'homophone' lists, only the earlier orthoepists record *ă*; the short variant obviously became rare in the seventeenth century.

Variation is also common, in words from French, in closed syllables before *r* plus consonant, where in native words only ME *ă* would occur. Hart has *ā* in *tart*, Mulcaster in *sarce* 'to shift' (OF *saas*; but see § 8, Note 2) and *parce* 'parse?'; Bullokar gives *ā* alone in *marl, parsing*, and *scarce* (in which it survives in PresE), *ă* alone in *charm, largely*, and *scarcity*, and *ă* beside *ā* in *art, charge, guard, garden, large, scarcely*, and *part*. Butler has *ā* in *card*, *The English Scholemaster* (1646) in *guard*, and Willis in *card* and *guard* (but *ă* in *ward*). Poole appears to have ME *ā* in *card, guard, lard, nard, reward*, and *scarce* (see Vol. I, pp. 431-2). Cooper, followed by Brown, pairs *card* with *car'd* in his 'homophone' list. But such words are more often given with *ă*, as by Hart, Gil, and Hodges, and the present pronunciation (except in *scarce*) descends from the short vowel.

Note 1: As Bullokar and other sources give a long vowel, which they do not distinguish from ME *ā*, in certain native words in which it must be developed by lengthening of ME *ă* before *r* plus consonant, it might be argued that this new lengthened sound is also what is shown in the originally French words above. But (*a*) sources which do not show the lengthening in native words show ME *ā* in words from French, and (*b*) in native words Bullokar (as is pointed out by Zachrisson, *Bullokar*, pp. 33-35) shows the long vowel only before those *r*-groups which caused lengthening in OE, and not before others (as in the words cited above); the long vowel in the originally French words must therefore be due to a different cause than in the native words. For the explanation of the latter see § 43 below.

Note 2: Miège gives ME *ā* in *regard* (cf. Zachrisson, *Eng. Vowels*, p. 122). For other possible cases see § 43, Note 1.

Note 3: In certain words of French origin, such as *chamber*, earlier ME shows variation between *ă* and *au*, and in late ME the *au* variant commonly became *ā*; in the result late ME and early ModE show variation in such words between *ă* and *ā*. For evidence of early ModE *ă* in *chamber, chamberlain, angel, change, strange, stranger*, and *ancient* see § 62 (1).

VARIATION BETWEEN ME *ă* AND *ǭ*

§ 7. In ME there is a common variation, before OE lengthening groups beginning with a nasal, between unlengthened *ă* and ME *ǭ* < OE *ā* by lengthening (e.g. *hănd* beside *hǭnd*). But in ModE there is hardly any trace of this variation, except between words of different classes, and even so it survives not as a variation in quantity, but chiefly as one between ME *ă* and ME *ŏ* (on which see § 71 below); for in later ME the normal tendency to shorten vowels before consonant-groups asserted itself even before those which had caused OE lengthening, and ME *ǭ* was shortened to *ŏ* (thus *strŏng* < *strǭng* < late OE *strāng*). The original *ă* survives in ModE regularly before *nd*, except in *bond* beside *band*, but not before *ng* except in *hang*; in *comb* and *womb* there is no evidence of it, but in *lamb* it is invariable (< OE *lambru* pl.).

Note 1: ModE *ă* in *hand*, &c., may to some extent arise from ME reshortening of OE lengthened *ā* in dialects in which the latter did not become *ǭ*, or in which the reshortening preceded the change of *ā* > *ǭ*. *Fang* sb. and vb., which is evidently of Northern origin, seems a clear case of a word with reshortened ME *ā*.

Note 2: See further §§ 13 (3) and 15 on quantity-variation in *among*, *comb*, and *womb*.

VARIATION BETWEEN ME *ĕ* AND *ę̄*

§ 8. Variation between ME *ĕ* and ME *ę̄* was very common in the sixteenth and seventeenth centuries and affected a large number of words. In most of them PresE has generalized the short variant, though often the spelling with *ea* testifies to the former existence of the long variant. In the account of the evidence which follows, it should be understood that ME *ĕ* means a ModE vowel descended from ME *ĕ*, and that ME *ę̄* means one descended from ME *ę̄*; in the latter case it may be one of three vowels, [iː] (the PresE representative of ME *ę̄* in most words, though it will be argued in due course that it does not descend directly from ME *ę̄*), [eː], and [ɛː], according partly to date, partly to the influence of neighbouring sounds, as described in subsequent chapters. The variation in quantity occurs in both English and French words.

(1) *Native words*

(*a*) *OE lengthening before consonant-groups*

Lengthening of OE *ĕo* is primarily to OE *ēo* > ME *ę̄*, which subsequently may become late ME *ę̄* when it precedes *r* plus consonant; but unlengthened *ĕo* gives ME *ĕ*. *Earth* (OE *eorðe* with [rð]) has *ę̄* in Levins, Hart, and Gil, and *ĕ* in Hart and Gil (as a variant), Robinson, Hodges, and later sources. *Earl* is recorded with *ę̄* by Cooper, and with *ĕ* by Hodges, Price, Poole, Stringer, Brown, and *RS*. *Learn* has *ę̄* in Levins (beside *ĕ*), Hart (beside *ĕ*), Bullokar, and Cooper, and *ĕ* in Robinson, Gil, Hodges, Poole, Coles, Brown, and *RS*. *Earnest* has *ę̄* in Cooper and *ĕ* in the *Treatise of Stops*, Stringer, and *RS*. *Herd*, in spite of the spelling (which testifies to usual *ĕ*), is recorded with *ę̄* by Levins (beside *ĕ*) and Price. *Swerd* 'sword' has *ę̄* beside *ĕ* in Levins, *ĕ* in Bullokar.

(*b*) *ME lengthening in open syllables*

Early ME *ĕ* is sometimes lengthened, and sometimes kept short, in syllables which were evidently sometimes treated as open, and sometimes as closed. *Stretch* has *ę̄* in Levins but otherwise *ĕ*. *Breast* (OE *ĕo* > eME *ĕ*) has *ę̄* in Levins (beside *ĕ*), *The English Schole-Master*, and Poole, and *ĕ* in Robinson, Gil, Hodges, and later sources. *Nest* has *ę̄* in Bullokar but *ĕ* in

Gil and Hodges. This variation is very common when a syllabic consonant follows in the second syllable. *Nether* has $\bar{e}$ in Bullokar. *Feather* is normally recorded with $\breve{e}$ (e.g. by Hodges), but is put with *father* (which presumably in this case has ME $\bar{a}$) in Hunt's and Fox and Hookes's 'homophone' lists. *Leather* and *weather* are recorded only with $\breve{e}$. *Beaver* has $\breve{e}$ in Cooper followed by Aickin. *Heaven* has $\bar{e}$ in Cheke (beside $\breve{e}$), Hart, Gil (beside $\breve{e}$), Hodges, the *English Schole-master*, Wallis (beside colloquial $\breve{e}$), and the 'homophone' lists from Wharton's onwards; otherwise it has $\breve{e}$ (e.g. in Robinson, Price, and Wilkins). *Even* adj. and adv. has $\breve{e}$ in Bullokar and $\bar{e}$ in Robinson; Brown pairs it with *heaven* in his 'homophone' list, but this is ambiguous. On [i:] in *even* see § 10. *Seven* has $\bar{e}$ in Cheke, Hart (but *seventh* has $\breve{e}$ beside $\bar{e}$), and probably Laneham; but $\breve{e}$ in Bullokar, Gil, Hodges, and Brown. *Freckle* (ON *freknur* pl.) has $\bar{e}$ in Levins. *Yeoman* has $\breve{e}$ in Smith, Hunt (probably), Coles, Strong, Young, Lye, *WSC*, and Brown, but Jonson, and possibly Brown (as a variant), seem to give $\bar{e}$ (the evidence of other orthoepists is ambiguous); the variation may be due to occasional lengthening in the open syllable.

(c) Late OE or early ME shortening before consonant groups

Shortening before consonant groups is in certain cases irregular in occurrence. (i) When a syllabic consonant follows in the next syllable (cf. the preceding paragraph). *Weapon* has $\bar{e}$ in Bullokar (beside $\breve{e}$), Hodges, *The English Schole-master*, Coles, and *RS*; it has $\breve{e}$ in Bullokar and Brown. *Threaten* has $\breve{e}$ in Price and *RS*. *Heathen* is recorded with $\breve{e}$ in Wallis's transcription of colloquial pronunciation. *Beacon* has $\breve{e}$ in the 'homophone' lists of Hawkins and *WSC*. *Easter* has $\breve{e}$ in Hart, Strong, Young, and 'homophone' lists from Hodges ('near alike') onwards. *Leaper* is probably recorded with $\breve{e}$ by the 'homophone' lists (see Vol. I, p. 397). *Ever* has $\bar{e}$ once in Robinson, against usual $\breve{e}$. *Never* has $\breve{e}$, but *ne'er* has $\bar{e}$ (so in Robinson), as in PresE. *Together* has normally $\breve{e}$, but Gil gives $\bar{e}$ once beside $\breve{e}$ thrice. On variation between $\bar{e}$ and $\breve{e}$ by shortening in *heifer* and *(n)either*, see § 129: the two pronunciations seem about equally common, $\breve{e}$ being perhaps more colloquial; in *(n)either* $\breve{e}$ belongs especially to the conjunction, and weak stress may assist the shortening. (ii) Before *st*, which in oblique cases by forming a group which began the second syllable left the first syllable open and its vowel long, but which when final sometimes caused shortening. *East* has $\breve{e}$ in the *Welsh Hymn*, Bullokar, and the 'homophone' lists from Hodges ('near alike') onwards. *Yeast* has $\breve{e}$ in Willis and *RS*, and $\breve{\imath}$ from $\breve{e}$ in Smith and *WSC*. *Lest* (OE *þȳ lǣs þe*) is given with $\bar{e}$ by Levins, Laneham (but his transcription is perhaps ambiguous), Robinson, Hodges, Willis (beside $\breve{e}$), and the 'homophone' lists, which do not distinguish *lest* from *least* (this might mean $\breve{e}$ in *least*, but otherwise it is recorded with $\bar{e}$); but *lest* has $\breve{e}$ in other sources, e.g. Bullokar, Willis, and Wallis. Bullokar gives ẹ̄ beside ĕ in the *unleast* (*unlest*) variant of *unless*. (iii) Before other consonant groups, which normally cause shortening, though the conventional PresE spelling testifies to the continued existence of forms with ẹ̄ in the sixteenth century. An important case is a ME shortening before *r*-groups in words which had OE lengthening of *ĕa* to *ēa* > ME ẹ̄; shortening produces ME ĕ, which varies with unshortened ẹ̄. *Earn* is recorded with ĕ by Levins (against ẹ̄), Hodges, Poole, Coles, Stringer, Brown, and the 'homophone' lists from Wharton onwards; with ẹ̄ by Levins (beside ĕ), Price, and Cooper (followed by Aickin). *Fern* is recorded with ĕ by Levins (beside ẹ̄), Gil (1621 edition), Poole, Coles, and Brown; with ẹ̄ by Levins (beside ĕ) and Gil (1619 edition). *Shard* (spelt *sheard*) is recorded with ẹ̄ by Cooper and with ĕ by RS. *Yard* in Levins has ẹ̄ beside ă (< ME ĕ), the latter being regular in other orthoepists. *Bearn* 'bairn' has ĕ in RS (cf. the present Scotch pronunciation). *Beard* has ẹ̄ in Cooper (followed by Aickin), [iː] < ME ẹ̄ by raising of ẹ̄ in Levins (beside ĕ) and Hodges, and ĕ in Levins, Bullokar, Mulcaster, Price, and RS. In other words the ME ẹ̄ which is shortened does not originate from late OE *ēa* < earlier *ĕa*, and the shortening is more regular. ME ĕ is commonly recorded in, for example, *dearth*, *health*, *wealth*, *breadth*, and *meant*; but *health* has ẹ̄ in Gil. *Heard* regularly has ĕ (or ă derived from it) by shortening of OAngl *ē*, but late ME ẹ̄ by lowering before *r* of unshortened ME ẹ̄ occurs once in Gil (who twice otherwise has *ā* by lengthening of ă < ME ĕ) and in Butler; the retention, or reintroduction, of this late ME ẹ̄ is no doubt due to the influence of the infinitive. J. Smith similarly gives [iː] from ME ẹ̄ without lowering. (Compare the modern dialectal pronunciations with a long vowel recorded by Wright, *EDG*, Index, and Milton's rhyme in *Lycidas* between *heard* and *appeared*.) *Read* p.t. has ĕ, as in Hodges, Aickin, RS, and the 'homophone' lists; but the lists of Fox and Hookes and of Young, if they may be relied on, record ẹ̄. The comparative *greater* has ĕ in Hart (cf. ME *gretter*). *Nearer* has ĕ (derived from the ME *nerre* from OE *nēarra*, or by analogy with such comparatives as *greater*) in Hart and Gil, against ẹ̄ in *near*. (iv) Before *ch* (treated as a double consonant). The 'homophone' lists give ĕ for *reach*. Cooper, followed by Aickin, gives ĕ for *each*. Smith gives ĕ beside ẹ̄ for *breach* (which comes partly from OE *bryce*, partly from OF *breche*). But ẹ̄ is normal in such words.

(d) *Shortening in trisyllabic forms*

In some cases shortening occurs in oblique forms owing to their being trisyllabic in OE or ME, but not in the uninflected forms, which are disyllabic. *Early* has ẹ̄ in Cooper, followed by Aickin, and ĕ in Stringer and RS. *Heavy* has ẹ̄ in Gil and ĕ in Cooper, Brown, and RS. *Leavie* 'leafy' has ĕ in Hodges. *Steady* has ĕ in Hodges, Cooper, Brown, and RS. *(Al)ready* has ẹ̄ in Hart and *The English Schole-master* (but the latter is hardly reliable), otherwise ĕ. *Many* (spelt *meany*) has ẹ̄ in Levins; ĕ is not recorded by the orthoepists. *Pretty* (OE **prǣtig*; see *OED*) has ĕ < ME ẹ̄ in Levins, who rhymes it with *petty*; this is probably also the meaning of the *Welsh Hymn*'s transcription *preti* and the spellings *prety* and *preti* used respectively by Laneham and the shorthand-writer Hopkins, though these forms might show ME ẹ̄. (On this word see also § 11 below.) *Weary* has ĕ in Bullokar (so also *weariness*, beside—in *weary*—less frequent long vowels, both ẹ̄ by lowering and ē̞), in Gil (once, beside ẹ̄ five times), and in Price; ẹ̄ is also shown by Butler (beside ē̞). *Meadow* has ĕ in Levins, Bullokar, Brown, and *RS*. The existence of trisyllabic inflected forms, or the effect of the [n] in acting as a syllabic consonant and so closing the syllable (cf. (*b*) above), is the cause of the short ĕ in *weasand* recorded by *RS*. The original trisyllabic forms of OE cause the short ĕ of *reachless* 'reckless', recorded by Cooper and *WSC*; of *Reading*, recorded by *RS*; and of *cleanse*, recorded by Hodges (but only as a variant beside ẹ̄), Cooper, Brown, and *RS*. *Errand* (OE *ǣrende*) has usually ĕ, but Gil has ẹ̄ twice beside ĕ once.

(*e*) *Shortening in the first element of a compound*

Breakfast has ĕ in Coles and later sources. *Seamstress* has ẹ̄ in Price and ĕ in *RS*. *Mermaid* has ẹ̄ in Cooper.

(2) *Words from French*

Variation is especially frequent before *r* plus consonant. *Pearl* has ẹ̄ in Bullokar and Cooper, and ĕ in Wharton's 'homophone' list, Price, Poole, Brown, and *RS*. *Term* has ẹ̄ in Levins, ē̞ beside ĕ in Gil, and ĕ in Poole. *Perch* has ẹ̄ in Levins and Gil and ĕ in *RS*. *Search* has ẹ̄ in Levins, Bullokar (beside ĕ), Gil (1619 edition), and Cooper (followed by Aickin), and ĕ in Gil (1621 edition), Hodges, Price, Poole, Cocker, Brown, and *RS*. *Searce* 'a sieve' (see Note 2) has ẹ̄ in Levins (beside ĕ) and Bullokar and ĕ in Poole and *RS*. *Hearse* has ĕ in Robinson, Poole, and *RS*. *Rehearse* (*rehearsal*) has ĕ in Hart, Bullokar (beside ẹ̄), Poole, Brown, and *RS*, but ẹ̄ in Cooper. In this class also we should probably place *pierce*, which has ĕ in Bullokar, Mulcaster, and Poole, and the 'homophone' lists of Hodges and Strong, but ẹ̄ in Robinson, perhaps also in Laneham (who spells the word with *ea*; but *ea* sometimes stands for ĕ in this author); it is, however, not quite certain that *pierce* has original ME ẹ̄ (see § 122). *Fierce* (original ME ẹ̄ < AN ē̞ for OF *ie* in *fiers*) has ẹ̄ (by late ME lowering before *r*) in Bullokar (beside ē̞), Robinson, and Gil, while Laneham spells the word with *ea* (cf. *pierce* above); it has ĕ in Levins, Poole, Aickin, and *WSC*.

To those native words which show variation before the group *st* there correspond *beast*, *feast*, and *jest* (OF *beste*, *feste*, and *geste*). *Beast* has ĕ in the 'homophone' lists from Hodges's 'near alike' onwards and is rhymed with *divest* by Lye (though his quantity-marking inconsistently shows $\bar{e}$ in *beast*); otherwise it has $\bar{e}$. *Feast* has $\breve{e}$ in the *Welsh Hymn* (cf. Jonson's rhyme *feast : dressed*), but normally $\bar{e}$. *Jest* (*gest*) has $\bar{e}$ in Levins (beside $\breve{e}$) and Gil, but $\breve{e}$ in Bullokar and Hodges.

In other words from French variation occurs before a syllabic consonant in the next syllable, as in some native words. *Leaven* has $\breve{e}$ in Cooper, Brown, and *RS*, but $\bar{e}$ beside $\breve{e}$ in Hodges; Coles gives it as a homophone of *leaving* in his *Eng.–Lat. Dict. Heron* has $\bar{e}$ in Bullokar. *Reason(able)* has $\breve{e}$ varying with more frequent $\bar{e}$ in Bullokar, and $\breve{e}$ once beside $\bar{e}$ thrice in Gil. *Lever* (spelt *leaver*) has $\breve{e}$ in Cooper. *Eager* also has $\breve{e}$ in Cooper, followed by Aickin. The 'homophone' lists, by pairing *leper* with *leaper*, may show $\bar{e}$ in the former; but $\breve{e}$ in the latter is more likely. Laneham's spelling *mitter* 'metre' may show $\breve{\imath}$ by raising of ME $\breve{e}$. Variation also occurs before -$\bar{\imath}$ in the next syllable, as in native words; *easy* has $\breve{e}$ twice beside $\bar{e}$ twice in Hart, and *treaty* has $\breve{e}$ in Bullokar.

In the initial syllable of words which were trisyllabic in ME a short vowel is normal, but a long also occurs. *Leveret* is spelt with *ea* (which is perhaps indicative of earlier $\bar{e}$) but pronounced with $\breve{e}$ by Cooper. *Treachery* has $\breve{e}$ in Cooper, Brown, and *RS*, and *lechery* in Brown and *RS*; in these the affricative [tʃ] assists shortening. But *schedule* has $\bar{e}$ in Hodges (who says that the *sche* has the same sound as *sea* in *seated*) and apparently in Hunt and Cocker, who give the phonetic spelling *sedule* (cf. *se-dule* in Young's 1722 edition); but it has $\breve{e}$ in Coles, Strong, and Young 1682, whose spelling is *sed-dule*. *Measure* and its derivatives have $\bar{e}$ in Gil and perhaps in Brown (though he is more likely to mean $\breve{e}$); it has $\breve{e}$ in Bullokar, Robinson, Hodges, Price, Coles, Strong, Young (1682 edition), and *RS*. *Jeopard* (a back-formation from *jeopardy*) is spelt *je-pard* by Brown, which appears to show $\bar{e}$; Jonson has *jépard*, in which *é* should mean ME $\bar{e}$. Other orthoepists merely say the *o* is silent, without precisely indicating the quantity of the *e*; in at least several cases it is probably short.

Variation also occurs in open syllables before a single consonant, where in native words only a long vowel would be expected (cf. ME $\breve{a}$ beside $\bar{a}$ in words from French). (*a*) *Words with shift of stress. Present* has $\bar{e}$ once beside $\breve{e}$ twice in Gil. *Pheasant* has $\breve{e}$ in Brown and *RS*, and *peasant* probably $\breve{e}$ in Brown. *Pleasure* (OF *plaisir*) has $\bar{e}$ in Bullokar, Gil, and the 'homophone' lists from Hodges ('near alike') onwards, but normally $\breve{e}$ (as in Hart, Robinson, and Hodges). *Pleasant* shows similar variation. *Leisure* (OF *leisir*) has $\bar{e}$ in Price (and ME *ai* in other orthoepists); ME $\breve{e}$ is not recorded. *Treasure* (OF *tresor*) has $\bar{e}$ in Hart, Bullokar, and Gil (beside $\breve{e}$), and perhaps in Brown (though $\breve{e}$ is more probable); it has $\breve{e}$ in Robinson, Hodges, Price, Coles, Strong, and *RS*. *Zealot* and *zealous* have $\bar{e}$ in Lloyd and *RS*; so *zealously* in Hodges. *Jealous* has $\bar{e}$ in Gil (1619 edition only, beside $\breve{e}$), Hodges, Hexham, and Price, but *ĕ* in Hart, Bullokar, Robinson, Gil (1621 edition, and as a variant in 1619 edition), Strong, Young, and Brown. *Endeavour* has *ĕ* in Hart, Laneham, Bullokar, Cooper, and *RS*; it has *ẹ̄* in Gil, Hodges, Lloyd, Price, and apparently in Brown. *Cease* (OF *cesser*) has *ĕ* in the 'homophone' lists of Hodges, Young (beside *ẹ̄*), and Cooper ('near alike'). *Press* (OF *presser*) has *ẹ̄* in Levins, Cheke (beside *ĕ*), Poole, and Fox and Hookes. *Lessor* and *lessee* have [iː] < ME *ẹ̄* in *RS*; cf. the normal ME *ẹ̄* in *lease* vb. (OF *lesser*). (b) *Words with unchanged stress. Leash* (OF *lesse*) has *ĕ* twice beside *ẹ̄* once in Smith. *Phlegm* has *ẹ̄* in Levins, Gil, Butler, Wallis, Poole, and the 'homophone' lists of Aickin and Brown; the PresE *ĕ*, though not recorded, must go back to ME (cf. OF *flemme*).

Mess (OF *mes*) has *ẹ̄* in Levins (cf. ME *ā* in *ace* and *lace*). *Realm* (OF *reaume*) owes *ĕ* to shortening before the consonant-group of the form in which *l* was pronounced; it is shown by Bullokar, Coles (who rhymes with *whelm*), Cooper, Brown, and *RS*. On the other hand only *ẹ̄* is recorded in the form without *l*, which was used by most sixteenth- and seventeenth-century orthoepists (e.g. Laneham, Hart, Hodges, and Willis), though Coote describes it as a barbarism. Gil pronounced the *l* but nevertheless used *ẹ̄*; this must be regarded as a blend-form.

Note 1: *Pearl, perch, hearse, pierce,* and *fierce* also show variation between ME *ĕ* and ME *ẹ̄*, owing to the frequent interchange between ME *ẹ̄* and ME *ę̄* before *r*; see § 9 below.

Note 2: The *OED*'s etymology of *searce* is inadequate; it says that it is from OF *saas*, 'with unexplained insertion of *r*'. The ME *saarce* will explain Mulcaster's pronunciation (see § 7), but not the pronunciations cited above. Zachrisson's view (*Bullokar*, p. 37), that Bullokar by giving ME *ẹ̄* in what was originally ME *saarce* shows the identity of ME *ā* and ME *ẹ̄* before *r*, is an insufficient explanation of the forms of the word. There has clearly been contamination, probably in ME, of *saas* (possibly recorded in English; see *OED*) and *search*, as is shown by the agreements between the forms of the two words (for which see *OED*). The contamination was probably in the first place between *searce* vb. (i.e. *saasen in ME) and *search* vb., the meanings of which are very similar. The influence of *search* accounts both for the *r* and the vowel (*ĕ* or *ẹ̄*) of *searce*, a form which appears first in the sixteenth century. The sixteenth- to eighteenth-century form *sierce* may show ME raising of *ẹ̄* to *ę̄* in *searce* sb. and vb.

VARIATION BETWEEN ME *ĕ* AND *ẹ̄*

§ 9. Variation between ME *ĕ* and ME *ẹ̄* occurs in a few words, both native and adopted from French. In native words it occurs both before groups of consonants which cause late OE lengthening, and other groups which cause shortening. Of words subject to lengthening, *end* has *ĕ* in all orthoepists except Laneham, who gives ME *ẹ̄* beside *ĕ*; Cooper condemns *eend* as a barbarism. *Eld* has *ẹ̄* in Levins, as has *bield* sb. 'refuge' and vb. 'succour'. *Seld* and *seldom* have *ẹ̄* in Bullokar (the latter probably only by artificial quantity-marking, because of its being treated as a derivative of the former); Poole's rhymes seem to show variation in *seld* (see Vol. I, p. 430). In *fieldfare*, in which *RS* gives *ĕ* against Bullokar's *ẹ̄*, the fact that *field* is the first element of a compound has either inhibited lengthening or caused reshortening; the form with *ẹ̄* is probably due to a recognition of the etymological connexion with the simplex *field*. Smith has *ĕ* in *yeld* p.t. 'yielded' (late OE *geld* < *geald*); his variant *ĭ* is probably by raising of this *ĕ*. *Yearn* has *ĕ* in Poole, Cole, and the 'homophone' lists, but [iː] in *RS*.

Shortening of OE *ē* to *ĕ* occurs in a number of words beside forms that preserve the long vowel. The shortening is normal in *bless* and *brethren*, but for both of these Hart shows [iː] < ME *ẹ̄*. The comparative *liefer* (OE *lēofra*) has *ĕ* beside less frequent *ẹ̄* in Bullokar. In *friend* the shortening is probably due to derivatives (*friendly*, *friendship*) in which the vowel occurs before a group of three consonants in words which (in the case of *friendly* in oblique forms) were trisyllabic and had a secondary stress; but it might also sometimes occur in the simplex in cases in which the *n* and *d* were not separated by the syllable-division. ME *ĕ* is recorded by Levins and eleven later sources (including Robinson, Hodges, and Cooper); but *ẹ̄* is retained by Salesbury, Cheke, Laneham, Bullokar, Wharton (followed by J. Smith), and Price (followed by Lye and *The Protestant Tutor*). *Fiend* is not recorded with ME *ĕ*. *Devil* has *ĕ* in Brown but *ẹ̄* in Wharton (followed by J. Smith). On the common *ĭ* by ME shortening see § 11 below. *Heard* has [iː] < ME *ẹ̄* in J. Smith, but *ĕ* is normal (see also § 8 (1*c*)). OE (Anglian) *ēfen* explains the [iː] of *evening*, recorded by Bullokar, Gil, Price, and Lye; OAngl *ēfnung* (WS *ǣfnung*) should give ME *ĕ*, which Bullokar records beside [iː]. On *ĕ* in *weary* (produced by shortening in trisyllabic oblique forms) in Bullokar, Gil, and Price, see § 8 (1*d*); [iː] from ME *ẹ̄* is shown by Hart, Bullokar (beside *ẹ̄*), Butler (beside *ẹ̄*, which he prefers), and Cooper, and *ẹ̄* by lowering of *ẹ̄* before *r* by Bullokar, Gil, and Butler. In the compound *threepence* ME *ĕ* must have existed but is not recorded.

Variation between ME *ĕ* and *ẹ̄* also occurs in French words, and is especially frequent before *r* plus consonant. *Fierce* (AN *ẹ̄* for OF *ie* in *fiers*) has *ẹ̄* in Levins (beside *ĕ*), Bullokar (beside *ẹ̄*), Hodges, Coles, Hunt, and Cooper; it has *ĕ* in Levins, Poole, Aickin, and *WSC*. *Tierce* (AN *ẹ̄* for OF *ie* in *tierce* fem. of *tiers*) has *ĕ* in Cooper, followed by Aickin and Brown. Hodges has [iː] (< later ME *ẹ̄* < original ME *ẹ̄*) in *pearl*, *perch*, *hearse*, and *verse* (in part from OF *vers*, in part from OE *fers*); for the last word Hodges also gives *ĕ*. *Pierce* probably also belongs with these cases, though it is not certain that it has original ME *ẹ̄* (see § 122); it has ME *ẹ̄* in Levins, Price, Coles, Cooper, Brown, and *RS*, and in Hodges's 'near alike' list (his 'alike' list gives *ĕ*). For evidence of *ĕ* in words with original ME *ẹ̄* see § 8 (2), where is also given evidence of *ẹ̄* in *fierce*.

WSC records *ĕ* in *lieger*; it is a case of variation between short and long vowel in a syllable which was sometimes open, and sometimes closed, before a syllabic consonant (cf. above). *Lieutenant*, when the *u* is pronounced as [v] or [f] (as it is by all orthoepists except Bullokar who record the word), shows variation in the vowel. ME ẹ̄ is recorded by Gil, Butler, Hodges, Wharton, Hunt, Price, Coles, J. Smith, *The Protestant Tutor*, and *RS*; Merriott shows ĭ, probably by direct shortening of ME ẹ̄, saying that *liftenant* is a gross fault of spelling, and Brown uses exactly this form in his 'phonetically spelt' list. Short ĕ is shown only by *WSC* (against the [iː] of *RS*); this form, first recorded in Tyndale (see *OED*), may be due to some process of analogy or corruption (cf. *lift* beside *left* adj., *left* p.p.).

Note 1: Variation between ĕ and eME ẹ̄ is most frequent in native words before *r* plus a homorganic voiced consonant; but as eME ẹ̄ commonly develops to late ME ẹ̄ before *r* plus consonant, such cases are dealt with in the preceding discussion of variation between ĕ and ẹ̄. In *beard* the converse occurs; ME ẹ̄ (< OE *ēa*) becomes late ME ẹ̄ by raising, whence [iː] recorded by Hodges (see § 8 (1c) above).

Note 2: Even in ME, shortening of ME ẹ̄ results in ĭ as well as ĕ; indeed shortening to ĕ is to be regarded as typical of late OE or the earliest ME, and shortening to ĭ as the normal ME process (cf. the converse lengthening of ME ĭ to ẹ̄ in open syllables). ME shortening therefore sometimes results in variation between ME ĭ (by shortening) and ME ẹ̄ (the retained long vowel); on ĭ forms of *friend, fiend, field, devil,* and *threepence* see § 11.

VARIATION BETWEEN ME ĭ AND ẹ̄

(1) *Lengthening in open syllables*

§ 10. Variation between ME ĭ and ME ẹ̄ is most frequent in open syllables, in which in later ME there was irregular lengthening of ĭ to ẹ̄. *Evil* has ĭ in Smith, Hart, Butler, Hodges, and perhaps Wilkins (who does not mark the vowel long, but in other cases omits to do so when there can be no question of a short vowel); it has [iː] in Bullokar, Robinson, Gil, Wharton (followed by J. Smith), Coles, Young, Lye, and Brown. *Cripple* varies between ĭ and [iː] in Levins, and has ĭ in Butler and Hodges; Coles in his 'homophone' list pairs it with *creepl* among the ME ĭ words (this pairing is apparently due to Butler's spelling *creepple* 'cripple' and his inclusion of both spellings in a note in his 'homophone' list). On *little* see § 11. *Weevil* has ĭ in Butler (see Vol. I, p. 162), and *beadle* has ĭ in Brown (see Vol. I, p. 371). *Beetle* has ĕ by lowering of ME ĭ in Bullokar. *Stead* has ĭ (< OE *stȳde*) in Butler and [iː] (< ME ẹ̄ < ĭ < OE *ȳ*) in Hart, Laneham, and Hodges's 'near alike' list (which is followed by those of Fox and Hookes and Cocker); it also has ME ẹ̄ and ĕ (probably by shortening of ẹ̄) from OE *stĕde* (see § 30). *Week* is paired with *wick* in Hodges's 'near alike' list, followed by Wharton, Strong, and *RS* (but *wick* may have [iː]; see § 31). Wharton and *RS* also pair it with *weak* on [iː]. *Give* has [iː] in Hart (beside ĭ more often), Bullokar, and Gil (once, beside regular ĭ; he also says the 'Mopsæ' pronounce the word [giː]); other orthoepists give ĭ. *Live* regularly has ĭ. *Her* is spelt *heer* by Laneham, which probably shows [iː] < ME ẹ̄ developed in a stressed form of *hĭre* (though *ee* might be used as a symbol for ĭ); ME ĭ is shown (beside ĕ) by Hart, Bullokar, and Gil. Laneham also has [i:] probably in *women* and possibly in *merry*, and Gil has [i:] once against ĭ twice in *women*; otherwise *women* is recorded with ĭ (except that Bullokar has ŭ and another of Laneham's spellings may show ĕ by lowering of ĭ). *Even* adj. and adv. (which also has variation between ME ĕ and ẹ̄; see § 8 (1*b*)) has forms with ĭ and ẹ̄ which presuppose a ME variant **iven* (cf. OFris *ivin*); ĭ is shown by Hart and Gil (beside [i:]) and by Butler, and [i:] by Robinson, Sherwood, Hodges, Wharton, Price, Coles, Young, and Lye. *Sieve* has [i:] in Levins and *RS*; Brown's 'phonetic' spelling *sive* probably means ĭ (cf. the spelling of *give*). *Wherry* (etym. obscure, perhaps from *whirr*; see *OED*) has [i:] < ME ẹ̄ in Bullokar, as have the originally French words *chisel* and *cherries*; in the latter ME ẹ̄ must develop in the fourteenth-century variant *chĭry* (which is recorded by Smith beside the form with ĕ).

Note 1: Hart and Bullokar show ME ẹ̄ in *like* vb., in which it develops from earlier ĭ (recorded once by Bullokar) < OE ī by shortening. On this and other words which have late ME ẹ̄ from (and beside) ME ĭ by shortening of or as a variant to ME ī, see § 138. Gil's ẹ̄ in *repine* is probably a further instance.

Note 2: It may be here remarked that the phonetic process whereby ME ĭ and ŭ were lengthened in open syllables was a direct change from lax [ɪ] and [ʊ] to tense [e:] and [o:], just as ME ẹ̄ and ọ̄, when shortened, became directly ĭ and ŭ; the tongue-positions of English [ɪ] and [ʊ] are only slightly higher than those of 'cardinal' [e:] and [o:], with which ME ẹ̄ and ọ̄ must have been pronounced. To assume intermediate stages of the lengthening (and of the shortening), as is often done, is false; it is against phonetic probability and is supported by no evidence. A. J. Bliss, *English and Germanic Studies*, ii (1948–9), 40–47, rightly objects to such a view, but his own hypothesis seems to me still less acceptable.

(2) *Shortening*

§ 11. Variation also results from ME shortening of ẹ̄ to ĭ, the converse process to the lengthening in open syllables just discussed. *Friend* has ĭ in the *Welsh Hymn*, Mulcaster, Gil, Wallis, Lloyd, Poole, Coles, Lye (beside ẹ̄), *WSC* (beside ĕ), Price's 'homophone' list (though elsewhere he records [i:]), the rhymes of Poole and Coles, and perhaps in Ray; the evidence for [i:] < retained ME ẹ̄ and for ĕ is given in § 9. *Fiends* has ĭ in the *Welsh Hymn* and the 'homophone' lists of Hodges ('near alike'), Price, Coles (*Eng.–Lat. Dict.*), and *WSC* (the pairing is with *fins*); it has [i:] in Wallis. Bullokar rhymes *field* on ĭ (cf., probably, Chaucer's *hild* 'held' and *fil* 'fell' < earlier *hēld*, *fēll*). *Devil* has ĭ in Smith, Bullokar, Robinson, Butler, Hodges, Coles, and Cooper; [i:] is given beside ĭ by Wharton (followed by J. Smith). Levins records unshortened [i:] (doubtless a Northernism) in *nimble* and *swipple*; he also has [i:] in *nipple*, in which ĭ may be of similar origin. Shortening before [tʃ], treated as a double consonant, accounts for ĭ in *breech(es)*, recorded by Hodges, Poole, and Coles (cf. PresE [ɪ] in the plural). Shortening in the first element of a compound occurs in *threepence*, in which [ɪ] is recorded in the 'phonetically spelt' lists of Coles, Strong, and Young, and in *cheesecake*, in which it is shown only by that of Coles; as the latter is not recorded until the fifteenth century, the shortening may be later than the change of ME $\bar{e}$ to [i:], but the effect is the same. ME $\breve{e}$ by the alternative (early) process of shortening is not recorded by the orthoepists for *threepence*. Shortening in the first syllable of a word which is trisyllabic in oblique forms accounts for the normal $\breve{\imath}$ in *silly* (but Bullokar has [i:] < ME $\bar{e}$) and for $\breve{\imath}$ in *pretty* (OE *prētig*; see *OED*). Wallis gives the latter as *prity*, and says further that when we wish to exaggerate the meaning we protract the pronunciation to *pree-ty*, and compares *lee-tle* 'little'; these forms with [i:] could be explained (especially in view of the manner in which he records them) as due to ModE lengthening, under exaggerated stress, of [ɪ], but in *pretty* [i:] could well descend from ME $\bar{e}$. On [i:] in *little*, shown also by Gil and Strong, see Vol. I, pp. 351–2. In *weary* ME shortening of $\bar{e}$ to $\breve{\imath}$ precedes the rounding shown in the dialectal form *worry* (see § 85 below). The shortening to $\breve{\imath}$ recorded by Gil in *greenish* is probably due to the secondary stress of the suffix; cf. *Greenwich*. Analogous variation in words of French origin occurs in *feeble*, which has $\breve{\imath}$ in Smith and Levins (who rhymes it with *pebble*, elsewhere given with $\bar{\imath}$), and in *lieutenant*, in which the $\breve{\imath}$ recorded by Merriott and Brown (see § 9) is probably by direct shortening of $\bar{e}$.

VARIATION BETWEEN ME $\breve{\imath}$ AND $\bar{\imath}$

§ 12. Variation between ME $\breve{\imath}$ and $\bar{\imath}$ occurs both in native words and in those adopted from French.

(1) *Native words*

The variation occurs chiefly before OE lengthening groups. The most important class of word is those in *-ind*, which are normally recorded with ME $\bar{\imath}$; but there is some evidence of variation. Smith gives '*uīnd* or *uind*' for *wind* sb. Mulcaster has $\breve{\imath}$ in *wind* and *bind* against $\bar{\imath}$ in *kind*, *find*, *mind*, and *hind*. Bullokar transcribes *find* with $\bar{\imath}$ but rhymes it on $\breve{\imath}$. Coote says that some pronounce *blind*, *find*, and *behind* short, while others pronounce them long; Young's 'homophone' list shows variation in *find*. Hodges says that 'som men cal the *winde*, the *wind*'. It is clear that the variation was most common in *wind*, which has now come to have the short vowel; but in the sixteenth and seventeenth centuries it was more usually pronounced with ME $\bar{\imath}$, which is given by Levins, Bullokar, Robinson, Gil, Willis, Wharton, Poole, J. Smith, Cooper, and Brown. Short $\breve{\imath}$ (due probably to the originally disyllabic form of the suffix *-ere*) is apparently shown for *winder* by Fox and Hookes, who put it with *window* in their homophone list; but Bullokar has $\bar{\imath}$. Variation also occurs before *ld*. Smith and Hart have $\breve{\imath}$ beside $\bar{\imath}$ in *child*, for which other orthoepists, such as Bullokar, Gil, Hodges,

Wallis, Wharton, and J. Smith, give ī; but Bullokar, despite his transcription, rhymes the word on ĭ. *Children*, owing to the influence of the following consonants, has normally ĭ; Bullokar marks the ī long, but probably only to indicate the derivation from *child*. *Wild* regularly has ME ī. *Build* has ĭ from OE ȳ in Cheke, Bullokar, Robinson, Gil, Hodges, Richardson, Poole, and Cooper; it has ME ī from OE ȳ by lengthening in Cheke, Bullokar, and Gil, more often than the ĭ variant which they also give. *Guild* has ME ī, similarly developed, in Gil. *Climb* has ĭ beside less frequent ī in Bullokar; Gil gives ī.

In *chine* 'crack' sb. and vb. the PresE pronunciation with [ai] is from the verb (OE *cīnan*); the noun (OE *cĭnu*, from the weak grade of the verbal stem) should have ĭ, which is recorded by Brown. Similarly Gil's ī in *grisly* is due to the analogical influence of the verb *agrise*. *Withe* (OE *wĭðð e*) should have ĭ, as in Willis; the PresE variation between [ɪ] and [ai] is due to the influence of *withy* (OE *wīðig*), though the latter now has only [ɪ] < ME ĭ by shortening in trisyllabic oblique forms.

Shortening before the final consonant-group accounts for ĭ in *Christ*, which is recorded by Hart and Willis; Wallis, in his fifth edition, says that this is a Scotch pronunciation (though this would seem not the whole truth). In oblique forms the consonant group began the second syllable, and the long vowel was preserved; this, the present pronunciation, is recorded by the *Welsh Hymn*, Robinson, Hodges, Wallis, Wilkins, and Coles. In *Christian*, which is trisyllabic in ME, ĭ is normal; it is recorded, for example, by Gil and Hodges. *Grist* has ME ī in Coles; it is of course exactly analogous to *Christ*. *Ditch* (which owes its PresE [ɪ] to shortening before [tʃ]) retains ME ī in Salesbury. *Rich*, Gil says, has ME ī in the Northern dialect. *Bridle* has ĭ in Smith, which may be explained as due to shortening before the syllabic consonant of the second syllable. *Whiter* has ĭ in Bullokar (ME *whitter* < OE *hwītra*). Smith's ĭ in *like* adj. is by analogy from the ME comparative *likker*; his ĭ in *whiles*, which descends from ME (see Vol. I, p. 54), must be explained by shortening in the second element of the compounds (*sumehwiles, oðerhwiles, perhwiles*) in which the word is first found (see *OED*). *Fivepence* has ME ĭ in Coles (whose 'phonetic' spelling is *fĭp-ence*), followed by Strong, Young, and Brown.

(2) *Words from French*

Variation is also recorded in words from French, chiefly by early sources. Bullokar's ĭ in *assign* must be due to pronunciations in which the *gn* was [ŋŋ] or [gŋ] (cf. § 441 below). As I interpret his forms, Bullokar also has (according to Zachrisson's selective word-lists) ĭ four times beside ī six times in *strive*; ĭ once beside ī once in *price*; ī twice in *advice*, but ĭ once beside ī twice in *advise* and ĭ once in *advisedly*; ī thrice in *device*, but ĭ twice beside ī twice in *devise*; and he transcribes *despise* with ī but rhymes it on ĭ.

There is here a suggestion that the short vowel is originally appropriate to the verbs, in which it could develop in ME proparoxytone inflexional forms. Similarly Hart has ĭ in *derived*. The syllabic consonant in the next syllable accounts for Gil's ĭ in *cider*. An alternative explanation, especially for ĭ before [v] in *strive* and *derive*, would be fifteenth-century shortening; cf. § 32.

Variation occurs even in open syllables, where ī would be expected. In words in which the stress shifts, Hart has ĭ in *desirous* (once, beside ī twice) and *ivory*. *Vizor* (*vizard*) has ĭ in Hart and Bullokar. *Tyrant* has ĭ in Bullokar, as have *viage*, *lion* (but Hart has ī), and *Lyons*. *Image* has ME ī beside ĭ in Gil. On *diverse* and *divers* see § 289; the form with [z], presumably stressed on the first, has ĭ in Bullokar, Gil, and Hodges (once, beside ī once), but ī in Robinson. *Victuals* (OF *vitaille*) is clearly shown to have ĭ by Hodges, Wharton (followed by J. Smith), Coles, Strong, Young, Cooper, and the shorthand-writers T. Shelton and Everardt; the pairing with *vitals* in the 'homophone' lists from Hodges ('near alike') onwards, including Cooper's 'near alike' list, must be held to show ĭ in *vitals* (see § 23 (*b*) below). The variation also occurs in words in which the stress does not shift. Hunt pairs the variants *quit* and *quite* (< OF *quite*, &c.; see *OED*) as homophones. Hart gives ĭ once beside ī once in *vice*, which Bullokar rhymes on ĭ. Bullokar has ĭ once beside ī once in *nice*, and ĭ once beside ī once in *guise*. *Require* (< OF, but with $i <$ Latin?) has ĭ once beside ī thrice in Bullokar, and *isle* has ĭ once beside ī twice. Bullokar also seems to rhyme the word *rhyme* on ME ĭ. It should be observed that this evidence, though unexpected in view of PresE pronunciation and treated as erroneous by Jespersen, *Hart*, and Zachrisson, *Bullokar*, is parallel to that which shows variation in the quantity of the English vowels derived from OF *a*, *e*, and *o*; moreover in Hart, who writes *i* for ME ĭ but *ei* for ME ī, there is no question of the mere wrongful omission or inclusion of a mark of quantity.

Note: For further evidence of ME ĭ developed by shortening from and existing beside ME ī see § 138 below, under 'Alleged failure of the diphthongization of ME ī'; it is there also suggested that ME ĭ may have existed beside ME ī in *oblige* (from OF). Hart's transcription *uilī* (in the *Methode*) may well represent *wily* (for which *OED* records -*ll*- spellings from the fifteenth to the seventeenth century); it would then show shortening of ī to ĭ in trisyllabic forms. (Jespersen's guesses 'Willy' and 'will he' are improbable glosses for the word, but Danielsson's 'will ye' is possible.)

VARIATION BETWEEN ME ŏ AND ǭ

§ 13. Variation between ME ŏ and ǭ could arise in consequence of the OE treatment of WGmc ă before *mb*, *nd*, and *ng*, since (*a*) PrOE retraction causes a frequent development to ŏ, and (*b*) if this retraction fails, there can be later OE lengthening of the surviving ă to ā, which will become ME ǭ. But OE ŏ < WGmc ă before a nasal is predominantly Western and Northern, and it is therefore much better to explain StE ŏ in such words as *strong*, &c., and in *among*, *comb*, and *womb* as by ME shortening of Southern and Midland ME ǭ < OE ā by OE lengthening of unretracted PrOE ă (see further under (3) below and § 15); it should be observed that ŏ occurs only before OE lengthening groups, and not before other nasal combinations.

(1) *Lengthening in open syllables*

Variation occurs in a number of words as the result of ME lengthening in open syllables. In some cases the lengthening occurs in disyllabic oblique forms but fails in the monosyllabic nominative. Thus *broth* normally has ŏ from the nominative, as in Bullokar, Hodges, and Coles, but has ME ǭ in the Northerners Levins and Poole and in *WSC-RS* (cf. the spellings cited by *OED*). *Lot*, which normally has ŏ, is recorded with ǭ by Bullokar, again probably because of ME lengthening in the open syllable of oblique forms (cf. the spellings cited by *OED*). *Frost* has ME ǭ in *WSC-RS*. *On* has ME ǭ in Bullokar and apparently in Wharton's and Hunt's 'homophone' lists, and *off* has ME ǭ in *WSC*; on these pronunciations, which develop from ME extended adverbial forms *onne* [ɔnə] and *offe* [ɔfə], see further Vol. I, p. 108. Hart's ŏ in *hoped* (against ǭ in *hope*) is due to failure of lengthening in the ME trisyllabic form. Bullokar gives ŏ in *losing* beside ME ǭ regularly in *lose* vb. (OE *lŏsian*); in the verbal noun lengthening fails in ME trisyllabic forms. Failure of lengthening before a syllabic consonant (perhaps assisted by weak stress) accounts for the ŏ recorded in *over* and its compounds by Hart (twice, beside ǭ once), Bullokar (regularly), and Gil (fourteen times); but Robinson and Hodges have the normal ǭ both in the simple word and its compounds. Hart and Bullokar have ŏ in *open(ing)*; Gil has ŏ in *openly* but ǭ in *open* adj. and vb. *Nostrils* has [oː] in *WSC-RS*, which shows blending of the old word (with ME ŏ) and the new formation *nose-thirls* (cf. *OED*, s.v. *nosethirl*). On variation before *r* see below.

Similar variation occurs in words adopted from French, either because of ME lengthening in open syllables or because in them a shortening which might otherwise be expected fails. One or other of the words *host* has ŏ in Bullokar (beside ǭ), Robinson, and Poole; the stress-shifted *hostess* has ŏ in Robinson. *Boast* (probably from OF; see *OED*) has ŏ in Poole and Strong. *Toast* has ŏ in Coles and Cocker but ǭ in *WSC-RS*. *Cost* has ǭ in Fox and Hookes (see Vol. I, p. 408) and *WSC-RS*. *Reproach* vb. varies between ŏ and ǭ in Bullokar (but the noun has ǭ). Poole (a Northerner) has ŏ in *enthroned* and probably variation between ŏ and ǭ in *coll* (< OF *coler* or *acoler*); see further Vol. I, pp. 430–1. Gil has ŏ in *coll*. Brown, probably a Northerner, has ŏ in *cloak*. *Noble* and *nobleman* have ŏ in Hart (twice, beside ǭ once) and Gil (once, beside ǭ four times), *sober* has ŏ once (beside ǭ once) in Gil but ǭ in Newton, and *soder* 'solder' has ŏ in Gil; in these the syllabic consonant favours the short vowel. Bullokar has $\bar{\varrho}$ in *pomegranate*, despite its being in the first syllable of a trisyllabic compound.

(2) *Variation before* r-*groups*

The variation is most common before *r* plus consonant, where it occurs both in native words and in words adopted from French. In PresE the distinction between ME ŏ and $\bar{\varrho}$ is obliterated before *r*, both having become [ɒ:], but formerly they were distinguished (as they still are in many dialects), ME ŏ being [ɒ:] and ME $\bar{\varrho}$ [oə]; the phonetic transcriptions of *OED*, which are not based on StE (as is shown by the article on the letter *O*), preserve the distinction.

(*a*) *Native words*

These are past participles of verbs of OE second and fourth strong conjugations and analogous ME formations, in which lengthening in the open syllable sometimes occurred and sometimes failed because of the following syllabic *n* (or in the plural forms, e.g. *borne* in contrast to the sing. *boren*). *Forlorn* has ŏ in Gil; *RS* says that it has 'long o', but this probably means [o:] by lengthening of ME ŏ before *r* rather than ME $\bar{\varrho}$. *Torn* has ŏ in Bullokar (beside $\bar{\varrho}$), Gil, and Coles, and ŏ beside [u:] in Young's 'homophone' list (see Vol. I, p. 413); *RS* gives 'long o' (probably by lengthening of ME ŏ) beside [u:] from ME $\bar{\varrho}$ by raising of ME $\bar{\varrho}$. It has ME $\bar{\varrho}$ in Bullokar, Robinson, Hodges, and Cooper. *Shorn* has ŏ in Coles, and varies like *torn* in *RS*. *Born(e)* has ŏ in Robinson, Gil, Wilkins, and Coles, and ME $\bar{\varrho}$ beside ŏ in Hart and Bullokar. But Hodges distinguishes *born* with ŏ from an unglossed *born* (our *borne*) with $\bar{\varrho}$ (cf. Cooper and *WSC-RS*, who make a similar distinction between *born* with ŏ and *borne* with [u:] from late ME $\bar{\varrho}$ by raising of ME $\bar{\varrho}$). This distinction, like that of spelling which accompanies it in Cooper (but not in Hodges and *WSC-RS*), is of course arbitrary. *Sworn* has ŏ in Smith, but $\bar{\varrho}$ in Bullokar, Gil, and Coles. *Worn* has ŏ in Bullokar and Gil, and *RS* gives 'long o' (probably by lengthening of ME ŏ); it has ME $\bar{\varrho}$ in Coles. Similarly *before* (ME *bifŏren*) has ŏ once beside $\bar{\varrho}$ eleven times in Gil.

(*b*) *Words adopted from French*

Here there is some difficulty in distinguishing words which have original ME $\bar{\varrho}$ from those which have original ME $\bar{\varrho}$; but according to Jordan, §§ 227–8, and Luick, § 411, OF *o* when it becomes a long vowel in ME is normally $\bar{\varrho}$, except in the neighbourhood of labials, where it often becomes $\bar{\varrho}$, though even in these circumstances $\bar{\varrho}$ is also found. Applying this rule, we can divide the words as follows.

(i) Words with ME $\bar{\varrho}$ beside ŏ. *Cord* has ŏ in Hodges and $\bar{\varrho}$ in Bullokar, Willis, and Coles; *RS* has 'long o', probably by lengthening of ME ŏ. *Cork* has ŏ in Poole. *Corpse* (originally *corse*) has ŏ in Robinson (who pronounced the *p*), and ǭ in Bullokar and Gil; the 'homophone' lists from that of Hodges onwards equate it with *course*, which may show either [u:] or [o:], both of which in *corpse* ultimately descend from original ME ǭ. On *horde* see § 18; Willis and Poole show ME ǭ. *Sort* has ǒ in Hart, Laneham, Bullokar (beside rarer ǭ), Robinson, Butler, and Hodges, and ǭ in Bullokar and Coles. *Resort* has ǒ in Gil. *Scorn* has ǒ in Hart, Bullokar (beside ǭ), Gil, Hodges, and Coles, ME ǭ in Bullokar, and 'long o' (probably lengthened ME ǒ) in *RS*. The variation also occurs when the *r* is followed by a consonant which belongs to the next syllable (cf. *pierce*, which is disyllabic in ME but varies between ĕ and ẹ̄); *order* has ǒ in Bullokar, Gil, and Hodges, but ǭ in the Northerner Brown (see Vol. I, p. 418). It is this that accounts for the variation in *glory*, for in OF *glorie* the *i* was consonantal (as also originally in ME *glorie*). The word has ǒ in Hart, Bullokar, Robinson, Hodges, and probably Wilkins (Vol. I, p. 261), and ǭ in Gil and Lodwick. Cooper says that the word is pronounced with either '*o* or α'; the former means [o:] from ME ǭ, the latter either ǒ (as is more likely) or [ɒ:] by lengthening of ME ǒ. *RS*'s 'long o' is ambiguous, as it may either represent ME ǭ or be developed by lengthening of ME ǒ; but in this word the latter is unlikely, as *RS* otherwise shows the lengthening only before *r* plus consonant. On *glorious* see (3) below.

(ii) Words which in ME have either ǭ or ǭ beside ǒ. In these words, sixteenth-century evidence of [o:] shows ME ǭ, but seventeenth-century evidence (from that of Robinson and Gil onwards) is ambiguous, since in the seventeenth century [o:] may either represent ME ǭ or arise by lowering before *r* of earlier [u:] < ME ǭ. *Force* has ǒ in Hart, Bullokar, and Gil, beside ME ǭ in Hart and Bullokar and the ambiguous [o:] in Gil (once only in the 1621 edition, where 1619 has ǒ), Butler (possibly), Hodges, and Coles. *Forge* has ǒ in Gil and ǭ in Bullokar; [o:] occurs in Hodges and Coles. Bullokar gives ǭ in *form* vb. (beside much more frequent ǒ) and in *perform* (varying with both ǒ and ǔ). *Porch* has ǒ in Bullokar and [o:] in Gil, Hodges, and Coles; Cooper says that it varies between '*o*', i.e. [o:], and 'α', either ǒ (as is probable) or [ɒ:] by lengthening of ME ǒ before *r*. *Port* has [o:] in Hodges and Coles. *Report* has ǒ in Gil and [o:] in Hodges and Newton. *Sport* has ǒ beside ǭ in Bullokar, ǒ in Gil, and [o:] in Coles. *Fork* has ǒ in Poole. *Fort* has ǒ in Gil. *Pork* has ǒ in Poole and [o:] in Hodges and Coles. *Portion* has ǒ in Bullokar and [o:] in Hodges; cf. *glory* and *order* above.

(3) *ME shortening*

Variation between ǭ and ǒ because of ME shortening occurs in certain words. *Holy* has ǒ (by shortening in trisyllabic inflected forms) in Hart, Bullokar, and Hodges's 'near alike' list (which is followed by Fox and Hookes and by Brown), and ǭ in Gil, Hodges *EP*, and the 'homophone' lists of Strong, Cooper, and Aickin. Hart similarly gives ǒ in *wholly* but not in *whole* (Jespersen, *Hart*, § 39), but in these words he shows a *w*-glide; see further § 431 below. Hart (Jespersen, op. cit., § 26) and Gil give ŏ beside ǭ in *only*. *Homely* has ŏ in Hodges's 'near alike' list, followed by Fox and Hookes. *Lord* has ŏ (by shortening in trisyllabic forms of the uncontracted *loverd* rather than by shortening before the consonant-group) in Hart, Bullokar (beside more frequent ǭ), Gil, Robinson, and Hodges, [ʊ:] < ŏ in Coles, and 'long o', probably by lengthening of ME ŏ, in *RS*; but ME ǭ occurs in Smith and Bullokar and is the source of the long vowel (probably [o:]) shown by the rhymes of Willis and Poole. Shortening is almost invariable before the consonant-group *ng* in *strong*, *long*, &c., but Gil has ǭ once beside ŏ eleven times in *among*. Before *nd* pronunciations developed from ME ǭ are very rare, but ŏ by shortening occurs in *bond* and sporadically in other words (see § 71). Before *mb* shortening is not common; *comb* has ŏ in Bullokar, Butler, and Poole (see Vol. I, p. 430), but ǭ normally (as, for example, in Coles), and *womb* has ŏ in Bullokar and Butler, but [o:] < ME ǭ in Daines, Poole (beside [u:]), and Coles. *Most* has ŏ in Hart (regularly) and in Poole (cf. ĕ in *east*). Gil gives ŏ twice beside ǭ once in the second syllable of *Cotswold*, and says further that the name is vulgarly pronounced *Cotsal*. *Forehead* has ŏ by shortening in the first element of a compound in PresE, but Bullokar gives ǭ (perhaps only because of the etymological connexion with *fore*). The trisyllabic *glorious* is recorded only with ŏ, by Bullokar, Robinson, Gil, and Hodges; contrast *glory*, which shows variation (see 2 (*b*) (i) above). *OED* gives [oə] in *glorious*, but in view of the sixteenth- and seventeenth-century evidence this looks like an artificial pronunciation on the analogy of [oə] from the variant ME ǭ in *glory*.

Note 1: Of the words included under 2 (*b*) (ii) above, only *force*, *forge*, and *porch* are recorded with [u:], which is likely to descend from original ME ǭ. But in both native and French words ME ǭ is sometimes raised in ME to ME ǭ, and therefore in some of the words cited under 2 (*a*) and 2 (*b*) (i) above we also find variation between ME ŏ and ME ǭ; see further §§ 15–16 below. In the seventeenth century, in consequence of the lowering of [u:] < ME ǭ to [o:] (the equivalent of ME ǭ) before *r*, an apparent variation between ME ŏ and ME ǭ results in native words which in fact varied in ME only between ME ŏ and ME ǭ. On the other pronunciations of *form* and *perform* see §§ 17 and 19 below.

Note 2: Poole shows a long vowel which is probably due to the survival of a ME long vowel (but might be by lengthening of ME ŏ before *r*; see Vol. I, p. 432) in *accord*, *record*, *disgorge*, *scorn* (which in ME can only have ǭ as a long vowel) and in *afford*, *force*, *remorse*, and *forge* (which in ME can have ǭ beside ǭ).

Note 3: For the view that ŏ in *strong*, &c., *among*, *comb*, and *womb* is by ME shortening cf. § 7 above. For evidence of ModE [u:] in *comb* and *womb* (which is ultimately from ME ǭ) see § 15 below. Zachrisson and Eichler doubt respectively Bullokar's and Butler's ŏ in *womb*, but there is no reason why it should not be accepted.

VARIATION BETWEEN ME ŏ AND ME *ou*

§ 14. Shortening of ME *ou* produces ME ŏ, and occasionally there is variation between the two. *Forty* (ME *fourty* < OE *fēowertig*) has ŏ in Gil, Butler, Cooper (probably), *WSC-RS*, and Brown; but Hodges gives [o:] <

ME *ou* (perhaps owing to the analogy of [oː] < ME *ou* in *four*) and Cheke seems to have [uː] < ME *ū*, a special variant of ME *ou* in this word (see § 173). *Knowledge* has *ŏ* by shortening in Hart (twice only), Hodges, and Brown, but [ou] in Gil and [oː] < ME *ou* in Hart (six times). The evidence of Bullokar (whose spelling may be intended merely to show the derivation) and of Strong (who says that in *knowledge* the *ow* is pronounced as *o*, but so likewise in *know*) is of uncertain value. *Slothful* has *ŏ* in Hart but *ou* in Bullokar (as has *sloth*, spelt *slowth*; Willis has [oː] < ME *ou* in *sloth*).

Moth has ME *ŏ* (< OE *mŏððe*) in Butler and Hodges, but is rhymed on [oːþ] by Levins, followed by Willis and Poole; this pronunciation represents the fourteenth-century *mouȝthe* (with ME *ou*) < OE *mŏhðe* (see *OED*). A variant of the latter is the pronunciation [moːt] < fourteenth-century *moȝte, moughte* < OE *mŏhðe* (cf. *height* < *hēhðu*); this is shown by the 'homophone' list pairing with *mote* and *moat* given by Wharton, Fox and Hookes, Cooper ('near alike'), Cocker, and Brown (who gives '*moth* in the sun'; cf. the spelling *moth* 'mote' *Hen. V*, IV. i. 189 cited by *OED*, s.v. *mote* sb.[1], and see further Onions, *Shakespeare Glossary*, s.v. *mote*).

Note 1: On analogical ME *ou* (shown by Gil) beside *ŏ* and *ọ̄* in *fourth* see § 16 (*a*) below.

Note 2: ModE [oː] in *moth* is explained as above by Luick, § 555, Anm. 2, and by Onions, 'The Plural of Nouns ending in *-th*' (S.P.E. Tract LXI), p. 27, footnote 3. Onions regards the *oa* of the spelling *moath* (used by Lyly in *Euphues*) as 'extraordinary', but it shows identification of ME *ou* with ME *ọ̄* by monophthongization (cf. e.g. *shrode* 'shrewd' < ME *shrow(e)d*).

VARIATION BETWEEN ME *ŏ* AND *ọ̄*

§ 15. Variation between ME *ŏ* and *ọ̄* occurs before an OE lengthening-group in *gold*, for which Cocker gives [uː] < ME *ọ̄*, but which in other orthoepists has pronunciations descended from ME *ŏl*.

Late OE or early ME shortening under weak stress accounts for *ŏ* in *other*. See § 4 above on Hart's *ŏ* in *other* 'or' and in *nother* 'neither' (OE *nōðer*). Gil regularly transcribes (*an*)*other* with *ŏ*, saying that he is following the 'docti' but that we more frequently use *ŭ*; Hodges has *ŏ* in *another* and *other* (once in each word, beside *ŭ* 26 times in all), but in his case there may well be accidental omission of a diacritic. Gil's *ŏ* in *brother* (once, beside *ŭ* five times and once in *brotherhood*) might develop in the OE plural forms *brōðro* (nom.), *brōðra, brōðrum* by shortening before the consonant-group, but may well be an imperfect transcription influenced by the conventional spelling. Otherwise these words have ME *ọ̄* or ME *ŭ* by later (ME) shortening.

In *comb* and *womb*, which have variation between ME *ŏ* by shortening of *ǭ* before the consonant-group and unshortened *ǭ* < late OE *ā* by lengthening of PrOE *ă* (see § 13 above), there also develops in later ME a variant in *ọ̄* by raising of ME *ǭ*. *Comb* has [uː] < late ME *ọ̄* in Fox and Hookes and perhaps in *WSC-RS*, and *womb* has [uː] in Levins, Butler, Hodges, Poole (beside [oː] < late ME ǭ), Strong, Young, Cooper, *WSC*, and Brown.

Note: For evidence of ME ŏ and ME ǫ̆ in *comb* and *womb* see § 13 (3). It is highly unlikely that in either word the ModE [uː] goes back to late OE ō by lengthening of PrOE ŏ < WGmc ă before a nasal, since there is no evidence that StE has any pronunciations developed from such an OE ō. Raising of ME ǫ̆ to ǭ in the phonetic conditions of *womb* is a normal process; in such words as *comb* it is not normal in StE but was found in vulgar and dialectal speech, and both Fox and Hookes and *WSC-RS* give much evidence that is based on vulgar pronunciation.

Variation before r

§ 16. Apart from these cases, the variation is recorded only before *r*, in two classes of words: (1) those that have original ME ǭ, and (2) those that have later ME ǭ by raising of original ME ǫ̆. The variation between ME ŏ and ME ǭ has, in these words in which *r* follows, been obliterated in present StE, ŏ having been lengthened to [ɒː] and [uː] < ME ǭ lowered to [oː] and thence to [ɒː], but it survives as a distinction between [ɒː] and [oə] in many dialects, which *OED*'s phonetic transcriptions record (e.g. *sword* is recorded as having both [ɒː] and [oə], which shows the survival in this word of the ME variation between ŏ and ǭ).

(a) *Words with original ME* ǭ

From the early seventeenth century onwards [uː] from ME ǭ is often lowered to [oː], the equivalent of ME ǫ̆, because of the following *r*; in the seventeenth-century orthoepists (from Robinson and Gil onwards) cited below, [oː] must then be understood to show ME ǭ as influenced by the lowering, and not ME ǫ̆.

(i) Native words. *Board* has [uː] in Salesbury, Levins, Bullokar, Butler, Merriott, and Cooper, and [oː] in Gil, Hodges, Price, and Coles, and probably also in the 'homophone' lists from that of Wharton onwards, in which it is equated with *bor'd*. But Cooper relegates this pairing to his 'near alike' list, clearly because he himself used [uː] in *board* (which he spells *boord*) but [oː] in *bor'd*. *Hoard* has ŏ in Cheke (beside [uː]), [uː] in Cheke, Levins, Wharton, Price, and *WSC-RS*, and [oː] in Robinson, Willis, and Coles. *Ford* has [uː] in Mulcaster, Price, and *WSC-RS*, and [oː] in Hodges and Coles. *Sword* (see Note 3) has [uː] in Levins, possibly Laneham (but his spelling with *oo* is perhaps ambiguous, since he uses *oo* occasionally for ME ŭ), Butler, and Cooper; it has [oː] in Coles. *Word* has ŏ in Levins, Bullokar, and Gil (in the last two, beside ŭ; see § 18), but apparently [uː] in Salesbury, who spells it *woorde*. *Forth* has ŏ in Hart, Gil (1619 edition, once), and Daines, [uː] in Cheke, Laneham, Bullokar (beside ŭ), Mulcaster (beside ŭ), Gil, Butler, Cooper, and *WSC-RS*, and [oː] in Robinson, Gil (1621 edition, once, where 1619 has ŏ), Daines (beside ŏ), Hodges, and Coles; it has ŭ in Hart (beside ŏ), Bullokar, and Mulcaster (see § 92 below). The 'homophone' lists from Hodges onwards, which equate the word with *fourth*, are ambiguous, for *fourth* itself varies (see below). *Afford* (OE *geforðian*) has [u:] in Butler, Wharton (followed by J. Smith), Price, and *WSC-RS*, and [o:] in Bullokar; but this long vowel identified with ME *ǭ* is less likely to arise from [u:] < ME *ǭ* by lowering before *r* (for which there is no clear evidence in Bullokar) than by lengthening of ME *ŏ* (see §§ 45–48 below). Mulcaster and Poole give *ŭ*, which is open to the same alternative explanations as in *forth* (see § 92). *Thorn* has ME *ǭ* in Young (see Vol. I, p. 413), and *ŏ* beside the ambiguous [o:] in Bullokar. *Morn* has *ŏ* in Bullokar and Coles (cf. Hodges's *ŏ* in *morning*). In all these words the variation results from the operation or failure of OE lengthening; but in *fourth* it results from shortening in ME *fōrþe* < OE *fēorða*, *ŏ* being recorded by Hart, [u:] by *RS*, and [o:] by Hodges and *WSC* (see Vol. I, pp. 362–3). This [o:] is probably by lowering of [u:]; but it might be from ME *ou*, which Gil records and which is due to the analogical influence of *four*.

(ii) Words adopted from French. In the following words, [u:] probably represents ME *ǭ* (though it could be from original ME *ǭ*, raised to *ǭ* in later ME). *Border(er)* has [u:] in Hart and Laneham, but *ŏ* in Bullokar and perhaps also in Butler. *Force* has [u:] in Wharton (followed by J. Smith), Cooper, and *WSC-RS*, and possibly in Bullokar, who transcribes it with [o:] but rhymes it (on [u:]?) with *course*. *Forge* and *porch* have [u:] in *WSC-RS*. For the evidence of the *ŏ* variant in these last three words see § 13 (2b).

(b) *Words with original ME ǭ*

ME *ǭ* is sometimes raised to *ǭ* in later ME, so that a variation between ME *ŏ* and *ǭ* may become one between *ŏ* and *ǭ*.

(i) **Native words.** *Torn* and *shorn* have [u:] in *RS*, beside 'long *o*', probably by lengthening of ME *ŏ*; *torn* seems also to have [u:] (beside *ŏ*) in Young's 'homophone' list (see Vol. I, p. 413). Cooper and *WSC-RS* make the variation in pronunciation, as well as (in Cooper) in spelling, in *born(e)* correspond to a distinction of sense. Cooper twice distinguishes *borne* with [u:] from *born* with '*o* guttural', i.e. ME *ŏ* (whether or not lengthened); *RS* gives [u:] for *born* (so spelt; glossed 'supported') and 'long *o*' (ME *ŏ* lengthened) for *born* (glossed 'past birth'). (Cf. the distinction made by Hodges; see § 13 (2a).) *Sworn* and *worn* have [u:] in Hodges and Cooper; here the [w] aids the raising. For the evidence of ME *ŏ* in these words see § 13 (2a).

(ii) **Words adopted from French.** *Corpse* (originally *corse*) has [u:] in Hodges, and *sort* and *glory* seem to have [u:] in Cheke, if we may rely on his spellings with *oo*. For evidence of ME *ŏ* in these words see § 13 (2b). On *horde* (in which Levins has [u:]) see § 18.

Note 1: According to the accepted view, late OE lengthening does not occur before [rþ] as in *forth*, but the early ModE evidence, coming from so many different sources, leaves no doubt that ME ǭ did occur in this word, and there seems no other way of explaining it than by OE lengthening. The way out is doubtless to assume that the lengthening occurred in the verb *forth* < OE *forðian* (which would have [rð] and not [rþ]) and was thence extended by analogy to the adverb. On *forth* and *afford* see also § 92, Note 2.

Note 2: The rhymes of Willis and Poole show a long vowel (either [u:] or [o:]) descended from ME ǭ in the following words: *board, ford* (Willis), *morn* (Poole), *sword, word* (both authors). Similarly the 'homophone' lists from that of Hodges onwards show a long vowel in *morning* by pairing it with *mourning*.

Note 3: Jordan, § 66, Anm. 3, appears to regard ME *swǭrd* as derived from Old Northumbrian *swǭrd*, which shows the Northumbrian change of *weor* to *wor* and subsequent lengthening. In ME the form is rare in Southern and Midland texts, but occurs beside *swerd* in *Libeaus Desconnus* (in rhyme, ll. 168 seq.). On Jordan's view, the form with ME ǭ must show Northern influence on London English. (The lack of either a preceding palatal or a following *w* (see Bülbring, § 325) makes it improbable that OE stress-shift is the explanation.) Bullokar gives ME ĕ in the word; for evidence of ŭ see § 18.

Note 4: Seventeenth-century [u:] in *form* and *perform* is from ME ū rather than ME ǭ, though the latter is possible; see further § 17 below.

VARIATION BETWEEN ME ŏ AND ū

§ 17. Variation between ME ŏ and ū results, in a sense accidentally, in two words of French origin because of the existence of variants in OF. The variation between OF *forme* and *fourme* is reflected by greater variation in English (cf. *OED* and Pope, § 582); from *forme* can come ME forms with ŏ and ǭ (and possibly ǭ, in view of the preceding labial), and from *fourme* can come both ME ŭ and ū. Sixteenth- and seventeenth-century [u:] probably represents ME ū, retained undiphthongized before *r*, but it could represent ME ǭ; one cannot say, however, that there is clear evidence for the latter. The pronunciation with [u:] is shown for *form* by Hodges and Wharton, and was probably that of Cheke and Laneham, though their spelling *foorm* might possibly indicate ME ŭ. Bullokar (except for one transcription with ǭ), Hodges (in most cases), and Coles give ŏ. Attempts were made to make this variation between ME ŏ and [u:] conform to differences of meaning: Cooper would distinguish *foorm* (with [u:]) 'seat, hare's seat' from *fǫrm* (with ME ŏ, whether lengthened or not) 'shape' (*WSC* follows to the extent of glossing *form* with [u:] 'form to sit on'), and *OED* quotes Todd 1818—who is in fact following Walker (cf. Kauter, *Hodges*, § 46), Nares, and Elphinston—as giving [foərm] 'seat, class in a school, lair of a hare' and [fɒ:rm] (with [ɒ:] < ME ŏ) for all other senses. Mulcaster also seems to distinguish the pronunciation with ŏ from another variant, that with ME ŭ; see § 19 below. *Perform* shows the same variation in OF and ME as *form* (cf. the spellings cited by *OED*), but only *WSC* gives evidence of [u:] < ME ū; Bullokar has ŏ (beside ME ǭ and ME ŭ), as has Hodges.

Note: For the pronunciations of *form* and *perform* with ME ǭ and with ME ŭ see respectively § 13, under 2 (*b*) (ii), and § 19.

VARIATION BETWEEN ME ŭ AND ǭ

§ 18. Variation between ME ŭ and ME ǭ occurs chiefly in consequence of the irregular lengthening of ME ŭ to late ME ǭ in open syllables. *Love* has [u:] in Levins, Smith, Hart, Bullokar (beside ŭ), Butler (once, beside ŭ; Eichler regards this single case as an error, but without justification), and Newton (beside [ʌ]). It has ŭ in Mulcaster (see Vol. I, pp. 123-4), Bullokar, and sixteen seventeenth-century orthoepists. *Above* has [u:] in Levins and Hart (beside ŭ), but ŭ in Hart, Bullokar, Mulcaster, and eight seventeenth-century sources. *Dove*, which I take to have ME ŭ beside ū (see § 39, Note 3), has [u:] in Levins, Bullokar, and perhaps Butler (beside ŭ), but ŭ in Mulcaster, Robinson, Sherwood, Hodges, Willis, Coles, and *WSC-RS*. *Come* has [u:] in Levins (beside ŭ), Hodges (once only out of twenty-five occurrences), and Newton (beside [ʌ]), but ŭ in Levins, Hart, Bullokar, Coote, Robinson, Butler, and Hodges. *Some* has [u:] in Newton, otherwise ŭ. *Wood* has [u:] in the *ABC for chyldren* and Newton (beside [u]), but ŭ in Smith, Bullokar, and ten seventeenth-century sources.

Shortening of ME ǭ to ME ŭ is the converse of the lengthening of ŭ to ǭ in open syllables, and is to be regarded as the normal ME process when ǭ is shortened (cf. shortening of ME ẹ̄ to ĭ, discussed in § 11 above). In *month* shortening to ŭ before the consonant-group is regular; ŭ is recorded by, for example, Bullokar, Gil, and Butler. In *mother*, *brother*, and *other* the shortening may be explained either from the trisyllabic oblique forms (but there is no secondary stress) or from the influence of the syllabic consonant in the following syllable. *Mother* retains [u:] < ME ǭ in Hart (once, beside ŭ thrice), but has ŭ in Hart, Bullokar, Mulcaster, Robinson, and Gil. *Brother* is recorded only with ŭ, e.g. in Tonkis, Gil (who also has ŏ once, possibly by error), and Hodges. *Other* retains [u:] in Smith and Hart, but has ŭ in Smith, Hart (normally), Tonkis, Robinson, Gil (who says it is the common form, though he follows the 'docti', who say oðer, in his transcriptions), Hodges, and Cooper. (On other forms of the word see § 15 above.) Shortening in the first syllable of a compound occurs in *twopence* (given as *tuppence* in the 'phonetically spelt' lists of Coles, Strong, and Young), in which ME ǭ is from earlier wǭ.

In two native words the variation is due to special causes. *Sword* (see § 16, Note 3) has [u:] < ME ǭ in Levins, Laneham (possibly), Butler, and Cooper and [o:] by lowering in Coles (see § 16 (*a*) above), but ŭ (< late WS *swurd*; cf. Bülbring, § 268) in Mulcaster, Gil, Butler, Hodges, Poole (beside [u:] or [o:] < ME ǭ), and Price. *Word* seems to have [u:] in Salesbury (see § 16 (*a*), where is given evidence for ME ŏ), and has ŭ (< late WS *wurd*; cf. Bülbring, § 281) in Bullokar (beside ŏ), Mulcaster, and ten seventeenth-century sources. The evidence of Hart and Wharton (who is followed by J. Smith) is ambiguous, but probably refers to ŭ.

Variation between ME *ŭ* and *ǭ* is recorded only in one non-native word, *horde*, which comes immediately from French and shows much variation because in its ultimate source, Turkī, there was already variation (see *OED*). Turkī *urdu* must ultimately underlie a form with ME *ŭ* recorded by Mulcaster. Turkī *orda*, however, would ultimately give rise to an OF form with *o*, whence would arise either ME *ŏ* (not recorded) or ME *ǭ* (which may be taken to be the basis of the [o:] shown by Willis and Poole); and this *ǭ* could be raised in ME to *ọ̄*, which would account for Levins's *hoord*.

Note 1: For further instances of [u:] < ME *ǭ* by lengthening of ME *ŭ* (existing as a variant beside ME *ū*) see § 167 below (under 'Alleged cases of the failure of diphthongization of ME *ū*'). Butler mentions a Western form which he spells *stoor*' (i.e. [stu:r]) instead of StE *stur* 'stir'; it must develop by lengthening in the open syllable of a late ME (Western) *stüren* < OE *stўrian*.

Note 2: Hodges's [ʊ] (not [ʌ]), which he normally has for ME *ŭ*) in *month* and *mother* is to be taken as representing ME *ŭ*, preserved from unrounding by the preceding bilabial [m], and is not by late (ModE) shortening of [u:] < ME *ǭ*, since (a) the only evidence of failure of early shortening in these two words is Hart's [u:] in *mother*, and (b) Hodges himself has [ʌ] by early shortening in *brother*, which is exactly analogous to *mother* except for the lack of a labial consonant before the vowel. There are, it is true, no other instances in Hodges of [m] exercising a rounding influence on ME *ŭ*, but it is *a priori* not unlikely, the other bilabials [w], [p], and [b] all do.

Note 3: In *churl*, which normally has *ŭ* < Western ME [y] < OE *ĕo* (cf. Luick, § 397), Bullokar once gives a vowel identified with ME *ǭ* (beside *ŭ* four times). His long variant could be [o:] by lowering of [u:] < ME *ǭ* (< late OE *eō* by stress-shift < *ēo* by OE lengthening < *ĕo*), but there is no certain evidence in Bullokar of lowering of [u:] to [o:] before *r* (cf. the discussion of his [o:] in *afford*, § 16 (a) above). On the other hand there is undoubted evidence of a lengthening, in his speech, of ME *ŏ* before *r* plus consonant to identity with ME *ǭ* (see §§ 45–48 below), and it would therefore seem better to refer his long variant in *churl* to ME *ŏ*, which we could explain from unlengthened OE *ĕo* by assuming stress-shift to the *o*.

VARIATION BETWEEN ME *ŭ* AND *ū*

§ 19. Evidence of variation between ME *ŭ* and ME *ū* is given by the orthoepists in comparatively few words, though the spelling shows that there must formerly have been a long vowel in words which now have a short. In native words before OE lengthening groups ME *ū* is invariably recorded in *hound*, *pound*, *ground*, &c.; but *mourn* has *ŭ* in Willis and Poole (against normal ME *ū* in, for example, Bullokar, who has both [ʌu] and [u:], Robinson, who has [o:], and Hodges, who has [ʊ:]), and *young* has invariably *ŭ*. *Turn* (OE *turnian*, reinforced in ME by OF *tourner*) has normally *ŭ* (so Bullokar, Robinson, Gil, Hodges, and Newton), but seems to have [u:] in Young's 'homophone' list (see Vol. I, p. 413). On *coomb* see § 164; Butler probably has *ŭ*, in contrast to PresE [u:] < ME *ū*. Shortening occurs in the first element of the compound *housewife* (cf. *husband*), for which *ŭ* is recorded by Laneham, Hodges, and Brown; the pronunciation [hauswaif] is a re-formation. Shortening in trisyllabic forms (with secondary stress) accounts for Bullokar's *ŭ* in *thousand*, but ME *ū* is recorded by Hart, Robinson, Gil, Hodges, and Brown. *Curd* (ME *crud*, of unknown origin) and *bunch* (a ME word, probably echoic) have a long vowel in Levins, which suggests that originally they had ME *ū* and that the *ŭ*-forms show shortening.

In words adopted from French there is equally little variation in each word, but there is variation between words of the same type. *Found* vb. (< OF *fonder*) and *founder* have *ŭ* in Bullokar, but normal *ū* in Gil. Before *rn* the equivalent of ME *ū* is given in *adorn* by Laneham and in *bourn* by Bullokar, Hodges, and Cooper; but ME *ŭ* is given in *adjourn* by Price, Cooper, *The Protestant Tutor*, and *WSC-RS*, and in *sojourn* by Robinson, Hodges, Price, *WSC-RS*, and Brown. *Gourd* regularly has ME *ū*. Before [rdʒ], an OE lengthening-group, ME *ŭ* occurs in *scourge* in Butler, Newton, Cooper, *The Compendious School-Master*, *WSC-RS*, and Brown, but ME *ū* in Poole; ME *ŭ* is normal in *surge*, but Laneham has [ʌu] < ME *ū*. Before *rs* ME *ū* is recorded in *source* by Cooper and in *(dis-), (con-)course* by Hart, Bullokar, Gil, Butler, Hodges, Wallis, Poole, Cooper, and *WSC-RS*, but Brown has ME *ŭ* (see Vol. I, p. 418); *nurse* has normally *ŭ*, but Poole has [u:] beside *ŭ*. *Count* has regularly ME *ū*; *fount*, however, has *ŭ* in Poole. *Court* has ME *ū* in Bullokar, Robinson, Gil, Hodges, Coles, and Cooper, but *ŭ* in Poole. *Form* has *ŭ* in Levins, Mulcaster, and Poole; Mulcaster gives also what he treats as a distinct word with *ŏ*, but without gloss to explain the sense-distinction intended. *Perform* has *ŭ* in Bullokar and *conform* in Coles, *Eng.-Lat. Dict*. Evidence of ME *ū* in these last three words is given in § 17 above; they also have ME *ŏ* (see § 17). *OED* records ME spellings which show *ŭ* beside *ū* in *form* and *perform* (q.v.). When the syllable-division breaks the consonant-group, ME *ŭ* is the rule; it occurs invariably in *journey*, *journal*, and *attorney*. But before *n* ME *ū* occurs in *counter* and *countenance* (in spite of the latter's being trisyllabic); in *country* the fact that another consonant immediately follows causes the vowel to be ME *ŭ*, which is invariably recorded. Cooper's *ŭ* in *scoundrel* (a sixteenth-century adoption of unknown origin) is to be similarly explained; the present [au] is due to development on the model of *pound*, &c. In syllables that were sometimes treated as open and sometimes as closed, variation occurs in *touch*, which has the equivalent of ME *ū* in Levins (beside *ŭ*), Hart (beside *ŭ*), Laneham, Bullokar (once, beside *ŭ*), Gil (beside *ŭ*), Butler (beside *ŭ*; see Vol. I, p. 163), Poole (beside *ŭ*), Strong, and *RS* (against *ŭ* in *WSC*), and ME *ŭ* in Robinson, Hodges, Price, the *Welsh Breviary*, Coles, Richardson, *The Compendious School-Master*, Cocker, *WSC*, and Brown; but when the second syllable contains a syllabic consonant *ŭ* is almost invariable, as in *trouble*, *cousin*, and *dozen*, and similarly in *double* (which, however, has ME *ū* beside *ŭ* in Salesbury) and *couple* (which has ME *ū* in Smith). Words which in ME were trisyllabic normally have $\breve{u}$; so *courteous, courtesy* (but Laneham has [ʌu] beside [ʊ]; Bullokar uses his symbol for ME $\bar{u}$, but it may be merely to show the derivation from *court*—cf. his [ʌu] in *abundance*), and *courtesan*. *Courtier*, however, is recorded (e.g. by Robinson) with ME $\bar{u}$ owing to the influence of *court*. *Nourish(ment)* has usually $\breve{u}$, but Bullokar gives [ʌu] < ME $\bar{u}$ twice (beside $\breve{u}$ thrice). *Flourish* and *courage* have normally $\breve{u}$, but the former has [ʌu] beside $\breve{u}$ in Bullokar and the latter has [ʌu] beside $\breve{u}$ in Hart (once each) and [u:] beside [ʌu] (both from ME $\bar{u}$) in Gil; Wharton, followed by J. Smith, distinguishes these two words (in which *ou* is said to be pronounced *oo*, i.e. [u:] < ME $\bar{u}$) from those in which it is pronounced *u* (i.e. ME $\breve{u}$).

Note: Variation between ME $\breve{u}$ and $\bar{u}$ must be assumed in certain words which normally have ME $\bar{u}$ but in eModE are recorded with [u:] < late ME $\bar{o}$ < ME $\breve{u}$ by lengthening in open syllables; see § 167 below (under 'Alleged failure of diphthongization of ME $\bar{u}$').

VARIATION IN WORDS WITH OF [y], [yi], AND [oi]

§ 20. OF [y] normally gives ME [y:] or [iu], but in positions where English would commonly have a short vowel it can undergo shortening; thus OF *fust* 'a cask' gives ModE *fust* and *fusty* (see *OED*, s.vv.), and similarly OF *duc* 'duke' (which has a closed syllable) gives a form with ME $\breve{u}$ which is shown by the 'homophone' list pairing with *duck* (Young, Cocker, and Brown). Brown also gives *cure* as a homophone of *cur*.

OF [yi] in *fruit* normally gives ME [y:] or [iu], but Bullokar rhymes *fruit* on ME $\breve{\imath}$, either because of a process of shortening and unrounding or because of a ME development of [yi] to [wi]; see further Vol. I, p. 110.

Boistious, which is to be taken as having OF oi (see § 255, Note 1) has $\breve{u}$ once beside [ɔi] once in Bullokar; the form with $\breve{u}$ is best explained as being due to direct shortening of [oi] to [ʊ] (cf. ME shortening of [o:] (ME $\bar{o}$) to [ʊ]), though it might be due to the analogy of ME $\breve{u}$ beside analogical [ɔi] in *fust, foist* 'a winecask'.

QUANTITY VARIATIONS IN LEARNED ADOPTIONS

§ 21. Words adopted from Latin (including those of ultimately Greek origin) and 'learned' OF words (which for our immediate purpose are not distinguishable from words taken direct from Latin, and were probably regarded as if they were directly from Latin) show similar quantity variations to those of native words and words from OF; but the principles determining the quantity in individual words show some special features, and they therefore require separate treatment. It is of first importance to observe that the natural English quantities of such words bear no relation to the original Latin quantities; the determining factor is the quantities used in the traditional English pronunciation of Latin, and these really depend on the analogy of the quantities developed in native English words, or rather of those used in ME adoptions from OF (which in turn depend on native models, but show some special features, as we have seen). But in some words the natural English quantities are subsequently altered artificially owing to the influence of the original Latin quantities; in particular there is a tendency always to use ME ẹ̄ (i.e. PresE [i:]) as the representative of Latin *ae* and Greek *oe*. It is necessary to distinguish words in which the stress in English remains on the syllable which bore it in Latin (i.e. in the traditional English pronunciation of Latin) from those in which it is shifted to an earlier syllable. In each case, however, the general principle is that the vowel retains the quantity which it had had in the English pronunciation of Latin. In closed syllables the vowel was always short, and remained so in English; variation occurs only in open syllables.

(1) *Words in which the stress does not shift*

§ 22. (*a*) Disyllabic words normally have long vowels in open syllables, in accord with the analogy of most words from French (which largely depend on the analogy of the long vowel existing in open syllables in the great majority of native disyllables in later ME); thus Hodges gives ME ī in *finis*. But we have seen that words from OF can show a short variant in eModE even in open syllables of words which were disyllabic in ME; and the same applies, though comparatively rarely, to words adopted from Latin. In some cases it might be argued that this short variant is due to the original Latin quantity, but it also occurs in words which have a long vowel in Latin; we must therefore rather regard the short variant as showing a naturally developed pronunciation which is independent of Latin quantity and is strictly comparable to the similar short variant in words from OF. Thus ME ă occurs in *Cato* (Lat ă) in Bullokar (five times), *Naso* (Lat ā), *Thales* (Lat ă), and *Thraso* (Lat ă) in Bullokar, and *Plato* (Lat ă) in Gil (but ā in Bullokar). ME ĕ occurs in *Eva* 'Eve' (Lat ē) in Hart (twice; not understood by Jespersen), *Venus* (Lat ĕ) in Bullokar and Gil (but ẹ̄ in Robinson), *Ceres* (Lat ĕ) in Bullokar, *Caesar* in Gil (five times, beside ẹ̄ once; Robinson ẹ̄), and *Phoebus* in Gil. ME ŏ occurs in *Moses* (Lat ō) in Hart (but ǭ in Gil and Hodges), *folio* (Lat *fŏlĭō*, disyllabic) in Hart, and *Protheus* (Lat ō, disyllabic) in Bullokar. ME ŭ occurs exceptionally for Lat ū in *Cuma* 'Cumae' in Bullokar (thrice); cf. ŭ for OF [y] in Brown's *cure* (see § 20 above).

(*b*) Words with two syllables after that which bears the stress regularly have a short vowel, in accordance with native analogues. *Phalaris* (Lat ă) has ă in Bullokar, *Constantinople* (Lat *-ŏpŏlis*) has ŏ in Gil, and *Oedipus* and *Daedalus* have ĕ in RS. In the last two the modern pronunciation is due to the tendency, remarked on above, to use ME ẹ̄ as an automatic representative of Latin *ae* and Greek *oe*, regardless of phonetic context; Lye already has $\bar{e}$ in *Oedipus*. PresE [ou] < ME $\bar{\varrho}$ in *Constantinople* is due to the suffix being disyllabic in English; Gil's *ŏ* could also be explained from this anglicized form, short vowels being not uncommon, in native words and in words from OF, before a syllabic consonant in the following syllable.

Note: The vowel in *Venus, Ceres*, and *Caesar* might develop in the trisyllabic oblique forms (gen. *Věněris, Cěrěris, Caesăris*), in which case they would belong under (*b*). In *Cato, Plato, Thales, Naso*, and *Thraso* it might develop in the originally pretonic syllable of the oblique forms (gen. *Cătōnis, Plătōnis, Thălētis* beside *Thălis, Nāsōnis*, and *Thrăsōnis*), in which case they belong under 2 (*b*) below; as *Naso* and *Thraso* have [z] in Bullokar they might perhaps be better regarded as having pronunciations developed in oblique forms with the stress on the syllable following, but it seems possible that this [z] might develop in the nominative singular even though the stress there precedes the consonant.

(2) *Words in which the stress shifts*

§ 23. In these words the vowel, to begin with, keeps the quantity which it had when still pretonic in the English pronunciation of Latin; in general this results in a short vowel (and regularly in case (*a*) below). But long vowels are, in later use, often substituted, (i) because of the use of ME $\bar{e}$ to represent Latin *ae* and Greek *oe* (cf. PresE [iːkɒnɒmik] 'economic' in place of the popular [ekɒnɒmik], which is in accord with the normal rules and must be regarded as the traditional and naturally-developed pronunciation); and (ii) because, as the words became fully assimilated to the English vocabulary, it was often felt to be not in accord with natural ModE pronunciation to retain a short vowel in a *stressed* open syllable, where most native words and words from OF had long vowels because of ME lengthening in such syllables.

(*a*) In pretonic syllables which were separated by an unstressed syllable from the main stress the vowel, in the English pronunciation of Latin, was always short even when the syllable was open; the single exception was Latin *u*, which in open syllables, owing to its having been identified with OF [y] in the French pronunciation of Latin, was always 'long' (i.e. [yː] or [iu] > [juː]). This mode of pronunciation is preserved in English adoptions from Latin in which the stress does not shift (see §§ 269, 284 below). In consequence, in those words in which the stress is shifted in English to the syllable which originally had been pretonic, the vowel of this syllable was originally always short (again with the exception of [yː] or [iu] for Lat *u*), and in most words it remains so. The following eModE quantities, which differ from those used in PresE, are in accordance with the rule. ME *ă* occurs in *alien, alienate, rarify* (*RS*) and *rarity* (Cooper and *RS*). ME *ĕ* occurs in *obedient* and *experience* (second syllable; Hart), *predecessor* (first syllable; Hart, *RS*), *abbreviation* (Bullokar), *region* (Bullokar), *superior* (Bullokar, Gil), *ingenious* (Gil; cf. the 'homophone' list pairing with *ingenuous*), and *material* (Gil). ME *ĭ* occurs in *violence* and *violate* (Bullokar) and *triumphing* and *diamond* (Gil), in spite of its being in hiatus; but in this case ME $\bar{\imath}$ (which Gil gives in the name *Dyamond*) must be regarded as more regular (see § 270 below). When the vowel is not in hiatus ME $\breve{\imath}$ is normal (e.g. *diligent* has $\breve{\imath}$ in Bullokar, Gil, and Hodges). ME $\breve{o}$ occurs in *commodious(ly)* (second syllable; Hart), *overture* (Gil, Brown; Hodges $\breve{u}$; < OF *o(u)verture*), *probity, protoplast,* and *prototype* (*RS*; cf. his $\breve{o}$ in *protomartyr*, in which the first syllable remains pretonic). In *ominous, exonerate,* and *onerate,* which vary in PresE, *RS* and Brown give the regularly developed $\breve{o}$.

But long vowels (which in some cases are probably due to the influence of etymologically related words) are also recorded, sometimes in words in which PresE itself retains the original short vowel. ME $\bar{a}$ occurs in *supernatural* (Hodges), *alienate* (Hodges), *parity, satisfy, sacrament, sacrifice,* and *sacrilege* (Brown); ME $\bar{ę}$ in *edify, equity,* and *emulate* (Lye, followed by Cocker; probably artificial, and due to the use of ME $\bar{ę}$ to represent Lat *ae*) and in *Jesuit* (Brown); and ME $\bar{ǫ}$ in *prodigal* (Gil, probably owing to the influence of Lat *prōdigālis*; Robinson $\breve{o}$).

(*b*) In immediately pretonic syllables the English pronunciation of Latin (to judge from English words in which the stress does not shift; see §§ 284–91 below) normally had short vowels, but long also occurred; in consequence, in words in which the stress shifted, the newly stressed vowel was ordinarily short, but long variants were possible from the beginning and have since become more common because of the general English tendency to have long vowels in stressed open syllables. In accordance with this general principle, short vowels are recorded in the following words which now have long vowels (in one or two cases still varying with short). ME $\breve{a}$ occurs in *parents* in Bullokar (thrice) and Gil (once, beside $\bar{a}$ twice) and in *parentage* in Gil (once) and *RS*, in *papal* in Cooper, and in *patent(ee)* in *RS*; cf. $\breve{a}$ in *salary*, as in Brown. ME $\breve{e}$ occurs in *precept* (Hart), *Egypt* (Bullokar, Gil; but Hart $\bar{ę}$), *secret* (Bullokar, thrice; but Robinson and Hodges $\bar{ę}$), and *equal* (Bullokar four times, beside $\bar{ę}$ once; Gil once beside $\bar{ę}$ once; but Robinson and Hodges $\bar{ę}$). ME $\breve{\imath}$ occurs in *private* (Hart, Bullokar), *recite* (Hart), *provide* (Hart), *simony* (Gil), *Titan* (Gil), *triumph* sb. (Gil once, despite the *i* being in hiatus; but $\bar{\imath}$ twice), and *vital* (Gil, and the 'homophone' lists of Hodges ('near alike'), Fox and Hookes, Strong, and Cooper ('near alike'), which pair *vitals* with *victuals*). ME $\breve{o}$ occurs in *Roman* (Hart, Bullokar), *Trojan* (Robinson, Gil), *pronoun* (Hart, Bullokar), *poet* (Bullokar), *zodiac* (Gil), *notable* (Cooper, *RS*, Brown; but $\bar{ǫ}$ in Hart and Bullokar), *progress* (Brown), and *prologue* (Brown).

On the other hand long vowels occur, though rarely, in words in which PresE still has the normal short vowel. ME $\bar{a}$ is recorded in *Saturn* (Robinson, Gil) and consequently in *Saturday* (Brown); the original Latin quantity (*Sāturnus*) may influence all three (cf. Vol. I, p. 367 on Brown's form). Similarly Gil has ME $\bar{a}$ in *implacable* (second syllable), from Latin *im-*

plācābilis, and ME *ī* in *Tithon* (Lat *Tīthōnus*). But ME *ẹ̄* in *legible* (Hart) and *senate* (Brown) is contrary to the Latin quantity.

Note: On *Cato, Plato, Thales, Naso,* and *Thraso* see under 1 (*a*) above (§ 22); they are probably derived from the Latin nominative rather than from oblique forms. But *Titan* (Lat *Tītan, Tītānis,* also *Tītānus, Tītāni*; plural *Tītānes* or *Tītāni*) is here presumed to have been adopted from the oblique forms. Latin *zodiacus* was originally four-syllabled and a proparoxytone, but in the French (and therefore presumably the traditional English) pronunciation of Latin it would become trisyllabic (with the *i* pronounced as [j]) and a paroxytone; in either case, however, the *o* is immediately pretonic.

Part 2: Late ME and ModE Shortening

§ 24. The processes of shortening which are discussed in this Part are of three types. (1) Shortening of the types which occur in OE or ME, and which are responsible for many of the variations in quantity discussed in the previous part; i.e. shortening before consonant-groups, in words containing a syllabic consonant in the second syllable, in compounds, and in trisyllabic words including some which are disyllabic in ModE, but were trisyllabic while final *e* was still pronounced. These shortenings normally occur in OE or earlier ME, but in some words can be shown to belong to late ME or ModE; such cases are dealt with here. (2) Shortening in monosyllables before single final consonants. (3) An apparent shortening of final vowels. In the discussion below of the individual ME vowels and diphthongs, shortenings of types (1) and (2) are treated together; but shortening of type (3) is separately discussed in § 40.

Shortening of type (2) is far the most important for the history of ModE pronunciation. It occurs very commonly before final [f] (including late ME [f] < [χ]), [þ], [d], and [t]; fairly commonly, especially in the case of ME *ǭ*, before final [k] and [v]; and more rarely before other consonants. But though the consonants differ in their power to cause it, it is to be regarded as essentially due to a general tendency to shorten the vowels of closed syllables, of which shortening before consonant-groups is an earlier and more regular manifestation, and is therefore the counterpart of the lengthening of vowels in open syllables. The process affects chiefly the vowels *ẹ̄* and *ọ̄*, to a somewhat less extent the vowel *ǭ* and the diphthongs *au* and *ou,* less still *ū* and *ē* (but *ẹ̄* is more commonly shortened in the dialects), and only rarely *ā* and *ī*. Though the shortening is commonly regarded as a ModE sound-change, since its results are shown chiefly in ModE texts, it probably operated most fully in the early fifteenth century and may have already occurred occasionally in the fourteenth century, i.e. contemporaneously with lengthening in open syllables; it was, however, an irregular process, so that unshortened forms often survived beside the shortened in eModE, and indeed StE often retains unshortened forms to this day. The twofold result of shortening of ME *ọ̄* in later StE (i.e. [ʌ] and [ʊ]) shows that the process, so far as it affects this vowel, occurred both before and after the unrounding of ME *ŭ*, which seems to have taken place in some forms of English, notably in the Eastern dialects, in the fifteenth century and in vulgar London English in the sixteenth century, but was not accepted in correct StE until *c.* 1640. Thus it is probable that shortening of [u:] was still actively proceeding in careful StE in the seventeenth century, and in some words (e.g. *room*) it seems indeed to have undergone shortening in more recent times. It is possible, however, that the shortened pronunciations recorded from *c.* 1640 onwards are not the result of a process which took place in StE itself, but were adopted by it from other forms of speech; in this event it might be possible to hold that the whole shortening process was essentially confined to the fifteenth century, even though its results do not become fully apparent in StE until the seventeenth century. It is in any event clear that the shortening of ME *au* and of ME *ǭ* and *ou* to *ă* and *ŏ* respectively was completed before the commencement of the ModE lengthening of the latter sounds, since, for example, *laugh* and *cough* are affected by the lengthening; and as there are signs that lengthening of ME *ă* had already occurred in dialectal or vulgar speech in the early sixteenth century, possibly in the late fifteenth century in the Essex speech represented by the Cely Papers (but see § 50, Note 1), we must put the shortening of ME *au*, *ǭ*, and *ou* back to an earlier date, i.e. the earlier fifteenth century.

SHORTENING OF ME *ā*

§ 25. Shortening of ME *ā* is not a normal feature of StE. Early shortening to ME *ă* is shown by the Northerners Levins (who has *wadde* 'woad') and Brown (who has ME *ă* in *bake*), and apparently also by Bullokar, who gives *ă* thrice (against *ā* nineteen times) in *crave*, *ă* twice (against *ā* fourteen times) in *grave* vb., and *ă* once in *behave* (and once also in *behaviour*); but his *ă* might perhaps be due to failure of ME lengthening in the past tenses. Gil similarly has *ă* once (against *ā* ten times) in *gave*, but it could be explained from the ME p.t. sing. *gaf*. Later shortening of [ɛː] < ME *ā* to [e] (and therefore to identity with ME *ĕ*) is shown by *WSC*'s statement that *scarce* has *a* pronounced like '*e* short' (cf. the sixteenth-century form *skers* cited by *OED*).

SHORTENING OF ME *ai*

§ 26. ModE shortening of ME *ai*, after the first element has been raised to [ɛ] owing to the assimilatory influence of the second, produces [e], which is identified with ME *ĕ*. *Again* is rhymed on *ĕ* in Bullokar and also has ME *ĕ* in Lye and *RS*, but ME *ai* or its equivalent in Hart, Bullokar (in his transcriptions), Robinson, Hodges, Newton, and the rhyme-lists of Levins and Poole. ME *ĕ* is (significantly) rather earlier and more frequently recorded in *against*; it is given by Hart (who also has the equivalent of

§ 26]   PART 2: LATE ME AND MoDE SHORTENING   499

ME *ai*), Gil (who says that most people say *agenst*, though some say *against*), and *WSC*; but *ai* is given by Levins, Bullokar, Robinson, and Hodges. ME *ĕ* is recorded for *said* by Smith (who also gives *zed* as a rustic pronunciation), Gil (who says that *sed* for *said* is a Lincolnshire, or perhaps generally Northern, pronunciation), Daines, Cooper (whose Latin edition says that this pronunciation is 'facilitatis causa'; the English edition, less discriminatingly, says that it is a case of 'barbarous speaking'), the 'phonetically spelt' list of Brown, and the shorthand-writers Bridges and Hopkins. But ME *ai* or its equivalent is recorded by Smith (beside *ĕ*), Hart, Robinson, Gil, Hodges, the shorthand-writers Farthing and Coles, and the rhyme-lists of Levins, Poole, and Coles. The present tense forms *sayest*, *saith*, and *says* show the same variation; ME *ĕ* is recorded by Jonson (as a frequent variant beside *ai*), Daines (who remarks that *ĕ* is used 'for the most part'), Evelyn, Cooper (a pronunciation 'facilitatis causa'), the 'phonetically spelt' list of Brown, and the shorthand-writer Bridges; but ME *ai* is recorded by Robinson, the shorthand-writer Farthing, and the rhyme-lists of Poole and Coles. *Wainscot* is recorded with *ĕ* by Lye, followed by *WSC-RS*.

Note: Ekwall, § 16, explains *ĕ* in all these words as being due to shortening of ME *ai*: in *against* before the consonant-group (and by analogy in *again*; notice that *ĕ* is recorded later and less frequently in *again*); so also in *wainscot*; and in *said* and *says*, &c., because of weak stress in the sentence. This explanation is here adopted. But *against* might have *ĕ* by shortening of ME *ẹ̄* in the form *aʒęnst*, and *said* by shortening of ME *ẹ̄* in the form *sęde* (in both cases with Saxon and Kentish loss of OE *g* before *n* and *d* respectively); analogy might lead to the extension of this *ĕ* not only to *again*, but also to *says*, &c. But *wainscot* (a ME adoption from Low German) must have direct shortening of ME *ai* to *ĕ* (cf. the pronunciation of *waistcoat* with *ĕ*); and Gil's statement that *sed* 'said' is a Lincolnshire or Northern pronunciation tells against the view that it has *ĕ* by shortening in the form *sęde*, which should not occur in Northern dialects.

SHORTENING OF ME *au*

§ 27. Shortening of ME *au* has two results, according to the pronunciation of the diphthong at the time of shortening in the dialect concerned. If shortening proceeds from the pronunciation [au] (i.e. the unchanged ME pronunciation) the result is [a], which is identified with ME *ă*; if from [ɒu] (a pronunciation apparently already developed, by rounding of the first element under the influence of the second, in the early fifteenth century in some forms of English, notably the Eastern dialects; cf. § 237, Note 2), the result is [ɒ], which is identified with ME *ŏ*. In either case the process of shortening is that the length of the diphthongal glide is so reduced that only the first element remains.

(1) *Shortening to ME* ă

§ 28. Shortening of ME *au* to ME *ă* occurs before final *f* and consonant-groups beginning with *f*, and in Bullokar before [v]. In StE the words involved have late ME [f] < [χ], but there is also evidence of the shortening before original [f].

(a) Before final [f] *and* [v]

Shortening occurs in *laugh*, which has the pronunciation [laf] in Smith (as a variant), Gil (who gives it as a dialectal pronunciation), T. Shelton, Sherwood, Dix, Butler (who says that 'some' pronounce the word thus), Hodges, and many later sources; Ridpath marks it as an 'Anglicism'. But the pronunciation [lauχ] or [lɒ:(χ)] is still recorded by Smith (beside [laf]), Hart, Laneham, Bullokar, Gil, and Butler (beside [laf]). The past tense follows the infinitive; it is [laft] in Hodges and Poole. Before original [f] shortening is shown in *Ralph* (ME *Rauf*) by Poole, Price, *The Protestant Tutor*, and the shorthand-writer Bridges (the *l* being of course silent), and in *safe* (ME *sauf*) and *chafe(d)* (ME *chaufen*) by Poole (see Vol. I, p. 431). Bullokar has ă in the compound *safeguard* but ā in *safety*; it seems likely that the shortening in the former is due to the [v] of the original form *sauve-garde*, for in *save* vb. Bullokar has ă thrice (beside ā seven times). Shortening is rarely shown before *f* which had been preceded by an *l* which became silent in the fifteenth century; but the Northerner Poole has it in *calf* and *half*, and it is perhaps also shown by the spellings *haf* 'half' (used by the shorthand-writer Bridges and by Cooper) and *caf* 'calf' (used by Cocker); but probably in Cooper, and possibly in the other two sources, the vowel intended is [a:] developed direct from unshortened ME *au* (cf. Note 3 below). Strong has the 'phonetic' spelling *hafpenny* 'halfpenny'. Other sources which say that the *l* is silent in such words either show unshortened vowels or give no indication (or an insufficiently clear one) of the nature of the vowel.

(b) Before the group [ft] < [χt]

(i) In disyllables, in which the syllable-division separates [f] and [t]. *Laughter* has [auχ] in Smith, probably also in Levins (this seems the most likely explanation of his rhyme with *slaughter*), and [ɒ:] (with loss of the spirant) in the shorthand-writers Bridges and S. Shelton and in Aickin. But it has [af], by shortening, in Daines, Price, Lye, Cocker, and the shorthand-writers Metcalfe and Mason. *Daughter* has [auχ] (< ME [aχ] < earlier [ɔχ]), or its ModE equivalent without shortening, in Cheke, Hart, Bullokar, Gil, Butler (beside [af]), and twelve later sources. It has [af] in Butler (who says that 'some say *dafter*'), Daines, and Lye. *Slaughter* is recorded only with ME [auχ] or its equivalent; so probably in Levins (see above on its rhyme with *laughter*) and in Daines, Cooper, *WSC-RS*, Brown, and the shorthand-writers Metcalfe, Everardt, and Bridges.

(ii) When the group [χt] (or [ft]) ends the word. *Draught* has ME [auχt] or its equivalent in Mulcaster, probably Willis (who rhymes it with *naught*),

Price, Coles, Cooper, Cocker, *WSC-RS*, and Brown. It has [aft] in Sherwood, Hodges, Strong, and the shorthand-writer Mason. Words like *caught, taught,* and *naught* have the equivalent of ME [auχt] even in such seventeenth-century writers as Daines, Strong, Cooper, and *WSC-RS*. Hodges (followed by Fox and Hookes) pairs *caught* with *cough't* in his 'near alike' list; the pronunciation intended may be [kaft], but this cannot be certainly established (see Vol. I, p. 402). Poole rhymes *taught* with *laught* 'laughed' and *craft*, &c., probably showing [ft] in *taught* as well as in *laught*. Thus in the seventeenth century [aft] is the less common pronunciation of *draught*, and is only rarely (and not beyond doubt) recorded for the analogous *caught* and *taught*; its use in Present English in *draught* must be regarded as largely an accident due to the establishment of the spelling *draft* as a useful variant of *draught*.

Note 1: Richardson (1677) gives *h* as the value of *gh* in *draught, daughter, laugh* (and *rough* and *cough*); at this date these are probably Northernisms.

Note 2: Spellings appear to show shortening of *au* to *ă* in *sauce*, whence *ă* is transferred to *saucer* and *sausage* (or else independently developed in the latter words); see § 238, Note 3. If OF *au* in *chaudron* also gives ME *ă*, as seems likely (see loc. cit.), the process is similar, though the cause of shortening is different.

Note 3: The process of development is not that in *laugh*, &c. [χ] > [f] before ME *ă* > *au*; spellings with *au* occur before spellings with *f*, and there is also evidence (as we have seen; cf. also Note 2) of shortening of original ME *au* before original ME [f]. Nor is the process that ME *au* > late ME *ā* > *ă*; in *laugh*, &c., the development *au* > *ă* finds place in StE (among other dialects), and the development *au* > *ā* is an alternative one typical of a different dialect or dialects (including vulgar London English).

PresE [ɑː] in *laugh* is by southern lengthening of eModE *ă* by shortening of ME *au*, but in *half*, &c., it is developed directly from unshortened ME *au*; this is shown (*a*) by the seventeenth-century evidence, which frequently records *ă* in *laugh* but only rarely and uncertainly in *half*, &c., and (*b*) by the fact that [ɑː] occurs in *half, calf*, &c., in Northern dialects which do not show lengthening of ME *ă* and have short vowels (usually [a]) in *laugh*.

The preponderance of [af] in *laughter* and its survival in Present English is clearly due to the analogy of *laugh*; in *daughter* and *slaughter* the preference is for ME [auχ]. In such words as *haughty* and *naughty* there is no evidence for the change of [χ] to [f].

(2) *Shortening to ME ŏ*

§ 29. Shortening of ME *au* to ME *ŏ* is not typical of StE, and the orthoepists give evidence of it only in *austere* (stressed on the first syllable), which has *ŏ* in the 'homophone' lists of Price (see Vol. I, p. 406), Young, and Brown. It is, however, shown, from the early fifteenth century, by such spellings as *beholve* 'behalf', *y-fole* 'fallen', *Oggest* 'August', *ontt* 'aunt', &c. (see § 237, Note 2); it occurs in typical ME shortening conditions (before consonant-groups and in the first syllables of words, especially compounds, that have secondary stress; so *austere* when stressed on the first syllable), but there is a special tendency to shortening before *l*, including even final *l* in *oll(e)* 'all'. Modern dialects show similar shortening (see § 237, Note 2), and the shortened pronunciations have in some cases entered StE; so regularly in *sausage* (shortening in a word with secondary stress), and as a variant beside [ɒ:] in *austere* and in *halter*, *salt*, *Salter*, and *Salton* (shortening before *l*; see Daniel Jones, *Eng. Pron. Dict.*, s.vv.).

Note 1: For further examples of early spellings which show the shortening see Zachrisson, *Eng. Vowels*, pp. 81–82, and *Bullokar*, p. 67, and Wyld, *Coll. Eng.*, p. 252 (who, however, misinterpret these spellings; see § 237, Note 2); cf. also Luick, § 527, who rightly assumes shortening. Walker (1775) gives ŏ as the pronunciation of *au* in *holocaust* (cf. Milton's rhyme with *embost* in *Samson Agon.*, ll. 1702 seq.) and in *exhaust*.

Note 2: Hodges's ŏ in *laurel*, *Maurice*, and *Laurence* is not due to shortening of ME *au*, but represents OF ǫ < Lat *au*.

SHORTENING OF ME ẹ̄

§ 30. The shortening of ME ẹ̄ in monosyllables before a single final consonant is a very common process, and PresE has many words in which the shortened vowel alone survives; but the traditional spelling with *ea* bears testimony to the existence of the long variant in the sixteenth and early seventeenth centuries, when the words assumed their modern orthography. (*a*) Before [þ] shortening is shown in *death* by Robinson (beside ẹ̄), Price, Coles, Lye, Cooper, and Brown; but ẹ̄ remains in Levins, Hart, Robinson, Gil, Willis, and Poole. *Breath* has ĕ in Hart (beside ẹ̄), Robinson, Gil, Hodges, Price, Coles, Strong, Lye, Brown, and *RS*; but Levins, Gil (1619 edition, beside ĕ), Willis, and Poole retain ẹ̄; so perhaps Hunt, who seems not to distinguish *breath* from *breathe*. *Beneath* normally has ẹ̄, but has ĕ in Levins (beside [i:]) and Gil. (*b*) Before [f] shortening is shown in *deaf* by Cocker, but ẹ̄ is retained in Smith, Levins, Bullokar, Willis, Poole, Coles, and *RS*. (*c*) Before [d] (which, with [t], is the most frequent cause of the shortening) ĕ occurs in *head* in Cheke, the *ABC for chyldren*, Smith, Hart, Laneham (who perhaps also has ẹ̄), Robinson, Gil (beside ẹ̄), Butler, Hodges, Poole (beside ẹ̄), Price, Coles, Young, Cooper, the *Treatise of Stops* (which perhaps also has ẹ̄), Aickin, *WSC-RS*, and Brown; but ẹ̄ remains in Levins, Gil (beside ĕ; but 1619 edition only ẹ̄), Willis, Poole, and *The Protestant Tutor*, perhaps also as a variant in Laneham and the *Treatise of Stops*. *Bread* has ĕ in Hart, Gil (beside ẹ̄), Hodges, Hunt, Poole (beside ẹ̄), Price, Coles, Strong, Lodwick, Cooper, Aickin, *WSC-RS*, and Brown; it has ẹ̄ in Cheke, Levins, Smith, Tonkis, Gil (beside ĕ), Hayward, Daines, Willis, Wharton (followed by J. Smith), Poole, *The Protestant Tutor*, and the 'homophone' lists of Wharton, Young, *WSC*, and Cocker (which, however, also show ĕ). *Dead* has ĕ in Hart, Gil (beside ẹ̄), Hodges, Poole (beside ẹ̄), Wilkins, Coles, Cooper, Aickin, Cocker, and Brown; it has ẹ̄ in Smith, Levins, Tonkis, Gil (beside ĕ), Poole, and the 'homophone' lists of Young, *WSC*, and Cocker. *Dread* has ĕ in Poole (beside ẹ̄), Price, Coles, Cooper, Brown, and *RS*; it has ẹ̄ in Smith, Levins, and Poole. *Stead* has ĕ in Laneham, Robinson, Hodges, Poole, Price, Coles, Cooper, Brown, and *RS*; it has ẹ̄ in Levins, Bullokar, Gil, and Willis. *Spread* has ĕ in Laneham, Gil, Hodges, Willis (beside ẹ̄), Poole, Coles, Cooper, Brown, and *RS*; it has ẹ̄ in Cheke, Levins, Gil (1619 edition), Willis (as a variant), and Price. Hunt has ẹ̄ in the pres.t., ĕ in the p.t. (as in *read*). *Shred* has ẹ̄ in Levins but ĕ in Cooper and *RS*. *Tread* has ĕ in Hodges, Willis, Coles, Brown, *RS*, and Coles's 'homophone' list, but ẹ̄ in Smith and Levins. *Lead* sb. 'plumbum' has ĕ in Cooper, *WSC-RS*, and the 'homophone' lists, but ẹ̄ in Levins, Smith, Robinson, Gil, Willis, Poole, *The Protestant Tutor*, and the 'homophone' list of Strong (which also shows ĕ). (*d*) Before *t* shortening is shown in *sweat* by Gil (twice, beside ẹ̄ six times), Price, and *RS*, but ẹ̄ by Levins, Gil, Hodges, Poole, Cooper, and the 'homophone' lists; Smith makes an artificial distinction between the substantive, with ĕ, and the verb, with ẹ̄. *Threat* has ẹ̄ in Levins, Gil, Willis, Poole, and Coles, but ĕ in Brown. On ĕ in *teat* see Note 1. *Wheat* has ĕ in Fox and Hookes. The past tense *eat* is [et] in Cheke and in *WSC* (which pairs *eat* with *yet*). *Beat* has ĕ in Laneham. *Wet* has ĕ normally (as in Bullokar and Gil) but retains ẹ̄ in Levins and in Brown (beside ĕ); both men are Northerners. (In this word *OED* regards the shortened form as originating in the p.t. and p.p. of the verb, and the unshortened vowel as being appropriate to the adj. and infinitive; but shortening could, at least in theory, occur independently in the adj. and infinitive; Bullokar's ĕ occurs in the p.p., but Gil's in the adj.) *Neat* sb. 'ox' has ĕ in Coles, *Eng.-Lat. Dict*. *Plait* has ĕ (by shortening of ẹ̄ in the form *pleat*) in *WSC-RS*. In the word *jet*, adopted from OF, ModE ĕ may either represent a ME variant in ĕ or be by shortening of ẹ̄; Levins gives ẹ̄, and *RS* uses the spelling *jeat* but gives ĕ. (*e*) Before other consonants there is rare evidence of shortening. Gil gives ĕ in *shears* and in *swear* (once, beside ẹ̄ once).

Note 1: In those words (such as *red*) in which the short vowel was so early generalized as to be represented in the normal sixteenth-century orthography, ĕ is regularly shown by the orthoepists; but Levins has [i:] < ME ẹ̄ in *shed*, *shred*, *red* (beside ĕ), and *fret* (also in *wet*; see above). Bullokar's ĕ in *teat* is probably a ME variant; see *OED*.

Note 2: For rhymes, spellings, and present-day dialectal pronunciations showing shortening of original ME ẹ̄ to [ɪ] see § 116, Note 2. It is not clear what is the process involved: it could be (*a*) ME raising of ẹ̄ to ẹ̄ followed by normal ME shortening of ẹ̄ to ĭ, (*b*) ME shortening of ẹ̄ to ĕ followed by raising of ĕ to ĭ, or (*c*) fifteenth-century shortening of tense [e:] < ME ẹ̄ to [ɪ], which would be the same phonetic process as ME shortening of ẹ̄ to ĭ. Of these alternatives, (*a*) seems the most likely (and is in effect adopted by Kihlbom, p. 73).

SHORTENING OF ME ẹ̄

§ 31. Shortening of ME ẹ̄, whether in ModE (when it is [i:]) or in late ME (when it is still [e:]), gives [ɪ], which is identified with ME ĭ. Before a single final consonant such shortening is comparatively rare, but accounts for the PresE pronunciation of several words. *Sick* normally has ĭ in the orthoepists (as in Bullokar, Gil, and Hodges), but seems to vary between [i:] and ĭ in Levins. Levins seems also to show this variation in *rick* (which has late ME *ẹ̄* by raising of earlier *ẹ̄*; cf. Jordan, § 81, Anm. 1); but *ĭ* is normal, being given by Butler (despite his spelling *reek*) and Hodges. *Grit* (spelt *greet*) retains [i:] in Levins (probably a Northernism). *Wick* has [i:] in Cheke and in Levins (whose spelling is *weak*). In other words the shortening is less general, and was probably chiefly found in vulgar speech; it is not usually recorded in the best orthoepists and does not survive in present StE, though it is widespread in the dialects. That it was perhaps a little more common in good speech in the sixteenth century is suggested by Smith's giving *ĭ* in *retrieve, thief*, and *heel*; but he is unsupported. Thus *sheep* (in which *ĭ* is common in the dialects) has [i:] in Salesbury, Smith, Gil, and Robinson; Coote describes [ɪ] as a barbarism, and it is recorded otherwise only in the 'homophone' lists from Hodges (who relegates it to his 'near alike' list) onwards. Bullokar's rhymes, which often depend on vulgar or dialectal pronunciations, may show *ĭ* in *deed* and *mean* sb. 'medium' (of which the latter has late ME *ẹ̄* by raising of *ẹ̄*). Gil once has *ĭ* (beside [i:] thirteen times) in *seem*. The 'homophone' lists record *ĭ* in *creek* (Wharton), *green* (Wharton), *keen* (Hawkins, Cocker), *keel* (Hawkins, Brown), and *feet* (Fox and Hookes), probably also in *cleaver* (Coles, *Eng.–Lat. Dict.*; see Vol. I, p. 411). For spellings showing this shortening see § 132, Note (especially under (*f*)).

SHORTENING OF ME *ī*

§ 32. Shortening of ME *ī* is rare and does not affect StE, perhaps because diphthongization had normally begun before the shortening process became fully operative; but shortening to *ĭ* is occasionally shown in the modern dialects (see Wright, § 155), and is recorded by Bullokar in *five* (once, beside *ī* thrice), *life* (once, beside *ī* five times; but he rhymes the word on *ĭ*), *mile* (once, beside *ī* once), *rife* (once, beside *ī* once), and *thrice* (once). Cf. also § 12 (2). The statistics are derived from Zachrisson's word-lists.

SHORTENING OF ME *ǭ*

§ 33. Shortening of ME *ǭ* occurs in the same circumstances as that of ME *ẹ̄*, but is somewhat less common. (*a*) Before [þ] shortening is shown in *cloth* by Robinson, Gil, Butler, Hodges, and Coles; but *RS* and the Northerners Levins and Poole retain ME *ǭ* (which Gil gives as the Northern pronunciation). *Froth* similarly has *ŏ* in Gil and Butler (as has *frothy* in Hodges), but *ǭ* in Levins, Willis, and Poole. *Wroth* has *ŏ* in Hodges ('near alike' list) and Coles, but *ǭ* in Gil and *RS*. *Loath* has *ŏ* in Bullokar. *Both* has *ŏ* in Hart (beside *ǭ*), Bullokar (once, beside *ǭ* twelve times), and Gil (eight times, beside *ǭ* twice); normally, however, it has *ǭ*. (Hart always gives [ð] in this word; but normally it has [þ].) (*b*) Before [f] shortening is shown only in

§ 33]   PART 2: LATE ME AND MoDE SHORTENING   505

loaf, which has *ŏ* once in Bullokar (as has the plural *loaves*). (*c*) Before [d] shortening is shown in *woad* by Smith and Wharton (who says the *a* is silent), perhaps also by Hodges in his 'alike' list, which is followed by Fox and Hookes (but see Note 1 below); but Coles has *ǭ*. *Rode* has *ŏ* in 'homophone' lists from Hodges onwards. Similar shortening also occurred in *broad* and *abroad*, though it is not recorded by the orthoepists, who have either unshortened ME *ǭ*—so Smith, Hart, Levins, Laneham, Bullokar, Gil (1621 edition), *The English Schole-master* (1646), Willis, Poole, Price, and Ray (1691; see Vol. I, p. 189)—or [ɒ:] by ModE lengthening of eModE *ŏ* (see § 53 (2) below); but the shortened *ŏ* is shown by the fifteenth- and sixteenth-century *brod* recorded by *OED* and by such rhymes (ultimately of course traditional) as those with *God* (e.g. Milton, *Psalm* 135, ll. 5–6; *Psalm* 86, ll. 41–43), *rod* (Pope, *Epistle to Arbuthnot*), and *sod* (Keats, *Ode to a Nightingale*). (*d*) Before [t] shortening is shown regularly in *hot* and *wot* (as, for example, by Robinson and Gil), but the Northerner Levins has *ǭ*, as has Laneham in *hot*. *Wrote* has *ŏ* in 'homophone' lists from Hodges onwards. *Boat* has *ŏ* in Wharton. *Groat* has [o:] from unshortened ME *ǭ* in Levins, Butler, and Price, but *ŏ* in the 'homophone' lists of Young, Coles, *Eng.-Lat. Dict.* (which records vulgarisms), and *WSC-RS* (the word being paired with *grot*), and [ɒ:] by ModE lengthening of eModE *ŏ* in other sources (see § 53 (2) below). For shortening in this word compare the fifteenth- and sixteenth-century spellings *grott(e)* and *grot* recorded by *OED* for *groat* (the coin) and similar spellings of *groats*. (*e*) Shortening also occurred sporadically before other consonants. It accounts for the PresE pronunciation of *gone*, which has *ŏ* in Robinson, Hodges, and Strong; but ME *ǭ* is retained by Cheke, Smith, Levins, Mulcaster, Gil, Poole, and *RS*. Hodges records *ŏ* (as in PresE) in *shone*, but Poole *ǭ*; Coles varies. *Anon* has unshortened *ǭ* in Levins. *None* (as well as *nonce*) has *ŏ* in Poole, as also it has in Hodges (twice, against *ǭ* in *nonce* once, and *ǭ* in *once, one, ones*, and *only*). *Whom* has *ŏ* in Smith, Hart, Gil (once, in 1621 edition only; 1619 *ǭ*), and perhaps Poole (see Vol. I, p. 430). *Whose* has *ŏ* in Hart (thrice, beside *ǭ* once). *Those* seems to have *ŏ* in Laneham. Shortening in these last three words may be due to weak stress (cf. Hart's *ŏ* in *who*); but Wright records [ɒ] in many dialects, including those of the Home Counties, in *home*, which is closely analogous to *whom*.

Note 1: In *woad* Levins shows shortening of Northern *ā* to *ă*. Hodges (followed by Hunt and Fox and Hookes) pairs *woad* with *wad*, which shows shortening in *woad*; but we could only take it to be shortening to *ŏ* if we were to assume that in *wad* the *ă* has been rounded under the influence of the *w*, of which there is no certain evidence elsewhere in Hodges. The pairing may rather depend on the Northern form *wad* 'woad', made familiar to Southerners by the botanist Turner, who (being a Northerner) expressed a firm preference for it against *woad*; cf. Fuller's use of the form *wad*. Hart, in the *Methode*, gives *uoad* 'woad' as a word containing a 'triphthong' ([w] being counted as a vowel); his pronunciation is probably of dialectal origin (see § 145, Note).

Note 2: Coles knew some variant, perhaps *ŏ*, beside *ǭ* in *stone, one, none, once*, and *nonce*.

On shortening to *ŭ* in *whom*, *only*, and *none* see § 36. Normally the orthoepists show either ME *ǭ* or [u:] < ME *ǭ* in *whom* and *whose* (see § 153).

Note 3: That shortening before *d* affected other words than those cited above is shown by Milton's rhymes of *abode* with *God* (*Psalm* 81, ll. 37–39; *Psalm* 84, ll. 14–16, 37–39) and of *load* with *God*, *trod*, and *rod* (*Sonnet* XIV). See also Wright, *EDG*, § 122.

SHORTENING OF ME *ou*

§ 34. Shortening of ME *ou*, even before it is monophthongized, gives ME *ŏ* (cf. the ME shortening in *knowledge*). *Troth*, which retains *ou* in Bullokar, has *ŏ* in Coles. Hart has *ŏ* in *slothful* (see § 14 above), but would not necessarily have had it in the simplex *sloth*, which has *ou* in Bullokar and [o:] in Willis.

The shortening is commonest when late ME *ou* develops before an [χ] which subsequently becomes [f]; the diphthong is then as a rule shortened (but is retained if the change to [f] fails to occur). The sources of late ME [ouχ] are various.

(1) *Early ME ŏh*

Cough has [ou] (with retention of the spirant) in Smith, and [o:], probably with retention of a spirant, in Willis (see Vol. I, p. 427); Hodges (followed by Fox and Hookes) shows loss of the spirant by equating *cough't* with *coat* (see Vol. I, pp. 402–3). Mulcaster says the value of the *gh* is the same as in other words, i.e. it is not [f]. Price gives *coh* as a Western pronunciation. Retention of [o:], despite the change of [χ] to [f], is shown by Coles, who rhymes the word with *loaf* among his [o:] words. Shortening and the change of [χ] to [f] are shown by Sherwood, T. Shelton, Dix, Butler, Hodges (but contrast [ko:t] 'cough't' above), and many later sources, including Price. *Trough* has a long vowel in Wharton (see Vol. I, p. 338), Willis (probably with retention of a spirant; see Vol. I, p. 427), probably Price (who says that *gh* is pronounced as *h*; contrast his pronunciation of *cough*), and in Brown (who gives *trow* and *trough* as homophones). Coles shows retention of [o:] despite the change of [χ] to [f], by rhyming the word with *loaf* among his [o:] words (cf. the seventeenth-century spelling *trofe* recorded by the *OED*). Coles's form helps to explain Hodges's plural [tro:vz], in which the [v] is due either to the analogy of e.g. *knives* plural of *knife*, or to a direct change of ME [ʒ] to [v] (see Vol. I, p. 182). Cocker's 'phonetic' spelling *hoved* 'houghed' shows [o:] and perhaps the same [v] from ME [ʒ], but may be a formation on [ho:f] 'hough', which would be parallel to Coles's [tro:f] (see Vol. I, p. 366). Shortening of ME *ou* to *ŏ* and the change of [χ] to [f] are shown in *trough* by Hodges (in the singular), Wallis, Poole, and *WSC-RS*. *Lough* (for *loch*?) has [ɒf] in *WSC-RS*. *Though* (ME *þŏh*; cf. Orm's *þohh*) is not recorded with [f] by the orthoepists;

on its forms see § 4. *Slough* is put with *sloe* in the 'homophone' lists; Strong, Young, Cocker, and Brown do not indicate which of the words *slough* it is, but in Hodges it seems to be 'quagmire' (see (2) below), Fox and Hookes gloss it 'quagmire', and Coles glosses it 'old skin'. *Slough* 'cast skin' is of uncertain origin. If it is from early ME *slōh* it belongs here, and should in ModE become either [slou] (cf. Coles) or [slɒf]; the PresE [slʌf] would have to be explained as in § 39 (c) below. But if it is from OE **slōh* (Jordan § 197) it belongs with *slough* 'miry ground' under (2) below; if from OE **slūh* (Ekwall in *RES* ix (1958), 311) it belongs in § 39 (a) and Coles's gloss would have to be taken as an error, as [oː] < OE *ūh* is impossible. Shortening of *ou* to *ŏ* before *ft* < [χt] is shown by Cooper in *brought* and *sought*, which he says some pronounce [brɒft] and [sɒft], while others say [brɔːt] and [sɔːt]. Hodges pairs *ought* with *oft* in his 'near alike' list; Price and Fox and Hookes pair *sought* with *soft*. Other orthoepists do not show the change of pre-consonantal [χ] to [f] after ME *ou*.

(2) *Other sources*

Early ME *ǫh* < OE *āh* in *dough* appears as [ou] in Smith and as [oː] in Hodges, Willis (who probably retains the spirant; see Vol. I, p. 427), the shorthand-writer Cartwright, and the 'homophone' lists from Hodges onwards. On Brown's *duff* 'dough' see § 39 (c) below.

In four cases words in which late ME *ūh* is to be expected appear to be given with late ME *ouh*; except in one case the change of [χ] to [f] is not shown and the diphthong is unshortened. The first is *rough* (OE *rūh*); but Willis's inclusion of it in a list of words with late ME *ouh* is probably an error (see Vol. I, p. 427). *Through* (ME *þrūh*) has [oː] in a number of orthoepists (see § 4), whose evidence there is no reason to doubt. If Fox and Hookes are not in error in glossing *slough* as 'quagmire' when they pair it with *sloe* (see (1) above), the word has [oː] < late ME *ou* < eME *ǭ* before [χ] (OE *slōh*). Hodges in his 'near alike' list puts *slough* (glossed 'mud, &c.') with *slow* adj. (but the pairing is more likely to depend on [ʌu] in the latter), and a little later *sloughs* (plural of the same word?) with *sloes*. Willis rhymes *chough* (which has eME *ǭh*; see Vol. I, p. 23, note 5) on [oː], as if from ME *ou*; Lye and the shorthand-writer S. Shelton have [ɒf] (cf. the seventeenth-century spelling *choff* recorded by *OED*), of which the simplest explanation would be that it shows shortening of late ME *ou*.

Note: *Hough* seems clearly to belong with words which have early ME *ŏ*; see *OED*, s.v. *hough* sb., and compare especially the note there on the etymology. Though the word is probably connected with OE *hōh*, its ME and ModE forms all descend from an early ME form with *ŏ*; this early and general shortening is probably due to the influence of the compound *hōhsinu* (ME *hŏxene*, &c.), which probably also accounts for the Present English pronunciation of *hough* as [hɒk].

SHORTENING OF ME ọ̄

§ 35. Shortening of ME ọ̄, whether it occurs in later ME while the pronunciation of the unshortened vowel was still [oː] or in ModE after the change to [uː], results in the first instance in [ʊ]. If the shortening precedes the unrounding of ME ŭ the newly shortened vowel is identified with ME ŭ and shares with it its subsequent unrounding and lowering to [ʌ] (unless protected by the influence of rounding consonants, as perhaps in *book*); if, however, the shortening is later than the unrounding of ME ŭ the newly shortened vowel is unaffected by unrounding and remains [ʊ] in all phonetic contexts. In what follows, evidence is given (1) of early shortening, (2) of the survival of unshortened [uː] in the sixteenth and early seventeenth centuries, and (3) of later shortening, which appears in StE *c.* 1640. In the later seventeenth century any one word may have [ʌ], [uː], or [ʊ].

(1) *Early shortening to identity with ME* ŭ

§ 36. Early shortening accounts for the PresE pronunciation of *blood* and *flood* and of *glove*; but it was formerly more common, and before a greater variety of consonants. (*a*) Before [d] shortening is shown in *blood* by Cheke, Smith (beside [uː]), Levins (possibly), Bullokar, Coote, and many later sources. *Flood* has ŭ in Cheke, Bullokar, Coote, and many later sources. *Good* has ŭ in Cheke, Smith (beside [uː]), Hart (regularly, beside frequent [uː]), Bullokar, Robinson, Gil, Butler, Hodges (once, beside regular [ʊ] by the later shortening), Lloyd (possibly, beside [uː]), Newton, Poole, Price, Coles, Strong, Richardson, *The Protestant Tutor*, *WSC*, and Brown. *Hood* (and the suffix *-hood*) has it in Smith (beside [uː]), Bullokar (in *manhood*), Robinson, Butler, Poole, Price, Strong, Lye (who says that 'some mince' it thus), and *The Protestant Tutor*. *Stood* has ŭ in Daines, Poole, Price, Cooper's 'homophone' list of words of the same (and not merely 'near') pronunciation, *WSC*, and Brown's 'homophone' list; and *food* in *WSC*. (*b*) Before final *t*, the shortened ŭ was less common, and perhaps vulgar; it occurs in *foot* in Wilkins (beside both [uː] and [ʊ]), Coles, and Strong (in their 'phonetically spelt' lists), *The Protestant Tutor*, Cooper (in his list of 'barbarisms'), and *WSC* (in part following Cooper), and in *shoot* in the 'homophone' lists of Young, Cocker, and Brown. (*c*) Before [þ] the shortened ŭ occurs in (*for*)*sooth* in Robinson, Butler, Daines (who says only that 'some' use it), Strong, Young, and Brown. (*d*) Before [v] it is usual in *glove*, for which it is recorded by Mulcaster, Gil, Butler, and eight later sources. It occurs less frequently in other words: thus in (*re*)*move* in Mulcaster, Tonkis, Jonson, Daines, Price (followed by Hawkins), Coles, and *WSC-RS*; in (*ap*)*prove* in Hart (beside [uː]), Tonkis, Price, the *Welsh Breviary*, and *WSC-RS* (beside [uː]); in *behove* in Tonkis and Price; and in *hove* (presumably the verb meaning 'hover' < OE * *hōfian*; cf. *OED*) in

§ 36]   PART 2: LATE ME AND MoDE SHORTENING   509

Mulcaster. (e) Before other consonants the shortening is sporadic. It occurs in *book* and *took* in Hart (once in each word, beside [uː], which otherwise he gives regularly for *book*) and in *WSC*'s 'homophone' list; in *struck* p.t. and p.p. (< late ME *strǫ̆k* by raising of *ǭ* to *ọ̄* in the regular ME p.t. sing. *strǭk* < OE *strāc*) in Gil (beside the p.ts. *strāk*, *strōk*, and *strĭk* and the p.ps. *strĭkn* and *strŭkn*) and in Butler (who also gives [uː] in *strooke* p.t. and p.p. and in addition *strake* p.t., *stricken* p.p., and (in *Fem. Mon.*) *strooken* p.p.); in *look* in Newton (beside [uː]); in *roof* in Young's 'homophone' list (cf. shortening before [v], and in *deaf*); in *whom* in Price and Poole (late ME or early ModE *ŭ* < ME *ǭ* by raising of ME *ǭ*); and in *womb* in Poole, beside [uː] (ME *ǭ* by raising of ME *ǭ*). Hodges once has the symbol for [ʌ] in *only* (beside [oː] twenty times); there may very well be an error in the diacritic, as Kauter assumes, but not certainly, for the transcription represents a pronunciation which has actual existence (cf. Note 1 below). It results from shortening of ME *ǭ* by vulgar and dialectal raising of ME *ǭ* (see §§ 148 seq. below), a process which must be assumed to account for the ModE development of *one* (see under (2) below). If Hodges's transcription is accepted, then shortening is shown in the derivative *only* and not in *one*, and may be peculiar to the former (cf. Hart's [hwɔləi] 'wholly' against [hwoːl] 'whole'); but the PresE pronunciation of *none* shows early shortening to *ŭ* (of *ǭ* by raising of ME *ǭ*) before final *n* (cf. [nɒn] 'none', by shortening of *ǭ*, discussed in § 33 above). This pronunciation [nʌn] seems to be first recorded by Wm. Turner, *The Art of Spelling and Reading English* (1710), who significantly also has ME *ŭ* (by shortening of ME *ǭ* by raising of *ǭ*) in *home*, *stone*, and *whole* (see Gabrielson, *Studia Neophilologica*, ii. 158–9); it is clear that the conventional explanation of *none*, that it has an analogical pronunciation modelled on [wʌn] 'one', will not suffice to explain the facts in Turner, though the analogy of [wʌn] has undoubtedly assisted the acceptance by StE of the originally vulgar or dialectal [nʌn]. On unshortened [uː] in *one* and *none* see 2 (e) below.

Note 1: *Home* (which like *whom* has a late ME variant in *ǭ* by raising of *ǭ*) has [ʌ], according to Wright, in the modern dialects, including those of the Home Counties, and provides a close analogue to the shortening shown in *whom*; but in the latter weak stress may assist the shortening. *Only*, according to Wright, is [ʌnli] in Herefordshire and Oxfordshire (cf. [ʊnli] in Norfolk and Suffolk), which gives support to Hodges's transcription. *Stone* has [ʊ] in Norfolk and Suffolk (late shortening) and [ʌ] in Norfolk, Lincs., Oxon., Bucks., and Cumberland. On *whole* see § 431 below.

Note 2: *Wood* does not show shortening of ME *ǭ*; its *ŭ* (which is preserved as [ʊ] by the influence of the preceding [w]) is the normal ME vowel (< OE *wudu*); but the spelling represents a late ME variant with *ǭ* by lengthening in the open syllable, which is recorded by the *ABC for chyldren*. *Wool* (OE *wull*) has only ME *ŭ*, a variant in *ǭ* being impossible; its conventional ModE spelling is an inverted one on the analogy of *wood* and of words which had *ŭ* by shortening but preserved the *oo* spelling.

Note 3: In *prove* and *move* it is usual to assume ME *ǭ* as the starting-point (so Jordan, § 228), as I do above. Mr. A. J. Bliss rightly points out, however, that ME *ǭ* cannot be explained from OF, and himself would assume that both words originally had ME *ŭ* (which would be normal) and that they later developed ME *ǭ* by lengthening in open syllables; they would then belong with *love*, &c. (see § 18 above). But in *King Horn* (MS C, ll. 1267–8) there is a rhyme between *hove* (OE *hōfe* 2 sing. p.t.) and *proved* (so MS L; MS O has *3ove* for *hove*), which establishes ME *ǭ* in *prove* at a date too early for lengthening in open syllables. Also there is seventeenth-century evidence that ME *ǭ* could occur in *move* (see § 154 below). I take ME *moven* and *proven* to be semi-learned forms, with ME *ǭ* (varying with ME *ǭ*) in place of the expected [u] (< OF *ou*) owing to the influence, in OF or ME, of Latin *moveo* and *probo*. But the eModE variation between *ŭ* and [u:] (or [o:]) might well go back to a ME variation between ME *ŭ* from popular OF and ME *ǭ* (or *ǭ*) from semi-learned forms, and be independent of both open-syllable lengthening and fifteenth-century shortening.

(2) *Survival of unshortened* [u:]

§ 37. Unshortened [u:] < ME *ǭ* is recorded by the orthoepists, more or less often, for nearly all the words in which *ŭ* by early shortening is found, and for others which are exactly analogous; in many of these it survives in PresE. (*a*) Before [d], unshortened [u:] occurs in *blood* in Smith (beside *ŭ*), Tonkis, Lloyd (beside *ŭ*), possibly Wharton (who is followed by J. Smith), and in Lye (who seems to prefer it to *ŭ*, since he says of the latter that 'some mince it thus'). *Flood* has [u:] in Tonkis and Wharton (followed by J. Smith). *Good* has [u:] in the *Welsh Hymn* (possibly), Smith (beside *ŭ*), Hart (nine times, beside normal *ŭ*), Tonkis, Daines, *The English Scholemaster*, Willis, Lloyd (beside *ŭ*), *The Welsh Breviary*, and J. Smith. *Hood* has [u:] in Smith (beside *ŭ*), Hart, Gil, Willis, and Lye (who seems to prefer it to *ŭ*). It is recorded for *mood* by Smith, for *food* by Bullokar, Gil, Daines, and Lye, and for *stood* by Gil and Poole; in *mood* and *food* it of course survives in present StE. (*b*) Before [t], unshortened [u:] is recorded for *foot* by Gil, Butler, Wallis (see Vol. I, pp. 239–40), Price, Wilkins (beside both [ʌ] by early and [ʊ] by later shortening), Lye, and possibly Cooper (see Vol. I, pp. 289–90); for *shoot* by Bullokar, Butler, Hodges, and Coles; for *boot* by Smith and Coles; for *root* by Coles; and for *soot* by Willis and Price. (*c*) Before [þ], unshortened [u:] is recorded in (*for*)*sooth* by Hart, Daines, Hodges, and Price, and in *tooth* by Lye. (*d*) Before [v], unshortened [u:] is recorded in *glove* by Levins; in *move* by Levins, Bullokar, Robinson, Gil, Sherwood (in the infinitive), Butler, Hodges, Willis, Wallis, Wilkins, Cooper, and *WSC-RS* (beside *ŭ*); in (*ap*)*prove* by Levins, Hart (beside *ŭ*), Bullokar, Robinson, Sherwood, Hodges, Willis, Coles, *WSC-RS* (beside *ŭ*), and Brown; and in *behove* by Bullokar, Gil, and Sherwood. (*e*) Of other words which show shortening, either in the orthoepists or in PresE, or which are analogous to those which show shortening, the following may be noticed. *Book* has [u:] in the *Welsh Hymn*, Smith, Hart (regularly, beside *ŭ* once), Bullokar, Robinson, Gil, Hayward, Butler, Price, Lye, and Cooper (possibly; see Vol. I, pp. 289–90). *Took* has [u:] in the *Welsh Hymn*, Smith, Hart (beside *ŭ*), Robinson, and Gil. *Strook* p.t. 'struck' has [u:] beside *ŭ* in Butler. Similarly [u:] occurs in *brook* in Bullokar, Robinson, Gil, Butler, and Price;

§ 37]   PART 2: LATE ME AND MoDE SHORTENING   511

in *forsook* in Gil; in *cook* in the *Welsh Hymn* (MS A) and Smith; in *crook* in Price; in *hook* in Gil; in *look* in Smith, Bullokar, Hayward, Newton (beside [ʌ]), Ray, and possibly Cooper; in *nook* in Price and Coles; in *rook* in Smith and Coles; and in *shook* in Gil. *Whom* has [u:] in Bullokar, Gil, Daines, Cooper, and Brown's 'homophone' list. *One* is once transcribed with the diacritic for [u:] in Hodges, against that for [o:] some thirty-six times; there is probably an error in the use of the diacritic (especially as those for [u:] and [o:] are very similar), but the [u:] transcription gets some support from the (equally isolated) one which shows [ʌ] (by early shortening) in *only* (see § 36 above). We must in any event assume that this word and *none* had a variant in late ME ǭ by raising of ME ǫ in order to account for PresE [wʌn] 'one' and [nʌn] 'none' (see § 36 above) in contrast to the Midland [wɒn] and [nɒn], which develop more directly from ME ǫn and nǭn; and Cocker in fact records [u:] in *none* (see Vol. I, p. 417).

Note: Wright, Index, records the survival of the pronunciation [u:n] 'one' in Dorset and Somerset. Shakespeare rhymes *one* with *shoon* and Milton with *soon* (see § 150, Note 1).

(3) *Later shortening to* [u]

§ 38. In the seventeenth century only the best observers give evidence of the development of [u] by later shortening of the [u:] whose survival has been demonstrated above. The reason was apparently that the less competent orthoepists were unable to distinguish a short [u] as well as the unrounded [ʌ] (to which the name 'short *u*' attached) from [u:]; [u] and [u:] are commonly both spelt *oo*, and [u] was largely a contextual variant of [u:]. It appears further that [u:] continued to be heard in the same words as had [u] by shortening; this added to the confusion, from which even Wallis and Cooper are not entirely free (see above, Vol. I, pp. 239–40 and 289–90). But there is sufficient evidence of the occurrence of [u] by later shortening in the following cases. (*a*) Before [d] in *good*, for which it is given by Hodges, Wallis, Coles, Cooper, and possibly by Ray (see Vol. I, p. 188); in *hood*, for which it is recorded by Hodges, Coles, and Cooper; and in *stood*, recorded by Wallis, Poole (probably, beside [u:]), Coles, and Cooper. Cooper appears to give it for *blood* and *flood*; this is possible, as there is some evidence for the survival of [u:] in these words (especially the former) in the seventeenth century (see the preceding paragraph). (*b*) Before [t] in *foot* in Hodges, possibly Wallis (see Vol. I, pp. 239–40), Wilkins, Coles, and possibly Cooper (see Vol. I, pp. 289–90), and in *soot* in Coles and Cooper; but, as in PresE, not in *boot*, *root*, and *shoot*. (*c*) Before [þ] Coles gives [u] in *sooth* and *tooth*, which in PresE have normally [u:], though [u] exists as a variant in *tooth*. (*d*) Before [v] there is no evidence of later shortening to [u]. (*e*) Of other consonants, only [k] regularly causes later shortening; it seems by contrast only rarely to have caused early shortening (see under

1 (*e*) above). In *book* [ʊ] is recorded by Hodges, Coles, and possibly Cooper (see Vol. I, pp. 289–90); in *hook, look,* and *took* by Hodges and Coles; in *cook* by Hodges; and in *brook, crook,* and *shook* by Coles. But Coles has [uː] in *nook* and *rook*, which have [ʊ] in PresE (like the other words here cited). Before other consonants the shortening is sporadic; Hodges has [ʊ] in *hoop*, and Cocker seems to have [ʊ] beside [uː] in *fool* (see Vol. I, p. 417).

Seventeenth-century shortening of [uː] not derived from ME *ǭ* occurs in *youth*, which has [ʊ] in Coles and perhaps Newton; see § 178 below. Cf. the PresE variant [ʊ] in *room*, which has [uː] < ME *ū*.

SHORTENING OF ME *ū*

§ 39. Shortening of ME *ū* is confined almost entirely to words which have final [f] developed in the early fifteenth (or late fourteenth) century from final [χ]; and even in these words there survived in StE until the early seventeenth century forms which showed failure of the change of [χ] to [f] and consequent failure of the shortening of the vowel. The words involved may be classified as follows.

(*a*) ME *ū* from OE *ū* in *rough* is shortened to *ŭ*, in consequence of the change of [χ] to [f], in Butler (beside [ʌu] < ME *ū*), Hodges, Wallis, Poole, Coles, Strong, *WSC-RS*, Brown, the shorthand-writers Shelton, Bridges, and Hopkins, and the 'homophone' lists from Hodges onwards. But [ʌu] from ME *ū*, with no change of [χ] to [f], is retained in Bullokar, Laneham, Butler (possibly, beside *ŭ*; see Vol. I, p. 163), Daines, and the shorthand-writer Mason (see Vol. I, p. 391), and northern [uː] occurs in Levins and apparently in Mulcaster. Newton also retains [χ], and presumably therefore ME *ū* (> [au] in his speech).

(*b*) Late ME *ū* from OE *ō* before [χ] (cf. Jordan, § 125) is shortened to *ŭ*, with the change of [χ] to [f], in *tough* in Butler, Wallis, Wharton, Coles, *WSC-RS*, and Brown. But [ʌu], and the spirant developed from [χ], are retained in *tough* by Smith, Bullokar, Butler (possibly, beside *ŭ*; see Vol. I, p. 163), Daines (see Vol. I, p. 334), and Brown in his 'homophone' list (a very late instance—Brown's many dialectalisms should be borne in mind); Levins has Northern [uː] < ME *ū*. In *enough* the shortened *ŭ* and the [f] from [χ] are recorded by Robinson, Gil, Butler (beside [ʌu]), Hodges, Wharton, *WSC-RS*, and the shorthand-writers Shelton, Bridges, and Hopkins. Gil even gives short *ŭ* before the spirant developed from [χ] (which he retains as a variant) as well as before [f]; this pronunciation is a blend, and is probably due to the desire to distinguish *enough* from the plural *enow*, which has [ʌu] throughout the sixteenth and seventeenth centuries. But Laneham, Bullokar, and Butler retain [ʌu] in *enough* (in Butler, beside *ŭ*); this retention is regular before the spirant developed from [χ], which in their speech remains as the only means of distinguishing

§ 39] PART 2: LATE ME AND MoDE SHORTENING 513

enough from *enow*. Mulcaster appears to have northern [uː] < ME *ū*. Loss of the spirant, and consequent identity of *enough* with *enow*, seems to be shown by the pairing of the two words in Hodges's 'near alike' list; but we must allow for the possibility of grammatical confusion. *Chough* (which has ME *ǭh*; see Vol. I, p. 23, note 5) has [ʌ] by shortening before [f] < [χ] in Hodges, as in PresE. The PresE [au] in *slough* 'miry ground' develops from ME *ūh* < *ǭh* without shortening.

(c) Late ME *ūgh* seems occasionally to have occurred in words which normally have late ME *ough* from earlier *ǒh* or OE *āh* (see § 170 below), and this late ME variant *ū* is subject to shortening in consequence of the change of [χ] to [f]. *Hough* (ME *hǒgh*; see § 34, Note) is 'phonetically' spelt *huff* by Strong, and *hoof* (which probably shows Northern [u] < ME *ŭ*) by Brown. *Dough* (OE *dāh*) is 'phonetically' spelt *duff* by Brown (probably a Northerner), and *cough* (ME *cǒgh*) is given as *cuff* by Brooksbank and Brown.

The only case of shortening of ME *ū* before a consonant other than [f] < [χ] is *youth*, in which a number of orthoepists show ME *ŭ* (see § 178 below). In *dove* and *shove* the ModE *ŭ* is not developed by shortening of ME *ū* (see Notes 2–4 below).

Note 1: For other pronunciations of some of these words see § 34 above. The variant *duff* 'dough', originally a Northernism (see *OED*, s.v. *duff* sb.¹), is an example of the process described under (c) above. On *slough* 'cast skin' see § 34 (1).

Note 2: *OED* attributes ModE [ʌ] in *shove* to shortening of ME *ū*, and compares *dove* (*OED*, s.vv.); similarly Luick (see Note 4). But the resemblance between the two words is illusory. *Shove* (OE *scūfan*) must be considered with the other verbs of the same class, i.e. *brook* (OE *brūcan*), *louk* (OE *lūcan*), *lout* (OE *lūtan*), *suck* (OE *sūcan*), and *bow* (OE *būgan*). These verbs, originally strong, develop weak p.ts. and p.ps. by the thirteenth or the fourteenth century, and in the fourteenth century have spellings both in the new weak p.t. (or p.p.) and in the infinitive which indicate ME *ŭ* (see *OED*, s.vv.). The abnormal vocalism is associated with the change in conjugation. Although the weak p.t. and p.p. were often formed on the infinitive, the starting-point of the change in conjugation was probably the old strong p.t. pl. stem in *ŭ*; this stem, which shows some tendency to be generalized as the p.t. and to invade the p.p. even when the verb remains strong, was often the basis on which the new weak p.t. and p.p. were formed. In consequence the verbs, as a class, often had, when they became weak, an infinitive with a long vowel (ME *ū*) and a p.t. and p.p. with a short vowel (ME *ŭ*); they had clearly been assimilated to the common class of ME weak verb (e.g. *read*) which has a long vowel in the infinitive and a short vowel in the p.t. and p.p. But infinitives with ME *ŭ* were then formed on the analogy of the p.t. and p.p., whence the surviving short vowel in *shove* and *suck* and the fourteenth-century forms *luk(en)* 'louk' and *lote*, *lutte* 'lout'; in *brook* the new infinitive in *ŭ* was formed early enough for lengthening in the open syllable to follow, thus *brŭken* > *brǭken* > *brook* (with [uː], later shortened to [ʊ]). (Laȝamon's *broken* infin. (MS C), which is regarded by *OED* as showing ME *ǭ*, is too early, and is rather an error for *brouken*, the reading of MS O, or for *bruken*.) The same lengthening may have occurred in *shove*; *OED* cites the spelling *shoove* (1653), but at this late date *oo* might be used for ME *ŭ* by inverted spelling. The only verb of this class which shows no form in ME *ŭ* is *bow*, the reason being that its p.t.pl. stem *bŭg-* became ME *bū-* and was thus identical with the infinitive stem (ME *bū-* < OE *būg-*). Even in those words which have PresE [ʌ], regular forms in ME *ū* (from OE *ū* in the infinitive stem) long survived; Levins's [uː] in *suck* is rather a dialectal development of ME *ū* than from ME *ǭ* < *ŭ* by lengthening in the open syllable.

Note 3: The difficulty of explaining PresE [ʌ] in *dove* by shortening of OE *ū* is occasioned by the fact that the word has an eModE form in [uː] (see § 18 above), which must be from ME *ǭ*; this cannot be otherwise developed than by lengthening of ME *ŭ* in the open syllable. Unless we accept Luick's view (see Note 4) we must therefore assume an OE **dūfe*; but an OE **dūfe* (which would be in agreement with the forms of the cognate Gmc languages) must also be assumed to account for the ME forms in *ou* (*douve*, &c.). Such a variation could be explained (if we accept *OED*'s suggestion that the word is derived from the stem *dūb-* 'to dive') by assuming two formations, one on the infinitive stem *dūb-* (whence OE **dūfe*) and one on the weak grade *dŭb-* (whence OE **dŭfe*). The latter would explain not only the early ModE form in [uː], but also the PresE form in [ʌ], and there would be no necessity to assume shortening of ME *ū* in the alternative form (ME *douve*), which does not survive in StE.

Note 4: Luick, §§ 389 and 393 (2), assumes that in *dove* and *shove* (and some others) there was an eME shortening of *ū* to *ŭ*, which was succeeded by the lengthening of the new *ŭ* to late ME *ǭ* in open syllables. But, as Jordan, § 55, Anm. 3, remarks, there is no sufficient evidence of this; and the process is in itself unlikely. Ekwall in *RES* ix (1958), 311 explains *dove* and *shove* by assuming failure of diphthongization of ME *ū* before *v* (cf. § 164 below, and add as a further possible example *houve*, q.v. in *OED*), followed by shortening of [uː] to [u] > [ʌ]. But spellings suggesting *ŭ* occur in both words before 1400, and the explanation separates *shove* from the other verbs discussed in Note 2.

SHORTENING OF FINAL VOWELS

§ 40. The shortening of final vowels is a process which one would hardly expect to find in late ME or early ModE, since it seems flatly contrary to the general tendency of the language to shorten vowels in closed syllables and to lengthen them in open, but there is a body of sixteenth-century evidence which leaves little doubt that such a shortening occurred. In part this evidence consists of transcriptions in the spelling reformers which could be explained away by the assumption that the mark of length had been inadvertently omitted (and are so explained by Jespersen, *Hart*, and Zachrisson, *Bullokar*); but the transcriptions are consistent with statements on pronunciation which cannot be so easily dismissed and which support them. The *ABC for chyldren* (c. 1555) has statements which show ME *ĕ* in *fle* 'flay' (OE *flēan*) and *sle* 'slay' (OE *slēan*) and ME *ŏ* in *do* 'doe', *ro* 'roe', and *go* (see Vol. I, pp. 18–19). The most notable case is Smith's argument in *De ... linguæ Græcæ pronunciatione* (written 1542, published 1568) that two short vowels are the equivalent of one long vowel, which he illustrates by equating the English words *buy it* (transcribed βὶ ἰτ) with *bite* (transcribed βῖτ) and *go on* (transcribed γὸ ὸν) with *gone* (transcribed γῶν); it is essential to his argument to assume (what indeed his transcriptions show) that *buy* and *go* had ME *ĭ* and *ŏ* respectively. Mulcaster (see Vol. I, p. 124) says that *ò* (i.e. ME *ŭ*), which is 'still naturallie short' (always short by nature), occurs not only in *to* and *do* (which have weak forms), but also in *two*, which must therefore have ME *ŭ* (pronounced still as [u]). Bullokar not only fails to mark certain final vowels as long, but also rhymes *flee*, *dry*, and *lie* on short [ɪ], i.e. ME *ĭ* (see Vol. I, pp. 109–10). Gil, in a discussion of metre (ed. Jiriczek, p. 137), says that the vowel of *going* is short, like those

§ 40] PART 2: LATE ME AND MoDE SHORTENING 515

of *doing* (which has a weak form), *any*, *spirit*, and *body*; this confirms his invariable transcription of *go* with *ŏ*. It seems beyond doubt that in most cases the transcriptions which show a short vowel in final position (and in derivatives of words with final vowels, especially inflexional forms) are both deliberate and correct. The detailed evidence is as follows.

ME *ā* does not normally occur in final position. But Smith gives the names of the letters *k* and *h* as *ka* and *ha* (with ME *ă*); as, however, the name of *h* is clearly his own invention, that of *k* may also be a new formation and not the traditional ME *kā* (PresE [keɪ]).

ME *ẹ̄* in final position is shortened to *ĕ* in *fle* 'flay' and *sle* 'slay' in the *ABC for chyldren*. Smith transcribes with *ĕ* the English word *sea* and Latin *sē* (which he equates) and Latin *tē*. Bullokar has *ĕ* in *yea* (twelve times, against [iː] once, according to Zachrisson's word-list). But Hart's isolated *dez* 'days' (beside normal *dē(z)*) is almost certainly a mere error.

ME *ẹ̄* is shortened to *ĭ* in *bee* (which Smith once identifies with the name of the letter *b*, transcribed with the symbol for ME *ẹ̄* but without long mark, which means [ɪ]; see Vol. I, p. 55) and in *thee* vb. 'thrive', which he similarly transcribes; but *bee* also has [iː] (once). Smith indeed gives the names of all the letters *b*, *c*, *d*, *ð*, *g*, *p*, *t*, *þ* as the consonant plus [ɪ]; if these names are modelled on the traditional names of, for example, *b* and *d*, Smith's [ɪ] is by shortening of ME *ẹ̄*. Bullokar rhymes *flee* on [ɪ] (see Vol. I, p. 109). Gil gives *ĭ* once (against [iː] six times) in *tree*. For spellings which appear to show similar shortenings see § 132, Note, under (*d*).

ME *ī* is shown as *ĭ* by Smith in *buy* (see above) and in *dyed*, which is transcribed as *died* [drəd] or *dĭd* [dəɪd]. Bullokar (cf. Vol. I, p. 114) has *ĭ* in *appliable* and *applied* (from *apply*, not recorded), *buying* (against *ī* in *buy*), *bye*, *cry*, *denying* and *denyeth* (against *ī* in *denied* twice), *die* sb. and its plural [dɪz], *die* vb. and *died* p.t., *dry*, *fly*, *fy*, *lie* sb., *lie* vb., *liar*, *slyly* (first syllable), *spy* vb. (against *ī* in *spy* sb.), *tie*, *trial*, *trier*, *try* (against *ī* in *trying* and *tried*), *why*, and *wry*. He also rhymes *dry* and *lie* vb. on *ĭ* (see Vol. I, p. 109).

ME *ǭ* is rather more generally shortened. The *ABC for chyldren* has *ŏ* in *do* 'doe', *ro* 'roe', and *go*. Smith has *ŏ* in *go* (see above) and in the transcriptions of LA in *doe* (once, beside *ǭ* once), *toe* (once, beside *ǭ* thrice), and *wooed* pronounced [wɔəd] (which has *ŏ* by shortening of ME *ou* < OE *wōgian*; cf. Hart below). Hart has *ŏ* in the interjection *o* (which might perhaps have a weak form) and once in *ro* (glossed 'row?' by Jespersen, but perhaps *roe*; otherwise *row* has *ǭ* thrice); ME *ou* in *show* is twice *ŏ*, thrice *ǭ* (i.e. [oː] by monophthongization). Bullokar has *ŏ* in *ago*, *foes*, *forego*, *go* (six times), *ho* interjection (four times), *lo* interjection (once, beside *ǭ* thrice), *toe*, *wo* interjection, and *woe* sb. (twice). Gil has *ŏ* in *forego* (twice, beside *ǭ* twice; but *forgo* has *ǭ* once), *go* (eight times), *ho* interjection, *lo* interjection, *mo* 'more' (once, beside *ǭ* once), *tho* 'then', and *woe* (once, beside *ǭ* seven times).

ME ǭ (by raising of ME ǭ after [w]) is shortened to ME ŭ in *two* in Mulcaster (see above).

There is no evidence of shortening of final ME ū. On final ME [y:] (and eModE [y:] < ME *iu*) see Note 1 below.

It might perhaps be argued that the shortening was a dialectal one which attained a limited currency in StE, for of the sources of evidence Mulcaster was a Northerner, Smith a native of Essex, Bullokar of Sussex, and Gil of Lincolnshire. But it would seem a truer interpretation to say that the shortening was a widespread tendency which affected pronunciation in the sixteenth and early seventeenth centuries, after which the normal unshortened forms were again generalized. Danielsson (*Hart*, ii. 154) has suggested that Smith and Gil may have been influenced by the Classical rule that *vocalis ante vocalem corripitur*; and both he and Koziol (*English Studies*, xxxix (1958), 140) have drawn attention to the tendency in present StE for a long vowel or diphthong to be shortened before an immediately following unstressed vowel, and have suggested that the short vowel shown in such a word as *go* might have been generalized from *going*. Such explanations, and the influence of reduced stress, would certainly account for much of the evidence, but hardly for all of it; and to argue from an inflected to an uninflected form does not seem to me typical of these early sources. I prefer to think that in late ME, before the diphthongization of ME ī was far advanced, there was a tendency to shorten vowels in absolute finality which contrasted with the earlier and more general lengthening of vowels that were final in the first syllable of disyllabic words, and that the shortened variants persisted in educated use until the early seventeenth century.

Note 1: Smith frequently omits the long mark from final *v* (i.e. ME [y:] or *iu*, in, for example, *due*, *blue*, *brew*, &c.); but this is a vowel without short equivalent, and the omission is therefore better not taken as a sign of shortening. His name of the letter *q* is given as *quu*, which should mean [kwu]; but it is to be regarded as an invented name, and not as a development of the traditional [ky:] or [kiu] (PresE [kju:]).

Note 2: Smith in *LG* represents the monophthongal pronunciation of ME *ai* in *day*, *pay*, and *way* as *da*, *wa*, and *pa*, but it seems unlikely that he has any intention of indicating shortening; *LA* has *dā*, &c.

Note 3: Words with short final vowels which develop in weak forms are deliberately excluded from the evidence set out above. But it seems doubtful whether the regular final ŏ recorded by Smith, Hart, Bullokar, and Gil for *so* and *no* is sufficiently accounted for by the supposition that it develops under weak stress, for weak forms of these two words are comparatively rare in PresE (cf. Daniel Jones, *English Pronouncing Dictionary*, s.vv.); all four orthoepists give evidence of shortening of final ME ǭ (and/or in Hart's case final ME *ou*) in words which cannot have weak forms.

Note 4: In the nature of things confirmation of the orthoepists' evidence on this point cannot ordinarily be provided by spellings, since the conventional English orthography has no means of indicating a short final vowel; see, however, § 132, Note, under (*d*). And confirmation from rhymes can be had only if ME ī and ME ḝ are rhymed together, as they are by Bullokar, by virtue of their both being shortened to [ɪ]; theoretically one might also look for parallel rhymes of ME ū with ME ǭ, but the orthoepists themselves give no evidence of shortening of final ME ū.

Part 3: LENGTHENING

§ 41. In the sixteenth and seventeenth centuries, lengthening in Standard English affects only the vowels *ă* and *ŏ*, and occurs (1) before *r*, especially when it is followed by another consonant; (2) before one of the voiceless spirants [s], [f], and [þ], especially when it is followed by another consonant; and (3) in certain other circumstances. In this Part I shall first set out and analyse the evidence for the lengthening in each of the three cases, and then discuss the phonetic process whereby it occurred.

LENGTHENING BEFORE *r*

(1) *Lengthening of ME ă before* r

§ 42. The first evidence of lengthening of ME *ă* before *r* plus consonant occurs in Bullokar, who shows it in native English words before the consonant groups which had caused lengthening in OE, i.e. before *rn* in such words as *barn, warn,* and *yarn* (beside short *ă*) and before *rl* in *carl*; he identifies the lengthened sound with ME *ā*. Gil gives ME *ā* in *heard* twice, against ME *ę̄* once; it develops by lengthening of ME *ă* in the well-known *hard* form (see further Vol. I, pp. 145–6). Butler has a long vowel (again identified with ME *ā*) in *barm*. Daines shows a long vowel, which he attempts to distinguish from ME *ā*, in *barn, carp, sharp, smart, art,* and *marsh* (see Vol. I, pp. 330–3). Newton shows (dialectal) lengthening to [a:] in *care* and *mare* (see Vol. I, p. 250). Poole's rhymes appear to show lengthening (to identity with ME *ā*) before *rd* and *rs*, and in the plurals of two words in final *r*, *bars* and *cars* (see further Vol. I, pp. 431–2). Coles in his *Syncrisis* says that the *a* of *arm*, &c., like that of *father*, has a sound midway between those of *all* and *ale*; lengthening to [a:] is certain. But in the *Schoolmaster* he shows no lengthening (see Vol. I, p. 442). Cooper says that the letter *a* always has the value of the long equivalent of ME *ă* (i.e. a front vowel [a:]; see § 54 below) before *r* plus consonant, except before *rsh* (contrast Daines; Cooper has dialectal loss of *r* before *sh*); he gives as examples *barge, carp, dart,* and *tart*. *WSC* may distinguish the vowel of *part* from that of *car*, though neither is 'long *a*' (ME *ā*); the former would then have [a:], as in Cooper (see further Vol. I, p. 361). Cocker's 'homophone' list (see Vol. I, p. 417) shows a lengthened vowel, identified with ME *ā*, in *war* (cf. Poole's rhymes, and those cited in § 43, Note 3 below).

Note: Bullokar also shows a long vowel, identified with ME *ā*, in words adopted from French, whatever the consonant that follows the *r*; in such cases it seems necessary to regard the long vowel as showing a ME variant in *ā* (see § 6 above), and not as being due to lengthening in ModE, as assumed by Luick, § 530, Anm. 1.

§ 43. The confusing feature of this evidence is that it shows two results of lengthening, for Bullokar, Gil, Butler, Poole, and Cocker identify the lengthened sound with ME $\bar{a}$. Horn, § 45, Anm. 3, assumes that this shows that there was a distinct process of lengthening of ME $\breve{a}$ whereby it became identical with ME $\bar{a}$; Zachrisson, *Bullokar*, p. 33, suggests that the process may have occurred in ME times. But here we meet the central difficulty; as ME $\breve{a}$ and ME $\bar{a}$ diverge in quality in ModE (the latter being fronted more rapidly), it is hard to see how there can be a ModE lengthening process which would directly produce from ME $\breve{a}$ a sound identical with ME $\bar{a}$; but on the other hand we can hardly put the process back into ME times because Bullokar shows the lengthened sound in *barn* and *quarn* 'quern', which have $\breve{a}$ only by late ME lowering of ME $\breve{e}$ to $\breve{a}$ before *r*. As Bullokar and Butler are both of them poor phoneticians, it might be possible to assume that they simply failed to distinguish between the old $\bar{a}$ and the new lengthened sound; but their evidence is supported by that of Gil (a good observer) and of foreign orthoepists (see Note 1 below) and by occasional sixteenth- and seventeenth-century rhymes between ME $\breve{a}$ before *r* and ME $\bar{a}$ (see Note 3 below). The solution seems to be to assume that there was only one process of lengthening, the immediate result of which was [a:], but that it occurred at different dates and therefore gave different results in various dialects. In some southern dialects which influenced StE but were distinct from it (including presumably vulgar London English and the dialect of Sussex, evidenced by Bullokar) the lengthening occurred before ME $\bar{a}$ was fronted from [a:], so that the lengthened sound was identified with ME $\bar{a}$; this must mean that the lengthening, though later than the change of ME $\breve{e}$ to $\breve{a}$ before *r* (which occurred *c*. 1400), nevertheless had been completed before the later fifteenth century, since fronting of ME $\bar{a}$ must by then have begun. Poole, who was a Northerner, is doubtless evidence of a similar development in the North. In StE itself, on the other hand, the lengthening did not occur until long after ME $\bar{a}$ had been fronted from [a:]; the new seventeenth-century [a:] was therefore kept distinct from ME $\bar{a}$. A similar double development affects ME $\breve{o}$ before *r*; see further below.

Bullokar's evidence, as Zachrisson points out, seems to show that the lengthening occurred first (or rather most commonly) before the OE lengthening groups; Daines's shows it extended to all cases of *r* plus consonant. Bullokar's use of a lengthened vowel would seem to have been a vulgarism; all the other sixteenth-century orthoepists, and indeed most of those of the seventeenth century, show unlengthened $\breve{a}$. Daines appears to have [a:] in *bars* (see Vol. I, pp. 332–3), and one would think it unlikely that the singular *bar* would not have the same vowel. It is true that Daines says that *are* has 'short' *a*, but this means no more than that it is not ME $\bar{a}$; *bars* likewise is said to have a short vowel, though it seems clear from the terms Daines uses to describe the pronunciation of its *a* that it has [a:]. Similarly Poole shows lengthening in *bars* and *cars*. Cooper still gives short ă in *bar, car*, and *tar*; on *WSC* see § 42. Cocker, however, shows lengthening in *war*. Despite the lack of evidence, it is probable that lengthening before final *r* occurred at the same time as before *r* plus consonant; foreign observers record it in *far* in 1672 and 1678 (see Note 1). But it must have been less frequent before final *r*, and therefore made its way into careful speech more slowly. Lengthening before intervocalic *r* does not occur in seventeenth-century StE nor in PresE.

Note 1: Luick, § 550, Anm. 1, cites the evidence of the *Alphabet Anglois* (1625) identifying *a* in *harp* and *part* with ME *ā* (but *part* being an adoption from French may vary in ME between ME *ă* and ME *ā*), and of the Swede Bolling (1678) identifying with ME *ā* the *a* of *far, darkness, are*, and *enlarge* (but *are* has ME *ā* in the strong form, and *enlarge* being from French may vary in ME). Festeau (1672) probably also knew lengthened [aː] both before *r* plus consonant and before final *r*; see § 44, Note 4 below.

Note 2: The rhyme *after : carter* (*Rede me and be not wroth*, 1527), cited by Wyld, *Coll. Eng.*, p. 257, has been taken to show lengthening to [aː] in both words; but the loss of *r* at so early a date is a sure sign of dialectalism. Furthermore, all rhymes involving *after* are to be regarded as special cases, in view of the surviving dialectal pronunciations [ɑːtə(r)] (widespread in the Midlands and South) and [ɒːtə(r)] (Northamptonshire); these are to be explained as showing a development of pre-consonantal [f] to [u], analogous to that of pre-consonantal [v] in *havk-* > *hawk* (see § 423 below for a fuller discussion). The spelling *auternoone* 'afternoon' is recorded in an account of a visit by the Vice-Chancellor of Cambridge to Queen Elizabeth at Audley End in Essex in 1578 (cited by Lord Braybrooke, *History of Audley End* (1836), p. 75). The rhyme must depend on a pronunciation [kɒːtə(r)] for *carter*, i.e. on the dialectal lengthening of ME *ă* to [ɒː] before *r* which is discussed immediately below; cf. especially Brown's 'phonetic spelling' *chauter* 'charter'. Brown, it is to be noted, is probably shown by his language to have been a Northerner; and the forms of *Rede me* (e.g. *-is* for *-es*, which is common, and *thou ware* 'thou wast') suggest that its author (W. Roy or J. Barlow) was also a Northerner. See also § 53, Note 6, under (*d*).

Note 3: Rhymes, in view of their frequent ambiguity, are unsatisfactory evidence of lengthening, and indeed can never give evidence of the StE lengthening of *ă* to [aː] until, with the loss of *r*, it becomes possible to rhyme, for example, *path* with *hearth*. But there are many sixteenth- and seventeenth-century rhymes which show a lengthening of ME *ă* to identity with ME *ā* before *r*. (Words of OF origin should of course be excluded from consideration, since they may vary in ME between *ă* and *ā*.) Early rhymes of *heard* on ME *ā* are cited in Vol. I, p. 145; here we may add that Dryden rhymes *heard* with *prepar'd*. Spenser commonly has such rhymes (e.g. *mard* 'marred' : *stared, unbard* 'unbarred' : *far'd*, *hard : far'd : prepar'd*; cf. Bauermeister, *Zur Sprache Spensers auf Grund der Reime in der F.Q.*, § 81), and they survive as late as Pope (who has *hard : dared*). This lengthening is also shown by rhymes before final *r*: Jonson has *far : air*, Dryden *care : war*, and Pope *star : air : bear*. In view of their agreement with the orthoepistical evidence cited in the text above and in Note 1, such rhymes are to be accepted as accurate; they do not involve a licence of rhyming short vowels with long.

Dialectal lengthening to [ɒː]

§ 44. ME *ă* when lengthened before *r* occasionally became not [aː] but [ɒː], i.e. the vowel was rounded (by the lip-protrusion of [r]) as well as lengthened. This process is the explanation of Fox and Hookes's pairing of *barm* with *balm* (see Vol. I, p. 408); they record many vulgarisms, but show no special connexion with any regional dialect. Brown, who records many Northernisms, has *chauter* 'charter'; cf. the rhyme *after : carter* discussed in Note 2 above. Cooper describes *Chorles* 'Charles' as 'barbarous speaking'.

The Welsh orthoepist Jones in his *Practical Phonography* (1701) says that *a* is pronounced like *au* in *arrand*, *arrant*, *arrears*, and *arrest* and in eight other words before intervocalic *r*; see further § 55, Note 2 and § 427. Note. The pronunciation seems to have been particularly common in the West, owing to a special pronunciation of the [r] (see § 55, Note 2 (*b*)); Wright records [ɒ:] in *barley*, *park*, and *part* for Gloucestershire, and in *cart* for Worcestershire; Ekwall, *Jones*, p. lxxix, records [ɒ:] in *lard* for Somerset; Wyld, *Coll. Eng.*, p. 205, for the place-name *Charlbury* in Oxfordshire. But it also occurred in Northern dialects, as Brown's evidence suggests; Wright records [ɒ:] in Scottish dialects in *barley* and *darn*. Cooper and Fox and Hookes are evidence of its occurrence as a vulgarism in the Home Counties, and Wyld, loc. cit., observes that in the nineteenth century [tʃɒ:lz] 'Charles' (represented in writing as *Chawles*) was 'hyperfashionable or vulgar'. The pronunciation survives in *Marlborough*.

Note 1: Daines does not give evidence of [ɒ:] for ME *ă* before *r*, as alleged by Luick, § 550, Anm. 2; see Vol. I, p. 332 footnote.

Note 2: Spellings to illustrate this pronunciation are cited by Luick, § 550, Anm. 1 and 2; Wyld, *Coll. Eng.*, p. 205; and Zachrisson, *Eng. Vowels*, pp. 62–63. A fifteenth-century form *laurd* 'lard' cited by *OED* cannot, according to Luick, be confirmed. A 1525 print of Tyndale (who was significantly a Gloucestershire man), has *chaurge* 'charge' twice. The Diary (1615–22) of Richard Cocks (a merchant and probably a native of Coventry; see *Diary*, ed. Maunde Thompson (Hakluyt Soc., 1883), pp. xii–xiii) has *yorn* 'yarn', *yord* 'yard', and *Chorles*; similarly Mrs. Basire (a Shropshire lady) has *Chorles*. In the seventeenth century, according to Luick, interchange of the spellings *au(r)* and *ar* is frequent, e.g. *hawser* spelt *harser* and *haurser*, *Haughton* spelt *Harton* (the latter by Henslowe, a native of Sussex). The spellings of Cocks and Mrs. Basire certainly show the development to [ɒ:]. But the *au* spellings are perhaps less certain. Zachrisson suggests that they may show (i) the lengthening of ME *ă* to [a:] before *r* and (ii) the development of ME *au* to [a:] in *dance*, &c., so that we may have inverted spelling with *au* in place of *a*. This argument may reduce a little the value of these spellings with *au* for *a*, but not much weight can be allowed to it, for the English have never regarded *au* as a spelling-symbol for [a:]; since the early seventeenth century, in StE itself, they have used it as the most convenient representation of the sound [ɒ:] (of which ME *au* is the main source)—so much so that in those words with following nasal in which the spelling *au* has been able to maintain itself the [ɑ:] pronunciation has now been almost completely abandoned in favour of [ɒ:] (e.g. *vaunt*, *launch*, &c.). The odds are strongly that if an Englishman spells with *au* a word of which the traditional spelling is *a*, his intention is to show [ɒ:] (or whatever vowel in his dialect is used for ME *au* in its free development).

It may again be noticed that spellings which involve a silent *r* are in the seventeenth century reflections of vulgar or dialectal pronunciation.

Note 3: Zachrisson, loc. cit., points out that the spellings with *au* for ME *ă* before *r* occur in French words and suggests that they may show English substitution of [ɒ:] < ME *au* for French [ɑ]. But this explanation will not cover *yord* and *yorn*; and as *charge* and *lard* are ME adoptions, they should show identification of ME *ă* or *ā* with OF *a* and be independent of French influence by the fifteenth century.

Note 4: Luick, § 550, Anm. 2, cites foreign orthoepists as showing [ɒ:] for ME *ă* before *r*. Festeau (1672) says that *far* and *hard* are pronounced with French *a* 'fort long'; this could indicate [ɒ:], since the monophthong developed from ME *au* is often identified with French *a*, but might equally well (indeed, better) be interpreted (with Zachrisson) as showing the ordinary lengthening to [a:]. Nyborg (1698) says that the sound of *all* occurs in *pardon* and *parson*; Nicolai (1693), Tiessen (1705), and Beuthner (1711) say that the sound of *salt* occurs in *far* and *hard*. These statements are better evidence for [ɒ:].

(2) *Lengthening of ME ŏ before* r

§ 45. In PresE it is difficult to tell which words contain ME ŏ lengthened before r and which ME ǭ (or ọ̄ or ū); for the new long vowel ultimately became identical with the old ones, and many words, as we have seen, varied in early ModE between ŏ on the one hand and ǭ or ọ̄ on the other. In the seventeenth century this difficulty does not arise when the lengthening of ŏ resulted in open [ɒ:] (the StE development), for [ɒ:] was carefully distinguished from [o:] even before r; but there is, as we shall see, evidence that the lengthened vowel in one development became identical with ME ǭ, and when this occurs it may be very difficult indeed to determine whether we have to do with eModE lengthening or with a ME long variant. The criteria which tend to show that there has been lengthening are: (1) the absence of evidence of a pronunciation [u:] in the word in question, since such a pronunciation is certain evidence of original ME ọ̄ or of later ME ọ̄ by raising of ME ǭ; (2) the presence in the orthoepist concerned of evidence of lengthening of ME ŏ in other words, or of the analogous lengthening of ME ă before r (which is shown, as we have seen, by Bullokar, Gil, Butler, Daines, Poole, Coles, Cooper, and *WSC-RS*); and (3) best of all, in a native word, the impossibility of either late OE lengthening before consonant-groups or of ME lengthening in open syllables.

§ 46. On the analogy of lengthening of ME ă before r, we should expect to find evidence of the lengthening of ME ŏ earliest before the r-groups that had caused late OE lengthening. But it is precisely here that the fact that some observers identify the new lengthened sound with ME ǭ is most inconvenient; criterion (3) fails us, and it is hard to tell whether we have to do with lengthening or with a ME long variant. But nevertheless there appears to be lengthening in the following words, which may be disposed in two groups. (1) *Corn* has ŏ in Gil and Coles, but a long vowel identified with ME ǭ in Bullokar and 'long o' in *RS*. *Horn* has ŏ in Hart, Gil, and Hodges, but a long vowel identified with ME ǭ in Bullokar, 'long o' in *RS*, and open [ɒ:] in Cooper, who says that o is 'almost always' [ɒ:] before rn. *Morn* has [ɒ:] in Newton. *Churl* (OE cĕorl > ceŏrl > ME chŏrl or chǫ̆rl) has a long vowel identified with ME ǭ in Bullokar. It should be observed that in none of these words is there evidence of [u:] < ME ǭ, and that the long vowel is given only by observers who show lengthening of ME ă; *RS* and Cooper (but not Bullokar) also show lengthening of ME ŏ before other r-groups. (2) *Lord*, which varies between ŏ and ǭ (see § 13 (3) above), has [ɒ:] by lengthening of ME ŏ in Coles and 'long o' in *RS*. For *shorn, torn*, and *born(e)* two pronunciations are given by *RS*, of which [u:] is from late ME ǭ by raising of ME ǭ (and in *born(e)* is made to correspond to the sense 'supported'; see § 13 (2a)), and the other, 'long o', must be developed by some other process, presumably lengthening (note that he makes this pronunciation correspond to the sense 'past birth', for which Hodges and Cooper give ME ŏ). Similarly *RS*'s 'long o' in *forlorn* and *worn* and in the originally French words *cord* and *scorn* is likely to be by lengthening; in this author both ME ǭ and original ME ǭ are normally [u:] before *r*.

Of the orthoepists who give this evidence of eModE lengthening before the *r*-groups which had caused OE lengthening, only Bullokar (who is by far the earliest) fails to show it before other *r*-groups; there is, however, a clear suggestion that it occurred earlier (or more regularly) before the former.

Note 1: On *churl* see also § 18, Note 3. Bullokar's long vowel identified with ME ǭ in *scorn* (recorded once, beside ŏ twice) might well be by lengthening, since no other orthoepist records ME ǭ in this word (except for *RS*'s 'long o'); but in such a word from French a ME variant in ǭ is always possible.

That Bullokar's long vowel in the words of group (1) in the text above is due to lengthening of ME ŏ, and is not derived from ME ǭ < OE ō by OE lengthening before consonant-groups, is strongly suggested by his failure to show lowering of [u:] < ME ǭ (or < ME ū) before *r*. The only possible cases of this lowering are (i) the rhyme of *course* (transcribed with [ʌu]) with *force* (transcribed with ME ǭ), but it should be held to depend on the variant [u:] in both words and not on [o:] by lowering of [u:] < ME ū in *course*; (ii) the long vowel identified with ME ǭ which Bullokar gives in *afford*. But this should rather be considered a further example of lengthening of ME ŏ to identity with ME ǭ; it is not cited among the words of group (1) in the text above only because there is, in this case, evidence in other orthoepists of a ModE variant in [u:] < ME ǭ.

Note 2: Poole's rhyme of *morn* with *mourn*, and the 'homophone' list pairing (found from Hodges onwards) of *morning* with *mourning*, show ME ǭ in *morn* and *morning* rather than lengthening of ME ŏ in these two words and lowering of ME ū in *mourn(ing)* (see § 16, and Note 2 there).

§ 47. In other circumstances the evidence is less difficult to interpret. Before consonant-groups other than those which cause OE lengthening it is as follows. (*a*) Before *rm* : *storm* has ŏ in Bullokar, Gil, Hodges, and Coles, but 'long o' in *RS*; *reform* has ŏ in Hart and Bullokar, and *deform* has ŏ in Bullokar, but *transform* and similar words have 'long o' in *RS*. (*b*) *North* has ŏ in Hart, Bullokar, and Gil, but [ɒ:] in Cooper and 'long o' in *RS*. (*c*) *Orb* has [ɒ:] in Coles. (*d*) Before *rt*, Cooper says, *o* is almost always long guttural α ([ɒ:]), and *WSC-RS* gives 'long o' in *short*, which has ŏ in Hart, Gil, and Coles. (*e*) Before *rs* in *horse* Bullokar, Robinson, Gil, and Hodges have ŏ, but Poole's rhymes (see Vol. I, p. 432) seem to show lengthening to identity with ME ǭ. (*f*) Before other *r*-groups lengthening is (by chance) not recorded; thus ŏ alone occurs in *fork* in Bullokar and Hodges, and in *stork* in Gil, and it is uncertain whether Newton intends ŏ or [ɒ:] in *York*.

Before an *r* which is final in the word or syllable there is no fully satisfactory evidence of lengthening. Bullokar once shows a long vowel in *for*, and Poole rhymes *or*, *dor*, and *nor* with *fore*; but conceivably there might in both cases be cross-influence between *for* and *fore*. Bullokar regularly shows ME ǭ in *former*, but because the word is, as he supposes, derived from *fore* (cf. Zachrisson, *Bullokar*, pp. 33–34); the words are ultimately related, of course, and Bullokar often gives completely false quantity-markings in what he regards as 'derivatives'. Poole seems to rhyme *abhorred* (first recorded early in the fifteenth century) on ọ̄ (see Vol. I, p. 432), but though one would expect only ŏ in *abhor* it might perhaps have ME ọ̄ (since it seems to come in part through OF). The *Welsh Breviary* (1670) identifies with Welsh *o* the vowels of both *for* and *call*; but this is likely to mean that short [ɒ] occurs in the former and the corresponding long vowel [ɒ:] in the latter, rather than that both words have the same vowel. Gil is able to distinguish *forgo* from *forego* by the vowel-quantity. Smith, Hart, Robinson, Daines, Hodges, Wallis, and Wilkins all show retention of a short vowel before final *r*; so do Cooper and *WSC-RS* (the latter has, for example, short [ɒ] in *forty*), though they show lengthening before *r* plus consonant. Holder says that the English pronunciation of *forma* and *mortem* is with a short vowel, whereas foreigners use a long *o* (see Note 2 below). But in spite of this evidence it is probable that lengthening occurred at the same time before final *r* as before *r* plus consonant; it must, however, have been less common before final *r*, and so have made its way into careful speech more slowly. In PresE lengthened [ɒ:] occurs as regularly before final *r* as before *r* plus consonant.

Before intervocalic *r* there is no lengthening in PresE (so *sorry*, *morrow*, &c.); PresE [ɒ:] in *glory* and *story* is by lowering of ME ọ̄, recorded as a variant beside ŏ in the former and probable for the latter. Though some seventeenth-century observers give ambiguous evidence on *glory* (see § 13 (2) above), it is best to interpret their statements as meaning that the word has either ŏ or ME ọ̄, not lengthening of ME ŏ.

Note 1: Cooper's 'guttural *o*' in *porch* and *form* (as also in *born*) may be either short [ɒ] or [ɒ:]; he does not specify the quantity.

Note 2: Holder seems to have confused quantity and quality. Foreigners (he is most likely to know the French pronunciation of Latin) would use a short tense [o], which he has identified with the long tense [o:] developed from ME ọ̄, and which he contrasts with the short lax [ɒ] developed from ME ŏ. But his evidence shows both that ME ọ̄ was in his speech unlowered before *r*, and that the English used a short vowel in the two words. He represents the foreign pronunciations as *foorma* or *forema*, *moortem* or *moretem*.

§ 48. The evidence set out above shows two results of the lengthening process, as in the case of ME ă; Bullokar, the Northerner Poole, and *RS* identify the lengthened vowel with ME ọ̄ (as they identify ME ă, when lengthened, with ME ā), but Coles and Cooper show [ɒ:], identical with the monophthong developed from ME *au* (just as they show [a:] for lengthened ME ă). But the twofold result is likely to depend not on two distinct processes of lengthening, but on the date at which lengthening occurred. The actual vowel resulting from lengthening may be assumed to have been in the first instance approximately 'cardinal open [ɔ:]' (or somewhat lower), but if lengthening occurred early, before ME ọ̄ had been raised to [o:], the new long vowel was identified with the old one; on the other hand if lengthening occurred late (i.e. in the seventeenth century itself in StE), after ME *ǭ* had been raised to [o:] and a new open [ɒ:] had developed from ME *au*, the new long vowel was identified with the latter sound. It is the second development which is typical of StE and has alone remained a feature of its pronunciation; the former must have been native to vulgar or dialectal speech (by which Bullokar, Poole, and *RS* are in other respects greatly influenced), and affected StE but little. The date of the early lengthening is likely to have been the same as that of ME *ă*, i.e. in the fifteenth century.

Note 1: Sporadic evidence of lengthening of ME *ŏ* to identity with ME *ǭ* is provided by rhymes. Chapman in 1594 has *horse* : *course*. Daniel rhymes *short* with *sort* and *court*, and Dryden (*Fables*, 1700) rhymes *short* with *court*; these rhymes probably depend on [o:], but it is just conceivable that *court* may have ME *ŭ* and that the rhymes may be of ME *ŏ* with ME *ŭ* (a type found in both Daniel and Dryden). Later examples of such rhymes are Pope's *horse* : *coarse* (1717) and *short* : *court* (1734) and Gray's *horse* : *course* (1757). Shakespeare rhymes *abhor* with *more* and *adore* (Viëtor, pp. 234, 235); cf. Poole's rhyme, discussed above. In *The Two Noble Kinsmen*, *nor* is rhymed with *hoar* (cf. Poole's rhyme of *nor* with *fore*); but *hoar* might have a pronunciation [hwɒr] owing to the development of ME *ǭ* to [wɒ] (cf. Midland [wɒn] 'one' and *OED*'s note on the *wh* digraph).

Note 2: Lengthening of ME *ŏ* to identity with ME *ǭ* is shown by the present dialects, which have [ɔə] and [uə] (typical dialectal developments of ME *ǭ* before *r*; cf. Wright, § 126) in *fork*, *horse*, *storm*, and *short* (see Wright, § 87 and Index). The development is shown almost entirely by Northern dialects, but occurs sporadically in others (including Hertfordshire in the case of [ɔəs] 'horse').

(3) *ME* ă *preceded by* w *and followed by* r

§ 49. When ME *ă* is subject to the rounding influence of a preceding *w* as well as the lengthening influence of a following *r*, the result in PresE is [ɒ:], i.e. the same as lengthening of ME *ŏ*. But this result is not because the *w*-influence causes a change to *ŏ* before the lengthening operates; evidence even of the StE lengthening of ME *ă* to [a:] before *r* is somewhat earlier than that of rounding of unlengthened *ă* to *ŏ* (except in special words). If there were successive stages, they would rather be (*a*) lengthening to [a:] and (*b*) rounding of [a:] to [ɒ:]. But in fact in no case where ME *ă* becomes [ɒ:] do we find evidence of any stage intermediate between unlengthened and unrounded [a] and [ɒ:]; evidently the lengthening and the rounding were simultaneous processes. But if lengthening fails there can be rounding to [ɒ], as Coles's evidence shows; this, however, is hardly a StE development, and the inconsistency in Coles's evidence (see Vol. I, p. 442) suggests a mixture of two modes of pronunciation characteristic of different dialects. When there is early lengthening to identity with ME *ā* (as in Bullokar and Butler) the rounding fails.

Bullokar shows lengthening to identity with ME *ā* in *quarn* and in *warn* (once, against unlengthened *ă* thrice), but unchanged ME *ă* occurs in *warm*, *wharf*, and *quartern*. Butler shows lengthening to identity with ME *ā* in *swarm*. The StE lengthening to [ɒ:] is shown first by Daines (see Vol. I, pp. 331–3), who gives evidence of it in *ward, warm, swarm, warn, wharf, dwarf, swarve, warp, wart, quart, swart,* and *thwart*. Coles is more conservative; he shows both lengthening and rounding in *ward, dwarf,* and *wharf,* but rounding alone in *warm, swarm, warn, wart, quart,* and *thwart,* and neither lengthening nor rounding in *warp* and *warble* (see Vol. I, p. 442 and p. 443). Cooper shows [ɒ:] in *ward, warden,* and *warm*; he is followed (perhaps indirectly) by *WSC-RS*, with the addition of *warn, warner,* and *wart* to his examples (see Vol. I, pp. 301–2). It would appear from the evidence of Bullokar that in this case, as with ME *ă* uninfluenced by *w*, the lengthening was at first most common before the *r*-groups which had caused late OE lengthening.

Before final *r* (as in *war*) neither lengthening nor rounding is shown by Bullokar and Coles. Daines has [ɒ:] in *wars*, and we may perhaps deduce that he would have it also in the singular *war*, as have Cooper and *WSC-RS*. Of these three authors, Cooper and *WSC-RS* do not show lengthening before final *r* of ME *ă* uninfluenced by *w* or of ME *ŏ*; Daines has [a:] in *bars*, and we may perhaps deduce that he would have it also in the singular *bar*. Cooper and *RS* show lengthening before intervocalic *r* in *warren* (see Vol. I, pp. 301–2), though they do not show lengthening in this position of ME *ă* uninfluenced by *w* or of ME *ŏ*. The reason why lengthening of ME *ă* after *w* and before final or intervocalic *r* is apparently more frequent than that of ME *ă* uninfluenced by *w* or of ME *ŏ* in these positions, is that the *w* not only causes rounding, but also reinforces the lengthening influence of the *r*. In PresE lengthening is found before final *r* but not before intervocalic *r*.

Note 1: Miège, undoubtedly following Cooper, gives [ɒ:] in *war* and *warren* and in the other words of Cooper's list, to which he adds *warn, quart,* and *quarter* (see Vol. I, pp. 301–2). Elphinston (1765, 1786), like Coles, seems to have [ɒ] with rounding but without lengthening in *war, ward, sward,* and *wharf*.

Note 2: On lengthening before intervocalic *r* see § 55, Note 2.

Note 3: For a connected summary of the influence of a preceding *w* in causing the appearance of rounded [ɒ:] in place of eModE [a:] of various origins see § 195 below.

LENGTHENING BEFORE VOICELESS SPIRANTS

(1) *Lengthening of ME ă before Voiceless Spirants*

§ 50. The lengthening of ME *ă* before the voiceless spirants [s], [f], and [þ] is revealed by our evidence only towards the end of the seventeenth century. Short vowels are shown in such words as *pass, path, laugh, last,* and *ask* by Smith, Hart, Robinson, Gil, Butler, Hodges, Willis, and Coles; perhaps also by Ray, who says that *laugh* is pronounced *laff* (a spelling conceivably intended to show that the vowel is short by its doubling of the consonant), and by Brown (see Vol. I, p. 367). The statement of Daines that *staffe* has 'long *a*' does not show lengthening (see Vol. I, p. 333). The 'phonetically spelt' lists may be the first to show lengthening, but their evidence is most uncertain; for that of Young see Vol. I, p. 353, and for that of Cocker, Vol. I, p. 366. The only certain evidence is that of Cooper, who says that a long vowel, which (he asserts) is qualitatively the same as ME ă, occurs in *cast*, *past*, *last*, and other words when *s* is followed by another consonant, and in *path*; but not in *pass* (see Vol. I, p. 304). The lengthening may have been known to the author of *WSC*, who (though he restricts the term 'long *a*' to ME ā and has no means of describing a lengthened ă) seems to separate *blast* and *part* from the other examples which he gives of 'short *a*'.

Cooper's evidence supports the usual assumption that the original quality of the lengthened vowel was the same as that of unlengthened ME ă. It is generally thought that ME ă was by this time pronounced as [æ] and that the lengthened sound was therefore [æ:], and it is further assumed that this [æ:] was subsequently lowered to [ɑ:]. But if the explanation of the lengthening process given below (§ 54) is correct, the lengthened sound was originally [a:], from which both the Standard English [ɑ:] and the dialectal [æ:] can easily develop. Lowering of [æ:] to [ɑ:], assumed by the usual theory, seems an unlikely process, since the gap between the two sounds is large and the normal direction of change in ModE is towards the further fronting of front vowels.

The lengthening was not uniformly carried through, and the old unlengthened vowel continued to exist beside the new lengthened one. Considerable fluctuation in usage resulted; Walker (1791) and Batchelor (1809) speak as though the unlengthened pronunciation was at that time gaining ground at the expense of the lengthened one; see Jespersen, *ModE Gr*, § 10. 62 (whose explanation of these statements—that they show a new process of shortening—should certainly not be followed). Present StE generally accepts the lengthened pronunciation, but not in some words (e.g. *lass*), while in others there is variation (e.g. *hasp*, *alas*, *asp*, *ass*, *mass*, &c.), with a preference in some cases for [ɑ:], in others for [æ] (cf. Luick, § 555). In Northern English and in American English [æ] (or [a]) is normally preferred. The variant [æ:] of the lengthened sound occurs in the dialects (especially those of the South-west; see Wright, § 26) and as a variant in American English, and was formerly in-use in Standard English (see Ekwall, *Laut- und Formenlehre*, § 43; it was still known to Ellis). Long palatal [a:] occurs in American English (cf. Luick, § 555 end); it represents the original lengthened sound and is not to be taken as a 'compromise pronunciation', as it is by Luick (an improbable hypothesis; cf. Note 2 below). That this pronunciation is regarded as artificial is in no way inconsistent with its being a genuine survival in conservative speech of the original lengthened sound; conservatism is often artificial.

Note 1: The lengthening probably occurred much earlier than the time at which it was accepted into careful speech (an acceptance shown by Cooper's evidence); but reliable evidence of it is lacking before Cooper. The *Cely Papers* have been reported to have the spellings *marsters* 'masters' and *farder* 'father' (so Zachrisson, *Eng. Vowels*, p. 62, and Wyld, *Coll. Eng.*, pp. 204, 257, 298), which Wyld took as showing lengthening (and, by implication, loss of *r*), though Zachrisson was uncertain whether they were phonetic. But I am informed by Miss A. H. Forester that the true readings are *maistres* 'mistress' and *faider* 'father'; and in consequence there is no question of ModE lengthening of ME *ă*. On the rhyme *after : carter* see § 43, Note 2; it depends on a dialectal pronunciation of *after* which is in no way connected with lengthening before voiceless spirants. Wyld, op. cit., p. 204, to make Shakespeare's rhyme of *past* with *waste* 'intelligible', assumes lengthening to [æ:] in *past*, inexactly rhymed with ME *ā* in *waste*; but the rhyme is exact and depends on the normally developed variant of *waste* with ME *ă* (see § 6). Rhymes can in fact give no evidence of lengthening to [a:] before voiceless spirants until, with the loss of *r*, it becomes possible to rhyme, e.g., *path* with *hearth* (as is pointed out above); but the loss of *r* is much later than the lengthening, and there is in consequence no point in looking for such rhymes.

Note 2: In old-fashioned speech *after, ask*, &c., are (or were until recently) pronounced with short [a] even in educated Southern English, instead of the usual Southern English [ɑ:] or the [æ] which would be employed in words in which no lengthening occurs; cf. Daniel Jones, *Outline of English Phonetics*, §§ 294–5; Nicholson, *Introduction to French Phonetics*, p. 21. This [a] is first recorded by Smart 1838 (see Luick, § 555, Anm. 1). Luick would regard it as a compromise between [ɑ:] and [æ], but this view may be rejected (*a*) because such 'compromise pronunciations' are extremely unlikely except as isolated slips of the tongue when one hesitates between two pronunciations, and (*b*) because it is unthinkable that a sound which on Luick's hypothesis was otherwise unknown in Southern English should have been invented to act as a compromise between two other well-known sounds [æ] and [ɑ:], especially as most Englishmen to whom this sound [a] is not native have the utmost difficulty in learning to articulate it. We must rather regard this pronunciation as showing the survival before a voiceless spirant of the value [a] which at one time ME *ă* possessed in all positions; and it follows that the voiceless spirant must have exercised an influence on ME *ă* which was unfavourable to fronting. It is obviously preferable to assume that the voiceless spirant prevented the change from [a] to [æ] than that it caused the retraction of an already developed [æ] to [a].

Note 3: The pronunciation [ɑ:] in *father, rather, paths*, and *baths* requires a somewhat different explanation, since the following spirant is voiced, not voiceless; see § 53 below.

(2) *Lengthening of ME ŏ before Voiceless Spirants*

§ 51. Lengthening of ME *ŏ* before the voiceless spirants [s], [f], and [þ] is recorded at the same date as that of ME *ă*. There is no sign of it in Hart, Bullokar, Robinson, Gil, Hodges, and Wallis (who gives *loss* and *lost* as examples of the short vowel which corresponds to the long one in *laws* and *cause*). Even Coles, though he knew lengthening of ME *ŏ* (as of ME *ă*) in other circumstances, shows it for neither vowel before voiceless spirants. The only evidence comes from Cooper, who shows lengthening in *lost, frost*, and in other words before *st*, and in *off*, but not before final *s* in *loss*; his evidence on the lengthening of ME *ŏ* and ME *ă* before voiceless spirants is thus exactly parallel (see Vol. I, p. 305). Cooper further shows clearly that the lengthened sound developed from ME *ŏ* was identical with the monophthong developed from ME *au*, for *lost*, &c., are said to have 'long o guttural', which is also the sound of *laws*, &c. For once *WSC-RS* gives no evidence comparable with Cooper's.

The unlengthened pronunciation continued in use beside the new lengthened one, for which there is a considerable body of eighteenth-century evidence (cf. Luick, § 555, Anm. 1). Walker (1791) gives evidence of a reaction against the lengthened pronunciation, which he describes (probably not truthfully) as 'everyday growing more and more vulgar', like the lengthened pronunciation of ME ă in *castle*, &c. (cf. Jespersen, *ModE Gr*, § 10.76). The lengthened pronunciation, however, remained common throughout the nineteenth century. It is now heard chiefly among speakers of the older generation, and is much less common than the unlengthened pronunciation.

Note: It is probable that the lengthening took place much earlier than the time of its acceptance into careful speech, as shown by Cooper; but there is no reliable evidence before his. Zachrisson, *Eng. Vowels*, p. 82, thinks that the fifteenth-century spellings *auffer* 'offer' and *sauft* 'soft' may show the lengthening; but the former is a misreading and the latter may be otherwise explained (see § 237, Note 2). Wyld, *Coll. Eng.*, p. 257, cites *crooft* 'croft' (1422) and *toossed* 'tossed' (from *Euphues*, 1578), but Luick, § 555, Anm. 2, rightly rejects these two isolated spellings as 'too uncertain'; it is hardly natural to represent [ɒ:] by *oo*, which normally stands for two ME sounds (ME ǭ and ǭ̣) which are kept distinct from [ɒ:]. These may be inverted spellings due to the many words in which variation occurs between ME ŏ and either ME ǭ or ME ǭ̣, and which may therefore be spelt either with *o* or with *oo*. Wyld also cites the spellings *moathes* 'moths' and *geestes* 'guests', but these show the ME variants *ou* and *ẹ̄* which existed in these words (and in any case there is no question of lengthening of ME ĕ before a voiceless spirant); and Latimer's spelling *clausset* 'closet', which if it is not due to the ultimate etymon (Latin *clausum*) may be explained in the same way as the spelling *sauft* cited by Zachrisson (see above).

(3) ME ă preceded by w and followed by a voiceless spirant

§ 52. When ME ă is preceded by *w* and followed by a voiceless spirant there is added to the lengthening influence of the latter the rounding influence of the former; the interaction of the two tendencies produces various results.

(1) The lengthening alone occurs. Cooper clearly describes [a:] in *wasp*, which he does not distinguish from *last*, &c. In PresE *waft* and *quaff* normally have [ɑ:].

(2) The lengthening is accompanied by retraction and rounding to [ɒ:]. The orthoepists give no examples (see, however, Note 1 below). In PresE *swath* has normally [ɒ:], as have *waft* and *quaff* occasionally (cf. Wyld, *Coll. Eng.*, p. 202).

(3) Lengthening fails, and *w*-influence alone operates. Cooper gives 'gutural *o*' ([ɒ]) in *wast* (but we must allow for lack of stress in this word). *OED* records [ɒ] as a second pronunciation for *swath*, and *quaff* occasionally has [ɒ] (cf. Wyld, loc. cit.). *Wasp* in PresE has only [ɒ] (cf. failure of lengthening in *asp*). On this development see further § 54, Note 1.

(4) Neither lengthening nor *w*-influence operates. Wyld, *Universal English Dictionary*, records [æ] as a second pronunciation of *swath*, and Jespersen, *ModE Gr*, § 10.95, records [æ] as a variant pronunciation of *quaff*. I doubt whether these pronunciations may be regarded as showing a StE development.

Note: Coles and *WSC-RS* record [ɒ:] in *was*, where it might develop in the strong form with [s]; in this case it belongs under (2) above. The strong form with [s] is recorded until the time of Gil (see § 4), but it is much less frequent. Explanation should rather proceed from the weak form with the voiced spirant [z], which the word certainly has in Coles's pronunciation. The plural [swɒ:ðz] 'swaths' requires a different explanation from the singular [swɒ:þ], in view of the following voiced spirant. *Wrath*, though usually taken as an example of (2) above, requires a different explanation (see § 53 (6) below). On *was* and *swaths* see further § 53 (3).

OTHER CASES OF LENGTHENING OF ME *ă* AND ME *ŏ*

§ 53. Lengthening of ME *ă* and occasionally of ME *ŏ* occurs sporadically in other circumstances than directly before *r* or the voiceless spirants [s], [f], and [þ]. This fact has not explicitly been observed (though Ekwall, *Laut- und Formenlehre*, § 47 end and § 75 end, shows some suspicion of it), and various ingenious explanations are offered of the pronunciations concerned. Lengthening occurs occasionally in StE before other front consonants, namely the voiceless spirant [ʃ], the voiced spirants [z] and [ð] (especially in the combination [ðz]), the nasal [n], and the stops [t] and [d]. It is powerfully assisted by, and perhaps in the dialects may occur merely because of, an [r] (especially when syllabic) in the following syllable. It is also assisted by a preceding bilabial or labio-dental consonant and by a preceding [r], especially if itself preceded by a bilabial consonant. Lengthening is especially likely to occur when two or more of these influences are operative in the one word; and when a bilabial or labiodental (especially [w]) precedes ME *ă*, there is commonly rounding and retraction to [ɒ:]. The dialectal evidence (see Note 1 below) suggests that lengthening because of the conditions described above was especially frequent in Scottish and South-western English dialects, and that the distribution of the lengthened sounds among the dialects is not always the same in these circumstances as when the lengthening is due to a following [s], [f], or [þ].

(1) In StE, lengthening is rare if only one of the factors mentioned above occurs in the word in question. Lengthening before [n] accounts for the variant [ɒ:] beside more regular unlengthened [ɒ] in *gone* in PresE; but the orthoepists record only unlengthened eModE *ŏ* or ME *ǭ* (see § 33). Jespersen, *ModE Gr*, § 10.81, refers to [ɒ:] in *shone*, I do not know on what authority; it seems never to occur in PresE, and is not recorded by seventeenth-century orthoepists (who give either unlengthened eModE *ŏ* or ME *ǭ*; see § 33). Purely dialectal lengthening of ME *ă* before *n* is shown

by Newton (see Vol. I, p. 250). Lengthening before *d* occurs in *God*, which has the variant [ɒ:] beside normal [ɒ] in PresE; no seventeenth-century orthoepist records [ɒ:], but it had already developed, at least in vulgar speech, by Cooper's time (Wyld, *Coll. Eng.*, p. 253, cites the spelling *Gaud* from Otway (1681) and Pope's rhyme with *unawed*; but such rhymes as Pope's *God: road* depend on shortening of ME ǭ to ǒ before *d* in *road*, &c.). The eighteenth-century Scottish orthoepists Johnston and Buchanan show lengthening of ME ă before the group [vz] in [stɑ:vz] 'staves' but not in the singular *staff*; see Vol. I, p. 178, note 2.

(2) When two of the factors are present in one word, lengthening is much more common, and affects ME ă as well as ME ǒ. An important example, and one of the earliest recorded, is the pronunciation [ɒ:] in the words *(a)broad* and *groat*, which can be satisfactorily explained only if we regard it as due to lengthening of eModE ǒ by shortening of ME ǭ (see § 33 for evidence of shortening of ME ǭ in these and other words with final *d* and *t*, and cf. *gone* for the later lengthening of eModE ǒ by shortening). In these two words the lengthening influence of *d* and *t* (cf. lengthening in *God* and in the dialectal pronunciations cited in Note 1 (*d*) below) is reinforced by that of a preceding *r* (which in *broad* is further preceded by a bilabial). In *(a)broad* [ɒ:] may be recorded in one instance by Gil 1619 (the printed text has the symbol for ME *au*, but it is corrected by hand to ǭ in the copy of the 1619 edition formerly possessed by Luick (see *Archiv*, cxv. 230–4) and is ǭ in the 1621 edition), and is certainly shown by Hodges, Coles, Cooper, Aickin, *WSC-RS*, Cocker, and Brown. In *groat* [ɒ:] is recorded by Hodges, Cooper, Aickin, *WSC-RS*, and Brown. Beside this pronunciation there survived unshortened ME ǭ, recorded for both words by Price (1665) and for *broad* by Ray (1691), to mention only two sources of later date than the first certain record of [ɒ:] (in Hodges); in the latter part of the eighteenth century [o:] < ME ǭ is still shown by Walker (cf. Luick, § 535, Anm. 2), and in *groat* it has reasserted itself and alone survives as the present StE pronunciation. See further Note 3 below.

(3) The cases remaining for discussion are those in which ME ă is lengthened (often with rounding to [ɒ:]) under the influence of two or more of the factors set out at the beginning of this section. *Paths*, in which ME ă is preceded by a bilabial and followed (in Hodges as in present StE) by [ðz], is twice transcribed by Hodges (in *EP*) with the sign for ME *au*, in contrast to the singular *path*, which has unlengthened ME ă. Hodges's distinction is paralleled in the eighteenth-century orthoepist Johnston (a Scot), who gives [ɑ:] in the plural but ă in the singular, and in Murray's entry in *OED* (see Vol. I, p. 178). But Hodges's transcription is not to be taken as an inexact representation of [a:]; he was a first-rate observer, and his evidence must be accepted at its face value as meaning [ɒ:], which shows rounding by the preceding bilabial (cf. *father*, under (4) below).

Nevertheless Hodges records unlengthened ME *ă* in *baths*, in which the phonetic conditions are closely comparable; the lengthening and rounding were evidently irregular changes. The distinction between the two words may be due to *paths* being the more common plural, and so more liable to show changes developed in the first place in popular speech. *Was* (which has a preceding [w] and a following [z]—but see § 52, Note) has [ɒ:] by lengthening and rounding in Coles's *Schoolmaster* (Vol. I, p. 443) and *WSC-RS* (Vol. I, pp. 301–2). *Wattle* and *watch* (which have a preceding [w] and a following [t]) have [ɒ:] (by lengthening and rounding) in Cooper (Vol. I, pp. 301–2); *WSC-RS* follows Cooper with regard to *watch*, but not *wattle* (which is simply omitted from his list). *Wash* (preceding [w] and following [ʃ]) has [ɒ:] in Daines (see Vol. I, pp. 331–3) and in *WSC-RS* (see Vol. I, pp. 301–2). In Present English similar pronunciations occur only in the plurals *paths*, *baths*, and *swaths* in their forms [pɑːðz], [bɑːðz], and [swɒːðz]. These pronunciations obviously owe their currency in the South to the analogy of the singulars, in which [ɑː] or [ɒː] develops because of the following voiceless spirant; but that they are not purely analogical forms is shown by their [ðz], in contrast with the [þs] of the analogical plurals. See further Note 4 below.

(4) The influence of a following syllabic [r] is seen in *father*, *rather*, *lather*, and *gather*. In *father* three factors operate—the initial labiodental, the following [ð], and the [r] of the next syllable. It has [ɑ:] in Coles (who does not show lengthening before a voiceless spirant); in the *Schoolmaster* (1674) he puts *father* between *fall* and *fame* when giving examples of the different values of the letter *a*, and in the *Syncrisis* (1677) he says that it has a value of *a* intermediate between those of *a* in *all* and *ale* and identical with that of *a* in *arm*. Eighteenth-century orthoepists also show [ɑ:] in *father* with some regularity. But Jones (1701) says that *a* is pronounced like *au* in *father*; the labiodental has evidently caused rounding to [ɒ:], as occasionally in present-day American English (cf. Hodges's evidence on *paths* above). *Rather* (in which preceding [r], following [ð], and [r] in the next syllable all operate) is not recorded with [ɑ:] until Buchanan (1766), who was significantly a Scot (cf. Scottish [ɑ:] in *gather* and *lather*; see Note 1 below, under (*f*)); Walker (1791) still gives only the pronunciations with ME *ā* and unlengthened ME *ă*, of which he prefers the former. Both these words normally have either unlengthened ME *ă* or ME *ā* in seventeenth-century orthoepists (see § 6 above). In present-day usage, [ɑ:] is general in *father*, but in *rather*, though [ɑ:] is general in Standard Southern English and in Australian English, unlengthened ME *ă* ([a] or [æ]) is common in Scottish and American English; the ME *ā* variant is now only dialectal. In *lather* (on which there is no early evidence) the preceding [l], by its lip-protrusion, acts as a third factor favouring lengthening, in addition to the following [ð] and [r]; Daniel Jones, in his *English Pronouncing Dictionary*, gives

precedence (rather surprisingly) to the pronunciation with [ɑ:], but only [æ] is recorded by *OED* and Wyld, *Universal English Dictionary*; it would seem that the use of [ɑ:] in this word in StE has increased in recent times. In *gather* only two factors, the following [ð] and [r], operate, and StE has only the unlengthened [æ]. The acceptance of [ɑ:] in *rather* and *lather* in StE, and in *gather* in educated Scottish English, was probably facilitated by its occurrence in *father*, where it was accepted earlier and more generally, obviously because it was a more common development in this word than in the others. See further Note 5 below.

(5) Next comes a group of words in which a preceding [w] operates in addition to a following [t] or [d] and an [r] in the next syllable (which was syllabic, while still pronounced, in the word in which lengthening was most regular, and may sometimes have been syllabic in one or more of the others). In all these cases the [w] causes rounding to [ɒ:] in addition to aiding the lengthening (but see Note 6 below, under (*f*)). The most important case is *water*, in which [ɒ:] is found quite early. Robinson transcribes the word with his symbol for [ɒ:] thrice (see Vol. I, p. 211), and Gil does so once (beside unlengthened ME *ă* thrice and ME *ā* six times). Daines says that *Walter* (in which the *l* was commonly silent from ME onwards because of the OF variant without *l*—cf. ModF *Gautier*) is pronounced 'quasi *water*'. Cooper and *WSC-RS* say that in *water* the *a* is pronounced like *au* (see Vol. I, pp. 301–2). *Water* is paired with *Walter* by the 'homophone' lists of Hodges ('alike'; but this is one of the few cases in which the 'alike' list of *SH-PD* is not in conformity with the transcriptions of *EP*, which thrice give ME *ā* in *water*), Wharton, Fox and Hookes, Strong, Cooper, and Brown. Other evidence of [ɒ:] in *water* is given by eighteenth-century orthoepists, from Jones (1701) onwards. In the sixteenth century Levins and Hart give ME *ā* or unlengthened ME *ă* (see § 6). Turning to other words, we find that Robinson gives [ɒ:] in Spanish *quatro* (in which the [r] cannot be syllabic), though in all other words Spanish *a* is identified with ME *ā*; there is no reason to doubt that Robinson's pronunciation of Spanish was merely a reflection of his pronunciation of English. At the end of the eighteenth century, Elphinston (1790) and Walker (1791) give [ɒ:] in *squadron* (in which [r] could perhaps have been syllabic (cf. § 328 below), though normally the [n] would be); Walker gives it also in *quadrant* (in which also syllabic [r] is conceivable) and in *quadrate* (in which syllabic [r] is hardly possible unless in the form—indicated by the spelling *quadrat*, for which see *OED*—in which the second syllable was fully unstressed). It is of some importance to observe that Elphinston was a Scot; but the other orthoepists cited in this paragraph, with the exception of Brown (whose speech was marked by pronunciations characteristic of the North), are evidence for StE pronunciation. In Present English [ɒ:] occurs only in *water*, which is by far the commonest of the words here cited and the only one

in which syllabic [r] would have regularly occurred in eModE. See further Note 6 below.

(6) *Wrath* is usually assumed to owe lengthening only to the following [þ], and rounding to the influence of the [w] acting over the [r]. But the word has [ɑ:] in Scottish and American English, in which lengthening before a voiceless spirant does not normally occur, and (a less important point) the rounding, though not the lengthening, is regular in StE, whereas in such words as *swath*, *waft*, and *quaff* it may fail. The factors producing lengthening in this word are apparently more complex than is usually supposed. To the influence of the voiceless spirant (which must be the chief factor) there is added that of the preceding consonant group, consisting of a bilabial consonant followed by [r]; the latter not only causes rounding in Southern English, but also assists the lengthening process. Seventeenth-century evidence tends to show that the [ɒ:] produced by lengthening and rounding was accepted in this word almost as early as [ɒ:] in *water* and earlier than [a:] in *past*, [ɒ:] in *frost*, or [a:] in *wasp*; on the other hand there is no seventeenth-century evidence of [ɒ:] in such words as *waft* (see § 7 (*b*)). The earliest evidence of [ɒ:] in *wrath* is Milton's (see Note 7); Young gives the 'phonetic' spellings *rawth* and *rawthful*; and Cooper and *WSC-RS* say that in *wrath* the *a* is pronounced like *au* (see Vol. I, pp. 301–2). In other sixteenth- and seventeenth-century orthoepists the word has unlengthened ME *ă* or ME *ā* (see § 6). See further Note 7 below.

Note 1: The validity of the statements above can be very largely demonstrated from the evidence of the modern dialects, as recorded by Wright, Index. Lengthening occurs (*a*) before [ʃ] in *ash*; (*b*) not before unassisted [z] or [ð] (but see under (*f*) below); (*c*) before [n] in *hand* and *gone*; (*d*) before [t] and [d] in *cat*, *lad*, *blot*, *cot*, *God*, and *rod*; (*e*) before [r] in the next syllable in *acorn* and *apron* (which have [ɑ:] in Scottish dialects, presumably from ME *ă* preserved from open-syllable lengthening by a syllabic consonant in the next syllable); (*f*) in association with a combination of lengthening factors in *fashion* (preceding labiodental and following [ʃ]), *wash* (preceding [w] and following [ʃ]), *fathom* (preceding labiodental and following [ð]), *bother* (preceding bilabial and following [ð] and syllabic [r]), *bad* (preceding bilabial and following [d]), *fat* (preceding labiodental and following [t]), *what* (preceding [w], in the dialects concerned, and following [t]), *watch* (preceding [w] and following [tʃ]), *pan*, *bond*, *wander*, and *want* (preceding bilabial and following [n]); to these may be added *gather* and *lather* (following [ð] and syllabic [r]), which have [ɑ:] in educated Scottish speech (not recorded by Wright). The result of the lengthening of ME *ă* is normally [ɑ:] or [æ:], of ME *ŏ* [ɒ:] or [ɑ:]; but in some dialects ME *ă* becomes [ɒ:] after [w], and also in *fashion* and *fathom* in Scottish dialects. Wright records the lengthening chiefly for Scottish and Southern (especially South-western) English dialects, but also more sporadically for Antrim, Isle of Man, Westmorland, Northumberland, Lancashire, Yorkshire, and various Midland dialects (Shropshire, Staffordshire, and Leicestershire; Oxfordshire, Buckinghamshire, Bedfordshire, and Hertfordshire), and for Suffolk and Essex. For dialectal evidence on *father* and *rather* see Note 5, and on *water* see Note 6, under (*f*).

Note 2: The dialects also show lengthening in cases for which there is no StE evidence, thus (*a*) before [p] in *top*, *crop*, and *drop*; (*b*) before [g], [k], and [ŋ] in *bag*, *wag*, *dog* (widespread, of course), *facts*, *axe*, *box*, *flock*, *ancle*, *bang*, *bank*, *hang*, *thank*, *tong*, and *wrong*;

(c) before [l] in *follow* and *swallow* (note the preceding labial). The long close [oː] and the diphthong [uə] which occur in Scottish and Northern dialects in *blot, cot, God, cock, cog, frost, sop*, &c. (and in Devon in *God*) may develop by ModE lengthening of ME ŏ, but in many cases are probably due to a ME variant in ǭ developed by lengthening in the open syllable of the oblique forms. *Sod* (apparently adopted from MD or MLG *sode*) may also have ME ǭ.

Note 3: (a) The earliest evidence of [ɒː] in *broad* seems to be Spenser's rhyme with *fraud* (cf. Ekwall, § 80). It is recorded by the foreign orthoepists Mauger (1685) and Miège, 1688; see Horn, § 96 (2); Luick, § 535, Anm. 2.
(b) Other explanations of [ɒː] in *broad* and *groat* are unsatisfactory. It can hardly be due to lowering of ME ǭ under the influence of the preceding *r*, for there is no sufficient evidence that a preceding *r* possessed the power of lowering ME long vowels, and there is no sign of an [ɒː] pronunciation of *grove, groan, grope*, &c., or of *broke*. Horn, § 96 (2), and Luick, § 535, adopt the explanation that [ɒː] in (a)*broad* and *groat* comes into StE from South-western dialects in which ME ǭ was still so pronounced. But there is no evidence that the South-western dialects influenced StE in the modern period, nor is there the slightest likelihood that South-western influence would affect the pronunciation of these common StE words; such an hypothesis is a confession of failure. Luick would add as a further instance of this supposed South-western influence the eighteenth-century [ɒː] in *loath*; Horn, loc. cit., Anm. 1, is inclined to agree, but points out that in this word [ɒː] may be due to lengthening of eModE ŏ by shortening of ME ǭ—an explanation which should certainly be accepted, in view of Bullokar's ŏ in the word.
(c) *OED* gives [ɒː] as a variant pronunciation not only for *groat* (the coin), but also for *groats*, which is not recorded by the seventeenth-century orthoepists (unless Hodges's *groats* with [ɒː], which is unglossed, is meant as this word and not as the plural of *groat* (the coin), which in both instances immediately precedes); eighteenth-century orthoepists give [ɒː].

Note 4: It is important to observe that the seventeenth-century evidence for [ɒː] in *paths, was, wattle*, &c., is excellent; Daines and *WSC-RS* are not, it is true, very reliable authorities, but only *wash* relies on their unsupported testimony, which is in harmony with the evidence of the modern dialects (see Note 1, under (*f*)). Hodges, *EP*; Coles, *Schoolmaster*; and Cooper are in the highest class, with Robinson and Gil (who also show [ɒː] from ME ă in other words; see above), and Wallis. *OED* records a seventeenth-century spelling *wauch* 'watch'.

Note 5: (a) The reported spelling *farder* 'father' in the *Cely Papers* is a misreading for *faider*, which merely shows ME ā spelt *ai*; see further § 50, Note 1 above.
(b) Ellis, p. 1007, cites Wilkins as showing [æː] in *father*, but wrongly; Wilkins does not recognize the existence of a sound [aː] or [æː], and transcribes *father* with his symbol for ME ā, which Ellis must have misunderstood. He also wrongly interprets Jones as showing [ɑː].
(c) In the modern dialects, *father* has [ɑː] in many Scottish and English dialects, [æː] in Scottish and some English dialects (chiefly WMidland and South-western), and pronunciations developed from ME ā and unlengthened ME ă. Wright records no [ɒː] forms. *Rather* has [ɑː] in the dialects of six English counties (Northern, Midland, and Southern), and [æː] in those of five (Midland and South-western), but otherwise pronunciations developed from ME ā or unlengthened ME ă. Wright does not record either [ɑː] or [æː] in *rather* in Scottish dialects, but neither does he for *gather*, for which [ɑː] certainly occurs in educated Scottish pronunciation. He shows no lengthening in *gather* in any dialect, and does not record *lather*.

Note 6: Other possible evidence of lengthening and rounding in *water* is as follows:
(a) The *OED* cites the Scottish spellings *walter* (fourteenth to seventeenth centuries), *waltir* (fifteenth to sixteenth centuries), and *valter* (sixteenth century); but these are ambiguous, since Scottish spelling often used *al* for ME ā.
(b) Davies, *English Pronunciation from the Fifteenth to the Eighteenth Century*, p. 62, cites a letter dated 1481 from the *Stonor Papers* which contains the spelling *Water* 'Walter' twice.

This letter (written from Modbury, Devon) is clearly dialectal in spelling and grammar; but *Water* 'Walter' occurs elsewhere in the fifteenth century and later (cf. Withycombe, *English Christian Names*, p. 278). The pronunciation, however, need not have been [wɒːtər]; it may well have been [watər] (cf. *Wat, Watson*, &c., with ME ă). If so, the evidence of Daines, Hodges, &c. cited under (5) above is uncertain.

(*c*) Wyld, *Coll. Eng.*, p. 202, cites the spelling *woater* 'water' from the *Verney Memoirs* (of date 1688); we may accept this as evidence of open [ɒː], the spelling being based on the value of *oa* in *broad* and *groat* (though ordinarily *oa* then represented close [oː]).

(*d*) Viëtor, *Shakespeare's Pronunciation*, p. 94, cites the rhyme *hereafter : water* from Sylvester (1621), which may be accepted as showing that *water* has a vowel identical with that developed from ME *au* (cf. § 43, Note 2). But Sylvester came from Southampton and his rhyme might depend on dialectal pronunciation, though at this date there is no need to assume so as far as *water* is concerned.

(*e*) Miège (1688) follows Cooper in giving [ɒː] in *water* (see Vol. I, pp. 301–2, and Zachrisson, *Eng. Vowels*, p. 122).

(*f*) In the modern dialects, *water* has [ɑː] in Midland and South-western dialects and in Kent, and [ɒː] in Scottish, Midland (including SEMidl), and Southern (especially South-western) dialects, in addition to pronunciations derived from unlengthened ME ă and from ME ā, which occur in many dialects.

Note 7: (*a*) The contrast between *wrath* and *waft*, &c., can only be explained if we assume, as I do above, that the group consonant-plus-*r* has influence over the vowel, for otherwise the conditions favour lengthening and rounding in *waft* (in which the [w] immediately precedes the vowel) rather than in *wrath* (in which it does not). I assume that explanation should proceed from the variant with ME ă and [þ], not from those with ME ā and [ð] or ME ā and [þ] (for which see § 6).

(*b*) Milton uses the spelling *wrauth*. It occurs first in the autograph Trinity MS (1637), though here it is corrected to *wrath*. Later Milton deliberately adopted the spelling, and caused his scribe's *wrath* to be corrected to *wrauth* in the Morgan MS. *Wrauth* is the usual spelling of the first edition of *Paradise Lost*. See Wyld, *Coll. Eng.* (3rd edit.), p. 400, who in part follows Darbishire, *The MS of Book I of 'Paradise Lost'*, pp. xxix, xxxvi.

(*c*) Hodges in his list of words pronounced 'near alike' and Coles in his careless *Engl.-Lat. Dict.* pair *wroth* with *wrath*, but we cannot use this pairing to determine the pronunciation of the latter, because (i) it is not certain whether *wroth* has short [ɒ] or lengthened [ɒː], (ii) in these lists words with ME ă in which there can be no *w*-influence are often equated with words with ME ŏ, owing to the unrounding of the latter.

THE PHONETIC PROCESS WHEREBY LENGTHENING OCCURS

(1) *Nature of the process*

§ 54. It is evident from the foregoing that the factors which cause lengthening of ME ă and (to a less extent) of ME ŏ are varied. But the process may be assumed to have been the same in every case. It is primarily a process of rounding and retraction; the consonants which affect the vowels arrest, in the first place, the tendency to change in the pronunciation of ME ă and ME ŏ. Then in the normal course of events the difference between the vowels in their free development and in their arrested development is accentuated by the lengthening of the latter. The second part of the process is thus dissimilatory.

(1) In the case of ME ă, the normal direction of change is from its ME pronunciation [a] (see § 59 below) to [æ]. The retraction which is the first step in the lengthening process therefore consists in holding the

vowel at palatal [a] while ME *ă* in free position goes on to [æ]. This is shown by Cooper's evidence, for his lengthened vowel is a front vowel when the retractive agent is a following [r] or a voiceless spirant unassisted by any other factor. The same conclusion follows from the consideration of the unlengthened but retracted [a] formerly used before voiceless spirants in StE (see § 50, Note 2); the vowel was held back at palatal [a], though free ME *ă* was [æ]. In cases in which the result of the process is [ɒ:] it would be possible to believe that the first stage consisted not merely in holding ME *ă* as [a], but in retracting it from palatal [a] to back [ɑ]; in this case there would be no necessary connexion between the retractive process and the fronting of free ME *ă*. But the chronology of the changes in StE (for which alone we have full evidence) suggests that this is not so; evidence of [ɒ:] by lengthening (first recorded, among the orthoepists, by Robinson and Gil in *water*) is a little earlier than that of [a:] by lengthening (first recorded by Daines), but the gap (between 1617 and 1640) is not so great as to suggest that the processes were different—especially when we remember that [ɒ:] by lengthening, being identical with the monophthong developed from ME *au*, was a distinct phoneme from ME *ă*, whereas [a:] by lengthening was merely a contextual variant of ME *ă* until StE accepted [a:] < ME *au* in *dance*, &c., and *half*, &c. (which was not until the time of Coles, who is the first to distinguish clearly as a separate phoneme, as Daines did not, the lengthened [a:]). When this factor is taken into account it seems clear that we may, and should, regard the [ɒ:] of, for example, *water* and the [a:] of, for example, *hard* as being divergent results of what was initially a single process.

(2) In the case of ME *ŏ* the direction of change was from its ME pronunciation as a relatively high vowel, approximately 'cardinal open [ɔ]' (which, with the lengthened sound *ǭ* produced from it in open syllables, was identifiable with OF *ǫ*, itself a relatively high vowel) to the ModE lowered and partly unrounded vowel [ɒ], which is more closely akin to French back [ɑ] than to French open [ɔ] and is differentiated from the former more by its lip-rounding than by its tongue-position; in some dialects, indeed, the lowering and unrounding proceeds so far as to produce back [ɑ]. In StE the lowering had occurred, in at least the less correct forms of speech, before 1600, for about that date we begin to get evidence that ME *ŏ* had become a sound akin to foreign [ɑ] sounds, with which it is (inaccurately) identified (see § 86 and Note 1 there). But the vowel [ɒ:] produced by lengthening of ME *ŏ* is in PresE little below the tongue-position of 'cardinal open [ɔ]' (cf. the diagram given as a frontispiece in D. Jones, *English Pronouncing Dictionary*, and his *Outline of English Phonetics*, § 305), and the lips are more closely rounded even than for 'cardinal open [ɔ]' (and much more than for PresE [ɒ]); and there is no reason to believe that it was ever essentially different from what it now is. The effect of the 'lengthening' consonants

was therefore primarily to arrest the lowering and especially the unrounding process, while ME ŏ in free position went on to its ModE pronunciation.

(3) To the theory advanced above the objection might be raised that it assumes a difference in quality between the new lengthened sounds and ME ă and ŏ in their free development, whereas Cooper states definitely that the unlengthened and lengthened sounds are qualitatively identical, and Newton's vowel-system assumes this. But Cooper's statement may well be somewhat inexact; for the sake of the symmetry of his vowel-system he makes [ɪ] and [ʊ] the short equivalents of tense [e:] and [o:] (see Vol. I, pp. 289-91), and to identify as short and long equivalents [æ] and [a:], lowered [ɒ] and the higher [ɒ:], is a lesser inaccuracy. Similar arguments are applicable in Newton's case. To make a distinction between [ɒ] and [ɒ:] is indeed held to be unnecessary in modern 'broad' phonetic transcriptions, and the more elementary books on phonetics gloss over the difference; it is only in the 'narrow' transcription, and more accurate textbooks, that it is made explicit. But Newton and Cooper may perhaps have had a justification which a present-day phonetician would lack; it is quite possible (indeed, in the case of ME ă probable) that beside the more advanced pronunciation in which ME ă and ME ŏ had become [æ] and lowered [ɒ] in their free development and had been held back and lengthened when influenced by consonants, there existed a more conservative pronunciation in which they were still [a] and approximately 'cardinal open [ɔ]' in all circumstances and no lengthening had occurred. An individual might indeed mix in his speech the conservative values of the freely developing vowels with lengthened forms; and the conservative values of the unlengthened vowels would be qualitatively identical with the new lengthened vowels. A further consideration which applies to ME ă is that when lengthened it did not remain at the value [a:]: in one development (that preserved in Present StE) there was further retraction to guttural [ɑ:]; in the other (which formerly affected StE) there was fronting to [æ:], the retractive influence having obviously ceased to operate. It is possible that Newton and Cooper, both of whom are influenced by dialect, may have used such an [æ:] (see Note 3).

Note 1: In StE lengthening occurs only when one or more of the retractive factors *follows* the vowel. When [w] precedes ME ă and no retractive factor follows the vowel, the fronting of the vowel is arrested, but no lengthening occurs; instead, the dissimilation consists in the rounding of the vowel to short [ɒ] (as in *want*). When the factor following the vowel is one of the voiceless spirants [s], [f], and [þ], the dissimilatory lengthening sometimes fails in StE, even though the retraction has occurred (see § 50, Note 2); and in this event, if [w] precedes the vowel, rounding to short [ɒ] results (see § 52). Coles shows occasional failure of lengthening, but dissimilatory rounding to short [ɒ], even when [r] follows (in *warm*, &c.; see § 49).

Note 2: It follows from this argument that when lengthening is shown, ME ă in its free development must already have reached [æ]. This means that in those dialects (e.g. probably vulgar London English and the Sussex dialect, as represented by Bullokar and *RS*, and the Northern dialects, as represented by Poole) in which the lengthened vowel was identified with ME *ā* (see §§ 42–43 above), ME *ă* must have reached [æ] during the fifteenth century, and must have been fronted before ME *ā* was; this, though different from the sequence of changes in StE, is not at all improbable (since there is no connexion between the ModE fronting of ME *ă* and ME *ā*). The dubious occurrence of [ɒ:] in *water* in Scotland as early as the fourteenth century might suggest that ME *ă* had already been fronted by that date, but this would be consistent with the known rapid development of Northern pronunciation; it may be significant that fronting of ME *ă* as far as [e] occurs in a number of words in Scottish and Northern dialects (Wright, § 23). But in careful StE there is no evidence of either [ɒ:] in *water*, &c., or of [a:] before the early seventeenth century (Robinson, Gil, Daines, Hodges), and only after 1670 is lengthening at all fully shown (Coles, Cooper); we may conclude that in StE [æ] for ME *ă* in free position, though it may have occurred in less careful speech in the second half of the sixteenth century, was accepted more widely only in the first half of the seventeenth century, and quite generally after 1670.

It similarly follows that ME *ŏ* in its free development must have reached its lowered and unrounded position by the time that lengthening occurs. In those dialects in which the lengthened vowel is identified with ME *ǭ* and in which the lengthening must be dated to the fifteenth century (i.e. vulgar London English and the Sussex dialect, represented by Bullokar and *RS*, and the Northern dialects represented by Poole; see §§ 45–48), the change of ME *ŏ* in free position must also have occurred during the fifteenth century. For StE there is, rather surprisingly, no evidence of lengthening before *r* and spirants until Coles (1674) and Cooper (1685), who first show the StE lengthening to [ɒ:], though in *broad* and *groat* it is recorded earlier (indeed before 1600 in Spenser's rhyme); this must indicate that the new pronunciation of ME *ŏ*, like the lengthening which was the by-product of the process of change, was not fully accepted in careful StE until the later seventeenth century, despite the existence of evidence for it from about 1600.

Note 3: Cooper's evidence, of course, shows that the lengthened vowel developed from ME *ă* before *r* and a voiceless spirant was a front vowel; indeed, it is highly probable that his description of the articulation was based on the long and not the short vowel. Ekwall, *Laut- und Formenlehre*, § 43, quotes early eighteenth-century evidence which shows [æ:] as the value of the lengthened vowel developed from ME *ă* (and of ME *au* in *aunt, calf*); and he rightly regards this [æ:] as explaining why later orthoepists (Johnston, 1764; Elphinston, 1765; Batchelor, 1809) make no qualitative distinction between unlengthened ME *ă* and the lengthened sound.

(2) *Frequency of lengthening*

§ 55. If this account of the lengthening process is correct, it follows that lengthening must occur in any one dialect at one and the same time in all cases (except possibly in those in which [ɒ:] develops from ME *ă*); but there may of course be differences between dialects not only in the date at which lengthening occurs (see above), but also in the frequency with which it occurs in different cases. Thus the early lengthening of ME *ă* to identity with ME *ā* and of ME *ŏ* to identity with ME *ǭ* is recorded only before *r*, and though this may be fortuitous (in view of the small amount of evidence there is for this early lengthening even before *r*) it need not be; note that Bullokar and Butler have lengthening to identity with ME *ā*, and not retraction and rounding to [ɒ:], in *warn*, *quarn*, and *swarm*, which shows that in the dialect to which this early lengthening was native the detailed working-out of the process was different from that of StE. But though the lengthening must in any one dialect have occurred at one time in all cases to which that dialect is subject, it nevertheless appears at different dates in different cases in careful StE. The explanation, as between [a:] and [ɒ:], is at least in part that the latter was recognizable as a distinct phoneme earlier than the former, as is pointed out above; but as between the various cases of lengthening to [a:] or of that to [ɒ:], it is the relative commonness of lengthening in various phonetic circumstances. The more frequent the lengthened vowels were, the more quickly they arrived in careful speech; and their frequency depended on the strength of the retractive influences operating in the word or words in question.

We must therefore turn to a more detailed examination of these retractive influences, in order to determine how it was that they affected the vowels and why they differed in their power to do so. The evidence of StE and of the dialects (for the latter see especially § 53, Notes 1 and 2 above) shows that lengthening can occur before almost any consonant. But it is especially apt to occur, in descending order of likelihood, before: (1) [r], especially a group of *r* plus consonant (early lengthening to identity with ME *ā* and *ǭ* only occurring before [r]); (2) the voiceless spirants [f], [þ], and [s], especially (at least in the case of [s]) if they form part of a group of spirant plus consonant (cf. Cooper's evidence); (3) a group of consonants, especially if the second member of the group is syllabic or non-syllabic [r] (so in *father*, &c., *water*, *quadrant*, &c., and (without [r]) *paths* and *baths*). In the case especially of ME *ă* (but also in that of ME *ŏ*) a preceding bilabial or labiodental consonant (especially [w]) obviously assists the lengthening; this assistance is of particular importance in case (3) above. In *groat* and *rather* the preceding [r], owing to its lip-protrusion, seems to have the same effect; so probably the [l] in *lather*, since [l] also has some lip-protrusion, though less than [r]. Certainly an [r] which is itself preceded by a labial (as in *broad*) powerfully assists the lengthening; and *wrath* suggests that the group [wr] has greater power than simple [w].

In the lengthening process tongue-position does not seem to be involved. The change from 'cardinal open [ɔ]' to [ɒ] is one of lowering, that of [a] to [æ] of raising; [g] has back tongue-position, [f] none, and the other consonants before which lengthening occurs are point consonants. The prime cause seems, on the contrary, to be the difference in degree of mouth opening between the consonants and the vowels affected; the consonants all have the teeth fairly close together, the vowels have wide mouth-opening. The change from [ɔ] to [ɒ] definitely widens the opening, and as the PresE [ɒ:] has a less wide opening than the PresE [ɒ], the effect of the lengthening process has clearly been to preserve a vowel with narrower mouth-opening. Similarly PresE [ɑ:] in, for example, *hard* [hɑːd] has distinctly narrower mouth-opening (less distance between the upper and lower teeth) than PresE [æ] in, for example, *had* [hæd]; the lengthening process has again had the effect of preserving a narrower mouth-opening.

Evidently in both cases the following consonants with their narrow mouth-opening have by assimilation favoured the retention of the vowel which had narrower mouth-opening. But the extent to which this occurred has depended on the duration for which the mouth was to be held in its position of narrow opening; hence the greater effect of spirants against stops and of groups of consonants against single consonants (thus *r* plus consonant and *s* plus consonant caused more regular lengthening—so that it was earlier recorded—than simple *r* and *s*).

As for the difference between voiceless and voiced consonants (other than [r]), the fact that lengthening does sometimes occur before voiced consonants proves that lack of voice is not a prerequisite; it is rather that the presence of voice detracts from the consonant's power to cause the lengthening. Now voiced consonants have tenser articulation than voiceless, and the difference is especially marked in the spirants. Also PresE [ɑ:] and [ɒ:] are tenser than [æ] and [ɒ], and the changes from [a] to [æ] and from [ɔ] to [ɒ] were therefore accompanied by a reduction of tension. Evidently one of the operative factors was a subconscious desire to avoid a tense vowel before a tense consonant; therefore the changes of the vowels from tense [a] and [ɔ] to lax [æ] and [ɒ] tended to proceed before the tenser (i.e. the voiced) consonants (especially the voiced spirants). But this factor in favour of vowel-change (and therefore against the initial stage of the lengthening process), being in conflict with the factor of mouth-opening which was opposed to the changes of the vowels (and therefore produced the initial differentiation which lengthening exaggerated), was apt to be negatived when the latter was specially strengthened (e.g. by the existence of a consonant group, as in *paths* or *father*).

It is clear that [r] is a special case, as it causes so much more regular lengthening than the rest of the consonants. It brings about lengthening not only by its quality as a continuant with narrow mouth-opening (from which its voiced nature detracts), but also by virtue of special properties of its own. These are twofold: (*a*) its retractive and lowering power due to the conformation of the tongue in the articulation of the ModE [r]—a power which is one of the most obvious features of ModE phonology; this is what in this connexion affects ME *ă*, preventing fronting and raising of its tongue-position; (*b*) its rounding power due to its lip-protrusion (exhibited in other connexions), which is what affects ME *ŏ*, inhibiting its change from the more rounded [ɔ] to the less rounded [ɒ]. It should further be observed that the power of [r] (syllabic or non-syllabic) greatly to reinforce the effect on the vowel of a consonant which it follows (as in *father, water, quadrant*) is probably not merely because it forms with that consonant a group of fairly long duration, but because it modifies the articulation of the preceding consonant by anticipation of both the position of the back of the tongue and the lip-protrusion used for the articulation of [r] (cf. OE *i-*

mutation and back-mutation, in which a sound in the following syllable affects the development of the vowel of the preceding syllable). The special influence of eModE syllabic [r] (as in *father, water*, &c.) is due to its greater duration and emphasis in comparison with non-syllabic [r]. But intervocalic [r] has little power to cause lengthening (see, however, Note 2 below), just as it has little power to bring about other vowel-changes (e.g. unchanged vowels survive in *Wirral, merry*, and *hurry*); the reason is that in intervocalic position [r] usually remains in ModE as some species of trilled [r] (of which the present StE representative is the so-called 'flap' [r]) with little guttural quality and lip-protrusion and correspondingly little power to cause retraction, lowering, or rounding.

The reason why a preceding labial consonant assists the influence on ME *ă* is clear enough; it favours lip-rounding, which is ordinarily associated with back tongue-position, and so is opposed to fronting. It would still more obviously oppose the unrounding of ME *ŏ*, and so assist the lengthening; this factor comes into account in the case of *broad*. The close association between rounding and lengthening is illustrated by the direct change, in such words as *water* and *wrath* (and in Hodges's pronunciation of *paths*), from ME *ă* to lengthened and rounded [ɒː].

Note 1: It is probably no accident that Cooper, Miège, and *WSC-RS* show lengthening before final [r] in *war* but not in *car* and *for*; in *war* the lengthening (primarily retractive) influence of [r] is reinforced by the strong retractive influence of [w]. It may also be no accident that lengthening before final [r] is shown by the *Alphabet Anglois* and Festeau in *far*, in which the labiodental may assist the lengthening.

Note 2: The evidence for lengthening before intervocalic [r] is as follows. (*a*) Cooper, Miège, and *WSC-RS* show lengthening in *warren*; the weak influence of intervocalic [r] is doubtless reinforced by that of [w]. (*b*) Jones (1701) shows lengthening of ME *ă* to [ɒː] in *arrand, arrears*, &c. (see § 44); his evidence must reflect a Western dialectal pronunciation in which the retractive influence of [r] is especially strong, as is shown by the development of ME *ă* to [ɒː] in this pronunciation. Cf. Wright, § 259, on the special nature of [r] in Pembrokeshire, Herefordshire, Gloucestershire, Oxfordshire and 'all the south and south-western dialects' and its 'great influence upon a preceding vowel'. (*c*) In the modern dialects (see Wright, Index) lengthening before intervocalic [r] occurs in *barrow, marrow, harrow, arrow, carrot*, and *borrow*, chiefly in Northern (especially Scottish) dialects and in south-west England, though Antrim and Kent each have it in two words. The occurrence in the south-west confirms the inference drawn from the evidence of Jones (see above). Lengthening seems a little less uncommon after a bilabial, though the evidence is too slight to be significant. We should of course exclude cases in which the [r] becomes final in the dialects, and in which lengthening is more common (so *harrow* [aː(r)], *barrow* [baː(r)], and *carry* [kaː(r)]); also those in which by syncope of the unstressed vowel the [r] is brought into juxtaposition with another consonant (so *carrot* [kaːt], *barrel* [baːl], *warrant* [wɑːnd] and [wɒːn]), as the lengthening may not precede the syncope; and perhaps finally the south-western [kwɒːdl] 'quarrel', in which the intrusion of [d] may precede the lengthening. Wright gives no evidence on *morrow, sorrow, sorry*, and *lorry*.

(3) *Distribution of lengthening*

§ 56. If this view of the lengthening process is correct, lengthening should occur only in those dialects in which ME *ă* and *ŏ* undergo in free position the changes from [a] to [æ] and from [ɔ] to [ɒ] of which the inhibition is the first stage of the process. Unfortunately there are no sufficiently accurate and extensive records of dialectal pronunciation to enable such a correspondence to be demonstrated in detail. Wright's helpers were unable to distinguish accurately between [a] and [æ] (see *EDG*, § 22), and for ME *ŏ* he does not distinguish (§ 82) between dialects which have [ɔ] (his mid-back-wide-round) and those which have [ɒ] (his low-back-wide-round); and his evidence of lengthening itself does not seem very systematic or complete. But lengthening belongs chiefly to Southern England and to Scottish dialects, though it occurs sporadically elsewhere in the North and Midlands (cf. § 53, Note 1); and correspondingly ME *ă* is raised (even as far as [e] in some instances) and ME *ŏ* is unrounded (even as far as [ɑ]) in the South of England, in certain Scottish dialects, and sporadically in Northern and Midland dialects (which agree closely with those that show sporadic lengthening). Conversely lengthening (otherwise than before *r*) is lacking in Northern and Midland dialects which retain [a] for ME *ă* and show no signs of the unrounding of ME *ŏ*. But lengthening before *r* (Wright, §§ 37, 87) does occur, or appear to occur, even in Northern and Midland dialects in which ME *ă* and *ŏ* remain unchanged in free position. The explanation would seem to be that there are two distinct processes of lengthening where *r* is concerned. (*a*) In StE the lengthening occurs while the consonant is still pronounced; thus *ăr* > [a:r] > [ɑ:r] and *ŏr* > [ɒ:r], and these groups subsequently, with the vocalization of [r] to [ə], become [ɑ:ə] > [ɑ:] and [ɒ:ə] > [ɒ:]. This is clearly also the process in those Scottish and Northern dialects which still have [ɑ:r] for ME *ăr* and [o:r] (so recorded by Wright, § 87; erroneously?) < [ɒ:r] for ME *ŏr*. (*b*) In other dialects of the North and Midlands, in which free ME *ă* and *ŏ* do not change, the lengthening fails while [r] is retained (hence the surviving pronunciations [ar] and [ɔr] of certain dialects); but when [r] is vocalized there arise the groups [aə] and [ɔə] (also recorded by Wright, §§ 37, 87), which may further develop to [ɑ:] and [ɒ:]. This process is therefore analogous to that in StE by which [ə:] arises during the eighteenth century from [ər] < ME *ĭr*, *ĕr*, and *ŭr*.

Thus, though Wright's evidence is an imperfect basis for argument, it does show a general agreement between the dialectal distribution of lengthening of ME *ă* and *ŏ* and that of their tendency to change by raising in the one case and unrounding (with lowering) in the other. This, taken together with the firmer argument that it is only these two vowels subject to change in their free position which are liable to ModE lengthening, may be held to support the view here advanced of the nature of the lengthening process.

Note: Other explanations of the lengthening of ME *ă* and *ŏ* are proposed by Jespersen and Luick. Jespersen, *ModE Gr*, §§ 10.66, 10.67, 10.69, 10.81, gives a somewhat confused discussion. But in general he would regard lengthening except before *r* (i.e. before voiceless

§ 56]   PART 3: LENGTHENING   543

spirants and in *father, water, gone*, &c.) as being due to blending ('preservative analogy'): since many of the words in question vary in ME and in early ModE between ME *ă* and *ā*, or ME *ŏ* and *ǭ*, he assumes that new pronunciations arose which combined the length of the long variant (on which primarily they were based) with the quality of the short variant. These blend pronunciations were therefore with [æ:] (blend of [æ] from ME *ă* and [ɛ:] from ME *ā*) and [ɒ:] (blend of [ɒ] from ME *ŏ* and [ɔ:] from ME *ǭ*). This theory seems to me inherently improbable, and we may note (*a*) that in such words as have a variant in ME *ā* or *ǭ*, these sounds so long as they survive are not distinguished from ME *ā* or *ǭ* in other words in which no 'blending' occurs; and (*b*) that many words in which lengthening of ME *ă* or *ŏ* occurs have no normal ME variant in *ā* or *ǭ* (e.g. *ass* and *off*). Jespersen admits this, and has to fall back on the theory of analogical extension of lengthened [æ:] and [ɒ:] from words which did have ME variation to others 'of a similar phonetic structure'. It is much better to explain the lengthening from the phonetic structure in the first place. Lengthening before [r] Jespersen regards as 'compensation length', 'though [ɑ:] certainly was found before the total disappearance of *r*'. But we may object (*a*) that the lengthening is found much earlier than the loss of [r], and occurs in Scotch and Northern dialects in which [r] is still retained; (*b*) that it does not explain the development of [ɒ:] in *Chorles*, &c.; and (*c*) that it involves a different explanation for the lengthening before [r] from that given for lengthening before a voiceless spirant. [Jespersen, we may further note, would explain [ɒ:] in *broad, groat* as a blend pronunciation between ME *ǭ* and the short variant [ɒ]; and [ɑ:] in *answer, branch*, &c., as a blend between ME *ă* and ME *au* (but *can't* and *shan't* have 'compensation length').] I doubt very much these theories of 'compensation length' and 'compromise pronunciations'.

Luick multiplies hypotheses still further. He accepts the 'blend pronunciation' explanation of early ModE [æ:] (PresE [ɑ:]) in *father, rather*, and *water* (see § 494, and for the further development of the theory § 537 and Anm., § 539, and § 560 and Anm. 2). To explain why the [ɑ:] of *father* has such general currency, he assumes that the [r] of the next syllable causes a general retraction of earlier [æ:] to [ɑ:], whereas in *grass*, &c., this retraction is confined to Southern English. He explains lengthening before voiceless spirants (§ 555, Anm. 5) thus: to pass from the low tongue position of ME *ă* and *ŏ* (which he thinks were at the time pronounced [æ] and [ɑ]) to the position of the lengthening consonants [s], [f], and [þ] is a difficult operation [?] requiring more exactitude and energy of articulation than other operations, and the time required for the organs to take up their new position is therefore longer than usual; a glide-vowel is thus able to develop, and is later absorbed by the preceding vowel; thus half-long vowels arise, for which either short vowels or fully long vowels are later substituted. This theory (for which there is no scrap of evidence) seems to me both ingenious and incredible. He explains lengthening before [r] (§ 549 (1)) as due to the development (while [r] was still retained) of a glide [ə] before it; this glide then coalesced with the preceding vowel and was absorbed into it, giving as a result a long vowel. But there is no evidence of such a glide [ə] after a short vowel; in eModE a glide [ə] develops only in limited phonetic circumstances (see § 218 below), and is less frequent than in PresE. Luick assumes, both in the case of lengthening before [r] and before the voiceless spirants, that the lengthened sounds are [æ:] and [ɑ:], and that these were later retracted to [ɑ:] and [ɒ:]; this view depends largely on his assumption that at the time of lengthening ME *ă* was [æ], ME *ŏ* was [ɑ], and ME *au* was [ɑ:], and partly on his view of the nature of the lengthening process. But ME *ŏ* and ME *au* were not (except in dialectal speech) [ɑ] and [ɑ:]; see §§ 86 and 235 below.

It is commonly assumed that [ɒ:] in *war, quaff*, and *water* develops by rounding to [ɒ] followed by lengthening; but Jespersen, § 10.91, is nearer the truth in regarding these words as showing the retraction of a long sound (which he gives as [ɑ:]) to [ɒ:]. Luick, § 539, regards [w] as preventing fronting of long [ɑ:] (ME *ā*) in *water*, but would regard the rounding as preceding the lengthening in words of the type of *war* (§ 550) and *quaff* (§ 555); this is contrary to the evidence.

DIALECTAL LENGTHENING OF ME ĭ AND ME ĕ

§ 57. In Welsh transcriptions of English pronunciation, ME ĭ is transcribed by *u* or *y* (see § 79 below); but before *nk* and *ng* it is transcribed *i* (which otherwise is used regularly for ME ẹ̄) by the *Welsh Hymn*, Salesbury, the *Welsh Breviary*, and T. Jones. Salesbury also transcribes ME ĭ by Welsh *i* before [n] in *ginger*; the *Welsh Hymn* and Salesbury do so for ME ĭ before [ç]; and Salesbury does so for ME ĭ before [l]. These transcriptions indicate at least a tensing, and probably a dissimilatory lengthening, of ME ĭ before [ŋ], [n], [ç], and [l]. That lengthening occurred before [ŋ] is made almost certain by the observation of the Welsh-born orthoepist Price (who is thoughtlessly followed by the English Lye) that *e* in *English* and *England* is pronounced *ee*. The phonetic process involved is one of assimilation; it is purely Welsh, and before [ŋ] merely reflects a similar change in Welsh itself.

Newton shows a dialectal lengthening of ME ĕ to [ɛː] in *end* and *health* (see Vol. I, p. 253).

VII

THE FREE DEVELOPMENT OF THE STRESSED VOWELS

Part 1: THE SHORT VOWELS

§ 58. In this chapter we shall consider the development of the vowels when it was not influenced, in the period between 1500 and 1700, by adjacent sounds. We shall start from the position which may be assumed to have applied before the commencement of our period in 1500; ME vowels which before that time had been influenced by the phonetic context and had developed abnormally are treated either in this chapter or in Chapter IX, according to their fifteenth-century pronunciation. Thus the change of ME ă before *l* to *au* is not treated in Chapter VIII, which deals with the development of the vowels under the influence of adjacent sounds, because the influence belongs to late ME, and not to our period; nor will more than a cross-reference be given in this Part. The account of the development of ME *au* in Chapter IX will be held to cover later ME *au* from ME ă before *l* as well as earlier ME *au* from other sources.

ME ă

§ 59. ME ă is usually held to have been, in the ME period, the back vowel [ɑ] as in German *mann*. This assumption, however, does not appear to be based on any special evidence, and is certainly wrong, at least as far as late ME is concerned. For ME ă must be held to have been, in late ME, the exact short equivalent of ME ā (since the latter develops from the former by lengthening in open syllables); and ME ā, though in its turn usually held to have been a back vowel (obviously since it arises from ME ă), develops in ModE as if it had been a front vowel, being raised (like ME ẹ̄ and ẹ̈) towards the front of the mouth and not towards the back (as are the undoubted back vowels ǭ and ọ̄). We must therefore assume that ME ā was a front vowel, and it follows that at the time when lengthening in open syllables occurred ME ă was also a front vowel; this is consistent with the fact that it represents OE ǽ (an undoubted front vowel) as well as OE ă (which may but need not have been a back vowel). But ME ă and ā were certainly not [æ] and [æ:]; they must rather be taken to have been, at and after the time of lengthening in open syllables, the vowels [a] (as in French *Paris*) and [a:], the lowest possible of the front vowels (see further below).

In ModE the late ME pronunciation [a] of ME ă remains unchanged in many dialects, especially those of the North, but in others (notably Southern dialects and StE itself) it is fronted to [æ] (and even in some dialects to [e]). The rate of the StE development, and the nature of the sound used in the sixteenth and seventeenth centuries by educated speakers, have been the subject of considerable controversy; but it seems not to have been realized that this controversy has depended to some extent on a difference of opinion on theoretical phonetics. It was the view of Sweet that PresE [æ] was the lowest possible of the front vowels (*Primer of Phonetics*, § 34), and that the French [a] in *Paris* was 'low-out-back-wide' (§ 237), i.e. a vowel for which the tongue was formed into the shape appropriate to a back vowel, slack ('wide') and as low as possible in the mouth, but was bodily thrust forward ('out') to the position of the 'mixed' (central) vowels, without losing the slope from front to back which is characteristic of a back vowel (§ 37). H. C. Wyld accepted Sweet's general phonetic system (*A Short History of English*, § 20, and Chapter III generally) and in particular his view of the nature of [æ] (§§ 44 and 45); the French sound [a] in *Paris* is not described, to my knowledge, in Wyld's writings, but from private correspondence I learned that he accepted Sweet's analysis of its formation. Most other modern phoneticians and phonologists have abandoned Sweet's artificial and over-elaborate vowel-system, and have also rejected his view of the nature of [æ] and [a]; the latter is regarded as a front vowel, the lowest possible (and therefore a 'cardinal' vowel), and [æ] as another front vowel for which the tongue is raised slightly higher. This, the generally accepted view, seems to me to be undoubtedly better founded.

From this difference of opinion on a matter of phonetic analysis arises a difference of method in determining the value of ME $ă$ in eModE. To Sweet and Wyld it was sufficient to show that ME $ă$ had become a front vowel; it followed, from their phonetic theory, that it must then be [æ] (but see Note 1 below). To other phonologists who accept the rival phonetic theory the proof that ME $ă$ was at any given period a front vowel does not end the matter; it is necessary to look for further evidence whether it is [a] or [æ].

There are no descriptions of the articulation of ME $ă$ until the seventeenth century, when we find them in the works of the systematic phoneticians; the spelling reformers clearly did not need to describe a sound which presented, from their point of view, no difficulty, and the writers of grammars equally do not seem to have found any necessity for such descriptions. The first description is that of Wallis (see Vol. I, pp. 238–9); its value is doubtful, as it covers both ME $ă$ and $ā$ and is probably based on the latter, but as far as it goes it shows that $ă$ and $ā$ were both front vowels. The description given by Wilkins (see Vol. I, pp. 254–5) again covers both ME $ă$ and $ā$; it is not very clear in its implications, but seems to indicate a front vowel, without perceptible raising of the tongue (though we may doubt this with regard to $ā$). Holder (Vol. I, p. 264) is more useful, though again the one description does duty for both ME $ă$ and $ā$; they are shown to be front vowels and to be removed from e (i.e. ME $ĕ$ and $ẹ̄$) by such a space that Holder thinks it possible for there to be an intermediate vowel, which he would designate æ. The most likely values are [a] and [æ:] for ME $ă$ and $ā$, [æ] and [ɛ:] for the hypothetical vowel æ (short and long), and [e] and [e:] for ME $ĕ$ and $ẹ̄$. Newton and Cooper restrict their description to ME $ă$ and the lengthened sound derived from it before various consonants; Newton says that the 'lips and chaps' are 'a little opened', which is too vague to be of use, but in Cooper ME $ă$ is shown to be a front vowel, with the tongue a little raised. From these descriptions of articulation it appears clearly that ME $ă$ is a front vowel, but there is no evidence that it is [æ] rather than [a]; indeed the evidence of Wilkins, in its vague way, and that of Holder quite clearly, favours [a]. We must turn to our other evidence.

Identifications of ME $ă$ with foreign vowels are relatively frequent. It is said to be the same as French a by Palsgrave, Hart, and Cooper (who would even identify it with French nasalized a in *demande*; this, however, seems unlikely). It is identified with Welsh a by the *Welsh Hymn*, Salesbury, Wallis, the *Welsh Breviary*, T. Jones, and Cooper; with Spanish a by Percival, Minsheu, and Owen; and with Italian a by Florio and Wallis. Instances could be multiplied. An identification of more special interest is that with French nasalized e in *entendement* given by Wallis; as Lehnert shows, French nasalized e in the seventeenth century was identical with nasalized a and pronounced with back [ɑ], but Wallis may be repeating sixteenth-century identifications (which depend on a more forward pronunciation of nasalized e) or be basing his description on the pronunciation of the Northern French dialects. It is interesting to notice that *rendezvous* is transcribed *randyvooz* in the 'phonetically spelt' lists of Coles and Young. This identification of ME $ă$ with the continental pronunciation of a may of course be an inexactitude (cf. the failure of most Englishmen today to realize the difference), but if it shows anything at all, it favours the value [a] rather than [æ] even in Cooper. Tonkis, Jonson, and Daines, on the other hand, say that ME $ă$ as well as ME $ā$ is 'less broad' than French a; but they refer not to the French front [a] but to the back [ɑ], as is shown by their identification of 'French a' with the vowel developed from ME au. However, the contrast which they draw would be more pointed if ME $ă$ were [æ].

Our available evidence does not then get us very far. We can, however, fall back on indirect evidence drawn from other eModE developments. (1) The palatalization of [g] and [k] before ME $ă$ shown by Robinson in one word, and by Wallis more generally, proves that by the beginning of the seventeenth century ME $ă$ was a palatal vowel; but it does not necessarily show that it was [æ] rather than [a], though palatalization of the consonants would be a good deal more likely before [æ]. (2) If my theory of the lengthening of ME *ă* (see § 54) is correct, it follows that evidence of the lengthening is also indirect evidence that ME *ă* in free position had developed to [æ]. It would appear then that ME *ă* had become [æ] in vulgar or dialectal speech in the fifteenth century (perhaps even in the fourteenth century in Scottish speech), in less careful StE in the late sixteenth century, and in correct educated English to an increasing degree during the seventeenth century; after about 1670 it was the normal pronunciation (see § 54, Note 2). But the comparative scarcity of evidence of lengthening in the early part of the seventeenth century implies that [a] was still a common, and perhaps at that time the normal, pronunciation. (3) No argument, however, can be based on the failure of most seventeenth-century observers to distinguish ME *ă* after [w] in, for example, *want* from ME *ă* in free position, even though the former was probably never fronted to [æ] but remained [a] until it was retracted and rounded to [ɒ]; for even if ME *ă* in free position were [æ] and ME *ă* after [w] were [a] the two sounds would be merely contextual variants of the one phoneme, and the differentiation would not be observed until ME *ă* after [w] was rounded to [ɒ] and so became identical with ME *ŏ*.

The evidence is slight, but is, I think, sufficient to show that in the sixteenth and seventeenth centuries there were two pronunciations of ME *ă* in use in StE: a more conservative [a], generally used by careful speakers until 1600 and probably still the more usual pronunciation among such speakers until 1650, which may have continued in occasional use until the end of the century; and a more advanced [æ], vulgar or popular in the sixteenth century, gradually winning wider acceptance in the first part of the seventeenth century, and generally accepted by careful speakers by about 1670 (cf. Note 4). We shall find reason to believe that very similar situations applied in the cases of ME *ā*, ME *ę̄*, and ME *ǭ* (see Part II of this chapter).

Hunt apparently refers to the dialectal over-raising of ME *ă* to [e] discussed in the notes below when he gives, as his example of the fault of speaking too 'mincingly', the sounding of *e* for *a* as in *weter* 'water' and *lerd* 'lard'; for the dialectal fronting before *r* in the latter compare Note 2 (*c*).

Note 1: Sweet and Wyld's view was in fact less logical than it seems, for if modern phoneticians can (erroneously, as it must have seemed to Sweet) believe that French [a] is a front vowel, Wallis and Cooper may have committed a similar 'error' in describing a seventeenth-century [a]. Zachrisson, though his views are generally similar to Wyld's, rejects Sweet's view of the nature of [a] and accepts the usual analysis (*Eng. Vowels*, p. 7 footnote).

Note 2: Attempts have been made to prove the early existence of [æ] for ME *ă* by the use of spellings.

(*a*) Horn, § 40; Zachrisson, *Eng. Vowels*, pp. 58–60, and *Englische Studien*, lii (1918), 316–18; Wyld, *Coll. Eng.*, pp. 198–9; Jordan, § 265; and Kihlbom, p. 119, cite alleged spellings with *e* for ME *ă*. These are subject to grave objections, as Zachrisson eventually apparently realized, though he was not altogether prepared to forgo the use of such evidence.

The most important objection, and it alone is a decisive one, must be that no Englishman could conceivably use *e* as a means of representing [æ]. It may seem natural to a foreign scholar to suppose that the sound [æ], which almost all foreigners have difficulty in distinguishing from [e], might be spelt *e*; but it is little short of incredible that native English-speaking scholars should have accepted this view. No English-speaking child learning to spell, whatever other errors he might make, would write *ket* for [kæt]; the distinction between [æ] and [e] is an absolute one for him (since otherwise he could not distinguish, for example, *man* from *men*), and the value of the symbol *a*, when it expresses a short vowel, is [æ]. The view that in the fifteenth and sixteenth centuries the sound [æ] might be expressed by the letter *e* instead of *a* depends on the fallacious assumption that there is an absolute phonetic value for each letter, and that the value of *a* is [ɑ] or [a]. But in fact letters have no absolute values, nor even conventional international values; in each language the phonetic values of the letters depend on the history of the pronunciation of that language, and they change as the pronunciation changes. Moreover letters can have more values than one; in particular vowel-letters, in any language which makes distinctions of quantity as well as of quality, normally have at least two values, a long and a short vowel, and there need be no phonetic (though there is usually a historical) relationship between the two (cf. the values [æ] and [ei], and the more specialized value [ɑː], of the letter *a* in PresE). In ME the English letter-values were to some extent controlled by the French, so that changes in pronunciation sometimes brought about changes in the spelling of words and not changes in the values of the letters; but after about 1350 this situation ceased entirely to apply, and English orthography developed according to its own conventions. When therefore ME *ă* changed from [a] to [æ] the short value of the letter *a* also changed from [a] to [æ], so that the sound [æ] would always be expressed by the letter *a*; to expect to find, in English writers, spellings which will establish the pronunciation [æ] is therefore a notable futility.

If spellings with *e* for ME *ă* could really be shown to exist, they would and could prove only one thing—that ME *ă* and ME *ĕ* had become identical. (Provided, that is, that the *e*-spellings were such that they could not be explained as inverted spellings on the model of *many* pronounced [menɪ] and similar instances.) Such identity would be due to fronting of ME *ă* to [e], which is recorded by Wright, §§ 23 and 198, for Scottish and Northern English dialects and in the neighbourhood of London; it occurs, for example, for OE *ă* in *cat*, ON *ă* in *happen*, and OF *a* in *carrot*. Batchelor (1809) clearly describes this pronunciation as a vulgarism, saying that in it *man* comes to be like *men* and so on. See also Horn, § 41, who cites a little eighteenth-century evidence. That this development of ME *ă* had already occurred by the last quarter of the sixteenth century is shown by certain rhymes of ME *ă* with ME *ĕ* (see Note 3 below) and probably by the foreign spellings discussed in this note under (c), and it may also account for some of the sixteenth-century *e*-spellings said to occur in native writers (e.g. the Northerner Machyn's *Crenmer* 'Cranmer' (1554) and Henslowe's *ectes* 'acts' (1598), if these are genuine). Admittedly the identity of ME *ă* with ME *ĕ* shows that the former has been fronted not merely to but past [æ], but the pronunciation is plainly dialectal and no valid conclusions on the StE development can be drawn from it.

But it seems highly unlikely that many of the alleged *e*-spellings for ME *ă* do in fact exist. They are in the printed texts, but often are not in the manuscripts, as Zachrisson, *Bullokar*, pp. 139–41, was driven to admit. The reason is that in fifteenth- and sixteenth-century English hands the letters *a* and *e* are closely similar, and the editors of the texts which have been used (who were neither trained palaeographers nor philologists, and never dreamt that anything would turn on the question whether a fifteenth-century scribe used *e* or *a* when so many of his spellings seemed unintelligible aberrations) have often misread and misprinted *a* as *e*. Zachrisson, *Bullokar*, attempted to demonstrate, by the use of facsimiles, that some *e*-spellings were genuine; but Professor N. Davis, in his important article 'The Text of Margaret Paston's Letters', *Medium Ævum*, xviii (1949), 12–28, has shown (p. 24) that in fact none of the *e*-spellings for stressed ME *ă* hitherto cited from the Paston Letters really exist; either the symbol used is *a*, or the word is one in which not ME *ă* but one of the ME *e*-vowels is to be expected, or the vowel is unstressed. Similarly

Miss A. H. Forester informs me that alleged instances of *e* for *a* (e.g. *seke* 'sack', *semend* 'salmon') in the *Cely Papers* are all misreadings. As the two letters are so alike, it is important to observe that the intention of the writer must be taken into account; thus I often write what is undoubtedly the shape appropriate to *n* when I mean *u*, or that appropriate to *a* when I mean *o*, but I should not expect my *u*'s to be read as *n*'s or my *o*'s as *a*'s, still less to be told that I must really pronounce *u* as [n] or *o* as [æ]. This being so, it is doubtful whether we should accept as evidence of pronunciation any alleged instances of *e*-spellings for ME *ă* unless we are assured they come from scribes whose hand is such that their *e*'s and *a*'s are always quite clearly distinct; in practice this might well mean scribes who use the Italian hand, and would restrict us to documents written after 1550, when evidence of fronting of ME *ă* and *ā* would not be at all remarkable.

Furthermore, as *o* and *e* are so frequently confused in fifteenth-century documents because of the close similarity of the letters in the hands of that time, all alleged *e*-spellings for ME *ă* which occur in words in which a ME *o*-variant is possible should be excluded from consideration unless we are assured that a careful collation of the manuscripts rules out the possibility that what the scribe really intended was *o* and not *e* (as well as the possibility that he intended *a*). Such assurances are hitherto lacking. Zachrisson admitted (*Bullokar*, p. 140) that in some of the instances which he had cited the manuscripts either have, or may have, *o* and not *e*; and the same may well apply in some of Wyld's cases (e.g. *cress* for *cross*, *thenking* for *thonking* 'thanking').

Apart from these palaeographical considerations, there are objections of a philological sort to many of the *e*-spellings that have been adduced; only Kihlbom, of the writers named above, has been really careful to exclude *e*-spellings in words which may have a ME variant in *ĕ*. Such cases (assuming for the purposes of discussion that the scribes really intended to write *e* and not *a*) may be classified as follows.

(i) Many of the spellings occur in words which have (as Wyld admits) a ME variant in *ĕ* developed from OE *ǣ* (or *ĕa*; see Jordan, § 76); originally such an *ĕ* variant was WMidl or Kentish, but may later have become more widespread (see Jordan, § 32, Anm. 3). Examples are Wyld's *wessh* 'wash' and *eddres* 'adders' cited from Palladius (Jordan, § 15, Anm. 2, states that a WMidl scribe has left traces in the manuscript), and Jordan's *fethem* 'fathom' cited from the Londoner Gregory and *gled* from the NWMidl *Torrent of Portyngale*; perhaps also Wyld's *sedness* 'sadness' cited from Mrs. Basire (a Shropshire lady) in the seventeenth century. It is safest to reject all words which have OE *ǣ* or *ĕa*; this would rule out Zachrisson's *beck* 'back' cited from Rutland documents of 1485. (ii) The *e* forms of *sack* 'a bag' which occur from the thirteenth to the seventeenth century in East Anglian texts (e.g. *Genesis and Exodus*, *Promptorium Parvulorum*, and Margaret Paston) and in Northern and Scottish texts (e.g. *Cursor Mundi*, *Scottish Legends of the Saints*, and Dunbar) are to be explained from ON *sekkr* from Prim. Gmc. *sakkiz (whence perhaps OE *sæcc* beside *sǎcc* from Latin *saccus*); see *OED*. (iii) Some of the words cited may have ME *ā* (cf. Zachrisson, *Engl. St.*, p. 316); so the *pek* 'pack' in seventeenth-century Suffolk records (*OED* cites a fourteenth- and fifteenth-century spelling *pake*), and Mrs. Basire's *Frencis* 'Francis' (cf. ME *ā* in *ancient*, and see § 104 and Note 2). (iv) In some of the cases cited by Wyld, ME *ă* appears as *e* in syllables which either certainly or possibly are unstressed, or in words which are frequently unstressed in the sentence and so develop weak forms; all such cases should be excluded. (v) Some of the words cited have OF variants in *e* which certainly or possibly give rise to *ĕ* variants in English. Raising because of the preceding palatal (see Pope, §§ 413–17) occurs in *charity* (which has *e*-forms from the fourteenth to the sixteenth century, because of ME *cherte* from OF *chierte* beside *charite*), *chesible* (the normal ME form, replaced after 1700 by latinized *chasuble*; see *OED*), *January* (which has *e* forms from the thirteenth century onwards because of ONF *Jenever*, *Genever*, which was later gradually made to conform to Latin *Januarium*), and *jasper*; so possibly in *gallon* (ONF *galon*, in which raising should not have occurred, but which may have been influenced by Central French *jalon*, in which raising is possible). Raising because of the preceding *s* might occur in *satisfy* and (despite the inhibiting influence of the following *l*) in *salary*, which have English *e* forms from the fifteenth to the seventeenth century. (In *gallon*, *satisfy*, and *salary* ME *ā* is not impossible; nor can we be certain, especially in the last word, that the first syllable was always accented.) Raising because of the following [dʒ] or [tʃ] (Pope, § 423) occurs in French in *tragedy* (which has *e* forms in English from the fourteenth century) and may occur in *bachelor* (which has English *e* forms in the fifteenth century). *Renk* 'rank' is a common ME variant, derived from OF *renc* beside *ranc* (the French word is supposed to be an adoption of OHG *hrinc, hring*).

Of the cases which remain outside these categories, Palladius's *sedness*, which Wyld takes to be a spelling of *sadness*, is admitted by Zachrisson, *Bullokar*, p. 36, to mean 'sowing' and to be derived from OE *sǣd*. A legal paper among the *Paston Letters* (of date 1451; the scribe seems to belong, as one would expect, to Norfolk) has twice a form *excercary*, which Zachrisson, *Bullokar*, p. 141, establishes beyond doubt as the manuscript reading. Gairdner, followed by Zachrisson, took it as a form of *accessary* (a sense which would fit the context). Zachrisson interprets it as showing the word stressed on the first syllable (and therefore with *e* for stressed ME *ă*), and with unstressed [ə] spelt *er* in the second. One could, however, explain it as having the stress on the second syllable and a redundant *r* in the spelling on the analogy of *horse* pronounced *hoss*. I doubt whether the word is *accessary*; I would rather regard it as *exercary 'an employer, a maintainer', from *exerce* 'to employ' (in the second occurrence, the context is: 'Sir T. Todenham maynteynyth hym, and therefore he were worthy to be indyted as excercary'). *Ravish*, according to *OED*'s list of forms, has *e* beside *a* from the fourteenth to the sixteenth century (but in its quotations *e* occurs first in the fifteenth century, and is restricted to Northern or Scottish texts); Zachrisson, *Englische Studien*, lii. 316, suggests that the word may have an OF variant in *e*, but there seems no warrant for this assumption, as there is no palatal influence operative. If, however, *e* did occur in the fourteenth century (as stated by *OED*), we could hardly regard it as a development of stressed ME *ă*; the word might be stressed on the second syllable. In a letter by Thomas Pery dated 1539 (cited by Wyld), *examine* has *e* in the second syllable nine times; *OED* cites the spelling *exemnyt* from the Scotch *Complaynt of Scotlande* (1549). As *examine* is an adoption of Fr. *examiner*, itself a fourteenth-century adoption from Latin which should not have been subject to raising under palatal influence, we must I think assume original *a*; but it is a suspicious circumstance that Pery should be reported to have *e* regularly in this word and not once in any other (except *cherity*, which has a ME variant in *ĕ* derived from OF). Possible explanations are (*a*) that the word has ME *ā* (the vowel being in an open syllable, and the original Latin vowel being also long), which has been shortened to *ĕ*; (*b*) that the *a* is unstressed, the English system of stressing on the first syllable being applied even though it is a prefix. If these special explanations were rejected we should have to take it that in this one word Pery shows the vulgar raising of ME *ă* to [e]; this, however, would in him not be surprising. His speech was clearly Cockney; there are many striking parallels in his spellings to the evidence of the 'homophone' lists (which set out to teach the avoidance of exactly such 'mistakes' in spelling as he commits); and in particular he uses *w* for *v*, as in *wery* 'very', *dywers* 'divers', *ewery* 'every', and *hawe* 'have' (over fifty examples in all). The evidence of such a writer clearly does not relate to educated StE.

On the whole one may safely conclude that the evidence, like much of this alleged evidence from spellings, melts away under criticism.

(*b*) Wyld, loc. cit., cites spellings with *a* for ME *ĕ*, which he would explain as inverted spellings which show that ME *ă* has become [æ]. But if they are inverted spellings, they should depend on identity of the two sounds. This may arise either by fronting of ME *ă* to [e], or by lowering of ME *ĕ*. Zachrisson, *Eng. Vowels*, p. 59, adopts the latter explanation; see also Wright, § 51, who shows that ME *ĕ* becomes [æ] in 'East and South-west Country' (*inter alia*). Wyld's examples are from Margaret Paston (Norfolk), Gregory (Suffolk), Machyn (a Yorkshireman), and Elyot (South-west); the agreement with Wright's evidence is so close as to suggest the correctness of Zachrisson's view. These spellings therefore also depend on dialectal pronunciation and cannot be used as evidence for StE. Zachrisson, *Bullokar*, p. 140, admits further that *zastyrday* 'yesterday' is probably a misreading for *ʒustyrday*, a clearly dialectal form (which Professor Davis informs me is certainly the manuscript reading); and *massage* 'message' and *massynger* might depend on variation between *mass* and *mess* (the sacrament).

(*c*) Luick, § 538, Anm. 2, refers to evidence adduced by Barnouw, *Echoes of the Pilgrim Fathers' Speech*, pp. 24–25. This consists of spellings by a Dutch scribe of names of

English emigrants preserved in the town records of Leyden and dated 1611. The scribe seems to spell according to the sound and appears to have done his work carefully. ME ă (except before *l*) varies between *a*, *ae*, and *e*. Luick ignores the *a*-spellings, which are against [æ] for ME ă (which could hardly be identified with Dutch *a* if it were so pronounced), and concentrates attention on the *e*-spellings, which are in favour of a fronted pronunciation. But the *e*-spellings may indicate the dialectal pronunciation established above (see under (*a*)), since ME ĕ is equally transcribed *e*. The emigrants may have been dialect speakers; some of them came from Spalding and appear to have used an East Anglian form of the name (see Barnouw, p. 44, who cites information supplied to him by Sir William Craigie). Wright, § 23, records [e] for ME ă in *after* in Lincolnshire. It is important to observe that *e* is equally used for ME ă before *r* in *Hardy* and *Harding* (beside *a*-forms); but fronting in such circumstances is purely dialectal, being found chiefly in Scotch and Northern dialects, but also in Rutland, Buckinghamshire, and Dorset in *barley* and in Buckinghamshire in *harvest*. If these Dutch spellings really indicate [æ] or [e] for ME ă in free position, they must also do so for ME ă before *r*; and we then have no alternative but to regard them as reflecting dialectal pronunciation.

Note 3: Horn, § 40, and Wyld, *Coll. Eng.*, p. 199, cite Shakespeare's rhyme of *back* with *neck* (also *scratch* with *wretch*, but this depends on the variant *wratch*). Horn takes it to show [æ] for ME ă (which would make it an inexact rhyme), but Wyld (p. 198 top) seems to treat it (correctly) as an exact rhyme showing [e]. Bullokar has rhymes which seem to be best interpreted as rhymes of ME ă with ME ĕ (see Vol. I, p. 110). Similar rhymes may occur sporadically in other poets; thus Wyatt has *chamber*: *danger*: *remember* (which looks like, but is not certainly, an ă : ĕ rhyme), Daniel has *cracks*: *checks* (but there is a ME *chak* form; see *OED*), and Drayton has *pennyfather* : *together* (but *OED* records a seventeenth-century form *togather*). Undoubted instances are few; when they occur they must depend on the dialectal and vulgar development described in Note 2 above by which ME ă becomes [e]. For the evidence of Wright and of Batchelor (1809) see Note 2.

Note 4: Zachrisson, *Englische Studien*, lii. 317, argues that the form *sack* (the wine) arises from French *sec* through French [ɛ] (which is lower than English [e]) being identified with [æ] from ME ă, and that therefore ME ă must have been [æ] in the early sixteenth century. But *OED*'s explanation (which Zachrisson reports not altogether fairly) is sufficient, and much sounder—that *sack* arises beside *seck* because of the variation between dialectal *seck* and StE *sack* 'a bag'.

Note 5: Zachrisson, *Eng. Vowels*, pp. 120–1, cites French orthoepists who say that ME ă is pronounced like French *a*, i.e. as [a]. But Festeau (1672 and 1693) and Miège (1688) seem to know [æ]; the former says that ME ă 'approaches a little' French *a*, the latter that it is '*ai* bref ou *e* ouvert'. Miège may of course refer to the dialectal or vulgar [e] for ME ă, but it seems unnecessary to believe so.

Note 6: A good indication that [a] was ceasing to be the normal pronunciation of ME ă during the seventeenth century is the treatment of foreign [a] in words adopted from languages of which the orthography could not influence English orthography. While ME ă was [a] the foreign sound would of course be correctly heard and would be spelt in English as *a*; but after ME ă had become [æ] and ME ŭ had become [ʌ] a foreign [a] would be liable to be confused with [ʌ] and to be spelt *u* (cf. the inability of most untrained speakers of Southern English, at the present day, to distinguish [a] from [ʌ]). This situation applies with adoptions from Hindī. *Punkah* (Hindī *pankhā*) has the form *punkaw* in Finch 1625 (twice), but is *panhah* in 1672 (but in a translation of Bernier's *Great Mogul*). *Bungalow* (Hindī *banglā*) has *u*-forms in 1676 and 1711; *OED* records no *a*-forms. *Pundit* appears first in this form in 1698 and continues so throughout the eighteenth century; in the nineteenth century *pandit* comes in beside it as a more learned form which represents more closely the Hindī original. In its earliest occurrence (in 1672) it has the form *pendet*, which must reflect a French form (cf. French *Pendjab* 'Punjab').

Note 7: Luick, § 538, regards the change of ME ă to [æ] as occurring in the sixteenth century, since in his view ME ŏ becomes [ɑ] and ME *au* becomes [ɑ:] at that time; and in

Anm. 1 he therefore uses evidence which contrasts ME *ă* and ME *au* as showing the pronunciation [æ] for the former. But (i) front [a] can be kept distinct from back [ɑ(:)], as modern French shows; and (ii) Luick's theory that ME *ŏ* was [ɑ] and ME *au* [ɑ:] cannot stand.

ME *ă* BEFORE *l*

§ 60. In late ME, about or shortly before 1400, ME *ă* developed to *au* before a back ('dark') [l], i.e. before *ll* or *l* plus consonant. It subsequently shared the development of ME *au* both generally and in special phonetic circumstances (as in *half* and *calm*). The diphthong, or sounds developed from it, are shown by all orthoepists from the writer of the *Welsh Hymn* onwards. But in certain circumstances the diphthongization failed either generally or occasionally, apparently because ME did not use, or did not regularly use, a back [l] in those circumstances. The orthoepists' evidence is particularly interesting when it shows this failure of diphthongization, which occurs as follows:

(1) Before a single *l* in intervocalic position, as in *palace, balance, salary, palate*, and (despite the modern spelling with *ll* where ME had originally *l*) in *alley, challenge, dally, dalliance, tally, stallion, gallop, wallop* (which has later *w*-influence), *pallet*, and so probably *mallet* and *allegory*. The orthoepists regularly show ME *ă* in such words; a few examples will suffice. Hart gives it in *allegory* and *palate*, Bullokar in *callet, gallant, tallage*, and *talon*, Robinson in *challenge*, Gil in *valley* and *value*, and Hodges in *alley, dally, balance, palace*, and *valley*. Words like *fallow* constitute a special case; they probably belong here, since the *l* was originally single, but might be regarded as showing the influence on the *l* of a following bilabial consonant (see below). Bullokar gives *ă* in *shallow* and *wallow* (which in PresE shows later *w*-influence), Butler in the same two words, Gil in *mallow* and *wallow*, Hodges in *hallow*, and Price in *shallow, tallow*, and *wallow*.

(2) Before an *l* which is followed by a bilabial consonant the development varies. PresE has ME *ă* in *alb* and *scalp*; Hart gives *ă* (beside more frequent *au*) in *almighty* and *always* (but the first has unstressed *al*), Bullokar in *Almain* (perhaps unstressed; contrast *au* in *almond*), Robinson in *Albion* (but the reason may be late adoption, as in PresE *Alps*), and Gil in *almost*. On the other hand Daines and Hodges have ME *au* in *scalp(s)*. (Hodges's [ɒ:] in *alp(s)* probably does not indicate the pronunciation of the word *Alps*; it is merely a syllable-ending, of which *scalps* is the example.) A development similar to that of PresE *alb* explains ME *ă* in *alms*, which is recorded by Robinson and was apparently known to Butler, who says that the *a* is short 'if *l* have his proper sound' (cf. Robinson, who shows retention of [l]) but who also knew the pronunciation *aums*. Bullokar and Hodges have only ME *au* in *alms*, and some orthoepists show the development of this *au* to later ME *ā* (see § 104 (2)). See further Note 1 below.

(3) Before an *l* which is followed by an *f* which begins a new syllable the

diphthongization fails in PresE *Alfred*; further examples may be *alpha* (recorded in ME, but perhaps readopted later) and *alphabet* (not recorded until 1513). Hart gives *ă* in *alphabet*.

(4) Before an *l* which is followed by other voiceless consonants there is occasional failure of diphthongization. To this cause may be due PresE [æ] in *altitude* (recorded in ME, but perhaps readopted in ModE with *ă*). Smith gives *ă* in *salt*, Hart in *alter*, Bullokar in *alter* (four times) and *halter* (once) but *au* in *altar*, *psalter*, and *halt*, Gil in *malt* and *salt* (twice, beside *au* thrice). Hart has *ă* in *chalk*, Bullokar in *walk* (once, against *au* thrice) but *au* in *talk*, and Gil in *walk* (once, against *au* once); Wallis, though he teaches that *a* before *ll* is pronounced like ME *au*, nevertheless says that '*walk, talk,* &c. rectius per *a* Anglicum [i.e. ME *ă*] efferuntur; quae tamen negligentius loquentibus sonantur *wau'k*, *tau'k*, *etc.*'—a remark which, though his preference for ME *ă* shows the typical influence on him of the conventional spelling, is shown by its agreement with the earlier transcriptions (which it confirms) to relate to real and not to fictitious pronunciations. A final case is Hart's *ă* in *Walsh* 'Welsh'; Gil's *ă* in *exalted*, an early fifteenth-century adoption, may belong under (6) below rather than with *salt*, &c.

(5) In unstressed syllables the pronunciation in which the diphthongization failed was common and eventually displaced that in which it occurred (see § 273 below). Lack of stress explains the *ă* of the weak form *shall* and of the first syllable of *salvation* (recorded by Robinson, Gil, and Hodges; but Strong has *au* developed under secondary stress). It probably also explains Hart's *ă* (beside *au*) in *almighty*; but it seems unlikely to account for Hart's *ă* in *always* and Gil's in *algate* and *almost*. The PresE pronunciation of *alchemy* and *algorism* might arise in forms stressed on the second syllable, but could be explained by readoption of the words in ModE.

(6) Diphthongization naturally fails in words adopted after the process was complete. In *halberd* (first recorded in the late fifteenth century) Gil gives *ă* beside *au*; PresE has [æ], but *OED* records that the pronunciation was formerly [ɒ:]. Apparently this word was adopted just about the time when the change occurred, so that it sometimes showed it and sometimes did not; but other possible explanations are (*a*) that despite the late date of *OED*'s first instance the word was a ME adoption and varies because it is of type (2) above (see further Note 2 below), (*b*) that the *au* pronunciation is a deliberate anglicization. Lack of diphthongization in words which are not of the types set out above is exemplified in PresE by *fallacy* (recorded 1483), *callous*, and *recalcitrant*. Other possible examples are mentioned under the previous headings. The fact that PresE uses the sound developed from ME *au* in *waltz* must be due to an attempt to imitate the German back [ɑ] (cf. *vase* pronounced [vɒ:z]). Diminutives like *Hal* (which has *ă* in Gil and Butler) and *Mal* 'Mary' (which has *ă* in Butler) probably lack diphthongiza-

tion because they are ModE formations (or reformations) from *Harry* and *Mary* (of which the latter could have eModE *ă*).

Note 1: The failure of diphthongization in *alms* is probably, and retention of [l] is certainly, assisted by the fact that a disyllabic pronunciation survived into the sixteenth century; Levins rhymes *almes* with *less, chess*, &c. An *m* which belongs to the same syllable as the *l* does not prevent diphthongization (cf. ME *au* in *calm, psalm*, &c.); the monosyllabic ME form *alms* (which arises owing to the word being treated formally as if it were a plural—cf. *riches*) accounts for the development of ME *au* and its ModE descendants in this word. Bullokar's *ă* (once, beside *au* four times) in *bald* may be due to the ME disyllabic form *balled*, in which the *l* might conceivably be single; but the transcription is probably erroneous.

Note 2: Gil also gives *ō* in *halberd*; this must represent the sixteenth- and seventeenth-century forms *holberd*, &c. (see *OED*), and it is therefore probable that his [o:] is really from ME *ou*. This makes it appear more likely than not that the word is a fourteenth-century adoption, in which case we should be obliged to explain its variation between *a* and *au* as an example of type (2) above. But the *o*-form of *halberd* is unexplained; indeed, the relation of the English forms cited by *OED* to the French forms is not at all clearly made out. Gil's *ă* in *thrall* and *wall* (once in each case, beside *au* once) seems to be an error of transcription, as it is unsupported by other evidence.

Note 3: The variant pronunciations of *Mall* (for which Gil and Butler give *au*) and *Pall Mall* seem to depend on direct adoption of Latin *malleus* as well as of OF *mail*.

Note 4: For similar failure of the development of ME *ŏ* to *ou* or *ū* before *l* followed by certain consonants see §§ 88, 169.

ME *ă* BEFORE [χ]

§ 61. ME *ă* before [χ] develops, in the ME period, to *au*, as in *slaughter* (cf. Jordan, § 122). Some words, such as *laugh*, appear in StE in the seventeenth century with the pronunciation [af] instead of ME [auχ]; this might seem to show that when ME [χ] became [f] the diphthongization of ME *ă* to *au* did not occur. But we have seen reason to suppose that the process was that ME *ă* was first diphthongized to *au* and then directly shortened to *ă* when subsequently [χ] changed to [f] (see § 28, Note 3).

VARIATION BETWEEN ME *ă* AND *au* BEFORE A NASAL

§ 62. In words adopted from French variation occurs in ME between *ă* and *au* before a nasal consonant. The *au* variant subsequently shows diverse development; in certain phonetic circumstances it becomes, during the late ME period, ME *ā* (see § 104 below) but otherwise it develops in the Modern period either to [ɒ:] or to [ɑ:] (see §§ 238–9 below). The variation between ME *ă* and ME *au* (or sounds developed from it) continues into the seventeenth century; in most words ME *au* or its descendants are now used in StE, but ME *ă* survives in dialectal and in American and Australian English. The cases may be classified as follows.

(1) Words in which ME *ă* varies with ME *au* which often becomes ME *ā* in late ME. Here we shall examine the evidence for the *ă* pronunciation;

for that showing ME *au* and *ā* see § 104 below. *Salmon* (ME *sa(w)mon*, &c.), which retains [æ] in PresE, has ME *ă* in Coles (who gives the 'phonetic spelling' *sam-mun*) followed by Young; so probably Strong, whose spelling is *samon* (but this may perhaps mean ME *ā*). It is not clear what Cooper's pronunciation was; he includes the word in a list of those which have silent *l* and fails to mark it with a dagger (thereby showing that it has not got [ɒ:] < ME *au*); but it is not certain that it has ME *ă* (as is probable) rather than [a:] < ME *au* (which is the probable pronunciation of the other words which are left unmarked). *WSC-RS* includes *salmon* in a list of words in which *al* is pronounced *au*, but this list is merely an unintelligent copy of Cooper's and it is doubtful whether we should assume from it that *salmon* had [ɒ:]. *Chamber* has *ă* in Bullokar (beside *au*) and in Gil; so *chamberlain* in Hart. *Angel* has *ă* in Robinson (beside *ā*) and in Gil (who also gives *ă* in *angelical*). *Change* has *ă* in Smith, Hart (thirteen times, beside *au* seven times and *ā* once), Robinson (beside *ā*), and Gil. *Range* has *ă* in Bullokar. *Strange* and *stranger* have *ă* in Hart and *ă* beside *au* in Bullokar. *Ancient* has *ă* in Robinson and perhaps also in Tonkis and Jonson; the 'phonetic spelling' *an-shent* in Coles (followed by Strong, Cocker, and Brown) probably means *ă*, but its significance is somewhat uncertain. The Northerner Levins perhaps has *ă* (beside *ā*) in *change* and *strange*; see Vol. I, p. 27.

(2) Words in which ME *ă* varies with ME *au* which becomes (in the Modern period) [ɒ:] or [ɑ:]. Here we shall give the evidence for the *ă* pronunciation; for that showing ME *au* and the sounds derived from it see §§ 238–9 below. *Dance* has *ă* in Gil (beside [ɒ:], which is his usual form; in the Errata he says that such words as *dance* vary between *ă* and [ɒ:]), and in Hodges (beside [ɒ:]). *Chance* has *ă* in Smith, Robinson (beside [ɒ:]), and Gil, who also gives it in *chancellor*. *Lance* has *ă* (beside [ɒ:]) in Hodges. *Branch* has *ă* in Gil. *Example* has *ă* in Hart and Gil. *Transitory* and *translating* have *ă* in Hart. *Chanter* has *ă* in Smith, as have *advantage* and *Flanders* in Bullokar. *Plant* has *ă* in Gil and Hodges. Of the rhyme-lists, that of the Northerner Levins shows *ă* in a number of words which now have [ɒ:] or [ɑ:] (see Vol. I, p. 27). Willis shows it in *plant*, and probably also in *blanch, branch, haunch, paunch,* and *staunch*; other words have ME *au* (see Vol. I, pp. 424–5). Poole's pronunciation probably varied between ME *ă* and *au* in some words at least (see Vol. I, p. 436). Coles shows *ă* in *blanch, branch, haunch, launch, paunch,* and *staunch* (see Vol. I, p. 442). In *fancy* Bullokar, like PresE, has ME *ă*; but in two other words which have [æ] in PresE the orthoepists show ME *au*—Bullokar in *andiron* and Mulcaster in *stamp*.

(3) In some words of English or Norse origin the same variation occurs between ME *ă* and *au* as in words of French origin; whether it is due to the analogy of the latter, or to an occasional ME development of ME *ă* to *au*, is

uncertain, but the rarity of pronunciations developed from ME *au* in native words suggests that analogy is much the more likely explanation. The orthoepists normally record ME *ă*, but [ɒ:] occurs in *anger* in Daines and in *ant* in Hodges and Daines; *ant* is placed with *aunt* (presumably because the former has a sound descended from ME *au*, rather than because the latter had ME *ă*) by 'homophone' lists from Hodges's 'near alike' list onwards (Coles, it should be noticed, pairs the two words in his *Lat.–Eng. Dict.*, but not in the more careful *Schoolmaster*). The variation is especially common in *answer*. It has *ă* in Laneham (beside *au*), Bullokar, Tonkis, Gil (who expressly rejects Hart's pronunciation with ME *au*), and Hodges, but ME *au* in Laneham and Hart, and [ɒ:] from ME *au* in Robinson. The 'phonetic spelling' *anser* given by Coles, Strong, Young, and Brown, and the shorthand-writers Bridges and Hopkins, seems to show ME *ă*, but might possibly mean [a:] from ME *au*.

Note 1: Daines says that *a* is pronounced short before *n* except in *ancient*, *anger*, *ant*, words in which [dʒ] follows *n*, and words in -*ance*; if his rule is reliable, he must have used *ă* in words like *example*, *plant*, *branch*, &c., but he may simply have forgotten such words. The 'phonetic spellings' *hant*, *vant* (Strong), *hansh*, *lansh* (Brown) seem to show *ă*, but they may be a faulty way of writing [a:]. The shorthand-writer Farthing would omit the *u* from *taunt*; this may show *a*, but is ambiguous not only in the same way as the 'phonetic spellings', but also because *au* is reduced to *a* by shorthand-writers even when pronounced [ɒ:].

Note 2: Luick, §§ 519, 521, explains the words of class (2) as having [æ] because of a special process of monophthongization of ME *au* to [æ:] with subsequent shortening to [æ]. This explanation could be extended to words of class (1), since they also have an eModE pronunciation with ME *au* (see § 104). But this complex process need not be assumed unless we regard ME as having only *au* in such words (as appears to be assumed by Luick, § 414 (2) and Jordan, § 224 (III)). It is much simpler to assume that there was in ME variation between *ă* and *au* (the latter being an AN development of French nasalized *a*); so Horn, § 132. On the AN process see A. J. Bliss, *Archivum Linguisticum*, iv (1952), 142–5.

DIALECTAL *ai* < ME *ă*

§ 63. A development of ME *ă* to ME *ai* is shown before [ʃ] in *ash* 'ask' by the *Welsh Hymn* and in *ash* sb. by Salesbury, before [tʃ] in *watch* and [dʒ] in *domage*, *heritage*, and *language* by Salesbury, before [ntʃ] in *branch* by the *Welsh Hymn*, and before [ndʒ] in *oranges* by Salesbury and in *change*, *range*, *danger*, *strange*(*r*), and *angel* by Butler. This development is apparently dialectal, being shown only by the two Welsh sources, by Butler (who lived for most of his life in Hampshire), and probably by Cooper (see Note 2), who has other dialectalisms; ME evidence agrees with ModE in showing it as chiefly but not solely Western.

Note 1: In ME the same or similar developments are fairly widespread, but with a tendency to predominate in the West; see Jordan, §§ 102, 103, 224 Anm.; Luick, §§ 404 and 436. Luick's statements that the changes also occurred in the North (§§ 404 and 436, Anm. 1) are erroneous, being based solely on Northern spellings in which *ai* is really only the common graphic representation of ME *ā*. If the Folio's spelling *raing'd* 'ranged' *A &C*, I. i. 34, represents Shakespeare's pronunciation, he also used this dialectalism.

Note 2: Cooper's [ɛ:] in such words as *age* and *strange* probably develops from ME *ai*, not ME *ā* (see Vol. I, pp. 307–8), and therefore shows the currency of this dialectal development in Hertfordshire.

Note 3: Jordan, § 224 Anm., and Luick, § 436, treat *ai* in *change*, &c., as being developed from ME *ā* < earlier *au* for OF *a* before a nasal, but there is no valid evidence for this view; the *ai* occurs only in words which also have ME *ă*, and is much more likely to develop from the short vowel. The process in all cases is the diphthongization of ME *ă* before a following alveolar consonant or consonant-group.

Note 4: Luick, § 436, says that Levins shows diphthongization in words in *-aynge*, *-aynche* and in *-ayge*. But Levins knows no distinction of ME *ai* and ME *ā*, and freely employs the Northern spellings *ai* and *ay* for ME *ā* without phonetic significance.

VARIATION BETWEEN ME ă AND ME ĕ

(1) *Words with ME ĕ before* r

§ 64. ME *ĕ* before *r* began to change to *ă* in the early fourteenth century in the North, and by the end of the century the new sound had begun to appear in the South, though it did not become at all common until the fifteenth century. In StE the changed pronunciation never became entirely general, and its spread seems in particular to have been inhibited by the retention of the old *e* spelling, especially in words derived directly or indirectly from Latin. Late adoptions were of course not affected. The retention of the old pronunciation with *ĕ* beside the new pronunciation with *ă* led to a variation in late ME and in ModE in individual words or between words of the same class.

Note 1: On the late ME development see Luick, § 430, and Jordan, §§ 67, 270. Wyld, pp. 212–22, gives a full account of the situation in ME and early ModE, with much valuable evidence. But his account of the ME situation, and his theory that the change began in the South-east, is incorrect. Some of the early forms cited by Wyld do not in fact show the late ME change of *ĕ* to *ă* before *r* (cf. Luick, § 430, Anm. 2 and Jordan, § 67 Anm.); the *ă* forms go back either to OE variants with *ĕa* (so *dark*) or *ǣ* (so *mar*), or to OF variants in *ar* besidè *er* (so OF *sarmon* beside *sermon*, *marchant* beside *merchant*). It is these forms which lead Wyld to give a false account of the ME development. *Dark* in early ME is from OE **dĕarc* from WGmc **dark-* (cf. thirteenth-century ME *dearc*, and the OHG weak verb **tarchanjan*, &c., from WGmc **darknjan*; see *OED*). On the *ă* forms of the *Ancrene Wisse* group (which go back to OE variants) see d'Ardenne, *St. Iuliene*, 'Language', § 3, Note 3.

Note 2: The lowering was probably in the first instance to [æ], and subsequently to [a] (cf. Wyld, *Coll. Eng.*, p. 212); for evidence of an analogous lowering of *ĕ* to [æ] in early ME in the WMidl dialect of the *Ancrene Wisse* group see d'Ardenne, op. cit., § 3 (*b*).

Note 3: Horn, §§ 32–34, regards ME *ĕ* as having invariably become *ă* before *r*. In his view, it is only eModE *ĕ* by ModE shortening (in e.g. *learn*) or in ModE adoptions from foreign languages which is unaffected by the change to *ă* and which, by a later lowering process, becomes [ə]. Thus he would explain the *ăr* variant in *heard* from ME *hẹrde*, the [ər] variant as due to an eModE *hērde* by ModE shortening of *hẹrde* (he should say of late ME *hẹrde*, since shortening of ME *ẹ̄* gives [ɪ] not [e]); similarly in *learn* we have, in his view, (*a*) unshortened *ẹ̄r* < earlier *ẹ̄r*, (*b*) [ər] < eModE *lērn* by ModE shortening of *lẹ̄rn*, and (*c*) *ăr* < ME *lĕrn*, which *ĕ* either because of the failure of OE lengthening or because of ME shortening. In other words, such as *certain*, &c., Horn would regard the [ər] as being due simply to a spelling pronunciation. But though the spelling does undoubtedly influence the ModE pronunciation from the eighteenth century onwards (if not indeed earlier), the sixteenth- and seventeenth-century evidence makes it improbable that *ĕ* in such words is due simply to the spelling. Horn's theory, which depends on the assumption of a ModE shortening process which in itself is not improbable but for which there is no evidence, is justified only if we are to regard all sound-changes as being without exceptions. But though this classical doctrine may be true of an individual dialect (provided it is rigidly enough defined), it is demonstrably untrue of modern StE, which is not a pure dialect but a mixed language and in consequence shows great variety of pronunciation in words which are clearly of the same class. It would be a fair guess in the present instance that the lowering was not at all typical of educated London English but was regular in more vulgar speech, and that the lowered forms made their way into educated speech gradually and inconsistently from this dialect which had regular lowering. The lowered pronunciation is less freely accepted in words of Latin origin, obviously owing to the influence of Latin orthography and probably also pronunciation.

(a) ME ĕ before r followed by a tautosyllabic consonant

§ 65. Some words with ME *ĕ* before *r* followed by a consonant belonging to the same syllable now have [ɑː] by lengthening of late ME *ă*. Of these, *heart* has *ă* in all sixteenth- and seventeenth-century orthoepists (except possibly Poole; see Note 2) from Salesbury onwards, including the short-hand-writers, the 'homophone' lists, and the 'phonetically spelt' lists. *Hearth* has *ă* in Hodges, Coles, Lye, Cooper, *WSC*, Aickin, and Brown, but *ĕ* in Gil, Price, and Cocker, and most probably in the 'homophone' lists of Price, Young, Cocker, and Brown, where it is equated with *earth*, which has regular *ĕ*. *Hark* and *hearken* have normally *ă*, from Hart and Laneham onwards; see also the Note below. *Sheard* has *ă* in Hodges. *Clerk* has *ă*, as in Cooper. Other words, in which the spelling changes to *a*, such as *yard* and *farm*, have normally *ă* (as in Hart, Bullokar, Robinson, Gil, and Hodges); the change of spelling is of course itself due to the early predominance of *ă* pronunciations in these words. But some such words seem to have had an *ĕ* variant in the North (see Note 2).

Words which now have [əː] from early ModE *ĕr*, such as *earth*, *earl*, *earn*, and *learn*, have usually *ĕr* in the orthoepists, as in Hart, Bullokar, Robinson, Gil, and Hodges. But the shorthand-writer Hopkins gives *ă* in *earl* and *learn*, and similar pronunciations are recorded by the 'homophone' lists, as follows: *earn* is equated with *yarn* by Hodges's 'near alike' and later lists; *herd* with *hard* and *pert* with *part* from Wharton's list onwards; and *yearn* with *yarn* from Ellis's list onwards. Rather better evidence for StE *ă* where PresE has [əː] occurs for *desert* 'merit', which has *ă* in Robinson and twice in Gil (once when the rhyme requires it and once unrhymed); *swerve*, which has *ă* beside *ĕ* in Gil and *ă* in Hodges; *serve*, which has *ă* in Hodges (but it may descend from the OF variant in *a*; see Luick, § 430, Anm. 2), beside *ĕ* in Hart, Robinson, and Gil; *serge*, which has *ă* in Price (followed by Lye), Poole, and Coles; and *yerk*, which has *ă* in Smith. ME *ă* is most commonly recorded in *heard*, which has it in Cheke (beside *ĕ*), Laneham, Coote, Robinson (beside *ĕ*), Hayward, Daines, Wharton, Poole, Price,

Cocker, and the 'homophone lists' from that of Hodges onwards. Butler knows the ă pronunciation, but says that it is not generally accepted (he himself prefers a pronunciation with a long vowel). Gil twice shows lengthening of this ă to identity with ME ā (see Vol. I, pp. 145–6), as Bullokar does of late ME ă < ME ĕ before r in *barn* and *quarn* 'quern' (see § 43 above). But ME ĕ is recorded for *heard* by Cheke (beside ă), Bullokar, Mulcaster (but his evidence is of uncertain value), Robinson (beside ă), and *RS*; so possibly Merriott, who equates *herd* with *heard*, and Brown, who gives *herd* as a 'phonetic' spelling of *heard*.

In the verb *pierce* and the name *Pierce*, which now have [iː] from late ME ẹ̄, pronunciations derived from ME ĕ formerly occurred; eModE ĕ occurs in Bullokar, Mulcaster, and Poole, and the 'homophone lists' of Hodges and Strong equate the verb and the name with *parse*, thus showing late ME ă.

Note 1: Butler regards the ă pronunciation of *hearken* as a corruption, and says that the true pronunciation is with ME ẹ̄; so perhaps Brown, who 'phonetically' spells the word *heark'n*. This pronunciation, like the spelling, must be due to the analogy of *hear*, for OE lengthening should not occur before *rc*.

Note 2: The Northerner Poole possibly shows [ər] from ĕr as a variant beside ăr (which he has beyond doubt) in *clerk, hark, heart,* and *carve*; see Vol. I, pp. 434–5. Earlier, in the sixteenth century, Mulcaster (also a Northerner) appears to have ĕr in *farm*; cf. the present Scottish pronunciation [ferm] and the Lancashire [fəːm] (see Wright, *EDG*, Index).

Note 3: Some of the words cited above also had pronunciations with a long vowel descended from ME ẹ̄ or ẹ̄; see § 8.

Note 4: The Northerners give especially full evidence of the lowering of ME ĕr to ăr in words of the type of those cited above. Levins has ăr in *jerk, convert* and similar words, *serve,* and *conserve* (see Vol. I, pp. 26–27). Poole shows ăr in a long list of words; but [ər] from ĕr occurs certainly or possibly as a variant in many of them, while others of precisely the same type are only recorded with [ər]. See Vol. I, pp. 434–5, for a detailed discussion and summary of Poole's evidence. The pronunciations of these two men cannot be regarded as typical, in this matter, of StE.

Note 5: For spellings illustrating the ă pronunciation of all the words cited above see *OED* and Wyld, *Coll. Eng.*, pp. 217–22; *a*-forms are frequent in *serve* and its derivatives and in *swerve*, and also occur in *earn, learn,* and *search*, though apparently less often; on the other hand *e*-forms occur in words which now have [ɑː] (cf. Wyld, op. cit., pp. 221–2).

(b) ME ĕ before r followed by a heterosyllabic consonant

§ 66. Words which now have [ɑː] by lengthening of eModE ă (most of which are now spelt with *a*) vary more in the orthoepists than the corresponding words under (*a*) above. *Harvest* has ĕ in Cheke against ă in Hart and Bullokar. *Darnel* has ĕ beside ă in Cheke; this word is of unknown origin, and occurs in the fourteenth century as *dernel*, in the fifteenth century as *darnelle*; it is also found in a Walloon dialect as *darnelle*, but may perhaps be assumed to have original ME ĕ. *Farther* has ă in Bullokar. *Marvel* has ă in Robinson, Gil, and Hodges, but ĕ six times beside ă thrice in Bullokar. *Particular* has ĕ in Hart, ă in Bullokar. *Varnish* has ĕ in Gil. *Sergeant* has ĕ in Bullokar and Gil, but ă in Hodges. To these words we may add *person*, which is now pronounced with [ə:] and spelt with *ĕ*, but which formerly was commonly pronounced with [ɑ:(r)] from eModE *ăr*. It has *ĕ* in Hart, Bullokar, and Robinson, but *ă* in Laneham, Butler, Hodges, and Brown. During the seventeenth century the distinction according to the meaning of the two spellings *person* and *parson* became fairly well established (cf. the forms cited by *OED*), but the distinction of pronunciation was not well established. The 'homophone' lists from that of Wharton onwards pair together the two spellings *person* and *parson* (but Cooper includes them only in his 'near' list; the distinction of pronunciation must have been coming into use in his time). Wharton similarly pairs the two forms *perboiled* and *parboiled*; the former is a latinized form, the latter the OF, probably already understood as 'part-boiled'.

Some words which are now pronounced with [ə:] and spelt with *e* vary frequently in pronunciation in the orthoepists. *Certain* and its derivatives have *ĕ* in Hart, Bullokar, Robinson, and Gil, but *ă* thirteen times (beside *ĕ* once, probably by error) in Hodges; Coote describes *ă* as the 'barbarous speech of your country people', and is followed by Hunt. The name *Gervase* has *ĕ* beside *ă* in Gataker (cf. *Jervis*). *Kerchief* has *ĕ* in Young; Coote describes *ă* as 'barbarous', but Hunt reverses this and gives *ĕ* as dialectal. *Pernicious* has *ĕ* in Strong, but *ă* in Young. *Serpent* has *ĕ* in Bullokar and Robinson, but *ă* in Hodges. *Servant* has *ĕ* in Hart, Bullokar, Robinson, and Gil, but *ă* in Hodges (who also gives it in *service*) and Brown; Cooper, however, describes *ă* in *service* as 'barbarous speaking', and is followed by RS. *Verdict* has *ĕ* in Young, *ă* in Strong (followed by Cocker), and *ĕ* beside *ă* in Brown. *Verjuice* has *ă* in Hodges and Coles (followed by Strong and Young), but perhaps *ĕ* in Aickin. Lily further tells us of pronunciations *argo* for Latin *ergo* (cf. Shakespeare's *argal*), and *sparma* for *sperma*. Coles in his careless *Eng.–Lat. Dict.* pairs *kernel* with *carnal*. The Londoner Hodges, it should be observed, gives most evidence of *ă* in these words which now have [ə:]. The comments of Coote and Cooper are not fully justified, but they show an opposition (on the part of schoolmasters at least), both in the late sixteenth and in the late seventeenth century, to the spread of the *ă* variant in place of the original *ĕ* in words of this class; and to this opposition we may attribute the eventual displacement of the *ă* variant.

Note 1: In *merchant* the variation between *e* and *a* already existed in OF. In the orthoepists *ă* is normal (cf. modern French) and is recorded by Cheke, Robinson, Gil, Coles (followed by Strong and Young), and Cooper. Cooper says (correctly enough) that *e* is a mere etymological spelling. But *ĕ* is recorded by Price. *Market* similarly varies in OF; Cooper again gives *ă* and says that *e* is an etymological spelling. The spelling is primarily responsible for the PresE pronunciation of *merchant*; in the name *Marchant* and in *market*, where the etymological spelling with *e* did not gain acceptance, the pronunciation with [ɑ:] remains.

Note 2: *Varlet* has *ĕ* in Bullokar. It is an adoption of the fourteenth-century French *varlet*, and occurs in English from the fifteenth century onwards in the form *varlet*. Spellings with *e*, which must be regarded as inverted, occur in the sixteenth and seventeenth centuries; Bullokar's pronunciation, which I see no reason to doubt, is an artificial result of this spelling with *e*, and is closely paralleled by the PresE [ə:] in *merchant*.

Note 3: *Perfect*, which has a common *a* variant in OF and ME (cf. modern French *parfait*), has *ă* seven times in Hodges (including its derivatives). Coote nevertheless says that *parfit* is 'barbarous'. The variant *ĕ*, which was supported by Latin spelling and pronunciation, is given by Cheke, Hart, Bullokar, Robinson, Gil, and the shorthand-writers J. Willis and Everardt (who often reflects less educated pronunciation). Even Hodges gives *ĕ* in *perfection*, presumably because it is a later adoption from Latin (whence also we may explain the fact that Hart and Hodges show [k] pronounced in *perfection* but not in *perfect* or its derivatives). See further § 442 below.

Note 4: For spellings illustrating the pronunciation of the words cited under (*b*) above see *OED* and Wyld, *Coll. Eng.*, pp. 212–21. Forms with *a* are common in *servant*, *service*, *certain*, and *person*, and (of words not cited above) in *mercy*; they also occur in *fervent*, *guerdon*, *herbage*, *universal* (cf. '*Varsity*'), and the names *Merton*, *Derby*, *Herford* 'Hereford', &c. On the other hand *e*-forms occur in *farther*, *harbour*, and *marvel* in the sixteenth century.

(c) ME ĕ before intervocalic r

§ 67. Late ME *ă* developed from ME *ĕ* before intervocalic *r* is comparatively rare, but survives in PresE in *Harry*, *arrant*, *farrier*, and *quarrel* (see further Note 3). Of the orthoepists, Lily tells us of Latin *perago* pronounced as *parago*. Bullokar has *ă* four times in *imperative(ly)*. Hodges gives *ă* in *errand*, and the 'homophone' lists from Hodges's 'near alike' list onwards pair *errand* with *arrant*. Wharton, followed by Cocker and Brown, adds to this equation *errant*, thus showing that a distinction of spelling between *errant* and *arrant* has been made to correspond to the difference of meaning, though as yet there is no distinction of pronunciation. *Sirrah* has *ă* from earlier *ĕ* (see Note 1) in Cooper, followed by *WSC-RS*. Cooper also says that *miracle* is pronounced with *ă* 'facilitatis causa' (so the more discriminating Latin text; the English text says that this pronunciation is 'barbarous speaking'); again ME *ĕ* is the basis (see Note 1). *RS* follows the English text of Cooper. For other possible cases of late ME *ă* for ME *ĕ* before intervocalic *r* see under (*d*) below.

Note 1: *Sirrah* is first recorded in the sixteenth century, when there are found (see *OED*) the forms *serea*, *serray*, *serrha*; the *ĕ* shown by these forms goes back to the thirteenth- to sixteenth-century form *ser(e)* of *sir*, in which *ĕ* probably develops by early lowering of *i* under weak stress. *Miracle* has a fourteenth-century form *maracle*, which must be regarded as developed from the fourteenth- and fifteenth-century form *meracull*, &c. (see *OED*); the latter should be explained from a popular or semi-popular OF *meracle (cf. Pope, § 640 (3)) beside learned *miracle* from Latin *miraculum*.

Note 2: For spellings illustrating late ME *ă* for ME *ĕ* in the words cited above see *OED* and Wyld, *Coll. Eng.*, pp. 218–19. *Peril* may be added to the list; it has *a*-forms in the fifteenth and sixteenth centuries.

Note 3: Luick, § 430, Anm. 3, would explain the change of *ĕ* to *ă* in *arrant* and *Harry* as being due to the geminated *r*, and would regard *herring*, *very*, *merry*, and *peril* as showing that the change did not occur before single intervocalic *r* (so Jordan, § 270). But though it is clear that the change was more regular before geminated *r*, late ME *ă* does occur in *peril* (see Note 2), and its occurrence also in *miracle* tells further against Luick's view. Luick, loc. cit., Anm. 2, regards *quarrel* as 'unklar'; Jordan, § 270, explains it from a syncopated form *querle*. Jordan's explanation could be extended to cover *ă* in *peril* (which might get it from *parlous*) and *miracle* (cf. the fourteenth-century syncopated *mercle* cited by *OED*). But it is simplest to regard all these words as showing the change before single intervocalic *r*—especially as it is doubtful to what extent geminated *r* was still distinguished from single *r* in Northern dialects in the early fourteenth century and in London English about 1400.

Note 4: ME *ă* in *harald* 'herald' (shown by Hodges's 'homophone list' pairing with *Harold*) is due to medieval Latin *haraldus* beside *heraldus*. *OED* cites *a*-forms of the English word from the fifteenth to the eighteenth centuries, including examples from *Richard II* (stage-directions at 1. iii. 6 and 25), and Wyld cites an *a*-form from Machyn. *Harald* is of course one of Milton's special spellings, occurring, for example, in *P.L.* i. 518, 752; there is no necessity to regard it as an Italianate spelling, though Italian influence may have been a factor in Milton's choice, since Hodges's evidence shows that the *a*-form was current in contemporary pronunciation.

(*d*) ME *ĕ* before final r

§ 68. *War*, *far*, and *star*, in which the PresE form goes back to late ME *ă* from ME *ĕ*, have regularly *ă* in the orthoepists, except that *star* has *ĕ* in Cheke. Levins, who rhymes *star* with *her* and *err*, probably has *ă* in all three words (see Note 1). These words, however, may strictly belong under (*c*) above; *war*, *star*, and *err* have originally geminated intervocalic *r*, as has *far* in the (originally comparative) form *ferre*, and *her* has originally single intervocalic *r*; it is, however, uncertain whether the final *e* was regularly pronounced when the change from *ĕ* to *ă* occurred. The name of the letter *r*, which was originally *ĕr* (cf. the names of *f*, *l*, *m*, *n*, *s*, and *x*), is a clear case of the change before final *r*; Daines says that 'infantuli' pronounce the name *ar*, though it should be *er*.

Words which have [ə:] in PresE have regularly *ĕ* in the orthoepists, except for Levins's forms of *her* and *err* mentioned above.

Note 1: *OED* records the seventeenth-century form *arr* for *err*, and the sixteenth-century forms *harre*, *hare*, *are* for *her*; the *a*-forms of *her* develop under strong stress, and are uncommon because the word is normally weakly stressed.

Note 2: Chaucer's *harre* 'hinge' (OE *hĕorr*), *C.T. Prol.* 550, provides an early instance of the change of *ĕ* to *ă* in London English; as the word comes at the end of the line, it is impossible to say with certainty whether the final *e* is pronounced, though it may be, for the word is feminine as well as masculine in OE and thus may add a final *e* in eME, and in any case is here a dative. The rhyme-word is *knarre* (LG *knarre*), which may have a final *e*. The *ă*-form of *herre* is evidently used for the sake of rhyme.

Note 3: For spellings illustrating the change of *ĕ* to *ă* in such words see *OED* and Wyld, *Coll. Eng.*, pp. 217–21. In addition to the words cited above, *a*-forms occur occasionally in the fifteenth and later centuries in *defer* and *prefer* (late fourteenth-century adoptions) and in *infer*. As *infer* was not adopted until the early sixteenth century, it should not show the change of *ĕ* to *ă*; presumably it is influenced by the analogy of *defer*, &c., and by such pronunciations of Latin words with *ĕ* before *r* as Lily describes. At its first appearance in Skelton's *Magnificence* (1526), l. 61, it rhymes with *debarre*. Variation between *ĕ* and *ă* occurs in the name *Ker* (*Kerr*, *Carr*). *Far* has *e*-forms until the sixteenth century.

(*e*) Summary

§ 69. The evidence of the orthoepists goes to show that *ă*-forms were most common in the sixteenth and seventeenth centuries in words in which they now survive, though there was more variation. The comments of Coote and Cooper show a certain opposition on the part of schoolmasters (and doubtless other literate people) to the *ă*-forms, while the evidence of the 'homophone' lists suggests that *ă*-forms were more common among less well-educated people—in this case not only because of their tendency to use more advanced pronunciations, but also because they lacked knowledge of the traditional spelling, which supported the *ĕ*-forms. Northern orthoepists show predominantly *ă*-forms, though they often retain the traditional spelling. There are hints that *ă*-forms were more common in London speech than might be judged from our evidence. The change of *ĕ* to *ă* seems to be most common before *r* followed by a consonant, but occurs also before final and even before intervocalic *r*, generally but not always in words in which it was originally geminated.

(2) *Other Cases of Variation between ME ă and ME ĕ*

§ 70. *Any* (OE *ǣnig*) had ME *ă* by early shortening of *ǣ* to late OE *ǽ*, but ME *ĕ* by later shortening of ME *ę̄* (when not from OK *ē*). *Many* (OE *mănig*) gets ME *ę̄* and *ĕ* from *any* by analogy. ME *ă* is recorded in *any* by Hart and Gil and by Robinson twice (beside *ā* by ME lengthening five times), and in *many* by Hart, Gil, and Hodges (but ME *ā* by lengthening in Robinson and Cooper). The orthoepists do not record ME *ĕ* in either word; unshortened ME *ę̄* is, however, shown by Levins in *many*. Smith records ME *ĕ* in *catch*; this represents the ME form *kecchen*, an analogical variant of *kacchen* < ONF *cachier* on the model of *lecchen* (itself probably analogical) beside *lacchen* < OE *lǣccan*. He also gives ME *ĕ* in *mass*, where it represents ME *messe* (which is from either OF *messe* or popular Latin *messa*) beside ME *masse* < OE *mǽsse* (itself < pop. Lat. *messa*). *Thanet* (OE *Tĕnet* beside *Tǽnett*) is given as *Tennet* in the 'phonetically' spelt list of Coles, who is followed by Strong, Young, and Cocker.

The variation is especially often recorded in the case of the word *than*, which is transcribed *ðen* by Hart (commonly, but also *ðan*) and regularly by Robinson and Gil, and which is identified with *then* in the 'homophone' lists of Hodges, Hunt, Fox and Hookes, Coles, Strong, *RS*, and Brown; Cooper makes the modern distinction of spelling between *than* and *then*, but may be suspected of not making a distinction of pronunciation. The two words are in origin mere variant forms which have been distinguished in meaning in ModE (cf. *OED* and Luick, § 363, Anm. 4); it seems that even when the distinction of spelling was fairly generally observed, the pronunciation often remained undistinguished. But other orthoepists than those named (e.g. Bullokar and Hodges, *EP*) make the present distinction of pronunciation as well as of spelling.

Note 1: Laneham has *ony* 'any', which is from OE *ānig* by ME shortening of *ǭ* to *ŏ*.

Note 2: For evidence from other sources of variation between ME ă and ME ĕ in various cases see § 59, Notes 2 and 3; § 64, Note 1; § 66, Notes 1-3.

VARIATION BETWEEN ME ă AND ŏ

§ 71. Modern StE does not preserve the OE variation between ŏ and ă for WGmc ă before nasals. But London English about 1400 showed variation, before the OE lengthening groups *ng* and *nd*, between ME ă from OE unlengthened ă and ME ŏ by shortening of earlier ME ǭ from late OE ā by lengthening (cf. § 7). The orthoepists show almost invariable ă before *nd* in *stand*, *hand*, &c., but ŏ sometimes occurs (e.g. in *stand* in Laneham, beside ă; in *brand-iron* in Bullokar; in *strand* in Poole). *Bond* survives beside *band*, in differentiated senses; Hodges pairs them in his 'near alike' list, doubtless because they were confused in use. Before *ng* in *strong*, *long*, &c., there is, on the other hand, invariable ŏ, except in *hang*, which has equally regular ă. It would appear that in the OE dialect from which modern StE derives the lengthening was comparatively rare before *nd* but common before *ng*. The survival of unlengthened ă in *hang* can easily be explained by the assumption that lengthening was rare in OE *hăngian*, short vowels tending to develop (and therefore no doubt also to be preserved) in the first syllable of trisyllabic words with secondary stress (as verbs of this class originally had); the influence of ON *hănga* (cf. Kihlbom, p. 124) may have aided the retention of ă, but need not be assumed. *Lamb* has only ă (so Hart, Bullokar, and Gil). Coote, Hunt, and Cooper record, as a dialectalism, ME ŏ in *stamp* (probably < OE *stămpian*; see *OED*).

On ME ă by unrounding beside original ME ŏ see § 87.

ME ĕ

§ 72. ME ĕ was a lax sound, and retained this value in eModE as in PresE; lax quality is clearly shown by the evidence of Robinson (see Vol. I, pp. 207–8) and Cooper, who describes ME ĕ as the short equivalent of ME ā (in this he is followed by Aickin) and says that it is identical with German short *e*, but is rare in French. The not infrequent identifications of ME ĕ with short tense *e* of other languages are merely inexact.

Note: ME ĕ in *Thames*, which is given by Gil, Butler, Coles, Young, and Brown, is normally developed from the OE form *Tĕmes*. The ModE spelling is due in part to the ME Essex form *Tames* < OE *Tǣmes*, but more to the Latin form *Tamesis*. Hart gives a transcription *Thāms* (in which *th* represents aspirated *t*, thus [th]), and Strong gives the 'phonetic' spelling *Tames*; these might both be imperfect transcriptions due to concentration on the representation of the consonant (Hart's comes in a passage in which he is specially considering aspirated stops; but note that he marks the vowel long), but support each other. If they truly represent a variant pronunciation, they might show the survival of the Essex form (aided by the spelling), or be a mere spelling-pronunciation; the latter alternative does not seem at all likely in Hart's case.

VARIATION BETWEEN ME ĕ AND ŏ

§ 73. In *yon* and *yonder* the normal forms (found in Bullokar, Robinson, and Gil) descend directly from OE ŏ < Gmc ă (Campbell, § 172); ME ĕ (shown by Cheke's *ien* 'yon' and Smith's '*ionder* vel *iender*') is either a Gmc ablaut variant or from the OE 'rising' diphthong *eo* with stress-shift.

Yolk (OE *gĕolca*) has normally developed ĕ in Gil, Daines (who says that the pronunciation is 'commonly' *yelke*), Newton, and Cooper (who prefers the spelling *yelk*); but *yelk* is nevertheless condemned as the 'barbarous speech of your country people' by Coote, followed by Hunt. The variant pronunciation, which is due to OE stress-shift after the palatal, is recorded by implication by Coote and by Price (who says that in *yolk* the *l* is silent) and Brown (who gives the 'phonetic' spelling *yoke*).

Note: Another word which varied similarly was *yellow* (OE *gĕolu*); see *OED*, and compare Lodge's rhyme *follow* : *yellow*. The form *yallow* shows ME unrounding of the ŏ variant to ă.

VARIATION BETWEEN ME ĕ AND ŭ

§ 74. A few words retain ME variation between ĕ and ŭ, which is due to various causes. *Sword* has (among other pronunciations) ME ŭ < late WS ŭ in Mulcaster, Gil, Butler, Hodges, Poole (beside ME ǭ), and Price, but ĕ in Bullokar. *Worry* normally has ŭ < late WS *wŭrgan*; its pairing with *weary* in Hodges's 'near alike' list may depend on SE ĕ < OE ȳ in *wyrgan*, but is more likely to be due to the dialectal form *worry* 'weary' recorded by Cooper (see Vol. I, p. 401). *Churl* has ŭ < Western ME [y] < [ø] < OE *ĕo* in Bullokar, Hodges, and Poole, but Poole also records a word *charl* which may represent ME *chĕrl*. *Jeopardy* retains ME ŭ in Hart, against ĕ (or ḗ) in other orthoepists (cf. § 8 (2) above).

VARIATION BETWEEN ME ĕ AND ME ĭ

(1) Words with OE ў

§ 75. In PresE, South-eastern ĕ < OE ў survives in the words *fledge* adj., *bury*, *merry*, and the suffix *-bury* in place-names; its survival chiefly before *r* is due to the fact that in ME ĕ < ў before *r* is not limited to the South-east, but is spread over a wider area. These words are normally recorded with ĕ, but ĭ is given by Salesbury in *bury* and by Smith in *fledge*.

ME ĕ also occurs sporadically in other words in which PresE has ĭ; it is given in *business* by Cheke, in *bridge*, *evil*, and *thin* by Smith (beside ĭ), in *list* vb. 'listen' and in *ridge* by Smith, in *mirth* by Gil (beside ĭ) and Coles, in *shirt* by Hart and Bullokar, in *skirt* and *birth* by Coles (see Vol. I, p. 347 and p. 442), and in *build* by Fox and Hookes. Coote, the headmaster of a grammar school at Bury St. Edmunds, records ĕ in *mill*, *hill*, *knit*, and *bridge* as the 'barbarous speech of your country people'; Daines, another Suffolk schoolmaster, also mentions the dialectal *mell* 'mill'; and Hunt, following Coote, gives *bredg* 'bridge', *mell* 'mill', and *hell* 'hill' as dialectal forms.

Note: *Skirt*, a ME adoption from ON, is best explained as having $\breve{e}$ owing to the analogical influence of the native *shirt*. On $\breve{e}$ in *worry* see § 74; on ME $\bar{e} <$ SE $\bar{e} <$ OE $\bar{y}$ by lengthening of original $\breve{y}$ in *build* see § 135 below. Rhymes depending on SE $\breve{e} <$ OE $\breve{y}$ are found in sixteenth- and seventeenth-century poets.

(2) *Raising of ME $\breve{e}$ to $\breve{i}$*

§ 76. Raising of ME $\breve{e}$ to $\breve{i}$ is a fairly common process which begins in ME (first in the thirteenth century in the South-east; see Luick, § 379, Anm. 1) and continues into the fifteenth century (possibly even into the sixteenth); it is perhaps to be regarded as a general tendency to change, but is powerfully affected by neighbouring consonants and is regularly shown only in certain special circumstances. Both in ME and ModE, $\breve{e}$ remains as the more common variant except in these special cases. The earlier (pre-1400) raising is shown only in limited circumstances; the later raising occurs sporadically before various consonants.

Note 1: Wyld, *Coll. Eng.*, p. 222, treats the raising as a combinative change, a view justified by its especial frequency before certain consonants. But its sporadic occurrence before consonants of varied type suggests rather that it is a general tendency which is aided by and is therefore most apt to occur in specified phonetic contexts.

Note 2: ME $\breve{o}$ shows a similar and parallel tendency to be raised; see § 92 below.

Note 3: Beside the raising of ME $\breve{e}$ to $\breve{i}$, there was also an opposite tendency to lower ME $\breve{i}$ to $\breve{e}$ (see § 80 below); it is therefore often impossible to decide whether rhymes or 'homophone' lists show a pronunciation [e] or [I]. But where it seems possible, an attempt is made below to indicate what pronunciation is likely to be intended.

Note 4: The raising of ME $\breve{e}$ to $\breve{i}$ (and the lowering of ME $\breve{i}$ to $\breve{e}$) seem to have been especially common in Northern English; the evidence of Levins and Poole cited below relates to Northern rather than to StE pronunciation.

§ 77. The detailed evidence of the raising is as follows.

(a) *Early raising*

Early raising of ME $\breve{e}$ (cf. Luick, § 379; Jordan, § 34) occurs in the following cases. (i) Before *ng* [ŋg] the raised vowel became general before 1500 and the $\breve{e}$ variant disappeared from pronunciation; it remains only in the spelling of *England* and *English*, which were especially influenced by the tradition of the orthographical system. In *wing* and *fling* no sign of ME $\breve{e}$ remains, and *England* and *English* themselves have [I] in all orthoepists who record them (the first being Hart). But Bullokar and Price (who is followed by Lye) give the *e* in these two words as being pronounced *ee*; in Bullokar the explanation is probably that he did not trouble to invent a special diacritic to show that in this special case *e* was pronounced [I], and in Price it is almost certainly that he (like other Welsh sources) showed lengthening of ME $\breve{i}$ to [i:] before [ŋ] (see § 57 above). (ii) Before *n* plus consonant the change to $\breve{i}$ is regular in StE in *hinge* and *singe* (in both of which Hodges records *ĭ*), but otherwise is chiefly Northern. Thus [ɪ] is shown in *bench* by Levins and Poole, in *stench* by Levins, and in *revenge* by Poole. But the equation of *quench* with *quince* in the 'homophone' lists of Hawkins and Cocker doubtless relates to vulgar Southern English; similarly Bullokar rhymes *end* with *find*, apparently on *ĭ*. (iii) Between *r* and a dental the change, though less regular, is more widespread in ME, but the orthoepists give little evidence of it. In the 'homophone' lists *thread* is paired with *thrid* (Coles, *Schoolmaster*) and *wrest* and *rest* with *wrist* (Wharton). Levins gives *ĭ* in *wretch*. (iv) Between [g] and [j] and a dental the raising is much more common in eModE. *Together* has *ĭ* in Cheke, Laneham, and Hodges (six times, beside *ĕ* once). *Get* has *ĭ* in Levins; Cooper says that *ĭ* is used 'facilitatis causa' (so Latin edition; but the English edition condemns it as 'barbarous speaking'). *Yes* has *ĭ* in Smith (beside *ĕ*), Gil, Butler, Newton, and Coles. *Yesterday* has *ĭ* in Gil, Cocker, and (with loss of [j]) in the short-hand-writer Bridges. *Yeast* has *ĭ* in Smith and is equated with *is't* by *WSC* (thus showing loss of [j]). *Yeld* p.t. sing. 'yielded' (OE *gĕald*) has *ĭ* beside *ĕ* in Smith. *Yet* has *ĭ* in Smith (beside *ĕ*), Gil (thirteen times, beside *ĕ* once), Gataker (who quotes Smith, apparently with approval), and Newton, and is equated with *it* (which shows loss of [j]) in the 'homophone' lists of Hodges ('near alike'), Price, Merriott, and *WSC*. But even in these words *ĕ* seems to have been the more common variant in educated StE; thus it is recorded in *together* by Hart, Bullokar, Robinson, and Gil, and in *get* by (e.g.) Bullokar, Robinson, Gil, and Hodges. (v) The raising occasionally occurred in late ME in other circumstances than those set out above. Thus *cherry* varies between *ĕ* and *ĭ* from the fourteenth century onwards; as the word is probably from OF *cherise* (see *OED*), the *ĕ* may be presumed to be original and the *ĭ* to be due to raising, probably because of the preceding palatal. Smith records variation between *ĕ* and *ĭ*, and Bullokar has [iː] < late ME *ē*, presumably by lengthening of ME *ĭ* in the open syllable (unless he has again used the symbol for [iː] as an inaccurate representation of [ɪ]).

(b) Later raising

Later raising of ME *ĕ* (cf. Luick, §§ 540–1) is on the whole less common, but occurs in PresE in *nib*, *limpet*, and *trivet* and is recorded by the orthoepists in the following cases. (i) Before a single nasal: *ken* is equated with *kin* in the 'homophone' lists of Hawkins and Cocker, and *yeoman* has *ĭ* (developed from the *ĕ* shown by various sources) in Hodges. (ii) Before dentals (cf. the earlier raising between [g] or [j] and a dental): *ĭ* is shown in *weasel* by Butler, in *largesse* by Gil, in *melons* in the 'homophone' lists of Fox and Hookes, Strong, and Young (which equate the word with *millions*; but the latter might have *ĕ* by lowering), and in *neither* (in which unraised *ĕ* is recorded by other sources) in Strong's 'phonetically spelt' list. The raising is especially common before *l* plus consonant, where it may belong to ME. *Helve* has *ĭ* in Bullokar (but perhaps < WS *ie*). Levins has *ĭ* in *stealth*; so may Poole in *stealth*, *health*, and *wealth*, but it is more likely that *tilth*, with which they rhyme, has [e] by lowering. Cooper's English edition condemns *ĭ* in *held* as a 'barbarous' pronunciation; but it may not arise by raising of *ĕ* (cf. § 11 above). (iii) Before other consonants: *ĭ* is shown in *reck* by Smith, in *theft*, *persevere* (second syllable), and *dregs* by the Northerner Levins, and in *ever* by Newton. But in *pebble* the common *ĭ*-form (recorded by Levins and Coles) is probably from OE *ў*, and the PresE *ĕ* either by lowering or an instance of SE *ĕ* < *ў* (cf. *ODEE*, s.v.).

Note 1: Jordan, § 34, includes as examples of early raising a good many words which have ME *ĭ* not by raising of *ĕ* but by direct shortening of ME *ę̄*; so, for example, *riddle*, *sick*, *rick*, and the forms *briþren* 'brethren', *find* 'fiend', and *prist* 'priest'. Cf. § 11 above.

Note 2: It is probable that regular raising occurred not only before *ng* [ŋg] but also before *nk* [ŋk], and in part accounts for the fusion of ME *thenken* with ME *thinken*.

Note 3: Gil records *fitch* 'vetch', which would have to be taken as showing raising if it is from ONF *veche* (so *OED*). But the frequent and widespread occurrence of *f*-forms of this word suggests that there may have been an unrecorded OE adoption of Latin *vicia*, whence might also arise the *i*-forms (recorded from the late fourteenth century onwards; see *OED*, s.v. *fitch*).

Note 4: Though I follow Luick in treating the raising in the cases under (*b*) as later, it may well be that it is only rarer. The fact that the evidence is later than 1400 does not necessarily mean that the tendency is not older; to a large extent it is probably a case of dialectal forms gradually obtaining wider acceptance.

(3) *Other cases*

§ 78. Bullokar shows *ĕ* in *whirl* beside *ĭ* in *whirl-pool*; the verb should only have *ĭ*, but the sb. has *ĕ* from MDu *wervel* (cf. *OED*). Poole shows *ăr* < ME *ĕr* in *girth* (ON *gĕrðu*, but influenced by *gird* or *girdle* with *ĭ* < OE *ў*; Butler gives *ĭ*), *quirk* (sixteenth-century *quirk* and *querk*, of obscure origin), and in a word *quirp* or *querp* (perhaps a dialectal alteration of *quirk*). In *girl* he has [ər], which may represent either ME *ĭr* or *ĕr*. On variation in *her* see § 4 above. On *ĕ* by lowering of *ĭ* see § 80 below.

Note 1: For Poole's *ăr* in *girth*, which is a Northernism, cf. *OED*, s.v. *garth* sb.² He also gives *ăr* in *chirp*, which is probably an alteration of *chirk*, itself a variant of *chark* < OE *cĕarcian*.

Note 2: If *girl* is from OE *gўr(e)le*, *gўr(e)la* (cf. *OED*) it belongs under (1) above. But this etymology does not easily explain the PresE variants [gɛəl], [geəl], [giəl], which point to late ME *gę̄rl* varying with (and probably developed from) *gĕrl*. The latter could be a South-eastern development with OE *e* < *y* and lengthening before *rl*.

ME *ĭ*

§ 79. ME *ĭ* was a lax open vowel (as lengthening to *ę̄* in open syllables proves), and retained this quality in eModE. The best evidence comes from Welsh sources. The manuscripts of the *Welsh Hymn* identify ME *ĭ* either with Welsh *y* or with Welsh *u* and distinguish it from Welsh *i*, which is identified with ME $\bar{e}$. Salesbury identifies ME $\breve{\imath}$ with both Welsh *u* and Welsh *y*, and the *Welsh Breviary* and T. Jones with Welsh *y*; all three agree in distinguishing it from Welsh *i*, identified with ME $\bar{e}$. The distinction in quality between open [ɪ] < ME $\breve{\imath}$ and close [i:] < ME $\bar{e}$ is thus consistently observed. The only English orthoepist to show clearly the difference between these two sounds is Robinson, who, though he does not say in so many words that ME $\breve{\imath}$ is lax, does show that its articulation is less fronted than that of ME $\bar{e}$. That ME $\breve{\imath}$ was open [ɪ] also appears on balance from the evidence of Cooper, who says that it is the short equivalent of ME $\bar{e}$ (an inexactitude, but only possible if ME $\breve{\imath}$ is the low PresE sound), is the same as French and German *i* and French *é* (inconsistent identifications, none of which is altogether exact), and is less far forward than ME $\bar{e}$.

Note: The orthoepists normally say that ME $\breve{\imath}$ is the short equivalent of ME $\bar{e}$ and often identify it with French, Italian, and German *i*; these are of course inexactitudes, and do not show that ME $\breve{\imath}$ was close in the sixteenth and seventeenth centuries.

LOWERING OF ME $\breve{\imath}$ TO $\breve{e}$

§ 80. Lowering of ME $\breve{\imath}$ to $\breve{e}$, like the parallel change of $\breve{u}$ to $\breve{o}$ (see § 97 below), occurred before 1300 (cf. Jordan, § 36, against Luick, §§ 542–3); it is clearly shown by spellings, and probably accounts for some of the ME rhymes between original $\breve{\imath}$ and $\breve{e}$. Characteristic particularly of Northern and South-western dialects, it seldom affected StE. But before intervocalic *r* it accounts for our form of *sheriff* < earlier *shiref* and possibly of *wherry*, for the common variant *sperit* of *spirit* (recorded regularly by Hodges), and for sporadic $\breve{e}$ variants in other words such as *syrup*, *miracle*, and *mirror* (see § 213 below); it also probably accounts in part for the disappearance of the expected East Midland $\breve{\imath}$ forms of *bury* and *merry* (cf. § 75).

In the word *lemon* the $\breve{e}$ has ousted $\breve{\imath}$ in both spelling and pronunciation; Butler says that *limon* is 'commonly pronounced *lemmon*', *WSC* that *limon* is pronounced *lemon* (without any suggestion of a variant pronunciation with $\breve{\imath}$), and *The Compendious School-Master* equates the surname *Liman* and *lemon* with *leman* (perhaps because they all had [e], but more likely the series depends on variation in *lemon*). Similarly if *clever* has original $\breve{\imath}$ (as is probable), its ModE form is due to lowering; but Coles, *Eng.–Lat. Dict.*, probably shows $\breve{\imath}$ (see Vol. I, p. 411). *Whither* (which has $\breve{e}$ from the late thirteenth century onwards; see *OED*) has $\breve{e}$ in Robinson, Butler, and probably in the 'homophone' lists of Hodges ('near alike'), Price, Fox and Hookes, and Coles, *Eng.–Lat. Dict.* (which is based on vulgar pronunciation), where it is equated with *whether* and *weather*. *Spindle*, *wrist*, and apparently also *women* (see § 10) have $\breve{e}$ in Laneham, and *beetle* (which has ME $\breve{\imath}$) and *pick-axe* have $\breve{e}$ in Bullokar; these two sources record less correct pronunciations. *Since* has $\breve{e}$ beside $\breve{\imath}$ (once each) in

Robinson (but it may be from ME *sĕpen* < OE *sĕoppan*), and *hither* has *ĕ* in Gil (once, beside *ĭ* thrice) and Butler. Butler also shows *ĕ* in *spit* (beside *ĭ*), *wring*, *milt* sb., and in *Billingsgate* pronounced *Belinsgate* (a common seventeenth-century form, probably of the dialect of London; cf. Eichler, § 56). Levins has *ĕ* in *inch*, *fringe*, *shiver*, *spit*, *rivet*, *cricket*, *minnow*, and *resh* (OE *risc*, ME *rish*) 'a rush', and Poole has it in *film* and probably also in *tilth* (which rhymes with *stealth*, *health*, and *wealth* among the *e* lists); cf. also Poole's note (among the *i* lists) '*ilm* vide *elm*, *ilth* vide *elth*'.

Note 1: The *ĕ* variant in *spirit* was very common and survives in vulgar pronunciation still; it accounts for the conventional rhyming of *spirit* with *merit* and *inherit*. It is sometimes explained (as by Horn, § 26, Anm.) as a ME variant form from OF *esperit*, but lowering of *ĭ* is more likely.

Note 2: The evidence of Butler may show South-western dialectal influence on his speech (cf. Eichler, § 56); that of Levins and Poole certainly reflects Northern pronunciation. Often it is doubtful whether rhymes and the identifications of 'homophone' lists show lowering of *ĭ* to *ĕ* in one of the words concerned or raising of *ĕ* to *ĭ* in the other; the cases cited above are those in which lowering seems the more probable explanation.

Note 3: For further ModE evidence see Wyld, *Coll. Eng.*, pp. 226–9 (but Luick's account of the distribution of the *ĕ*-forms is more accurate). Some of the *e*-spellings cited by Luick, § 551, Anm. 1, in the attempt to prove the ModE identification of ME *ĭr* and *ĕr* are probably to be explained by ME lowering of *ĭ* to *ĕ*. The common *e*-forms in Machyn reflect Northern pronunciation. Wyld suggests hesitantly but rightly that in London English the *e*-forms belong to a lower-class dialect; they are common in the letter of Thomas Pery, who was certainly a Cockney. Wyld, *Rhymes*, p. 82, has some good evidence, including rhymes of *spirit*. See also Kihlbom, p. 19, on lowering to *ĕ* as a feature of the Eastern dialects (represented by the *Paston Letters*, the *Cely Papers*, and de la Pole), with which vulgar London English is allied. Jordan, § 271, cites similar fifteenth-century evidence.

VARIATION BETWEEN ME *ĭ* AND *ŭ*

§ 81. In words of four classes, as listed below, there occurs variation between ME *ĭ* and *ŭ*. The fact that this variation is common before *r* has led some phonologists to give a false account of the ModE development whereby ME *ĭr* and *ŭr* became identical (as [ər]); the occurrence of evidence of *ŭr* in words conventionally spelt *ir* has caused them to date the general identity of ME *ĭr* and *ŭr* too early. The general ModE sound-change is discussed in Chapter VIII below; for the present we may note merely that it can be proved to have occurred only when there is evidence that ME *ĭr* is identified with ME *ŭr* in words other than those discussed here, which had a variant in *ŭr* from late ME onwards.

(1) *Words with OE ў*

§ 82. Words with OE *ў* appear with *ŭ* in ModE when the *ў* occurs in conjunction with rounding consonants which caused it to become *ŭ* either in late OE or in ME; in most cases the *ŭ*-forms show the influence on StE of the OE Saxon (ME Southern) dialects. (*a*) Before consonants other than *r*, ME *ŭ* is normal in *much* (late OE *mўcel* < *mĭcel*, in which both [m] and [tʃ] exercise rounding influence); but *ĭ* occurs in Salesbury (in *mychgoditio* 'much good do it you'), Cheke, Smith (beside *ŭ*), and Hart (beside *ŭ*). *Such* (late OE *swўlc* < *swĭlc*) also has normal *ŭ*, but ME *ĭ* in MS A of the *Welsh Hymn* (against ME *ŭ* in other manuscripts) and in Cheke; cf. the present-day vulgarism [sitʃ]. *Shut* and *shuttle*, in which rounding (of original OE *ў*) is due to the preceding [ʃ], normally have *ŭ* in ModE (so *shut* in Bullokar, Robinson, and Gil), but the former has *ĭ* in Cheke and the latter in Smith. But *busy* and *business*, despite their South-western spelling, are regularly recorded with *ĭ*; so by Salesbury, Laneham, Gil, Hodges, the *Welsh Breviary*, Cooper, *WSC-RS*, and the 'phonetically spelt' lists of Coles, Strong, and Young. (*b*) Before *r* ME *ŭ* is regularly recorded in *worm* (OE *wўrm*), which shows late OE rounding to *ŭ* under the combined influence of [w] and [r]; similarly in *worry* (cf. § 74). *Church* (late OE (Southern) *cўrice* < *cĭrice*), in which the preceding [tʃ] aids the rounding, has normal *ŭ* (so in Hart, Bullokar, Robinson, and Gil), but the original *ĭ* remains in Salesbury, Smith (beside *ŭ*), and the Northerner Poole (beside *ŭ*); Poole similarly gives *ĭ* beside *ŭ* in *churn* (late OE *cўrin* < *cĭrn*). Words conventionally spelt *i* are those in which only the [r] exercised rounding influence and in which the development to *ŭ* presumably belongs only to late ME (in Southern dialects); in these Midland *ĭ* is normally recorded, and in what follows I give only the evidence for *ŭ*. It is particularly these cases which have led to the too early dating of the general identity of ME *ĭr* and *ŭr*; but that a special explanation is required is shown by the facts that early orthoepists (i) give evidence of *ŭr* only in words with OE *ўr* or in others to which a special explanation applies, (ii) give no evidence of that unrounding of ME *ŭ* to [ʌ] which precedes the identification of ME *ĭr* and ME *ŭr*. *Stir* has *ŭ* in Levins, Laneham, Butler (who probably also knew *ĭ*), and Poole; Hodges, Wilkins, and Cooper show [ʌr], but these authors know the general identification of *ĭr* with *ŭr*. *Thirst* has *ŭ* in Butler (who perhaps also knew *ĭ*) and Coles; Cheke has, with metathesis, *thrusti* 'thirsty'. *First* has *ŭ* in Robinson, Wharton (followed by J. Smith and Young), Newton, Price *Eng. O.* (but apparently *ĭ* in *VO*; see Vol. I, p. 343), Coles, and Strong (in both his 'homophone' and 'phonetically spelt' lists); Butler says that 'soom, in soom places', use ME *ŭ*. Hodges gives ʌr, but this may represent either ME *ĭr* or ME *ŭr*. *Fir* (OE **fўre* or ON *fўri-*) may also have a variant in ME *ŭ*, though none of the evidence is decisive (since it comes from authors late enough to have known the general identity of ME *ĭr* and *ŭr*); ME *ŭ* seems to be shown by the evidence of Young and Lye (who do not appear to have recognized the general identity of ME *ĭr* and *ŭr*) and by the identification of *fir* with *fur* in many 'homophone' lists. Of these the most noteworthy case is the first, Hodges's 'near alike' list; the relegation of the pairing to this list is con-

§ 82]   PART 1: THE SHORT VOWELS   573

sistent with the evidence of *EP*, in which *fir* is transcribed with *ĭr* not *ʌr* (for [ər]); but on the other hand Hodges does give *ʌr* [ər] for other words which can have only ME *ĭr*. Price says that *fir* has *ir* pronounced like *er*, obscurely; but he says the same of words which can only have ME *ĭr*. Cooper says that *ir* in *fir* is pronounced like *ur*; but he knows the general identity of ME *ĭr* and *ŭr*. *Shirt* has *ŭ* in Hunt.

Note 1: The ME variant *trist* 'trust', recorded by Salesbury, is of obscure origin, but perhaps represents an OE verb *trystan formed on OE *trust adj. (see *OED*, s.v. *trust* adj.).

Note 2: Cooper gives *dud* 'did' and *tunder* 'tinder' as examples of 'barbarous speaking'; this presumably relates to the dialect of Hertfordshire. Earlier Daines, a Suffolk schoolmaster, had given *tunder* as a variant (which he seems to prefer) of *tinder*. *OED* records for *did* a twelfth-century *dude* (in which the *u* undoubtedly represents [y]) and a fourteenth-century *dud* and a fifteenth-century *dode*; the last of these at least probably shows [ʊ]. The plural has *u*-forms from the twelfth to the fifteenth century; after 1400 these spellings must mean [ʊ]. The modern Northern dialects have [ʊ], and Somerset and Devon have [ʌ] (see Wright, Index). In this word late ME *ŭ* must develop from OE *ў̆* under weak stress; the rounding to *ў̆* in OE is itself a special development due to weak stress. *Tinder* has *u*- and *o*-forms from the thirteenth to the seventeenth century and in the modern dialect of Lincolnshire; see *OED*, which suggests that these forms are due to ON *tundr* against OE *tynder*. Contrariwise *sister* is from ON *systir*, and *suster* (recorded by Coote and Hunt as a dialectalism) is from OE *s(w)uster*.

Note 3: For fifteenth-century evidence see Kihlbom, pp. 21–25.

(2) *Words with OF* [y] *and* [ø]

§ 83. OF [y], when it gives rise to a short stressed vowel in English, usually becomes ME *ŭ*, but sometimes is unrounded to ME *ĭ*. Similarly, OF [ø] gives either *ĕ* or *ĭ*, whence *kever* and *kiver* < OF *cuevre* beside *cover* < OF *co(u)vrir*; Gil records *kiver* as an Eastern pronunciation, and Cooper (a native of Hertfordshire) says that he prefers the spelling *cover* to *kiver*. In the modern dialects *kiver* occurs in those of the East, but is not restricted to them (see Wright, § 219).

Note: Wright also shows that [ɪ] (or [e] < ME *ĭ*) is widespread in *just* (OF *juste*). The [e] which occurs in *judge* in South Oxfordshire may be similarly developed from ME *ĭ* < OF [y], but could be due to a South-western change of ME *ŭ* to [ɪ] or [e] (see § 96).

(3) *Words with ME* rĭ

§ 84. In late ME (*c*. 1400) metathesis of *r* occurs in words which have *rĭ* preceded by a consonant and followed by a dental (e.g. *brid*); the result was ordinarily *ĭr*, but a variant *ŭr* seems to have arisen at the same time (cf. Luick, § 432). The conventional ModE spelling of the words in question is with *ir*, and the pronunciation [ɪr] is that ordinarily recorded by the orthoepists, e.g. Hart (Jespersen, *Hart*, § 5) and Bullokar (see word-list in Zachrisson, *Bullokar*). But the variant *ŭ* is recorded for *bird* by Laneham, Robinson, Gil (eight times, beside *ĭ* once), Butler (who says it is used by 'soom, in soom places'), Wharton (followed by J. Smith and Young), Poole, Price, the *Welsh Breviary*, and Strong's 'phonetically spelt' list of monosyllables; for *dirt* by Coote (as the 'barbarous speech of your country people'), Butler, Poole (beside *ĭ*), Strong (as before), and Lye; for *third* by Butler (who says it is used by 'soom, in soom places') and Wharton (followed by J. Smith and Young); and for *thirty* by Cheke (beside *ĭ*), Robinson, and Young.

Note 1: Wilkins gives [ʌ] in *third*, and Cooper and *WSC-RS* say that *ir* in *bird* is pronounced *ur*; but these authors recognize the general identity of ME *ĭr* and *ŭr*.

Note 2: Luick, loc. cit., would regard the ModE forms *burn* and *burst* as developed from ME *brinnen* and *bristen* in accordance with this sound-change; but Jordan, § 269, Anm., explains them as analogical forms with *ŭ* from the p.t. pl. Luick's view seems the better; but the early generalization of the *ŭ*-form probably owes something to the analogy suggested by Jordan. *Burn* regularly has *ŭ* in the orthoepists (so in Bullokar, Robinson, Gil, Hodges, and Wallis); *burst* is rarely recorded, but has *ŭ* in Wallis (who distinguishes *ŭr* [ʌr] clearly from *ĭr* [ɪr] and even from *ĕr* [ər]) and in Price and Coles, who seem to have the form *bust* (see Vol. I, pp. 344 and 441 note 2).

(4) *Rounding of ME ĭ*

§ 85. After *w*, and in isolated words after *b* and before *m*, there occurs in ME a rounding of *ĭ* to *ŭ*. The one case which affects StE is the word *woman*, in which ModE accepts the rounded vowel in the singular but retains unrounded [ɪ] in the pronunciation (though not in the spelling) of the plural. This distinction was already established in the seventeenth century, and is recorded by Robinson, Gil, and Hodges. In the singular ME *ŭ* is also shown by Hart, Price, and the 'phonetically spelt' lists of Coles, Strong, and Young; in seventeenth-century orthoepists the vowel may be either [ʌ] or [ʊ] (cf. *OED*, s.v. *woman*). Bullokar shows [ʊ] in the plural as well as in the singular; this pronunciation, though at variance with PresE usage, is of course as easy to explain in the plural as in the singular, and is in agreement with the ModE spelling.

In other cases the rounded vowel is now only dialectal. It is recorded in a single word by Bullokar (who has many dialectal or vulgar pronunciations), in another single word by Hodges (but not as a feature of his own speech), and more fully by Cooper (followed by *RS*), who describes it as 'barbarous speaking'. That Cranmer and Latimer used the rounded pronunciation (see Note 2) does little to modify this impression that it was avoided in good StE of the later sixteenth and seventeenth centuries; there is much to suggest that educated persons used occasional dialectalisms in the early sixteenth century which they would have avoided at its close.

The process is one of rounding of the vowel, presumably through a stage [y], to [ʊ], where it becomes identical with ME *ŭ* and develops with it; after *c.* 1640 we might expect to find either unrounded [ʌ], or rounded [ʊ] retained because of the influence of the labial. Cooper's evidence does not indicate whether the sound is [ʌ] or [ʊ]. (See further Notes 2 and 3.) Luick, § 543, Anm. 3, explains *ŭ* in *bishop* by this process of rounding of [ɪ] to [ʊ]; but in other words, where the modern dialects have [ʌ] for ME *ĭ* after *w*, he would adopt a different explanation (§ 542), namely that there has been direct lowering of [ɪ] to [ʌ]. That this explanation is wrong is shown not only by the unnecessary duality of hypothesis, but also by the occurrence of *u*-spellings for ME *ĭ* after *w* in the fifteenth century and even earlier, before ME *ŭ* was unrounded to [ʌ]. *Bishop* does not in fact have *u*-forms earlier than the other words, as Luick apparently believes (cf. § 543, Anm. 3).

The rounding is shown in the following cases. (*a*) In words with original ME *ĭ*: Bullokar transcribes *whirling-wind* with *ŭ*, and Cooper records the dialectal forms *bushop* 'bishop', *wull* 'will', *wuth* 'with' (also *wumme*, *wuth me* 'with me'), and (before *m*) *frankumcense* 'frankincense'. In the last word the substitution of *m* for *n* (on which the rounding depends) is unexplained; the lack of stress assists the rounding. (*b*) In the word *weary* there is rounding of *ĭ* by ME shortening of *ẹ̄* (cf. the fourteenth-century spelling *wiry* cited by *OED*), whence the form *wurry* given by Cooper; Hodges in his 'near alike' list pairs *weary* with *worry*, which probably shows the same pronunciation of the former as Cooper records (see Vol. I, p. 401). (*c*) Cooper's *whuther* 'whether' (which *RS* glosses 'wither') shows rounding in the form *whither*, in which ME *ĭ* is probably by raising of ME *ĕ* (but see Note 2 below).

Note 1: On [iː] < ME *ẹ̄* by lengthening of ME *ĭ* in *women* see § 10, where also is mentioned a spelling of Laneham's which appears to show [e] by lowering of *ĭ*. For early spelling-evidence see *OED*, s.v. *woman*; in both singular and plural *u*-forms occur from the early thirteenth century (*Ancrene Wisse*) onwards.

Note 2: *Bishop* has *u*-forms from the fourteenth century (e.g. in Langland) until the seventeenth century (see Luick, § 543, Anm. 3; Wyld, *Coll. Eng.*, pp. 229–30; and *OED*, s.v.). Wyld, loc. cit., cites Jones (1701), who says that some pronounce the word *Booshop*, and comments (correctly) that this spelling shows retention of rounded [ʊ]. Wyld shows that Cranmer used the form *bushop*. The present tense forms of the verb *will* have *u*- and *o*-forms from the twelfth to the sixteenth century, and *wull* 1st person sing. occurs in dialectal English from the seventeenth to the nineteenth century (see *OED*); the early (twelfth- to fourteenth-century) *u*-forms must often refer to a pronunciation [y], but the later *u*- and *o*-forms must show complete rounding and retraction to ME *ŭ*. *OED* provides evidence on the other words cited above as follows. *Will* sb. has *u* in the fifteenth century and in nineteenth-century Scotch dialects. *Whirl* vb. has sixteenth- and seventeenth-century *o* and *u* forms. *With* has a sixteenth-century Scotch spelling *wutht* and a Northern dialectal form *wud* from the seventeenth to the nineteenth century. *Frankincense* has a sixteenth- and seventeenth-century form *fran(c)kumsence*, which occurs in Latimer's *Sermons*. *Whether* has *i*-forms once in the *Cura Pastoralis* and from the fourteenth to the seventeenth century; it has *o*-forms in the fourteenth century (in the *Northern Passion* and Robert of Gloucester's *Chronicle*). (Cf. *whither*, which has *y* in the *Blickling Homilies*, *u* in Laȝamon, and *o*-spellings from the thirteenth to the sixteenth century.) No *u*- or *o*-spellings are recorded for *weary*, but see Note 4 below.

Note 3: In the modern dialects, *will* has [ʊ] (less frequently [ʌ]) in many dialects (including Cooper's Hertfordshire, and Norfolk and Essex); *with* is [wʌd] in Sussex; *weather* has [ʌ] in Norfolk, and *wether* has [ʌ] in Norfolk and Suffolk. So with other analogous words (*which*, *wind* sb. and vb., *window*, *wish*, *witch*; *well*, *wench*, *wet*; *bellows*, *besom*, *better*; *bill*, *bind*); the rounding of original ME *ĭ* is chiefly Scotch and Northern, that of original ME *ĕ* chiefly South-western, but both occur sporadically in other dialects. See Wright, Index.

Note 4: The U.S. (dialectal) verb *worry* 'make weary' (see *OED*, s.v. *worry* vb., 5 (*e*)) is clearly not in origin a form of *worry* < OE *wyrgan*, but the seventeenth-century dialectal form of *weary* recorded by Hodges and Cooper.

Note 5: In *bishop* the rounding influence of the [b] is reinforced by that of the [ʃ]; cf. § 196 below.

ME ŏ´

§ 86. The quality of ME *ŏ* during the sixteenth and seventeenth centuries is a matter of some dispute. The evidence which we are required to interpret is as follows. (*a*) Earlier orthoepists, down to Gil and Butler (i.e. orthoepists representative mainly of sixteenth-century pronunciation), regard ME *ŏ* as the short equivalent of ME *ǭ*. (*b*) But later (seventeenth-century) orthoepists regard it as the short equivalent of the monophthong developed from ME *au*; so Waad (1602; see Vol. I, p. 130), Robinson, Hodges, Wallis (plagiarized by Price, *VO*), Newton, Wilkins, Holder, Coles, Lodwick, Cooper, Ray, and the shorthand-writer Dix. (*c*) Certain writers give evidence of a more individual sort. Waad transcribes ME *ŏ* by *A*; this suggests an affinity (but equally a difference) between ME *ŏ* and ME *ă*. Robinson (see Vol. I, pp. 207–8) implies that ME *ŏ* is formed with the tongue further forward than for ME *ǭ*, but less far forward than for ME *au* (a monophthong). Wallis (see Vol. I, p. 225, and for fuller details Lehnert, *Wallis*, § 99) says that ME *ŏ* is a back ('guttural') vowel, and identifies it with German *a* when the latter is short, though he also says that it is between German *a* and *o*. Cooper identifies it with German *a* in *Mann*. (*d*) But ME *ŏ* is usually identified with *o* of foreign languages; thus Welsh orthoepists (the *Welsh Hymn*, Salesbury, the *Welsh Breviary*, and T. Jones) identify it with Welsh *o*, Palsgrave, Florio, Minsheu, and Percival, amongst others, identify it with French, Italian, or Spanish *o*.

There can be no doubt that the pronunciation of ME *ŏ* has changed since the fourteenth century from a somewhat higher back vowel to a very low one (see § 54 (2)); and if my theory of the nature of the process whereby ME *ŏ* was lengthened (see §§ 54–56) is correct, this lowering was proceeding during the sixteenth and seventeenth centuries. The evidence of the earlier orthoepists who regard ME *ŏ* as the short equivalent of ME *ǭ* may depend on a pronunciation in which ME *ŏ* had not yet been lowered very far; but it should be remembered that until ME *au* was monophthongized, ME *ǭ* was the only long vowel to which ME *ŏ* could be compared, and that at this time ME *ǭ* itself may have had lower tongue position than it had in the seventeenth century. Robinson's evidence is perhaps a better indication that ME *ŏ* had not yet been lowered, for he describes it as being further back in the mouth (i.e. higher) than [ɒː] < ME *au*, whereas it is now lower than [ɒː]; but we should remember that in his system the short vowels are always further back than the long vowels, and that for the sake of maintaining this system he may possibly (but not very probably) have depended on the now dialectal pronunciation in which ME *au* was monophthongized to [ɑː], a sound slightly lower than the PresE [ɒ]. That seventeenth-century orthoepists regard ME *ŏ* as the short equivalent of [ɒː] < ME *au* may show that it has been lowered; but they may have been obliged to use [ɒː] < ME *au* as the nearest long equivalent because ME *ǭ* had been so raised as to make it no longer suitable in that function. The identification of ME *ŏ* with *o* of foreign languages, which continues in the seventeenth century, must show that it is a rounded vowel, but need not show that it has not been lowered; for the lowered [ɒ] of PresE is similarly substituted for the higher foreign sounds. The identifications with foreign *a*, on the other hand, are definite evidence of a lowered [ɒ]; such identifications are not found in English orthoepists before Wallis.

The theory set out in the previous chapter on the nature of the process of lengthening of ME *ă* and ME *ŏ*, if accepted, enables us to draw important conclusions on the pronunciation of unlengthened *ŏ* (see § 54, Note 2), for lengthening shows that in free position ME *ŏ* has become lowered [ɒ] and failure of lengthening that the lowering has not yet occurred to any significant degree. The lack of evidence of lengthening (which would be immediately noticed and recorded once ME *au* had been monophthongized, as lengthened ME *ŏ* and monophthongized ME *au* are identified and constitute a recognizably distinct phoneme) shows that lowering of ME *ŏ* had not been accepted in the early seventeenth century by the educated language; indeed, evidence of lengthening is not found before Newton (*c.* 1661), Coles (1674), and Cooper (1685), so that lowered [ɒ] cannot have been generally current in StE until *c.* 1670. But in the vulgar and dialectal speech represented by Bullokar and *RS* and by the Northerner Poole the lowering had apparently occurred in the fifteenth century. This agrees well with our other evidence—Robinson's that ME *ŏ* was still higher than [ɒː] < ME *au* and the lack of comparisons with foreign [ɑ] until the time of Wallis (except for the foreign evidence cited in Note 1, which may well refer to vulgar speech). The evidence, then, leads to the same conclusion as in the case of ME *ă*: that the new pronunciation was vulgar or dialectal in the sixteenth century, gradually entered StE during the first part of the seventeenth century, and became normal among educated speakers about 1670.

On early lowering and unrounding of ME *ŏ* to identity with ME *ă* see the following section.

Note 1: Zachrisson, *Eng. Vowels*, pp. 134–6, cites the evidence of foreign orthoepists who identify ME *ŏ* with foreign *o*; others (Bellot, 1580; Festeau, 1693; Miège, 1691) notice a *resemblance* of ME *ŏ* to French *a* (i.e. back [ɑ]), but only Mauger, 1679, identifies the two sounds. Zachrisson rejects the view that ME *ŏ* was generally [ɑ] (see Note 2), but holds that it may have been 'more open and somewhat less rounded' than it now is. It could hardly have been so without becoming [ɑ]. A very relevant remark here is that of Nicholson,

Introduction to French Phonetics, p. 24: 'In French ears it [PresE [ɒ]] sounds, as it really is, akin to the *a*-vowels.' Luick, § 534, Anm. 1, cites an anonymous Dutch grammar as saying that the English mostly pronounce their *o* like the 'aldergroofste *a*' of the Netherlanders; and the Leyden documents of 1611, which represent ME *ŏ* regularly by *a*. But Dutch [ɑ] is a particularly retracted vowel, easily confused with PresE [ɒ]; thus a modern grammar (*Teach Yourself Dutch*, by H. Koolhoven) observes (p. 13) that 'English speakers are apt to confuse it with the vowel of *cot*, *rod*', and the reverse is true.

Note 2: Luick, § 534, following Viëtor, holds that ME *ŏ* was not only lowered, but also unrounded to [ɑ], and that this was the StE pronunciation from the later sixteenth until the late eighteenth century. This view depends on (i) the identification of ME *ŏ* with German, Dutch, and French *a*, (ii) the failure of the seventeenth-century English phoneticians to describe the lip-rounding of [ɒ], and (iii) Luick's theory that ME *au* when monophthongized became [ɑ:] (which in turn depends in part on his theory that ME *ŏ* became [ɑ]). This view is undoubtedly false. As for his argument (iii), ME *au* did not become [ɑ:] in StE (see § 235, Note); even if it had, the identification of ME *ŏ* as its short equivalent might be inexact, as the evidence of Robinson shows. As to (ii), it is to be observed that PresE [ɒ] has what is termed 'open' lip-rounding (cf. Daniel Jones, *Outline of English Phonetics*, §§ 297–8), i.e. lip-rounding different in degree, and to some extent in nature, from 'close' lip-rounding, possessed by the vowels [u(:)] and [o:]; that the seventeenth-century phoneticians should describe the lip-rounding of [u(:)] and [o:] and not that of [ɒ(:)] is in no way surprising. Moreover as there was in the seventeenth century no back [ɑ:], but instead only a front [a:] (in those writers who used a lengthened sound in *part*, &c.), the rounding of [ɒ(:)] lacked the significance it now has in distinguishing [ɑ:] from [ɒ:]; the distinction of [a:] in *part* from [ɒ:] in *port* or *taut* was sufficiently marked by the tongue-position. In any case Wallis's remark that ME *ŏ* was between German *a* and *o* implies some degree of lip-rounding and is an exact enough description of the PresE sound. As to (i), the identifications with foreign *a*, cf. Note 1 above; in several cases it is indeed not identity, but merely resemblance, which is remarked upon. As is pointed out in Note 1, PresE [ɒ], owing to its very low tongue-position (which Daniel Jones, loc. cit., describes as that of 'cardinal [ɑ]', though perhaps it is a little higher) and its 'open' lip-rounding, appears to foreigners at the present time as an [ɑ] sound; and conversely foreign [ɑ], being generally more retracted even than PresE [ɑ:] (and still more so than seventeenth-century [a:]) in *fast*, *cart*, &c., commonly seems to present-day Englishmen to be a sort of [ɒ:] sound. In other words, the same comments on resemblances and the same identifications as were made in the late sixteenth, seventeenth, and early eighteenth centuries are to be met with today when English [ɒ] is compared with foreign [ɑ]; and a trained phonetician today knows them to be false. Sweet's interpretation of these earlier identifications as showing the same error as untrained observers make at the present day is obviously right. Luick is further obliged to assume that in the eighteenth century there was a change from [ɑ] to PresE [ɒ], for which there is no evidence; and this duplication of hypotheses (one to account for the early evidence, another to account for the known PresE pronunciation) betrays the essential weakness of the theory.

IDENTIFICATION OF ME *ŏ* WITH ME *ă*

§ 87. In the preceding section we have seen that there was in StE during the sixteenth and seventeenth centuries a tendency to lower ME *ŏ* and to reduce its lip-rounding. This tendency in some dialectal forms of English operated so fully and so early that ME *ŏ* became completely unrounded and lowered, and in consequence identical with ME *ă* before the latter had been affected by ModE fronting; when this occurred, ME *ŏ* developed with ME *ă* from [a] to [æ]. This identification of ME *ŏ* with ME *ă* made its way into vulgar London English and thence occasionally into more correct speech

§ 87] PART 1: THE SHORT VOWELS 579

(cf. Wyld, *Coll. Eng.*, pp. 240–2, who cites spellings and rhymes which show this development from the sixteenth, seventeenth, and eighteenth centuries). But despite the currency of *Gad* for *God* and the by-forms *strap* < *strop* and *plat* (*OED*, sb.³) < *plot*, it seems unlikely that an educated man would ever have used this pronunciation in careful speech (whatever he may have said in his unguarded moments). Significantly, nearly all the evidence in the orthoepists occurs in 'homophone' lists, which often record vulgarisms; all the lists (with the partial exceptions noted below) have examples, ranging in number from one in Butler to six or more in later lists. Even in the 'homophone lists' the identification of ME *ŏ* with ME *ă* is treated with some reserve. Hodges puts only one case into his list of words which are 'alike' (perhaps even then by error), though he gives more numerous examples in his list of words which are 'near alike'; Coles gives no example in his most careful list (that of the *Schoolmaster*), one in his *Eng. Dict.*, and a fair number (probably adopted from Strong) in his careless *Eng.–Lat. Dict.*; Strong gives the example from Coles's *Eng. Dict.* in his 'alike' list, and adds those adopted by Coles's *Eng.–Lat. Dict.* in a 'near alike' list; and Cooper gives no example in his 'alike' list, though some are admitted to his 'near alike' list. It seems clear that these authors think that ME *ŏ* will be identified with ME *ă* only by the most careless speakers. Outside the 'homophone' lists the only orthoepistical evidence comes in Bullokar's rhymes (see Vol. I, p. 110), which are based on vulgar or dialectal speech; in the Northerner Poole's rhyme-lists (*orb : barb, torch : arch*); in the well-known passage in Gil in which he compares the speech of the *Mopsæ* with that of the Eastern dialects, and gives *skalerz* 'scholars' as one of the affected or careless—at any rate reprehensible—pronunciations used by the *Mopsæ*; and in Hunt, who gives *gad* as a Northern form of *god*.

The identification of ME *ŏ* with ME *ă* is due to a ME and not an early ModE development. It is earlier than the fronting of ME *ă*, and earlier than the diphthongization of ME *ă* and ME *ŏ* before [χ], since it gives rise to the variation between ME *au* and ME *ou* in *daughter*, &c. (see § 240); it must therefore go back to the thirteenth century, since diphthongization before [χ] occurs from the early thirteenth century (cf. Jordan, § 121). In Western and South-western texts the unrounding is found very early; but though it is perhaps most typical of such texts in ME and is found most commonly in South-western dialects at the present day, it is unlikely that (as is usually assumed) the pronunciation made its way into StE from these dialects. StE vulgarisms in ModE times come almost without exception from the dialects to the East of London, and Gil's evidence suggests that it is here that we should seek the origin of the identification of ME *ŏ* with ME *ă* in London English. Jordan, § 272, cites fifteenth-century spellings which show the unrounding not only from Western texts, but also from *Palladius* (Essex); see also Kihlbom, pp. 142–4, who cites *a*-spellings from the South, London, and the East, and rightly regards the unrounding as a sporadic tendency which in London English is to be regarded as indigenous and 'shared with the surrounding dialects', and as primarily vulgar. Still more significant (especially for date) is the evidence of place-names (see Note 3 below); original ŏ is unrounded to ă in various names in Bedfordshire, Hertfordshire, Essex, Middlesex, Surrey, and Sussex, the change being shown in thirteenth-century documents for Bedfordshire and Essex. This early evidence of the unrounding in the South-eastern area strengthens the case for supposing that the rhymes of *oi* with *ai* in the *Alexander* group (Essex) depend on unrounding of the first element of the diphthong contemporaneously with (and in consequence of) the change of ŏ to ă (see § 261, Note 2); there is similarly an unrounding of ME *ou* (< OE āw, āg) which is especially characteristic of Essex (cf. Jordan, § 105, Anm., and see § 241 below). A case which may well show the early intrusion of the unrounding into the educated language of London is in *The Hous of Fame*, l. 1940, where the three authorities for the text at this point (MSS F and P, which constitute an α-group, and the Caxton edition, which represents a β-group) all read *hattes* for *hottes* 'panniers' (to which Skeat and later editors emend; cf. *OED*, s.v. *hot, hott* sb.). The unrounding also occurred early in the North; *OED* records *ʒalow* 'yellow' (< earlier *ʒolow*) from Northern texts from 1375 onwards.

Note 1: The lowering and unrounding of ME ŏ until it is identical with ME ă is not affected by 'lengthening' (primarily retractive) consonants. Thus Hodges's 'near alike' list pairs *form* with *farm, former* with *farmer,* and *loft* with *laugh't*; neither the following *r* nor the voiceless spirant, which in ModE would cause lengthening, has prevented unrounding. Contrast also *Gad* and *Gawd* 'God'; in the former we have lowering and unrounding, in the latter lengthening. As the 'lengthening' consonants exercise their influence *after* ME ă has begun to be fronted, and as the unrounding of ME ŏ must occur *before* the fronting of ME ă, it is easy to see why the 'lengthening' consonants do not inhibit the unrounding; their operative period had not yet come.

Note 2: Wright, §§ 82–83, records [æ] for ME ŏ in Kent, Devon, and Dorset in *cross*, in Devon and Dorset in *crop*, and in Devon in *clot*. ME ŏ is more often [a] (or back [ɑ]), but in most dialects which have these pronunciations ME ă is [æ] (or [e]), and the two sounds are thus kept distinct. ME ŏ before voiceless spirants (Wright, §§ 84–85) and *r* (§ 87) is often [ɑː], but this sound may be a later development of [ɒː] by lengthening rather than evidence of an earlier ă from ME ŏ. *Cross* has [æː] (which looks like lengthening of early ModE ă from ME ŏ) in Wiltshire (Wright, Index). I have heard [læri] 'lorry' in South-western dialectal speech.

Note 3: The volumes of the English Place-name Society show *a*-forms for ME ŏ in Hertfordshire, Surrey, and Sussex in the ModE period. In Middlesex *Talington* 'Tollington' appears in 1336. In Bedfordshire occur *Balnherst* 'Bolnhurst' 1202, *Clapham* 1247 (< *Cloppham*), *Claphull* 'Clophill' 1287, *Calworthe* 'Colworth' thirteenth century, and *Kakeswell* 'Cogswell' 1407. In Essex such forms occur 'frequently in early ME' (Reaney, *Place-names of Essex*, p. xxxvi); I have observed *Radyngas* tempore Henry I (?) and *-rathynges* 1282 'Roding' (< OE *Hrōða*), *Brakeshaved* 'Broxted' 1198, *Barham* 'Borham' 1216 (probably not from OE *bār* 'boar'; cf. Reaney, s.n.), *Galdhangr(e)* 1218 and *Caldhangre* thirteenth century 'Goldhanger', *Taleshunt* 1237 and *Talishunte* 1285 'Tolleshunt', *Wakenden* 1272 'Ockendon' (< *Woccandūn), *Bakkyng* 1272 'Bocking', and *Capford(e)* 1309 and 1401 'Copford'.

Note 4: On spellings with *o* for ME *ă* in Eastern documents which may be, and in the Northerner Machyn which almost certainly are, inverted spellings depending on the unrounding of ME *ŏ* to identity with ME *ă* see § 194, Note 3. Gradation variants may ultimately explain *chop* vb. beside *chap* vb. (cf. also *chip*, in which may originate the OE palatalized *c*).

ME *ŏ* BEFORE *l*

§ 88. ME *ŏ* before back ('dark') *l* develops in late ME to *ou* and at times further to *ū*; subsequently (i.e. in the ModE period) it shares the development of these sounds. The diphthongization is however not found in certain words; the explanation is that they were adopted into English after it was complete, and therefore retain unchanged their *ŏ*. *Absolve* has *ŏ* in Gil and Hodges, as has *resolved* in Robinson; but *dissolve* (a ME adoption) has properly [ou] in Mulcaster, though in PresE it has [ɒ], presumably because of analogy. *Extol* (a late fifteenth-century adoption) has *ŏ* in Bullokar, Hodges, and (as it seems) in Price, but a pronunciation developed from late ME *ou* in Levins. *Revolt* (a sixteenth-century adoption) has *ŏ* in Hodges; in PresE [ou], which must be due to analogy, is more common.

Failure of diphthongization before an *l* which is followed by a voiceless consonant is rather less common than in the case of ME *ă* (see § 60); but Smith has *ŏ* in *colt* and Bullokar in *folk* (twice, against [oː] < ME *ou* once), *dolt, doltish,* and *holpen* p.p. (against ME *ou* in *holp*).

Failure of diphthongization is regularly shown in such words as *follow* (ME *folwen*), in which the single *l* at the end of the syllable was apparently not 'back' [l], and before single intervocalic *l* in such words as *choler* (for which, for example, Hart has *ŏ*) and *holly* (which in OE and ME has single *l*). Hart's *ŏ* in *Polz* '(St.) Paul's', which is exceptional (ME *ou* being normal in this word), may perhaps be compared with the retention of ME *ă* in *Hal* and *Mal*; but Laneham's spelling *Polles* is to be regarded as showing ME *ou*.

Note: For the failure of diphthongization cf. the parallel case of ME *ă*, § 60 above.

ME *ŏ* BEFORE [χ]

§ 89. ME *ŏ* before [χ] usually develops in late ME either to *ou* (which sometimes becomes late ME *ū* > eModE [ʌu]; see § 170 below) or to *au*, according as the real starting-point of the development is ME *ŏ* itself or ME *ă* by unrounding of ME *ŏ*; for evidence of these pronunciations see § 240 below. But the *Welsh Hymn* transcribes *ought* as *ocht*, and Hart and Gil also show occasional failure of the diphthongization. In *(al)though*, in which they have regular *ŏ*, it is clearly due to weak stress in late ME. Otherwise Hart has *ŏ* thirteen times in the *Orthographie* (in *brought, nought, ought* vb., and *thought*; I exclude *oh* interjection) against ME *ou* once in the *Methode* (in *brought*) and late ME *ū* < *ou* four times in the *Orthographie* (in *brought, ought* vb., and *sought*). Apart from *though*, Gil has *ŏ* only once, in *boht* 'bought' (where the 1619 edition has *ou*), against *ou* (ME *ou*) over twenty times (including two other occurrences of *bought* itself) and ME *ū* < ME *ou* nine times; that the isolated example of *ŏ* is an error is obviously possible, but in view of Hart's evidence it seems better to regard it as a chance record of a real variant pronunciation. Hart's and Gil's evidence of *ŏ* is supported by that of the modern dialects; Wright, § 90 and Index, shows that in Scottish dialects (in which alone [χ] is now preserved, as it is in Hart and Gil) *ŏ* is more widespread than [o:] < ME *ou*, and *ŏ* also occurs occasionally in English dialects in which [χ] does not become [f] but is lost without trace (so [bɒt] 'bought' in S. Lancashire, S. Staffs., and Shropshire, [ɒt] 'ought' in Oxfordshire).

Note: In words in which ModE shows the change of [χ] to [f] (e.g. in *cough*) the vowel is [ɒ]; in view of Hart's and Gil's evidence this could represent undiphthongized ME *ŏ*, but as diphthongization is the normal StE process and is earlier than the change of [χ] to [f] it is preferable to assume that normally this ModE [ɒ] is by shortening before [f] < [χ] of late ME *ou* < *ŏ* (see § 34 (1)). Similarly [af], shown in *daughter* by certain sources, is to be regarded as developed by shortening before [f] < [χ] of late ME *au* < *ă* < *ŏ* (and not by unrounding of the *ŏ* of an earlier *dŏfter*, as assumed by Wyld, *Coll. Eng.*, p. 241, the unrounding being in fact earlier than the change of [χ] to [f]).

VARIATION BETWEEN ME *ŏ* AND ME *ŭ*

(1) *Variation descended from OE*

§ 90. Certain words preserve in ModE a variation between *ŏ* and *ŭ* that arose in late OE. In *world* the OE development was that the original *weorold* became *worold* in eWS and in ONb (cf. Bülbring, §§ 268 and 266), but late WS had *wuruld, wurld* (see *OED*, s.v., and Jordan, § 73, Anm. 1) beside retained *worold*. The *ŏ* form is recorded by Hart, Bullokar, Gil, Butler, Hodges, and possibly by Young (who gives *worling* as a phonetic spelling of *worldling*; but see Vol. I, p. 352); the *ŭ* form by Robinson, Poole, Price, Strong (who gives *wurling* 'worldling'), Cooper (who has [ʊ] not [ʌ]), and *WSC-RS* (as Cooper). *Worse* and *worth* are from late WS **wursa* < *wyrsa* < *wiersa* and late WS *wurð* < *weorð* (cf. Bülbring, §§ 280 and 268), and are normally recorded by the orthoepists with *ŭ*. But in ONb *weorð* > *worð* (cf. Bülbring, § 265), whence we can explain the form with *ŏ* recorded by the Northerners Levins and Poole; the Southerner Willis follows Levins, perhaps inadvertently. Cooper (followed by *WSC-RS*) has ME *ŭ* in *beyond*, where it represents the OE (late WS) *beiundan*, ME *beʒunde* (cf. Bülbring, § 299, and *OED*, s.v. *beyond*); see Vol. I, p. 306.

Note 1: Willis may have followed Levins in regard to *worth* because he knew a Southern pronunciation of the word with ME *ŏ* by lowering of ME *ŭ* < late WS *ŭ*; cf. Note 2.

Note 2: Levins gives *ŏ* in *worse*, but the OAngl form was *wyrsa* (cf. Bülbring, § 262), whence, with retraction of the *y*, arises a form with late ONb *ŭ* (Bosworth-Toller cites *wurresta* from the Lindisfarne Gospels); Levins's *ŏ* must be due to lowering of this *ŭ*. Similarly Levins and Poole give *ŏ* in *work*, where it cannot be due to the late ONb change of *wĕor* to *wŏr*, since the OAngl form should be *werc*. The late ONb form is in fact *wærc*, from which by retraction there might arise **worc*. But the modern dialectal pronunciations cited by Wright show that Northern dialects have forms developed from ME *ūr* (either because of adoption of the Southern ME form, or because of the analogy of the verb, with **wurcan* < *wyrcan*); and Levins's and Poole's *ŏ* may be by lowering of ME *ŭ*. Wright records [wɒːk] for South Northumberland and [wɒk] for Leicestershire.

(2) *Variation in words from OF*

§ 91. Latin countertonic *ŏ* becomes [u] in OF, whence normal ME *ŭ* in *stomach*; but Bullokar has *ŏ* once (beside *ŭ* once), which may show the influence of Latin *stomachus*. Similarly *companion* has *ŭ* in Laneham and Bullokar but *ŏ* in Hodges, probably because of the Latin form. In *colony*, *polish*, and *fornication* the normal ME *ŏ* is due to these words being 'learned' OF adoptions from Latin, so that they lack the development of Latin countertonic *ŏ* to [u]; but there seem to have been OF variants which had been 'popularized' to the extent of the substitution of [u] for the Latin *ŏ*, whence the ME *ŭ* recorded in *polish* by Bullokar (cf. the late ME *u*-forms cited by *OED*, which compares Italian *pulire*, *pulito*), in *fornication* by Strong, and in *colony* by *RS* (cf. *Cullen* 'Cologne', recorded by Coles and Young, from Latin *Colonia*). *RS* also records *ŭ* in *colonel*; the PresE pronunciation [kəːnəl] descends from ME *ŭ* in the variant form *cor(o)nel*.

Latin tonic *ŏ* before *n* in *front* also becomes OF [u], whence normal ME *ŭ*; but Hodges has *ŏ* in *frontlets*, probably owing to the influence of the original Latin form. Latin countertonic *ŭ* becomes OF [u] in *sovereign*, whence ME *ŭ* in Robinson and Hodges; but ME *ŏ* is recorded by Gil and perhaps by Butler (whose transcriptions are of doubtful value), probably owing to the influence of Italian *sovrano*.

On variation between ME *ŭ* and ME *ŏ* in *form* see § 17, and on *horde* see § 18.

Note: The *o*-forms recorded for *stomach*, *frontlets*, and *sovereign* may be due to lowering of ME *ŭ* to ME *ŏ* and to the acceptance of the normally vulgar lowered pronunciation under the influence of the spelling and (in the first two cases) of the Latin etymon; this is especially likely in the case of *stomach*, since the *ŏ*-form is recorded by Bullokar, who gives other evidence of lowering to *ŏ* of ME *ŭ*. See further § 97 (1).

(3) *Raising of ME ŏ to ME ŭ*

§ 92. (a) By the late twelfth century OE *ŏ* before *ng* was raised to *ŭ* (cf. the raising of *ĕ* to *ĭ* before *ng*, § 79 above). The change does not affect late ME *ŏ* < *ǭ* < OE *ā* by lengthening of *ă*, and therefore does not occur in dialects (including London English) which ultimately had OE *ă* for WGmc *ă* before a nasal; it can occur only in those which had OE *ŏ* for this sound. It is therefore characteristic of the West and especially the North-west Midlands (cf. Jordan, § 31), but ME evidence shows it also in the North (*Towneley Plays*) and South-west (*The Owl and the Nightingale*, if the rhyme at ll. 1071–2 is due to SW influence on the author's language, as is probable); modern dialectal evidence (Wright, § 32) shows it not only in the West Midlands, but also in Northern, East Midland, and SW dialects. Its occurrence in StE in the related words *mongrel, monger,* and *among*(*st*), and sporadically earlier in other words, must be due to dialectal influence; the natural StE pronunciation is with late ME ŏ by shortening of ǭ.

It is only for words with PresE [ʌ] that good evidence of the raising is found in the orthoepists. *Monger* has ME ŭ in Gil. *Among* has ME ŏ in Hart, Bullokar (thrice, against ŭ once), and Gil (eleven times), but ME ŭ in Bullokar (once), Robinson (thrice), Butler, Hodges, Poole, Cooper, and Brown; the change from the ŏ type to the ŭ type would appear to have occurred in StE about 1600. The 'homophone' lists may show ME ŭ in other -*ong* words. *Tongs* is paired with *tongues* by Hodges, Ellis, Fox and Hookes, Young, Richardson, Cooper ('near alike'), *The Compendious School-Master*, Cocker, and Brown; but in Coles's *Schoolmaster* the pairing depends on ŏ in both words, and may do so in other lists. Fox and Hookes pair *longs* with *lungs*. Coles (in his least careful list, that of the *Eng.–Lat. Dict.*) pairs *wrong* with *wrung* and *rung*. Bullokar rhymes *longs* with *tongues*, and the Northerner Poole probably shows, by his rhymes, that all these -*ong* words have ŭ. But the fact that the most plentiful evidence, both in the 'homophone' lists and in the rhymes of poets, comes from pairings or rhymes with *tongue*, shows that the spelling of the latter is a factor; it would appear that a pronunciation of *tongue* with ŏ by lowering of ŭ had been assisted to common currency by the spelling and is often the basis of the pairing or the rhyme (as it certainly is in Coles's careful *Schoolmaster*).

(*b*) Raising also occurs before [v], where it affects StE pronunciation. *Coventry* (OE *Cōfantrēo*) has ŏ in Laneham and Waad, as in the normal PresE pronunciation; but there is a variant pronunciation with [ʌ]. *Oven* (OE *ofen*) has, on the other hand, ME ŭ in Bullokar and Hodges as in PresE; Butler gives ŏ, but his transcription may be imperfect. *Shovel* (OE *scofl*) has ME ŭ in Bullokar, Butler, Hodges, and Hunt. *Hovel* may be a further case if it is from LG **hovel* (as seems most likely); it has ME ŭ in *RS*, as in modern Northern and North Midland dialects, but retains ME ŏ in present StE.

(*c*) Raising between a labial and *r* (cf. Jordan, § 35, Anm. 2) seems to occur in several cases. The only clear example is *word*, in which ŭ occurs in late WS (Bülbring, § 281) and becomes more widespread in ME (Jordan, loc. cit.); it has ME ŏ in Levins, Bullokar (ten times, beside ŭ thrice), and Gil (once, beside ŭ thrice), and in Willis ME ǭ < OE ō by lengthening; but ŭ is more commonly recorded—by Salesbury (probably), Hart, Bullokar (thrice), Mulcaster, Robinson, Gil (thrice), Butler, Hodges (who has [ʌ]), Wharton (followed by J. Smith), Newton, Poole (who also has ME ǭ, following Willis), Price, Coles, Cooper (who has [ʊ] not [ʌ]), *WSC-RS* (as

Cooper), and Brown. *Murder* (OE *morðor*) regularly has *ŭ* in the orthoepists. *Forth* has *ŭ* in Hart (beside *ŏ*), Bullokar, and Mulcaster, and *afford* has *ŭ* in Mulcaster and Poole; but otherwise these words have forms derived from OE *ŏ* (see § 16 above). See further Note 2 below.

(*d*) The raising shown by Newton in *frog* and *dog* is dialectal (see Vol. I, p. 249).

   Note 1: The modern dialectal distribution of ME *ŭ* in *along, song,* &c. is probably a pointer to the OE distribution of *ŏ* for WGmc *ă* before nasals, if allowance is made for the influence of StE [ʌ] in *among* &c. Luick, § 429.1, explains WMidland *ŭ* before *ng* by ME shortening of *ǭ* < OE *ō* < *ŏ* for *ă* plus nasal; this is possible, but seems unlikely.

   Note 2: Raising before *r* is an unlikely process, and in the words discussed under (*c*) above the phonetic process would rather be one of increased rounding, which obviously is most likely after *w*. Other explanations are possible for *murder* (in which ME *ŭ* may be attributed to the influence of AF *murdre* and Law Latin *murdrum*, which also probably influence the consonantal development; cf. Luick, § 379, Anm. 3, and *OED*) and for *forth* and *afford* (in which ME *ŭ* may be by shortening of ME *ǭ* or more probably be due to the analogy of *fŭrðor*; cf. Jordan, loc. cit.). It may be granted that there are also alternative explanations possible for ME *ŭ* in *oven* (which might be from OE **ōfen*; cf. Luick, loc. cit., Anm. 3), *shovel* (which might be influenced analogically by *shove* vb.), *Coventry* (which might have ME shortening or an analogical pronunciation because of words like *love*, *shove*, &c., in which *o* is pronounced *ŭ*), and *hovel* (which may not be from LG **hovel*); but these seem less likely than those available for ME *ŭ* in *murder, forth,* and *afford*.

   Note 3: *Hover*, which has ME *ŭ* in Hodges, Cooper, and *RS* but [ɒ] in PresE, is to be taken as an iterative form of *hove* vb. < OE **hōfian* (see *OED*), and has *ŏ* by late OE, *ŭ* by ME, shortening (cf. Mulcaster's *ŭ* by fifteenth-century shortening in *hove* itself, whence indeed ME *ŭ* may arise in *hover* by analogy). In the sixteenth and seventeenth centuries *hover* commonly rhymes on ME *ŭ* (so in Lodge, Shakespeare, and Drayton).

   Note 4: *Poverty* varies between ME *ŏ* (so Bullokar once and Butler) and ME *ŭ* (so Bullokar thrice and Hodges). As OF *povrete* has *ǫ* (cf. Pope, § 674), one would expect ME *ŏ*, and the variant in *ŭ* might well be due to raising. But OF *o* in the vicinity of labials gives either ME *ǭ* or ME *ǭ* when the vowel is made long (as in ME *povre* itself), and the *ŭ* variant in *poverty* may be by ME shortening of ME *ǭ*, which in its turn would be due, in the sb., to the analogy of the ME adj.

ME *ŭ*

§ 93. ME *ŭ* was originally the high-back rounded vowel [u]. In PresE in most words it has been unrounded and lowered to [ʌ], but in some words [u] is retained because of labial and other influences (see § 196 below). Orthoepistical evidence of the unrounding begins *c.* 1640 (except for certain evidence of Coote's which relates to 'barbarous' speech and not to StE; see below) and is as follows. (*a*) Certain orthoepists distinguish the *ŭ* of *cut* from that of *put*; so Hodges (see Vol. I, pp. 168, 170), Wallis, Newton (see Vol. I, pp. 248–9), Wilkins (Vol. I, p. 255), Cooper (Vol. I, pp. 287–8), and Ray (Vol. I, p. 188). Price (see Vol. I, p. 342, note 1) follows Wallis in distinguishing [u] from [ʌ] in the introductory part of *The Vocal Organ*, but elsewhere in this and his other book shows no recognition of the distinction; and Daines and Willis, though they both show changes dependent on the unrounding of ME *ŭ* to [ʌ] in free position (see Vol. I, pp. 336, 427–8) do not distinguish from 'short *u*' the vowel of such words as *wool*, *wood*, and *wolf*, let alone others spelt with *u* in which [ʊ] must have remained. (*b*) The original text of the late fifteenth-century *Welsh Hymn* and Salesbury (1547) equate ME *ŭ* in all positions with Welsh *w* (i.e. [ʊ]), but in the later seventeenth century T. Jones and the *Welsh Breviary* equate it with Welsh *y* (i.e. it is [ʌ]); so occasionally certain manuscripts of the *Welsh Hymn*, which date from 1587 onwards. (*c*) ME *ŭ* is regarded as the short equivalent of ME *ǭ* by Smith, Hart, Waad, Robinson, Gil, and Butler, but not by later orthoepists, except in such words as preserve [ʊ] (e.g. *put*); Newton keeps the traditional pairing of ME *ŭ* with ME *ǭ*, but is confused (see Vol. I, pp. 248–9). (*d*) It is identified with [ʊ] in foreign languages by (among others) Hart, Percival, and Sherwood (who says that it is like French *ou* pronounced very short), but with the sound of French *eur*, or French feminine *e*, by Wallis. (*e*) Hodges, Wilkins, Coles, and Cooper fail to distinguish ME *ŭ* in free position from stressed and unstressed [ə] (cf. Vol. I, pp. 180–1 and 241–3 above, § 214 below); this is only possible if ME *ŭ* is [ʌ]. (*f*) Descriptions of articulation accord with the conclusions which we draw from other evidence. Hart used a rounded back vowel (see Vol. I, p. 73) and Robinson a high-back vowel, which *may* have been unrounded but certainly had not been lowered (see Vol. I, pp. 203, 207–8). Wallis, Wilkins, and Cooper (see Vol. I, pp. 287–8) describe ME *ŭ* as a 'guttural' vowel, unrounded and lowered. Holder's vowel *oo*, which is ME *ŭ*, is described as having tongue-position closely similar to that of [o:] but (to interpret his terms) with a rather wider passage between soft palate and tongue, and without lip-rounding; this description is very suitable to the PresE [ʌ] (see Vol. I, pp. 265, 267–9).

Indirect evidence of the unrounding of ME *ŭ* is provided by two other developments, both of which depend on it; these are the identity of ME *ŭr* with ME *ĕr* and *ĭr* (see § 214), and of ME *ui* with ME *ī* (see § 262). The English orthoepists record both these developments about the same time as they record the unrounding of ME *ŭ* itself. Coote in 1596 shows that ME *ŭr* has become identical with ME *ĕr* in 'the barbarous speech of your country people', and it follows that in such speech ME *ŭ* in free position must have become [ʌ]. But for evidence relating to StE we have to wait until 1640, when Daines records the identity of ME *ŭr* with both *ĭr* and *ĕr*, and may therefore be assumed to have used [ʌ] for ME *ŭ* in free position (cf. § 214). Daines also used a pronunciation of ME *ui* which resembled, but was not identical with, that of ME *ī* (see Vol. I, pp. 333–4); this is the pronunciation [ʌi] (recorded a little later by Wallis), which depends on the unrounding of the first element of the diphthong, contemporaneously with the unrounding of ME *ŭ*. Thus both types of indirect evidence show that Daines used unrounded [ʌ] for ME *ŭ*; he is narrowly the first English orthoepist to give evidence of the unrounding in StE

(Hodges being the next; see above). Later orthoepists give similar evidence of the development of ME ŭr to identity with ME ĕr and ĭr, and of ME ui to [ʌi] or more commonly to [əi] and identity with ME ī.

The direct and indirect evidence of the development of ME ŭ given by the orthoepists is self-consistent and must be accepted as a correct picture of careful StE pronunciation. But occasional rhymes show that both the identity of ME ŭr with ĭr and ĕr, and of ME ui with ME ī, may already have been known in StE after c. 1570, though rarely; this evidence agrees with that of foreign and Welsh orthoepists (see Note 1), who show unrounding of ME ŭ from 1580 onwards, and with occasional transcriptions in the extant manuscripts of the *Welsh Hymn* (see above). The evidence of spellings on the identity of ME ŭr with ME ĕr and ĭr, and of ME ui with ME ī, is of more doubtful significance, but it may show both developments from the early fifteenth century in scattered dialects (possibly first in Northern and next in Eastern dialects), in Cockney pronunciation from c. 1525, and in StE from c. 1550; it would follow that ME ŭ was occasionally unrounded in dialectal speech from the early fifteenth century, in Cockney speech from c. 1525, and in StE from c. 1550. This conclusion in no way affects the validity of the evidence of the English orthoepists that careful StE did not accept unrounding of ME ŭ and the associated changes until 1640, though it does demonstrate the conservatism and resistance to change of the consciously 'correct' standard speech.

A final question remains: although the present unrounded and lowered vowel does not make its appearance in StE until 1640, it is possible that the unrounding (as distinct from the lowering) of the vowel may have occurred earlier. The only possible evidence of this comes from Lily's *Grammar* and from Cheke. Lily includes among the faults of the English pronunciation of Latin 'Ichnotes', which is 'a certain slenderness of speaking: . . . as, for *nunc* . . . pronouncing *nync, tunc,* . . . *tync, aliquis* . . . *eliquis, alius* . . . *elius*'. Now to unround ME ŭ might fairly be described as making it more 'slender'; but it does not seem to be this of which Lily is thinking. His point as regards *aliquis* and *alius* seems to be the English use of ME ā (now fronted, and therefore written *e*; see § 101 below) for Latin *a* in an open syllable; and he probably also means to condemn the English use of ME [y:] for Latin ū (or, in these words, for Latin *u* long by 'position'). Lily, then, gives no evidence of the unrounding of ME ŭ. Cheke's evidence is to be similarly explained (see Vol. I, p. 43). Hart, on the other hand, describes the vowel *u* (i.e. both ME ŭ and ME ọ̄, and the corresponding sounds in other languages) as being formed with the tongue retracted and the lips 'so neare together, as there be left but space that the sounde may passe forth with the breath' (*Orthographie*, f. 30ᵛ). We may conclude that in StE during the sixteenth century ME ŭ was still normally a fully rounded vowel, and that the unrounding did not precede the lowering by any great interval. But it would easily be possible for rounded and unrounded allophones of the ME *ŭ* phoneme to exist unnoticed side by side; indeed Price, Daines, and Willis show that fully unrounded and lowered [ʌ] could still be treated as an apparently unobserved variant of rounded [ʊ] by any man whose speech was unaffected by the later shortening of [uː] < ME *ǭ*, since it was only this shortening that made the difference between [ʌ] and [ʊ] phonemic. Our chief guarantee that there was not a much older allophonic distinction in educated speech is that the indirect evidence of the associated changes does not lead to different conclusions (except in these three individual sources) from those based on the direct evidence of the articulation of ME *ŭ* itself.

Note 1: Florio's identification of ME *ŭ* with Italian 'close o' probably indicates that it was still [ʊ]. Foreign orthoepists quoted by Horn, § 61; Wyld, *Coll. Eng.*, p. 232; Zachrisson, *Eng. Vowels*, pp. 133–4, show the unrounding to have occurred rather earlier than the English orthoepists do. Bellot 1580, Mason 1622, *Alphabet Anglois* 1625 compare ME *ŭ* with French *o*; they must refer to unrounded [ʌ] (see further Note 4 below). Erondelle in 1606 identifies ME *ŭ* 'as the common [i.e. the vulgar] sound it' with French feminine *e*. This evidence of Erondelle's, which emphasizes that the unrounded [ʌ] for ME *ŭ* was vulgar in 1606, is valuable confirmation of Coote's similar comment in 1596, and of the general correctness of the evidence of the English orthoepists. But (as Professor A. J. Bliss has kindly informed me) John Davies, *Antiquæ Linguæ Britannicæ . . . Rudimenta*, 1621, identifies ME *ŭ* in *hunt* and *stir* with Welsh 'obscure' *y*, i.e. he gives it without qualification as [ʌ].

Note 2: Attempts have been made to use spellings to show that [ʌ] developed from ME *ŭ* very early in certain dialects, by citing fifteenth- and sixteenth-century spellings with *a* for ME *ŭ* (so Wyld, *Coll. Eng.*, p. 233; Zachrisson, *Eng. Vowels*, p. 81; and Kihlbom, pp. 185–6). The theory underlying the citation of such evidence is that because a certain sound (here [ʌ]) is similar to another (here [a] or [æ]), therefore the letter that ought to represent the latter is likely to be used by 'phonetic' spellers for the former. This certainly happens when the speaker of one language or dialect is representing the sounds of another language or dialect, for he actually hears the strange sound as being identical with his native sound; thus at the present time Southerners hear the Northern English [a] for ME *ǎ* as [ʌ], and foreigners hear the StE [ʌ] for ME *ŭ* as [a], so that we might expect a Southern Englishman to use the letter *u* to represent his conception of the Northern pronunciation of ME *ǎ* and a foreigner to use the letter *a* to represent his conception of the English pronunciation of ME *ŭ*. But to suppose that anyone would interchange the letters *a* and *u* in representing the sounds of his own dialect is to ignore the whole concept of the phoneme theory (which, though not under that name, has long been familiar to scholars); though ModE [ʌ] may bear a resemblance to [a], ME *ŭ* and ME *ǎ* in ModE normally remain distinct phonemes and no Englishman speaking a dialect in which they remain distinct could ever confuse them, whatever *resemblance* they may have come to have to each other when heard by foreigners or judged by abstract phoneticians; to the speaker of a language, distinct phonemes of that language do not normally even seem to resemble each other. And if the sounds remain distinct elements in meaning (so that, for example, the distinction of *run* from *ran* depends entirely on the distinction between [ʌ] < ME *ŭ* and [æ] or [a] < ME *ǎ*), it is inconceivable that any English scribe would use *a* to represent [ʌ]. If *a*-spellings for ME *ŭ* really exist, then they must depend not on mere resemblance, but on actual *identity*, of ME *ŭ* and ME *ǎ* in the dialect in question; the evidence of the seventeenth-century spelling-books, and their 'homophone' lists intended to warn pupils against errors of spelling on phonetic grounds, shows that there must be identity (albeit in careless speech) and not mere resemblance. The detailed consideration of these real or alleged spellings with *a* for ME *ŭ* (and of rhymes or puns between ME *ǎ* and ME *ŭ*) therefore belongs under the discussion of the identification of ME *ŭ* with ME *ǎ* (see § 97, Notes 6 and 7).

Note 3: *Punkah, bungalow,* and *pundit,* with [ʌ] for the 'impure' Hindī *a*, show that ME *ŭ* had become [ʌ] at the time when the *u*-forms of these words appear; the earliest such form recorded by *OED* is dated 1625. Cf. § 59, Note 6.

Note 4: Luick, §§ 529–30, gives the following account of the development of ME *ŭ*. It became in the first place, with lowering and advancing of the tongue-position, an advanced and half-unrounded *o* sound ('ein vorgeschobenes und halbentrundetes *o*'); this sound Luick believes to have been used in StE from at latest the end of the sixteenth century until the early eighteenth century. But as ME *ŭ* lost all its rounding, it became more and more an [ə] sound, and then finally became (§ 563) the present [ʌ] sound about 1800. This elaborate theory is unjustified; it is due to an attempt to interpret too literally the vague descriptions in early sources of a sound of which the exact analysis is extremely difficult. The view that ME *ŭ* first developed to a sort of *o* is based entirely on identifications by *foreign* orthoepists (cf. Note 1) of the English sound with foreign *o*; but foreigners still falsely substitute an *o* sound for PresE [ʌ] (cf. French *lonch* for English *lunch*). The view that later the pronunciation was [ə] is based (i) on descriptions of ME *ŭ* which might mean [ə] but might equally mean [ʌ], and (ii) on the failure of certain seventeenth-century sources, and their eighteenth-century successors, to distinguish between the two sounds. But (i) the precise distinction of [ə] and [ʌ] is a matter of some nicety, and we should not therefore depend too closely on the vague descriptions of early sources (which we are very liable to misinterpret); and (ii) from the seventeenth century onwards [ə] and [ʌ] might legitimately be regarded as contextual variants of the one phoneme (the former being used in unstressed syllables and in stressed syllables before [r] and as the first element of the diphthong [əi], the latter in stressed syllables for ME *ŭ* (except before *r*) when unrounded and as the first element of the diphthong [ʌu]), and are in fact so regarded by those sources which do not distinguish between the two sounds (see especially Vol. I, pp. 241–3).

Luick's distinction of his seventeenth-century 'advanced half-unrounded *o*' from PresE [ʌ] is itself artificial; PresE [ʌ] is, as regards its tongue-position, 'an advanced variety of [ɔ]', but is 'pronounced with lip-spreading' (D. Jones, op. cit., § 334)—a description which differs from Luick's of his hypothetical and different vowel only in the distinction between a half- and a fully unrounded vowel. Ekwall, § 97, believes, with Luick, that the first stage in the unrounding was a sort of *o*-sound, but that by a direct change this became [ʌ], perhaps already in the seventeenth century and certainly by 1750. Here again there is a distinction finer than the evidence will allow. From the late sixteenth century onwards all the evidence can well refer to the PresE sound as described by Jones; to postulate some variant is obviously possible, but unnecessary.

Special words with ME *ŭ*

§ 94. The orthoepists record ME *ŭ* in various words which now have unhistorical (chiefly spelling-) pronunciations. *Bombast* (OF [u]) has *ŭ* in Gil; *Cologne* (OF [u]) is 'phonetically spelt' *Cullen* (*-in*) by Coles and Young; *coney* (OF [u]) has *ŭ* in Gil, Hodges, Wharton (followed by J. Smith), Strong, and Cooper; (*ale-*)*conner* (OE *ŭ*) has *ŭ* in Laneham, as has *grovelling* (ON *ŭ*) in Bullokar and RS. *Poniard* (ME *ŭ* < OF *ui*) has *ŭ* in *WSC*. *Wont* 'custom' (OE *ŭ*) has *ŭ* in Hart, Laneham, Bullokar, Gil, Butler, Brooksbank, Price, Wharton, Coles, and *WSC*; but *WSC* records *ŏ* as the vulgar pronunciation. Compare also the words cited in § 91 above.

ME *ŭ* BEFORE *ld*, *lt*, AND [χ]

§ 95. ME *ŭ* before *ld* (as in *shoulder*) and *lt* (as in *poultice*) normally becomes, during the ME period, *ou*, and shares its subsequent development (see §§ 248–51 below), but in a few orthoepists there is evidence of pronunciations descended from late ME *ū* (see § 174). On ME *ŭ* before [χ] see § 175; it normally becomes ME *ū*, but sometimes ME *ou*. See further § 97 below.

Note: PresE *won't* [wount] 'will not' is an instance of late ME *ou* < ME *ŭ* before *l*; see further § 425, Note 4, below.

ME *ŭ* BECOMES [ɪ] OR [e]

§ 96. Luick, § 532, maintains that there was a general tendency for ME *ŭ* to become [ɪ] or [e] by development in a horizontal direction through the value [y], and cites orthoepistical evidence which he believes reveals this change and various PresE pronunciations which may be due to it. But the change is not general, and certainly not Standard English. Wright, *EDG*, § 100, shows that OE *ŭ* becomes [ɪ] or [e] (especially before a nasal) in Scotland, Antrim, Somerset, and Devon. So § 173 in *but, dust, hussy, us,* and §§ 218-19 in French words in the same dialects, with the addition of Northern English dialects (*bushel*), Berkshire (*brush*), and Wiltshire (*touch*). This modern dialectal evidence shows that the change is Northern and South-western, and does not occur elsewhere. Widespread [ɪ] and [e] in *just* and *cover* are to be differently explained (see § 83); so perhaps the South Oxfordshire [e] in *judge*. There is (with one exception) no evidence of this change in StE. Many cases cited by Luick from the orthoepists, and all the PresE cases cited, show ME variation between *ĕ* and *ŭ* (§ 74) or between *ĭ* and *ŭ* (§§ 81-85). Comparisons by seventeenth- and eighteenth-century orthoepists (chiefly foreign) of ME *ŭ* with French *u* or German *ü* are probably attempts to find equivalents for the unrounded English vowel developed in the seventeenth century, and are not to be taken literally as showing the intermediate value [y] assumed by Luick.

The one case in which this pronunciation is recorded for London English is in Gil, who gives *biccherz* 'butcher's' as one of the pronunciations of the *Mopsæ*. He compares it with the 'Eastern' *kiver* 'cover', but the obvious resemblance disguises a difference of origin; *kiver* has ME *ĭ* < OF [ø], but *butcher* can have in OF only [u], whence ME *ŭ*; the pronunciation with [ɪ] must develop from ME *ŭ* and must have entered vulgar London speech from either the Northern or the South-western dialects, of which the former alternative is the more probable.

Note: Daniel, a native of Somerset (see § 97, Note 1), rhymes *touch* with *rich*; [ɪ] < ME *ŭ* in *touch* would be closely comparable to *biccherz* 'butcher's'. Wright, Index, records [tɪtʃ] 'touch' for Somerset, Wiltshire, and Devon.

LOWERING OF ME *ŭ* IN ME DIALECTS

§ 97. Lowering of ME *ŭ* to *ŏ* is parallel to that of ME *ĭ* to *ĕ*, which is shown by spellings from the late thirteenth century (see § 80 above), and itself also belongs to the thirteenth century. The existence of this lowering to *ŏ* in ME has, it seems, escaped recognition, for the reason that ME spelling cannot show it (*o* being a frequent graphic representation of [ʊ]); but it is clearly shown by ModE evidence and by associated changes, is exactly parallel to the known lowering of *ĭ* to *ĕ*, and like the latter is due to a dialectal exaggeration of the normal lowering from OE tense short [u] (or [i]) to ME lax [ʊ] (or [ɪ]). There is some suggestion in the ModE evidence that *ŏ* < *ŭ*, like *ĕ* < *ĭ*, was especially common in Northern and South-western dialects.

The existence, and the dating, of the lowering of *ŭ* to *ŏ* are made clear by the consequential changes, which are as follows. (i) Before *l* ME *ŭ* became *ŏ* and so developed to normal late ME *ou* in *shoulder*, &c. (see § 174 below); similarly before [χ] ME *ŭ* became *ŏ* and so developed to rare late ME [ɔuχ] in *through* and *drought* (see § 175). (ii) Sometimes ME *ŭ* seems to have developed to ME *ŏ* early enough to share the change of ME *ŏ* itself to identity with ME *ă* (see (2) below). (iii) In consequence of (ii), ME *ŭ* before [χ] could become ME *ă*, whence late ME [auχ] in *drought* (see Note 5 below).

The varying results, in different classes of words, will be explained if we assume that the sequence of the sound-changes involved is this. (*a*) Before [χ] there tends to develop a [u] glide which gives rise to the ME diphthongs *au*, *ou*, &c. and to *ūgh* [uːχ] < OE *ŭh* [uχ] in *drought*. This glide develops by the early thirteenth century in some dialects, but is not fully generalized until after 1300 (cf. Jordan, § 121). (*b*) During the thirteenth century there proceed the two changes (both of them dialectal) *ŭ* > *ŏ* and *ŏ* > *ă*; sometimes the former is apparently earlier in date and its results are affected by the latter, so that finally ME *ŭ* > late ME *ă*. (*c*) About 1400 there develops a [u] glide before *l*, giving the diphthongs *au*, *ou*, &c. and *ūl* [uːl] < earlier *ŭl* [ʊl]. As the changes described under (*b*) are earlier than this diphthongization before *l*, its results always build on theirs; thus if ME *ŭ* > *ŏ*, the final result is [ɔul], as in *shoulder*. But as (*a*) normally precedes the changes under (*b*), its results are normally not dependent on theirs—in particular if OE *ŭh* in *drought* has already become *ūgh* [uːχ] the vowel is not further affected; but apparently in some dialects the glide [u] before [χ] developed late and after the changes under (*b*), so that in these dialects the sequence was *ŭh* > *ŏh* > *ough* [ɔuχ] (as occasionally in the seventeenth century and in present-day dialects in *drought* and *through*) and even sometimes *ŭh* > *ŏh* > *ăh* > *augh* [auχ] (whence rare [ɒː] in *drought*). It is the particular merit of this hypothesis that it enables us to explain why in *drought* late ME *ū* is normal and late ME *ou* is abnormal, whereas in *shoulder*, &c., late ME *ū* is dialectal and rarer and late ME *ou* gives the normal StE pronunciation.

(1) *Identification with ME ŏ*

The identification of ME *ŭ* with ME *ŏ* is shown by the rhymes of the Northerners Levins (see Vol. I, p. 23) and Poole (Vol. I, p. 432); it is also shown apparently by the Midlander Tonkis (when the conventional spelling has *o*; see Vol. I, p. 314) and by Brown, probably a Northerner (Vol. I, p. 370). Bullokar, a native of Sussex, may show it by his rhyming of the word *must* (see Vol. I, p. 110), and more doubtfully by one or two transcriptions (admittedly influenced by the conventional orthography) in which he gives *ŏ* (so *wort*, and *coney* with *ŏ* once beside *ŭ* once); cf. also his *ŏ* in *stomach* (§ 91 above). Butler gives *ŏ* in *covetous* (first syllable), but the transcription may be imperfect. Coles, in his *Schoolmaster*, certainly shows *ŏ* in *tongues* (where Brown also has it), and 'homophone' list pairings of -*ŭng* with -*ŏng* may sometimes depend on lowering of *ŭ* > *ŏ* (see § 92). The *ŏ*-forms recorded in certain words adopted from French may in part be due to lowering (see § 91, Note); the ModE development of 'spelling-pronunciations' in such words as those discussed in §§ 91 and 94 (note especially the *ŏ* recorded by *WSC* as the vulgar pronunciation of *wont*) may have been strongly aided by the existence of *ŏ* by lowering of ME *ŭ* (especially in view of the observable tendency in the orthoepists, e.g. Tonkis, Coles, and perhaps also Gil in *sovereign*, to record the lowered pronunciation in words in which the conventional spelling suggests it). For other possible or probable instances of the lowering see § 90, Notes 1 and 2, and see also Notes 1–4 below.

(2) *Identification with ME ă*

The identification of ME *ŭ* with ME *ă* was rare and dialectal, and except before [χ] (see Note 5 below) not certainly evidenced (but see Notes 6 and 7). No orthoepist shows it clearly, though one of Bullokar's rhymes may depend on it (see Vol. I, p. 110). Coles in his *Eng.–Lat. Dict.* pairs *muster* with *master*, but probably because the latter had a vulgar form *muster* (recorded by *OED* for the sixteenth century).

Note 1: Rhymes of ME *ŭ* with ME *ŏ* are not uncommon in sixteenth- and seventeenth-century poets; they are a special feature of Daniel's rhyming, who has, for example, *top* : *up*, *born* : *return*, *sorrows* : *furrows*, *records* vb. : *words* (but the latter may have *ŏ*), *scorn* : *mourn* (probably an *ŏ* : *ŭ* rhyme), *forced* : *worst* (cf. § 90, Note 2), &c. Daniel seems to have been a native of Somerset; it is believed that he was born near Taunton, and he farmed at Beckington in Somerset and was there buried. He shows the parallel lowering of ME *ĭ* to *ĕ*, and also the South-western change of *ŭ* > [ɪ] (see § 96, Note).

Shakespeare rhymes *sun* with *gone* (*Venus and Adonis*, l. 188) and has a number of (ambiguous) rhymes of *tongue(s)* with words in ME -*ŏng* (see Viëtor, *Shakespeare's Pronunciation*, §§ 555–6).

Note 2: Wright, § 101, shows [ɒ] for ME *ŭ* in various words in scattered dialects (including Northern and South-western dialects); it is especially common in *tongue*, in which also it seems to have been most common in the seventeenth century (cf. § 92 above).

Note 3: Certain orthoepists make use of a dialectal word *mother* 'puella' for the sake of contrast with *mother* 'mater'; Mulcaster (a Northerner) gives ME *ŏ* for the former and ME *ŭ* for the latter. Butler puts the two words together in his list of 'words like and unlike', spelling the former *moðð̆er* and the latter *moð̆er*; presumably they are unlike. Wharton follows by putting them together in his 'homophone' list; the 'puella' word is spelt *modder* and is said to be a Norfolk word (cf. *OED*). Gil's statement that *mother* is pronounced

§ 97] PART 1: THE SHORT VOWELS 593

'*moðer* vel *muðer*' may be due to his confusing the two; elsewhere he gives *muðer* 'mater' thrice.

The etymology of the dialect word is dubious (see *OED*, s.v. *mauther*), but all the early forms show ME *ŏ*, as do the orthoepists; spellings with *au* or *or* are late and intended to show [ɒ:] by lengthening of ME *ŏ*. In the circumstances the suggestion that the dialect word is the ordinary word *mother* used in a different sense (thus 'female parent' passing into 'female' and so 'female child', probably jocularly to begin with) seems to me not improbable; it would then have ME *ŏ* by lowering of ME *ŭ*, a process which, as we have seen, is recorded for some of the areas in which the dialect word is chiefly current (E. Anglia and adjoining counties, Gloucestershire, Herts., and Sheffield). There has evidently been early differentiation of the pronunciation in accordance with the meaning (the dialectal pronunciation with *ŏ* by lowering being assigned to the dialectal sense), but the evidence of Gil, Butler, and Wharton may show that this differentiation was in the seventeenth century still imperfect.

Note 4: In the modern dialect of Essex the place-name *Notley* (OE *Hnutlea*) is pronounced [nɒ:tli] (see Reaney, *Place-names of Essex*, s.n.); this shows lengthening (presumably not later than the seventeenth century) of eModE *ŏ*, which at so early a date is unlikely to be a spelling-pronunciation and must arise by ME lowering of OE *ŭ*.

Note 5: The development of OE *ŭh* to late ME *augh* [auχ], in consequence of the change of ME *ŭ* to *ă*, is shown by Brown's 'phonetic spelling' *drawt* 'drought'; Wright, Index, records [drɒ:t] 'drought' for South-east Kent and Wiltshire.

Note 6: As is pointed out in § 93, Note 2, spellings with *a* for ME *ŭ* must depend on identity of ME *ă* with ME *ŭ*. But few of the spellings cited by Zachrisson, *Eng. Vowels*, p. 81, and Wyld, *Coll. Eng.*, p. 233, are genuine. The form *warsse* 'worse' represents ME *wĕrse* not *wŭrse*. The spelling *apon* 'upon', which occurs as early as Richard Rolle and is used by Cheke, must depend on lack of stress and reduction of both unstressed ME *ă* and unstressed ME *ŭ* to [ə]. Zachrisson, *Bullokar*, pp. 125–30, admits that in certain supposed fifteenth-century cases the manuscripts have *o*, not *a*, and concludes that there are no established fifteenth-century instances (see, however, Kihlbom, pp. 185–6, who, with doubts whether they are 'correctly rendered', refers to certain spellings of William Cely's, of which he says (p. 181) that *camyth* 'cometh' is certain). Zachrisson, loc. cit., claims two certain cases in the *Diary* (1550–3) of Machyn, a tailor resident in London who was probably of Northern (Yorkshire) origin (see Axel Wijk, *The Orthography and Pronunciation of Henry Machyn*). One of these spellings, the regular *Chamley* 'Chomley' (recorded thirteen times), is rightly explained by Wijk (p. 157) as representing a ME variant in *ă*; he refers to EPN Society, vol. ix, p. 377. Wijk (p. 162) agrees that the manuscript has 'an apparently very distinct *a*' in *Saper Lane* (once, beside *Soper Lane* once) and in *Samersett* (once, beside *Somersett* thirty-eight times); the facsimile of the latter given by Zachrisson makes Wijk's 'apparently' seem unnecessarily cautious. Wijk nevertheless thinks that these two *a*-spellings are errors for *o*, but it does not seem likely that they should be, and it is unnecessary to assume that they are.

Reaney, *The Place-names of Essex*, records the forms *Ramford* 1466 'Romford' (PresE [rʌmfəd] < OE *rūm+ford*), *Westharrock* 1568 'West Thurrock' (OE *þurruc*), *Ragwold* 1777, 1805 'Rugwood' (OE *rug* 'rye'), *Bramley* 1494 'Bromley' (late OE *Brumlea*; but OE *brōm* 'broom' may well also have given eME *ŏ* > *ă*), and *Staremere* 1260 'Sturmer' (OE *Stūrmere*). This place-name material from Essex connects well with that cited by Kihlbom from William Cely (whose connexions were with London and Essex).

Note 7: Shakespeare's rhyme *shudder : adder* (*V. & A.*, l. 880) must show identity of *ŭ* and *ă* if it is exact; if it is imperfect, as feminine rhymes often are, it has no value as evidence and cannot be cited to prove that *ŭ*, by becoming [ʌ], had approximated to *ă*. The spelling *shadyr* in *Ludus Coventriæ*, doubtfully cited by *OED* as a form of *shudder*, is better explained as one of *shatter* in the sense 'scatter' (Kökeritz in *Moderna Språk*, xliii (1949), 159; *Sh. Pron.*, p. 241).

Part 2: THE LONG VOWELS

THE DEVELOPMENT OF ME ā

(1) *General Outline*

§ 98. ME ā is usually assumed to have been the back vowel [ɑː], but wrongly; for in ModE it develops like the ME long front vowels ẹ̄ and ę̄ (which are raised towards the front of the mouth) and not like the ME long back vowels ǭ and ọ̄ (which are raised towards the back). It seems therefore certain that ME ā must have been a front vowel, namely front [aː]; and it is a further argument in favour of this view that ME ă, from which in native words it develops, descends in most native words from OE ǣ, which was certainly a front vowel.

The subsequent history in eModE of ME ā makes it certain that in StE its fronting began earlier than that of ME ă; indeed, it must have begun in the fifteenth century, though little satisfactory evidence has yet been produced to prove that it did (see § 100, Note). During the sixteenth and seventeenth centuries we find in StE three pronunciations of ME ā, representing three successive stages of the fronting: [æː], open [ɛː], and close [eː]. Of these, [æː] seems to have been the normal pronunciation in careful speech before 1650, and [ɛː] after 1650; but [ɛː] had existed already in the sixteenth century in less careful forms of StE, while [æː] still occurred after 1650. The third pronunciation, close [eː], existed in StE from the beginning of the seventeenth century, but was rare before 1650 and was still not accepted in good speech in the second half of the seventeenth century; it became normal in StE early in the eighteenth century. The existence side by side of these different StE pronunciations, and especially of the two pronunciations [æː] and [ɛː] (to which corresponded the two pronunciations [ɛː] and [eː] for ME ẹ̄), leads to some confusion in our evidence; some orthoepists record developments which depend on the more advanced pronunciations who normally seem to have used the more conservative ones.

It is important to observe that the development of ME ā in StE was much slower than in Northern and Eastern dialectal speech. In the North ME ā had perhaps already been fronted as far as [ɛː] before 1400, for by this date we find evidence that Northern ME ā had become identical with the monophthong developed from ME *ai*. In the sixteenth century Smith still records [ɛː] as the Northern pronunciation of ME ā, but by this time Northern English already showed the development to the final stage [eː] (see under (3) below). In the Eastern dialects ME ā had become identical with [ɛː] from ME *ai* in the fifteenth century, and spellings show that it had already reached the further stage [eː] during the course of the same century (see under (3) below).

(2) *The Pronunciations* [æː] *and* [εː]

§ 99. The evidence of the sixteenth- and seventeenth-century orthoepists on the pronunciation of ME ā is of two sorts: direct evidence consisting of statements concerning the articulation of ME ā or its relation to ME ă or to foreign sounds, and indirect evidence deduced from developments which depend on the fronting of ME ā. In some ways the indirect evidence is the more revealing, though it is chiefly here that we meet with signs of a certain inconsistency of pronunciation, or at least of recording pronunciation, in some orthoepists; and we shall consider it first.

(a) *Indirect evidence*

§ 100. There are three changes associated with the fronting of ME ā which have to be considered:

(i) When ME ā was fronted to open [εː], it overtook ME ẹ̄ before *r*, in which position ME ẹ̄ was never fronted (see §§ 203–4); evidence of the identity of ME ār and ME ẹ̄r is therefore indirect evidence that ME ā has reached the value [εː], while evidence of a distinction between ME ār and ME ẹ̄r is evidence that ME ā has not reached [εː], i.e. that it is still [æː]. After 1650 the identity of ME ār and ME ẹ̄r is normal, and it follows that [εː] for ME ā is normal; but Wallis, Price (in his text; but not in his 'homophone' list, which reflects the more advanced pronunciation), and the *Treatise of Stops* (1680) still do not distinguish ME ẹ̄ before *r* from ME ẹ̄ in free position, and accordingly must still have [εː] for ME ẹ̄ in all positions and [æː] for ME ā. Before 1650 it is normal to distinguish ME ār from ME ẹ̄r, and it follows that ME ā is normally [æː]. We may notice that Robinson makes this distinction, which depends on the preservation of [æː] for ME ā, though he gives other evidence which depends on [εː] for ME ā; either ME ẹ̄ has been fronted in spite of the influence of the following *r* (see § 204), or there is inconsistency. Bullokar, Daines, and Hodges are also inconsistent, for they normally distinguish between ME ār and ẹ̄r, and thus give evidence of [æː] for ME ā, but in special circumstances give evidence of the identity of ME ār and ẹ̄r, which depends on fronting of ME ā to [εː] (see § 204). Hodges shows the identity of ME ār and ME ẹ̄r chiefly in his 'near alike' list in *SH-PD*, which depends on a less careful pronunciation than that on which the transcriptions of *EP* are normally based.

(ii) When ME *ai* was monophthongized to open [εː], it was identified with ME ẹ̄ by those persons who used [εː] for ME ẹ̄, and with ME ā by those persons who used [εː] for ME ā (see §§ 225, 227–9 below). Thereafter it shared the fronting of ME ẹ̄ or of ME ā as the case might be. Evidence of the identification of ME ā with this monophthong [εː] developed from ME *ai* is therefore evidence that ME ā had passed beyond the stage [æ:] in the speech of persons who make the identification. It may be either [ɛ:] or [e:]; in the case of most of the seventeenth-century orthoepists who identify ME *ā* with ME *ai* the latter possibility is ruled out by the fact that they still distinguish ME *ā* from ME *ẹ̄* in free position, as they would not do if they used [e:] for ME *ā* (see under (3) below, and §§ 106 seq.). The earliest StE orthoepist who shows the identity of [ɛ:] < ME *ai* with ME *ā* is Robinson; he gives such frequent evidence of the identity that we must assume that [ɛ:] is his normal pronunciation of ME *ā* (contrast his evidence on ME *ār* and *ẹ̄r*; see under (i) above). Gil (see Vol. I, p. 151) probably shows the identity of ME *ā* with ME *ai* by two isolated transcriptions: *āerj* 1619 and *aerj* 1621 'airy' and *rāzing* 1621 'raising' against *raizing* 1619. These two transcriptions depend on a pronunciation [ɛ:] for ME *ā* which is wholly inconsistent with Gil's other evidence (see below); we must assume that although he normally used [æ:] for ME *ā* and [ɛ:] for ME *ẹ̄*, he makes use on these two occasions of transcriptions based on a pronunciation which he condemns, and which our evidence shows was really less correct at his time than his normal pronunciation. The other orthoepists who show the identity of ME *ā* with ME *ai* before 1650 are Daines; the 'homophone' lists of Butler (whose list would appear to represent a less conservative pronunciation than his own) and Hodges (in his 'near alike' list only, which is based on less careful pronunciation than *EP* and the 'alike' list); and the shorthand-writers T. Shelton 1620, Dix 1633, and Rich 1646 (whose abbreviations make use of most careless pronunciations). This evidence shows that ME *ā* was [ɛ:] before 1650, but not normally in good speech. After 1650 the identity of ME *ā* with ME *ai* is shown by Wallis in his representation of popular pronunciation (but not in his own speech), Merriott, Strong, Richardson, Lodwick, Cooper, Aickin, *WSC-RS* (who may have had [e:] for ME *ā*), Cocker, and Brown, in shorthand-writers from Farthing 1654 onwards, and in 'homophone' lists from Wharton 1654 onwards (but some of these lists show identity of ME *ā* and ME *ẹ̄*, and therefore [e:] for ME *ā*). It is evident that [ɛ:] for ME *ā* was normal after 1650 in StE. In Northern English, identity of ME *ā* with ME *ai* is found already before 1400, and if the process of monophthongization was the same as in StE (see § 229, Note 1) it would follow that ME *ā* had already become [ɛ:]; but another explanation is possible. Smith records the identity of ME *ā* with ME *ai* as a feature of Northern and Scottish English; it is shown by the Northerners Levins, Mulcaster, Hume, and Poole (of whom Levins and Hume show the further fronting of ME *ā* and the monophthong from ME *ai* to close [e:]; see under (3) below). In the 'Eastern dialects' identity of ME *ā* with ME *ai* is found in the fifteenth century, and in the North-west Midlands perhaps by 1425 (see § 229, Note 1).

(iii) The fronting of ME *ā* proceeded for a time step by step with that of ME *ẹ̄*: while ME *ā* was [æ:], ME *ẹ̄* was [ɛ:]; but when ME *ā* became [ɛ:],

ME $\bar{e}$ became [e:]. Conversely it follows that orthoepists who have [ɛ:] for ME $\bar{e}$ must have [æ:] for ME $\bar{a}$, and that orthoepists who have [e:] for ME $\bar{e}$ may have, and probably will have, [ɛ:] for ME $\bar{a}$ (but Smith and Holder appear to be exceptions; see below). Evidence independent of that here adduced on the development of ME $\bar{a}$ shows that ME $\bar{e}$ was certainly or probably still pronounced as open [ɛ:] by Cheke, Hart, Gil, Butler, Wallis, Price, and Wilkins, all of whom therefore must be assumed to have pronounced ME $\bar{a}$ as [æ:]. But ME $\bar{e}$ was [e:] in the speech of Bullokar (at least sometimes), Florio, Tonkis (who was a Midlander), Robinson, Gataker, *The English Schoolmaster* (1646), and normally after 1650; the same pronunciation is recorded by the shorthand-writers from Folkingham (1618) onwards and by the 'homophone' lists from Hodges ('alike') onwards—sources which usually rely on less careful pronunciation. It may be remarked that Hodges's 'alike' list for once differs from *EP* in recording the identity of ME eu with ME iu (on the basis of which we can assume that ME $\bar{e}$ was [e:]); here again there is a certain inconsistency in the evidence, for normally *EP* depends on a pronunciation in which ME $\bar{e}$ was still [ɛ:]. It follows that ME $\bar{a}$ could have been [ɛ:] in the speech represented before 1600 by Florio, between 1600 and 1650 by Tonkis, Robinson, Gataker, *The English Schoolmaster*, the shorthand-writers, and Hodges's 'alike' list (but not by his *EP* as a rule; see under (i) above), and after 1650 in the speech of most orthoepists (but not Wallis, Price, and Wilkins).

Note: Wyld, *Coll. Eng.*, pp. 194–5, cites rhymes of ME $\bar{a}r$ words with *were*, *there*, and *where* to prove that in the fifteenth and early sixteenth centuries ME $\bar{a}r$ was identical with ME $\bar{e}r$, and consequently that ME $\bar{a}$ had been fronted in StE in the fifteenth century and possibly earlier. But these rhymes depend on the ME variants *ware* (an unstressed development of ON *várum*), *thare*, and *whare* (see *OED* and cf. § 105). The rhyme *square* : *bere* 'bear' vb. (fifteenth century) cited by Dibelius, *Anglia*, xxiii (1901), 188 depends on the variant *bare* (see § 204, Note 3). Spellings cited by Dibelius, loc. cit.; Zachrisson, *Eng. Vowels*, pp. 64–66; Wyld, *Coll. Eng.*, pp. 195, 248; and Kihlbom, p. 132, show that ME $\bar{a}$ was identified with the monophthong [e:] developed from ME ai in the fifteenth and sixteenth centuries, but refer mostly to the 'Eastern dialect' (Paston Letters, Cely Papers), in which ME $\bar{a}$ was fronted early and rapidly. One or two, however, may represent StE and show rare [ɛ:] for ME $\bar{a}$ in StE in the fifteenth century. Jordan, § 284, regards early identity between ME ai and ME $\bar{a}$ as characteristic of the 'East Midlands' (more precisely, his evidence refers to Essex, Norfolk, and Lincolnshire); he erroneously believes that the result of monophthongization of ME ai was [æ:] and that ME $\bar{a}$ was consequently [æ:] in the 'East Midlands' (cf. his § 276).

(b) Direct Evidence

§ 101. The direct evidence of the fronting of ME $\bar{a}$ to [æ:] and [ɛ:] is as follows.

(i) Certain orthoepists identify ME $\bar{a}$ as the long equivalent of ME $\breve{a}$. This identification is most significant in the phoneticians Wallis, Wilkins, and Holder, who make one description of articulation cover both ME $\bar{a}$ and ME $\breve{a}$. It is somewhat less significant in the spelling reformers Smith, Hart,

Bullokar, Waad, Gil, and Hodges; it is often forgotten (though it is an obvious point) that these men realized that their reformed systems of spelling would have more chance of acceptance if they kept as close as possible to the unreformed spelling, and that they therefore were prepared to make concessions to ordinary views of the relations between the vowels. Robinson, who recognized the qualitative difference between ME *ā* and ME *ă*, nevertheless in his phonetic script used the same symbol for ME *ā* and ME *ă*, merely reversing it (in accordance with his general practice) to indicate the long vowel; and Robinson did not intend his script for ordinary use. Thus the mere use of the same symbol for ME *ā* as for ME *ă* is not in itself very significant, especially in Bullokar and Hodges, whose method is merely to add diacritics to the ordinary spelling. But the fact remains that all these men do describe ME *ā* as differing only in quantity from ME *ă*. The statement clearly involves some inaccuracy; it would only be true if the conservative pronunciation [æ:] of ME *ā* were compared with the advanced pronunciation [æ] of ME *ă*. But it would be impossible for any orthoepist with a reasonable knowledge of phonetics (which all these men except Bullokar possessed) to identify ME *ā* as the long equivalent of ME *ă* after it had become [ɛ:] unless, like Robinson, he had a theory that the long vowel was always more forward in the mouth than its short equivalent. The identification of ME *ā* as the long equivalent of ME *ă* therefore points to the conclusion that all these orthoepists normally pronounced ME *ā* as [æ:]. This conclusion is supported by the indirect evidence cited under (*a*) above, though with the qualification that Bullokar, Gil, and Hodges very occasionally and inconsistently give evidence of pronunciations which depend on [ɛ:] and not [æ:] for ME *ā* (see under (*a*) (i) and (ii) above). On the other hand there are orthoepists who distinguish between the quality of ME *ā* and ME *ă*; these are Robinson, Butler, Newton, Lodwick, and Cooper. The distinction in itself does not necessarily mean that they did not use [æ:] for ME *ā*, since it may only depend on more accurate observation; but it is shown by indirect evidence in the case of Robinson, and by indirect and direct evidence in the cases of Newton, Cooper, and Lodwick, that these four had [ɛ:] for ME *ā*. There is, however, no evidence to prove that Butler had [ɛ:] for ME *ā*; his 'homophone' list indirectly shows this pronunciation (see under (*a*) (ii) above), but differs from his text.

(ii) No distinction is made between ME *ā* and foreign [ɑ(:)] by the *Welsh Hymn*, Palsgrave, Salesbury, apparently Smith, and T. Jones (who as late as 1688 identifies ME *ā* with Welsh *a*). The identification is inaccurate, but on grounds of general probability one would suppose that none of these orthoepists can have pronounced ME *ā* as [ɛ:], for it would have then been comparable with foreign *e* (e.g. French *ę*) rather than *a*. But Robinson, whose evidence in general shows that he used [ɛ:] for ME *ā*, nevertheless identifies Spanish *a*, except in *quatro*, with ME *ā*. Robinson must have relied for this identification (as for his distinction between ME *ār* and ME *ẹ̄r*; see under (*a*) (i) above) on the pronunciation [æ:] for ME *ā*; but it is evident that he is treating Spanish pronunciation as if the words were being adopted into English and using what seem to him the nearest native equivalents in the given phonetic context. Gil similarly has ME *ā* for Spanish [ɑ:] in *bravada* (first adopted in the form *bravado* in 1583; but Gil has the Spanish form, cited explicitly as such in a discussion of the adoption of foreign words), though he treats German [ɑ:] differently (see below). Robinson's evidence, which is not self-consistent, perhaps shows a faulty knowledge of Spanish pronunciation; but the other orthoepists who identify ME *ā* with foreign [ɑ:] all had reason to know the real pronunciation of the foreign languages in question, and we may assume that their identifications mean that they used [æ:] and not [ɛ:]. Palsgrave adds to his evidence an important qualification; French *a* is like English *a* (ME *ā*) 'where the best englysshe is spoken'. We may take it that he knew a less correct pronunciation of ME *ā* which invalidated his identification, and that this pronunciation was [ɛ:]. On the other hand there are orthoepists who distinguish between ME *ā* and foreign [ɑ(:)]; this distinction of course does not necessarily mean that the authors who make it did not use [æ:] for ME *ā*, for even if they did there would still be a sufficient difference between the English and the foreign pronunciation of 'long *a*'. Lily in his Latin grammar says that the English pronounce the *a* in Latin *aliquis* and *alius* too slenderly, as if the words were *eliquis* and *elius*; as this remark refers to the English use of ME *ā* for Latin *a* in an open syllable (see § 93), it appears to show [ɛ:] for ME *ā*. Lily's transcription is a rough one and may exaggerate the degree of the 'slenderness' of the English vowel. Hart (who sometimes does not distinguish ME *ā* from foreign [ɑ(:)], and who is shown by other evidence to have used [æ:] for ME *ā*) says that *a* in some German words is 'broader' than the English sound. Tonkis says that ME *ā* is 'exilius' than French *a*. Gil identifies German *aa* in *maal* and *haar* not with ME *ā* (as Wyld, *Coll. Eng.*, 3rd edition, Appendix I, mistakenly supposes) but with the monophthong developed from ME *au*. Wodroephe says that ME *ā* is less open than French *a*. Sherwood identifies English *a* in *all* (i.e. the monophthong developed from ME *au*) with French *a*, and ME *ẹ̄* with 'French *é* masculine'; ME *ā* he says is pronounced *ae*, which probably means [æ:], for if he had used open [ɛ:] he could have indicated it more clearly by identifying it with French *ę* (but see § 114, Note 1 (*b*)). Jonson follows Tonkis (or an unidentified common original). Daines implies that ME *ā* is less broad than foreign *a*. Hexham's identification of ME *ā* with 'Dutch *ea*' certainly refers to a pronunciation [ɛ:] (see Vol. I, pp. 383–4). Coles in his *Syncrisis* says that ME *ā* is too 'narrow' to be used for Latin *a*. The *Welsh Breviary* identifies ME *ā* with Welsh *e*; the pronunciation indicated is probably open [ɛ:] (see Vol. I, p. 345). Cooper compares ME *ā* with French *ę* (see

Vol. I, p. 286, note 2). Richardson's evidence, like Hexham's, shows a pronunciation [ɛ:] (see Vol. I, pp. 383-4). This evidence for the most part shows merely that ME *ā* has been fronted, without revealing its exact quality; but Sherwood may be attempting to represent [æ:], and [ɛ:] is shown possibly by Lily early in the sixteenth century and certainly by Hexham, the *Welsh Breviary*, Cooper, and Richardson.

(iii) Descriptions of articulation are given by certain orthoepists. They are often simply of 'the vowel *a*', and cover both ME *ā* and ME *ă*; but in such cases the description is normally based on the long vowel, which gives the vowel-letter its name. Smith says that *a* 'labiis diductis aperto profertur ore'—a description which suits [æ:] rather than [ɛ:]. Hart (see Vol. I, p. 73) says that *a* is pronounced with the tongue taken clean away from the teeth or gums and the mouth open wide; since Hart is a good observer, this is clear evidence against [ɛ:] and for [æ:]. Robinson's evidence (see Vol. I, pp. 207-8) merely shows that ME *ā* is further forward than ME *ă*, and less far forward than ME *ĕ*. Either [æ:] or [ɛ:] would suit the conditions; a part of Robinson's evidence seems to depend on [æ:] for ME *ā* (see under (*a*) (i) and (*b*) (i) above), but some of it certainly shows [ɛ:] (see under (*a*) (ii) above). As he had tense [e:] for ME *ẹ̄*, it is probable that his normal pronunciation of ME *ā* was [ɛ:]. Wallis's description of the articulation of the English *a* shows that ME *ā* was a front vowel, with the middle of the tongue a little raised (see Vol. I, p. 226); [æ:] is more likely than [ɛ:], for which the raising of the tongue is considerable, and Wallis's other evidence shows that he must himself have used [æ:]. Newton gives ME *ā* as the long equivalent of ME *ĕ*. Wilkins (Vol. I, p. 254) says that the vowel *a* (i.e. ME *ā* as well as ME *ă*) is pronounced, not with the tongue 'convex' (as it is for the vowels *e* and *i*), but merely 'less concave [than for the back vowels] or plain'; he must have used [æ:] (for which the tongue is raised towards the front, but not very far, so that his inaccuracy is not great), and not [ɛ:], for which the tongue is definitely 'convex'. Holder (Vol. I, p. 264) describes the vowel *a* as a front vowel; that it was [æ:] appears from a special feature of his evidence (see under (iv) below). Lodwick (Vol. I, pp. 276-7) does not give ME *ā* as the long equivalent of ME *ă*; this position is filled by the vowel of *demand*. He says that ME *ĕ* is a short vowel with no long equivalent, and that ME *ā* and ME *ẹ̄* are long vowels with no short equivalent. ME *ẹ̄* must therefore be closer than ME *ĕ*, i.e. close [e:]; ME *ā* must be more open—a condition satisfied by both [æ:] and [ɛ:], of which the latter is much the more likely, in view of the close resemblance between Lodwick's pronunciation and Cooper's. Cooper (Vol. I, p. 286) makes ME *ā* the long equivalent of ME *ĕ*, and from this fact and his descriptions of the articulation of the front vowels it is clear that he used [ɛ:] for ME *ā*—that is, when he did not use the dialectal pronunciation [ɛə] discussed in Vol. I, pp. 307-8. Aickin follows Cooper's vowel-system.

(iv) Special factors enable us to determine the value of ME $\bar{a}$ in the speech of certain orthoepists. Smith, in discussing MSc $\bar{a}$, appears to show that its pronunciation was intermediate between ME $\bar{a}$ and ME $\bar{ę}$ (see Vol. I, p. 58); this would appear to show that MSc $\bar{a}$ was open [ɛ:], which would be intermediate between [æ:] for ME $\bar{a}$ and [e:] for ME $\bar{ę}$. Smith's other evidence suggests that he used [æ:] for ME $\bar{a}$; but he also uses $\bar{a}$ to transcribe Northern [ɛ:], and must therefore have known [ɛ:] beside [æ:] for ME $\bar{a}$. Gil's transcriptions of and comments on the pronunciation of the 'Eastern dialect' and the speech of the *Mopsæ* show that he must have used [æ:] for ME $\bar{a}$ (see Vol. I, pp. 145–7); the *Mopsæ*, however, used [ɛ:] (and even [e:]; see under (3) below). This evidence is in general consistent with the rest of Gil's evidence; but two transcriptions of ME *ai* as $\bar{a}$ (see § 100) inconsistently depend on the pronunciation [ɛ:] for ME $\bar{a}$ which he condemns in the *Mopsæ*. Similarly Gil, like Smith, uses $\bar{a}$ to transcribe Northern [ɛ:] < ME *ai* (see Vol. I, p. 151); and he is misled by the normal spelling *creance* of the hawking-term into giving [krɛ:nz] as the pronunciation of the *cranes* variant, which has late ME $\bar{a}$ < ME *au* before *n* (see § 104, Note 2). Holder (Vol. I, p. 264) gives evidence closely similar to Smith's, saying that between the vowels *a* and *e* there is a gap which allows room for a hypothetical vowel *æ*; this would appear to mean that he used [æ:] for ME $\bar{a}$ and [e:] for ME $\bar{ę}$, and that the hypothetical 'long *æ*' would be [ɛ:]. Holder's other evidence suggests that he had [æ:] for ME $\bar{a}$ (see under (i) above). But this evidence of Smith's and Holder's on the gap between ME $\bar{a}$ and ME $\bar{ę}$ presents difficulties; see § 114 (iii) below.

Note 1: Zachrisson, *Eng. Vowels*, pp. 120–1, brings forward evidence from foreign orthoepists which shows [ɛ:] for ME $\bar{a}$ as early as 1528, and commonly from the beginning of the seventeenth century (cf. Lily's evidence from the early sixteenth century). The same evidence is cited by Horn, § 90; Luick, § 493, Anm. 1 (who adds evidence of [æ:] for ME $\bar{a}$ from an anonymous Dutch grammar of 1568); and Ekwall, § 29.

Note 2: Luick, § 493, Anm. 2, points out that as late as the sixteenth century ME $\bar{a}$ is used to replace foreign *a* in words adopted from foreign languages; this would hardly have been possible if ME $\bar{a}$ had been generally [ɛ:].

Note 3: Some scholars, interpreting too literally the orthoepists' identification of ME $\bar{a}$ as the long equivalent of ME $\breve{a}$ or their failure to distinguish ME $\bar{a}$ from foreign *a*, believe that in the sixteenth century there was a conservative pronunciation in use in which fronting of ME $\bar{a}$ had not begun earlier than that of ME $\breve{a}$ (cf. Ekwall, § 29), or in which ME $\bar{a}$ was still [ɑ:] (cf. Luick, § 493, Anm. 3; Luick himself comes near this view in Anm. 1). These theories are highly improbable; our other evidence shows that there is some inaccuracy in this evidence of the orthoepists, though it is slight and venial. Ekwall, § 29, and Luick, § 493, Anm. 1 (*b*), suggest that there may have been a palatal [a:] for ME $\bar{a}$ in the sixteenth century—an assumption which would fit admirably some of the orthoepistical evidence, but which seems in general improbable. Ekwall, § 29, would take Cooper's evidence that ME $\bar{a}$ is the long equivalent of ME $\breve{e}$ as showing a 'half-open [e:]' midway between [ɛ:] and [e:]; but this is to interpret Cooper's evidence too literally (especially in view of the fact that he identifies, for example, [ʊ] as the short equivalent of [o:]). Luick, § 493, Anm. 1 (*b*), suggests that this identification means [ɛ:] (as it should be taken) 'or perhaps [e:]'; but in authors who like Cooper had [e:] for ME $\bar{ę}$ and kept ME $\bar{ę}$ distinct from ME $\bar{a}$, it is not possible for ME $\bar{a}$ to be [e:]. (Luick misinterprets Cooper's evidence on ME $\bar{e}$, following J. D. Jones's suggestion that Cooper shows lax [ɪː] for ME $\bar{e}$.) Luick, § 493, is in doubt whether Cooper's [ɛə] for ME $\bar{a}$ is a dialectalism personal to himself or a StE pronunciation; but it is certainly the former. Horn, § 90, would explain the occurrence side by side in eModE of the two pronunciations [æː] and [ɛː] as due to the influence of different dialects, the former being due to Midland and the latter to Eastern and Southern influence. There is no need for this hypothesis; the two pronunciations represent two stages in the StE development; we have to do with 'class' rather than 'regional' dialect.

(3) *The Pronunciation* [eː]

§ 102. The only direct orthoepistical evidence, before 1700, of [eː] for ME $\bar{a}$ in StE is Gil's, when he says that the *Mopsæ* pronounce *capon* not only as *kēpn* (i.e. with [ɛː], equivalent to Gil's pronunciation of ME $\bar{e}$), but also 'almost *kīpn*'; this transcription is as near a representation of [keːpn] as he can manage, for the sound [eː] did not exist in the speech which his alphabet was designed to represent, and therefore was not provided with a symbol (see Vol. I, p. 145). Indirect evidence is provided by evidence of the identity of ME $\bar{a}$ with ME $\bar{e}$, for this did not come about until ME $\bar{a}$ had reached the value [eː], where it overtook ME $\bar{e}$. For detailed evidence of this identity see § 115 below. It is shown in the fifteenth century for the 'Eastern dialect', in the sixteenth century for Northern English, for StE by rhymes after 1600 and spellings after 1630, and by the orthoepists in some 'homophone' lists after Wharton's (1654). But it is recorded by no sixteenth- or seventeenth-century orthoepist in the text of his work, and it is evident that the 'homophone' list pairings are based on a less correct pronunciation than that of the compilers of the lists. Until 1700, then, [eː] for ME $\bar{a}$ seems to have been confined to vulgar, or at least careless, speech; after 1700 rhymes show it to have been in more general use. PresE [ei] develops from it about 1800.

Note 1: When ME $\bar{a}$ in free position became close [eː] it became distinct from ME $\bar{a}$ before *r*, which was never fronted beyond open [ɛː]. No sixteenth- or seventeenth-century orthoepist remarks on this distinction, evidently because, in the pronunciation which they describe, ME $\bar{a}$ in free position had not yet been fronted beyond open [ɛː]. But it may be observed that in the eighteenth century there was equally no distinction drawn between [eː] < ME $\bar{a}$ in free position and [ɛː] < ME $\bar{a}$ before *r*, the two sounds being regarded as contextual variants of one phoneme, 'long *a*'.

Note 2: Luick, § 493, Anm. 1 (*a*), says that [eː] for ME $\bar{a}$ is shown by Miège 1685 and by a Welsh source of 1670. The latter is the *Welsh Breviary*, and its evidence should rather be interpreted as meaning [ɛː]; see Vol. I, p. 345. Miège 1685, according to Luick, identifies ME $\bar{a}$ with 'French *é*'; but 'French *é*' in the seventeenth century covered both French *ę* and French *ẹ* (see § 114, Note 1). Miège's *English Grammar*, 2nd edition, 1691, says that English '*a* long' is pronounced like '*e* open' or the diphthong *ai*; this clearly means [ɛː] and not [eː].

Note 3: Ekwall, § 29, takes rhymes of ME $\bar{a}$ with ME $\bar{e}$ and spellings with *a* for ME $\bar{e}$ and *e* for ME $\bar{a}$ as showing [æː] for ME $\bar{a}$—why, it is difficult to see, unless these spellings and rhymes are to be regarded as approximate, for ME $\bar{e}$ was never [æː]. Luick, § 493, Anm. 2, refers to them only as showing that ME $\bar{a}$ has been fronted; he does not regard them as showing identity (see § 499, Anm. 1, end).

Note 4: LG *greven* is adopted into English in the early seventeenth century as *graves*

(1631 onwards; see *OED*, s.v. *greaves, graves*); it is evident therefore that by 1631 ME *ā* was [e:], at any rate in the probably vulgar speech in which this fisherman's term is likely to have first become current.

Note 5: Gil, and possibly Smith, give evidence of [ɛə] in Northern speech (see Vol. I, pp. 146–7), and this seems to presuppose an earlier [e:] from which it develops. Cooper gives [ɛə] as his normal pronunciation of ME *ā*, but this is a dialectalism and not StE. One would expect that, in the dialect which affected Cooper, ME *ẹ̄* (when not represented by [i:] from a ME variant *ẹ̄*) would also be [ɛə], but Cooper keeps the two sounds distinct; his [ɛə] < ME *ā* is dialectal, but his [e:] for ME *ẹ̄* is apparently due to StE influence (it being the current StE pronunciation).

Special Words with ME ā

§ 103. The interjection *ah* seems for some time to have been pronounced with ME *ā*; thus Bullokar and Robinson transcribe it simply as *ā*. But Hart and Bullokar show the *a*'s of *ahha* to be short. Lengthening of this short *ă* would explain the modern pronunciation, evidently used by Hexham (see Vol. I, pp. 380–1). *Jaques* is identified with *jakes* in the 'homophone' lists of Hodges and Strong. On possible ME *ā* in *Thames* see § 72 Note. On ME *ā* beside ME *ai* in *pair* see Vol. I, p. 176; Hodges shows ME *ā* both in *EP* and in *SH-PD*, equating *pair* with *pare* in the 'homophone' list of the latter; Ellis follows Hodges.

ME *ā* DEVELOPED FROM, AND VARYING WITH, ME *au*

§ 104. In certain words ME *au* develops in some forms of speech to ME *ā* in late ME; these words fall into various classes, as set out below. But ME *au* survives, sometimes as a more common variant, beside ME *ā*.

(1) The most important class is words which have ME *au* before *n*. (*a*) Before *n* followed by [dʒ], *change* has *au* in Hart (seven times, beside *ă* and *ā*), Bullokar, Daines, and Willis, and *ā* in Levins, Hart (once), Robinson (beside *ă*), and Hodges. *Grange* has *au* in Bullokar and Willis, and *ā* in Levins and Cooper. *Range* has *au* in Laneham and *ā* in Levins and Robinson. *Strange* has *au* in Laneham, Bullokar (beside *ă*), Daines, and Willis, and *ā* in Levins, Robinson, and Cooper. *Danger* has *au* in Bullokar and Daines, and *ā* in Robinson and Hodges. *Manger* has *ā* in Cooper; *RS* gives [a:] < ME *au*, but see Note 1 below. *Stranger* has *au* in Bullokar but *ā* in Robinson, Hodges, and Cooper; *RS* gives [a:] < ME *au*. *Angel* has *ā* in Robinson (beside *ă*) and Hodges. *Mangy* has *ā* in Cooper; *RS* gives [a:] < ME *au*. (*b*) Before [n] followed by [tʃ] late ME *ā* < *au* is recorded in *staunch* by Levins. (*c*) The word *ancient* has *au* in Hart, Bullokar, and Daines, but *ā* in Hodges and either *ā* or *ă* in Tonkis and Jonson. It will be observed that sixteenth-century orthoepists (with the exception of Levins, who is probably influenced by his Northern dialect) generally record ME *au*; but ME *ā* becomes more common than ME *au* in the seventeenth century. It is apparent that a pronunciation of another (lower-class) dialect is making its way into StE (see Note 2 below).

(2) Other cases show ME *ā* developed from ME *au* when the latter is not followed by *n*. (*a*) *Gauge* has ME *ā* in Cocker. (*b*) Before *m*, PresE has [ei] < ME *ā* in *chamber*; I have not observed this pronunciation in the orthoepists, who give ME *au* (Bullokar and Hodges) or ME *ă* (Hart, Bullokar, and Gil). *Flame* regularly has *ā* (so Bullokar). *Lamp* has *ā* in Cheke (see Vol. I, p. 45). *Balm* (OF *bame* > ME *baume*) has *au* in, for example, Bullokar (who apparently pronounces the *l*), Jonson, and Wharton, but *ā* in Price (see Vol. I, pp. 342–3) and Coles (see Vol. I, p. 442). On *salmon* see § 62 above. *Almond* (for which OF should have forms without *l*, in which case the *au* would immediately precede *m*) has *ā* in Coles, Strong, Young, and Cocker, who give the 'phonetic' spelling *a-mun*. Price and Coles give *ā* in *calm*, which is similar to *almond*. ME *au* also develops to *ā* in English words in which *l* becomes silent before *m* in late ME (a development which at that date was restricted to vulgar forms of speech); for the sequence of the sound-changes, see the note below. *Haulm* (< OE **halm*) has *ā*, and no *l*, in Bullokar. *Psalm* (late ME *psaulm*) has *ā* in Coles, Hawkins (see Vol. I, p. 416), Cocker (see Vol. I, p. 366), and Brown (beside *au*). *Alms* (late ME **aulms*) has *ā* in Coles, and is put with *aims* in the 'homophone' lists of Price, Hawkins, and Cocker. *Palm*, *qualm*, and *shalm* 'shawm' have *ā* in Coles. All orthoepists except those mentioned give ME *au* for these words; the pronunciation with ME *ā* was evidently vulgar (or dialectal), and could not develop in educated Standard English, in which the *l* was still pronounced until late in the sixteenth century. (*c*) ME *au* is regularly shown to have become late ME *ā* in *safe* < *sauf* and *save* < *sauve*, and in their derivatives. Similarly ME *Rauf* 'Ralph' > *Rafe*, a form recorded by Hart, Bullokar, Hodges, Willis, Wallis, Poole, Price, Coles, Strong, Cocker, and Brown. In *half* ME *ā* is recorded by Coote (who describes it as 'the barbarous speech of your country people'), Poole, Price, Coles, and Cocker; this development accounts for the PresE pronunciation of *halfpenny*, which is 'phonetically' spelt *hafpenny* by Strong but *ha-penny* by Young. *Calf* has ME *ā* < *au* in Poole, Price, Coles, and Cocker. *Salve* (OE *sealf*) is shown to have ME *ā* by Butler, Price, and Cocker and is equated with *save* (which must mean that both words have ME *ā*) by Fox and Hookes. *Laugh* has ME *ā* < *au* in Cocker (Vol. I, p. 366) and Brown (Vol. I, p. 418); cf. unshortened [oː] < ME *ou* in *cough* and *trough* in Coles.

(3) Three final cases are quite foreign to present StE, and were evidently always vulgar. (*a*) Before *k* late ME *ā* < *au* occurs in *talk*, which Bullokar rhymes with *spoke* (for *spake*), and in *hawk*, which Aickin pairs with *hake* in his 'homophone' list. (*b*) Before *l* (retained), late ME *ā* is shown by Hart's *ā* in *false*, Bullokar's rhymes of *all* and *small* with *frail* and *fail*, by Poole's rhyme of *balls*, *calls*, &c. with *ails* and *bails*, and by 'homophone list' pairings (only in careless lists), thus *aul* 'awl?': *ale*, *tall* : *tale*, *hall* : *hale* : *hail*

(Butler), *all : awl : ale, tall : tale* (Wharton), *ball : bale : Baal* (*Comp. Sch. M.*), *awl : ale : ail* (MS list of *c.* 1700). (*c*) In final position late ME *ā* is shown in *law* by Merriott's condemnation of *la* as a 'gross fault of spelling' and by Cocker's 'phonetic' spelling *layer* 'lawyer'; similar spellings in shorthand-books can hardly be adduced as evidence, in view of the common rule that the second letter of a digraph might automatically be omitted, but Ridpath's marking of the omission of *u* from *au* (*adience* 'audience') as an Anglicism implies that he knew an English pronunciation which justified the practice. See further Note 4 below.

It appears, in the light of all the evidence cited above, that we have to do here with a late ME change of *au* to *ā* which could occur in any position, but which did in fact occur much more frequently before certain consonants (above all before [ndʒ]) than in other positions. It was evidently a change characteristic of vulgar, even dialectal speech; Gil (see Note 2 below) gives evidence of its occurrence not only in the speech of the *Mopsæ*, but also in his 'Eastern dialect', and Coote, a Suffolk schoolmaster, describes *ā* in *half* as the 'barbarous speech of your country people'. But it is also shown by Bullokar, who was a native of Sussex, with his *ā* in the unexpected words **awn* 'own' (cf. Gil's evidence on *lawn*), *haulm, talk, all,* and *small*. Except in such words as have [ei] < ME *ā* in PresE the evidence comes only from sources which reflect vulgar pronunciation, chiefly the 'homophone' and 'phonetically spelt' lists; the one notable exception is Coles, who was a most careful observer (especially in his *Schoolmaster*, in which occurs the rhyming list which gives evidence of ME *ā* in *chant*, &c., *half*, &c., *alms*, *qualm*, and *shalm*), but who seems certainly to have been influenced by vulgar or dialectal speech. From such speech the form with ME *ā* has made its way into StE in those words in which it most frequently developed; in some it had already been accepted during the sixteenth century, in others it was accepted in the seventeenth.

Note 1: RS follows Cooper's list of examples, but gives a different pronunciation from Cooper's for *stranger, manger,* and *mangy*. This pronunciation is theoretically possible; but it may be that instead of making a conscious and intelligent alteration, on which we can rely, he has merely made a mistake in an uncomprehending imitation of Cooper, and did not really use [aː] in the three words in question. Daines lays down a general rule that *a* is pronounced 'full and broad' (i.e. with the sound descended from ME *au*) before *n* followed by a *g* pronounced as *j*; his examples (as indicated above) are *danger, change,* and *strange*.

Note 2: In vulgar and dialectal speech the development of ME *au* to *ā* before *n* was more common than PresE pronunciation would suggest. Bullokar (who records vulgar pronunciation, especially in his rhymes) has *own* (for **awn*) rhyming with *pain* (see Vol. I, p. 111). Cocker in his 'homophone' list equates *pawn* with *pane*, &c. (see Vol. I, p. 417). Gil records [ɛə] < ME *ā* in *dance* in his account of the 'Eastern dialect' (see Vol. I, pp. 147–8) and [ɛː] < ME *ā* in *lawn* as a pronunciation of the '*Mopsæ*', whose speech he compares with the 'Eastern dialect'. The hawking-term *creance* (a line attached to a hawk's leash) has a form *cranes*, recorded by *OED* from Florio, 1598, onwards, which seems to develop from ME *creaunce* (< OF *creance*) (i) by syncope of the originally pretonic *e*, and (ii) by the change of ME *au* > *ā* before *n*; Gil says that the word (which he regards as a plural without a singular; cf. *OED*) is pronounced *krēnz* [krɛːnz] or *kreanz* [krɛənz], of which the former certainly represents the *cranes* form. Coles shows a more general use of late ME *ā* < *au* before *nt* in *chant, grant, plant, aunt, daunt, haunt, taunt,* and *vaunt* (see Vol. I, p. 442); this must reflect Midland pronunciation, since he tells us that he was born in 'the very heart of England' and educated in 'her very eye' (Oxford) before coming to live in 'her very head' (London). Wright, *EDG*, § 202, shows [ɛə] or [e:] in *dance, chance, aunt,* and *chant* in scattered dialects (including Midland dialects, but not Eastern).

Note 3: Butler says that ME *au* in *change, strange, angel,* and *danger* is Northern; but it is shown by orthoepists who are not Northerners, and Levins has *ā*. Butler himself used the (chiefly Western) dialectal pronunciation with ME *ai* < ME *ă*; see § 63.

Note 4: With the pronunciations recorded in paragraph (3) compare Spenser's rhymes of *call* and *all* with *tale* and of *baude* 'bawd' with *roade* 'road', i.e. with the Northern form *rade* (cf. Bauermeister, *Zur Sprache Spensers auf Grund der Reime in der F.Q.*, §§ 83, 180). Dryden rhymes *ball* with *ale* in *MacFlecknoe*.

Note 5: In the native words cited above, ME *au* is shown by all orthoepists who record the words except those specified as showing *ā*. In Coles ME *ā* in all cases varied with some other pronunciation; see Vol. I, p. 442, note 4.

Note 6: In the native words (and in *almond* and *calm* if they do not go back to OF forms without *l*), the development of *au* to *ā* is clearly later than the loss of the *l* or the change of [χ] to [f], since the frequency with which it occurs is greater in words in which *l* is lost or [χ] becomes [f]. The sequence of the sound-changes is therefore as follows: (*a*) ME *ă* becomes *au* before *l* or [χ]; (*b*) loss of [l], change of [χ] to [f]; (*c*) *au* becomes *ā*; (*d*) fronting of ME *ā* (including the new *ā*). The whole sequence must occur within a comparatively short period (*c*. 1375–1425 in southern English, rather earlier in the North). Trevisa already has *straange* (Jordan, § 224 (III)). But in words from OF the development may be earlier; it certainly is in such as have *au* before a labial (e.g. *safe, save, flame*), where the change of *au* > *ā* is dated *c*. 1300 by Jordan (§ 240). In native words the process, though analogous, is not simultaneous.

Note 7: In the *Cely Papers*, I am informed by Miss A. H. Forester, there is a group of spellings with *a* for ME *au*, some at least of which (e.g. *akys* 'hawks', *faturs* 'fautors', *clase* 'clause', *Ajust* 'August') seem to me to be closely analogous to the evidence cited under (3) above and therefore probably to show late ME *ā* < ME *au*.

Note 8: Jordan, § 292, simplifies and falsifies the development by assuming that (e.g.) ME *ălf* became either *āf* directly by loss of *l* and compensatory lengthening ('Ersatzdehnung'—a most dubious process) or else *auf*. He cites fifteenth-century spellings showing the change. Analogous changes are *fŏlk* > **foulk* > **fouk* > *fǭk* (*Cursor Mundi*, MS Cot., 12054), *scŭlk* > **scūlk* > *scūk*.

Note 9: The explanation given above means that forms like *save* 'salve', *cafe* 'calf', and *same* 'psalm' are not evidence of the development of ME [au] to the precursor of PresE [ɑ:] in these and other words (as wrongly taken by Luick, § 521, Anm. 1).

VARIATION BETWEEN ME *ā* AND ME *ę̄*

§ 105. Smith records ME *ā* beside ME *ę̄* in *there*; the variation is due to that in OE between *þăra* (weak form of *þāra*) and *þǣr* (cf. § 100, Note). On ME *ā* in *swear* (Cheke) and *tear* (Smith) see § 204, Note 1.

THE DEVELOPMENT OF ME *ę̄*

(1) *General Discussion*

§ 106. We have seen that ME *ā* began to be fronted before 1500, and developed comparatively slowly but uninterruptedly through the stages [æ:] and [ɛ:] to [e:], the last of which had not yet been accepted in careful speech before 1700, though it had already become common in less careful speech. Before 1500, as we shall see, ME ẹ̄ had already become [i:] and remained fixed in that value. In the narrowing gap between ME ā and ME ẹ̄ was ME ę̄. At first it seems to have remained in its ME value of open [ɛ:], but when (in some forms of StE in the sixteenth century, and in more careful speech about 1650) ME ā reached this value, ME ę̄ had moved on to close [e:], thus for the time escaping identification with ME ā (see under (2) below). But ME ā continued to advance towards close [e:], and one of two things could then happen to ME ę̄: it could retain its value of close [e:] and thus become identical with ME ā, or it could assume the value [i:] and become identical with ME ẹ̄.

That the former of these developments did in fact occur is shown by seventeenth-century and still more commonly by early eighteenth-century evidence (see under (3) below); identity between ME ā and ME ę̄ was in the seventeenth century found in the more 'advanced' speech in which ME ā had become close [e:], and in the early eighteenth century it was accepted in careful speech. Identity between ME ā and ME ę̄ is recorded still earlier in Northern speech and in the Eastern dialects (see § 115, Note 1), in consequence of the rapid rate at which the fronting of ME ā proceeded in those dialects. On the other hand in PresE ME ę̄ appears to have developed to [i:] and to identity with ME ẹ̄ in the great majority of words, and a similar situation occurs already in *WSC-RS* at the end of the seventeenth century, and perhaps in certain other seventeenth-century sources (see under (4) below). This apparent development of ME ę̄ to [i:] is shown still earlier by Northern orthoepists.

The usual theory of the development of ME ę̄ is that after passing through the stages [ɛ:] and [e:] it developed by a phonetic change from [e:] to tense [i:], where of course it would become identical with ME ẹ̄. This theory seems the natural one in view of the PresE pronunciation. Support for it has been found in the view of J. D. Jones, set forth in his edition of Cooper's *Grammatica*, pp. 23*–36*, that in Cooper's speech (and his contemporaries') ME ę̄ had the value of lax [ɪ:], and was therefore clearly in process of development from tense [e:] to tense [i:]. This view depends on a literal interpretation of Cooper's statement that ME ę̄ was the long equivalent of ME ĭ; but this statement is erroneous and is due to an attempt to make the English vowel-system more symmetrical than it in fact was in Cooper's time, and there can be no doubt that Cooper's pronunciation of ME ę̄ was tense [e:] (see Vol. I, pp. 290–1, and § 114 below). Newton's similar evidence is due to the same causes (Vol. I, pp. 248–9). There is no other evidence of a pronunciation with lax [ɪ:] intermediate between [e:] and [i:]. It might further be argued that the development of ME ęu, which certainly proceeds from [ɛu] through [eu] to [iu], shows that ME ę̄ equally proceeded by phonetic development from [ɛ:] through [e:] to [i:]; but the parallel will not stand examination, and it is clear that after ME ęu had reached the stage [eu] the change to [iu] was due not to the first element changing in accordance with a change of ME ẹ̄ to [i:], but to the second element exerting a raising influence on the first element (see §§ 243–4 below). ME ęu becomes [iu], in fact, not because ME ẹ̄ becomes [i:], but because it becomes [e:] (cf. § 113 (iv)).

§ 107. The theory that ME ẹ̄ became [i:] as a result of a gradual phonetic change in StE itself was elaborated before Wyld, *Coll. Eng.*, pp. 209 seq., had shown that ME ā and ME ẹ̄ became identical. (Wyld believes that this identity came about at the stage open [ɛ:], and not close [e:], as stated above; that he is wrong on this point is shown by the evidence of such late seventeenth-century orthoepists as Cooper and Lodwick, who have close [e:] for ME ẹ̄ but open [ɛ:] for ME ā.) Now it is manifestly impossible that in a single dialect ME ẹ̄ should both remain at the stage [e:] to be overtaken by ME ā, and go on to the stage [i:], as the ordinary theory assumes it did; in other words, the identity of ME ā and ME ẹ̄ is incompatible with the ordinary theory that ME ẹ̄ passed by a phonetic change from [e:] to [i:]. The ordinary theory might be upheld if we were to assume that the pronunciation which made ME ā identical with ME ẹ̄ was not native to StE, but was imported from dialects which did not show the change of ME ẹ̄ from [e:] to [i:]; but this assumption is made improbable by the fact that rhymes and spellings which tend to show identity of ME ā and ME ẹ̄ appear earlier than any valid evidence that StE used the pronunciation [i:] generally in words containing ME ẹ̄. Luick, who is prepared to see in the PresE pronunciation of *great*, &c. the influence of the south-western dialects (see under (3) below), nevertheless is apparently unwilling to extend this explanation to cover the sixteenth- and seventeenth-century rhymes between ME ẹ̄ and ME ā. The most systematic of Modern English phonologists, he appears to realize that the identity of ME ẹ̄ and ME ā is incompatible with the theory, which he accepts (§ 499), that ME ẹ̄ became [i:] in StE by a phonetic change; and eludes the difficulty by assuming that the rhymes cited by Wyld are inexact rhymes of open [ɛ:] with close [e:]. But there is no warrant for the assumption that poets would use inexact rhymes of this sort; and in any case the evidence for the identity of ME ā and ME ẹ̄ is not rhymes alone (see under (3) below). Zachrisson, *Bullokar*, p. 40, attempts to resolve the difficulty by assuming that the 'advanced' pronunciation of ME ā became identical with the 'conservative' pronunciation of ME ẹ̄, but does not appear to realize that in the case of associated changes like the fronting of ME ā and of ME ẹ̄, it is highly improbable that those who maintained a conservative pronunciation of ME ẹ̄ would accept an advanced pronunciation of ME ā and thus obliterate a distinction which was maintained, on Zachrisson's view, both in fully conservative speech and in 'advanced' speech. It is true that Smith and Holder appear to combine the conservative pronunciation of ME $\bar{a}$ with the advanced pronunciation of ME $\bar{e}$ (see § 114 below); but the effect of this combination is to increase the difference between the two sounds, not to obliterate it.

Thus Wyld's proof that ME $\bar{a}$ and ME $\bar{e}$ were identical in StE at one time makes it very difficult to accept the ordinary theory of the StE development of ME $\bar{e}$. And there are other objections to it. The development after 1400 of the ME front vowels ME $\bar{\imath}$ and $\bar{e}$ is paralleled by that of the back vowels ME $\bar{u}$ and $\bar{o}$: ME $\bar{\imath}$ and ME $\bar{u}$ became diphthongs, ME $\bar{e}$ and ME $\bar{o}$ were raised to the places [i:] and [u:] left vacant by ME $\bar{\imath}$ and ME $\bar{u}$. One would expect that ME $\bar{e}$ and ME $\bar{o}$ would show the same parallelism of development, and it appears that to begin with they do: for after remaining unchanged in their ME values [ɛ:] and 'cardinal open [ɔ:]' for some time they then are raised to the values [e:] and [o:] left vacant by ME $\bar{e}$ and ME $\bar{o}$. The analogy of ME $\bar{o}$, which remains [o:] until, late in the eighteenth century, it is diphthongized to [ou], would lead us to expect that ME $\bar{e}$ would also remain as [e:] until, late in the eighteenth century, it was diphthongized to [ei]. The ordinary theory asks us to believe that the parallelism was not exact, and that ME $\bar{e}$ developed to a stage further than ME $\bar{o}$ did. This is perhaps not a grave weakness (especially as appeal may be made to the influence of a desire to keep ME $\bar{e}$ distinct from ME $\bar{a}$, whose development from [a:] towards [e:] might upset the parallelism between the front and back vowels), but it is undoubtedly a weakness. Finally there is an argument against the ordinary theory which seems decisive. It has hitherto escaped general notice that when ME *ai* was monophthongized to [ɛ:], it did not always become identical with ME $\bar{a}$: many people did not yet use [ɛ:] for ME $\bar{a}$, but used it instead for ME $\bar{e}$; and when such people accepted the monophthongal pronunciation [ɛ:] for ME *ai*, the result was that in their speech ME *ai* became identical with ME $\bar{e}$ (see further §§ 225 seq. below). This situation is shown by Hart, and by many sixteenth-century rhymes between ME *ai* and ME $\bar{e}$. (Wyld and Zachrisson, it may be noted, would explain such rhymes as showing that ME *ai* has become identical with ME $\bar{a}$, which in turn has become identical with ME $\bar{e}$; see § 115, Note 3.) The evidence leaves no doubt that the identity of ME *ai* with ME $\bar{e}$ was a StE development, and on phonetic grounds it is clear that it came about only in forms of StE in which the fronting of ME $\bar{e}$ had not yet begun; if then ME $\bar{e}$ was subsequently fronted in StE by progressive stages to [i:], ME *ai* should equally have been fronted to [i:] in the mode of speech which identified ME *ai* with ME $\bar{e}$. Of such a pronunciation [i:] for ME *ai* in StE there is no trace; Watts's rhyme (1720) of *day* with *bee* can hardly be accepted, in such a rhymer, as exact. Similarly (to modify slightly an argument of Wyld's in *Coll. Eng.*, pp. 211–12), ME $\bar{a}$ became identical with ME $\bar{e}$ (in some forms of speech before the end of the sixteenth century, and in careful StE about 1700) while ME $\bar{e}$ was still [e:] and had therefore not completed the change to [i:] assumed by the normal theory; if therefore ME $\bar{e}$ had changed to [i:] by a phonetic change which occurred in StE, ME $\bar{a}$ should also have become [i:]. This conclusion can only be rebutted by denying that the identity of ME $\bar{a}$ with ME $\bar{e}$ was a StE development; but the nature of the evidence leaves little doubt that it was. Of such a pronunciation [i:] for ME $\bar{a}$ in StE there is no evidence; Wyld is mistaken in his belief that Gil records it in the speech of the *Mopsæ* (see Vol. I, p. 145, note 2). It follows that the phonetic development of ME $\bar{e}$ from [e:] to [i:] was at any rate not a StE development. Another detail which points to this conclusion is the fact that though StE in the sixteenth century knew two developments of ME *ai*, or rather one development which had two results (its identification with ME $\bar{e}$ in conservative speech, and with ME $\bar{a}$ in more advanced speech), PresE knows only one pronunciation of ME *ai*, [ei] developed from eighteenth-century [e:]. This apparent disappearance of one mode of pronunciation (that in which ME *ai* was identified with ME $\bar{e}$) might be explained by assuming that the other mode of pronunciation, in which ME *ai* was identified with ME $\bar{a}$, simply displaced its rival; but actually it seems to be due to the fact that ME $\bar{e}$ in StE became identical with ME $\bar{a}$, so that the pronunciation which identified ME *ai* with ME $\bar{e}$ became the same as that which identified ME *ai* with ME $\bar{a}$.

A final important argument is that if the ordinary theory of a ModE sound-change were true, there should be a period (in StE about 1700, on the ordinary view) when we pass rapidly from sources of evidence which regularly show [e:] for ME $\bar{e}$ in all words to sources which show [i:] in all words. Now it is true that about this date we pass from sources which still recognize ME $\bar{e}$ as a distinct vowel [e:] to sources in which it has lost its identity; but it is not true that there is a sudden displacement of [e:] by [i:]. During the whole of the sixteenth and seventeenth centuries there is evidence of [i:] pronunciations in 'ME $\bar{e}$ words', especially in sources which reflect vulgar seventeenth-century speech; this [i:], it will be argued, represents a ME variant in $\bar{e}$ existing beside the (usually) more normal $\bar{e}$ (for details see §§ 117–27, 'Variation between ME $\bar{e}$ and ME $\bar{e}$'). In general, as the seventeenth century advances, the evidence for [i:] from a ME variant $\bar{e}$ progressively increases, i.e. the [i:] variant is recorded in more and more words (especially in vulgar sources) and there begins to be evidence of it, though very sporadically, in cases in which a ME variant is comparatively ill authenticated. The whole impression is that the mode of pronunciation appropriate to one dialect is gradually being supplanted by that appropriate to another; this is a process which occurs in other cases in ModE (cf. the introduction of late ME $\bar{a}$ in place of ME *au* in *change*, &c.; see § 104 above), and the evidence relating to [i:] and [e:] in 'ME $\bar{e}$

words' is of exactly the type which we find in the other cases in which the pronunciation of one dialect supplants that of another.

§ 108. We thus reach the conclusion (with Wyld, op. cit., pp. 211–12) that the theory that ME $\bar{e}$ in StE itself became [i:] by a gradual phonetic change is false. How then did the pronunciation which apparently identifies ME $\bar{e}$ and ME $\bar{e}$ as [i:] arise? Wyld suggests that StE has adopted a pronunciation developed in some other dialect, in which presumably ME *ai* was not monophthongized to [ɛ:] until after ME $\bar{e}$ had left this value and had gone on to [e:], and in which ME $\bar{a}$ never overtook ME $\bar{e}$ because the latter developed by a phonetic change to [i:] before ME $\bar{a}$ became [e:]. This theory would avoid the difficulties inherent in the ordinary one, and would satisfactorily explain the situation in StE. The difficulty is to find the dialect in which the development occurred which it is necessary to assume. As far as we can judge from the evidence of the modern dialects (cf. Wright, *EDG*, §§ 58, 137), in those dialects most likely to influence StE the normal development of ME $\bar{e}$ is to [e:] and identity with ME $\bar{a}$. In the present dialects [i:] occurs in ME $\bar{e}$ words most commonly in the North, though some such words have [e:]; similarly Northern orthoepists in the sixteenth and seventeenth centuries, though they show [i:] in most ME $\bar{e}$ words, also show signs of the identity of ME $\bar{e}$ with ME $\bar{a}$. The 'Eastern' dialects (i.e. the dialects of Essex, Suffolk, and Norfolk) show early identity of ME $\bar{e}$ and ME $\bar{a}$. It is by the Eastern dialects, especially that of Essex working through its close connexion with Cockney speech, that StE is most likely to be affected; and Gil's evidence on the resemblance of the speech of the *Mopsæ* to that of the Eastern dialects may perhaps be held to show that [i:] instead of [e:] in ME $\bar{e}$ words was a feature of both forms of speech (see Vol. I, p. 149). But it is of no assistance to solve the problem of the development of ME $\bar{e}$ in StE by saying that there is 'dialectal influence', if when we turn to the Eastern and Northern dialects we find the same problem confronting us there—the fact that ME $\bar{e}$ is sometimes identified with ME $\bar{a}$ and sometimes apparently developed to [i:] and identity with ME $\bar{e}$.

The solution of the problem seems paradoxically to be that neither in StE nor in the Eastern and Northern dialects did ME $\bar{e}$ develop to [i:] by a ModE phonetic change from an earlier pronunciation [e:]. The [i:] pronunciation in 'ME $\bar{e}$ words' does not go back to ME $\bar{e}$ at all; it goes back to a late ME $\bar{e}$ variant, commonly developed from ME $\bar{e}$ in ME times, but often older still. In ModE times ME $\bar{e}$ became [i:] as ME $\bar{o}$ became [u:]; ME $\bar{e}$ was fronted from open [ɛ:] to close [e:], and there stopped, as ME $\bar{o}$ was raised from 'cardinal open [ɔ:]' to close [o:], and there stopped; ME $\bar{a}$ was successively fronted from [a:] through [æ:] and open [ɛ:] to close [e:], where it became identical with ME $\bar{e}$. But throughout the ModE period there was a struggle going on between two ways of pronouncing 'ME $\bar{e}$ words'; the ME variant with ME $\bar{e}$, now become ModE [i:], gradually displaced the more normal variant with ME $\bar{e}$ whose development stopped at [e:] and which became identical with ME $\bar{a}$. There was in a sense a change of pronunciation from [e:] to [i:], but it was not a ModE phonetic change; it was simply the displacement of one mode of pronunciation by another which had developed from it before the ModE period began.

This theory assumes that all 'ME $\bar{e}$ words' had a ME variant in ME $\bar{e}$. How is this variation to be explained? In many words it results from differences between the Saxon and Anglian dialects of OE, both of which affect modern StE. In others it is the result of more particular causes—for example, the analogical influence of a verb with OAngl $\bar{e}$ by i-mutation on a noun with OE $\bar{e}a$. But such influences would bring about variation only in a comparatively small number of words. The variation in the great majority of words is due to a much more general cause—a certain instability of OE $\bar{æ}$ and ME $\bar{e}$ themselves (i.e. in both cases, in all probability, of the sound [ɛ:]). In OE, only the Saxon dialects preserve both $\bar{æ}^1$ < WGmc $\bar{a}$ and $\bar{æ}^2$ < WGmc ai with i-mutation. In OK (which does not, however, seem to have influenced StE in this regard) both $\bar{æ}^1$ and $\bar{æ}^2$ became $\bar{e}$. In OAngl $\bar{æ}^1$ became $\bar{e}$, and $\bar{æ}^2$ normally remained as $\bar{æ}$; but in certain circumstances even $\bar{æ}^2$ showed signs of instability in OAngl and developed often to $\bar{e}$ (cf. Bülbring, § 167, Anm., and his article 'OMerc. $\bar{æ} > \bar{e}$ before d, t, s, l, n, r' in *A Miscellany presented to Dr. Furnivall*). In the ME dialects descended from OAngl, ME $\bar{e}$ of whatever origin was still unstable and tended to become $\bar{e}$; the instability was apparently especially well marked in the Northern dialects of ME (cf. Bradley in *Camb. Hist. Eng. Lit.* i. 396), and this explains why sixteenth- and seventeenth-century Northern orthoepists give fuller and much earlier evidence of the pronunciation [i:] in 'ME $\bar{e}$ words' than Southern orthoepists do. The 'Eastern' dialects (especially Essex), from which we have assumed that the [i:] pronunciation in large measure came into StE, also seem to have had a common raising of ME $\bar{e}$ to ME $\bar{e}$ (see Note 2 below). The date of the main period of operation of the ME tendency to raise $\bar{e}$ to $\bar{e}$ must be set, according to dialect, in the thirteenth and early fourteenth centuries, after the lengthening of ME $\breve{e}$ in open syllables, and before (i) the late thirteenth-century texts in which rhymes depending on raised $\bar{e}$ occur (see Note 2 below) and (ii) the commencement of lowering before r, which occurred about 1300 in the North and in the latter part of the fourteenth century in the South.

Note 1: The view that ME $\bar{e}$ tended to be raised to ME $\bar{e}$ is strongly supported by the parallel case of ME $\bar{o}$, which is shown by seventeenth-century evidence and by that of the modern dialects to have been raised to ME $\bar{o}$, ModE [u:] (cf. §§ 148–52). This raising of ME $\bar{o}$ seems to have been common in Northern and Eastern dialects.

Note 2: The tendency of ME $\bar{e}$ to become ME $\bar{e}$ in Northern and Eastern dialects, which must be assumed to enable us to explain the ModE developments (which are themselves the chief evidence of this tendency), has only been observed sporadically. It is possible that a review of the ME evidence might show that this tendency was more common than is generally supposed. Rhymes between 'ME $\bar{e}$ words' and ME $\bar{ę}$ words, when they occur, are apt to be passed over as anomalous and 'inexact'; what is needed is a complete collection of such rhymes. The tendency of ME $\bar{ę}$ < OE $\bar{æ}^2$ < WGmc $ai+i$ to become ME $\bar{ẹ}$ before dentals in the East Midlands and the North is well established (cf. Jordan, § 48, Anm. 2; Luick, § 361, Anm. 2). ME $\bar{ę}$ in final position frequently rhymes with ME $\bar{ẹ}$ (cf. Luick, loc. cit.); such rhymes are commonly regarded as inexact (as by Luick), but though they may be granted to be due largely to the difficulty of finding 'true $\bar{ę}$ rhymes', it seems more likely that the poets are making use of a comparatively rare $\bar{ẹ}$ variant than that they are rhyming together two sounds which are really quite dissimilar in their acoustic effect and were distinct phonemes. Bradley, as cited above, remarks on the frequency of rhymes between 'ME $\bar{ę}$' and ME $\bar{ẹ}$ in Northern texts, and suggests that the difference between the sounds was less in the North than in the South; it is more probable that in the North ME $\bar{ẹ}$ variants of the 'ME $\bar{ę}$ words' were particularly common. Of special interest are two articles by Miss Barbara Mackenzie, 'A Special Dialectal Development of OE $\bar{e}a$ in ME', *Englische Studien*, lxi (1927), 386–92, and Miss Erna Fischer, 'Ae. $\bar{e}a$ im südostmittelenglischen und die Heimat des südlichen "Octovian" ', *Englische Studien*, lxiv (1929), 1–19. Miss Mackenzie maintained that rhymes from Essex and Suffolk texts from the late thirteenth century (*Alisaunder* group) to the late fifteenth century (Hawes) show that OE $\bar{e}a$ becomes $\bar{ẹ}$ in these dialects. Miss Fischer, in a well-reasoned article, had no difficulty in disposing of this suggestion; she showed that in the South-eastern texts in question ME $\bar{ę}$ of all origins (and not merely OE $\bar{e}a$) rhymes with ME $\bar{ẹ}$. Most cases are of ME $\bar{ę}$ before dentals (including *r*), and show raising of ME $\bar{ę}$ to $\bar{ẹ}$. Miss Fischer points out that before *s* the raising is not found in these texts; cf. the ModE evidence cited in § 123 below, which shows the raising less commonly before *s*. There are also rhymes between ME $\bar{ę}$ and ME $\bar{ẹ}$ in final position. Other rhymes cited depend on analogical pronunciations (see § 120, Note). But both in texts dating from *c*. 1300 and in fifteenth-century texts (Lydgate and *Palladius*) there are rhymes of ME $\bar{ę}$ and ME $\bar{ẹ}$ before consonants other than dentals. Miss Fischer would regard all the rhymes except those before dentals as inexact or analogical. To this almost traditional explanation of inconvenient ME rhymes I can only reply that I do not believe that ME poets, writing at a time when poetry was recited aloud and not read silently, would have used 'inexact' or 'analogical' rhymes. A survey of ME rhyming technique as a whole which would allow us to judge this issue has not yet been produced. In sixteenth- and early seventeenth-century poetry there are exceedingly few instances of poets giving up the attempt to rhyme truly, but numberless cases of rhymes which are justified, not by the common pronunciations of sixteenth- and seventeenth-century StE, but by comparatively rare variant pronunciations (sometimes vulgar pronunciations) which are proved to have existed by other evidence. It seems probable that we should find, if we had equally detailed evidence of the various modes of pronunciation current in ME, that what we are now inclined to dismiss as 'inexact' or 'analogical' rhymes are in fact justified by variant pronunciations. Our prejudice ought to be in favour of accepting the rhymes as true, even if this involves our formulating exceptions or additions to the laws of phonology which describe the normal development of ME.

Note 3: A somewhat similar view to the above was put forward by Kökeritz, *The Phonology of the Suffolk Dialect*. In this dialect, according to Kökeritz, the sound [e:] occurs for ME $\bar{a}$ and *ai* and for ME $\bar{ę}$ (the situation I assume as the normal result of ModE developments), but also for ME $\bar{ẹ}$; on the other hand the sound [i:] is used for ME $\bar{ẹ}$, for ME $\bar{ę}$, for ME *ai*, and (rarely) for ME $\bar{a}$. Kökeritz well argues that this strange situation cannot be the result of ModE phonetic changes, and would set the beginnings of the process in ME. His view is that in ME in the Suffolk dialect the native $\bar{ę}$ for OE $\bar{æ}^1$ < WGmc $\bar{a}$ was displaced by $\bar{ẹ}$ from the Anglian area, and the native $\bar{ę}$ < OE $\bar{æ}^2$ < WGmc $ai+i$ was displaced by $\bar{ẹ}$ from the Kentish area; that this invasion of alien pronunciations caused a general tendency for $\bar{ę}$ of whatever origin to be displaced by $\bar{ẹ}$, and that in the result $\bar{ę}$ more or less disappeared (he is rather vague as to the extent of the disappearance) from the late ME dialect of Suffolk. Hence in eModE the Suffolk dialect had only [i:] for both 'ME $\bar{ę}$' and ME $\bar{ẹ}$ (the sound being in fact always derived from ME $\bar{ẹ}$). But StE in eModE used a distinct pronunciation for ME $\bar{ę}$, and the attempt to adopt this StE pronunciation without realization that it should be restricted to a part only of the words for which the Suffolk dialect used [i:] caused a free alternation in the dialect between [i:] and [e:] for both ME $\bar{e}$ and ME $\bar{ę}$ (Kökeritz, op. cit., §§ 30, 49, 258–68).

S. Karlström, in a review of Kökeritz's book in *Studia Neophilologica*, v (1932–3), 128–48 (see especially pp. 138–43), accepts the view that the explanation of the dialect's pronunciation of ME $\bar{e}$ and $\bar{ę}$ must be sought in ME, but himself proposes to explain the facts by assuming that owing to the conflict between Saxon $\bar{ę}$ and Anglian $\bar{e}$ for OE $\bar{æ}^1$ < WGmc $\bar{a}$, and between unraised $\bar{ę}$ and raised $\bar{e}$ for OE $\bar{æ}^2$ < WGmc $ai+i$ before dentals, there arose in the dialect a fluctuation between ME $\bar{e}$ and ME $\bar{ę}$ which first spread to the other classes of 'ME $\bar{ę}$ words' (i.e. those with OE $\bar{e}a$ or early ME $\check{e}$) and then apparently (in the dialect) to ME $\bar{e}$; he would extend this explanation to StE to account for its [i:] for ME $\bar{ę}$.

These two explanations have in common that they explain a general fluctuation between ME $\bar{e}$ and $\bar{ę}$ as an analogical extension of a fluctuation appropriate only to special classes of ME $\bar{ę}$ words. But such explanations are unsuitable for Northern English, in which there occurs at an early date the same puzzling situation as in StE; for in the North we cannot look to fluctuation between Saxon $\bar{ę}$ and Anglian $\bar{e}$ for OE $\bar{æ}^1$ < WGmc $\bar{a}$, and are left only with Karlström's variation between $\bar{ę}$ and $\bar{e}$ for OE $\bar{æ}^2$ < WGmc $ai+i$ before dentals. Kökeritz and Karlström both accept it as significant, and as an argument in favour of their explanation from analogy, that [e:] does not occur in the Suffolk dialect in words (e.g. *meece* 'mice') which have ME $\bar{e}$ < OE $\bar{y}$; these, unlike other ME $\bar{e}$ words, have only [i:], according to Kökeritz. But there can have been nothing to distinguish them from other ME $\bar{e}$ words at any date after about 900.

While agreeing that we must seek an explanation in the ME period and that the dialect shows an analogical extention of a fluctuation in pronunciation, I should explain the original fluctuation differently from either Kökeritz or Karlström: namely, by the development within the dialect itself of a variant in ME $\bar{e}$ for ME $\bar{ę}$ of all origins (including ME $\bar{ę}$ < OF, which Kökeritz and Karlström neglect) by the tendency to raising discussed above. Thence the variation would spread first to ME $\bar{ę}$ words, and later (probably in ModE times, after ME $\bar{a}$ and ai had become [e:] and so identical with one of the variant pronunciations used in 'ME $\bar{ę}$' and 'ME $\bar{e}$' words) to ME $\bar{a}$ and ME ai words in rare instances. It may be doubted, despite Kökeritz, whether [i:] is significantly commoner in the dialect for ME ai than for ME $\bar{a}$; for the supposed ME ai words which he cites (§ 49) have all a ME variant in $\bar{ę}$, either because they are French (*chain, grain, rein*) or for special reasons (*drain*, on which see § 115, Note 9, and *key*, which has [i:], ultimately from ME $\bar{e}$, in StE itself).

Kökeritz's final statement of his view, as it applies to StE, is in his *Shakespeare's Pronunciation*, pp. 194 ff., where he abandons the theory of a variation between ME $\bar{ę}$ and $\bar{e}$ produced by a clash of dialectal types (except in the case of OE $\bar{æ}^1$) and assumes a general raising of ME $\bar{ę}$ of all origins to $\bar{e}$ (with the qualification, in the case of ME $\check{e}$ in open syllables, that it may have been lengthened directly to $\bar{e}$—an improbable hypothesis). This explanation, in its essentials, anticipated my own, except that I do not think that the ME raising of $\bar{ę}$ to $\bar{e}$ can have been confined to the South-east.

§ 109. The struggle of the raised ME $\bar{e}$ to replace the normal ME $\bar{ę}$ was in StE a long-drawn-out process. Chaucer has already rhymes which show ME $\bar{e}$ in 'ME $\bar{ę}$ words' in final position (ten Brink, *Language and Metre of Chaucer*, § 23 (*d*); cf. Wild, *Die sprachlichen Eigentümlichkeiten der wichtigeren Chaucer-Handschriften*, § 21), before dentals (ten Brink, op. cit., § 25 (2)), and before *v* (*evere, nevere, greve* 'grove' with OE $\bar{æ}^2$, *leve* 'leave' sb. and *bileve* 'belief'; cf. ten Brink, § 25 and Note, who suggests that the last two words may be influenced by the analogy of the related verbs). It seems to me improbable that these are inexact rhymes, as is often assumed (as by Miss Fischer, op. cit.); so cultivated a poet is not likely to have held on occasion that a rhyme between the markedly different sounds [ɛ:] and [e:], which were distinct elements in meaning (*mẹten* 'measure' with [ɛː], *mẹten* 'meet' with [eː]), was near enough. I would rather hold that these rhymes show Chaucer making occasional use of ME ẹ̄ variants in 'ME ę̄ words'— variants which had already begun to come into the language of London from that of Essex, where the *Alisaunder* group shows them to have been not uncommon a hundred years earlier. But up to and during the sixteenth century the old pronunciation with the normal ME ę̄ on the whole maintained its position. (For details, see under 'Variation between ME ę̄ and ME ẹ̄' below.) About the beginning of the seventeenth century the pressure, from the vulgar forms of London English and from the related Eastern dialects, to substitute the raised ME ę̄ variant for the normal ME ę̄ seems to have become stronger; Gil shows consciousness of this pressure in 1619, and in the 'homophone' lists from 1640 onwards we are given much evidence of the currency of the raised vowel in vulgar speech, though the authors of the spelling-books in which these lists appear still teach (in the text of their works, as against the lists) a distinct pronunciation for ME ę̄. But in *WSC-RS* at the end of the century we see the complete victory of [iː] < raised ME ę̄; it has ousted [eː] < normal ME ę̄ so fully that the author of these books does not realize that the digraph *ea* was intended to represent a different sound from the digraph *ee*. It must be granted that on other grounds it appears that the author of *WSC-RS* used a not very correct speech; but his evidence shows us the beginning of the end. During the early eighteenth century this wholesale substitution of the originally vulgar [iː] for [eː] became general. It was probably no accident that the more careful varieties of StE finally succumbed to the pressure of the vulgar pronunciation when ME ę̄, having been overtaken at the stage [eː] by ME ā, lost its separate identity; thereafter the *ea* spelling, which had previously been a symbol of the separate identity of ME ę̄, became meaningless, and would even suggest that it was more correct to pronounce words so spelt with [iː] (the pronunciation associated with the *ee* spelling) than with [eː] (the pronunciation now associated with 'long *a*').

Thus in the great majority of 'ME ę̄ words' the pronunciations developed from ME ę̄ were displaced by [iː] from a ME ę̄ variant. But in a few words pronunciations developed from unraised ME ę̄ survive. PresE has [ei] from early eighteenth-century [eː] in *great*, *steak*, and two or three other words discussed under (3) below. Before *r*, as in *bear*, *pear*, *wear*, &c., open [ɛː] from unraised ME ę̄ is fairly common beside [iː] from raised ME ę̄ (which occurs, for example, in *rear*, *gear*, *shear*). The reason why unraised ME ę̄ survives in PresE comparatively often before *r*, though very rarely in other positions, is not far to seek. The consonant, from the later fourteenth century, exercises a marked lowering influence in London speech, especially, it seems, in its more vulgar forms (see Chapter VIII, Part 3). One of the first vowels to be subjected to its influence was ME ę̄, which tended to be lowered to late ME $\bar{e}$ (see § 126 below). Thus in the vulgar forms of speech from which the ModE pronunciation of 'ME $\bar{e}$ words' ultimately comes, the effect of the raising of ME $\bar{e}$ to ME $\bar{e}$ in earlier ME tended to be neutralized, before *r*, by the late ME tendency to lower ME $\bar{e}$ to ME $\bar{e}$ in that position. But it was only before *r* that the earlier ME tendency to raise ME $\bar{e}$ to ME $\bar{e}$ was so neutralized, and it is therefore only before *r* that PresE pronunciations derived from unraised ME $\bar{e}$ are at all numerous. It is further to be observed that even before *r* [ɛ:] < ME $\bar{e}$ is preserved chiefly in words in which $\bar{e}$ arises by lengthening of $\breve{e}$ in an open syllable, i.e. when the $\bar{e}$ was comparatively late-developed and had had less time to be subjected to the raising influence before the retractive power of *r* asserted itself.

§ 110. In words adopted from foreign languages in the early ModE period, we cannot explain a PresE pronunciation [i:] in contrast to a sixteenth- or seventeenth-century pronunciation [ɛ:] or [e:] from a variation in ME between ME $\bar{e}$ and ME $\bar{e}$. These words therefore present a problem. In words adopted from Latin (e.g. *supreme* 1523, *sincere* 1553, *scheme* 1550, *obscene* 1593) educated StE in the sixteenth and seventeenth centuries used [ɛ:] or [e:] representing ME $\bar{e}$; but if the theory of the development of ME $\bar{e}$ in ModE which I have advanced is correct, the PresE [i:] cannot develop from this [ɛ:], [e:] pronunciation. The explanation, as regards Latin words (and Greek and Hebrew words treated as though they had been adopted through Latin), seems to be as follows. The educated eModE pronunciation was based on the 'reformed' pronunciation of Latin introduced, in accordance with the teachings of Erasmus, by his English disciples; in this pronunciation Latin $\bar{e}$ and Latin $\breve{e}$ in open syllables were identified with ME $\bar{e}$. But in the earlier 'unreformed' pronunciation of Latin, ME $\bar{e}$ had often been substituted for Latin $\bar{e}$ and Latin $\breve{e}$ in open syllables; early adoptions from Latin were commonly pronounced in accordance with this 'unreformed' pronunciation even in educated StE (see § 127), and later adoptions might also be pronounced in accordance with it. The 'unreformed' pronunciation of Latin seems to have survived throughout the sixteenth and seventeenth centuries, doubtless in less well educated circles; in 1670 we get evidence of it in the *Welsh Breviary*, which tells us that though English *e* in *the* (i.e. ME $\bar{e}$) was pronounced like Welsh *e*, the English pronounced Latin *e* like Welsh *i*, i.e. [i:] (see Vol. I, p. 345). Thus English words adopted from Latin would vary between [ɛ:] or [e:] on the one hand and [i:] on the other according as the speaker was influenced by the 'reformed' or the 'unreformed' pronunciation of Latin itself. The orthoepists, who are strongly influenced by the 'reformed' pronunciation, afford no evidence of this variation. But we may contrast the $\bar{e}$ shown in *extreme* (adopted 1460) by Hart and Butler with Shakespeare's rhymes of *extremes* with *deems* and *seems* (cf. Viëtor, *Shakespeare's Pronunciation*, p. 120), and we may notice Sackville's rhyme of *Thrasimene* (in which an orthoepist would certainly have shown ME ẹ̄) with *seen* (*Oxford Book of Sixteenth Century Verse*, p. 125; of date 1563). The PresE pronunciation of these words adopted from or through Latin clearly depends on the 'unreformed' pronunciation, of which we get only occasional glimpses after Lily and Cheke had imposed their 'reformed' pronunciation on the educated classes in the South (Hume shows the survival of the 'unreformed' pronunciation in Scotland; see Vol. I, p. 318).

In the case of words adopted from modern foreign languages, [iː] for foreign [eː] requires a different explanation. In the fifteenth, sixteenth, and early seventeenth centuries, careful educated StE had no close [eː] sound; ME ẹ̄ was already [iː] and ME ę̄ was still open [ɛː] (see under (2) below). Speakers who used these pronunciations would then have to adopt an approximate pronunciation of foreign words containing close [eː], and they might often identify the especially tense foreign [eː] with the rather lax English [iː] from ME ẹ̄ (cf. Gil's description of the *Mopsæ*'s [keːpn] 'capon' as 'almost *kīpn*' [kiːpn]). The history of seventeenth-century adoptions from Dutch suggests that the [iː] pronunciations of words with Dutch [eː] did arise in this way (see Note below).

In both classes of words (those adopted from the classical languages, and those adopted from modern foreign languages) we must also allow for the influence of analogical and spelling pronunciations. It is quite normal for the pronunciation of words adopted from foreign languages to be 'anglicized' after models already existing in the language, and in this way words pronounced originally with [eː] might be given an analogical variant with [iː] because native words similarly varied. It would also be quite natural for 'spelling pronunciations' of these originally exotic and unfamiliar words to arise in the vulgar seventeenth- and early eighteenth-century speech whence, it is clear, the PresE pronunciation of 'ME ę̄ words' originates. This would almost inevitably occur after ME ę̄ had lost its separate identity (as it had done in the North by the middle of the sixteenth century at latest and in the East and in vulgar London speech probably by the late sixteenth century); for thereafter [eː] was the principal member of the 'long *a*' phoneme and was especially associated with ME ā and with the name of the letter *a*, whereas [iː] was associated with ME ẹ̄ (both original and by raising of ME ę̄) and therefore with the name of the letter *e* and the symbols *ee*, *ea*, and *e-e* (as in *mete*). In consequence it would be more natural to pronounce Latin and other foreign words (e.g. *supreme*) with [iː], which seemed in conformity with the spelling, than with the 'educated' [eː], which to speakers who no longer had ME ę̄ as a distinct sound would suggest 'long *a*'; and schoolmasters themselves would find it expedient to teach [əi] for Latin ī, [iː] for Latin ē (and *ae*), and [eː] for Latin ā, thus preserving a distinction between the sounds which would help to ensure accuracy in spelling Latin words and their English derivatives. The pronunciation of words from Greek and Hebrew would of course conform to that of words from Latin; and originally 'literary' words from modern foreign languages (and most foreign adoptions are in origin literary) would follow suit.

> *Note*: The history of seventeenth-century adoptions from Dutch, referred to above, is as follows. *Tea*, probably adopted from Dutch *thee*, varies between [i:] and [e:] from its first appearance in English; it rhymes either on [i:] or (in the seventeenth century and in the eighteenth century until 1762; see *OED*) on [e:], and it vacillates between the forms *tay* (representing [te:]) and *tee* in two of the earliest quotations (those dated 1658 and *c.* 1660) given by *OED* (but *tay* occurs alone in the quotation dated 1655). It is evident that the pronunciation [ti:] cannot develop from the pronunciation [te:] by a ModE sound-change (even if we date it earlier than 1700, the usually accepted date among those who believe in such a sound-change), for the two pronunciations appear together from the beginning. MDu. *splete*, *spleet* occurs as *spleet* from 1609 onwards—significantly it first occurs (in this form) in the *Feminine Monarchy* of the orthoepist Butler, who we know had [ɛ:] for ME ẹ̄ and had no tense [e:] in his own speech; later, when [e:] for ME ẹ̄ was common in educated speech, we find a form *spleat* (1657). On the other hand, LG *greven*, being a fisherman's word, was first adopted into a more vulgar form of speech which already possessed the sound [e:] for ME *ai* and ME *ā*; it occurs in 1614 as *graives*, in 1631 and later as *graves*, and not until 1735 (possibly because of renewed LG influence) as *greaves* (see *OED*, s.v. *greaves*, *graves*). Du. *ezel*, a less popular word, appears from the first as *easel*, but probably varied in the same way as *tea* between [e:] and [i:]. Du. *leeman*, adopted later in the century (1688) when even conservative educated StE was on the point of adopting tense [e:] for ME *ā* and *ai*, occurs only in the form *layman* (whence PresE *lay figure*); a pronunciation [i:] for foreign [e:] does not occur because no speakers at this date lacked the sound [e:] in their pronunciation of English. But perhaps we must allow for possible association with the other sb. *layman* 'a member of the laity'.

§ 111. I shall now proceed to discuss in more detail the evidence of the orthoepists on the sixteenth- and seventeenth-century pronunciation of 'ME ẹ̄ words'. Under (2) I shall examine the evidence on the development of ME ẹ̄ while it was still distinct from ME *ā*; under (3) the evidence for the identity of ME ẹ̄ with ME *ā*; under (4) the seventeenth-century evidence of the general substitution of [i:] < the ME ẹ̄ variant for [e:] < ME ẹ̄. Sixteenth- and seventeenth-century evidence of the existence of a ME variant ẹ̄ beside ME ẹ̄ in various classes of words will be given under 'Variation between ME ẹ̄ and ME ẹ̄', §§ 117 seq.; under this head will be found the eModE evidence for the raising of ME ẹ̄ to ME ẹ̄, as well as that for the late ME (early fifteenth-century) lowering of ME ẹ̄ to ME ẹ̄ before *r*.

(2) *The Development of ME ę̄ as a Distinct Sound*

§ 112. The development of ME ẹ̄ while it was a distinct sound (as it was in the speech of all sixteenth- and seventeenth-century orthoepists, with the exceptions noted under (3) below, § 115) may be traced, like that of ME *ā* (see §§ 99 seq.), from two sorts of evidence: direct evidence such as descriptions of the articulation of ME ẹ̄, and indirect evidence deduced from the development of related sounds and from sound-changes dependent on the fronting of ME ẹ̄.

(a) Indirect Evidence

§ 113. There are five developments in ModE pronunciation which are associated with the fronting of ME $\bar{ę}$ and provide indirect evidence of its progress.

(i) In forms of speech in which ME $\bar{ę}$ was still kept distinct from ME $\bar{a}$ and in which it can be shown that ME $\bar{a}$ had reached the value [ɛ:], we may conclude that ME $\bar{ę}$ had been fronted from [ɛ:] to [e:]. Evidence independent of that to be derived from statements concerning ME $\bar{ę}$ itself shows that ME $\bar{a}$ had reached the value [ɛ:], whence we assume that ME $\bar{ę}$ had reached the value [e:], possibly in Northern dialects in the late fourteenth century, in the North-west Midlands perhaps by 1425, in Eastern dialects in the fifteenth century, in some forms of London English perhaps in the fifteenth century and certainly in the sixteenth century; but in careful StE [ɛ:] for ME $\bar{a}$, and consequently [e:] for ME $\bar{ę}$, was not normal until after 1650. Before 1650 evidence of [ɛ:] for ME $\bar{a}$, and consequently of [e:] for ME $\bar{ę}$, is given by Lily, Robinson, and Hexham, the 'homophone' lists of Butler and Hodges (but this evidence refers to less careful speech than their own), and the shorthand-writers T. Shelton, Dix, and Rich. Even of these few orthoepists, Robinson is inconsistent; for one feature of his evidence depends on [æ:] for ME $\bar{a}$ and [ɛ:] for ME $\bar{ę}$ (see § 99 (*a*)). On the other hand, Smith, Bullokar, Gil, Daines, and Hodges, who normally have [æ:] for ME $\bar{a}$, give very occasional evidence of [ɛ:] for ME $\bar{a}$ and must therefore have known [e:] for ME $\bar{ę}$, though (except for Smith and Bullokar) they did not normally use it themselves. After 1650 almost all orthoepists show [ɛ:] for ME $\bar{a}$; but Wallis (except in a description of more popular speech than his own), Price (except in his 'homophone' list), Wilkins, and Holder give evidence of [æ:] for ME $\bar{a}$ and may therefore have had [ɛ:] for ME $\bar{ę}$ (though we cannot conclude that they necessarily had it; Holder indeed seems certainly to have had [e:]).

(ii) When ME $\bar{ę}$ in free position was fronted to [e:], it became distinct from ME $\bar{ę}$ before *r*, which remained as [ɛ:] (see §§ 203–4). This distinction is not explicitly recorded by any orthoepist before 1650, nor by Wallis, Price, and the *Treatise of Stops* (1680) after 1650. Some orthoepists (notably Smith, Robinson, and Newton) should have recorded it, since they appear from other evidence to have themselves used [e:] for ME $\bar{ę}$ in free position; but they have evidently followed the suggestion of the traditional spelling because there still existed (even after 1650) a mode of pronunciation in which ME $\bar{ę}$ in free position had not been fronted from [ɛ:]. But most orthoepists after 1650 remark on the distinction, thus showing that ME $\bar{ę}$ in free position had been fronted in the normal pronunciation of the time; and there is some evidence of identity of ME $\bar{ę}r$ with ME $\bar{a}r$ in Bullokar, Daines, and Hodges.

(iii) ME *ai* when it was monophthongized became [ɛ:], and was identified by some speakers with ME *ē̞*. It follows that at the time when the monophthongization occurred (it was very rare in StE in the fifteenth century, but more common in the sixteenth), ME *ē̞* must have still been [ɛ:]. But subsequently both ME *ē̞* and the monophthong were fronted, and we cannot assume merely from their identification that they were both still [ɛ:] among those speakers who (like Hart) identify them. Hume, indeed, seems to give [e:] as the Southern pronunciation of ME *ai* and consequently of ME *ē̞* (see §§ 228, 230); and the pairings of Hodges's 'near alike' list also depend on [e:] for both ME *ai* and ME *ē̞* (see § 230).

(iv) The development of ME *e̞u* to [iu] follows as a secondary consequence of the fronting of ME *ē̞* from [ɛ:] to [e:], for the first element of the diphthong, after being fronted from [ɛ] to close [e] when ME *ē̞* was similarly fronted, then became subject to the assimilatory influence of the second element and was raised to [i]. Evidence of the identity of ME *e̞u* and ME *iu* as [iu] is therefore indirect evidence that ME *ē̞* has been raised to [e:]. Such evidence (see § 244) is given by Tonkis (who was a Midlander), by the Northerner Levins, in one or two exceptional but significant instances by Bullokar (now known to be a native of Sussex), by shorthand-writers from Folkingham (1618) onwards, by Hodges in his 'alike' list (which for once differs from the speech—presumably his own—recorded in *EP*), by Gataker, and normally after 1650, even by careful orthoepists like Coles and Cooper. But after 1650 ME *e̞u* is kept distinct from ME *e̞u* by Wallis (who knows [iu] for ME *e̞u* but regards it as a less correct pronunciation), Wharton, Price, and Wilkins; these orthoepists may therefore not have known the raising of ME *ē̞* from [ɛ:] to [e:].

(v) The identity of ME *ā* and ME *ē̞* comes about when ME *ā* has overtaken ME *ē̞* at the stage [e:], and evidence of the identity is therefore evidence that ME *ē̞* is [e:]. Such evidence (see under (3) below) begins in StE in spellings and rhymes from *c.* 1600, and occurs in the 'homophone' lists after 1650. It may occur in the fifteenth century in Northern and Eastern dialects. The fact that ME *ā* and ME *ē̞* are not identical does not of course prove that ME *ē̞* is not [e:]—merely that both sounds are not [e:].

(b) *Direct Evidence*

§ 114. Descriptions of the articulation of ME *ē̞* do not in themselves allow us to decide between the values [ɛ:] and [e:]; the orthoepists who give such descriptions merely show that the vowel is a front one, with the tongue raised to an appreciable extent. To determine which of the two sounds they employed we have to rely on their comparisons of the English sound with foreign vowels, and the relation in which they put it to ME *ĕ*.

(i) Identifications of ME *ē̞* with foreign vowels show both the values [ɛ:] and [e:]. Hart shows the former by identifying ME *ē̞* with German *ä* and

French $ę$; he transcribes Fr. *père* as *pērah* ($ē$ being his symbol for ME $ẹ̄$), but uses a special mark (as in *volunté* 'volonté') for Fr $ę$ (see *Orthographie*, f. 66ʳ). Butler identifies French $ę$ with ME $ẹ̄$ by transcribing French *bois* (pronounced [bwɛ(z)] as *bwoës*. On the other hand Florio identifies ME $ẹ̄$ with (in his own term) Italian 'close *e*', in contrast to the monophthong developed from ME *ai*, which he identifies with Italian 'open *e*' (see Vol. I, p. 32). *The English Schoolmaster* (1646) and Richardson identify ME $ẹ̄$ with Dutch *ee*, and Hexham identifies it with Dutch *e*; all three show the value [e:] (see Vol. I, pp. 383-4). Other identifications of ME $ẹ̄$ with foreign vowels are in themselves indecisive (see Note 1 below).

(ii) ME $ẹ̄$ is said to differ only in quantity from ME $ĕ$ by Cheke, Hart, Gil, Butler, Hodges, Wallis, Price, and Wilkins. Strong and *The Protestant Tutor*, who merely follow Price, cannot be counted as independent witnesses. This identification should mean a pronunciation with [ɛ:], since ME $ĕ$ was an open sound; but it cannot be pressed too far. Smith and Holder (see under (iii) below) give evidence which seems to mean that they used [e:] for ME $ẹ̄$, in spite of their identification of it as the long equivalent of ME $ĕ$. But it would be going too far to discredit this evidence entirely; all the authors who give it have [æ:] as their normal pronunciation of ME $ā$, and so may have (and ordinarily would have) [ɛ:] for ME $ẹ̄$. On the other hand Robinson's evidence shows that ME $ẹ̄$ was a more fronted sound than ME $ĕ$, and he must therefore have used [e:] (see Vol. I, pp. 207-8). Lodwick, who says that ME $ĕ$ is a short vowel with no long equivalent, and that ME $ẹ̄$ is a long vowel with no short equivalent, must also have used [e:]. Newton and Cooper (see Vol. I, pp. 290-1) identify ME $ẹ̄$ as the long equivalent of ME $ĭ$ (as Cooper identifies ME $ọ̄$ as the long equivalent of [ʊ]); Cooper's evidence has been too literally interpreted as meaning that he used lax [ɪ:] for ME $ẹ̄$, but he is obviously over-systematizing, as is shown by his retention of the identification of ME $ẹ̄$ with 'French *é* masculine'. It is as certain that he used [e:] and not lax [ɪ:] for ME $ẹ̄$ as that he used [o:] and not lax [ʊ:] for ME $ọ̄$. Aickin follows Cooper.

(iii) That Gil used [ɛ:] for ME $ẹ̄$ follows from a comparison of his own speech with that of the *Mopsæ*; it is evident that [e:] was not ordinarily used in his pronunciation, and he provides no symbol for the sound (see Vol. I, p. 145). But it also appears (e.g. from his evidence on ME *ai*) that he knew [ɛ:] as a pronunciation of ME $ā$ (and *ai*), and accordingly must also have known [e:] as a pronunciation of ME $ẹ̄$ (see Vol. I, p. 151, and § 101). We may assume from the fact that the *Mopsæ* used [ɛ:] and even [e:] for ME $ā$ (see Vol. I, p. 145, and § 102) that they regularly used [e:] for ME $ẹ̄$, though Gil gives no evidence of this pronunciation; instead, he singles out their use of [i:] (< ME $ẹ̄$) in *leave* sb. for attention. Probably Gil's lack of a symbol for [e:] accounts for his failure to record what was clearly a common pronunciation in rather less careful speech than his own. On the reasons for believing that Smith and Holder combined [æ:] for ME *ā* with [e:] for ME *ẹ̄* see § 101. This combination of the conservative pronunciation of ME *ā* with the advanced pronunciation of ME *ẹ̄* is unexpected, but not impossible in a time when both sounds varied in pronunciation. But Smith's and Holder's evidence presents difficulties. In the first place, if Smith did use [e:] for ME *ẹ̄* in free position, he should have shown a difference between ME *ẹ̄* in free position and ME *ẹ̄* before *r*, since the latter was not normally fronted from [ɛ:]. In the second, he mentions MSc *ā*, the sound which is intermediate between ME *ā* and ME *ẹ̄* (see Vol. I, p. 58) and which I assume to have been [ɛ:], as though it were one which did not exist in English. Similarly Holder speaks of the vowel which is intermediate between ME *ā* and ME *ẹ̄*, and which again I assume to be [ɛ:] (see Vol. I, p. 264), as hypothetical. But both Smith and Holder must have known the sound [ɛ:]; many of Smith's contemporaries and some of Holder's used it for ME *ẹ̄* in free position, others for ME *ā* (Smith himself uses *ā* as a symbol for Northern [ɛ:]); and both men must have used it (as everyone did) for ME *ẹ̄* before *r*. The explanation is doubtless that, insofar as [ɛ:] occurred in their own speech (before *r*), it was merely a contextual variant of the 'long *e*' phoneme, of which [e:] was for them the dominant member; and that insofar as it occurred in the speech of their contemporaries it was merely a 'diaphonic' variant of either 'long *a*' or 'long *e*' (which both men regard as being normally [æ:] and [e:] respectively). It would be natural for persons whose concern was simply to isolate the essential vowel-sounds (i.e. the vowel phonemes) of contemporary English to overlook these contextual and diaphonic variants; and Smith might nevertheless recognize as a distinct entity Scottish [ɛ:] for MSc *ā*, especially when it occurred in words for which he himself used [o:] < ME *ǭ*.

Our evidence, both indirect and direct, shows that for over a century there were two pronunciations of ME *ẹ̄* in use in StE, as there were of ME *ā* (see §§ 98–101). Until about 1650 the more common pronunciation in careful speech, used by those persons who had [æ:] for ME *ā*, was [ɛ:]; this pronunciation, like [æ:] for ME *ā*, survived into the third quarter of the seventeenth century. But there had long existed beside this pronunciation another with [e:], which about 1650 began finally to displace, even in careful speech, the older pronunciation, just as [ɛ:] began to displace [æ:] for ME *ā*. The advanced pronunciation [e:] for ME *ẹ̄* might be combined with the conservative pronunciation [æ:] for ME *ā*, as by Smith and Holder, but one would not expect this to be a common state of affairs. The two sounds, ME *ā* and ME *ẹ̄*, are shown by the evidence to have remained distinct so long as ME *ā* had not been fronted beyond [ɛ:] to [e:]; there is no evidence to suggest that any speakers combined the advanced pronunciation [ɛ:] for ME *ā* with the conservative pronunciation [ɛ:] for ME *ẹ̄* and thus identified the two sounds at the stage [ɛ:].

§ 114] PART 2: THE LONG VOWELS 623

Note 1: The following identifications of ME ẹ̄ with foreign vowels are indecisive and must ordinarily be rejected as evidence.

(a) With Welsh e, as in the *Welsh Hymn* and Salesbury, since the evidence of the *Welsh Breviary* suggests that in the seventeenth century (and presumably also in the sixteenth) Welsh e might be used as a transcription for either [ɛ:] or [e:] (see § 115, Note 5).

(b) With French e, as in Palsgrave (whose rule covers both Fr ẹ and Fr ę), Sanford and Colson (who give no examples), Tonkis, Wallis, and Cooper (who say that ME ẹ̄ is the same as 'French é masculine'). These identifications are generally assumed (as by Luick, § 499, Anm. 1) to mean close [e:], since the phrase 'French é masculine' is taken to be synonymous with the present 'é acute'. But it is not so; it covers both ẹ and ę, in contrast to 'e feminine'. Pope, §§ 735-7, shows that the acute was first used merely to mark those e's which were not feminine, and might be applied (as by Ronsard) to both ẹ and ę; and that the grave was not proposed as a mark of ę until 1660 nor adopted by the Academy until 1740.

(c) With foreign e generally, as in Daines and Coles (who says that the English pronunciation of Latin ē does not need reforming, from which we may assume that it was the same as the foreign pronunciation); 'foreign e' may obviously be either [ɛ:] or [e:].

(d) With Latin or Greek ē. German philologists are apt to search out the presumed pronunciation of ē in classical Latin and Greek, and (attributing this knowledge to sixteenth- and seventeenth-century scholars) to assert that this must also have been the pronunciation of ME ẹ̄. But statements that ME ẹ̄ is pronounced like Latin or Greek ē merely mean that Englishmen substituted ME ẹ̄ for ē in their pronunciation of Latin and Greek, and tell us nothing about its value.

Note 2: Zachrisson, *Eng. Vowels*, pp. 125-7, cites evidence from Bellot and Delamothe which confirms Hart's identification of ME ẹ̄ with Fr ẹ. He cites no reliable evidence (except Florio's) for the value [e:]. Zachrisson thinks that Miège shows this value, as indeed he does, but not merely by his identification of ME ẹ̄ with 'French é masculine' (see Note 1 (b) above); it is his other identification of ME ā with Fr ę which shows that he must mean to identify ME ẹ̄ with Fr ẹ.

Note 3: There is some possibility that Florio's choice of ME *ai* instead of ME *ā* as the English equivalent of Italian 'open e' may mean that he regarded ME *ā* as still normally [æ:] (as the evidence shows it to have been at his time), and in that case he distinguishes ME *ā* as [æ:], ME *ai* as [ɛ:], and ME ẹ̄ as [e:]. This distinction would be artificial, as there is no other evidence of ME *ai* pronounced as a monophthong and yet kept distinct from both ME ẹ̄ and ME *ā*. But he would in this case make a third to Smith and Holder in showing [æ:] for ME *ā* and [e:] for ME ẹ̄.

(3) *Identity of ME ę̄ and ME ā*

§ 115. The ModE fronting of ME ẹ̄ itself stopped at [e:] (the commoner pronunciation after 1650), and it was therefore overtaken by ME *ā*, which after 1650 began to pass from the value [ɛ:] (the commonest pronunciation in correct speech at that time) to [e:]. The resulting identity of ME ę̄ and ME *ā*, which was common in early eighteenth-century StE and still exists in many forms of dialectal speech, would have remained in Present StE if the pronunciation developed from ME ę̄ had not been replaced, in most 'ME ę̄ words', by the pronunciation [i:] developed from a ME ẹ̄ variant.

Apart from Northerners (see Note 1 below), the only orthoepists who give evidence of the identity of ME ę̄ and *ā* in the seventeenth century are the authors of certain 'homophone' lists, and even these in their general discussions of the sounds of English clearly distinguish between ME *ā* and ME ę̄. It is remarkable that there is no evidence of the identity in the rhyme-lists of Willis and Coles, though during the seventeenth century poets increasingly rhyme ME $\bar{a}$ with ME $\bar{ẹ}$. Similarly there is no evidence in the 'phonetically spelt' lists; and even of the 'homophone' lists little more than half show the identity (otherwise than before r). The lists which show it are those of Wharton 1654 (the first), Hunt, Price, Fox and Hookes, Coles (only in the careless *Eng.–Lat. Dict.*), Young, Cooper (who has one example only, in his 'near alike' list; the pairing is of *steak* with *stake*, which might be, but probably is not, a special case), *The Compendious Schoolmaster*, Hawkins, *WSC-RS*, Cocker, and Brown. The most careful lists avoid the pairing of ME $\bar{a}$ and ME $\bar{ẹ}$ (otherwise than before r). Thus Hodges has no examples even in his 'near alike' list, to which he admits many pairings based on pronunciations less correct than his own, and Coles has none in his more careful lists (those of the *Schoolmaster* and the *Eng. Dict.*). Cooper has none in his 'alike' list; Wyld, *Coll. Eng.*, p. 210, is in error in saying that this list pairs *meat* with *mate*, for the pairing is of *meat* 'cibus' with *mete* 'metior' (Latin text, ed. Jones, p. 78). The pairing in the same list of *flea* 'pulex' with *flay* or *flea* 'excorio' obviously depends on ME $\bar{ẹ}$ in the latter word.

Since the identity of ME $\bar{ẹ}$ and ME $\bar{a}$ is shown only in 'homophone' lists published after 1650, and even so with many exceptions, we are entitled to assume that even in more careless forms of StE the identity was rare before 1650 and was far from universal after that date. We cannot then regard poets' rhymes between ME $\bar{ẹ}$ and ME $\bar{a}$ during the seventeenth century as depending on the best forms of speech, especially as Willis and Coles do not include such rhymes in their lists; rhymes between ME $\bar{a}$ and ME $\bar{ẹ}$ before 1650 (at earliest) must be regarded as being a departure from the best rhyming by hard-pressed poets. But we may nevertheless expect to find evidence of the identity of ME $\bar{ẹ}$ and ME $\bar{a}$ before 1650, in view of Gil's evidence (1619 and 1621) that the *Mopsæ* used for ME $\bar{a}$ not only [ɛː] but also [eː], the value at which ME $\bar{a}$ overtook ME $\bar{ẹ}$ in free position. This is little later than the earliest valid evidence of the identity of ME $\bar{ẹ}$ and ME $\bar{a}$ in StE so far produced; but Gil does not himself actually record that the *Mopsæ* identified ME $\bar{a}$ and ME $\bar{ẹ}$. It is evident that in this matter at least his strictures on the pronunciation of the *Mopsæ* were well justified; the evidence shows that Wyld, *Coll. Eng.*, p. 169, is grievously mistaken in declaring that the pronunciations of the *Mopsæ* show 'the way in which most decent speakers pronounced at that time'.

PresE preserves the identity of ME $\bar{ẹ}$ with ME $\bar{a}$ in positions other than before r in the words *great*, *break*, *steak*, and *yea*; to these we should probably add *lay figure* (see § 110, Note above). No satisfactory explanation of the PresE pronunciation of these words has been offered except Wyld's (*Coll. Eng.*, p. 212) that they preserve the normal StE development whereby ME $\bar{ẹ}$ became identical with ME $\bar{a}$ (see further Note 6 below). There is nothing in the early evidence to suggest that these words had a special development. On early rhymes of *break* with ME *ā* words see Note 2 below. The sixteenth- and seventeenth-century orthoepists do not distinguish *great, break, steak*, and *yea* from other ME *ẹ̄* words. *Yea* has eModE [i:] from ME *ẹ̄* beside ME *ę̄* (see § 119). *WSC-RS*, which has [i:] in 'ME *ẹ̄* words', has it also in *great* and *break*; Brown and the early eighteenth-century MS 'homophone' list have [i:] in *great*. Eighteenth-century evidence commonly shows [i:] (a pronunciation which survives in present-day dialects) beside [e:] in *great, break*, and *steak*. The only possible seventeenth-century evidence of one of these words being distinguished from other ME *ẹ̄* words comes in two 'homophone' lists. The one pairing of ME *ẹ̄* with ME *ā* in Cooper's 'near alike' list is of *steak* with *stake* (but in the text of his grammar Cooper does not distinguish *steak* from other ME *ẹ̄* words, and keeps it, like them, apart from ME *ā* words). Similarly the only pairing of this sort in *RS*'s list is of *great* with *grate* (but elsewhere *RS* does not distinguish *great* from other 'ME *ẹ̄* words', and gives [i:]); on the other hand *WSC*, which is by the same author and has a much less brief 'homophone' list than *RS*, includes several pairings of ME *ẹ̄* with ME *ā*. It seems that these two pairings have no special significance; Cooper's choice of *steak*, and *RS*'s of *great*, may be purely fortuitous, or may, more probably, show that in the careless speech on which these two lists were based the situation at the end of the seventeenth century was essentially that of PresE—the [i:] pronunciation derived from a late ME *ẹ̄* variant had become established in all but a few 'ME *ẹ̄* words', of which *steak* and *great* happened to be two. A similar conclusion is suggested by the evidence of Wm. Turner (1710), recorded by Gabrielson, *Studia Neophilologica*, ii. 158–9; Turner, despite Gabrielson, preserves a true distinction between [i:] < ME *ẹ̄* and [e:] and [ɛ:] < ME *ę̄* (but has ME *ẹ̄* in *these* and by lowering of ME *ẹ̄* before *r* in *beer*, &c.), and says that *ea* is pronounced [e:] in *great* and *break* 'very often (if not most commonly)'; it is true that this implies a variant pronunciation, but it would be [i:] (and not the 'ME *ā*' which many scholars, including Gabrielson himself, falsely assume to develop in these words). See further Notes 6–9 below.

Note 1: Northern orthoepists show the identity of ME *ā* and ME *ẹ̄* much earlier than Southerners, the reason being the earlier fronting of ME *ā* in the North. Levins records it in a few words (Vol I, p. 26), so does Hume (Vol. I, p. 319). Gil records it in his account of the Northern dialect (Vol. I, pp. 146–7); both sounds have the pronunciation [ɛə] developed from [e:]. But there is no adequate evidence of the identification in the rhyme-list of the Northerner Poole (Vol. I, p. 436). On the Scot Ridpath see Vol I, p. 393. The two sounds were also identified early in the 'Eastern dialect', as is shown by spellings (see Note 4 below) and by rhymes (Dibelius, *Anglia*, xxiii (1901), 188 cites *beheue* 'behave' sb. rhyming with *beleue* 'belief' from the late fifteenth-century Suffolk manuscript of *St. Patrick's Purgatory*, ed. Toulmin Smith, *Englische Studien*, ix, lines 49–50; his other examples are less decisive, but *mad* 'made' : *stede* 'stead' in the London skinner Lovelich's *Graal* may show early identity of ME *ā* and *ẹ̄* in Cockney, if it does not depend on shortening in both words). Gil's evidence may also show identity in his 'Eastern dialect', for he gives ME *ā* in that dialect as [ɛə], a pronunciation which normally develops after ME *ā* and *ẹ̄* have become identical with the value [e:] (see Vol. I, pp. 146–7); we may assume that he also knew [e:] for ME *ā* in the 'Eastern dialect', though he does not record it. Newton in three words appears to show the dialectal [ɪə] or [eə] for ME *ẹ̄*, but not for ME *ā* (see Vol. I, p. 251).

Note 2: Horn, § 75, and Ekwall, §§ 51–54, ignore the identity of ME *ā* with ME *ẹ̄* in seventeenth- and eighteenth-century StE; it was pointed out by Wyld, *Coll. Eng.*, p. 209 seq. (cf. Note 3), who is followed by Zachrisson, *Bullokar*, p. 38 seq. Wyld, p. 209, believes that ME *ā* (and ME *ai*) caught up with ME *ẹ̄* at the stage [ɛ:]; that this theory is false is shown by the evidence of the late sixteenth- and seventeenth-century orthoepists cited in §§ 113–14 above, who have [e:] for ME *ẹ̄* and [ɛ:] for ME *ā*, so that it is clear that ME *ā* did not overtake ME *ẹ̄* until the [e:] stage.

Note 3: Not all the sixteenth- and seventeenth-century rhymes cited by Wyld, *Coll. Eng.*, p. 196 and p. 211, and *Rhymes*, pp. 53–54, to prove the identity of ME *ā* and ME *ẹ̄* bear this interpretation. Some we may exclude summarily. Rhymes of *hair* with ME *ẹ̄* words depend on the common variant with ME *ẹ̄* representing OE *hǣr*. Rhymes of ME *ai* with ME *ẹ̄* do not by inference show identity of ME *ā* and ME *ẹ̄*; for when ME *ai* was monophthongized it had two developments, to identity with ME *ā* or to identity with ME *ẹ̄* (see §§ 225 seq. below), whereas Wyld assumes (as is usual) that it had only one, to identity with ME *ā*. Rhymes of *great* and *break* with other ME *ẹ̄* words merely prove that these two have not yet been differentiated. It is difficult to see why Wyld cites the rhyme *straight* : *height*, which depends on the ME *ai* variant in the latter word. Others of the rhymes should probably be excluded; at best they are liable to other interpretations, and ambiguous evidence is valueless. Early sixteenth-century rhymes of *break* with ME *ā* words, which are too early to be credible as examples of the general identity of ME *ā* and ME *ẹ̄* in free position, are discussed in Note 7 below. Rhymes of *Thames* with ME *ẹ̄* words clearly depend on ME *ẹ̄* by lengthening in the open syllable of ME *Tĕmes*. Suckling rhymes *Seine* with *clean*, but this merely shows that ME *ẹ̄* in *clean* is identified with French *ę* in *Seine*; the rhyme is not even a case of ME *ai* rhyming with ME *ẹ̄*, which in any event would be inadmissible (see above). Rhymes of *feature* with *nature* (Spenser, Shakespeare; cf. Shakespeare's *defeated* : *created*) depend on the OF and ME variant *ai* in *feature* (*defeated*). The rhyme of *speak* with *make* may depend on the analogical infinitive *spake* (see Note 4 below), which is due to the variation in eModE in the p.t. between *spake* (the normal form) and *speak* (from the OE and ME plural); this alternative explanation is indeed the more probable in the case of Sackville (cf. his rhyme of *break* with *make* discussed in Note 7 below), but in Waller and Cowley the rhyme is more likely to depend, as Wyld believes, on identity of ME *ā* and ME *ẹ̄*. Spenser's rhyme of *retrate* 'retreat' with *late* depends on the ME variant *retrait* (cf. *OED*).

There remains, of Wyld's lists, only one sixteenth-century rhyme, Spenser's *seates* with *states*. But Zachrisson, *Bullokar*, p. 39, cites certain other Spenserian *ẹ̄* : *ā* rhymes collected by Gabrielson; cf. Bauermeister, *Zur Sprache Spensers*, § 82. I have found no sixteenth-century *ẹ̄* : *ā* rhymes in any other poet in *The Oxford Book of Sixteenth Century Verse*. Spenser seems, in this as in other matters, to stand alone; his rhyming is based either on advanced London speech or on Northern pronunciation. (In favour of the latter hypothesis it could be argued (i) that his family is supposed to have been of Northern origin, (ii) that he spent a year in the North after going down from Cambridge, (iii) that he was a pupil of a school in which the influence of Northern masters is reported to have adversely affected the boys' pronunciation, and (iv) that in the *F.Q.* VII. vii. 41 (and thrice elsewhere; see Bauermeister, § 180) he rhymes *rode* on the Northern form *rade* (in the case cited, with *maid*). Spenser's rhymes, in any event, are certainly not evidence of correct StE pronunciation at his time.) At the beginning of the seventeenth century I find the rhymes *creature* : *nature* in Breton, 1604 (*Oxford Book of Sixteenth Century Verse*, p. 422 and p. 425) and *greatly* : *lately* (*Anon.*, 1610; op. cit., p. 872); it is possible but unlikely that these rhymes show the influence of a preceding *r* on ME *ẹ̄*. Gil's evidence (see above) shows that about this time general identity of ME *ẹ̄* and ME *ā* was possible in the speech of the *Mopsæ*. Wyld cites from Habingdon (whose first work is dated 1634) the rhymes *leave* : *crave* and *great* : *state*; from his contemporary Waller the rhyme *speak* : *make* (see above); from

Cowley the rhymes *ease* : *paraphrase* and *speak* : *make* (see above); from Dryden rhymes of *shame* with *dream* and with *theme*. Other examples could be added, from Drayton's *sea*: *Virginia* (*Odes*, 1619) onwards; but it is not until after 1700 that rhymes between ME ā and ME ẹ̄ become really numerous and clearly reflect the normal careful pronunciation of StE. Later in the eighteenth century they again become rare, doubtless because [i:] was establishing itself more and more in 'ME ẹ̄ words'; but Cowper has *tread* : *shade* in 1773 (*Oxford Book of Eighteenth Century Verse*, p. 562).

Note 4: Wyld, *Coll. Eng.*, p. 248, would interpret certain early spellings as showing (*a*) monophthongization of ME *ai* to ā, and (*b*) identity of ME ā (and consequently ME *ai*) with ME ẹ̄. But spellings with *ei* for ME ẹ̄ may satisfactorily be explained as inverted spellings due to the common use of the spelling *ei* and the pronunciation ẹ̄ (representing ME variants) in *receive*, &c.; and spellings with *ea* for ME *ai* show the direct identification of the monophthong developed from ME *ai* with ME ẹ̄ instead of with ME ā (see §§ 225, 228 below). Neither class proves the identity of ME ā and ME ẹ̄. But other spellings, if correctly reported, would show the identity of the two sounds: these are *a* for ME ẹ̄ and *ea* or *e* for ME ā. The difficulty is that as *a* and *e* are very similar in fifteenth- and sixteenth-century hands (see § 59, Note 2 (*a*)), it is possible that supposed cases of *e* for *a* and vice versa are merely errors of the transcribers of the manuscripts; and in fact N. Davis has shown (*Medium Ævum*, xviii (1949), 24) that none of the alleged *e* spellings for ME ā hitherto cited from the *Paston Letters* has real existence (the letter being in fact *a*, or the word one in which *e* is to be expected). Similarly I am informed that the alleged *Cely Papers* instances of *e* for ME ā (e.g. *ceme* 'came') and *a* for ME ẹ̄ (e.g. *grat* 'great') are all misreadings. Until there has been a careful re-examination of the manuscript evidence, therefore, we must regard with suspicion all alleged spellings of this sort. Here one can do no more than record that, excluding the *Paston Letters* and *Cely Papers*, spellings which would show the identity of ME ā and ME ẹ̄ have been cited as follows. (i) Alleged fifteenth- and sixteenth-century spellings are cited by Wyld, *Coll. Eng.*, pp. 194–5; Zachrisson, *Eng. Vowels*, pp. 56–58; Dibelius, *Anglia*, xxiii (1901), 188; Jordan, § 276; and Kihlbom, p. 119. If we exclude those spellings which can be accounted for by special causes (cf. Zachrisson, loc. cit.), the number which may show identity of ME ā and ME ẹ̄ otherwise than before *r* (a special case) is extremely small, and the sources are Eastern (de la Pole, Capgrave), except for two isolated instances in Zachrisson, Rymer's *teke* 'take' (which would relate to Cockney English) and *rether* 'rather' from a Northern source. But it is suspicious that both de la Pole and Rymer have *t(h)eke* 'take'; surely we have to do with an analogical formation *tẹ̄ke*, p.t. *tọ̄k* on the model of *nẹ̄me* (OE *niman*), p.t. *nọ̄m*? The two synonyms would be certain to be associated. Wyld's *yeate* 'gate' (Shillingford) has ME ẹ̄ not ā (see Jordan, § 76, Anm.). Dibelius cites from Tyndale *mate* 'meat' (but it is ON *matr* rather than OE *mete*), *spake* (an analogical form; cf. Zachrisson, op. cit., p. 58), and *mane* 'mean' (also analogical, or perhaps due to the influence of OE *manian*). Thus the fifteenth- and early sixteenth-century evidence is slight and unsatisfactory, and in any case would relate to dialectal (Northern and Eastern) speech (as Jordan, § 276, realized, for he took the supposed *Paston Letters* spellings to refer to a special East Midland development). Kökeritz, *Phonology of the Suffolk Dialect*, § 267, cites *a nape* 'an heap' from a document of date 1470, but clearly not from the manuscript, since his reference is to a periodical, *The East Anglian*; *whaeth* 'wheat' (1539), again not from manuscript, is not a phonetic, but merely a confused spelling; and *sade-leppe* 'seed-lip' (1583, from an Ipswich document) is more likely to show the dialectal survival of the so-called 'Essex' ā < OE ǣ. (ii) Spellings that seem certainly valid evidence of the identity are cited by Kökeritz, op. cit., for the Suffolk dialect from the early seventeenth century (e.g. *banes* 'beans' 1617 and *visitteacon* 'visitation' 1608; see §§ 248 and 267). Diehl, *Anglia*, xxix (1906), p. 160 and Wyld, *Coll. Eng.* (3rd edit.), p. 211 footnote and p. 401, cite late sixteenth- or early seventeenth-century spellings (*a* for ME ẹ̄ and *ea* for ME ā) which show identity of ME ā and ME ẹ̄ in more advanced types of StE; not until about 1700 do such spellings become at all frequent. (See also Zachrisson, *Bullokar*, p. 40 footnote.) The Northerner Machyn, in his *Diary* (1550–3), has *a*-spellings for ME ẹ̄ (e.g. *sale* 'seal') and also *ay*-spellings (e.g. *rayme* 'realm' and *say* 'sea') which probably (though perhaps not beyond all doubt) depend on a general identification of ME *ai* with ME ā and of the latter with ME ẹ̄ (see Wijk, *Machyn*, p. 99). The evidence of spellings, when sifted, tends to confirm that of rhymes and the orthoepists: the identity of ME $\bar{a}$ with ME $\bar{ę}$ was rare before 1650 and not common until c. 1700.

It should be noted that only Wyld and Kökeritz realize the obvious point that these spellings depend on identity of the sounds; before Wyld they had been explained by the untenable supposition that fronting of ME $\bar{a}$, by merely decreasing the gap between the two sounds, would lead to the interchange of the methods of representing them.

Note 5: Some orthoepists who have been, or might be, held to show a general identity of ME $\bar{a}$ and ME $\bar{ę}$ do not do so. Hart, *Methode*, f. Aiiii[r] identifies the name of the letter *h* with the noun *ache* (formerly pronounced with [tʃ]), and goes on to say that with the names of the letters as they are, *t h r* (*te ache er*) can reasonably be held to spell *teacher*. This does not mean that the *each* of *teacher* is the same in pronunciation as the word *ache*; Hart is obviously thinking of the visual appearance of the letter-names and of the word *teacher* in ordinary orthography. The *Welsh Breviary* equates both ME $\bar{a}$ and ME $\bar{ę}$ with Welsh *e*, but similarly equates both ME *au* [ɒ:] and ME $\bar{ǫ}$ [o:] with Welsh *o*; the author has clearly failed to distinguish [ɛ:] from [e:], [ɒ:] from [o:]. Cooper shows the identity only in the one word *steak* in his 'near alike' list, though Wyld, *Coll. Eng.*, p. 210, argues that as Cooper refers in his Part I (the phonetic part) to *a* in *cane* as 'e longa', and in his Part II (the spelling-book part) to ME $\bar{ę}$ in a large number of words as 'e longa', therefore ME $\bar{a}$ and ME $\bar{ę}$ must be identical. But Wyld has failed to observe a change in Cooper's nomenclature between the two parts, from scientific to popular, which affects other sounds as well (see Vol. I, pp. 297–8, and note 1 to p. 298); in reality ME $\bar{a}$ and $\bar{ę}$ are carefully distinguished, in Part I in scientific terms and in Part II in popular terms. On Cooper's $\bar{a}$ in *scream* see Vol. I, p. 291, note 1. Wyld, op. cit., p. 196, states that Wallis, as well as Cooper, 'intend[s] to imply that in [his] day, the three original ME sounds *a*, *ai*, and $\bar{ę}$ had been levelled under what [he] call[s] "long *e*"'; as Wyld makes no mention of Wallis in the place to which cross-reference is made (pp. 209 seq.), it is impossible to discover the reason for this wholly erroneous statement, unless it be a mistaken belief that Wallis's evidence is the same as Cooper's. Wallis in actual fact gives [æ:] for ME $\bar{a}$, [ɛ:] for ME $\bar{ę}$, and [ai] for ME *ai*. Zachrisson, *Bullokar*, pp. 39–40, interprets Brown's 'phonetic spellings' *fane* or *feane* 'feign', &c., as showing that in Brown's speech *ea* and 'long *a*' were different ways of expressing the same sound, i.e. that ME $\bar{ę}$ and ME $\bar{a}$ were identical. This view is possible, but it is more likely that the alternative transcriptions represent alternative pronunciations, and that the *ea* transcriptions represent ME variants in ME $\bar{ę}$ (see Vol. I, pp. 368–9). (Zachrisson, *Eng. Vowels*, p. 200, has another even less acceptable explanation.) Zachrisson, *Bullokar*, p. 40, also refers to certain rules on the pronunciation of *ea* and *ei* given by Strong and Dyche, and cited in his *Eng. Vowels*, p. 200. Strong says that *ea* and *ei* are improper diphthongs in which *i* and *a* lose their sounds, and Zachrisson would assume that *ea* and *ei* are therefore pronounced alike; but Strong's confusions on the nature of proper and improper diphthongs, which have no relation whatever to pronunciation (cf. the list of examples of *ei* cited by Zachrisson, *Eng. Vowels*, p. 200, from Strong), are best disregarded. Strong simply does not understand the distinction originally intended between 'proper' and 'improper' diphthongs, and applies the terms haphazard (see Vol. I, p. 373). Dyche's rules (*Eng. Vowels*, p. 201) depend on a *distinction* between ME $\bar{a}$ and ME $\bar{ę}$; *neighbour* and *heir* are said to have *ei* pronounced 'like long *a*', and *convey*, *veil*, *either*, *key*, &c. have *ei* pronounced 'like long *e*'. The latter group of words has pronunciations descended from a ME variant in ME $\bar{ę}$ (whence may arise ME $\bar{ę}$ by raising; cf. PresE [i:] in *either* and *key*).

Note 6: Jespersen, *ModEGr*, § 11.75, suggests that the PresE pronunciation of *break*, &c. is due to 'preservative analogy' (e.g. that eighteenth-century [e:] in *great* is due to blending of [i:] developed in *great* itself and [e] in the ME comparative *gretter*); it is extremely doubtful whether all the words in question had quantity variation at the end of the seventeenth century, and in any case 'preservative analogy' seems to be a purely fictional process. Horn, § 81, and Luick, § 500, believe all these words to have pronunciations adopted by StE from the South-western dialects; but there is no evidence of South-western influence on StE in ModE times, and one would not expect it to affect such common words. A more probable explanation is put forward by Ekwall, § 54. He would explain [e:] in *break* and *great* as showing the influence of the preceding *r* (but see Note 8); in *steak* as showing the survival of ME *ai* (the word is from ON *steik*); and in *yea* as due to the analogy of *nay*. But *ai, ei* forms of *steak* are not found after the fifteenth century in StE, and *ā*-forms are not found before the late seventeenth century (1694 *stakes* cited by *OED*; so in the eighteenth century); the gap is too wide to allow us to connect the *ā*-forms with the *ei, ai*-forms. (Similarly *bleyke* 'bleak' adj. and vb., from ON *bleikr*, does not occur after the fifteenth century, and *ai*-forms of *weak* occur only rarely in Southern English in the early sixteenth century.) The analogy of *nay* might preserve the pronunciation of *yea* which identified ME *ẹ̄* with ME *ā* and *ai*, but could hardly lead to its development. Zachrisson, *Bullokar*, p. 40, who rejects Wyld's hypothesis, says rather vaguely that the PresE [ei] 'may go back to early variants with *ā, ai*, or be due to the influence of related words with *ai, ě*'; he is evidently thinking partly of Ekwall's and partly of Jespersen's explanation, but with the difference (shown by a reference to *Eng. Vowels*, p. 58) that he would explain [ei] in *break* from the eModE analogical infinitive *brake*. But this infinitive, though it explains early rhymes of *break* (see Note 7), does not seem to have survived after 1600.

Note 7: Wyatt in his 'Blame not my Lute' and Sackville (cf. Wyld, *Rhymes*, p. 53) rhyme *break* with *sake* and *betake* at a time when ME *ẹ̄* and ME *ā* were not yet identical in educated StE. But these rhymes do not show a special development of ME *ẹ̄* after *r*; they depend on an analogical infinitive *brake* modelled on the eModE past tense *brake* beside the variant *break* from the ME plural *brēken*, OE *bræcon*. Cf. Sackville's rhyme of *speak* with *make* (Note 3) and *ā*-forms of verbs of the *tear* class (§ 204, Notes 1 and 3).

Note 8: Both those who would explain PresE [ei] in *break* and *great* by 'preservative analogy' or by the influence of preceding *r* and those who would regard it as due to South-western dialectal influence have seen a parallel in the [ɒ:] of (*a*)*broad* and *groat*; but the analogy does not hold. In the first place, *broad* and *groat* are shown to have [ɒ:] by a succession of seventeenth-century evidence which perhaps begins with Gil and certainly begins with Hodges, whereas no seventeenth-century orthoepist gives clear evidence of a special development in *break* and *great*. In the second place, the [ɒ:] developed in *broad* and *groat* is the same sound as is developed by ModE lengthening of ME *ŏ* in, for example, *God* pronounced [gɒ:d], *loss* pronounced [lɒ:s], whereas the PresE [ei] in *great* and *break* is significantly different from the [ɛ:] developed from ME *ẹ̄* in *bear* (which is also the sound which would be expected as the result of a ModE lengthening of ME *ě*).

Note 9: It is possible that we should add the names of the letters *j* and *k* to the instances of PresE [ei] for seventeenth-century [e:] < ME *ẹ̄*, for normally the names of consonant-letters are formed by prefixing ME *ě* (so *f, l*) or suffixing ME *ẹ̄* (so *b, c, d*). The normal procedure was sometimes adopted with *j* and *k*; the name of the former is said by Coles and Lye to be *jea*, by Aickin *je*, and by Cocker *jee*, and that of the latter is said by Lloyd (1654) to be *key*, the word *key* in its turn being said to be pronounced *kea* (cf. *OED*, which records that the letter-name was formerly [ki:]). The PresE [dʒei] and [kei] might therefore represent **jẹ̄* and **kẹ̄*. But [kei] is more likely to represent ME **kā* (cf. the modern German name [ka:]), and [dʒei] is probably modelled on it to avoid confusion with [dʒi:] for *g*. *Drain* vb. is not an instance, as has been claimed, for (despite Murray in *OED*) it is a more normal form, not a spelling, of eModE *drean*: OE **drēagnian* > **drēgnian* > late ME **drainen* (cf. Jordan, § 97 (1*a*)). ME **drẹ̄nen* is difficult but may be < Saxon **drēanian* < **drěagnian* < **drěagnian*. OE recorded forms are late and rare, with graphic *h* for PrOE *g*.

(4) *General Substitution of* [i:] *for* [e:] *in* '*ME ę̄ Words*'

§ 116. There is little seventeenth-century evidence for the general substitution of the pronunciation [i:] derived from a ME variant in ME *ẹ̄* for [e:] derived from ME *ę̄*. The *Welsh Breviary* does not show [i:] for ME *ę̄*, as was assumed by J. D. Jones (see Vol. I, p. 345). The evidence of Young's 'phonetically spelt' list (see Vol. I, p. 352) may prove no more than that he knew [iː] as one value of the digraph *ea*; but though, like his sources, he normally keeps *ea* and *ee* distinct (as in *reak* 'wreak'), his use of *ea* to express [iː] in *intrigue* may show that ME *ẹ̄* had in his own speech already lost its separate identity. *WSC-RS* (see Vol. I, pp. 364–5) gives clear evidence of the general substitution of [iː] for [eː]; in the author's pronunciation all 'ME *ẹ̄* words' have [iː] and *ea* has the same significance as *ee*. This evidence does not appear to refer to a very correct pronunciation; the speech of the author of *WSC-RS* appears to have been at least somewhat 'advanced', and was indeed probably vulgar. Brown, whose dialectal pronunciations connect him with the North (see Vol. I, pp. 369–71, pp. 417–19), cannot be accepted as providing valid evidence of the StE pronunciation of ME *ẹ̄* words; but it is clear that ME *ẹ̄* had ceased to have a separate existence in the speech represented in his 'phonetically spelt' list, which uses *ea* as a symbol for [iː] in *fatigue* and *intrigue* (see Vol. I, p. 368); that his own speech was similar is suggested by his comment on the pronunciations of the spelling *tear*, though in his general rules he follows Cooper in distinguishing two sets of *ea* words, one with [eː] from ME *ẹ̄* and the other with [iː] from ME *ẹ̄*. Certain 'homophone' lists give hints of a mode of pronunciation in which all 'ME *ẹ̄* words' had [iː]; but the nature of the evidence makes it unjustifiable to use it to show more than that [iː] occurs in the particular words involved, especially as the authors of the lists all distinguish ME *ẹ̄* from ME *ẹ̄* in the text of their spelling-books.

Eighteenth-century evidence commonly shows the PresE situation in which all 'ME *ẹ̄* words', with certain definite exceptions, have [iː].

Note 1: The general substitution of [iː] for [eː] in 'ME *ẹ̄* words' occurred early in the North; it is shown by Levins (Vol. I, pp. 24–26), by Hume (Vol. I, p. 320), and by Ridpath (see Vol I, p. 393). Brown's evidence (see above) probably depends on this Northern pronunciation. But Poole does not clearly show the general use of [iː] in 'ME *ẹ̄* words' (see Vol. I, p. 436). Gil's evidence on the 'Eastern dialect' unfortunately fails to show whether it used [iː] in 'ME *ẹ̄* words' (see Vol. I, p. 149).

Note 2: Zachrisson, *Eng. Vowels*, pp. 68–69, and Wyld, *Coll. Eng.*, p. 209, and *Rhymes*, p. 60, who accept the usual view that ME *ẹ̄* passed from [eː] to [iː] by a ModE sound-change (though Wyld would regard it as a dialectal and not a StE change), believe that there is evidence which shows this change at an earlier date than that usually assigned to it (*c.* 1700). The evidence which they adduce consists of spellings and rhymes. On the theory which I have put forward, such evidence cannot show that there has been a general substitution of [iː] for [eː] in 'ME *ẹ̄* words'; even if it really showed [iː], it would be evidence of the pronunciation [iː] only in the particular word concerned. But it is worth while to take this occasion of pointing out that even on the assumption that ME *ẹ̄* passed from [eː] to [iː] by a ModE sound-change, the evidence of Wyld and Zachrisson does not prove this change to have occurred.

(1) The evidence of many of the rhymes must be rejected for various reasons. Some of the rhymes cited really have ME *ẹ̄* in both words; so Wyld's *stepe* 'steep' : *lepe* 'leap' (Skelton), both of which have OE *ēa*, and *seas* : *these*, &c., which depend on sixteenth- and seventeenth-century StE *ẹ̄* in *these*. Very many of the rhymes cited by J. D. Jones in his edition of Cooper's *Grammatica*, pp. 32*–34*, depend on ME *ẹ̄* in both words. A large number of the other rhymes cited by Wyld and Jones depend on a well-established ME *ẹ̄* variant in the supposed 'ME *ẹ̄*' word; we may particularly mention words which have ME *ẹ̄*

before a dental, e.g. *clean, beat, great*, in which raising to ME ẹ̄ occurs in ME. Most of the remaining rhymes certainly or probably depend on shortening. Shortening of ME ẹ̄ will of course give [i]; normally [e] results from ME ẹ̄, but [i] often occurs (cf. the spellings cited below; on the phonetic process involved see § 30, Note 2). The mere possibility that the rhymes may depend on shortening makes them inconclusive as evidence. Shakespeare's rhymes of *beseech* with *impleach, beseech thee* with *teach thee*, certainly depend on shortening; cf. his *beseech'd* : *enrich'd* (see Viëtor). Lodge's *aggrieved* : *deceived*, Shakespeare's *relieveth* : *upheaveth*, and seventeenth-century rhymes of the type *believe* : *conceive* (Jones, loc. cit.) may well depend on shortening; cf. such rhymes as *give* : *receive* (Jones, loc. cit.). Shortening is also possible before *p* and *k*, and would explain such rhymes as *threap* : *keep* (*Oxford Book of Sixteenth Century Verse*, p. 156) and *speak* : *seek* : *peak* (Jones, loc. cit.). Rhymes between ME ẹ̄ and ME ę̄ in final position (e.g. Pope's *see* : *flea* cited by Jones, loc. cit.) can hardly be used as evidence of a ModE development of ME ẹ̄ to [i:] by those who reject ME rhymes of this sort as inaccurate. Rhymes between *stream(s)* and *seem(s)* in Spenser and Raleigh are perhaps the best evidence of a sixteenth-century change of ME ẹ̄ to [i:] so far produced; but apart from the fact that *stream* vb. (used in Spenser's rhyme) might have ẹ̄ from an OE *strēman* and might analogically influence the sb. (used in Raleigh's rhyme), we must again point out that similar rhymes are found in ME.

(2) Wyld and Zachrisson cite spellings with *i* or *y* for ME ẹ̄. Zachrisson (but not Wyld) would reject pre-1550 cases on the ground that the spelling shows shortening (so Kihlbom, p. 73); after 1550 he would join with Wyld in interpreting these spellings as showing [i:]. But in ModE the letters *i* and *y* have only two values, short [i] or the diphthong [əi] (PresE [ai]); and it would therefore be altogether surprising if they were used for [i:]. To argue that because *i* and *y* represent [i] they ought also to be used to represent [i:] is not characteristic of a plain man, but of a phonetician; if it were otherwise, there would have been no need for the sixteenth-century spelling reformers, and they would not have failed. The various writers cited by Wyld and Zachrisson (and similarly in connexion with ME ę̄; see § 132, Note) were striving as best they could to follow the conventional StE orthography, and it is unthinkable that they would use the vowel-letter *i* in any but its traditional values; even Smith and Bullokar, who set out to reform or to supplement the traditional spelling, and of whom the former was a most learned linguist, were unable to rid themselves of the idea that ME ī was the long equivalent of ĭ and should be so written. In point of fact all the words cited have [i] by shortening (see under (1) above); Zachrisson should have dismissed them as he dismissed the pre-1550 cases (as is realized by Wijk, *Machyn*, pp. 97–99, who adds to Zachrisson's instances from Machyn one or two others, e.g. *grit* 'great' and *myllman* 'mealman'). (i) Shortening before *ch* [tʃ] is common in ME and continues in eModE, and accounts for the spelling *prych* 'preach' as for Shakespeare's rhyme of *teach* (see under (1) above). (ii) Before [k] shortening occurs in late ME or eModE in, for example, *sick, rick, struck* < *strook*, &c.; similar shortening accounts for *bryking* 'breaking', *bryke-fast* 'breakfast' (in this word note the ME shortening preserved by the PresE pronunciation), *spyking* 'speaking', *spike* 'speak'. (iii) Before [v] shortening occurs in late ME or eModE in *glove*, &c.; similar shortening accounts for *berive* 'bereave' (Ascham) and *bequived* 'bequeathed' (Queen Elizabeth). If it be argued that the Queen's spelling should be explained from the normal form with [ð] the problem is little more difficult; final [ð] does not normally cause shortening in StE, but Hart gives ŏ in *both* (in which he has [ð]); the dialect of Northumberland shows analogous shortening of Anglian ē in *breathe* (Wright, *EDG*, § 132). (iv) *Lipe* 'leap' shows shortening of ME ẹ̄ (< sb. and p.t.), not of ę̄; such spellings occur before 1400 (see *OED*). The evidence of modern dialects confirms that we have to do with shortening in all the words cited by Zachrisson and Wyld. Wright shows that ME ẹ̄ of various origins appears as [i] in many dialects in the following cases: (i) before *ch* [tʃ] in *breach* (§ 61), *each, bleach, reach, teach* (§ 138), *preach* (§ 220); (ii) before [k] in *break* (§ 61) and *beak* (§ 220); (iii) before *v* in *deceive* (§ 220); (iv) before [ð] examples fail, but cf. shortening of ME ę̄ referred to above. The dialects also show shortening of ME ẹ̄ to [i] before *d, t, l, m, n,* [þ], and *s*. The parallelism between the spellings and the dialectal pronunciations listed under (i), (ii), and (iii) is very close. The retention of final *e* in many of the spellings does not show that the vowel is long (if it did, it would be 'long *i*'); it is an unintelligent graphic addition (such as was common in the fifteenth and sixteenth centuries) due to the

influence of the traditional spelling, and after *v* is absolutely necessary, according to the conventional rule, even when the vowel is short.

VARIATION BETWEEN ME ẹ̄ AND ME ẹ̄

§ 117. If the theory of the development of ME ẹ̄ advanced above is correct, it follows that all 'ME ẹ̄ words' had developed, before or during the ME period, a variant pronunciation with ME ẹ̄. On the other hand many 'ME ẹ̄ words' have a variant in ME ẹ̄. In the following section we shall examine the evidence for the existence of ME ẹ̄ beside ME ẹ̄ in various classes of words.

(1) *Words containing OE ǣ¹ (WGmc ā)*

§ 118. OE ǣ¹ (WGmc ā) is ǣ in WS and ē in Anglian and Kentish; this variation between the OE dialects affects ME and leaves fairly numerous traces in StE pronunciation during our period. In the following, no attempt is made to exhaust the list of words which have OE ǣ¹; the object is merely to illustrate the variation. (*a*) *Leech* is said by Smith to have either ẹ̄ or ẹ̄; it has ẹ̄ in Willis. But *speech* regularly has ẹ̄, as in Hart and Willis. (*b*) The variation is commonest in *read*. It has ẹ̄ in Hart, Laneham, Robinson, Jonson, Price, Cooper, the 'homophone' lists of Hodges ('near alike'; contrast *EP*), Price, Coles, Strong, Young, Cooper, *WSC-RS*, Cocker, and Brown. It has ẹ̄ in the *ABC for chyldren*, Smith, Bullokar, Gil, Hodges *EP* (contrast his 'near alike' list in *SH-PD*), Wallis, Wilkins, the *Treatise of Stops* (possibly with a variant ẹ̄), *The Protestant Tutor*, and Willis's rhyme-list (see Vol. I, p. 426). *Deed* always has ẹ̄, as in Butler and Hodges. *Mead* has ẹ̄ in the *ABC for chyldren* and Willis. *Thread* (usually with a short vowel) has ẹ̄ in Laneham. *Dread* (also usually short) has ẹ̄ in Willis, followed by Poole. (*c*) *Fear* shows frequent variation; it has ẹ̄ in Hodges, Cooper, Aickin, Brown, the shorthand-writer Bridges, and the rhyme-lists of Willis and Coles, but ẹ̄ in Hart, *The English Schole-Master* (1646), and the 'homophone' lists of Price, Hawkins, *WSC-RS*, and Cocker, which equate the word with *fare* and *fair*. *Bier* has normally ME ẹ̄, but 'homophone' lists from that of Fox and Hookes onwards equate it with *bare* and *bear*. *Where* and *there*, however, always have ME ẹ̄ except in the *Welsh Hymn* (MS A only, in *where*) and in the Northerners Levins and Poole (see Vol. I, p. 436), who naturally have Anglian ē. Mulcaster, also a Northerner, may have ME ẹ̄ in *where* and *there*, since in his speech they have the same vowel as *mere*, for which only ẹ̄ is recorded (see § 126) though ẹ̄ is possible. (*d*) *Breath*, when it has a long vowel, has in StE always ME ẹ̄, as in Hart, Bullokar, Gil (1619), and Willis (followed surprisingly by the Northerner Poole); but Levins has [iː] from ME ẹ̄. (*e*) *Meal* 'a repast' has ME ẹ̄ in Salesbury (see Vol. I, p. 16). A special case is *cheese*, which varies in Smith between ẹ̄ and ẹ̣̄. The form with ẹ̄ goes back to Anglian cēse < WGmc *kāsi < Lat. cāseus. The form with ẹ̣̄ cannot, however, go back to the normal WS form, which is cīese (with WS palatal diphthongization). But in the 'Saxon patois' palatal diphthongization sometimes fails (cf. Bülbring, § 153), and so a form *cǣse might be found, which would give ME chẹ̣̄se (cf. the twelfth-century spellings cease and cæse recorded by OED).

(2) *Other words which have OE dialectal variants*

§ 119. Variation between ME ẹ̄ and ME ẹ̣̄ deriving ultimately from OE also occurs in a certain number of other words, in which it is due to a variety of factors.

(a) *Variation between Anglian and WS because of Anglian smoothing*

Eke (Anglian ēca, WS ēaca) has ẹ̣̄ in Robinson (once, beside ẹ̄) and Gil, but ẹ̄ in Bullokar and Robinson (once). Near (Anglian nēr < *nēhur, WS nēar < *nēahur) has ẹ̣̄ in Smith, Laneham, Bullokar (thirteen times, beside ẹ̄), Robinson, Gil (once, beside ẹ̄), Willis, Wallis, Price, Coles, and Cooper (followed by Aickin); but ẹ̄ in Hart, Bullokar (nine times), Gil (twice), and probably Hunt (who gives it as a homophone of *ne'er* 'never').

(b) *Variation between Anglian and WS because of WS palatal diphthongization*

Year (Anglian gēr, WS gēar) has ẹ̣̄ in Laneham, Bullokar, Robinson, Butler, Hodges, Willis, *The English Schole-Master* (1646), Price, Coles, Cooper (followed by Aickin), and the shorthand-writer Bridges; but ẹ̄ in Gil. Yea (Anglian gē, WS gēa) has ẹ̣̄ in Bullokar (once) and Hodges (*EP* and the homophone list of *SH-PD*), but ẹ̄ in Salesbury, Hart, Robinson, Gil, Lane, Richardson, Coles's 'homophone' and rhyming list (in his *Schoolmaster*), and Willis's rhymes. See further Note 1 below.

(c) *Variation because of back-mutation*

Pease (oblique and plural forms pĭsan > ME pẹ̣̄sen beside pĕosan > ME pẹ̄sen) and glede 'kite' (glĭda beside *glĕoda and ON glĕða) may vary between ẹ̄ and ẹ̣̄ (see Vol. I, p. 426); similarly *cleave* 'haerere' and by analogy *cleave* 'findere' (see Vol. I, p. 56).

(d) *Variation because of late WS palatal mutation*

Cheap vb. has ẹ̄ beside ẹ̣̄ in Smith. OE cēapian normally gives rise to the ẹ̣̄ form; but WS palatal mutation causes ēa to develop to ē (Bülbring, § 315), whence cēpian, which gives rise to the ẹ̄ form.

(e) *Kentish* ē < ǣ²

There is little or no evidence to show variation between Kentish ẹ̄ and non-Kentish $\bar{e}$ from OE $\bar{æ}^2$ (Gmc $ai+i$); but it may occur in *sleave* (§ 124 and Note 2) and in *sea* (§ 125 and Note).

Note 1: The 'homophone' lists equate *yea* with *ye*, which is ambiguous, except in the cases of Hodges (who spells *ye* as *yee*), and Coles (who adds rhymes with $\bar{ẹ}$). Levins rhymes *yea* with $\bar{ẹ}$, but in his speech $\bar{ẹ}$ was generally [i:]; he should have $\bar{ẹ}$ in *yea*. Poole also should have $\bar{ẹ}$, and rhymes *yea* with *fee*; but he also rhymes it with $\bar{ẹ}$ words, which in his speech may be, but are probably not, pronounced as [i:]. (He is, however, following Willis in these $\bar{ẹ}$ rhymes.)

Note 2: Variation in OE may arise from other causes than those set out above, which are designed to show only the most frequent examples. *Sere* adj. 'withered' is OE *sīere*, *sēre beside *sēar*; Coles has ME $\bar{ẹ}$ in *seir*, presumably *sere* adj.

(3) *Special conditions*

§ 120. In some words variation between ME $\bar{ẹ}$ and ME $\bar{ẹ}$ arises because of special conditions. Shortening under weak stress and lengthening because of restressing accounts for early ModE $\bar{ẹ}$ beside normal $\bar{ẹ}$ in *he* (§ 4) and *the* (§ 4). *Even* varies between ME $\breve{e}$ and ME $\bar{ẹ}$ (§ 8), ME $\breve{i}$ and ME $\bar{ẹ}$ (§ 10). *Stead* (OE *stede* and *styde*) similarly varies between ME $\breve{e}$ and ME $\bar{ẹ}$ (§ 8), ME $\breve{i}$ and ME $\bar{ẹ}$ (§ 10). Rhymes on these two words are hopelessly ambiguous. *These* varies in ME because of the circumstances of its formation (see *OED* for the forms; but Murray's explanation of them is unfortunately confused); in ME *pĕs* and *pĭs* were originally used as plurals, but were later extended by the addition of the plural ending *e*, giving *pĕse* (whence *pẹ̄se* with lengthening in the open syllable) and *pĭse* (whence *pẹ̄se*). The word usually has ME $\bar{ẹ}$ in the orthoepists; thus Smith, Hart, Bullokar, Robinson, Gil and Hodges transcribe it *ðēz*, and likewise Strong says that it has ME $\bar{ẹ}$. But Laneham and Newton have ME $\bar{ẹ}$ (cf. the eModE spelling *theese*). (*Be*)*smear* (OE *sme(o)ru* sb., *smerian* beside *smirian* vb.; see *OED*) has $\bar{ẹ}$ < eME $\breve{e}$ in Willis but $\bar{ẹ}$ < eME $\breve{i}$ in Coles, Cooper (followed by Aickin and Brown), and the shorthand-writer Bridges. *Leam* (OE *lēoma*) should have $\bar{ẹ}$, but Laneham has $\bar{ẹ}$, and the forms recorded by *OED* suggest that the word has $\bar{ẹ}$ from the fourteenth century onwards (cf. the rhymes cited in the Note below); it may be that OE had **lēam-* beside *lēoma* (see Vol. I, p. 91). In certain cases analogical processes appear to cause variation between ME $\bar{ẹ}$ and ME $\bar{ẹ}$. *Reek* vb., which should normally have ME $\bar{ẹ}$, seems to have ME $\bar{ẹ}$ in Willis, because of the influence of the OE preterite (see Vol. I, p. 426). *Steam* sb. (OE *stēam*) has ME $\bar{ẹ}$, but the verb (OAngl *stēman*) should have ME $\bar{ẹ}$, as in Cooper; the verb, however, might be influenced by the substantive and come to have ME $\bar{ẹ}$ (cf. Horn, § 79, Anm. 3, on *dream* vb.) or the substantive might be influenced by the verb and come to have ME $\bar{ẹ}$. *Stream* vb. is not recorded until ME, and seems likely to be a ME formation from the substantive (OE *strēam*), which would have ME $\bar{ẹ}$; but it might go back to OAngl *strēman or be influenced by the analogy of *stẹ̄men*, *tẹ̄men*, &c. beside *stẹ̄m*, *tẹ̄m*, &c., and in either event would develop a form with ME $\bar{e}$ which might react on the substantive. This may be the explanation of Spenser's and Raleigh's rhymes referred to in § 116, Note 2. The occurrence in ME of $\bar{e}$ beside $\bar{ę}$ in *leave* sb. 'permission' and *belief* (OE *lēaf* and *bi+lēafa*) is commonly attributed to the analogical influence of the related verbs (OAngl *lēfan, bi+lēfan*), as by ten Brink, *Language and Metre of Chaucer*, § 25, Note. Gil records ME $\bar{e}$ in *leave* sb. in the speech of the *Mopsæ*. But it is possible, especially as in eModE there is only this record of ME $\bar{e}$ in *leave*, that we have to do not with analogical influences but with raising of ME $\bar{ę}$ to $\bar{e}$ before *v*; raising of ME $\bar{ę}$ before other consonants was especially common in the sort of speech which Gil calls that of the *Mopsæ*. On Smith's $\bar{e}$ in place of normal $\bar{ę}$ in *cleave* 'findere' see Vol. I, p. 56.

Note: Many of the rhymes cited by Mackenzie, *Englische Studien*, lxi (1927), pp. 387–8, may depend on pronunciations similar to those discussed above. Thus *lem* (OE *lēoma*) rhymes with *rem* 'cream' (*Arthur and Merlin*), *strem* sb. (*St. Patrick's Purgatory*), *beme* 'beam' (*Floris and Blancheflour*, Lydgate, Hawes); Fischer, *Englische Studien*, lxiv (1929), p. 14, cites also Chaucer's *lemes* : *dremes* (*C.T.*, B 4119). All these may depend on $\bar{e}$ in *leam*, as in Laneham. Mackenzie cites also the following rhymes. *Dreme* 'dream' rhymes with *ʒeme* (*Floris*) and *seme* 'seem' (Lydgate); it may have analogical $\bar{e}$ owing to the influence of OE **drēman*. *Heved* 'head' rhymes with *cleued* 'cleft' (*St. Alexius*), perhaps because *cleave* 'split' has $\bar{e}$ as in Smith; but both words probably have $\bar{ę}$. The rhyme *lepe* 'leap' vb. with *weep* (*Arthur and Merlin*) may show the influence of the sb. (OAngl **hlēp*) on the verb, or of the preterite (OE *hlēop, hlēopon*) on the infinitive. *Leped* 'leapt' : *creped* 'crept' (*King Alisaunder*) doubtless depends on shortening. *Hepe* 'heap' : *leep* pret. sing. (*Richard Cœur de Lion*), *hepe* : *lep* pret. pl. (*Seven Sages*), and *chepe* 'bargain' : *lepe* pret. sing. (*Octovian*) may show ME $\bar{e}$ in the preterite owing to the influence of the infinitive. *Beme* 'beam' : *ʒeme* (*St. Patrick's Purgatory*) may possibly depend on ME $\bar{e}$ in *beam* owing to the influence of *leam* (OE *lēoma*).

These ordinarily rhymes on $\bar{ę}$ in the sixteenth and seventeenth centuries (cf. Wyld, *Rhymes*, p. 60), but Greene rhymes it with *'grees* 'agrees' (*Oxford Book of Sixteenth Century Verse*, p. 391).

(4) *Raising of ME $\bar{ę}$ to ME $\bar{e}$*

§ 121. Raising of ME $\bar{ę}$, which is characteristic of Northern and Eastern dialects, is usually regarded as a combinative change, occurring before dentals 'in the widest sense' (Luick, § 187; cf. § 361, Anm. 2; Jordan, § 48, Anm. 2). But evidence, both in ME (see § 108, Note 2) and eModE (see below), shows it to have occurred before other consonants than dentals and in final position; moreover it is very common before *r*, which, though in one sense a dental, can hardly have exercised a raising influence: there are parallels enough for isolative raisings occurring in spite of, but hardly any for a combinative raising because of, a following *r*. The greater frequency with which evidence of the raising is recorded before *r* and dentals must be attributed simply to the statistical accident that in English it is much more common for a vowel to be followed by *r* or a dental than by other consonants or no consonant. Raising of ME $\bar{ę}$ to $\bar{e}$ (like the parallel raising of ME $\bar{ǫ}$ to $\bar{o}$; see §§ 148–52 below) must then be an isolative tendency, analogous to (and a continuation of) the early OE changes whereby $ǣ^1$ < WGmc $ā$ became $ē$ in Anglian and Kentish and $ǣ^2$ < WGmc $ai+i$ became $ē$ in Kentish and (less generally) in Eastern Mercian. The tendency affects ME $ẹ̄$ of all origins, including even the latest developed, ME $ẹ̄$ < $ĕ$ in an open syllable (cf. the rhymes cited by Miss Fischer, *Englische Studien*, lxiv. 1–19).

In deference to the usual view, the evidence is set out below in accordance with phonetic context; but that cited under (*c*) and (*d*) must indicate that an isolative change is involved. In what follows, it is assumed that evidence of eModE [iː] in authors who do not generally identify ME $ẹ̄$ with ME $ę̄$ is *ipso facto* evidence of late ME $ẹ̄$.

(a) Raising before r

§ 122. Evidence of raising of ME $ę̄$ to $ẹ̄$ before *r* occurs in the earlier ME period, and the process must cease to operate at latest about 1400 in Southern English, for by that time even in the South *r* had begun to exert a strong lowering influence (in particular, by the early fifteenth century, on ME $ẹ̄$; see § 126 below). Evidence of raising before *r* is fairly common, obviously because ME $ę̄$ precedes *r* in many common words.

Raising before final *r* occurs as follows. (i) Words with OE $ǣ^2$ (Gmc $ai+i$). *Ere* adv. has [iː] from $ẹ̄$ in *RS*. *Rear* vb. has $ẹ̄$ in Smith but $ę̄$ in Coles. (ii) Words with OE $ēa$. *Ear* (of corn) has $ę̄$ in Bullokar, and so has *ear* (of the head) in Bullokar, Robinson, Butler, Hodges (once, beside $ẹ̄$), and Price; but the latter word has $ẹ̄$ by raising in Butler (who merely admits that 'some' say it thus), Hodges (four times, beside $ę̄$), Coles, Cooper, and Brown. *Sear* has $ę̄$ in Willis, but $ẹ̄$ in Coles and Cooper (followed by Aickin). *Tear* 'lacrima' has $ę̄$ in Smith, Robinson, and Gil, but $ẹ̄$ in Bullokar, Butler, Hodges, Willis, Cooper, Brown, and *RS*. To these we might add *shears*, if it owes its vowel to OE *scēar*; but OE has a distinct formation *scērero* pl. (see *OED*). The word is only recorded with $ẹ̄$, by Laneham, Cooper, and Brown's 'homophone' list (which equates the word with *shire*, pronounced [ʃiːr] as in compounds). (iii) OE (and ON) $ĕ$ in an open syllable. *Bear* vb. seems to have $ę̄$ in Johnson (1662), but has $ẹ̄$ in all other orthoepists. *Gear* has $ẹ̄$ in Bullokar, Coles, Cooper, and Aickin. *Shear* vb. has $ẹ̄$ in Butler, Willis, and Strong's 'homophone' list, but $ę̄$ (identified with ME $ā$) in Cooper (Latin edition) and in Brown's 'homophone' list, which equates the word with *share*; these two orthoepists thus distinguish the verb from the substantive, perhaps because of the OE distinction between *scĕran* and *scērero* pl. Other 'homophone' lists put *shear* with both *shire* (which shows [iː] from ME $ẹ̄$) and *share* (which shows [ɛː] from ME $ę̄$); so Wharton, Price, Fox and Hookes, Coles (*Eng.–Lat. Dict.*), and *WSC*. It seems probable that this is the verb, with variation; but their *shear* may cover both the sb. and the vb., and they may have known but failed to make clear the distinction made by Brown in his list. *Spear* has $ẹ̄$ in Price but $ę̄$ in Willis,

Coles, and Cooper. *Tear* vb. (and the derived sb.) have ẹ̄ in Smith, Bullokar, Gil, Cooper (who equates ME ẹ̄ in *tear* vb. with ME ā, and contrasts *tear* 'lacrima'), and *RS*. *Wear* has ẹ̄ in Bullokar, and *weir* has ẹ̄ in Willis. To these words we should possibly add *blear-eyed* (ME ĕ?), which has ẹ̄ in Willis and ẹ̄ in Coles and Cooper (followed by Aickin).

It will be noticed that there is variation not only between analogous words, but also in the pronunciation of individual words. Raising is shown chiefly in native English words, but there are two which (as far as is known) did not form part of the OE vocabulary, *gear* (ON *gervi*) and *blear* (of unknown origin; first recorded in ME). The raising before final *r* seems less frequently recorded in the sixteenth and early seventeenth centuries than it is later; it may have come into StE from the 'Eastern dialects', in which it appears to have been common in ME, or from vulgar London English, as represented by the 'homophone' lists (see Notes 1 and 3 below).

Raising of ME ẹ̄ to ME ẹ̄ before *r* plus consonant occurs as follows. (i) The native English word *beard* has [iː] in Levins (probably a Northernism) and Hodges, against ẹ̄ in Cooper and Aickin (who identify this ME ẹ̄ with ME ā). Other native words have regularly ẹ̄. (ii) *Verse* (ME vẹ̄rs, but also evidently vẹrs, in part from OE *fers* and in part from OF *vers*, whence the long vowel must arise) has [iː] in Hodges. (iii) Words adopted from French. *Pearl* (pop. Lat *pĕrla*) and *perch* (Lat *pĕrtica*) have normal ME ẹ̄ (< OF ę < Lat ĕ blocked); this is recorded for *pearl* by Bullokar and Cooper. But raising to late ME ẹ̄ is shown by Hodges's [iː] in both words. *Hearse* (Lat *hĭrpicem*) and its derivative *rehearse* have ME ẹ̄ (< OF ę < ę < Lat ĭ blocked); this is recorded by Bullokar and Cooper, but Hodges has ME ẹ̄ by raising. The etymology of *pierce* is dubious, and it cannot therefore be determined whether it should normally have ME ẹ̄ or ME ẹ̄; Luick, § 411, Anm. 2, apparently regards ME ẹ̄ as normal and ME ẹ̄ as an unexplained irregularity. We can now explain ẹ̄ (if ẹ̄ is normal) as due to raising. The word has ẹ̄ in Robinson, but ẹ̄ in Levins, Price, Coles, Cooper, Brown, and *RS*, and in Hodges's 'near alike' list.

Except in *pierce* (which may not have original ME ẹ̄) the raising is less commonly preserved before *r* plus consonant than before final *r*, but affects words of French origin as well as (indeed, apparently more than) native English words. The reason is that before *r* plus consonant there is normally, in native words (less often in French words), a late ME lowering of earlier ẹ̄ to ẹ̄ (see § 126 below).

PresE uses the pronunciation [iː] in a good many words for what is usually described as 'ME ẹ̄' before *r*. This [iː] should always be explained as developed from a late ME variant ẹ̄, either by raising of ME ẹ̄ before the following *r*, or (as in *fear*) representing OAngl ē for WS ǣ. We then get a coherent picture of the development of ME ẹ̄ and ME ẹ̄ before *r*: (*a*) late ME ẹ̄ before *r* develops, like ME ẹ̄ in all other positions, to ModE [iː];

(*b*) late ME ẹ̄ before *r* (which includes the ẹ̄ developed by lowering of ME ẹ̣̄ in this position) retains the value [ɛ:], being held back by the influence of the following *r* (see §§ 203-4 below), and becomes identical with ME *ā* when the latter reaches this value, the two sounds then remaining unchanged as [ɛ:], whence (after the loss of *r*) the PresE [ɛə]. The latter now occurs chiefly in words (e.g. *bear*, *tear* vḅ., *wear*) with early ME *ĕ* in an open syllable (though [i:ə] occurs even in such words; cf. *gear*, *shear* vb., *spear*), the exceptions being *were* pronounced [wɛə] (the obsolescent strong form), *there*, *where*, *ere*, *e'er*, and *ne'er*; this suggests that the unraised pronunciation was most likely to maintain itself in words in which ME ẹ̄ was of comparatively recent development (cf. further Note 5 below and § 109 above).

Note 1: The evidence of the 'homophone' lists is necessarily often ambiguous, for ME ẹ̄r words can only be put with ME ẹ̣̄r words (except when *shear* is put with *sheer* and *shire*) or ME *ār* words. The latter pairing shows retention of ME ẹ̄, but the former does not necessarily show raising to ME ẹ̣̄, for ME ẹ̄ can, and often does, become ME ẹ̣̄ before *r*. But when ME ẹ̄r and ME ẹ̣̄r words are paired the pronunciation [i:] generally seems more likely. Such pairings are given in many lists (usually the same pairings repeated) and may show [i:] in *tear* vb., and more doubtfully in *pear* and in *bear* vb. These three words are also put with ME *ār* words, so if they did have [i:] from ME ẹ̄, they also had [ɛ:] from ME ẹ̄.

Rhyme-lists are similarly ambiguous. Levins seems to have [i:] generally for free ME ẹ̄, and also for ME ẹ̄ before *r*; this is a Northernism. Poole, also a Northerner, does not certainly have [i:] for free ME ẹ̄, but he has it always for ME ẹ̣̄ before *r*. On Willis see Vol. I, pp. 425-6.

Note 2: Raising of ME ẹ̄ to ME ẹ̣̄ before final *r* cannot be shown by spellings in ME, since both sounds were represented by *e* or *ee*. Gower does often distinguish ẹ̣̄ as *ie*, but affords no evidence of the raising, as ME ẹ̣̄ for both OE *ǣ*¹ and *ǣ*² may in his speech be a Kenticism. From the fifteenth century onwards we may look for non-Kentish *ie* spellings as evidence of ME ẹ̣̄ by raising of ME ẹ̄; and *ee* spellings in the sixteenth century may often, and in the seventeenth century must almost always, show ModE [i:] from ME ẹ̣̄. Such spellings are fairly plentiful, to judge from the evidence of *OED*: see under *ere*, *ear*, *sear* vb., *shear(s)*, *gear*, *pear*, *spear*, *weir*, *blear*, *tear* sb. 'lacrima'.

Note 3: Rhymes of ME ẹ̄ with ME ẹ̣̄ before final *r* in ME are not infrequent in Eastern texts. See Mackenzie, *Englische Studien*, lxi (1927), 386-92 and Fischer, ibid. lxiv (1929), 1-19. Cf. also *Havelok*, 11-12, 731-2, 824-5, 1640-1. Sixteenth- and seventeenth-century rhymes between ME ẹ̄ and ME ẹ̣̄ before final *r*, which are comparatively frequent, are necessarily ambiguous, for they may depend either on the raising of ME ẹ̄ to ME ẹ̣̄, or on the later lowering of ME ẹ̣̄ to ME ẹ̄ before *r* (see § 126 below); but at any rate they reveal the variation in pronunciation. On the development of ME ẹ̄ and ME ẹ̣̄ before *r* see Wyld, *Rhymes*, pp. 63-67, and especially pp. 65-66, for a list of rhymes between ME ẹ̄ and ME ẹ̣̄ before *r*. Wyld fails to understand and to explain the ModE development of ME ẹ̄ and ME ẹ̣̄ before *r*; he can only assume that there are 'two streaks of different dialectal influence in our present Standard' (p. 64).

Note 4: The following spellings recorded by *OED* seem to show the raising of ME ẹ̄ to ME ẹ̣̄ before *r* plus consonant: sixteenth-century *beerd(e)* 'beard', *peerle* 'pearl'; seventeenth-century *hierce* 'hearse'. *Pierce* has *ie* from the sixteenth century onwards, beside sixteenth- and seventeenth-century *ea* and sixteenth- to eighteenth-century *ei* forms which show ME ẹ̣̄.

Note 5: Even in some of the 'exceptions' cited above we could assume late ME ẹ̄ by open-syllable lengthening of earlier *ĕ*, e.g. *wĕre* could be from an earlier *wĕren* by restressing of an eME weak form, [ðɛə] could be from late ME *ðĕre* < *ðĕre* < a weak form *ðĕr* plus adverbial *-e* (similarly for *where*, and perhaps though not very probably for *ere*); but such an explanation will hardly apply to *e'er* (ME *ẹ̄r* < *ẹ̄ver*; cf. Laȝamon's *ær*) and *ne'er* (Laȝamon *ner*).

Note 6: Horn, §§ 86-87, adopts very much the same explanation as that set out in the preceding paragraph of the development of ME *ẹ̄* before *r* in ModE. He regards PresE [ɛə] as the normal development before *r* of eModE [ɛ:] from ME *ẹ̄* (though he unnecessarily assumes that this [ɛ:] was at one stage fronted to [e:] and then retracted again to [ɛ:], both these developments occurring in the ModE period); and he explains PresE [iə] in *tear* sb. 'lacrima' and such words with original ME *ẹ̄* as being always derived from an eModE [i:] which the retracting influence of the *r* was powerless to affect. But as he does not recognize the OE and ME raising of OE *ǣ*, ME *ę̄* before *r*, he can find no better explanation for this early ModE [i:] in *tear* than that *tear* varied in early ModE between [ɛ:] and [i:] on the analogy of such words as *year* or *fear*, in which the variation goes back to OE dialectal variants. On Luick's elaborate and improbable view of the development of ME *ę̄* before *r* in eModE see § 203, Note.

(b) Raising before other Dentals

§ 123. There is little evidence of the raising of ME *ę̄* to ME *ẹ̄* before other dentals than *r* outside the 'homophone' lists. *Mean* vb. has *ẹ̄* in Smith but *ę̄* in other orthoepists. *Clean* has [i:] from ME *ę̄* in Hart, Laneham (beside *ę̄*), and Strong's 'phonetically spelt' list, but *ę̄* is normal (it occurs, for example, in Price and Aickin among seventeenth-century spelling-books). *Hele* 'cover' (OE *hĕlan*), perhaps already dialectal, has *ẹ̄* in Bullokar. *Deal* has ME *ẹ̄* in Laneham but *ę̄* in Hart; the latter is normal. *Metre* has ME *ẹ̄* (probably beside *ę̄*) in Laneham, and *ẹ̄* twice beside *ę̄* once in Bullokar; but the reason may be rather the variation between *ẹ̄* and *ę̄* for Latin *ĕ* in open syllables than ME raising. *Feat* adj. (if this, and not *fit*, be the word intended; see Vol. I, p. 90) has *ẹ̄* in Laneham. *Said* (i.e. ME *sẹde* < OE (Saxon) *sǣde*) is twice rhymed on [i:] < ME *ẹ̄* by Bullokar. *Please* has ME *ẹ̄* beside ME *ę̄* in Newton. *Weasel* has ME *ẹ̄* (represented by *ee*) in the 'phonetically spelt' lists of Coles and Young. It should be noticed that Laneham, a London merchant, and the 'phonetically spelt' lists, which were based on less careful pronunciation, give most of the little evidence cited above; the raised pronunciation was evidently avoided in good speech. Gil would then appear to be justified in his inclusion of *mīt* 'meat' (with ME *ẹ̄*) among those pronunciations of the *Mopsæ* which he condemns.

Plentiful evidence of the raising is provided by 'homophone' lists after that of Wharton (1654). (a) *Knead* has *ẹ̄* in Price and Coles (*Eng.-Lat. Dict.*). *Bread* has *ẹ̄* in Wharton and Cocker, *dead* in Young and Cocker, and *head* in Young. (b) *Meat* has *ẹ̄* in Wharton, Price, Ellis, Fox and Hookes, Coles (*Eng.-Lat. Dict.*), Strong, Young, Richardson, *The Compendious Schoolmaster* (which also gives *ẹ̄* identified with ME *ā*), and Cocker. *Mete* has *ẹ̄* in the same lists. *Sweat* has *ẹ̄* in Wharton. (c) *Heal* has *ẹ̄* in Fox and Hookes, Strong, Young, and Cocker (who also gives *ẹ̄* identified with ME *ā*). *Steal* has *ẹ̄* in Fox and Hookes, Strong, Coles (*Eng.-Lat. Dict.*), and Brown. *Seal* ('sigillum'?) has *ẹ̄* in Strong. *Wheal* (presumably 'pustula') has *ẹ̄* in Wharton, Coles (*Eng.-Lat. Dict.*), and Cocker; on Young see Vol. I, p. 413.

Weal has $\bar{\varrho}$ in Coles (*Eng.–Lat. Dict.*), Young (who also gives ME $\bar{\varrho}$ identified with $\bar{a}$), and Brown. *Ceiling* has $\bar{\varrho}$ in Cocker. (*d*) *Quean* (which throughout the sixteenth and seventeenth centuries is usually employed by the orthoepists as a stock example, in contrast to *queen*, of the distinction between ME $\bar{\varrho}$ and ME $\bar{e}$) is nevertheless identified with *queen* in the 'homophone' lists of Hunt, Price, Ellis, Fox and Hookes, Coles (*Eng.–Lat. Dict.*), Strong, Young, *The Compendious Schoolmaster*, Hawkins, and Cocker. *Wean* and *bean* in Coles (*Eng.–Lat. Dict.*), and *mean* in Cocker, also have ME $\bar{\varrho}$. (*e*) *Peace* has $\bar{\varrho}$ in Ellis and Strong, who identify it with *piece*; for a parallel, cf. Coles's [i:] in *weasel* mentioned above. *Press* has [i:] in Fox and Hookes. (*f*) *WSC-RS* pairs *breaches* with *breeches*; but *breach* may have ME $\bar{\varrho}$ from OE *brȳce*, *brĭce*, or there may be shortening.

Thus the 'homophone' lists show the raising before *d*, *t*, *l*, *n*, and *s* (consonants before which raising occurred in OE; cf. Bülbring in *A Miscellany presented to Dr. Furnivall*), and perhaps before [tʃ]. The words affected are native English words, with the exception of *ceiling*, *metre*, *seal* (if it be 'sigillum'), and *peace*; and the vowels affected are OE $\bar{æ}^2$ < WGmc $ai+i$, ME $\bar{\varrho}$ < OE $\bar{e}a$ and < OE $\breve{e}$ in open syllables, and ME $\bar{\varrho}$ < OF ϱ. Clearly the process, though it began in OE, continued in ME; the greater susceptibility of native words is due to their having been longer exposed to the raising tendency.

The evidence as a whole shows that the use of the raised sound was a vulgarism, which might occasionally make its way into the speech of higher classes, as is shown by Smith and Hart in single cases, and perhaps by Laneham (but he seems not to represent educated speech) and by Coles's spelling of *weasel* in his *Schoolmaster* (but these 'phonetic spellings' are often based on vulgarisms; Coles's list on the other hand is the most careful). Gil's attack is a tacit admission that people of pretensions might occasionally use this pronunciation; but it was obviously not a mere prejudice that caused him to regard it with disfavour. The raised vowel is avoided even by some 'homophone' lists, including the best; Hodges and Cooper admit it neither to their 'alike' nor to their 'near alike' lists, and Coles only to his least careful one (that of the *Eng.–Lat. Dict.*).

Note 1: In the sixteenth and still more in the seventeenth century there are rhymes which depend on the raising of ME $\bar{\varrho}$ to $\bar{e}$ before dentals; see § 116, Note 2. It seems probable that the raised pronunciation made its way into London English from the dialect of Essex and neighbouring districts; ME texts from these districts give frequent evidence of the raising (cf. § 108, Note 2).

Note 2: Some scholars have declined to accept the view that there was a raising of OE $\bar{æ}^2$ < WGmc $ai+i$ to ME $\bar{e}$ before dentals, including *r*, and have sought to explain rhymes of OE $\bar{æ}^2$ with OE $\bar{e}$ (e.g. Chaucer's rhyme of *deel* 'deal' with *weel* 'well', *Pardoner's Tale*, ll. 669–70) by the influence of Kentish $\bar{e} < \bar{æ}^2$. But (*a*) such rhymes occur in texts from areas remote from Kentish influence (cf. Jordan, § 48, Anm. 2); (*b*) they involve ME $\bar{\varrho}$ from sources other than OE $\bar{æ}^2$; (*c*) the eModE evidence, which shows [i:] to have been used in the same phonetic contexts by orthoepists who still distinguished ME $\bar{\varrho}$ as [i:] from

ME $\bar{e}$ as [ɛː] or [eː], shows that the ME rhymes are not inexact; and (*d*) eModE evidence supports ME rhymes in showing a parallel raising of ME $\bar{\varrho}$ to ME $\bar{\rho}$ before dentals, especially *r*.

(c) Raising before consonants other than dentals

§ 124. That ME $\bar{\varepsilon}$ was raised to ME $\bar{e}$ before other consonants than dentals cannot be held to be well established; it would be desirable for the ME evidence of the development of ME $\bar{\varepsilon}$, especially in the Eastern dialects, to be re-examined with the object of discovering whether there is much indication of the process. Certain rhymes (see Note 2) suggest that it did occur. The ModE evidence on the development of ME $\bar{\varepsilon}$ can hardly be explained unless we assume that there was such a raising (see § 108 above), and support for the assumption comes from the analogy of ME $\bar{\varrho}$ (cf. § 151 below). The orthoepistical evidence is slight, but would tend to show that [iː] existed in certain 'ME $\bar{\varepsilon}$ words' in vulgar speech at a time when the great mass of our evidence still shows that ME $\bar{\varepsilon}$ was kept distinct from ME $\bar{e}$.

(i) Before *v* raising may be shown in *leave* sb. 'permission', of which Gil says that the *Mopsæ* pronounce it *līv* instead of *lēv*, and in *sleave* (silk) (OE $\bar{æ}^2$ < WGmc *ai+i*), which Hodges *SH-PD* pairs with *sleeve* (OAngl $\bar{e}$, WS *īe*) in his 'near alike' list, which is based on a less careful pronunciation than his own. The evidence is, however, unsatisfactory. *Leave* may have analogical $\bar{e}$ (see § 120). *Sleave* may be influenced by the analogy of *sleeve* itself, or Hodges may be influenced by Kentish pronunciation (see Note 3).

(ii) Before *m* raising appears to be shown by the pairing of *team* with *teem* in the 'homophone' lists of Young and (following him) Coles in the careless *Eng.-Lat. Dict.* and Cocker. But again analogy may account for this equation of two related words; cf. § 120 above.

(iii) Before *k* raising is shown by Wharton's pairing (adopted by *WSC-RS*) of *weak* and *week* as homophones. But the 'phonetic spelling' *reek* 'wreak' in Young 1722 is altered from *reak* 1681, and Willis's rhymes of ME $\bar{\varepsilon}$ words with *reek* may rest on analogical $\bar{e}$ in the latter (see § 120).

The evidence is thus slight and mostly rather doubtful; except for Gil's condemnatory reference (evidently well justified), it is all found in 'homophone' lists and a late (eighteenth-century) version of a 'phonetically spelt' list. We should perhaps add to the evidence cited above that of authors who show a general substitution of [iː] for [eː] in 'ME $\bar{\varepsilon}$ words', for if the theory which I have advanced to account for the ModE development is correct, this [iː] pronunciation is always due to a ME $\bar{e}$ by raising; this evidence is set out in § 116 above, and comes from *WSC-RS* and Northerners. But confining our attention to the evidence here cited, we may notice that only Gil, Hodges, Wharton, and Young originate evidence of [iː] in these words, and that only six authors, out of the eighteen studied who give 'homophone' lists, give pairings which show [iː], though the lists are mostly uncritical and based on vulgar pronunciation. The careful lists (Hodges's 'alike' list, Coles's list in the *Schoolmaster*, and Cooper's lists) avoid such pairings entirely. There can be no doubt that [iː] in these words was very far from being a correct pronunciation.

Note 1: ME rhymes which appear to depend on raising of ME ẹ̄ are cited by Mackenzie, *Englische Studien*, lxi (1927), 387–8 and Fischer, ibid. lxiv (1929), 4 (footnote) and 7. These rhymes come from texts written in the dialects to the east of London. Mackenzie cites *stepe* 'steep' (OE *stēap*) : *depe* 'deep' (*Arthur and Merlin, King Alisaunder, Palladius*), *stepe* : *kepe* 'keep' (*Palladius*), *hepe* 'heap' : *kepe* (*Richard Cœur de Lion, Seven Sages*, Lydgate, *Palladius*); Fischer cites *heved* 'head' : *weved* 'weaved' : *agreved* 'aggrieved' : *cleved* 'cleft' (*Octovian*), *slep* 'sleep' : *wep* 'weep': *kep* 'keep' : *hep* 'heap' (*Arthur and Merlin*), *slep* : *crepe* 'creep' : *wepe* : *hepe* 'heap' (*Octovian*). Other possible examples may depend on analogical pronunciations rather than on raising (see § 120, Note). On similar examples in Chaucer see § 109.

Early ModE rhymes which may depend on raising before labials and *k* are ambiguous; thus in particular rhymes of *receive*, &c. with ME ẹ̄ words may depend on shortening, not on ME raising of ẹ̄ to ẹ̄ (see § 116, Note 2). Such rhymes are rare. Wyatt's rhyme of *leave* sb. with *believe* and *preve* 'proof' (*Oxford Book of Sixteenth Century Verse*, p. 62) might seem to depend on [iː]; but he also rhymes *believe* with *give* (p. 65), probably with shortening in *believe*. In any case ME ẹ̄ in *leave* sb. may be analogical. Swift's *cheap* : *meet* may show raising to ME ẹ̄ in *cheap*.

Note 2: There is some possibility that Hodges may be influenced by Kentish pronunciation. He lived in Southwark (Vol. I, p. 166). His [v] in *troughs* appears to have a parallel in the modern dialects of Kent and Essex (Vol. I, p. 182). The 'alike' list in *SH-PD* (in general based on the same speech as *EP*) has [ʌu] in *low* vb. (of a cow); so *low* adj. in the modern dialect of Kent. Similar pairings showing [ʌu] for ME *ou* occur in the 'near alike' list. But modern Eastern dialects, including Essex, show this development, as well as Kent. The 'near alike' list shows [uː] in *boat* (as now in Hertfordshire and Kent) and in *both* (as in Hertfordshire); and [s] for [ʃ] in *wished* (cf. MKentish *ss* for *sh*). But the 'near alike' list includes vulgarisms that have their counterparts in other dialects near London as well as Kent; in particular, Essex influence is shown (see Vol. I, pp. 614–15). Thus [iː] in *sleave* need not be a Kenticism, but may show a vulgar pronunciation adopted (like these other pronunciations in the 'near alike' list) from Essex. If this is so, Hodges's evidence shows exactly what is implied by Gil—that the vulgar [iː] was adopted from the 'Eastern dialect'.

(d) *Raising in final position*

§ 125. Raising of ME ẹ̄ to ME ẹ̄ in final position seems to be well evidenced by ME rhymes (see Note below) and is supported by the analogy of raising of ME ǭ (cf. § 152 below). But there is extremely little orthoepistical evidence of it. Strong (followed by Young, Coles in his careless *Eng.–Lat. Dict.*, *WSC-RS*, and Cocker) pairs *flea* with *flee*, and *WSC-RS* (followed by Cocker) pairs *sea* with *see*. Thus the evidence is confined to 'homophone' lists, and only five of the eighteen authors who give such lists show the raising, of which there is no evidence in the more careful lists; only Strong and *WSC* initiate examples. It is clear that the raised pronunciation was not accepted in any but careless speech in the seventeenth century.

Note: Rhymes between 'ME ẹ̄' and ME ẹ̄ in final position are not uncommon in ME. Mackenzie, *Englische Studien*, lxi (1927), 387–8, cites *sle* 'slay' : *me* (*Arthur and Merlin*), and Fischer, ibid. lxiv (1929), 5 (footnote), says that there are other examples of *sle* rhyming on ME $\bar{e}$ in *Arthur and Merlin* and *Richard Cœur de Lion*, and adds *stre* 'straw' rhyming with *be* in *Palladius*. Ten Brink, *Language and Metre of Chaucer*, § 23 (*d*), regards $\bar{e}$ for final ME $\bar{e}$ in *sle* 'slay' as the normal development in Chaucer; his opinion is based of course on rhymes. Early ModE rhymes showing raising of final $\bar{ẹ}$ to $\bar{e}$ are not very common; but Wyld, *Rhymes*, p. 60, cites examples of *sea* and *flea* rhyming with ME $\bar{e}$ from Waller, Milton, Cowley, Dryden, and Pope, and for an earlier example we may add the rhyme *sea* : *safety* Hall, 1597 (*Oxford Book of Sixteenth Century Verse*, p. 729).

(5) *Late ME Lowering of ME $\bar{ẹ}$ to ME $\bar{ę}$ before* r

§ 126. After *r* had begun to exert lowering influence in Southern English, ME $\bar{ẹ}$ before *r* was sometimes lowered in late ME (probably in the early fifteenth century, certainly not later), and variation resulted between the original $\bar{ẹ}$ and the lowered $\bar{ę}$. The effect of this later combinative lowering was to some extent to neutralize, before *r*, the earlier isolative raising of ME $\bar{ę}$. The lowering, like the raising, was ultimately not restricted to vulgar speech, though it seems clear that all lowering before *r* was originally much more common in vulgar than in careful speech. It occurs in the following cases.

(*a*) *ME $\bar{ę}$ before final* r

(i) *Native English words.* *Dear* has $\bar{ę}$ in sixteen sources, but $\bar{ẹ}$ in Smith (beside $\bar{ę}$), Mulcaster (as it seems), Gil (once only, beside $\bar{ę}$ ten times; Spenser's rhyme in the passage Gil is transcribing requires $\bar{ę}$), and Butler (beside $\bar{ę}$; see Note 1). *Hear* has $\bar{ę}$ in fourteen sources, but $\bar{ẹ}$ in Hart, Bullokar (as is shown by his comparing it with *hair*, which has ME $\bar{ę}$, as well as with *here*; but his transcriptions have only $\bar{ę}$), Butler (who prefers it, but admits that 'some' use $\bar{ę}$), Hodges (in *SH-PD*, but not in *EP*, which gives his own pronunciation), and Daines. *Here* also varies; it has $\bar{ę}$ usually, as in Bullokar (eighteen times, against $\bar{ẹ}$ in compounds), Robinson, Gil (against $\bar{ẹ}$ in compounds), Price, Wilkins, Coles, and *RS*, but $\bar{ẹ}$ in Hart (see Note 2), Bullokar (five times, in compounds only), Mulcaster (apparently), and Gil (in compounds only).

(ii) *OF words.* *Appear* has $\bar{ę}$ in eleven sources, and $\bar{ẹ}$ only in Robinson (once, beside $\bar{ę}$ four times). *Cheer* has $\bar{ę}$ in Smith (beside $\bar{ẹ}$), Hart, Price, Coles, and Cooper (followed by Aickin), and $\bar{ẹ}$ in Smith (beside $\bar{ę}$), Gil, and Hodges *SH-PD* (identified with ME $\bar{a}$; not in *EP*). *Arrear*, *rear* sb., and *rearward* have $\bar{ę}$ in Bullokar, Coles, and Cooper (followed by Aickin and *RS*), but $\bar{ẹ}$ in Willis. *Clear* (ten sources), *peer* (three sources), and *sphere* (three sources) are recorded only with $\bar{ẹ}$. (iii) *Mere*, a late ME adoption from Latin, probably has original $\bar{ẹ}$ in English (for early adoptions from Latin took $\bar{ẹ}$ for Latin *e* in the neighbourhood of labials, though later adoptions took $\bar{ę}$), and is recorded with $\bar{ẹ}$ in Bullokar, Willis, and Coles, and probably in Mulcaster; but Newton has ME $\bar{ę}$.

(b) ME ẹ̄ before intervocalic r

Weary has ẹ̄ in Hart, Bullokar (beside ẹ̣̄), Butler (who only admits that 'some' pronounce it thus), and Cooper, and ẹ̣̄ in Bullokar (twice, beside ẹ̄), Gil, and Butler (who prefers this). *Dreary* has ẹ̣̄ in Robinson.

(c) ME ẹ̄ before r plus consonant

(i) Native English words. These normally show lowering to ẹ̣̄. *Earl* has ẹ̣̄ in Cooper, as has *earnest*. *Earth* has ẹ̣̄ in Levins, Hart, and Gil. *Learn* has ẹ̣̄ in Levins (beside ĕ), Hart, Bullokar, and Cooper. *Herd* has ẹ̣̄ in Price (Vol. I, p. 343, note 6), but ẹ̄ in Levins (perhaps a Northernism). PresE shows failure of the lowering in *beard*, in which late ME ẹ̄ is itself due to raising of eME ẹ̣̄ (see § 122); [iː] is recorded by Levins and Hodges (against ẹ̄ in Cooper and Aickin).

(ii) Words adopted from OF. There is only one certain example in the orthoepists, *fierce* (with ME ẹ̄ < AF ę for Central Fr *ie* < Lat *ĕ* in an open syllable; cf. Luick, § 415), which has ẹ̄ in Levins, Bullokar (beside ẹ̣̄), Hodges, and Cooper, and ẹ̣̄ in Laneham, Bullokar (beside ẹ̄), Robinson, and Gil. *Pierce* may possibly be another example (see § 122). Hodges shows retention of ẹ̄ by raising of original ẹ̣̄ in *verse, pearl, perch, hearse,* and *rehearse* (see § 122).

The evidence from all sources shows that ẹ̣̄ by lowering is on the whole rarer than the retained ẹ̄, except in native words before *r* plus consonant; ẹ̣̄ is commonest in early orthoepists (though even in these ẹ̄ is about as frequent as ẹ̣̄) but is rarely found after Butler, and never after 1650, except in the 'homophone' lists, which show [ɛː] < ẹ̣̄ surviving (probably as a vulgarism) beside [iː] < ẹ̄. Probably the lowering was always commoner in vulgar speech. None of these words has in PresE a pronunciation derived from the ẹ̣̄ variant (though *earl*, &c. doubtless would have if the long vowel had not been ousted by the short), but many of them retain the *ea* spelling which is a witness to the existence of ẹ̣̄ as a fairly common variant in the sixteenth century.

Note 1: Butler makes an artificial distinction between *dear* 'charus', with ME ẹ̣̄, and *deere* 'carus', with ME ẹ̄. The distinction in the spelling of the Latin word is paralleled in other writers of the time; in Butler's case the first 'word' is shown to have the meaning 'beloved' by his statement that *dearling* 'darling' is derived from it, and the second therefore presumably means 'costly'.

Note 2: Hart's transcription of *here* in the *Orthographie* is *hier*, which might be interpreted as showing [iː] from ẹ̄ followed by an [ə]-glide before *r*; in the *Methode* it is *hiĕr*, which might be explained as an error due to hesitation between *hĕr* (with ME ẹ̣̄) and *hīr* (with ME ẹ̄). But in each case these explanations should be rejected, in favour of one which assumes that Hart's pronunciation was [hjɛːr], with a [j]-glide after the *h* (see Vol. I, p. 84).

Note 3: The 'homophone' lists cannot give unambiguous evidence for the pronunciation [iː] < ME ẹ̣̄, as they can only put ME ẹ̣̄ words spelt *ea* with ME ẹ̄ words spelt *ee*; but they

§ 126] PART 2: THE LONG VOWELS 645

probably mean [i:]. The lists contain (of the words cited above) *appear, dear, hear*, and *cheer*.

But the lists can give unambiguous evidence for ME ẹ̄ by pairings with ME ā words; and many lists (from Hodges's 'near alike' list onwards) give such pairings for *cheer, steer, hear, weary*, which thus have (probably as a variant only) ME ẹ̄ by lowering from ME ẹ̄. So possibly has *peer*, which is put with *pear* and *pair*; but this grouping may depend on variation between ẹ̄ and ẹ̄ in *pear*. It should be noticed that pairings of words spelt *ea* with words spelt *ee*, and pairings of either of these types with ME ā words, are avoided by Hodges in his 'alike' list, and by Cooper altogether; Coles in his *Schoolmaster* only pairs *dear* with *deer*, *hear* with *here*, and two differentiated spellings of *cheer* with each other, and in any case these pairings in Coles certainly depend on [i:].

The evidence of rhyme-lists is similarly difficult to interpret. Levins seems always to have [i:] for ME ẹ̄ before *r* (as he has for ME ẹ̄ before *r* and normally for free ME ẹ̄); so has Poole (as for ME ẹ̄ before *r*, but not certainly for free ME ẹ̄). In both men the absence of ẹ̄ variants is a Northernism. Willis probably has [i:] in *cheer, clear, dear, hear, steer*, and *jeer* (all these words are spelt *ea* in his lists) and in *beer* and *deer*; but *here* probably has ME ẹ̄ by lowering (see Vol. I, p. 426). Coles has [i:] in *clear, fleer, jeer, leer, peer*, and *steer*, as is shown by the arrangement of his list.

Note 4: The lowering of ME ẹ̄ to ẹ̄ before *r* cannot be shown by spellings in the ME period because ME ẹ̄ and ME ẹ̄ were both represented by *e, ee*; it can be clearly shown only by the use of the digraph *ea*, which was used solely for ME ẹ̄. This digraph was in only occasional use in the late fifteenth century, but already in the fifteenth century *ea* spellings occur for *steer* vb. (see *OED*) and *hear* (see Jordan, § 277, Anm. 2, who cites two examples; the suggestion of Holthausen, recorded in Matthes's appendix to the second edition of Jordan's book, that the lowering had occurred not before final *r* in the infinitive, but before *r* followed by a consonant in the p.t. *heard*, whence transference to the infinitive, is possible but unnecessary). During the early part of the sixteenth century the use of the *ea* digraph became gradually more common; and from this time onwards ME ẹ̄ before *r* is frequently *ea* (thus at a comparatively early date in this century, 1535, *OED* cites many *ea* spellings from Coverdale). Sixteenth- and seventeenth-century *ea* spellings occur, according to *OED*, in *dear, here, appear, cheer, clear, peer, sere* adj. (from ON *sér*), *arrear, rear* sb. and adj., *sphere, mere, weary, dreary, earl, earnest, learn*, and *herd* (fifteenth- and sixteenth-century *heerd*, sixteenth- and seventeenth-century *heard*; but the latter might be an inverted spelling due to *heard* p.t. pronounced with ĕ). Several of these words also occur with *ei, ey* spellings, from the fourteenth century onwards; but these spellings are described by *OED*, or shown by its quotations, to be from Scottish texts, in which the *i* is added to the *e* merely as a graphic device to show that it is long. The prose *Merlin*, though not remarkably Northern in its linguistic forms, uses *ei* fairly frequently for ME ẹ̄ before *r*, as in *heiren* 'hear', but also uses this digraph for ME ẹ̄ in *beheilde* 'beheld', so that it is clear that the *ei* spelling has no more phonetic significance than in the Scottish texts. The spelling *beire* 'bier' in the *Mirror for Magistrates*, if not due to Northern influence, would seem to show lowering of ME ẹ̄ to ME ẹ̄, since this spelling would depend on either the monophthongization of ME *ei* to [ε:] or the variation between ME *ei* and ẹ̄ in such words as *perceive*.

Laȝamon has *dære* 'dear', *hæren* 'hear', and *wærie* 'weary' (see *OED*). In the school of orthography to which Laȝamon (or his scribe) belonged, the letters *a, æ*, and *e* had probably distinct values originally, thus [a(:)], [æ(:)], and [e(:)]; but by the date of the Cotton MS the distinction seems to have been lost, at any rate in regard to the short vowels, so that æ was used interchangeably with *e* and less often with *a*. This development was probably due to the change of short [æ] to [e], less often to [a]; cf. the *Ancrene Wisse*'s use of *ea* (see d'Ardenne, *St. Iuliene*, 'Language', §§ 1-3). The uncertainty in the use of the symbol æ may have affected it when it represented a long vowel, and we can hardly rely on these spellings; but if they were phonetic, they would show a lowering of ME ẹ̄ to [æ:]. This would be a specifically WMidl development and distinct from though analogous to the later StE lowering.

Note 5: Rhymes of ME ẹ̄ before *r* with ME ẹ̄ are fairly frequent in the sixteenth and seventeenth centuries, but are ambiguous, since they may depend on the raising of ME ẹ̄ to ẹ̄ rather than on the lowering. Rhymes of ME ẹ̄r words with *hair*, it should be noticed, are ambiguous in this way, for they depend on the commoner ME variant hẹ̄r of *hair*, in which raising of ME ę̄ is possible. But lowering of ME ẹ̄ to ę̄ is shown clearly by the following rhymes cited by Wyld, *Rhymes*, p. 66—*dear* : *air* (Drayton), *clear* : *fair* (Suckling), *here* : *prayer* (Cowley). See also § 204, Note 4 below.

Note 6: Horn, § 85, recognizes that ME ẹ̄ before *r* becomes in eModE either [iː] or [ɛː]; he regards the two developments as belonging to different dialects. He does not date the change of ME ẹ̄ to [ɛː] before *r*, but would seem to regard it as belonging to the ModE period. On this point, and on Luick's more elaborate view, see § 201, Note.

(6) *Variation between ME ę̣ and ME ẹ̣ in eModE Adoptions from Foreign Languages*

§ 127. On variation between ME ẹ̄ and ME ę̄ in words adopted into English from foreign languages before 1700, and on the reasons for this variation, see § 110 above. Such variation would appear to have been more common than appears from the evidence of the orthoepists. Here we shall do no more than examine one or two points of the orthoepists' evidence.

In words adopted from Latin, Greek, and Hebrew (all of which appear to have been treated as if they had come into English through Latin), educated StE in the sixteenth and seventeenth centuries substituted [ɛː] or [eː] < ME ę̄ for *ē* and *ĕ* in open syllables; it treated similarly *ae* and *oe* in Latin words or latinized forms of Greek words. In so doing it followed, as was natural, the 'reformed' pronunciation of Latin which had been introduced in the early part of the sixteenth century by Lily and Cheke, following the teaching of Erasmus, and which had clearly been accepted by the overwhelming majority of well-educated Southerners. This development is so regular that it is unnecessary to cite individual orthoepists to illustrate it, except perhaps for Hebrew words and names, of which *pharisee*, *Galilee*, *Ezekiel*, &c. have ME ẹ̄ in Butler, Hodges, Wallis, and Cooper. We may notice also that there is evidence of the disyllabic pronunciation of *dirge* until the end of the seventeenth century, in Cooper and *RS*; Cooper pronounced the final *e* as [eː] (< ME ę̄), but *RS*, representing a less well-educated pronunciation, pronounced it as [iː]. Butler seems to have pronounced *creature* as three syllables, but it has only two (the *ea* being pronounced as ME ę̄) in Robinson, Gil, Hayward, and Cooper. The pronunciation of Latin *ae* and *ē* as ME ę̄ affected of course the prefixes *e-*, *pre-*, and *re-*.

The 'unreformed' pronunciation of Latin, which represented the historical development of the pronunciation in use in England in the later Middle Ages (in effect a French pronunciation of Latin), seems to have survived beside the reformed pronunciation during the sixteenth and seventeenth centuries, doubtless in less well-educated circles (see § 110); in the neighbourhood of labials, if not elsewhere, it identified Latin *ē* and *ĕ* in open syllables with ME $\bar{e}$. Early adoptions into English from Latin tend to follow the 'unreformed' pronunciation even among educated speakers; thus *Peter* in Coles and Young and *Eve* in Coles have [i:] < ME $\bar{e}$. But *Eden* has ME $\bar{e}$ in Hodges. On *mere* with ME $\bar{e}$ see § 126.

VARIATION BETWEEN ME $\bar{e}$ AND ME $\bar{\imath}$

§ 128. Variation can arise before *r* between ME $\bar{e}$ and ME $\bar{\imath}$ when original ME $\bar{e}$ is (*a*) raised in ME to $\bar{\imath}$ (see § 136 below) and (*b*) lowered in late ME to $\bar{e}$ (see § 126 above). In some cases there was already in eME an $\bar{e}$ variant beside the $\bar{e}$ which is raised to $\bar{\imath}$; so in *brere* 'briar', which has $\bar{e}$ < WS $\bar{æ}$ beside $\bar{e}$ < Anglian $\bar{e}$ (WGmc $\bar{a}$), and in ME develops a form *brīr (> ModE *briar*) from the *brēr* variant. An example of the variation is Milton's rhyme of *quire* 'choir' with *heir* (*Christ's Nativity*, ll. 115–16), which, despite the spelling of *quire*, must depend on ME $\bar{e}$ in both words.

VARIATION BETWEEN ME $\bar{e}$ AND ME ai ($ęi$)

(1) *Native English words*

§ 129. Variation between ME $\bar{e}$ and ME ai ($ęi$) occurs only occasionally in native words, in special circumstances. (*a*) In three words it seems to arise as a result of the occasional loss, beside normal retention, of OE *h* at the end of the first element of a compound (cf. Luick, § 516, Anm. 5); they are *heifer*, *neighbour*, and *either* (*neither*). In *heifer*, OE *hēahfore* becomes *hēafor*, whence ME *hēfer*. In *neighbour*, OE *nēahgebūr* becomes *nēahbūr and then *nēabūr, whence ME *nēbūr. In *either*, OE *ǣghwæðer* becomes *ǣgþer* and then *ǣhþer; with loss of the *h* we get *ǣþer and ME *ēther*. When the *h* (in the third case, the *g*) was retained, diphthongization to early ME *ęi*, later *ai*, occurred. *Heifer* has ME $\bar{e}$ in Price and Lye; Cooper says merely that the *i* is silent, but he probably had $\bar{e}$, as most of the words in the list in which *heifer* occurs have $\bar{e}$. Cooper is followed by Aickin; *WSC-RS* and Brown show $\breve{e}$ developed from $\bar{e}$. *Neighbour* has *ai* in Strong, Young, and the shorthand-writers Dix and Hopkins. It has $\bar{e}$ beside *ai* in Price, and $\bar{e}$ in Coles, Brown, and the shorthand-writers Bridges, Mason, and Stringer (cf. Holofernes's comment in *Love's Labour's Lost*, v. i. 25–26). (*N*)*either* has *ai* in Smith, Bullokar (in (*n*)*either* pron. and *either-or*), Gil, Richardson, and *RS* (the last-named only in *neither*). It has $\bar{e}$ in Hart (when stressed), Robinson, Hodges *EP*, Price (followed by *The Protestant Tutor*), Strong, Lye, the *Treatise of Stops*, Cooper, Cocker, Brown, and *RS* (the last-named only in *either*). It has $\breve{e}$ developed from $\bar{e}$ in Hart (mostly unstressed), Bullokar (in (*n*)*either* conj. and once in *either-or*), Butler, the 'phonetically spelt' lists of Young and Cocker, 'homophone' lists from that of Hodges ('near alike'; contrast *EP*) onwards, and the shorthand-writers T. Shelton and Bridges; and ĭ by raising of this ĕ in Strong. The evidence of some authors is ambiguous, as they merely say that the *i* is silent without indicating the quantity of the *e*; such are Brooksbank, Cocker, and the shorthand-writer Everardt, and strictly also Cooper, whose list however is of words which mostly have undoubted *ẹ̄*.

(b) *Key* and *lea* (*OED*, sb.²) vary because the normal Southern pronunciation has gradually been ousted by a Northern pronunciation (see *OED*, s.v. *key*, and cf. Luick, § 516, Anm. 5, who rightly rejects the explanation of Jordan, § 94, Anm. 1). The sources of the two words are OE *cǣge* (beside *cǣg*) and the adjective *lǣge; in Southern English the intervocalic *g* in these two words is vocalized and becomes part of a diphthong *ęi*, but in Northern English it remains consonantal until it finally disappears without affecting the development of the vowel (Jordan, § 101). *Key* has *ai* in the *Welsh Hymn*, Price *VO* (but not *Eng.O.*), and the Northerner Poole (as a variant beside *ẹ̄*), but *ẹ̄* in Hodges, Lloyd (who says it is pronounced *kea*), Price (*Eng.O.*), Strong, Young, Lye, *The Compendious Schoolmaster*, *WSC-RS*, Brown, and the rhyme-lists of Willis, Poole (beside *ai*), and Coles. *Lea* sb.² and *lea* adj. retained *ey* and *ay* spellings until the nineteenth and eighteenth centuries respectively, but began to be spelt *lea* in StE in the seventeenth century (see *OED*); the substantive has *ai* in Smith and [i:] from late ME *ẹ̄* by raising of ME *ẹ̄* in *RS*. The Northern pronunciation with *ẹ̄* was evidently formerly current in other words than these two in which it survives in PresE. Newton has *ẹ̄* in *weigh*; Price, *Eng.O.* (but not *VO*) in *grey* (OE *grǣg*); Coles in *whey* (OE *hweg*) and *weigh* (OE *wegan*) (see Vol. I, p. 444); Brown, who was probably a Northerner, in *neigh* (OE *hnǣgan*), *whey*, and *weigh* (in the last case beside *ai*). For *neigh* compare Holofernes's comment in *Love's Labour's Lost*, v. i. 26.

(c) *Flay* should normally have *ẹ̄* in the infinitive (from OE *flēan*); the form *flay* is due to the analogical influence of the p.p. (OE *flægen). The orthoepists use the spelling *flay* but only the pronunciation with *ẹ̄* is recorded, by the *ABC for chyldren*, Levins, Smith, and the 'homophone' lists from that of Hodges onwards. The *ABC for chyldren* similarly shows *ẹ̄* in *slay* (OE *slēan*, p.p. *slægen*).

Note 1: *Neighbour* might be explained under (*b*), i.e. as showing Northern loss of intervocalic ȝ from the ME form *neȝȝebur* without vocalization; in modern dialects it is [niːbə(r)] chiefly in the North and North Midlands, but the widespread [neːbə(r)] might represent ME *ẹ̄* as well as ME *ei*.

Note 2: I have observed no evidence in orthoepists before 1700 for the pronunciation [əiðə(r)] from ME *īðer*; such evidence seems to begin with Jones in 1701 (see *OED*). The ME *īðer* develops from *īhþer* < *ēhþer* < *ǣhþ·r* (Jordan, § 94, Anm. 2). It occurs in Lydgate, and in modern dialects in Suffolk and Norfolk, and in addition in Shropshire, Dorset, and Devon. It seems clear that Standard English adopted it from the 'Eastern dialect'. Scattered dialects (Northern, Midland, and Southern) have [iːðə(r)]; the widespread [eːðə(r)] may represent either ME *ẹ̄* or ME *ai*. *Neighbour* has ME *ī* in the shorthand-writer Folkingham; see § 139.

Note 3: The introduction of the Northern forms discussed under (*b*) may have been assisted by the variation of *ai* and *ẹ̄* in French words, even in final position. For Northern influence on StE about this time compare the introduction of the -*s* form of the 3rd sing. (and not infrequently in Shakespeare for the 3rd plural) present indicative, and the spread of the form *are* (found, however, as early as Chaucer and Gower); in the sphere of pronunciation compare the *Mopsæ*'s *biccherz* 'butcher's', which is introduced either from Northern or South-western dialects, of which the former is more probable (see § 96).

Note 4: The consonant in the cases discussed under (*b*) is a 'secondary palatal' (derived from an OE guttural *g*, in many cases originally appropriate to oblique forms in which a back vowel followed) and is lost when it becomes final in word or syllable in ME; see Jordan, § 101. There is perhaps some suggestion in the ModE evidence that in ME the development may not have been confined to the North, as is usually assumed.

Note 5: *Weir*, despite its spelling, has ME *ẹ̄* (shown, for example, by *RS*), being derived from the stem of *werian*. On eModE *drean* beside *drain* vb. see § 115, Note 9.

(2) *Native English words reinforced by French*

§ 130. In two words variation occurs because native English words were reinforced in ME by French words with different vowels. The modern *hair* is in part from OE *hǣr*, in part from OF *haire* 'a hair-shirt'; in the sixteenth and seventeenth centuries the spelling derived from the latter is much commoner, though not invariable (*hear* still occurs), but the pronunciation usually derives from the native word. The PresE pronunciation could derive from either, but is more likely to go back to ME *ẹ̄*. ME *ai* (< OF) is shown by Levins (beside *ẹ̄*), Robinson, and *The English Scholemaster* (1646); so perhaps by Poole, who rhymes *hair* with *are*, *bare*, *prayer*, &c. ME *ẹ̄* (< OE *ǣ*) is shown by Cheke, Levins (beside *ai*), Laneham, Bullokar, Hodges (Vol. I, pp. 175–7), and Daines (Vol. I, p. 335). 'Homophone' lists which do not show the general identity of *ai* and *ā* nevertheless equate *hair* with *hare* (thus showing the identity of ME *ẹ̄r* and ME *ār*); so in Hodges, Merriott, Johnson, and Ellis. *Seine* 'a fishing-net' develops in the seventeenth century a form *sean*, which is included by *RS* in a list of words in which *ea* is pronounced as if it were *ee*; this, in *RS*, is clear evidence of a ME variant in *ẹ̄*. Such a variant must arise by the adoption of OF *seine* in a monophthongized form **sẹ̄ne* (cf. the words cited under (3) below); the cognate OE *segne* should regularly give a ME form in *ẹi* > *ai*.

(3) *Words adopted from French*

§ 131. In Anglo-Norman the diphthong *ei* was monophthongized to *ẹ̄*, and both the earlier diphthongal and the later monophthongal pronunciations passed into English. Though cases of variation owing to this cause are common, the extent of it does not seem to have been generally realized (but compare Luick, § 516, Anm. 6). Miss Pope shows (§§ 1157–9; 1326, §§ ii, iii, vi) that in AN and Western French OF *ai* and *ei* were monophthongized to *ẹ* both before a consonant and in final position, and that OF nasalized *ai* and *ei* were similarly monophthongized to nasal *ẽ*. Thus variation between

ME *ai* (*ẹi*) and ME *ẹ̄* can in theory occur in any word adopted from AN, whatever the position of the vowel. The cases of variation recorded by the orthoepists can be arranged as follows.

(a) Before a consonant

Before *v*, ME *ai* is shown in *conceive* by *RS* (and Daines implies its existence); in *deceive* by Levins and *RS*; in *perceive* by Levins; and in *receive* by Daines (beside *ẹ̄*), Wallis (beside *ẹ̄*), and *RS*. Otherwise ME *ẹ̄* is commonly recorded in each of these words. Before *t*, ME *ai* is recorded in *conceit* by Robinson and *RS*; in *deceit* by Robinson (beside *ẹ̄*), Wallis (beside *ẹ̄*), and RS; in *receipt* by Levins and *RS*; and in *retreat* by Levins. Otherwise ME *ẹ̄* is commonly recorded. In words in which the syllable containing the original OF *ei* becomes unstressed, variation is also shown. *Forfeit* has *ai* in Levins, but *ẹ̄* in Price and Strong, and shortening to *ĕ* in Robinson; *counterfeit* has *ẹ̄* in Price, and shortening to *ĕ* in other sources; *surfeit* is said to have silent *i* by Cooper (although the remark is in itself ambiguous, most of the words in Cooper's list have *ẹ̄*, which is thus more likely than *ĕ* in this word also). *Dais* has *ẹ̄* in Levins. *Leisure* has *ai* in Cheke, Levins, and *RS*, but *ẹ̄* in Price. *Raisin* has *ai* in Young, but *ẹ̄* in Coles, Strong, Lye (who, however, may mean *ĕ*), and the 'homophone' lists of Hodges and later authors. *Seize* has *ai* in Wallis (beside *ẹ̄*), but *ẹ̄* in Hodges and many later authors. *Domain* (spelt *demain*) has *ẹ̄* in Price followed by *The Protestant Tutor*. *Rein* is said by Daines to be 'usually and better sounded *quasi rean*'; Coles rhymes it on *ẹ̄*. *Skein* has *ẹ̄* in Poole (Vol. I, p. 436), Price, and *The Protestant Tutor*. *Vein* has *ai* beside *ẹ̄* in Coles and *ẹ̄* in Brown and the shorthand-writer Ridpath (a Scot, who marks this as an Anglicism; see Vol. I, p. 393). To these we may probably add *feign*, shown with *ẹ̄* beside *ai* by Brown, *heinous*, shown with *ai* by Cocker and *ẹ̄* by Brown, and *chain*, shown with *ẹ̄* by Levins; but it should be noticed that Brown and Levins are both Northerners. *Heir* is equated with *hare* by Ellis, who shows identity of ME *ẹ̄r* and ME *ār*, but not identity of ME *ai* and ME *ā*; it therefore has ME *ẹ̄* (cf. Luick, § 416 end). *Inveigle* has ME *ẹ̄* in Cooper, *WSC-RS*, and Brown; cf. the Present English variation between usual [i:] and less common [ei]. *Veil* has *ẹ̄* in Levins. *Ceiling* has [i:] from late ME *ẹ̄* by raising of ME *ẹ̄* in Cocker.

(b) In final position

Rey (*OED*'s *ray* sb.[4]?) has *ẹ̄* in Coles. *Prey* has *ẹ̄* in Coles (*Schoolmaster* and *Shorthand*) and the shorthand-writer Ridpath (a Scot). *Prey* and *pray* have *ẹ̄* beside *ai* in the 'phonetically spelt' lists of Brown; he also gives *ẹ̄* in *survey*. There is little evidence of this development, which must have been comparatively uncommon, perhaps because among native English words

ME $\bar{e}$ is rarer in final position than ME *ai*, so that in French words the diphthongal pronunciation was preferred.

> *Note* 1: Levins is not altogether satisfactory evidence for the pronunciation of these words (see Note 2), but his form of *veil* seems to be supported by Shillingford's *feale* 'fail', which (since it may well go back to a ME variant with $\bar{e}$) should not be used to show monophthongization of ME *ai* to $\bar{a}$ and raising of the consequent $\bar{a}$ until it is identical with $\bar{e}$, as it is by Wyld, *Coll. Eng.*, p. 248, followed by Jordan, § 284. Spenser regularly spells *veil* as *vele* (owing, at least in part, to the influence of Latin *velare*) and rhymes it on $\bar{e}$. Levins's $\bar{e}$ in *chain* is supported by Queen Elizabeth's spelling *chean* (which is again misused by Wyld, loc. cit., as evidence of monophthongization of ME *ai*).
>
> *Note* 2: Brown and Ridpath, being Northerners, are not the best evidence for StE; Coles however is reliable, and his contractions in his *Shorthand* are always based on actual pronunciations. On Brown's evidence see Vol. I, pp. 368-9. It may seem strictly unjustifiable to quote Levins as evidence for variation between *ai* and $\bar{e}$ in any of the words cited in this section, since he knew (*a*) monophthongization of ME *ai* to $\bar{a}$, and (*b*) identity of ME $\bar{a}$ and $\bar{e}$, as appears from his evidence on a few words. But his evidence on words which vary between *ai* and $\bar{e}$ seems altogether credible, and it appears that he knew also a pronunciation which kept these two sounds apart (or at least inherited a spelling, not always orthodox, which still marked the distinction between the two sounds).
>
> *Note* 3: Whenever *WSC-RS* is said to show ME $\bar{e}$, it must be understood that the pronunciation is [i:]; the words cited occur in a list which is said to show *ei* pronounced '*e* long as if *ee*'.

THE DEVELOPMENT OF ME $\bar{e}$

§ 132. In ME the vowel $\bar{e}$ was pronounced as tense [e:], but already by 1500 it had been raised to [i:]. There is almost complete unanimity among the orthoepists on this development. ME $\bar{e}$ is identified with *i* in foreign languages throughout the sixteenth and seventeenth centuries—with Welsh *i* by the *Welsh Hymn* (late fifteenth century) and later sources, with French *i* by Hart and later orthoepists, with Italian *i* by Florio and others, with Spanish *i* by Percival and others. It is said to be the long equivalent of ME *ĭ* by orthoepists from Hart onwards, with the few exceptions mentioned below. Only four early orthoepists do not show the development to [i:]. Palsgrave (see Vol. I, pp. 8-9) hesitates to identify ME $\bar{e}$ with French *i*; he is influenced by the spelling, and only obscurely indicates a difference between ME $\bar{\imath}$ and French *i*, but his hesitation in part might be due to the fact that the French sound is tenser than the English. Smith (see Vol. I, pp. 59-60), under the influence of the spelling, regards ME $\bar{\imath}$ as the long equivalent of ME *ĭ* and a pure vowel, and describes ME $\bar{e}$ as a distinct sound midway between ME $\bar{e}$ and ME $\bar{\imath}$. Bullokar similarly regards ME $\bar{\imath}$ as the long equivalent of ME *ĭ* and ME $\bar{e}$ as being intermediate between 'the old sound of the letter *e*', i.e. ME $\bar{e}$, and ME $\bar{\imath}$ (cf. Zachrisson, *Bullokar*, p. 45). Waad's spelling rests on similar assumptions (see Vol. I, p. 130). None of these orthoepists is to be taken seriously; the influence of the spelling has led them into error with regard to ME $\bar{\imath}$ (see further § 137), and their failure to identify ME $\bar{e}$ as the long equivalent of ME *ĭ* follows as a matter of course.

We must look a little more closely at evidence which proves that ME $\bar{e}$ was not in fact exactly identical in quality with ME $\breve{\imath}$, but tenser. The *Welsh Hymn* identifies ME $\bar{e}$ with Welsh i, but ME $\breve{\imath}$ is identified either with Welsh u or with Welsh y. Salesbury follows (or rather independently confirms) these identifications, and the *Welsh Breviary* and T. Jones give similar evidence. The distinction made by these Welsh sources can only mean that ME $\bar{e}$ is tense [i:] and ME $\breve{\imath}$ is lax [ɪ]. Robinson (Vol. I, pp. 207–8) shows that ME $\bar{e}$ is formed further forward in the mouth than ME $\breve{\imath}$, and is the extreme vowel-position. Newton regards it as a long vowel without short equivalent. Holder (Vol. I, p. 264) clearly describes i (i.e. ME $\bar{e}$) as a tense vowel; he comments on the tension of the muscles of the tongue, its stiffness, and its nearness to the palate. Cooper (Vol. I, pp. 286, 290–1) does not make ME $\bar{e}$ the long equivalent of ME $\breve{\imath}$; he (erroneously) regards ME $\bar{e}$ as the long of ME $\breve{\imath}$, and is compelled arbitrarily to split ME $\bar{e}$ into two sounds, short and long, according to slight variations of quantity which depend on the following consonant. He shows that it is tenser than ME $\breve{\imath}$ and ME $\bar{e}$, being the 'closest of all the vowels' and 'nearest the nature of consonants'. But Daines very correctly observes that in its articulation the tongue is 'not so restrained' as it is for i in Italian and other European languages. Obviously throughout the sixteenth and seventeenth centuries ME $\bar{e}$ had very much its present value, except that it lacked the slight diphthongization of present Southern English.

Note: Zachrisson, *Eng. Vowels*, pp. 69–71, and Wyld, *Coll. Eng.*, p. 206 (cf. also Kihlbom, pp. 63–64), cite spellings designed to prove that ME $\bar{e}$ has become [i:]. Words which normally have ME $\bar{e}$ often have fifteenth- and sixteenth-century spellings with i. Zachrisson admits that in many cases this i-spelling is to be explained from ME, OE, or OF variants (op. cit., pp. 70–71), but argues that in at least the majority of the cases cited in his list at the foot of p. 69 and the top of p. 70 the i is a phonetic spelling which shows that ME $\bar{e}$, by becoming [i:], has displaced ME $\breve{\imath}$ as the long equivalent of ME $\breve{\imath}$ and is therefore represented by the same graphic symbol (i.e. the letter i). Wyld's list is less critical than Zachrisson's but for convenience the two are conflated in what follows. It is extremely doubtful whether these spellings are to be explained in the way suggested by Zachrisson and Wyld. They require more careful classification than Zachrisson and Wyld give, and may be arranged as follows:

(*a*) In some words we may have to do with the ordinary late ME and ModE digraph *ie* or its variant *ye* used as a symbol for ME $\bar{e}$ (as in the PresE spelling *chief*); these digraphs are purely conventional and in no sense phonetic. Thus we have *sien* 'seen', *indied* 'indeed', *agryed* 'agreed', *fried* 'freed'. See also under (*d*) below.

(*b*) In words of the types in which ME quantity variation occurred (see Chapter VI, Part 1, above), an OE variant $\breve{e}$, susceptible of raising to $\breve{\imath}$, or a ME variant $\breve{\imath}$ certainly or probably existed, and the i-spelling should be regarded as a representation of ME $\breve{\imath}$. Such are *hyrde* 'heard', *wyry* 'weary', *stypylle* 'steeple', *liver* 'liever', *priste* 'priest' and probably also *spidye* 'speedy', *grivous* 'grievous', *pivishly* 'peevishly' (see further (*f*) below). *Ivel* 'evil' (cited by Wyld) preserves original ME $\breve{\imath}$.

(*c*) In the following words we have to reckon with shortening under weak stress, either directly to $\breve{\imath}$ or to $\breve{e}$ (in which case unstressed $\breve{e}r$ and $\breve{\imath}r$ have probably been identified as [ər]): *thir* 'there', *hyrafter* 'hereafter', *whir* 'where', *wi* 'we'.

(*d*) Some are words with ME $\bar{e}$ in final position, or inflectional forms of such words: *tri* 'tree', *si* 'see', *syying* 'seeing', *fye* 'fee' (cf. also *sien* 'seen', *agryed* 'agreed', *fried* 'freed' under

(a) above, and *wi* 'we' under (c) above). The evidence of sixteenth-century orthoepists (e.g. Smith, Hart, and Bullokar) shows shortening in final position (see § 40), and these spellings may therefore show *ĭ*.

(e) Before *r* we find the following: *Dyrham* 'Dereham' (*Paston Letters*), *hire*, *hyre* 'hear' (Zachrisson cites four examples from the *Paston Letters*, and Wyld from the *Siege of Rouen*, c. 1420, Shillingford, Gregory), *hiresay* 'hearsay' in a letter to James VI of Scotland, *hyre* 'here' (*Paston Letters*), and *dyre* 'dear' (Gregory). On these forms see § 136, Note 2 below; here we may merely note that they are subject to other interpretations than that they mean [i:].

(f) Words in which ME *ẹ̄* occurs before a single final consonant or compound consonant, and derivatives of such words. (i) Before [v]: *belyve* 'believe', *prive*, &c. 'preve', &c. (prove), *lyve* 'leave' sb. (which Zachrisson would take as having here [i:] from ME *ẹ̄* introduced into the sb. in place of ME *ę̄* because of the analogy of the vb.), *ryves* 'reeves', *slyves*, *slyvys* 'sleeves', *myve* 'meve' (move). (ii) Before [m]: *dymeth* 'deemeth', *symyth* 'seemeth'. (iii) Before [p]: *kype* 'keep', *kypith* 'keepeth', &c., *shype* 'sheep', *wypyng* 'weeping'. (iv) Before [d]: *hyde* 'heed', *spyde* 'speed', *nideful* 'needful', *dides* 'deeds', *briding* 'breeding'. (v) Before [t]: *myte* 'meet'. (vi) Before [tʃ]: *besyche*, &c., 'beseech'. (vii) Before [z]: *lyse* 'leese' (lose). (viii) Before [n]: *quin* 'queen'. (ix) Before [l]: *fyle* 'feel', *style* 'steel'. (x) Before [k]: *besyking* 'beseeking', *mykely* 'meekly'. In all these cases we have to do with shortening to [ɪ]. Shortening of other ME long vowels is recorded by eModE evidence before all the consonants here concerned except [z] (see Chapter VI, Part 2), and there is the closest correspondence between this spelling-evidence and that of the modern dialects as recorded by Wright, §§ 132, 142, 146, and 220; the latter shows [ɪ] by shortening of ME *ẹ̄* before all the consonants concerned above, including [z] (in *cheese*), in over thirty words in all, some of which are the same as those cited by Zachrisson and Wyld (*believe*, *seen*, *keep*, *sheep*, *speed*, *need*, *meet*, *queen*, *feel*, *steel*, and *seek*), and also before [f], [ð], [þ], and [s]. A special explanation may be possible in the case of *steel*, for *stile* and *style* (cited by *OED* from the fourteenth to the sixteenth century) may be from the OE variant *stȳle*; but the fifteenth- and sixteenth-century *still* (and perhaps the fourteenth-century *styl*) shows shortening. The use of 'final *e*' in many of the spellings cited is not a serious objection to the view that they show shortening (cf. § 116, Note 2, end).

Thus most of the *i*-spellings represent short [ɪ]. But it does not follow that ME *ẹ̄* had become [i:] before the shortening occurred; for even in ME, when *ẹ̄* was still [e:], the result of shortening was [ɪ] (see §§ 11 and 31 above, and cf. Luick, §§ 385-7).

There is of course no objection to Zachrisson's and Wyld's view that ME *ẹ̄* became [i:] in the fifteenth century; but the evidence on which they rely is invalid. The importance of the point is that similar evidence is used to establish [i:] for ME *ę̄*, where it leads to false conclusions (cf. § 116, Note 2, under (2), where the general theory underlying the use of such spellings is discussed).

ME ę̄ in words adopted from foreign languages

§ 133. (1) ME *ę̄* is common in words adopted in ME from French; it is used both for general OF *e* and for AN *e* < OF *ie*. A special case of the latter is *Dieppe*, which in the seventeenth century was pronounced with [i:], being equated with *deep* in the 'homophone' lists of Hodges, Hunt, Fox and Hookes, Strong, Cooper, and Brown. The PresE pronunciation [di(:)ep] or [djep] is a reformation after Modern French—an all-too-common process in foreign place-names.

(2) In early adoptions from Latin ME *ę̄* is used for Latin *ē*; but most such words have ME *ẹ̄* for Latin *ē* (see § 127).

(3) In ModE adoptions from French (and other foreign languages), ME *ẹ̄* (that is, [i:]) is used to represent foreign *i*. *Genteel* (first recorded

1599) has [iː] in Coles, though he gives *gentile* as the normal and *genteel* only as a 'phonetic' spelling. *Intrigue* (vb. 1612, sb. 1647) has [iː] in Coles, Young, and Brown; so *fatigue* (1669) in Brown, *magazine* (1583) in Coles and *RS*. These words retain [iː] in Present English. But there are others which differ. *Oblique* (a fifteenth-century adoption, but not common until the late sixteenth century) might be expected to have [iː], as normally in PresE; but [əi] is recorded by Hodges and Brown, and as a variant by *OED*. Similarly Hodges has [əi] in *sardine* (first recorded *c*. 1430). *Pique*, which as a substantive is first recorded in 1632, and as a verb in 1664, has [əi] in Brown; this must be an anglicization, as the present [iː] is to be expected in a word adopted after 1500. On *oblige* see § 138 (3).

Note: Luick, § 581 (1), shows that fifteenth- as well as sixteenth- and seventeenth-century adoptions from foreign languages have ME ẹ̄ for foreign *i*. *Oblique* and *sardine* do not tell seriously against this view, as they may be adopted direct from Latin as well as from French, and Latin *ī* until the late nineteenth century was invariably identified with ME *ī* in the English pronunciation of Latin. But so long as it was possible for men like Palsgrave and Smith to fail to recognize the difference between ME *ī* and French *i*, it was possible for ME *ī* to be substituted for foreign *i* (the pronunciation being thus anglicized); and occasional cases may then arise of fifteenth- or early sixteenth-century adoptions in which foreign *i* is not replaced by ME ẹ̄ but by ME *ī*. Luick's general statement of the situation, which is well supported by evidence, holds good.

VARIATION BETWEEN ME ẹ̄ AND ME ī

§ 134. Variation between ME ẹ̄ and ME ī occurs (*a*) in certain words with OE ȳ, in which SE ē > ME ẹ̄ survives beside East Midland *ī* into the seventeenth century; (*b*) before *r* and other consonants, in consequence of a dialectal raising of ME ẹ̄ to ME *ī* which occasionally affects StE; (*c*) in certain late adoptions from foreign languages, dealt with above; and (*d*) in certain words in which eME *ĭ*, existing as a variant to ME *ī*, is lengthened in late ME to ẹ̄ (see § 138 below). Here we shall deal in more detail with the first two of these cases.

(1) *Words with* ẹ̄ < *OE* ȳ

§ 135. Bullokar has [iː] in *dive*. *Fire*, to judge from an unusual 'homophone list' pairing, may have [iː] in Coles (see Vol. I, p. 410, note 6); Gil says that [iː] in *fire* was a feature of the 'Eastern dialect'. Gil himself has [iː] twice in his transcriptions of *build* (OE *býldan*), beside the three pronunciations ([yː], [əi], and [ɪ]) which he mentions in a separate discussion of the word. Jonson gives *keen* beside *kine* as the plural of *cow*; Wallis follows, and adds *mees* beside *mice* and *leece* beside *lice*. *WSC* describes *meece* 'mice' as 'barbarous speaking'. Wallis, it should be noticed, was born and received his early education in Kent, Jonson was a Londoner, and Bullokar a native of Sussex; but Gil was born in Lincolnshire and therefore came from outside the 'South-eastern area'.

Note: Coles gives the 'phonetic spelling' *Yeeldhall*, and Hodges, Strong, Cooper ('near alike'), and *WSC* put *Guildhall* beside *yield* in their 'homophone' lists; but the word has ME ē̞ from Anglian *(ge)géld*, not late WS *(ge)gýld* < *(ge)gield*.

(2) *Raising of ME ę̄ to ME ī*

§ 136. ME ę̄ appears to have been subject to a comparatively rare process of raising to ME ī, whence arises PresE [ai] in *briar, friar, quire, choir*, and *contrive* (cf. Luick, § 481); to these we may add (with Jordan, § 225, Anm. 1, who, however, adopts a different explanation) *umpire, dice* (cf. Note 3), and *grise* < *grece* 'steps'. The change occurs before a few consonants only (*r*, less often *s*, *v*, and perhaps *k*; see Note 2 below), but can hardly be combinative, since raising because of a following *r* is improbable. It must rather be considered an isolative tendency (as apparently by Luick, loc. cit., who attributes it somewhat vaguely to 'factors of sentence phonetics') which is found only in a few phonetic contexts merely because it is itself rare; it probably originated in dialects in which ME ę̄ tended to be raised to ē̞, and would then be due to an unconscious attempt to preserve the distinction between ME ē̞ and ME ę̄ (e.g. between *grē̞ce* 'grease' and *grę̄ce* 'steps') even at the expense of losing that between ME ē̞ and ME ī. The earliest evidence comes in *dice*, which has ī in rhyme in *King Alisaunder* and in Chaucer (cf. Luick, § 481, Anm. 2). Luick considers *dice* not to be comparable to the other words here cited, because in it ME ī appears a century earlier, as he believes; but the argument seems mistaken, since in all words the raising must have occurred before 1400, even if the evidence appears later. In any case there is fourteenth-century evidence for ME ī < ę̄ in other words, probably in the *Ayenbite* and certainly in *Gamelyn* (see Note 2). Further evidence comes from the early fifteenth century onwards (cf. Zachrisson, *Eng. Vowels*, p. 71). The raising may have originated in the East and North, for *King Alisaunder* is an Essex poem and *Gamelyn* is East Midland, and in the fifteenth century there is evidence from the *York Plays* and the *Paston Letters*. But the raised pronunciation was accepted early into London English, as Chaucer's rhyme of *dice* indicates; and in eModE the *i*-spelling was rapidly generalized in the words that now have [ai].

It will be noticed that all the words which in PresE show the apparent raising are of French origin, except *briar*. Jordan, § 225, Anm. 1, to account for this fact, would assume that OF ę was tenser than ME ę̄, and therefore was sometimes equated with ME ī and not ME ę̄. He would explain *briar* by the analogy of *friar*, but (as Matthes points out in his note in the appendix to the second edition of Jordan's book) the analogy is not a convincing one; and if Jordan's view were correct we should expect to find sporadic *i*-forms in all words adopted from French which had OF ę. It has not previously been observed in this connexion that in words adopted from French ME $\bar{ę}$ is much less often lowered to $\bar{ę}$ than it is in native English words (see § 126 above). But though this confirms Jordan's view that native and French words are differently treated, it cannot be directly due to any difference between OF $ę$ and ME $\bar{ę}$ such as he suggests; for when words of one language are adopted into another, the native variants of the sounds used in them are substituted for the foreign variants (here ME $\bar{ę}$ for OF $ę$). Moreover the evidence cited below proves that in vulgar or dialectal speech native $\bar{ę}$ was raised more freely than StE would suggest; and there is reason to suspect that in such speech, in which lowering of ME $\bar{ę}$ before r was also more common than in StE, it did not spare words of French origin. The problem is rather to explain why educated English accepted, from the vulgar or dialectal speech in which the developments seem to have occurred, the raising of ME $\bar{ę}$ more freely in French words and its lowering before r less freely. One may suggest that the determining factor was the recognition by educated persons, in the late fourteenth and fifteenth centuries, of the French origin of the words. Their knowledge of French pronunciation, with its specially tense $ę$, might predispose them (before and for a short while after 1400, while ME $\bar{i}$ was still [iː] and ME $\bar{ę}$ [eː]) in favour of [iː] (ME $\bar{i}$) by raising, owing to confusion such as Jordan suggests between a lax and open English [iː] and a tense and close French [e]; and it would certainly make them oppose (in the fifteenth century) the acceptance of open [ɛː] (ME $\bar{ę}$) by lowering before r, which would be an obvious departure from the French pronunciation.

It so happens that the words which in PresE have [ai] are rarely recorded by the orthoepists; *dice* has ME $\bar{i}$ in Levins and Smith (so *die* and *dies* in Bullokar), and *choir* (spelt *quire*) and *briar* have $\bar{i}$ in Butler. But there are indications that in vulgar or dialectal speech ME $\bar{i}$ by raising of ME $\bar{ę}$ occurred in words other than those that show it in StE. Hart says that 'countrie men' say *heier* (i.e. [həiər], as if *higher*) for *heare*. Bullokar has ME $\bar{i}$ in *flȳs* 'fleece' (see Vol. I, p. 106); it seems to me more likely to be due to raising of ME $\bar{ę}$ than to late WS $\bar{i} < \bar{ie}$. The 'homophone' lists of Young and Cocker have ME $\bar{i}$ in *here* and/or *hear*, Cocker's also in *spear* and *sphere* (see Vol. I, pp. 413, 417), and Brown's in *deer* and/or *dear*; cf. the spellings cited in Note 2 below. Coles may show ME $\bar{i} < \bar{ę} (< \bar{i}$ in an open syllable) in *fir* (see p. 410, note 6). The most plentiful evidence comes from spellings (see Note 2 below). Such evidence is always difficult to interpret, and I have been at pains in the Note to draw attention to possible alternative explanations; but the evidence of the spellings is consistent with the development shown sporadically by PresE pronunciation, with the orthoepists' evidence here cited, and with rhymes (see Note 3), and must be held to show that the raising at one time (probably in dialectal speech) had fairly widespread currency.

Note 1: Luick, loc. cit., cites as further examples the early ModE forms *relive* 'relieve', *retrive* 'retrieve', and *reprive* 'reprieve'; but these spellings might show ME *i* by shortening (cf. the spellings discussed § 132, Note). Luick also cites *clive* 'cleave' ('divide'), which may also show ME *i* by shortening, but may have ME *ī* because of the analogy of *cleave* 'adhere', which in the speech of Smith had given ME *ẹ̄* to *cleave* 'divide' (see Vol. I, p. 56), and might equally give it ME *ī* (from the OE form *clīfan*).

Note 2: The hypothesis of a raising of ME *ẹ̄* to *ī* is possibly supported by forms other than those cited by Luick. An interesting case is the word *sick*, which has thirteenth- to sixteenth-century forms *sike*, &c. which suggest ME *ī* (see *OED*) and rhymes on ME *ī* in Chaucer (*T. & C.* iii. 1360–3; v. 1352–4). Jordan, § 84, Anm. 3, would explain this *ī* form as a blend of the *i* form (developed by shortening of ME *ẹ̄*, perhaps in the noun *sickness*) and the *ẹ̄* form; in other words, a new form arises having the *i*-quality of *sick* but the long quantity of *seek*. This explanation seems entirely unacceptable. Luick, § 282, assumes an OE **sīec* by WS palatal mutation of *ēo* to *īe*. But the ME *ī* form is not merely South-western; it might, however, have spread through the agency of London English. Or Mercian *ē* may have become *ī* because of the preceding *s*, as Mercian *ĕ* becomes *i* after *s* and Mercian *ē* becomes *ī* before *ht*, *hs*. One should perhaps resist the temptation to explain the form as showing ME raising of *ẹ̄* to *ī*, though this in some ways would be easiest.

As Professor J. R. R. Tolkien has suggested, raising of *ẹ̄* to *ī* would be the simplest solution of the *Ayenbite*'s spellings *clier*, *clyer*, and *clyre* 'clear'; other suggestions (cf. Wallenberg, *The Vocabulary of Dan Michel's Ayenbite of Inwit*, s.v. *hyer*) are unconvincing. The same explanation could very well apply to the *Ayenbite*'s forms of *here* and *hear* and to the still earlier (late thirteenth-century) Kentish *hier* 'here' in MS Arundel 248 (cf. the evidence of ME *ī* in these words cited below), but in them we also have to reckon with the possibility of a glide [j]; see further § 430, Note 2, where the words are more fully discussed. The *Kentish Sermons* have *apierede* 'appeared', which though isolated might be a very early instance of the change of ME *ẹ̄* to *ī* in a word of French origin and so parallel to the *Ayenbite*'s forms of *clear*.

The poem *Gamelyn*, which dates from about the middle of the fourteenth century and is East Midland in its forms, rhymes *sire* with *hire* 'here' (ll. 221–2) and *fire* with *spire* 'shut' vb. (ll. 503–4); the latter is ME *speren* < MLG *speren* (see *OED*, s.v. *spear* vb.²). In such a word ME *ẹ̄* might be expected, but *Cursor Mundi* rhymes it on ME *ę̄*; if this be the original vowel, then ME *ę̄* must have been raised to *ẹ̄* before undergoing the further change to *ī*. *Cursor Mundi* itself has *spird* p.p., but it is uncertain whether *OED* is right in assigning this form to *speren* rather than *sperren* (ModE *spar*).

Other possible support is given by forms cited by *OED* and by Zachrisson, Wyld, and Kihlbom in another connexion, but unambiguous evidence is rare. Thus spellings with *ie* for ME *ẹ̄* are either the common and unphonetic digraph used, for example, in PresE *chief* or are the Kentish diphthong < OE *ēo*; and most *ye* spellings are probably only variants of these *ie* spellings (as certainly in Kentish for OE *ēo*). But raising of ME *ẹ̄* to *ī* is the likeliest explanation of the fourteenth- and fifteenth-century *spire* and fifteenth-century *sphyre* 'sphere', the fourteenth- to sixteenth-century *lyre* 'leer' (OE *hlēor*), and the sixteenth-century *styre* 'steer' sb. ('young ox'). Other similar forms are subject to more various explanations. Sixteenth-century *besmire* 'besmear' may be connected with fourteenth-century *smired*, *smyrede* 'smeared', which probably show ME *ĭ* descended from the OE variant *smĭrian* (see *OED*, s.vv. *besmear*, *smear*). Fifteenth- and sixteenth-century *tyer* 'tear' ('lacrima') may (*a*) only show *ye* as a graphic symbol for ME *ẹ̄*, or (*b*) be connected with the thirteenth-century *ti(e)r* and the twelfth-century *tiar*, of which the former at least shows ME *ī* from OE *ēa* before the guttural [ȝ] in *tēagor* (cf. ME *hye* plural of *high* from OE *hēage* pl. of *hēah*). Sixteenth-century *pyre* and sixteenth- and seventeenth-century *pire* 'pier' may represent the OF variant *pire* (see *OED*, s.v.). The fifteenth- and sixteenth-century *styre*, *stire* 'steer' vb. may show the survival of ME *ī* from OE (WS) *ī* beside *ȳ* from early WS *īe* in *stīeran*. The fifteenth-century *dire* 'dear' (cited by Wyld, *Coll. Eng.*, p. 206; see § 132, Note above) may similarly show ME *ī* from OE (WS) *ī*, *ȳ*, *īe*. *Hear* has fairly common *i*, *y* forms; *OED* gives *hire* as a fourteenth- and fifteenth-century form (an example is quoted from the *Boke of Noblesse*, 1475), and *hyre* as a fourteenth- to fifteenth-century form (an example is quoted from More, *Dyaloge*, 1529); Zachrisson cites four instances from the *Paston Letters*, and Wyld three, from the *Siege of Rouen, c.* 1420, Shillingford, and Gregory respectively (see § 132, Note above, under (*e*); on *hiresay* 'hearsay' see below). Again these forms may show ME *ī* from OE (WS) *ī*, *ȳ*, *īe*. But such ME forms should be South-western, for *i*-mutation to *īe* seems in OE to be restricted to pure WS; it might, however, have occurred in other Saxon dialects, or have been extended owing to the currency of WS as a standard literary language to dialects which did not originally have it. On ME *ī* (and [y:]) from Saxon *ī*, *ȳ*, *īe* see Jordan, § 83, Anm., § 86, Anm. 1 and 2; in ME itself the *ī* forms of Saxon dialects might have made their way into the 'mixed' language of London and in the fifteenth century have gained wider currency (e.g. in the Norfolk speech of the Pastons) because of the influence of the developing standard language. The form *diʒere* 'dear' which occurs twice in *Genesis and Exodus*, l. 3483, might afford thirteenth-century evidence of the currency in Norfolk of forms derived from WS *dīere*, *dȳre*; but it could be taken as showing the 'Kentish' diphthongization (also found in the Essex *Vices and Virtues*, and *Hatton Gospels*) of OE *ēo* (OK *īo*) in *dēore* (*dīore*). But the theory of South-western influence will not serve for *hirs* 'hears' in *Cursor Mundi*, l. 4192; this form, if it shows a long and not a short vowel (see below), would have to be taken as showing raising of ME *ẹ̄* < OAngl *ē* to ME *ī*. *Hyre* 'here' cited by Zachrisson, *Eng. Vowels*, p. 70, from the *Paston Letters* might be an inverted spelling due to the oscillation between ME *ī* derived from the South-western dialects and ME *ẹ̄* in *hear*. But when all is said that can be for the doctrine of South-western influence, it remains true (*a*) that there are words which this hypothesis will not cover, (*b*) that it is improbable that South-western dialectal forms should have had such wide currency as these *i*-spellings appear to have done; and though it may be correct to use this explanation for forms found in South-western writers (so Kihlbom, op. cit., p. 64), I would reject it in other cases.

An alternative possibility is that the *i*-spellings show shortening of ME *ẹ̄* > *ĭ* and that the final *e* is an unintelligent graphic addition (cf. the spellings cited in § 116, Note 2 and § 132, Note), though such an addition does not seem likely after *r*. Gil shows shortening of ME *ẹ̄* in *shears* and *swear* (see § 30), but there is no orthoepistical evidence of shortening of ME *ẹ̄* before final *r*. It seems, however, to be shown in *steer* vb. by the seventeenth-century *sterre*, sixteenth-century *stir*, and sixteenth- and seventeenth-century *stirre* forms cited by *OED* (but see Note 3). Cf. the fourteenth- and more conclusively the sixteenth-century spelling *ster* of *steer* 'young ox', and possibly *Cursor Mundi*'s *hirs* 'hears' and the fourteenth-century *dir* 'dear'. But the evidence of modern dialectal pronunciation, as recorded by Wright, fails to support the theory that shortening was not uncommon in such words. In the form *Dyrham* 'Dereham' cited by Zachrisson, op. cit., p. 69, however, there can be little doubt that shortening in the first element of the compound has occurred; so possibly in *hiresay* 'hearsay', a late sixteenth-century spelling cited by Wyld, loc. cit. The fourteenth- and fifteenth-century forms *wiry*, *wyry* 'weary' (see *OED*, Wyld, loc. cit., Zachrisson, loc. cit.) have shortening, probably in the first instance in the trisyllabic inflected forms of the adjective (cf. § 85).

Wright cites practically no dialectal forms which would support the theory that ME *ẹ̄* was raised before certain consonants to ME *ī*, except in words that have [ai] in Standard English; but *clear* is [klæiə(r)] in Shropshire.

The fifteenth- and sixteenth-century spellings with *i* for ME *ẹ̄* discussed in § 132, Note under (*f*) seem certainly to show [ɪ] by shortening; but if they referred to a long vowel, they would most naturally be interpreted as showing ME *ī*, which we should have to explain as due to raising.

Note 3: Spenser has a curious form *stire*, rhymed regularly on ME *ī*; it appears to represent both *stir* (so in most instances) and *steer*. In either case it must have late ME *ī* < ME *ẹ̄* (derivation from the WS form *stīeran* being improbable); in so far as it is from *stir* (OE *stȳrian*) it shows that ME *ẹ̄* < *ĭ* in an open syllable was subject to the raising (cf. late ME *ī* in *fir* < OE *fȳre or ON *fȳri* apparently recorded by Coles). Contact between the verbs *stir* and *steer* may be a factor in explaining the spellings of the latter which appear to show shortening (see Note 2 above); they might be inverted spellings, or more probably representations of an analogical form.

Note 4: On a parallel raising of ME *ǭ* to ME *ū* see § 158 below.

THE DEVELOPMENT OF ME ī

§ 137. The diphthongization of ME ī is ignored by certain orthoepists. Palsgrave only obscurely indicates that he recognized any difference between ME ī and French i, and explicitly identifies ME wī with French [wi] (see Vol. I, p. 9). Smith regards ME ī as the long equivalent of ME ĭ, and as being identical with Latin ī, which (he says) is the long equivalent of Latin ĭ; he further identifies it with French i and describes it as a very tense front vowel. On his evidence on Norman *my* 'moi', which is not relevant to ME ī, see Vol. I, p. 59. Bullokar, like Smith, regards ME ī as the long equivalent of ME ĭ, and Waad uses *i* as his symbol for both ME ī and ME ĭ (see Vol. I, p. 130). To this list we may perhaps add Hodges, who says that ME ī is a long vowel without a short equivalent. But he regards ME ẹ̄ as the long equivalent of ME ĭ and is apparently willing to allow *ei* as an alternative means of writing ME ī; his evidence therefore clearly shows diphthongization, and even after we have allowed for the influence of words like *eye* it seems likely that he himself recognized the diphthongization and would have described the sound as a diphthong *ei* but for the obvious advantages to a schoolmaster of keeping its traditional designation as a 'long vowel'. As late as 1686 Lodwick counts ME ī as a pure vowel.

To interpret the evidence of Palsgrave, Smith, Bullokar, Waad, and Lodwick as showing that ME ī was still [iː] (as has been done) would be a grave mistake. All contemporary evidence—as early as the *Welsh Hymn* (before 1500) and Lily (*c.* 1521), who says that among the English faults in pronouncing Latin is 'iotacism', the pronouncing of *i* too 'broad'—shows that diphthongization has occurred. Luick, § 483 and Anm. 1, sets the beginnings of diphthongization about 1400 on the ground that from the early fifteenth century onwards foreign *i* was replaced by ME ẹ̄ in words adopted from foreign languages; he is undoubtedly correct. The failure of these orthoepists to record the diphthongization, it should be noticed, is not due to their being ignorant of the theoretical distinction between a pure vowel and a diphthong; Smith was especially clear on this point, and some of his evidence which shows that he did not recognize the diphthongization of ME ī comes when he is arguing that Latin ī and ME ī are pure vowels which differ from ĭ only in length. The failure was one of practical phonetic analysis (for which there are special reasons in Lodwick's case; see Vol. I, pp. 277–8) and not of theory. An exact parallel is provided by Australians and Cockneys at the present time, who are quite unaware that they often pronounce [əi] for StE [iː] (or rather [ɪi]); theoretical training in phonetics does not always improve their acoustic perception. See further Note 1 below.

The most common way in which the diphthongization is shown by sixteenth- and seventeenth-century orthoepists is by the transcription *ei*, or by statements that ME *ī* is like Latin *ei* or Greek ει or foreign [ɛi]. In these cases the identification does not mean merely that Latin *ei* or Greek ει were identified with ME *ī* in the English pronunciation of these languages (Latin *ei* was not), but that an attempt is being made to find means of expressing the degree of diphthongization; such statements are a pseudo-learned variation on the ordinary transcription *ei*. The orthoepists who adopt this transcription or identify ME *ī* with foreign [ɛi] are Hart, Baret, Minsheu, Robinson, Gil, Sherwood, Daines, Gataker, J. Smith, and (identifying ME *ī* with Dutch *ij* or *ey* pronounced [ɛi]) *The English Schole-master* (1646), Hexham, and Richardson; cf. also Note 2 below. Of these, the evidence of Robinson, Gil, Daines, and Gataker presents special features; see further below.

A common theory, relying on the evidence which we have just reviewed and on that cited in Note 2 below, is that ME *ī* developed through the stages [ei], [ɛi], and [æi] to [ai]. This view is altogether impossible. If the development had been that suggested, ME *ī* would have crossed the path of ME *ai* developing to [æi] and [ɛi] (see §§ 225–6 below); most of the orthoepists who say that ME *ī* was *ei* still pronounced ME *ai* as a diphthong. Yet the two sounds are always kept distinct, as they are still. ME *ī* can never have been [ɛi], and we must therefore admit that the orthoepists' transcription of ME *ī* as *ei* and their comparison of it with foreign [ɛi] sounds were not exact; this point is well made by Zachrisson, *Eng. Vowels*, p. 130 foot, pp. 205–6. There are indeed indications in various orthoepists that the transcription *ei* was only approximate. The identification of ME *ī* with Welsh *ei* in the *Welsh Hymn* and Salesbury may well mean [əi] (see Vol. I, p. 4). Robinson (see Vol. I, p. 209) shows that the diphthong was a glide ending in the position of tense [i]; he says nothing of the exact position of the first element. Gil says that the diphthong is almost *ei*, but 'sono exilior quam si diffunderemur in *e*'; i.e. the first element is not the ordinary *e* [e], but a thinner (more obscure) sound, which must be [ə] or some closely related 'mid-mixed' ('central') vowel. Gil further refers to Lipsius, who praises the English for pronouncing (Latin) *ī* as *ei*, which Lipsius evidently thought was the original pronunciation. The terms of Gil's reference seem to mean that he will not as a rule use *ei* as a symbol for ME *ī* because (*a*) the sound is not exactly *ei*, and (*b*) we should then be no longer able to claim that we pronounced the symbol *i* (he uses the variant form *j* himself) in the distinctive way which won the applause of Lipsius. His expression is not altogether clear, except in that part in which he says that ME *ī* is not exactly *ei*. Daines says that the Southern pronunciation of ME *ī* is like, but not so full as, Latin *ei*; his evidence thus repeats Gil's. Gataker, in an obscure reference to the name of *w* (he seems rather to mean the name of *y*), says that in our pronunciation it is 'almost' *wei* rather than *wii*; it is clear that he also hesitates to express ME *ī* as *ei*. Ray (Vol. I, p. 189) says most significantly that the nature of the first element of the diphthong is doubtful and that 'one that did not curiously observe it, would think it to be *e*'.

If then we are given these hints that the transcription *ei* and the comparisons with foreign [εi] are only approximate, we are free to turn to another hypothesis. What this hypothesis should be is indicated by the development of ModE [iː] (from ME *ẹ̄*), which in present Southern English has been slightly diphthongized to [ɪi], and when the diphthongization is more pronounced (as in Cockney or Australian English) becomes not [ei] but [əi]. We may similarly assume that ME *ī* first became [ɪi], and that the first element then became a mid-mixed or central vowel. This central vowel was obviously comparable to some *e* sound, as is shown by the orthoepists' transcriptions. Two explanations are possible. The central vowel may have had the tongue raised to the same height as [e]; it would then be a little, but only a little, higher than the present [ə] (some common varieties of which are in fact as high as [e]; see Daniel Jones, *Outline of English Phonetics*, §§ 356–9). Or the orthoepists may be thinking of the pronunciation of *e* in unstressed syllables, where we may assume that it was already [ə]; none of those orthoepists who transcribe ME *ī* as *ei* have a separate symbol to express the pronunciation of unstressed *e*. If this second explanation be accepted, ME *ī* was already [əi], and not merely approaching it. Thus the *ei* transcriptions, whichever of these two explanations we adopt, mean [əi] or some closely related diphthong. Wallis gives an exact description of such a diphthong [əi], saying that ME *ī* is pronounced as a diphthong beginning with '*e* foemininum', i.e. [ə] (see Vol. I, pp. 233–4, and Note 3 below).

Orthoepists later than Wallis are less precise: thus Wilkins (see Vol. I, p. 256) and Cooper (Vol. I, p. 293) describe a diphthong [ʌi], and the two Welsh sources, the *Welsh Breviary* (Vol. I, p. 345) and T. Jones (Vol. I, p. 355), use a transcription which is doubtless intended for [əi] but could mean [ʌi]. Coles (see Vol. I, p. 439) regarded the first element of ME *ī* as a 'guttural' sound. These orthoepists are not to be taken as attempting to describe a different sound from Wallis's; none of them distinguishes [ə] from [ʌ] as a separate phoneme (see Vol. I, pp. 241–3 above), and there is clear evidence that the *Welsh Breviary* confused [ə] and [ʌ]. Thus the sound they heard was, beyond any real doubt, still [əi]—though as the difference between [əi] and [ʌi] is so slight it is not of great importance which sound they actually used. It should be noticed that both the Welsh sources identify the second element as tense [i] (transcribed with Welsh *i*), whereas T. Jones gives the second element of ME *ai* as lax [ɪ] (transcribed as Welsh *u*). Robinson, it will be remembered, also gave the second element as tense [i]; but he did not distinguish ME *ai* in this respect as T. Jones does. The present Australian and Cockney [əi] < ME *ẹ̄* similarly ends with tense [i].

The transition from this seventeenth-century [əi] to PresE [ai] is slight and easy. Indeed, the exact nature of the first element of the Present English diphthong is not easy to determine; most people use [a], but some use sounds nearer [æ] or [ɑ], and 'others again, especially in the North of England, use a sound nearer to [ʌi] or [əi]' (Daniel Jones, op. cit., § 407), and *OED* adopts [əi] as its transcription for the diphthong—perhaps because Sir James Murray was Scottish. Little change has occurred since the seventeenth century; but it is unlikely that the sound [ai] was ever heard in careful Southern English speech before 1700, since a diphthongal pronunciation of ME *ai* survived (in old-fashioned speech) practically until that date, and there is no trace of confusion between ME *ī* and this diphthongal pronunciation of ME *ai* (except by the Yorkshireman Richardson; see Vol. I, pp. 382–3). But in the North the development was more rapid and the [ai] stage was reached by 1600. Lily, in remarking on the English fault of 'iotacism', says that it is especially noticeable among 'our English Northern people'. Gil gives the Northern pronunciation of ME *ī* as *ai*; this is the same as his transcription of the StE (Southern) pronunciation of ME *ai* and different from the approximate value *ei* which he gives for Southern ME *ī*. Daines shows clearly the identity of Northern ME *ī* and Southern ME *ai*, saying that in the North *fire* is pronounced like *faire* (see further Note 4). Richardson, as remarked above, confuses the (Northern) pronunciation of ME *ī* with the diphthongal pronunciation of ME *ai*. Newton gives as his own pronunciation the purely dialectal [ɒi], which must develop from [ai]. So in the seventeenth century [ai] was a dialectal (especially Northern) pronunciation, which cannot have appeared in StE until the diphthongal pronunciation of ME *ai* had finally disappeared; it was probably adopted during the eighteenth century.

Note 1: Some scholars (e.g. Viëtor, *Shakespeare's Pronunciation*, § 18) have held such evidence as Smith's to relate to a conservative style of pronunciation in which ME *ī* had not passed beyond the first stage of its diphthongization, [ɪi]. But (*a*) other evidence shows [əi] at a still earlier date, (*b*) it is inconceivable that both [ɪi] < ME *ī* and [i:] < ME *ẹ̄* can have coexisted, as Viëtor assumes, for the difference between the two sounds is too slight to enable them to be held apart as separate phonemes, as ME *ī* and *ẹ̄* continued to be, and (*c*) the hypothesis is unnecessary to explain Smith's error, for [əi], especially if pronounced with a short first element (on-glide) and a long second element, can be mistaken for a pure vowel, as is pointed out above.

Note 2: Evidence apparently showing [ei] or [ɛi] for ME *ī* is found in other sources than those cited above, as follows:

(*a*) In foreign orthoepists; see Zachrisson, *Eng. Vowels*, pp. 129–30.

(*b*) 'Occasional spellings' with *ei* for ME *ī*; but these need not be parallel to the orthoepists' transcriptions, for (as Jordan, § 279, Anm., points out) they may be due to the variation between *ei* and *ī* in a number of common words such as *eye* and *height*—an explanation which is inherently more likely for such spellings when they occur in conventional orthography than the hypothesis of phonetic intention. On spellings with *ai* for ME *ī* see Note 4 below.

(*c*) Alleged rhymes of *ẹi* words with *ī* words, cited by Jordan, § 279. All except one of those cited from the Wiltshire *Legends of St. Editha and St. Etheldreda* are cases of ME *ī* rhyming with OE *ĕg* (*side* : *leyde*, *by* : *wey*, &c.). Wright, *EDG*, § 64, shows that OE *ĕg* is commonly [ai] in modern dialects, especially those of the West Midlands and the South; it is clear that in these dialects OE ĕg > ig > ī. These rhymes are not therefore rhymes of ME ī with ME ẹi. The exception is the rhyme *enmie* : *obeye*, which is admittedly a rhyme of etymological ME ī with ME ẹi. But *enemy* has fourteenth-century forms *ennymei*, *en(e)me* and fifteenth-century *enmei* (see *OED*), which must be due to alteration of the final vowel on the analogy of words adopted from French with (in English) final -*ey*, such as *valley* and *alley*. The two rhymes cited from Lydgate must be struck out. *Peyse* 'weight' : *paradise* depends on the twelfth- to fifteenth-century form *parais*, &c., which is derived from the French 'early semi-popular form *paraïs*, *pareïs*' (see *OED*). *Arise* : *praise* depends on the variant *prise* < OF *prisier*, a reformation on the French strong form *prise* (1 sing. pres. indic.) beside *praise* < OF *preisier* (cf. *OED*, s.vv. *praise* vb. and *prize* vb.[1]; the use of *prize* in the sense 'extol' is only recorded in Northern texts, but theoretically it might have all the meanings of *praise* in all parts of the country).

Thus there are no true cases of rhymes of ME ī with ME ẹi; nor are any to be expected, for exact rhymes of ME ī and ME ẹi are impossible, since the two sounds did not ever become identical.

Note 3: Wyld, *Coll. Eng.*, p. 224, seriously misrepresents Wallis, making it appear that his 'e foemininum' may either be [ə] or [ʌ]. Actually Wallis is the only orthoepist to distinguish the two sounds; [ʌ] is called '*u obscurum*' (see Vol. I, pp. 225–6, 241–3).

Note 4: Luick, § 482, Anm. 3, gives further evidence of the identity of Northern ī with Southern *ai*. But he says that it may be explained either as showing Northern [ɛi] for Southern [əi], or Northern [ai]; in view of the present pronunciations in North and South he prefers the former alternative, which he says means that the North was more conservative. This view depends on the mistaken theory that ME ī became [ɛi] before developing to [əi] or [ai], and is to be rejected on that ground alone. But in any case it cannot be reconciled with Gil's evidence, since his *ai* does not represent [ɛi]. Nor is it probable that the North, which had more advanced pronunciations for ME ā, ME ẹ̄, and ME *ai*, would have a more conservative pronunciation for ME ī. The development of all these sounds is closely related; and Lily's evidence means, obviously, that the diphthongization in the early sixteenth century was more pronounced in the North.

Rapid diphthongization to the stage [ai] also seems to have occurred in the East and to have led to the same confusion between dialectal [ai] < ME ī and StE [ai] < ME *ai* as Richardson displays in the seventeenth century. Zachrisson, *Eng. Vowels*, p. 72, and Kihlbom, p. 36, cite *whrayt* 'write', with *ay* for ME ī, from the (Essex) *Cely Papers*, which seems to depend on the identification of an advanced pronunciation of ME ī with a conservative one of ME *ai*. But it is not clear on what grounds Kihlbom, p. 38, regards de la Pole's spellings *tame* 'time' and *mat* 'might' as showing diphthongization of ME ī— unless they involve the mechanical omission of a letter and are intended for *taime* and *mait*. It is strongly to be suspected that many of de la Pole's mis-spellings are non-phonetic. (*Vayage* 'voyage', cited by Zachrisson, loc. cit., and Wyld, *Coll. Eng.*, p. 224, merely represents the ME and OF variant *veiage*; see *OED*, s.v. *voyage*.)

Note 5: When ME *ui* became [ʌi] by the unrounding of the first element it quickly became identical with [əi] < ME ī; proof of the identity of the two sounds is thus proof that ME ī had become [əi]. It is possible that in some dialects the identity had already come about in the fifteenth century, though the evidence is unsatisfactory (see § 262, Note 2); in general evidence of it is later than evidence of other sorts for [əi] < ME ī, and this is especially true of StE, in which the identity of ME *ui* and ME ī is not shown until the seventeenth century (see § 262).

Note 6: Hayward perhaps attempts to describe a diphthong [əi] for ME ī; see Vol. I, p. 322. But most of his descriptions of articulation are adopted from Pierre de la Ramée, and do not apply to English pronunciation; it is safer therefore to exclude him from our list of authorities for [əi].

Note 7: The hypothesis put forward by A. J. Bliss, *English and Germanic Studies*, ii (1948–9), 40–47, that ME ī was diphthongized to [ẹi] in the thirteenth century and so became identical with ME ẹi in *eye*, is based on the false view of the process of diphthongization of ME *ī* rejected above; his parallel hypothesis of the development of ME *ū* falls with it, and is equally based on a false view of the process of diphthongization. Bliss takes no account of the eModE evidence on the nature of the sounds.

ALLEGED FAILURE OF THE DIPHTHONGIZATION OF ME *ī*

§ 138. Luick, § 485, argues that before certain consonants the diphthongization of ME *ī* fails.

(1) *Before* [tʃ]

The words cited as examples are *weech-elm* (a seventeenth-century form of *wych-elm*), *sleech* (a by-form of *slitch*; see *OED*), *screech* (a by-form of *scritch*), and *meech* vb. (a nineteenth-century form of *miche*). To these we may add *meecher* (a seventeenth-century form of *micher*, the substantive derived from *miche* vb.) and *seech* (a nineteenth-century form of *sitch*). Luick would regard these as having ME *ī* preserved as [iː]. But in every case (see Note 1) the [iː] pronunciation is to be explained from late ME *ē̜* developed from ME *ĭ* by lengthening in an open syllable (a process which does occur before [tʃ]).

(2) *Before* k

Luick's example is *shriek*. The etymology of this and related words is not altogether clear; if it be from *shrike*, as Luick assumes, it probably owes its [iː] to a late ME *ē̜* developed in an open syllable from earlier *ĭ* by shortening of *ī*. This shortening of *ī* to *ĭ* may occur not in *shrike* itself but in *shritch* (ME *shrichen*), which is probably a variant of *shrike* (both being developed from OE **scrīcan* (?); see *OED*); but it could occur in trisyllabic forms of the verb such as *shrikeden*. In early ModE there are words which parallel *shriek* (see Note 2); Hart (as Zachrisson, *Eng. Vowels*, p. 76, points out) has [iː] once in *liked* (beside [əi] often in *like*), and Zachrisson's word-list to Bullokar shows [iː] seven times, [əi] twice, and *ĭ* once in (*mis*)*like* vb. Some modern dialects have [iː] in *dike* (see Vol. I, p. 108), though Bullokar gives [əi]. In all these words ModE [iː] is from ME *ē̜* by lengthening of *ĭ*; in *like* and *dike* ME *ĭ* is by shortening of OE *ī* in the verbs (OE *līcian, dīcian*; cf. Bülbring, § 349), whence it was extended, as Zachrisson's evidence shows, to the adjective *like* (cf. Raleigh's rhyme *seek : alike*) and the noun *dike*. Bullokar actually records ME *ĭ* once (in *liketh*), and Hart uses [iː] in the past tense, in which the OE shortening is most likely. A similar case appears to be Gil's [iː] in *repine*, if the word is from OE *pīnian* (see *OED*); again OE shortening to *ĭ* has been followed by ME lengthening to *ē̜*.

(3) *Before* [dʒ]

The example cited by Luick is *oblige*. This word is a fourteenth-century adoption, and therefore is not an example of French *i* being represented in

English by fifteenth-century [iː] < ME ẹ̄; it should in eModE have [əi] < ME ī. But in the seventeenth and eighteenth centuries [iː] was common; it is recorded among the orthoepists by Coles, Strong, and Young. Luick's explanation is that ME ī in this word was sometimes diphthongized, but sometimes remained as [iː] because of the influence of the following consonant. *OED* explains the [iː] pronunciation as due to French influence; Luick's objection to this view, that the word remained in continual use and therefore was not likely to be subject to foreign influence, is not conclusive (especially as the foreign influence might have been a result of the introduction into English of the senses marked III in *OED*—'confer a favour on', &c.), but has some force. An alternative explanation would be that [iː] developed from a late ME ẹ̄ by lengthening of an earlier ĭ, which could easily occur as a variant to ī in such a position in a word of French origin; this lengthening to ẹ̄ may be shown by the fourteenth-century spelling *oblege* cited by *OED* (but the spelling could show lowering of ĭ to ĕ). The influence of Modern French would, however, account for the vogue of the pronunciation in the eighteenth century.

We may conclude that there is no satisfactory evidence to show that the diphthongization of ME ī failed in the circumstances alleged by Luick.

Note 1: There is no reason to suppose that *wych-elm* has ME ī, since it is from OE *wĭc*, *wĭce* (see *OED*, s.v. *witch* sb.³); from the latter form we get ME *wĭche* which may become *wẹ̄che*. *Slitch* is from OE **slīc* (whence also *slike*; see *OED*); early ME shortening before *ch* gives *slĭch*, and late ME lengthening of the ĭ so developed to ẹ̄ in the open syllables of oblique forms (e.g. the plural) gives *sleech*. Similarly develop *sitch* and its variant *seech* from OE *sīc*. *OED* unnecessarily assumes 'echoic modification' to explain the development of *screech* from *scritch*; lengthening in the open syllable of ME *scrĭchen* gives late ME **scrẹ̄chen*. *Miche* vb. and *micher* sb. are from ME **michen* and *mycher* (from OF *muchier* and **muchere*); in these ME forms lengthening in the open syllable can occur.

Note 2: Luick, § 485, Anm. 6, allows that [iː] in *shriek* and in the forms *deek* for *dike* and *leek* for *like* (Zachrisson, *Eng. Vowels*, pp. 75–76, cites many spellings showing the latter) may develop in the variants with *ch*, but even so he would apparently regard the process as being the failure of diphthongization of ME ī before *ch*. Zachrisson, however, adopts the explanation given above, that in every case the [iː] develops from late ME ẹ̄ by lengthening of ĭ by shortening of OE ī. This explanation is supported by the fourteenth-century rhyme of *deke* 'dike' with *eke* (which has ME ẹ̄); Luick cites this rhyme as an admitted objection to his theory. In *like* and *dike* [iː] was probably originally dialectal; see Vol. I, p. 108 above.

Note 3: Luick similarly alleges that diphthongization of ME ū fails before [tʃ] and [dʒ], but the evidence is again unsatisfactory; see § 167.

VARIATION BETWEEN ME ī AND ME ẹi (LATE ME ai)

§ 139. In *height* and *sleight*, in which OE ē undergoes late OE shortening, there develops in ME either ME *ai* (in Saxon areas, where these words were assimilated to *ĕhta* < *ĕahta* 'eight') or ME ĭ (in Anglian areas, where, in the absence of words with ĕ before *h*, they were assimilated to the type of *cnĭht*, *rĭht* < earlier *cnĕht*, *rĕht*; see Jordan, § 96); from the latter in late

ME there develops a variant in *ī* by absorption of [ç] (see the following section). In *height* ME *ī* sometimes occurs with retention of [ç] (so in Gil) owing to the analogy of *high* (< OAngl *hēh*). In *weight* (OE *gewiht*) there should be only ME [iç] > late ME *ī*; the spelling with *ei* and the pronunciation with ME *ai* may be due to the influence of the ON cognate (so Jordan, loc. cit.), but is more likely to arise from the analogy of the verb (OE *wegan*, whence ME *ẹi* > *ai*). *Freight* (probably < MDu *vrecht*) should have only ME *ai*, but appears to be affected by the variation in *weight*. *Eight* should have ME *ẹi* > *ai* in the South (< OE (Saxon) *ĕhta* < *ĕahta*) and ME *au* in the Midlands and North (< OE (Anglian) *ǣhta*) (cf. Jordan, § 63), but modern Northern (and Midland) dialects have pronunciations descended from ME *ī*, as if from OE **ihta* < **ĕhta* beside *ǣhta* (either analogical, on the model of *mĕht*, *nĕht* beside *mǣht*, *nǣht*, or of *sĕx* 'six', or in accordance with R. Girvan, *Angelsaksisch Handboek*, § 92, Aanm. 2—but see Bülbring, § 210, and Sievers–Brunner, § 122 (3), who deny that the Anglian change of *ǣ* > *ĕ* occurred before *ht*).

The evidence of the orthoepists is as follows. *Height* has ME *ai* in Cheke, Laneham (?), Willis (see Note below), Cooper (who also gives the form *heightth* [sic] pronounced *haitth*), and *WSC-RS* (but *WSC* admits that 'some' use *ī*). It has *ī* in Gil (whose transcription with *ei* stands for ME *ī*), Butler, Poole, *WSC* (who says that 'some' use this pronunciation), and Cocker. *Sleight* has *ai* in Willis (who also gives this pronunciation for *slight* adj., of which the phonology is identical; see also Note below), but ME *ī* in Hodges, Coles, Strong, and Brown. *Weight* has *ī* in Richardson and Cocker (cf. Chaucer's *wight*), but otherwise *ai*, as in Bullokar, Gil, and Hodges. By the reverse analogy Brown has ME *ī* in *weigh* (a Northernism). *Freight* has *ī* in Fox and Hookes's 'homophone' list, but otherwise *ai*, as in Hodges. *Eight* has *ī* in the Yorkshireman Richardson, but otherwise *ai*.

In *eye* the unstable eME diphthong *ẹi* (< OE *ē* (Anglian and late WS; cf. Bülbring, § 317) before *g*) regularly becomes late ME *ī* except in the North (cf. Jordan, § 97 (1*b*)), despite the common retention of the spelling appropriate to the diphthong; only ME *ī* is recorded (by Hart and later sources), except for Levins's [i:], an obvious Northernism.

In *neighbour* (OE *nē(a)hgebūr*) shortening in the first element of the compound produced *ĕ*, which diphthongized to *ẹi* > *ai*, shown by Strong, Young, and the shorthand-writers Dix and Hopkins; but the influence of *nīgh* (< *nẹigh* < *nēh*) and *nȳe* gave rise to a form with ME *ī*, shown by the spelling *nibor* used by the shorthand-writer Folkingham (cf. fourteenth-century *nyebore* recorded by *OED*). On pronunciations of this word with ME *ę̄* see § 129.

Note: Levins rhymes together *height*, *sleight*, *slight* adj., *fight*, *weight*, *eight*, and *straight*; these rhymes reflect Northern pronunciation, which still has both [ai] < ME *ī* and [ei] < ME *ai* in all these words; see Vol. I, p. 22. Willis uses Levins's list without following it automatically; his evidence may be treated as independent. Brown puts *eight* and *height* together in his 'homophone' list; as he has many Northernisms, it is not unlikely that the pairing depends on ME ī in *eight*, as in Richardson (see Vol. I, p. 382).

VARIATION BETWEEN ME ī AND ME *ĭgh* [ɪç]

§ 140. Variation occurs in late ME and early ModE between ME ī and ME *ĭgh* [ɪç] in such words as *night*, and also by analogy in such words as *nigh* (with ME *īgh* [iːç]). This variation is the result of the divergent development of ME *ĭgh* in late ME—a development which has not been accurately traced by phonologists. ME *ĭgh* gave rise, in late ME and early ModE, to three pronunciations.

(*a*) The original pronunciation [ɪç] survives. The PresE pronunciation [ai] cannot go back to this [ɪç], which in the modern period can develop in only two ways: (i) to short lax [ɪ], by simple effacement of the [ç] (a pronunciation which occurs in some dialects, chiefly Northern, in *night*; see Wright, *EDG*, Index); (ii) to [iː], by vocalization and absorption of the consonant (as in ME; see under (*b*)); this pronunciation is common in the dialects (chiefly Northern).

(*b*) In late ME [ɪç] developed to [iː] and shared the subsequent development of ME ī to the diphthong [əi] (Present English [ai]). The process was that the [ç] became voiced [j], and the group [ɪj] was then assimilated to [iː]; it must have been complete by about 1400. In the fifteenth century this pronunciation was predominantly Eastern; thus in Jordan, § 295, Anm., the majority of the texts cited are Eastern. Among them is the *Ludus Coventriae*, which is a Norfolk text; cf. my article, 'The Etymology and Meaning of *Boy*', *Medium Ævum*, ix (October 1940), pp. 152-3, where Furnivall's opinion, that the loss of *gh* is especially frequent in Norfolk texts in the fifteenth century, is quoted. Gower's rhymes which show the development to ME ī may be Kenticisms. We should regard the retention of [ɪç] as the characteristic development of educated StE, and the [əi] pronunciation as being introduced into London English probably from the Eastern dialects.

(*c*) There is evidence, though not all of it is satisfactory, for a third pronunciation [əiç] developed from ME *ĭgh*. It could be explained in any one of three ways: (i) as a blend of the first two pronunciations; (ii) as due to the analogy of the development of ME *īgh* in *nigh* (see below); (iii) as due to the lengthening of ME ĭ to ī before [ç] in late ME through the development of a glide [j] between the ĭ and the [ç].

Note 1: Wyld, *Coll. Eng.*, p. 305, and Jordan, § 295, ignore the evidence for the survival of the original pronunciation, believing apparently that only one pronunciation is possible at any one time; they would doubtless argue that the sixteenth- and seventeenth-century orthoepists who show retention of the [ç] are giving artificial pronunciations based only on the spelling, but this in the case of Gil at least is demonstrably not so (see below).

Note 2: Explanation (iii) described under (*c*) above is that put forward by Luick, § 403; some support is to be found in the pronunciation [iːç] recorded by the *Welsh Hymn* and

Salesbury (see below), in which ModE *ĭ* is similarly lengthened before [ç]. But this Welsh pronunciation [i:ç] seems to develop in the course of the loss of [ç], since there is no modern dialectal pronunciation [i:ç]. On the other hand certain Scotch dialects have [aiçt], &c. (cf. Wright, § 77), for which Luick's explanation would seem to be the most suitable. But Luick is in error in explaining the PresE pronunciation from a fifteenth- and sixteenth-century [əiç], since there is no continuous tradition of unambiguous evidence for such a pronunciation in StE. Luick does not recognize the existence of the pronunciation [əi] in the eModE period.

Note 3: ME *ŭght* in *drought*, &c. shows analogous divergent development to [uχt] and [ʌut]; there may also have been a pronunciation [ʌuχ], similar to [əiç] < ME *igh*, as assumed by Luick, § 403, but there is hardly any evidence for it. See § 177 below.

(1) *Words with ME ĭgh*

§ 141. The sixteenth- and seventeenth-century orthoepistical evidence for these three pronunciations of ME *ĭgh* (which only occurs before *t*) is as follows.

(a) The pronunciation [ıç]

The pronunciation [ıç] is recorded by Smith (six times, against [əi] twice; see below), Hart, and Sherwood, who expresses a definite preference for the 'older and true pronunciation' of *igh* as it is written, i.e. as [ıç], as against [əi] (see further under (*b*) below). To these we may add Coote, whose evidence implies that there was still a pronunciation [ıç] (see under (*b*)). Jonson repeats Smith's opinion that the *g* should be omitted from such words as *night*, but it is doubtful whether this means that he preserved the pronunciation recorded by Smith. Other orthoepists show retention of the spirant, but leave the quantity of the vowel doubtful. Daines perhaps had short [ı] in *sight*, for he is careful to say that the vowel of *sigh* is 'long *i*' [əi] but says nothing of that of *sight*; yet some suspicion attaches to his evidence (see below). Price in large measure follows Daines; he preserves the spirant but says nothing of the vowel. Similarly the shorthand-writer J. Willis (the only shorthand-writer to show retention of the spirant) says nothing of the vowel. The evidence of others again is subject to suspicion. Bullokar regularly transcribes [ıç] as *ih* (with short [ı]), but he puts this *ih* into his transcriptions *deliht* 'delight' and *kiht* 'kite'. Yet this need not mean that he is being guided only by the spelling. If he were, how should he know that the *i* ought to be short? To know this, he would at least have to hear other people say [ıç]. He has either made a mistake in attempting to record a pronunciation which he did not himself use, or analogical pronunciations of *delight* and *kite* have developed because of the variation between [əi] < ME *ī* and [ıç] in words which have etymological [ıç]. Tonkis, though he says nothing of the vowel, gives a very circumstantial description of a spirant not only in *light*, but also in *spright*; perhaps he also used an analogical pronunciation for the latter. As he was born in Wolverhampton, he may have been confused by differences between Midland

and Southern speech. Daines, like Bullokar, includes *delight* among words having the spirant. It may be that the survival of the *gh* spelling in *delight* (and in *spright* beside *sprite*) was due to the existence, when English orthography was becoming settled, of analogical pronunciations with [ɪç].

(*b*) *The pronunciation* [əi]

The pronunciation [əi] < late ME *ī* is recorded by Smith (twice, in each case explicitly as a variant beside [ɪç], which is recorded six times in all), Coote, Robinson, Sherwood, Butler, Hodges, *The English Schole-master* (1646), Willis, Wallis, Merriott, Hunt, Wilkins, Coles, Strong, Young, Lye, Richardson, *WSC-RS*, Cocker, and the shorthand-writers T. Shelton, Cartwright, Richardson, and Farthing. Coote's evidence is to the effect that *gh* is 'of most men but little sounded', so that *might* and *fight* become *mite* and *fite*; we may assume that some men sound the *gh*, and Coote himself observes that 'the truest is, both to write and pronounce' it. Sherwood's evidence is even more important; he expresses a preference for the older and true pronunciation of such words as *light* as they are written, but says that there is another pronunciation as *ei* [əi], 'prononciation moderne, et fort usitée à Londres et ailleurs', thus *leit* 'light'. It is worth noticing that Robinson and Hodges, who about Sherwood's time invariably record [əi], were both Londoners. Two other orthoepists who probably used [əi] are Cheke (a native of Cambridge), who uses the spelling *unperfight* for *unperfect*, and Laneham (a Londoner), who uses the spelling *indighted* for *endited*. On Bullokar, Tonkis, and Daines see above.

(*c*) *The pronunciation* [əiç]

Evidence for [əiç] comes from Gil and less clearly from two Welsh sources. Gil's evidence does not depend on the orthodox spelling, for in transcribing a passage from *The Faerie Queene*, IV. x. 24, he writes *deljtful* (*j* means [əi]) for Spenser's *delightful*, thus showing that his speech really preserved the distinction between ME *ī* in *delight* and ME [ɪç] in *night*, &c. MS A of the *Welsh Hymn* uses regularly, and MSS P and L3 use commonly, the transcription *eich* (or more often *eigh*) for ME [ɪç]; but they are altering an original which had the transcription *ich*, and are evidently influenced partly by this and still more by the ordinary English orthography, so that their scribes may well have intended only to record the pronunciation [əi]. T. Jones says that *i* before *gh* is pronounced like Welsh *yi* [əi], but describes Englishmen as drawing out the breath 'like a gasp, a sigh, or a cough', in *bright* and *fight* as well as in *bought*. On the face of it this means [əiç] in *fight*, but he may be confused; thus he might be describing the two pronunciations [əi] and [ɪç], and not one pronunciation [əiç]. It should be noticed that his evidence of the survival of [ç] is forty-eight years later than the last evidence of it given by a Southern Englishman

(Daines in 1640); Jones may well be influenced by dialectal pronunciation. Those orthoepists who show survival of [ç] without giving any information on the nature of the vowel may of course have possibly used this [əiç]; they are Coote, J. Willis, Tonkis, Daines, Jonson (?), and the Welshman Price (see under (1) above).

Note: The *Welsh Hymn* (see Vol. I, p. 4) and Salesbury (see Vol. I, p. 15) show a pronunciation [i:ç] for ME [ɪç]; this pronunciation is a dialectal development of eModE [ɪç] in which the spirant has tensed and lengthened the vowel but not yet itself disappeared.

(2) Words with ME īgh

§ 142. Variation between [əi] < ME ī and short [ɪ] also occurs in words with ME *īgh*, such as *high, nigh, sigh*, and *thigh*. These words should have only two pronunciations, [əiç] with the spirant retained and [əi] with it lost; but (probably because of the analogy of the variation in ME *ĭgh* words) they come also to have a pronunciation with [ɪç]. The evidence for the three pronunciations is as follows.

(a) The pronunciation [əiç] is recorded by Gil in *high* (fourteen times, beside [əi] four times) and *nigh* (three times, beside [əi] once); by Daines in *sighes* pronounced *siihes* with 'an aspiration' and '*i* long'; and by *The English Schole-master* (1646) in *sigh* pronounced as Dutch *sijh* (though *right*, &c. have [əi] without a spirant, as if Dutch *rijt*, &c.). So perhaps Price, who follows Daines but does not repeat his evidence on the nature of the vowel.

(b) The pronunciation [əi] is recorded by the *Welsh Hymn* in *nigh*, by Gil in *high* (four times, beside [əiç] fourteen times) and *nigh* (once, beside [əiç] thrice), and by all orthoepists who show [əi] for ME *īgh* (see § 141 (*b*)) except *The English Schole-master* (see under (*a*) above). Observe that Gil shows occasional apparent loss of final [ç] (but never of medial), because of the influence of oblique forms with [j] < OE *g*.

(c) The analogical pronunciation [ɪç] is recorded by Smith in *sigh* (twice), by Hart in *high* (but compare his *heier* [həiər] 'higher'), and by Bullokar in *high, nigh, sigh*, and *thigh*. There is some room for suspicion in Bullokar's case (see § 141 (*a*)), but none in Smith's and Hart's.

Note: Salesbury records [i:ç] (transcribed as Welsh *ich*) in *nigh* (Ellis, p. 754); this pronunciation is a development of eModE [ɪç] (see § 141, Note).

(3) Summary

§ 143. Reviewing the evidence on both ME *ĭgh* and ME *īgh*, we may remark that Hart and Gil are the best of the orthoepists in preserving the historically correct pronunciations whatever the indications of the conventional spelling. Daines seems to preserve the historical distinction of [ɪç] in *sight* and [əiç] in *sigh*, but his evidence is much less clear than

Gil's and he does not preserve the historical distinction between *sight* and *delight* as Gil does. The evidence shows that during the sixteenth century the 'Eastern' pronunciation [əi] for ME *ĭgh* was replacing the [ɪç] pronunciation; from the very beginning of the seventeenth century it gets the upper hand, though [ɪç] survived until about 1650 (but after Sherwood in 1632 the evidence is more confused). Probably during the sixteenth century and especially in the early seventeenth century there was very real confusion in actual speech among those who attempted to preserve the [ɪç] pronunciation, resulting not only in inverted spellings but also very probably in analogical pronunciations. In the circumstances Gil's retention of the historical distinctions is remarkable. Forms of *high* and *nigh* without [ç], in sources which normally retain it, go back to late OE oblique cases with analogical *g* (cf. Sievers–Brunner, § 295, Anm. 2) or to ME forms in which intervocalic [ç] appears to have been voiced to [j] (so Hart's *higher*; cf. the ME forms *heʒer* > *heier* > *hier*, recorded by *OED*). Before *t* there is no evidence at all of pronunciations developed in modern StE by vocalization or mere loss of the [ç] in the pronunciation [ɪç], which is simply displaced by the alternative [əi] pronunciation developed from late ME *ī*.

ANALOGICAL [ui] AND [ɔi] FOR ME *ī*

§ 144. A few words which by etymology should have only ME *ī* develop by analogy pronunciations with [ui] and [ɔi] and spellings with *oi*; the chief cases are *boil* 'ulcer', *groin*, *hoist*, and *joist*. For evidence and fuller discussion of these analogical pronunciations see § 259 below.

THE DEVELOPMENT OF ME *ǭ*

§ 145. The development of ME *ǭ* in eModE is parallel to that of ME *ę̄*. In discussing the development of ME *ę̄* between 1500 and 1700 we saw that it had two pronunciations, a conservative one which retained the ME value of open [ɛ:] and a more advanced one with close [e:]. ME *ǭ* seems similarly to have had two pronunciations, but the evidence is not altogether clear; there is, however, evidence of vacillation between a more open and a closer sound. Zachrisson's conclusion comes near the mark, that the pronunciation was with 'an intermediate sound [between open [ɒ:] as in Present English *awe*, and close [o:]], which in the course of the seventeenth century may have been narrowed into [o:], at least in the pronunciation of some speakers' (*Eng. Vowels*, p. 142). But this view needs to be modified slightly; the two sounds co-existed. The 'intermediate sound' must have been essentially the ME pronunciation, and have differed from the very open ModE [ɒ:] developed by the monophthongization of ME *au* and the ModE lengthening of ME *ŏ* by being produced with a slightly less open mouth, higher tongue-position, and probably greater tenseness and lip-rounding; that is, it must have been about, or slightly higher than, what modern phoneticians call 'cardinal open [ɔː]', whereas the PresE [ɒː] is lower. Thus we must allow for three long guttural vowels in addition to [uː]: (1) a low open [ɒː] developed from ME *au* and by ModE lengthening of ME *ŏ* (and of ME *ă* after *w* and occasionally in other positions); (2) a higher, less open 'intermediate vowel' (somewhere about or above the position of 'cardinal open [ɔː]'), which was the conservative pronunciation of ME *ǭ*, and probably essentially its ME value; (3) close [oː], the more advanced pronunciation of ME *ǭ* which for some time coexisted with, and eventually replaced, the more conservative pronunciation. But these last two were never distinct phonemes; they were only variants (partly 'diaphonic', partly contextual) of 'long *o*'.

The evidence for this twofold pronunciation of ME *ǭ* is as follows.

(1) Comparisons of ME *ǭ* with foreign vowels. Florio compares ME *ǭ* with Italian 'open *o*'; this comparison must be based on the 'intermediate' vowel. J. Smith also compares ME *ǭ* with 'Italian *o*', but his evidence lacks Florio's preciseness. On the other hand ME *ǭ* is compared with close [oː] in various languages, e.g. with French *au* by Sanford, Cotgrave, Butler (all of whom compare the pronunciation of *au* in *Paul's*, i.e. of the ME variant *ou*, with French *au*), and Wallis; and with Dutch *oo* by *The English Scholemaster* (1646), Hexham, and Richardson, a comparison which depends on the value tense [oː] (see Vol. I, p. 384). See further Notes 1–3 below.

(2) The relation in which ME *ǭ* is placed to ME *ŏ*. Sixteenth- and early seventeenth-century orthoepists—Cheke, Smith, Hart, Bullokar, Gil, and Butler—regard ME *ǭ* as the long equivalent of ME *ŏ*; but this view is given up by later orthoepists—Waad (see Vol. I, p. 130), Robinson, Hodges, Wallis, Newton, Wilkins, Holder, Lodwick, and Cooper—who regard ME *ǭ* as a long vowel with no short equivalent, except for Robinson and Cooper, who give [ʊ] as its short equivalent, and Newton, who is confused (see Vol. I, pp. 248–9). But this change may have no significance for the pronunciation of ME *ǭ* or ME *ŏ*; none of the earlier orthoepists record the monophthongization of ME *au* (except that Gil admits its existence as a more usual variant, though often retaining the diphthong in his transcriptions as the more formal pronunciation) and ME *ǭ* was therefore the only long vowel to which ME *ŏ* could be compared; when the new monophthong was established, it may well have provided a more satisfactory 'long equivalent' of ME *ŏ* without any change having taken place in the pronunciation of ME *ŏ* and ME *ǭ*. Cooper, however, certainly had close [oː] for ME *ǭ*, and Robinson probably had; the terms of Cooper's identification of ME *ǭ* as the long equivalent of [ʊ] leave no doubt that the gap between the two sounds was narrow, and though Robinson allows that there is some difference, it is clearly not great.

(3) Descriptions of the articulation of ME *ǭ*. Robinson says no more than that ME *ǭ* is the long equivalent of ME *ŭ* but is produced through a 'longer organ', i.e. further forward in the mouth (cf. the difference which he describes between ME *ŏ* and [ɒ:] < ME *au*, ME *ă* and *ā*, &c.). A vowel with well-marked lip-rounding is described by Wallis, Newton, Wilkins, Holder, and Cooper; both the 'intermediate vowel' and close [o:] would have lip-rounding, but it would be more marked in the latter.

(4) Wallis and Richardson give evidence which appears to show that the 'intermediate vowel' was the first element of the diphthongal pronunciation of ME *ou* (see § 248); as all our evidence (except that of Wallis) shows that this first element was identical with ME *ǭ*—a state of affairs which must in any event be assumed to explain the monophthongization of ME *ou* to identity with ME *ǭ*—it follows that the 'intermediate vowel' was also used for ME *ǭ* itself.

In spite of the vague evidence, I think that we may conclude that ME *ǭ*, like ME *ẹ̄*, had two pronunciations during the sixteenth and seventeenth centuries, a more advanced pronunciation with close [o:], and a more conservative one with the 'intermediate vowel' [ɔ:]; and that the latter survived perhaps as long as open [ɛ:] for ME *ẹ̄*, i.e. until the third quarter of the seventeenth century, though only in very conservative speech.

Note 1: Palsgrave compares French *au* with both ME *ou* in final position and ME *au* in final position; these comparisons probably depend on diphthongal pronunciations in both languages, and the latter is not to be interpreted (with Pope, § 536) as showing open [ɔ:] for Fr. *au*.

Note 2: Variation between a more open and a closer sound seems to be shown by the evidence of foreign orthoepists quoted by Zachrisson, *Eng. Vowels*, pp. 141–2.

Note 3: Other comparisons of ME *ǭ* with foreign sounds are vague or ambiguous. These are (*a*) with foreign *o* generally, as in Daines, Coles, and Ray; (*b*) with Welsh *o*, as in the *Welsh Hymn*, Salesbury, the *Welsh Breviary*, and T. Jones (Welsh long *o* is [ɔ:]; but the W.B. identifies Welsh *o* with both the monophthong developed from ME *au* and with ME *ǭ*, so that we can hardly argue with assurance from comparisons with Welsh *o*); (*c*) with French *o* in Sherwood, who probably means [o:]—his example is *rose*—though French *o* is more often open than close; (*d*) rather off-hand comparisons of ME *ǭ* with Spanish *o* in Percival and Minsheu, Owen, and J. Smith.

Note 4: In widespread dialects ME *ǭ* becomes [ɔə] (cf. [ɛə] < ME *ẹ̄*); this pronunciation is mentioned by Gil as characteristic of Lincolnshire, where, he says, they use *toaz* for *tōz* 'toes' and *hoaz* for *hōz* 'hose'. Wallis would prefer this pronunciation to the StE [o:] in words conventionally spelt *oa* (see Lehnert, *Wallis*, § 124), obviously because of the influence of the spelling (as in the case of *ea*, to which Wallis explicitly refers). In one word this dialectal pronunciation seems to have occasionally influenced StE, namely in *woad*, which Hart transcribes *uoad* [wɔəd] and cites as an example of a 'triphthong' ([w] being a vowel in Hart's view), and for which Nares, 1784, records a disyllabic pronunciation (see Horn, § 96).

ME *ǭ* BEFORE *ld*

§ 146. ME *ǭ* before *ld* was diphthongized in late ME to *ou*. The orthoepists regularly show the diphthong in such words as *gold* so long as a diphthongal pronunciation of ME *ou*, distinct from ME *ǭ*, survived. Before final *l*, as in *whole*, no diphthongization occurred, and none is shown by the orthoepists. The process was probably that before *ld* ME *ǭ* was first shortened to *ŏ* (cf. rhymes between such words as *holde(n)* and *wŏlde(n)*, e.g. in *Sir Orfeo*), and that this *ŏ* > *ou c.* 1400 by the process described in § 88 above; before final *l* the preliminary shortening would not occur.

VARIATION BETWEEN ME *ǭ* AND ME *ǭ*

§ 147. Variation between ME *ǭ* and ME *ǭ* occurs in eModE (1) in consequence of ME raising of ME *ǭ* to ME *ǭ*, (2) in words which have OF *o* in the neighbourhood of labials, and (3) occasionally in special words.

(1) *Raising of ME ǭ to ME ǭ*

§ 148. Raising of ME *ǭ* to ME *ǭ* is an isolative change parallel to that of ME *ę̄* to *ē* (see §§ 121-5 above) and occurs in similar circumstances, namely before *r*, before other dentals, before *m*, *v*, and *k*, and in final position; ME *ǭ* of all origins is affected, but the older *ǭ* < OE *ā* apparently more than the later *ǭ* < OE *ŏ* in open syllables. The raising is not characteristic of StE but seems to have been common in Northern and Eastern dialects; but it made its way early into London English, in which it was found chiefly in vulgar but occasionally in educated speech. The raising also occurs as a combinative change after *w*, owing to the rounding influence of the consonant; in this instance (which has of course no parallel in the case of ME *ę̄*) the raised pronunciation has wider currency in StE.

Note: Rhymes which depend on raising of ME *ǭ* to ME *ǭ* are not uncommon in ME texts, at least of the South-eastern area, and occur, for example, in *Havelok* and the *Alexander* group. In a valuable note in *English and Germanic Studies*, ii (1948-9), 3-9, G. V. Smithers shows that such rhymes occur before [m] (in *home*), the dentals [d], [n], and [þ], and in final position; he appears to regard them as depending on a licence of rhyming, but in view of the almost exact correspondence with the sixteenth- and seventeenth-century evidence cited below of [uː] for ME *ǭ* before [t], [n], [þ], [m] (and other consonants), and in final position it is clear that the rhymes depend on real pronunciations and are exact. But it may be granted that the difficulty of finding rhymes for the words in question is a factor influencing the ME poets in favour of pronunciations which were obviously abnormal. The early occurrence of the raised pronunciation in London English is shown, for example, by Chaucer's rhymes *anon : agon* p.p. : *don* infin. (*T. & C.* ii. 410), *forsothe : bothe* (*T. & C.* iv. 1035), *hoom : doom* (*C.T.*, B 3127). Gower also rhymes *hom* 'home' on ME *ǭ*. The explanation of the well-known series of rhymes in *T. & C.* v. 22-26 (where *lore* < OE *lār* and *more* adv. < OE *māre* serve as the *a*-rhymes and *forlore* p.p. : *more* 'root' < OE *mŏru*, and *bifore* as the *b*-rhymes) might possibly, in view of eModE evidence, be that the earlier *ǭ* < OE *ā* had been raised to *ǭ* (i.e. the *a*-rhymes would then be on *ǭ* < *ǭ* < OE *ā*) but later ME *ǭ* by lengthening in open syllables had not been raised (i.e. the *b*-rhymes would be on *ǭ* < *ŏ*). But this hypothesis, which I formerly preferred, no longer seems satisfactory. The explanation is rather that in the educated London dialect spoken by Chaucer and Gower lengthening of ME *ę̆*, *ă*, and *ŏ* in open syllables was not yet phonemic because (i) ME *ę̆* and *ŏ* differed in quality from ME *ę̄* and *ǭ*, so that their lengthened allophones were distinguishable from the older long vowels, (ii) final

-*e* was preserved. Hence Chaucer and Gower could still distinguish open-syllable *ẽ* and *õ* from *ẹ̄* and *ọ̄*. But in other dialects *ẽ* and *õ* had undergone phonemic lengthening and identification with the older long vowels, and could be rhymed with them; such rhymes Chaucer and Gower sometimes inconsistently adopt. For further details see *Trans. Phil. Soc.*, 1962, pp. 124–48. Raising of lengthened *ẽ* and *õ* must have occurred in those dialects in which phonemic lengthening was early.

(a) Raising before r

§ 149. Late ME *ọ̄* by raising of ME *ǭ* is rather more frequently recorded in London English before *r* than in other phonetic contexts (except after *w*), though there are no traces of it in PresE. Raising is found both in native words, where it affects both ME *ǭ* < OE *ā* and ME *ǭ* < OE *ŏ*, and in words adopted from French; and occurs before final *r* and *r* plus consonant.

(i) **Native English words.** *Boar* (OE *ā*) has [u:] < ME *ọ̄* in Cooper and probably also in Hodges, who relegates to his 'near alike' list the pairing of *boar* with *bore* (which probably depends on [o:]); Cooper likewise puts this pairing in his 'near alike' list, and it is clear in his case that he does so because in his own pronunciation *boar* had [u:] and *bore* had [o:], so that the pairing could not be admitted to the 'alike' list. *Hoar* (OE *ā*) and *hoarse* (OE *ā*) have [u:] in Hodges, but not in Cooper, who has [o:]; Cocker has [u:] in *hoar*. *More* (OE *ā*) has [u:] thirteen times against [o:] twice in Hodges. The remaining cases have OE *ŏ*. *Torn* seems to have [u:] beside *ŏ* in Young's 'homophone' list (see Vol. I, p. 413). *Borne* has [u:] in Cooper and *RS*, *worn* in Hodges and Cooper, and *shorn* and *torn* in *RS* (beside a pronunciation described as 'long *o*', i.e. [o:] by eModE lengthening of ME *ŏ* before *r*). *Sworn* has [u:] in Hodges and Cooper; but in this word the influence of the preceding *w* comes into play.

(ii) **Words adopted from French.** *Sort* has [u:] in Cheke, if we may judge from his spelling *soort*. *Corpse* has [u:] in Hodges (for whom the *p* is still silent). *Glory* (ME *glorie*, with consonantal *i*, i.e. [j]) has [u:] in Cheke.

Note 1: The 'homophone lists' are necessarily ambiguous, as they can only pair ME *ọ̄r* words with ME *ǭr* words, which may have lowering; the pronunciation [o:r] seems generally more probable, and is certain in Coles's *Schoolmaster*. But Cocker's equation *hoar* : *hour* : *whore* may depend on [u:] in all three words. Rhyme-lists are similarly ambiguous in the seventeenth century.

Note 2: Luick, § 511, regards eModE [uə] for ME *ọ̄* before *r* as a development in the seventeenth century of eModE [oə]; he holds that it later disappeared again because of the lowering of the first element to [o], giving [oə]. He regards the [uə] as probably a dialectal development of an earlier [oə]. But the [uə] (or [u:]) pronunciation, which is recorded earlier than Luick realizes, must be associated with the ME rhyme-evidence and with the evidence of [u:] for ME *ọ̄* in other phonetic contexts; the single hypothesis of ME raising to cover all the facts is to be preferred to Luick's complex processes. The disappearance of the [u:] variant before *r*, it may be granted, was probably due to the ModE lowering which affected [u:] of all origins; in any event it was rare in London English. Horn, § 105, Anm. 3, would explain [u:] beside [o:] in *more* and *boar* as due to the analogy of the variation in *moor* and *boor* in the seventeenth century; this explanation should also be rejected.

(b) Raising before other Dentals

§ 150. *Throne* (ME *trone* < OF) is [truːn] in the *Welsh Hymn* and Salesbury. Hodges's isolated transcriptions of *one* as [uːn] and of *only* as [ʌnli] (as if with ME *ŭ* by shortening of *ǭ* < *ǭ*) may be errors, but the pronunciations have or had existence (see §§ 36–37 above and Note 1 below). Cocker has [uː] in *none* (see Vol. I, p. 417) and also in *foal*. Brown, a Northerner, has [uː] in *stole* and perhaps in *pole* and *mole* (see Vol. I, p. 419). Hodges in his 'near alike' list pairs *boats* with *boots* and *both* with *booth* (cf. Chaucer's rhyme *bothe : forsothe*). Newton varies between [oː] and [uː] in *both*. *WSC-RS* has [uː] in *ghost*, *most*, *post*, *roast*, and *engross*. Laneham has [uː] in *those*. Levins shows frequent raising before dentals (see Vol. I, p. 22).

Note 1: *Pearl* rhymes *trone*, and other words with *ǭ* before dentals, with *ǭ* (ed. Gordon, p. xlix). Shakespeare's rhyme of *one* with *shoon* (*Hamlet*, IV. v. 25) and Milton's with *soon* (*March. Winchester* ll. 7–8) appear to rest on a pronunciation [uːn]. Marlowe's of *stood* with *abode* seems to show [uː] < ME *ǭ* in the latter word.

Note 2: ME raising of ME *ǭ* to *ǭ*, whence ModE [uː], explains why, when 'parasitic' *w* develops by the over-rounding of the beginning of the vowel, the result is often [wʊ] > [wʌ] even when ME *ǭ* is the original basis; so in [wʌn] < [wʊn] 'one' (contrast [wɒn] in many dialects), Brown's [wʊl] 'whole', and the dialectal *wuts* 'oats' and *whutter* 'hotter' recorded by Cooper. See further § 431 below.

(c) Raising before other Consonants

§ 151. The other consonants before which raising of ME *ǭ* to ME *ǭ* is recorded are the labials *m* and *v*, and *k*. The Northerner Levins shows raising before these consonants (see Vol. I, p. 22). Fox and Hookes have [uː] in *comb*; so perhaps Coles (beside *ǭ*) and *WSC-RS*. Poole, a Northerner, seems to have [uː] in *drove*, *grove*, &c. (see Vol. I, pp. 433–4). Bullokar, who was a native of Sussex, records [uː] in *poke* and once (beside [oː] twice) in *stroke* sb. In the p.t. of the verb *strike*, OE *strāc* > ME *strǭk*, whence by raising to *ǭ* arises the eModE *strook*; early shortening of ME *ǭ* to *ŭ* gives *struck* p.t. and p.p., which is recorded by Gil (beside *strōk* p.t. < ME *strǭk*) and by Butler. Both Gil and Butler also have a p.p. [strʊkn], a blend of *struck* and *stricken* (for their other forms see § 36 above). But Bullokar still has *stroke* p.t. and *stricken* p.p. *Smoke* has [uː] in Levins and varies in Smith, who arbitrarily assigns [oː] to the substantive and [uː] to the verb.

Note 1: *OED*, s.vv. *smook* sb. and vb. (which are chiefly Scottish and Northern) suggests that they are probably adoptions of Flemish *smuik* sb. and *smuiken* vb. But this hypothesis is unnecessary; they are simply dialectal forms of the ordinary English words.

Note 2: Raising before [v] is the justification for such rhymes as *strove : above* and *groves : loves* (Milton, *Il Penseroso*, ll. 19–20, 133–4); all the words have [uː]. The paucity of rhyme-words for *love* and *above* drives poets to rely on dialectal and vulgar variant pronunciations.

Note 3: *Home* has [uː] or [uə] in many dialects, including those of Lincolnshire, Norfolk, and Hertfordshire; this is the explanation of its rhymes on ME *ǭ* in *Havelok*, Chaucer, and Gower. But there is no certain evidence of this pronunciation in the orthoepists; the 'homophone' list grouping *home* : *whom* : *holme* (Hodges 'alike', Fox and Hookes, Coles's *Eng.–Lat. Dict.*, *WSC*) depends on [oː] and the simpler *home* : *whom* (Wharton, Ellis, Strong, Brown) may also depend on [oː]. But Coles's *Schoolmaster* shows variation in both *home* and *whom* between [oː] and some other vowel, probably [uː]; see Vol. I, p. 440, note 1.

Note 4: It has been suggested to me by Mr. M. G. de St. V. Atkins that in *Havelok*, l. 1101, one should emend *shop* to *swok* 'betrayed', which would give excellent sense; the rhyme with *hok* 'hook' would then require a form *swǭk* < *swǭk* < OE *swāc* which would be parallel to eModE *strook* < OE *strāc*.

(d) Raising in final Position

§ 152. Bullokar (who is influenced by dialect) rhymes *go* on *too* and once spells it *goo* (but normally *go*); Price gives the pronunciation [guː], departing from Wallis, who had said that [goː] was more correct than [guː]. Daines (a Suffolk schoolmaster) probably pronounced *toe* as [tuː] (see Vol. I, p. 335). The Northerners Levins and Poole commonly have [uː] for final *ǭ* (see Vol. I, pp. 22 and 434).

Note: On rhymes in Chaucer and Gower between *to* and *do* and words with final ME *ǭ* (whether or not preceded by *w*) see Macauley, *Works of John Gower*, vol. ii, pp. cv–cvi. Such rhymes may depend on ME *ǭ* in *to* and *do* (see § 4 above) or on raising of final *ǭ* to *ǭ*; on the whole the latter seems more likely to be the usual explanation, and in the case of *soth* 'sooth' : *goth* 'goes' it is the only one possible (cf. the ModE evidence cited above). Macauley adopts the explanation of inexact rhyming, on which see § 148, Note.

(e) Raising after w

§ 153. After *w*, ME *ǭ* by raising of ME *ǭ* is a combinative change, and is much more common in the sixteenth and seventeenth centuries than it is in other positions; in PresE [uː] < *ǭ* alone survives in most words. Indeed, even in the sixteenth and seventeenth centuries only [uː] is found in *two*, which is commonly recorded, and only Bullokar shows retention of the [w]. Early shortening to *ŭ* occurs in *tuppence* (Coles, Strong, Young). In other words there is variation. *Who* has [uː] in Bullokar, Gil (often), Butler, Hodges, Daines, Price, Wilkins, Coles, Cooper, and Brown's 'homophone' list; but [oː] is retained by Robinson and Willis. Hart has *ŏ* and Gil twice has *ŭ*—shortenings under weak stress of [oː] and [uː] respectively. *Whom* has [uː] in Laneham, Bullokar, Gil (eleven times, beside other forms), Daines, Cooper, and Brown's 'homophone' list, but [oː] is retained by Mulcaster, Robinson, Gil (thrice; stated to be a variant beside [uː]), Hodges (*EP* and his 'alike' list), Merriott, Coles (beside some variant), and most 'homophone' lists, after Hodges (see § 151, Note 3). It has *ŏ* by shortening of [oː] in Smith, Hart, Gil (1621 once, where 1619 has [oː]) and probably in Poole, and *ŭ* by shortening of [uː] in Price and Poole. *Whose* has [uː] in Laneham, Gil, Hodges's *EP*, and Coles; but [oː] is retained by Hart (once), Robinson, Willis, Poole, Hodges's 'near alike' list (contrast *EP*), and most 'homophone' lists (following Hodges). Hart thrice gives *ŏ* by shortening of [oː]. *Womb* has [uː] in Levins, Butler, Hodges, Poole,

Strong, Young, Cooper, *WSC*, and Brown, but [oː] is retained by Daines; Poole and Coles vary. *Ooze* sb. 'slime' (< OE *wāse*) varies in the sixteenth and seventeenth centuries between ME ǭ and ME ọ̄ (cf. the spellings cited by *OED*); Gil gives [oːz] (in contrast with [uːz] 'flow' < ME *wǭsen* < OE *wōs* 'sap'). Hodges has [uː] in an unglossed *ooze* which may be either word. *Woe* is paired with *woo*, which must show a pronunciation [wuː], in the 'homophone' lists of Strong, Richardson (a Northerner), Cooper (a native of Hertfordshire), and Brown (a Northerner); but [oː] is retained by, for example, Smith, Robinson, Gil, Hodges, and Newton, and ŏ by shortening in final position is given by Bullokar (twice) and Gil (once). *Worn* and *sworn* (see § 149 above) may be further examples of the combinative raising.

The raising is most frequent when the *w* is preceded by another consonant (OE *twā*, *hwā*, &c.). Absorption of the *w* often accompanies it—regularly in *ooze*, almost always in *two*, commonly in *who*, &c. (as in PresE), and sometimes in *sworn*—but is a secondary consequence and not an essential part of the process (cf. *womb*, and sixteenth- and seventeenth-century pronunciations of *two*, *who*, &c., and *sworn* with raising but retention of [w]).

Note: Variation from PresE pronunciation in such words is shown by Campion's rhyme *so* : *woe* : *two* and by Greene's rhymes *so* : *woo* and *so* : *woe*; probably all the words involved have ME ǭ. On rhymes of such words with *to* and *do* in Gower and Chaucer see § 152, Note.

(2) *Words with OF* o *in the neighbourhood of labials*

§ 154. In words adopted from French, OF *o* if it becomes long is usually represented by ǭ, but in the neighbourhood of labials it is often, though not invariably, ọ̄. Variation between ǭ and ọ̄ is shown in the following words. *Move* (on whose ME forms see § 36, Note 3) has normally [uː] or (with shortening) ŭ from ME ọ̄ (cf. § 36); but Sherwood says that the pronunciation varies (*to move* having *o* pronounced like French *ou*, and *he move* (?) having *o* pronounced like French *o*), and Wallis (influenced by the spelling) says that it is pronounced 'more correctly' with [oː] than with '*u* pingue' ([uː] or [ʊ]). *Poor* (ME *povre*) also has normally ọ̄, recorded as [uː] by Smith, Hart, Bullokar, Gil (twice), Hodges, and Price. But ǭ also occurs (see Note 1), though there is no certain orthoepistical evidence; for though [oː] is recorded by Gil (once, when required by a rhyme in the text which he is transcribing), Daines, Coles, and *WSC-RS*, this seventeenth-century [oː] may be due to lowering of [uː] before *r* rather than to ME ǭ. *Border*(*ers*) has [uː] in Hart and Laneham. *Force* has [uː] in Wharton (followed by J. Smith), Cooper, and *WSC-RS*, but [oː] from ME ǭ in Hart and Bullokar, and the ambiguous seventeenth-century [oː] in Robinson, Gil (1621 edition, where 1619 has ŏ), Butler (possibly), Hodges, and Coles. *Forge* has [uː] in *WSC-RS*, but [oː] < ME ǭ in Bullokar; seventeenth-century [oː] in Hodges and

Coles is ambiguous. *Sport* has [o:] < ME ǭ in Bullokar, and ambiguous [o:] in Coles. *Form* has [o:] < ME ǭ once in Bullokar, against ŏ twelve times; so has *perform*, against ŏ once and ŭ once. The ambiguous [o:] alone is shown in *port* and *pork* (Hodges and Coles) and in *report* and *portion* (Hodges). On *tome* see Vol. I, p. 407.

A special case of this variation is *Rome*, from OE *Rōm* reinforced by OF *Rome*. In this word [u:] is normal in the sixteenth and seventeenth centuries, as in Bullokar, Robinson (see further below), Willis, Price (contrast his 'homophone' list; see below), Poole, Lye (following Price), *WSC-RS*, Brown's 'phonetically spelt' list, and the 'homophone' lists from Butler's onwards, including those of Hodges, Coles's *Schoolmaster*, and Cooper (which are the best), but with two exceptions (see below). The word has [o:] only in Hart, Price's 'homophone' list (paired with *roam*; contrast his text, which gives [u:]), and Coles's least selective list, that of the *Eng.–Lat. Dict.* Cooper in 'editing' the material of earlier 'homophone' lists removes the pairing of *Rome* with *roam* to a list of words which are pronounced 'differently' (and not even 'near alike'). Robinson, though he gives [u:] in transcribing *Rome* in an English text, gives [o:] in *Romam* in his Latin poem; this important evidence shows that the usual view, that the [o:] pronunciation (whence PresE [ou]) in *Rome* is due to French or Italian influence, is inexact; it is more immediately derived from the English pronunciation of Latin, in which [o:] in *Roma* may show ME substitution of ǭ for ō even in the neighbourhood of a labial, but is more likely to be due to the 'reformed pronunciation', which was based to some extent on foreign models.

Note 1: ME ǭ in *poor* is shown by such rhymes as *povre* : *Dover* (*Havelok*), and probably by the fourteenth- to seventeenth-century spelling *pore*. Cf. Luick, § 411.

Note 2: In the words cited above in which *r* follows the vowel, it is possible (but less likely) that [u:] may go back to original ME ǭ with raising (cf. § 149 above) rather than original ME ǭ.

Note 3: Seventeenth-century [u:] in *form* and *perform* is from ME ū rather than ME ǭ; see §§ 17 and 19. But ME ǭ is possible.

Note 4: The rhymes of Willis and Poole are ambiguous; they may depend on either [o:] or [u:]. So too are such 'homophone' list pairings as *poor* : *pore*, though [o:] generally seems more likely.

Note 5: Many of the words cited above also have a variant pronunciation with ŏ; see § 13 (2).

Note 6: It is here assumed that the 'homophone' list pairing of *Rome* with *roam* depends on [o:] < ME ǭ, but only because, in giving this pairing, Price and Coles are departing from the original one with *room*. In itself the pairing with *roam* is of dubious significance. The etymology of the word is uncertain (see *OED*), and it may have had ME ǭ beside ǭ (especially if it were of Romance origin, in view of the following labial); *OED* uses Gower's rhyme of *roam* with *home* as 'decisive' proof that the former has ME ǭ, but in fact it is not so, for Gower rhymes *home* on ME ǭ (see *Works*, ed. Macauley, vol. ii, pp. ci–cii, and cf. § 151, Note 3 above). Bullokar uses the spelling *rowm*, as if the word has ME *ou*; it is doubtful whether *OED* is on safe ground in dismissing this *rowm(e)* spelling, which occurs from the fourteenth century onwards, as due merely to scribal confusion, though in Bullokar's case it is likely enough that his pronunciation had [o:] < ME $\bar{\varrho}$, despite his spelling (cf. his *owerz* 'oars'). Shakespeare's rhyme *roaming* : *coming* must depend on [u:] in both words; in *roam* it may be from an original ME variant in $\bar{\varrho}$ or from late ME $\bar{\varrho}$ by raising of $\bar{\varrho}$. The 'homophone' list pairing could therefore depend on normal seventeenth-century [u:] in *Rome* and this variant [u:] in *roam*.

(3) *Variation between ME $\bar{\varrho}$ and $\bar{\varrho}$ in special words*

§ 155. Variation between $\bar{\varrho}$ and $\bar{\varrho}$ occurs in a number of words owing to conditions more restricted in their application than those discussed above.

(*a*) In words which receive weak stress in the sentence, ME $\bar{\varrho}$ is sometimes shortened to $\breve{o}$, which if restressed in late ME or eModE is lengthened to [o:]; examples are *do* and *to* (see § 4).

(*b*) *Door* shows variation because of its twofold origin (see *OED*). OE *dŭru* becomes normally ME *dŭre* and (with lengthening in the open syllable) late ME *dōre*. OE *dŏr* becomes ME *dŏr* and by blending *dŏre*; from the latter form arises *dōre* by lengthening in the open syllable. The form *dore*, according to *OED*, 'prevailed in the sixteenth century and is found as late as 1684'; it probably still survives in pronunciation, in which however the variant with ME $\bar{\varrho}$ would become identical with it when lowering of [u:] to [o:] took place before *r* in the early seventeenth century. The evidence of the orthoepists is as follows. The pronunciation [u:] is recorded by Salesbury, Smith, Bullokar (four against five times), Gil (once, when he is free to give his own pronunciation; contrast below), and Hodges. The pronunciation with unambiguous ME $\bar{\varrho}$ is recorded by Hart and Coote and by Bullokar (beside [u:]). It will be noticed that sixteenth-century evidence does not show any marked prevalence of the *dore* form in pronunciation. The ambiguous seventeenth-century [o:], which may either represent ME $\bar{\varrho}$ or be due to lowering of [u:], is recorded by Robinson, Gil (twice, when required by the rhymes of the poets whom he is transcribing; contrast above), Coles, Strong, and *RS*.

(*c*) In *lose* vb. ModE [u:] is due to the influence of *loose* adj. (and the derived verb); OE *lŏsian* should normally give ME $\bar{\varrho}$ (which might be raised to $\bar{\varrho}$ in vulgar or dialectal speech and thus assist the confusion with *loose*). The verb has ME $\bar{\varrho}$ in Bullokar (six times) and in *RS* in the p.p.; Bullokar also gives unlengthened $\breve{o}$ once in *losing*. Analogical ME $\bar{\varrho}$ occurs in Bullokar (once), Robinson, and Hodges (whose spelling is *loose* but who shows that the *s* is pronounced [z]). By the reverse analogy Bullokar has ME $\bar{\varrho}$ in *loose* adj. (twice) and variation between ME $\bar{\varrho}$ (twice) and the regular ME $\bar{\varrho}$ (thrice) in *loose* vb.; cf. the rhyme *foes* : *loose* vb. (*Oxford Book of Sixteenth Century Verse*, p. 876).

Note: Rhymes of *door* with, for example, *oar* and *ore* (as in Poole) probably depend as a rule on [o:], but not certainly, as ME $\bar{\varrho}$ may be raised to ME $\bar{\varrho}$ before *r* (cf. § 149 above). The 'homophone' lists pair *door* with *doer*, which seems generally to show [u:ə]; but it should be noticed that Cooper, who gives this pairing, shows [o:] in *do*.

THE DEVELOPMENT OF ME ọ̄

§ 156. ME ọ̄ had by 1500 already been raised from its ME value of tense [o:] to [u:]. This latter value is shown by the *Welsh Hymn* (before 1500) and all sixteenth- and seventeenth-century orthoepists, who equate ME ọ̄ with [u:] in foreign languages (thus Welsh *w*, French *ou*, Spanish *u*, and Dutch *oe*) and who regard it as the long equivalent of English short [ʊ]— i.e. in early orthoepists ME *ŭ*, and in later ME *ŭ* when protected from unrounding by a labial (as in *push*). The only exceptions are Robinson and Cooper, for whom [ʊ] is the short equivalent of [o:] (ME ọ̄), and Newton, whose vowel-system is confused (see Vol. I, pp. 248–50). Robinson's transcription of ME ọ̄ as *uw* does not mean that it has become diphthongal (see Vol. I, p. 208). The descriptions of the articulation of ME ọ̄ given by Hart, Wallis, Newton, Wilkins, Holder (see Vol. I, pp. 265–9), and Cooper show that it was produced with marked lip-rounding, and Cooper's shows that it had more lip-rounding and was tenser than [ʊ]. This is also shown by the frequent analysis of [w] as a vowel, for [w] is thus identified with ME ọ̄.

ME ǭ in Words adopted from Foreign Languages

§ 157. In words adopted later than 1400 from foreign languages, foreign [u:] is replaced not by ME *ū*, as had been the case before that date, but by ME ọ̄, which has become the English equivalent of foreign [u:] (cf. Luick, *Hist. Gram.*, § 581 (2)). Thus *rendezvous*, a seventeenth-century adoption, is 'phonetically spelt' *randyvooz* by Coles, followed by Young. (The identification of French nasalized *ẽ* with ME *ă* is normal in the sixteenth and seventeenth centuries.) *Accoutred* (the verb is a seventeenth-century formation, but *accoutrements* is recorded from the sixteenth century) has [u:] < ME ọ̄ in Cooper. But *rouge* and *gouge*, both late fifteenth-century adoptions, show variation between [u:] (as if < ME ọ̄) and [ʌu] (as if < ME *ū*); see § 167 below. The variation between *bouse* (for which Willis and Coles give [ʌu]) and *booze* is probably due to adoption both in ME (with ME *ū* > [ʌu]) and after 1500 (with [u:], as if < ME ọ̄); cf. *OED*, s.vv.

VARIATION BETWEEN ME ọ̄ AND ME *ū*

§ 158. Variation occurs between ME ọ̄ and ME *ū* in certain words in which there existed (*a*) a ME variant in *ū*, and (*b*) a ME variant in *ŭ* which underwent late ME lengthening in an open syllable to ọ̄ (see § 167 below).

The analogy of raising of ME *ẹ̄* to late ME *ī* (see § 136 above), and the general parallelism of development between the front and back vowels in ME and eModE, would lead us to expect a similar raising of ME ọ̄ to late ME *ū* (so Luick, § 481), probably in those dialects which raise ME ǭ to ọ̄. Such a raising does seem to have occurred in dialectal or vulgar speech, though there is less evidence of it than of raising of ME *ẹ̄* to *ī* (perhaps in part because ME *ū* commonly remains undiphthongized before *r* and thus becomes identical with ME *ǭ*, so that in this position the effects of a raising in, say, the early fourteenth century would largely be obliterated in the early fifteenth). But Bullokar, whose speech shows many signs of dialectal influence, records [ʌu] < ME *ū* in *roof, booth*, and *bruise* (< OE **brōsian*?; see Vol. I, pp. 114–15); Luick, § 481, says that *ouze* 'ooze' (< OE *wōs* 'sap') and *ouzel* are recorded with ME *ū*, without citing his evidence, and it is presumably the former word (spelt *owze*) for which *WSC* (another representative of vulgar speech) gives [ʌu].

Note 1: In *ooze* the influence of the original initial *w* has to be allowed for.

Note 2: Spellings with *ou* for ME *ǭ* (cf. Zachrisson, *Eng. Vowels*, p. 77; Wyld, *Coll. Eng.*, p. 234; and Kihlbom, p. 151) are of uncertain value, since (*a*) in the later sixteenth century, if not earlier, *ou* was used as a symbol for *ŭ* by shortening in, for example, *bloud* and may have been so used in the fifteenth century (this usage was doubtless based on the fact that many words from OF were spelt with *ou* but pronounced with ME *ŭ*); and (*b*) some words with ME *ū* (e.g. *roum* 'room', *wound* sb. 'vulnus', *pour* vb.) were commonly or regularly spelt with *ou* but pronounced with undiphthongized [uː], so that by inverted spelling *ou* might be used to represent [uː] < ME *ǭ* (cf. Zachrisson, op. cit., p. 78). But these *ou* spellings from Eastern texts could well show raising of ME *ǭ* to ME *ū*. OED records *flour(e)* 'floor' (cf. § 165, Note 4) from the fourteenth to the seventeenth century (unfortunately without quoting fourteenth-century instances) and *gouse* 'goose' (which looks a certain enough indication of ME *ū*) for the sixteenth century.

Note 3: Rhymes and 'homophone' list pairings (which are so often our main sources of evidence for vulgar and dialectal pronunciations) can unfortunately not provide satisfactory evidence, since (*a*) before *r* rhymes or pairings of ME *ǭ* with ME *ū* (e.g. Marlowe's *floor : tower* and Raleigh's *floors : bowers*) will normally if not always depend on [uː] by failure of diphthongization of ME *ū* before *r* (see § 165 below), and (*b*) in other cases both ME *ǭ* and ME *ū* may have been shortened to *ŭ*. For the 'homophone' list evidence see § 165, Note 4.

Note 4: See Wright, §§ 162, 164, 169, on dialectal [ʌu] < ME *ǭ*. It occurs in *tool* in Durham. In the North-west Midlands (especially Derbyshire and Staffordshire, but also in some words in Shropshire, Cheshire, Leicestershire, and Northants.) he records pronunciations which appear to arise from a more general ME change of *ǭ* to *ŭ*; cf. such spellings as *goud* 'good' in *Pearl* and *Sir Gawain and the Green Knight*.

VARIATION BETWEEN ME *ǭ* AND ME [yː] OR *iu*

§ 159. *Choose*, which in eModE has a common variant spelling *chuse*, varies also in pronunciation; so likewise does *shoot*. The variant with a vowel identified with ME [yː] or *iu* is recorded in *choose* by Bullokar (four times, against [uː] < ME *ǭ* twice), Robinson, Gil, and Willis (who rhymes *chuse* with *use* and *muse*). Jonson says that to pronounce *choose* and *shoot* as *chewse* and *shewte* is 'Scottish-like' (he is thinking, clearly, of Scottish [yː] < ME *ǭ*). Hodges in *SH-PD* pairs *choose* with *cheweth* (pronounced *chews*) but in *EP* gives [uː]; this pairing probably depends on the variant with [yː], but might show reduction of [juː] < ME *eu* to [uː] in *chews*. The *Welsh Breviary* says that in *chuse* the *u* is pronounced like Welsh *w*; this probably shows the variant with ME *ǭ*, but again may show reduction of [juː] to [uː] after [tʃ]. Butler, however, gives [uː] < ME ǭ. Coles probably has [yː] in *shoe* (see Vol. I, pp. 391–2). As a consequence of the reduction of [juː] to [uː] after [ʃ] and [tʃ], the two forms became identical, and the spellings *chuse*, *shute*, and *shue* (*shew*) went out of use during the eighteenth century (see *OED*).

The reason for the [yː] variant is disputed. Sweet, *HES*, § 682, explains it as being due to the introduction into StE of a South-western form. In this case we must assume that South-western [øː] from OE *ēo* developed in the fourteenth century to [yː]. Such a development is not allowed by Luick, § 357, and Jordan, § 84, who would explain the occurrence of *u*-spellings for South-western [øː] as being due to the adoption of French means of representing the sound. Alternatively it would be possible to assume that StE speakers, having no [øː] sound at their command, substituted the other front-rounded vowel [yː], which some hold they did possess, for the SW sound. But it seems a fatal objection to this view that in the OE forms *sceōs* 'shoes' and *sceōc* 'shook' the *e*, when used, was purely graphic, and the words therefore did not contain the diphthong *ēo*. Luick, § 486, rejecting Sweet's explanation, would assume that the influence of the preceding palatal causes fifteenth-century [uː] < ME ǭ to become [yː], and this theory is much sounder; better still one could assume that a glide [i] developed between the palatal and fifteenth-century [uː], giving [iuː] > [iu] (= ME *iu* and *ęu*), from which [yː] may arise as a variant. There is some suggestion that the change was originally more typical of the West.

Note 1: Luick does not distinguish this palatal influence on [uː] < ME ǭ from the palatal influence which causes ME *ū* to become [yː] (see § 178). But it is most unlikely that we should have to do with merely one change. If we accept Luick's general argument, we must modify it by assuming two analogous changes, thus: (*a*) ME *ū* becomes [yː], probably before it had begun to be diphthongized, i.e. while it was still [uː] (see § 178, Note 1); (*b*) later, [uː] < ME ǭ becomes [yː]. On a probable analogous change of [ʊ] to [iu] or [yː] after [dʒ] see Vol. I, p. 83.

Note 2: Except in *chuse*, the *u*-spellings seem not to be common in StE in the words cited. Such spellings in Tyndale cannot be unconnected with the fact that he was a Gloucestershire man (see § 185, Note 2).

Note 3: Shakespeare's pun on *suitor* and *shooter* does not depend on [yː] in the latter, as assumed by Luick, § 486, Anm. 1; both words are pronounced [ʃuːtər]. Luick's explanation is forced on him by his incorrect view that ME [yː] was pronounced [iy] or [jy:] in the sixteenth century, so that *suitor* was pronounced [siytər], [sjyːtər], and then [ʃyːtər]. See further § 186.

Note 4: Northern [yː] < ME ǭ is commonly recorded, e.g. by Smith, Hart, and Sanford; Hunt records *gid*, which shows shortening and unrounding, as a Northern form of *good* (it is in fact Scottish).

THE DEVELOPMENT OF ME *ū*

§ 160. The diphthongization of ME *ū* is shown by all English orthoepists except the Northerners Levins (see Vol. I, p. 22), Mulcaster (see Vol. I, p. 126), and Poole (who has [uː] in *boughs* and also in *dough*, with late

ME *ū* < *ou* before [χ]; see Vol. I, p. 434). It is recognized even by those who fail to observe that of ME *ī*; the reason is clearly that the *ou* spelling suggested the analysis of the sound as a diphthong. The only possible exceptions among Southerners are Palsgrave, who will go no further than to say that ME *ū* is pronounced 'almost' as French *ou*, and Tonkis, who can describe it no more precisely than as being 'apertius' than French *ou*. But the Dutchman Lodwick explicitly (and erroneously) denies that ME *ū* is a diphthong; see Vol. I, pp. 277–8.

The diphthongization is shown both by comparisons with foreign sounds and by analyses and descriptions. ME *ū* is compared with Welsh *ow* by the *Welsh Hymn* and Salesbury (which should strictly mean [əu], but [ʌu] is more probable; see Vol. I, p. 4); with Dutch *ou* by Hexham, and with French *aou* by Sanford, Sherwood, and J. Smith. Sherwood says that it is '(presque) comme *eu*'; it seems probable that we should take the *e* of this transcription as being '*e* feminine', and the value intended is then [əu]. Analyses of the sound are of even greater value. Cheke says that it is a 'sonum coniunctum', as if Greek *ου*. Smith follows, though with some uncertainty (see Vol. I, pp. 56–57); but he is clear in saying that ME *ou* differs from ME *ū* 'granditate vocis', and he transcribes the former as *ōu* (with a long first element) and the latter as *ou*. Hart says that ME *ū* is a diphthong with a long second element, thus *oū* (this transcription is usually simplified to *ou*), whereas ME *ou*, when still diphthongal, has a long first element, thus *ōu*; Hart's analysis would fit very well if ME *ū* were a rising diphthong with an obscure first and a tense second element. Gil's method of transcription follows Smith's. Jonson (Vol. I, p. 325) follows Smith's distinction of ME *ū* from ME *ou*. The pronunciation [ʌu] is shown beyond doubt by Wallis, Wilkins, and Cooper, who identify the first element with 'guttural *u*', i.e. unrounded [ʌ] < ME *ŭ*; Coles evidently analysed the diphthong in the same way (see Vol. I, p. 439). But Newton gives [au], which at this date must be dialectal (see below).

It is often argued, on the basis of some of these identifications with foreign sounds and some of the analyses and transcriptions, that ME *ū* was diphthongized in the first instance to [ou], as it is similarly argued that ME *ī* was diphthongized to [ei] (see § 137). But in this event ME *ū* would have become identical with ME *ou*, which remained as a diphthong long after ME *ū* had become one. It is obvious that they did not become identical; alleged rhymes between the two sounds are to be otherwise explained (see Note 2 below). Identifications and analyses which seem to show [ou] are simply inexact, and may be due to three causes: (*a*) the ordinary spelling *ou*; (*b*) the fact that in unstressed syllables the letter *o* often had the value [ʌ] or [ə]; (*c*) the difficulty of describing the centralized vowel [ʌ], which in any case has in PresE the tongue raised almost exactly to the same height as 'cardinal open [ɔ:]', which as we have seen was still used as the conservative pronunciation of ME $ọ$. The process of diphthongization must certainly have been this: in the first stage the beginning of the vowel [uː] became lax, thus [ʊu] (cf. the present Southern English pronunciation of the former [uː] < ME $ọ$); then this lax [ʊ], now become the first element of a slight diphthong, was gradually lowered and centralized until it reached the value [ʌ], giving a diphthong [ʌu]; the final transition to PresE [au] is slight and easy. The last stage [au] already existed in the sixteenth and seventeenth centuries (cf. Newton's evidence and the identification with French *aou* cited above, and Note 3 below); but Cooper says definitely that the diphthong [au], of which he recognized the existence in theory, was not actually used in English. The explanation is that it was not in use in StE, though it occurred in the dialects, especially in the North; Gil says that Northerners pronounced ME $ū$ as *au*, and it seems that the Northern pronunciation of ME $ū$ was identical with the conservative Southern pronunciation of ME *au*, i.e. they were both [au]. Compare the Northern pronunciation of ME $ī$ (see § 137).

Note 1: Luick, § 483, argues that the diphthongization began soon after 1400, since after this date foreign [uː] is no longer identified with ME $ū$ but with ME $ọ$. Though it seems that the replacement of foreign [uː] by ME $ọ$ was not invariable in fifteenth-century adoptions (cf. *rouge*, § 167(*b*)), Luick's view is undoubtedly in general correct. With the exception *rouge* may be compared *oblique* (see § 133 and Note).

Note 2: Jordan, § 280, cites alleged cases of rhymes between ME *ou* and ME $ū$. Such rhymes are inherently improbable, and all the 'ME *ou* words' involved are in fact ones which may have a variant pronunciation with ME $ū$, owing to the influence of a following *w* (*growe, flowe, knowe*) or [χ] (*nought, brought*). For variation in such words between ME *ou* and ME $ū$ see §§ 170, 172–3 below.

G. V. Smithers, *English and Germanic Studies*, ii (1948–9), 62–64, argues that fifteenth-century *row* 'to make rough' is an adoption of MDu *rouwen*, and would explain the PresE pronunciation [rau] as showing that in the fifteenth century ME $ū$ was [ou] and so could be identified with MDu *ou*. But for the reason stated above no [ou] stage of ME $ū$ can be admitted, and PresE [rau], if the word is an adoption of MDu *rouwen*, is to be explained from the analogy of the native adjective *row* < OE *rūw-* 'rough' (which Smithers himself points out is a likely explanation). His interpretation of the transcriptions used by the *Welsh Hymn* and Hart as meaning [ou] cannot be accepted.

It may further be observed, in view of Hexham's seventeenth-century identification of Du *ou* with ME $ū$, that the determining factor in these identifications of diphthongs in our language with those of another is probably the nature of the diphthong rather than the precise points of beginning and ending the glide. If MDu *ou* < Gmc $ū$ before *w* was a rising diphthong in which the second element predominated (as seems virtually certain in view of the origin of the sound and modern Dutch pronunciation) it would tend to be identified with the rising diphthong [ʌu] < ME $ū$, in spite of the difference in the starting-points of the glides, rather than with ME *ou*, a falling diphthong in which the first element predominated and which was of the type of the Modern Dutch diphthongs with a long first element.

Note 3: Spellings with *au* for ME $ū$ (see Zachrisson, *Eng. Vowels*, pp. 78–79) seem probably to be phonetic, though they might be due to a complicated analogical process. They are based on an advanced pronunciation, probably dialectal (in view of the texts in which they occur), in which ME $ū$ was pronounced [au] and was thus identical with the conservative pronunciation of ME *au*. Zachrisson, op. cit., p. 79, points out that *au* is used in early plays to denote the Northern pronunciation of ME $ū$. Rare spellings in the *Paston Letters*

(Norfolk) which have *ew* for ME *ū* (Kihlbom, p. 191) must, if correctly reported, show the dialectal pronunciation [ɛu] recorded by Cooper (see Vol. I, p. 302) and by Wright for 'East Country' dialects; but Miss A. H. Forester informs me that the instance cited from the *Cely Papers* is not in fact *hew* 'how' but *here*, despite Zachrisson, *Bullokar*, p. 142.

Note 4: Foreign orthoepists show the diphthongization by identifications of ME *ū* with foreign diphthongs similar to those cited above from English orthoepists; see Zachrisson, op. cit., pp. 132–3.

Note 5: After *w*, and before *m* and *r*, ME *ū* often, but not always, remains as [u:]; see below.

Special words with ME ū

§ 161. *Bowl* 'a sphere' (OF *boule*) has [ʌu] in Cheke, the *ABC for chyldren*, and twelve later sources. It is a commonplace to contrast it with *bowl* 'a vessel' (OE *bolla*). But the two words are equated in the 'homophone' lists of Hodges ('near alike' only), Price, Fox and Hookes, Strong ('near alike'), WSC, Cocker, and Brown. In Price's case the equation certainly depends on the pronunciation [ʌu] developed from late ME *ū* < *ŏ* before *ll* in *bowl* 'a vessel', and the same may be the explanation in the other cases; Hodges's 'near alike' list has a number of pairings of ME *ou* words and ME *ū* words which probably depend on variant pronunciations of the former. It is, however, possible that some of these 'homophone' lists show the beginning of the analogical process (itself probably due to the identity of the words in the type of speech represented by Price) which led to *bowl* 'a sphere' losing its etymologically true pronunciation and assuming, probably at first as a hyper-correct form, that of *bowl* 'a vessel'.

Uncouth has [u:] in Laneham and Cooper but [ʌu] in Butler; the latter is of course normally developed from ME *ū*. The former has puzzled scholars, but it represents a ME unstressed form *uncŭp*, with restressing and lengthening of the vowel to late ME *ǭ* in the open syllable of the plural; compare the variation between [ʌu] and [u:] in *could* (see § 4), which probably influences *uncouth*.

FAILURE OF THE DIPHTHONGIZATION OF ME *ū*

§ 162. The influence of certain consonants, acting during the fifteenth century, prevents the diphthongization of ME *ū*. These consonants are: (1) a preceding *w*; (2) a following *m* or *p*; (3) a following *r*, especially if it is followed by another consonant. There are also to be considered here (4) an apparent failure of diphthongization in words which are often weakly stressed, and (5) certain alleged further cases of consonantal influence inhibiting diphthongization. In no case is the failure of diphthongization regular, though it is almost so in the second; but the diphthongal pronunciation is less frequent in each of the first three cases in the seventeenth century than in the sixteenth. In *wound* 'vulnus' and before final *r* we do not find evidence of the undiphthongized [u:] until the seventeenth century, except once in *pour* (which is, however, an uncertain case; see § 165, Note 5). There appears to be a conflict between the diphthongized and the undiphthongized pronunciation, in the course of which the latter becomes increasingly common; this suggests that the failure of diphthongization was more characteristic of vulgar speech.

(1) ME ū *after* w

§ 163. *Wound* 'vulnus' and the derived verb have [ʌu] in Smith, Bullokar, Willis, Poole, Strong, and *RS*. Gil says that [ʌu] is a Northern pronunciation, but the evidence shows that though it may have been more common in Northern speech it was not confined to it. The [u:] pronunciation occurs in Gil, Butler, Hodges, and the shorthand-writer Bridges. *Wound* the past tense of *wind* is not often recorded; it seems regularly to have [ʌu] owing to the analogy of other verbs of its conjugation. Butler in his 'homophone' list pairs it with *wound* 'vulnus', probably because [ʌu] can occur in both. In *swound* 'swoon' [ʌu] is usual; Willis rhymes it with *sound*, and this pairing occurs in most 'homophone' lists from that of Butler onwards. But the form *swoon* is shown by three 'homophone' lists, which pair the word with *soon*—those of Hodges (who uses the spelling *swoun*), Young (who uses the spelling *swoon*), and Coles in his least careful list, that of the *Eng.–Lat. Dict.* (which follows Young). All these three authors also give [ʌu]. In *woo* (late ME *wou(w)e* &c.) [u:] is the normal form.

(2) ME ū *before* m *or* p

§ 164. Before *m* or *p* the failure of the diphthongization of ME *ū* is regular in PresE (except for one pronunciation of the name *Cowper*) and I have found only two cases of the occurrence of [ʌu] in the orthoepists. (*a*) Before *m*, [u:] is regular in *tomb*, as in Bullokar and eleven later sources. PresE has regularly [u:] from ME *ū* in *coomb* 'valley' and *coomb* 'dry measure'; the former has [u:] in Fox and Hookes, and one or other of the words has probably [u] in Butler, but rather by failure of late OE lengthening of OE *ŭ* than by ModE shortening of [u:] < ME *ū*, as assumed by Eichler, §§ 85 and 90. *Room* has [ʌu] in Laneham (the one instance of diphthongization in this class of word), but otherwise regularly [u:], as, for example, in Bullokar, Robinson, Butler, Willis, Poole, and the 'homophone' lists from that of Hodges onwards, in which the word is equated with *Rome*. (*b*) Undiphthongized [u:] is regular before *p* in *coop*, *croup* 'rump', *droop*, *hoop* 'whoop', and *stoop* vb. Examples of [u:] occur in the orthoepists in *coop* (Bullokar, Hodges), *droop* (Robinson, Butler), *hoop* 'whoop' (Bullokar, and Hodges if the word which he records be this one), and *stoop* (Cooper). But Bullokar has [ʌu] twice in *poop*. On ME *ū* before *v* see § 39, Note 4.

(3) *ME* ū *before* r

§ 165. The failure of the diphthongization of ME *ū* is common before *r* plus consonant, but rare before final *r*. The few cases of ME *ū* before intervocalic *r* show variation.

(a) Before r *plus consonant*

[ʌu] occurs in *mourn* in Bullokar (beside [u:]); in *bourn* in Bullokar; in *adorn* in Laneham; in *court* and its derivatives (including *curtsies*) in Laneham (beside [u:]) and Bullokar; in *course* in Bullokar (see also Note 2) and Gil; in *fourth* in Price (see below); and in *surge* in Laneham. Wallis says that *court* and *course* should be pronounced with [ʌu], 'vulgo tamen negligentius efferri solent per *oo*'; he is undoubtedly influenced by the spelling in his preference, but should not be supposed to have invented an artificial pronunciation with [ʌu] (see Vol. I, p. 369, note 1). Otherwise he gives [u:] in these and other words (see below). The undiphthongized pronunciation appears either as [u:] or (in the seventeenth century) as [o:] because of the lowering influence of the following *r*, and is commonly recorded (both in the sixteenth and in the seventeenth century) in *mourn, bourn, court*, and *courtier, course* (and its by-form *coarse*; but Bullokar distinguishes *coarse* with [u:] from *course* with [ʌu]), *source, form* and *perform*, and *gourd*; for the detailed evidence see § 208 below. *Fourth* is influenced by *four*, and so can have ME *ū* (see § 173); but though Price's [ʌu] (see above) is certainly from this ME *ū*, *RS*'s [u:] and Hodges's and *WSC*'s [o:] are open to other and more probable explanations. See further Notes 1–3 below.

(b) Before intervocalic r

Before intervocalic *r*, there is variation: *courage* has [ʌu] in Hart, [ʌu] beside [u:] in Gil, and [u:] in Wharton (followed by J. Smith); *nourish(ment)* has [ʌu] in Bullokar; and *flourish* has [u:] in Wharton (followed by J. Smith). Such words normally have ME *ŭ* in eModE as in PresE (see § 19).

(c) Before final r

Before final *r*, the diphthongization is not as a rule prevented; thus *our, hour, flour*, and *flower* normally have [ʌu] (but compare the 'homophone' list evidence set out in Note 4). *Four* (see § 173) has [ʌu] in the *ABC for chyldren*, Hart, Laneham, Gil (once, beside [ou]), Butler (beside [ou]), Willis, and Poole; there is no evidence of [u:] from ME *ū*, and the [o:] recorded by some orthoepists is to be explained from earlier [ou] (also often recorded) < the ME variant *ou*. *Your* (see § 4) has [ʌu] in Bullokar, Gil (thrice, beside [u:]), Daines, Brooksbank, and Poole, possibly in *RS*; [u:], recorded by Levins, Laneham, Gil, Hodges, Lye, and the shorthand-writer Hopkins, is not necessarily to be taken as evidence of the prevention of diphthongization by final *r*, since it may be due to the analogy of [u:] in *you* (see § 4 above). Two probable cases are *pour* and *tour* (but see Note 5). *Pour* has [ʌu] in Laneham, Hart, Bullokar, Gil, Butler, Willis, Hunt, Poole, Coles, *RS*, and probably the 'homophone' lists (see Note 4), but is explicitly stated to vary between [u:] and [ʌu] by Smith, and in PresE has [ɒə] < [o:] by lowering of earlier [u:]. *Tour* has [ʌu] in Salesbury but [u:] in PresE. See further Notes 4–6 below.

Note 1: There is other evidence which shows the undiphthongized pronunciation before *r* plus consonant, though we cannot tell with certainty whether the exact sound was [u:] or [o:]. (*a*) Strong says that *course, court*, and *mourn* have the 'improper diphthong' *ou*, by which he means the digraph *ou* when it does not represent [ʌu]. (*b*) Rhymes with ME ǭ or ME ǭ words may show either [u:] or [o:] in *gourd* (Willis), *course, source, discourse, recourse, mourn, court, nurse*, and *scourge* (Poole). (*c*) Similarly 'homophone' list pairings with either ME ǭ or ME ǭ words may show either [u:] or [o:]. These are as follows: from Hodges's 'alike' list onwards, *course* with *corpse* (in *EP* the latter word has [u:]), *mourning* with *morning*; from Strong's list onwards *bourd* with *board* and *bor'd*; from Cooper's 'alike' list onwards *bourn* with *borne* (in Cooper himself, this pairing depends on [u:] in both words).

Note 2: Bullokar rhymes *course* (transcribed with [ʌu]) with *force* (transcribed with [o:]); as the transcriptions clearly afford no guide to the basis of the rhyme, it is reasonable to assume that it depends on the variant [u:] in both words, especially as he has [u:] in *coarse* (spelt *coorc'*).

Note 3: For fifteenth-century spellings showing [u:] for ME *ū* before *r* plus consonant see Luick, § 488, Anm. 1; but *sword* must be deleted from Luick's list of examples, since it has a ME variant with ǭ.

Note 4: The 'homophone' lists from those of Hodges onwards equate *pour* with *poor* (thus showing either [u:] or [o:]) and with *power* (which probably shows [ʌu], though if *pour* can have [u:] *power* also might have it). In Hodges the equation with *power* comes in the 'alike' list, which reflects his own pronunciation, and that with *poor* in the 'near alike' list; later authors ignore this distinction, except that Cooper admits only the pairing with *power* in his Latin edition, whereas the later English edition has both pairings. The 'homophone' lists show undiphthongized pronunciations (either [u:] or [o:]) in other words than *pour*. Hunt (followed by later lists) pairs *flour* with *floor*; Cooper 'near alike' pairs *sour* with *swore, sower,* and *sore*, and is followed by *The Compendious Schoolmaster* and the manuscript list (see Vol. I, p. 419; this list adds *sewer*); Cocker pairs *hour* with *hoar* and *whore*, and is followed by the MS list, which adds *our* and *wooer*. Price and *WSC* pair *your* with *yore*, which shows either [u:] or more probably [o:].

Note 5: Luick, § 488, Anm. 2, is of opinion that diphthongization never fails before final *r*. He would explain PresE [ɒə] in *pour* (which is of unknown origin) from the unexplained ME forms *poer* and *pore*; fifteenth-century *poar* and *pore* certainly seem to point to a ME variant with ǭ, from which it is obviously possible not only to explain PresE [ɒə], but also Smith's [u:], if we assume raising of ME ǭ to late ME ǭ. He would follow Zachrisson in explaining eModE *shore* 'shower' as showing failure of diphthongization and lowering before *r* followed by a consonant in the plural *showers*. This ingenious argument from inflected forms could obviously be applied to *tour* and all the words cited in Note 4 except *sour*, but is unsatisfying. We may argue against it that monosyllables like *tour* would at least commonly have had disyllabic inflected forms like *toures* at the time (about or soon after 1400) that the diphthongization began; and above all that as intervocalic *r* causes failure of the diphthongization in rather more than half of the few cases that occur, there is no very good reason to suppose that final *r* might not have the same effect at least occasionally.

Note 6: Daniel's rhyme *ours* : *stores* : *shores* must show failure of diphthongization in *ours* and either raising of ME ǭ to ǭ (> ModE [u:]) in *stores* and *shores* or ModE lowering of [u:] > [o:] in *ours*. An anonymous poem of 1593 has *sour* : *endure*, which confirms the 'homophone' list evidence cited in Note 4.

(4) *Apparent Failure of Diphthongization in Weakly Stressed Words*

§ 166. In words which are frequently weakly stressed, eModE often has [uː] beside [ʌu] < ME *ū*; but this [uː] is not strictly due to failure of the diphthongization, but to shortening in early ME of *ū* to *ŭ*, and to re-lengthening (under restored stress) of [u] to [uː] either (*a*) through late ME *ǭ* developed in an open syllable in *could* (see § 4) and *uncouth* (see § 161) or (*b*) in final position after ME *ū* had become a diphthong but before ME *ŭ* was unrounded, in *through* and *you* (see § 4).

(5) *Other alleged Cases of the Failure of Diphthongization*

§ 167. Luick, § 485 (2), argues that diphthongization of ME *ū* also occasionally fails before [tʃ] and [dʒ]; but the evidence is to be interpreted otherwise.

(a) *Before* [tʃ]

The words cited as examples by Luick are *mooch* (late ME *mouche*), and *couch* sb. and vb., *crouch*, *pouch*, and *vouch*, which though mostly fourteenth-century adoptions from French have sixteenth- or seventeenth-century forms with *oo* (see *OED*). *Couch* is recorded with [uː] by Price in *Eng. O.* (against [ʌu] in *VO*) and by Lye. But in all these words eModE [uː] is to be explained from a late ME *ǭ* by open-syllable lengthening of a ME variant *ŭ* beside ME *ū* (see Note 1).

(b) *Before* [dʒ]

The words cited as examples by Luick are *gouge* and *bouge*. The latter is unglossed; Luick may mean the substantive meaning 'wallet' and the derived verb 'to stave in a ship's side or bottom'. According to Luick, *bouge* has [uː] in the eighteenth and nineteenth centuries (loc. cit., Anm. 1). *Gouge* sb. and vb. have fifteenth- to seventeenth-century spellings with *oo* (see *OED*). We may add to Luick's examples the word *rouge*, which has now [uː] (though *WSC* gives [ʌu]). Of these three words, *gouge* is first recorded in 1495–8 and *rouge* in 1485 (see *OED*); in them [uː] from ME *ǭ* is to be expected as a substitute for French [u] (cf. § 157), and *WSC*'s [ʌu] in *rouge* and the present variant [au] in *gouge* are due either to subsequent anglicization or to the words' being adopted at a time when it may still have been possible to identify (though inexactly) the already diphthongized ME *ū* with OF [u]. *Bouge*, if it be the 'wallet' word, is a fourteenth-century adoption, and its [uː] should then be explained from a late ME *ǭ* by open-syllable lengthening of a ME variant *ŭ* beside ME *ū*; but if it be a form of *budge* vb., which is a sixteenth-century adoption, [uː] is to be expected as a substitute for French [u] when it is made a long vowel in English.

§ 167] PART 2: THE LONG VOWELS 691

Thus in neither of these cases (*a*) and (*b*) is there any sufficient reason to believe that the [uː] pronunciation in ModE shows the failure of the diphthongization of ME *ū*.

Note 1: The ME variant *ŭ* is shown in *couch* by the fifteenth-century spelling *cuche*, in *crouch* by the fourteenth-century *cruchen*, in *pouch* by the fifteenth-century *poche*, in *vouch* by the fourteenth-century *vochen* (see *OED*). All these words (including *couch* sb. from OF *couche*) are disyllabic in ME, so that the *ŭ* variant occurs in an open syllable and may be subject to lengthening to late ME *ǭ*. The variation between ME *ŭ* and ME *ū* is easy to explain before [tʃ], especially as all the words are probably adoptions from OF (see *OED*; *mooch* is from 'some dialectal variety of pronunciation' of OF *muchier*; *crouch* is perhaps somewhat doubtful).

Note 2: *Mooch* is first recorded in the fifteenth century (see *OED*) and may therefore have [uː] through the identification with French [u] of [uː] < ME *ǭ*; cf. § 157.

Note 3: Luick, § 485 (2)b, adduces *touch* with *ŭ* as a further example of the failure of diphthongization before [tʃ]; he would apparently regard *ŭ* as due to eModE shortening of [uː] retained as the pronunciation of ME *ū*. But the word must be assumed to have rather a ME variant *ŭ* beside *ū*; Luick, loc. cit., Anm. 1, shows himself aware of this possibility.

Note 4: Compare Luick's view that diphthongization of ME *ī* fails before [tʃ] and [dʒ] —also before [k]; but Luick himself is unable to argue that there is any evidence for a comparable failure of the diphthongization of ME *ū* before [k] (§ 485 (4) and Anm. 5). In point of fact there is also no evidence of the failure of the diphthongization of ME *ī* (see § 138).

VARIATION BETWEEN ME *ū* AND ME *ou*

§ 168. Variation between ME *ū* and ME *ou* is more common than has been supposed. It occurs in native English words, in circumstances in which during the ME period the development of certain vowels was influenced by the consonants *l*, *w*, and [χ].

(1) *ME ǭ or ŏ (late ME ou) before* l

§ 169. The usual development is to late ME *ou*, eModE [ou] > [oː]. But sometimes this late ME *ou* is assimilated to *ū* by the raising influence of a back *l*. (*a*) For both ME *ǭ* and ME *ŏ* before *ll* or *ld*, [ʌu] is shown by the *Welsh Hymn* (Vol. I, p. 5), Salesbury (Vol. I, p. 12), Smith, beside [ou] (Vol. I, p. 55), Robinson (Vol. I, p. 211), Brooksbank (who says that *o* is pronounced like *ou*, by which he seems to mean ME *ū*, in *old*, *bold*, &c.), Price (Vol. I, pp. 343–4), the *Welsh Breviary* (Vol. I, p. 345), and Lodwick (Vol. I, p. 277). (*b*) For ME *ŏ* before an *l* which is final in the word or syllable, [ʌu] is shown by Salesbury in Latin *sol* pronounced *sowl* (*ow* means ME *ū*) and by Price in *bolster* and *bole* (ON *bolr*). But when ME *ǭ* < OE *ā* precedes final *l* neither diphthongization to late ME *ou* nor assimilation to ME *ū* occurs (cf. § 146); thus Robinson and Price give [oː] in such circumstances. (*c*) Wharton appears to have [ʌu] in *folk* (see Vol. I, pp. 337–8). (*d*) The assimilation does not occur before *lt*; thus Robinson and Price have [oː] < late ME *ou* in *colt* and *molten* respectively. In this case the *l* must have had less back quality; it may be recalled that before *lt* there is sometimes failure of the diphthongization of ME *ă* and *ŏ* (see §§ 60, 88). Price's [ʌu] in *dolt* is no exception to the rule here stated; the assimilation is due to the earlier form *dold*. (*e*) The assimilation to ME *ū* does not occur in *soldier* (which has [oː] in Robinson and Price) nor in *scaffold* (which has [oː] in Price), because of the earlier forms without *l*. Neither does it occur in late adoptions; thus *extol* lacks [ʌu] in Price.

Note 1: PresE [au] in *prowl* (ME *prollen*) is a survival of this development of ME *ŏ* to *ū* before *ll*, not a spelling pronunciation (as assumed by Luick, § 518, Anm. 5, and Jordan, § 273). Dr. C. T. Onions informed me that *thole* (OE *þoll*) was pronounced [þaul] by oarsmen until *c.* 1925; cf. the earlier spellings *thoul, thowl,* &c.

Note 2: Laneham and Brown record a comparable later change of eModE [ou] to [uː] before *l*. For Levins, who has [uː] for ME *ou* before *ll* and *ld*, and also before *lt* (contrast Robinson and Price) and in *extol* (contrast Price), the explanation might be either the ModE change recorded by Laneham and Brown, or the ME change, with [uː] for ME *ū* (recorded by Levins in other circumstances); see Vol. I, p. 22. Poole, also a Northerner, has ME *ū* beside [oː] < ME *ou* in *poll* and *toll* (see Vol. I, p. 434).

Note 3: Examples of [ʌu] for ME *ou* before *l* may be found in the rhymes of poets; thus Wyatt rhymes *behold* and *gold* with *should*, the most likely explanation being that all three words have [ʌu]. Spenser rhymes *enrolled, fold,* and *hold* with *howled*. Milton's special spelling *rowl* 'roll' indicates a pronunciation [rʌul] (cf. the rhyme of *roul* and *soul*, which can also have [ʌu] < ME *ū*, with *foul* in Ps. vii (1653), ll. 13–18); it is, however, not an example of the process here described, for it descends from ME *roulen < OF *rouler* < *rotuláre* (whereas the surviving variant *roll* is from ME *rollen* < OF (*je*) *rolle* < *rótulo*). But as Milton seems to insist on [ʌu] < ME *ū* in *rowl*, it may be assumed that this is also the basis of the rhymes of, for example, *old* with *rowl'd* (Ps. lxxxiii. 37–39) and *scrowle* with *enrowle* (Ps. lxxxvii. 21–23). *Scroll* and *control* follow the analogy of *roll* (cf. *OED*, s.vv.); Poole varies between ME *ū* and ME *ou* in all three, Robinson has [ʌu] in *control*, and Price has [ʌu] in *control* but [oː] in *scroll*.

Note 4: Some of the pairings of the 'homophone lists' seem to depend on ME *ū* < ME *ou* before *l*. Hodges ('near alike'), Price, Fox and Hookes, Strong ('near alike'), *WSC*, Cocker, and Brown pair *bowl* 'a sphere' with *bowl* 'a vessel' (see § 161); Price and *WSC* add as a third homophone *bole*. In Price at least this pairing depends on [ʌu]. Price also pairs *cold* with *could*; again both words probably have [ʌu]. Hodges ('near alike') pairs *hole* (OE *hŏl*) with *howl*; this appears to show [ʌu] for *ŏ* before final *l* as in Price's *bole* (ON *bolr*).

Note 5: Wright shows that this [ʌu] occurs in the dialects. The evidence is rather scanty, but shows that it must once have been a widespread variant; it occurs in Midland dialects, including Norfolk and Essex, in *bold*, &c. (§ 41), in a number of scattered dialects for *ŏ* before *ld* and *lt* and in *bolster* (§ 86), and before final *l* in *coal* in one dialect, Northamptonshire (§ 93).

(2) ME *ǭ* or *ŏ* (*late ME* ou) *before* [χ]

§ 170. Normally ME *ǭ* and *ŏ* before [χ] develop to late ME *ou* (eModE [ou] > [oː]) and (in the case of ME *ŏ*) to late ME *au* (eModE [au] > [ɒː], whence the PresE pronunciation of words in which a *t* follows the [χ]). But the influence of the [χ] sometimes causes assimilation of late ME *ou* to late ME *ū*, eModE [ʌu]. *Bought, sought,* and *nought* have [ʌu] in Smith; so has *caught*, in which it develops in late ME *cought* (a fourteenth- and fifteenth-century analogical p.t. and p.p. recorded by *OED*; compare also fifteenth-century *coght*). But in *cough* Smith has ME *ou* (with retention of [χ]). *Brought, ought* vb., and *sought* have [ʌu] in Hart (four times in all, beside forms representing late ME *ou*). *Daughter* has [ʌu] in Laneham. *Brought, ought* vb., *thought*, and *nought* 'nothing' have [ʌu] in Gil (nine times in all, beside ME *ou* over twenty times). *Bought, sought, thought*, and *wrought* have [ʌu] (beside ME *ou*) in Butler. *Fought* has [ʌu] in Daines (see Note 1). *Moth* has a form *mouth* (with [ʌu]) < OE *mohðe* in Coles, *Eng.– Lat. Dict.* (see Vol. I, p. 411). *Though* has [ʌu] in Laneham and once in Robinson; Hodges in his 'near alike' list pairs it with *thou*. The rhymes of the Northerner Poole show ME *ū* in *ought, bought, fought, nought, sought, thought, wrought*, and *taught* (in the last word apparently from a late ME analogical form *toght*; see Vol. I, p. 433 above, and compare Smith's [ʌu] in *caught*); in Poole this is no doubt a dialectalism. Shortening of late ME *ū* < *ou* to the equivalent of ME *ŭ* occurs in *dough* in Brown, in *cough* in Brooksbank and Brown, and in *hough* in Strong; Brown's 'phonetic' spelling *hoof* 'hough' probably shows Northern [ʊ] for ME *ŭ*. (For shortening of the normal late ME *ou* to *ŏ* see § 34.) The shortening to ME *ŭ* survives in PresE in the originally Northern form *duff* 'dough'.

Note 1: Daines's [ʌu] in *fought* may show the survival of the past tense plural developed from OE *fuhton*, but this explanation seems less likely than that given above, in view of the evidence of other orthoepists on words in which ME *ŭ* is impossible.

Note 2: Laneham also gives spellings *methooght, bethooght*. These, if they represent OE *þōhte*, probably show an eModE assimilation of [oυ] to [u:] (cf. the similar change of eModE [oυ] to [u:] before *l* in Laneham and Brown; see § 169, Note 2); if they represent OE *þūhte*, they probably show a pronunciation [υχ], since *oo* commonly represents ME *ŭ* in Laneham as well as ME *ǭ* (ModE [u:]).

Note 3: Jordan, § 280, cites fifteenth-century rhymes of *nought* and *brought* with ME *ū* words; he explains these as showing [oυ] for ME *ū*, but this explanation is impossible (see § 160 and Note 2 above), and we should rather interpret them as depending on late ME *ū* < *ou* in *nought* and *brought*.

Note 4: Mulcaster seems to have pronunciations developed from late ME *ū* in all words with earlier ME *ǭ* before [χ], but this is in him certainly a northern dialectal feature (see Vol. I, pp. 126–7). On Poole's [u:] in *dough* see Vol. I, p. 434.

(3) *Early ME ǭ before* [χ]

§ 171. Early ME *ǭ* before [χ] at first developed to a diphthong *ǫu*, which then was normally assimilated to ME *ū*; but occasionally it becomes late ME *ou* by a direct dissimilatory change of *ǫu* to *ǭu*. The evidence for this late ME *ou* is very slight. Hodges in his 'near alike' list pairs *bough* with *bow* 'arcus', and *slough* (glossed 'mud, &c.') with *slow*; but these pairings probably depend on [ʌu] in *bow* and *slow* (see § 172 below). A little later he pairs *sloughs* (unglossed; is it the plural of the same word?) with *sloes*. Fox and Hookes pair *slough* (glossed 'quagmire') with *sloe*; but there is perhaps some suspicion that the gloss is an error. Willis rhymes *chough* (which has eME *ǭh*; see Vol. I, p. 23, note 5) as if it had [oː] < ME *ou* (see Vol. I, p. 427).

Note: Wright, § 167, shows that [ou], [oː], or (with shortening) [ɒ] < ME *ou* occur for early ME *ǭ* before [χ] in *bough, enough*, and *tough* in scattered dialects (chiefly but not entirely Northern).

(4) ME ǭ before w

§ 172. ME *ǭ* before *w* usually becomes late ME *ou* (the *w* being vocalized and coalescing with the vowel to form a diphthong); but occasionally the result is late ME *ū*, by raising of the vowel under the influence of the *w* and eventual absorption of the *w*. *Soul* has [ʌu] in the *Welsh Hymn* (so originally; but MS H only once against [oː] twice), Robinson, the *Welsh Breviary*, and Poole (cf. Note 3 below), but not in Price (though he shows the raising of late ME *ou* to *ū* before *l*). *Own* has [ʌu] in the *Welsh Hymn* and in Hart (*Orthographie*, against [ou] thrice in the *Methode*). Hodges in his 'near alike' list pairs *sow* vb. (of seed) with *sow* 'female pig' and *sower* 'one who sows' with *sour*. Young pairs *sown* with *sound*. Hunt and *The Compendious Schoolmaster* give the series *sew* vb., *sow* vb. (of seed), and *sow* 'female pig', which probably depends on variation in *sow* vb. Hodges in the same list also pairs *bow* 'arcus' with *bough* (cf. Note 4 below) and *slow* with *slough* (glossed 'mud, &c.'); these pairings might depend on [oː] < ME *ou* (see § 171 above), but [ʌu] seems more likely. Again in this list Hodges pairs *low* adj. with *low* vb. (which has [ʌu]—see § 173 below), and *lower* (comparative of *low*) with *lour* vb. (OE **lūrian*?); in this case [ʌu] seems certain. Price, and probably Hexham (see Vol. I, p. 381), have [ʌu] in *froward*.

Note 1: Rhymes show similar pronunciations: thus Jordan, § 280, quotes a fifteenth-century rhyme of *know* with *bow* vb. (OE *būgan*)—a rhyme which does not show, as Jordan assumes, that ME *ū* was pronounced [ou]. Spenser rhymes *soul* with *owl* and *howl*; Daniel *know* with *vow*, *own* with *renown*, *showed* and *sowed* (of seed) with *allowed*, *know* and *owe* with *allow*, *show* with *now*, *knows* with *brows*, &c.; Shakespeare *mow* vb. with *brow*; Drayton *known* with *town*; Milton *soul* with *foul*; Dryden *own* with *crown* and *shown* with *gown*; and Pope *own* with *gown*.

Note 2: Wright, § 127, shows that [au] and [ʌu] occur for ME *ǭ* before *w* in a great variety of dialects, including Norfolk (commonly), Suffolk and Essex (less commonly), and Kent (commonly).

Note 3: The Northerner Levins seems regularly to have ME *ū* for ME *ǭ* before *w* (see Vol. I, p. 23); so Mulcaster in *owe*, and Poole regularly (see Vol. I, p. 434). But in them the pronunciation is dialectal.

Note 4: Levins also shows ME *ū* in *bow* 'arcus' (OE *bŏga*) and Poole in *flown* (OE *flŏgen*), *tow* (if the verb, OE *tŏgian*), and *strow* 'strew' (eME *strŏwen* < OE *strēowian*); similarly Brown, another Northerner, pairs *tow* vb. with both *toe* (on [oː]) and *tough* (on [ʌu] < ME *ū*). To explain this late ME *ū* it is best to assume lengthening, in the open syllable, of eME *ŏ* to *ǭ* (which was developed early in the North), and thereafter the change of *ǭw* to late ME *ū* as in the words cited above; there seems no reason to suppose that eME *ŏw* could directly become late ME *ū*. Similar rhymes are found in the poets; thus Daniel rhymes *bow* 'arcus' with *brow*.

(5) *Early ME ǭ before* w

§ 173. Early ME *ǭw* usually becomes late ME *ou*, and is thus identified with early ME *ǭw* (cf. Jordan, § 106); but it is also assimilated to late ME *ū*, which is not infrequent in *four* and its derivatives. *Four* (OE *fēower*) has [ʌu] in the *ABC for chyldren*, Hart, Laneham, Gil (once, beside [ou] five times), Butler (beside [ou]), Willis, and Poole. It has the normal ME *ou* ([ou] or [o:]) in Bullokar, Gil (beside [ʌu]), Butler (beside [ʌu]), Hodges, Wharton, Coles, Strong, Cooper, Aickin, *WSC-RS*, Brown, and the 'homophone' lists. *Fourteen* (OE *fēowertēne*) has [ʌu] in Laneham and Butler but [ou] in Gil and [o:] in Hodges. *Forty* (OE *fēowertig*) appears to have [u:] in Cheke (which would represent ME *ū* retained unchanged before *r*) and has [o:] in Hodges; in both orthoepists the word is probably influenced by *four*, as ME shortening of *ou* to *ŏ* normally occurs in it (see § 14 above). In *fourth* (ME *fǫrþe* < OE *fēorþa*) the influence of *four* accounts for [ʌu] < ME *ū* given by Hart (beside *ŏ*) and Price and for [ou] < ME *ou* given by Gil. *Low* vb. (of cattle) is transcribed by Salesbury with Welsh *ow* (elsewhere used for ME *ū*, and so also, we should assume, here); Hodges in his 'alike' list (followed by Strong's 'alike' list; see Vol. I, p. 412) pairs *low'd* p.t. with *loud*. Price gives [ʌu] in *toward*, where it develops from ME *ǭw* in the contracted form **tǭwrd*.

Note 1: Jordan, § 280, cites fifteenth-century rhymes of *grow* and *flow* with ME *ū* words; these do not, as Jordan supposes, show [ou] for ME *ū*, but depend on variant pronunciations of *grow* and *flow* with ME *ū*. Earlier instances are *bure* 'bower': *foure* 'four' in *King Horn*, *growe* 'grown': *rowe* 'rough' (< OE *rūw-*) in *Sir Orfeo*, and *tru* 'true' (< *trǫw* < OE *trēowe*): *nu* 'now' in *Cursor Mundi*. A further example is the rhyme *grown: crown* in the carol 'The Holly and the Ivy', which, though recorded in modern times, dates from the fifteenth century at latest. *The Nutbrown Maid* rhymes *trow* (OE *trēowian*) both with *grow, know*, and *bow* 'arcus' (on ME *ou*?) and with *now, you*, and *avow* (on ME *ū*). Shakespeare rhymes *grow* with *brow* and *growing* with *bowing*, and Daniel *grown* with *renown*.

Note 2: The Northerner Levins has [u:] < ME *ū* in *glow* and *trouth* 'truth' (see Vol. I, pp. 22–23). Poole, also a Northerner, has [ʌu] in *flow, glow, grow, bestow*, and *trow*, and their derivatives (see Vol. I, p. 434).

Note 3: Wright, § 168, shows that [au] and [ʌu] occur for OE *ōw* in a number of dialects, chiefly Northern, but including Kent.

(6) *ME ŭ before* ld *or* lt

§ 174. Before *ld* or *lt*, ME *ŭ* usually develops to late ME *ou* (see Luick, § 502 (2), Jordan, § 274, Anm.); thus in *shoulder, coulter, poultice*, and *poultry*, for which [ou] or [o:] < late ME *ou* is recorded by, for example, Cooper followed by Aickin, and probably in *won't* 'will not' (see § 425, Note 4). On the nature of the process involved see § 97 above. But the development to late ME *ou* is not invariable; the [u] glide which develops before the *l* sometimes coalesces with unchanged preceding ME *ŭ* to give [u:], which is identified with ME *ū* and develops to eModE [ʌu], recorded in *shoulder* by Laneham and Bullokar and in all the words mentioned above by *WSC-RS* (see Vol. I, p. 364). On *should* and *would* see § 4 above.

Note 1: *WSC-RS* also gives [ʌu] in *mould*, which seems to be the word meaning 'pattern' and may have ME *ŭl* beside *ŏl*, and in an unglossed *moulter*; see Vol. I, p. 364. *Moult* (OE *mūtian*) should have only ME *ū*, but was modified, as its variant *moulter* shows, by contact with *moulder* (*moulter*) 'decay', in which [oul] is probably < ME *ŭl*.

Note 2: The development discussed here should not be regarded as a special case of that dealt with in § 169 above, i.e. of the change of late ME *ou* to late ME *ū* before *l*, because (*a*) *WSC-RS* shows [ʌu] only in words which have ME *ŭ* before *ld* and *lt*, and not in words which have ME *ŏ* or *ǭ* (see Vol. I, p. 364, note 2), and (*b*) late ME *ou* from other sources is not usually shown as [ʌu] before *lt* by the orthoepists (but see § 169, Notes 2 and 5).

Note 3: Brown gives [uː] in *shoulder*, *poultice*, *poultry*, *mould*, and *moulter* (*WSC-RS*'s list of words) and Laneham in *moulding* 'pattern-work'; but this [uː] is a special development of late ME *ou* before *l*, and occurs in both authors in words in which there can be no question of their having eME *ŭ*; it is therefore dealt with under ME *ou* in § 251 below.

Note 4: For dialectal evidence showing [au] or [ʌu] in the words dealt with above see Vol. I, p. 364, note 4.

(7) ME *ŭ* before [χ]

§ 175. ME *ŭ* before [χ] is analogous to ME *ŭ* before *ld* and *lt*, but whereas in the latter case late ME *ou* is normal in StE and late ME *ū* is apparently vulgar or dialectal, in the former the reverse applies; for the reason see the discussion of the process involved, § 97 above. In *through* (early ME *þrŭh*) pronunciations developed from late ME [þrouχ] are recorded by a number of sources (see § 4 above), chiefly of a sort which reflect vulgar pronunciation ('homophone' and 'phonetically spelt' lists and the shorthand writers). *Drought* has ME *ou* in Wharton, who includes it in a list of words in which *ou* is pronounced as *ow* in *know*, not as *ou* in *thou*. (On Brown's [ɒː] < late ME *au* see § 97 and Note 5.) See Wright, Index, for similar pronunciations of both words in modern dialects.

(8) *Words adopted from French*

§ 176. *Vowel* has normally [ʌu] < ME *ū* from later OF *vouel*, but Hart regularly transcribes the word *voel*; the *o*, though not so marked, is probably long, for Hart frequently omits the mark of length from it when it is final in the syllable. In Hart [oː] may develop from either ME *ou* or ME *ǭ*. Hodges in his 'near alike' list pairs *prowess* with *prose*; the first word must have [oː], which again may represent either ME *ou* or ME *ǭ*. If we were to accept Jordan, § 229, Anm., both words might have Central French *ou* beside AN [u] for Late Latin 'free' *o*; but Pope, § 225, says that the diphthongization of 'free' *ǫ* (< Latin *ō*) to [ou] occurs only when it is tonic, so that it could occur in *prow* adj. (whence *prowess*), which comes from Late Latin **prōdis* (see *OED*), but not in *vowel* (from Latin *vōcālem* or *vōcāle*). Hart's [oː] must then be explained in some other way. It may be a mere spelling-pronunciation; it may be due to the analogy of words spelt with *ow* which varied in pronunciation between ME *ou* and ME *ū*; it may be due to the influence of Latin *vōcālis*. The last seems to me the most probable reason, but the others may also have had some influence. On the variation between *ou* and *ū* recorded by Cooper in *rowen* see § 245 below.

VARIATION BETWEEN ME *ū* AND ME *ŭgh* [uχ]

§ 177. Variation between ME *ū* and ME *ŭgh* [uχ] occurs in a few words, in which it is due to the divergent treatment of ME *ŭgh* in later ME, when two (perhaps three) pronunciations developed. (1) The pronunciation remained unchanged as [uχ], which survived into the sixteenth century. (2) The [χ] was vocalized to [u] (doubtless through the intermediate stages [ɣ] and [w]) and coalesced with the preceding *ŭ* to give ME *ū*, eModE [ʌu]. It is this type which survives in PresE; the present [au] could not develop from the sixteenth-century [uχ]. (3) There was also (at least in *through*) a pronunciation with late ME *ūgh* [u:χ], eModE [ʌuχ], which is either a blend of the first two, or shows the lengthening of ME *ŭ* to *ū* before [χ] through the development of a glide [w] between the *ŭ* and the [χ] (so Luick, § 403).

The evidence for these pronunciations is slight, as there are few words which exemplify ME *ŭgh*—*drought, doughty, mought* 'might', ME *thoughte* 'it seemed' (OE *pūhte*), and (in final position) *through*. Hart shows retention of [uχ] in *mought* 'might', which he regularly transcribes *muht*. Hodges shows [ʌu], with no spirant, in *drought*. Laneham and Butler have [ʌu] in *mought* and *drought* respectively; as both authors retain the spelling *gh*, it is possible that their pronunciation was with [ʌuχ] (the third type), but the retention of the *gh* may in each case be purely graphic and due to the conventional orthography. There is rather more evidence on *through*, but we should remember that the development of *ŭgh* in final position may have been special and that in this word abnormal pronunciations may develop under weak stress. Gil seven times gives [uχ], which may show retention of the ME pronunciation, as in Hart's *muht*; but Gil's may be a weak form. Laneham and Butler may also show this pronunciation (see § 4). Daines gives [ʌu], without spirant; this is a strong form, and is parallel to Hodges's pronunciation of *drought*. Bullokar (three times) and Gil (four times) give (beside other forms) the pronunciation [þrʌuχ], which is of the third type described above. (The pronunciation [þroː(χ)] recorded by some orthoepists also represents ultimately ME *ŭgh*; see § 175.) The fact that the third type of pronunciation certainly occurred in *through* does not, however, prove that it existed in *drought*, &c., in which the *ŭgh* was not final.

Note 1: Compare the development of ME *ĭgh* [iç] (see §§ 140–3). Luick's explanation of the PresE pronunciation, that it develops from late ME *ūgh*, is not to be accepted, as there is so little evidence for this late ME form; cf. § 140, Note 2.

Note 2: Further evidence of the first type of pronunciation, [ʊχ], may perhaps exist in Laneham's spellings *methooght* and *bethooght*; for in Laneham *oo* is often used for ME *ŭ*, and *methooght* may be the etymologically correct descendant of OE *þūhte* (cf. the fifteenth-century form *thught* cited by *OED*, s.v. *think* vb.¹), while *bethooght* may show the analogical influence of *þūhte* on (be)*þōhte*. But the spellings may show late ME *ou* (from OE *þōhte*) assimilated in eModE to [u:] because of the influence of the following [χ]; see § 251 below.

VARIATION BETWEEN ME *ū* AND ME [y:] OR *iu*

§ 178. Variation between ME *ū* and ME [y:] occurs in two groups of words. (1) In native words, ME *ū* when it follows a palatal consonant has a tendency to develop to either [y:] or [iu] (see Note 1), but not regularly, so that there arises a variation between the original and the altered sound (cf. Luick, § 486) which persists until the seventeenth century.

The words which show the variation are *you*, *your*, and *youth*. In *you* and *your* ME *ū* develops to [ʌu] under strong stress and to [ʊ] (whence later [u:]) under weak stress; for the evidence see § 4. ME [y:] (i.e. eModE [y:] or [iu]) is shown in *you* by Robinson, Richardson (see Vol. I, p. 382), Cooper (who says that in this word *ou* is pronounced 'like *eu*'), Brown (who follows Cooper), and *WSC* (which says that *ou* in this word is pronounced '*u* long or *eu*'); so probably in Butler, who says that *you* should be written *yu* (cf. his evidence on *your* below). ME [y:] is shown in *your* by Robinson, Butler (who says that *your* should be written *yure*), Willis, Strong (who gives the 'phonetic' spelling *yure*), Cooper, Brown, and *WSC*. The evidence of the 'homophone' lists on *your* is ambiguous (see § 4). In *youth* ME *ū* is not shown except by the Northerners Levins (who rhymes it with ME *ū* words; but all are pronounced [u:]) and Poole (who follows Levins in rhyming it with *south*, &c., but gives two other sets of rhymes; see below). ME *ŭ* by shortening of ME *ū* occurs in Hart (see Vol. I, p. 80), Gil (twice, against [y:] five times; see Vol. I, p. 145), Butler (beside [y:]), and probably other orthoepists (see Note 2). ME [y:] (i.e. [y:] or [iu]) is shown by Robinson, Gil (five times, against *ŭ* twice), Butler (beside *ŭ*), Poole (who rhymes the word with *ruth* and *truth*, but also gives other sets of rhymes), Lye, and Cooper, followed by Brown and *WSC*. A pronunciation with [u:] (by simplification of [ju:] < [iu] < ME [y:]) is given by Hodges, and probably by the shorthand-writers J. Willis, Everardt, and Mason, who reduce the word to the spelling *uth* on the ground that in it the *you* is pronounced like the name of the letter *u*. Seventeenth-century shortening of this [u:] accounts for the [ʊ] given by Coles, who rhymes *youth* with *sooth* and *tooth* in the section of his lists which is devoted to [ʊ] words. It is not certain whether Newton means [ʊ] or [u:].

(2) In words adopted from French, normal OF [y] is sometimes represented by ME *ū*, especially in the North and North Midlands, but also sometimes in the South; the reason may in part be OF variants with [u].

Huge has [ʌu] in Laneham (see Vol. I, p. 93). *Cucumber* has [ʌu] in the seventeenth century; it is recorded by Coles, Cooper, and *RS* (cf. also *OED* for further evidence). Compare the thirteenth-century French form *coucomber*.

> Note 1: Luick, § 486, Anm. 2, dates the change of ME *ū* in the fifteenth century, because spellings and rhymes which show it first occur then. He is therefore compelled to assume as a starting-point a diphthongal pronunciation [uu] of ME *ū*, which he says develops first to [ʏʏ] and then (with [ʏʏ] < ME [y:]) to [iy]. The following considerations tell against this theory. (*a*) The diphthongal pronunciation of ME *ū* in the fifteenth century was probably already [ʌu] rather than [uu], since ME *ū* is kept well separate from ME *ǭ*, which had become [u:]; it would hardly be possible to maintain so fine a distinction as [uu] and [u:], and ME *ū* must then have become [ʌu] before ME *ǭ* became [u:]. It is impossible to believe that [ʌu] could have become [ʏʏ] or [y:]. (*b*) Luick's assumption of a sixteenth-century [iy] < ME [y:] is false (see § 186), and therefore there is no reason to assume an intermediate fifteenth-century stage [ʏʏ]. On phonetic grounds a better explanation would be that ME *ū* when still pronounced [u:] was palatalized directly to [y:] because of the influence of the preceding consonant; cf. the development of ModE [ju:] discussed in § 187 below. But the simplest and best explanation (though rejected by Luick, § 486, Anm. 2) is the assumption that fourteenth-century [u:] for ME *ū* became [iu:] and then [iu] by the development of a glide-vowel after the palatal consonant, and thus identical with ME *iu* and *ęu*, from which a variant [y:] may later have developed (see § 188 below). Either of these last two explanations assumes that the change begins in the fourteenth century, when ME *ū* was still [u:]; the lack of fourteenth-century evidence is not a serious objection, since the tendency to palatalization (which would inhibit the tendency to diphthongize [u:] to [ʌu]) may have taken some time to reach fulfilment, and in any case the palatalized pronunciation was never more than a variant.
>
> Note 2: Poole's rhyme of *youth* with *sooth* and *tooth* (beside other sets of rhymes) shows either [u:] as in Hodges (as is more probable) or [ʊ] as in Coles.
>
> Note 3: Some orthoepists give ambiguous evidence on *youth*. Daines says that it is pronounced as if *yuth*, which may mean ME *ŭ* or ME [y:]; in his case the latter seems more probable, as he gives a rule that *-uth* as in *Ruth* 'hath ever *u* long'. Wharton similarly says that it is pronounced *yuth*; the other words in his list have *ŭ*. J. Smith, Strong, and Young follow Wharton directly or indirectly, giving the pronunciation as *yuth*. Hawkins slightly varies the statement by saying merely that the *o* in *youth* is silent. Some of these may have ME [y:], but ME *ŭ* seems generally more likely.
>
> Note 4: The rhymes of poets also show ME [y:] in these words. Thus *you* rhymes with *view* (Lodge), *true* (Breton, Drayton, Davies), and *hue* (Daniel); *yours* with *procures* (Daniel); *youth* with *ruth* (Surrey, Greene, Marlowe) and *truth* (Greville, Daniel, Drayton). But Milton, like Hodges, has [u:], for he rhymes *youth* with *sooth* (*On a fair Infant* (1625), ll. 53–54).
>
> Note 5: The spellings *yow* 'ewe', 'yew', *youseful* 'useful', *youmare* 'humour', *ashoure* 'assure' are not inverted spellings which show that the letters *ou* had the value [y:] after *y* or *sh*, as assumed by Luick, § 486, Anm. 1. The basis of Luick's view is his belief that ME *ęu*, *iu* and [y:] were pronounced [iy] and [jy:] in the sixteenth and seventeenth centuries, so that, for example, *use* was [jy:z] and *sure* was [sjy:r] which became [ʃy:r]; but this belief is false (see § 186).

THE DEVELOPMENT OF ME [y:], ME *iu*, AND ME *ęu*

§ 179. Many scholars have held that there was in late ME, in the London dialect from which StE grew, a sound [y:] developed in SW (Saxon) dialects from various native sources (cf. Luick, §§ 399, 486) and/or used as a substitute for OF or AN [y] in Romance words. The use throughout this book of the notation 'ME [y:]' (corresponding to Luick's *ü*), particularly but not only with reference to the sound substituted for OF [y], is in deference to this view, but is not intended to prejudge the widely held opinion that in East Midland dialects and in London English foreign or dialectal [y(:)] was regularly replaced by the diphthong [iu] in adopted words or forms. ME *iu* arises, in the East Midlands and elsewhere, chiefly from OE *īw*, and ME *ęu* from OE *ēow*.

(1) *Theories of the development of ME* [y:], iu, *and* ęu

§ 180. Ellis (*EEP*, pp. 163–84) regarded [y:] as the normal pronunciation of these ME sounds in the sixteenth century; he considered that [iu], developed from [y:], appeared beside it in the first half of the seventeenth century or perhaps earlier, and that [y:] went out of use about 1650, Wallis giving 'practically the last' evidence for it. In effect [y:] and [iu] were successive but overlapping stages of a single development.

Other philologists (e.g. Viëtor, *Sh. Pron.*, pp. 28–31; for full references see Luick, *Hist. Gram.*, § 490, Anm. 7) held that throughout the sixteenth and seventeenth centuries there were two pronunciations [iu] and [y:], representing divergent developments of the ME sounds. Viëtor is inclined also to admit the existence of pronunciations [iy] and [yi], but would regard these as mere compromises between the main types [y:] and [iu].

Jespersen (*Hart*, pp. 44–59; *ModE Gr*, pp. 102–5), Zachrisson (*Eng. Vowels*, pp. 146, 155, 220; *Bullokar*, pp. 79–96), and Ekwall, § 63, held that after 1500 (and indeed in late ME itself in London English) there was only one pronunciation of these sounds, [iu]. This is now the dominant view.

Wyld, *Short History*, pp. 193–5, and *Coll. Eng.*, pp. 242–4, set out a theory that there were in eModE three pronunciations, all in use at the one time, but representing different stages of development: (*a*) [y:], the original ME pronunciation of OF [y]; (*b*) [iy] or [jy:], the next stage in its development; (*c*) [iu] or [ju:], the final stage. He also held that late ME [iu] < ME *iu* and *ęu* (also from ME *ęu*, but here he is in clear error) became [iy] or [jy:] in the fifteenth century, and thus were identified with ME [y:] in the second stage of its development and so shared its further development to [iu]. We may at once point out two weaknesses of this theory: (*a*) it leaves unexplained the occurrence of [y:] for ME *iu* and *ęu*, since according to it these sounds never passed through an [y:] stage (Wyld might, however, perhaps have argued, though he did not, that ME *iu* and *ęu* assumed the [y:] pronunciation by analogy from ME [y:], with which they were identical in other pronunciations); (*b*) it involves the assumption that ME *iu* and *ęu* passed from [iu] through [iy] back to [iu]—a suspicious complication.

Luick's theory (*Anglia*, xlv. 132–81; *Hist. Gram.*, § 490) elaborated

Wyld's. He allowed that the incipient Standard English of late ME had at least two pronunciations, [y:] and [iu], and probably a third [yu], for ME [y:], *iu*, and *ęu*. But by the sixteenth century [y:] had displaced the other pronunciations and formed the sole starting-point of further developments. It first became [iy] (later [jy:]), which was the typical eModE pronunciation until the second half of the seventeenth century. During the seventeenth century this [iy] became [iu], which became general about the beginning of the eighteenth century and itself developed to [ju:], earlier in some positions (e.g. initially) than in others but generally during the eighteenth century. During the seventeenth century [iy] also showed a tendency to develop to [y:]; and the various pronunciations co-existed.

Note: Luick's theory led him into extraordinary subtleties in his dealings with the evidence. (*a*) Sixteenth-century evidence for [iu] or [yu] he regarded as showing dialectal pronunciations used by people who had not learnt 'die feinere Aussprache der Hauptstadt'; these go back to ME developments. But seventeenth-century evidence for [iu] shows a StE development of earlier [iy]. (Actually there is no evidence for a sixteenth-century [yu], as alleged by Luick; see § 182 below.) (*b*) Sixteenth-century evidence that the name of the letter *u* was [iu] was accepted, but this letter-name was asserted to be a special case. Actually it is not; see below. (*c*) Sixteenth-century evidence for [y:] was rejected as mistaken, [iy] being according to Luick the sound which the orthoepists really heard. But seventeenth-century evidence for [y:] was accepted and explained as showing a variant seventeenth-century development of the sixteenth-century pronunciation [iy]. (*d*) ME [y:] was assumed to become [iy] and then by this seventeenth-century development to revert to [y:]—a suspicious complication, like Wyld's similar assumption concerning ME [iu].

(2) *The evidence*

(*a*) *Identity of the sounds*

§ 181. From at least as early as 1500 ME [y:], *iu*, and *ęu* were identical. The best orthoepists make no distinction whatever between them; it is only those who are influenced by the spelling (including Wallis) who in any way treat these sounds differently, and in such cases what distinction there is is based on the conventional orthography and does not accord with the etymology of the words except when the conventional spelling does so.

(*b*) *Evidence for a pronunciation* [y:] *for ME* [y:], &c.

§ 182. The evidence is of two sorts. (i) There are identifications of ME [y:], &c., with foreign sounds. Palsgrave, Cheke, Smith, Cotgrave, Colson (1620), and Robotham (1643) identify it with French [y]. Smith also identifies it with Scottish and Northern English [y:] < ME $\bar{\varrho}$. Similar evidence is given by other orthoepists who seem to waver between two pronunciations (see § 184 below). (ii) There are descriptions of the articulation of ME [y:], &c. Cheke says that the English pronunciation of ME [y:] agrees with the descriptions of classical grammarians of Greek *v*, which is 'sonus simplex' combining the characteristics of *u* and *i* (see Vol. I, p. 42). Holder describes most accurately (in spite of Jespersen's cavils) a sound [y:] used in *rule* (see Vol. I, pp. 265–6). Hart also describes [y:], but seems to waver between two pronunciations (see § 184 below). (iii) Gil also probably used [y:], for he rejects Hart's spelling *iu* as representing the pronunciation of the *Mopsæ* and instead uses a single letter for ME [y:] as though it were a simple vowel; that he also uses a single letter for ME *ī* is not an overwhelming objection, for in this case he is careful to say that ME *ī* is really a diphthong. Gil may be proved not to have used [ju:] (see further Vol. I, pp. 144–5).

Against this evidence must be set that of Salesbury (Vol. I, p. 16) and Lodwick (Vol. I, p. 276), who do not recognize [y:] as an English sound, and of Wilkins (Vol. I, p. 260) and Cooper (Vol. I, p. 293), who explicitly deny the existence of [y:] (which they knew from French) in English.

Note 1: Smith's use of his symbol for [y:] as his transcription of the word *yew* does not discredit his evidence, for if ME *iu* and *ęu* generally became [y:], the word *yew* (OE *īw* and *ēow*) would also be pronounced simply as [y:].

Note 2: Laneham spells French *vu* as *vieu*, which may show that ME *ęu* is identical with French [y] but may also represent an anglicized pronunciation of the French word.

Note 3: Hume (Vol. I, p. 318) seems to show that [y:] was used in the Scottish pronunciation of Latin, but makes it certain that the English pronunciation which he knew was [iu].

Note 4: Hayward and Jonson give descriptions of a sound [y:], but these are adopted from the French writer Ramus (Pierre de la Ramée); and repetition by such unoriginal and uncritical authors is insufficient evidence that the descriptions apply as well to English as to French pronunciation.

Note 5: Zachrisson, *Eng. Vowels*, pp. 143–6, cites (and rejects) evidence from foreign orthoepists in favour of a pronunciation [y:]. Delamothe (1592) and Gres (1636) identify the English pronunciation of ME [y:] with French [y] and the Scottish [y:] < ME *ǭ* (they perhaps follow Smith). Festeau (1693) and Miège (1688) identify English *u* (i.e. ME [y:]) with French [y], but say that English *eu* (i.e. ME *ęu*, probably also at this date ME *ęu*) is pronounced *iu*; the distinction may have been suggested to them by Wallis, who to some extent wavers between two pronunciations (see § 184 below).

(c) *Evidence for a pronunciation* [iu] *for ME* [y:], *&c.*

§ 183. The *Welsh Hymn*, Salesbury (Vol. I, pp. 15–16), and the *Welsh Breviary* (Vol. I, p. 345) transcribe ME [y:], &c. as *uw*; as these Welsh sources use *u* as a transcription for ME *ĭ*, this should mean a pronunciation [ɪu], with a lax first element (and not [yu] as assumed by Ellis followed by Viëtor and Luick); but the purpose may have been to avoid the suggestion of the 'rising diphthong' [ju(:)] which the transcription *iw* would give. T. Jones, however, gives this transcription *iw*. Tonkis (Vol. I, p. 315) analyses ME [y:] as *iu* and identifies the second element with ME *ŭ* (still [ʊ] in his speech). Hume shows that [iu] was the English pronunciation of Latin 'long *u*', which is identified with ME [y:] in the English pronunciation of Latin (see Note 3 to § 182, and Note 3 below). Robinson may be proved to have had [iu] (and certainly not [ju:]) for ME [y:], &c.; see Vol. I, pp. 208, 210 above. Sherwood (Vol. I, p. 377) analyses the English pronunciation of ME [y:] as *iu*. Butler used [iu] (see Vol. I, p. 160). Newton includes [iu] < ME *iu*, &c. among his diphthongs. Wilkins (Vol. I, p. 260) and Cooper (Vol. I, p. 293) give descriptions of [iu] and deny the existence of [y:] in English. *WSC* follows Cooper. Neither Cooper nor *WSC* can have had [ju:], since in *you* they can still distinguish between the sound descended from ME [y:] and [u:] < ME *ǭ*. The pronunciation [iu] is shown probably by Hodges *EP* (beside [ju:] initially and sometimes in unstressed syllables), though *SH-PD* show the more advanced pronunciation [ju:]; see Vol. I, p. 179. Other orthoepists who give similar evidence seem to waver between two pronunciations; see under (*d*) below.

Note 1: Baret, whose evidence is taken as certainly showing [iu] by Jespersen, *Hart*, pp. 53–54, and Zachrisson, *Bullokar*, p. 87, but as showing [iy] by Luick, *Hist. Gram.*, § 490, and who is in reality extraordinarily confused, has probably unintelligently plagiarized Hart (see Vol. I, p. 80, note 1). His evidence should be entirely left out of account.

Note 2: Luick takes Sherwood's transcription *iu* as showing [iy]; see § 186 below.

Note 3: There is evidence to show that the letter-name *u* was pronounced [iu] from 1528 onwards (Luick, § 490, Anm. 1 (*d*)). Luick regards it as a special case, and explains that the names of the letters *u* and *q* are perhaps Latinisms, since the 'Schulaussprache' of Latin at that time used [iu] for Latin *u* in an open syllable. But Luick fails to understand why Latin *u* in an open syllable was (and still is in the 'old' pronunciation of Latin now dying out) pronounced as [iu] or [ju:]. The reason is that in ME the English pronunciation of Latin followed the French, and that Latin *u* in an open syllable was accordingly pronounced as [y:]. The English pronunciation of Latin *u* in an open syllable therefore develops with ME [y:], with which it is identical, and is by no means a special case. For evidence of the identity of Latin 'long *u*' with ME [y:] see Cheke (Vol. I, p. 43 above) and Hart (Vol. I, p. 79) as well as Hume (cf. § 182, Note 3 above).

Note 4: Zachrisson, *Eng. Vowels*, pp. 143–6, cites evidence for [iu] from foreign orthoepists, which dates from as early as 1528.

Note 5: Jespersen, *Hart*, pp. 58–59, cites rhymes to prove the existence of the pronunciation [iu], but many of them do not show this. (*a*) Rhymes of *you* and *youth* with ME [y:] or *iu* words depend on the late ME variant pronunciation of *you* and *youth* with [y:]; see § 178. (*b*) On the other hand, the rhymes of *you* with *do* and *thereto* depend on the pronunciation [ju:] of *you* developed by re-stressing from the ME weak form *yŭ* of the ME variant with *ū*. (*c*) The rhymes *yew* : *rue* vb., *ewe* : *hue*, *true* : *adieu*, *true* : *view* merely show the identity of ME [y:], *iu*, and *eu*, which is not in question.

But there remain the rhymes *suing* : *wooing* and *abuse it* : *lose it*, cited from Shakespeare, which do depend on the pronunciation [iu] or [ju:] (the latter would make the rhymes exact).

(d) Orthoepists who waver between the two pronunciations [y:] *and* [iu]

§ 184. A notable and much discussed case is Hart, who gives what I take to be a clear and accurate description of a rounded high-front vowel, i.e. of [y:], which applies to the English pronunciation of ME [y:], &c. as well as to Northern [y:] < ME *ǭ* and French, Spanish, and German [y(:)], but yet analyses both the English and the foreign sounds as a diphthong [iu] (the second element is identified with ME *ŭ*) and always transcribes them by the digraph *iu*. The confusions of Hart's account (which contrast oddly with the penetration of some of his detailed remarks and especially his description of the articulation of the sound [y:]) may perhaps be due to his knowing two pronunciations of ME [y:] which he did not properly distinguish; see further Vol. I, pp. 79–81, and § 185 below. Bullokar identifies ME [y:] with French [y] (cf. Jespersen, *Hart*, p. 51) but also describes a diphthongal pronunciation [iu] (cf. Zachrisson, *Bullokar*, p. 96). Sanford (1604) follows Beza's description of the French sound [y] and identifies it with Scottish *u* in *gud* (i.e. *good*) and English *u* in *lute* (following directly or indirectly Smith?); but in his *Italian Grammar* (1605) he says that Italian *gl* is pronounced like English *l* in *lute*, which we must therefore assume was pronounced [lju:t] or at least [liut]. Yet in his Spanish grammar (1611) he uses a less simple (but less ambiguous?) method of indicating the pronunciation of Spanish *llu*. He would seem to have known two pronunciations of ME [y:]—the one [y:], the other [iu] or more probably [ju:]; see further Vol. I, p. 376. Wallis in *De Loquela* includes in his vowel-system a labial vowel which is clearly [y:]; he explicitly says that it, like French *u*, is 'sonus simplex' and contrasts it with [iu], 'sonus compositus'. Here he gives it for ME *iu* and *ęu* as well as for OF [y], but in the *Grammatica* proper he describes a pronunciation [iu] for ME *ęu* (and as a variant for ME *ęu*). He seems to have known both [y:] and [iu], but characteristically to have admitted to the latter only in words spelt with the digraph *eu*; see further Vol. I, p. 239. Howell, a very poor phonetician, says in his *English Grammar* (1662) that the English pronunciation of ME [y:] is like 'French *u*', which in its turn is like the diphthong *ew*; similarly in his earlier revision of Cotgrave (1650) he had said that 'French *u*' was like English *ew* in *crew*, &c. or like English *u* in *flute*. It is possible that he is confused between [iu] and [y:], but even more likely (remembering how bad a phonetician he was) that he has heard the French sound as [iu], the pronunciation that he used for ME [y:] and ME *ęu*. Price (Vol. I, p. 341) follows Wallis in including in his vowel-system (plagiarized without understanding from Wallis) a labial vowel [y:] and also in describing a pronunciation [iu], which seems more likely to have been his own.

Note: That good (as well as bad) phoneticians should seem to confuse the two sounds [y:] and [iu] is at first sight surprising. But it should be remembered, in view of the fact that the evidence shows there was no distinction in pronunciation between ME [y:] on the one hand and ME *iu* and *ęu* on the other, that if there were two pronunciations [y:] and [iu] in Southern English they would have been mere 'diaphonic' variants of each other (used by different speakers or by the same man in different styles of speech) and no distinction of meaning would ever have depended on the difference between them. To distinguish between different members of one diaphone is always difficult. For this reason we should not lay too much stress on the identifications of the StE pronunciation of ME [y:], &c. with Scottish or foreign [y(:)] (cf. the common failure of Englishmen and Frenchmen at the present day to distinguish between the [ju:] of the one language and the [y] of the other); it is the descriptions of articulation that really matter, and these show (*a*) a pronunciation [y:], (*b*) a pronunciation [iu], and (*c*) confusion between the two. (On 'diaphones' see D. Jones, *Outline of English Phonetics*, pp. 52–53.)

(e) Evidence of the development of [iu] *to* [ju:]

§ 185. The diphthong [iu] seems originally to have been a falling diphthong, with a short second element; it then changed to a rising diphthong, and the second element, being stressed, was lengthened, giving a pronunciation [iu:] which quickly developed to [ju:]. The pronunciation [iu:], with vocalic first element, might have been expected in StE during the later sixteenth or earlier seventeenth century, but there is no clear evidence of it and it must be regarded rather as a theoretical than as an actual stage. Such rhymes as those referred to in § 183, Note 5 might depend on [iu:], but could equally be on [ju:], and the latter seems more likely. Hart identifies his 'diphthong' *iu* with the word *you* and the beginning of *youth*, respectively transcribed *iu* and *iuþ*, but this does not mean that his *iu* was [ju:]; both words are shown by other evidence to have had ME *ŭ* (see § 178), and he is identifying [iu] with [ju] because of his denial of a distinction between the vowel [i] and the consonant [j]. The evidence for the final stage [ju:], which seems to develop first in initial position, may be set out as follows.

(i) ME [y:], &c. in initial position in a word. Butler says that the word *yew* should be written *iw* but is pronounced *yiw*, and that *ewe* is pronounced *yew*. Gataker records [ju:] for ME [y:]; his evidence may refer only to initial position, or may apply more generally (Vol. I, pp. 217–18). Wilkins may perhaps have known the pronunciation [ju:] for ME [y:], at least in initial position, for he transcribes the word *you* with his digraph for ME [y:]; but this may not be significant, for he regards [j] as a vowel, in no way distinct from [i], and therefore would admit no distinction between [ju:] and [iu] unless in the length of the second element, on which he makes no comment. Richardson says that *use* is pronounced as if it were *yuwz*. Cooper, followed by *WSC*, says that the pronunciations *yeusless* 'useless' and *yeusary* 'usury' are 'barbarous speaking', though he recognizes as correct pronunciations which develop through combinative changes which depend on the pronunciation [ju:] even in medial position; it would appear, however, that [iu] was held preferable in careful speech even in initial position. Good evidence of the pronunciation [ju:] is provided by statements that the name of the letter is so pronounced; such statements are made by Hodges, Hexham, Richardson, and the shorthand-writers J. Willis, Everardt, Hopkins, and Mason, who reduce the word *you* to *u* and *youth* (now pronounced [ju:þ]; see § 178) to *uth*, on the ground that *u* stands for [ju:]. The 'homophone' lists give adequate evidence. From Hodges's 'alike' list onwards *ure* is paired with *your* (*ewer* with ME *ęu* is also added); from Wharton onwards *yew* is paired with *ewe* (but both words might lack [j]; see § 182, Note 1 above). Cooper will admit the pairing *your*: *ewer* only to his 'near' list, and as ME *ęu* is not distinct from ME *iu* and ME [y:] in his speech, the reason can only be that he did not fully accept the pronunciation [juː] for these sounds (cf. above).

(ii) ME [yː], &c. in initial position in a syllable. The 'homophone' lists from Hodges's 'alike' list onwards pair *inure* with *in ure* and *in your*; but Cooper will admit this pairing only to his 'near' list.

(iii) ME [yː], &c. in medial position in word or syllable. Hart's two alleged transcriptions of *true* and *virtues* with *iū*, which would have meant either [iuː] or [juː], were misreported by Jesperson; Danielsson has shown the true readings to have *iu*. Sanford (see § 184) may have used [juː] in *lute*. Gataker (see under (i) in this subsection) may have known [juː] not only initially, but generally. T. Jones's transcription *iw* may mean either [iu] (with tense first element) or [juː], of which the latter is more probable. The rhymes cited by Jespersen (see § 183, Note 5 above) probably show [juː] in medial position.

For more certain evidence than this we have to consider combinative changes which depend on the development of [iu] to [juː]: thus [siu] becomes [sjuː] and then [ʃuː], and [ziu] similarly becomes [ʒuː]. In unstressed syllables these changes are recorded in Robinson, where, however, they depend on the development of a glide [j] and not on the development of [iu] to [juː] (see Vol. I, p. 210), in Hodges *EP* (where, however, only [siu] becomes [ʃuː], [ziu] being unaffected), and in Cooper, who includes *usual* among words pronounced with '*sh* or *zh*'. In stressed syllables Cooper says that the use of '*sh* for *s*' in *sure* and *sugar* is 'facilitatis causa' (so the Latin text, here more discriminating and dependable than the English text, which says that these pronunciations are 'barbarous speaking'); *RS*, elaborating Cooper, says that *sh* in *shugar*, &c. is 'after the West-Countrey-dialect'. Brown (a Northerner) gives a rule that *s* is pronounced *sh* before 'long *u*' as in *sure*. In *youth* the pronunciation [juːþ] develops as a result of the inevitable reduction of [juː] to [uː] after [j] (see § 178): it is first recorded by the shorthand-writer J. Willis (1602) and is given by Hodges in *EP*; Coles in his careful *Schoolmaster* gives a later development of it; and Newton means either [juːþ] or Coles's pronunciation. The most plentiful evidence of these combinative changes occurs in the 'homophone' and 'phonetically spelt' lists. The change of [siu] to [ʃuː] is shown by Hodges's pairing *suit* : *Shute* : *shoot* in *SH-PD* (contrast *EP*, which does not show this change in stressed syllables). Later 'homophone' lists (but not all) follow Hodges. Merriott says that *shute* for *suit* is 'a gross fault of spelling'. Brown, perhaps following Hunt (whose intention is uncertain), adds the pairing *sue* : *shoo*. The 'phonetically spelt' lists of Coles, Strong, and Young give *shoogar* 'sugar'. Brown gives *ashure*, &c., in which I assume that the vowel is [uː] in spite of the spelling with *u* (which is due to the conventional orthography); after original [ʃ] the combination [juː] < [iu] for ME [yː] has been reduced to [uː] (cf. the PresE pronunciation of *chute*), and so the letter *u* can represent [u:] after *sh*. Brown also gives the spelling *shoot* 'suit' (cf. his 'homophone' list pairing cited above). The analogous changes of [diu] to [dʒu:] and [tiu] to [tʃu:] are shown only in Brown's 'homophone' list, which pairs *due* (and *dew*, with ME *ęu*) with *Jew*, *duel* with *jewel*, and *tulip* with *julip*. The reduction of [ju:] to [u:] after certain palatal consonants through the loss of the [j], which is difficult to pronounce in such circumstances, is shown by various 'homophone' lists. After original [ʃ] reduction to [u:] is probably shown by the pairing of *Shute* with *shoot*, given by many lists after Hodges; but *shoot* may have late ME [y:]. After [r] reduction is shown by the pairing *rheum* : *room* given in lists from Wharton onwards, and by Brown's *rude* : *rood*; after [d], by the pairing *adieu* : *ado* given by Cooper ('near alike') and Brown; after [dʒ], by Brown's pairings of *Jew* with *dew* and *due*, *jewel* with *duel*, and *julip* with *tulip*. It will be observed that these reductions are most frequently shown by the Northerner Brown at the very end of the seventeenth century, although there is continuous evidence for them in the 'homophone' lists after 1640.

Note 1: Luick interprets Hexham's and Richardson's transcription *yu* for ME [y:] as showing [iy], but wrongly; see § 186 below. He similarly interprets spellings like Brown's *ashure* as showing a pronunciation [ʃy:] developed from [s] before [jy:] from earlier [iy] for ME [y:]; it may be granted that if there had been a seventeenth-century pronunciation [jy:] in normal use much of the evidence cited above could be explained in the light of it. (Thus the grouping *suit* : *Shute* : *shoot* could rest on a pronunciation [ʃy:t], in *shoot* representing the variant with ME [y:], in *suit* developed < [sjy:t]; the pairing *duel* : *jewel* might rest on a pronunciation [dʒy:əl], in *duel* developed from earlier [djy:əl]; and so on.) But (*a*) some of the evidence cited is not susceptible of explanation in this way (e.g. the pronunciation [ju:þ] 'youth' and the 'phonetic' spelling *shoogar*), and it is best to have a single hypothesis to cover all the facts; (*b*) the evidence for a pronunciation [jy:] for ME [y:] is insufficient (see below); and (*c*) as the evidence is satisfactorily explained by assuming that it depends on the pronunciations of PresE, it is false method to seek for other explanations without good cause.

Note 2: Spellings *shue* 'sue' and *shooter* 'suitor', which show the change of [siu] to [ʃu:], occur in *Love's Labour's Lost* (cf. Zachrisson, *Eng. Vowels*, p. 85); Wyld, *Coll. Eng.*, p. 293, cites *ishu* from Gabriel Harvey, and similar spellings, dating mostly from after 1640. Zachrisson, op. cit., p. 86, attempts to explain the spellings *shute* 'shoot', *shuke* 'shook', *shue* 'shoe' (cited from fifteenth- or early sixteenth-century authors) as inverted spellings giving very early evidence of the change of [siu] to [ʃu:], but they are to be otherwise explained. In the *Catholicon Anglicum* they show Northern isolative [y:] < ME *ǭ*. In Tyndale, a Gloucestershire man, they show the survival of combinative [y:] < ME *ǭ* (which occurs in all the words cited; see § 159). The one case cited from Skelton shows the spread of this spelling (and possibly the pronunciation which it represents) into StE.

Note 3: Cheke's spelling *broosed* 'bruised' does not show reduction of [ju:] to [u:] by loss of [j] after a difficult consonant combination. The form *broose* for *bruise* occurs from the fourteenth to the sixteenth century and undoubtedly represents a ME variant with *ǭ* (see *OED*, and Vol. I, p. 115).

Note 4: The spelling *quewre* 'cure' (dated 1653) probably means [kju:r], as suggested by Wyld, *Coll. Eng.*, p. 244, but need have no special significance.

Note 5: Foreign orthoepists cited by Zachrisson, op. cit., pp. 143–6, often appear to teach [ju:] rather than [iu] even as early as Desainliens (1566).

Note 6: Rhymes which depend, or probably depend, on [ju:] for ME [y:], &c. seem to be rare even at the end of the sixteenth century. Shakespeare has *suing* : *wooing* and *abuse it* :

lose it (see § 183, Note 5), Davies in 1596 has *servitude* rhyming with *blood* and *food* (which presumably have [uː]), and an anonymous poem of 1593 (*Oxford Book of Sixteenth Century Verse*, p. 502) rhymes *endure* with *sour* (which must have undiphthongized ME *ū* before *r*). The rhymes *utter* : *suitor* (Raleigh) and *scum* : *fume* (Marston) may show [jʊ] by shortening of [juː] for ME [yː], but might depend on a ME variant in *ŭ* beside [yː].

(*f*) *Evidence for the supposed pronunciation* [iy] *or* [jyː]

§ 186. That this pronunciation existed is assumed by Wyld and Luick; the latter regards it as typical of the sixteenth and seventeenth centuries. The evidence which he alleges for its existence (cf. *Hist. Gram.*, § 490, Anm. 1 (*a*) and (*b*)) is as follows. (i) Evidence of interlingual grammars, &c. Luick takes Sherwood's transcription *iu* and Hexham's and Richardson's transcription *yu* as using the letters in their French or Dutch values, and therefore as meaning [iy]. But all three authors are English, and the transcriptions, in my view, are certainly English transcriptions and therefore mean [iu] or [juː]; they are so taken in §§ 183 and 185 above. (ii) Luick would assume that the diphthongal pronunciation confusedly described by Hart, Baret, Bullokar, Butler, and Price was really [iy]. But we have seen (in § 184 above) that Hart, Bullokar, and Price waver between [iu] and [yː]; Butler certainly has [iu] (see § 183 above); and Baret clumsily plagiarizes Hart and has no value as evidence (see § 183, Note 1 above). (iii) Luick literally interprets late seventeenth-century French transcriptions *chure* 'sure' and *chugar* 'sugar' as showing [ʃyː] < earlier [sjyː] < [siy]. But such transcriptions are rather to be regarded as incompletely phonetic; the pronunciation of the consonant, but not of the vowel, is shown. Similar English transcriptions give even less support for Luick's view; see § 185, Note 1 above. (iv) Luick very naturally relies greatly on the evidence of Ray (Vol. I, p. 189), who agrees with Wilkins that ME [yː] is a diphthong but explicitly denies that the 'subjunctive vowel' is [uː] and identifies it with French [y]. He says that there is 'nothing of the sound of' *loose* in *luce*. Ray is so clear that we cannot regard him as hesitating between the pronunciations [yː] and [iu]; we must admit that he used, or thought that he used, a pronunciation [iy] or more probably [jyː]. I would reject all the other evidence brought forward by Luick in favour of the pronunciation [iy] or [jyː]. As Ray's then stands alone, it is insufficient to establish that [iy] or [jyː] was the typical sixteenth- and seventeenth-century pronunciation, for Ray wrote at the end of the seventeenth century (in 1691), and even if we allow full weight to his age his testimony cannot take us back before 1650 at the earliest. For an explanation of Ray's evidence see § 187 below.

Note 1: Evidence similar to Sherwood's occurs in grammars written by foreigners (cf. Zachrisson, *Eng. Vowels*, pp. 144–5; *Bullokar*, pp. 87–92). But we should notice (*a*) that the methods of transcription employed in such grammars are frequently faulty and ambiguous, and (*b*) that their authors freely plagiarize each other and the works of English grammarians and spelling reformers; it may therefore well happen that a transcription *iu*, though given by a Frenchman for whom it ought to mean [iy], may be adopted uncritically from an English author for whom it certainly meant [iu]. The transcription *iu*, of which Hart gives the earliest evidence among the authors we have examined, seems in fact to have been a commonplace; it is employed by the not very original Tonkis. Are we to interpret it as [iu] in Tonkis (who was writing for Englishmen, and who definitely identifies the second element with ME *ū*) and as [iy] in Sherwood because he was writing for Frenchmen? For further criticism (very well founded) of Luick's argument see Zachrisson, *Bullokar*, loc. cit.

Note 2: It is possible, though unlikely, that some of the late seventeenth-century foreign orthoepists cited by Luick heard the sound described by Ray and intended to represent it by the transcriptions which they adopt.

(3) *Review of the evidence*

§ 187. The evidence makes it certain that the pronunciation [iu] existed from at latest the beginning of the sixteenth century. This pronunciation began to develop to [juː] at least as early as the last decade of the sixteenth century (and probably as early as the 1560's); [juː] was at first most common initially. The nature of the evidence for [juː] in English sources makes it clear that though this pronunciation was fairly common after 1640, in careful speech [iu] was still preferred until the time of Cooper. But certain combinative changes depending on [juː] were accepted by Cooper, and still earlier by Coles in the careful *Schoolmaster* and as early as the forties by Hodges both in *EP* and in his 'alike' list, which seem to record pronunciations which he accepted as correct. Ray's evidence (see § 186 above) is best interpreted as showing a further development of the pronunciation [juː]. According to Daniel Jones, *Outline of English Phonetics*, § 326, in present StE the [uː] of the combination [juː] (as in *muse*) is a fronted sound, different in articulation from the [uː] of such words as *lose*; the 'fronting' is of course due to assimilatory influence exercised by the [j]. An acute observer will notice, as Ray did, a difference between the vowels used in *loose* and *luce*, provided that the [j] is kept in the latter word. In Cockney English (cf. Wyld, *Coll. Eng.*, pp. 243-4) and occasionally in Australian English the vowel is fronted until it comes almost or entirely to the [yː] position. Ray may have heard the 'fronted' [uː] of present StE and have confused it with French [y], to which it is somewhat similar in acoustic effect; he may even have heard a variety of it which made it identical with the French sound. In either case Ray's evidence shows a sound developed from [juː] and thence from [iu], and not a sound which (as Wyld and Luick assume) was the source of [iu] and [juː].

It is possible to argue, as do Jespersen and Zachrisson, that all the evidence for the existence, in the sixteenth and seventeenth centuries, of a pronunciation [yː] should be rejected. The arguments which may be put forward are as follows. (*a*) It may be said that it is inherently improbable that there should have been throughout so long a period two distinct pronunciations due to divergent development. But in the course of this chapter we have met with several examples of distinct pronunciations of what was originally only one sound, and we shall find others in following chapters. It is therefore quite possible that there should have been two pronunciations in this case, in which we have to do with two distinct ME sounds, [iu] < earlier ME *iu* and *ęu*, and the sound which we have so far described as ME [y:], i.e. the sound used in ME for OF [y]. (*b*) It may be argued that the identifications of the eModE pronunciation with Scotch [y:] and French [ȳ] involve the same error as the present-day Englishman's identification of his [ju:] with French [y]. (*c*) It is more difficult to reject the descriptions of the articulation of an English sound [y:], but it is possible to discredit each of these descriptions in turn; Jespersen and Zachrisson have found no difficulty in disbelieving the orthoepists. The reason in every case is the same. The sound [y:] is not easy to describe, and sixteenth- and seventeenth-century orthoepists did not have at their command an accepted technical vocabulary as the modern phonetician has. Their attempts therefore always give some opportunity for cavilling, and if we concentrate attention on the phrases which might have a double meaning, we can easily persuade ourselves that they were trying to say something different from what in fact they do say. In any case Wallis's evidence of a labial [y:] is unambiguous and explicit; and it seems a perverse disregard of the historical context to argue that Holder really meant a diphthong [iu] when he was intervening in a discussion whether the English sound was a pure labial vowel or a diphthong and, despite a theoretical qualification, was siding with Wallis (with whom he was on bad terms) against Wilkins (with whom he seems to have been on good terms). (*d*) On the other hand, some orthoepists, of considerable authority, do not recognize or explicitly deny the existence of [y:] in English. Such denials are most telling when they come from native speakers; and the clearest cases are Wilkins, deliberately setting himself against Wallis's view that 'English *u*' was a pure labial vowel, and Cooper, who knew his predecessors' work and must have been equally deliberate in his confirmation of Wilkins. But we must remember both the common failing of sixteenth- and seventeenth-century orthoepists of denying the existence of well-established pronunciations which they did not happen to use themselves, and the fact that [y:], if it existed, was only a 'diaphonic' variant of [iu] (see § 184, Note); Wilkins rejected Wallis's valid distinction of [ə] and [ʌ] because it was not phonemic in his own speech, though it certainly was in Wallis's, and Smith and Holder failed to recognize the existence of [ɛ:] in English, though it was a common contextual and diaphonic variant of both ME *ę̄* and ME *ā* (see § 114 above). Moreover, [y:] (again if it existed) was obviously always the rarer variant, and by the second half of the seventeenth century may have been obsolescent. Authors of interlingual grammars, and especially foreigners, would tend to concentrate their attention on the common English [iu] diphthong and its difference from foreign [y], and might well forget to notice, or indeed not know, the rarer pronunciation which was identical with the foreign sound. It is the native evidence which is the more significant.

We can, in my view, legitimately reject, if we wish, the identifications of the English sound with foreign [y]; if sixteenth-century observers could identify foreign [ø] with English [ɛu], as they did, they could equally be guilty of identifying foreign [y] with English [iu]. What we cannot legitimately do is to twist evidence for an English pure vowel [y:] into descriptions of a diphthong [iu]. If we do not want to accept the evidence of Hart, Gil, Wallis, and Holder in favour of [y:] we must simply reject it outright. We cannot even argue that they are trying to describe Ray's [iy] (or [jy:]), for he is describing a diphthong, they a pure vowel. We might argue (though I know of no proof) that because they falsely identified English [iu] with foreign [y], they uncritically accepted descriptions of the articulation of the foreign sound as if they were also valid for English; such an explanation would be particularly suitable for Hart. But in the lack of proof I prefer to accept the evidence in favour of [y:] and to believe that there was a variation in pronunciation which causes the variation, and in some cases (as in Hart's) the confusion, in the evidence.

(4) *Explanation of the late ME and early ModE development*

§ 188. The difficulty in tracing the early ModE development of OF [y], ME *iu*, and ME *eu* arises from the uncertainty about what happened in ME itself. With Luick, §§ 399(2) and 407(3), I should hold that in the East Midland dialects and in the language of London ME *eu* became [iu], and so identical with ME *iu*, about 1300. The problem is to decide how OF [y] and sounds identified with it were treated in adopted words. On grounds of general linguistic theory it is undoubtedly easiest to assume that it was simply replaced by the diphthong [iu] as the only available native substitute in the East Midland dialects; and this certainly was what occurred in popular speech. But that this was the only development is difficult, though not impossible, to reconcile with the rarity, in the fourteenth century, of the inverted spelling *u(e)* for the native diphthong [iu] and with the fact that cultivated poets like Chaucer and Gower rhyme OF [y] with native [iu] comparatively seldom, especially considering the usefulness of such rhymes. Jordan, § 230, therefore suggests that in highly cultivated speech a pronunciation [y:] was maintained. The objection to this view is that it is very rare for an exotic sound to be adopted from one language or dialect into another. But in medieval England the contact between AN and ME was unusually close, and part of the population was for a considerable time bilingual; ME adopted from AN the diphthongs [ɔi] (which in the native vocabulary occurred, exceptionally, only in *broiden* and the place-name *Croydon*) and [ui] (which as far as is known did not occur in any native word). On Luick's hypothesis (§ 399) that OE *īw* and *ēow* had developed through [yu] to [y:] in Saxon dialects and that this pronunciation had currency in the incipient standard language, there was a native [y:] in these forms of speech with which OF [y] could be identified; and this indeed is what he himself assumes (§ 412).

If we agree that OF [y] could become, in fourteenth-century London speech, not only the popular [iu] but also [y:], then it varied in English from the start. On Luick's view, earlier ME *iu* and *ęu* also varied between [iu] and [y:]; alternatively we could assume a tendency for [iu] to develop to [y:] early in the fifteenth century, when the spellings *ew* and *u(e)* begin to interchange more freely (e.g. *Tuesday* for earlier *Tiwesday*, &c.). In this case the sixteenth- and seventeenth-century variation between [y:] and [iu] would be merely a continuation of a late ME variation both in adopted and native words. But if we assume that late fourteenth-century London English had only [iu], even in words from French, then the occurrence of [y:] as a variant to [iu] in the sixteenth and seventeenth centuries could be explained only by assuming a restricted tendency of [iu] to become [y:] by assimilation of the two elements, probably in the fifteenth century.

That the normal pronunciation in London English was always [iu] there can be no doubt. It is the sole source of the PresE pronunciation, and [y:], if it existed, died out at the latest in the eighteenth century (see Note 3 below). The normal [iu] developed gradually to [ju:]; and towards the end of the seventeenth century there was a tendency, which persists in PresE, for the second element of [iu] or more likely [ju:] to be fronted in the direction of [y:]. After the development of [ju:], combinative changes occurred in which the [j] disappeared and the vowel remained as [u:], as in *sure*; similarly after the consonant [j] the diphthong [iu], in tending to become [ju:], was reduced to [u:] by the coalescence of the two [j]'s; and after certain consonants or combinations of consonants there was a tendency to eliminate the [j] for greater ease of pronunciation, as in *chute, Jew, rheum, sewer, lute*, and (in some forms of seventeenth-century English and in present American English) in *duke* and *tune*.

Note 1: Jordan, § 109, regards the change of ME *ęu* to [iu] as occurring about 1400 in consequence of the incipient raising of ME *ę̄* to [i:], and is obliged to hold that OF [y] was replaced by native [eu] in the East Midlands. Luick's view is much sounder, that ME *ęu* became [iu] about 1300 owing to the raising influence of the second element on the first. An exact parallel is the rapid development of ME *ęu* to [iu] in the seventeenth century once ME *ę̄*, and with it the first element of the diphthong, had become [e(:)], so that ME *ęu* became [iu] while ME *ę̄* was still [e:] (see §§ 243–4). Luick's hypothesis that in the SW the diphthong [øu] < OE *ēow* became [yu] relies on the parallel of the change of East Midland [eu] to [iu], and is not improbable in theory. But there is little evidence, apart from *uw* and *u(e)* spellings, for his view that OE *īw* and *ēow* both became [yu] and then [y:]; Jordan (§ 109, Anm. 1) rejects it in the case of *ēow*. Assimilation of [iu] to [y:] is in itself a credible process; and it is by no means true that English has, since the OE period, shown a uniform tendency to reject [y:] from its sound-system.

Note 2: In Northern English OF [y] was identified with the new [y:] < earlier ME *ǭ*.

In Southern and West Midland English it was identified with ME [y:] < OE ȳ (Luick would add, < OE īw and ēow as well; see Note 1 above).

Note 3: Wyld, *Short History*, p. 194, draws attention to Voltaire's statement, in his *Dictionnaire Philosophique* (1764), that the English, though they mispronounce other vowels, pronounce *u* as the French do, i.e. as [y]. This statement may refer to the pronunciation of a rather earlier period; Voltaire was in England between 1726 and 1729. Jespersen, *Hart*, p. 53, in discussing Luick's view that Steele 'still' knew the pronunciation [y:] in 1775, points out that Steele actually says that the French pronunciation of *u* is not used in English 'except in the more refined tone of the court, where it *begins* [Jespersen's italics] to obtain in a few words'. Jespersen interprets this remark as referring to a new fashion 'seizing only upon a few words, probably those felt to be recent loans' (i.e. recent adoptions from French). This view may very well be right; but we should remember that persons unacquainted with the history of pronunciation commonly mistake unfamiliar *old* pronunciations for neologisms, and that (at least in more recent times) court pronunciation has been remarkable rather for conservatism than for 'new fashions'.

Special words with ME [y:]

§ 189. Gil, in discussing the word *build*, says that it is pronounced with ME [y:] as well as [əi] < ME *ī* and [ı] < ME *ĭ*; in his transcriptions he twice shows a fourth pronunciation with [i:] < ME *ē̦*. The form with [y:] is South-western. Other orthoepists show only [ı] or [əi] (see § 12). Smith gives ME [y:] in *church*, and Hart in *bury*. It would be easy to explain their transcriptions as due to the influence of the conventional spelling, but (*a*) they are both good observers, and (*b*) it would be remarkable if they had independently made this error in words so closely comparable, for in both the South-western dialects should have had short [y] from OE ȳ (OE (late WS) *cyrice*, OE *byrigean*). We may explain Smith and Hart's long [y:] (if we accept it) by assuming either that in the South-western dialects [y] was occasionally lengthened in open syllables, or preferably that StE speakers, having no short [y] sound, substituted their own long [y:] for it when they adopted the South-western pronunciation (as the spelling of these two words proves them to have occasionally done). Chaucer's rhyme *Mercurie*: *murie* 'merry' (*Kn. T.*, ll. 1385–6) closely parallels and confirms Hart's evidence on *bury*.

The word *juice*, which normally has ME [y:] from OF [y], also has in eModE a pronunciation with [əi] developed from ME *ī* (which arises by unrounding of ME [y:]) and a pronunciation with [wəi]; this [wəi] is an eModE development from either ME *ui* or OF *ui* [yi], and its occurrence in *juice* can be explained only by analogy (see further § 259, Note 1).

Note 1: The occasional lengthening, even in the South, of ME *ī* and *ŭ* in open syllables provides an analogy for the lengthening of ME [y] suggested above. But on this analogy the lengthened sound should have been, not [y:], but the lower rounded vowel [ø:].

Note 2: *Bruise* is not an example of the survival of South-western [y:] into PresE, as stated by Wyld, *Coll. Eng.*, p. 242; OE *brȳsan* coalesces with OF *brisier*, *bruser*, and the modern pronunciation may be explained either from the last of these forms (see *OED*; cf. Wyld, *Short History*, p. 195) or from the eModE and ME *broose* (< OE *brōsian?; see Vol. I, p. 115).

VIII

THE INFLUENCE OF CONSONANTS ON THE DEVELOPMENT OF THE STRESSED VOWELS

§ 190. It is the purpose of this chapter to describe connectedly the influence of the consonants on the development of the stressed vowels in ME (especially late ME) and in early ModE, in such a way as to present a systematic picture of this influence and to attempt, where possible, a phonetic explanation. It should be noticed that shortening and lengthening influences have already been dealt with in Chapter VI, and only incidental reference will be made here to them; for the chief concern of this chapter is with qualitative and not quantitative changes. When the consonantal influence acted on the vowel before 1500, and especially when it resulted in variation in pronunciation between 1500 and 1700, the detailed evidence has already been given above in Chapter VII; here I shall merely refer to the place where this evidence is given, summarize its chief features, and proceed to point out analogies to other changes and to discuss the phonetic explanation. When, however, the evidence has not already been given (because the consonantal influence on the vowel did not operate in StE until after 1500), it will be set out in detail in this chapter.

PART 1: RAISING INFLUENCES

RAISING OF ME ĕ, ŏ, AND ĭ BEFORE *ng*

§ 191. Before *ng*, ME ĕ, ŏ, and in dialectal speech ME ĭ, are raised.

(*a*) Raising of ME ĕ to ĭ before *ng* occurs in ME (see § 76; Luick, § 379; Jordan, § 34) and apparently begins in the North, though it soon became general. Raising of ME ĕ before *ng* is distinguished by its regularity from the other cases of raising of ME ĕ to ĭ dealt with in §76 above and discussed in § 192 below.

(*b*) Raising of ME ŏ before *ng* occurs in ME (see § 92; Jordan, § 31); this change is often regarded as specifically West Midland (as by Jordan), but ME rhymes and modern dialectal evidence show that it also occurred at least sporadically in widespread Northern, Midland, and Southern dialects. It is found in PresE in *among*, &c., and seventeenth-century rhymes suggest that in all words of this class the raised pronunciation was a not uncommon variant in StE.

(c) The evidence of Welsh orthoepists (see § 57) shows that ME *ĭ* was raised from lax [ɪ] to tense [i] before *ng* and *nk*; dissimilatory lengthening probably followed. This development is purely dialectal and belongs to the West; it is analogous to the raising of ME *ĕ* and *ŏ* before *ng* but is apparently later, for the lengthening (if it did occur) must be subsequent to the diphthongization of ME *ī*, which begins about 1400, whereas the raising of ME *ĕ* and *ŏ* is established in fourteenth-century documents.

The phonetic reason for these raisings is that the tongue-position of the vowels is made higher to anticipate the raised tongue-position of the consonant [ŋ]; only the smallest movements of the tongue are necessary to pass from [ɪ] and [ʊ] to the position of [ŋ] after front and back vowels respectively, while the tongue-position of tense [i] is very nearly that of [ŋ] after a front vowel.

RAISING BEFORE DENTALS AND OTHER CONSONANTS

§ 192. Before dentals, and to a lesser extent before other consonants, ME *ĕ*, *ŏ*, and *ĭ* (in dialectal speech) are raised, and the ModE lowering of ME *ŭ* is counteracted.

(a) Raising of ME *ĕ* to *ĭ* takes place in ME and perhaps, in certain cases, in eModE (see § 77; Luick, §§ 379, 540–1; Jordan, § 34); it occurs chiefly before dentals in a wide sense (including *n*, *l*, and intervocalic *r*), also before labials (fairly often before *v*, but rarely before *b*), and occasionally before *g* and *k* (which are front palatal consonants after a front vowel). The raising is assisted (or perhaps sometimes primarily caused) by a preceding *r*, *g*, [j], or [tʃ]. It seems to be most common in the North, but is not uncommon in London English (chiefly in its more vulgar varieties); it perhaps comes into StE from the Eastern dialects.

(b) Raising of ME *ŏ* is not so well established, but occurred in ME before *v* (see § 92 above).

(c) The evidence of Welsh orthoepists (see § 57) shows that ME *ĭ* was raised from lax [ɪ] to tense [i] before the dental and palatal consonants *n*, [ç], and *l*; dissimilatory lengthening probably followed in the fifteenth century. The process is dialectal.

(d) On the influence of dentals on eModE [ʊ] < ME *ŭ* see § 196 below.

All these changes are obviously related. The raising influence of the dentals on front vowels is easy to account for; a vowel with the front of the tongue raised further towards the front palate is substituted for one with lower tongue-position, in order to anticipate the high tongue-position of the following consonant. The labials, which have less influence, must affect the vowels in a different way, by tending to reduce the lip- and mouth-opening of the vowel in order to anticipate the position required for the consonant. The labiodentals [v] and [f] might be expected to have most influence, as the teeth almost close in their articulation. The influence of [k] and [g] on front vowels must be because after front vowels they are front palatal consonants, and thus approximate to the nature of dentals.

PART 2: THE ROUNDING INFLUENCE OF LABIALS

§ 193. In the preceding section we saw that labials, when they follow a vowel, occasionally exert a raising influence. This, however, is not their normal effect, which is to cause greater lip-rounding, especially when the consonant precedes; this influence is clearly due to their method of articulation, and especially that of the bilabials *w* (which exerts the most influence), *m*, *b*, and *p*.

In ME the influences exerted by labials are as follows: (*a*) ME *ǭ* when preceded by *w* is rounded and raised to *ō* (see § 153). (*b*) ME *ǭ* when followed by *w* shows two developments: either the *w* is vocalized and coalesces with the unchanged *ǭ* to form the diphthong *ou*, or the *ǭ* is first rounded and raised, so that when vocalization of the *w* eventually occurs the result is ME *ū* (see § 172). (*c*) Similarly ME *ō* before *w* gives a diphthong *ǫu* which becomes either *ou* or (by rounding and raising of the first element, perhaps before the *w* is vocalized) ME *ū* (see § 173). (*d*) ME *ū* after *w* or before *p* or *m* is frequently not diphthongized, because the influence of the bilabial prevents the unrounding, and consequently the lowering, of the first part of the long vowel (see § 163).

In eModE, a preceding labial assists the lengthening of ME *ă* and *ŏ*; this lengthening is primarily a process (in the case of ME *ă*) of retraction and rounding or (in the case of ME *ŏ*) of prevention of unrounding (see §§ 54–55).

We come to the eModE cases of rounding, or prevention of unrounding, which have not already been discussed in Chapters VI or VII. These are the rounding of unlengthened ME *ă* to [ɒ] after *w*; rounding and lengthening to [ɒː] after *w*, and to some extent after other labials; and the prevention of the unrounding and lowering of ME *ŭ* because of labial influence.

Note: The influence of a following labial on the diphthong [au], both in ME and in eModE, is quite different, for it consists in causing the elimination of the rounded second element. For the evidence and a fuller discussion see §§ 104 and 238–9.

ROUNDING OF ME *ă* AFTER *w*

§ 194. All sixteenth-century, and most seventeenth-century, orthoepists do not show the rounding of ME *ă* after *w*; such are Levins, Smith, Hart, Bullokar, Mulcaster, Gil, Butler, Hodges *EP* (for *SH-PD* see below), Willis, Poole, Price, Wilkins, and Young. The first evidence comes in Robinson, who always has *ŏ* in the unstressed words *was* and *wast* and normally in *what* (though unrounded *ă* occurs once in *somewhat*), but who

§ 194] PART 2: INFLUENCE OF LABIALS 717

in stressed words has normally unrounded *ă*, except that [ɒ] occurs once in each of the words *warrant* and *want*. Newton has [ɒ] in *what* but not in *was* and *quarrel*. Coles in his *Schoolmaster* does not normally show rounding, but has [ɒ] in *what* rhyming with *wot* and *trot*. Between *w* and *r* Coles shows more regular rounding to [ɒ] if lengthening fails (see Vol. I, p. 442); so in *warm*, *swarm*, *warn*, *wart*, *quart*, and *thwart*. Cooper shows [ɒ] in *was* and *watch* (the latter has also [ɒː]; see § 53(3)), but not in *wan*, *wasp*, and *quality*; Wyld, *Coll. Eng.*, p. 202, is in error in saying that Cooper shows rounding in these last three words. *WSC* uses *want* as a spelling to indicate the vulgar pronunciation of *wont*; as the reference must be to a pronunciation with [ɒ] in the latter, it follows by implication that ME *ă* has been rounded in *want*.

Rounding after *wr* is a special case, in which the rounding influence of the *w* reinforces that of the *r* (see under *r*-influence below). Hodges, *SH-PD*, equates *wroth* and *wrath*, but this equation, though it may possibly show rounding of ME *ă* to *ŏ* in the latter word, is essentially ambiguous (see § 57, Note 7). Coles in his careless *Eng.–Lat. Dict.* follows Hodges. A certain case is shown by Strong's 'phonetic' spelling *rossler* 'wrestler', in which ME *ă* (the more normal variant) has been rounded to [ɒ], presumably before the loss of *w* shown by Strong's spelling.

The evidence clearly suggests that the rounded pronunciation, which began as a vulgarism (cf. Note 3 below), made its way into StE very slowly indeed (cf. Wyld, *Rhymes*, pp. 68–69). It was most common, and was first accepted in StE, in the normally weakly stressed *was* and *what*. Unrounded forms apparently still survived in *wan*, *quality*, &c. in the late eighteenth century (see Ekwall, *Laut- und Formenlehre*, § 27); Luick's explanation that these were literary words, and so not fully subject to the normal processes of phonetic change (Luick, § 538), is possible, but unnecessary.

Rounding fails before [g], [k], and [ŋ] in such words as *wag*, *wax*, *twang*, *wangle*, and *swank*; stated more positively, the normal change of ME *ă* from [a] to [æ] is so strongly encouraged by these consonants that the retractive and rounding influence of *w* cannot operate. As the normal change is one involving raising of the tongue-position, we must have here a further instance of the raising influence of the palatal varieties of [g], [k], and [ŋ] used after front vowels. In *swam* we should expect [ɒ]; PresE [æ] must be due to the analogy of other verbs of the same conjugation, such as *began* (see Jespersen, *ModE Gr*, § 10.95; Ekwall, op. cit., § 23).

Note 1: Hodges, *SH-PD*, followed by Fox and Hookes, pairs *wad* with *woad*; this equation, however, may not mean that rounding of ME *ă* had occurred in *wad* (see § 33, Note 1).

Note 2: Some words which now have short [ɒ] by rounding of ME *ă* had in the seventeenth and eighteenth centuries long [ɒː] by lengthening and rounding; see § 53 (3).

Note 3: Wyld, *Coll. Eng.*, p. 202, cites fourteenth-century spellings and a rhyme which he believes show rounding of ME *ă*: his examples are *swolwe-bridde* (*E.E. Prose Psalter*,

p. 180), *swolʒ* sb. 'throat' (*Patience*, l. 250), *swolʒed* p.t. 'swallowed' (*Patience*, l. 363), and *swalowe* infin. rhyming with *holowe* (Chaucer, *Hous of Fame*, ii. 527-8). It is a suspicious circumstance that all the cases concern the various words *swallow*. The explanation proceeds from the verb, which in the infinitive and present stem has original ĕ (retained until the sixteenth century, and in dialectal forms until the nineteenth century); forms with ă and ŏ begin in the twelfth century (see *OED*), and those with ŏ continue until the seventeenth century. The weak past tense and past participle have *o*-forms from their first appearance in the fourteenth century until the seventeenth century. As *OED* points out, the ă-forms are due to the influence on the infinitive and present stem of the original strong past tense, and the ŏ-forms to that of the original strong past participle, which retains ŏ until its last appearance (in the form *swolwe*) in the fifteenth century. *OED* remarks that this analogical extension may have been 'furthered by association with *swallow* sb.¹' (the bird); this would, however, apply only to the ă-forms. *Swallow* sb.² 'throat', &c. is from OE *geswelg*, and has only ĕ-forms until the fourteenth century, when ă- and ŏ-forms (due, as *OED* again points out, to the analogical influence of the verbal forms) first appear; ŏ-forms survive until the seventeenth century. *Swallow* sb.¹ (the bird) has original ă; ŏ-forms appear in the fourteenth century and, though they are not explained by *OED*, are clearly due to the analogical influence of *swallow* vb. and *swallow* sb.² There is no reason whatever for assuming a fourteenth-century change of ME ă to [ɒ] after *w* to explain these forms.

Zachrisson, *Eng. Vowels*, p. 62; Wyld, *Rhymes*, p. 68; and Kihlbom, p. 121, cite fifteenth-century spellings with *o* for ME ă from the *Paston Letters* and the *Cely Papers*; those from the *Cely Papers* concern only the weakly stressed *was*, but those from the *Paston Letters* occur in other words, and after other labials (*b*, *v*, and *f*) as well as *w*. This rounding is clearly dialectal, and appears to be assisted by a following *l* or *r*. But it is probably from the Eastern dialects represented by the *Paston Letters* and the *Cely Papers* that the rounded [ɒ] made its way into StE. (Luick would interpret Zachrisson's fifteenth-century examples as inverted spellings showing the unrounding of ME ŏ. This is possible; but I would accept them as showing rounding of ME ă.) Machyn in the sixteenth century has *wosse* 'wash', but as he has *o* for ă in other words which have no ME variant in ŏ (thus *Ovenon* beside *Avenon*, *grovel* beside *gravel*; see Wijk, *Machyn*, pp. 55, 132) it is very doubtful whether this spelling shows *w*-influence on ME ă (though Wijk, p. 61, seems to take it so, following, for reasons that will not bear examination, Luick's view that the result of *w*-influence was to cause retention of [a]); like the other spellings with *o* for ME ă, it should be interpreted either as showing identification by Machyn of his own Northern dialectal pronunciation of ME ŏ as [a] with Southern [a] (against Northern [æ] or [e]) for ME ă (so Wijk, p. 55) or more simply, and preferably, as an inverted spelling due to ME unrounding of ME ŏ to identity with ME ă. Spellings with *o* for ME ă after *w* are in fact not common until the seventeenth-century *Verney Memoirs*. In the seventeenth century rhymes on unrounded ME ă are still much more common than rhymes on rounded [ɒ], and in the early eighteenth century ă-rhymes are still normal (see Wyld, *Rhymes*, pp. 69-70). At some time such ă-rhymes became traditional and ceased to represent the ordinary pronunciation; the evidence leaves no doubt that this occurred during the course of the eighteenth century.

Note 4: Luick, §§ 536 and 538, assumes that the process was not that ME ă was rounded to [ɒ], but that it was retained unchanged as [a]. His only reason, as appears clearly from § 537, Anm. 2, is his assumption that in eModE the regular development of ME ŏ was to unrounded [a], which was later (after ME ă following *w* had become identical with this [a] < ME ŏ) rounded again to the PresE [ɒ]. But if we reject this theory of the development of ME ŏ (as we should), we must assume that ME ă after *w* was not merely held back, but also rounded, by the influence of the consonant. Luick admits that there is no objection to this assumption, in itself (§ 536, Anm. 2).

ROUNDING AND LENGTHENING TO [ɒ:]

§ 195. After *w*, and to a less extent after other labials, there sometimes occurs rounded [ɒ:] in place of eModE [a:], as though [a:] had been rounded to [ɒ:]. In fact, however, it is impossible to prove that an [a:] stage had preceded the [ɒ:] stage; the influence of the preceding labial seems to cause direct development to [ɒ:] instead of to [a:]. The regularity of the rounding varies according to the phonetic circumstances, which must therefore be distinguished.

After *w*, rounding occurs in the following circumstances:

(*a*) Instead of eModE [a:] (by lengthening of ME *ă*) before *r* [ɒ:] regularly appears in such words as *ward, war* (see § 49).

(*b*) Instead of eModE [a:] (by lengthening of ME *ă*) before a voiceless spirant [ɒ:] is found only occasionally in PresE (see § 52); no example of the rounded vowel is recorded by the orthoepists.

(*c*) In the special cases of lengthening of ME *ă* discussed in § 53, it is always the rounded [ɒ:] which is recorded when the vowel is preceded by *w*. Thus *was, wattle, watch,* and *wash* have occasional [ɒ:] in seventeenth-century orthoepists, and *swaths* has [ɒ:] in PresE. *Water* has regular [ɒ:] when lengthening occurs, as in Robinson, Gil, and later orthoepists; Robinson gives [ɒ:] in the analogous Spanish *quatro*, and late eighteenth-century orthoepists give [ɒ:] in *squadron, quadrant,* and *quadrate*. In *wrath* Present StE normally has rounded [ɒ:], though Scottish and American English have unrounded [a:] or [ɑ:]; seventeenth-century orthoepists record [ɒ:]. It is sometimes explained that in this word the rounding influence of the *w* operates 'over' the *r*, but in point of fact it reinforces that of the *r*, which itself exercises the primary rounding influence; the lip-protrusion, and therefore the rounding influence, of the *r* is especially strong because it in turn is preceded by *w*.

(*d*) When eModE [a:] < ME *au* before a nasal (see the following chapter) is preceded by *w*, rounding may perhaps occur; *qualm* has [ɒ:] beside [ɑ:] in PresE. But it is impossible to say with certainty that this [ɒ:] is developed by rounding of earlier [a:] rather than by direct normal monophthongization of ME *au*. In the orthoepists, only Lodwick and Cooper give evidence of [a:] < ME *au*, and neither gives any evidence of the development after *w*.

(*e*) Jespersen, *ModEGr.*, § 10.91, who believes that there was a ModE process of rounding [a:] to [ɒ:] after *w*, cites as examples *memoir* pronounced [memwɒ:] (cf. *OED*, which gives this pronunciation) and *je ne sais quoi*, which, according to evidence in Thackeray in 1841 (see Jespersen), was also pronounced with [ɒ:]. But we have seen that in native words there is no real evidence that there was ever a stage [a:] before rounding occurred to [ɒ:], and it would be dangerous to assume such a process merely to account for the pronunciation of two words which have been incompletely anglicized. In the sixteenth century, when *memoir* was adopted, StE possessed no [a:] or [ɑ:]; French [a:] in *memoire* must then have been identified either with ME *au* (already sometimes pronounced [ɒ:]), which would immediately explain the [wɒ:] pronunciation, or with ME *ă* [a], which seems more probable; then in the seventeenth century the normal lengthening and rounding direct to [ɒ:], under the combined influence of *w* and *r*, would ensue. In *je ne sais quoi* (recorded from 1656, but always recognized as a French phrase) the pronunciation with [wɒ:] seems to represent a late (early nineteenth-century) anglicization on the model of [wɒ:] in, for example, *water* or *war* (in which *r* was by then silent).

Other labials than *w* occasionally cause lengthening to be accompanied by rounding to [ɒ:]; the rounded vowel occurs in *paths* in Hodges (§ 53), in *father* in Jones (1701) and occasionally in present American English (§ 53), and perhaps in other words (notably *pardon* and *parson*) in late seventeenth-century pronunciation (see § 44, Note 4).

Note 1: See § 194 for rounding of unlengthened ME *ă* after *wr*. Compare also the rounding of *ĭ* to [y] or *ŭ* in *wruxled* p.p. of **wruxlen* from OE *wrixlan* (*Sir Gawain and the Green Knight*, l. 2191).

Note 2: Except in *paths*, the [ɒ:] discussed in the last paragraph above may be due solely to the retracting influence of the *r*; but in *father* it does not seem likely that the *r* alone would cause retraction and rounding to [ɒ:], separated as it is from the vowel.

ME *ŭ* REMAINS [ʊ] AFTER LABIALS

§ 196. When ME *ŭ* was unrounded to [ʌ] about 1640, it remained in certain words as rounded [ʊ] (cf. Luick, § 531; Horn, §§ 66–67). This retention of [ʊ] occurs after the labial consonants *w*, *p*, *b*, and *f*, and in the seventeenth century (though not in PresE) apparently also after *m*. The influence of the preceding labial requires to be assisted by that of a following consonant; this may be either the bilabial *m* (as in *woman*), or the dentals *d* (as in *wood*), *t* (as in *put*), *s* (as in *puss*), more frequently [ʃ] (as in *push*, *bush*), and above all *l* (as in *pull*, *bull*, *wool*, and *full*). In the seventeenth century the dentals *r* and *n* also assist the prevention of unrounding; *Worcester* and *worsted* may show the survival into PresE of [ʊ] thus retained before [r], though in these words forms without *r* existed before the time when ME *ŭ* was changing its pronunciation and the PresE [ʊ] may then develop before [s]. PresE shows retention of [ʊ] before [ʃ] in a word where no labial influence operates in *cushion*; similarly the Welsh orthoepist Jones shows [ʊ] retained by the influence of the dental *n* alone, without labial influence (see Note 1). But the PresE pronunciation of *cuckoo* is due merely to continued imitation of the bird's note, which has prevented the normal phonetic development.

The reason why a preceding labial tends to prevent unrounding of ME *ŭ* is clear: the lip-position of the consonant operates against the spreading of the lips found in [ʌ]. The dentals assist, or even alone cause, the retention of [ʊ] not as a rule because they favour rounded vowels, but because they favour vowels with high tongue-position. The dental *l* has special power to aid retention of [ʊ] because of its lip-protrusion and because for the English 'dark' *l* (used before consonants and finally) the back of the tongue is raised (see Daniel Jones, *Outline of English Phonetics*, §§ 668–9); in the case of [ʃ] (which also assists the ME rounding of *ĭ* to [ʊ]; see § 85, Note 5) the influence of the high tongue-position is reinforced by the rounding influence of the lip-protrusion which accompanies its articulation (cf. Daniel Jones, op. cit., § 727). On *r* see § 198 below.

The PresE distinction between words with [ʊ] and words with [ʌ] shows no regularity; [ʌ] occurs in positions that should favour [ʊ] in *won, wonder, pun, puff*, the golfing term *putt* (a differentiated form of *put*, which probably owes its pronunciation to Scottish), *pulp, pulse, but, bulk*, and *bulb*. A following consonant clearly limits the rounding power of *l* (cf. §§ 60 and 88). Luick, § 531, and Ekwall, *Laut- und Formenlehre*, § 98, suggest that the failure to retain [ʊ] in some of these words is due to their more literary and less popular character, but this explanation is unnecessary; the rounding influence acted sporadically and produced inconsistent results, as is evident from the common words *put, but, butcher*, and *butter*.

In sixteenth-century orthoepists, and such early seventeenth-century orthoepists as Tonkis, Robinson, and Gil, there is naturally no distinction between the vowels of *but* and *put*, as ME *ŭ* was in all positions the rounded [ʊ]. Daines and Price seem to have treated [ʊ] and [ʌ] as contextual variants of the one phoneme. The distinction is shown only by Hodges, Wallis, Newton, Wilkins, Holder (see Vol. I, pp. 266–9), Coles (see Vol. I, p. 440), Cooper, T. Jones, and *RS* (*WSC* is confused, but *RS* distinguishes [ʊ] from [ʌ] though not from [uː]; see Vol. I, pp. 360–1).

In the seventeenth century there was evidently some variation and uncertainty in pronunciation. Hodges gives [ʌ] once against [ʊ] twice in *pull*, Wilkins gives [ʌ] beside [ʊ] in *pull* and *full*, and Holder gives [ʌ], probably as a variant to [ʊ], in *full* (see Vol. I, pp. 268–9). Other words also seem to have varied (see the evidence cited below), and from the difference between the recorded seventeenth-century and the PresE pronunciations we can assume that there must also have been variation in *wont, put, punish*, and *bulk*. This variation and uncertainty probably explains why so excellent a phonetician as Cooper, though he lays down in his Part I a clear rule that certain words have [ʊ], nevertheless includes the same words in a list of which the other members now have, and must certainly have also had then, the sound [ʌ]. Cooper has been careless, but his carelessness was probably condoned by the existence of a variant [ʌ] in the words which according to his rule had [ʊ] (see Vol. I, p. 298, note 3). *RS*, in part following Cooper, shows variation in some of these words (see Vol. I, p. 360). Willis rhymes *bull, full, pull, wool, bush, push*, and *put* with words that now have [ʌ] (see Vol. I, pp. 427–8); it is evident that he, like Daines and Price, did not recognize a phonemic distinction between [ʊ] and [ʌ], so that one cannot tell which occurs in any word, and I exclude him from the following list of evidence. This list includes only those words recorded by the orthoepists which have [ʊ] in PresE, or which certainly or possibly had [ʊ] in the seventeenth century in the speech of persons who pronounced ME ŭ in free position as [ʌ].

(1) *ME ŭ after w*

Wolf and its derivatives have [ʊ] in Hodges, Coles, Cooper (apparently beside a variant with [ʌ]; see above), and *RS*. *Wool* (which has ME *ū̆*; its *oo* is due to inverted spelling) has [ʊ] in Hodges and Newton; the evidence of *WSC* is vague, but from *RS*'s silence we may assume that it refers to [ʊ] (see Vol. I, p. 361). *Wood* has [ʊ] (from ME *ŭ*, not from the ME variant in *ǭ* which explains the spelling; see § 36, Note 2) in Hodges, Wallis (followed without understanding by Price), Newton, and Coles; *WSC*'s evidence is again vague, but may be assumed to refer to [ʊ] (see Vol. I, p. 361). *Woman* has [ʊ] in Hodges but [ʌ] in *RS* (though the evidence of *WSC* may show that this author recognized the variation of pronunciation; see Vol. I, p. 360); Coles's 'phonetic' spelling *wum-man* perhaps suggests [ʌ], but does not rule out [ʊ]. *Wonder* and its derivatives have [ʊ] in Hodges and Cooper (who apparently also knew a variant with [ʌ]; see above), and [ʌ] in *RS* (see Vol. I, p. 360). *Wont* (which has ME *ŭ*; the PresE [ou] is a spelling pronunciation) has [ʊ] in Hodges. *Worsted*, according to Cooper's rule, has [ʊ], but he apparently also knew a variant pronunciation with [ʌ]; *RS* also shows variation between [ʊ] (stated to be the more common pronunciation) and [ʌ]. The PresE pronunciation probably develops not from Cooper's, in which the *r* was still pronounced, but from the pronunciation which is represented as *wusted* and described as 'barbarous speaking' by Cooper (followed by *WSC-RS*); whether this transcription refers to a form with [ʊ] or [ʌ] it is not possible to say. Coles similarly gives a 'phonetic' spelling *Wuster* for *Worcester*; this again is ambiguous. Words in which ME *ŭ* came between *w* and a pronounced [r], such as *word, work, worship, worry,* and *worts,* have [ʌ] in Hodges, but according to Cooper's general rule have [ʊ] in his speech (though he seems also to have known the variant pronunciation with [ʌ]; see above); *RS* (and more obscurely *WSC*) shows the same variation, the [ʊ] pronunciation being described in *RS* (which is partly following Cooper) as the more common. Lye says that *wourts* 'worts' (one of Cooper's words) has *ou* pronounced *oo*; in the other words of the list which includes *wourts* this means a pronunciation [uː], but in this case must mean [ʊ] (since *worts* cannot have ME *ū*). Lye's evidence is however of little value, as he is here influenced by Price (who did not distinguish [ʊ] and [ʌ]) and shows no sign elsewhere of himself recognizing this distinction.

(2) *ME ŭ after p*

Pull has [ʊ] twice in Hodges, besides [ʌ] once (see *EP*, edited Kauter, p. 14, l. 7, where *pul* is given as [pʌl] and [pʊl] to illustrate the two word-endings [ʌl] and [ʊl]); Wilkins similarly shows variation between [ʊ] and [ʌ] (see Vol. I, p. 261); but only [ʊ] is recorded by Wallis (followed without understanding by Price), Coles, and Cooper. *Pulse* has [ʌ] in Hodges. Cooper in his 'near alike' list pairs *pulse* and *pulls*; such pairings in this list of Cooper's depend on variant pronunciations which he himself did not use, but it is impossible to determine whether in this case the pairing depends on the recorded variant [ʌ] in *pulls* (as is more probable) or an unrecorded variant [ʊ] (which phonetically is quite possible) in *pulse*. *Put* has [ʌ] in Hodges, though it has [ʊ] in PresE; on the other hand *punish* has [ʊ] in Hodges but [ʌ] in PresE.

(3) *ME ŭ after* b

Bull has [ʊ] in Hodges, Coles, and Cooper. *Bulk* has [ʊ] in Hodges, though it has [ʌ] in PresE. *Bush* and its derivatives have [ʊ] in Hodges and Coles.

(4) *ME ŭ after* f

Full and its derivatives have [ʌ] in Hodges, Newton, and Holder, but [ʊ] in Wallis (followed without understanding by Price), Wilkins (beside a variant [ʌ]; see Vol. I, p. 261), and Cooper. PresE has regular [ʊ] except in *fulsome*, which varies. Comparable but unrelated words, such as *fulminate*, have [ʌ].

(5) *ME ŭ after* m

ME *ŭ* in *mother* and *month* is normally not distinguished from ME *ŭ* in other words by the orthoepists; but Hodges gives [ʊ], which is rather to be explained from ME *ŭ* by shortening than as a late (seventeenth-century) shortening of [uː] < ME *ǭ* (see § 18, Note 2), though it must be granted that there is no other evidence of failure of unrounding after *m*.

Note 1: The Welsh orthoepist T. Jones, who normally shows [ʌ] for ME *ŭ*, shows [ʊ] in *undo*, *until*, and *unwise*, in which the dental *n* has prevented unrounding in spite of the lack of labial influence. This pronunciation must be dialectal (see Vol. I, p. 355); it is similar to the tensing, and probable lengthening, of ME *ĭ* before *n* and other palatals (see § 57).

Note 2: Some of the words discussed above still varied in pronunciation in the eighteenth century. Luick, § 531, Anm. 1, and Horn, §§ 66–67, cite the evidence of Walker (1791), who knew and disapproved of [ʊ] in *bulk* and *punish*; of Sheridan (1780), who gives [ʊ] in *wont*; and of Johnson (1764) and Nares (1784), who give [ʌ] in *put*. These eighteenth-century pronunciations of *bulk*, *punish*, *wont*, and *put*, it will be noticed, are the same as those of Hodges in 1644.

Note 3: The pronunciation of *would* with [ʊ], which might be explained as due to failure of the unrounding of eModE *ŭ*, is rather due to late (seventeenth-century) shortening of eModE [uː], since this latter explanation is the only one possible for the analogous *should* and *could*. For the evidence on *would* see § 4.

ROUNDING OF ME ĭ BY LABIALS

§ 197. After [w], and in isolated words after [b] and before [m], there is rounding of ME ĭ to ME ŭ. The process belongs, however, to the ME period itself, and is therefore treated in Chapter VI above (§ 85).

PART 3: THE INFLUENCE OF *r* ON THE DEVELOPMENT OF VOWELS

§ 198. No consonant exercises greater or more varied influence on the development of the vowels in ME and ModE than *r*. In the following discussion it will be necessary to distinguish under separate headings three different ways in which *r*-influence operates, thus rounding influence, lowering influence, and the development of a glide-vowel [ə] before *r*. In each of these cases except the last it will be necessary further to distinguish the influence of a following from that of a preceding *r*. When a following *r* is concerned, it is generally of importance to distinguish the influence of final *r*, intervocalic *r*, and *r* plus consonant. In many of the cases to be discussed, the detailed evidence has already been set out in Chapter VII (or sometimes in Chapter VI); here we shall discuss the processes involved and other general questions of which the consideration was not previously relevant.

The rounding influence of *r* is due to the lip-protrusion which accompanies the articulation of the consonant (see Daniel Jones, *Outline of English Phonetics*, § 749) and may operate at any time in the history of English (cf. Bülbring, § 275, for an OE example). The lowering influence operates in late ME (in the fourteenth century in the North, in the late fourteenth century and particularly in the fifteenth century in the South) and in ModE, and perhaps reflects a change in the nature of the consonant, from point-trilled to a variety of the PresE point-fricative; for the latter the body of the tongue is held low (Daniel Jones, op. cit., § 747) and the sound is practically a vowel (Sweet, *Primer of Phonetics*, § 211)—often indeed a frictionless continuant (Jones, op. cit., § 796), a class of consonant which is in fact a vowel (Jones, op. cit., § 183 footnote). This point-fricative *r* is closely allied to the vowels [ə] and [əː], and 'the sound [of the frictionless continuant variety] is equivalent to a weakly pronounced "retroflexed" [ə]' (Jones, op. cit., § 796). It is its tongue-position which accounts for its lowering influence, and its resemblance to the vowel [ə] which explains why the latter often appears as a glide before it. The influence of *r* on seventeenth-century [ʌ] < ME ŭ, which, though treated here under 'lowering', really involves a slight raising and fronting of the vowel, is similarly due to the inherent quality of the ModE [r]; for [ʌ] changes to [ə], the vowel to which the consonant is so closely allied.

Note: Luick, §§ 505–11, regards lowering as being in most cases subsequent to and due to the development of an [ə] glide before the *r*. Against this assumption we may point out the following facts. (1) Most of the eModE evidence on the development of an [ə] glide shows it after the high vowels [iː] or [uː] or diphthongs ending in [i] or [u], and before final *r*; there is evidence for it after other ME long vowels and before *r* plus consonant, but it is doubtful whether we are justified in assuming that it was general after ME *ā*, *ẹ̄*, and *ǭ* and before *r* plus consonant until the time when *r* was lost in final position and before consonants by being vocalized into [ə]. After the ME short vowels there is, as Luick admits, no evidence that a glide-vowel ever developed (see Luick, loc. cit., Anm. 2); Luick would assume that there was such a glide-vowel in order to conform to his general theory, but it is surely better to fit one's theory to the facts than the facts to one's theory. (2) Lowering does not occur before an [ə] developed otherwise than before *r* in such words as *real*, *fealty*, *payer*, *rowan*, *rower*. In *prayer* and *mayor* the lowering is due to the ME forms *praire* and *maire* (cf. Horn, § 118); in *boa* and *Noah*, which have [ɒə] and [ɒː] beside [oə] (or [ouə]), we have to do with analogical pronunciations of comparatively recent origin (see § 210). (3) Luick's chronology of the lowering of ME *ẹ̄* is wrong; before final *r* as well as before *r* plus consonant it seems to antedate the development of a glide [ə] before *r*. Luick would divorce the lowering of ME *ẹ̄* before *r* plus consonant from its lowering before final *r*, and would explain the lowering of ME *ẹ̄* before *r* plus consonant and of ME *ĕ* before *r* from the influence of the consonant itself, whereas all the other cases of lowering are to be due to the glide [ə]. It is much preferable to regard all cases of lowering as due to the direct influence on the vowel of the consonant itself; this explanation involves us in no difficulties or inconsistencies. The glide before *r* is a by-product of its quasi-vocalic quality, and not the means whereby that quality influenced the preceding vowel.

THE ROUNDING INFLUENCE OF *r*

(1) *Rounding due to a following* r

§ 199. A following *r* exercises rounding influence in the following cases:

(*a*) The diphthongization of ME *ū* tends to be inhibited before *r* plus consonant, comparatively rarely before final *r*; before intervocalic *r* variation occurs (see § 165).

(*b*) Similarly a following *r* occasionally assists in the retention of [u] for ME *ŭ* (i.e. it assists the inhibition of unrounding of ME *ŭ*) in the seventeenth century (see § 196).

(*c*) Before *r* ME *ŏ* is not lowered and unrounded, but remains with approximately its ME value as 'cardinal open [ɔ]' and then undergoes dissimilatory lengthening (see §§ 54–55). This result is primarily due to the lip-protrusion of [r], which inhibits the tendency to unround ME *ŏ* (see § 55). On the other hand the influence of *r* in preventing the fronting of ME *ă* is primarily due to the retractive power of ModE [r], though its rounding power may help.

(*d*) A following *r* assists lengthening and rounding of ME *ă* direct to [ɒː] (see §§ 49 and 195), and in certain dialects it is alone responsible for it (see § 49 and cf. § 55, Note 2).

(2) *Rounding due to a preceding* r

§ 200. A preceding *r* exercises rounding influence in the following cases:

(*a*) About 1400, in words in which ME *ĭ* was preceded by a group consisting of a consonant plus *r* and was followed by a dental, metathesis of the *r* and the vowel occurred, and the vowel either remained as *ĭ* or was rounded to *ŭ* (see § 84 above and Luick, § 432). As no such rounding occurred in words in which ME *ĭ* was originally followed by *r*, it is evident that the rounding occurs while the *r* precedes the vowel, though there appears to be some obscure connexion between the rounding and the metathesis. The part played by the succeeding dental is not clear; it would favour a vowel with high tongue-position, but not [u] as against [ɪ], and is perhaps connected with the metathesis rather than the rounding.

(*b*) A preceding consonant group consisting of *w* plus *r* (in which the lip-protrusion of the [r] is accentuated by that of the [w]) causes rounding of unlengthened ME *ă* to [ɒ]; see § 194.

(*c*) Similarly a consonant group consisting of *w* plus *r* causes lengthening and rounding of ME *ă* direct to [ɒː] in *wrath*; see § 195.

(*d*) A preceding consonant group consisting of consonant plus *r* assists the lengthening of ME *ŏ*, primarily by preventing the tendency to unround the vowel. On the other hand the influence of a similar group on a following ME *ă* is primarily retractive, but a comparison with the influence on ME *ă* of a preceding labial suggests that the lip-protrusion of [r] was the cause of the process (see § 55).

THE LOWERING INFLUENCE OF *r*

(1) *Lowering due to a following* r

§ 201. A following *r* begins to exercise lowering influence in late ME; more precise indications of the date are given by the history of ME *ĕ* before *r*. Lowering before 1500 occurs in the following cases.

(*a*) *ME ĕ before* r

ME *ĕ* before *r* tends to become late ME *ă*; see §§ 64–69. Late ME *ă* appears in the North and North Midlands from comparatively early in the fourteenth century, and occurs in Chaucer, but is not common in the South and South Midlands until the fifteenth century. The lowered sound never became entirely general in StE but was formerly more common than now, especially in less well-educated speech. The lowering is most common before *r* plus consonant, especially if the consonant belongs to the same syllable; it is not uncommon before final *r*, but is rare before intervocalic *r* (though it does occur even here and was formerly more common than now).

(*b*) *ME ę̄ before* r

ME *ę̄* before *r* tends to become *ę̄* (see § 126); the change is earlier than that of surviving ME *ę̄* to [iː], which was complete by *c.* 1450. The lowered pronunciation seems to have been more common in the sixteenth century than it was in the seventeenth; it does not remain in PresE. Before *r* plus consonant in native words the lowering is regular in the orthoepists, except that Levins has [i:] in *herd* and that Levins and Hodges have [i:] in *beard* (in which early ME $\bar{ę}$ is raised to ME $\bar{ẹ}$, which then escapes the later lowering back to $\bar{ę}$). In Levins these pronunciations may be Northernisms. PresE happens to preserve a long vowel only in *beard*, in which it has the unlowered pronunciation. Before *r* plus consonant in words adopted from French, before final *r*, and before intervocalic *r* the lowering, though occasionally recorded, is rarer than the retention of ME $\bar{ẹ}$; lowering in all circumstances is rarer in words adopted from French than in native English words (see § 136, where an explanation is suggested). The lowering was probably not characteristic of educated StE, or at least was less common in it than in vulgar or dialectal English, from which the lowered pronunciations were sometimes adopted.

Insofar as ME $\bar{ẹ}$ escaped this late ME lowering to $\bar{ę}$ [ɛ:], the normal fifteenth-century change to [i:] occurred before *r* as in other positions; the sixteenth- and seventeenth-century orthoepists, when they do not show $\bar{ę}$ by late ME lowering, consistently identify ME $\bar{ẹ}$ before *r* with ME $\bar{ẹ}$ in other positions and show that its pronunciation is [i:]. (See § 126 above, where 'ME $\bar{ẹ}$' means that the orthoepists named record [i:] < ME $\bar{ẹ}$ in the word in question.) PresE has [iə] < late fifteenth-century [i:] < unlowered ME $\bar{ẹ}$ in all words in which ME $\bar{ẹ}$ stood before final and intervocalic *r*, and before *r* plus consonant in the native *beard* and in *fierce* (to which *pierce* may be parallel; see § 122) adopted from French.

Note: Luick explains the lowering of ME $\bar{ẹ}$ to ME $\bar{ę}$ before *r* plus consonant as a ME change (§ 431) and the lowering before final and intervocalic *r* as an eModE change, consisting in the lowering of [iə] from ME $\bar{ẹ}$ to [ɛə], equivalent to ME $\bar{ę}$ before *r* (§§ 507-8). His reasons for thus divorcing lowering before *r* plus consonant from lowering before final and intervocalic *r* are as follows. (i) Lowering before *r* plus consonant is regular, lowering before final and intervocalic *r* only occasional (§ 431, Anm. 3). On my view, there are exceptions to the lowering before *r* plus consonant; Luick would give up *pierce* as 'unklar', would regard the [iə] pronunciation of *fierce* as due to the analogy of the variant *fier*, *feer*, and because of his (in my view incorrect) theory of the ModE development of ME $\bar{ẹ}$ before *r* does not need to assume that *beard* had a ME variant in $\bar{ę}$ by raising. But even so the greater regularity of the lowering before *r* plus consonant is sufficiently accounted for by the different phonetic circumstances and is paralleled in all cases of lowering before *r* (cf. the lowering of ME $\breve{e}$ discussed under (*a*) above); we need not assume that it occurred at a different time by a distinct process. Further, the evidence for the lowering before *r* plus consonant is no earlier than the evidence for the lowering before final and intervocalic *r*; in either case the evidence consists of rare fifteenth-century and common sixteenth-century *ea* spellings (see § 126, Note 4) and the evidence of sixteenth-century orthoepists. (ii) Luick also depends on the analogy of ME $\bar{ọ}$, which became [u:] before being lowered, in the ModE period, to [o:] (equivalent to ME $\bar{ǫ}$) before *r*. But this analogy does not hold. Sixteenth-century orthoepists who show the lowering of ME $\bar{ẹ}$ before final and intervocalic *r* (as well as before *r* plus consonant) do not show the lowering of ME $\bar{ọ}$ before final and intervocalic *r* or before *r* plus consonant. Luick, § 508, Anm. 1, is in error in citing Hart and Bullokar as showing the lowering of ME $\bar{ọ}$, for they give the equivalent of

ME ǭ only in *door*, which is a special case with a ME variant in ọ̄ (see § 155). The first valid evidence of the lowering comes in Robinson and Gil in the early seventeenth century. Similarly, though *ea* spellings occur for ME ẹ̄ before *r* from the late fifteenth century, *oa* spellings for ME ǭ before *r* do not occur until the seventeenth century, and then rarely at first, except that *whore* is recorded as having an *oa* spelling in the sixteenth century by *OED* (see further.§ 207, Note 1).

If we are not to force the evidence to a false symmetry, we must distinguish two changes. (i) In late ME lowering of ME ẹ̄ to ME ę̄ occurs before *r* plus consonant (where it is most common) and before final and intervocalic *r*; it is a direct lowering from [e:] (the ME value of ME ẹ̄) to [ɛ:] (the ME value of ME ę̄). (ii) After ME ǭ has become [u:], there occurs, apparently about or just before 1600, a lowering of [u:] from ME ǭ and from other ME sounds to [o:], the contemporary value of ME ọ̄.

The different treatment of the front and back vowels is not surprising. The two changes are of course comparable, and are due to the same quality in the pronunciation of [r], but they are not contemporaneous nor effected by exactly the same phonetic stages.

§ 202. The remaining cases of lowering before *r* belong to the ModE period after 1500, and no detailed evidence or discussion of them has been given in Chapter VII above. In what follows I shall treat the lowering first of the ModE long front vowels, then of the long back vowels, and finally of the short vowels.

(c) Failure of fronting of ME ę̄

§ 203. Late ME ę̄ (i.e. original ME ę̄ and the lowered vowel occasionally developed from ME ẹ̄ before *r*; see under (*b*) on pp. 726–7 above) is retained as open [ɛ:] and is not fronted to [e:] before *r* (with the doubtful exception that before final *r* fronting to [e:] may occasionally have been permitted; see below). Ekwall, § 56, assumes that the process was that in the sixteenth century there was a lowering of ME ę̄ in *bear*, &c. from [ɛ:] to [æ:] (which was later, we must conclude, raised to [ɛ:] as ME ā passed from [æ:] to [ɛ:]). But it is improbable that the *r*-influence would cause retraction to [æ:] only to allow fronting again very shortly afterwards. Horn, § 86, however, puts forward a contrary (and more usual) theory, that there was first fronting to [e:], succeeded by retraction to [ɛ:]; but it is improbable that *r*, which had already caused occasional retraction of ME ẹ̄ to ME ę̄ (i.e. of [e:] to [ɛ:]), would allow fronting of ME ę̄ from [ɛ:] to [e:] only to cause retraction again shortly afterwards. No valid parallel for such a process can be drawn from the back vowels. It is true that ME ǭ is raised to [u:] before *r* in the fifteenth century in accordance with its normal change in free position, but the parallel to this is the raising of ME ẹ̄ to [i:] before *r* as in free position. The parallel to ME ę̄ is ME ǭ, which there is no sufficient reason to believe was ever raised before *r* from its ME value of approximately 'cardinal open [ɔ:]' (see § 206 below). The later stages of the development of the long back vowels before *r* (lowering of sixteenth-century [u:] about 1600 to identity with ME ǭ before *r*, and the change of [ɔə] to [ɒə] about 1800) have no parallel among the front vowels, as is sufficiently shown by the fact that

§ 203]   PART 3: INFLUENCE OF *r*   729

sixteenth-century [iː] before *r* remains unchanged in the seventeenth century; the development of ME ọ̄ therefore gives no justification for assuming that the lowering influence of *r* on ME ẹ̄ came into play late, after a period in which the normal fronting had proceeded unchecked.

PresE [iə] and eModE [iː] in *tear* 'lacrima', *year*, &c. is not developed from late ME ẹ̄ but from late ME ẹ̄, which arises sometimes from raising of original ME ę̄ (as in *tear*), sometimes from OE variants (as in *year*); see also § 122 above.

Note: Horn's view of the development of ME ę̄ before *r* has already been discussed (see § 122, Note 6). Luick, §§ 509–10, sets forward a most elaborate theory. He assumes that the process of development of ME ę̄ is different before final *r* and before *r* plus consonant. Before final *r* he argues that ME ę̄ became first [ɛːə] as a consequence of the development of a glide [ə] before *r*; this [ɛːə] then was fronted (as regards the first element) to [eːə], a sound which then underwent a double development, either with retraction of the first element to [ɛːə] as in PresE *tear* vb., or with fronting of the first element to [iːə] as in *tear* sb. 'lacrima'. In the former case (when retraction to [ɛːə] occurs), ME ę̄ became identical with ME ā (*ai*) before *r*, and all three sounds then shared the fronting of ME ā (*ai*) in free position to [eː(ə)], so that ME ę̄ before *r* was back to where it was before it was retracted. Then in the eighteenth century (see Luick, § 568 (1)) the three ME sounds, now [eːə], were before *r* retracted once more to [ɛːə], the PresE value, because the retractive influence of the [ə] glide was at that time strengthened, probably as a consequence of the final disappearance in the eighteenth century of the consonant [r] in final position and before consonants. (On Luick's view of the development of ME ā (*ai*) after the stage at which they overtook ME ę̄ before *r*, see § 205, Note.) But Luick says that before *r* plus consonant (as in *earn*, *early*, &c.), eModE [ɛːə] had quite another development than before final *r*: the first element was shortened, giving [eə], which, being identical with the [eə] which Luick believes (falsely) to have developed from ME ĕ before *r*, shared its supposed development to [əː]. This ingenious theory covers the facts of PresE pronunciation, but must be rejected on the following grounds. (1) The very diversity of the processes assumed, the swift succession of fronting, retraction, fronting, shortening, and so on, is a source of grave weakness. (2) The whole theory depends on the view that a glide vowel had developed after both ME ę̄ and ME ĕ, and that it was this glide vowel which determined the subsequent development of the vowels; on this point see § 198, Note. (3) It takes no account of variant pronunciations existing in ME and eModE which explain the variety of PresE pronunciation that Luick tries to bring under one hypothesis. PresE [əː] in *earn*, *early*, &c. descends not from ME ę̄, but from the ME and eModE variant ĕ. *Early*, if it retained the variant developed from ME ę̄, would be [ɛəli] not [əːli]; cf. the present Scottish pronunciation, and Cooper's [ɛːrli] (see below). PresE [iə] in *tear* sb. 'lacrima' has been explained above, from late ME ẹ̄, not late ME ę̄. Except possibly before final *r* (see below), there is no need to assume for ME ę̄ before *r* more than one extremely simple development: that it remained as [ɛː] throughout the eModE period without any raising, because of the retractive influence of the *r*, and became [ɛə] with the vocalization of *r*. The possible abnormal and occasional special development before final *r* has left no traces in PresE.

§ 204. If the process assumed above, that ME ę̄ before *r* was never fronted from its ME value of open [ɛː], is correct, then identity between ME ę̄ and ME ā before *r* will result not from any change in the pronunciation of ME ę̄ before *r*, but from the fronting of ME ā, before *r* as well as in free position, through [æː] to [ɛː]. We saw above (§§ 98 seq.) that from other evidence it appears that ME ā was pronounced [æː] in good speech until about 1650, but that it was [ɛː] in some forms of speech during the sixteenth century and that this pronunciation [ɛː] became the normal one after 1650. On my theory of the development of ME $\bar{e}$ and ME $\bar{a}$ before r, then, we should expect that identity before r will be shown in some forms of speech during the sixteenth century and will become common after about 1650; and this is precisely what we do find.

The detailed evidence is as follows. ME $\bar{ẹ}$ before r is not explicitly distinguished from ME $\bar{ẹ}$ in free position by any orthoepist before 1650, and Wallis (1654), Price (1665), and the *Treatise of Stops* (1680) still make no distinction; the reason is that in careful speech before 1650 ME $\bar{ẹ}$ had not been fronted from open [ɛː] and that this pronunciation was still in conservative use after 1650 (see §§ 112–14). But there did exist varieties of speech in which ME $\bar{ẹ}$ had in free position been fronted to [eː] and had left behind ME $\bar{ẹ}$ before r at the value [ɛː], which in these varieties of speech had been reached by ME $\bar{a}$; and of the resulting identity before r we get occasional hints. Bullokar uses the transcriptions *bār* 'bear' sb., *āring* 'earing' ('ploughing'), and *tār* beside *tẹ̄r* 'tear' vb., which depend on this identity; but it is identity in other and less careful speech than he normally chooses to represent, for he distinguishes ME $\bar{ẹ}$ before r from ME $\bar{a}$ in all other words. In two of these cases he has departed from his stricter standard for the special purpose of getting a visual distinction between the transcriptions cited and *bær* 'bear' vb., *ær* 'ear' (of the head) and *eer* 'ear' (of corn) respectively. Daines (see Vol. I, p. 335) knew a pronunciation in which ME $\bar{ẹ}$ in *hair* was identical with ME $\bar{a}$ in *hare*, but also one in which the two sounds were still distinct, and perhaps regarded the latter as more correct. Hodges, *EP* (see Vol. I, pp. 175–7), also shows identity of ME $\bar{ẹ}$ in *hair* with ME $\bar{a}$, though otherwise in *EP* ME $\bar{ẹ}$ and ME $\bar{a}$ are carefully distinguished even before r. In *SH-PD* Hodges gives the following pairings in his 'homophone' lists: the 'alike' list (which generally gives the same pronunciation as *EP*, but admits a few less careful pronunciations) has *hare* paired with *hair* (cf. *EP*) and *bare* paired with *bear* sb. and vb.; the 'near alike' list (which is based on less careful pronunciation) repeats the identification of *bare* with *bear* and adds *chare* paired with *cheer* (the latter has late ME $\bar{ẹ}$ by lowering of ME $\bar{ẹ}$). It looks as though the *bare*: *bear* pairing, which gets into both lists, was intended only for the 'near alike' list and is included in the 'alike' list by error. The position in Hodges is thus essentially the same as in Bullokar and Daines, and these three orthoepists do no more than give us hints, when there is some special reason (Bullokar's desire to make visual distinctions, or the conventional *ai* spelling of *hair*), that beside the more conservative and 'correct' pronunciation in which ME $\bar{ẹ}$ was [ɛː] and ME $\bar{a}$ [æː] in all positions, there existed a more advanced pronunciation in which ME $\bar{ẹ}$ was [eː] in free position but [ɛː] before r, where it had been overtaken by ME $\bar{a}$ as it reached that value.

After 1650 the most important evidence is Cooper's; for him ME $\bar{a}$ is [ɛː]

§ 204] PART 3: INFLUENCE OF *r* 731

in free position (when not diphthongized to [ɛə]), and has overtaken ME *ẹ̄*, as his lists show, in *bear, beard, early, earn, rehearse, search, sheard, swear, tear* vb., *wear*, and (in the Latin text) *shear* vb. He expresses a preference for the spelling *mare-maid* against *mair-maid* 'mermaid'; both forms imply the identity of ME *ẹ̄* before *r* (OE *mĕre*) with ME *ā*. It will be noticed that in this last and other words Cooper preserves ME *ẹ̄* where PresE has only [ə:] from ME *ĕ* (cf. § 203, Note). WSC-RS, in part following Cooper, shows that ME *ā* is identical with ME *ẹ̄* before *r* in *there, were, where, bear, swear, tear* vb., and *wear*. Cooper's evidence confirms that of other sources which often depend on a less correct pronunciation but which in this case must show the normal post-1650 pronunciation. The shorthand-writer Bridges (1659) gives *sware* 'swear'. The 'phonetically spelt' lists of Strong (1676) and Brown (1700) give similar *a*-spellings for *bear, their* (Strong) and *bear, pear, swear, tear* sb. 'rent', and *wear* (Brown). 'Homophone' lists, following and adding to those of Hodges (see above), give pairings of ME *ẹ̄r* and *ār* words from Wharton onwards, including those that do not show (as many do) a general identity of ME *ā* and *ẹ̄* in all positions. Thus the extremely careful list of Coles, *Schoolmaster*, has the pairings *bare* : *bear*, *sware* : *swear*, *pare* : *pear*, and *ware* : *were* : *wear* and also shows [ɛ:] in *their* and *there*, and Cooper in his 'alike' list gives similar evidence. Certain lists seem to show open [ɛ:] identical with ME *ā* in many words which now have [iə] < eModE [i:] < late ME *ẹ̄*; thus in *tear* 'lacrima', *shear* vb., and *peer* (first recorded thus in Wharton's list), *weir* (first in Price), *rear* vb. and adj. (first in Strong), *pier* and *sphere* (first in Young). Cooper follows these lists as regards *rear* vb. and *shear*, but relegates to his 'different' list the pairing of *tear* 'lacrima' (which he says is pronounced *teer*) and *tear* vb. (pronounced *tare*). Coles, on the other hand, avoids these pairings altogether, except in the careless list of the *Eng.-Lat. Dict.*, and even in this he adopts only the pairing *share* : *shear*. It would seem that in good seventeenth-century speech the PresE distinctions between words with [iə], earlier [i:] < late ME *ẹ̄*, and words with [ɛə], earlier [ɛ:] < late ME *ẹ̄*, had already, for the most part, been established.

There is no valid evidence of the failure of the retraction. It is true that Robinson, whose evidence shows that he normally used [ɛ:] for ME *ā* and [e:] for ME *ẹ̄* in free position, and who would therefore be expected to show that ME *ẹ̄* before *r* was identical with ME *ā* and different from ME *ẹ̄* in free position, does not do so; he identifies ME *ẹ̄* before final *r* (as in *bear*; so also in the plural *bears*) and intervocalic *r* (as in *dreary*) with ME *ẹ̄* in free position. Similarly Newton, though he had [e:] for ME *ẹ̄*, fails to distinguish the vowel of *mere*. This evidence might show [e:] for ME *ẹ̄* before *r*; but it is more likely that Robinson and Newton, in giving these transcriptions, have been influenced by the ordinary spelling and by the fact that, in what was still in Robinson's time the normal careful pronunciation of StE and in

Newton's a surviving pronunciation, ME $\bar{e}$ in free position as before *r* was still [ɛ:] and ME $\bar{a}$ was still [æ:]. In other words, these transcriptions of ME $\bar{e}r$ words are based on a more conservative pronunciation than is most of Robinson's and Newton's evidence on ME $\bar{a}$ and ME $\bar{e}$; the inconsistency is easy to understand at a time when pronunciation varied considerably in this connexion. Similarly Smith and Holder, who appear to have [e:] for ME $\bar{e}$ in free position and should therefore distinguish it from ME $\bar{e}$ before *r*, appear to deny the existence in English of a sound [ɛ:]; the explanation is that for them [ɛ:], used for ME $\bar{e}$ before *r*, was simply a contextual variant of the 'long *e*' phoneme, of which the principal member was [e:] (see § 114 (iii) above).

There is, however, a slight possibility that before final *r* retraction might sometimes exceptionally fail; for in general final *r* exercises a weaker retractive power than preconsonantal *r*. The normal development would then be for the vowel, after fronting from [ɛ:] to [e:], to remain fixed at the latter value until diphthongization and the development of *r* to [ə] gave a PresE pronunciation [eiə] (thus *[beiə] 'bear' to rhyme with *payer*, &c.). No such pronunciations are found in Present StE, but Wright, §§ 65 and 134, records [eiə] for ME $\bar{e}r$ in a few isolated cases in scattered dialects. The orthoepists give no hint of a special development before final *r* except for two dubious cases in Cooper. In dealing with the pronunciations of the digraph *ea*, he puts most words which have ME $\bar{e}$ before final *r* either in a list illustrating the pronunciation *ee* ([i:] < late ME $\bar{e}$) or in one illustrating 'long *a*', i.e. ME $\bar{a}$ ([ɛ:] < late ME $\bar{e}$ without fronting); but *forswear* appears in a list illustrating 'long *e*' ([e:] < late ME $\bar{e}$ with fronting in free position), though *swear* is in the 'long *a*' ([ɛ:]) list. But Cooper is here apparently using material drawn from Price, who did not recognize a distinction between ME $\bar{e}$ in free position and ME $\bar{e}$ before *r* (except by implication in his 'homophone' lists) and naturally includes *forswear* in the same list as other ME $\bar{e}$ words. The second case comes in Cooper's English text (not in the Latin text), in which there is added to the list of 'barbarous' pronunciations an entry '*their, there* (*thare*)'. But it is probable that the addition was hasty and ill-considered, and that Cooper meant to protest not against the pronunciation of *their* and *there* as if they were *thare*, but against spelling them *thare* because they were so pronounced. This is how *RS* (p. 133) took Cooper's meaning, for though it gives in its list (largely taken from Cooper) of words 'vulgarly spoken, and grossly mistaken in writing' the entry *thare* '*their, there*', it adds that 'though both have the same sound of *thare*; yet we never write *thare* with an (*a*)'. Cooper has evidently been careless in both cases, and we must, I think, conclude that there is no sound evidence to show that before final *r* fronting was occasionally permitted.

PresE shows [ɛə] < earlier [ɛ:] by retention of the original value of ME $\bar{e}$ (i) before final *r* (*pear*, &c.), (ii) before intervocalic *r* (*wearing, bearish*, &c.;

§ 204]   PART 3: INFLUENCE OF *r*   733

but we must allow for the influence of the words from which these are formed), and (iii) before *r* plus consonant in *girl* pronounced [gɛəl], from the ME variant *gẹrl(e)* (in all other cases StE has lost the long vowel, as it has in the normal pronunciation of *girl*).

Note 1: Cheke gives *sware* 'swear' infin. and Smith *tār* 'tear' infin. These forms may, however, be explained as analogical, with ME *ā* derived from the p.t. in place of the original ME *ẹ̄* of the infinitive. *Tear* has a p.t. (sing. and pl.) *tāre* from the fourteenth to the seventeenth century, beside the old p.t. pl. *tẹ̄ren* (to the fourteenth century; fifteenth century *ter*, *terre*) and perhaps a p.t. sing. **tẹ̄r* (cf. *bẹ̄r* p.t. sing. of *bear*; such forms are of course derived from the plural). *Swear*, which passes into the *tear*, *bear* conjugation, has a p.t. (sing. and pl.) *sware* from the fourteenth to the seventeenth century, beside fourteenth- and fifteenth-century *swere* (sing. as well as pl.). Variation between *ā* and *ẹ̄* in these two and similar verbs in the p.t. might well influence the infin.; such analogical influence of the p.t. on the infin. of strong verbs is common. Smith, it is true, has [e:] for ME *ẹ̄* and so could in theory have [ɛ:] for ME *ā* and therefore identity of ME *ẹ̄* and *ā* before *r*; but actually he has [æ:] for ME *ā* (see § 101 (iv)) and identity of ME *ẹ̄* and *ā* before *r* is therefore impossible in his own speech. But in the advanced Northern and Eastern pronunciation (in which the fronting of ME *ẹ̄* and *ā* was much more rapid than in StE) identity of ME *ẹ̄* and *ā* before *r* would occur early, and this circumstance may have influenced both Cheke (who was born in Cambridge) and Smith (who was born in Essex of a Lancashire mother).

On Gil's long vowel, identified with ME *ā*, in *heard*, see Vol. I, pp. 145–6; it is not ME *ẹ̄* become identical with ME *ā* before *r*, for this explanation, though possible, would be contrary to the whole tenor of Gil's evidence.

Note 2: *Searce* 'a sieve' is not developed normally from OF *saas*, and its spellings and the pronunciations given for it by the orthoepists do not show that ME *ẹ̄* has become identical with ME *ā* before *r*. See § 8, Note 2.

Note 3: Spellings to illustrate the identity of ME *ẹ̄* and *ā* before *r* are not cited by Zachrisson, *Eng. Vowels*; Wyld, *Coll. Eng.*; and Kihlbom, who do not deal with this development despite its important bearing on the development of ME *ẹ̄* and *ā* in free position, nor by Horn, § 86, and Luick, § 510. *OED* provides little evidence of *are* spellings for late ME *ẹ̄r*, except in the verbs *shear* (see under *share* vb.), *bear*, *tear*, *swear*, *wear*, in all of which *a*-forms in the infinitive stem are recorded at some time or other between the fifteenth and the eighteenth centuries; in each of these cases we must reckon with the analogical influence on the infinitive of the variation between ME *ẹ̄* and *ā* in the strong p.t. (cf. Note 1 above), and such cases therefore have no value as evidence. *Ere* has *a*-forms from the thirteenth to the sixteenth century, but these are due to an OE **ār* or ON *ár*, or to OE unstressed *ǣr* beside stressed *ǣr*. *Gear* has fourteenth- and fifteenth-century *gare*, fifteenth- and sixteenth-century *gayre*, *gaire*, *geyre*; these are Northern and Eastern forms which show the analogical influence of *gare* adj. from ON *gørr*, *geyrr*, &c. *Weir* has fifteenth- and seventeenth-century *ware* and modern dialectal *wair*, *ware* forms, but as this noun is from the stem of the OE verb *werian*, we must allow for the possible analogical influence of the vb. *ware* < OE *warian*. *Shear(s)* sb. has a sixteenth-century *share* sing. and a seventeenth-century *shares* pl., but we must allow for the possible analogical influence of the verb *share*, itself a variant of the verb *shear* developed by analogical and not phonetic processes.

There are apparently few spellings which certainly show identity of ME *ẹ̄* and *ā* before *r*, but such are the sixteenth- and seventeenth-century *pare* 'pear' and the sixteenth- to eighteenth-century *mare*- and *mair*- forms of *mermaid*. In the sixteenth century there occur the Scottish forms *baird* 'beard' and *pairse* 'pierce', but Scottish pronunciation was more advanced than StE in this respect. Early *ei* and *ai* spellings, e.g. in fifteenth- and sixteenth-century forms of *spear* and fifteenth- to eighteenth-century forms of the infinitive and strong p.t. of *wear*, are Scottish and Northern, and show the use of *ei* and *ai* as graphic symbols for ME *ẹ̄* and *ā*. The interchange in these spellings between *ei* and *ai* may show Northern identity of ME *ẹ̄* and *ā*, but is of no significance for StE. In the South we could have *ei* used for ME *ẹ̄* by inverted spelling on the model of words like *deceive* which vary between ME *ẹ̄* and ME *ei*; cf. the PresE spelling of *weir*. *Spear*, which has *ei* in the fifteenth-century Bodleian MS of Trevisa, *De Prop. Rerum* (see *OED*, s.v.), may be an example of this use of *ei* for ME *ẹ̄* in the South; but the language of this manuscript does not represent Trevisa's own dialect, and seems Northernized.

Words which have late ME *ẹ̄* by lowering of earlier ME *ẹ̄* generally are not recorded with spellings that show identity of late ME *ẹ̄* and *ā* before *r*, but *clear* has an eighteenth- and nineteenth-century dialectal form *clair*, and *fierce* has a sixteenth-century form *fayrse*, which may represent StE pronunciation (*OED* does not describe the form as Scottish or Northern, but such information is not always given in the early volumes; the form is not illustrated by a quotation). Other forms are of no significance for the identity of ME *ẹ̄* and *ā* before *r*. Fourteenth- and fifteenth-century *pare* 'peer' is obviously due to Italian *pare* or Latin *parem*. Thirteenth-century *bare* 'bier' is probably from ON *barar* fem. pl. 'funeral bier'. *Ei*, *ey* forms of *dear*, *here*, *steer*, *pier*, &c. are Scottish or Northern, and occur from the fourteenth century onwards.

Note 4: Rhymes between ME *ẹ̄* and ME *ā* before *r* do not seem to be common before 1650. Willis (1651) includes no such rhymes in his lists. But I have found in the *Oxford Book of Sixteenth Century Verse* eleven *ẹ̄r* : *ār* rhymes, of which eight are dated before 1600, but none before 1590 (except perhaps an undated example on p. 160). The late ME *ẹ̄r* words involved include *fear* (five times), *ear* sb., *tears* 'lacrimae', *dear*, and *year*. Wyld, *Rhymes*, pp. 65–66, cites no examples earlier than Drayton, who has *cares* : *tears*. Similarly Cowley has *ear* : *share*, *there* : *declare*, Waller *fear* : *care*, Dryden *spares* : *tears*, *fear* : *share*, and Swift *shares* : *ears*. Rhymes between ME *ẹ̄* and ME *ai* do not provide certain evidence that ME *ẹ̄* has failed to be fronted before *r* and has become identical with ME *ā*, for Hart's and other evidence shows that ME *ai* when monophthongized sometimes became identical with ME *ẹ̄* and not with ME *ā*; this development probably explains Sackville's rhyme *despair* : *fear*. But such rhymes from Cowley onwards without doubt depend on the normal development, whereby ME *ai* becomes identical with ME *ā*, which in turn becomes identical with ME *ẹ̄* before *r*. But it should be observed that rhymes between ME *ẹ̄* words and *hair* are of no significance, for the latter has a more common variant pronunciation with ME *ẹ̄*.

(d) *Limitation of fronting of ME* ā *and* ai

§ 205. Fronting of ME *ā* before *r* proceeded simultaneously with fronting of ME *ā* in free position until the value [ɛː] was reached, where ME *ā* became identical both with ME *ẹ̄* before *r* (see under (*c*) immediately above) and with the monophthong developed from ME *ai* (see the following chapter). Thereafter no further fronting occurred, and before *r* ME *ā* and the monophthong developed from ME *ai* remained as [ɛː] while in free position they advanced to [eː] and ultimately were diphthongized in StE to [ei]. But because before 1700 ME *ā* and *ai* had been fronted in free position from [ɛː] to [eː] only in dialectal or advanced (and probably vulgar) speech, and because the fronting is recorded only in the most careless and least phonetic of our sources (see § 102), there is no evidence before 1700 of any distinction between the sounds in free position and before *r*; this is also the case in eighteenth-century books on pronunciation, and it is evident that [ɛː], after it had ceased to be the pronunciation of ME *ā* and *ai* in all positions, came to be generally (and legitimately) regarded as merely a contextual variant, not requiring separate description, of the 'long *a*' (or *ai*) phoneme, of which the dominant member was [eː]. The silence of late seventeenth-

and eighteenth-century sources on any distinctive pronunciation of 'long *a*' and *ai* before *r* does not mean that fronting to [e:] had occurred before *r* as in other positions; the description of contextual variants was no part of the purpose of these writers, nor was their understanding of phonetics exact enough to permit it (see further the Note below). We must judge of what occurred *c.* 1700 from the evidence of nineteenth-century phoneticians and of the pronunciation of PresE, which regularly has [ɛə] < earlier [ɛ:] for ME *ā* and *ai* before *r*, and shows that the check to fronting beyond [ɛ:] occurred before *r* plus consonant (*scarce*; examples of *ai* are lacking), intervocalic *r* (*vary, fairy*), and before final *r* (*pare, pair*).

> *Note*: Luick assumes that ME *ā* (*ai*) before *r* shared the fronting of ME *ā* (*ai*) in free position not only till they reached the value [ɛ:], where they became identical with ME *ẹ̄* before *r*, but until they (and ME *ẹ̄* before *r* with them) had gone on again to close [e:]; from this they were retracted to [ɛ:] in the eighteenth century when the assimilatory influence of the [ə] glide (to which, and not to the *r* itself, Luick attributes the retractive power) was increased, probably in consequence of the disappearance of the consonant [r] in final position and before consonants. See Luick, § 568 (1). In Anm. 4 to this section Luick claims that chronology is against the assumption that ME *ā* (*ai*), and ME *ẹ̄* before *r* which had become identical with them, remained at the value [ɛ:] without being fronted, with ME *ā*(*ai*) in free position, to [e:]; he argues that ME *ā* in free position was [e:] in the second half of the seventeenth century, and that therefore orthoepists at this time should have noticed that 'long *a*' had a different pronunciation before *r* than in free position, whereas in fact no evidence of such a difference is found before the middle of the eighteenth century. But Luick (who fails to interpret rightly Cooper's important evidence) is wrong in saying that ME *ā* was already [e:] in the second half of the seventeenth century; this was true only of the advanced pronunciation recorded in spelling-books, 'homophone' lists, and the like, which are not interested in, and have no adequate means of describing, such details as the variant pronunciations of 'long *a*' before different consonants. Good orthoepists like Cooper, who might have recorded such a difference had it existed in their speech, still used [ɛ:] for ME *ā* (*ai*) in free position; and so may some early eighteenth-century orthoepists. In any case the silence of early eighteenth-century orthoepists on the matter is of little significance, as is pointed out above, for their works are in general of poor quality, being mostly of the type of seventeenth-century spelling-books, and often mere plagiarisms of seventeenth-century works. Jones (1701), who is a valuable authority, is precluded by his method (the 'phonetically spelt' technique invented by Coles) from expressing any differences in the value of 'long *a*' in different circumstances.
>
> Luick's view is an elaboration, with closer argument, of that of Horn, § 92, and Ekwall, § 30, both of whom regard ME *ā* before *r* as having been fronted to close [e:] before being retracted in the eighteenth century to [ɛ:]. The chief objection to this view is the unlikelihood that the following *r*, which had been exercising a retractive influence since *c.* 1400, would ever have allowed the fronting to [e:], especially as ME *ẹ̄* had already been affected by the retractive influence while ME *ā* was reaching the value [ɛ:]. The view adopted by these three scholars involves the highly improbable assumption that ME *ẹ̄* was retracted to become identical with ME *ā* as [ɛ:], then allowed to be fronted to [e:], and then for a second time retracted to [ɛ:]. It is obviously preferable to assume that the following *r* never permitted either ME *ẹ̄* or ME *ā* to get further forward than [ɛ:].
>
> On Luick's view that the lowering of ME *ā* &c. is later than, and probably indirectly due to, the loss of *r* in the eighteenth century see § 210, Note 2 (end).

(e) The Development of ME ǭ before r

§ 206. The theory of the development of ME *ǭ* before *r* presents some points of difficulty, owing to a certain imprecision of our evidence. No sixteenth- or seventeenth-century orthoepist distinguishes ME $\bar{\rho}$ before *r* from ME $\bar{\rho}$ in free position. Later evidence to the same effect must be briefly mentioned. Walker in 1775 says that *forge* is pronounced nearly as the words *foe urge* (see Jespersen, *ModE Gr*, § 13.352). It is clear that the only difference he recognizes between ME $\bar{\rho}$ in free position in *foe* and ME $\bar{\rho}$ (or its equivalent developed from ME $\bar{\rho}$ before *r*; see § 13 (2*b*)) in *forge* is that in the latter case it is followed by [ə]; and as it is inconceivable that ME $\bar{\rho}$ in free position was not close [o:] by raising at this time, it follows that Walker regards the *o* in *forge* as being also [o:]—more precisely, that on his evidence the word contains the diphthong [oə]. What must be the same pronunciation as Walker's continued in use in careful StE speech in the nineteenth century and is still occasionally heard from conservative speakers, and is the normal Northern dialectal pronunciation of ME $\bar{\rho}$ before *r*. Wright, *EDG*, § 126, gives this dialectal sound as either [oə] (with tense, close [o]) or (in some Northern and most Scottish dialects) close [o:] with no [ə] glide. The old-fashioned StE pronunciation is usually similarly described as [oə]. But *OED*, which gives this old-fashioned pronunciation for ME $\bar{\rho}$ before *r*, uses a different symbol for its first element than for close [o:] in French *chose* and the first element of the PresE diphthong in *no*. Jespersen, loc. cit., describes it as a more open sound than close [o:], though less open than PresE [ɒ:] in *awe*, *horse*, &c.

Now we have seen (§ 145) that ME $\bar{\rho}$ was probably originally a variety of open *o*, approximately 'cardinal open [ɔ:]' (or a little higher), and that it was raised in the course of the sixteenth and seventeenth centuries from this value to [o:]. Obviously the evidence on ME $\bar{\rho}$ before *r* could be interpreted as showing that it at first underwent the normal raising to [o:] and was at a later date again lowered; this is in fact the usual theory (so Horn, § 98; Ekwall, § 78; Luick, § 511). But the analogy of ME $\bar{e}$ tells against this view, for ME $\bar{e}$ was never raised before *r*; and though the development of the front and back vowels before *r* is not parallel in its later stages, it seems to be in its earlier (ME $\bar{e}$ and $\bar{o}$ both undergo normal raising to [i:] and [u:], but ME $\bar{e}$ and $\bar{\rho}$, it will be here argued, remain unchanged). Moreover, modern observers, as we have seen, differ in their analysis. The obvious explanation, which would accord with the known fact that *r* was already exercising its lowering influence by the relatively late date at which ME $\bar{\rho}$ was changing, in StE, from 'cardinal open [ɔ:]' to [o:], is that before *r* the change never occurred; but that [ɔ:] and [o:] were in the sixteenth and early seventeenth centuries merely diaphonic and contextual variants, and from about 1650 onwards merely contextual variants, of the 'long *o*' phoneme. The older sound came to be used only before *r*, the new sound in free position; [o:] was therefore the dominant member of the phoneme, but both it and [ɔ:] stood sharply contrasted to the lower open [ɒ:] < ME *au* and ME *ŏ* by lengthening (the '*au*' phoneme). In consequence, the distinction between

ME ǭ before r and ME ǭ in free position was, so long as the r was pronounced, a nicety of phonetic analysis of no practical significance in English, and was therefore not made by seventeenth- and eighteenth-century observers (nor, less justifiably, by Wright in *EDG*); but the evidence of such observers need not be interpreted literally.

I should conclude, then, that in all probability there developed, during the late sixteenth and seventeenth centuries, a differentiation within the 'long o' phoneme, ME ǭ remaining at or about cardinal [ɔː] before r but becoming [oː] elsewhere, but that this distinction, being contextual and of no significance, passed unobserved until the development of precise scientific phonetics in the later nineteenth century. On the late identification of ME ǭ before r with [ɒː] < ME ŏ by lengthening, which is most easily explained in accordance with the view here expressed, see § 210 below.

Note 1: It follows from the view here put forward that when, about 1600, eModE [uː] was lowered before r to identity with ME ǭ, it must have assumed immediately, or at least very quickly, the value 'cardinal open [ɔː]' and not close [oː]; but this would be natural, for once it was identified with ME ǭ it would of course take on that value of the latter which was used before r.

Note 2: Jespersen, *ModE Gr*, § 13.351, argues that ME ǭ before r was subject to two conflicting tendencies: (*a*) raising, which resulted in its becoming [oː], a pronunciation which explains sixteenth-, seventeenth-, and eighteenth-century evidence, and (one could add further) the more modern StE and dialectal evidence; and (*b*) lowering before r, which tended to keep the vowel where it was or even to lower it still further, and so gave the normal PresE pronunciation with fully open [ɒː]. Jespersen himself would appear to regard the conservative pronunciation of the nineteenth century as having a fairly low vowel which was produced by the tendency to keep ME ǭ before r more or less where it had always been, though his meaning is not altogether clear. This view combines the two alternatives discussed above. The objection to it is that it assumes two different directions of change at the same time. Jespersen argues that the raising of ME ǭ before r with ME ǭ in free position is shown by the pronunciation [fouksl] 'forecastle'; but the early loss of r, which must be assumed (with Ekwall, § 131) to explain why diphthongization is permitted, must also account for the failure of the retractive influence of r to prevent the raising.

(f) Lowering of sixteenth-century [uː] *before* r

§ 207. About 1600 late sixteenth-century [uː], developed either from ME ǭ or from ME ū (diphthongization of which often failed before r) and occasionally also from ME [yː], &c. (see § 209 below), was lowered because of the influence of a following r until it became identical with the sound developed before r from ME ǭ, i.e. approximately 'cardinal open [ɔː]', a contextual variant of the [oː] phoneme (see immediately above). The lowering is first shown by the orthoepists in the seventeenth century; spellings and rhymes support this evidence, though there are one or two cases of possible sixteenth-century evidence of the lowering. The lowering of ME ẹ̄ to ę̄ before r does not provide an exact analogy (see §§ 201 above): lowering of ME ẹ̄ is earlier, and belongs to the late ME period; it is a direct lowering from [eː] to [ɛː], not of eModE [iː] < ME ẹ̄; it occurs almost without exception in native English words before r plus consonant, whereas in the seventeenth century unlowered [u:] was still common in such words; and before final *r* the lowering of ME *ẹ̄* is recorded most commonly in the sixteenth century and tends to disappear in the seventeenth, whereas the lowering of [u:], not found in the sixteenth century, becomes increasingly common in the seventeenth.

Note 1: Evidence in Bullokar which might possibly be held to show the lowering is open to other and preferable explanations. *OED* does not record *oa* spellings, which show the lowering, until the seventeenth century (when they are still rare, even in such words as *coarse* and *hoard*; cf. Luick, § 508 (2) and Anm. 1), except that *whore* has *oa* in the sixteenth century—a more precise date cannot be given, for *OED* unfortunately cites no examples. Horn, § 105, Anm. 1, refers to sixteenth-century *oa* spellings of *floor* and *course*, again without examples or precise dates. (It may be observed that Bullokar, using *course* in the sense of the PresE *coarse*, has the spelling *coorc'*, which shows a pronunciation [ku:rs].) The *oa* spelling in *coarse* and *hoard* becomes common only after 1700. Levins provides a sixteenth-century rhyme which might show lowering, but equally may depend on the ME raising of ME *ǭ* to ME *ọ̄*; in any case his evidence would refer to Northern dialectal and not StE pronunciation (see further § 208, Note 2(*a*)). Foreign orthoepists appear not to show [ɔ:] until the seventeenth century (see Horn, loc. cit.), and even then their evidence refers mostly to *poor*, which had ME *ǭ* beside *ọ̄*.

Note 2: The lowering presumably affected eModE [u:] < late ME *ọ̄* by raising of ME *ǭ* in such words as *more*, but evidence cannot of course be found, since the effect of the lowering was to produce a pronunciation identical with that developed from the normal unraised ME *ǭ*. But the disappearance of the raised [u:] variant in such words may have been assisted by the lowering, as Luick, § 511, suggests (see § 149, Note 1 above).

§ 208. Evidence of the lowering is as follows:

(i) Sixteenth-century [u:] < ME *ǭ* before *r* plus consonant. *Hoard* has unlowered [u:] in Wharton, Price, and *WSC-RS*, but [ɔ:] by lowering in Robinson and Coles. *Sword* has [u:] in Butler and Cooper, but [ɔ:] in Coles. *Word* has [u:] possibly in Salesbury. *Forth* has [u:] in Cheke, Laneham, Bullokar, Mulcaster, Gil (beside [ɔ:]), Butler, Cooper, and *WSC-RS*, but [ɔ:] in Robinson, Gil (once, beside [u:]), Daines, Hodges, and Coles. *Afford* has [u:] in Butler, Wharton (followed by J. Smith), Price, and *WSC-RS*. *Fourth* has [u:] (probably developed from ME *ǭ* in *fǭrþe* < OE *fēorða*) in *RS*, but [ɔ:] in *WSC* (see Note 1 (*e*) below). *Toward* is 'phonetically' spelt *toard*, which shows [ɔ:], by Strong; but the explanation may be that *to* itself varies between [o:] and [u:]. The unlowered [u:], it will be seen, remains common in the seventeenth century.

(ii) Sixteenth-century [u:] < ME *ǭ* before final *r*. *Floor* has [u:] in Bullokar and Price, but [ɔ:] in *RS*. *Moor* (tract of land) has [u:] in Price, and [ɔ:] in *RS*. *Whore* has [u:] in Cheke, Smith, Bullokar, Verstegan, Butler, Hodges, Price (followed by Lye), and Cooper, but [ɔ:] in Daines, Coles, Brown, and *RS*. *Boor* (with Dutch [u:] identified with fifteenth-century [u:] < ME *ọ̄*) has [ɔ:] in Robinson. *Moor* (the race) has [ɔ:] in Coles, probably also in Cooper (who says that the pronunciation is 'the same or near' to that of *more*, in which he has [ɔ:]; but his hesitancy may mean that either *Moor* or *more* varied in pronunciation). The evidence shows that the lowering occurs as early before final *r* as before *r* plus consonant; and though the amount of evidence is hardly sufficient, it would seem that it was as common in the seventeenth century before final *r* as before *r* plus consonant.

(iii) Sixteenth-century [uː] < undiphthongized ME *ū* before *r* plus consonant. *Bourn* has [uː] in Hodges and Cooper. *Course* and its derivatives (including the by-form *coarse*) have [uː] in Hart, Laneham, Bullokar (in *coarse*), Butler, Hodges, Wallis, Price, Lye, Cooper, *RS*, and Brown (beside [ɔː]), and [ɔː] in Coles, *WSC*, and Brown. *Court* has [uː] in Laneham, Gil, Hodges, Wallis, Price, the *Welsh Breviary*, Lye, Cooper, and *RS*, but [ɔː] in Robinson, Coles, and Brown. (*Per*)*form* has [uː] in Cheke, Laneham, Hodges, Wharton, Cooper, Coles, and *WSC-RS*. *Gourd* has [uː] in Lye and *RS*, but [ɔː] in Daines, Price, Coles, Strong, *The Protestant Tutor*, and Brown. *Mourn* has [uː] in Cheke, Bullokar, Butler, Hodges, Wallis, Young, and Cooper, but [ɔː] in Robinson, Coles, Strong, and Brown; Newton varies between the two. *Source* has [uː] in Wallis, Lye, and Cooper, but [ɔː] in Coles. Unlowered [uː] is in general more common.

(iv) Sixteenth-century [uː] < undiphthongized ME *ū* before final *r*. *Pour* is recorded only with [uː] (or diphthongized [ʌu]). Lowering to [ɔː] is probably shown in *your* by its equation with *yore* in the 'homophone' lists of Price and *WSC*, but it is possible that the latter word has [uː] from late ME *ǭ* by raising of ME *ǭ*. There is thus no certain evidence (for further possible evidence see Note 4 (*a*)) of the lowering before final *r* in the orthoepists, and it would seem, though there are too few instances for us to speak with assurance, that the lowering of [uː] < ME *ū* was less common before final *r* than before *r* plus consonant.

Note 1: The following notes relate to sub-section (i) above.
(*a*) The words cited have also a variant in ME *ǒ*; see § 16.
(*b*) Words adopted from French cannot be cited as examples, for such words normally have ME *ǭ* except when a labial precedes the vowel, and even then ME *ǭ* may occur as a variant to ME *ǭ*: cf. § 13 (2*b*).
(*c*) The evidence of rhymes and rhyme-lists is necessarily ambiguous, since rhymes between ME *ǭ* and ME *ǭ* may depend on ME raising of the latter as well as on ModE lowering of the former. Levins may have [uː] in *hoard* and *sword*. Willis and Poole rhyme many of the words cited above with ME *ǭr* words; for Willis at least the more probable explanation is that eModE [uː] has been lowered to [ɔː].
(*d*) Bullokar gives a long vowel, identified with ME *ǭ*, in *afford* and *churl*, where it might show lowering (in the sixteenth century, earlier than our other evidence) of [uː] < ME *ǭ*; but a more probable explanation is that the words show lengthening before *r* of ME *ǒ* (see § 46, Note 1).
(*e*) Hodges shows [ɔː] in *fourth* (contrast *RS* above), but it may be due to the analogical influence of *four* with [ɔː] < ME *ou*.
(*f*) The word *board* is a special case, for the OE words from which it primarily descends and which give ME *ǭ* (beside *ǒ*), are reinforced in ME by a word (ultimately Germanic) adopted from French, which affects the meanings considerably (see *OED*) and may affect the pronunciation, for it would have in ME both ME *ǭ* and (since a labial precedes) ME *ǭ*. Such influence from French no doubt accounts for the occurrence of *oa* spellings in this word in the sixteenth century, as early as More. But the evidence of the orthoepists seems to show only the early seventeenth-century lowering: [uː] occurs in Salesbury, Levins

(probably), Bullokar, Butler, Merriott, and Cooper, but [ɔ:] in Gil, Hodges, Price, Coles, and probably in the 'homophone' lists from Wharton's onwards, in which it is equated with *bor'd* (which might however have [u:] < late ME *ǭ* by raising of ME *ǭ*).

Note 2: The following notes relate to sub-section (ii) above.

(*a*) Rhymes are ambiguous evidence (cf. Note 1 (*c*) above). Levins rhymes *whore* with *bore*, but the latter may have [u:] by raising in ME of ME *ǭ* to ME *ǭ*, especially as raising was particularly common in Northern dialects; in any case his evidence cannot hold for StE. Seventeenth-century rhymes, however, probably depend for the most part on lowering of eModE [u:]; Willis rhymes *whore* with *oar* (see Vol. I, p. 428) and Poole rhymes *floor* and *moor* with *oar* and *ore*, *floors* and *moors* with *oars* and *course*, and *whor'd* with *snor'd*. 'Homophone' list pairings are similarly ambiguous, but probably depend as a rule on lowering; from Wharton's list onwards we find the pairings *whore* : *hoar*, *moor* : *more*, *boor* : *boar*. However, Cocker's *whore* : *hoar* : *hour* seems more likely to depend on [u:] in all three words, though [ɔ:] by lowering is possible in *hour* as in *whore*; this case at least shows how unreliable these pairings are as evidence.

(*b*) *Door* and *poor* cannot be cited as evidence of lowering, for both words had ME *ǭ* as well as ME *ǭ*; on *door* see § 155, and on *poor* see § 154.

Note 3: The following notes relate to sub-section (iii) above.

(*a*) Rhymes provide only ambiguous evidence. Poole rhymes *bourn*, *course*, *nurse*, *scourge*, and *source* (all of which in his speech must have had a long vowel from ME *ū*) with ME *ǭ* words; these rhymes may well show lowering, but might depend on [u:] by raising to ME *ǭ* of ME *ǭ*. Earlier, Willis rhymes *gourd* with ME *ǭ* words. A special case is Bullokar's rhyme of *source* with *force*, which almost certainly depends on [u:] (in the latter word from the ME variant *ǭ*), though Bullokar himself unintelligently transcribes *source* with his symbol for [ʌu] and *force* with his symbol for [o:] (from the ME variant in *ǭ*). In view of the ambiguity of rhymes, there is little point in citing those of poets; but one which seems likely to depend on lowering of [u:] (and if so gives early evidence of it) is Barnfield's of *mourn I* (ME *ū*) with *scorn I* and *forlorn me* (ME *ǭ*) in 1597.

'Homophone' list pairings are also ambiguous. Hodges's pairing of *course* with *corpse* depends on [u:], which is recorded for both words in his *EP*. Other pairings may show lowering.

(*b*) Bullokar gives [ɔ:] in (*per*)*form*, but it represents a ME variant in *ǭ* (see § 13 (2 *b*)) and not lowering of [u:] < ME *ū*.

Note 4: The following notes relate to subsection (iv) above.

(*a*) Cocker's pairing of *hour* with *hoar* (and *whore*) may show lowering of undiphthongized [u:] in *hour* to [ɔ:], but *hoar* seems more likely to have [u:] by raising of ME *ǭ*.

(*b*) *Pour* is in reality a special case, for fifteenth-century spellings *poar* and *pore* seem to point to an unexplained variant with *ǭ* (cf. the fourteenth-century forms *pore* and *poer*). Cf. *OED*, and see § 165, Note 5.

§ 209. Summing up the evidence, we may say that there is just a hint that the lowering influence was more powerful when *r* was followed by a consonant than when it was final. The lowering is shown most often by Robinson, Coles, and Brown, and sporadically by Gil, Daines, Hodges, Price, Strong, *The Protestant Tutor*, Cooper, and *RS*. The evidence is thus continuous throughout the seventeenth century, but unlowered [u:] seems to remain more common than lowered [ɔ:]; several of the authors who occasionally show lowering have more frequent [u:] in comparable words. The lowered pronunciation later became more common, but PresE pronunciation still shows variation. Sixteenth-century [u:] < ME *ǭ* before *r* plus consonant has been regularly lowered in *hoard*, *forth*, *afford*, and *fourth*, for which *OED* gives the conservative pronunciation [ɔ:ə] and Daniel Jones,

English Pronouncing Dictionary, the later and now more normal [ɒ:]. *Sword*, according to *OED*, varies in the conservative pronunciation between lowered [ɔ:ə] < ME ǭ and [ɒ:] by lengthening of ME ǒ; the normal PresE [ɒ:] (recorded by Jones, op. cit.) may represent either of these. Sixteenth-century [u:] < ME ǭ before final *r* is regularly lowered in *floor* and *whore*, for which *OED* gives [ɔ:ə] and Jones [ɒ:]. The different *moor* words vary; *OED* and Jones both give preference to unlowered [u(:)ə] over the lowered variants [ɔ(:)ə] (recorded by *OED* and by Jones), [ɒə], and [ɒ:] (recorded by Jones). *Boor* is recorded by *OED* and Jones only with unlowered [u(:)ə]. Sixteenth-century [u:] < ME ū before *r* plus consonant is regularly lowered in *court* and *source*, for which *OED* gives [ɔ:ə] and Jones [ɒ:]; so normally it is in *mourn*, for which *OED* gives only [ɔ:ə] though Jones records the rare [uə] beside normal [ɒ:]. *Bourn* is given by *OED* only with [ɔ:ə], but Jones gives [uə] preference to [ɔə], [ɒə], and [ɒ:], which he also records. *Gourd* has both [u(:)ə] and [ɔ(:)ə] in both *OED* and Jones, but *OED* gives preference to the latter and Jones (who does not record [ɒə] or [ɒ:] in this word) to the former. *OED* gives only [ɒ:] by lengthening of ME ǒ in *perform*; Jones's [ɒ:] is presumably to be similarly explained, though it could go back through [ɔ:ə] to sixteenth-century [u:] and ME ū. Sixteenth-century [u:] < ME ū before final *r* is regularly lowered in *pour*, for which *OED* gives [ɔ:ə] and Jones [ɒ:]; but this word is a special case (see § 165, Note 5). *Your* varies; *OED* rather uncatholically gives only [u:ə] for the strong form, but Jones records [ɒ:], [ɒə], [ɔə], and [uə], in that order of priority. The predominance of the lowered pronunciations over the unlowered [uə] seems to depend on two factors in PresE. (*a*) Lowering is more likely before *r* plus consonant than before *r* in final position. (*b*) It is most common in frequently used words. Unlowered [uə] occurs more or less often in *boor, moor, bourn, gourd, your,* and *mourn*; all these words, except for *your* (which is liable to the analogical influence of *you*) and *mourn* (in which [uə] is rare and artificial and generally confined to theatrical and clerical pronunciation, which seeks a distinction from *morn*), are in less frequent use than those in which unlowered [uə] has been lost.

The evidence of PresE shows that the lowering affected a class of word other than those already dealt with, i.e. such as *sure, lure,* and *pure*. ME [y:], *iu*, and *eu* (and at times also ME *ęu*) had already developed in some forms of speech to [ju:] by the late sixteenth century; in some phonetic contexts this [ju:] was reduced to [u:] in the seventeenth century, and perhaps earlier (see § 185). In this last development, there was nothing to distinguish [u:] in *sure* from [u:] in *floor* and *pour*; and even when reduction had not occurred and the fuller [ju:] was used, it was still true that in, for example, *pure* a late sixteenth-century [u:] preceded *r* and was thus exposed to its lowering influence. PresE does in fact show [ɔə], [ɒə], and [ɒ:] in such words (see Daniel Jones, *Outline of English Phonetics*, §§ 462–3), but though Jones, loc. cit., says that 'it is quite usual to hear good speakers' employ these lowered pronunciations, the best speech is still careful to retain unlowered [uə]; and this fact, in contrast to the position with ME $\bar{\varrho}$ and ME $\bar{u}$ words, is best explained by the hypothesis that early in the seventeenth century, when the lowering took place, fewer speakers pronounced words of the *sure, pure* type in such a way as to render them liable to lowering, so that the lowering took longer to affect careful StE. It is most frequent in common words (cf. Jones, loc. cit.). For possible seventeenth- and early eighteenth-century evidence of the lowering see § 244 (last paragraph).

That the lowering of sixteenth-century [uː] depends on the *r* itself, and not on a glide-vowel [ə] developed before it, is shown by the fact noted by Jones, op. cit., § 463, that the lowered pronunciations of [juː] < ME [yː], &c. are not used 'in words which have no *r* in the spelling, such as *influence* [ɪnfluəns], *arduous* [ɑːdjuəs]'. So also in *ewer, fewer*, in which the *r* was originally separated from the [juː] < ME *eu* by a vowel; but in *steward* and *Stuart*, for which Jones, loc. cit., records lowered pronunciations, early syncope of [ə] may have brought the *r* into direct contact with [juː] < ME *iu*.

Note 1: The view set out above is essentially that of Luick, §§ 507–8, except that Luick ascribes the lowering influence to the [ə] glide and not to the *r* itself; he describes the change as reaching completion before the end of the seventeenth century, and as being from [uːə] to [oːə]. Luick improperly cites *door* and *poor* as examples of the lowering (§ 508 and Anm. 1). So also does Horn, who in §§ 105, 109 describes the lowering process thus: early ModE [uː] was lowered in the sixteenth century to ϱ (his symbol for [ɒː]), which was raised in the seventeenth century to $\bar{\varrho}$ ([oː]), which later (in the nineteenth century, as Horn believes) was lowered again to ϱ ([ɒː]). This hypothesis is evidently highly improbable, for it assumes that in the first instance the lowering was to a lower position than that subsequently obtaining; if *r* had caused lowering as far as [ɒː] by the sixteenth century, is it likely that it would have allowed raising to [oː] in the seventeenth century, only to cause lowering again later? Horn's reason is his belief that the lowering occurred in the sixteenth century, and that the lowered sound was from then on identical with ME $\bar{\varrho}$, which he believed to be only [ɒː] in the sixteenth century and [oː] in the seventeenth. But in the advanced type of pronunciation in which the lowering would have first become evident, ME $\bar{\varrho}$ was already [oː] by the latter half of the sixteenth century (see § 145).

Note 2: Mutschmann, *Anglia Beiblatt*, xix (1908), 180, would explain the PresE retention of [uə] as a variant in certain words (see above) as due to the influence of a preceding bilabial. In theory a bilabial might indeed favour retention of a following [uː], which has close lip-rounding, as against lowered vowels with decreased lip-rounding. But the facts hardly support Mutschmann's hypothesis. *Gourd* has no preceding bilabial, yet [uə] is common (Mutschmann would fall back on the suggestion that the pronunciation is influenced by French, but this is most unlikely); *pour* has no [uə] variant, despite the preceding bilabial (but this word is a special case), and in *mourn* the [uə] variant is extremely rare. Mutschmann has not taken into consideration ME [yː] words, in which lowering or retention of [uə] is clearly uninfluenced by the nature of the preceding consonant (see above and Jones, loc. cit.).

(g) *Lowering of* [ɔə] < *seventeenth-century* [ɔː] *before* r

§ 210. No further lowering before *r* of seventeenth-century [ɔː] (< ME ϱ and *ou* (in *four*) and in part < late sixteenth-century [uː]) is recorded by seventeenth- or eighteenth-century observers; thus Walker in the later eighteenth century still distinguishes ME ŏ before *r* (though it had been lengthened) from ME ǭ, &c. before *r*, and the same is true of other writers of the time. But PresE has [ɒə] or [ɒ:] both for ME ŏr and for ME ǭr, &c. *OED*, in its list of phonetic symbols, still keeps the old distinction; but Murray's article on the letter *o* (which has been overlooked in this connexion) shows that its distinction was not based on the normal speech of 'London and the South of England' (i.e. on StE), in which ME ǭr was identified with ME ŏr, but on conservative, dialectal, and American English. His article on *o* was written in 1908, but its statements were probably equally true of some thirty years before, when Murray may be presumed to have first considered the representation of these sounds in the Dictionary.

On the whole it appears that the change of [ɔə] to [ɒə] and [ɒ:] in StE can be dated to the early nineteenth century (cf. Horn, § 98); Luick, § 568, would apparently assign it to the eighteenth century, though saying (§ 568 (2)) that it was not observed until the second half of the nineteenth century, but this is contrary to the evidence, which shows that in the eighteenth century the correct etymological distinctions could still be recognized. The change therefore lies well outside the limits of this inquiry, but it seems relevant to examine its nature, for it confirms the view taken above of the eModE development of ME ǭ before *r*.

This was that ME ǭ (and sixteenth-century [u:] when affected by lowering) were, in the later seventeenth century, approximately 'cardinal open [ɔ:]' before *r* in contrast to close [o:] for ME ǭ in free position. But this [ɔ:] was merely a contextual variant, used solely before [r], of the 'long *o*' phoneme, of which the principal member was [o:], and was therefore not separately described. The situation changed, however, when [r] was vocalized to [ə]. Then [ɔ:(ə)r] < ME ǭ, &c. before *r* became [ɔ:ə] > [ɔə], [ɒ:r] < ME ŏ before *r* became [ɒ:ə] > [ɒə] > [ɒ:], and both these developments were distinct from [o:ə] > [oə] in *boa* and *Noah*. That is to say, the distinction between, for example, *boar* and *boa* depended, when final [r] became [ə], solely on the distinction between [ɔə] in *boar* (with 'cardinal open [ɔ]' as its first element) and [oə] in *boa* (with close [o] as its first element); [ɔə] and [oə], being used in the same phonetic context (here in final position) to express a distinction of meaning, had become distinct phonemes, and English now possessed three phonemes [ɒə] (> [ɒ:]), [ɔə], and [oə] where before it had had only two ('short *o*' lengthened before *r*, and 'long *o*', which covered both [ɔ:] and [o:]). But English, in common with other languages, resists the tendency to develop too many phonemes dependent on over-fine phonetic distinctions, as these three do (cf. the assimilation of the retracted form of ME ă in *fast* to [a:] < ME *au* in *demand*, in *wan* to [ɒ] < ME ŏ, and in *war* to [ɒ:] < ME *au* in free position). If this tendency to reduce the number of phonemes be applied to [ɔə] < ME ǭr, it can be (*a*) assimilated again to the 'long o' phoneme and become [oə], identical with the sound used in *boa* [boə], a pronunciation of ME *ǭr* which can still occasionally be heard in StE, or (*b*) assimilated to the '*or*' (or '*au*') phoneme and become [ɒə] or even (by a further assimilation, involving the absorption of the [ə]) [ɒː], as in the normal PresE pronunciations [bɒə] and [bɒː] of *boar*.

The truth of this hypothesis is established by dating and by the dialectal distribution of the pronunciations involved. (*a*) As far as our evidence goes, loss of [r] by vocalization precedes the loss of the distinction between ME *ǭr* and ME *ŏr*. It seems that [r] was still maintained in good speech throughout the eighteenth century, to judge from the evidence of native English orthoepists; not until Batchelor (1809) is there clear evidence of its loss from good StE (cf. Wyld, *Coll. Eng.*, p. 299), and the loss of the distinction between ME *ǭr* and *ŏr* is certainly not earlier (see above). (*b*) It is in those dialects (above all in StE) in which [r] is regularly lost in final position and before consonants that ME *ǭr* becomes identical with ME *ŏr*; the sounds remain distinct in those in which [r] commonly remains (notably in Scottish dialects; cf. Murray's distinction in *OED*).

The hypothesis has the further advantage that it enables us to explain satisfactorily the occurrence in PresE of a variant [ɒə] beside normal [oə] in *boa* and *Noah*. *OED*, consistently with its avoidance of the lowered [ɒə] in all words, does not give it in these two; Daniel Jones, *English Pronouncing Dictionary*, gives [ɒə] or [ɒː] as the rarer pronunciation in both, but Wyld, *Universal English Dictionary*, gives [ɒə] priority in *boa* and records [ɒː] alone for *Noah*; my experience confirms Jones's that the abnormal [ɒə] is much rarer than the normally developed [oə] in both words. However this may be, it is certainly late; in the seventeenth century *Noah's* is paired with *nose* in the 'homophone' lists of Strong and of Cooper (who puts the pairing in his 'same or near' list, devoted to pairings of common nouns and proper names), and there is no evidence of a special pronunciation of ME *ǭ* in these words until the late nineteenth century. The fact that in them [ɒə] is only a (more or less rare) variant beside normally developed [oə], whereas in *boar* and *Nore* [ɒə] or [ɒː] is almost universal in Present StE, shows that a different explanation applies. Clearly [ɒə] in *boa* and *Noah* is analogical; the variation between [oə] (by re-assimilation to the 'long o' phoneme) and [ɒə] > [ɒː] (by assimilation to the '*or, au*' phoneme) in *boar* and *Nore* has affected these two isolated words in which ME *ǭ* precedes a final [ə] which is not developed from *r*, and has caused them to assume, beside their proper pronunciation [oə], the analogical [ɒə] > [ɒː]. The analogical pronunciation probably originated among speakers native to dialects in which ME *ǭr* was [ɔə] or [oə] in the course of their adoption of the StE pronunciations [ɒə] and [ɒː] in *boar, Nore*, &c.

Note 1: On dialectal pronunciations see Wright, §§ 126 and 260. The pronunciation [ɒə] (as in StE) occurs in dialects in which *r* > [ə] in final position even when the word 'is used alone or stands at the end of a sentence' (Wright, p. 219, end of second paragraph). But [ɔə] (Wright's inaccurate notation, which covers [ɔə]; see § 206 above) is kept in Northern and North Midland dialects (ibid., § 126), in which final *r* in words used alone or at the end of a sentence is 'still lightly trilled' (ibid., p. 219), and in Herefordshire, Oxfordshire, Berkshire, and southern counties in which *r* is pronounced (usually as a 'reverted or retracted' *r*; ibid., § 259). But [ɔə] is also recorded for Norfolk and Suffolk (§ 126), where (as Wright says nothing specific on their pronunciation of *r*) it must be assumed that final and preconsonantal *r* is treated as in StE; here [ɔə] < ME *ǭr* has evidently been re-assimilated to the 'long o' phoneme and become a true [ɔə] (with close first element).

Note 2: On Luick's theories of the lengthening of ME *ŏ* before *r* and the lowering of seventeenth-century [o:] (as he regards it) before *r*, their identity in PresE as [ɒə] in careful speech and [ɒ:] in less careful in such words as *for, short* and *more, force* presents a difficulty. According to his theory, the lengthening of ME *ŏ* was due to the absorption of a glide [ə] developed before *r*, thus [ɒr] > [ɒər] > [ɒ:r], and with the loss of the *r*, the result in PresE should be [ɒ:] (Luick, § 567). On the other hand the lowering of seventeenth-century [o:] was according to Luick, § 568 (2), due to an unabsorbed [ə] glide, the assimilatory power of which had been increased in the eighteenth century probably as a consequence of the loss of [r] in final position and before consonants: thus [o:ə] > [ɒ:ə]. Words like *for* and *short* should then have simply [ɒ:] without addition of [ə], but words like *more* and *force* should have the addition of [ə], thus [ɒ:ə] (in Luick's notation; I normally follow Daniel Jones's [ɒə]). Luick, § 568 (3), would explain the failure of PresE to show such a distinction by the hypothesis that the two classes of words influenced each other analogically, so that on the one hand *more* and more especially *force* (where a consonant follows) lost the [ə], while on the other hand in careful speech *short* and more especially *for* (where the vowel is final) took on a light [ə]. The essential weakness of this theory is its assumption that the lengthening of ME *ŏ* was due to an [ə] glide developed after it, of which there is no evidence; the lengthening was directly produced by the [r] itself, and the immediate result of lengthening was [ɒ:r]. The [ə] of PresE in words of the *for, short* class is quite simply explained; it is not a glide-vowel, but represents the [r], which was not merely lost but vocalized to [ə], so that late seventeenth-century [ɒ:r] (< ME *ŏr*) becomes PresE [ɒ:ə]. In the *more, force* type, on the other hand, the [ə] developed by vocalization of the [r] coalesced with the pre-existing glide which occurred after ME long vowels. In PresE [ə] in fact occurs very rarely indeed before a consonant in words of either type (*short, force*); the reason is clearly recent absorption of the [ə] into the preceding [ɒ:] when a consonant follows—a process which also occurs, though less regularly, in final position in, for example, *for* and *more*.

On Luick's view of the process whereby [o:ə] (in his notation) became [ɒ:ə] the latter pronunciation ought to be as regular in *boa* and *Noah* as in *boar* and *Nore*, for it is absurd to suppose that the [ə] of the two former words was, even before the loss of *r* (and certainly not after it), in any way different from the [ə] of the two latter. A further difficulty is that he treats the retraction of ME *ā, ai,* and *ę̄* before *r* to [ɛ:ə] as a parallel eighteenth-century change to the supposed lowering of [o:ə] to [ɒ:ə]; but apart from other objections to his view of the development of ME *ār*, &c. (see § 205, Note), the evidence of nineteenth-century English is against his assumption that the two processes were contemporaneous, for it regularly had [ɛə] (in his notation [ɛ:ə]) for ME *ār*, &c. at a time when it had not fully accepted the lowered [ɒə] (Luick's [ɒ:ə]) for seventeenth-century [ɔ:r].

Note 3: Evidence of the pronunciation [ɒ:] from the seventeenth century onwards in words which varied between ME *ŏ* and ME *ǭ, ō,* or *ū*, is not evidence of the lowering, for this [ɒ:] develops by lengthening of ME *ŏ*, not from the ME long variant. Thus *born*, &c. have [ɒ:] in Cooper.

(h) *Lengthening of ME ă*

§ 211. Before *r*, ME *ă* was lengthened. The process seems to have been in the first instance one of prevention of fronting beyond the value [a], i.e. it was due to the retractive influence of *r* (see §§ 54 seq.). The [a:] developed as a result of the lengthening was later retracted to [ɑ:], and there was even (in dialectal speech) a direct lengthening to [ɒ:]; this latter change was primarily due to the rounding influence of *r* (see § 199), but its retractive influence probably assisted.

(*i*) *ME ĕ becomes* [ə] *before* r

§ 212. Stressed ME *ĕ*, when it escaped the lowering which occurred *c*. 1400 to *ă*, remained before *r* with the same value as in other positions (i.e. as [e]) until the early seventeenth century in StE (not so long in the dialects; see Note 2), but was then retracted because of the influence of the following *r* to the central vowel [ə]; here it became identical with ME *ĭ*, which had been similarly retracted, and commonly also with ME *ŭ*. The change occurs before *r* plus consonant and final *r*, but not normally in StE before intervocalic *r*. The reason for the retraction was to anticipate the pronunciation of the *r*, for [ə] is a vowel closely allied to the ModE [r]. This seventeenth-century [ə] developed before *r* from ME *ĕ* (and from ME *ĭ* and *ŭ*) must have been of approximately the same quality as PresE [ə:], which later develops from it when the *r* is vocalized to [ə]; it must then have been a member of the [ə] phoneme very similar to that described by D. Jones, *Outline of English Phonetics*, § 356 (the [ə] of *admit* [ədmit], *breakfast* [brekfəst], *forward* [fɒ:wəd]), and distinctly higher in articulation than that described op. cit., § 361 (the [ʌ]-like variety of [ə] used in final position, for example, in *villa* [vɪlə], *over* [ouvə]). But being stressed it would be more tense than any member of the PresE short [ə] phoneme, which is used only in unstressed position.

The evidence of the retraction of ME *ĕ* to [ə] before *r* is as follows. Coote gives as examples of 'the barbarous speech of your country people' the pronunciations *gurth* 'girth' (ME *gĕrth*), which shows identity of stressed ME *ĕr* and *ŭr*, and *hur* 'her' (an unstressed form). Robinson (Vol. I, p. 209) does not distinguish stressed ME *ĕ* before *r* from stressed ME *ĕ* in other positions; his regular transcription *hur* 'her' and the single transcription *katùrva* 'caterva' (in which the second syllable is marked as unstressed) show a simple reduction of unstressed *ĕ* to [ə] which is independent of the influence of the *r*. Daines, however, shows that ME *ĕr* is identical with both ME *ĭr* and ME *ŭr*; it must then be [ər]. Hodges (Vol. I, pp. 180–1) shows the development of unstressed *ĕ* in *her, manner, ranker, saver* to [ə] (which he identifies with [ʌ] < ME *ŭ*); but stressed *ĕr* is regularly transcribed *ĕr*, and is therefore not retracted to [ər] (contrast ME *ĭr* in Hodges; see below). Wallis is the first, apart from Daines, to show the retraction of stressed *ĕ* to [ə] before *r*, and his evidence is fuller and more exact. He says that *e* before *r* is pronounced as '*e* feminine' [ə], 'and not indeed so much because it ought to be pronounced thus, but because it can hardly be conveniently pronounced otherwise; for it is permissible, if it can be done without the appearance of affectation, to use even in this position the clear, i.e. the masculine, sound' ('atque hoc quidem non tam quia debeat sic efferri, sed quia vix commode possit aliter; licet enim, si citra molestiam fieri possit, etiam illic sono vivido, hoc est mascule, efferre'). We may conclude that [ə] was in Wallis's view the normal pronunciation, but unretracted [e] still existed (cf. the evidence of Hodges a little earlier, and of Wilkins and Coles later) and was recognized by Wallis as a permissible variant if it came naturally to the speaker. Again in a later passage Wallis says that *e* is pronounced '*e* feminine' before *r* 'where the sound is not so much required as avoided with difficulty, for the tongue passes with greater difficulty from *e* masculine to *r*' ('ubi non tam requiretur sonus ille quam aegre evitatur; difficilius enim transit lingua ab *é* masculino ad *r*'); here Wallis recognizes the phonetic reason for the sound-change. His examples are *vertue, liberal, liberty*, and *stranger*, of which only *vertue* has stressed *ĕr*; but that the retraction occurred regularly in stressed syllables is shown by a list of Latin words (see Vol. I, p. 241 above) which in accordance with English custom he would have pronounced as if they were English words. Wallis, though he shows the retraction of *ĕr* to [ər], carefully distinguishes *ĕr* from *ŭr* (see Vol. I, p. 241). Hunt, though he perhaps had [ər] for ME *ŭr*, nevertheless explicitly denies that stressed ME *ĕr* is identical with *ur*, and so must have retained [er]. Poole shows the identity before *r* of ME *ĕ* and ME *ĭ* (which at this date must be due to retraction to [ə]) in many words, but does not rhyme ME *ĕr* and *ĭr* with ME *ŭr* (see Vol. I, p. 435); the distinction between ME *ĕr, ĭr* and ME *ŭr* may in his speech be a Northernism. Price *VO* and *EO* (see Vol. I, p. 343) shows that ME *ĕr* and *ĭr* are identical; in *VO* he follows Wallis in describing an '*e* obscure' which is used both for ME *ĕ* before *r* (so Wallis) and for ME *ĭ* before *r* (here he differs from Wallis). But Price keeps ME *ŭr* distinct from ME *ĕr* and *ĭr*, except in unstressed position. The *Welsh Breviary* uses Welsh *y* (i.e. [ə]) as a transcription for ME *ĕ* in *her*; but this development may have occurred in unstressed position. Wilkins preserves *ĕ* in *earth* (twice) but has [ə] (identified with [ʌ]) in *firmament*. Coles, *Schoolmaster*, says that *e* in *her* has a value distinct from that of the first *e* in *ever*, and in the *Shorthand* he says that *e* in *her* is the same as *u*; this evidence, however, refers only to *her*, in which [ə] develops under weak stress. The rhyme-lists of the *Schoolmaster* keep ME *ĕr* distinct from ME *ĭr* and *ŭr*, which are identical as [ər], except once more that *her* rhymes with *ŭr* (see Vol. I, pp. 441–2); Coles then agrees with Hodges in showing retraction to [ər] of *ĭr* but not of *ĕr*. Lodwick gives evidence of a pronunciation [jərþ] 'earth' (see Vol. I, p. 279), of which the starting-point could be either [jerþ] or [jɪrþ]; *r*-influence is certain, but not on what vowel it acted. Cooper shows retraction of *ĕr* to [ər] in stressed syllables (in *err, prefer, fern*) as well as in *her*. Probably following Wallis, he says that it is hardly possible to pronounce *e* otherwise than [ə] in these words because of the 'tremulous motion' of *r*. He identifies ME *ĕr* with *ĭr* and both of these with *ŭr*. *WSC* shows that *ĕr* is identical with *ŭr* in *prefer, refer, pertain*, &c., as well as in *her* and in unstressed syllables. In *prefer, refer*, &c., says *WSC*, the vowel 'bears hard upon the *r* sounding sharp' (i.e. stressed), but the *e* is 'apparently sounded'. His meaning is hard to discover; does the passage show that *WSC* vaguely realized that [ə] was a vowel closely related to the ModE [r] and found it difficult to distinguish the vowel from the consonant? Brown in his 'phonetically spelt' list shows identity of ME *ĕr* with *ŭr* by the transcription *surch* 'search'. The 'homophone' lists from that of Hodges onwards pair *her* with *Hur*; Wharton alone pairs *pearl* with *purl*.

ME *ĕ* before intervocalic *r*, which remains as [e] normally in StE and invariably in PresE, is nevertheless occasionally shown with retraction to [ə]. Wallis includes *terris* (contrasted with *turris*) in his list of Latin words which is intended to illustrate the difference between '*e* feminine' [ə] and [ʌ] < ME *ŭ* as in *but*, &c. (see Vol. I, p. 241); it follows that [ə] must occur in *terris* before intervocalic *r*. *WSC* says that *bury* and *Canterbury* are pronounced with short *u*; as their pronunciations are much more likely to descend from ME *ĕ* than ME *ŭ*, it follows that in his speech ME *ĕ* has become identical with ME *ŭ* before intervocalic as well as preconsonantal and final *r*.

Note 1: Some words vary in ME between *ĕr* and *ĭr* (see §§ 75-8), and the interchange of *ĕr* and *ĭr* forms in such words is of course not valid evidence of general identity between *ĕr* and *ĭr* and of the retraction to [ər]. *Her* varies in this way in Gil, but it is probable that the pronunciations cited above develop (in unstressed position) from the *ĕr* form, which is the more common in Gil and regular in other orthoepists.

Note 2: The evidence of spellings is of uncertain value in this matter of the retraction of *ĕr* to [ər]. Examples of *ir* spellings for original ME *ĕr* are *firk* for *ferk* (OE *fercian*) and *firkin* (see *OED*). In *virtue* for *vertue* and *firm* for *ferm* the *ir* forms are due to readoption direct from Latin. On *er* spellings for ME *ĭr* see § 213, Note 1 (*c*), below. Spellings with *ur* for ME *ĕr* appear to be rare except in words where special conditions apply. Thus *churl* for *cherl* does not depend on general identity of ME *ĕr* and *ŭr* (as it is taken by Horn, § 33), but on a ME (South-western) *ŭr* variant. Similarly *hurth* 'hearth' (OE *heorð*), which Mr. R. E. Alton kindly informs me occurs in the account-books of Magdalen College for 1506-7 and 1515-16, may be a Western spelling, with *u* for [ø] < OE *ĕo*; the word also appears as *hirth* (1509-10). Early spellings with *er* for ME *ŭr* again appear to be liable to special explanations. Thus *serlyn* 'sirloin' (OF **surloigne*) is cited by *OED* from an *Old City Account Book* of 1525, but in this word we have to reckon with a fictitious etymology *Sir Loin* (see *OED*), and the *ser-* form, like the more usual *sir-* form, may be due to the analogy of *sir*, which varies in the fifteenth century between *sir, ser, scher*, and *sur*. The analogy of this variation in *sir* might perhaps also account for the sixteenth- and seventeenth-century *ser-, scher-* forms of *surplice* and of its Northern variant *surpcloth* (see *OED*). A certain case of an *er* spelling for original *ŭr* which depends on retraction to [ər] is the *g(h)erkin* form of *gurken* from Du. **gurkkijn*; but the word is not recorded until a later date than that at which the orthoepists show the retraction to [ər] (*OED*'s first quotation is from Pepys, 1661).

Diehl, *Anglia*, xxix (1906), 150, cites *surmon* 'sermon' from Machyn, a form which may well depend on general identity of ME *ĕr* and *ŭr*, though here again we must reckon with the possibility that it is due to the analogy of variation in *sir*. *Fur* for *far*, also cited by Diehl, is a ME variant form (see Vol. I, pp. 410-11). Diehl's spellings with *ir* for *ĕr* (op. cit.,

p. 150) and *er* for *ir* (ibid., p. 153) are not conclusive evidence of retraction to [ər]; several of the *er* spellings, and the two *ear* spellings cited on p. 153, occur in words which have OE or ON ȳ.

Spellings with *o* for ME ĕ before *r* in Machyn (cf. Zachrisson, *Bullokar*, p. 53), insofar as they really exist (cf. Wijk, *Machyn*, p. 89), are not to be interpreted as showing *or* = *ur* = *er* but as being further examples of Machyn's use of *o* for ME ă (here < ME ĕ before *r*); so Wijk, p. 89 (see further § 194, Note 3). It seems likely that Machyn did identify ME ĕr and ŭr, though most of the spellings cited by Wijk, pp. 89 and 121, are explicable from ME variants (so *cherche* 'church'); *Burgany* (once) and *Borgane* (once) 'Bergavenny' and *sercotte* 'surcoat' seem reasonably safe evidence, in addition to *surmon* (six times), on which see above. But Machyn's evidence does not relate to StE.

On the whole the spellings suggest that ĕr may have been identical with ŭr from the early sixteenth century in certain dialects, and in Cockney from 1525 (*City Acc. Bk.*); but the evidence is rather unsatisfactory.

Note 3: Sixteenth-century rhymes tend to confirm the orthoepists' evidence that retraction of ĕr to [ər] was not accepted in good StE until the seventeenth century. The following is the evidence of the rhymes of pieces included in the *Oxford Book of Sixteenth Century Verse*. (a) Apparent rhymes of ME ĕr with ME ĭr. The rhyme *girl(s)* : *pearl(s)* (Lyly, &c.) depends on ME ĕ in *girls*. The rhymes *stir* : *gear* (Golding), *stir* : *err* (Warner), *first* : *reversed* (Daniel), *birth* : *earth* (Daniel, &c.), *mirth* : *earth* (Anon., op. cit., p. 866) depend on ĕ < OE ȳ in *stir*, *first*, *birth*, and *mirth*. The rhymes *spirits* : *merits*, &c. (Greville, &c.), *mirror* : *error* (Lodge) depend on ĕ in *spirits* and *mirror* (cf. § 80). We are left with the rhyme *birds* : *herds* (Shakespeare), and even this may depend on lowering of ME ĭ to ĕ (a change which is independent of the following consonant). (b) Apparent rhymes of ME ĕr with ME ŭr. The rhyme *clerk* : *work* (Harington) depends on ME ĕ in *work*. Sidney (1580–1) has *nourish* : *cherish* : *flourish*, which, if it be a true feminine rhyme, must depend on *r*-influence on ME ĕ and ŭ, and would then be the only certain evidence of retraction of ME ĕr to [ər] among the rhymes of the whole book. It will be observed that in this instance we have to do with intervocalic *r*.

Note 4: See Luick, § 551, Anm. 1, for the evidence of foreign orthoepists. From c. 1660 ME ĕ or ME ĭ before *r* (Luick does not clearly distinguish the cases) is identified with French 'feminine e' or with French *eu* or the [ø] sounds of other languages. Luick, § 551, interprets this evidence as referring to 'a "mixed vowel" which to judge from its sound was not far different from [e]'. But we may with confidence take the identification with [ø] as referring to [ə] (or later to the [əː] developed from [ər] by vocalization of the *r*); PresE [əː] is generally mistaken by foreigners for a rounded front vowel (cf. D. Jones, *Outline of English Phonetics*, § 347) and Englishmen commonly make the reverse mistake (cf. Nicholson, *Introduction to French Phonetics*, p. 29 foot, p. 31 foot). For the reason see Sweet, *Primer of Phonetics*, § 62. Luick's 'mixed vowel not far different from [e]' would in fact be indistinguishable from PresE [ə]; the chief members of the English [ə] phoneme have tongue-height practically the same as that of [e] (D. Jones, op. cit., §§ 335 seq.).

Some foreign orthoepists identify ĕ (or ĭ) before *r* with [e]. Thus Festeau, 1693, does not distinguish ĕ before *r* from ĕ in free position. Such authors may often be plagiarizing earlier French–English grammars written before the retraction of ĕr to [ər], or they may fail to distinguish [ə] from [e]; Miège, 1688, &c. fails to distinguish properly these sounds (see § 213, Note 1(a) below). Luick, § 551 (beginning), correctly takes such identifications by foreigners as being somewhat inexact; we may compare the tendency of some foreigners to substitute varieties of [e] for PresE [əː] (cf. D. Jones, op. cit., § 351, and the much-ridiculed [sɛːr] 'sir'). The evidence of Festeau and Miège and other similar evidence need therefore not be held to show retention of an unretracted [e] before *r*, though for some time in the seventeenth century this is not impossible.

Note 5: Wright, § 56, shows that [əː] and its modification [ʌː] occurs for ME ĕr in many dialects. Retraction of ME ĕ occurs also before intervocalic *r* in the dialects (see Wright's Index, s.vv. *berry*, which certainly has ME ĕ, and *bury* and *merry*, in which the [ə] pronunciation may be from ME ĕ or ME ĭ). American pronunciation often has [ə] for ME ĕ before intervocalic *r*, as in *America*.

5571.2   X

Note 6: Luick, § 551, regards the process of development in StE as being due to an [ə] glide before the *r*. He considers that the [eə] which developed in this way became, by assimilation of the two elements, a 'mixed' (central) vowel similar to [e]; this vowel was short (somewhat surprisingly, since on Luick's theory it was a blend of two short vowels), and subsequently changed to [ə], where it became identical with ME *ŭ* (see § 214, Note 6). But there is no valid evidence for a 'mixed' vowel similar to [e] as distinct from [ə] (see Note 4 above), and none at all that a glide [ə] ever developed between ME short vowels and *r*. ME *ĕ* must therefore be considered to have been retracted directly to [ə] by the influence of the *r* itself.

Ekwall, § 50, assumes a double development of ME *ĕ* before *r*, thus (i) ME *ĕ* before *r* becomes [ə] in the seventeenth century and thus identical with ME *ŭ* before *r*; (ii) ME *ĕ* before *r* remained [e] and in the eighteenth century became a 'mixed vowel' which was not identical with ME *ŭ* before *r*, and was probably similar to German *e* in *Gabe*. Ekwall adopts this theory to explain the distinction made by some eighteenth-century orthoepists between ME *ĕr* and ME *ŭr*, but it is unnecessary for this purpose (see § 214, Note 6, end). It is also in part based on the failure of some eighteenth-century orthoepists to distinguish ME *ĕ* before *r* from ME *ĕ* in free position; these are presumably foreign orthoepists of the sort mentioned in Note 4 (end), whose evidence may be inaccurate (though it is possible that unretracted [er] remained for some time before its final disappearance) and bad English observers who saw no point in distinguishing between contextual variants of 'short *e*'.

(*j*) ME *ĭ* becomes [ə] before r

§ 213. ME *ĭ* before *r* remains at first as [ɪ], identical with ME *ĭ* in free position. But *c*. 1600 it underwent lowering and retraction to the central vowel [ə] described in § 212 above.

From the fact that ME *ĭ* and ME *ĕ* both undergo this retraction to [ə], it has been assumed that they had already become identical before the change to the central vowel occurred, and that this identity must have been the result of lowering of ME *ĭ* before *r* to [e] (so Horn, § 26; Luick, §§ 550–1). But it is evident that the identity might be the result merely of both ME *ĭ* and ME *ĕ* independently becoming [ə] before *r*. The evidence of Hodges, Wallis, and Coles, less decisively of Wilkins and possibly of Brown, leaves no doubt that the second explanation is the correct one, and that *ĭr* and *ĕr* did not become identical until each had separately made the change to [ər]. See further Note 1 below.

The evidence for the lowering and retraction of ME *ĭ* to [ə] because of the influence of a following *r* is as follows. Sixteenth-century orthoepists and the early seventeenth-century orthoepists (Robinson, Gil, and Butler) do not distinguish ME *ĭ* before *r* from ME *ĭ* in other positions; it follows that *ĭr* was still pronounced [ɪr]. The only possible sixteenth-century orthoepistical evidence of the retraction of *ĭr* to [ər] is in Bullokar and Coote. On Bullokar's *ĕ*-form in *whirl* vb. see Note 1 (*b*) below. He also gives *ŭ* in *whirling-wind*, in which, however, it is due to rounding of ME *ĭ* to *ŭ* (see § 85). Coote gives *sur* 'sir' as an example of the 'barbarous speech of your country people'; but if he intended to indicate the general identity of *ĭr* and *ŭr* his example is a bad one, for *sir* has a ME form in *ĕ* and a fifteenth-century *sur* form (see *OED*, which suggests that it may be from

OF *sor, sieur*) and is moreover commonly used in unstressed position in the sentence. We get no valid evidence until the seventeenth century. Daines seems to have retraction of both *ĭr* and *ĕr* to [ər], for he says that '*er* is the same in pronunciation as *ir*', and though his examples in this place are *err'd* and *bird* (the latter of which has a common ME *ŭ* variant) he later says that *nerve* is pronounced *nirve*, clearly by way of explaining that its pronunciation is [nərv] (in contrast apparently to the preceding word *serve*, for which Daines presumably used the common pronunciation [sarv]). Both *ĕr* and *ĭr* in Daines's speech seem further to have been identical with *ŭr*. Hodges (see Vol. I, pp. 180–1) shows lowering and retraction of ME *ĭ* before *r*, in stressed and unstressed syllables, to [ə], a sound which Hodges regularly identifies, whatever position it comes in, with unrounded ME *ŭ* [ʌ]. Hodges shows retention of unlowered [ɪr], recorded in his transcriptions eleven times, beside lowered [ər], recorded nineteen times; but the only word which varies between the two pronunciations is *virgin*, which has [ɪr] once and [ər] thrice. There is not sufficient support in the transcriptions for the view that [ɪr] was used by Hodges in formal speech and [ər] in ordinary speech; he shows rather a state of affairs in which the [ər] pronunciation had made its way into good speech but had not yet finally ousted the [ɪr] pronunciation. It is noteworthy that Hodges does not show retraction of stressed ME *ĕr* to [ər]; he therefore shows clearly that ME *ĭr* developed to [ər] independently of ME *ĕr*. Wallis, in contrast, shows retraction to [ər] of ME *ĕr* but not of ME *ĭr*; Lehnert's suggestion (*Wallis*, § 91) that he has been influenced by the spelling is unnecessary, in view of the reverse position in Hodges. Newton seems to be able to distinguish ME *ĭr* from ME *ŭr* (see Vol. I, p. 252). Wilkins agrees with Hodges in showing lowering to [ər] (identified, as by Hodges, with [ʌr]) of stressed ME *ĭr* in *firmament*, but does not show retraction of stressed ME *ĕr*; his evidence is, however, less valuable than that of Hodges, since he gives much fewer transcriptions. Merriott (1660) says that *sur* for *sir* is a 'gross fault of spelling'; the example is indecisive. Hunt's statement that *ir* is pronounced *ur* in *shirt* and *chirp* probably applies only to these two words; he condemns *sur* 'sir' as dialectal. Poole rhymes *ĭr* with *ĕr*, presumably because both are retracted to [ər] (see Vol. I, pp. 434–5). Price (see Vol. I, p. 343) shows that both *ĭr* and *ĕr* are [ər], but distinguishes them from ME *ŭr*. Coles, *Schoolmaster*, says that *i* has a different value in *irk* from that in other words, and in his *Shorthand* says that *i* in *irk* is pronounced *u*; the rhymes of the *Schoolmaster* show that *ĭr* is identical with *ŭr* as [ər] (see Vol. I, pp. 441–2). But Coles, like Hodges, shows no retraction of stressed ME *ĕr*. Lodwick's [ə] in [jərþ] 'earth' may develop from earlier [ɪ] (see Vol. I, p. 279). Cooper gives [ər] for *ĭr* as well as for *ĕr*. *WSC-RS* shows general identity of *ĭr* and *ŭr*. Brown's evidence has points of difficulty. In his text, he says that *ĭr* is identical with *ŭr* only in *birth, first, fir,* and *bird*, all of which have a ME *ŭr* variant. In his 'phonetically spelt' list *ur* spellings for *ĭr* occur chiefly in such words as had a ME *ŭr* variant (thus *churn* glossed 'chirn' and eight others); but we also find *furm* 'firm', which has no *ŭr* variant (though the [ər] pronunciation may develop from the ME *ĕr* form). In the 'phonetically spelt' list we again find *er* spellings for *ĭr* in words which have or may have a ME *ĕr* variant (*merth* 'mirth', *berth* 'birth', *berch* 'birch', *ferm* 'firm', *serk'l* 'circle'; so also perhaps *cherp* 'chirp', *serkit* 'circuit', *merr* 'myrrh'). But we also find *berd* 'bird', which can have no ME *ĕr* form. The evidence may perhaps mean that in Brown's own speech (he was apparently a Northerner) ME *ĭr* was kept distinct from ME *ŭr* and perhaps from ME *ĕr*, but that in other forms of speech known to him, and represented by occasional entries in his 'phonetically spelt' list, ME *ĭr* was identical with ME *ĕr* and therefore (see § 212 above) with ME *ŭr*. The 'phonetically spelt' lists of Strong and Young give *surkit* 'circuit'; Strong's 'homophone' list gives '*sir* : *Sur* (a place); *answer*', and Coles, *Eng.-Lat. Dict.*, has *confirm* : *conform*, which depends on ME *ŭ* in the latter.

PresE does not show retraction of ME *ĭ* to [ə] before intervocalic *r*, but it probably occurred occasionally in StE in the seventeenth century, though none of the evidence is entirely conclusive. Hodges in his 'homophone' list pairs *sirra* with *Surrey*. Cooper says that *ir* is identical with *ur* in *syrup*, *miracle*, *mirror*, *squirrel*, *stirrup*, and *whirry* 'wherry' (glossed 'linter' in the Latin text). *WSC-RS* follows Cooper with regard to *miracle*, *mirror*, and *stirrup*. Both Cooper and *WSC-RS* say that *ir* is not pronounced as *ur* when it is for Latin *in-*, as in *irrational*. Brown's 'phonetically spelt' list gives *surrop* 'syrup' and *sorra* or *surry* 'sirrah'. It is probable that in many of these words we have [ə] < ME *ĭ*, but in none is it certain. *Syrup*, *squirrel*, and perhaps *sirrah* (< *sir*) have ME *ŭ* variants, and *syrup*, *miracle*, *mirror*, and perhaps *squirrel* have ME *ĕ* variants (see *OED*, s.vv.); *wherry* is of obscure origin and even if < *whirr* vb. might have rounding of *ĭ* to [u] after the bilabial; and *stirrup* certainly has a ME *ĕ* variant (surviving in PresE pronunciation as [e] beside normal [ɪ]) and perhaps also one in ME *ŭ* (see Note 3 below), both of which may be due to the influence of the various stems of *sty* vb. (q.v. in *OED*), though ME lowering of *ĭ* to *ĕ* might also account for the former. Those words which have ME *ŭ* variants may then simply have the pronunciation [ʌ], without *r*-influence, in the orthoepists cited; and those which have no *u*-variants may owe [ər] to retraction of *ĕr*, not of *ĭr*. But it seems likely that Cooper at least knew the change of ME *ĭ* to [ə] before intervocalic *r*. His exception (followed by *WSC-RS*) that [ɪr] was still used for *ir-* when it represented Latin *in-*, as in *irrational*, shows the conservative influence of the educated pronunciation of Latin. It is a similar conservative pronunciation of English which has regularly preserved [ɪ] for ME *ĭ* before intervocalic *r* in present StE.

Note 1: The evidence cited in support of the hypothesis that ME *ĭ* was lowered to [e]

§ 213]   PART 3: INFLUENCE OF *r*   753

before *r* as a preliminary to the retraction to [ə] does not bear examination. It is as follows (see Luick, § 551, Anm. 1).

(*a*) The statements of the foreign orthoepists Mason, 1622, and *Alphabet Anglois*, 1625, that *ĭ* before *r* was pronounced as *e* in certain words. But the nature of this *e* is not made clear; it may well be the French 'feminine *e*', so that this evidence may refer to the complete retraction to [ə] and not to a preliminary lowering to [e]. Cf. also § 212, Note 4, on the failure of some foreign orthoepists to distinguish ME *ĕ* before *r* from ME *ĕ* in free position. Further, in each case the words cited in illustration are special words which varied in pronunciation in ME. *Sir* (Mason) has ME *ĕ* and *ŭ* beside ME *ĭ*. *First* (Mason and *Alph. Angl.*) and *girdle* (Mason) have ME *ĭ*, *ĕ*, and *ŭ* from OE *ў*. *Third* and *bird* (*Alph. Angl.*) have a common *ŭ* variant. It is not improbable that in all words the authors may refer to the pronunciation with ME *ŭ*, unrounded before *r* as in free position to [ʌ], a sound commonly identified with French 'feminine' *e*, and that their evidence is not at all relevant to the retraction of ME *ĭ* before *r*. Mauger, 1679, says that when *i* is joined to *r*, it is pronounced like French '*e* masculine', e.g. *sir* pronounced *ser*. But Mauger's rules are often generalizations from a special case, and so may this one be; *sir* has a ME *sĕr* variant capable of the pronunciation [ser] before retraction of *ĕr* to [ər]. Or there may be false identification of [ər] with [er] (see § 212, Note 4). Miège, 1688, &c. says that in a number of words *i* is pronounced like 'open *e*'; but he clearly fails to distinguish [ə] from [e]. His use of the terms '*e* masculine', '*e* open', and '*e* feminine' is entirely without rational basis; thus *e* in *left* is 'masculine', in *care*, &c., *maker*, &c., *wet* and *red* 'feminine', in *certain*, *vertuous*, and *met* 'open'. If short [e] can be 'masculine', 'feminine', and 'open', unstressed [ə] can easily be 'feminine' and stressed [ə] 'open'. In any event Miège's examples of *i* pronounced as '*e* open' in his *English Grammar* (2nd edit. 1691) are *virtue*, *sir*, *girl*, and *dirt*, of which the first three have a ME variant in *ĕ*. These and other late seventeenth- and eighteenth-century statements that *ĭr* is pronounced *ĕr* might in some cases at least mean no more than that ME *ĕr* and *ĭr* had become identical in consequence of the completed development of both to [ər].

(*b*) Occasional *ĕ* forms recorded by the orthoepists in words which varied in ME between *ĕ* and *ĭ* (e.g. *shirt*, with OE *ў*) are clearly not evidence of lowering of ME *ĭ* to [e] in consequence of the influence of the following *r*. Bullokar's *ĕ* in *whirl* is subject to a special explanation; the verb, which should have only *ĭ*, is analogically influenced by *whirl* sb., which has original *ĕ* (from MDu. *wervel*; cf. *OED*, which cites fifteenth- and sixteenth-century forms for the substantive, and sixteenth-century Scottish *quherle* for the verb).

(*c*) Spellings with *er* for ME *ĭr*, which are frequent in the diary of R. Cocks (1615–22), a merchant and probably a native of Coventry, may depend not on lowering of ME *ĭ* to [e] because of the influence of the following *r*, but either on a spontaneous lowering of *ĭ* to [e] in all positions, or on identity of ME *ĭr* and *ĕr* in consequence of the completed retraction to [ər]. Sixteenth-century spellings with *er* for *ĭr* are perhaps best explained as showing the spontaneous lowering of *ĭ* to [e] in all positions. So Berners 1523 *erk* 'irk' and Greene 1593 *yerksomeness* 'irksomeness'; but in this case it is possible that there may have been a ME *erk, as the etymology is unknown (see *OED*; the two suggested etymologies could each give rise to a ME *erk), though only *irk* is recorded in ME. Machyn has *cherche* (twenty-eight times) and *cheyrche* (five times), but these represent ME variants; the latter is apparently a Northernism (cf. *weird* < OE *wyrd*, and see Jordan, § 148). Similarly *ser* 'sir' (eighty-five times) is the ME variant *sĕr*; and *serkutt* 'circuit' (once), though it may well show identification of ME *ĕr* and *ĭr* (both of which Machyn appears to identify with ME *ŭr*), could be an inverted spelling on the model of *ser* beside *sir*. (For the forms cited see Wijk, *Machyn*, p. 121.)

(*d*) Rhymes of ME *ĕr* with ME *ĭr* may depend on both being [ər].

The lowering mentioned under (*c*) of ME *ĭ* to [e] in all positions may indeed explain all the evidence on which Luick relies. This lowering could influence ME *ĭ* before *r*, but only before intervocalic *r* does it seem to be directly assisted by the consonant. Even in this position it is by no means regular; elsewhere it is very sporadic, and it occurred chiefly in vulgar speech (cf. § 80 above). The regular StE retraction of *ĭr* to [ər] should not be made dependant on this irregular and non-standard lowering to [e].

Note 2: Words which vary in ME between *ĭ* and *ĕ* (see §§ 75–78) and those which vary between $\breve{\imath}$ and $\breve{u}$ (see §§ 81–85) do not provide valid evidence of a general identity of $\bar{\imath}r$ and $\breve{e}r$ or of $\bar{\imath}r$ and $\breve{u}r$ as [ər]. Horn, §§ 25–27, though he recognizes that *first* varies in ME (see § 27, Anm. 1), fails to realize that *bird* also varies, and regards its $\breve{u}r$ form in Gil and Butler as evidence of a general identity of $\bar{\imath}r$ and $\breve{u}r$. So Lehnert, *Wallis*, § 90. On Wyld's theory, which involves a similar error, see Note 7.

Note 3: Spellings do not provide very satisfactory evidence. On *ir* spellings for ME $\breve{e}r$ see § 212, Note 2. On *er* spellings for ME $\bar{\imath}r$ see Note 1 (c) above. *Ir* spellings for ME $\breve{u}r$, and *ur* spellings for ME $\bar{\imath}r$ (except in words of the type mentioned in Note 1) would be more conclusive but are rare. Horn, § 26, cites *urchin* as an example, supposing it to be an inverted spelling of ME *irchoun*; but *OED* shows that *urchin*, &c. occurs from the fourteenth century onwards, being 'a variant of *hurcheon* and *irchin*, agreeing in vowel with the former and with the latter in the dropping of *h*'. *Sir-* forms of ME *surloin* (OF *surloigne), which occur from the seventeenth century onwards (*OED*'s first example is from the 'Water Poet' J. Taylor, 1630), may be explained from the fictitious etymology *Sir Loin* (to which *OED* believes that 'the final prevalence of the *sir* form may have been largely due') and from the analogy of the variation between the *sur* and *sir* forms of *sir* itself. The spellings *sirname* (sixteenth to nineteenth century) and *sirename* (fourteenth and fifteenth centuries) of *surname* (OF *surnom*) 'are due to etymologizing alteration on *sir* sb., *sire* sb., quasi "father's name"' (*OED*) and are made possible by the existence of the *sur* form of *sir*, *sire*. The *sir-* forms of *surplice* and its Northern variant *surpcloth* may also be due to the analogy of the variation in *sir*; a very early example is from the *Paston Letters* (1459), *sirples wise* 'surplice-wise', and from York *Churchwardens' Accounts* (1525) comes *syrpe clothe*, from Phaer's *Æneid* (1558) *syrpleys*, from Greene (1592) *cirples*. Similar forms occur in the seventeenth century. If they depended on general identity of ME $\bar{\imath}r$ and $\breve{u}r$, they would show that this identity came about during the fifteenth century in Northern and Eastern dialects and by the latter half of the sixteenth century in StE; this conclusion is not inconsistent with our other evidence. *Whirr* vb., *whirry* vb., and *wherry* sb. have *ur* forms, the earliest being in Udall, *Roister Doister* (before 1553), but in these words the preceding bilabial may cause rounding of $\breve{\imath}$ to [u]. The London-born diplomat Chaloner has *urksome* 'irksome' 1549, and *urke* 'irk' occurs in the *Mirror for Magistrates*, 1577 (see *OED*, s.vv.); ME has only *ir* forms, but if *irk* be < ON *yrka* a ME *urk is perhaps possible. Machyn has *syrcott* 'surcoat' (once), but this may depend on the analogy of *sur* beside *sir*, and *durge* 'dirge' (thirty-six times); the frequency of the latter is itself suspicious, and suggests that we may have to do with a Northern form < late ME *durge < *drige (cf. fifteenth-century *dorge* and sixteenth- to eighteenth-century Scottish *drudgy* cited by *OED*). The other spellings cited by Wijk, *Machyn*, p. 121 (*Fanchurche*, *furst* and *forst* 'first', *hurt* and *hort* 'hurt', *shurt* 'shirt', *thurd* 'third'), certainly represent ME variants in $\breve{u}r$ < OE $\breve{y}r$ or < $r\breve{\imath}$, and are largely Southernisms alien to Machyn's Northern dialect.

The *ir* forms of *gherkin* from Dutch *gurkkijn certainly depend on general identity of $\bar{\imath}r$ and $\breve{u}r$ as [ər], but the word is not recorded until after the English orthoepists show the retraction of $\bar{\imath}r$ to [ər]; *OED*'s first quotation is from Pepys (1661), who uses the spelling *girkin*.

Before intervocalic *r*, *u* spellings occur in *squirrel* and *syrup*, but go back to a ME variant in $\breve{u}$ (see above). *OED* records a fifteenth-century *murrour* 'mirror' (without quotation, so that no exact date can be given) and a sixteenth-century Scottish *murrur* (from Gau, *Richt Vay*, 1533); but there may be rounding of $\breve{\imath}$ to [u] after the preceding bilabial, and even if the spelling shows [ə] it may derive from the ME $\breve{e}$ variant rather than from ME $\breve{\imath}$. *Stirrup* has *o*-forms in the S. Lancs. *Torrent of Portugal*, c. 1435, in records from Northants., 1474, and in records relating to Windsor Castle, 1536–7; Captain Smith, 1626, has *sturrop* (see *OED*). These forms might, however, depend on a late ME $\breve{u}$ variant (see above).

The spellings cited by Diehl, *Anglia*, xxix (1906), 153, refer entirely to words which varied in ME between $\bar{\imath}r$ and $\breve{u}r$.

The evidence of spellings is thus unsatisfactory. They may show sporadic dialectal retraction of ME $\breve{\imath}$ before *r* to [ə] in the fifteenth and sixteenth centuries; for StE there is no possible evidence before 1549 at earliest.

Note 4: No rhymes occur in the *Oxford Book of Sixteenth Century Verse* which depend on a general identity of ME *ĭr* and *ŭr* as [ər]. The rhyme *first* : *worst* (Campion) depends either on ME *ŭ* < OE *ў* in *first* or on ME *ĕ* in *worst*. The rhymes *first* : (*ac*)*curst* (Shakespeare, recorded in Viëtor's lists), *stur* 'stir' : *door* (Surrey), *stir* : *incur*, *spur* (Shakespeare) depend on ME *ŭ* < OE *ў* in *first* and *stir*. *Work* : *kirk* (Drayton) may depend on *ĭ* in *work* or on *ŭ* (on the analogy of *church*) in *kirk*. *Bird* : *afford* (Breton) depends on late ME *ŭr* < *rĭ* in *bird* and on *ŭ* in *afford*. *Dirt* : *hurt* (Spenser) depends on *ŭr* < *rĭ* in *dirt*.

Note 5: For the evidence of foreign orthoepists see Luick, § 551, Anm. 1, and Horn, § 26, and see Note 1 above.

Note 6: Wright, § 76, shows that English dialects have [əː] or its variant [ʌː] for *ĭr* plus consonant. Before intervocalic *r* [ə] or [ʌ] occurs in *spirit* (but it may be from ME *ĕ* and not from ME *ĭ*); Wright does not record other words with ME *ĭ* before intervocalic *r* (but *bury* and *merry* may in many dialects derive their [ə] from ME *ĭ*; cf. § 212, Note 5). Kemp Malone, 'Notes on *WSC*', *MLN*, xxxix. 502–4, says that [ə] occurs in *stirrup*, *squirrel*, and *syrop* in U.S. dialects.

Note 7: Horn, §§ 26–27, and Luick, § 551, regard the process of development of ME *ĭ* before *r* as being lowering to [e] (see Note 1 above), after which it was the same as that of ME *ĕ* (on Luick's view of this process see § 212, Note 6). Wyld, *Short History*, § 256, fails to distinguish the late ME change whereby, for example, ME *brĭd* becomes either *bĭrd* or *bŭrd* from the ModE development whereby *ĭr* becomes [ər]. He believes that all *ĭr* words, 'perhaps' in the sixteenth century, became *ŭr* [ʊr] (he would assume, unnecessarily, an intermediate stage with a high-flat vowel; but [ɪ] could be rounded directly to [ʊ] under the influence of *r*); and that this [ʊr] later became [ʌr] and then (apparently by a direct change) [əː]. This view is largely invalidated by his failure to notice that *bird* is a special case; and it is inconsistent with seventeenth-century evidence that *ĭr* was identical with ME *ĕr* while both were still distinct from ME *ŭr* (on Wyld's view, ME *ĭr* should be identical with ME *ŭr* and both should for some time be distinct from ME *ĕr*).

The evidence of the sixteenth- to eighteenth-century orthoepists (both native and foreign) on the development of ME *ĭ* before *r* is carefully considered by A. Gabrielson in *Minnesskrift . . . tillägnad Professor Axel Erdmann*, pp. 68 ff. (Uppsala, 1913), supplemented by his 'Early Modern English *i*/*r* (+cons.)', *Studia Neophilologica*, iii (1930), 1–10. The account given above is independent of his, from which it differs in detail.

(*k*) *Early ModE* [ʌ] *becomes* [ə] *before* r

§ 214. Stressed ME *ŭ* before *r* remains for some time in early ModE as [ʊ] and is then unrounded, with stressed ME *ŭ* in most other positions, to [ʌ]. In Scottish and Irish dialects it remains as [ʌ] before *r* to the present day (cf. Wright, *EDG*, § 107), and there is evidence that the same situation commonly applied in StE during the seventeenth and eighteenth centuries (see below). But by another development [ʌ] before *r* quickly changed to [ə], so that ME *ŭr* became identical with ME *ĕr* and *ĭr*, which had also developed to [ər] (see above); this development is recorded for StE during the seventeenth century (when it was probably more common than the pronunciation which retained [ʌr] for ME *ŭr*) and is the basis of the Present StE pronunciation, which makes no distinction of ME *ŭr*, *ĕr*, and *ĭr*.

The development of [ʌ] to [ə], though treated here for convenience, is neither a retracting nor a lowering process. It consists in slightly advancing and raising the tongue-position, [ə] being somewhat higher and more forward than [ʌ] (cf. D. Jones, *Outline of English Phonetics*, p. 63, fig. 34). But the reason for this change is the same as for the retracting and lowering influences dealt with in the preceding sections; it is to anticipate the tongue-position and quality of the ModE fricative [r], which is closely allied to the [ə] vowel (see § 198 above). The raising and fronting of [ʌ] to [ə] is thus the exception which proves the rule that since 1400 [r] has possessed a lowering and retracting influence by virtue of its resemblance to the [ə] vowel.

As the identity of ME *ŭr* with ME *ĭr* and *ĕr* is dependent on the unrounding of ME *ŭ* to [ʌ], we should not expect evidence of this identity from orthoepists who do not show the unrounding. This is in fact the situation. Bullokar's form of *whirling-wind* does not prove that in his speech ME *ŭr* and *ĭr* were identical because of *r*-influence (see § 213 above). Coote's evidence on *sir* (§ 213) and on *her* (§ 212) is insufficient to show that ME *ŭr* is idential with *ĭr* and *ĕr*; but his *gurth* 'girth' (§ 212) does show that ME *ŭr* and ME *ĕr* were identical in the 'barbarous speech of your country people', and therefore that in such speech ME *ŭ* had by his time been unrounded to [ʌ] and further become [ə] before *r*. Robinson's evidence refers only to unstressed syllables (§ 212). Daines says that *u* before *rr* in *demurred* 'hath a flat or dull sound and short', and speaks further of '*u* flat, as in *ur*'. If this means, as it seems to, that ME *ŭ* before *r* is different from ME *ŭ* in other positions, it would most naturally be taken as showing that before *r* ME *ŭ* had passed through [ʌ] to [ə], and that in free position it was [ʌ]. In this case ME *ŭr* should be identical with ME *ĭr* and *ĕr*, and Daines appears to show this identity by his entries 'herne, hirne, (or corner) which is rather *hurne*' and '*snirle* (which some write *snurle*)'. It is true that OE *hȳrne* gives ME (South-western) *hŭrne* beside *hĕrne* and *hĭrne*, and that the etymology of *snirl* (a variant of *snarl*) is uncertain (though it may be a ME *snĕrlen, as Rösler–Brotanek, § 44, suggest); but the terms of his remarks suggest that he recognized only a graphic distinction between the *er*, *ir* forms and the *ur* forms, and I would conclude (with Rösler–Brotanek) that he shows the development of ME *ŭr* to [ər] and identity with ME *ĭr* and *ĕr*. Hodges identifies ME *ŭr* with ME *ĭr*, though he fails to distinguish [ə] from [ʌ] because they were for him merely variant members of a single phoneme (see Vol. I, pp. 180–1); and similar evidence is given by Wilkins (see § 213), Coles (see Vol. I, pp. 441–2), and Cooper (see Vol. I, pp. 291–2), except that the last-named identifies ME *ŭr* with both ME *ĭr* and ME *ĕr*. Hunt uses *ur* as a transcription for [ər] < unstressed ME *ĕr*; his evidence thus resembles Robinson's.

Wallis, however, does not show the development of ME *ŭr* from [ʌr] to [ər]; he carefully describes both the sounds [ʌ] (used for ME *ŭ*) and [ə], and distinguishes *ĕr* pronounced [ər] from *ŭr* pronounced [ʌr] (see Vol. I, p. 241). Lehnert, *Wallis*, § 91, suggests that he is influenced by the spelling, but there is no reason to believe that this is so (at any rate in the sense that Wallis has invented a distinction that did not actually exist); even in StE [ʌr] must have existed, at least for a short time, before passing into [ər], and it was just at this time that it should have existed. Wallis's evidence is in fact confirmed by that of Poole and Price (and of much later orthoepists; see Note 4). Poole does not rhyme ME *ŭr* with ME *ĕr* and *ĭr*, though he rhymes ME *ĕr* and *ĭr*, but the distinction may in his speech be a Northernism. Newton's evidence probably does not show a special development of ME *ŭr* (see Vol. I, p. 249). Price (see Vol. I, p. 343) gives [ər] for ME *ĕr* and *ĭr*, but keeps these sounds distinct from ME *ŭr*, though he must have used [ʌ] for ME *ŭ* in free position (see Vol. I, p. 342, note 1). On Brown (whose own probably Northern speech perhaps preserved ME *ŭr* as a distinct sound, but who gives some evidence of its identity with both ME *ĕr* and ME *ĭr*), and for the evidence of other 'homophone' and 'phonetically spelt' lists, see §§ 212 and 213 above.

Summing up, we may observe that from Daines onwards there is fairly plentiful evidence of the development of [ʌr] to [ər]. Of the retention of [ʌr] for ME *ŭr* in contrast to [ər] for ME *ĭr*, *ĕr* evidence is given by Wallis, Poole, and Price, perhaps supported by Brown. The [ʌ:] recorded by Wright, §§ 56 and 76, for ME *ĕr* and *ĭr* as well as for ME *ŭr* in certain dialects may possibly develop directly from earlier [ʌr] and show that in these dialects [ər] < ME *ĕr* and *ĭr* changed to [ʌr] while [ʌr] < ME *ŭr* remained unchanged; but the present StE [ə:] used for all three ME sound-groups shows (since it must develop from earlier [ər]) that in StE it was ME *ŭr* which changed from [ʌr] to [ər], and for this reason it must be assumed that it was the [ə] variant of their [ə]–[ʌ] phoneme that Hodges, Wilkins, Coles, and Cooper used for ME *ŭ* before *r* (cf. Vol. I, pp. 241–3).

Before intervocalic *r* [ʌ] remains in PresE, and this must have been the normal pronunciation in the seventeenth century. But the evidence cited in §§ 212 and 213 shows that in some words at least certain orthoepists knew pronunciations in which ME *ĕ* or *ĭ* before intervocalic *r* had become identical with ME *ŭ* before intervocalic *r*; and unless we assume that seventeenth-century StE sometimes used the [ʌ] for [ə] shown by some modern dialects (see immediately above), it follows that this identity results from the change of ME *ŭ* from [ʌ] to [ə] before intervocalic as before final and preconsonantal *r*.

Note 1: Identity of ME *ĭr* and *ŭr* in consequence of their development to [ər] is not shown by the interchange of *ĭr* and *ŭr* forms in words which varied between these sounds in ME; see § 213, Note 2.

Note 2: On spellings with *ur* for ME *ĕr*, and *er* for ME *ŭr*, see § 212, Note 2. On spellings with *ur* for ME *ĭr*, and *ir* for ME *ŭr*, see § 213, Note 3. Such spellings, though in many ways unsatisfactory as evidence, tend to show that ME *ŭ* before *r* may have passed through [ʌ] to [ə] as early as *c.* 1435 in Northern dialects, and somewhat later in more southerly dialects (Norfolk, *Paston Letters*, 1459; Northants., 1474); Cockney documents show the change in the early sixteenth century (*City Account Book*, 1525), and StE writers occasionally from 1549 (Chaloner) onwards.

Note 3: On rhymes between ME *ĕr* and *ŭr* see § 212, Note 3, and on rhymes between

ME ĭr and ŭr see § 213, Note 4. These sixteenth-century rhymes show that identity of ME ŭr with ĭr or ĕr was practically unknown in StE in the sixteenth century; only one rhyme (of Sidney's) shows the identity of ME ĕ and ŭ—as it happens, before intervocalic *r*.

Note 4: Miège, 1685, &c. (I have used his *English Grammar*, 2nd edit., 1691) says that in some words *ir* is pronounced as *er*, in others as 'a sort of mixt sound, coming near that of the English *o*'; these latter words (*bird, shirt, fir*) have all a ME variant in ŭr, and it is evidently [ʌ] < ME ŭ which Miège describes as a 'mixt sound'. His distinction of the two groups shows that in the form of English on which he based his teaching ME ŭr was distinct from ME ĕr (ĭr); his evidence thus confirms that of Wallis, whose first edition was some thirty years earlier than Miège's first work. Similar evidence is given by the eighteenth-century orthoepists Buchanan, Thomas Sheridan, Scott, Walker, and Smith (see Luick, § 551, Anm. 1); but it should be noticed that of these Buchanan is a Scot and Sheridan an Irishman, so that their pronunciation may be influenced by that of Scottish and Irish dialects, which still distinguish [ʌr] from [ər]. Walker describes the pronunciation which makes *ir* always the same as *ur* (i.e. which makes [ʌr] into [ər]) as 'vulgar', but this is hardly the whole truth; we may suspect an actor's prejudice. It is further to be observed that these eighteenth-century writers, in seeking to differentiate between ĭr, ĕr, and ŭr, give an impression of much confusion, as though they were attempting artificially to maintain a distinction which had long ceased to have validity in ordinary speech. The seventeenth-century evidence that ME ĭr, ĕr, and ŭr had all become identical as [ər] must be held to represent the normal StE development.

Note 5: Wright, *EDG*, § 107, records [ʌr] for ME ŭr in Scottish and Irish dialects, [ʌ:] or [ə:] in English. His Index shows that [ər] for ŭr before a vowel occurs in *borough* and *furrow* in English dialects.

Note 6: Wyld, *Short History*, § 252, appears to believe that [ʌr] became PresE [ə:] by a direct change. But the seventeenth-century evidence shows that ME ŭr had become identical with ME ĕr, ĭr before the loss of *r*, so that we must assume an intermediate [ər] stage.

Luick, § 551, assumes that ME ŭ before *r*, in spite of the presence of an [ə] glide which he believes (wrongly) to have developed after the vowel, had what he regards as its normal free development to [ə], where it became identical with ME ĕ and ĭ before *r*, which had made a combinative change to [ə] (see § 212, Note 6). The [ə] which then represented ME ĕ, ĭ, and ŭ before *r* was, says Luick, lengthened when *r* was finally lost and lowered [*sic*] to its present value [ə:], whereas the [ə] < ME ŭ in free position became 'an *a*-sound' (by which he means the PresE [ʌ]—see § 563, Anm. 2). But if we reject his view that ME ŭ in free position ever became [ə] and hold instead that it became directly [ʌ] (as we should; see § 93, Note 4), but agree that ME ĕr and ĭr when retracted became [ər] (and not [ʌr]; for the dialectal [ʌ:] < earlier [ʌr] is a side-development, not a stage in the StE development): then it follows that the identity of ME ŭr with ME ĕr and ĭr must be due to a combinative change in the former (from [ʌr] to [ər]) as well as in the two latter. The final stage is agreed to be a direct development of [ər] to [ə:] (though the PresE tongue-positions make it very doubtful whether any 'lowering' was involved) in consequence of the loss of [r]. A curiously late example of the failure of older phoneticians to distinguish [ə] from [ʌ] (which is what has misled Luick) occurs in Ellis (cf. Luick, § 551, Anm. 1), who regards ME ĕ, ĭ, and ŭ before *r* as having the same sound as ME ŭ in free position; but it seems incredible that Ellis, who was born in 1814 and was educated and lived in Southern England, should have retained [ər] in place of the normal nineteenth-century [ə:].

Ekwall, § 99, does not recognize that before ME ŭr became [ər] it had passed through a stage [ʌr] (still preserved in Scottish and Irish pronunciation) and that this [ʌr] is the explanation of the attempted eighteenth-century distinction (see Note 4) between ME ŭr and ME ĕr, ĭr pronounced as [ər].

Summary of the development of ME ĕr, ĭr, and ŭr

§ 215. Our evidence shows that before final *r* and *r* plus consonant ĕ, ĭ, and [ʌ] < ME ŭ became a relatively high [ə] sound. With the vocalization of [r] to [ə] in these positions the [ər] thus developed becomes [əə], i.e. [əː], in PresE. The development of the three sounds to [ə], though contemporaneous, was independent; thus in the seventeenth century we find persons who use [ər] for *ĕr* and not for *ĭr* (so Wallis; there is a hint of this situation in Brown), or vice versa (so Hodges, Coles, less decisively Wilkins), and as late as the end of the eighteenth century there were some speakers who (like Wallis, Poole, and Price in the seventeenth century) used [ʌr] and not [ər] for ME *ŭr*, if we may trust their evidence. Intervocalic *r* is shown to have occasionally exercised the same influence on all three vowels as final and preconsonantal *r* by seventeenth-century orthoepistical evidence, by the evidence of isolated spellings and rhymes, and by the pronunciation of modern English and American dialects; but it must have had this effect much more rarely, since the change to [ə] before intervocalic *r* is less often recorded and leaves no trace in present StE.

The evidence of spellings, though subject to many objections, suggests that *r* began to cause the development of all three vowels to [ə] in some dialects early in the fifteenth century (possibly first in Northern and next in Eastern dialects). This state of affairs need not surprise us, since the lowering of ME *ĕ* to *ă* and of ME *ẹ̄* to *ę̄* shows that soon after 1300 in the North and by 1400 in the South the nature of [r] was such that it could cause the development to [ə]. But the [ə] pronunciation made its way into StE very slowly; it is found in Cockney speech early in the sixteenth century (according to the evidence of spellings) and occasionally in educated speech from 1549 onwards (according to spellings and an isolated rhyme), but was not accepted as normal in educated StE speech until 1640—and even after this date we find Wallis and (apparently in imitation of him) Cooper saying of the [ə] pronunciation for ME *ĕ* before *r* that it is one which can hardly be avoided rather than one which ought to be used. The resistance to [ə] in place of [ʌ] before *r* was prolonged until much later, though many good speakers accepted it after 1640. There could hardly be a better example of the resistance to change of the educated and consciously 'correct' Standard language in the sixteenth and seventeenth centuries; nor of the eighteenth-century attempt to preserve in speech the distinctions suggested by the conventional spelling.

(2) *Alleged lowering caused by a preceding* r
(a) *Lowering of ME ǭ*

§ 216. ModE [ɒː] in (a)*broad* and *groat* has been explained as showing lowering of [oː] < ME *ǭ* to [ɒː] under the influence of the preceding *r*; but comparable words show no sign of an [ɒː] pronunciation, and the explanation should rather be that eModE *ŏ* (developed in both words by shortening of ME *ǭ* before *d* or *t*) has been lengthened to [ɒː]. See § 53 (2) and Note 3 above.

(b) Retraction of ME ę̄

§ 217. If an *r* preceded by another consonant possessed retractive influence over a succeeding ME ę̄, we should expect that influence to operate by causing ME ę̄ to remain as [ɛ:] and not to take part in the fronting of ME ę̄ in free position to [e:]; ME ę̄ after *r* would then be overtaken by ME *ā* at the same time as ME ę̄ before *r* was similarly overtaken. Of such a development of ME ę̄ after *r* there is practically no evidence. The PresE pronunciation of *great* and *break*, and sixteenth-century rhymes of *break* with ME *ā* words, are not due to the retractive influence of the preceding *r* (see § 115). There remains only one isolated case of possible retraction due to a preceding *r*. Cooper, who is the first orthoepist to give full evidence of the identity in good StE of ME ę̄ before *r* with ME *ā*, also shows that the equivalent of ME *ā* occurs in the word *scream*. In the sixteenth century there occurs a form *shrame* of the related *shream* (see *OED*). It is possible that we have here an example of *r*-influence which has not survived in StE; but a more likely explanation is that *scream* and *shream* have a ME variant in ME *ā*, of which an explanation is suggested in Vol. I, p. 291, note 1.

Note: After *c.* 1700 (even earlier in some sources of evidence) ME *ā* was generally identified with ME ę̄ in free position as [e:]; and it is therefore of no special significance if ME ę̄ in *great*, &c. is at that date identified with ME *ā*. But in Cooper this situation does not apply; ME ę̄ is [e:] in free position, and is kept distinct from ME ę̄ before *r* and ME *ā*, which are [ɛ:] (or in the latter case [ɛə]).

THE DEVELOPMENT OF A GLIDE [ə] BETWEEN A VOWEL OR DIPHTHONG AND *r*

§ 218. Either during the fifteenth century or at the beginning of the sixteenth century, there develops between certain vowels and diphthongs and a following *r* a glide [ə]. This glide is in effect given off by the *r*, for the reason that the ModE [r] is closely allied to the vowel [ə] (see § 198). The evidence of the orthoepists is as follows.

(1) After ME *ī*, eModE [əi], the glide is shown by Cheke in *fier* 'fire', by Levins in *fyer* 'fire', *hyer* 'hire', &c., by Hart in *meier* 'mire' and *feiër* 'fire' (the latter in a passage illustrating hiatus, where it is not distinguished from *beiër* 'buyer', *heiër* 'higher', and *deiër* 'dyer'), by Laneham in *fier*, &c. (beside *firie*) and *entier*, by Gil in *hjer* 'hire' and *attier* 'attire' (*i* is an error for *j*), by Poole (who rhymes *fire*, *ire*, *dire*, &c. with *buyer*, *higher*), by Merriott (*fier* 'fire' and *Iarland* 'Ireland' are 'gross faults of spelling'), by Coles's 'phonetic spellings' *admier* 'admire' and *conspier* 'conspire', by Strong and Young (who follow Coles, except that Young 1722 regularly has *-ur* for Coles's *-er*), by Cooper (who says that *fire*, *inspires*, &c. are pronounced *fi-ur*, *inspi-urs*, &c.), by *WSC-RS* (following Cooper), by Cocker's

'phonetic spellings', and by Brown. The 'homophone lists' give the pairings *ire* : *eyer* (Fox and Hookes, and others) and *hire* : *higher* (Coles and others).

(2) After ME *ū*, eModE [ʌu], Hart shows no glide in *flour*. Bullokar shows the glide in *showers* and *towers* but not in *flowers*. Butler records variation in *flour, tower*, and *shower*. Hodges gives no glide in *towers*. The 'homophone lists' from Hodges onwards pair *flour* with *flower*. In general the orthoepists follow the indications of the ModE spelling, which from the middle of the sixteenth century onwards shows the glide in most of these words.

(3) After ME [y:], Cheke shows the glide in *pleasuer* 'pleasure' (which has analogical [y:r]). Levins puts *sure* in an -*er* list. Hart, in illustrating hiatus, gives *siuër* 'sure' and *piuër* 'pure' beside *viuër* 'viewer', but twice elsewhere has *siur* 'sure' (without [ə] glide). Bullokar has *puer* 'pure'. Sherwood says that -*ure* as in *pure* is pronounced *uer*. Cooper says that -*ure* as in *lure, cure*, &c. is pronounced *eu-er*; so *WSC-RS*. The 'homophone lists' of Strong and Cooper have the pairing *suer* : *sure*.

(4) After late ME *ẹ̄*, eModE [i:], the glide is shown by Hart's *diër* 'dear' (but not in *here*; see Vol. I, p. 84), by Gil's *dier* 'deer', *apier* 'appear' (twice, against *apīr* twice), *bier* 'beer', *dier* or *dīer* 'deer', *pīerles* or *pierles* 'peerless', by Coles in an extensive list of words (e.g. *ear, year, cheer, here, spear, steer, fierce*, and *pierce*) which he treats as containing a diphthong [iə] (see Vol. I, pp. 439–40), and by *RS*'s *re-ur* 'rear'.

(5) After ME *ai*, eModE [ai], the glide is shown by Laneham's *faer* (beside *fair*), by Gil's *aerj* 'airy', *aier* 'air', *fāeri, fāerī* (for Spenser's *Faerie*), *fāierlj* (once, beside *fāirlj* once) 'fairly', *faier* twice, *fāier* twice (beside *fair* eleven times, *fāir* ten times), and by Cooper's statement that in *lair* the *ir* is pronounced as if it were *ur* (i.e. the pronunciation is [lɛ:ər]).

(6) After ME *ā, ẹ̄*, and *ǭ* the glide is seldom shown. Hart has *ēer*, apparently for *e'er* (ME *ẹ̄r*) 'ever', and *ōer* 'oar' and Bullokar *owerz* 'oars' (with *ow* for [o:] < ME *ǭ*); Gil has *earl* (a phonetic spelling, in which the *a* is intended to represent the glide [ə]) beside the pronunciations *ērl* and *erl* which he says others use; and *RS* has *mo-ur* 'more' and *ma-ur* 'mare'. Hunt pairs *lore* and *lower, ore* and *ower* as homophones.

(7) After ME *ǭ* and undiphthongized ME *ū*, eModE [u:], the only evidence of the glide comes in Cooper's pairing in his 'near alike' list (which is based on less careful pronunciation than his own) of *door* with *doer*.

The evidence shows that the [ə] glide was common after ME *ī* and *ū*, which in ME were high-front [i:] and high-back [u:] and in eModE the diphthongs [əi] and [ʌu] ending in a probably stressed and prolonged second element, high-front [i] and high-back [u] respectively. It was also common after ME [y:] (high-front-round), ME *ẹ̄* (in ME the moderately high-front [e:] and during the fifteenth century fully high-front [i:]), and ME *ai* (a diphthong ending in the high-front [i]). This situation is what we should expect; to pass from these vowels and diphthongs to [r] the tongue has to make a large adjustment which gives full opportunity for the development of a glide-sound. After the other long vowels (ME $\bar{\varrho}$ and ME $\bar{a}$, which in eModE were low-front vowels, and ME $\bar{\varrho}$, a moderately low-back vowel) the tongue has to make a slighter adjustment to pass to [r], and the chances of a marked glide-sound developing are correspondingly reduced; the evidence of the [ə] glide after these vowels is infrequent and would tend to show that the glide was originally rarer or less noticeable. We may notice that Hart's *ēer* 'e'er' is perhaps a special case; that Gil, who shows the glide after ME $\bar{\varrho}$, was tempted to do so by a desire for completeness in his account of the glide-diphthongs and had to admit that there were other modes of pronunciation; that Bullokar, who shows it after $\bar{\varrho}$, commonly represents dialectal or vulgar pronunciation; and that *RS*, who shows it after both ME $\bar{a}$ and ME $\bar{\varrho}$, also represents vulgar or advanced speech. After ME $\bar{\varrho}$ and undiphthongized ME $\bar{u}$, i.e. eModE [u:], we should expect the glide to be fairly frequent, though perhaps not so frequent as after the corresponding front vowel (ME $\bar{\varrho}$, eModE [i:]); the extreme paucity of evidence for a glide [ə] after early ModE [u:] may be accidental.

The orthoepists' evidence shows that the glide developed chiefly before final *r*, but also before intervocalic *r* and once (in Gil's *earl*) before preconsonantal *r*.

In PresE preconsonantal *r* and final *r* (except when the following word begins with a vowel) have been vocalized to [ə], and this [ə] has coalesced with and reinforced the [ə] glide (so *scarce, fierce, beard*; *fair, dear, poor*, &c.). PresE retains intervocalic *r*, but shows the [ə] glide before it after all the ME long vowels and diphthongs, as in *fairy, vary, weary, fiery*, &c.

After the ME short vowels there is no eModE evidence of a glide [ə], and PresE does not show it (e.g. in *carry, berry, mirror, borrow*, and *hurry*).

Note 1: The spellings cited by Wyld, *Coll. Eng.*, p. 300, show the [ə] glide chiefly after ME $\bar{\imath}$ (from 1528 onwards), but also after ME [y:] (so *duaring* 'during' 1581, and possibly *youers* 'yours', Gabriel Harvey) and ME $\bar{u}$ (*devower*, Gabriel Harvey; so possibly *youers* 'yours'). Rhymes from the sixteenth century onwards occasionally show the glide, chiefly after ME $\bar{\imath}$. Wyld, loc. cit., cites Watts's *door : to her* (cf. Cooper's evidence above). Luick, § 506, Anm. 1, cites some additional spellings, showing [ə] after ME $\bar{\imath}$ (*hire*, &c.), ME $\bar{\varrho}$ (*herein*), and ME $\bar{u}$ (*bower, tower* in the late fifteenth and early sixteenth centuries; but *power*, from OF *pouer*, &c., should be excluded). Luick also cites the evidence of foreign orthoepists showing [ə] after ME $\bar{\imath}$ and ME $\bar{\varrho}$ from 1580 onwards.

Note 2: Luick, §§ 505–6, assumes that the [ə] glide develops after all ME vowels, long or short, without differentiation. This is contrary to phonetic probability. He admits (§ 506, Anm. 2) that there is no evidence of the glide after the ME short vowels, but says that it must be assumed to have existed (though it was probably weaker after short vowels) to explain the later development of the short vowels before *r*. But the special development of the eModE vowels, long and short, before *r* is due to the direct influence of the *r* itself and not (as Luick assumes) to the [ə] glide; cf. § 198, Note. It is strongly against Luick's view that no glide [ə] occurs before intervocalic *r* in PresE after ME short vowels, though it does after ME long vowels and diphthongs.

Part 4: VARIOUS OTHER CONSONANTAL INFLUENCES

THE INFLUENCE OF *l*

§ 219. Before 'dark' *l* there occurs in late ME diphthongization of ME *ă* (see § 60), ME *ŏ* (see § 88), and ME *ǭ* (see § 146) as a result of the *l* giving off before it a glide [u]; ME *ŭ*, by a similar process, becomes late ME *ū* or *ou* (see § 174); and ME *ou*, by a process of assimilation, tends to become ME *ū* (see § 169).

In ModE a following *l* assists the preservation of [u] for ME *ŭ* (see § 196). Some evidence shows that eModE [ou] occasionally became [u:] before *l* (see § 251).

DENTAL OR PALATAL INFLUENCE

§ 220. In ME, chiefly in Western dialects, a following palatal caused diphthongization to *ai* of ME *ă* (see § 63). A following [dʒ] causes monophthongization of ME *au* to late ME *ā* in *gauge* (see § 104 (2)). A preceding palatal produces [y:] or [iu] from fifteenth-century [u:] < ME *ǭ* (see § 159) and from ME *ū* (see § 178). But palatal influence does not cause the failure of the diphthongization of ME *ī* (see § 138) and ME *ū* (see § 167), as Luick has suggested.

In ModE a preceding [j] affects the pronunciation of [u:], causing it to tend towards [y:] (see §§ 186-7). Various palatals in a wide sense (*d, t, l, r*, [ʃ], [tʃ], [dʒ], and [j]) cause simplification to [u:] of a following [ju:] < earlier [iu] < ME [y:], *iu, ęu*, and *ęu*, and the consonants [s] and [z] coalesce with the [j] of a following [ju:] to become [ʃ] and [ʒ] (see §§ 185, 244).

See also Part 1 (on raising) for further details of the influence of dentals and palatals on the vowels.

GUTTURAL INFLUENCE

§ 221. In ME there occurs before [χ] diphthongization of ME *ă* to *au* (see § 61) and of ME *ŏ* to *ou* (see § 89), as a result of the giving off of a glide [u] before the [χ]; ME *ou* by a process of assimilation tends to become *ū* (see § 170); early ME *ǭ* becomes *ū* or *ou* (see § 171); and ME *ŭ* normally becomes *ū* but appears occasionally as *ou* (see § 175).

In ModE there is some evidence of an occasional development of eModE [ou] to [u:] before [χ] (see § 251).

On the raising influence exerted by a fronted [g] preceding the vowel, and by [g] and [k] following it, on ME *ĕ*, see §§ 76-77.

LABIAL INFLUENCE

§ 222. In late ME a following *m, f,* or *v* causes monophthongization of ME *au* to late ME *ā* (see § 104); similarly in ModE these three consonants cause monophthongization of eModE [au] (< retained ME *au*) to [aː], later [ɑː] (see §§ 238–9).

For further details of labial influence see Parts 1 and 2 of this chapter on raising and rounding respectively.

NASAL INFLUENCE

§ 223. In late ME a following *n* in certain circumstances causes monophthongization of ME *au* to late ME *ā* (see § 104); similarly in ModE it causes monophthongization of eModE [au] (< retained ME *au*) to [aː], later [ɑː] (see §§ 238–9 below). On the similar influence of *m* see immediately above.

On the raising influence of *ng* and *n* see Part 1 of this chapter.

IX

THE DEVELOPMENT OF THE STRESSED DIPHTHONGS

§ 224. In this chapter we shall consider the development of the stressed ME diphthongs until 1700, both in free position and when influenced by neighbouring consonants.

ME *ai* AND ME *ęi*

(1) *General outline*

§ 225. In the second half of the thirteenth century early ME *ęi* became *ai* (cf. Jordan, § 95) and thereafter the two diphthongs developed together, though to some extent the spelling preserved the earlier distinction. The orthoepists give no valid evidence of a distinction between ME *ęi* and ME *ai*; they sometimes attempt to follow that suggested by the ordinary spelling, but break down whenever the spelling does not correctly represent the etymology. These attempts are therefore artificial, but not entirely so; they depend on different modes of pronouncing late ME *ai* (including early ME *ęi*), even though they do not show the preservation of a distinction between early ME *ai* and early ME *ęi* (see further below).

The ModE development of ME *ai* is parallel to that of ME *au*; the two diphthongs are closely analogous in their nature (the one rising from [ɑ] or [a] to high-front [i], the other to high-back [u]) and in their origins. The ModE development of ME *au* is in some respects less controversial than that of ME *ai*, which it helps us to understand. The first stage in the development of ME *au* was that the second element exercised an assimilatory influence on the first, which it attracted from [a] or [ɑ] through 'dark' [ʌ] to open [ɒ]; the second stage was that the first element, thus modified, assimilated the second to itself and absorbed it, giving the long vowel [ɒː]. On this analogy, we should expect that in the first stage of the development of ME *ai* the second element would exercise an assimilatory influence on the first, attracting it through [æ] to [ɛ]; and that in the second stage the first element, thus modified, would attract the second element to itself and absorb it, giving the long vowel [ɛː]. Our evidence confirms this explanation of the development of ME *ai*; but it should be noticed that what are here spoken of as two distinct stages, the raising of the first element and the lowering of the second, were in fact often contemporaneous—the two elements gradually approached each other. After ME *ai* had been monophthongized to open [ɛ:] its development ceased to be parallel to that of ME *au*; the latter became a vowel significantly different from the existing back vowels (being lower than even the conservative pronunciation of ME *ǭ*, which was in process of giving place to close [o:]) and so was not identified with them nor affected by the raising processes to which they had been subjected but which were now reaching fulfilment; but ME *ai*, becoming [ɛ:], was identified with existing front vowels (normally with ME *ā*, occasionally with ME *ę̄*) and was therefore affected by the raising processes to which they were still subject. In consequence it was itself raised to [e:], and about 1800 was diphthongized once more to [ei].

The orthoepists, as we shall see, give evidence of all the stages in the monophthongization of ME *ai*. They show the progressive raising of the first element, giving pronunciations [ai], [æi], and [ɛi]; the lowering of the second element to some sort of *e* sound, and its weakening acoustic effect; and the eventual monophthongization to [ɛ:]. It must be observed that the various pronunciations overlapped to a considerable extent. Spellings and rhymes prove that the monophthong was already in use even in StE from early in the sixteenth century, and the orthoepist Hart records it as his own pronunciation in his earliest work, the manuscript of 1551. It follows that the modified diphthongal pronunciations [æi] [ɛi], &c. must have been developed during the fifteenth century. But we find evidence of diphthongal pronunciations, both the original [ai] and the modified forms, as late as the end of the seventeenth century, though by this time they were comparatively rare. It is clear that until 1650 or 1660 careful speech preferred the diphthongal pronunciation (Hart is the only orthoepist before this time who regularly gives evidence of the monophthong); but the pressure of the monophthongal pronunciation, which must for long have been the normal form of less careful speech, continually increased, and during the second half of the seventeenth century it made swift progress towards displacing the diphthongal pronunciation even from the most careful speech. There is evidence that the monophthongal pronunciation was commoner, and was earlier accepted, in final position and before *r* (cf. the evidence of Robinson, Daines, Coles, Cooper, and *WSC-RS* cited below).

No clear account has yet been given of what happened to ME *ai* after it was monophthongized to [ɛ:], for scholars have been inclined to minimize or to forget the extent to which the pronunciation of ME *ā* and ME *ę̄* vacillated in the sixteenth and seventeenth centuries. There were in fact two things which could happen to the monophthong [ɛ:] < ME *ai*. Careful speakers in the sixteenth century and in the first half of the seventeenth century still commonly pronounced ME *ę̄* as [ɛ:]; it is obvious therefore that if such speakers were to accept [ɛ:] for ME *ai* it would be identical, in their speech, with ME *ę̄*. This not uncommon development has not hitherto been properly demonstrated or explained (see Note 1 below, and see further § 228). But more advanced speakers already pronounced ME *ā* as [ɛ:] in the sixteenth century and used [e:] for ME *ẹ̄*; such speakers therefore identified [ɛ:] < ME *ai* with ME *ā*. This development, probably already the commoner in the sixteenth century, was certainly so in the seventeenth; the reason is obviously that the more advanced speakers (who would identify [ɛ:] < ME *ai* with ME *ā*) were more willing to accept the monophthong in the sixteenth and early seventeenth centuries, and that the most conservative speakers did not accept it until the second half of the seventeenth century, when they had also accepted [ɛ:] in place of [æ:] for ME *ā*. It was only when the advanced monophthongal pronunciation of ME *ai* was accepted by speakers who retained the conservative pronunciations [æ:] for ME *ā* and [ɛ:] for ME *ẹ̄* that ME *ai* was identified with ME *ẹ̄* instead of ME *ā*. After the seventeenth century we get no further evidence of the two distinct identifications of monophthongized ME *ai*; this fact can only be explained by the hypothesis (to which other evidence also leads) that the normal StE development of ME *ẹ̄* and ME *ā* was to become identical about 1700 as [e:], so that the two developments were merged into one. The identification of the monophthong from ME *ai* with ME *ẹ̄* does not result in a PresE pronunciation [i:].

Note 1: Horn, § 114; Luick, §§ 515–16; Wyld, *Coll. Engl.*, pp. 247–9; Zachrisson, *Eng. Vowels*, pp. 64–68, 124–5, 150, 190–201; and Jordan, § 284, all assume that ME *ai* when monophthongized had only one development, to identity with ME *ā*; the evidence for its identity with ME *ẹ̄* is either neglected or misinterpreted. The reason is partly a failure to consider carefully the phonetic processes involved and a tendency to speak of 'monophthongization to ME *ā*' rather than to a ModE sound; and partly the failure to recognize that ME *ẹ̄* and ME *ā* became identical about 1700 (for if they did not, it would be difficult to explain the disappearance of the pronunciation which identified ME *ai* with ME *ẹ̄*). Wyld and Zachrisson leave rather uncertain the question (an important one) whether the immediate result of the monophthongization was [æ:] or [ɛ:]. Jordan believes that it was [æ:]; in this event the identification of the monophthong with ME *ẹ̄* would be impossible, and we should have to explain away the evidence which shows the identification. But in fact there is plentiful evidence for [ɛ:] as the result of the monophthongization, and none of an earlier [æ:] stage. The most careful account of ME *ai* in the ModE period is Luick's, who recognizes that it had various overlapping pronunciations, and fails only to recognize that the monophthong was sometimes identified with ME *ẹ̄*. His failure to do so has two causes. Firstly, it would be difficult to reconcile with his view that ME *ẹ̄* became [i:] by a ModE sound-change *c*. 1700. Secondly, he regards the fronting of the first element of ME *ai* as proceeding step by step with that of ME *ā*; on this hypothesis monophthongization cannot occur until after ME *ā* has reached [ɛ:]. But though the hypothesis will explain the eModE diphthongal pronunciations [æi] and [ɛi] for ME *ai* (which appear to correspond to [æ:] and [ɛ:] for ME *ā*), it will not explain the survival until late in the seventeenth century of a diphthongal pronunciation [ai] (unless we assume that ME *ā* also retained in the seventeenth century a pronunciation [a:]). It is also open to the serious objections (*a*) that the first element of ME *ai* originally develops from ME *ă* or ME *ĕ*, not from ME *ā* (in this it differs from ME *ẹu*, the first element of which commonly develops from, and in eModE is fronted with, ME *ẹ̄*); (*b*) that it ignores the parallel case of ME *au*.

Viëtor, *Shakespeare's Pronunciation*, § 43, and Ekwall in his edition of Jones's *Practical Phonography*, pp. cv–cviii, and in his *Hist. ne. Laut- und Formenlehre*, §§ 31–33, do argue that ME *ai* had two developments, to identity with ME *ẹ̄* as well as with ME *ā*; but their exposition of the theory was such as to invite the rejection which it has received from other scholars (e.g. Zachrisson, *Eng. Vowels*, pp. 197–201). They failed to explain the double development, cited false evidence in favour of the identification of ME *ai* with ME *ẹ̄*, and mistakenly connected with the sixteenth- and seventeenth-century identification of ME *ai* and ME *ẹ̄* the PresE pronunciation [iː] in *neither*, *key*, &c., which in fact is from a ME *ẹ̄* variant.

Note 2: The PresE diphthongal pronunciation of ME *ai* is not a survival of the eModE diphthongal pronunciations. It is a different diphthong from any in use in the sixteenth and seventeenth centuries, and is used for ME *ā* and ME *ẹ̄* in *great*, &c. as well as for ME *ai*. In any event there is no eighteenth-century evidence to prove a continuity between the seventeenth- and the nineteenth-century diphthongs.

(2) *Diphthongal pronunciations*

§ 226. In view of the amount of the evidence given by the orthoepists for the diphthongal pronunciations of ME *ai*, it will be convenient to treat it under various sub-headings.

(*a*) *General evidence of a diphthong, and evidence for* [ai]

The *Welsh Hymn* transcribes ME *ai* as *ae*, the conventional Welsh digraph, which has no special significance beyond showing that the sound is diphthongal. Palsgrave probably knew two diphthongal pronunciations, [ai] and [ɛi] (see Vol. I, p. 10), possibly beside monophthongal [ɛː]. Salesbury transcribes ME *ai* by the Welsh letters *ay* (see Vol. I, p. 12). Smith (see Vol. I, p. 57) represents ME *ai*, in both *PG* and *LA*, as *ai*, which probably shows [ai]; he also records a pronunciation [ɛi], transcribed as *ei*, which he tries to distinguish according to the usual spelling (see under (*b*) below). He further shows reduction of the second element and a monophthongal pronunciation in Northern English, which he may have occasionally used himself (see below). Hart occasionally transcribes ME *ai* words with *ai*, which may show a diphthongal pronunciation but is more likely to be an error due to the influence of the normal spelling. Bullokar records diphthongal pronunciations [ai] and [ɛi] transcribed as *ai* and *ei*; he tries to distinguish them according to the ordinary spelling. Mulcaster (see Vol. I, p. 125) says that *ai* is the man's diphthong and *ei* the woman's; he probably means [ai] and [ɛi]. But he also shows monophthongization and identification with ME *ā*; this was probably his own pronunciation (he was a Northerner). Tonkis identifies ME *ai* with Italian *ai*, thereby showing [ai]; he also tries to make a distinction between *ai* and *ei*. Robinson shows variation between a diphthongal and a monophthongal pronunciation. The diphthong is transcribed *aī*, the first element being identified with ME *ă* and the second with tense [i] (since Robinson's *ī* represents ME *ẹ̄*); the value is therefore probably [ai], for it is unlikely that Robinson regularly had [æ] for ME *ă*, since he does not show lengthening of ME *ă* before *r* and voiceless spirants (though he does show it in *water*). Gil (see Vol. I, pp. 150–1) varies in his transcriptions. His normal form is *ai* representing [ai], but he also commonly uses *āi* representing [æi], and *ei* representing [ɛi] in words ordinarily spelt with *ei*.

He transcribes the Northern pronunciation [ai] of ME *ī* as *ai*, thus confirming the assumption that this is the value of the digraph. But he also shows monophthongization in the Northern dialects, in the speech of the *Mopsæ*, and in two isolated and exceptional cases in his own speech (see further below). Hayward, 1625, describes ME *ai* as a 'proper' diphthong—a term which he uses correctly to mean a diphthong in contrast to a digraph. Butler says that ME *ai* is a diphthong, being 'rightly pronounced with the mixed sound of the two vowels'; he gives no clear evidence of the precise sound. His evidence on *change*, &c., which in spite of the *a* spelling he says are pronounced with *ai* (a Westernism), shows that he really did use a diphthong in his own speech. But he also records a monophthong [ɛ:] (see below). Daines (see Vol. I, p. 329) may be proved to have used a diphthong for medial ME *ai* even before *r* by his evidence that the Northern pronunciation [fai(ə)r] of *fire* was the same as the Southern pronunciation of *fair*; but in final position he shows monophthongization. Hodges used a diphthong transcribed *ai*, probably representing [ai] (see Vol. I, pp. 175–7); in *EP* he gives no evidence of monophthongization except in *their* transcribed *ðēr* (probably an unstressed form). Monophthongization in less careful speech than his own is shown by the 'near alike' list of *SH-PD*. Gataker probably used a diphthong, though his evidence is not very certain (see Vol. I, p. 217). *The English Schole-master* (1646) identifies ME *ai* with Dutch *ay*, i.e. [ai]. Willis does not rhyme ME *ai* words with either ME *ā* or ME *ẹ̄* words. Wallis says that ME *ai* is a diphthong which consists of '*a* exile correptum' (ME *ă*) and *i*; this probably means [ai], for Wallis shows no lengthening of ME *ă* and therefore probably normally pronounced it as [a] and not [æ]. He also gives evidence of [ɛi] (see under (*c*) below), but makes no mention of the monophthongal pronunciation except in his representation of the forms of colloquial language. The value of Price's definition of ME *ai* as a proper diphthong is uncertain (see Vol. I, p. 341). Wilkins transcribes ME *ai* by the digraph *ai*, probably meaning [ai]; he denies the existence in English of a diphthong *ei* [ɛi] and gives no evidence of the monophthongal pronunciation. In the speech taken as a basis by Coles's *Schoolmaster* ME *ai* was apparently still normally a diphthong of which the first element was a front vowel, though there is monophthongization before *r* (see Vol. I, pp. 439–40); but his less careful works show monophthongization to identity with ME *ā*. Strong, who distinguishes *ey* pronounced as *ay* from *ei* pronounced as '*e* long' (as in *conceive* with ME *ẹ̄*), may well have known a diphthongal pronunciation; but his 'phonetically spelt' lists show identification of ME *ai* with ME *ā*. The Yorkshireman Richardson (see Vol. I, pp. 382–3), though he himself used a monophthong, speaks of a diphthongal pronunciation used in some parts of England which he seems to regard as more correct; he identifies this sound with Dutch [ai] and confuses it with his Northern [ai] for ME *ī*. Cooper's evidence (see Vol. I, pp. 292–3) is most important. He says that ME *ai* is ordinarily the monophthong [ɛː], but he also shows two diphthongal pronunciations, of which the second is certainly [ɛi] and the first is described as beginning with the vowel of *can* or *cast*. Cooper may well have had [æ] for ME *ă* (he shows lengthening), but would be expected to have [aː] (though [æː] is possible) in *cast*; the first diphthong may then have been either [ai] or [æi], of which the latter value is perhaps the more likely. Of the two diphthongal pronunciations, Cooper says that [ɛi] is the commoner; indeed, [æi] is said to occur only in *bait, caitiff, ay* 'yea', and *eight* pronounced *ait*, 'which are all I know in our tongue'. Further, he says that ME *ai* when 'more strongly sounded' (i.e. when more carefully and deliberately pronounced) is a diphthong, but when 'more gently sounded' is a monophthong, which is used 'for the most part in common discourse'. In final position and before *r* ME *ai* seems always to be a monophthong in Cooper's speech, except in the special word *aye* 'yes' (see § 233). His evidence therefore shows the restriction of the diphthongal pronunciations to medial position in formal and careful speech; their end is obviously in sight. T. Jones, *Welsh Dictionary* (1688), identifies ME *ai* with Welsh *au*. *WSC-RS* gives evidence similar to, and in part derived from, Cooper's. ME *ai* is a monophthong when pronounced 'more gently', especially in final position and before *r*; but apparently there is also a diphthongal pronunciation of an unspecified nature. *RS*, in explaining that *ai* and 'long *a*' are apt to be mistaken, makes the important comment that 'the Londoners affecting (as they think) a finer pronunciation' do not pronounce *ai* as a diphthong, 'but the honest countryman, not to say our universities will (by no means) part with the authentick custom'. Other evidence from the last decade of the seventeenth century shows only a monophthong.

(b) Evidence for the pronunciation [æi]

Our discussion of the evidence cited above shows that the transcription *ai* used by some orthoepists is ambiguous and may mean [æi] if we take it that ME *ă* was [æ] in their pronunciation. This is most likely to be the case with Robinson and Cooper, and these two orthoepists, especially the latter, may then give evidence of the pronunciation [æi]. Smith also gives possible evidence of this pronunciation. He says that the rustics of his Essex pronounce ME *ai* as *āi*; this transcription might be held to indicate [æi] if we took it as showing that the first element of the diphthong had the same quality as ME *ā*, but Smith's comments show that he intends it rather to represent a drawling prolongation of the first element. This being the purpose of the sign of length, it is possible that Smith intends no comparison of the quality of the first element of the diphthong with ME *ā*. But when Gil in representing his own pronunciation commonly (though not in the majority of cases) transcribes ME *ai* as *āi*, there is little doubt that his purpose is to indicate not a prolongation of the first element, but the identity of its quality with that of ME *ā* as he pronounced it (i.e. as [æ:], normally); the transcription thus means [æi]. Gil also shows [ai] and [ɛi].

(*c*) *Evidence for the pronunciation* [ɛi]

Palsgrave probably knew a diphthongal pronunciation [ɛi] beside [ai] (see Vol. I, p. 10). Smith gives evidence of [ɛi] in a manner which is unconsciously followed by Bullokar, Tonkis, Gil, Gataker, and Wallis. He tries to distinguish *ai* [ai] from *ei* [ɛi] in accordance with the ordinary spelling (see Vol. I, p. 57), but admits that 'fœminæ quædam delicatiores' (so *PG*) or 'mulierculæ et nonnulli qui volunt isto modo videri loqui urbanius' (so *LA*) pronounce *ai* as *ei*. This is clear evidence of a pronunciation [ɛi] for all ME *ai* words, irrespective of their spelling, used by more advanced speakers; and it shows that Smith's attempted arbitrary distinction between *ai* and *ei* words is based on a real variation between the more conservative pronunciation [ai] (which he has to admit some people use even in *ei* words; cf. Wallis below) and the more advanced [ɛi]. We may assume that the same is true of the other orthoepists who silently try to make this distinction between *ai* and *ei*—Bullokar, Tonkis, Gil (who often but not always uses *ei* when the ordinary spelling has it), and Gataker; they all give implicit evidence of a variation between [ai] and [ɛi] in all ME *ai* words. Gil explicitly says that *they* can be pronounced either ð*ei* or ð*ai*. Tonkis, who identifies *ai* with Italian *ai* [ai], identifies *ei* with Latin *ei*; this, however, tells us nothing except that whatever sound he used for English *ei* (we may assume that it was [ɛi]) he also used to pronounce Latin *ei*. Mulcaster, perhaps taking a hint from Smith, says that *ai* is the man's diphthong and *ei* the woman's; there is no attempt to distinguish them according to the spelling, and he himself probably used the monophthongal pronunciation. Wallis distinguishes from *ai* pronounced [ai] the *ei* of *receive* (ME *ęi* beside *ę̄*), which he says is pronounced as a diphthong consisting of '*e* masculine' plus *i*, i.e. [ɛi] (his '*e* masculine' was an open vowel); but he also admits that *ei* is pronounced 'plenius' as if *ai*. The distinction based on the spelling is therefore arbitrary, but the evidence of the diphthong [ɛi] as a variant to [ai] remains. Newton, who normally shows ME *ai* as a pure vowel, gives [ɛi] when hunting for examples of diphthongs (see Vol. I, p. 250). But Wilkins explicitly denies that *ei* [ɛi] occurs in English; we may take this as meaning no more than that he himself did not use it. Cooper (see Vol. I, pp. 292-3) describes two diphthongal pronunciations, of which the second is certainly [ɛi], since it is said to begin with *e* as in *ken* or *a* as in *cane* (i.e. [ɛ(:)]) and to end with *i*. Cooper says that this diphthong is in more common use than the first ([ai] or [æi]), but that the normal pronunciation is the monophthong [ɛ:].

(d) *Lowering and weakening of the second element*

Certain orthoepists give evidence of the lowering of the second element of the diphthong or of its weakening. This weakening should be regarded rather as an indication that the acoustic effect of the second element became less marked as it approached the quality of the first element, than as showing that it was pronounced with less force and was about to vanish without trace (as is usually assumed). The process of monophthongization was that the two elements gradually approached each other, so that the diphthongal glide gradually became shorter (as in the PresE pronunciation of [ai] < ME $\bar{\imath}$; see Daniel Jones, *Outline of English Phonetics*, § 410), until eventually the beginning and the end of the sound had become the same; it was not that the first element increased in quantity and force of articulation while the second element simply became weaker and ultimately dropped off.

Evidence of a slight lowering of the second element of the diphthong is perhaps given by Welsh transcriptions, which (in contrast with Robinson's transcription of the second element as tense [i]) identify it with Welsh *y* or *u*, with which they also identify the lax English [ɪ] from ME $\bar{\imath}$; but they may be unthinkingly using conventional Welsh digraphs. Palsgrave regards it as being the nature of French and English diphthongs that the second element is pronounced 'shortly and confusedly'; this is evidence of the weak acoustic effect of the second element, though as the remark is a general one and not applied specifically to ME *ai* it cannot be pressed too far. Smith (see Vol. I, p. 57) describes in *PG* the pronunciation of *ai* in Scotland and Northern England as being *ae*; by this he means a diphthongal pronunciation in which the second element is lowered either to tense [e] or more probably to lax [ɛ] (see further Note 1 below). But in *LA* he says that this pronunciation is used by those 'qui valde delicate voces has [ME *ai* words] pronuntiant, mulierculæ præsertim', i.e. by advanced speakers of StE. Hart's isolated transcription *aehtþ* 'eighth' may indicate a diphthongal pronunciation with a lowered second element, but is probably an error (see Vol. I, p. 78). Gil says that in the English diphthongs the first element seems to sound more acutely and clearly, and in *ai* and *ei* so to fill the ears that it would be more reasonable for the *i* to be subjoined to than put beside the *a* or *e* ('ut i. subiungi æquius esset, quam ad latus adhærere'). This observation may merely depend on the fact (which is true of the PresE diphthongs [ai] for ME $\bar{\imath}$ and [ei] for ME $\bar{a}$) that English diphthongs are pronounced with a decreasing impulse of breath; but it may mean that in ME *ai* the second element, being lowered, had come to possess a less distinct acoustic value.

Note 1: Ellis, *EEP*, i. 121, followed by Viëtor, § 42, and Zachrisson, *Eng. Vowels*, pp. 190–1, mistakenly supposes that Smith, in saying in *LA* that the pronunciation of those who 'valde delicate pronuntiant' is the 'Roman diphthong *ae*', means to indicate a monophthongal pronunciation; he argues that Latin *ae* was ordinarily pronounced by Englishmen as a monophthong identical with ME $\bar{\rho}$. But no one who has studied Smith's arguments in *PG* can for one moment suppose that by the 'Roman diphthong *ae*' he means the sound used for Latin *ae* in the 'unreformed' English pronunciation of Latin; he means the classical Latin sound, or rather what he himself conceived it to be, and he would certainly suppose that it was a true diphthong composed of *a* as the first element and *e* as the second. That Smith does not mean a monophthong is in any case abundantly clear from the context in *LA* itself; for the following reference to the 'improper Greek diphthong ǫ' (with which he here identifies the Northern pronunciation of ME *ai*) would be entirely meaningless if he thought that the 'Roman diphthong' was in reality a monophthong and therefore itself 'improper'.

Note 2: Foreign confirmation of the diphthongal pronunciations of ME *ai* comes from early seventeenth-century Dutch transcriptions of English personal names in which ME *ai* is transcribed *aey*, *ey*, *ai*; see Luick, § 516, Anm. 1.

Note 3: The use by Southerners of the digraph *ai* to express the Northern pronunciation [ai] of ME $\bar{\imath}$ is evidence of the diphthongal pronunciation of ME *ai*, *c*. 1600 (for such spellings compare Luick, § 482, Anm. 3). The spelling *ae* occasionally found for ME *ai* (e.g. in *pae* 'pay') is usually interpreted as showing monophthongization to identity with ME $\bar{a}$, but Luick, § 516, Anm. 1, very reasonably suggests that it may show a lowered second element ('reduced', Luick's term, is less accurate than 'lowered').

Note 4: An analysis, with accurate statistics, of the rhyming practice of sixteenth-century poets would show the prevalence of the diphthongal pronunciation. Such an analysis is outside the scope of this survey, but the following approximate figures of rhymes in the *Oxford Book of Sixteenth Century Verse* may prove suggestive; for a reason to be given below I exclude from consideration rhymes in poems by Spenser. (1) ME *ai* in words not derived from French rhymes with ME $\bar{\rho}$ thirteen times (seven times in free position, six times before *r*). I include Daniel's *fair* : *repair* : *her*, since *her* can have ME $\bar{\rho}$ (cf. Chaucer, *C.T.*, F 790). I exclude *their(s)* rhyming twice on ME $\bar{\rho}$ and Raleigh's rhyme of *again* with *mean*. ME *ai* in words adopted from French in which a variant $\bar{\rho}$ is not authenticated by other evidence, but in which it is a theoretical possibility, rhymes with ME $\bar{\rho}$ twenty-one times. I exclude all cases of French or English words which are known from other evidence to have varied in ME between ME *ai* and ME $\bar{\rho}$. (2) ME *ai* rhymes with ME $\bar{a}$ thirty-seven times (twenty-three times in free position, fourteeen times before *r*). I include Fairfax's *faith* : *hath* and the anonymous *deceive me* : *have me* (p. 871), since *have* and *hath* have ME $\bar{a}$ beside ME $\breve{a}$; but I exclude Drayton's *bare* : *hair*, since *hair* may well have ME $\bar{\rho}$ (the more common variant), and rhymes of *waist* on ME $\bar{a}$ (Davies and Campion), which depend on ME $\bar{a}$ in *waist* itself. Thus there are fifty certain monophthongal rhymes, or seventy-five if we include all the cases mentioned as excluded (except words in which ME $\bar{\rho}$ is well established by other evidence, so that the rhyme is clearly on ME $\bar{\rho}$, and the *waist* rhymes). All the monophthongal rhymes come from within twenty years of 1600 (except Heywood's *Penelope* : *say* 1534 and the anonymous *ears* : *despairs* in Tottel 1557); but it must be granted that most of the poems in this book are later than 1580. Excluding the part devoted to Spenser, the book has 781 pages; thus if the figures are anything near accurate (I do not guarantee their absolute accuracy), there is on the average one monophthongal rhyme every ten pages (if we include the doubtful cases). But in the ten pages 500–9 there are 14 rhymes of *ai* with *ai* (and nine of $\bar{a}$ with $\bar{a}$); in pp. 600–9 (all devoted to Drayton, who makes frequent use of monophthongal rhymes and has six certain and one possible case in these pages) there are 12 rhymes of *ai* with *ai* (and 12 of $\bar{a}$ with $\bar{a}$); in pp. 700–9 there are 9 *ai* with *ai* rhymes (and 10 $\bar{a}$ with $\bar{a}$). The tendency is clearly to keep *ai* apart from $\bar{a}$. The same is even more true of *ai* and $\bar{\rho}$.

Shakespeare in the poems examined by Viëtor, pp. 217–26, has only one *ai* : $\bar{a}$ rhyme (the rhyme *remain* : *dame* cited from the *Passionate Pilgrim* is non-Shakespearian, and *gait*, which rhymes on $\bar{a}$, has ME $\bar{a}$, being from ON *gata*); but there are, as I estimate, about 300 rhymes of *ai* with *ai*. Viëtor's lists are incomplete, it is true; but in all Shakespeare there are barely a dozen certain rhymes of *ai* with $\bar{a}$. Such rhymes, however, are frequent in Spenser (cf. Horn, § 114, Note 3), but he is influenced in his rhyming by some advanced form of speech, either Northern or less correct London English (or a combination of the two influences).

Wyld, *Rhymes*, pp. 56–57, argues that the unwillingness of sixteenth- and seventeenth-century poets to rhyme ME *ai* with ME *ā* is due to the influence of the spelling, but this seems contrary to all that we know of their rhyming habits (whatever their mentors like Puttenham may have advised); the evidence for the survival of the diphthongal pronunciations is so strong that we need have no doubt that they are the influence which restrained the poets.

Note 5: Luick, § 516, gives in outline an interpretation of the orthoepistical evidence which is closely similar to that given above. The interpretations of the evidence of certain orthoepists given by Zachrisson, *Eng. Vowels*, pp. 190–7, who by special pleading seeks to minimize the evidence for the diphthongal pronunciations, are not to be relied on.

(3) *Monophthongal pronunciations*

(a) *Evidence of monophthongization to* [ɛ:]

§ 227. Under this heading we shall examine only such evidence as shows clearly that the immediate result of monophthongization in StE in the sixteenth and seventeenth centuries was [ɛ:]. Evidence of the identification of this monophthong with either ME ẹ̄ or ME ā, and of the later raising from [ɛ:] to [e:], will be given under separate headings below.

Palsgrave uses the digraph *ey* to transcribe French ę [ɛ(:)] in *royne* 'reine' pronounced (as he says) *reyne*. Hart (see Vol. I, pp. 78–79) carefully and explicitly identifies ME *ai* as the long equivalent of ME ĕ, thus showing the value [ɛ:], and transcribes it as *ē*, a symbol which he also uses for French ę in *père*. Florio identifies ME *ai* with (in his own phrase) Italian 'open *e*', i.e. [ɛ:]. Gil (see Vol. I, pp. 148, 151) identifies the *Mopsæ*'s pronunciation of both ME *ai* and ME *ā* (which obviously they identified) with his pronunciation of ME ẹ̄ (normally [ɛ:]); it has been argued that he shows that the *Mopsæ* identified ME *ai* with their own pronunciation of ME ẹ̄, but this is a misinterpretation. Butler, who normally used a diphthongal pronunciation, says that the 'corrupt' English monophthongal pronunciation is 'in imitation of the French'; we may conclude that the English pronunciation of the digraph *ai* was the same as the French, which was [ɛ(:)] (except in final position, where it was [e:], as now). Newton and Cooper regard the monophthongal pronunciation of ME *ai* as the long equivalent of ME ĕ, i.e. [ɛ:]; Cooper is followed by Aickin.

Note 1: Zachrisson, *Eng. Vowels*, p. 150, takes Palsgrave's identification of ME *ai* with French *ai* as showing [ɛ:], though he admits there is room for doubt; but Palsgrave's terms (see Vol. I, p. 10) suggest that he means diphthongal pronunciations, which existed in many cases in French (see Pope, §§ 527–32).

Note 2: The foreign orthoepists cited by Zachrisson, op. cit., pp. 124–5 (cf. Luick, § 516, Anm. 2 (*b*)), give reliable evidence of [ɛ:] for ME *ai*; they are Desainliens 1566, Bellot 1580, Delamothe 1592, Erondelle 1605, Mason 1622, Mauger 1679, and Miège 1688. On Luick's different interpretation of the evidence of Miège see § 230, Note.

(b) *Identification of* [ɛ:] < *ME* ai *with ME* ẹ̄

§ 228. Conservative speakers who retained the pronunciation [ɛ:] for ME ẹ̄ must, if they accepted the monophthongal pronunciation [ɛ:] for

ME *ai* (as they usually did not), have identified ME *ai* with ME *ẹ̄*. The clearest and most regular evidence of this development is provided by Hart, both in his manuscript of 1551 and in the later *Orthographie* and *Methode* (see Vol. I, pp. 78–79); in the manuscript he speaks of both *ai* and *ẹ̄* as being merely the long equivalents of ME *ĕ*, and in the *Orthographie* and *Methode* he uses the symbol *ē* to transcribe both *ai* and *ẹ̄* (cf. the symbol *ee* used in a trial transcription in the manuscript; see Vol. I, p. 79, note 4). There is no certain evidence in Hart of a diphthongal variant, though occasional transcriptions (probably errors) may give evidence of the pronunciations [ai] and [ae]. Waad, who seems (from the scrap of his phonetic writing which we possess) to have been influenced by Hart, agrees with him in identifying ME *ai* with ME *ẹ̄* (see Vol. I, p. 130). Hume's evidence (see Vol. I, pp. 318–19) shows that the Southern pronunciation of ME *ai* was [e:] and different from the Southern pronunciation of ME *ā*; it is a safe assumption that it was identical with the Southern pronunciation of ME *ẹ̄*. Gil, as remarked above (see § 227), does not give evidence that the *Mopsæ* identified ME *ai* with ME *ẹ̄*; but he objects to Hart's treatment of *ai* on the ground that it represents an improper pronunciation, not that it is a bad spelling. Butler says that ME *ai* is sometimes 'corruptly sounded as *e* in imitation of the French'; in other words, ME *ai* in this 'corrupt' pronunciation is identical with ME *ẹ̄*. Hodges in *EP* transcribes *their* as *ðēr*, but this word shows special development under weak stress. In his 'near alike' list in *SH-PD*, however, Hodges gives definite evidence of the identification of ME *ai* with ME *ẹ̄*; he equates ME *ai* in free position with ME *ẹ̄* five times, and with ME *ā* only twice (*lead : laid* pp., *meads : maids, please : plays, plead : played, sea : say,* against *place : plaice, raze : raise*). In this list, it is important to note, ME *ā* is kept distinct from ME *ẹ̄* except before *r*; the pairings quoted therefore show two distinct developments of ME *ai*. On the treatment given to ME *ai* before *r* by this list see § 231 below.

Note 1: Scholars have been unwilling to accept at its face value Hart's clear evidence identifying ME *ai* with ME *ẹ̄*. Jespersen, *Hart*, pp. 33–41; Zachrisson, *Eng. Vowels*, p. 192; and Luick, § 516, Anm. 2 (*a*), offer various explanations of Hart's transcription of ME *ai* as *ē* in the *Orthographie* and the *Methode* (the evidence of the manuscript is largely ignored), but they agree that whatever Hart may say, the explanation of his transcription was certainly not that he pronounced ME *ai* in the same way as ME *ẹ̄*. But Hart's evidence, in reality unassailable in itself, is strongly supported by the evidence of other orthoepists (as we have seen), by spellings, and by rhymes (see Notes 4 and 5 below), and is easily explicable.

Note 2: The 'homophone' lists of Wharton, Young, *WSC-RS*, and Cocker pair *play* with *plea*, and Brown pairs *say* with *sea*; both pairings are adopted from Hodges's 'near alike' list. But these later seventeenth-century orthoepists show in their 'homophone' lists the identification of ME *ā* with ME *ẹ̄*, of which in their case the identification of ME *ai* with ME *ẹ̄* may be a secondary result.

Note 3: Many words preserve in eModE a ME variation between ME *ai* and ME *ẹ̄* (see §§ 129–31 above); such words of course cannot be used as evidence of a ModE identification of the monophthong developed from ME *ai* with ME *ẹ̄* (cf. Luick, § 516, Anm. 5 and 6).

In particular all words adopted from French which have OF *ei* are theoretically capable of a ME variant *ẹ̄* even when only *ai* is clearly established by our evidence (cf. Luick, § 516, Anm. 6). This consideration affects the following sources of evidence:

(*a*) Many spellings certainly or possibly depend on a ME variant in *ẹ̄*. Such are the *Paston Letters*' *nebers* 'neighbours' (cited by Zachrisson, *Eng. Vowels*, p. 67), and *ea* or *e* spellings in words adopted from French, e.g. Shillingford *feale* 'fail', Queen Elizabeth *cheane* 'chain', Buckingham *fethful* 'faithfull', Paston Letters *pre* 'pray' (Wyld, *Coll. Eng.*, p. 248, Zachrisson, loc. cit.) and *leaman* 'layman' (see *OED*, s.v.). Cf. §§ 129–31 above.

(*b*) Many sixteenth- and seventeenth-century rhymes of words spelt *ei* (e.g. *deceive*) with either ME *ai* or ME *ẹ̄* words depend on ME variation between ME *ei* (*ai*) and ME *ẹ̄* (though Ellis, iii. 872, cites some such rhymes as evidence for the ModE pronunciation of ME *ai*). Even such rhymes as *ears : despairs* (Anon. 1557) and *faith : death* (Sidney) may depend on ME *ẹ̄* beside *ai* (though evidence of it is lacking), since the words involved are from French.

(*c*) Evidence of ME *ẹ̄* in individual words normally spelt with *ai* is given by many orthoepists, but depends on a ME variant. In addition to the evidence cited in §§ 129–31 above, Jones (1701) frequently records this *ẹ̄* variant; cf. Ekwall's edition, pp. xcviii–cv.

(*d*) ModE [iː] in *key, neither*, &c. develops from a late ME *ẹ̄* by raising of the ME variant *ẹ̄* beside *ai*.

Note 4: Some spellings do appear to give evidence of the identity of ME *ai* with ME *ẹ̄*. Dibelius, *Anglia*, xxiii (1901), 189 cites *ressyng* 'reising' ('travelling') and *gayt* for *gẹ̄t* 'get' from the *Paston Letters*. Kihlbom, p. 76, cites *ayme* < OE *ēam* 'uncle' from the *Cely Papers*; but the correct reading is (*n*)*eyme*, Miss A. H. Forester informs me, and *ei, ey* is a common spelling of Richard Cely junior for ME *ẹ̄*. Diehl, *Anglia*, xxix (1906), 164, 174, adds sixteenth-century examples, thus *Hewode* 'Heywood' (Henslowe); but examples from Machyn should be rejected, since he (like other Northerners) seems to show the identity of ME *ai* with ME *ā* and of ME *ā* with ME *ẹ̄* (see Wijk, *Machyn*, pp. 64 (*a*-spellings for ME *ai*) and 99 (*a*-spellings for ME *ẹ̄*)), so that the identity of ME *ai* with ME *ẹ̄* (shown by *e*-spellings for ME *ai* and vice versa; see Wijk, pp. 65 and 99) probably does not result from direct identification of [ɛː] < ME *ai* with ME *ẹ̄*. Many others of Diehl's spellings are to be rejected, including all those which have *ei* for ME *ẹ̄*, since these could easily be inverted spellings on the model of, for example, *deceive* spelt with *ei* and pronounced with *ẹ̄* (cf. also the Northern use of a following *i* to show length). Wyld, loc. cit., cites similar spellings with *ey* for *ẹ̄*.

Note 5: Rhymes with ME *ẹ̄* of ME *ai* in words not adopted from French are evidence of ModE identification of the two sounds. Dibelius, loc. cit., cites *may : degre : be* from Audelay (Shropshire, 1426) and *waye : me : betraye* from *Generydes* (EMidl, fifteenth century), which must depend on [ɛː] < ME *ai* and on ME *ẹ̄* (by relengthening of ME *ĕ* by shortening of ME *ẹ̄*) in *degre, be*, and *me*. Ellis, iii. 872, cites rhymes of *ai* with *ẹ̄* from Sidney. Wyld, *Rhymes*, pp. 53–54, cites rhymes of ME *ai* (in native words) with ME *ẹ̄* from Surrey, Drayton, and later poets; Wyld would explain them as showing (*a*) identity of ME *ai* with ME *ā*, and (*b*) identity of ME *ā* with ME *ẹ̄*, but though the later poets do show (*b*) Surrey gives no evidence of it, and his rhymes must rather be interpreted as showing direct identification of ME *ai* with ME *ẹ̄*. I have myself noticed the following rhymes (see § 226, Note 4): *Penelope : say* (Heywood), *ear : fair, away : sea* (Greville), *fair : ear* (Ralegh), *fair : repair : her* (Daniel), *sea : lay* vb. (Constable), *sea : holiday, lean : swain, bear : fair, sea : play* (Drayton), *fair : repair : there* (Shakespeare), *fair : clear, sea : way* (Davies). These seem unambiguous rhymes of ME *ai* with ME *ẹ̄*. There is no valid evidence, as far as I know, of any of these poets except Drayton rhyming ME *ā* with ME *ẹ̄* (see § 115, Note 3); but Daniel and Shakespeare (as well as other late sixteenth-century poets) rhyme ME *ār* with ME *ẹ̄r*. It follows that though the *air : ẹ̄r* rhymes may depend on the normal identification of ME *ai* with ME *ā* and of ME *ār* with ME *ẹ̄r*, the rhymes in free position (seven of the thirteen cited) must depend on direct identification of ME *ai* with ME *ẹ̄*.

Note 6: Delamothe, 1592 (cf. Zachrisson, op. cit., p. 124), identifies French *ai* [ɛ(ː)] both with ME *ai* and with ME *ē̦*; it therefore appears that he regarded ME *ai* and ME *ē̦* as identical.

Note 7: Wright, *EDG*, §§ 48, 64, and 206, gives evidence of a dialectal pronunciation [i:] in ME *ai* words; but the same or related dialects have also [i:] for ME *ā* (ibid., § 43).

(c) Identification of [ɛ:] < *ME* ai *with ME* ā

§ 229. More advanced speakers, who were more likely to accept the monophthongal pronunciation [ɛ:] for ME *ai*, already pronounced ME *ā* as [ɛ:] in the sixteenth century, and later, when conservative speakers also accepted the monophthongal pronunciation, they too had come to use [ɛ:] for ME *ā*; the normal result of monophthongization was therefore the identification of ME *ai* with ME *ā*. Smith (see Vol. I, p. 57) says that in Scottish and Northern English neither *e* nor *i* is heard after *a* unless most obscurely, and ME *ai* is therefore *ā*. Levins, a Northerner, identifies the two sounds. Mulcaster, another Northerner, though he records diphthongal pronunciations, also says that *i* is either silent or very gentle in *daie*, &c., and himself seems to have identified ME *ai* with ME *ā* (see Vol. I, p. 125). The first evidence for StE is that of Robinson, who shows identity of ME *ai* with ME *ā* in seven cases in stressed medial position (about one-twentieth of all the cases in this position), forty-six times in final position (where he uses a diphthongal pronunciation thirty-three times and in addition an uncounted number of times in the word *they*), and frequently before *r* (see § 231 below). In unstressed medial position ME *ai* is identified with ME *ā* in about one-third of the cases. Gil (see Vol. I, p. 151) shows monophthongization of ME *ai* to identity with ME *ā* in the Northern dialect and in the speech of the *Mopsæ*. In two isolated instances, which are incompatible with the great bulk of his evidence, he shows identification of ME *ai* with ME *ā* in his own speech, once before *r* (1619 *āerj*, 1621 *aerj* 'airy') and once in free position (1621 *rāzing*, but 1619 *raizing* 'raising'); this evidence of monophthongization, which depends on a mode of pronunciation different in several respects from that which is the normal basis of his transcriptions, is probably to be accepted, though some doubt is possible in the case of *raising*. Daines shows identification of ME *ai* with ME *ā* in final position (*say* is pronounced *sa*) but a diphthong medially. Wallis shows identification of ME *ai* with ME *ā* only in his transcript of the forms of colloquial language (*da* for *day*); otherwise he gives diphthongal pronunciations. The Northerner Poole rhymes ME *ai* with ME *ā*. Merriott says that *hallida* 'holiday' is a gross fault of spelling which follows the sound. Strong's 'phonetically spelt' list shows *ā* for *ai*. Newton identifies ME *ai* with ME *ā*. The Northerner Richardson shows monophthongization to *ā* in his own speech. Lodwick identifies *ai* and *ā* as [ɛ:]. Cooper gives [ɛ:] for ME *ai* as the normal pronunciation, used 'for the most part in common discourse', and also uses [ɛ:] for ME *ā* in the words (strictly only two) in which he did not use the dialectal [ɛə]. Aickin, following Cooper, identifies ME *ai* with ME *ā*. *WSC-RS* shows that this identity is normal, especially in Londoners' speech. The 'phonetically spelt' lists of Cocker and Brown use *a* for *ai* (Brown also gives *ea* spellings for *ai*, but only in words which have a ME variant *ẹ̄*). Identity of ME *ai* with ME *ā* in less correct forms of speech than those normally represented by the orthoepists in the text of their books is shown by T. Shelton, 1620 (in all positions), and twelve later shorthand-writers, including the Scot Ridpath, who marks the use of *a* for *ai* as an anglicism (though the monophthongal pronunciation was very much earlier in the North), perhaps because in Northern spelling the *i* was used as a sign of length which he would not willingly omit. It is similarly shown for less careful speech by the 'homophone' lists of Butler (once, against monophthongization to ME *ẹ̄* or a diphthongal pronunciation in his text), Hodges's 'near alike' list in *SH-PD* (twice in free position, and twice before *r*), and normally in Wharton, Price, Fox and Hookes, Coles (once in the *Eng. Dict.* and often in the *Eng.-Lat. Dict.*; only before *r* in the more careful *Schoolmaster*), Strong, Young, Richardson, Cooper (once, perhaps by error, in his 'same' list, and five times in his 'near' list), *The Compendious Schoolmaster*, Hawkins, *WSC-RS*, Cocker, and Brown. The 'homophone' list of Ellis (1670) does not admit any pairings of ME *ai* with ME *ā*, probably deliberately.

The evidence seems to show that educated StE did not accept the identification of ME *ai* with ME *ā* in careful speech until the seventeenth century, and generally avoided it until after 1650 or 1660, when it was more readily accepted.

Note 1: Identification with ME *ā* of ME *ai* occurs in the second half of the fourteenth century in the North (cf. Jordan, § 132) and in the fifteenth century in the East (cf. Jordan, § 284; but Jordan's view that the result of monophthongization was [æː] is contrary to the StE evidence). Dibelius, *Anglia*, xxiii (1901), 189, cites the rhymes *attaine* : *blame* from Brompton's *Penitential Psalms* and *breyne* : *pelicane* from the *Stasyons of Jerusalem*; both these are EMidl or NEMidl texts. Zachrisson, *Eng. Vowels*, pp. 64–66, cites spellings from the *Paston Letters* (Norfolk) and *Cely Papers* (Essex). Wyld, *Coll. Eng.*, pp. 195, 248, cites a spelling dated 1421 (*maid* 'made') from a Coventry text, and Dibelius, loc. cit., cites the rhyme *wait* : *algat* from Audelay (Shropshire 1426); these appear to show very early identification of ME *ai* with ME *ā* in the North-West Midlands, but *ai* in *maid* 'made' may be the conventional use of *i* to mark a long vowel and *wait* (in which *a* is found as early as *Cursor Mundi*) may be analogically influenced by the cognate and synonymous *wake* and *watch*.

It is possible that in the North the process of monophthongization was different from that of StE, and consisted not of an assimilation of both elements to each other, but merely of the second element to the first, thus [ai] > [ae] > [aɛ] > [aː] (and not [ai] > [aə] > [aː], as stated by Jordan, § 132); cf. Daniel Jones, *Outline of English Phonetics*, § 410 (for [ae] and [aɛ] forms of PresE [ai] < ME *ī*), and Wright, § 154 (for Yorkshire and Lancashire [ɑː] < [ai] for ME *ī*). This would accord with the Northern development of *ui* > *ū* and *oi* > *ǭ* (cf. Jordan, loc. cit.) and would make it unnecessary to assume that ME *ā* had already become [ɛː] by the second half of the fourteenth century in the North; it should be observed, however, that the Northern development of ME *ā* was undoubtedly very rapid, having reached [eː] by the sixteenth century and perhaps by the fifteenth, so that fronting to [ɛː] may have occurred as early as the second half of the fourteenth century.

In general it seems better to assume that the process of monophthongization in non-Northern dialects (which do not show $ui > \bar{u}$ and $oi > \bar{\varrho}$) was the same as in StE, even though this involves the assumption that ME $\bar{a}$ had already become [ɛ:] by the date at which it is identified with ME *ai*; it would follow of course that in these dialects ME $\bar{ę}$ had become [e:], ME $\bar{ẹ}$ [i:], and ME $\bar{\imath}$ [əi] before 1450, and in the NWMidlands perhaps before 1425, but such a conclusion does not seem to conflict with other evidence on dialectal developments.

Note 2: Spellings show the identification of ME *ai* with ME $\bar{a}$ in StE. Dibelius, loc. cit., cites *grane* 'grain' from an official document of Edward VI dated 1483; Zachrisson, op. cit., p. 64, cites spellings with *a* for *ai* or *ai* for $\bar{a}$ from Gairdner, *Letters and Papers Illustrative of the Reigns of Richard III and Henry VII*, i. 80 (of date 1484), and Ellis, *Original Letters*, II. ii. 161 (1484), II. ii. 162 (1485), and III. i. 102 (1483). All these spellings come from documents written or issued by Richard III as protector or king, so that they may depend on a personal peculiarity and show Northern (less probably Eastern) influence on Richard's or his secretary's speech. Wyld, loc. cit., cites Lady Margaret Beaufort's *sa* 'say' in a letter to her son Henry VII (Ellis, op. cit., I. i. 47), which is apparently later than 1500, though the year is not given. Such spellings become more frequent later in the sixteenth century (cf. Diehl, *Anglia*, xxix (1906), 160 and 173).

Note 3: StE rhymes showing identity between ME *ai* and ME $\bar{a}$ begin in the sixteenth century, though diphthongal rhymes are the norm (see § 226, Note 4). Ellis, *EEP*, iii. 872, cites two *ai* : $\bar{a}$ rhymes from Sidney (in whom *ai* : $\bar{ę}$ rhymes are, however, more usual). Spenser has frequent *ai* : $\bar{a}$ rhymes (cf. Horn, § 115, Anm. 3), but in his case we must allow for the influence of Northern or advanced speech on his rhyming practice (as of Northern dialects on his vocabulary). In *The Oxford Book of Sixteenth Century Verse* I have observed, in poets other than Spenser, thirty-seven *ai* : $\bar{a}$ rhymes (twenty-three in free position, fourteen before *r*); they all date from after 1580, but so do most of the poems in this book. Of these rhymes eleven, a high proportion, come from Drayton (who also has *ai* : $\bar{ę}$ rhymes; see § 228, Note 5); he is perhaps influenced in this respect, as in many others, by Spenser. Wyld, loc. cit., cites only seventeenth-century *ai* : $\bar{a}$ rhymes, all of them before *r*.

(d) *Raising of* [ɛ:] < *ME* ai *to* [e:]

§ 230. The monophthong [ɛ:] from ME *ai* was affected by the same raising tendencies as other eModE long front vowels, and became [e:].

(i) When ME *ai* was identified with ME $\bar{ę}$, it was raised to [e:] when ME $\bar{ę}$ advanced to that value. Hume (see Vol. I, pp. 318–19) identifies ME *ai* as pronounced in the South with MSc $\bar{a}$, which was [e:]; the Southern pronunciation of ME $\bar{a}$ is different, according to him, from the Southern pronunciation of ME *ai*, which must then have been monophthongized to identity with ME $\bar{ę}$ and raised with it from [ɛ:] to [e:]. Hodges in his 'near alike' list identifies ME *ai* with ME $\bar{ę}$ in five of the seven pairings which show monophthongization in free position. But in this list, ME $\bar{ę}$ is distinct from ME $\bar{a}$ in free position though identical with it before *r*, and it follows that ME $\bar{ę}$ in free position has been raised from [ɛ:] to [e:], though held back as [ɛ:] before *r*; ME *ai* therefore, when identified with ME $\bar{ę}$, must also have been raised from [ɛ:] to [e:] in free position. But in Hodges's own speech, ME *ai* was diphthongal and ME $\bar{ę}$ still normally [ɛ:] in all positions.

(ii) When ME *ai* was identified with ME $\bar{a}$, it was raised to [e:] when ME $\bar{a}$ was raised to that value. There is no evidence of this raising in careful speech before 1700, but certain 'homophone' lists, which identify

ME *ai* with ME *ā̈* and ME *ā* in free position with ME *ẹ̄*, give evidence of a less careful form of speech in which [e:] was used for all three sounds in free position (since it was as [e:] that ME *ā* and ME *ẹ̄* became identical). The lists which show both developments are those of Wharton (1654), Price, Fox and Hookes, Coles (only in the careless *Eng.–Lat. Dict.*), Young, Cooper's 'near' list, *The Compendious Schoolmaster*, Hawkins, *WSC-RS*, Cocker, and Brown. More careful lists, though they show identity of ME *ai* and ME *ā̈*, do not show identity of ME *ā* and ME *ẹ̄* (see § 115), i.e. they do not show the raising of ME *ā* (and ME *ai* identified with it) from [ɛ:] to [e:].

Note: Miège, 1688 (according to Luick, § 516, Anm. 2 (*b*)), identifies ME *ai* with 'French *é* masculine'; Luick interprets this as showing [e:], but 'French *é* masculine' was an ambiguous term which might mean either [ɛ(:)] or [e(:)] (cf. § 114, Note 1 above). In his *English Grammar* (2nd edit., 1691), Miège identifies French *ae, ai* with ME *ai*; this also is ambiguous, but is more likely to mean [ɛ:] than [e:]. Miège has [ɛ:] for ME *ā*, and not [e:] as Luick believes (see § 114, Note 2); it is therefore probable that he has [ɛ:] and not [e:] for ME *ai*.

(4) *ME* ai *before* r

§ 231. The development of ME *ai* before *r* differs from that of ME *ai* in free position in two respects.

(*a*) Monophthongization was earlier before *r*. The reason is that the diphthong [ai] and its variants are articulated by the tongue gliding from a low to a high position in the mouth; but when the ModE [r] follows, the body of the tongue must return to a low position. The influence of *r* since *c.* 1400 has operated against high tongue-position in a preceding vowel (see Chapter VIII, Part 3 above); and its influence on a preceding ME *ai* tended to cut short the upward glide, i.e. to cause lowering of the second element of the diphthong and so to hasten monophthongization. The evidence is as follows. Robinson transcribes ME *ai* before *r* as *ā* twelve times and as *aī* fourteen times; but in medial stressed position before other consonants than *r* the ratio of *ā* to *aī* transcriptions is as one to twenty. Gil identifies ME *ai* with ME *ā* in *airy* in both 1619 and 1621, but in *raising* only in 1621 (possibly by error; no error is possible in the case of *airy*). Hodges in *EP* shows *ẹ̄* for ME *ẹi* in *their* alone, but this word has a special development under weak stress; he does not show monophthongization of ME *ai* in *hair* and *pair* in *EP*, as has been thought (see Vol. I, pp. 175–7). In *SH-PD* in the 'near alike' list he shows monophthongization both in free position and before *r*. Ellis in his 'homophone' list equates *pair* with *pare*, though he shows no other *ai* : *ā* equations; but he is following Hodges, and we should not regard *pair* as necessarily having *ā* by ModE monophthongization of ME *ai*. Coles in his careful *Schoolmaster* shows monophthongization (to identity with ME *ā*) only before *r*. Cooper shows regular monophthongization before *r*, but before other consonants shows the survival of diphthongal pronunciations beside the monophthongal. In his list of words pronounced alike (not 'near alike') he gives five pairings of ME *ai* with ME *ā* before *r*, but only one before another consonant. The text of *WSC-RS* gives similar evidence to Cooper's, but the 'homophone' lists show identity of ME *ai* and ME *ā* in all positions without distinction. Other orthoepists show either diphthongal or monophthongal pronunciations without regard to the following consonant.

(*b*) In free position [ɛ:] < ME *ai* is raised to [e:] (see § 230 above), but before *r* it is held back at [ɛ:], as are both ME *ẹ̄* and ME *ā*. The only evidence of this in the seventeenth century comes from Hodges's 'near alike' list, in which he shows two distinct developments of ME *ai* in free position (identification with *ẹ̄* and with *ā*; see §§ 228 and 229), but before *r* only one, for in that position ME *ai*, *ā*, and *ẹ̄* are all [ɛ:]: thus he equates *chare*, *chair*, and *cheer* (the last word has late ME *ẹ̄* by lowering), and *fares* and *fairs*. The other 'homophone' lists which identify ME *ai* with ME *ā* and show [e:] for both sounds in free position (see § 230) must also have known a pronunciation [ɛ:] used before *r*, but the 'homophone list' method ordinarily affords no means of indicating such a distinction; it is only the chance that Hodges shows two developments in free position against one before *r* which enables us to deduce that ME *ai* in free position, when identified with ME *ẹ̄*, was different from ME *ai* before *r*.

(5) *Summary*

§ 232. The chief feature of the orthoepists' evidence on ME *ai* is the variety of pronunciations it records. Several orthoepists, and in particular Gil, seem to have employed more than one diphthongal pronunciation; others employed a diphthongal pronunciation in one position and not in another (e.g. Daines and Coles); others again employed both diphthongal and monophthongal pronunciations without regard to phonetic circumstances (so Gil, and more particularly Robinson), though the frequency of the diphthongal or monophthongal pronunciation varied according to the context. The survival of the diphthongal pronunciations in careful speech (especially in medial position), long after monophthongal pronunciations had come into use in StE, is one more example of the tenacious conservatism of the educated spoken language.

Special words with ME ai

§ 233. The ModE pronunciations of the words *aye* 'yes', *plait*, and *plaid* present problems.

Aye is recorded with ME *ai* by Wilkins and Cooper (who glosses the word 'I or yea' and gives the pronunciation as the diphthong which begins with *a* as in *can* or *cast*, i.e. [ai] or [æi]). Modern dialects have pronunciations descended from ME *ai* (see Wright, *EDG*, Index). 'Homophone lists' show ME *ī* by equating *aye* with *I* or *eye*; Price in his list says '*yea* or *yes* we sound *I*'. Gil's evidence appears to show variation between ME *ai* and ME *ī*, though it is rather confused, probably because of the variation (see Vol. I, p. 141). Sixteenth- and seventeenth-century spellings also show variation. Explanation is made more difficult by the obscurity of the origin of the word, which appears first in 1576 but rapidly becomes common. Derivation from *ay* 'ever' (the hypothesis seemingly preferred, though with doubts, by Murray in *OED*) would account for the modern spelling (found from 1637, according to *OED*, but probably implied by Gil's *ēi* in 1619) and for the seventeenth-century pronunciation recorded by Wilkins and Cooper, but not for the modern pronunciation or the normal early spelling *I*. On the other hand, derivation from the pronoun *I* (accepted by Onions in *Oxf. Dict. Eng. Etym.*), though it accounts for the modern pronunciation and the early spelling, leaves unexplained the modern spelling and the seventeenth-century variant pronunciation. Probably we have to do with two synonyms of different origin that have been confused, both of them back-formations from negatives: (1) from *nich* 'not I', used to mean 'no', the positive *ich*, *I* used to mean 'yes'; (2) from *nay* 'never', used as a strong negative 'no' (cf. *no* itself < OE *nā* 'never'), the positive *ay* used in affirmation. For the parallelism in ME of *nich* and *nai* cf. *The Owl and the Nightingale*, l. 226: *Thar to ne segge ich nich ne nai*. Only a double origin will convincingly explain the variation in both spelling and pronunciation.

PresE [æ] < ME *ă* in *plait* is shown (beside [ɛː] < ME *ai*) by Price's equation of *plait* sb. and vb. with *plat* (and with *plate*) in his homophone list; similarly *WSC-RS* equates it with *plat* and *plot* (with *ă* < *ŏ* by unrounding). The ultimate source of *ă* in *plait* (which occurs late in the sb.; see *OED*) is the past stem of the vb. (Wycliffe 1382, *platte* p.t., *plattid* p.p.), where it is clearly analogical; *threat* (p.t. *thratte*), &c. have affected the conjugation of *pleat*, itself a variant of *plait*. The apparently analogous PresE [æ] in *plaid* goes back to the sixteenth century (see *OED*), when the word was adopted from Gaelic; the abnormalities of its variant forms are doubtless due to Gaelic itself.

Note 1: *OED* connects with the *ă*-form of *plait* the fifteenth- to seventeenth-century form *plate* of the verb and the sixteenth-century *plate* (Coverdale 1535) of the noun. But these show normal monophthongization of ME *ai* to identity with ME *ā*.

Note 2: On *waist* (in which ModE *ai* is purely graphic) see Vol. I, p. 409, note 2, and § 6 above.

THE DEVELOPMENT OF ME *au*

§ 234. ME *au* shows two developments in ModE. In its free development it is monophthongized to [ɒː]. Before certain consonants, however, there is also monophthongization to [aː] > [ɑː], which in most of the words concerned finally prevails over the normally developed [ɒː].

(1) *The free development of ME* au

(a) *General outline*

§ 235. The process whereby ME *au* was in its free development monophthongized to [ɒ:] was that in the first stage the second element exercised a retractive and rounding influence over the first, which passed from [a] through 'dark' [ɑ] to [ɒ]; in the second stage the first element assimilated the second to itself, until the two elements became identical and the result was the long vowel [ɒ:].

The evidence of the orthoepists shows that diphthongal pronunciations, at least in some words, survived in conservative speech until late in the seventeenth century. In the sixteenth century careful speech seems only to have used the diphthongal pronunciations, though the monophthongal pronunciation had already developed. In the sixteenth century, and perhaps sometimes in the seventeenth century, the diphthongal pronunciation was [au] (or perhaps rather [ɑu]); but in the seventeenth century, when a diphthong was used, the first element was normally not [a] but [ɒ]—i.e. it had been influenced by the retractive and rounding influence of the second element. The monophthongal pronunciation is recorded by English orthoepists from the beginning of the seventeenth century, and is clearly the more common even in careful speech throughout that century. Some of the evidence (e.g. that of Salesbury and Daines) suggests that monophthongization proceeded more quickly in final position. There is definite evidence that the *au* spelling helped to preserve the diphthongal pronunciation in the seventeenth century even after the monophthongal pronunciation was in common use; and the evidence of the *Welsh Breviary* and especially of Cooper shows that it was retained longest in words of a learned type, undoubtedly by a deliberate exercise of conservatism.

The orthoepists show the same development for late ME *au* from ME *ă* before *l* (see § 60) as for earlier ME *au*. Occasionally we find transcriptions which appear to show retention of ME *ă* in certain definite circumstances; there is, however, no evidence of a general failure of the late ME diphthongization. But the difference in spelling between, for example, *all* and *awl* sometimes influenced orthoepists who know both the old diphthongal and the new monophthongal pronunciation of ME *au*.

Note: Luick, §§ 519–20, regards the process of monophthongization as consisting merely in the loss of the second element without any change in the first, giving [ɑ:], which later (in the eighteenth century; see § 558) became [ɒ:]. His reasons for regarding [ɑ:] as the sixteenth- and seventeenth-century monophthongal pronunciation of ME *au* (see § 520, Anm. 1 (*c*)) are: (*a*) the monophthongal pronunciation is identified with [ɑ:] in foreign languages; (*b*) the articulation is described as being with wide-opened mouth, and lip-rounding is not mentioned (but see § 237 below); (*c*) late eighteenth-century orthoepists identify with ME *ŏ* or the monophthong from ME *au* the first element of the diphthongs developed from ME *ī* and ME *ū*; (*d*) open [ɔ] sounds in other languages (e.g. French and Italian) are not compared with ME *au* (but this is not entirely true; cf. the *Welsh Breviary* (1670), § 237 below).

The real basis of this theory is the comparison of ME *au* with foreign [ɑ:]. But the nature of PresE [ɒ:] must be considered: in its articulation, the mouth is wide open and the tongue only slightly raised, being lower than for 'cardinal open [ɔ]'; the lip-rounding is usually slight and may easily be disregarded (indeed Nicholson, *Introduction to French Phonetics*, p. 24, declares that 'the lips are idle'). In consequence, English [ɒ:] 'differs widely' (Nicholson, loc. cit.) from French [ɔ:] (and similar foreign sounds); and it is a commonplace of modern phonetic textbooks to point out that to foreigners it sounds like their [ɑ:] (so Ellis, *EEP*, p. 72; Nicholson, loc. cit.) and conversely that foreign [ɑ:] sounds to Englishmen like their [ɒ:] (so Passy, cited by Zachrisson, *Eng. Vowels*, p. 139). There has in fact been this tradition of identifying English *au* with foreign [ɑ:] from Delamothe (1592) to our own times (beside other identifications: earlier, of foreign [ɑ:] with ME *ā*; later, and somewhat rarely, of ME *au* with foreign [ɔ:] and, probably from Festeau (1672) onwards, of foreign [ɑ:] with lengthened ME *ă*). But equally, from Coles (1674) onwards, there has been a tradition of saying, with increasing clarity and authority, that the identification of ME *au* with foreign [ɑ:] is inexact; this evidence significantly begins when the lengthening of ME *ă* (even though originally to a palatal [a:], not to back [ɑ:]) was providing an alternative substitute for foreign [ɑ:]. I can see no grounds for believing that an identification which we know to be wrong now was nevertheless perfectly accurate, and therefore a reason for assuming that the pronunciation of ME *au* was different, before such-and-such a date (whether 1800, 1750, or 1670).

The value of the late eighteenth-century evidence of Elphinston and his successors is very doubtful. The identification with ME *au* of the first elements of the diphthongs < ME *ī* and *ū* may rest, at least in part, on dialectal pronunciations in which they really were retracted towards [ɒ], for Elphinston was a Scot and Sheridan Irish (cf. Jespersen, *ModE Gr*, § 8.21, who suggests that Sheridan's analysis of ME *ī* refers to the Irish pronunciation [ʌi]—which also occurs in Southern Scotland; see Wright, § 6). Jespersen, loc. cit., actually himself analyses a Scottish pronunciation of ME *ū* as beginning with an [ɔ] sound. Moreover these analyses must be considered in relation to the similar one of ME *oi*, which is taken to begin with *au* (not unlengthened *ŏ*)—an analysis which is true if the sounds are as in PresE (in which the first element of ME *oi* is the higher sound of [ɒ:] < ME *au*, not that of [ɒ] < ME *ŏ*), but is pointless if we assign Luick's values (in which ME *oi* is [ɑi] and ME *au* and *ŏ* have identical quality [ɑ], differing only in quantity). But though the *au* sound is said to be full and clear in *oi*, in *ou* (ME *ū*) it is indistinct; similarly Elphinston says that in ME *ī* the *au* sound is rapid, whereas in *oi* 'the composition is clear'. Any eighteenth-century orthoepist attempting to analyse what he knew only as *oi* and *ou* would be tempted by the spelling to exaggerate the acoustic resemblance of their first elements; and similarly the fact that the digraph *oi* in many words (e.g. *join*) was still commonly pronounced as 'long *i*' undoubtedly induced them to suppose that there was a general affinity between the 'diphthong *oi*' (in *all* words) and ME *ī*. Nevertheless Elphinston is constrained to admit, in effect, that there is some difference. The evidence is at least so liable to variant interpretations that it cannot bear the weight of proof.

Only by assuming that eModE had no [ɑ:] sound can we satisfactorily explain its treatment of words then adopted from foreign languages. If ME *au* had really been [ɑ:], foreign [ɑ:] should regularly have been identified with it; but in fact the identification is either with ME *ā* (even though it had been fronted at least to [æ:]) or with ME *au*, and the double treatment shows that English had to choose between two approximations to the foreign vowel. Thus Robinson and Gil (see § 101 (ii)) substitute ME *ā* for Spanish [ɑ:] (except that Robinson has in *quatro* the same sound as in *water*, i.e. the reflex of ME *au*). *Hurricane*, adopted in various forms from 1555 onwards, never has *au* in the third syllable (see *OED*); similarly with *ambuscade* (1582–8), *ambuscado* (1592), and *desperado* (1610). *Gauze*, at its first appearance in 1561, has the form *gais* (admittedly in a Scottish text). *Vase* (adopted 1563) seems to have been more commonly pronounced with ME *ā* (a pronunciation which survives in America) than with ME *au* (see *OED*, which cites eighteenth-century rhymes on ME *ā*). *Spa* (adopted 1565) has forms with both ME *ā* and ME *au*: the normal spelling in the late sixteenth and early seventeenth centuries is with *au* or *aw* (see *OED*), but Spenser, *F.Q.*, I. xi. 30, obviously pronounced the name with ME *ā* (though he, or his printer, used the common spelling *Spau*), for he rhymes it with *away*, &c. But when, in the later seventeenth century, StE accepted [a:] > [ɑ:] for lengthened ME *ă* and for ME *au* before nasals, &c. (as in *dance*), foreign [ɑ:] could be more exactly reproduced; after this date arise reformed pronunciations such as [vɑ:z] and [spɑ:].

Lehnert, *Wallis*, §§ 149–51, arguing against Luick's view, shows (*a*) that German *a*, with which ME *au* is commonly compared, itself had a tendency to rounding (cf. Gil's identification of German [ɑ:] in *haar* and *maal* with ME *au*, but Spanish [ɑ:] in *bravada* with ME *ā*; see § 101 (ii) above), and (*b*) that in one passage Wallis, influenced by the spelling, appears to identify ME *au* with French *au* (open [ɔ:]); but it is not certain that Wallis intended this comparison.

The theory elaborated by Luick was first put forward by Viëtor, *Shakespeare's Pronunciation*, pp. 65–67, who is followed by Horn, § 128; it is rightly rejected by Jespersen, § 10.71, Zachrisson, *Eng. Vowels*, pp. 138–9, and Ekwall, § 36. On Luick's similar view that ME *ŏ* was not [ɒ] but [ɑ] from the late sixteenth to the eighteenth century see § 86, Note 2.

(*b*) Diphthongal pronunciations of ME au

§ 236. ME *au* was originally pronounced [au], but in the course of its development towards a monophthong became [ɒu]. In the following paragraph I shall give definite evidence of the latter value; here I shall give evidence which refers either to the pronunciation [au] or to some insufficiently defined diphthong. The *Welsh Hymn* transcribes ME *au* as Welsh *aw*, i.e. [au]. Palsgrave (see Vol. I, p. 9) identifies ME *au* with French *au*; he probably means to indicate a diphthongal pronunciation in both languages. Salesbury identifies ME *au* with Welsh *aw*, but in final position also shows a monophthongal pronunciation. Smith, Hart, and Bullokar, by transcribing ME *au* as *au*, apparently identify the first element with ME *ă*, and must have used [au]. Sanford (1611) seems to show a diphthongal pronunciation by saying that Spanish *ao* 'pawseth most vpon the *a*', as in English *fawn* and French *paon*, but his meaning is not clear; the second element is apparently not distinctly audible, at all events. In 1604 he had shown a monophthongal pronunciation. Tonkis shows variation: under the influence of the spelling, he identifies English *au* with Italian *au* [au], but *a* in *call* with French *a*. Hume (see Vol. I, pp. 319–20) is confused, but may have known a diphthongal beside a monophthongal pronunciation. Hayward (1626) says that ME *au* is a 'proper diphthong'—a term which he defines, and apparently also uses, correctly. Butler says that ME *au* is properly a diphthong with the mixed sound of the two vowels; he may also have known a monophthongal pronunciation. Daines (see Vol. I, pp. 330–1) gives a diphthong in medial position when the spelling is *au*. Gataker (see Vol. I, p. 217) is vague; his evidence ought to mean that ME *au* was still a diphthong. Wallis says that ME *au* 'recte pronunciatum' consists of '*a* exile' (ME *ă* rather than ME *ā*) plus *w*, i.e. [au], but otherwise gives only the monophthongal pronunciation; it is possible but unlikely that the diphthongal pronunciation which he describes is arrived at only by theoretical deduction. Price says that ME *au* is a 'proper diphthong' (which he defines correctly), except when he is following Wallis. The *Welsh Breviary* identifies ME *au* in *author* with Welsh *aw* [au], but in *call* and *cause* with Welsh *o* (i.e. with [ɔː] in this case). Cooper, however, says that the diphthong composed of *a* as in *can* or *cast* plus [u] (i.e. [au] or [æu]) does not exist in English, though he recognizes its theoretical possibility.

The diphthong [ɒu], in which the first element is retracted to open [ɒ], may be the basis of Palsgrave's comparison of ME *au* with French *au*, but is first certainly shown by Robinson, who, though he normally shows monophthongization, retains this diphthongal pronunciation [ɒu] before [χ] (see Vol. I, p. 210). Gil, who shows monophthongization, says that if a diphthong is used, the first element 'deducitur in *â*', i.e. is retracted to [ɒ] (see Vol. I, p. 152). Wilkins, who also shows the monophthongal pronunciation, gives transcriptions of *awe* and *yaw* which show [ɒu]. Holder (see Vol. I, p. 269) shows [ɒu] once, against normal [ɒː]. Cooper gives [ɒu] in fifteen words of a learned type—but *laurel* is included—derived from Latin (cf. the *Welsh Breviary*'s diphthong in *author*), but admits that careless speakers use [ɒː], the pronunciation of all other ME *au* words, even in these fifteen. This appears to be the last evidence of the diphthongal pronunciation. Cooper similarly gives almost the last evidence of the diphthongal pronunciation of ME *ai*, the development of which is parallel to that of ME *au*.

Note: Of the sixteenth- and seventeenth-century French orthoepists cited by Zachrisson, *Eng. Vowels*, pp. 136–8, the only one who possibly shows a diphthongal pronunciation is Bellot; Zachrisson rightly rejects the view that Mason also shows a diphthong. But foreign orthoepists commonly record rather less correct pronunciations than native orthoepists, and this may account for their failure to show diphthongal pronunciations in the sixteenth century.

(c) *Evidence of Monophthongization*

§ 237. Monophthongization of ME *au* is shown by Salesbury, Waad (see Vol. I, p. 130), Sanford (1604), Verstegan (1605), Tonkis, Robinson, perhaps Hume (who is confused), Gil, Wodroephe, Sherwood, Jonson, Daines, Hodges, Wallis, Merriott, Newton, Price, Wilkins, Holder, the *Welsh Breviary*, Coles, Richardson, the *Treatise of Stops*, Lodwick, Cooper, Aickin, Ray, *WSC-RS*, and Cocker. The practice of shorthand-writers from J. Willis (1602) onwards, of writing *a* for ME *au*, may depend on monophthongization, but does not certainly do so, for Willis established a rule that all 'diphthongs' might be simplified by omitting the second letter. Dix (1633), who says that *au* is to be written *o*, since it is 'almost like' short *o*, certainly had a monophthongal pronunciation.

Of the authors cited, some require more detailed comment. Salesbury (see Vol. I, pp. 12–13) describes monophthongization in final position (giving *awe* as a single example), but otherwise shows [au] both in final position (once) and medially (always). Sanford may give a diphthong in 1611 (see § 236). Tonkis gives the monophthong only when the spelling suggests

§ 237] ME au 787

it (as in *call*), not when the spelling is *au*. Robinson gives the monophthong in all positions except before [χ]. Gil normally gives the monophthong, but records the existence of a diphthong [ɒu]. Daines shows the monophthong in final position always, but in medial position only when the spelling is *a*; when it is *au* in medial position he gives a diphthong. Wallis normally gives the monophthong, though he mentions [au] as a more correct (but perhaps only theoretical) pronunciation. Price shows the monophthongal pronunciation in that part of *VO* in which he plagiarizes Wallis, but otherwise says that ME *au* is a 'proper diphthong' (see Vol. I, p. 341). Wilkins and Holder give some evidence of [ɒu] beside [ɒː]. Cooper gives [ɒu] as a more correct pronunciation (beside less correct [ɒː]) in some learned words (see § 236), but otherwise gives only [ɒː].

The nature of the monophthong is indicated in three chief ways. (i) It is described as the long equivalent of ME *ŏ* by Robinson, Hodges, Wallis, Newton, Price (when plagiarizing Wallis), Wilkins, Holder, Coles (*Schoolmaster*—the arrangement of his rhyme-list shows that he so regarded it), Lodwick, Cooper, and Ray (following Wilkins); cf. also the evidence cited above of the shorthand-writer Dix. This is consistent with our assumption that ME *ŏ* and *au* had their PresE values. But the evidence of Robinson introduces a complication. His theory that the long vowels were produced through longer organs (see Vol. I, pp. 203, 207–8) ought to mean that ME *ŏ* was further back in the mouth, or higher, than ME *au*, if we may argue from the analogy of the relation between [u] for ME *ŭ* and [oː] for ME *ǭ*, which Robinson also pairs as short and long. But in PresE ME *ŏ* is lower than ME *au*, i.e. [ɒ] is lower than [ɒː]. It is possible that Robinson used dialectal [ɑː] for ME *au*, but more likely that ME *ŏ* in his speech was higher than it is now, approximating still to its ME value of [ɔ] and therefore higher than [ɒː] < ME *au*.

(ii) ME *au* is identified with [ɑː] in foreign languages. It is identified with Welsh *a* by Salesbury, who transcribes *awe* as *a*; with French *a* by Sanford, Tonkis, Wodroephe, Sherwood, Jonson (following Tonkis or his source), Daines, Wallis, and Cooper; with German *a* by Verstegan, Gil, Wallis, and Cooper; and more vaguely with 'foreign' *a* by Holder. But there are indications that this identification is not exact. Gil uses it for German [ɑː] but not for Spanish [ɑː] (see § 101 (ii) and § 235, Note (end)). The *Welsh Breviary* uses Welsh *o* for both ME *au* and ME *ǭ*; Welsh *o* has two values (Morris Jones, *Welsh Grammar*, § 13), closer and more open (cf. Welsh *e*, used by the *Breviary* for both [ɛː] and [eː]). Coles in *Syncrisis* (1677) says that *a* in *all* is too 'broad' to be used as the pronunciation of Latin *a*; as his object is to reform the English pronunciation of Latin on Continental models, this must mean that ME *au* is 'broader' than foreign [ɑː]. Richardson says that 'some would have Dutch *a* to be like' ME *au*; this implies dissatisfaction with the identification of the monophthongal pronunciation of ME *au* with Dutch [ɑ:] rather than that he pronounced ME *au* as a diphthong.

(iii) Descriptions of the articulation are given by some orthoepists. Wallis classifies the reflex of ME *au* as a guttural vowel. Newton says that in its articulation the 'lips and chaps' are 'wide open', and Wilkins that it is the 'most apert' of the vowels and that the tongue is 'concave' (i.e. raised towards the back). Holder says that ME *au* has 'a kind of natural Articulation without Art, onely by opening the Mouth'. Cooper describes ME *au* as a guttural vowel, produced with the tongue retracted. None of these phoneticians describe any lip-rounding, but it is normally only slight in PresE [ɒ:]. Moreover in Wallis, who influences both Wilkins and Cooper, the failure to mention such rounding as there is may well be due to his classifying the vowels in the three categories of palatals, labials, and gutturals, of each of which there were, he said, three examples; the three labials were [u(:)], [y:], and [o(:)], all of which have greater lip-rounding than [ɒ(:)], and so the latter had to be classed as a guttural. Luick makes no allowance for this systematizing tendency in Wallis and other seventeenth-century phoneticians. Moreover Wallis's identification of the first element of ME *ou* with '*o* guttural' (ME *ŏ* and *au*), though inexact, must imply that the latter had lip-rounding; it would be incredible if '*o* guttural' were [ɑ]. Newton's and Wilkins's view (apparently shared by Holder) that [ɒ(:)] was the most open of the vowels was natural (and correct) when [a:] > [ɑ:] had not yet developed; of these men, only Cooper shows [a:] by lengthening of ME *ă*. Wilkins's mention of tongue-raising tells strongly in favour of [ɒ:] for ME *au* against Luick's supposed [ɑ:].

Note 1: The analogy of ME *ai*, the development of which is parallel to that of ME *au*, may suggest that monophthongization (and therefore the preliminary rounding of the first element) of ME *au* might occur before 1400 in the North, in the fifteenth century in the East, and occasionally from 1500 onwards in less correct London English.

Note 2: The spellings cited by Zachrisson, *Eng. Vowels*, pp. 81–82, and *Bullokar*, p. 67, and by Wyld, *Coll. Eng.*, p. 252, are claimed to show rounding of the first element of ME *au* (by the spelling *ou*) or monophthongization (by the spelling *o*), but are in fact to be otherwise explained. It is altogether improbable that any Englishman would use *ou* and *o* as representations of the '*au* phoneme', whatever its pronunciation, since it is always kept distinct from both the '*ou* phoneme' (i.e. ME *ou*) and the 'long *o*' phoneme (i.e. ME *ǭ*), which become identical; *ou* and *o*, so far from seeming phonetic spellings for [ɒu] and [ɒ:] (as they might to a modern phonetician thinking of his phonetic alphabets), would seem to an Englishman, thinking in terms of the conventional English spelling, entirely unphonetic and misleading. In fact other and more natural explanations of these spellings (assuming that they are indeed present in the manuscripts) are available.

Many of them depend on fifteenth-century shortening of ME *au* to ME *ŏ*; as this is a shortening of [ɒu] to [ɒ], it follows that the rounding of the first element of the diphthong must have occurred, but the spellings directly show only the shortening (cf. Luick, § 520, Anm. 1 (*a*)). We may distinguish three main classes of these spellings. (*a*) Those which have *au* for ME *ŏ* (*sauft* 'soft', so perhaps *Hawpe* 'Hope', assuming that *Hope* has ME *ŏ*) might perhaps depend on (i) lengthening of ME *ŏ* to [ɒ:] (but we should have to assume anomalous lengthening before *p* as well as regular lengthening before a voiceless spirant) and (ii) monophthongization of ME *au* to [ɒ:]; but they could also depend on shortening of ME *au* to *ŏ* and the consequent use of *au*, by inverted spelling, as a symbol for *ŏ*. But the alleged *caumplet* 'complete' is *clumplet* in Machyn's MS, presumably by error for *cumplet*; and the *Cely Papers*' supposed *auffer* 'offer' is certainly *ansfor*, an unexplained spelling of 'answer', as Miss Forester and Professor Davis agree, despite Zachrisson, *Bullokar*, pp. 137–8. (*b*) The spellings *oggest* 'August', *ontt* 'aunt', and *monde* 'maundy' certainly show shortening of ME *au* in the first syllable of words with secondary stress or before consonant-groups; cf. Wright, § 202, on [ɒ] in *aunt*, &c. in the present dialects. So probably in *loful* 'lawful' and *oful* 'awful' (shortening in the first syllable of a compound with secondary stress). (*c*) The use of *o* before *l* in *beholve* 'behalf', *y-fole* 'fallen', and *Wolsingham* 'Walsingham' (which does not show *w*-influence, despite Zachrisson) in the fifteenth century, and in *defolte* 'default' and *oll(e)* 'all' in the sixteenth century, is clearly a special case, as it is the most common. The simplest explanation, which is certainly correct, is that it shows shortening of *au* to [ɒ]; cf. [ɒl] 'all', [fɒl] 'fall', &c. in modern dialects (Wright, § 40) and [ɒ] in *halter*, *malt*, and *salt* (Wright, § 39 and Index) and in *calf* (with loss of *l*; Wright, Index), and StE [ɒ] beside [ɒ:] in *halter*, *salt*, *Salter*, and *Salton* (see D. Jones, *Eng. Pron. Dict.*, s.vv.).

The use of *ou* (*ow*) for ME *au* (*couses* 'causes', *defowts* 'defaults', *commowndment* 'commandment') should not be explained either as showing rounding of the first element of ME *au* or as due to an attempt to imitate the French pronunciation of *au* (which is highly improbable), but as an inverted spelling modelled on words in which the conventional spelling was *ou* (*ow*) but the pronunciation was ME *au* (e.g. *brought*). A particular source of these inverted spellings in Eastern writers (who provide most of them) is their use of the conventional spelling *ow* but the Eastern (especially Essex) pronunciation with ME *au* in words with OE *āw* and *āg* (cf. Jordan, § 105, Anm., and § 241 below); we may compare Bullokar, who spells *own* in the conventional way but rhymes it on a pronunciation developed from ME *au* (see Vol. I, pp. 107, 111). A pretty reverse instance is the spelling *awnly* 'only' cited by Zachrisson from the *Paston Letters*, in which the 'Essex' form *awn* replaces *own* as a representation of [oːn] < ME *ǭn*.

Wyld is, of course, in error in citing words of the type of *taught*, *wrought*, *caught* as evidence; the spellings and rhymes of such words depend on late ME variation between *au* and *ou* in *wrought*, &c.

Note 3: Sixteenth- and seventeenth-century foreign orthoepists identify ME *au* with foreign [ɑː]; cf. Zachrisson, *Eng. Vowels*, pp. 136–8; Luick, § 520, Anm. 1 (*c*). The earliest example is cited by Horn, § 128, from Du Wes (misnamed Dugres by Horn) in 1536.

Note 4: The existence of the monophthong [ɒː] for ME *au* as a common sixteenth-century pronunciation is shown by its substitution for foreign [ɑː] in *gauze*, *vase*, and *Spa* (adopted in 1561, 1563, and 1565 respectively); see § 235, Note.

Note 5: The statement of Davies, *Eng. Pron.*, p. 10 (cf. p. 11), that ME *au* was 'levelled under' ME *ou* during its development, is patently absurd as applied to StE at least, since it is evident that StE does not now identify, and therefore can never have identified, ME *au* with ME *ou*. The assertion is based on inverted spellings with *ou* for ME *au* (see Note 2 above). On the spelling *thawgh* 'though' see § 240, Note 3 below.

(2) *Combinative development of ME* au *to* [ɑː]

(*a*) *General outline*

§ 238. In certain circumstances, where the influence of consonants affects its development, ME *au* shows not only the normal development to open [ɒː], but also a special one to palatal [aː], which in StE later becomes back [ɑː]. The special development occurs (i) before *n* plus consonant (as in *dance*, *branch*, *demand*, *aunt*) but not before final *n* (as in *lawn*); (ii) before the labial continuants *m* (as in *balm*, *calm*, *almond*), *f* (as in *half*, *calf*), and *v* (as in *halve*, *calve*, *salve*); (iii) possibly before the dentals [s] and [d] (see Note 3 below). This eModE development of [au] to [aː] is exactly analogous to the late ME development of ME *au* to ME *ā* before *n, m, f,* and *v* discussed in § 104 above. The process is evidently that the second element of the diphthong is assimilated to the first before the latter has undergone any change whatever (contrast the free development of eModE [au] < ME *au*; see § 235 above). When [n] follows the reason is clear: in pronouncing the series [aun] the tongue has to rise from a low-front to a high-back position, and then move directly to high-front; the elimination of the intermediate high-back position is to permit a direct passage from low-front to high-front. The special development fails before final [n] probably because in this position after the diphthong [au] a retracted variety of [n] was used; but before the palatal consonants [s], [tʃ], [d], and [t] the [n] must have been well fronted. When a labial continuant follows the phonetic reason for the special development is not so clear: the operative factor may be rather the position of the jaws than the tongue-position; for the labial continuants the jaws are closed, and the elimination of the second element of the diphthong may serve the purpose of allowing a quicker passage to this closed jaw-position.

The ME parallel shows that ModE [aː] in *dance, calm, half,* and *salve* is developed from the diphthong [au], since late ME *ā* in *danger, safe,* &c. must be directly from ME *au*; thus [aː] < [au] is an alternative to [ɒː] not a secondary development from it. And as [au] was not in normal use for ME *au* in the seventeenth century (when [ɒu] or [ɒː] were more common), the development to [aː] must be earlier than 1600. On the other hand it is later than the loss of *l* in *half*, &c., which is not recorded until the late sixteenth century for StE; indeed there is little reliable evidence of earlier loss of *l* in other forms of English (except in conjunction with the late ME monophthongization of ME *au* to *ā*), but there is some suggestion of it in the Eastern dialects in the fifteenth century. The development of ME *au* to eModE [aː] could then have occurred in the Eastern dialects in the fifteenth century, though reliable evidence of it is lacking (cf. § 239, Note 3 below), but probably belongs chiefly to the sixteenth century, and rather to the late than the early sixteenth century. But there is no reliable orthoepistical evidence of it before 1650, and not until Coles in the 1670's and Lodwick and Cooper in the 1680's do we get evidence of its use in educated speech; and of these three, indeed, neither Coles nor Cooper is entirely free of dialectal influence and Lodwick is a foreigner. It therefore appears that the combinative development of ME *au* to [aː] was not native to educated StE, which at first knew only the isolative development to [ɒː] in *dance, half,* &c. as in all other ME *au* words. The combinative development to [aː] must have been characteristic of some other form of English, probably vulgar London speech (Cockney) or the Eastern dialects, from which, a century or more after its full development, it made its way into educated StE. Then followed a conflict between the originally vulgar [aː] (later [ɑː]), developed combinatively, and the hitherto normal [ɒː], developed isolatively—a conflict now largely settled, though some words (e.g. *launch*) still vary between the two pronunciations. In general [ɑː] is now used when the spelling is *a* (*dance, half*, &c.), but [ɒː] where the *au* spelling has maintained itself (*haunt, vaunt,* &c.); but there are exceptions, e.g. *aunt* with [ɑː], *halm* (also *haulm*) with [ɒː] beside [ɑː]. It seems probable that the more frequently used words were more likely to take on the originally vulgar [ɑː] pronunciation.

The view held by most scholars that the seventeenth-century pronunciation of *dance*, &c. was with [æː], which later became [ɑː], depends on their assumption that the immediate result of lengthening of ME *ă* was [æː] (for the vowel of *dance* is identified with that of *past*, &c.). But we have already found reason to believe that the latter was [aː], not [æː]. That the combinative monophthongization of ME *au* in *dance*, &c. was also in the first place to [aː] is inherently much more probable than that it was to [æː]; for the first element of the ME diphthong was certainly [a] (cf. PresE [au] < ME *ū*) rather than [æ], and it would be impossible to explain how the result of monophthongization could be a vowel further forward than the first element of the diphthong, especially as the ModE tendency was for this first element to be retracted under the influence of the second. But the vowel (in *dance*, &c. as in *past*, &c.) subsequently showed divergent development, on the one hand to [æː] (as in many PresE dialects, and formerly also in StE) and on the other to back [ɑː] (as in present StE).

In *dance, chant*, &c. ME *au* develops from OF nasalized *ã*. But ME *au* before a nasal, as a variant to ME *ă*, is not confined to words adopted from OF (see § 62); it is sometimes found in native English or in Norse words (whether because of the analogy of OF words or by reason of a ME sound-change is not clear, though the former is more likely). This ME *au* gives rise to the PresE [ɑː] in *answer* and to a variant pronunciation [ɑː] (beside normal [æ] from ME *ă*) which was previously in use in *ant*. A similar explanation may account for PresE [ɑː] in the contracted forms *can't* 'cannot', *a'n't* (now usually spelt *aren't*) 'am not', &c., and the (now obsolete) *ha'n't* 'has not' or 'have not'. These are not recorded, according to *OED*, before the seventeenth century, but might be much older than the time when they appear in writing; if they existed in ME, we could assume that there also existed variant forms *caunt, *aunt, *haunt (on the model of *aunt* for *ant*), in which the PresE [ɑː] pronunciation was developed. But [kɑːnt], [ɑːnt], and [hɑːnt] are more simply and better explained as analogical pronunciations. [ɑːnt] 'am not', though probably not developed from *aren't* (as assumed by *OED*), is certainly influenced by it; this influence is probably aided by the fact that *aren't* in dialectal speech gave rise to *ănt* < *ărnt* (cf. ME *ăr*, weak form) by assimilatory loss of *r* without influence on the preceding vowel (see § 401 (c) below, and cf. [eint] 'ain't' <

late ME *ānt* by loss of *r* in *ārnt* from ME *ār*, the strong form), so that in *aren't* itself there would be variation between [ænt] < late ME *ănt* and StE [ɑ:nt] < eModE [a:rnt], by late loss of [r] after lengthening. A further, and perhaps the main, model for [kɑ:nt], [hɑ:nt], and [ɑ:nt] 'am not' is [ʃɑ:nt] < *shaunt* < *shaull not* (the eModE strong form < ME *shăll*) beside [ʃænt] < *shănt* < *shăll not* (the eModE weak form); [ʃɑ:nt] itself is of course exactly similar to [tʃɑ:nt] 'chant' in its ModE development.

Many of the words with eModE [a:] or PresE [ɑ:] < ME *au* also had pronunciations derived from a ME variant in *ă* (see § 62). At the present day [a] or [æ] from the ME variant *ă* is normal in *dance*, &c. in Midland, Northern, and Scottish pronunciation, in America, and frequently in Australia in words which have the spelling *a* before *n* plus consonant. Others of these words have or had pronunciations derived from the late ME variant *ā* < ME *au*; on this variation between ME *ā* and ME *au* see § 104. Some words varied in the sixteenth and seventeenth centuries between ME *ă*, ME *ā*, and the pronunciations derived in ModE itself from ME *au* (see § 62).

Note 1: Horn, §§ 131–6, and Ekwall, §§ 44–45, give accounts similar to the above of the development of ME *au* before labials and *n* plus consonant, except that Horn regards the primary result of the combinative monophthongization as [æ:]. Horn regards the development, at least before labials (see § 131 (2)), as especially Eastern, Ekwall (whose general argument is excellent) as possibly dialectal.

Luick, § 521, gives a different explanation. He regards PresE [ɑ:] as from earlier [æ:], which in its turn is a secondary development, under consonantal influence, of still earlier [ɑ:], which he believes (see § 235, Note above) is the normal result of monophthongization of ME *au*. In §§ 519, 521 he explains dialectal and earlier StE [a] or [æ] in *dance*, &c. as due to shortening of eModE [ɑ:] or [æ:]. This attempt to explain all ModE pronunciations from one eModE development of one ME pronunciation is typical of Luick, and undoubtedly wrong; the [a] or [æ] in *dance*, &c. goes back to ME *ă* (so Horn, § 132) and existed in StE in the sixteenth century, before any monophthongization of ME *au* had been accepted by the orthoepists who record the *ă* forms. Luick's view that the normal result of monophthongization of ME *au* was [ɑ:] is not acceptable (see § 235, Note above); and we have already rejected the view that the combinative development to [ɑ:] was subsequent to the normal monophthongization. Luick's phonetic explanation of the combinative development (see his § 521) is similar to mine above, when allowance is made for the fact that he starts from a monophthongal pronunciation of ME *au*. He regards the combinative development as originally vulgar and most common in words which were much used in vulgar speech.

Wyld, *Short History*, follows Luick in explaining [ɑ:] in *half*, &c. (§ 260), but would explain it in *dance*, &c. from ME *ă* (§ 259, Note); but in this case, as Ekwall points out, why do we not find [ɑ:] in *scant*, *hand*, *stand*, &c.? Jespersen, *ModE Gr*, § 10.68, explains [ɑ:] in most of these words as a compromise between [a] < ME *ă* and [au] or [ɒ:] < ME *au* (!). But in § 10.69 he explains [ɑ:] in *can't*, &c. and in *ma'am* as due to compensatory lengthening; this explanation, possible in all these words, is most probable in *madam*, in which with the loss of the *d* the two short *a*'s coalesce into [a:], PresE [ɑ:].

Note 2: Luick, § 519, Anm. 1, sees in Gil's *lēn* 'lawn' a hint of dialectal [æ:] < ME *au* before a nasal; but it shows [ɛ:] < late ME (dialectal) *ā* (see Vol. I, p. 148 above).

Note 3: Luick, § 521 (3), would explain the earlier pronunciation [a:] or [ɑ:] in *hawser*, *saucer*, *sauce*, and *sausage* (for the evidence see Luick, § 521, Anm. 3) and the PresE pronunciation [tʃɑ:drn̩] beside [tʃɒ:ldrn̩] of *chaldron* as showing that the combinative development of ME *au* occurred before [s] and [d]. This is inherently quite possible. But [aː] in *hawser*, &c. may be due to lengthening of eModE *ă*, itself developed by shortening of ME *au* (cf. the seventeenth- and eighteenth-century *hasser* 'hawser', the sixteenth-century *sasser* 'saucer', the vulgar nineteenth-century *sass* 'sauce', and the seventeenth-century and vulgar nineteenth-century *sassage* 'sausage' recorded by *OED*). Similarly [ɑː] in *chaldron* (in which the *l* is not etymological; cf. OF *chauderon*) may be due to lengthening of eModE *ă* (cf. the lengthening and rounding of *ă* in *squadron* discussed in § 53 (5) above); *OED* records no *chadron form, but shortening of ME *au* to *ă* may easily occur in the phonetic conditions of this word.

Note 4: PresE [ɑː] in *laugh* and *laughter* and earlier [aː] in *daughter* (in the form *dafter*) are due to lengthening of eModE *ă* by shortening, before [f] < ME [χ], of ME *au*; see § 28 above.

(b) *The evidence*

§ 239. (i) Before *n* plus consonant the normal developments of ME *au* are shown by most orthoepists. Diphthongal pronunciations (either [au] or [ɒu]) are recorded by the *Welsh Hymn*, Salesbury, Hart, Bullokar (in *ancestor, andiron, ancient, change*, &c., as well as in *advance*, &c.), Mulcaster, Gil (in *aunt, demand*, and *grant*, beside the monophthong [ɒː]), and Butler; the normal monophthong [ɒː] is recorded by Robinson, Gil (in, for example, *dance* and *lance*), Daines (in *anger, ant, ancient, danger*, &c. as well as in *France*, &c.), Hunt, and *WSC-RS* (in *mangy, stranger*, &c. as well as in *branch, haunch*, &c.). Price shows either the diphthongal or the normal monophthongal pronunciation (it is not possible to determine which) in *haunt, glance*, &c. The combinative development to [aː] may possibly be intended by J. Smith's equation of *aun* with French *en*; but he also equates English *a* in *call* with French *a*. Lodwick gives certain evidence of [aː], saying that *a* in *demand* is the long equivalent of *a* in *man*. Cooper gives the same evidence independently. But Cooper's detailed evidence on the use of the pronunciations [aː] and [ɒː] and the spellings *a* and *au* in individual words is very confused, doubtless because there was so much variation in pronunciation between [aː] and [ɒː]; a summary of it is given in Vol. I, p. 304. We may notice that he gives, and appears to prefer, [aː] in such words as *haunt, daunt, jaunt*, and *maunder* as well as in *demand* and before *nch* (as in *launch* and *gaunch* beside *branch*, &c.). Cooper clearly relates the [aː] pronunciation to the *a* spelling, and would prefer to spell, for example, *gaunt* as *gant* in order to make the spelling accord better with the pronunciation. The subsequent history of these words has shown the same association of the *a* spelling with the [aː] pronunciation (in reality, of course, the *a* spelling originally represented ME *ă* and not [aː] < ME *au*), but working in the other direction; the conventional spelling determines the choice made between the rival modes of pronunciation.

(ii) Before the labial continuants *m*, *f*, and *v* most orthoepists show the normal development of ME *au*. A diphthongal pronunciation is given by Salesbury, Laneham, Bullokar (in *chamber* as well as in *salve* and *example*),

Mulcaster, and Butler; the normal monophthong [ɒ:] is given by Tonkis, Robinson, Gil, Jonson, Daines, Hodges, Howell, Wallis, *WSC-RS*, and Brown. Either a diphthong or the normal [ɒ:] (it is uncertain which) is given by Wharton (followed by J. Smith) and Price. The combinative development to [a:] is first shown by Coles in his *Schoolmaster* by the 'phonetic spellings' *hah-peny* 'halfpenny', *hahputh* 'halfpenny-worth'; the development to [a:] must be earlier than the loss of *f*, though later than that of *l*. Gil, it may be noticed, gives *hâpeni* 'halfpenny' (with normal [ɒ:] < ME *au*); the PresE pronunciation with [ei] descends from late ME *ā* < ME *au* developed once more after the loss of *l* but before that of *f*. J. Smith says that *aum* (as in *exaumple* 'example'?) is pronounced like French *em*; this may mean [a:], but does not certainly do so (see above). Lye may intend to show some other pronunciation than the normal [ɒ:] in *calf*, *half*, &c. by omitting the circumflex which is usually placed over *a* to show that it is [ɒ:], and if this is so the 'other pronunciation' is doubtless [a:]; but the omission may be accidental (see Vol. I, p. 354). Cooper's English text indicates that he used [a:] for ME *au* before *f*, *v*, and *m* in most words (see Vol. I, p. 304).

Note 1: Price, *EO*, says that '*aw* soundes broader than *au*, as *dawb*, *haunt*'; Luick, § 521, Anm. 2, not unnaturally assumes this to mean that [a:] (he would say [æ:]) occurs in *haunt*. But three years earlier in *VO* Price had made the same remark, with *saught*, *paw*, and *claw* as his examples; it is clear that he has invented an imaginary distinction of pronunciation to correspond to the two digraphs used for ME *au* by the conventional spelling. The 'phonetic spellings' *hant* 'haunt', *tant* 'taunt', *vant* 'vaunt' used by Strong and *hansh* 'haunch', *lanse* 'launch' used by Brown may perhaps mean [a:], but would more naturally mean [a] or [æ] < ME *ă*. Luick, § 521, Anm. 2, assumes from *RS*'s remark that certain words are better spelt *a* than *au* that the author pronounced them with [a:]; but the remark is plagiarized from Cooper, and *RS*'s other evidence shows rather that he used the normal [ɒ:].

Note 2: The evidence of Mason, 1622 (cited by Zachrisson, *Eng. Vowels*, pp. 137–8), though too vague to be a safe basis of argument, may mean that [a:] occurs in *advance*. Horn, § 133; Zachrisson, op. cit., p. 138; and Luick, § 521, Anm. 2, cite Miège, 1688, as providing evidence of [a:].

Note 3: Zachrisson, op. cit., p. 62, cites from the *Cely Papers* the spelling *arnswer* 'answer', which he interprets as showing [a:]. But the true reading, Miss A. H. Forester informs me, is *aunswer*, which is unremarkable.

Note 4: Luick, § 521, Anm. 1, states that Cooper shows the normal development of ME *au* in *half*, &c.; but the English text (which Luick did not use) seems to have been revised on this point, and gives indications of [a:] which are not present in the Latin.

Note 5: Some evidence which shows late ME *ā* < ME *au* before labials (see § 104 (2) above) has been wrongly interpreted as showing eModE [a:] < eModE [au] (as by Luick, § 521, Anm. 2; cf. § 104, Note 9 above).

VARIATION BETWEEN ME *au* AND ME *ou*

(1) *Before ME* [χ]

§ 240. Variation between ME *au* and ME *ou* occurs before the ME consonant [χ] in such words as *daughter*, *bought*, *sought*, and *thought*, i.e. in words which have late OE *ŏ* before [χt]; in *ought* we must assume ME shortening of earlier *ǭ*. The ultimate reason for the variation is the tendency of ME *ŏ* to be unrounded, in certain dialects, to ME *ă* (see § 87 above). From the normal *ŏ* variant there develops, in later ME, a diphthong *ou* when a glide [u] appears before the [χ]; but if the earlier unrounding to *ă* had occurred the result of the diphthongization was late ME *au*. It follows that the latter must have developed in the same dialects as show unrounding of *ŏ* (among them the Eastern dialect; cf. the early evidence cited in § 87 above). In StE unrounded *ă* < ME *ŏ* was originally a vulgarism which occasionally made its way into more correct speech; and so was its by-product, the *au* variant of *bought*, &c., with the difference that the latter came ultimately to be accepted (perhaps because the basic unrounding had been specially common before [χ]). For some reason it was adopted earlier in *daughter* than in other words and became the basis of the spelling; this fact influences the evidence of the orthoepists, of whom only Cheke records the *ou* form, while Hart, Bullokar, Gil, Butler, and other less important authors record *au* in *daughter* but in no other word. In the rest of the words involved, the *au* variant established itself only very slowly in correct speech: the only sixteenth-century evidence of it comes from Smith, a native of Essex; and though it is recorded quite often in the seventeenth century (most fully, before 1650, by the Londoners Robinson and Hodges), the *ou* variant remained the commoner in the first half of the century and perhaps later and was still in quite vigorous life at the end of the century. PresE invariably has the *au* variant except (*a*) in *though*, which owes its PresE pronunciation to a ME weak form; and (*b*) in words in which ME [χ] changes to [f] and ME *ou* is shortened in consequence to [ɒ] (as in *cough*). But Robinson records the *au* variant, with retention of [χ], in a strong form (which he normally uses) of *though*.

The *ou* variant is shown by Smith in *cough* (with retained [χ]) and by Hart in *brought* in the *Methode*. It is regular or normal in Bullokar (cf. Zachrisson, *Bullokar*, p. 13), Mulcaster, Coote, Gil, Butler, Jonson, Daines, Evelyn, and Wallis. Even in the later seventeenth century it is still shown by Wharton, Lloyd, Brooksbank, Price, Coles's *Schoolmaster* (which rhymes *ought*, &c. on both *ou* and *au*), Strong in his 'phonetic' spellings of *bought* and *brought* (beside *au* in *thought* and *wrought*), *The Protestant Tutor* (following Price), Cocker (beside *au*), and *WSC-RS* (beside [ɒ:] < *au*; see below). It also occurs in the 'homophone' lists of Hodges ('near alike', only in *cough't*), Fox and Hookes, Coles (*Schoolmaster* and *Eng. Dict.*), Richardson, Cooper ('near alike'), *WSC-RS*, Brown (beside *au*), and the anonymous manuscript list (beside *au*).

The *au* variant is shown in the sixteenth century by Smith (twice) and by Hart and Bullokar in *daughter*. Robinson has it regularly, either as a diphthong [ɒu] or as [ɒ:]; it occurs in *though* as well as in *ought*, &c. Gil and Butler show it only in *daughter*, but it is regular in Hodges (except for the one pairing in his 'near alike' list). Wallis has it in *sought*, beside more frequent *ou*. In the later seventeenth century it is recorded by Wilkins, Coles (beside *ou*), Strong (beside *ou*; see above), Young, Lye, Cooper, and Brown. *WSC-RS* says that the pronunciation of *ou* in such words as *bought* varies between 'o long' ([o:] < ME *ou*) and 'o broad'; the context, and the dependence on Cooper, show that the latter means [ɒ:] < ME *au*. It also occurs in the 'homophone' lists of Hodges, Hunt, Strong, Cooper ('alike', in contrast to ME *ou* in the 'near alike' list), Brown (beside *ou*), and the anonymous MS list (beside *ou*). The pairing of *naught* with *nought* in certain lists probably depends on the *au* variant in the latter.

> Note 1: Cooper gives, beside [ɒ:] < ME *au*, a pronunciation with [ɒf] for *bought*, &c.; see § 34. On ME *ū* < ME *ou* before [χ] in certain of the words cited above see § 170; it is recorded by Smith, Hart, Laneham, Robinson, Gil, Butler, Daines, and Hodges ('near alike' list) as an occasional variant in individual words, and is apparently regular in the Northerner Poole. On undiphthongized ME *ŏ* in the *Welsh Hymn*, Hart, and Gil (once) see § 89 above.
>
> Note 2: Rhymes show the variation between *au* and *ou*. The earliest *au* rhyme which I have discovered is Surrey's *ywrought : taught* (ante 1547); Horn, § 142, points out that such rhymes are frequent in Spenser (by birth a Londoner). Rhymes showing the *ou* variant also occur; thus Daniel has *thoughts : notes* in 1615. Seventeenth-century foreign orthoepists who show the *au* variant are cited by Horn, loc. cit. Spellings usually show only the *ou* variant, except in *daughter*, for which *OED* records a spelling *dahtorrs* in 1531 and *daughter* from 1532 onwards. But *sought* has earlier *au* forms: *OED* records the fourteenth-century *saʒte*, fourteenth- and fifteenth-century *saght*, and sixteenth- and seventeenth-century *saught* (used by Price in *VO*; see § 239, Note 1).
>
> Note 3: It is unlikely that Robinson's *au* in *though* goes back to ME *þäh*, &c. < OE *þēah* instead of ME *þŏh* < ON **þŏh*, for forms derived from OE *þēah* do not survive in literature (and therefore presumably not in StE speech) after the fifteenth century (see *OED*). But the spelling *thawgh* cited by Davies, *Eng. Pron.*, pp. 11, 65, from a printed text dated c. 1482 of a much earlier work, may represent ME *þäh* < OE *þēah*, and if so it may not confirm Robinson's evidence, though at first sight it seems to.
>
> Note 4: Horn, § 142, explains the *au* pronunciation as a special dialectal development of the group *-ouχt*, whether in ME or ModE is not made clear. Luick, § 535 (2), regards it as due to the adoption by StE of a dialectal pronunciation [ɑ:] (later developed to PresE [ɒ:]) of ME *ǭ* (with which ME *ou* is identified when it is monophthongized); i.e. he adopts the same explanation for [ɒ:] in *ought*, &c. as he does for *broad*. But the evidence of sixteenth-century orthoepists, notably Smith, and of Robinson shows that PresE [ɒ:] develops from ME *au*, the diphthongal pronunciations of which they record in *ought*, &c., and is not consequent on the monophthongization of ME *ou* to identify with ME *ǭ*. Luick's explanation of [ɒ:] in *broad* as due to dialectal influence on StE is in any event not acceptable (see § 53, Note 3 (*b*)). Ekwall, § 90, explains [ɒ:] in *ought*, &c. from a late ME *au* developed from ME *ou*; his only fault is in not finding the origin of the variation between *au* and *ou* at a stage earlier than ME diphthongization before [χ]. A. J. Bliss, *English and Germanic Studies*, ii (1948–9), 47–53, argues for the view here put forward.

(2) *In words with OE* āw *and* āg

§ 241. In the North, where OE *ā* did not become ME *ǭ*, OE *āw* became ME *au*; Ridpath implies Scottish *au* in *slow* (see Vol. I, p. 393).

§ 241] ME au

In many dialects OE āw, after becoming ǫw > ou, reverted to au (see Jordan, § 105, Anm.); later evidence than that cited by Jordan shows that the same development occurred to ME ou < OE āg, and in some dialects (e.g. the NW Midlands) it affected ME ou of other origins (cf. Jordan, § 109, Anm. 2). In the south-east it is especially characteristic of the dialect of Essex, in which there is much evidence of the change of ME ŏ > ă (see § 87, Note 3) and in which ME oi is shown by rhymes to have become ai (see § 261, Note 2); it is evident that the change of ou to au is parallel to that of oi to ai, and both must be due to the same tendency in pronunciation as led to the unrounding of ŏ to ă. When the ME short vowel was unrounded, the first element of the two diphthongs, evidently identical in quality with ME ŏ, was also unrounded. This explanation fits the chronology, for the unrounding of ME ŏ to ă belongs to the thirteenth century, whereas OE āw and āg gave ME ou at or before the beginning of the thirteenth century; rhymes showing both au < ou and ai < oi occur in Essex texts (the *Alexander* group) from the end of the thirteenth century. The change of ou to au evidently affected other Eastern dialects than that of Essex (including vulgar London English); Kihlbom, pp. 177–8, cites evidence from Suffolk, Norfolk (*Paston Letters*), and from the modern dialect of south-east Cambridgeshire, as well as from south-western sources. Bullokar, who was a native of Sussex and whose evidence on this point certainly represents dialectal speech, has ME au once beside ME ou twice in *crow* vb. (OE āw) and rhymes *own* (OE āg) on late ME ā < au (see Vol. I, pp. 107 and 111). Butler and Hodges (in his 'near alike' list) pair *know(n)* (OE āw) with *gnaw(n)* (see Vol. I, p. 398); this in Hodges is evidence for vulgar London English, but the pronunciation must by the seventeenth century have been rare even in such speech, for on this one point no later 'homophone' list follows his.

(3) *In special words*

§ 242. The variation between *nought(y)* and *naught(y)* goes back to OE (*nōwiht* beside *nāwiht*, with shortening in the first element of the compounds). The arbitrary distinction in sense between the variant forms, with the restriction of the *au* spelling to the sense 'wicked', leads the orthoepists to record only *au* in this sense as a rule; but Cheke gives *ou* in spelling and pronunciation, and Merriott gives evidence of a pronunciation [oː] < *ou*, saying that bad spellers do not distinguish *naught* from *note*. *Thaw* has [ou] < ME *ou* in Smith, whose evidence is supported by the spelling *thowe* from the fourteenth century onwards; the variant must represent an OE *pōwan or *pāwan beside *pāwian* (so *OED*). *Paul* has variation between ME *ou* derived from the OF form *Pol* and ME *au* from the Latin form. ME *ou* is recorded by Laneham (a London merchant), Sanford, Cotgrave, Butler (who describes it as a pronunciation of Londoners, 'after the French manner', i.e. like the French pronunciation of *au*), Coles, *Schoolmaster* (which gives the 'phonetic spellings' *Polesteeple* 'Paul's steeple', *Poles Churchyard*, *Poles-wharf*), Strong (who gives *Poles Church*), Young (after Strong), and the 'homophone' lists of the Londoner Hodges ('near alike') and of Strong; Hart gives undiphthongized ME ŏ. Hunt's 'homophone' list has *pall* : *Paul*; Brown adds *pole*, which shows variation between ME *au* and *ou*. The conventional spelling leads usually to a preference for the *au* form, which eventually prevailed; we may notice that Robinson, though a Londoner, gives [ɒ:] < ME *au*. *Vault* varies in consequence of the variation in OF between *voute* and *vau(l)te*; it has ME *ou* in Smith (who transcribes it *vōut*) and in the 'homophone' list of Fox and Hookes (who pair it with *vote*), but otherwise ME *au* (so Hodges, Hunt, Brown, and probably Aickin, all of whom give the *l* as silent).

THE DEVELOPMENT OF ME *ęu*

(1) *General outline*

§ 243. ME *ęu* was originally pronounced as [ɛu]. In eModE the first element develops at first in the same way as ME *ẹ̄*, from which it is in large part derived: while ME *ę̄* retained its ME value of [ɛ:] ME *ęu* remained as [ɛu], but when ME *ę̄* was raised to [e:] ME *ęu* became [eu]. The second element of the diphthong then exercised an assimilatory raising influence on the first, causing [eu] to change rapidly to [iu]. That the final development to [iu] was independent of any further change in ME *ę̄* is a necessary assumption if we are to believe, as I do, that in its free ModE development ME *ę̄* never advanced from [e:] to [i:]; its correctness is shown by the fact that, of all the seventeenth-century orthoepists who make no distinction between ME *ęu* and ME *iu*(*ęu*), only *WSC-RS* fails to recognize the separate existence of ME *ę̄* as a sound distinct from ME *ẹ̄* (and ME *ā*). An exact parallel to the spontaneous eModE development of ME *ęu* from [eu] to [iu] is provided by ME *ęu*, which develops from its original ME value of [eu] to [iu] (where it became identical with ME *iu*) a century before ME *ę̄* develops from [e:] to [i:] (see § 188 above). When it reached the stage [iu] ME *ęu* became identical with ME *ęu*, *iu*, and [y:], and developed with them to [ju:], which is reduced to [u:] in *shrew*, *strew*, and occasionally (in careless or dialectal English) *dew*, *lewd*, and *sewer*. The [u:] of [ju:] is liable to lowering before *r* in *sewer*, though the lowered pronunciation is not accepted in correct StE.

In careful StE, the distinction between ME *ęu* and ME *iu* (*ęu*) was maintained until *c.* 1640, but during the next thirty years it was gradually lost, the last satisfactory evidence of it coming from Price in 1668. Orthoepistical evidence of a mode of pronunciation which failed to distinguish ME *ęu* from *iu* is continuous from early in the seventeenth century, but it is clear from the nature of the evidence that until about 1660 it is based on careless or vulgar speech. As there is evidence of [e:] for ME $\bar{e}$ in more advanced StE in the sixteenth century, we may assume that [iu] for ME eu also existed in advanced StE in the sixteenth century; isolated pieces of evidence in Bullokar, and more frequent rhymes of poets, confirm this assumption. In the Northern and Eastern dialects, in which the development of ME $\bar{e}$ was rapid, we should expect early loss of the distinction between ME eu and ME iu—perhaps as early as the late fourteenth century in Northern English. Levins, a Northerner, shows no knowledge of the distinction in the sixteenth century.

Note: The ordinary view of the development of ME eu seems to be that the first element became [i] because ME $\bar{e}$ became [i:]. This is contrary to the evidence (which shows that [iu] for ME eu accompanies [e:] for ME $\bar{e}$), but seems to be assumed by Horn, § 126; Zachrisson, *Eng. Vowels*, p. 146; and Ekwall, § 62, though they do not make their belief at all explicit. Luick, §§ 546, 547, realizing that ME eu was already [iu] when ME $\bar{e}$ was still distinct from ME $\bar{e}$ (see § 546, Anm. 2), denies that the first element develops in association with ME $\bar{e}$ at all, and says that it develops in association with ME $\check{e}$ (see § 545); ME $\check{e}$, he says, had a tendency to become [i] which was stronger in the diphthong because of the raising influence of the high-back second element. But the evidence shows clearly that the acceptance of [iu] for ME eu was associated with the acceptance of [e:] instead of [ɛ:] for ME $\bar{e}$, and we must therefore reject Luick's view that the development of the first element of ME eu was independent of that of ME $\bar{e}$, though agreeing with him that it was affected by the raising influence of the second element.

(2) *The evidence*

§ 244. The orthoepists who recognize the distinct existence of ME eu give it in the following words: (*a*) native words with early ME $\bar{e}$: *dew, few, hew* vb., *lewd, shew* 'show', *shrew, shrewd, strew, tew* (< OE **tēawian*, a blend of *tēagan* and *tawian*; the latter gives *taw*); (*b*) native words with early ME $\check{e}$ in an open syllable: *ewe* (OE *eowu*), *sew* (OE *seowan*), *Newton* (see below), and *newt* (OE *efeta*); (*c*) the echoic ME formation *mew* (of a cat); (*d*) words adopted from French or from Latin and Greek (usually through French): *Beaumont, beauty, Eustace, ewer, fewtered* 'featured' (see Vol. I, p. 93), *neuter, pewter, pleurisy,* and *sewer*. Hodges (four times) and Price give ME eu in *feud*, which is of dubious origin; their evidence is supported by Holland's spelling *feaud* (1601). On Price's eu in *brewis* see § 246 below.

The distinction between ME eu and ME iu (eu) is made by Palsgrave (see Vol. I, p. 9), Smith in both *PG* and *LA* (for further details see below), Laneham, Hart (who also shows a special development; see Note 5 below), Bullokar (except for a rhyme and a transcription which show the loss of the distinction), Robinson, Gil, Butler, Daines, Hodges, Wallis (beside less correct [iu]; see Vol. I, p. 239, and Note 5 below), Wharton, Price (*EO*, 1668), and possibly Wilkins (but see below). On *RS*'s evidence see below. Of these authors, the majority certainly or probably used [ɛ:] for ME $\bar{e}$, and may then be assumed to have used [ɛu] for ME ęu. But Bullokar, Gil, Daines, and Hodges, though the great bulk of their evidence is based on a form of speech in which ME ẹ̄ was [ɛ:], on isolated occasions give evidence that rests on a form of speech in which ME ẹ̄ was [e:]; and Smith and Robinson, though some of their evidence depends on the more conservative form of speech in which ME ẹ̄ was [ɛ:], seem normally to have used [e:]. These six authors may then have known or have used a pronunciation [eu] instead of or beside [ɛu]. Of more direct evidence on the precise value of the diphthong there is little. Palsgrave's comparison of ME ęu with French sounds is so mistaken that we can hardly use his more accurate comparison with Italian *eu* to determine between the values [ɛu] and [eu] (see Vol. I, p. 9). Smith (see Vol. I, pp. 57–58) compares one pronunciation of the diphthong in *mew* with French *eau* in *beau*, which was still commonly pronounced with a diphthong of which the first element appears to have been tense (see Pope, § 539); that he means [eu] is confirmed by his identification of the first element with his pronunciation of ME ẹ̄. But though it seems possible that this [eu] could be used for ME ęu in other words, Smith does not say so; the alternative sound used in *mew*, which was evidently [ɛu], is what he in fact says was used for ME ęu in *dew, few*, &c. In any case the transitional [eu] stage was obviously evanescent; no orthoepist whose evidence is consistently based on the form of speech in which ME ẹ̄ was [e:] records a pronunciation of ME ęu which distinguished it from ME *iu*. Gil transcribes ME ęu as either *eu* or *ēu*; this probably does not reflect any variation in either the quality or the quantity of the first element, but that it could be regarded as long shows that it bore the stress.

The following is the evidence for the pronunciation [iu] (or its developments) and the consequent identity of ME ęu with ME *iu, ęu*, and [y:]. The Northerner Levins does not distinguish ME ęu from ME *iu*, &c. Bullokar (who by contrast was born in Sussex) rhymes *shew* with *too*; this rhyme, like many of Bullokar's, depends on a much less careful pronunciation than that which he takes as the normal basis of his transcriptions, but it probably represents his own natural pronunciation, for he once uses *eu* (his symbol for ME ęu) in *lukewarm* (which has ME ęu), thus betraying a confusion of the two sounds. Tonkis (who was a Midlander) does not distinguish ęu from *iu* (ęu) (see Vol. I, p. 314). Though Hodges generally is most careful to distinguish ME ęu from ME ęu, it might be argued that some hesitancy is revealed by his transcribing *Newton* four times with ęu, against *new* (*news, newly*) twelve times and *Newman* thrice with ęu; but he repeatedly gives *Newton* as a specially chosen example of ęu in deliberate contrast to *Newman* as an example of ęu, and we cannot doubt that he did really use ME ęu in *Newton*. The explanation must be that in the OE compound place-name *nēowa(n)tūn(e)* shortening occurs in the first element, giving late OE *nĕowa(n)tūn(e)*, whence ME *Nęwton* (cf. *ęwe* from OE *ĕowu*); this ęu form may be shown by thirteenth-century spellings with *ew*, *eu* (cf. Ekwall, *Oxford Dictionary of English Place-Names*, s.n. *Newton*). But in the personal name *Newman*, a later formation, there is no shortening and we find the normal development of OE *nēowe*, *nīwe* to ME *nẹw*, *niw*. The evidence of Gataker (see Vol. I, p. 217) shows the breakdown of the distinction between *ẹu* and *ęu*. Willis rhymes *ẹu* and *ęu* together. Wallis gives evidence of a less correct [iu] beside [ɛu] for ME *ęu*, and is somewhat uncertain about the distinction between ME *ẹu* and ME *iu* and *ęu* (see Vol. I, p. 239). Brooksbank, who says that *a* is silent in *Beaumont*, *Beawley*, and *Beauchamp*, must know no distinction between ME *ęu* and *iu*, for earlier authors had welcomed and extended the use of this *eau* spelling in order to distinguish ME *ęu* spelt *eau* from ME *iu* spelt *eu*. The Northerner Poole rhymes *ęu* and *iu* together. Merriott says that bad spellers do not distinguish *due* from *dew*. Newton gives [iu] for both ME *ęu* and ME *iu*. Wilkins seems to show a distinct pronunciation of ME *ęu* when he gives [ɛu] as an English diphthong with *hew* as his example; but trust in his evidence is reduced by his giving, as an example of the 'triphthong' [iɛu], the word *yew*, which has ME *iu*. Wilkins may have been led into this error by his desire to find an example to support a special argument in favour of the existence of 'triphthongs'; but it is to be suspected that he did not have any real knowledge of the old distinction between ME *ęu* and *iu*. No spelling-book later than Price's *EO* (1668) distinguishes ME *ęu* from ME *iu*. Coles in his careful *Schoolmaster* rhymes the two sounds, and Cooper identifies them as [iu] (see Vol. I, p. 302) and describes [fɛu] 'few' (transcribed *fâw*) as 'barbarous'. *RS* says that to distinguish *eu* in *eucharist* and *rheubarb* from 'long *u*' in *unity* and *rumour* would require 'a very critical ear' and a pronunciation involving 'an apparent, and too affected constraint, contrary to the usual pronunciation observed by the generality, which (in this case) would sound very pedantick'. This sentence might perhaps be held to show the survival of a conservative pronunciation in which ME *ęu* was still distinct; but as *RS* gives *rheubarb* (with ME *ęu*) as an example beside *eucharist* (with ME *ęu*) it is obvious that at best he has no personal knowledge of where ME *ęu* ought to be used, and it is possible that he has merely imagined a difference in pronunciation between '*eu*' and 'long *u*' in order to rebut it. Shorthand-writers regularly reduce *eau* (as in *beauty*) and *ew* (as in *dew*) to *u* (thus *buti*, *du*); so Folkingham (1618), E. Willis (1618), Dix, Farthing, Everardt, Coles, and Ridpath. But it should be remembered that their contractions are commonly based on careless speech. The 'homophone' lists pair ME *ęu* with ME *iu*, &c.: so Hodges (once, *ure* : *ewer*, in the 'alike' list, which here exceptionally shows a pronunciation different from that of *EP*; the 'near alike' list adds *shoe* : *shew*), Wharton and Price (contrast the distinction between ME *ęu* and ME *iu* preserved by these two authors in the text of their spelling-books), Hunt, Fox and Hookes, Coles even in the careful *Schoolmaster*, Strong, Richardson, Cooper (the 'same pronunciation' list has *shoe* : *shew*, *ewer* : *ure*; the 'near alike' list has *your* : *ewer*), *The Compendious Schoolmaster*, *WSC*, Cocker, Brown, and the anonymous manuscript list.

The development of ME *ęu* from [iu] to [ju:], and the later combinative developments of this [ju:], are shown only by a rhyme of Bullokar's, by Gataker, and in the 'homophone' lists. The pronunciation [ju:] is shown (in initial position at least) by Gataker (see Vol. I, pp. 217–18) and by the equation *your* : *ure* : *ewer* given in Hodges's 'alike' list, Wharton, Price, Fox and Hookes, Coles (*Schoolmaster*), Strong, Cooper (in the 'near alike' list, which has *ewer* : *your*; but Cooper evidently disapproved of this [ju:] pronunciation, for the 'alike' list has only *ure* : *ewer*), and *WSC*. Bullokar's rhyme *shew* : *too* seems at least to show [ju:] in final position, and may depend on reduction of [ju:] to [u:] after [ʃ]; but it is based on a less correct pronunciation than his transcriptions. Reduction of [ju:] to [u:] may in some cases be the basis of the pairing of *shew* with *shoe*, given in Hodges's 'near alike' list, Hunt, Fox and Hookes, Strong, Cooper's 'same pronunciation' list, *WSC*, and Brown; but it must be remembered that *shoe* can have a variant pronunciation with eModE [iu] beside [u:] < ME *ǭ* (cf. § 159 above). The manuscript list (which is later than 1700; see Vol. I, p. 419) shows reduction to [u:] after [s] by pairing *sewer* with *sour* and *sore*; there may also be lowering of [u:] (developed in *sour* from undiphthongized ME *ū*) to [ɔ:] before *r*, if *sore* does not have [u:] < late ME *ǭ* by raising of ME *ǭ*. Price much earlier pairs *ewer* with *your* and *yore*, and is followed by *WSC* (with the addition of *ure* to the equation); again lowering of [u:] to [ɔ:] in *ewer*, *your*, and *ure* is possible, though *yore* may have [u:] < late ME *ǭ* by raising of ME *ǭ*. The development of [dɛu] through eModE [diu] and [dju:] to [dʒu:] is shown by the Northerner Brown's pairing of *dew* with *due* and *Jew*.

Note 1: The evidence of *The English Schole-master* (1646) is uncertain (see Vol. I, p. 380), though it may show the identity of ME *ęu* and *iu*.

Note 2: French orthoepists (*Alphabet Anglois* (1625), which gives [ju:]; Mauger (1679), Miège (1688), and Festeau (1693), who give [iu]) show the identity of ME *ęu* and ME *iu* (Zachrisson, *Eng. Vowels*, p. 145), though they distinguish ME *ẹ̄* from ME *ę̄* (op. cit., p. 146).

Note 3: Zachrisson, op. cit., pp. 84–85, cites from the *Paston Letters* the spelling *shuyd* 'shewed', which he unnecessarily regards as a scribal error because it is isolated; as the Eastern dialects had [e:] for ME *ę̄* in the fifteenth century, they could also have [iu] for ME *ęu* and identity of ME *ęu* with ME *iu* and [y:]. *OED* records a fifteenth-century spelling *ryweyne* for ME *rewayne* (OF **rewain*, which should give ME *ęu*), from Caxton's print (c. 1470) of Lydgate's *Horse, Sheep and Goose*; the form may then be Eastern.

Note 4: Horn, § 126, cites from Spenser and Shakespeare the rhymes *few* : *true* and *beauty* : *duty*, which he wrongly regards as inexact. In the late sixteenth century the rhyme *beauty* : *duty* is not uncommon, though other such rhymes (e.g. Drayton's *dew* : *shoe*) are rare. It is evident that most late-sixteenth-century poets avoided rhymes which depended on [iu] for ME *ęu*, doubtless because it was still not the correct StE pronunciation, except in the case of *beauty*, a word much used in Elizabethan poetry for which no rhyme was available unless one took advantage of the less correct pronunciation and rhymed it with *duty*. Spenser, who freely rhymes ME *ęu* with ME *iu*, &c., may in this as in other cases have been influenced by Northern pronunciation, in which [iu] for ME *ęu* must have developed very early, or by advanced London English.

Note 5: A special development is shown by Hart's transcriptions—both in the *Orthographie* and in the *Methode*—*mieu* 'mew' (of a cat), *ieu* 'ewe', and *fieu* 'few' (in contrast with *feu* 'few', *šeu* 'shew', and *neuter*, which show the normal [ɛu]); these *ieu* forms represent a pronunciation [jɛu] developed by the introduction of a glide [j] before the first element. It exists in modern dialects, and is not to be explained (as by Horn, § 126, Anm. 2; Luick, § 546) as a blend of [juː] and [ɛu], for the same glide [j] develops before ME *ẽ* (see §§ 429–30). Hart's *beautifi* and *eaur* 'ewer' are merely inconsistent transcriptions which show the influence of the conventional spelling; cf. his occasional use of *ea* instead of *ẽ* for ME *ę̃* itself (see Jespersen, *Hart*, § 16). Wallis's transcriptions *niewter*, &c. beside *niwter*, &c. have been taken to show either a diphthong, with the first element a sound intermediate between *e* and *i*, or a 'triphthong', i.e. Hart's [jɛu] (see Horn, loc. cit.); but they involve merely the use of *ie* as the conventional digraph for ModE [iː] < ME *ę̃*, and indicate a pronunciation [iu].

VARIATION BETWEEN ME *ęu* AND ME *ou*

§ 245. Variation between ME *ęu* and ME *ou* occurs in native English words which in OE contain the groups *ēaw* or *ěow*; these normally develop to ME *ęu*, but with shift of stress in OE to *eāw* or *eǒw* they develop in ME to *ou* (except that in the North OE *eāw* becomes *au*). ME *ęu* occurs in *sew* (OE *sěowan*) in Butler (beside *ou*), Poole, and the 'homophone' lists of Hunt and *The Compendious Schoolmaster*; in *shew* 'show' (OE *scēawian*) in Smith, Hart (beside *ou*), Levins, Bullokar, Robinson (thrice, beside *ou* twice), Gil (six times, beside *ou* once), Butler (beside *ou*), Willis, Poole (beside *ou*), Cooper, *WSC* (beside *ou*), and the 'homophone' lists of Hodges, Fox and Hookes, Strong, Cooper, *WSC*, and Brown; in *shrew* (OE *scrēaw*) in Palsgrave, Levins (beside *ou*), Butler (beside *ou*), Daines (beside *ou*), Willis, Poole (beside *ou*), Cooper, and *WSC*; in *shrewd* in Cooper. ME *ou* occurs in *sew* in Hart, Butler (beside *ęu*), and the 'homophone' lists of Hunt (probably, beside *ęu*), Fox and Hookes, Coles, Strong, Richardson, *The Compendious Schoolmaster* (beside *ęu*), and *RS*; in *show* in Hart (beside *ęu*), Robinson (twice, beside *ęu* thrice), Gil (once, beside *ęu* six times), Hodges (despite the spelling with *ew*), Poole (beside *ęu*), *WSC*, Brown, and the shorthand-writer Bridges; in *shrew* in Levins (beside *ęu*), Butler (beside *ęu*), Daines (who prefers the spelling *shrew* to *shrow*), Hodges (despite the spelling with *ew*), and Poole (beside *ęu*); in *shrewd* in Coles, *Schoolmaster* (rhyming with *toad*, &c.; cf. the spelling *shrode* recorded by *OED*).

Variation between ME *ęu* and ME *ou* is also recorded in *rowen*, a word adopted from French. Cooper (see Vol. I, p. 302) records the two forms *rewain* (with ME *ęu* from ONF **rewain*) and *rowen*, and says that the former is pronounced '*reu-in*' (i.e. with [iu] < earlier [ɛu]) and the latter either '*ro-en*' (i.e. with [oː] < ME *ou*) or '*rou-en*' (see § 246 on this pronunciation with [ʌu]). The ME *ou* form goes back to (Western?) OF **rowain* developed from **rewain* by rounding of counter-tonic *e* before *w* (see Pope, § 484 (i)).

Note 1: Hart's transcriptions *šiō* (once) and *šio* (twice), beside *šo* thrice, give evidence of an occasional glide [j] developed in the *show* form of OE *scēawian*.

Note 2: Similar variation between ME *ęu* and ME *ou* occurred in *strew* (OE *strēawian*) and *ewe* (OE *ěowu*), which in earlier English had the forms *strow* and *yowe*. The pronunciations indicated by these forms are not recorded by the orthoepists, though Hart has the spelling *yowe*; but Newton gives ME *ou* in an unglossed *yow* which is probably 'ewe' (see Vol. I, p. 251).

VARIATION BETWEEN ME *ęu* AND ME *ū*

§ 246. *Rowen* has in PresE the pronunciation [au] < ME *ū*; it is recorded by Cooper (see immediately above) and by *WSC*. ME *ū* is probably from OF [u] < earlier *ǫw* (cf. the modern Picard *rouain* cited by *OED*, s.v. *rowen*), though the development of *ǫw* to *ū* could occur in ME itself. Price records ME *ęu* in *brewesse* 'brewis', of which the normal form is *browis*. Its *ew*-forms are difficult to explain, and *OED* suggests that they may be due to 'some popular association' with OE *brīw* (pl. *brīwas*) 'soup' or 'even with the verb *brew*'. The latter is the more hopeful hypothesis; the analogy may have been furthered by the point of formal contact provided by the p.t.pl. stem (OE *bruw-*). In this event we should expect that the *brewis* form of *browis* would normally have ME *ęu* (as apparently in Hodges's 'near alike' list) from the infinitive stem (OE *brēowan*), as seems to be established by the eModE variation between *ew* and *u* spellings (see *OED*); but from the p.t.sing. stem (OE *brēaw*) an occasional ME *ęu* variant might arise, as Price seems to show.

ME *ęu* AND ME *iu*

§ 247. On the development of eME *ęu* (> *iu*) and eME *iu*, which from late ME onwards are identified with ME [yː], see §§ 179–88 above.

THE DEVELOPMENT OF ME *ou*

(1) *General outline*

§ 248. ME *ou* was originally a diphthong of which the first element, identical in quality with ME *ǒ* and ME *ǭ* (from which it was derived), was the 'intermediate vowel' (approximately 'cardinal open [ɔː]') discussed, with reference to ME *ǭ*, in § 145 above. This diphthong continued in use until late in the seventeenth century. It is possible that the quality of the first element remained unchanged throughout (our evidence is not clear on this point; see below); but it would have been quite natural for it to be raised to close [o] (as Cooper's evidence may show), either when ME ǭ changed to [o:] or as a result of the raising influence which the second element was capable of exerting. But beside the diphthongal pronunciation there developed a monophthong, owing to the assimilation of the second element of the diphthong to the first, with which it coalesced; the result was a long vowel identical with ME ǭ. This monophthongal pronunciation had already developed in StE before ME ǭ was raised to [o:]; it therefore shared the latter's raising and subsequent development (at some time about 1800) to the PresE diphthong [ou].

The evidence of many orthoepists shows that the monophthongal pronunciation of ME *ou* developed more rapidly in final than in medial position. Laneham, Sherwood, Cooper (in his 'homophone' lists), and Aickin show that it was for some time more common in medial position in words which were recognized as derived forms of others in which ME *ou* was final (e.g. *known* and *grown*); according to the evidence of Sherwood and Cooper, we must reckon among these *own*, which must have been felt as closely related to *owe* (in the sense 'own, possess'). The diphthongal pronunciation survived in the seventeenth century chiefly in medial position, though Cooper records its occasional use in final position as late as the 1680's.

The evidence is rather vague as to the exact quality both of the first element of the diphthong and of the monophthong (cf. the vagueness concerning ME ǭ; see § 145). The first element is marked as long by Cheke, Smith, Hart, and Gil; this shows not only that it was stressed, and therefore preponderant, but also that it was identical with ME ǭ. Wallis, however, gives 'o guttural' (i.e. [ɒ(:)] < ME ŏ or ME *au*) as the first element; his evidence can hardly be accurate (see Vol. I, p. 233 footnote), but tells in favour of open [ɔ] rather than close [o]. Richardson identifies ME *ou*, when a diphthong, with Dutch *ou*, of which the first element is open; this again is in favour of the 'intermediate vowel'. But Cooper gives 'labial *o*' as the first element; this evidence, if accurate, is in favour of [o]. Palsgrave probably, and Sherwood certainly, mean to show a diphthongal pronunciation of ME *ou* by their identification of it with French *au*; but in the absence of knowledge of the precise quality of the first element of the French diphthong (which had obviously been rounded, and may—or may not—have been raised to [o] as an immediate preliminary to monophthongization) this identification does not assist us. From the fact that from late in the fifteenth or early in the sixteenth century the monophthong was identical in StE with ME ǭ we must assume that it was originally the 'intermediate vowel' and later [o:]. It is identified with Welsh *o* by the *Welsh Hymn*, Salesbury, and the *Welsh Breviary* (1670), and with French *o* by Sherwood; but these identifications are imprecise (see § 145, Note 3). The identification with French *au* given by Sanford, Cotgrave, and Butler would probably show [o:] (though French *au* is sometimes open [ɔ]) if it referred to a monophthongal pronunciation; but in view of Sherwood's contemporary evidence we cannot be sure that it does.

Note 1: Horn, § 137, gives an account of the monophthongization similar to that above. Luick, §§ 517–18, regards the second element as merely disappearing, while the first develops with ME *ǭ*; i.e. the first element, while ME *ou* was still a diphthong, was raised to close [o], from which monophthongization to [oː] could immediately develop. But there is no need to assume that this occurred, since the monophthong developed before ME *ǭ* was raised. The view that the second element merely fell off is somewhat loose; by being assimilated to the first it becomes merged in and indistinguishable from it.

Jespersen, §§ 11.41–11.43, regards PresE [ou] as a survival of the ME diphthong, which he believes was never monophthongized, its identity with ME *ǭ* resulting from the diphthongization of the latter. This view, which is contrary to all the evidence, has rightly not found acceptance (cf. Luick, § 518, Anm. 2). Davies, *Eng. Pron.*, p. 11, makes the extraordinary statement that ME *ou* 'fell together with ME *au* and ME *oi* (*ui*) during its development'—a state of affairs which obviously never applied in StE, since the sounds remain distinct. Her view is based on spellings with *ou* for ME *au* and with *aw* in *though* (see § 237, Notes 2 and 5, and § 240, Note 3) and on others with *oi* for ME *ou* and ME *ǭ* and with *ow* and *o* for ME *oi* (*ui*) (see § 261, Note 3).

Note 2: It is to be observed that the diphthongal pronunciation of ME *ou* in which the first element was the 'intermediate vowel' [ɔ] was distinct from that diphthongal pronunciation of ME *au* in which the first element was the ModE open [ɒ], and that the monophthongal pronunciation of ME *ou* with the 'intermediate vowel' [ɔː] was distinct from the monophthongal pronunciation of ME *au* with the ModE open [ɒː]. The difference was probably much the same as that between the French 'open [ɔ(ː)]' in *comme, port* and PresE 'open [ɒ(ː)]' in *comma, port*. Both pairs of sounds could be used, and kept distinct, in the speech of a single person (the difference between them need be no less than that between PresE [æ] and [e], which native speakers easily distinguish); and this situation may often have applied in the sixteenth and seventeenth centuries. To avoid confusion I normally transcribe the pronunciations of ME *ou* as [ou] and [oː], since the distinction between the 'intermediate vowel' and close [o(ː)] is not of great importance, especially in view of the vagueness of our evidence on the point.

(2) *The evidence*

(a) *Evidence of the diphthongal pronunciation*

§ 249. Cheke transcribes ME *ou*, which he describes as a diphthong, as ωυ. Similarly Smith describes a diphthong which he transcribes in *PG* as ωυ and in *LA* as *ōu*. Laneham shows a diphthong (beside a monophthong) in medial position (see Vol. I, p. 92). Hart in the *Orthographie* does not record a diphthongal pronunciation, because he has not yet invented a symbol for it which will distinguish it from ME *ū* (which he transcribes *ou*); but in the *Methode* he uses for ME *ou* a transcription *ōu*, regularly in medial position and once (beside the monophthongal pronunciation twice) in final position. The *Methode* should be regarded as representing better the pronunciation which Hart regarded as correct. Gil normally gives a diphthong (transcribed *ōu*) even in final position, and attacks Hart's transcriptions (in the *Orthographie*) which represent the monophthongal pronunciation; this Gil stigmatizes as the speech of the *Mopsæ*. But he himself used a monophthong even in medial position when the spelling was *o* (as in *gold*); only in the *Errata* to the second edition of 1621 did he point out that *ōu* (i.e. [ou]) could be used beside *ō* ([oː]) in *gold*, &c. This correction does, however, prove that there was a real diphthong in use, and that Gil's transcriptions are not based solely on the conventional spelling, even though it affects his choice between variant pronunciations. Sherwood (see Vol. I, p. 377) shows a diphthong medially in *bowl*, *soul*, and *mould*; he identifies it with French *au* (still pronounced as a diphthong in Western French dialects in the seventeenth century; see Pope, §§ 537 and 1328 (3)). Butler regularly transcribes ME *ou* as a diphthong, but perhaps knew a monophthongal pronunciation even in medial position (see below). Daines teaches a diphthongal pronunciation, which he calls '*ou* diphthong aspirate', even when the spelling is *o* (as in *roll*). Wallis, though he admits that others use [oː], prefers the diphthong, perhaps because of the spelling, by which he is strongly influenced. Wharton uses a diphthongal pronunciation in medial position when the spelling is *ou* (*ow*). Newton retains a diphthong medially except in *though*, and varies in final position. Wilkins does not recognize the existence of [ou] as an English diphthong. Richardson shows a diphthongal pronunciation (identified with Dutch *ou*) beside a monophthongal both in medial and final position (see Vol. I, p. 383). Cooper gives [ou] in medial position, even when the spelling is *o* (as in *bold*), with only two exceptions—*disown*, in which *w* is said to be silent, and *rowen* transcribed *ro-en*; in final position he shows monophthongization, but says that some people use [ou] even here. *The Compendious School-Master* says that *w* is 'softly sounded' in *grow*, &c.; whether this means a diphthongal pronunciation, or is an unwilling admission that the *w* is silent, cannot be determined. Aickin, following but adding to Cooper, teaches a diphthongal pronunciation in medial position (even when the spelling is *o*) but a monophthongal in final position and in derived forms of words with final *ou*, e.g. *grown*, *known*, and *sown* (see Vol. I, p. 357).

Note: Welsh sources (the *Welsh Hymn*, Salesbury, and the *Welsh Breviary*) use Welsh *ow* to transcribe the English diphthong in *old*, &c., and *soul*; but as Welsh *ow* is [əu] and is also used in transcriptions of English words which can only have ME *ū*, we must assume that *old*, &c., and *soul* have a variant in ME *ū* (see §§ 169, 172) and not the normal ME *ou*.

(b) *Evidence of the monophthongal pronunciation*

§ 250. The *Welsh Hymn* transcribes both ME *ou* and ME *ǭ* as Welsh *o*; ME *ou* was so treated in final position in the original, and in medial position in MS H (*c.* 1610) in the word *soul*. But it is doubtful whether this transcription shows monophthongization (see Vol. I, p. 5). Palsgrave identifies ME *ou* in final position with French *au*, but probably means a diphthongal pronunciation (see Vol. I, p. 10). Salesbury identifies ME *ou* with Welsh *o*; all the cases are in final position. His evidence probably does show monophthongization (see Vol. I, pp. 12–13). Laneham shows a monophthong, identical with ME ǭ, in final position and in derived forms of words with final *ou* (thus *known, elbows, followeth*); in medial position a diphthong is normal (see Vol. I, pp. 90, 92). Hart (see Vol. I, p. 78) bases his transcriptions in the *Orthographie* on the monophthongal pronunciation, identifying ME *ou* with ME ǭ and representing the two sounds as ō or *o*; but in the *Methode* he shows a diphthong, except in final position, where the diphthong occurs once only against the monophthong twice. Bullokar betrays the fact that his own pronunciation was normally a monophthong by his use of *ow* as a symbol for ME ǭ in *owerz* 'oars' and probably also in *rowm* 'roam'. Mulcaster perhaps means to describe a monophthong (see Vol. I, p. 127). Sanford and Cotgrave compare the pronunciation of *au* in *Paul's* (i.e. of ME *ou*) with French *au*; but this may not show a monophthong (cf., in § 249 above, the evidence of Sherwood). Tonkis identifies ME *ou* with ME ǭ; all the examples are in final position. Robinson shows regular monophthongization to identity with ME ǭ in medial and final position. Gil knew a monophthong beside a diphthong even in medial position (see § 249 above). Sherwood (1632) shows a monophthong, identified with French *o*, in final position and in derived forms (e.g. *known* and *sown*; so also *own*). Butler normally shows a diphthong, but may have known a monophthong even in medial position if his statement that the Londoners' pronunciation of *au* (i.e. ME *ou*) in *Paul* is 'after the French manner' rests on the normal seventeenth-century French monophthongal pronunciation of *au* (but compare Sherwood). Hodges shows only a monophthong, identified with ME ǭ, in medial and final position. Gataker shows this monophthong in final position (there are no medial examples), Willis in both medial and final position. Wallis admits that some people pronounce ME *ou* like ME ǭ. Wharton (see Vol. I, p. 337) shows the monophthong in final position; in medial position he uses the diphthongal or the monophthongal pronunciation according as the spelling is *ou* (*ow*) or *o* (cf. Gil). Lloyd shows the monophthong medially, Merriott finally, Newton finally (beside the diphthongal pronunciation) and in *though*, and Price both medially and finally. Wilkins identifies ME *ou* with ME ǭ. The *Welsh Breviary* has no examples of undoubted ME *ou* in medial or final position except *though*, which has a monophthong identified with Welsh *o*; but this may develop under weak stress. J. Smith identifies ME *ou* with ME ǭ both medially and finally; so do Coles (*Schoolmaster*), Strong, Young (finally; he gives no medial examples), Lye, and *The Protestant Tutor* (finally; no medial examples). Richardson shows a monophthong (identified with ME ǭ) both medially and finally, beside a diphthong. Cooper shows a monophthong [oː], identified with ME ǭ, in final position (though he says that some people even here use a diphthong), beside a diphthong [ou] in medial position (with two exceptions, in which he shows monophthongization; see § 249). In his 'homophone' lists he shows monophthongization in final position and in derivative forms (*thrown*, so also *own*) in his 'same pronunciation' list (which is based on the pronunciation which he regarded as correct); but monophthongization in medial position in other words is shown only in his 'near alike' list, which has *sold* : *sol'd*. Hawkins shows monophthongization in final position; he has no medial examples. Aickin (see Vol. I, p. 357), following but adding to Cooper, shows monophthongization in final position and in derivative forms (e.g. *grown, known, sown*) but retains the diphthong medially in other words. *WSC-RS* and Brown show monophthongization in all positions. The shorthand-writers regularly take advantage of monophthongization to allow them to abbreviate *ou* to *o*; so T. Shelton, Dix, Rich (followed by Botley), Bridges, Hopkins, Mason, Steele, and Ridpath. The 'homophone' lists show monophthongization both medially and finally (except for Cooper, on whose lists see above); so Hodges, Wharton, Price, Fox and Hookes, Coles, Strong, Young, Richardson, Cooper, Aickin, *WSC-RS*, Cocker, Brown, and the anonymous manuscript list.

Note 1: Horn, § 137, states that Salesbury shows the diphthong as well as the monophthong; this statement must depend on the transcription with Welsh *ow* given for *low* vb. 'mugire', but *ow* in Salesbury represents ME *ū*, which is recorded by other evidence for *low* vb. (see § 173).

Note 2: Zachrisson, *Eng. Vowels*, p. 83, cites fifteenth-century *o* and *oo* spellings for ME *ou*, which show monophthongization both medially and finally; most of his examples come from Eastern texts (*Paston Letters* and *Cely Papers*).

Note 3: Rhymes of ME *ou* with ME *ǭ* are common in sixteenth-century poetry. They occur most often when ME *ou* is final, in poets from Heath and Wyatt (*temp.* Henry VIII) onwards; but also in medial position, both in words recognized as derivative forms of others with final *ou* (from Churchyard 1575 and Bewe 1578 onwards, and perhaps earlier) and in other words (from Spenser, who rhymes *folk* with *cloak* in the *Shepheardes Calendar*, 1579, onwards).

LATE ME *ou* BEFORE [l] AND [χ]

§ 251. Late ME *ou* before [l] and [χ] usually shows the normal ModE development to [oː] (which is ultimately replaced, in the case of ME *ou* before [χ], by [ɒː] < ME *au*; see § 240). But sometimes in late ME there occurs assimilation of *ou* to [uː] because of the influence (chiefly a rounding, but also a raising, influence) of the following [l] or [χ]. This [uː] subsequently shows two developments.

(1) If [uː] develops early enough, it becomes identical with ME *ū* and is diphthongized with it to early ModE [ʌu]. On this development, for which there is a considerable body of evidence, see § 169 (ME *ou* before [l]) and § 170 (ME *ou* before [χ]).

(2) If [uː] develops rather later (in the fifteenth century), it becomes identical not with ME *ū* (already diphthongized), but with ME *ǭ* (now raised to [uː]). The evidence of this development given by orthoepists is as

follows. (*a*) Before [l], Laneham (see Vol. I, p. 90) has [uː] in *bold, hold,* and *told* (ME *ǭ* before *l*) and in *moulding* 'pattern work' (probably ME *ǒ* before *l*, but also perhaps ME *ŭ* before *l*; see Vol. I, p. 364); and Brown (see Vol. I, p. 370 and p. 419) has [uː] in *moulter* ('moulder'? with ME *ǒ* before *l*?), *mould* ('pattern'? probably with ME *ǒ* before *l*), *poll* (ME *ǒ* before *l*), *shoulder, poultice,* and *poultry* (ME *ŭ* before *l*). (*b*) Before [χ], Laneham has [uː] in *bethooght* 'bethought' and *me thoogt* 'me thought'—probably from ME *pŏhte* rather than *pŭhte*.

Note 1: Further possible evidence is given by the Northerners Levins, Mulcaster, and Poole (see § 169, Note 2, and § 170, Note 4), but their [uː] may be Northern undiphthongized ME *ū* developed as in (1) above and not fifteenth-century [uː] developed as in (2).

Note 2: The [uː] given by Laneham and Brown is not from undiphthongized ME *ū*, for they give no evidence of the failure of the diphthongization of original ME *ū* before [l] and [χ].

ME *oi* AND ME *ui*

(1) *Distribution of the two diphthongs*

§ 252. The conventional spelling *oi* conceals the existence in ME of two diphthongs, ME *oi* (pronounced [ɔi]) and ME *ui* (pronounced [ui]). Some words had only *oi*, others varied between *oi* and *ui*; some are recorded by the orthoepists only with pronunciations developed from ME *ui*, but the evidence of Gil (see Vol. I, p. 152) and Wallis (see Vol. I, p. 233) is to the effect that words which were pronounced with ME *ui* could also be pronounced with ME *oi*, and this evidence explains, and is confirmed by, the PresE pronunciation, which has [ɔi] < ME *oi* in all words spelt *oi*. The spelling has clearly been responsible for ME *oi* finally driving out pronunciations developed from ME *ui*, but the PresE pronunciation of 'ME *ui* words' is not a mere spelling-pronunciation; it represents the survival, assisted by the spelling, of one of the sixteenth- and seventeenth-century variants to the exclusion of the other, even in words in which ME *ui* was formerly much the more common. Gil's and Wallis's evidence also justifies the procedure of those orthoepists (some of them very dependable) who do not distinguish ME *ui* from ME *oi*; they have clearly relied on the variant with ME *oi* exclusively (doubtless because of the influence of the conventional spelling). The *Welsh Hymn* uses only the transcription *oe* (for ME *oi*). Smith does not distinguish ME *ui* from ME *oi* in his transcriptions (which are based on ME *oi*), though his comment shows that he knew both sounds without having clearly distinguished them (see Vol. I, pp. 58–59). Laneham does not normally distinguish ME *ui* (see Vol. I, p. 92). Robinson, an excellent phonetician, gives no hint of the existence of ME *ui*, and transcribes all words as having ME *oi*. Butler equally does not distinguish ME *ui*, but he is so poor a phonetician, and so much under the influence of the conventional orthography, that his evidence in itself is of no weight. Newton gives only a single diphthong [ɔi] (see Vol. I, p. 251). The arrangement of the rhyme-lists in Coles's *Schoolmaster* shows that all the words spelt *oi* which he gives were pronounced with [ɔi] < ME *oi*, whatever their etymology (see Vol. I, pp. 440–1).

Note 1: It might be argued that Gil's and Wallis's remarks on variation between ME *ui* and ME *oi* apply only to the examples which they give, but the general tendency of the evidence is such as to justify our extending them to mean that all words pronounced with ME *ui* can also be pronounced with ME *oi*. Gil, after referring to the diphthong *oi* as in *toiz* 'toys' and the 'triphthong' *uoi* as in *buoi* 'boy', proceeds: 'Aliquando per O. *indifferenter* [my italics] vsurpamus *u* ante i. Dicimus enim *toil*, aut *tuil* labos [*sic*, variant form of *labor*]; *broil*, aut *brūil* tumultus; *soil* aut *sūil* sordes.' Wallis (see Vol. I, p. 233 above) says in one place that some words which he has given with a diphthong beginning with 'ŏ obscurum' (i.e. unrounded ME *ŭ*) are pronounced by some people with 'ŏ apertum' (the distinction intended is between ME *ui* and ME *oi* in those words in his list which have the spelling *oi*), and in another, contrariwise, that in at least some words which he has given with a diphthong beginning with 'ŏ apertum' some people use 'ŏ vel *ŭ* obscurum' (again a distinction between ME *oi* and ME *ui*); the statements are less precise than might be wished, but make it clear that ME *ui* and ME *oi* are to some extent interchangeable. It seems to be implied, but is not made explicit, by both Gil and Wallis that there are some words in which ME *oi* cannot be replaced by ME *ui*; this is in fact what the evidence shows. On the other hand there is no reason to suppose that even Wallis means to imply that there are words in which ME *ui* cannot be replaced by ME *oi*.

Note 2: The important principle that all words which have ME *ui* were in English capable, from their first adoption, of a variant with ME *oi* has not been clearly recognized. Thus Luick, to whose researches (first published in *Anglia*, xiv. 294 ff.) the distinction between 'ME *oi* words' and 'ME *ui* words' is due (though most scholars have not accepted his results except with reservations), shows no recognition of it. In his *Historische Grammatik*, §§ 544–5, he divides words spelt *oi* into two mutually exclusive classes, one with ME *oi* and the other with ME *ui*; and he explains (§ 545) the present StE pronunciation of 'ME *ui* words' as being due to 'eine vom Schriftbild ausgehende Reaktion gegen die natürlich entwickelte Lautgebung', in consequence of which even these words 'die Lautung erhielten, die ursprünglich nur den alten *oi*-Wörtern [i.e. 'ME *oi* words'] zukam'. In § 545, Anm. 1, he records Gil's evidence that some words had both *oi* and *ui* without comment, but he comments on Wallis's evidence (that 'ME *ui* words' were also pronounced [ɔi] by some people) that it 'wohl als frühe Einwirkung des Schriftbildes zu deuten ist' (a view adopted by Lehnert, *Wallis*, § 139). Similar views of the general situation are taken by Horn, § 119 (but he recognizes that ME *oi* beside ME *ui* in 'ME *ui* words' may not always be due to the 'Einfluß des Schriftbildes'); by Ekwall, §§ 92–94; by Zachrisson, *Bullokar*, pp. 102–4 (who regards ME *oi* in 'ME *ui* words' as being due to the influence of the spelling, rejecting the view put forward by Slettengren that they are due to dialectal developments in 'Norman French, Continental French or Anglo-French itself'); and by others.

But Jespersen, *ModE Gr*, pp. 100–1, recognizes that though words which have Lat. *au* before *j* or which have earlier OF *ei* always have ME *oi*, the other classes 'are more or less uncertain' (by which presumably he means that they vary between ME *oi* and ME *ui*); Jordan, § 237, recognizes that the *oi* spelling of 'ME *ui* words' does not always stand for *ui* and that there must even in ME have been beside *ui* also the later *oi* form (which he would explain as arising from more southerly and central French dialects than Norman); and Slettengren (cf. Zachrisson, loc. cit.) puts forward a similar view to account for ME *oi* in 'ME *ui* words'. Jespersen's distinction of the various classes of words spelt *oi* got near to the truth, but (as often) he did not clinch matters. Slettengren's conclusions on the classification of the words (reported by Zachrisson, loc. cit.) are unacceptable.

Wyld, *Short History*, § 270; *Coll. Eng.*, p. 250; and *Rhymes*, pp. 73–75, shows no recognition that there were two distinct ME diphthongs involved.

§ 253. Whether a word has only ME *oi*, or varies between ME *oi* and ME *ui*, depends ultimately on its etymology. It seems useful to distinguish seven classes of words according to etymology, as follows; doubtful cases are discussed briefly in notes.

(*a*) *Words adopted from French which had OF* ǫi *from earlier* ei *or from Latin or Gmc* au *before* j

§ 254. These words have only ME *oi*. Here belong the following words, which are recorded with ME *oi* by the orthoepists named: *choice* (Hart (see Vol. I, p. 83), Mulcaster, Bullokar, Robinson, Butler, Hodges, Coles, and *RS*), *choice* vb. 'choose' (Levins), *cloister* (Price), *coy* (Smith, Hodges (*SH-PD*), Price, Coles, Cooper), *employ(ment)* (Bullokar, Poole, possibly Price—see Vol. I, p. 341), *exploit* (*RS*), *froise* (*WSC-RS*), *joy* (*enjoy*, *rejoice*) (Mulcaster, Bullokar, Robinson, Gil, Hodges, Cooper, and *WSC-RS*), the name *Joyce* (Hodges), *loy* (Cheke), *loyal* (Gil), *moiety* (*WSC*), *noise* (Bullokar, Hodges, Wallis, Coles, Cooper, and *RS*), *poise* (Coles, Cooper, and *RS*), *quoit* (Smith, *WSC-RS*), *roy* (Levins), *royal* (Bullokar, Robinson, Gil), *supploy* 'supply' (Levins), *voyage* (Cooper).

As so many words conventionally spelt with *oi* varied in pronunciation between ME *oi* and ME *ui*, it would not be at all surprising if words which by etymology should have only ME *oi* had come to have analogical pronunciations with ME *ui*. There is in fact some evidence of this, but remarkably little. Hodges's transcriptions of *royal(ly)* and *employ* are likely to mean that he pronounced these words with analogical [wəi] < ME *ui*, but in these two cases there is a special reason (see Vol. I, p. 175). Brown gives *froise* as a homophone of *fries* 3 sing. pres. indic. of *fry* verb; this equation must depend on an analogical pronunciation with [əi] < ME *ui* in *froise*, but again there is a special reason—the close connexion, in etymology and sense, between *froise* 'a fried cake' (probably < pop. Lat. *frixum, variant of *frīxum*, p.p. of *frīgere*) and the verb *fry* (< Lat. *frīgere*). Bullokar rhymes *noise* with *rise* and Brown gives it as a 'homophone' of *nice*. A certain amount of evidence for analogical ME *ui* in words which should have only ME *oi* comes from other sources (see Note 4 below).

Note 1: *Noise* is of doubtful etymology; Luick, § 545, groups it with words which have OF ǫi < Lat. or Gmc. *au* before *j*, and this seems probable. *Quoit* is also doubtful, but seems to belong here. On the etymology of *supploy* see Vol. I, p. 28.

Note 2: In *froise* Palsgrave gives [wɛː], which presents difficulties, especially if *OED* is right in deriving the word from popular Latin *frixum, as is here assumed. I have previously suggested (*Medium Ævum*, ix. 125, footnote 2) that it is due to adoption of the later [wɛ] pronunciation of OF ǫi (cf. *shamway* 'chamois', recorded by Daines). There are rhymes (see § 261, Note 2) which may well show a similar pronunciation [dʒwɛː] for *joy* (< popular Latin *gaudia*, which can give only OF ǫi). See further § 256, Note 1, where the date at which the French pronunciation [wɛ] exerted its influence is discussed.

Cooper's pairing (in his 'near alike' list) of *froize*, *phrase* 'cake fried' with *phrase* 'sentence' depends on the *fraise* variant of *froise* (which preserves the original OF *ei*); *OED*'s earliest evidence for this form is Johnson's entry in his dictionary.

In *coy* a pronunciation [wɛː] or [weː] is given by Palsgrave and Smith (in the latter as a variant beside [əi]), but the explanation is different; their pronunciation represents the earlier French *quei* < Latin *quetus < *quietus*. (Cf. *Medium Ævum*, ix. 121 and 125, footnote 2.)

Note 3: The equation of *employ* and *imply* in 'homophone' lists (those of Hodges ('near alike'), Coles (*Eng.–Lat. Dict.*), Strong, Young, Cooper ('near alike'), Hawkins, *WSC*, Cocker, and Brown) does not show analogical [əi] < ME *ui* in *employ*. The two words are doublets, being both descended from Latin *implicare*; *OED* records that *employ* was used in various senses now restricted to *imply* until 1626, and *imply* in the senses of *employ* until 1659. The evidence of the 'homophone' lists shows that in speech (probably chiefly in vulgar speech, for Hodges, Coles, and Cooper do not admit the pairing to their more careful lists) the confusion between the words continued later than *OED*'s datings suggest (in fact, until the end of the seventeenth century), though schoolboys were taught to distinguish them in writing; Dr. Denton's *implyment* 'employment', 1670 (Wyld, *Coll. Eng.*, p. 224) shows that the instruction was necessary. *Voyage* is sometimes recorded with [əi], but this arises from its ME variant *viage*; evidence of this form is given by Robinson, Strong, Young, and Cooper. *Royal* has a ME variant *rial*, which explains the [əi] pronunciation shown by the 'homophone' lists of Hodges ('near alike'), *WSC*, and Brown.

Note 4: Marston's rhyme *tryall : disloyal*, 1613, and Mrs. Basire's spelling *regis* 'rejoice', 1654 (cited by Wyld, *Coll. Eng.*, p. 224) may be accepted as showing analogical [əi] < ME *ui* in *disloyal* and *rejoice* (which should have only ME *oi*), though other explanations are conceivable. Jespersen, *ModE Gr*, p. 329, says that Dryden rhymes *joy* and Pope *enjoy* with ME *ī*, but gives no references nor the rhyme-words; such rhymes would show analogical [əi] < ME *ui* in (*en*)*joy*, which by etymology should have only ME *oi*.

Note 5: Wright, *EDG*, § 213, records in words of this group dialectal pronunciations which can hardly develop otherwise than from ME *ui*, which again would be analogical.

(*b*) *Words adopted from French which had OF* ǫi *from Latin and Gmc* ō *and* ŭ *tonic and countertonic, and* ŏ *countertonic, before* j

§ 255. Miss Pope, § 1161, records that AN seems to have varied between *ui* and *ǫi* (which became identical with *ǫi* in the later twelfth century) in these words; this would account for the ME variation, clearly shown by the orthoepistical evidence, between ME *ui* and ME *oi*. Here belong the words *anoint* (*oint, ointment*), *assoil, boil* vb., *boistious* 'boisterous', *cloy, coif, coil* vb. 'wind', *coin, destroy, disloined, essoin, foin* 'lunge', *join* (*joint, jointure*), *loin, moil, moist, point* (*appoint*), *poison, purloin, quoin, roil* vb. 'wander', *soil* sb. 'filth', 'ordure', &c. (and *soil* vb. 'stain', &c.), *spoil, toil, tortoise, Troy, turmoil*, and *voice*.

The orthoepists record variation between ME *oi* and pronunciations developed from ME *ui* in many of these words. *Anoint* (*oint, ointment*) has ME *oi* only in Mulcaster (in *oint*); ME *ui* is shown by Mulcaster (in *anoint*), Bullokar, Hodges, Cooper, Aickin, *WSC-RS*, and the shorthand-writer Farthing. *Boil* vb. (and derivatives) has ME *oi* in Bullokar (apparently; he transcribes it with *ui* but rhymes it on *spoil* with *oi*), Coles, and Ridpath; ME *ui* is shown by Bullokar, Gil (but he implies it has also *oi*), Hodges, Wallis, Price, Cooper, Aickin, *WSC-RS*, Strong's 'phonetically spelt' list, the 'homophone' lists of Hodges ('near alike'), Cooper ('same'), and Brown, and probably in Willis's rhyme-lists. *Cloy* has ME *oi* in Willis, Poole, Coles, and perhaps Price, but ME *ui* in Smith and Hodges. *Coil* vb. 'wind' has ME *oi* in Smith and the shorthand-writer Shelton. *Coin* (and its derivatives) has ME *oi* in Mulcaster, Robinson, Cooper, and Shelton, but ME *ui* in Bullokar, Hodges, and *WSC-RS*. *Destroy* has ME *oi* in Robinson, Daines, and Poole, but ME *ui* in Bullokar. *Join* (and derivatives) has ME *oi* in the *Welsh Hymn*, Salesbury, Bullokar (beside *ui*), Robinson, Gil (beside *ui*), Daines, and Coles; and ME *ui* in Hart (see Vol. I, p. 83), Bullokar, Mulcaster, Gil, Hodges, Price, Cooper, Aickin, *WSC-RS*, and the shorthand-writers Everardt, Mason, and Coles. *Loin* has ME *oi* only in Coles, and ME *ui* in Bullokar, Hodges, *RS*, and the 'homophone' lists of Hodges ('near alike'), Price, Fox and Hookes, Coles (*Eng.–Lat. Dict.*), Strong ('near alike'), Young, Cooper ('same'), Hawkins, *WSC*, Aickin, Cocker, and Brown. *Moist* (*moisture*) has ME *oi* in Gil, Hodges, Price, and Coles, and ME *ui* in *WSC*. *Point* and *appoint* have ME *oi* in Smith, possibly Hart (see Vol. I, p. 83), Bullokar (beside *ui*), and Coles; ME *ui* is given by Bullokar, Mulcaster, Gil, Hodges, Price, Cooper, Aickin, and *WSC-RS*. *Poison* (and derivatives) has ME *oi* only in Robinson; ME *ui* is given by Bullokar, Price, Cooper, Aickin, and *WSC-RS*. *Soil* sb. 'filth' and vb. 'stain', &c. have ME *oi* beside ME *ui* in Gil, and *ui* in Levins and probably in Willis; Coles gives *oi* in a word *soil* which may be this (since he is ultimately following Willis). *Spoil* has ME *oi* in Bullokar (but see under *boil* above) and Coles, and ME *ui* in Gil and Hodges, Strong's 'phonetically spelt' list, and probably in Willis. *Toil* has ME *oi* in Smith, Bullokar (who rhymes it with *soil* transcribed with *oi*), Gil (beside ME *ui*), Coles, and perhaps Mason, but ME *ui* in Levins, Bullokar (who so transcribes it), Gil, Hodges, Wallis, Cooper, Aickin, *WSC-RS*, the 'homophone' lists of Coles (*Eng.–Lat. Dict.*), Strong ('near alike'), Young, *WSC*, Cocker, and Brown, and probably in Willis. *Troy* has ME *oi* in Robinson and Willis and ME *ui* in Brown's 'homophone' list. *Voice* has ME *oi* in Hart (beside *ui*; see Vol. I, p. 83), Bullokar, Mulcaster, Gil, Hodges, Willis, Poole, Coles, and *WSC-RS*; it has ME *ui* apparently in Hart and in the 'homophone' lists of Young, Cocker, and Brown.

In certain of these words one or other pronunciation is clearly predominant, but the fact of variation is well established. Those in which no variation is recorded are both less numerous and less common. ME *oi*.alone is recorded in *assoil* (*Welsh Hymn* and Gil; but rhymes show ME *ui*—see Note 3 below), *boistious* (Bullokar), *coif* (Mulcaster, Bullokar, Hodges, Cooper, *WSC-RS*), *disloined* (Gil), and *turmoil* (Smith). ME *ui* alone is recorded in *essoin* (Coles, phonetically spelt *sine*), *foin* (Levins, Gil), *moil* (Cooper followed by Aickin and *WSC-RS*; the 'homophone' lists of Cooper, *WSC*, and Brown; and probably Willis), *purloin* (Daines), *quoin* (Levins), *roil* 'wander' (Levins), and *tortoise* (Price). But note the contrast between the etymologically related *disloin* and *purloin* and between *quoin* and its variant *coin* (preceding paragraph), perhaps also between *turmoil* and *moil* (which may be related); one should also remember Gil's and Wallis's proviso that words which have ME *ui* can also have ME *oi*. In the group as a whole records of ME *ui* outnumber those of ME *oi* by roughly five to three.

> Note 1: *Assoil* is from OF *as(s)oil* 1 sing. pres. indic. and *as(s)oille* pres. subj. of OF *as(s)oudre*. These are analogical forms; *solf < Lat *solvo* is replaced by *sol*, *soil* on the analogy of *tol*, *toil* 1 sing. pres. indic. of *toudre* (Pope, § 936); *toudre* in its turn owes its variant infinitive *tolir* and *toil* 1 sing. pres. indic. to the analogy of *bolir* < Lat. *bullire* and *boil* < Lat. *bullio*. As *boil* has OF *ǫi*, we may assume that *as(s)oil*, which is thus ultimately modelled on it, also has OF *ǫi*; so with the subjunctive forms. Luick, § 414, Anm. 1, takes OF *soil*, *soille* as having OF *ǫi*, arguing that they are formed on *solt* < Lat *solvit* on the analogy of *fail*, *faille* beside *falt* < Lat *fallit*; but as the English *assoil* varies between ME *oi* and ME *ui* (the latter being shown by rhymes; see Note 3 below) the OF word cannot have OF *ǫi*. *Boistious* is probably from OF *boisteux* (cf. Wallenberg, *The Vocabulary of Dan Michel's 'Ayenbite of Inwit'*, s.v. *boystoyse*) and so belongs here. *Cloy* is from *accloy*, from a by-form of OF *enclouer*, but also seems to belong here; Luick, § 545, is in error in associating *accloy* with words which have OF *ǫi* < Lat *au* before *j*, as is shown by its having ModE pronunciations which presuppose ME *ui*. *Destroy* is explained by Luick, § 417 (3), as being from an analogical ME *destroien* beside *destruien* (< OF *destruire* < late Lat *destrūgere) on the model of *anoien* beside *anuien*; he supposes it to have only ME *oi*. But as the word varies in ModE it seems better to follow Jordan, § 237, Anm., who takes *destroien* to be from late Lat *destrūcere [better *destrūgere?] against *destruien* < late Lat *destrūcere [better *destrūgere?]; in this case *destroy* would have OF *ǫi* and belong here. The ultimate etymology of *moist* is dubious, but it seems to have OF *ǫi*. *Turmoil* belongs here if it is connected with *moil*. The verbs *coil*, *moil*, and *spoil* belong here if derived from the OF infinitive forms, and the sb. *spoil* insofar as it is from the OF infinitive; the OF present tense forms (< Lat *colligo*, *mollio*, and *spolio*), and the sb. *spoil* insofar as it is from Latin *spolium*, belong however with group (c) below, in which Luick, § 415 (3), puts the derived English words *spoil*, *despoil*, and *moil*. ME *bile* 'boil' vb. seems to be a ME analogical formation; it does not lie behind the eModE pronunciation [bəil]. On *roil* vb. see Vol. I, p. 28. *Coil* sb. 'tumult', which seems to have ME *ui* in Willis, is of dubious origin.
>
> Note 2: Luick, § 545, puts *coif*, *moist*, and *voice* among words which have ME *oi* only. Reference to § 417 (2) shows that he realizes that they have by etymology OF *ǫi*, but believes that in them ME has 'at least predominantly' *ǫi*, probably from Central French. But in ModE *moist* and *voice* are recorded with pronunciations developed from ME *ui*; only *coif* has no record of ME *ui*, and this may be accidental.
>
> Note 3: Rhymes (see § 262, Note 3 below) show [əi] or [wəi] < ME *ui* in *assoil*, *boil*, *coil*, *coin*, *destroy*, *(en)join*, *loin*, *poison*, *purloin*, *spoil*, *toil*, and *voice*. Spellings which appear to show [əi] < ME *ui* (see § 262, Note 2 below) in *anoint*, *boil*, *destroy*, *join*, and *poison* are cited by Wyld, *Coll. Eng.*, p. 224.

(c) *Words adopted from French which have Latin or Gmc tonic ŏ before a palatal*

§ 256. In this class belong *annoy* and its derivatives, *boy*, *broil* (probably), *buoy*, *foil* (*milfoil*, *trifoil*), *oil*, *oyster*, *soil* sb. 'gound, earth', *toy*, and *void* and its derivatives. The class as a whole presents difficulties for English philology which have not been resolved. The normal OF vocalism was that tonic *ŏ* became *uo* > *ue* > *ö* before palatal *l* (Miss Pope, § 410), and the group *ǒj* became *uoi > *uei* > *üi* [yi] (Miss Pope, § 411); this [yi] became [y:] in AN and is represented in ME by [y:] or *ī* (Luick, § 417 (3)). But in northern and north-eastern OF dialects the 'breaking' of tonic *o* failed, and the result was *o̯i*; the influence of this development on AN and ME has been doubted, but it would most easily account for the *oi* forms of English *foil* (*milfoil*, &c.), *oil*, *soil* sb. 'ground' (cf. Jordan, § 232, Anm. 3), and perhaps *oyster* (but see Note 2). Many of the words here involved are, however, verbs or are subject to the influence of etymologically related verbs; and in the verbs there occur end-stressed ('weak') forms in which the *ŏ* is countertonic and therefore falls under case (*b*) above, i.e. there is variation in AN between *ui* and *o̯i* > *o̯i*, and in ME between *ui* and *oi*. But even if we explain ME *oi* in *foil*, &c. from the northern OF development, the *ui* forms of *foil*, *oil*, and *soil* remain a difficulty; for they are too frequently recorded in eModE to be comparable to the very rare analogical *ui*-forms of words of class (*a*) above. *Soil* 'ground' could be explained from the special analogy of *soil* 'filth', which comes under class (*b*). *Foil* might be explained from a verb < Lat *foliare (cf. *foliatus*), but the rare English verb is formed from the sb. The English verb *oil* is much later than the sb., from which it is formed, and it does not seem likely that ME *ui* in *oil* could be due to the influence of a verb < Lat *oleare. Probably the explanation lies simply in the fact that the OF diphthongs [ue] and [yi] were alien to the English system. It is remarkable enough that English should have accepted from French the diphthongs [ɔi], extremely rare in native words (cf. § 258), and [ui], unknown in native words; it is hardly to be expected that it should also have adopted [ue] and [yi]. For the former of these has been substituted ME [ui], quite often recorded in *foil*, *oil*, and *soil*; for the latter there was normally substituted AN (or ME) [y:] or *ī*, much more rarely but undoubtedly ME [ui] (as assumed by Luick, § 417(3)).

The orthoepists record variation in rather more than half the words here involved. *Boy* has ME *oi* in the *Welsh Hymn*, Cheke, Smith (beside [we:] < [wɛ:]), Bullokar, Mulcaster, Gil (as a so-called Northern pronunciation, beside his own [buɔi]), Hodges (*SH-PD*), Gataker, Willis, Wallis, Poole, Price, Wilkins, and Coles. ME *ui* is not certainly recorded: Strong rhymes *boy* with *hoy*, which he makes a homophone of *high* and *hie*, and *WSC* gives *boy* as a homophone of *buoy*, which in turn is equated (by both *WSC* and *RS*) with *buy* and *bye*; but there may be variation between [ɔi] and [əi] in *hoy* (in Strong) and *buoy* (in *WSC*). *Broil* has ME *oi* in Smith, Gil (beside *ui*), and Coles; it has ME *ui* in Laneham, Gil, Hodges, Cooper, *RS*, and Aickin, in Cocker's 'phonetically spelt' list, and probably in Willis. *Buoy* has ME *oi* in Price, and ME *ui* in Hart, Bullokar, Gil, Cooper, and *WSC-RS*. Fox and Hookes give it as a homophone of *boy* and Brown 'phonetically' spells it *boy*; this probably indicates ME *oi*. On *WSC*'s 'homophone' list see under *boy* above. *Foil* has ME *oi* in Smith, Mulcaster (beside *ui*), Price, Coles, and Shelton, probably also in Cooper (since he records *ui* only in his 'near alike' list, to which he relegates pronunciations different from his own); ME *ui* is shown by Mulcaster, Gil, Hodges, and the 'homophone' lists of Strong ('near alike'), Cooper ('near alike'), *WSC-RS*, and Brown, and probably in Willis. The derivatives *milfoil* and *trifoil* are recorded only by Levins, with ME *ui*. *Oil* has ME *oi* in Mulcaster, Bullokar, Hodges, Price, Coles, and Ridpath, but ME *ui* in Wallis, Cooper, *WSC-RS*, the 'homophone' lists of Coles (*Eng.–Lat. Dict.*), Cooper ('same'), *WSC*, Cocker, and Brown, and probably in Willis. *Soil* sb. 'ground' has ME *oi* in the *Welsh Hymn*, Smith, Bullokar (who so transcribes it), and Gil (beside *ui*), but ME *ui* perhaps in Bullokar (who despite his transcription rhymes it with *toil*, transcribed with *ui*), in Gil, in Strong's 'phonetically spelt' list (if this be the word intended), and probably in Willis.

Only ME *oi* is recorded in *annoy* (*noisome, noyous*) (Bullokar, Mulcaster, Robinson, Gil, Poole, and Price), *oyster* (Hart, Hodges), *toy* (Cheke, Smith (beside [wɛː] < [weː]), Mulcaster, Robinson, Gil, Willis, Wallis, Poole, Price, and Coles), and *void* (*avoid, devoid*) (Bullokar, Mulcaster, Robinson, Gil, Hodges, Daines, Poole, Coles, and *WSC-RS*). There are no words of this group which are recorded only with ME *ui*. In the group as a whole records of ME *oi* outnumber those of ME *ui* by roughly two to one (contrast class (*b*) above).

Note 1: The pronunciation [wɛː] for *oi* in *boy* (recorded by Palsgrave, Smith, Hart, Tonkis, and Butler, supported by other evidence; cf. *Medium Ævum*, ix. 121–5), in *toy* (Smith and Tonkis), and in *annoy* (Tonkis), is to be explained as due to the influence of the later French pronunciation [wɛ] (see A. J. Bliss, *English and Germanic Studies*, iv. 25–26); cf. *froise* and probably *joy* (see § 254, Note 2). The pronunciation [buɔi] for *boy* (Gil and Cooper) is a variant of [bwɔi], developed from [bɔi] with a *w*-glide (Bliss, op. cit., pp. 24–25); in my view (which differs from Professor Bliss's) it is more likely to be a side-development from [bwɔi] than an earlier stage. Bliss has shown conclusively that I was mistaken in associating these pronunciations with the earlier stages of the OF 'breaking' process. But certain puzzling features remain about the [wɛː] pronunciation: (i) it is not merely a 'pedant's pronunciation', for in *boy* at any rate it seems to have been quite widespread; (ii) the authors concerned single out as having [wɛː] for *oi* just these few common words, although the French origin of *boy* and *toy* is, to say the least, not immediately obvious; (iii) the evidence relates chiefly to final *oi* (but this may be accidental). The solution seems to be that [wɛː] is not primarily (if at all) due to sixteenth-century pedantic imitation of contemporary French pronunciation, as Bliss suggests (since this should affect all *oi* words, or if not, then learned words whose French connexions were especially obvious), but arises first in ME itself (i.e. in the period of adoption); it is normal enough for a ME variant to survive in certain words only, not in all those in which it is theoretically possible. OF [wɛ] < *oi* had already developed in the later twelfth century (Miss Pope, §; 519) and affected AN in the thirteenth century (§§ 1161 (ii) and 1223), so that it may have influenced the words involved from their first appearance in English or (in the case of *annoy* and *joy*, recorded in *Ancrene Wisse*) shortly thereafter.

Note 2: Luick, § 417, Anm. 2, followed by Jordan, explains ME *oister* as a blend of OF *uistre* and OE *ostre*; this is perhaps unnecessary, but the influence of the form descended from OE may account for the dominance of *oi* over *ui* in the word. In the seventeenth century it was still pronounced with ME *ŏ*, in spite of the spelling; this is the explanation of the pairing *austere* : *oyster* given in the 'homophone' lists of Price, Young, and Brown. Dialectal pronunciations recorded by Wright, *EDG*, Index, show ME *ui* in *oyster*; on Luick's hypothesis, they would be due to later analogy in English with 'ME *ui* words'.

Note 3: Latin tonic *ŏ* before *ng* does not break (Pope, § 426), so *disloined* and *purloin* belong in class (*b*) and not here; on the other hand certain words which are treated under class (*b*) may conceivably belong here (see § 255, Note 1, end). Certain words included here under class (*c*) are of doubtful etymology. *Broil* is a difficult word; it seems to be connected with an OF *bruillir* recorded by Godefroy (see *OED*), and if so probably belongs here. Wyld, *Universal English Dictionary*, gives OF forms *broiller*, *bruiller* (which he suggests may be connected with MHG *brodeln*); again these forms appear those of a class (*c*) word. Or is it possible that OF *bruler*, ME *brulen* have been blended with OF *boillir*, ME *boilen*? In that event *broil* would in effect belong with *boil* in class (*b*); Luick, § 545, associates *broil* with class (*b*) words, though connecting it with OF *bruillir* (§ 490, Anm. 6). I assume for *boy* and *toy* the etymologies proposed in my article in *Medium Ævum*, ix. 121–54, with the modifications shown to be necessary by A. J. Bliss, *English and Germanic Studies*, iv. 22–29; but *toy* especially remains doubtful.

Note 4: Luick, § 545, puts *annoy*, *void*, *avoid*, and *oyster* among words which have only ME *oi* (though he recognizes that by etymology they belong to class (*c*)); this is of course consistent with the bulk of the ModE evidence. He also gives *boy* among words which have only ME *oi*; but though orthoepistical evidence for ME *ui* is unsatisfactory, there are modern dialectal pronunciations which depend on it (cf. *Medium Ævum*, ix. 123).

(d) Words adopted from Dutch

§ 257. Words adopted from Dutch which in English have the digraph *oi* appear as a class to be assimilated to class (*b*) and show variation between ME *oi* and ME *ui* without regard to the nature of the Dutch diphthong (or vowel) represented by English *oi*. ME *oi* is recorded in *doit* (Dutch *ui*) by Hodges and in *loiter* (MDu *o*, ModDu *eu*) by Bullokar; on English *oi* in the latter see Llewellyn, *The Influence of Low Dutch on the English Vocabulary*, pp. 10–11. ME *ui* is recorded in *foist* 'cheat' (Dutch *ui*) by Hodges and in *roil* 'clumsy woman' (on its etymology see Vol. I, p. 28) by Levins. Variation is shown in the only word recorded more than once, *hoy* 'small vessel' (Dutch *oei*): Hart gives ME *oi* in his manuscript, but in the *Orthographie* a pronunciation developed from ME *ui* (see *Medium Ævum*, ix. 121, footnote 2); the latter is also given by Hodges, and Hunt's and Strong's 'homophone' lists give another pronunciation developed from *ui*, possibly (in Strong) as a variant to *oi* (see § 256 above, under *boy*).

(e) ME oi of native origin

§ 258. ME *oi* develops exceptionally from OE *ŏ* plus the OE voiced spirant *g* in the OE p.p. *brogden*; thus arises in ME the p.p. *broiden* (*broided*) beside normal *browden*, and from the former there is developed an infinitive *to broid*, whence in turn arise (by blending with ME (*em*)*brouder*, *embrouderie* < OF *bro(u)der*) the ModE *to broider*, *to embroider*, and *embroidery*. These words have of course only ME *oi* and not ME *ui*, and are thus assimilated to class (*a*). Price gives ME *oi* in *embroider*.

Note: The development in *brogden* is usually explained by assuming that from the infinitive *bregdan* the palatalized *g* has been analogically extended to the p.p.; but, as Professor J. R. R. Tolkien points out, it is probably a special development of the group *ŏgd* (cf. *Croydon* < *Crogdenu).

(*f*) *Analogical* oi *in words which have ME* ī

§ 259. The words *boil* 'ulcer', *groin*, *hoist*, and *joist* are from ME *bīle* (OE *bȳle*), *grīnde* (origin unknown), *hȳse* (and other forms; further relations uncertain), and *gīste* (OF *giste*). The ModE spelling and the PresE pronunciation with [ɔi] are clearly analogical; as the orthoepists show that *hoist* and *joist* also had pronunciations developed from ME *ui*, the most likely hypothesis is that they have been affected by the analogy of words of class (*c*), which vary in ME between ME ī (< OF [yi]) and ME *oi* and *ui*. *Boil* 'ulcer' is not certainly recorded with any analogical pronunciation by the orthoepists. Smith gives ME ī; Fox and Hookes pair *boyl* 'a sore' with *boil* vb. in their 'homophone' list, but the pairing probably depends on [əi] < ME ī in the former (despite its spelling) and [əi] < ME *ui* in the latter (cf. Strong's pairing *bile* 'a sore': *boil*); Willis rhymes *boil* 'ulcus' with 'ME *ui*' words, but the explanation is probably that suggested for Fox and Hookes (see Vol. I, p. 428); and in Coles, where [ɔi] would be certain, there is no gloss to the word *boil*, which may be only the verb (see Vol. I, p. 441). *Groin* is rhymed with 'ME *ui*' words by Poole, but the rhyme probably depends on [əi] < ME ī in *groin* and [əi] < ME *ui* in the other words (see Vol. I, p. 437); in Coles, however, analogical [ɔi] < ME *oi* is certain (see Vol. I, p. 441). Analogical pronunciations are recorded earlier and more fully in the other two words. *Hoise* (*hoist*), of which the first instance of the *oi* spelling in *OED* is dated 1509, has possibly ME *ui* in Hart (see Vol. I, p. 83), [wəi] < ME *ui* in Hodges, ME *ui* in Cooper (see Vol. I, p. 303), and ME *oi* in Levins, Poole, Coles, and *WSC*. *Joist* (or its by-form *joise*), of which the earliest *oi* (*oy*) spellings are dated 1453 (see N. Davis, *Medium Ævum*, xviii (1949), 23), 1477–9 (Luick, § 484, Anm.), and 1494 (*OED*), has [wəi] < ME *ui* in Bullokar (see Vol. I, pp. 115–16). Hodges pairs *joise* 'joist' with *juice* in his 'homophone' list (the 'alike' list), and is followed by Wharton, Hunt, Strong, and Cooper ('near alike'); this pairing may depend on [wəi] in both words (so probably in Hodges) or on [əi] in both words (see Note 1 below); in the former case *joise* would have analogical [wəi] < ME *ui*, in the latter [əi] < ME ī.

Note 1: *Juice*, which is paired with *joise* 'joist' in the 'homophone' lists referred to above, itself takes on analogical pronunciations. It has OF [y] and so should normally have ME [y:] or [iu] (whence the PresE pronunciation); ME ī by unrounding of ME [y:] is also possible in some dialects. ME **jīs* 'juice' clearly underlies Robinson's transcription *džeīs*, is probably shown by Butler (see Vol. I, p. 174, note 2), and may be the basis of the pairing with *joise* in some at least of the 'homophone' lists cited (though hardly in Hodges's, in which the pairing originates). But *juice* has been affected by the analogy of words with OF *üi* [yi], which vary in ME between ME [y:] (or *iu*), ME ī, ME [wi:] < [yi], and (especially in words of class (*c*) above) ME *ui* [ui]; it has in consequence taken on pronunciations with ME [wi:] and ME *ui* [ui], from either of which eModE [wəi] can develop. This [wəi] pronunciation is certainly shown by Bullokar (see Vol. I, pp. 115–16) and may underlie the pairing with *joise* in others of the 'homophone' lists, especially that of Hodges. Sir T. Smith, J. Smith (1674), and Cooper give the normal ModE pronunciation developed from ME [yː] or *iu*; Cooper puts the pairing *juice* : *joise* into his 'near alike' (instead of his 'alike') list obviously because it depended on a variant pronunciation, which he did not accept as correct, in one or both of the words involved. See also § 260, Note 3.

Note 2 : *Groin* for ME *grine* may be due to the analogy of *loin*; the earliest evidence for the modern spelling is in Shakespeare's *Venus and Adonis*, ll. 1115-16, where, however, the rhyme depends on ME *ī* (not on ME *ui* > [əi] as apparently assumed by Wyld, *Coll. Eng.*, pp. 224, 251). *Boil* 'ulcer' may be affected by *boil* vb., with its ME variant *bile*; the earliest evidence for the *oi* spelling occurs in 1529 (cf. *OED*). It is not clear whether any special words affected the development of ME *giste* and *hyse*; *joist* may be due to some contact with *join*. But words of class (*c*) above must be the main model, in that they exhibit variation between ME *ī*, *ui*, and *oi*.

Note 3: Horn, § 120; Wyld, *Coll. Eng.*, p. 250; Jordan, § 285, and others assume that in these words *oi* for *ī* is an inverted spelling due to ME *ui* becoming [əi] and so identical with ME *ī*, and that the pronunciation with [ɔi] is a spelling-pronunciation. But though there is a little evidence that in some forms of speech ME *ui* had become identical with ME *ī* before the appearance of these *oi* forms, Hart, Bullokar, and Hodges, who give evidence of pronunciations derived from ME *ui* in *hoist* and *joist*, do not show identity of ME *ui* with ME *ī* and are still able to distinguish ME *ui* even in these words; that is to say, we have to do not with inverted spellings and subsequently with spelling-pronunciations, but with true analogical forms (pronunciation and spelling together). (So Jespersen, *ModE Gr*, p. 330.) *OED*, rejecting Horn's view on the ground that the *oi* forms of *hoise* 'are earlier than the interchange of *oi*, *i*, in *oil*, *ile*, *boil*, *bile*, etc.' (which is roughly but not strictly true), says that these *oi* forms 'appear to arise from a broad pronunciation of *hyse*'. This view is made more precise by Luick, § 484, who supposes that in familiar speech or in certain classes of society ME *ī* had already by the end of the fifteenth century at least reached the stage [ai] and probably already gone beyond it to a sort of [ɒi] sound which became identical with ME *oi* and thereafter developed with it. This exceptional development is inherently most unlikely in StE; why should it affect only these words? (The other three cases cited by Luick are probably not parallel.) It is a decisive objection that on this view the words would have only ME *oi* (as is assumed by Luick, § 545), whereas the earliest evidence which discriminates between ME *ui* and ME *oi* shows ME *ui* and not ME *oi* in *hoist* and *joist* (Hart even seems to take *hoise* 'hoist' as his example of ME *ui*, in contrast to ME *oi* in *oyster*—see Vol. I, pp. 82-83).

(g) *Analogical* oi *in other words*

§ 260. Analogical *oi* forms occur in other words, thus *foil* for *foul* vb. < OF *fouler*, *defoil* for *defoul* vb. < OF *defouler* (there has perhaps been contact with *soil* vb. 'defile', but see Note 2 below), *recoil* for *recule* &c. < OF *reculer* (perhaps owing to the special analogy of *coil* vb. 'gather', which has a variant form *cull*), *foist* 'small galley' (fifteenth century to seventeenth century *fuste*, sixteenth century *fuyste*, sixteenth century onwards *foist*) < OF *fuste*, similarly *foist* 'cask' (contrast *fusty*), *roister* < OF *rustre*. It seems probable that words of class (*c*), which varied between ME *ui* and *oi* on the one hand and ME [yː] on the other, are the model for the analogical *ui*, *oi* forms in words of this group, as they are for such forms in words of class (*f*) (so Luick, § 490, Anm. 6). Of the words cited, *foil* has [əi] < ME *ui* (probably as a variant beside ME *oi*) in Cooper. *Foist* 'small galley' has ME *oi* in Levins; he is followed by Poole, who, however, omits to gloss the word (see Vol. I, p. 437). *Recoil* has either ME *oi* or ME *ui* in Poole; the latter is perhaps more likely (see Vol. I, loc. cit.).

On Levins's *grounsoyle* 'hypothyron' see Vol. I, p. 28; it has ME *ui*.

Note 1: *Loiter*, in which *oi* is an English substitution for unfamiliar Dutch sounds, is perhaps to be compared with the words discussed above; see under class (*d*).

Note 2: *Defoil* is not an inverted spelling of *defile*, as taken by Wyld, *Coll. Eng.*, p. 224. A likely explanation of *defuyle, defoyle* is analogical substitution (probably in OF itself) of '*l* mouillé' for etymological [l] in the 1 sing. pres. indic. and pres. subj. of OF *fo(u)ler* on the analogy of such forms as *bo(u)il* 1 sing. pres. indic. and *bo(u)ille* pres. subj. of *bo(u)lir* < Lat *bullīre* (which later becomes *bo(u)illir* by extension throughout the verb of the strong stem). For such analogical substitution of 'jod-forms' see Pope, § 948; cf. especially *aille* pres. subj. of *aller* and *doign* 1 sing. pres. indic. and *doigne* pres. subj. of *donner*. The form *defile* is the result of blending of *defoil, defoul* with *file* < OE *fȳlan* (see *OED*).

Note 3: *Juice*, which has spellings with *oi* and *oy* (see *OED* and Luick, § 490, Anm. 6), is apparently a further case of a word which has taken on ME *ui, oi* in place of OF [y]; this would explain Shakespeare's rhyme with *voice* (Viëtor, p. 164). See further § 259, Note 1.

(2) *The development of ME* oi

§ 261. The orthoepists normally use the transcription *oi* for ME *oi*, thus identifying the first element with ME *ŏ*. Hart (see Vol. I, pp. 82–83) transcribes it *ōi* in his *Methode*, but the marking of the first element long is probably of no special significance; it may show that it is a rounded vowel, but it does not show that it is tense, for in Hart's speech there was no distinction of quality between ME *ǭ* and ME *ŏ*. Smith's comment on the 'shortness of the sound' (*breuitatem soni*) is equally not to be pressed, for it is by way of apology for his uncertainty about the distinction between *oi* and *ui*; for what it is worth, it shows that the first element is 'short *o*' (*breuis o*). Wallis, Wilkins, and Cooper identify the first element, in quality, with ME *ŏ* and the monophthong developed from ME *au*, i.e. it is open. Robinson's transcription *oī* and his statement that 'all diphthongs end in the place of the last long vowel' identify the second element with ME *ẹ̄* so far as quality is concerned, but should not be taken to mean that the second element was long or that the diphthong was a rising one. The *Welsh Hymn* equates ME *oi* with Welsh *oe*, Salesbury with Welsh *oy*; the latter should mean that the second element is lax [ɪ], for he uses Welsh *y* to represent ME *ĭ* and Welsh *i* to represent ME *ẹ̄*, but the transcription may be conventional.

The evidence on the exact quality of the two elements of the diphthong is thus slight, but gives no ground for supposing that at any stage from ME onwards it was essentially different from the PresE sound. If, as seems probable, the first element was identical in quality with ME *ŏ*, it was presumably approximately 'cardinal open [ɔ]' in ME and underwent some degree of lowering during the late sixteenth and early seventeenth centuries when ME *ŏ* itself was similarly lowered; according to D. Jones,

Outline of English Phonetics, § 437, the PresE diphthong begins 'about half-way between ... [ɒ] and [ɒː]', i.e. is a little higher than ME *ŏ* now is, so that the lowering of the first element of ME *oi* would seem to have been more limited than that of ME *ŏ*.

Note 1: Luick, §§ 544–5, arguing (as I also assume) that the first element is identical with ME *ŏ*, deduces that at the end of the sixteenth century ME *oi* > [ɑi], which remained until the second half of the eighteenth century, when it became [ɒi] (§ 557 (3)). There is no evidence for this roundabout view: it depends solely on Luick's hypothesis that ME *ŏ* was [ɑ] not [ɒ] from the sixteenth century to the eighteenth century (and that ME *au*, when monophthongized, became [ɑː] not [ɒː] and remained [ɑː] until the eighteenth century); but we have already found reason to reject this theory (see § 86, Note 2 and § 235, Note).

Note 2: In some forms of speech (probably the dialects to the east and north-east of London, and thence vulgar London speech) ME *oi* seems to have become ME *ai* by unrounding of the first element of the diphthong in consequence of the unrounding of ME *ŏ* to *ă* (see § 87 above), a process which occurred in the thirteenth century. The orthoepists give no evidence of this *ai* for ME *oi* (Coles's pairing of *alloy* with *allay* in his *Eng.-Lat. Dict.* depends on the older *allay* variant of the former word). Wyld, *Coll. Eng.*, p. 224, cites *vayage* 'voyage' from the *Cely Papers* (but this common early form represents OF *veiage, vayage*) and *loay* 'lie' (i.e. presumably *lay* used for *lie*) from the *Verney Memoirs*, 1656; the latter, an obviously confused spelling, might conceivably reflect the identity of ME *ai* with ME *oi*.

Bullokar rhymes *joys* with *always* (see Vol. I, p. 10), and *The Oxford Book of Sixteenth Century Verse* has *joy : gainsay* (Anon., p. 43) and *joy : stay* (Proctor, 1578; p. 149); Spenser rhymes *joy* with the name of the letter *j*, presumably *jay* (Bauermeister, *Zur Sprache Spensers*, p. 8). These rhymes could, as Zachrisson claims in Bullokar's case, depend on the 'Essex' change of ME *oi* to *ai*, but it is suspicious that they all involve the word *joy*; they may rather depend on eModE [dʒwɛː], refashioned in later ME or eModE after contemporary French pronunciation (see § 254, Note 2).

The evidence for the ME change *oi* > *ai* in Essex comes chiefly from rhymes in the *King Alisaunder* group, but there are spellings which also suggest it; cf. the spellings *beye* (*K.A.*), *bay, bey* (*Promptorium Parvulorum*, *c.* 1440, Norfolk), and *bey* (*Ludus Coventriae*, *c.* 1460, Norfolk) for the word *boy* (see *Medium Ævum*, ix. 123–4), which could be most easily explained by assuming such a change (cf. *Medium Ævum*, xii. 76). There are also spellings *leyen* and *leyn* 'loin' in the *Cely Papers* in 1484, the writer being a William Maryon who had connexions with London, Essex, and Hertfordshire; but as he often uses *ei* and *ey* for ME *ī* Miss A. H. Forester, to whom I owe this information, would interpret the *ley(e)n* spellings as showing the identity of ME *ui* with ME *ī*. Mr. G. V. Smithers has suggested to me that the *K.A.* rhymes may be due to the imitation by the ME poet of the rhyming practice of his French original (rhymes between OF *oi* and *ai* being made possible by convergent development of the two sounds). But (*a*) I know of no parallel for an English poet's using, in the ME period, rhymes justified only by French pronunciation; (*b*) the unrounding of ME *ŏ* to *ă* is demonstrably early and common in exactly the area from which the *K.A.* texts come (see § 87, Note 3 above); (*c*) when in ModE there was unrounding and lowering of ME *ŭ* to [ʌ], the first element of ME *ui* was similarly affected, so that it seems reasonable to assume that when ME *ŏ* > *ă*, ME *oi* would similarly > *ai*; for a ME parallel cf. 'Essex' *au* < ME *ou* (see § 241). See also § 272, Note.

Note 3: In the North ME *oi* became identical with ME *ǭ* (cf. Luick, § 434(2) and Anm. 3; Jordan, § 238). Smith records this development, saying that for *oi* the Scotch use ωι with hardly any ι. Mulcaster may have used this pronunciation (see Vol. I, p. 127), and Brown (also a Northerner, it seems) gives *noise* and *nose* as 'homophones'. Levins, however, appears to have [ɔi] (see Vol. I, p. 28); so also Poole. The development appears to have occurred sporadically in other areas, notably in Essex: cf. Luick, § 545, Anm. 4; Davies, *English Pronunciation*, p. 11.

(3) *The development of ME* ui

(a) Normal development

§ 262. ME *ui* was, in ME, a falling diphthong [ʊi] with a rounded first element identical with ME *ŭ*. In the normal development this pronunciation remained in use for some time in eModE, but subsequently, when ME *ŭ* was unrounded, the first element of the diphthong was also unrounded, giving a pronunciation [ʌi]. But the distinction between [ʌi] < ME *ui* and [əi] < ME *ī*, being slight, soon broke down; ME *ui* took on the [əi] pronunciation of ME *ī* (with which it therefore became identical), just as ME *ŭr*, after becoming [ʌr], soon took on the pronunciation [ər] and became identical with ME *ĕr* and *ĭr*. ME *ui* and ME *ī* later (probably, in good StE speech, after 1700) became [ai]; this pronunciation was still to be heard for ME *ui* in the nineteenth century, but has now disappeared from StE in consequence of the replacement of ME *ui* by ME *oi* in all words in which *ui* formerly occurred. In general the evidence is that in good StE speech [ʊi] was retained until about 1640, that [ʌi] was then used for a time, and that [əi] was used from at latest 1685; in rather less correct speech [əi] was in use from at latest about 1640; and in some forms of speech, if the evidence of spellings is to be relied on (see Note 2 below), [əi] occurred as early as the fifteenth century. The evidence for the various stages of the normal development is as follows.

(i) The pronunciation [ʊi]. Smith, though he is confused between the two sounds (ME *oi* and ME *ui*) used in pronouncing the digraph *oi*, is clearly thinking of ME *ui* when he suggests that the transcription *vi* (by which obviously *ui* is meant—Smith or his printer has followed convention by using the *v* form initially) might be better than *oi*. Mulcaster says that some words spelt *oi* seem to have, and to sound on, a *u*. Cooper, when he retains [ʊi] (see below, under (iv)), identifies the first element with rounded ME *ŭ*, as in *full*, which he calls 'o labial' (he regards [ʊ] as the short vowel corresponding to close [o:] < ME *ǭ*). These three writers, then, give the first element as short [ʊ]; but other evidence identifies, or seems to identify, it with [u:] < ME *ǭ*. Thus Laneham uses the spelling *brooyled* 'broiled' (but in Laneham *oo* can stand for [ʊ] as well as for [u:]); Bullokar represents the first element by *oo* without diacritic (when *oo* stands for [ʊ] he uses a diacritic); and Gil's transcription is *ūi*, except once when it is erroneously *vi* (with italic *v*), which should mean [vi], and once when it is erroneously v*i* (with Roman v), which should mean [y:i]. But the first element cannot have been identical with ME *ǭ*, and this evidence is best taken as meaning that the diphthong was a falling one and that the first element therefore predominated and seemed long in comparison with the second; it does, however, show conclusively that the first element was still rounded. Hart in the *Methode* transcribes ME *ui* as *oi* (in contrast to ME *oi* as *ōi*); the significance of this distinction (if it was not merely arbitrary even in intention) is doubtful (see Vol. I, pp. 82–83).

We may conclude that in the sixteenth and early seventeenth centuries ME *ui* was still a falling diphthong [ʊi], i.e. that it had not changed from its ME pronunciation. Except after labials (and even there only in Cooper; see below) there is no conclusive evidence for [ʊi] after Gil's second edition (1621); but in good speech it probably remained in general use until *c.* 1640, since ME *ŭ* seems still to have been rounded [ʊ] up to that date (see § 93).

(ii) The pronunciation [ʌi]. Daines describes a pronunciation of *ui* which makes it like, but different from, ME *ī*, and must then mean [ʌi], which the terms of his description would well fit (see Vol. I, pp. 333–4); as he records the identity of ME *ŭr* with both ME *ĕr* and ME *ĭr* he may be presumed to have used [ʌ] for ME *ŭ* in free position (cf. § 214), which makes it possible for him to have used [ʌi] for ME *ui*. The only other evidence for [ʌi] is that of Wallis (see Vol. I, p. 233), which is much clearer. Wallis says that the first element in his pronunciation of ME *ui* was '*ŏ obscurum*' (otherwise called '*ŭ obscurum*'), i.e. the unrounded [ʌ] sound which he used for ME *ŭ* and as the first element of the diphthong developed from ME *ū*; in his pronunciation ME *ī*, the first element of which was [ə], was still distinct from ME *ui*.

(iii) The pronunciation [əi]. The pronunciation [əi], and consequent identity of ME *ui* with ME *ī*, may be shown by Bullokar's rhymes of *joined* with *find* and of *noise* with *rise*, but such rhymes would also be justified by the variant pronunciation [wəi] for ME *ui* which is discussed in § 263, and which Bullokar himself shows in one word. Willis rhymes 'ME *ui* words' on *boil* 'ulcus', a rhyming which probably (but not certainly) depends on [əi] (see Vol. I, p. 428). Unambiguous evidence comes from Price, *VO*, who says that *oy* is pronounced like *y* in a number of 'ME *ui* words'. Poole rhymes such words with *groin*, a rhyming which again probably depends on [əi] but need not (see Vol. I, p. 437). Cooper says that certain 'ME *ui* words' are, as a variant, pronounced with '*i* diphthong', i.e. [əi] (see Vol. I, pp. 302–3); he is the first orthoepist of front rank to show the development in a way that makes it appear that it was present in his own pronunciation. He is followed by Aickin and *WSC-RS*. Rather earlier evidence is given by the 'homophone' lists: ME *ui* is equated with ME *ī* by Hodges ('near alike'), Price, Fox and Hookes, Coles (only in the *Eng.–Lat. Dict.*, his least careful list), Strong ('alike' and 'near alike'), Young, Cooper ('same' in *boil*, *oil*, *loin*, *moil*, 'near alike' in *foil* 'setting' and *foil* 'repulse'), Hawkins, Aickin, *WSC-RS*, Cocker, and Brown. The identity of the two sounds is also shown by the 'phonetically spelt' lists; Coles in his *Schoolmaster* has one spelling (*sine* 'essoin') which shows it, and there are others in Strong (the 'monosyllabic list') and Cocker. The identity is also shown by the shorthand-writers Farthing, Everardt, Mason, Coles, and Nicholas.

The earliest evidence from any orthoepist is thus Hodges's in his 'near alike' list, but it should be observed that this is a list to which he seems to relegate pronunciations of which he disapproved or which were at least different from his own. The evidence comes mostly from sources which show vulgar, or at least advanced, pronunciations; it looks as though [əi] for ME *ui* was not adopted in good speech until almost the time of Cooper. Coles seems deliberately to avoid giving evidence of the identity of ME *ui* and ME *ī*, though he gives enough to show that he knew the pronunciation (see Vol. I, p. 441).

(iv) *Retention of* [ʊi] *under labial influence.* The retention of [ʊi] for ME *ui* under the influence of labial consonants, after the change of ME *ui* to [əi] in free position, is parallel to the retention of [ʊ] for ME *ŭ* in similar circumstances. It is shown, however, only by Cooper, in the words *boil*, *moil*, *point*, *poison*, apparently in *buoy* pronounced [bwʊi], and perhaps in *foil* (since he pairs it with *file* only in his 'near alike' list; but his preferred pronunciation is more likely to have been with ME *oi*). He says that the diphthong [ʊi] is rare, and from another passage it appears that it was only a variant beside [əi] even in these words (see Vol. I, pp. 302-3).

Note 1: The unrounding of ME *ŭ* to [ʌ], which led as a secondary consequence to the identity of ME *ui* with ME *ī*, also leads to the identity of ME *ŭr* with ME *ĕr* and *ir*; as the latter appears to be shown by spellings from the fifteenth century onwards in some forms of speech—as early as *c.* 1435 in Northern dialects, somewhat later in the fifteenth century in more southerly dialects, and from the early sixteenth century in Cockney documents (see § 214, Note 2)—we may expect evidence of the identity of ME *ui* with ME *ī* at similar dates from similar sources.

Note 2: As Luick, § 545, Anm. 2, points out, some of the spellings by which it is sought to demonstrate the identity of ME *ui* with ME *ī* represent ME variants in ME *ī*, and the others may be due to the analogy of the variation between the spellings *oi* (*oy*) and *i* (*y*) in words like *destroy*, *destrye*. Thus none of the spellings adduced by Wyld, *Coll. Eng.*, pp. 224, 250, and by Zachrisson, *Eng. Vowels*, pp. 73, 89, and *Bullokar*, p. 103, are fully satisfactory as evidence, but they may perhaps show that ME *ui* became [əi] in some forms of speech (but certainly not in StE) as early as the fifteenth century; Wyld's earliest example is from *St. Editha* (1420) and the next from Gregory's *Chronicle* (before 1467). On the spellings *leyen* and *leyn* 'loin' (*Cely Papers*, 1484) see § 261, Note 2.

Note 3: Rhymes are uncertain evidence of [əi] for ME *ui*, for rhymes between ME *ī* and ME *ui* may in theory as well depend on the variant development of the latter to [wəi] (discussed below) as on the normal development to [əi]. Such rhymes are, however, normally to be taken as depending on [əi] < ME *ui*. They are fairly common after about 1630 (cf. Wyld, *Rhymes*, p. 75) and a regular feature of poetry written in the latter half of the seventeenth century. They are comparatively rare in the sixteenth century. Spenser has the largest number, but he is clearly willing to depend on the most advanced pronunciations. Sackville has *while* : *toil*, 1563, Marlowe *destroy* : *harmony* (but cf. the ME variant *destrye*), Daniel *toil* : *while*, 1599 (and others on *toil*). See also § 263, Note 1.

Note 4: Wyld, *Coll. Eng.*, p. 250, is in error in saying that Wallis gives three pronunciations of the digraph *oi*, namely [ɔi], [ʌi], and a third one *ūi*, thus *tŭyl* 'toil', *ŭyl* 'oil'. Wallis marks the *u* short, not long (cf. Lehnert, § 138), and Wyld has misread the diacritic. Wallis's '*tôil*, *ôil*, vel *tŭyl*, *ŭyl*' are alternative transcriptions of the same pronunciation ([ʌi] < ME *ui*), not indications of alternative pronunciations.

Note 5: In the North ME *ui* became *ū* by the loss of the second element (Luick, § 434 (2) and Anm. 3). This development (with the *ū* retained as [u:], identical with ME *ǭ*) is shown by Levins (see Vol. I, p. 28); Mulcaster may also have it (see Vol. I, p. 127). The same development seems to have occurred sporadically in other dialects, notably in Essex; see Luick, § 545, Anm. 4, and Davies, *Eng. Pron.*, p. 10.

Note 6: As the loss of the distinction between [ʌi] < ME *ui* and [əi] < ME *ī* was one of the causes of [ʌ] and [ə] becoming mere contextual variants of a single phoneme (see Vol. I, pp. 241–3), it is possible that Wilkins, Holder, Lodwick, and Coles (who like Cooper do not distinguish [ə] as a distinct vowel) used [əi] for ME *ui*, as Cooper did; but they may have used [wəi] as Hodges did. Coles's apparent reluctance to give evidence of the identity of ME *ui* and ME *ī*, commented on above, is difficult to account for, in view of his identification of [ə] with [ʌ], unless he used Hodges's pronunciation; but he may have preferred the variant [ɔi] < ME *oi* in all 'ME *ui* words'.

(b) *Variant development to ME* [wi:], *early ModE* [wəi]

§ 263. By a variant development ME *ui* became, in ME times, a rising diphthong, and in consequence the first element became consonantal and the second element was lengthened, giving [wi:]; this developed, with the normal change of ME *ī* to [əi], into an eModE pronunciation [wəi] (cf. Ekwall, § 95). Smith shows this pronunciation in *cloy* (see Vol. I, p. 59), and Hart in *hoy* and *buoy* (see Vol. I, p. 83). Bullokar has it in *joise* 'joist' (see Vol. I, pp. 115–16) and it may be the basis of his rhymes of *joined* with *find* and *noise* with *rise*. Hodges has [wəi], and possibly a variant [ʊəi], in all words which in his speech have ME *ui* (see Vol. I, pp. 173–5). There is no satisfactory evidence in later orthoepists; Wallis says that [w] is sometimes pronounced after the *b* of *boy* and *boil*, but this is almost certainly a glide-consonant (see Vol. I, p. 235).

Note 1: Rhymes between ME *ui* and ME *ī*, especially in sixteenth- and early seventeenth-century poets, may sometimes depend on [wəi] not [əi] for ME *ui* (see § 262, Note 3). Such a rhyme as Spenser's *coynd* : *twynd* 'twined' (*F.Q.* III. xii. 14) suggests strongly but cannot prove that he pronounced *coined* as [kwəind]. The earlier the rhyme, the more likely it is to depend on [wəi] rather than [əi]; thus Sackville's *while*: *toil* (cf. § 262, Note 3) may well belong here.

Note 2: Wright, *EDG*, § 213, records [wai], [wəi], &c. for ME *ui* only after labials, where [w] is probably a glide (cf. op. cit., § 244). But [kwain] 'coin' (§ 262) may be from ME [wi:] < *ui* (though a [w] glide does occur after [k] in *coat* in widespread dialects, and more rarely in other words beginning with [k]—see § 244).

X

THE VOWELS OF SYLLABLES NOT BEARING THE MAIN STRESS

INTRODUCTION

§ 264. It is in their representation of the vowels of syllables which do not bear the main stress that the orthoepists are most open to criticism. It can be proved that in the everyday speech of the sixteenth and seventeenth centuries the vowel [ə] was freely used in unstressed syllables in place of the various ME short vowels, and obviously this state of affairs receives little attention either in the general discussions of the orthoepists or in their transcriptions; to that extent they admittedly do not present a true picture of contemporary pronunciation. It can also be proved, by selected examples, that they are from time to time led by the accepted orthography to describe pronunciations or to give transcriptions which are not in accord with the etymology and the phonetic history of the words in question; and that in other cases, of which the clearest example is Hodges's identification with ME *ā* of pretonic *a* in numerous words, e.g. *about*, they are led by the consideration of words syllable by syllable and by certain preconceived ideas—e.g. that all vowels that end a syllable are long—to invent artificial pronunciations which can hardly ever have existed. It is therefore easy to take the further step of denying that their transcriptions of unstressed syllables have any validity at all.

But such a general rejection is certainly wrong. It ignores above all the influence of secondary stress, which was still of high importance in the seventeenth century. There are many cases in which the conventional spelling is far from suggesting the orthoepists' transcriptions and in which it is inconceivable that anyone in the sixteenth or seventeenth centuries could have invented the pronunciation described (Robinson's *ŏ* for ME unstressed *ă* before *l* and *n* is perhaps the best example), but in which it can be shown that, granted the continued existence of secondary stress, the pronunciation is developed by known or intelligible processes from the ME original. In yet other cases they give evidence, supported by the rhymes of poets, that certain ME long vowels had undergone the same development as in stressed syllables (e.g. [ʌu] < ME *ū* in *emperour*, [əi] < ME *ī* in *presently*, &c.); in these also the survival of secondary stress would have to be assumed, even if there were no direct evidence of it, to account for the recorded facts. Again, some weight must be allowed to concurrent testimony; when for example Hart, Robinson (who seems not to have known

Hart's work), and Gil (who knew Hart's work but angrily criticized his pronunciation, and did not know Robinson's) agree in showing [əi] < ME $\bar{\imath}$ in disyllables like *daily* and *boldly* as well as in trisyllables, their evidence, though it cannot in this case be supported by rhymes, has nevertheless to be accepted; and it follows that the second syllable of a disyllable could also have secondary stress. But if secondary stress was thus prevalent, and had the effect of causing ME long vowels, diphthongs, and the short vowel ă before *l* and *n* to undergo the same development as in stressed syllables, it is to be supposed that it must also have often fallen on syllables containing a short vowel unaffected by neighbouring consonants. Transcriptions which purport to show unreduced short vowels in syllables which do not bear the main stress may then depend on surviving pronunciations in which secondary stress was maintained. That colloquial usage did not so systematically maintain secondary stress is of course obvious, though it certainly had much more of it in the sixteenth and seventeenth centuries than later; the speech which the orthoepists largely represent is formal, but not artificial, for it develops regularly from real ME pronunciations.

That the orthoepists were not merely guided by the conventional orthography is as easy to prove as that they were occasionally influenced by it. If on the one hand Bullokar is led by the spelling to give ŏ for ME unstressed ŭ, on the other Hart, Robinson, Gil (normally), and Hodges transcribe it by ŭ in spite of the conventional spelling. Far too many alterations (usually etymologically correct) are made in the spelling of unstressed syllables by the spelling-reformers to warrant the view that they are content in them to follow the usual orthography; thus Robinson (who regularly writes -ŏl for unstressed -al) and Hodges (who as regularly writes -âl) agree in treating *metal* as an exception which has syllabic [l] and are justified by the etymology (ME *metel* beside *metal*, &c.), which obviously they could not have known. Hodges uses a special diacritic to show that *e* in *Laurence* is pronounced ă, which again is etymologically correct. All these distinctions would be not merely pointless, but also impossible, if [ə] were the only vowel ever heard in unstressed syllables and was indifferently spelt *a*, *e*, *o*, or *u*. Moreover to argue that when for example Gil gives *ai* in *certain* but ĕ in *citizen* he is merely following the spelling (because both words have original *ai*) is to assume that there was no more connexion between the conventional orthography and the pronunciation about 1600 than there is today, which was certainly not the case; it may be inconsistent that secondary stress should have remained and should have preserved *ai* in *certain* but should have been lost in *citizen*, but the inconsistency was that of the language and not of Gil.

It remains to consider why the orthoepists, particularly the earlier ones who give extensive phonetic transcriptions, should have chosen so largely to ignore the more reduced pronunciations of unstressed syllables and instead to represent the more formal. The chief reason was doubtless the careful consideration of speech word by word and syllable by syllable; during this process pronunciations with secondary stress, provided they really existed, would more readily come to mind. Moreover the more formal pronunciations would naturally be regarded as the more correct; the others might be used *facilitatis causa*, as Cooper phrased it, but could hardly be considered so good a basis for a reformed spelling, which it may well be argued should not slur over distinctions which are made in careful speech even if they are commonly lost in less deliberate utterance. It is often forgotten that the majority of the writers who give extensive phonetic transcriptions were concerned neither to teach 'correct' pronunciation (as the unfortunate term 'orthoepist' implies), nor yet to give scientific records of all the varieties of pronunciation in use in their time; their object was to provide examples of a practical reformed spelling intended for general use which should adequately represent the important distinctions of pronunciation then made; and as the more formal pronunciations of syllables which do not bear the main stress often serve to make clear distinctions of meaning which are lost in less careful pronunciation, spellings which, by representing the more formal pronunciations, preserve the distinctions are of greater practical value than those which do not. Similar considerations account for *OED*'s choice of a system of transcription for unstressed syllables which represents their 'ideal' rather than their normal modern pronunciation. We must also allow for the fact that of the sixteenth- and seventeenth-century orthoepists, only Wallis clearly distinguished the vowel [ə]; the failure to distinguish [ə] was no doubt due to an excessive concern with syllables that had primary or secondary stress—Wallis himself is mainly concerned with [ə] as a stressed vowel—but in its turn affected the nature of the transcriptions. In any case spelling-reformers who hoped to secure the general adoption of their systems would probably have shrunk from introducing an additional vowel-symbol for a sound which it was not really necessary to represent. Again, both Hart and Gil allow that regard has to be paid, even in a reformed spelling, to etymology; and Gil explicitly applies this principle to unstressed syllables. 'In syllabis correptis, vbi vtrumuis indifferenter auditur, etymon sequendum esse statuemus'; he therefore uses the spellings *divjn* 'divine', *skolar* 'scholar', *onor* 'honour', *kungurer* 'conjurer' rather than *devjn, skoler, oner, kungerer*, but if the unlearned, 'suas aures sequutus', uses the latter spellings he (Gil) holds it of no moment.

The orthoepists' evidence, then, refers mostly to real, though often formal, pronunciations of syllables not bearing the main stress; that this is so will appear more fully from the discussion of the detailed evidence which follows. There is also, as will be seen, a reasonable amount of evidence for the more reduced pronunciations of entirely unstressed syllables. But before we examine the detailed evidence it is necessary to consider certain general factors which are here relevant.

GENERAL CONSIDERATIONS

SECONDARY STRESS

§ 265. The chief factor causing variation in the ModE pronunciation of the vowels of syllables which do not bear the main stress is the presence or absence, in late ME or early ModE, of some form of secondary stress. It seems necessary therefore to examine the chief cases in which secondary stress occurred in late ME and early ModE.

(*a*) In native compounds of more than two syllables there were two main types, thus *hóusehòlder* (/ \ ×) and *súmmertìme* (/ × \); in such words the secondary stress usually remains, but in some there is loss (consequent on the loss of the sense that the word is a compound), thus *bláckberry, hóliday* (contrast *bláck bérry, hóly dáy*). In derivative verbs with a two-syllabled prefix which preserves its identity the secondary stress precedes, and is separated from, the main stress (*ùnderstánd*).

(*b*) In words of three or more syllables of French and Latin origin there was commonly a secondary stress separated from the main stress by a fully unstressed syllable; this stress survives in Standard English in such words as *jústify*, and is very common in American English in such words as *témporàry*. In derivative verbs with a two-syllabled prefix the secondary stress precedes, as in *còntradíct*.

(*c*) In native compounds of two syllables secondary stress occurs on the second element, thus *spríngtìme*. It is lost only when the compound is no longer felt to be such, as in *húsband, hóusewìfe* pronounced [hʌzɪf], and *thréepence*.

(*d*) In OE all unstressed long vowels had been shortened; but in ME the OE ending *-iġ* (and the ON *ig* of the adjectival and adverbial ending *-lig(e)*) became *ī*, giving, for example, *hǫlī, bodī*, &c., *dailī*, &c., *hevenlī, worthilī*, &c. In words of three syllables the final syllable could (and did) bear a secondary stress, and its vowel remained long whenever this secondary stress was retained; it was, however, often lost in later ME, and the vowel was then shortened. In words of two syllables the *ī* would also have had some form of secondary stress in early ME in inflected and therefore trisyllabic forms, since the long *ī* would clearly predominate over a following unstressed short *ĕ* (as is proved by the early loss of final *ĕ* in such words); this secondary stress is shown by eModE evidence to have survived in later ME even after the oblique forms had been reduced to two syllables by the loss of inflexional *ĕ*. But the commoner late ME development in these two-syllabled words was for the secondary stress to be lost.

Similarly, when in ME a diphthong *ou* developed after the stress in words like *swallow, sparrow, follow, marrow* by means of (i) the intrusion of a glide-vowel before OE *w* and *g* and (ii) the vocalization of OE *w* and *g* to [u], this diphthong would naturally attract to itself a greater degree of stress than a following unstressed inflexional *ĕ*, and so would acquire secondary stress in all inflected forms. This secondary stress often remained after the loss of inflexional *ĕ*; but it was also often lost. See further Notes 1 and 2 below.

(*e*) Essentially similar are words of French (or Latin) origin, of two syllables in ME either originally or after the loss of final *ĕ*, in which the second syllable was originally stressed. In such words, especially if they were or became 'popular', shift of stress often led to the second syllable becoming totally unstressed, in which case its vowel (if not already short) or diphthong underwent radical alteration. But (i) the influence of French pronunciation, (ii) the coexistence in English of two modes of stressing, the earlier one which placed the stress as in French and the later one which shifted it to the first syllable, and (iii) the frequent coexistence of a noun in which the stress had been shifted to the first syllable and a verb in which it remained on the second, tended to prevent (especially in more careful and better-educated speech) the full unstressing of the second syllable. It therefore often retained a form of secondary stress much like that of native two-syllabled compounds and exactly like that of such words as *daily* and *follow*, which were obvious models; so *émpìre, íncrèase* sb., &c. In late ME and early ModE the number of words so stressed seems to have been very large; and though it was not the 'popular' one, the mode of pronunciation which retained secondary stress and full vowels and diphthongs should not be regarded as merely artificial, imitative of French, or 'literary' (as Luick, § 466, tends to consider it); the stress-pattern (╱╲) in two-syllabled words was by no means foreign to the native system.

(*f*) In OE the only words in which the first syllable was not stressed were derivative words (mainly verbs) in which this unstressed first syllable was a prefix; often there still corresponded to the prefix a living adverb, so that recognition of the identity of the prefix was easy, and in such cases the vowel-reduction which should normally occur in an OE unstressed syllable for the most part failed. Clearly the prefix had received a form of secondary stress (so Bülbring, § 455); and though the tendency to reduce the vowel of prefixes continued during the ME and ModE period, so also did the opposite tendency to place some degree of secondary stress on them and preserve the full vowel, as is shown by both the spelling and the more deliberate PresE pronunciation of such words as *fòrbíd*.

(*g*) In many words of French and Latin origin the English tendency to shift the stress to the first syllable failed; they were left with a pretonic syllable which was commonly a recognizable prefix containing a vowel which in French was pronounced clearly, though without stress. It was natural for careful English pronunciation to place on such syllables the same form of secondary stress as occurred in native words of the *forbid* type; when this was done reduction of their vowels was inhibited (e.g. some form of [o] vowel is still heard in *pròvíde*, &c.). But in less careful speech the pretonic syllable was unstressed completely, and its vowel underwent reduction.

Note 1: Luick, § 443, seems to regard the loss of secondary stress and the reduction of -*ī* to -*ĭ* as the exclusive development in words of two syllables; but this appears to contradict his § 597 (1). Jordan, § 136, Anm. 2, holds that -*ī* could remain long in such words.

Note 2: Luick, § 599, appears to regard the second syllable of *follow*, &c. as necessarily unstressed, and the normal ME development as having been to reduce the vowel; he is then forced to explain the normal ModE development [ou] > [o:] > [ou] as analogical. But if one does not prejudge the issue by assuming loss of secondary stress, there is no reason why one should not trace the ModE pronunciation directly back to the ME form.

§ 266. In words adopted into ME from French or Latin, the vowels of syllables bearing secondary stress took quantity according to the following rules. (1) Pretonic syllables separated from the main stress by an unstressed syllable always contained a short vowel even when the syllable was open (as in *mètaphýsics*), except that in an open syllable *u* was 'long', i.e. was [y:] or [iu] representing OF [y]. (2) In immediately pretonic syllables the vowel was short if the syllable was closed. It is not clear what was the position if the syllable was open, as in *obey*; a long vowel is a certain indication that secondary stress was present, but it is not certain that short vowels occurred only when it was absent. (3) In immediately post-tonic syllables which retain secondary stress there occur short vowels, long vowels, and diphthongs; these syllables were originally stressed, and retain the vowel or diphthong that had developed in them when they were stressed. (4) In post-tonic syllables separated from the main stress the vowel was short in a closed syllable and usually long in an open syllable; but there may have been variation, even when secondary stress was present, in some cases, e.g. in the ending *-ary*.

§ 267. The general tendency in late ME and ModE has been for secondary stress to be lost. In more detail the position is that the secondary stress of a pretonic syllable which is separated from the main stress always remains; that of an immediately pretonic syllable is lost in ordinary speech (except in special cases such as *rè-sígn* against *resígn*), but is often kept in deliberate speech; that of post-tonic syllables is generally lost in English—but not comparably in American—speech, but is kept in some cases, especially when the ModE development under secondary stress has resulted in a pronunciation which does not readily admit of the reduction characteristic of ModE unstressed syllables.

Loss of secondary stress has these results in the ME and ModE periods.

(1) In ME, long vowels are shortened and diphthongs are monophthongized and shortened; in particular OF *ai* (*ei*) becomes *ĕ*, ME *ou* becomes *ŏ*, and OF [y] becomes *ĭ*. On the other hand the absence of stress does not seem to have produced in ME significant differences in the pronunciation of the short vowels, except of ME *ĕ* (see further below, § 293). (2) In late ME and ModE, however, the unstressed short vowels diverged markedly from the stressed short vowels; loss of secondary stress then came to involve the substitution of the unstressed values for the stressed. (3) In ModE long vowels when they lost secondary stress were either shortened, or had substituted for them the sound which develops from the corresponding ME unstressed *short* vowel; the latter process is of course analogical and modelled on the clearly recognizable correspondences that had developed in ME. The PresE diphthongs [ou] and [ei] < ME *ǭ* and *ā* tend to be monophthongized when they lose stress.

Retention of secondary stress, on the other hand, causes the vowel or diphthong on which it falls to develop exactly as it would if it were fully stressed. PresE retains pronunciations developed under secondary stress in many words. Thus [ou] < ME *ǭ* occurs in immediately pretonic syllables in careful speech in words containing the prefix *pro-*, and in 'learned' words it may even be more common than the reduced [ə], e.g. in *pròlíxity* (a late ME adoption). In post-tonic syllables secondary stress is regular in such words as *prócèss* sb., *diàlògue* (with ME short vowels), *óccupỳ*, *émpìre*, *cónfìnes*, *íncrèase* sb., *cómpòund* sb., *cóncòurse* (with ME long vowels), and *státùre*, *éntràils*, *trávàil*, *cúrfèw*, *néphèw*, *réscùe*, and *fóllòw* (with ME diphthongs). In some of these cases, it is true, there are or were variant developments showing ME or ModE loss of secondary stress; these are discussed in the appropriate place below. On the other hand eModE often had pronunciations developed under secondary stress which have now been lost either because variants developed from ME forms without secondary stress have prevailed, or because the secondary stress was lost during the ModE period; these cases are also discussed below.

Note: For such direct evidence as the orthoepists give on the incidence of secondary stress in sixteenth- and seventeenth-century English see § 1.

§ 268. Reimposition of secondary stress in the ModE period is rare, but does occur in some circumstances; its result is to lengthen the vowel on which it is placed. Thus [ɪ] becomes [i:] in such words as *mónarchỳ*, which, for example, Shakespeare rhymes with *free*. In words of this type (i.e. words with more than one post-tonic syllable) the process is not merely artificial, even though in StE it is most clearly evidenced in verse—in which it is easy to say that the metrical pattern artificially imposes stress on syllables which otherwise would lack it; the final syllable of *monarchy* is never quite as weak as the preceding syllable, and in certain forms of English (e.g. Australian and Cockney English) it is the normal development for a slight secondary stress to be reimposed and the vowel lengthened to [iː], whence [əi] by more recent diphthongization. But in the case of immediately post-tonic syllables the reimposition, and even the retention, of secondary stress is an artificial process dependent largely on the spelling. Thus in consequence of an arbitrary distinction of spelling *travail* normally retains, but *travel* always loses, secondary stress; and it is possible (though extremely pedantic) to reimpose secondary stress and to substitute [ei] < ME *ai* for [ɪ] < ME *ĕ* in *captain*, *fountain*, &c. because the spelling suggests it, whereas it would be inconceivable to do this in *barren* (< OF *barain). But the existence side by side of deliberate and often somewhat artificial forms with secondary stress (and with long vowels or diphthongs) and 'popular' everyday forms without secondary stress (and with short unstressed vowels) has not infrequently given rise to purely artificial analogical spellings and to pronunciations in which secondary stress has been imposed without any historical justification. An exceptionally clear case is the spelling *taffrail* and the corresponding pronunciation [tǽfrèil], in which secondary stress is artificially imposed although the form is a nineteenth-century alteration of earlier *tafferel* < Du. *tafereel*; here we have to do with false etymology and the influence of *rail* sb., but the confusion is only possible because of ME variation between -*ail* and -*ĕl* in syllables which sometimes had and sometimes lacked a historical secondary stress. The same process was at work in late ME itself; examples are *curtain* (*OED* records an -*ey*- spelling from Wycliffe, 1382) for OF *curtine*, *pleasure* (from *c.* 1440) for OF *plaisir*, *leisure* (from *c.* 1400) for OF *leisir*. In the last two cases the analogical spelling so often led to the artificial imposition of secondary stress and substitution of late ME or early ModE [yː] or [iu] for [ə] that it has given rise to the invariable PresE pronunciation.

Note: The occurrence of vowel-sounds typical of stressed or secondarily stressed syllables in syllables which are not capable of any of the types of secondary stress described above is a sure sign of interference with the normal development. Thus [prɒrougeiʃn̩] for [prɒrəgeiʃn̩] 'prorogation' is an artificial pronunciation due to the analogy of the verb *to prorogue*.

WORDS ADOPTED IN THE LATE ME AND ModE PERIODS

§ 269. Late ME and ModE adoptions are so completely assimilated to the existing English stock of words that their phonology rarely shows special features; in respect of syllables not bearing the main stress there is perhaps only one feature to be noted which in any way constitutes a new principle. Variations in the pronunciation of individual words, or between different words belonging to the same class, arise, in these later as in earlier adoptions, from the varying incidence of secondary stress. The fact that a word is adopted later than the date at which any given change occurs does not affect the issue, for variations developed in comparable words at an earlier date are by analogy imported into later adoptions. Thus the ME variation between *ī* and *ĭ*, which became an eModE variation between [əi] and [ɪ], was imported into the seventeenth-century adoption *aquiline*, which in PresE still varies between a form with secondary stress and with [ai] in the final syllable and one without secondary stress and with [ɪ]. Similarly *ŏ* under secondary stress remains [ɒ] but when unstressed became [ə] at an early date; yet a twentieth-century adoption such as *moron* can vary between a form with secondary stress and with [ɒ] in the second syllable and one without secondary stress and with [ə] (or even syllabic [n̩]). But analogical substitution of a ME unstressed short vowel for a late ME or early ModE diphthong is rare; it perhaps occurs in *fountain*, first recorded in 1450, for which there are obvious parallels, but it does not occur in *detail* (first recorded 1603), despite the parallel of *battle*, which was still being spelt with *-ail* as late as the seventeenth century.

Secondary stress seems particularly to have been attracted to syllables of a type which had not previously been known in English words. Thus in post-tonic syllables it was placed on final *o*, as in *hèrò* (for which *fòllòw* was a parallel after the monophthongization of final [ou] to [o:]; cf. Luick, § 606 (4)); final *e* in Greek and Latin words such as *catástrophè*, *Círcè*; final *-os* in Greek words such as *cháòs*; and similarly *-on* (*phenómenòn*), *-od* (*trípòd*), *-ose* (*béllicòse*), *-oid* (*fúngòid*), *-eur* (*grándèur*) (cf. Luick, § 607). Vowels in open syllables (or syllables which would have been open in ME) are long when there is secondary stress, except that in the endings *-ery* and *-ory* the *e* and *o* seem always to have been short (on the model of such native words as *merry* and *sorry*, in which the *r* was originally single); vowels in closed syllables are short. But the failure to impose secondary stress, and the loss of secondary stress which once was imposed, are common, both in immediately post-tonic syllables and in syllables which are separated from the main stress.

The number of words in which the stress fell on the second syllable was much increased; in most the single pretonic syllable was still a recognizable prefix, but in a great many it was not (e.g. *càntéen*, *àntíque*, *hòstílity*, *àrmáda*, *sàrdónic*; see further Luick, § 609). But in all cases the ME type in which the pretonic syllable bore secondary stress served as a model, even though the ultimate reason for the development of this type was the stress attracted to a prefix. In such pretonic syllables with secondary stress the vowels of closed syllables (including vowels which are followed in the spelling by a doubled consonant) were short. The vowels of open syllables were long, except for *a*; the latter was short even when under secondary stress (ME rarely had *a* in immediately pretonic syllables, and in the few cases in which it occurred, such as *about*, it was short), unless in hiatus (e.g. in *chàótic*). But lack of secondary stress, and the substitution of the unstressed short vowels, is frequent except when the first syllable ends with a vowel in hiatus.

In pretonic syllables under secondary stress which were separated from the main stress the principle holds good, in more recent as in ME adoptions, that in both open and closed syllables all vowels are short (but see Note 1 below) except for *u*, which in open syllables is 'long', i.e. early ModE [y:] or [iu], which later becomes [ju:] or in some circumstances [u:]. But vowels in hiatus or before *h* constitute an exception (see below).

Syllables which come between the main and secondary stresses are necessarily unstressed, and in them the unstressed developments of the ME short vowels are substituted for the original vowels; thus [ɪ] (or less often [ə]) is used for *i* and *e*, [ə] for *a*, *o*, and *u* and for *i* and *e* before *r*, as in *épitàph, júvenìle* with [ɪ], *ability* (often with [ə] in the penult), *séparàte* vb., *càtalògue, phótogràph, còlumbáceous, ìnterférence, líbertìne*. In some words a syllabic consonant replaces the group of [ə] plus liquid or nasal; thus *sérpentìne*. But *u* in an open syllable presented difficulty. The 'popular' ME development was to reduce OF [y] to *ĭ* in unstressed medial syllables (Luick, § 462 (2) and Anm.; cf. § 466 (3) and Anm. 2); but the few words in which it occurred were mostly 'literary' and 'learned' and the attempt to reproduce French pronunciation seems to have prevented the unstressing of OF [y] in this position, so that beside the 'popular' form *singiler there also existed the 'learned' *singular* with ME [y:] or [iu] representing OF [y] (cf. Luick, § 462 (2)). Similar variation occurred in early ModE in *century, scrupulous*, &c.; cf. the vulgar *edicate* beside *educate*. See also Note 2.

Note 1: The prefix *retro-*, in such words as *rètroáct, rètrocéssion*, should according to rule have short *ĕ*, and this is the normal pronunciation; but [i:] also occurs owing to the analogy of the Latin adverb *retro*, which has ME *ē̆* (represented by PresE [i:]) in the first syllable in accordance with the rule that in stressed open first syllables of disyllabic words the English pronunciation of Latin used long vowels, regardless of the original Latin quantity.

Note 2: Failure to reduce fully a syllable which by position ought to be unstressed sometimes occurs when other vowels than *u* are involved, e.g. in learned words such as *anglophobe, photostat*; the explanation is that these words are still clearly recognizable as compounds and are given double stressing, so that the first element is pronounced as if it were a separate word and its second syllable is given secondary stress.

§ 270. In late ME and ModE adoptions there occurs one type of sound-combination which was rare in the earlier vocabulary, namely unstressed vowels in hiatus before a stressed or secondarily stressed vowel. In native words unstressed vowels in hiatus had regularly been elided either in OE or in ME, both in derivative words with prefixes ending in a vowel (*bufan* < *be-ufan*) and when words were brought together in a group within the sentence (*þōþer* 'the other') (cf. Luick, §§ 311, 451–3). They survived, however, if the sense of the separate identity of the words led to their being kept apart. To do this it was necessary to stress what would normally be an unstressed word, which in turn led to its final vowel being lengthened; so that beside *pōper* (with elision) there existed *pḕ ǭper*, whence the PresE pronunciation of such groups. This type, in which the normally unstressed vowel is, to prevent elision, kept lightly stressed and long (or half-long), is of great importance as a model for non-native words with vowels in hiatus. Another native model arose from the development of OE *byrgels*, which became *byrigels* (with intrusive *i*) > *biriels* (by vocalization of OE palatal *g*) > *birieles* (with intrusive *e* in the final syllable); this form was taken as the plural of a singular *biriel* (*beriel*, *buriel*), whence ModE *burial* (with analogical spelling). In this word the ME *i* from OE *ig* was of course originally long, and must have tended to remain so in the trisyllabic form *biriels*, in which it would predominate over the following short *e*; but in the four-syllabled form *birieles* the secondary stress would shift to the *e*, and it was doubtless in this form that the *i* became regularly short (cf. Luick, § 448; Jordan, § 147, Anm. 2). In any event the result was that in this word ME had a short unstressed *ĭ* in hiatus before a vowel which probably had a light secondary stress (though it was easily lost); and it served as a model for OF words in *-iel* (e.g. *especiel*), later respelt *-ial* after Latin, and thence for less directly comparable cases, such as OF words in *-ioun*, *-ious*. The consequence is that in all ME or ModE adoptions the vowel *i* in hiatus *after* the main stress is represented by ME unstressed *ĭ*, which becomes [j] when the following syllable loses its secondary stress. These words in turn were models for the reduction of post-tonic OF [y] in hiatus (as in other positions) to the popular *ĭ*, so that the ending *-uous* became identical with *-ious* (cf. Luick, § 462, Anm., § 608, Anm.); in the same way *-ual* (as in *usual*, *annual*) could become identical with *-ial*. But native models for unstressed *a*, *e*, and *o* in hiatus before a stressed vowel were lacking, and such words as *árchaìsm*, *pántheìsm*, *héroìsm* (which are clearly divisible) had therefore to be modelled on native word-groups such as *pḕ ǭper*; the first part of the word was treated as a separate unit, its second syllable received a light secondary stress, and the vowel (being final in the unit) was made long. In the 'learned' pronunciation, which avoided the reduction of OF [y] to ME *ĭ*, the same treatment was given to unstressed OF [y] (and to Latin *u*, which was identified with OF [y]) in hiatus; it was made 'long', i.e. identified with ME [y:] or [iu] > [ju:], as in the PresE pronunciation of *ingénuous*, *úsual*.

For unstressed vowels in hiatus immediately *before* the main stress the only native model was word-groups such as *pḕ ǭper*; in consequence the pretonic syllable is treated as a separate entity and is given secondary stress and a long vowel not only when it is a prefix (as in *prèéminence*) but in all cases (e.g. *chàótic*, *crèátion*, *pòétic*). There being no native models to justify a different treatment of unstressed *i* in hiatus in pretonic syllables, it also is regularly made long (as in *biólogy*, *quièscent*); and as a further consequence the 'popular' treatment of OF unstressed [y] and of Latin *u* is not found in hiatus in pretonic syllables, where they are always [y:] or [iu] > [ju:], as in *dùét, dùálity*.

Pretonic vowels before *h* were often similarly treated. If they occur in a syllable with secondary stress which is separated from the main stress they are regularly long, as in *rèhabílitàte, pròhibítion*; but variation occurs in immediately pretonic syllables, where either long vowels with secondary stress or short unstressed vowels are found (e.g. *prehénsile, prohíbit*; but only long vowels in such as *cò-hábit*). Native word-groups such as *the house* are again doubtless the models: in them the definite article was sometimes pronounced with light secondary stress and a long vowel in order to make sure of avoiding elision, but as elision was by no means so likely in such groups as when the noun began with a vowel the unstressed form of the article was more commonly used; and this variation in the pronunciation of the article seems to be reflected in the variable treatment of immediately pretonic vowels before *h*.

The orthoepists show the normal treatment of late ME and eModE adoptions, as described in the foregoing paragraphs; their evidence is cited in detail below only when some point of special interest is involved (e.g. variation between two modes of pronunciation in eModE).

VARIATIONS IN PRONUNCIATION CAUSED BY SECONDARY STRESS IN POST-TONIC SYLLABLES

VARIATION BETWEEN ME *ā* AND ME *ă*

§ 271. In syllables not immediately post-tonic, final *a* in the suffix *-ia* (*India*, &c.) is ME *ā* in Robinson but *ă* in Gil; *Cesarea* has *ă* in Hodges, who seems to stress it on the second syllable. The suffix *-able*(*-ably*) has *ă* in Hart, *ă* beside *ā* in Bullokar, and *ā* in Robinson and Hodges. Hodges also gives *ā*, which seems artificial, in *incommunicability*. The suffix *-age* (in *marriage*, &c.) has *ă* in Hart, Bullokar, Coles (who has [ɪ] < [ə] < *ă*), Strong, Young, Cocker, and Brown and the shorthand-writer Hopkins; it has *ā* in Hodges in *heritage*. The suffix *-ary* has *ă* in Hart and Bullokar but *ā* in Robinson and in Hodges (except for *ă* once in *ordinary*). The suffix *-ate* in adjs. and sbs. has *ă* in Laneham, Bullokar, Cooper, and the shorthand-writer Hopkins; Robinson gives *ă* in *graduate* and *immoderately* but *ā* in *magistrate*; Gil and Hodges have *ā*. In verbs it has *ă* in Bullokar but *ā* in Hodges; Hart gives *ă* in *recapitulate* but *ā* beside *ă* in *separate*. *Associate* (it is not stated whether vb. or sb.) has *ā* in Coles and Young but *ă* in Strong and Cocker. The suffix *-ation* has *ă* in Hart's *Orthographie* and Bullokar, but *ā* in Hart's *Methode*, Robinson, Gil (except for *ă* in *expectation*), Hodges (except for *ă* in *exclamation*), and Cooper. The suffix *-ator* has *ă* in Hart but *ā* in Gil. *Tabernacle* has *ā* in the third syllable in Hodges.

[§ 271]   VARIATIONS IN POST-TONIC SYLLABLES

In immediately post-tonic syllables final -a (*Eliza, Charissa*) is *ā* beside *ă* in Robinson, *ă* in Gil. Final -*ah* in Hebrew names and words (*Jehovah, Jeremiah, Sarah, selah*) is *ā* in Robinson, *ă* beside *ā* in Hodges. The suffix -*able* (-*ably*) as in *notable* has *ă* in Hart, *ă* beside *ā* in Bullokar, and *ā* in Hodges. The suffix -*age* has *ă* in Hart, Bullokar, Hodges, Coles, Young, Cocker, and Brown, but *ā* beside *ă* in Robinson and Gil (in the latter *ă* predominates). The suffix -*ale* has *ă* in Bullokar in *female*, &c. *Library* has *ă* in Bullokar. Hart has *ă* in *Pilate* but Gil *ā* in *prostrate* adj.; *ă* in -*ate* is also shown by the 'homophone list' pairing of *palate* with *pallet* (Ellis, Young, Cooper 'near alike', *Compendious School-Master*). *Algate* has *ă* (second syllable) in Gil. *Derivative* and others in -*ative* have *ă* in Bullokar and Hodges. *Terrace* has *ă* in Laneham, but *purchase* (vb.) has *ā* in Robinson. *Theatre* has *ă* in Hodges, and *diadem* in Cooper. *Ephraim* has *ā* in Hodges. *Extraordinary* has *ā* four times against *ă* once in the second syllable in Hodges; *contradict* has *ă* in Cooper.

Note: Salesbury shows dialectal *ai* < *ă* in the suffix -*age* and in *orange*; see Vol. I, p. 17. In *palace* (which has *ă* in Hodges) the ending -*ace*, with short or long *a*, is not to be regarded as a development of the original ME and OF ending -*eis*, but as showing the influence of Latin *Palatium*.

VARIATION BETWEEN ME *ai* (*ei*) AND ME *ĕ*

§ 272. In syllables not immediately post-tonic, ME *ai* is recorded in *sovereign* by Robinson (in the sb.) and Gil, without syncope; ME *ĕ* is shown by Robinson in the syncopated *suvren* (adj.) and *suvraneīz* (which shows confusion of unstressed *ĕ* and *ă*). ME *ĕ* is shown in *chamberlain* by *WSC-RS*; Hart transcribes it with *ai*, but this appears to be an imperfectly phonetic transcription (since ME *ai* normally is *ē*). *Apparel* has *ĕ* in Bullokar, Robinson, and Gil. *Counterfeit* is also recorded only with ME *ĕ*, in Hart, Robinson, and *WSC-RS*; the last-named actually says it has '*i* short', i.e. [ɪ] < [ə] < ME *ĕ*. *Citizen* has *ĕ* in Gil.

In immediately post-tonic syllables, Levins shows both ME *ai* and ME *ĕ* in *barren*. Hart shows ME *ai* in *certain* (thrice) and *travelling*, but *ĕ* in *certain* (normally), *traveller*, *foreigns* 'foreigners', and *perfet(ly)* 'perfectly'. But others of his transcriptions are imperfectly phonetic; examples are *auluais* 'always', *Germain* 'German', and *Romain* 'Roman'. Bullokar has ME *ai* in *Britain* and *money*, *ai* beside *ĕ* in *battle* and *carain* 'carrion' (see Note), and *ei* thrice beside *ĕ* once in *certain*; he has ME *ĕ* or forms from it in *carren* 'carrion', *certain*, *dozen*, *foreign*, *sloven*, *sudden*, and *travel*. Robinson has *ā* < ME *ai* in *captain* but *ĕ* in *surfeit*. Gil has *ai* in *bargain*, *battles* (transcribing Spenser's spelling *battails*), *Britain*, *certain*, *curtain* (fourteenth-century *cortayn*, &c. with suffix-substitution beside original *cortine*; see *OED*), *fountain*, *marvel*, *sudden* (transcribing Spenser's spelling *suddein*), *valley* and *journey* (ME -*eie* < AN -*eie*; see further § 275, Note 2(*b*));

but he has *ĕ* in *villainous* and *ă* in *villain* (probably showing confusion of unstressed *ă* and *ĕ*, but perhaps influenced by the ultimate etymon *villānus*). Hodges has *ai* in *(un)certain* and its derivatives and in *mountain*, but *ĕ* in *battle* and *cattle*. Price has *ai* in *foreign*, *ĕ* in *bargain*, *chaplain*, and *sudden*. Coles, Strong, Young, Lye, Cooper, *The Compendious School-Master*, Aickin, *WSC-RS*, and Brown show only *ĕ* forms in such words, except that Strong and Young appear to have *ā* < *ai* in *certain*. Coles gives [ɪ] < [ə] < *ĕ*, and Young *ĕ*, in *Cologne* (pronounced *Cullin*, *Cullen*), and Coles, Strong, Young, and Brown give *ĕ* in *carrion* (see Note). *The Compendious School-Master* gives [ɪ] < [ə] < *ĕ* in *Calais*.

Note: *Carren* 'carrion', *Bullen* 'Boulogne', and *Cullen* 'Cologne' all present the same problem. In each case we have to do with a Latin or Romance form in *-ōnia* (**carōnia*, *Bonōnia*, *Colōnia Agrippīna*), which regularly gives OF forms in [ɔɲə] > [uɲə]. But in ME the OF combination of vowel plus [ɲ] is regularly represented by the combination vowel plus [i] plus [n] (cf. *Spain* < *Espagne*); Lat *-ōnia* therefore becomes ME *-oine*. Hence the ME spellings *caroin*, &c., *Coloyne* (see *OED*, s.vv. *carrion*, *Cologne*), and *Bol(l)oyn(n)e* (*Hundred Rolls*, 1274), and the pronunciation [buloin]. But even in stressed syllables ME *oi* seems in certain dialects to have become *ai* by unrounding of the first element (see § 261, Note 2 above), and this tendency was perhaps more widespread in secondarily-stressed syllables; hence *caroin* > *careyn*, &c. (see *OED*), *Boloyne* > *Boleyn(e)* (cf. the Norfolk family name), and *Coloyne* > *Coleyn(e)* (see *OED*), the change having occurred by at latest the early fourteenth century. To secondarily-stressed forms in *-ein*, *-ain* there regularly correspond unstressed forms in *-en*, whence *caren* (fourteenth century onwards), *Bullen* (by the fifteenth century), and *Cullen* (not recorded by *OED* until the sixteenth century, but clearly developed earlier).

A parallel in a stressed syllable is afforded by the difficult word *prune* 'to trim the feathers, preen' (*OED*, s.v. *prune* vb.[1]), which must represent an OF original in *-ugne* < *-ǫgne* (cf. the Scottish forms *prunʒe*, &c.) and therefore regularly develops ME forms in *ui* and *oi* (see *OED*); from the latter the late ME form in *ai* (*ei*), recorded in Chaucer MSS (see *OED*), develops by a phonetic process, and not by blending with *preen* vb.[1] 'to pin', &c., as assumed by *OED* and Jordan, § 237, Anm. The later blending is rather dependent on the previous existence of the *preyne* form; *preen* vb.[2] 'trim the feathers' is not safely recorded until the later seventeenth century, for *OED*'s quotation dated 1486 is rather an example of *preen* vb.[1]. The form *prune*, despite Jordan, loc. cit., represents a ME analogical pronunciation (not a ModE spelling-pronunciation) modelled on the variation between ME [y:] and [ui], [ɔi] in words of the *annoy* class (§ 256 above).

VARIATION BETWEEN ME *au* AND ME *ă*

§ 273. Before *n* in syllables not immediately following the stress, in words like *countenance* and those ending in *-an*, ME *ă* is given by all sources except Robinson, who has normally *ă*, but *ǒ* < *au* in *Phrygian*, *politician*, and *physician*; similarly in syllables immediately following the stress ME *ă* is given by all sources, except that Robinson in one word (*Trojans*) gives *ǒ* < *au*.

Before *l* (in the suffix *-al*), in syllables not immediately following the stress in words like *capital*, *continual*, and *special*, ME *au* is given by Levins, Hart (beside *ă*, in the proportion of one *au* to two *ă*), Bullokar (beside *ă*, which predominates), Robinson (who normally has *ǒ* < *au* and has [ɒː] < au in *several* (with syncope) and *special* but has no *ă* forms), Gil (beside *ă*), Hodges (always), Daines, Wharton (in *admiral* and *several*), Price (in *musical* but not *perpetual*), and J. Smith (who follows Wharton, but adds *general* sb.). ME *ă* is given by Hart, Bullokar, Gil, Daines, Newton (in *especially*), Price (in *perpetual*) and Cooper (whose 'near alike' list pairs *principal* with *principle*), and is probably implied by those sources who make no comment on the pronunciation of *a* before *l* in unstressed syllables. In syllables immediately following the stress, in words like *denial, moral, mortal*, ME *au* is shown by Levins (if we may accept as evidence his rhymes of *coral*, &c. with *all*, &c.), Bullokar (beside *ă*), Robinson (who has *ŏ* < *au* except for a single case of *ă* in *royal*; but *royalty* has *ŏ*), Gil (beside *ă*; *denial* has *ă* in the 1619 edition, *au* in the 1621 edition), Hodges (always), Daines, and Price (in *eternal*, but *ă* in *moral* and *mortal*). ME *ặ* is given by Hart, Bullokar, Robinson (once only), Gil, and Price; it is implied by the silence of later sources. Price (1665, 1668) and J. Smith (1674) are the last orthoepists to give evidence of ME *au*. On the other hand Robinson shows *ă* only once, and Hodges never in *EP*.

Note 1: *Metal* has syllabic *l* in Robinson, Hodges, and Cooper (< ME *metel*).

Note 2: The 'homophone list' pairings of *vial* with *viol* (Price, Fox and Hookes, Strong, and Cooper 'alike') and of *coral* with *carol* (Wharton) may show *ŏ* < *au* as in Robinson, but are more likely to show confusion of unstressed *ă* and *ŏ* as [ə]. Cf. Cooper's *meddle* : *medal*.

Note 3: Cooper gives ME *au* in *herald* (ME *heraud*). Hodges, *SH-PD*, pairs it with *Harold*, which probably depends on [ə] < ME *ă* in the one word and < ME *ŏ* in the other. The pairing then shows that in the unstressed syllable the vowel is < ME *ă* and the *l* is pronounced; this pronunciation represents a new formation on MedLat *heraldus, haraldus* rather than a ModE spelling-pronunciation. Similarly *emerald* has a form with *ă* and pronounced *l* which is to be regarded as a re-formation on a MedLat **esmaralda, -us* (cf. OF *esmeralde*, Sp. *esmeralda*, It. *smeraldo*).

VARIATION BETWEEN ME *ẹ̄* AND ME *ĕ*

§ 274. Final *e*, in syllables not immediately following the stress, is *ẹ̄* in Robinson in *Andromache* and *Melpomene*, but *ĕ* in Hart in *apostrophe* and in Bullokar in *syncope*. In syllables immediately following the stress, *ẹ̄* is given by Robinson in *poetry*, *Orpheus*, and *Shakespeare*, and by Hodges in *Bartimeus* and *Jezreel*; *ĕ* is given by Gil in *Belphoebe, hideous*, and *righteous* (which has suffix-substitution) and by Hodges in *courteous, righteous*, and their derivatives.

Note 1: That the *e* in *righteous* was pronounced is also shown by the 'phonetic spellings' *riteyus* (Strong) and *ri-teus* (Young), but the quantity of the *e* is doubtful.

Note 2: Robinson gives *ẹ̄* once, *ĕ* once, and *ĭ* once in the third syllable of *variety*, in which *ĕ* would be expected. The *ĭ* form must develop from [ə] < *ĕ*; the *ẹ̄* form probably shows the influence of the English pronunciation of Latin, in which the *e*, being in an open syllable, might be pronounced long even though pretonic (in the oblique forms of the Latin word).

Note 3: Gil gives $\bar{e}$ in *avenger* (last syllable), perhaps by error; but rhymes of the agent-suffix *-er* with ME $\breve{e}r$ and $\bar{e}r$ are not uncommon (e.g. Shakespeare *worshipper : cheer : fear*, Nashe *executioner : hear*). In part at least they are due to confusion of *-er* with *-eer* (*-ier*), but this in turn probably rests on occasional lengthening of ME *-ĕre* to *-ēre* (> later *-ḗre* by raising) under secondary stress.

VARIATION BETWEEN ME ī AND ME ĭ

§ 275. Variation between ME *ī* and ME *ĭ* is freely shown by the orthoepists, whose evidence proves that ME *ī* (with secondary stress) occurred, before the date of diphthongization to [əi], as a variant beside unstressed *ĭ* in the following classes of words:

(1) Words with ME *ĭ* < OE, ON *ig* (OE *-īc*) in the suffixes *-y* (*bloody, body*, &c.) and *-ly* (*heavenly, boldly*, &c.).

(2) Words with French or Latin *i* (e.g. *determine, crocodile, Florentine, mercy, cherries, caitive*).

(3) Words with OF *-é(e)* (e.g. *destiny, dishonesty, majesty, university, pity, army, country*). In such words *ĭ* is always more common, but [əi] is fairly frequent in syllables not immediately post-tonic, and though rare is found in immediately post-tonic syllables; it is clear that in ME itself the OF *-é* ending must have been assimilated to the native *ĭ* < *ig*, and therefore shows the same variation between ME *ĭ* and ME *ī* (so Jordan, § 246, against Luick, § 597 (4)).

(4) Words with OF *-ie* (e.g. *history, injury, glory, copy*). These also show [əi] fairly often except in immediately post-tonic syllables, where it is very rare but occurs; again there has been assimilation in ME to the native type *-ĭe(s)* (in oblique cases of nouns and adjectives in *-ī*) and therefore variation between *ī* and *ĭ*. The assimilation to the native models is of course accompanied by a complete change of stressing (e.g. from OF *memórie* to ME *mémorìe*).

Detailed evidence on the various types of words is analysed below; here we may notice a few pieces of evidence of a more general sort. Levins's evidence is confusing, and is not cited below; in his rhyme-lists he at first does not distinguish secondarily stressed *-y* from stressed ME *ī*, rhyming not only polysyllables (e.g. *confederacy*) but also disyllables (e.g. *baby*) with stressed ME *ī*, but in words beginning with *l* and later letters he keeps stressed ME *ī* apart from unstressed. On the whole it would seem that he must have known [əi] in words of all classes, even when disyllabic. Tonkis (1612) lays it down as a general rule that final *-y* is pronounced 'anglice' (i.e. with the English 'long *i*', [əi]), not 'gallice' (i.e. with [i(:)]); his example is the last syllable of *ability*, which he contrasts with the *i*'s of the second and third syllables. Gil, in two important comments, says: 'Poetic number often stresses and lengthens the last syllable of a proparoxyton in [ɪ], as *mizerj, konstansj, destinj*; whence also in prose it is almost the case that they are indifferently written and pronounced, but are however not accented, with the last long or short' (ed. Jiriczek, p. 134), and further: 'Poets however freely shorten syllables ending in *j* [i.e. ME *ī*]; since in the flow of speech the accent on a neighbouring syllable absorbs its length [i.e. the length of the "long *i*"]. But if the syllable is subject to any grammatical or rhetorical stress, it is not shortened, as *mj moni* – ᴗ ᴗ' (p. 136). These comments show a clear recognition that [əi] is associated with secondary stress and is specially though not exclusively poetic, and that [i] is associated with lack of stress and is characteristic of 'flowing' speech; but they further show that the withdrawal of secondary stress in prose did not necessarily involve the abandonment of the [əi] pronunciation. *The English Schole-master* (1646) says that final *-y* is pronounced like Dutch *ij*, which is identified elsewhere with ME *ī*; the examples are *only* and *verily*. Richardson (1677), however, says that final *-y* is 'wat korter' than ME *ī*; as he says the same thing of the *i* of *live* vb., it is evident that his final *-y* is ME *ĭ*.

Hodges shows the same position as applies in PresE; so all later seventeenth-century spelling-books, including Cooper's. The rare evidence of [əi] after Gil comes from *The English Schole-master* (as above), Wharton, Newton, T. Jones, and two doubtful transcriptions of Lodwick's (see below, under (1)). Evidence of ME *ĭ* in the ending *-fy*, where PresE has [ai], is doubtful; but see under (2) below. In the analysis which follows no evidence later than Hodges's is cited unless it differs from PresE pronunciation.

(1) *Words from OE and ON*

In syllables not immediately following the stress [əi] < ME *ī* is shown by Hart (in the suffix *-ly* fairly often, but more commonly *ĭ*), Robinson (in the suffix *-ly*), Gil (in the suffix *-ly* with three exceptions, and in *every* six times against *ĭ* thrice), *The English Schole-master* (1646) in *verily*, Newton in *commonly* and *earnestly*, and T. Jones (1688) in *merrily*. ME *ĭ* is shown by Cheke (in the suffix *-ly*), Hart (as the more common variant in the suffix *-ly* and alone in *every*), Bullokar, Robinson (in *every* but not in the suffix *-ly*), Gil (thrice in *every*, twice in *heavenly*, and once in *privily*), Hodges (always), and all later orthoepists (including Newton in *soberly* and *especially*) except those mentioned above. See further Note 1 (*a*) below.

In syllables immediately following the stress, [əi] < ME *ī* is shown by Hart (in the suffix *-ly* in *boldly*, *namely*, *wholly*, and six others), Bullokar (in *bodies* once, *happy* once, and in others according to Hauck), Robinson (in *yearly* and *lady* once each), Gil (in *baby* once, *lady* once against *ĭ* eight times, and *many* once against *ĭ* eight times; in the suffix *-ly*, which is thrice said to be [ləi], and some thirty times in all in such words as *daily*, *deadly*, &c.; *only* has [əi] seven times, *ĭ* but once), *The English Schole-master* (1646) in *only*, Lodwick (*c*. 1685) in *daily* (but his *-y*, which should mean ME *ī*, may be an error; see Vol. I, p. 279), and by T. Jones (1688) in *only* and *truly* (but ĭ in *thirty*). Wharton's 'homophone' list, ignoring the difference of stress, pairs *belly* with *belie*. ME ĭ is shown by the *Welsh Hymn*, Cheke, Salesbury, Smith, Hart (in the suffix *-y* and as the more common variant in *-ly*), Bullokar (as the normal variant for *-y* and *-ly*; note also ĭ in the suffix *-wise* in *flatwise*, &c. and twice in *in no wise*), Mulcaster, Gil (as the normal form of the suffixes *-y* and *-ly*), Hodges (always), and later sources (including Newton in *truly*) with the exceptions mentioned above. See further Note 1 (*b*) and (*c*) below.

(2) *Words from French or Latin with French or Latin* i

In syllables not immediately following the stress, ME ī is normally shown in words which have it in PresE; so Hart in *Catherine*, Bullokar in *masculine* and *feminine*, &c. But [əi] < ME ī occurs in *avarice* and *covetise* in Robinson, and in *enemy*, *Mercury*, *sanctuary*, and *tympany* in Gil. The suffix *-ine* has [əi] in *Florentine* in Hart, ĭ in *Florentine* and *porcupine* as well as *masculine* in Bullokar, and [əi] in *Paladine* in Robinson. The suffix *-ite* has ĭ in *parasite* and *infinitely* in Bullokar, [əi] in *parasite* in Robinson, [əi] in *infinite*, *requisite*, *indefinite*, *perquisite*, *Jesuite*, *parasite*, and *tripartite* in *WSC-RS*. The suffix *-ive* (in *primitive*, &c.) has ĭ in Hart, Bullokar, and other sources; but Gil says it is [əiv] and gives *fugitive* as an example. Words of other types which have [ai] in PresE usually have [əi] in the orthoepists; so *paradise* in Bullokar, Robinson, and Gil, *merchandise* in Bullokar, *prophesyings* and *sacrifice* in Hodges. But Bullokar has ĭ in *crocodile* (against [əi] in Robinson), and Gil has ĭ in *multipliable* (against [əi] in *multiply*). The suffix *-fy* in *satisfy*, &c. normally has [əi] (so Hart, Robinson, Gil, and Hodges); but exceptionally Hart has ĭ in *beautify* and *signify* (in the latter case beside [əi]), Gil in *vitrifiable*, and Wilkins in *crucified*—probably not by error (cf. such rhymes as Donne's *wee*: *dignifie* in Elegy XIX 41–42).

In syllables immediately following the stress, e.g. in *cherry* (which in ME is from OF), *dally*, *active*, *service*, *doctrine*, &c., ME ĭ is normally shown in words which have it in PresE; so Smith, Hart, Laneham, Bullokar, Gil, and Hodges. But Cheke has [əi] in *determine* and *doctrine*, Hart in *missive* and *perfited*, Bullokar in *cherries* and once (against ĭ once) in *satyr*, and Gil once (against ĭ once) in *caitive*, once (against ĭ five times) in *mercy*, and in *ruin*. In words which have [ai] in PresE the orthoepists normally show [əi]; so Bullokar and Gil in *empire*. But Hart has ī in *chastising* (stressed on first), Bullokar in *supine*, and Hodges in *pristine* and (in *SH-PD*) in *saphire* paired with *safer* (cf. the early spellings *saphir* and *sapher* < OF *safir*). The suffix *-ile* is *il* in Levins in *docile*, *facile*, *fertile*, *sterile*, *subtile*, and *utensile*, in Hodges once (against [əi]) in *Gentile*, and in Brown in *sterile*. Hart's ĭ in *advertised* (which must be stressed on the second) is etymologically correct; see *OED*, s.v.

(3) *Words with OF* -é(e)

In syllables not immediately following the stress, [əi] is shown by Tonkis in *ability*, Robinson in *destiny*, and Gil in *commodities* (once, against ĭ twice in *commodity*), *destiny* (twice, against ĭ once), *dishonesty* (against ĭ in *honesty*), *vanity* (once, against ĭ once), and alone in seven other words (twelve occurrences in all). Many of Gil's examples of [əi] are not in rhyme; it may be noticed that he gives [əi] in the suffix *-ty* or its plural ten times, though he lays it down as a general rule that the English suffix from Latin *-tas* is *tĭ*. ME ĭ is shown by Cheke, Hart, Bullokar, Robinson (in the suffix *-ty*), Gil himself (in the majority of cases), Hodges, and later sources. See further Note 2 (*a*) below.

In syllables immediately following the stress, [əi] is recorded only by Bullokar in *country* (once, against ĭ thrice), by Gil in *army* (once) and *beauty* (1619 once; not 1621), and by the 'homophone' list pairing *alley* : *ally* (Wharton; Coles, *Eng.-Lat. Dict.*), which ignores the normal difference of stress; the pronunciation was obviously rare. ME ĭ is shown by Cheke, Smith, Hart, Laneham, Bullokar (with the one exception), Mulcaster, Robinson, Gil (with the two exceptions), Hodges, and later sources. See further Note 2 (*b*) and (*c*) below.

(4) *Words with OF* -ie

In words with OF *-ie* (and words from Latin assimilated to this type), [əi] < ME ī is shown, in syllables not immediately following the stress, by Cheke in *company* (perhaps); by Robinson in *harmony*, *injury*, *tragedy*, and *papistry* (once, against [i:] < ĭ once); by Gil in *melancholy* (once, against ĭ once), *misery* (thrice, against ĭ twice), *victory* (once, against ĭ once), and alone in *adultery* and seven other words (fourteen occurrences in all); and by T. Jones (1688) in *company*. It should be noticed that Robinson and Gil give [əi] in words which are not in rhyme. ME ĭ is shown by Hart, Bullokar, Robinson (in *company* and *courtesy*), by Gil (alone in six words, and in three beside [əi]; also in *vigilancy*, a sixteenth-century adoption), by Hodges always, and by later sources with the exception of T. Jones.

In syllables immediately following the stress, e.g. *copy*, *easy* (ME *aisie*), *dowry*, [əi] is shown by Gil in *glory* (once, beside ĭ ten times) and *frenzy* (1619 once; not 1621), both in verse but not in rhyme; Lodwick (1685) also gives a transcription of *glory* which should mean [əi] (see Vol. I, p. 279) but may be an error. Otherwise ME ĭ is shown, e.g. by Hart, Robinson, Gil himself, and Hodges.

Note 1: (*a*) *Every* < earlier *everich* should have only ĭ, but has been assimilated to the common type with ĭ < ĭg, as Gil's evidence shows; but the etymological ĭ clearly predominates. The origin of the *-y* in *baby* is doubtful, but as it is assimilated to the common type it is treated with it.

(*b*) Gil gives *ei* in the second syllable of *barley*; this may well be an unphonetic transcription due to the conventional spelling, but he may have had an analogical pronunciation with ME *ei* on the model of *valley, journey, alley*, &c. (see Note 2(*b*)).

(*c*) Welsh *i* (usually equated with ME *ẽ*) is used to transcribe -*y* by the *Welsh Hymn* in *lady, pretty,* and *mighty*, by Salesbury in *lady* and *lily*, and by T. Jones in *thirty*; but Salesbury uses Welsh *y*, which he equates with ME *ĭ*, for -*y* in *holy*.

Note 2: (*a*) Smith gives -*ĕ* in *charity* and Hart in *affinity, curiosity, discommodity, superfluity,* and *sichory* 'chicory'. As they give this -*ĕ* only in words with OF -*é*, it appears to represent a development in which OF -*é* was identified with ME -*ĕ* and not assimilated to the native type in -*ĭ*. *Easy* (< OF *aisié*) seems to have been assimilated to *copy*, &c. (OF *copie*, &c.) in ME.

(*b*) Words in OF -*ée* < Lat -*āta* have -*eie* in AN (Miss Pope, § 1171), and in ME have spellings in -*ei*, -*ai*, &c. which are shown to be phonetic by such rhymes as Chaucer's *aleyes* : *weyes* (T. & C., ii. 820–2). Gil gives *ei* in *valley* and *journey* sb. and vb., and the 'homophone' lists of Wharton, Fox and Hookes, and Coles (*Eng.–Lat. Dict.*), ignoring the difference of stress, pair *alley* with *allay*. But from Central Fr -*ée* (and perhaps in part from confusion with -*é* < Lat -*ātem*, -*ātum*) there arise ME forms in -*é* (cf. Jordan, § 247 (1)), and assimilation to the native type in -*ĭ* then follows; hence -*ĭ* and rare -*ī* in *country, army, valley, journey, alley*, &c. *Causey* 'causeway', it may be noticed, has *ī* in Bullokar and in the 'homophone lists' of Fox and Hookes, Coles (*Eng.–Lat. Dict.*), Strong, and Brown, which pair *causeys* with *causes*.

(*c*) Certain words which have ModE unstressed [ɪ] have in OF only *ei* or *ai*, e.g. *abbey, belfry, lamprey, money, palfrey, very*. In these [ɪ] is capable of developing in either of two ways. (1) By ME shortening of *ai* (*ei*) to *ĕ* (cf. Luick, § 466 (4*a*)), in which case they become indistinguishable from words in OF -*é* and are, like the latter, assimilated to the native type in -*ĭ*; this explanation must certainly apply in those words (*lamprey, money, very*) which have -*e*, -*i* forms from the fourteenth and fifteenth centuries, and may apply to all words of this class. (2) By ModE shortening of ME *ai* to [ɪ] (as in *Sunday, yesterday*); this explanation perhaps applies to those words (*abbey, palfrey, belfry*; also *cockney, kidney*, which have ME -*ei* of native origin) in which -*i* forms are not recorded until the sixteenth century or later, but if so one would expect that PresE would have pronunciations with [eɪ] as well as with [ɪ]. The orthoepists give [ɪ] (or [e] by ModE lowering of [ɪ]) in *money* (Robinson, Gil, Hodges, Price followed by Lye), *abbey* (Price, *WSC*), *lamprey* (Price), *palfrey* (*WSC*), and *very* (regularly). There is evidence of ME *ai* only in *money* in Bullokar, who is perhaps specially liable to follow unthinkingly the conventional spelling (but he gives *ĭ* or *ī* in *country, journey, valley*, despite the common -*ey* spelling); but the words are unfortunately seldom recorded (with the exception of *money* and *very*). In these words ME *ī* would not be expected, as it could arise only by the reimposition (in ME times) of the secondary stress whose loss is a necessary condition for the change from -*ai* (-*ei*) to -*ĕ* and -*ĭ*. See further § 343, Note 1.

VARIATION BETWEEN ME *ĭ* AND THE CONSONANT [j]

§ 276. One of the products of secondary stress and its absence is variation between [ɪ] and [j] in words of originally more than two syllables like *ancient, collier, Christian*, and *position*; when the final syllable receives secondary stress, the *i* remains a vowel and the word is three syllables (in the case of *ancient*, &c.) or four (in the case of *position*, &c.), and so on, but when the final syllable is fully unstressed the *i* becomes [j] and the word is reduced by one syllable.

The pronunciation of *i* in such words as [ɪ] is shown by Bullokar and Gil regularly; so probably Hart, though his *i* may stand for either [ɪ] or [j]. Salesbury has [ɪ] in *condition* but [j] in other words. Robinson shows retention of *i* as the vowel [ɪ] when the final syllable has secondary stress, in which case it is preceded by a glide [j], as in *oblivyión*, &c.; so before an unstressed final syllable in three personal names and in *glorious*, but normally he has [j] for the *i* before an unstressed final syllable. Bullokar (twice) and Gil show both [ʃ] and [ɪ] in *fashion* (ME *facioun*), in which [ʃ] is ordinarily regarded as being from [sj] for -*si*-; their transcription, however, is not merely based on the conventional spelling (which itself requires explanation), but is to be compared with several cases in Robinson (e.g. *akšion* 'action') in which [ʃ] develops from [s] plus the [j] glide developed before retained [ɪ] (cf. PresE [ʃ] in *associate, emaciate*, and occasionally in *nauseate, nauseous*). Hodges normally has [j] or pronunciations in which [s] or [z] plus [j] for *i* become [ʃ] or [ʒ]; but he gives [ɪ] in *Christian, barbarian*, in the suffix -*ion* after consonants other than *s*, *z*, or *x* (e.g. in *communion, companion* but not in *compassion, complexion*), and in *convenient*. Robotham (1643) says that *lectio* is pronounced *lecsio* (three syllables?) or *lecsho*. Wallis says that *nation, station*, &c. scan as either two or three syllables. Lye says that *e* is separately pronounced in *scutcheon* (ME *scochoun* but fifteenth-century *scoochion* with suffix-substitution), *gorgeous* (sixteenth- and seventeenth-century *gorgious*), *sergeant* (fifteenth- and sixteenth-century *sergiand, -iaunt*, sixteenth- and seventeenth-century *sergiant*; see also *OED*, s.v., sense 2*b*, for an apparent pun on *geaunt* 'giant'), *pageant* (fifteenth- and sixteenth-century *pagiaunt*, &c.), and *ocean* (which has -*ian* forms from the thirteenth-century). *WSC* and *RS*, which normally show [j] (even in *scutcheon*, in which *eo* is said to be pronounced *ye*), say that *ie* is divided into two syllables in *osier* and *soldier*.

Otherwise [j] is shown. Salesbury has it in *gracious, exhibition*, and *prohibition*. Sanford (1604 and 1605) identifies *lli* in *scullion* and *collier* and *ni* in *onion, companion*, and *spaniard* with French and Spanish *ll* and Italian *gl* and with French and Italian *gn* respectively; he is followed by Cotgrave (1611). Robinson normally shows [j] for *i*, or pronunciations developed from [j] in coalescence with a preceding consonant, when the following syllable is unstressed (see above); so Hodges, with the exceptions stated above. Price says *i* is silent in *cushion*; he is followed by Lye, whose example is *fashion*, and by *The Compendious School-Master*. The 'phonetically spelt' lists of Coles, Strong, Young, Cocker, and Brown show [j] or pronunciations developed therefrom (but see Note below). Others who show [j] regularly are Cooper, *WSC-RS*, and the shorthand-writer Ridpath (who shows [ʃ] < [sj] for -*si*-). It is to be remarked that Cooper shows [ʃ] < [sj] and [ʒ] < [zj], with loss of *i*, not only in *ancient, conscience*, &c., but also in *associate* (as do the 'phonetically spelt' lists), *ecclesiastical, enthusiasm, nauseate*, and *transient*, which now have normally [ɪ]; *RS* shows the same development as Cooper's in words in -*tiate* (e.g. *vitiate*) and in *nauseous*.

Note: Coles in *Mysia, submission, propitiation* (third syllable), *vitiate*, and *vicious* and Strong in *tuition* and *tradition* show [ʃj] (spelt *shy*, thus *vishyus* 'vicious'), in which [ʃ] is from [s] plus a glide [j] (as in Robinson) and [j] is by ModE reduction of the [ɪ] shown by Robinson.

VARIATION BETWEEN ME $\bar{\rho}$ AND ME $\breve{o}$

§ 277. In medial syllables ME $\bar{\rho}$ occurs in *innocent* and *sycophant* in Robinson, ME $\breve{o}$ in *Britomart* in Gil and in *innocent* and *violence* in Hodges. The suffix *-soever* has $\breve{o}$ in Gil and $\bar{\rho}$ in Hodges (in such words as *whatsoever*). The suffix *-ony* seems only to have $\breve{o}$ (so Hodges in *testimony*). The suffix *-ory* has $\breve{o}$ in Hart, Bullokar, and Gil (*victory*); Hodges has $\breve{o}$ in *supererogatory* but $\bar{\rho}$ in *supererogatoriously* (in which the *o* is stressed, whereas in the former word the *a* is; but the *a* is marked long in both); Robinson gives $\bar{\rho}$ in *memory* and *victory*.

In final syllables, Hart gives $\breve{o}$ in *echo* and *folio*, Bullokar $\breve{o}$ in *Cato*, *Naso*, *Thraso*, and *Apollo's*, Robinson $\breve{o}$ beside $\bar{\rho}$ (once each) in *Gnato*, Gil $\breve{o}$ in *echo*, *Apollo*, and *Cicero* but $\bar{\rho}$ in *Apollo's* and *Cicero's*. *Purpose* has $\bar{\rho}$ in the vb., $\breve{o}$ in the sb., in Hart, $\bar{\rho}$ twice in the sb. in Gil, and [ə] < $\breve{o}$ in the vb. in Hodges. The suffix *-most* has $\breve{o}$ in Gil (*undermost*, &c.). The suffix *-fore* in *wherefore*, &c. has always $\bar{\rho}$ (so Robinson, Gil, and Hodges). The suffix *-ion*, when it has not $\breve{u}$, has always $\breve{o}$ except in Gil in *fruition*, which has $\bar{\rho}$ once; the form may be an error, but Milton has rhymes in which *-ion* seems to have $\bar{\rho}$, e.g. *contemplation* : *throne* (*Il Pens.*, 53–54), and it is therefore probable that the long *o* of the Latin *-iōnem* sometimes affected English pronunciation when secondary stress was retained. Coles shows [ə] < $\breve{o}$ in *Jerome*.

Note: Gil once gives $\bar{\rho}$ (against $\breve{u}$ once) in *whilom*, but the form is artificial; it comes when he gives as an example of metathesis Spenser's '*lōm whjl* for *whjlōm*'.

VARIATION BETWEEN ME $\bar{\rho}$ AND ME $\breve{u}$

§ 278. ME $\bar{\rho}$, when shortened in ME, became $\breve{u}$. The suffix *-dom* is transcribed *-doom* by Cheke and Laneham, but probably to mean [dʊm]; Laneham also has *-dom* twice, but this is unphonetic. Otherwise the suffix has [ʊ] in Hart, Robinson, and Gil and [ʌ] once (against $\breve{i}$ once, probably by error) in Wilkins. The suffix *-hood* is not distinguishable in its forms from the word *hood* in the orthoepists, who would seem always to have given it secondary stress; it has [uː] in Gil, the equivalent of ME $\breve{u}$ in Bullokar, Robinson, and Brown (whose transcription *mannud* 'manhood' looks like a fully unstressed form, but he has *hud* 'hood'), and [ʊ] by later shortening in Hodges and Cooper; but both the earlier and the later shortening are probably caused by the following [d] rather than by unstressing. Laneham has *-hod* twice; cf. his *-dom*, discussed above.

ALLEGED VARIATION BETWEEN ME *oi* AND $\breve{o}$

§ 279. Luick, § 466 (4*b*), argues that ME *oi* was reduced, when unstressed, to $\breve{o}$; but the evidence he cites is doubtful. The form *ivor(e)* 'ivory' may derive from AN *ivurie* and not OF *ivoire*. *Devo(u)r* 'devoir' and *endeavo(u)r* appear in the fourteenth and fifteenth centuries respectively, when unstressed *ĕ*, *ŏ*, and *ŭ* may all have been [ə]; in the ME form *dever* there has been suffix-substitution (cf. Laneham's evidence, § 281 below). In *porpoise* the *u* and *o* forms do not appear until the sixteenth century and probably represent [ə] < ME *ă* or *ĕ* by shortening of the original ME *ai*, *ei* < OF *ei*.

There is little relevant evidence in the orthoepists. Unstressed *oi*, when it does occur, remains as *oi* (e.g. in *turmoil* in Smith). The form *emrods* 'haemorrhoids', which occurs in seventeenth-century spelling-books, may owe its *ŏ* to shortening of the ME (fourteenth-century) form in *au* (see *OED*).

VARIATION BETWEEN ME *ou* AND ME *ŏ*

§ 280. In words such as *follow* the late ME *ou* is comparatively rarely reduced to *ŏ* (the not infrequent seventeenth-century [ə] is not from *ŏ* but from a late ME variant in *ŭ*; see § 295 below). Hart has eight *ŏ* forms (five in *borrow*, two in *follow*, one in *morrow*) against *fellow* once with *ō* (ME *ou*) and the difficult *boroued* 'borrowed', in which *ou* (which normally in Hart means [ʌu] < ME *ū*) must here mean [ow] ([w] being written *u* by Hart); otherwise he has [u(:)] < ME *ŭ*. Laneham gives *folo* 'follow', &c., but the *o* may be long (< ME *ou*) not short. Gil has *ŏ* once against [ou] six times in *sorrow(ful)*; otherwise he has [ou] or [o:] < ME *ou*. Butler seems to have *ŏ*; he says that *ow* in *follow*, &c. has the same sound as in *bestow* but is short (see Vol. I, p. 162). Other orthoepists (e.g. Bullokar, Robinson, and Hodges) record pronunciations which represent ME *ou* without shortening.

Note: Gil records that *Cotswold* is vulgarly pronounced *Cotsal*, in which the *a* may represent [ə] < ME *ŏ* < ME *ou*, but may go back direct to OE *ă*. For the variation between late ME *ou* and *ŭ* in such words as *follow*, and the evidence for the *ŭ* variant, see § 295 below.

VARIATION BETWEEN ME *ū* AND ME *ŭ*

§ 281. In syllables not immediately following the stress, the suffix *-ion* has always *ŭ* (or *ŏ*, which probably often means [ə] < *ŭ*), never ME *ū* in the orthoepists. The suffix *-our* has [ʌu] < ME *ū* in the *Welsh Hymn* (in *saviour*), Laneham (in *trumpetors*), Hart (in *chancellor*, and thrice in *emperor*, once with syncope), Bullokar (*emperor*), Gil (in *emperor*, but *ŏ* otherwise), Poole (who rhymes *paramour* and *conqueror* with *our*, *bower*, &c.), and Price (*saviour*). Salesbury transcribes *emperor* with Welsh *w*, which can mean either [ʊ] < ME *ŭ* or [u:] < ME *ū* undiphthongized before *r*. ME *ŭ* is shown by Hart in *governors*, and by Daines, Cooper, and *WSC-RS* (of whom Cooper and *WSC-RS* probably mean [ə] < ME *ŭ*, as may Daines); those who do not show [ʌu] normally give ŏ, which however must often mean [ə]. The suffix *-ous* has [ʌu] in Laneham (in *umbragious, ceruleous, glorious,* and *adventurous*), Hart (in *commodious* and *dangerous*), and Bullokar (in *precious*). ME ŭ is shown by Salesbury, Laneham (in *(un)courteous, amorous*), Hart (in *commodiously* and five other words), and Bullokar (in *boistious* and *couragious* 'courageous'—for the form in *-ious* cf. *OED*), and regularly in Robinson, Gil, Butler, Daines, Hodges, and all later sources.

In syllables immediately following the stress, the suffix *-our* has [ʌu] in Laneham (in *actors, endeavour* (with suffix-substitution; see § 279 above), and *armour*) and Hart (once each in *favour, authors, error,* and *predecessors*). Robinson has [ɔ:] by lowering of [u:] < ME ū undiphthongized before *r* in *enamoured*. ME ŭ is shown by Hart (in *labour*, which has ŭr in the *Orthographie* and syllabic *r* in the *Methode*), Bullokar, Butler, Daines, and Hodges. All later sources give ŭ or ŏ (which probably means [ə] < ME ŭ); Hart also has frequent ŏ forms, which in him probably show the substitution of the Latin suffix *-or* for the OF suffix *-our*. The word *colour* requires special mention, since in this word ME ĕ appears to be shown by Laneham (in the sb.), Bullokar (in the sb., but ŭ in the vb.), and Gil (once in the sb., once in the vb., and once in a case which may be either, beside ŏ once); the *e* must represent [ə] < ME ŭ, but it is a remarkable coincidence that three orthoepists should show reduction to [ə] in this word and not in others of the same class. *Neighbour* has ŭ in Laneham, Hart, Bullokar, and Hodges; but in *harbour* Gil has analogical [ʌu] (from the ME *herbŭre* form, with fifteenth-century assimilation of the ending to the *-our* suffix; cf. the forms cited by *OED*). The suffix *-ous* normally has ŭ when immediately preceded by the stress (so Hart in *jealous* and twice, against [ʌu] once, in *desirous*, Bullokar in *grievous* and *jealous*, and later sources).

VARIATION BETWEEN ME [y:] OR [iu] AND ME ĭ

§ 282. OF [y] when subjected to secondary stress is represented in ME, as in stressed syllables, by [y:] or [iu], but when the syllable in which it occurs is made fully unstressed it becomes [ɪ] (later [ə], especially before *r*). The orthoepists give much evidence of the variation between the fuller and the reduced forms. In what follows, 'ME [y:]' is to be taken as meaning either [y:] or the variant [iu] (> [ju:]).

In syllables not immediately following the stress (e.g. *coverture, multitude, spiritual,* &c.), [y:] is ordinarily found; so in Robinson, Gil, Hodges, and *WSC*. But Cooper (followed in part by *WSC*) gives [ər] in *sepulture* (cf. the fifteenth- and sixteenth-century forms cited by *OED*), *portraiture* (cf. fifteenth-century forms in *-oure*), and *furniture* (a sixteenth-century adoption from French, anglicized on the model of earlier adoptions).

In syllables immediately following the stress, variation between [y:] and [ɪ] (or [ə] < ME *ĭ*) is common, especially in more vulgar seventeenth-century pronunciation; it affects not only words adopted in ME, but also some not recorded in English before the sixteenth century, which have evidently been anglicized on the model of older adoptions. The earlier orthoepists, however, give little evidence of ME *ĭ* or sounds derived from it. Hart, Robinson, and Gil (after account has been taken of erroneous transcriptions) have only isolated instances, even before *r*. Bullokar, who represents more vulgar sixteenth-century speech, states as a general rule that *-ure* is pronounced *-ŭr* (i.e. [ər]), but has some transcriptions which show [y:r], evidently because he has been influenced by more correct speech. Hodges in *EP* shows the reflex of ME *ĭ* in four words before *r* and in two others, but he still shows [y:] more commonly even before *r* (where it occurs in seven words); but his 'homophone list' in *SH-PD* shows ME *ĭ* more freely. After 1650 the evidence for it increases; the chief sources are the 'homophone lists', which in general are based on vulgar pronunciation, but Cooper regularly shows [ə] < ME *ĭ* for OF [y] before *r*, and it is evident that in the latter part of the seventeenth century pronunciations derived from ME *ĭ* were more widely current than they had been. Yet Coles does not show them (except in the one word *verjuice*) either in his 'phonetically spelt' list or in his 'homophone lists' (except the careless one in the *Eng.-Lat. Dict.*); he evidently did not use them in his own speech even before *r*.

(*a*) In words in which OF [y] is not followed by *r* it is normally represented by ME [y:], both in medial syllables when prevocalic (as in *continual, virtuous, mutual*) and preconsonantal (*scrupulous, occupation, particular, singular*) and in final syllables when preconsonantal (*Neptune, fortune*) and final (*ague, continue, virtue*); it may be particularly noted that even in *minute* sb., in which PresE has [ɪ] < ME *ĭ*, Gil has ME [y:]. But ME *ĭ* is exceptionally shown in the following cases. Hart has *ĕ* in *scrupulous*, where it must represent [ə] < ME *ĭ*; Cooper's Latin text says *scrupelous* is 'facilitatis causa', his English text that it is 'barbarous speaking'. This word (a fifteenth-century adoption) is doubtless influenced by *scruple*, but the latter is itself from *scrupule*. Robinson gives [j] < ME *ĭ* in *virtuous*, Hodges *ĭ* in *manuscript* (a late sixteenth-century adoption from medieval Latin) and *verjuice*; the latter also has *ĭ* in Coles, *Schoolmaster* (the 'phonetically spelt' list), followed by Strong (whose 'phonetic spelling' has *u* for [ə]), Young (with *e* for [ə]), and Aickin. The 'homophone lists', which are based on vulgar speech, show ME *ĭ* in non-final position in *lettuce* paired with *Lettice* (Fox and Hookes), *ingenuous* paired with *ingenious* (Hodges 'near alike', Ellis, Fox and Hookes, Coles (*Eng.-Lat. Dict.*), Young, Cooper 'near alike', *The Compendious School-Master*, Hawkins, Cocker, and Brown), and (with syncope of ME *ĭ*) in *annual* paired with *annal* (Young) and in *messuage* paired with *message* (Strong, Cooper 'alike', Aickin, and Brown); they also show it in final position in *value* paired with *volley* (Hodges 'near alike', Cooper 'near alike') and with *valley* (Wharton, Coles (*Eng.–Lat. Dict.*), Cocker, and Brown).

(*b*) Before intervocalic *r* in words which have no simplex in *-ure* [y:] was more usual, but [ə] < ME *ĭ* does occur. *Mercury* has [y:] five times in Bullokar, but is once transcribed with the symbol for ME *ŭ* (i.e. [ə]); it has [y:] in Robinson. Gil's *u* should mean [ʊ], but is probably an error for *v*, his symbol for [y:]. *Usurer* is four times transcribed with *ĕ* in the second syllable by Robinson; Cooper says that *yeusary* 'usury' is 'barbarous speaking'. *Century* is paired with *centaury* by the 'homophone lists' of Strong, Coles (*Eng.–Lat. Dict.*), Young, Cooper 'alike', Cocker, and Brown.

(*c*) Before final *r*, or in derivatives of words with final *r*, ME [y:] is shown by Hart (always), Bullokar (in *creature* once against [ə] thrice, *measurable*, *mixture*, *natural* once against [ə] thrice, *pastures*, and *picturing*), Robinson (normally, but [ə] in *venture*), Gil (normally, but [ə] in *venture*), Hodges (in *creature*, *measure*, *moisture*, *nature*, and *scriptures*), Coles, Schoolmaster (in *measure* in the 'phonetically spelt' list; cf. the absence of pairings on [ə] in his 'homophone list'), Strong and Young (following Coles in *measure*, but otherwise [ər]), and *WSC-RS* (which, for once not following Cooper, gives [iu] in *pressure*, *stature*, *texture*, and *verdure* but follows Cooper in giving [ər] in other words). Levins probably shows [ər] for OF [yr] by his *raysure* 'razor'; in this word there seems to have been suffix-substitution (*-ure* forms are found in Hampole and then from the late fifteenth century, according to *OED*), but the reason would be that [ʊr] and [yr] had become identical as [ər]. ModE [ər] is certainly shown by Bullokar (as his more usual form), Robinson (in *venture* sb., following Barnfield's spelling; the verb is twice *ventred*, with syncope of [ə], once following Barnfield's spelling and once despite it but on the same page as the previous instance), Gil (in *venture* once, transcribing Harington's spelling *venter*, and in *conjurer*, which he writes *kungurer* but says is really pronounced *kungerer*), Hodges (in *figure(d)* eight times, *venture*, *jointure*, and *ordure*), Strong and Young (in *nurture*, *torture*, and *venture*), Cooper in all *-ure* words (including, for example, *nature* and *measure*), *WSC-RS* (when following Cooper; see above), Cocker (in *creature*), Brown (in *picture* spelt *pikter*), and the shorthand-writer Bridges (who gives *kretrs* 'creatures', *ordr* 'ordure', *mesr* 'measure', *fetr* 'feature'). The most plentiful evidence is provided by the 'homophone lists'; there is none in Coles's two more careful lists, but Hodges and Cooper, who so often agree with Coles in avoiding pronunciations that were evidently vulgar, do in this case provide evidence. The pairings are as follows: *bordure* : *border* (Coles, *Eng.–Lat. Dict.*), *censure* : *censer* : *censor* (Hodges, Wharton, Strong, Coles (op. cit.), Young, Cocker, Brown), *gesture* : *jester* (Hodges 'near alike', Strong, Coles (op. cit.), Young, Aickin), *jointure* : *jointer* (Hodges, Wharton, Hunt, Strong), *lecture* : *lector*

(Brown), *mature* : *matter* (Brown; see Note 4 below), *ordure* : *order* (Hodges (*EP*), Wharton, Hunt, Fox and Hookes, Coles (op. cit.), Young, Cooper, Cocker, Brown), *pasture* : *pastor* (Hodges, Hunt, Fox and Hookes, Strong, Coles (op. cit.), Cooper, Aickin, Brown), *picture* : *pickt her* (Cooper, Aickin, Brown), *tenure* : *tenor* (Hodges, Price, Strong, Cooper, Aickin).

(*d*) *Pleasure* and *leisure* (ME *plaisir*, *leisir*) have analogical [y:r] because of its variation with *ĭr* in words with OF [yr]; similarly *treasure* (ME *tresur*), when *ŭr* and *ĭr* became identical as [ər] in the fifteenth century, assumed [y:r] beside [ər] because of variation between [y:r] and [ər] in words with OF [yr]. *Measure* was probably the chief model for all these three. The evidence is that they are not inverted spellings to which in late ModE a spelling-pronunciation was made to correspond, but are true analogical forms, involving both spelling and pronunciation, from late ME (when the -*ure* spellings first appear). The orthoepists do not distinguish them from words with OF [yr]. Indeed, Bullokar, who gives [ər] for most true OF [yr] words, somewhat remarkably gives only [y:r] in *pleasure* and *leisure* (but [ər] in *treasure*); similarly in *EP* Hodges, who has [ər] in some true OF [yr] words, gives only [y:r] in *pleasure* and *treasure* (he does not record *leisure*). In the three words [ər] is shown only by sources which also commonly have it for OF [yr]. The detailed evidence is as follows. In *pleasure* [y:r] is shown by Hart, Bullokar (thrice), Robinson, Gil, Hodges, Coles (followed by Strong and Young); [ər] by Cooper (followed by *WSC-RS*), as in all -*ure* words, and by the 'homophone list' pairing with *pleaser* (Hodges 'near alike'; Coles, *Eng.-Lat. Dict.*). In *leisure* [y:r] is shown by Hart, Bullokar, and Gil, [ər] by Cheke, Laneham, and Cooper (followed by *WSC-RS*) and the 'homophone list' pairing with *lesser* (Cooper 'near alike', Aickin, Brown). *Treasure* has [y:r] in Salesbury, Hart, Robinson, Gil, Hodges, and Coles (followed by Strong and Young), [ər] in Bullokar, Cooper, and the shorthand-writer Bridges. A further case of analogical [y:r] is *manure* (ME *manour* < OF *manouvrer*), in which the -*ure* ending is found in the fifteenth century (see *OED*); it is paired with *manner* by Hodges (*EP*) and by Wharton, Fox and Hookes, Strong, Young, Cooper 'near alike', *The Compendious School-Master*, Cocker, and Brown. On the stressing of this word see *OED*, s.v. *manure* sb.; Dryden stresses it on the second, and Cooper's relegation of the pairing with *manner* to his 'near alike' list probably shows that he regarded the old stressing on the first as less correct. On *raysure* 'razor' in Levins see the previous paragraph.

(*e*) The same variation between ME [y:] (or [iu] > [ju:]) and ME *ĭ* occurs in words which have OF [yi], namely *circuit* and *conduit*. It is possible that OF [yi] originally gave ME [y:i] (*circuit* is three syllables in Chaucer, *C.T.*, A 1887, but there may be Latin or Italian influence); if so, syncope would explain the development from this of [y:] (with secondary stress), to which there normally corresponds an unstressed form in ME *ĭ*. *Circuit* has [y:] in

Levins and Hodges (contrast their evidence on *conduit*) and in Lye, but *ĭ* in Wharton, Price, and later sources (including Coles and Cooper). *Conduit* has *ĭ* in Levins, Coote, Hodges, and later sources (including Cooper). Brooksbank (1654) says that in both words the *i* is not silent as it is in *fruit*; presumably the *u* is silent.

Note 1: (*a*) Hart writes *u* in both the first and third syllables of *superfluity*, which ought to mean [ʊ]; the transcription is certainly unphonetic. Similarly Hodges writes *u*, which ought to mean [ʌ], in *opportunity*; the diacritic which indicates [y:] has been omitted by error.

(*b*) Hart gives transcriptions with *u* (which ought to mean [ʊ]) in *figured*, *natural*, *singular(ly)*, *argument*, and *instruments*, but these are probably imperfectly phonetic and have 'etymological' spelling with *u* in place of the normal *iu* for ME [y:]; *instruments* comes in a confused passage in which Hart says that the *u* is ordinarily pronounced *iu*, but that out of 'observasion for derivasions' he does not think it meet to write *iu*, since the sound of the simple vowel ('ðe voël onli') may be as well allowed in our speech as the diphthong— meaning apparently that in these words the pronunciation (rather than the spelling) should be reformed by the use of a simple vowel to accord with the etymology, and not that a simple vowel was in fact used (as Jespersen, *Hart*, p. 28, assumes). Similarly Gil in certain words (*salutation*, *sanctuary*, *scripture*, and *virtuous*) uses the symbol *u*, which should mean [ʊ], certainly by error (probably the printer's) for *v* = ME [y:]. Hodges has *u*, which should mean [ʌ], in *attributed*, but the circumflex that indicates [y:] has been omitted by error.

Note 2: ME *construen* > *constrien > (with change of *ĭ* to *ĕ*, or by syncope) *constre*; *constur* (*-er*) 'construe' is given by Coles, Strong, Young, and *WSC-RS*, and is implied by Bullokar, who treats *construction* as if it were a derivative of *constR 'conster'. *Eunuch* has [y:] in the second syllable in Hodges and Strong (followed by Young and Brown); this is due to the influence of the English pronunciation of Latin *eunūchus*, in which *ū* would regularly be represented by ME [y:]. Bullokar's *ĕ* in *porcupine* is < ME *ĕ* < OF *ĕ*, not OF [y]. On Gil's *tempesteus* 'tempestuous' see *OED*, s.v. *Moniment* (recorded by Coles) is from Latin *monimentum* beside *monumentum*.

Note 3: The forms cited in paragraph (*c*) above throw some doubt on the simple view that OF [y], when unstressed in ME, regularly becomes, as a first stage, ME *ĭ*; for (*a*) unstressed ME *ĭ* more often remains [ɪ] than it becomes [ə] when it is not subject to *r*-influence, and (*b*) in stressed syllables intervocalic *r* only occasionally influences a preceding *ĭ*, and one might therefore expect that in the words cited above ModE would show [ɪ] as well as (perhaps more often than) [ə], as is the case in, for example, *manuscript*. It may be that in the neighbourhood of *r* OF [y], when unstressed, became directly [ə] rather than *ĭ* (cf. Jordan, § 246); but the evidence is hardly decisive. In all the cases the final syllable receives somewhat greater stress than the second, and it is in such circumstances that unstressed ME *ĭ* is most likely to become [ə] (see § 294, Note 3 and § 303 below).

Note 4: Kauter, *Hodges*, § 67, treats ME *ŭ* in *murmur* (which Hodges spells *murmure*, with the *e* marked silent) as showing [ər] developed from OF [yr]. But the word varied in ME between *murmur (fourteenth-century *mormur*, *-or*, *-our*) < Latin *murmur* and *murmure* < OF (see *OED*); Hodges's pronunciation derives from the former and his spelling from the latter. The variation between *-ur* and *-ure* in this word may have been a particular model for the development of the analogical *-ure* variant of words like *manure*. At a later stage *manure* and *mature* seem to have influenced each other; the stressing of the former on the second syllable is probably due to the analogy of the latter, and Brown's stressing of *mature* on the first would seem to show the reverse process.

Note 5: *OED* records spellings that show [y:] from the fourteenth century in *conduit* and from the fifteenth in *circuit*, and spellings that show ME *ĭ* from the fourteenth century in *conduit*. The sixteenth-century forms *cyrquite*, *-quet* probably have [wi] or [wə] < [yi], the [y] having become consonantal (cf. Modern French *huile*).

VARIATION BETWEEN ME [y:] OR [iu] AND ME ŭ

§ 283. In the neighbourhood of [m] OF [y], when unstressed in ME, becomes either ME ĭ or ME ŭ (cf. Jordan, § 246); only the latter is recorded by the orthoepists. Bullokar has ŭ thrice in *volume*. *Common* has ŭ in Bullokar and Hodges; Hart, Robinson, and Gil, misled by the conventional spelling, give ŏ, but must really have used [ə] < ME ŭ. *Common* is paired with *commune* (a pairing of doublets) in the 'homophone lists' of Hodges, Wharton, Strong, Coles (*Eng.–Lat. Dict.*), Young, Cocker, and Brown. (*Ac*)*custom* has ŭ in Hart, Bullokar, and Hodges; Gil gives ŏ but must really have used [ə] < ME ŭ.

QUANTITY VARIATIONS IN PRETONIC SYLLABLES

§ 284. In pretonic syllables variations of quantity occur which are comparable to those produced by secondary stress in post-tonic syllables. Where long vowels are recorded, secondary stress must be assumed; but it may be doubted whether in pretonic syllables the short variant is necessarily always unstressed (as would normally be the case in post-tonic syllables). Other considerations than secondary stress affect the quantity of pretonic vowels; but it is probably true that stress remains the most important factor.

In pretonic syllables separated by an unstressed syllable from the main stress the orthoepists show the same pronunciations as PresE, i.e. all vowels are short except *u*, which is [y:] (or [iu] > [ju:]); but Hodges has artificial ẹ̄ in *reconciliation*, and conversely *RS* has regular ŏ in *protomartyr* where PresE has abnormal [ou]. Other variations from PresE usage (which alone are noticed below) all occur in immediately pretonic syllables. Gil, we may here observe, lays down a general rule that 'every syllable before the accent is short . . . unless nature forbids as in *foregoing*'; his transcriptions, with very few exceptions, conform. Others, and in particular Robinson and Hodges, show long vowels more freely; but in at least some cases the pronunciations with long vowels are likely to have been artificial, and there can be little doubt that Gil's rule is well founded on normal pronunciation.

PRETONIC *a*

§ 285. In immediately pretonic syllables the vowel *a* is shown as short except as follows. Robinson has ME ā in *chameleon*, in *lament* vb. (five times), and in *variety* (thrice). Gil gives ME ā once against ă once in *apply* (which is transcribed with single *p*) < ME *aplie* < OF *aplier*, in which the syllable (as in Robinson's words) is open; but the ā form in Gil is isolated.

Hodges normally gives *a* as long (i.e. ME *ā*) when it occurs in an immediately pretonic open syllable (as in *abased, abound, about, above, adultery,* &c.); there are in all some seventy cases, against thirteen with ME *ă* (including *maliciousness*, in which his transcription is doubtless influenced by *malice*). He also has ME *ā* six times in *supererogatorious(ly)*, where again it occurs in an open syllable immediately before a marked stress, and once (against *ă* twice) in *lascivious*, perhaps in this case by error (since otherwise he gives only *ă* before *sc* as in *ascend, ascent,* &c.). But he gives *ă* not *ā* in *abuse* sb. and vb., where the *b* belongs to, and closes, the first syllable.

It is difficult to decide the exact significance of this evidence. It clearly does not rest on normal English pronunciation; the only question is whether the transcriptions rest on a faulty analysis of speech, or truly represent artificial pronunciations actually used by the orthoepists who give them (and if so, presumably by other people open to the same influences). Robinson's transcriptions may perhaps be accepted as showing real though artificial pronunciations due to the influence of the English pronunciation of Latin; Gil's isolated case is probably an error of transcription (or printing); Hodges's are probably entirely artificial transcriptions, due to his having set up (as it seems) a rule that *a* when final in a syllable is long, and it is only occasionally that he follows the evidence of his ears and leaves the *a* unmarked (i.e. short)—a strange lapse in so good an observer.

PRETONIC *au*

§ 286. ME *au* is regularly shown as [au] or [ɒː] in *augment, Augustus,* &c. But diphthongization of ME *ă* to late ME *au* seems sometimes to fail in a pretonic syllable (see § 60 (5) above); failure of the diphthongization indicates absence, and its occurrence presence, of secondary stress in late ME.

PRETONIC *ai*

§ 287. *Maintain* has ME *ai* (or *ā* < ME *ai*) in Hart (but his *ai* is probably an unphonetic transcription, since he normally represents ME *ai* by *ē*), Bullokar, Robinson (who has *ai* four times, *ā* once), and Hodges; but a ME unstressed variant in *ĕ* is shown by Cooper (followed by Aickin and *WSC-RS*) and by Brown, who gives the 'phonetic spelling' *mantane* (indicating [ə] < *ĕ* in the first syllable.)

PRETONIC *e*

§ 288. Pretonic *e* occurs chiefly in words of classical origin, in which considerations of classical quantities have much influence. But ME *ĕ* is nevertheless shown, as a rule, by Hart, Bullokar, and Gil; only rarely does the last-named forget his doctrine that pretonic vowels are short. On the other hand Robinson and Hodges, who are the chief but not the only sources for ME $\bar{e}$, are so influenced by classical quantities that they give some forms which are unlikely ever to have had real existence in English.

The prefix *de-* has $\breve{e}$ in Hart, Bullokar, Robinson (once each in *defend, undeserved, deceit,* and *describe,* against more usual $\bar{e}$), and in Gil (about sixty times); it has $\bar{e}$ in Robinson (normally, including *deceit* once and *describe* twice), Gil (twice in *deceive,* once each in *declare* and *desire*), Hodges (always, including *demonstrated,* which he perhaps stressed on the second, *despise, destroy,* &c.), and Lodwick. (On certain instances of ME $\breve{\imath}$ in this prefix see Note 1.) The prefix *e-* (as in *elect, erect*) has $\bar{e}$ in Robinson, Hodges, and Coles. The prefix *pre-* has $\breve{e}$ in Hart, Bullokar (with one exception), Gil (four times, including once each in *prevent* and *unprevented*), and Hodges (once, against ME $\bar{e}$ thrice, in *incomprehensible (-bility)*); it has ME $\bar{e}$ in Bullokar (once, in *pre-joiningly*), Robinson (always), Gil (once, in *prevent*), Jonson, and Hodges (with one exception). The prefix *re-* has $\breve{e}$ in Smith, Hart, Bullokar, and Gil, but ME $\bar{e}$ in Robinson, Jonson, and Hodges.

Few words with pretonic *e*, apart from those formed with these prefixes, occur more than once in the orthoepists' transcriptions. *Create (creator)* has $\breve{e}$ in Gil, ME $\bar{e}$ in Bullokar, Robinson, and Hodges. *Eternal (eternity)* has ME $\bar{e}$ in Robinson, Hodges, and Lye. *Esteem* has $\breve{e}$ in Bullokar and Gil, as one would expect, but ME $\bar{e}$ (apparently used as being the equivalent, in the English pronunciation of Latin, of Latin *ae* in *aestimare*) in Robinson and Hodges. *Peculiar* has $\breve{e}$ in Hart. Robinson gives ME $\bar{e}$ in *Severus, pecunia, Hesione, Zenobia,* and *Jehovah,* also in *descry* and *espy* (as if from *describo, e-* + *spy*), but $\breve{e}$ in *Erasmus.* Gil gives $\breve{e}$ in *Æneas* and *secure,* regardless of classical quantities. It is also to be observed that although in *where* he gives ME $\bar{e}$ always, in the derivatives *whereat,* &c. $\breve{e}$ occurs twice (against ME $\bar{e}$ five times); and that although in *there* ME $\bar{e}$ occurs thirteen times against $\breve{e}$ twice, in the derivatives *therein,* &c. the preponderance is reversed (ME $\bar{e}$ thrice, $\breve{e}$ five times). Hodges gives $\breve{e}$ in *benevolence,* but ME $\bar{e}$ in *Bezaleel* and *Cesarea* (in each word both the first and second *e* are ME $\bar{e}$ and the *a* is ME $\bar{a}$; Hodges stressed each on the second?), *Ephesians* (twice, against $\breve{e}$ once), *Ezekiel, Jerusalem, petition, Theophrastus;* also in *escape* (once) and *establisht* (once, against $\breve{e}$ in *establish*), as if they were from *e-* + *scape* and *e-* + *stablish,* but $\breve{e}$ in *especial.*

Note 1: Robinson, Gil, and Hodges give $\bar{\imath}$ in the prefix *de-* in certain words, but this $\bar{\imath}$ is not developed by raising from ME $\breve{e}$; it is due to confusion between the prefixes *di-* and *de-* (see further § 292 below).

Note 2: It seems unlikely that in these pretonic syllables the symbol for ME $\bar{e}$ is used, by the orthoepists who give it, to indicate a short tense [e] by lowering of [ɪ] which they have confused with long tense [e:] < ME $\bar{e}$, though Robinson certainly does so use it in the inflexional ending *-es* (see § 338 below). In pretonic syllables Robinson is rather influenced, as Hodges clearly is, by considerations of etymology and of classical quantity (cf. their evidence on pretonic *a*).

Note 3: On Robinson's use of the reflex of ME *ę̄* in the native prefix *be-* and in *enough* see § 294, Note 2 below.

PRETONIC *i*

§ 289. The most noteworthy feature is the lack of a clear distinction between *diverse* and *divers* (cf. *OED*, s.vv.). The form with final [s] (presumably stressed on the second) has *ĭ* frequently against [əi] thrice in Hart; *diversely* (with [s]) has *ĭ* twice against [əi] once in Hart and *ĭ* in Bullokar. The form with final [z] (presumably always stressed on the first; certainly so in Robinson) has *ĭ* in Bullokar and Gil, [əi] in Robinson, and *ĭ* once against [əi] once in Hodges.

In other words pretonic *i* is normally short; so Hart in *directing*, Bullokar in *Diana*, *divide*, and *divine* (and apparently in *Lysander*), Gil in *Diana*, Hodges in *idolaters* and *idolatry* (against [əi] in *idol*). But Robinson has [əi] twice against *ĭ* twice in *divine(ly)*. Considerations of classical quantity probably account for his [əi], as indeed they may for Bullokar's and Gil's *ĭ* in *Lysander* and *Diana*. Smith has [əi] beside *ĭ* in *iwis*, and Gil gives [əi] in transcribing Spenser's *bynempt*; in both cases [əi] is clearly a spelling-pronunciation for an archaism of which the traditional pronunciation was unknown (in *iwis* perhaps assisted by the false etymology which took *iwis* as *I wis* 'I know').

PRETONIC *o*

§ 290. The prefix *pro-* has *ŏ* in Hart, Bullokar, Gil, and Hodges, but ME *ǭ* in Robinson (again influenced by classical quantities?). *Possess(ion)* has *ŏ* in Hart but ME *ǭ* twice against *ŏ* once in Robinson (whose transcription has single *s*). Hart has *ŏ* in *notoriously*. *Obey* (*obedience*, &c.) has *ŏ* in Hart, Gil, and Hodges but ME *ǭ* in Robinson. Bullokar has *ŏ* in *Prometheus* and *nobility*; but Robinson has ME *ǭ* in *molest* and *Orestes*, and Hodges in *coequal*, *coeternal*, and *sobriety*.

The prefix *to-* in *together*, *towards* would be expected to have ME *ŏ* if it was uninfluenced by the preposition *to*, and *ŏ* is given by Bullokar (in *toward*) and by Gil (twice, against *ŭ* once, in *together*, once in *altogether*, eleven times in *towards*). Otherwise the influence of the preposition is shown; Bullokar has [uː] in *together*, and [ʊ] by ModE shortening of [uː] is given by Hart in *together* and *towards*, by Robinson in *together*, and by Gil once (against *ŏ* twice) in *together*. Hodges uses a symbol which may mean either [ʊ] or [uː] in *altogether*, *heretofore*, and *together*; in the last of these he once uses a symbol which should mean [ʌ], but it is probably a misprint for that for [ʊ] or [uː].

PRETONIC u

§ 291. In words of Latin origin *u* in pretonic open syllables is always [y:] (or [iu] > [ju:]) representing OF [y]; so in Bullokar, Robinson, Gil, and Hodges in *superior, humanity, tumultuous, usurp,* &c. Gil once has *u* (which should mean [ʊ]) in *superior*, but it is probably an error for *v* (i.e. [y:]); so his *u* in *fruition*.

OTHER VARIATIONS IN PRONUNCIATION IN UNSTRESSED SYLLABLES

§ 292. Certain prefixes and suffixes show variations in pronunciation which are due to other causes than English phonetic developments. The prefix *com-* varies between ME *ŭ* (representing the OF form) and ME *ŏ* (which is due to direct Latin influence): ME *ŭ* is given by Bullokar (in *companion, complain*), Robinson (once, against *ŏ* fourteen times, in *complaint*), Hodges (with the exceptions noted below), Coles (regularly), and Young (in *compassion*, following Coles); but ME *ŏ* is given by Bullokar (in *command, commit, commodity, communication, compare, composer,* and related words), Gil, Hodges (once each in *communication, compounded,* and *companion*—perhaps errors due to the omission of the diacritic which shows that *o* is pronounced [ʌ]), Wilkins (in *communion*), Strong, and Young (when following Strong). The prefix *con-* has (properly) only ME *ŏ*, except that Young gives *u* (which must mean [ə]) in a 'phonetic spelling' of *convince*. The OF and ME variation between the 'popular' *de-* and the 'learned' *di-* from the Latin prefix *di-* (cf. *OED*, s.v. di- prefix¹) accounts for the *ĕ* recorded in *divide* by Hart and Gil and in *division* by Bullokar (once, against *ĭ* twice, but only *i* in *divide*), and for Hodges's pairing of *divisor* with *deviser*. Conversely the prefix *de-* appears sometimes as *di-* in words in which, by misdivision of the prefix from the stem, *des-* has been altered to *dis-* on the model of the variation between the 'popular' OF *des-* and the 'learned' *dis-* from the Latin prefix *dis-* (cf. *OED*, loc. cit.); Robinson has *ĭ* in *despair* and once (beside ME *ē̢* twice) in *despise*, and Gil once (beside *ĕ* once) in *despair*; Hodges pairs *descension* (which has ME *ĭ*-forms) with *dissension*. Similar variation occurs between the prefixes *em-* and *en-* (from OF) and *im-* and *in-* (from Latin): the *ĕ*-forms are given by Hart (in *encouraged*), Bullokar, Robinson (with three exceptions), and Gil (in four cases, against *ĭ* in five); the *ĭ*-forms are given by Hart (in *incline* and *increase*), Robinson (in *enjoin* and *enveigh* and once beside *ĕ* once in *enforce*), Gil (in five cases), and Hodges (always). Gil similarly varies between *enter-* in *enterfere* and *inter-* in *interchange, intermeddle*.

The suffix *-ion* has ME *ŭ* (< OF) in Salesbury, Mulcaster, Howell,

Coles, and *WSC-RS* (but *WSC-RS* at least must mean [ə]); but under Latin influence ME ŏ is given (but [ə] was doubtless used in pronunciation in most if not all cases) by Hart, Bullokar, Robinson (even in *surgeon* from AF *surjien* with ME substitution of the suffix *-ioun*), Gil, Hodges, and Wilkins. The suffix *-our* (*-or*) has ME ŭ (< OF) in the sources listed in § 281; under Latin influence ŏ is given (but [ə] was doubtless the usual pronunciation) by Bullokar (in *savour*), Coote, Robinson, Gil (in *auditor, author*, &c.), Wharton, Brooksbank, Price, J. Smith, the *Treatise of Stops*, and Ray. The suffix *-ous* is surprisingly given as [oːs] by Lye, Cocker, and Brown (in his 'phonetically spelt' list, in which *-ous* is commonly *-ose*); cf. *OED*, s.v. *-ose*, for the artificial tendency to substitute this form (< Latin *-osus*) for *-ous* < OF. It is significantly recorded, among the orthoepists, only by three minor seventeenth-century schoolmasters, who in this matter are obviously pedantic.

Note: The alternation between *de-* and *di-* for Latin *di-* also occurs in OF *devin, divin* 'divine'; Gil gives ĕ in *divine*. The prefix *di-* is 'phonetically' spelt *de-* by Strong (followed by Young) in *direction* (spelt *derecshun*), *division, digression*, and *distinction*; these spellings are likely to rest on the ME and OF variants in *de-*, but it is possible that the *e* represents [ə] developed in vulgar speech (on which the 'phonetically spelt' lists are often based) from ME ĭ.

CHANGES OF QUALITY OF UNSTRESSED VOWELS IN MIDDLE ENGLISH

ME POSITION: GENERAL CONSIDERATIONS

§ 293. Luick, § 460 and elsewhere, assumes special values for the ME vowels in unstressed position—values which are for the most part not accepted by Jordan, §§ 134–6. Luick assumes, in the first place, a parallelism between the front and back vowels. (*a*) ME ĭ and ME ŭ were, he argues, in closed syllables very open sounds, approaching the nature of unstressed ĕ and ŏ; the only qualification allowed to this parallelism is that in post-tonic syllables ĭ assumed this open quality rather later than ŭ. ME ĭ in pretonic open syllables actually became identical with unstressed ĕ (e.g. in *begin*), and so also in post-tonic syllables before a non-palatal consonant (*penis* > *penes* > *pence*); ME ŭ did not occur in pretonic open syllables, but in post-tonic syllables before *s* it became identical with unstressed ŏ (*rightwis* > *rightwus* > *rightos*, ModE *righteous*). (*b*) ME ĕ and ŏ became, in unstressed syllables, raised sounds, respectively 'a middle sound between ĕ and ĭ' (which Luick denotes by *ė*) and 'a middle sound between ŏ and ŭ' (denoted *ȯ*), both in pretonic syllables (where ĕ occurred only in words from French and Latin, but ŏ in native words such as *together* as well as in words from French) and in post-tonic syllables, whether open or closed (except for ME ĕ in final position; see Note 1 below). But before *r*, whether in pretonic or post-tonic syllables, open or closed, unstressed ĕ and ŏ became open sounds, ę̆ and ǫ̆. Later (Luick seems always to assume in the ME period, and in this case presumably in the fifteenth century) this ę̆ before *r* became [ə]. (*c*) ME unstressed ă, to which there is no parallel, is assumed to have had the same quality in unstressed as in stressed syllables.

Luick's view seems unacceptable. In general, ModE developments of the unstressed vowels do not show any parallelism comparable to that of the stressed *long* vowels (the stressed *short* vowels do not exhibit any marked parallelism in ModE), and Luick's parallel system seems imposed on, rather than derived from, the evidence. With regard to the particular pairings, the following observations apply.

(*a*) ME ĭ and ŭ. PresE pronunciation does not support the view that there is any essential difference between the pronunciation of ĭ and ŭ in stressed and unstressed position in closed syllables (except in post-tonic syllables in which reduction to [ə] has occurred); the assumption that a specially open pronunciation is regularly used for ME ĭ in unstressed closed syllables receives no confirmation from present-day usage. PresE has many shades of the [ɪ] sound, and some speakers use lowered varieties which are of the nature of [e] in unstressed positions generally, but others make no distinction between stressed and unstressed [ɪ] (cf. Daniel Jones, §§ 260–4). The fifteenth-century *e* spellings for ME unstressed ĭ cited by Luick (e.g. *lyeng* 'lying', *hole* 'holy') are capable of other explanations than Luick's (that ME ĭ had been lowered to his *ė* sound): *lyeng* may be an inverted spelling dependent on the development of unstressed ĕ to ĭ (see below) or on the raising of stressed ĕ to ĭ before *ng*, and in any case -*eng* is used mainly after *i* (or *y*) to avoid spellings such as *liing* (*lying*); and *hole* 'holy' may be an inverted spelling on the model of *cite* 'city'. Similarly *penes* for *penis* 'pence' may be by reverse analogy from -*is* for original -*es*; and there seems no reason to assume (with Luick, § 471) that the reduction to *pence* proceeds rather from *penes* than *penis* (it certainly originates in the compounds *twopence*, &c.); in any case the spelling with *e* may represent a pronunciation with [əs], which can develop from -*is* (see below). The ME use of *o* to represent unstressed ŭ in post-tonic closed syllables is capable of other explanations than that unstressed ŭ had become a very open sound approximating to unstressed ŏ. Before *m* in *whilom*, &c. the use of *o* for ŭ is the common graphic substitution; *u* spellings occur in the fourteenth century, and the orthoepists (Hart, Bullokar, Robinson, Gil, and Hodges) regularly give ŭ in (*ac*)*custom, seldom, bosom, blossom, whilom*, &c. (cases in which ŏ is given being rare and either mechanical errors or due to the ModE confusion of both ŭ and ŏ in [ə]; see further § 302, Note 1 below). In *bullock*, &c. it is better to accept Jordan's view (§ 136 (1)) that OE ŭ became ŏ than Luick's (§ 440) that ŭ remained; *o* was not regularly substituted graphically for *u* before *k*, *ck* in ME spelling, and Bullokar gives ŏ in *bullock* and his own name. Luick argues (§ 460, Anm. 1) that the fact that in PresE in careful speech the second syllable of *wedlock* is distinct from that of *bishop, bullock*, &c., shows that original ME unstressed *ŏ* was in late ME 'no real *ŏ*'; but the distinction is rather to be explained from the survival in early ModE and in careful speech in PresE of the secondary stress appropriate to the second element of the obvious compound *wedlock*. There is no ground whatever for Luick's view that *rightwus* > *rightòs*; it clearly became *rightus*, in which the ending was identical with the suffix *-ous* < OF, so that the way was opened for the substitution of the suffix *-eous*.

It seems best to conclude that ME *ĭ* and *ŭ* in unstressed syllables were generally of the same quality as in stressed syllables until reduction to [ə] occurred (which was only rarely in the case of *ĭ*). But in two cases there does seem to have been a special development of ME unstressed *ĭ*. In post-tonic syllables before *r* it regularly became identical with ME *ĕ*; thus *leisir* > *leiser*, (*aventure* >) *auntyr* > *aunter* (see Note 3 below). In pretonic syllables unstressed *ĭ* commonly (but not regularly) became *ĕ* (*begin*, &c., *enough*), so that there resulted variation between *ĭ* and *ĕ* in this position. These two cases are further discussed below, §§ 294 and 300.

(*b*) ME *ĕ* and *ŏ*. Objection must be taken to Luick's view (accepted by Jordan, § 135) that ME unstressed *ĕ* was 'a middle sound between *ĕ* and *ĭ*' which still remains in PresE. The view that in PresE unstressed *ĕ* is 'a "raised" variety of (*e*) which approaches (i)' (*Introduction* to *SOD*, p. ix), which Luick accepts (and which indeed seems to be the prime reason for his theory), is an erroneous compromise between regard for the spelling and observation of the sound. In fact PresE does not distinguish ME unstressed *ĕ* and *ĭ*; both are pronounced with a variety of sounds (ranging from a not very close [e] to the lowered [ɪ] which is also used for ME stressed *ĭ*) which are all regarded as members of the [ɪ] phoneme. As there is no reason to suppose that in ME stressed *ĭ* was pronounced much differently from the PresE sound, one would expect that unstressed *ĕ*, if it had already developed in ME its present pronunciation (as Luick assumes), would have been regarded then as now as a member of the [ɪ] phoneme and have been freely spelt *i*. This is the case in the North, where, it is clear, the change of unstressed *ĕ* to some variety of [ɪ] sound and so to identity with unstressed *ĭ* occurred (like many other changes of pronunciation) very early; but the *e* and *i* spellings do not interchange freely in Southern ME. On the other hand, as Luick points out, there are some *i* spellings for unstressed *ĕ* in the fourteenth century in the South, and unstressed *ĕ* rhymes with ME *ĭ* occasionally (but far from freely) in late fourteenth-century Southern writers, e.g. Chaucer. Luick's explanation is that, except in pretonic open syllables, ME unstressed *ĕ* and *ĭ* were distinct (he hesitates somewhat on this point—see § 460, Anm. 1, end), but that the boundaries between the two sounds must have been fluid ('fließend'). But this seems contrary to principle: sounds are either distinct or identical. The idea that unstressed ĕ, being pronounced with a raised sound midway between ĕ and ĭ, might sometimes be heard as ĕ and sometimes as ĭ and so vary in spelling and rhyming (even in the same author), is contrary to the whole idea of the phoneme; any individual speech-sound is interpreted as a member of a group of sounds which are regarded as being for practical purposes identical, though in fact they may differ greatly, and it does not rest with individual speakers of a language to decide the groupings; specially trained or acute observers may become aware of distinctions not ordinarily noticed and may make corresponding distinctions in specially designed phonetic transcripts (cf. Daniel Jones's transcription (§ 263) of the style of PresE pronunciation in which ME unstressed ĕ and ĭ are regularly [e] not [ɪ]), but their observations have no influence on the generally accepted phonematic groupings or on the conventional spelling. 'A middle sound between ĕ and ĭ' would be assigned either to the ĕ or the ĭ phoneme and would accordingly be spelt either e or i, and it would not rest with individuals to decide which phoneme it belonged to and how to spell it. If variation in spelling occurs within a linguistic group, the explanation must be either that different spelling conventions are competing (which cannot be the case here, as there is in ME no need to hesitate how to represent ĕ and ĭ) or that different pronunciations are competing—not that there are competing interpretations of one and the same sound. Variation in rhyming must also show variation in pronunciation.

The solution to the difficulty seems to be discoverable from a consideration of the process whereby ME unstressed ĕ became ĭ in some forms of ME—in the North by 1300, in East Anglia also by 1300 (*Trinity College Homily* and *Havelok*; see Jordan, § 135, Anm. 1), in other Midland dialects during the fourteenth century. It is usually assumed (e.g. by Luick, § 460 (2a); Jordan, § 135; Ekwall, § 110) that the process was a direct raising of some form of [e] to [ɪ]—which is of course easy to parallel. But if this view is adopted it is necessary further to assume (as does Luick, § 597 (6), for some of the words involved) a different ModE process whereby ModE [ə] > [ɪ], for in ModE [ɪ] occurs not only in unstressed syllables which had ĕ in ME, but also in syllables which had ă and ŭ; moreover there are cases in which ModE [ɪ], though occurring in syllables which had ME ĕ, seems to develop by a ModE change (which must be from [ə] to [ɪ]) rather than a ME change (see further §§ 333-7 below). Against this theory of two distinct processes, a ME raising of unstressed [e] to [ɪ] and a ModE change of [ə] to [ɪ], it is much better to hold that there was only a single phonetic tendency, of [ə] to become [ɪ], which operated both in late ME and in ModE, and which, at various times or among various classes of speakers, was favoured by certain following consonants. It is in favour of this assumption that we find (*a*) that in those dialects (especially the Northern) which in ME itself show early *ĭ* for unstressed *ĕ* there is also evidence that unstressed *ĕ* had become [ə] by at latest 1300 (cf. especially the discussion of the development of syllabic consonants, §§ 318 seq. below); (*b*) that *ĭ* for unstressed *ĕ* appears towards the end of the fourteenth century in South Midland dialects, at about the same date as developments that presuppose [ə] for ME unstressed *ĕ*; and (*c*) that the evidence of Levins (who, for example, has regularly [ɪl] < [əl] < syllabic [l] < ME -*le*) shows that the 'ModE' change of [ə] to [ɪ], like ME *ĭ* < original ME unstressed *ĕ*, was common and early in Northern dialects. On this view ModE unstressed [ɪ] and its lowered variants would not, as Luick assumes, be an unchanged survival of the later ME pronunciation of unstressed *ĕ*; it would in all cases (including those in which it represents ME unstressed *ĕ*) develop directly from [ə], of which ME unstressed *ĕ* is only one source. But as *i* spellings occur earlier for ME unstressed *ĕ* than for unstressed *ă* and *ŭ*, it would appear that ME unstressed *ĕ* began to change to [ə] earlier than these vowels; this conclusion would be consistent with the evidence on related developments, for example syllabic consonants. We thus reach the position that ME unstressed *ĕ* during the ME period itself became [ə], and that this [ə] then tended, both in later ME and in ModE, to become [ɪ]. See further Notes 4–6 below.

Before *r* Luick assumes that ME unstressed *ĕ* was an open sound, *ę̆*. His reason is that when, in verse, a stress is placed on the suffix of such words as *fishere* they can be rhymed with words with ME *ę̄*. But the argument cannot be allowed; such stressing of the suffix (whether purely artificial or due, as seems to me more likely, to hesitancy caused by the conflict between the English and French stress-systems in 'literary' ME) would have as its immediate result the substitution of stressed *ę̆*, which was always in ME an open sound, for unstressed *ĕ*; and the rhymes with ME *ę̄* (whether exact rhymes showing lengthening in the open syllable as a secondary consequence of the shifted stress, or inexact rhymes of short and long) are no evidence for the quality of unstressed ME *ĕ*. It seems unlikely that unstressed *ĕ* before *r* was differentiated from unstressed *ĕ* in other positions at any period of ME; by later ME it had become [ə] by a change which affected unstressed *ĕ* in all positions and which the evidence does not suggest was either accelerated or retarded by the influence of the *r*.

As for ME unstressed *ŏ*, there is no evidence at all which enables us to decide its late ME pronunciation; Luick's view is based merely on the supposed parallel of unstressed *ĕ*, and must therefore fall with his theory of the ME development of the latter. There is in fact no parallel development, and in the absence of any other arguments in favour of Luick's assumption it is safer to take it that unstressed *ŏ* was in ME not essentially different from stressed *ŏ*. This is true even of unstressed *ŏ* in pretonic open syllables; early ModE pronunciations of *together* (see § 290 above) are to be explained from the influence of the preposition *to*, and not as showing a ME change of pretonic $\ostrokeshort$ to [u]. Before *r* ME $\ostrokeshort$ was not distinct from $\ostrokeshort$ in other positions in stressed syllables, and there seems no reason to assume that there was any distinction in unstressed syllables; in ModE unstressed $\ostrokeshort$ before *r* has the same development as in other positions, i.e. it becomes [ə].

(*c*) ME $\abreve$ may be assumed, with Luick, to have had the same pronunciation in unstressed as in stressed syllables in ME.

Note 1: ME $\ebreve$ in final position, according to Luick, became (probably early) a murmur-vowel distinct from the sound used in closed syllables. It may be accepted that final ME $\ebreve$ was [ə], at least in the later ME period; the sound was probably a central vowel with relatively high tongue-position, and must originally have developed from an earlier tense vowel, to which it would appear to have been in some measure related. The following considerations, though inconclusive, support this assumption: (*a*) OF *é*, in some early adoptions, was identified, when it lost stress, with ME final $\ebreve$; (*b*) OF final unstressed *e* ('feminine' *e*), which itself had an affinity with OF *é* (cf. Pope, § 275), is identified with ME final $\ebreve$.

Note 2: The account given above is of Luick's view of southern English. He recognizes, of course, that in the North ME unstressed $\ebreve$ became $\ibreve$ (see further below), and in the NW Midlands a sound spelt *u*, which he interprets as meaning an obscurer sound which probably had a certain lip-rounding. Wyld, *Coll. Eng.*, p. 261, interprets the Western *u* spelling as meaning [ə], and may well be right; if so, and if the argument set forth above is correct, there was no difference in pronunciation, but only in spelling-convention, between the NW Midlands and the East. On the geographical distribution of the *u* spellings see Jordan, § 135, Anm. 1.

Note 3: *OED* records *er* spellings for *leisir* 'leisure' from the early fourteenth century. It is not clear whether the identity of ME $\ibreve r$ and $\ebreve r$ results from their both becoming [ər] by a direct change (which is by no means impossible), or from a lowering of $\ibreve$ to $\ebreve$ before *r* followed by the change of $\ebreve$ to [ə], as Luick assumes. If ME unstressed $\ebreve$ had been [ə] from an early period in ME we should have to assume that unstressed $\ibreve$ became identical with unstressed $\ebreve$ by virtue of a direct change to [ə].

Note 4: It should be observed that the change from [ə] to [ɪ] is comparatively slight; even the lowest variety of PresE [ə] has a tongue-position rather higher than that of 'cardinal' open [ɛ] (see Daniel Jones, § 335 seq.), and though [ə] is of course a central vowel, PresE short open [ɪ] is also articulated with the tongue some way retracted from a front towards a central position (cf. Daniel Jones, § 254).

Note 5: Ekwall, § 110, treats the change of unstressed $\ebreve$ to [ɪ] as though it were altogether a ModE change; but clearly it is not.

Note 6: It might well be argued that unstressed $\ebreve$ was pronounced [ə] from late OE onwards; this would account for the fact that the OE unstressed back vowels, when reduced at the end of the OE period, became identical with OE unstressed $\ebreve$. But such an argument is irrelevant to my purpose.

VARIATIONS IN PRONUNCIATION ARISING IN ME

(1) *Variation between ME $\ebreve$ and ME $\ibreve$ for original pretonic $\ibreve$*

§ 294. As remarked above (§ 293(*a*)), ME $\ibreve$ in pretonic open syllables tended in later ME to become $\ebreve$, but the change was not regularly carried through, and in consequence late ME and early ModE show variation between ME $\ibreve$ (retained) and ME $\ebreve$. On the nature of the phonetic process see Note 3 below. The orthoepists' evidence shows that $\ibreve$, despite the conventional ModE spelling with *e*, was the more common variant. The prefix *be-* has ME ĭ in Hart (in *because* and six other words; *before* and *begin* vary), Bullokar (in *because*), Robinson (once in *before*), Gil (about sixty times), and Hodges; it has ME ĕ in Smith, Hart (*becomes* and eight other words), Robinson (once in *begot*), and Gil (twelve times). *Enough* has ME ĭ in Bullokar, Gil, and Hodges. *Iwis* has ME ĭ (beside artificial [əi]) in Smith. On other forms given by the orthoepists see Notes 1 and 2.

Note 1: The prefix *be-* has [i:], as if < ME ẹ̄, in Bullokar (except in *because*, in which there is probably association with the preposition *by*, as is etymologically correct) and five times in Gil. Hodges's symbol may mean either [ɪ] or [i:], but the former seems more likely. The [i:] variant is doubtless due to ModE reimposition of secondary stress (probably when the pronunciation was considered syllable by syllable rather than in ordinary speech), and consequent lengthening of [ɪ] < ME ĭ to [i:]; but formal association with the verb *be* may have played a part.

Note 2: The prefix *be-* (with the two exceptions noted above) and the word *enough* have frequent ē (as if < ME ẹ̄) in Robinson. Hodges once gives ME ẹ̄ in *besiege*, but it is probably an error due to the use of the wrong diacritic. Robinson's transcriptions could be taken as showing confusion between a short tense [e] by lowering of unstressed [ɪ] and a long tense [e:] < ME ẹ̄, but it seems more likely that there has been an artificial reimposition, in ModE, of secondary stress and a consequent lengthening of ME ĕ to the equivalent of ME ẹ̄. In the case of *enough* there is probably also some association with the Latin prefix *e-*. See further Note 3.

Note 3: Since we have seen reason to suppose that ME ĕ was [ə] by later ME, the most natural explanation of the development of pretonic ME ĭ to identity with ME ĕ would be, not lowering of [ɪ] to [e] and a subsequent change to [ə], but a direct change of [ɪ] to [ə]. This change does occur in post-tonic syllables (see § 303 below), but not in good speech except (in PresE) in such cases as the penultimate *i* of *ability*, which occurs in an open syllable before a syllable with greater stress and is therefore closely comparable with the pretonic ME ĭ of *become*, *enough*, &c. If, as this argument makes probable, the late ME and ModE *e-*spellings and the orthoepists' *ĕ*-transcriptions represent the PresE pronunciation with [ə], then Robinson's forms with *ē* show not merely an artificial lengthening, but a substitution of a vowel typical of a stressed syllable for the [ə] of an unstressed syllable. His forms do indeed strongly suggest that he has argued from the analogy of Latin prefixes containing *ē*; for his evidence on these prefixes see § 288 above.

Note 4: For variation between late ME unstressed ĭ and ĕ (i.e. [ɪ] and [ə]) for original ME unstressed ĕ see § 334 below.

(2) *Variation between late ME ou and ŭ from ME -we*

§ 295. In words such as *folwe(n)* 'follow' there were variant developments in ME: either a glide-vowel *o* developed before the *w*, which then vocalized to [u], giving the diphthong *ou*; or the *w*, after final ĕ had become silent in late ME, vocalized to [u], which was identified with ME ŭ. PresE has regularly [o(:)] < ME *ou*, but formerly [ʊ] (or, by reduction, [ə]) < ME ŭ was common in *follow*, *narrow*, *sparrow*, *borrow*, *morrow*, *yellow*, &c. ME *ou* (or sounds developed from it) is shown by Hart (who has *boro*, &c. with [o] < [o:] < *ou* and *felō* with [o:] < *ou*; in all six forms < ME *ou*, against more than twice as many < ME ŭ), Laneham (*folo*, &c., but also ŭ), Bullokar, Robinson, Gil (who has both [ou] and [o:] < ME *ou*), Butler,

Hodges, Newton, Lye, Lodwick, Cocker, Brown, and the shorthand-writers T. Shelton, Everardt, Bridges, Heath, and Hopkins. The pronunciations [ʊ] and [uː] (by lengthening of [ʊ]) < ME *ŭ* are shown by Salesbury, Hart (commonly), Laneham (*yelloo* 'yellow'), Mulcaster, Jonson (apparently; he says *o* loses its sound in *willow* and *billow*), Howell (1662), Price, Richardson, and *WSC-RS*. Gil gives *fula*, in which the *a* must represent [ə] (probably < ME *ŭ*) as a Northern form of *follow*. In the seventeenth century these words also had pronunciations with [ə] and perhaps with [ɪ] (see Note 2 and § 302 below), which are likely to be derived from the ME *ŭ* rather than the ME *ou* variant.

Note 1: Smith gives the digraph *ou*, which ought to mean [ʌu], in *yarrow* and *yellow*; the transcription must be an error. Hart also has *ou*, which would normally mean [ʌu], in *boroued* 'borrowed', but the explanation seems to be that in this word the *u* stands for [w] (see § 280 above). There seems to be no sufficient reason to accept Smith's and Hart's transcriptions at their face value as showing [ʌu], which could only be developed if late ME *ŭ* < *w* were lengthened to *ū* before the diphthongization of ME *ū*.

Note 2: 'Homophone lists' pair *marrow* with *marry* (Fox and Hookes), *hollow* with *holly* (Wharton), and *gallows* with *galleys* (Young, Brown). Of these, *marrow* is a special case, since it has -*i* forms from the early thirteenth century (*Ste. Iuliene*) to the sixteenth (see *OED*); the normal OE *o*-stem noun with guttural *g* must have been blended with a *jo*-stem noun (Angl. *merg) with palatal *g*, whence ME *i*. The other two pairings seem to depend on a development now dialectal (Wright, *EDG*, § 229, and Index, s.v. *follow*, records final [ɪ] in Scottish and South-western dialects, including that of Berkshire) which was apparently to be heard in vulgar London speech in the seventeenth century, to judge from these 'homophone' lists. *OED* records *gallies* 'gallows' in the sixteenth century (from the *Thesaurus* of Cooper, a native of Oxford). In this development [ɪ] appears to be from late ME *ŭ* < *w*; the phonetic process might be [ʊ] > [y] > [ɪ], or [ʊ] > [ə] > [ɪ]. As both the stages [ʊ] > [ə] and [ə] > [ɪ] are common features of the ModE changes in unstressed syllables, the latter process, though at first sight the less direct, is the more likely.

REDUCTION OF THE ME UNSTRESSED SHORT VOWELS TO [ə]

§ 296. Direct evidence of the reduction of the ME unstressed short vowels to [ə] is infrequent, in comparison not only with what was possible, but also with the amount of evidence the orthoepists give of some changes (notably the development of syllabic consonants) which are secondary consequences of the change to [ə]. The identity of the vowel [ə] is indeed not recognized by any orthoepist before Wallis, and even he, surprisingly, says that it is a sound almost unknown among the English, except when (stressed) short *e* precedes *r*; his failure to consider unstressed syllables is typical. There are a few, but only a few, comparisons of English unstressed *ĕ* with foreign [ə] sounds. In the earlier orthoepists there are occasional confusions which suggest that the various ME unstressed vowels were often all [ə], and in the later seventeenth-century writers there is a frequent explicit or implicit identification of unstressed vowels with unrounded *ŭ*, i.e. of [ə] with [ʌ].

In setting out such evidence as there is, I distinguish cases in which the various vowels are followed by *r* (other than intervocalic *r*) from those in which they are not. But except in the case of ME unstressed *ĭ* (which regularly becomes [ə] before an *r* which forms part of the same syllable, and only irregularly otherwise), the development to [ə] seems to have been neither earlier nor more regular before *r*; the reason would seem to be that the tendency for reduction to [ə] is as early as (if not earlier than) the lowering influence of *r*, which does not cause the stressed short vowels *ĭ*, *ĕ*, and *ŭ* to change to [ə] before the fifteenth century at earliest (see § 212 seq.).

Note: ME unstressed *ĭ* is not influenced by a following intervocalic *r*.

(1) *Before* r (*other than intervocalic* r)

(*a*) *ME ĕ*

§ 297. Reduction of ME *ĕ* to [ə] before *r* is shown by the use of *y* in MS H (*c.* 1610) of the *Welsh Hymn* to transcribe *e* in *father* and *mother*. Salesbury gives [ə] in *paper* (see § 301 below). Hart does not distinguish unstressed *ĕ* before *r* from stressed *ĕ*; but his *ŏ* in *acorns* suggests that both *ĕ* and *ŏ* are [ə] before *r*, and his syllabic [r̩] < unstressed *-ĕr* presupposes an [ər] stage. Bullokar clearly used [ər] for ME *ĕr* (unstressed), for he confuses the suffixes *-er*, *-or*, and *-our* (i.e. *-ŭr*), and uses his 'half-vowel' *r* to represent both ME unstressed *ĕr* and the combination [ə]-glide plus *r* (e.g. in *fire*). Waad (see Vol. I, p. 130) gives *Mistur* for 'Mr.' Robinson transcribes unstressed *ĕr* by *ŭr* in two words (see Vol. I, p. 209), but otherwise follows the conventional spelling. Gil uses *ĕ* as the symbol for the reduced vowel from ME *ŭ* in *oner* 'honour'. Hodges marks unstressed *ĕ* before *r* with a diacritic of which the effect is to identify the sound with unrounded ME *ŭ*, but does not always use it; thus in *differ* the diacritic is used twice but not in a third occurrence of the word. (Unstressed *ĕ* in other positions is left unmarked, i.e. is not distinguished from stressed ME *ĕ*, so that Hodges makes a distinction between unstressed *ĕ* before *r* and in other positions; but this distinction seems invalid.) Hodges also identifies unstressed *ĕr* and *ŭr* by pairing, e.g., *saver* with *savour*, *ranker* with *rancour*. Howell (1662) says that *e* 'passeth obscurely' in *coffer* (and in *spoken*, *broken*, *brewes*). Hunt, Coles, Strong, Young, Cooper, and *WSC-RS* identify unstressed *ĕr* with unstressed *ŭr*, and the 'homophone lists' from Hodges onwards have pairings that depend on [ər] for ME *ĕr*. It is further to be observed that all orthoepists (from Cheke, Levins, and Hart onwards) who show a glide-[ə] before *r* (see § 218) identify it implicitly with ME unstressed *ĕ* before *r*, which must therefore also have been [ə].

(*b*) *ME ŭ*

§ 298. Reduction of ME *ŭ* to [ə] before *r* is implied by the identifications of ME unstressed *ĕr* with *ŭr* (see immediately above) and of ME unstressed

§ 298]   EARLY CHANGES OF QUALITY   869

ĭr with *ŭr* (see § 300 below). It is also shown, for example, by Laneham's *cooller* 'colour' and *Saterday* 'Saturday', by Hart's *labr* 'labour' (*Methode*), Bullokar's *ĕr* in *colour*, Gil's *ĕr* in *colour* (thrice, against *ŏr* once) and in *scissors*, Strong and Young's *humer* 'humour' and *horrer* 'horror', Strong's *favar* 'favour', and 'homophone list' pairings of unstressed *ŭr* with *ĕr* from Hodges onwards.

(c) ME ă *and* ŏ

§ 299. Reduction of unstressed *ăr* and *ŏr* to [ər] is shown chiefly by the use of *ar* or *or* as spellings of [ər] < ME *ĕr*, *ŭr*, and *ĭr*. Laneham has *currars* 'couriers', Hart *ĕr* in the first syllable of *particular* (i.e. *ĕr* is used to transcribe [ər] < ME *ăr*), Bullokar *lubbar* (which has originally ME *ĕr*) and conversely *ĕr* in *collar*, Robinson *ăr* in *traveller* (altered from *-er* to conform with Barnfield's spelling) but *ĕr* (which is etymologically correct) in *skoler* 'scholar', Gil *skolar* (but he says it is really pronounced *skoler*) beside *musterd*, Strong *favar* 'favour', and Young *familyur* (1722 edition). Cooper says that *ar* is pronounced *ur* in *pillar*, *vulgar*, &c., and also commonly in *scholar* (the partial exception is surprising, especially as the word has ME *ĕr*, but it has doubtless been in part remodelled after Latin); *WSC-RS* follows, giving as examples *auricular*, &c., *scholar*, *custard*, *mustard*, *bustard*. The 'homophone lists' pair *altar* with *alter* (Hodges onwards), *collar* with *choler* and *collier* (Wharton onwards). Reduction of *ŏr* to [ər] is shown by Cheke's *leisor* 'leisure' (ME *ĭr*), by Levins's impartial placing of *stubborn* (ME *ŭr*?) in both his *ŏ* and *ŭ* lists (with appropriate variation of spelling), by Hart's variation between *-ĕr* and *-ŏr* in *correctors* and *inventors* (but there may be really two formations, in *-er* and *-or*) and his *ŏ* in *acorn* (ME *ĕ*), by Bullokar's complete confusion of the suffixes *-er* and *-or* and his variation between *-ŏr* and *-ŭr* in *soldier*, by Waad's transcription of *Oxford* with *ŭr*, and by Gil's statement that *onor* 'honour' is really pronounced *oner*, his *ŏr* (once) beside *ĕr* (thrice) in *colour* (ME *ŭr*, but there may be re-formation after Latin), and his *-ŏr* in *endeavour* (ME *ĕr*, but there may be suffix-substitution). It is more directly shown by Hodges, who identifies with stressed [ʌ] < ME *ŭ* the *o* of *comfort* (and of *liquor* and *stubborn*); by Hunt, who says that *-or* is 'commonly' pronounced *-ur*; by Coles, who gives the 'phonetic spelling' *cumfurt* 'comfort'; by Strong, who follows Coles and adds *Bangger* 'Bangor' and is in turn followed by Young; by Lodwick, who writes *o* as *ŭ* in *forgive*; by Cooper, who says *-or* is pronounced *-ur*; and by *WSC-RS*, in which *eo* in *meteor* is said to be pronounced *ye*. The sources which use the suffix *-or* in preference to *-our*, or say that *-our* is pronounced *-or* (see § 292 above), probably as a rule used [ər]; in *WSC-RS* it is laid down clearly that *-or* is variable at will with *-our*, and that both are pronounced *-ur*. The 'homophone lists' from Hodges onwards pair *censor* with *censer*; Wharton and Strong pair *discomfort(ed)* with *discomfit(ed)*; Coles (*Eng.–Lat. Dict.*) and Young pair *exercise* with *exorcise*.

(d) ME ĭ

§ 300. In almost all words which have ME ĭ before *r* it develops from OF [y] and the conventional spelling is -*ure*, and in others with original -*ĭr* there developed an analogical variant in -*ure*; the reduction of ĭr to [ər] is therefore generally shown in the orthoepists by statements that in such words -*ure* is pronounced -*ur*, or by transcriptions with ŭr. Such statements and transcriptions are found from Laneham and Bullokar onwards (see § 282 above). Cheke uses the spelling *leisor* 'leisure', which equally shows [ər]. Cooper, followed by *WSC-RS*, says that -*yr* in *satyr* is pronounced -*ur*.

Note: OED records -*ur* spellings of *pleasure* from the early fifteenth century; also fifteenth-century -*our* spellings.

(2) *In free position*

(a) ME ĕ

§ 301. Reduction to [ə] of ME unstressed ĕ in free position had already occurred before late ME (see § 293 (*b*) above), but there is comparatively little evidence of it in the orthoepists, except in such words as show the further development of syllabic consonants. In some words adopted from French or Latin secondary stress may have preserved [e], but in most it is to be assumed that unstressed ĕ was [ə] and that the orthoepists were inaccurate in not distinguishing it. The use of *y* in MS H of the *Welsh Hymn* to transcribe the vowel of the second syllable of *maiden* means [ə], but this manuscript is dated *c.* 1610. Salesbury says that unstressed ĕ is pronounced 'obscurely, or as our [Welsh] *y*', meaning [ə], and gives transcriptions with Welsh *y* for unstressed ĕ in *ditches, oranges, trees* (which is disyllabic), *double,* and *paper*; he has *i* for unstressed *e* in *ginger*, and *e* in *faces, honest,* and *velvet*, all of which are probably mere errors of transcription. Bullokar gives ŏ in *emot* (which has ME ĕ); ŏ and ĕ have been confused as [ə]. Sanford (1604) and Cotgrave (1611) identify with French feminine *e* the English *e* in *is he come* and in the second syllable of the Latin *facere* (pronounced of course in the English fashion). Tonkis (1612) says that the possessive singular ends in -*us* (beside two cases with -*is*), obviously meaning [əs]. Robinson has *elafant* 'elephant', *kurant* 'current', and *suvraneiz* 'sovereignize' (which has ME ĕ in the penult < ME *ai*; cf. his own *suvren* 'sovereign'). Gil gives ŏ in *wagon* (Du *wagen*) and ă in *villain* (ME ĕ < *ai*). On Howell (1662) see § 297 above. Price, Cooper, Lye, *WSC-RS*, and Cocker say of *parliament* (ME *parlement*) merely that the *i* is silent; clearly ĕ and ă are confused as [ə]. Coles gives *alevn* as a 'phonetic spelling' of *eleven*; so Strong and Young. Young has *conshunce*, and Lye, followed by

WSC-RS, says that *-en* is pronounced *-un*. The 'homophone lists' pair *essays* and *assays* (Wharton), *pallet* and *palate* (Hunt, Ellis, Young, and Cooper 'near alike'). Reduction of ME unstressed *ĕ* to [ə] is also shown by the frequent use of *ĕ* as a symbol for [ə] developed from the other ME unstressed vowels (see below).

(b) ME back vowels

§ 302. The unstressed back vowels seem not to have been reduced to [ə] as early as ME *ĕ*, but the evidence cited by Wyld, *Coll. Eng.*, pp. 273–5, 278, shows that reduction had occurred by the middle of the fifteenth century, and it may well have been earlier. Again the orthoepists do not provide plentiful evidence, but there is enough to show that [ə] must have been the normal pronunciation.

ME *ŭ* is transcribed by Welsh *y* (indicating [ə]) by Salesbury in *season*. Bullokar shows that unstressed *ŭ* is [ə] by his spelling *savery* 'savoury' and his statement that the 'half-vowels' *l*, *n*, and *m* sound as *ul*, *un*, and *um* (which can only mean [əl], [ən], and [əm]). Gil says that he writes *person*, though the word is really pronounced *persn*, because in *personality* the *o* 'does not yet vanish', and has *rankerus* 'rancorous'. Jonson says that *o* 'loses its sound' in *person* and *action*, *WSC-RS* that *eo* is pronounced *ye* (i.e. [jə]) in *scutcheon*. The use of *u* as a symbol for [ə] developed from other unstressed vowels (e.g. by Coles, Strong, and Young in their 'phonetically spelt' lists; see also § 301 above) implies that ME unstressed *ŭ* has also become [ə]. Further evidences are the development of syllabic [n̩] < ME *un*, which is shown, for example, by Hart and Bullokar in *capon*, and occasional errors of transcription in which ME *ŭ* is falsely given as *ŏ* because of the influence of the traditional orthography; such spellings occur in Hart (in *second*, beside *ŭ*, and in *reason(able)* and *common*), Bullokar (in *bosom*, beside *ŭ*; but the *ŏ* form may be due merely to accidental omission of a diacritic), Robinson (in *common*), Gil (in *second*, *common*, *accustom*, and in *Abington* (1621, not 1619); cf. also *person* above), Hodges (in *second*; cf. *ŏ* twice beside *ŭ* twice in *Gifford*), and Strong (in *salmon*, but Young has *ŭ*). But on the other hand it is to be observed that in the great majority of cases ME unstressed *ŭ* is transcribed *ŭ* by the orthoepists, despite the traditional spelling with *o*; this seems to show that pronunciations in which unstressed *ŭ* and *ŏ* were not confused in [ə] still existed, i.e. pronunciations in which [ʊ] or [ʌ] for ME unstressed *ŭ* was preserved by some form of secondary stress.

A special case of the reduction to [ə] of ME unstressed *ŭ* occurs in such words as *arrow*, *follow*, &c., which have a ME variant in *-ŭ* (see § 295 above). Gil doubtless shows [ə] from this *ŭ* when he says that in the Northern dialects *follow* is pronounced *fula*. *WSC-RS* says that in *arrow*, *pillow*, &c. *ow* is pronounced like '*oo* or *u* obscure'; by *oo* is meant [u(:)], and by '*u* obscure' [ʌ] or [ə]—in this case clearly the latter. Otherwise the development is shown only in the 'homophone' and 'phonetically spelt' lists: *arrows* is paired with *arras* by Hodges ('near alike') and Young, *window* with *winder* by Fox and Hookes (but this probably rests on the analogical *windo(o)r(e)* form), and *pillows* with *pillars* by Fox and Hookes. Strong, Young, and Cocker give *gallus*, Brown *gallos*, as a 'phonetic spelling' for *gallows*; the first form certainly, and the latter probably, shows [ə]. The nature of the sources shows clearly that [ə] for -*ŭ* in these words was in the seventeenth century a vulgarism; the reason is probably that in them [u] developed from -*w* later than the change of original ME unstressed *ŭ* to [ə], and the seventeenth-century [ə] is the result of a second (ModE) process of reduction.

Reduction to [ə] of ME *ŏ* is shown by Levins's rhyme of *riot* with *quiet*, by Hodges in the second syllables of *purpose* and *historiographer* (see Vol. I, p. 183), by Coles's *Jerum* 'Jerome' and *issup* 'hyssop' (followed by Young), Strong's *Ling-cun* 'Lincoln' (ME *ŏ*?) (followed by Young), Young's *dimund* 'diamond' (if it has [ə] < ME *ŏ* < ME *au*; but [ə] is probably < ME *ă*), and by the 'homophone' list pairing of *society* with *satiety* (Price). It is more often shown by the use of *o* to transcribe [ə] derived from the other ME unstressed vowels, notably *ŭ* (see above), but also *ĕ* and *ă*.

Reduction to [ə] of ME *ă* is shown by Hart's *emong(st)*, *Nikles* 'Nicholas', and *palet* 'palate', by Laneham's *terres* 'terrace' and *obrayds* 'abraids', by Bullokar's *seperated*, Robinson's *avereīs* 'avarice' (twice, against *avareīs* once), Waad's *tAmuz* 'Thomas', Hodges's *inseperable*, Newton's *e*- in *again*, Coles's *Crismus* 'Christmas', *Miclmus* 'Michaelmas', *wummun* 'woman' and *yemmun* 'yeoman' (followed by Strong and Young), Strong's *assoshot* 'associate', Cooper's statement that *pageant* has, in the second syllable, '*e* short', and by the 'homophone list' pairings *assays* : *essays* (Wharton), *satiety* : *society* (Price), and *palate* : *pallet* (Ellis, Young, Cooper 'near alike'). The reduction is also shown by the use of *ă* to represent [ə] developed from the other ME unstressed vowels. On the other hand Hodges uses a special diacritic to show that *e* in *Laurence* is pronounced *ă*, so he must—at least in this word—have been able to distinguish *ĕ* from *ă* (by virtue, no doubt, of secondary stress); and similarly *WSC-RS* says that *except* for *accept* is a vulgarism.

Note 1: The occurrence of transcriptions with *ŏ* as well as with *ŭ* for ME unstressed *ŭ* should not be used as evidence for Luick's assumption that ME unstressed *ŭ* was a lowered sound between [u] and [o], since it is not the case that the orthoepists give indifferently *ŭ* or *ŏ*; *ŭ* is the normal transcription, *ŏ* is exceptional and occurs only in words which are traditionally spelt with *o* and in which it is probable that no vowel at all (but instead syllabic [n̩] or [m̩]) was ordinarily used (cf. Gil's comment on *person*, and Hart and Bullokar's syllabic [n̩] in *capon*).

Note 2: *Seldom* (ME *selden*, analogically reformed after *whilom*) has *ŭm* in Hart, Bullokar, and Hodges.

Note 3: Hodges identifies *o* in *uttermost* with [ʌ], which must mean it is [ə]; Kauter regards the transcription as erroneous, but cf. the sixteenth-century spelling *uttirmuste* recorded by *OED*. It is possible that in this word [ə] develops from ME *ĕ* in the original suffix *-mest* (which is still evidenced in the fifteenth century; see *OED*).

(c) ME ĭ

§ 303. When not followed by an *r* which forms part of the same syllable, ME unstressed *ĭ* is not regularly reduced to [ə]; indeed in PresE it is normally preserved, and it need not be doubted that this has in general been true of StE throughout the modern period. But present StE commonly has [ə] in certain cases, and [ə] < ME unstressed *ĭ* is frequent in Australian English, in the English dialects, and in vulgar speech, and there is corresponding evidence of [ə] in the sixteenth and seventeenth centuries.

Some words (e.g. *garden*) which show an early change of original unstressed *ĭ* to (in spelling) *e*–which must mean [ə]–are regularly given with *ĕ* by the orthoepists. The 'homophone list' pairing of *garden* with *guardian* depends on ME *ĕ* < *ei* in the latter. Similarly *curtain* (ME *ĭ*) is given with *-en* in Strong and Young's 'phonetically spelt' lists; Gil gives *ai*, which may show a genuine analogical pronunciation with ME *ai*, but may disguise a pronunciation with [ən]. In words which normally remain spelt with *i* the reduction to [ə] is shown by Hart's *medesin* 'medicine', Bullokar's *femenin* 'feminine', Robinson's *determened* 'determined' and *sivel* 'civil', Gil's *ĕ* (once, beside *ĭ* twice) in the second syllable of *destiny* and his *laberinths* 'labyrinths', and Strong and Young's 'phonetic spellings' *vardet* 'verdict', *varjus* (*varjes*) 'verjuice' (ME *ĭ* < OF [y]), and *medsun* 'medicine'. Cooper's English text says that *terrable* 'terrible', *possable* 'possible', and *scrupelous* 'scrupulous' (ME *ĭ* < OF [y]) are 'barbarous speaking', his Latin text that they are 'facilitatis causa'; both texts condemn as 'barbarous' *yeusary* 'usury' (ME *ĭ* < OF [y]). In *possible* and *terrible* there has been confusion of the suffixes *-ible* and *-able* in consequence of both unstressed *ĭ* and *ă* becoming [ə]; *OED* records *-able* in both words in the sixteenth century. WSC-RS, following Cooper, says that *impossable* and *terrable* are vulgarisms. WSC says further that in *gossip* the *i* is pronounced *u*, RS that it is 'obscure'; both mean [ə] (which they do not condemn). Reduction of unstressed *ĭ* to [ə] is shown by the 'homophone list' pairing *discomfit(ed)* : *discomfort(ed)* (Wharton, Strong), and perhaps by *president* : *precedent* (Coles, *Eng.–Lat. Dict.*). But *Surrey* : *sirra* (Hodges 'near alike') depends on the form *surry* (later *sirree*) of the latter, and *Barbary* : *Barbara* (Fox and Hookes, Strong, Young, Cocker, and Brown) on a variant of the Christian name.

It is observable that sources which reflect better speech show the reduction to [ə] only in circumstances in which it is admissible in present StE, i.e. (*a*) in penultimate open syllables that follow immediately the main stress and precede a secondary stress (e.g. [ə] is common in present StE in the penultimate syllable of *ability*), and (*b*) before *n* and *l* (i.e. where syllabic [ṇ] and [ḷ] can develop). The vulgar nature of the reduction in certain other cases is made clear by the evidence.

Note 1: Hart has *verelei* 'verily', but this represents a variant with ME *ē* < ME *ai* which is more regularly developed than that with *ī*.

Note 2: On the development of ME *ī* in pretonic open syllables see § 294 above. When not retained as [ɪ] it probably makes a direct change to [ə] by what appears to be the same process as that discussed here (see further loc. cit., Note 3); the only difference is that in pretonic position the change is more common in good speech than in post-tonic position.

SYNCOPE

§ 304. Syncope of unstressed vowels is a process that occurs at all stages of the history of English, and in Middle English and early Modern English it seems to occur in much the same circumstances. No attempt is made in the discussion which follows to distinguish cases in which the syncope dates from ME from those in which it occurs in early ModE; in many, and perhaps in most, it is in fact ME.

IN WORDS OF TWO SYLLABLES

§ 305. Syncope of the unstressed vowel of a disyllable is shown only in *Alice*, said to be pronounced *Al'ce* by Coles (*Schoolmaster*) and Brown (after Coles) and rhymed by Poole with words in [ls] and [lz].

IN MEDIAL UNSTRESSED SYLLABLES OF WORDS OF MORE THAN TWO SYLLABLES

(1) *Words with two syllables after the main stress*

§ 306. Syncope in such words is common; perhaps largely by accident, the orthoepists show it especially before the consonants *r*, *n*, and *s*, but also in other cases. Before *r* it is shown in *every* by Hart (thrice, against retained *e* thrice), Robinson (six times, against retained *e* twice), Gil (twice, against retained *e* five times, in addition to the entry '*ev'rj* pro *everj*'); in *watery* by Robinson; in *battery* by Gil; in *mystery* by the shorthand-writer Folkingham; in *century* and *centaury* by the 'homophone lists' of Young, Cocker, and Brown, which equate the words with *sentry*; also in *emperor* by Hart (once, against retained *e* twice), in *several* by Robinson (twice, against retained *e* once), in *sovereign* adj. by Robinson (but not in the sb.; see below), and in *furtherance* by Hodges (once, against retained *e* twice). Before *n* syncope is shown by Bullokar in *covenant*, by Robinson in *poisonous*, by Gil in *business*, *evening*, and *prisoner*, by Wharton in *summoner*, by Price in *scrivener*, by Coles (followed by Strong and Young) in *personal*, and by Cooper (followed by Cocker) in *falconer*. Before [s] or [z] it is shown in *medicine* by Laneham, Bullokar, Wharton, Brooksbank, Price, J. Smith, Coles, Strong, Young, Cooper, *WSC-RS*, Cocker, Brown, and the shorthand-writer Bridges; in *damosel* by Brooksbank, Price, Coles, Strong, Young, Lye, Cooper, *The Compendious School-Master*, and Cocker; in *venison* by Price, Coles, Strong, Young, Lye, *WSC-RS*, Cocker, and Brown; and in *Wednesday* (pronounced *Wens-*) by Brown. The specially favourable circumstances account for the syncope in *Worcester* (shown by Hodges, Lye, and the shorthand-writer Everardt), *Leicester* (shown by Hodges, Coles, and Everardt), and *Gloucester* (shown by Strong, Young, Lye, and the shorthand-writers J. Willis and Everardt). Before other consonants syncope is shown in *enemies* (Cheke), *Nicholas* (Hart), *captain* and *crocodiles* (Robinson), *chancellor* (Gil), *judgement* (regularly; so Gil and Hodges), *regiment* (Coles), *scrupulous* (Brown), *Exeter* (Everardt), *excellent* (Folkingham, a shorthand-writer), and *homily* (paired with *homely* in Hodges's 'near alike' list).

Failure of syncope is shown (in addition to the cases noted in the previous paragraph where the one orthoepist sometimes shows and sometimes lacks it) by Hart in *medicine*, Bullokar in *Leicester*, Gil in *courtesy*, and Hodges in *every* (eight times) and *several* (six times). Two especially interesting cases are *commandment* and *sovereign*. *Commandment* is given as *commandement* (with the original *e* still unsyncopated) by Hart (once, against the syncopated form thrice) and by Hodges (eight times); Wallis in his first edition (1653) says it is four syllables, but in his fifth (1699) is constrained to qualify this by saying that it was formerly so pronounced by everyone, though some now pronounce it as only three syllables. He is of course inaccurate in speaking of the three-syllabled form as though it was only of recent development, since it is shown much earlier by Hart and by Bullokar (see also Note 1 below). In *sovereign* Robinson has syncope in the adjective but thrice has *e* retained in the substantive (though once the *e* is a later insertion); Gil and Hodges show no syncope (in Gil the word is the adjective, in Hodges it may be either adjective or substantive).

A case requiring separate notice is syncope in the inflected forms of verbs in *-en*, &c., and *-er*, &c. In the present tense, syncope of the medial vowel is shown by Gil in *happeneth* and *strengtheneth* and by Hodges in *openest* and *strengtheneth*; in the present participle by Robinson in *labouring* and *ravening*, Gil in *reckoning*, and the shorthand-writer J. Willis in *reckoning*; and in the p.t. and p.p. by, for example, Hart in *considered*, Laneham in *sweetened*, Robinson in *ventred* 'ventured', Gil in *hastened*, and Hodges in *happened*. From these cases we should strictly distinguish others in which unstressed *e* may never have developed in the inflected forms. OE syncope after a long stem syllable in *hindrian*, *punrian*, and *wandrian* may account for the lack of medial *e* shown by Laneham in *thundered* and

Gil in *hindereth, thundering,* and *wandered*; Hodges has no medial *e* in *enlightening,* which may perhaps be a similar case if from an OE **lihtnian*. Verbs derived from OF verbs in *-rer* or *-rir* or formed from ME sbs. in *-re* may likewise in their inflected forms show the survival of the original ME forms without medial *e*; lack of medial *e* is shown by Cheke in *entred*, Hart in *disordering*, Laneham in *lettered* and *remembered*, Gil in *attempered*, and Hodges in *chambering* and *suffering*. Cooper says that such words as *numbered* are mostly written *numbred*, but are pronounced *numburd* merely 'sometimes by some'. But Hart's lack of medial *e* in *ciphering* is due to ModE syncope, as the verb is not recorded before the sixteenth century.

Syncope in phrasal groups is shown rarely. Hart has *tu ð' spesiaul* 'to the special' and *ōvr-it* 'over it', but his intention in the latter case may be to show syllabic [r].

Note 1: *OED* shows that the syncopated form of *commandment* occurs as early as the thirteenth century, but that the four-syllabled form was used regularly by Spenser and occasionally by Shakespeare. Cf. *changeling*, which Shakespeare scans as three syllables (*MSND*, II. i. 23) or two (ibid., IV. i. 56). The unsyncopated *capitain* seems to have survived continuously, though rarely, into the early seventeenth century (see *OED*, s.v.; its last example is from the Douai Bible of 1609). It seems doubtful whether the unsyncopated form of *judgement* survived into the sixteenth century. In this word and in *commandment* the syncope was supported by the tendency to reform the nouns after the verbs from which they were derived.

Note 2: A new formation on the infinitive is shown by Hodges's trisyllabic *suffered* (in a transcription of the Creed). In some cases (e.g. Hart's four-syllabled *considered* and Hodges's trisyllabic *waterest*) it is impossible to say whether there is a failure of syncope or a new formation on the infinitive; but Hodges's disyllabic *straitened* with syllabic [n] must certainly be the latter.

(2) *Words with three syllables after the main stress*

§ 307. In such words syncope of the immediately post-tonic vowel is shown by Hart in *indifferently* (once, against *e* retained once), Robinson in *sovereignize*, Hodges and Coles in *Salisbury*, Cocker in *seasonable*, and Brown in *ordinary*. Coles also has *Bartl'mew-Fair* 'Bartholomew Fair' (cf. *OED*, s.v. *Bartholomew*); in this case the form is mainly derived from Fr *Barthélemy*, and the syncope again affects the vowel immediately after the (in English) stressed syllable, giving *Bartlemy* (in which the *-le-* subsequently becomes syllabic [l]). Cocker's *Feberary* 'February' shows blending of ME *feverer* with the syncopated **febrary* < *February*. Laneham has *fiznamy* 'physiognomy', and Coles (followed by Strong and Brown) has *dixnary* 'dictionary'; these forms, which show loss of both the vowels in hiatus, probably develop in two stages, the first being the loss of the first vowel (see below, on the syncope of vowels in hiatus, and cf. Young's *dixonary*), and the second the loss of the surviving vowel, now immediately post-tonic in a word that has come to have three syllables after the stress.

Note: In *Salisbury* the syncope is probably older than lengthening in open syllables, and certainly older than the change of ME *ǎ* to *au* before back [l], which took place *c.* 1400.

OF VOWELS IN HIATUS

(1) *Syncope of the pretonic vowel*

§ 308. When two vowels occur in hiatus there is a marked tendency towards syncope of the less stressed vowel, especially when it is the first of the two. The commonest case in ModE is in words with the ending *-iage* (*carriage*, &c.), in which syncope of the *i* occurs; the surviving vowel is ME *ă* (see § 271 above), which becomes [ə] and then unstressed [ɪ] (see below, § 336). This syncope is not shown by Bullokar; but Gil has *marigabl* 'marriageable', Price, Lye, Cooper, *The Compendious School-Master*, Cocker, and Brown say that *i* is silent in *marriage*, &c., and Coles (followed by Strong and Young) has the 'phonetic spellings' *carridg*, *marridg*. *Pharaoh* has silent *a* in Hodges. *Atheist* and *atheism* have syncope of the *e* in Lye, *WSC*, Brown, and the shorthand-writer Everardt. *Geometry* is commonly said to have 'silent *e*' by seventeenth-century spelling-books; exceptions are Brooksbank, who says the *e* was not sounded 'till of late', and *The English Schole-Master* (1646), which says that in *geometry* and *George* the *eo* has the sounds of both vowels, but not so distinctly as when they are apart—a remark which, in this source, may mean no more than that the *e* serves to 'soften' the *g*.

Other cases are shown only in sources which usually reflect vulgar pronunciation. The 'phonetically spelt' lists show syncope of *i* in *Daniel*, *Ezekiel*, and *Christianity* (Strong, Young, and Cocker) and in *bullion*, *ruffian*, and *scullion* (Brown). The shorthand-writers show it in *Daniel* (Everardt, Bridges), *Ezekiel* (Everardt), *comprehend* (spelt *comprend* by Bridges), and *abbreviate* (Hopkins). The 'homophone lists' provide most evidence; syncope is shown in *meteor* (paired with *meter* by Hodges and Strong), *collier* (paired with *collar* by Wharton, Strong, and Young), *pannier* (paired with *banner* by Price), *palliate* (paired with *pallet* and *palate* by Ellis, Young, *The Compendious School-Master*, and Brown), *millions* (paired with *melons* by Fox and Hookes, Strong, Young, and Brown), *saviour* (paired with *saver* by Fox and Hookes, Coles (*Eng.-Lat. Dict.*), Young, Cocker, and Brown), *murrion* 'morion' (paired with *murrain* by Coles, *Eng.-Lat. Dict.*), and *galleon* (paired with *gallon* by Brown). In two words there is syncope of popular ME *ĭ* < OF [y]; these are *messuage* (paired with *message* by Strong and by Cooper in his list of words which are the 'same'), and *annual* (paired with *annal* by Young). It should be noted that these pairings are avoided by the most careful lists; Hodges and Cooper have only one each, and Coles none except in his *Eng.-Lat. Dict.*

Failure of syncope is shown in two personal names that now regularly have it: Coles gives *Eleanor* as four syllables, and *Michael* is said to have *ae* 'parted' by Lye followed by *WSC*.

Syncope in phrasal groups is shown fairly often by Hart, who gives *bōr'* twice for *borrow* before a vowel, *t'* 'to' and *d'* 'do' before vowels, and *ð'* 'the' before vowels, *h*, and *w* (which Hart regards as a vowel; theory seems here to triumph over observation).

> Note 1: *OED* cites spellings showing syncope in many of the words dealt with above.
>
> Note 2: Certain words recorded by the same or similar sources seem to, but do not, have syncope. Gil has *čaret* 'chariot' and Brooksbank and Brown show that in *chariot* the *i* is silent; but the source is ME *charette*. *Carrion* is given as *carren* or *carrin* by Coles, Strong, Young, and Brown; the source is ME *caren* < *careyn*, and ModE *carrion* is an analogical form on the model of variation between unsyncopated and syncopated forms of such words as *millions* and *galleon* (see above). Price says that *cushion* has silent *i*, but the source is ME *cusshyn*, &c. Laneham has *uncurtess* 'uncourteous' (ME *curtais*, &c.) and *currars* 'couriers' (ME *curour*). *Guardian* (late ME *gardeyn* < AF *gardein*) is paired with *garden* in the 'homophone lists' of Fox and Hookes, Strong, Young, Hawkins, and Brown; *soldier* (ME *souder*) with *solder* in those of Wharton and Price. *Righteous* (sixteenth-century *rightous* < *rihtwis*) is shown with 'silent *e*' by the shorthand-writers Folkingham and Ridpath.
>
> Note 3: In words such as *position*, *vision* the PresE pronunciation develops from ME forms in which the *i* was pronounced as [j]; ME [sj], [zj] > [ʃ], [ʒ], and there is no syncope. But there was also a variant mode of pronunciation in which the *i* was pronounced as [ɪ] and the following vowel had some degree of secondary stress (see § 276 above); in this case a glide [j] developed before the [ɪ] and then coalesced with a preceding [s] or [z], so that [-sɪʊn], [-zɪʊn] > [-sjɪʊn], [-zjɪʊn] > [-ʃɪʊn], [-ʒɪʊn]. These last forms could be a further source of PresE [-ʃən], [-ʒən] by syncope of the [ɪ], but the evidence suggests rather that the second mode of pronunciation was simply replaced by the first.

(2) *Syncope of the post-tonic vowel*

§ 309. Syncope of a post-tonic vowel in hiatus is not shown by the best authorities except in *power*, transcribed without *e* by Bullokar (once, beside *e* once), Robinson (thrice, beside *e* once), and Gil (four times, beside *e* twice); but Smith, Hart, and Hodges in *EP* retain *e*. Bullokar has no syncope in *vehemently*, though the *h* is shown as silent, nor have Robinson and Gil in *diamond*. But the 'phonetically spelt' lists of Strong, Young, and Cocker show syncope of the *a* in *diamond* (though Brown's does not); and similar syncope is shown by the shorthand-writers in *vehement* (spelt *vement* by J. Willis, Folkingham, Thomas Shelton, and Mason) and in *dialogue* (spelt *dilog* by Folkingham). The 'homophone lists' pair *prowess* with *prose* (Hodges 'near', Cooper 'near') and *Noah's* with *nose* (Strong, Cooper 'same or near').

Hart shows syncope in phrasal groups in *houb'īt* (for *houbī't*) 'howbeit' and *hierbei'tiz* 'hereby it is'.

> Note: Smith's *quīt* 'quietus' (in contrast with *quĭt* 'liberatus') is from ME *quīte*, *quĭt* < OF *quite* (in contrast with ME *quĭtte*, *quĭt* < OF *quitte*); see *OED*, s.v. *quit* adj. Smith has attributed to the variant forms of *quit* adj. the distinction of meaning normally marked by the formal distinction between *quiet* (< *quiētus*) and *quĭt* (< MedLat *quītus*).
>
> The ordinal numerals *twentieth*, &c. were in ME *twentith*, &c. (with *-ith* < OE *-igoða*), and forms with [ɪþ] are recorded by Hart, Bullokar, Gil, Butler, Young, and Brown; Levens and Strong have *twenteth*, &c. (rhymed by Levens on *loveth*, &c. and even *benethe*). The modern forms in *-ieth* are due to re-formation, the suffix *-eth* of, for example, *twenteth* being added to *twenty*.

LOSS OF ME UNSTRESSED *E*

IN FINAL POSITION

§ 310. The loss of ME unstressed *e* in final position is so regular that it is probably due to other causes than the processes of syncope in phrasal groups that account for the loss of non-final *e* in inflexional endings (see below); these must have affected it, but there must also have been a general tendency to evanescence (due to the sound being pronounced with decreasing force) which acted on final *e* even when words containing it were pronounced alone or came at the end of a sentence or phrase. The loss was completed, in educated London English, comparatively early in the fifteenth century. No survival of final unstressed *e* is shown by the orthoepists; thus in 1530 Palsgrave, giving examples of English mispronunciation of French, shows a regular failure to pronounce final *e*, and Smith says that to pronounce it is a French and not an English characteristic. The only possible exception is Wallis's statement that the pronunciations *baptis-me*, *beas-tes*, *cloth-es* were used 'parentum nostrorum ætate', 'aliaque istiusmodi (quæ a vetulis quibusdam etiamnum audies)'. By *parentes*, however, Wallis probably means ancestors; and though it is conceivable that he may have heard the plural *-es* still pronounced as a separate syllable (see below), it can hardly be credited that he knew, even from old men, pronunciations in which final *e* was still sounded. The general context of Wallis's remarks (see Vol. I, pp. 235–7) shows that final *e* had so long disappeared that it was only by a remarkable piece of philological deduction that he was able to argue that it had once been pronounced, and had then gradually become silent.

Note: In enclitic forms of pronouns (e.g. in *wiltu* 'wilt thou') the final vowel was apt to be reduced to unstressed *-e* (i.e. to [ə]); so *bi me* 'by me', &c. (which Gower would write as single words, *bime*, &c.) rhyming with *time*, &c., and even *fro ye* rhyming with *Troye* (*T. & C.*, i. 5). In the fifteenth century, by normal phonetic process, the final unstressed *e* of these enclitic forms was lost; hence the apparent omission, in eModE, of *thou* after *wilt* and *dost*, and Smith's [gou] 'go we' (see Vol. I, p. 49).

IN NON-FINAL POSITION IN INFLEXIONAL ENDINGS

§ 311. The loss of non-final unstressed *e* from the inflexions of nouns and verbs, though a characteristic difference between ModE and ME, appears not to be due to the operation of a general sound-change such as caused the loss of final *e*; the process was a protracted one, and appears to be due to a variety of factors. In general the loss of the *e* from the inflexions is only a special result of the action of syncope, and is largely a ME process. By the late fourteenth century syncope had frequently caused the loss of the vowel of the final syllable of words of three syllables or more, and in accordance with this tendency *husbandes* became *husbands*, *northwardes* became *northwards*, *maidenes* became *maidens*; in this way the inflexions of words of which the stem had two or more syllables were commonly reduced to mere consonants. The loss of the vowel from the inflexions of monosyllables, it is generally held (e.g. by Luick, §§ 475–6), is due to syncope in phrasal groups which have a unity within the sentence comparable to that of compounds and therefore have stress-patterns similar to those of words of three or more syllables, and in consequence show in late ME and early ModE syncope of the type discussed in §§ 306–7 above. Thus *mannes wit* is comparable in stressing to *medicine*, and as the latter is reduced to [medsɪn] so the former is reduced to *mans wit*; and similar considerations would apply to such groups as *othes grete*, *loved he*, *(he) loveth it*. Again, phrases like *grete othes* and *blacke birdes* would, especially after the loss of the final *e* of the plural adjective, have a stress-pattern similar to that of *husbandes*, and would be subject to the same form of syncope as the latter. In these ways merely consonantal inflexions would develop even for words with monosyllabic stems. A further influence, in the case of nouns, must surely be sought in the OF plural inflexion *-s* used for almost all masculines and some feminines, which would tend to be retained in French words adopted into English and which would reinforce the plurals in *-s* developed in ME itself by syncope. But syncope in words of two syllables (see § 305 above) was too rare, and probably too late, to be a factor of any importance.

The consequence of these developments was that by the fifteenth century the English inflexions had come to have two forms, the older one consisting of unstressed *e* plus a consonant (or two consonants) and a newer one which consisted of the consonant(s) alone; and the latter type has tended to be generalized, by a process of analogy, at the expense of the former. But the generalization was much less rapid and complete in some cases than in others. The verbal inflexion *-ed* was still often a separate syllable until the end of the seventeenth century, and in PresE survives as such in some adjectives and p.ps. used as adjectives (e.g. *naked*, *wicked*, *learned* adj., *blessed* adj.) and in derivatives such as *assuredly*, *composedness*. Similarly the verbal inflexions *-est* and *-eth* were commonly still a separate syllable while they remained in use. In adjectives the superlative inflexion *-est*, though sometimes reduced to *-st* by syncope, is now regularly a separate syllable. On the other hand, in the genitive and plural of nouns the inflexion *-s* was already much more common than *-es* by 1500, and now alone survives; and similarly when the Northern inflexion of the 3rd sing. pres. indic. of verbs appears in StE it is as *-s* and not as *-es*.

It is the merit of the theory set out above that it enables us to understand the differing rates at which the reduced inflexions were generalized. The greater rapidity of the extension of the reduced inflexions in substantives is doubtless in part due to the analogy of the French plural *-s*, but mainly to the fact that in substantives the conditions for syncope were especially favourable. The syncope of the vowel of the final syllables of words of three or more syllables (the *husbandes* type) occurs in words stressed on the first syllable; this means that it will occur in substantives rather than verbs (since native verbs with a stem of two syllables or more are usually not stressed on the first). Syncope in phrasal groups was again more likely to affect substantives, because of the closeness of the groups into which they enter; groups composed of genitive plus another substantive are so close that they often become virtual or real compounds (e.g. *bull's-eye, daisy*), and though a group of adjective plus substantive is rather less close, it can sometimes also give rise to a compound (e.g. *blackbird, blackberry*). But verbal groups such as *loved he, (he) loveth it* have less phrasal unity, and syncope was correspondingly rather less common. Of verbal inflexions *-s* for *-es* was the most rapidly generalized; the reasons are probably (*a*) that the dialects from which this form entered StE were more advanced in regard to syncope than was StE itself, (*b*) that it was supported by the analogy of the *-s* inflexion of substantives, already well established by the time the *-s* inflexion replaced *-eth* in spoken StE. The comparative rarity with which the superlative inflexion *-est* was syncopated to *-st* is probably due to the survival of the secondary stress which it had in OE.

Syncope of the *e* fails, and the full ending is retained, in cases where an impossible consonant group would be produced if a consonantal inflexion were added directly to the stem; thus *-es* is regular after [ʃ], [ʒ], [tʃ], and [dʒ] in *lashes, rouges, patches,* and *bridges*. The full inflexion is also normally employed when the consonant which ends the stem is such that a merely consonantal inflexion would be assimilated to it and lose its identity; thus in *kisses, loses, hunted,* and *hounded,* if the *e* were syncopated, the [z] or [d] of the inflexion would be assimilated to the preceding [s], [z] or [t], [d] and there would result apparently uninflected forms. In the genitive sing. of substantives ending in [s] such forms do occur in early ModE (thus Shakespeare has *my young mistress dog, his horse back*); but in late ME and early ModE the tendency of the language to maintain its surviving inflexions has successfully prevented the generalization of new uninflected forms (though uninflected genitives of personal names ending in *-s* have not been uncommon).

The evidence of the orthoepists on certain points of interest is set out below.

Note 1: The much greater rarity of the unsyncopated forms in Shakespeare's later plays has been regarded as reflecting the development of the language during his period of literary activity (cf. Schipper, *History of English Versification*, p. 227); but there is no warrant from other evidence for a rapid development between 1590 and 1615, and the change is probably due to his basing his scansion progressively on less 'literary' pronunciation.

Note 2: In such phrases as *for conscience sake* the *s* of the inflexion is to be regarded as absorbed into that of *sake*; see *OED*, s.v. *sake* sb. (heading II). The contracted p.ts. and p.ps. *read, led, put, cast, hurt*, &c. develop in OE and ME, and are not due to the late ME syncope discussed above.

(1) *The* -es *inflexion in substantives*

§ 312. The genitive sing. and the plural of substantives normally have -*s* in the orthoepists, except where PresE also preserves the full ending; this is the case even in so early an orthoepist as Smith. But there are certain exceptions. Salesbury gives *trees* as two syllables, [tri:ɪz]. Smith transcribes *Jews* with -*es*, [dʒy:əs], in contrast to *juice* (dʒy:s). Hart (cf. Jespersen, *Hart*, p. 83) has the full ending -*ez* or -*es* in *contraries*, *copies*, and twice in *enemies*, from which it would seem that he tended to preserve it after final *ĭ* (cf. Salesbury); he also has it in *modes* and once (against the reduced -*s* or -*z* four times) in *breaths*, both of which may be errors, and once in *examples* (against *exampls* once), where the explanation may be uncertainty in the representation of syllabic [l]. His evidence is slight and uncertain, but seems to suggest that he occasionally pronounced the -*es* inflexion without syncope. Bullokar uses a special sign, which he calls 'semi-vowel' *s*, for the genitive sing. and plural of sbs., because, he says, the pronunciation was 'formerly' -*es*. Gil even more clearly treats -*es* as an obsolete form; he says that Spenser's use of *wŭndes*, *kloudes*, *handes* for *wŭndz* 'woụnds' sb., *kloudz* 'clouds', *handz* 'hands' is a case of Diæresis, the separation of one into two, and by dealing with the matter in his chapter 'De Metro' he shows clearly that he views such forms as poetical. But it was apparently still a matter of common knowledge that poets might treat forms in -*es* as disyllables; Gil cites the Spenserian forms without any discussion, evidently feeling that it was not necessary to prove that they were disyllabic, and once elsewhere (ed. Jiriczek, p. 126, l. 22), in transcribing *F.Q.*, I. xi. 54, gives *cloudes* as a disyllable (thus *kloudez*) as if it were a mere matter of routine. Hodges normally shows the PresE position; an isolated transcription of *halves* with the *e* not marked as silent is almost certainly an error (cf. *kinde* with the *e* similarly left unmarked). Wallis says that *beas-tes*, *cloth-es* were pronounced as two syllables 'parentum nostrorum ætate', and that *mouth-es* is still so pronounced in the metrical psalms; this, like Gil's earlier evidence, shows that to pronounce -*es* as a separate syllable was still a known literary archaism (cf. the status of -*ed* at the present day). Wallis's further remark that such pronunciations could still be heard from some old people (see § 310 above and Vol. I, p. 236) seems to refer to -*es* (and not to final *e*); at this date (1653) the pronunciation of -*es* must, one would think, have been dialectal, and it is worth recalling that Wallis was a native of Kent, the dialect of which seems to have been unusually conservative. But at the very end of the century *RS* includes *Tuesday* in a list of words in which contiguous vowel-letters are said to be pronounced separately, i.e. the originally genitival -*es* is still a separate syllable. This piece of evidence seems difficult to believe, but the only other dubious case in *RS*'s list is *pageanty* [*sic*]; moreover *OED* cites sixteenth-century spellings which lend

§ 312] LOSS OF ME UNSTRESSED e 883

some support—thus *Tuesday* in the sixteenth century is spelt *Tewis-*, *Tewes-*, *Tuis-*, and *pageant* is spelt *pagia(u)nt, pagient, pagyant, pageyond* (and in the seventeenth century *pagiente*). On the whole it seems that we should accept the evidence, though *RS* is not a good source; but it would probably refer to vulgar or dialectal speech.

The position then seems to be that in the later sixteenth and the seventeenth centuries *-es* was not pronounced as a separate syllable in StE, though it may sometimes have been so pronounced in dialectal or vulgar speech until the end of the seventeenth century. The separate pronunciation of the *-es* was, however, well known as a poetic archaism and as a feature of former StE pronunciation; the contrast with final *-e* (the former pronunciation of which had been forgotten, and had to be rediscovered by deductive processes) suggests that in StE the final disappearance of the full pronunciation of *-es* was comparatively recent, and I am therefore disposed to accept the evidence of Salesbury, Smith, and Hart as showing its occasional survival in StE in the period 1540–70.

Note 1: In *pageant* (ME *pagyn*, Anglo-Latin *pagina*) there has been suffix-substitution.

Note 2: It is of course not only Spenser who in the late sixteenth century scans *-es* occasionally as a separate syllable, though with his archaizing tendency he does so unusually often; there are, for example, a number of cases in Shakespeare's early plays, thus *moones* (*MSND*, II. i. 7), *nightes* (ibid., IV. i. 93).

Note 3: Failure of syncope in *aloes* is shown by Price (who pairs the word with *alias* in his 'homophone list'), Coles, and *RS*, but not by Lye (whose pronunciation would rhyme with *woes*); the trisyllabic form must be due to the influence of Latin *aloë*. Similarly *RS* gives *series* as three syllables; this Latinate form still survives, but normally *series*, even when singular in function, is assimilated to native plurals in *-ies*.

(2) *The* -es *inflexion in verbs (3 sing. pres. indic.)*

§ 313. In contrast to their evidence on the inflexion *-eth* (see below), the orthoepists without exception show the alternative (originally Northern) form as *-s*, not *-es*. It occurs once only in Smith (in *smokes*) and a number of times in Hart (e.g. thrice in *methinks*). Bullokar, somewhat confusedly, says that in poetry *-z* may be substituted for *-eth*; this would be strictly true only of words with a stem ending in a vowel or voiced consonant. P.G. gives *hates* as a poetic contraction (see Vol. I, p. 33). Tonkis (1612) says *lov's* is a contraction of *loveth*. Gil twice gives *has* for *hath* as a Northern form, and a confused note (ed. Jiriczek, p. 69) seems to mean that in his view *hath* and *doth* [the original reads *did*, which is impossible] were the only forms of these words permissible in StE; otherwise he says that *-eth* can become *-s* or *-z* (*spēks, luvz* for *spēketh, luveth*), or *-ez* after *s, sh, x, z, ch,* and [dʒ]. He deals with this substitution not only when discussing inflexion, but also, as a poetic device, in his chapter on metre (ed. Jiriczek, p. 141); and he himself gives the transcription *waiz* 'weighs' in a prose example. Butler gives *loov's* as a variant to *looveth*; Ben Jonson says that *-eth* is 'sometimes shortned into *z* or *s*'. Hodges in *SH-PD* gives evidence closely similar to Gil's (by which his is perhaps influenced), but with the important difference that he explicitly says that whereas *-eth* is written, *-s* or *-z* (or after the specified consonants *-ez*) is ordinarily pronounced (see Vol. I, p. 168). Wallis says that *lightnes* 'lightens' (in contrast, apparently, to *lightneth*, for which he says it stands) is a monosyllable. J. Smith (1674) says that the inflexion *s* should be written '*s*, since it stands for *-eth*, which he would prefer as the written form. Cooper gives *-s* or *-th* as the inflexion of the 3rd sing. The 'homophone lists' from Hodges, *SH-PD*, onwards give freely such pairings as *boughs* : *boweth*. The shorthand-writer Bridges gives *ses* for *saith*.

Thus the evidence of the orthoepists gives no sign whatever that the inflexion of the 3rd sing. pres. could be pronounced as *-es* (except after the consonants specified by Gil and Hodges); there is presented a clear distinction between *-eth* (which they normally treat as a separate syllable; but see below) and a merely consonantal inflexion *-s* or *-z*, which Bullokar, and to a less extent Gil, associates with poetic use and which Hodges describes as colloquial—the familiar distinction between the *-eth* of literary prose and the *-s* of speech and of poetry based on speech. Syncope occurs in all cases in which it is possible.

Note 1 : Cases in which poets appear to scan the verbal inflexion *-es* as a separate syllable (cf. *MSND*, ed. E. K. Chambers, p. 186, § 8 (*b*)) must, in view of the evidence set out above, be regarded with suspicion; probably the form in *-eth* should be substituted.

Note 2 : The tendency of seventeenth-century printers to put an apostrophe before the *s* in the 3rd sing. is explained by the evidence set out above, which makes it very clear that *-s* was generally regarded as a contraction of *-eth* (cf. especially the evidence of J. Smith).

(3) *The* -eth *inflexion in verbs*

§ 314. The orthoepists normally show no syncope of the vowel of the verbal inflexion *-eth* (so, for example, Bullokar, Gil, and Hodges), and contrast the *-eth* inflexion with its 'contraction' *-s* or *-z* (see above). *Hath* and *doth* are of course shown as monosyllables; similarly *saith* (e.g. by Hart). But other words ending in a diphthong or vowel in the infinitive are shown in the 3rd sing. pres. as disyllables, e.g. *stayeth* (Hart), *crieth*, *lieth* (Hodges), and *seeth* (Butler). Syncope is, however, shown in such words by the shorthand-writer Farthing, who has *butifith* 'beautifieth' and *trith* 'trieth', and by Cooper, who distinguishes *seeth* from *seethe* by virtue only of [þ] in the former and [ð] in the latter. More general evidence of syncope is given only by Hart; though he transcribes the inflexion as [eþ] (once [ɪþ]) in some twenty-five verbs, he also has *servþ* 'serveth', *sitþ* 'sitteth', and *tākþ* 'taketh', and says (Chap. 11) that *cometh*, *runneth* are really only one syllable, *comth*, *runth*, in ordinary speech.

Note: The scansion of sixteenth-century poets shows very common syncope of the

§ 314] LOSS OF ME UNSTRESSED e 885

vowel of -*eth*, which would agree with Hart's evidence. But in many cases the form in -*s* may have been intended, even though -*eth* is printed (cf. the evidence of Hodges and J. Smith cited in § 313 above).

(4) *The* -ed *inflexion in verbs and adjectives*

§ 315. The orthoepists show much variation between the unsyncopated and the syncopated forms of the inflexion -*ed*; there is some suggestion, especially in the seventeenth century, that the unsyncopated forms are literary and perhaps even archaic. The evidence of the major writers is as follows.

Cheke shows many syncopated forms (e.g. *opend, offerd, laught*). Smith varies; thus he has -*ed* (or -*id*) in *brewed, vowed, wooed* but -*d* in *flayed, lied*, and says that *dyed* has -*ed* or -*d*. Hart's evidence is fuller; he shows the full -*ed* in thirty-eight words in which PresE has syncope, against -*d* or -*t* in forty-five words (as in PresE). The full -*ed* is found not only after consonants but also after ME vowels or diphthongs (e.g. *allowed, bestowed, continued, envied*). Syncope is shown in *learned* twice when it is a participle and five times when used as an adjective; otherwise it has the full -*ed* eight times when used as an adjective. In Chap. 11 Hart says that *supped, missed*, and *blissed* (blessed?) are really only one syllable in ordinary speech. Laneham has both the full -*ed* and some -*t* forms. Bullokar normally writes the full -*ed*, but in view of his system this is probably of no phonetic significance; syncope is shown in *fōr-opprest* 'fore-oppressed'. Tonkis regards *lov'd* as a contraction of *loved*. Robinson follows closely the forms of his exemplar Barnfield, departing from them only on four occasions, thrice in favour of -*d* and once in favour of -*ed*; he also follows Barnfield in giving *learned* as a disyllable when it is used adjectivally. Gil, when transcribing passages of verse, normally gives the forms required by the metre (most of his quotations are from Spenser, whose spelling is a clear guide to the forms he requires). In prose examples Gil commonly gives the full -*ed*, even after a vowel (e.g. in *busied* in a prose example and in *astonied* in verse against the requirements of metre); but he also gives in prose the contracted forms *dipt, fixt*, and *wisht*. It is interesting that *loved* has the full -*ed* twenty-seven times, -*d* only twice. The full -*ed* is given in *learned* used adjectivally and in its derivatives. Hodges normally gives -*d*, -*t*; but many of his transcriptions are of biblical passages, and in these he often retains the full -*ed*, e.g. in *clothed, loved, erred, passed, suffered, walked, witnessed*. Even in the biblical passages, however, syncopated forms occur; sometimes he seems to be guided by considerations of rhythm, as when, in the same verse, he gives *walked sometime* (/×/×) but *liv'd in them* (/×/), where *lived in them* (/××/) would be less regular. Occasionally the full forms occur (perhaps but far from certainly by error, through the omission of the diacritic that marks a silent letter) in normal prose; e.g. *used* is two syllables twice (against one syllable thrice) in normal prose. The full forms alone occur in *assuredly, naked, well-beloved, wicked* (*-ly, -ness*). The adjective *learned* is twice disyllabic; the verbal past tense is also disyllabic once, the p.p. monosyllabic four times. Hodges explicitly teaches that the forms in *-d, -t* are 'contractions' of the full forms in *-ed*; but it would appear from his evidence that his usage agreed closely with that of PresE. Hunt shows syncope not only in *delivered*, but also in *beloved*. Wharton (1654), however, says that *i* and *e* are sounded separately in *tied* and *lied*; Cooper says that words like *numbered* are mostly written *numbred* (which implies syncope of the medial vowel, not that of the inflexion), but 'sometimes by some' pronounced *numburd*, and that *-ed* is 'frequently' elided to *-d* or *-t* (from which it is obvious that he regards the unsyncopated form as the norm); and *WSC* in its 'homophone list' pairs *marred* with *married*. It would appear therefore that the full forms were until the end of the seventeenth century still sufficiently well known to be regarded as the ideal norm, and the syncopated forms, however common, were considered merely as 'contractions'. The distinction between, for example, *learn'd* p.p. and *learned* adj., though not absolute, was already developing by the time of Hart and was well marked by that of Hodges.

Note 1: That there continued to be a presumption in the late seventeenth century that the *-ed* would still be pronounced in full in the literary language is shown by the care of poets of the time, e.g. Dryden, to spell weak p.ts. and p.ps. in such a way as to indicate the pronunciation intended—and this in spite of the fact that Dryden almost invariably uses the syncopated forms.

Note 2: Smith's *yild* and *yeld* 'yielded' are not contractions of *yielded*, but ME analogical weak p.ps. (in place of the original strong form), and are in fact older than *yielded*.

(5) *The* -est *inflexion in verbs*

§ 316. Syncope of *-est* to *-st* is fairly commonly shown. Smith has *-est* in *liest* but *-st* in *layst*. Hart has only *-est* in his transcriptions, but in Chap. 11 says that *tellest* is really one syllable *telst* in ordinary speech. Tonkis says that *lov'st* is a contraction of *lovest*. Robinson shows syncope in *sayest, seest, singest*. Gil says that the 2nd sing. admits of syncope (thus *lovest* or *lov'st*), except after *s, sh*, &c. Hodges shows both the full *-est* and the syncopated *-st* in his transcriptions of biblical passages when the stem of the verb ends in a voiceless consonant; after a vowel or a voiced consonant he shows regular syncope, but a special problem seems to be involved (see Vol. I, p. 183).

Note: The scansion of sixteenth-century poets (e.g. Shakespeare) shows both forms, with the syncopated *-st* prevailing.

(6) *The* -est *inflexion of superlatives*

§ 317. I have observed no evidence of syncope of the vowel of the superlative inflexion *-est* in the orthoepists, though the scansion of poets indicates that syncopated forms did occasionally occur; cf. Abbott, *Shakespearean Grammar*, § 473.

SYLLABIC CONSONANTS AND RELATED DEVELOPMENTS

§ 318. It is a matter of common agreement that probably in late ME, and certainly in ModE, syllabic consonants develop in English by the loss of unstressed vowels; but the details of this development (when it occurred, in what circumstances, and by what processes) have not been properly worked out. Luick has recognized the problem and has set out to give a systematic answer; but his solution is unsatisfactory (see § 325, Note 3 below). Other writers (e.g. Horn, Jespersen, Wyld, and Ekwall), while making a series of often useful observations (Wyld's Appendix III to *Coll. Eng.* (3rd edition) is good on the phonetics of the cases he discusses) and gathering much evidence (some of which conflicts with Luick's view and is ignored by him), have not attempted a coherent theory.

GENERAL PHONETIC CONSIDERATIONS

§ 319. It is necessary in the first place to consider, from the point of view of English, in what phonetic circumstances syllabic consonants are possible and likely. The prerequisite is rapid and precise articulation; in slower utterance syllabic consonants, except perhaps in the positions where they are easiest to articulate, will either never develop or, if developed, will be replaced by a glide-vowel followed by a non-syllabic consonant (e.g. syllabic [l] by [əl]). It is improbable that at any period either type (the syllabic consonant or the vowel-consonant group) has entirely predominated to the exclusion of the other; in many phonetic circumstances there must always have been free variation between the two. This is the case in PresE, and we shall see in due course that the sixteenth- and seventeenth-century evidence is to the same effect.

But even in rapid and precisely articulated speech the occurrence of syllabic consonants is largely dependent on the nature of the preceding consonant. We may reasonably assume that the most reliable indication of what is likely to have occurred in earlier stages of English is what does actually occur in PresE, and a summary analysis of the circumstances determining the use of syllabic consonants in PresE follows.

After consonants other than liquids or nasals, the ease of articulation of syllabic consonants varies with the degree and nature of the articulatory movement involved; if no movement is necessary (e.g. when [m̩] follows a bilabial or [n̩] a dental) articulation is simple, as it also is for [l̩] or [n̩] after labial continuants. But any movement, even a slight one, makes possible the intervention of a glide-vowel between the one consonant and the other; after a voiced consonant it is in theory more likely than after a voiceless, since the vocal chords are already vibrating, and after a voiced continuant the extra sonority required for a syllabic consonant may also be rather more difficult to achieve. Nevertheless in practice syllabic consonants occur freely after almost any continuant, though varying with a group of [ə] plus non-syllabic consonant when movement is involved. When stops precede, the effect of articulatory position becomes more important: if a stop is followed by a homorganic liquid or nasal the 'plosive' part is usually omitted and the liquid or nasal follows immediately, but otherwise the tendency is to complete the stop by 'plosion'. When [l] or fricative [r] follows, the plosion can occur through the part of the oral passage which is left open; but when the nasals follow there must be an interval for plosion (if it is to occur) before the oral passage is closed, during which a glide-vowel may intervene (especially after a voiced stop). After non-alveolar stops syllabic [ṇ] (in contrast to syllabic [ḷ]) seems comparatively rare in PresE.

When a stop is preceded by a homorganic nasal the stopping process is in fact omitted and plosion alone occurs; but if certain other consonants are added to the group (as e.g. in *empty*) the plosion may also be omitted and the 'stop' come to be a period of silence or of mere voice (cf. Daniel Jones, *Outline of English Phonetics*, § 578). Comparable situations arise if syllabic consonants are used in such words as *hempen, sunken, Hamden,* and *Hamton*; but as both speakers and hearers are satisfied that the central consonant is indeed present, there is no occasion for avoiding such groups, and syllabic [ṇ] is in fact often used (beside perhaps more frequent [ən], the use of which permits plosion). But in such words as *wanton* and *London*, if syllabic [ṇ] is used, then either (*a*) plosion must be effected without the intervention of a glide [ə] before the [ṇ], which is somewhat difficult (especially after [d]), or (*b*) if plosion is omitted, then not only is the [t] or [d] reduced to a period of silence or voice, but also there is no movement of the vocal organs (as there is, for example, in *hempen* [hempṇ]) to correspond to either the beginning or the ending of the notional [t] or [d], so that the speaker is dissatisfied. Syllabic [ṇ] is therefore rare in such words (indeed Daniel Jones, *Eng. Pron. Dict.*, does not record it).

After a liquid or nasal, a syllabic consonant (which of course must itself be a liquid or nasal) can be employed if it can be made sufficiently sonorous to dominate the preceding consonant and so achieve 'syllabic lift'. This is very difficult when the preceding consonant is the same as itself, and therefore in such words as *linen* syllabic [ṇ] is not used. When the preceding consonant is different, the position depends largely on the relative inherent sonority of the two sounds. Syllabic [ḷ] is common after nasals, which are less sonorous, in such words as *runnel* and *camel*; and in eModE one would expect syllabic [r̩] to have been easily possible in, for example, *hammer*. Contrariwise, when a nasal follows [l] or (to a less degree) [r], more effort is required to make it dominate the inherently more sonorous preceding consonant, and so [ən] is more common than [ṇ] in, for example, *fallen* and *barren*; in some words (e.g. *sullen*) Daniel Jones, op. cit., does not record [n̩] after [l] even as a variant. After [r] syllabic [l̩] seems about as frequent as [əl] in, for example, *barrel*, and we need not doubt that in the reverse case in eModE syllabic [r̩] would have been possible in, for example, *caller*. Of the nasals, [m] seems the most and [ŋ] the least resonant; hence in PresE [ŋ̍] is rare after [m] in, for example, *common* (Daniel Jones, op. cit., records only [ən]), but in eModE did occur after [ŋ] in, for example, *condign* pronounced [kɒndɪŋŋ̍].

Syllabic consonants can readily be used in non-final position, e.g. in *riddles* [rɪdl̩z], *muttony* [mʌtn̩ɪ], and *bottomless* [bɒtm̩lɪs]; indeed reduction of [ən] and [əl] to [n̩] and [l̩] seems more rather than less likely in medial syllables (e.g. Daniel Jones gives regular [n̩] in *Gothenburg*, though in such words as *Nathan* he gives it only as a variant beside [ən]). In eModE, when [r] was not restricted to pre-vocalic position, syllabic [r̩] may well have occurred in such words as *gathers*, *thundery*, and *wonderment*.

Note 1: As syllabic [r̩] is possible before another consonant in eModE, and as [r] is inherently more sonorous than [n], there is no reason why at that time syllabic [r̩] should not have occurred, e.g., in *leathern*. Equally syllabic [n̩] could follow [r] if added sonority were imparted to the nasal. But it would in theory be easy for the combination [rn̩] to become [r̩n] by a shift of the emphasis to the naturally more sonorous consonant; so *children* [tʃɪldrn̩] might become [tʃɪldr̩n]. The reverse process, though less likely, could occur, especially if assisted by analogy; thus *leathern* [leðr̩n] > [leðrn̩].

Note 2: Though syllabic consonants can and do occur before a vowel (either of a suffix or of an independent word), the greater sonority of the following vowel is a considerable obstacle; see further § 330 below.

GENERAL REVIEW OF THE ORTHOEPISTS' EVIDENCE

§ 320. The evidence of the orthoepists makes it obvious that syllabic consonants were a commonly recognized feature of sixteenth- and seventeenth-century pronunciation; from the *Welsh Hymn* (which writes *hefn*, *efr*, *efrlasting*) onwards there is a constant succession of testimony, not confined to the major phoneticians, to their existence. Thus they are shown more or less clearly, in various classes of words, by the *Welsh Hymn*, Salesbury, Smith, Hart, Baret, Bullokar, Robinson, Hume, Gil, Butler, Daines, Jonson, Hodges, the *English Schole-Master* (1646), Wallis, Price, Coles (followed by Young, Cocker, and Brown, but not by Strong), Richardson, and Cooper; further evidence comes from the shorthand-writers T. Shelton, Metcalfe, Farthing, Everardt, Bridges, Hopkins, Mason, Coles, Ridpath, and Nicholas. The evidence of certain of these sources seems worth citing in more detail. Smith recognizes the existence of syllabic [n̩] and [l̩] when they are added to mutes (i.e. stops), but not otherwise, and does not clearly distinguish [l̩] and [n̩] from [əl] and [ən], for he says of both consonants that a sound is heard which is neither *a*, *e*, *i*, *o*, nor *u*, but a 'quasi vocalis'; but when discussing [l̩] he adds that this sound is 'tinnitus quidam, vocalis naturam habens, quæ naturaliter his liquidis inest'. Hart's transcriptions show syllabic consonants, but his general phonetic discussion shows no explicit theoretical recognition of their nature. He says that in *ordre* 'order' we pronounce the *e* before the *r*, 'or no perfite e, at al sounded', and that such words and *able*, &c. are not 'fully two sillables, but one and an addition of a half sillable softly aspired'; and he explains the term 'half-vowels' from the fact that *l, m, n*, and *r* have 'in maner the vertue of vowels'. Subsequently he identifies (falsely) the syllabic [l̥] of *able* with Spanish and Welsh voiceless [l̥]. Gil's account is clear beyond all doubt. He says that he will make only one point concerning syllables, that in our language (and in no other known to him) a syllable can consist of a consonant only, but in syllables of this sort some one of the liquids must be found, either with a mute (as in *bri-dle, ti-tle*) or alone (as in *ox-en*). Although it is customary to write *e* in such words, it is silent; in *oxen* nothing more is heard in the last syllable than in *nec* if the *ec* be subtracted, and so also in *bidden, open*, and *saddle*. Gil makes an advance on Smith in recognizing that syllabic [l̥] and [n̥] do not occur only after mutes, and in the clarity of his exposition. Hodges (perhaps influenced by Gil) says that to the rule that there are as many syllables in a word as there are vowels or diphthongs there is one exception, 'namely, that whensoever such consonants come in the end of any word that may bee pronounc't together, there will be one syllable more than there are vowels [e.g. *in-com-pre-hen-si-ble*, with the final *e* marked silent] . . . yea, sometimes one consonant alone must make a syllable; when it cometh after *x*, as in *ox-en, wax-en, flax-en*' (with the *e* again marked silent). Hunt gives the 'phonetic' spellings *muttne* 'mutton' and *fastne* 'fasten'. On Newton see Vol. I, p. 252. Price is unimportant, but it may be remarked here that he appears to be making a half-hearted attempt to describe syllabic consonants when he says that in words ending in *-le, -re*, and *-en* the *e* is 'obscure'; this must mean that it is silent, but that he shrinks from saying so because it would involve his admitting that a consonant could constitute a syllable. Coles, in his 'phonetically' spelt list, shows that he clearly recognizes the existence of syllabic consonants by regular spellings with *l* and *n*, as *weezl* 'weasel', *damzn* 'damson'; he does not usually write *-r* (having *-er* and *-ur* instead), but there does occur *ne-brr* 'neighbour'. In his *Shorthand* he says that a vowel is 'drowned' by a following liquid, as in *metal, eaten*, &c. Cooper, though recognizing that in such words as *able* the *e* was silent, did not understand the syllabic nature of the consonant, and counts the words as monosyllables.

But if the evidence of the orthoepists shows clearly that syllabic consonants existed, it also shows that there was free variation between [l̥] and [n̥] and [əl] and [ən]. This appears to some extent from the phonetic transcriptions of those authors who give them; they are not individually very consistent in their representation of syllabic consonants, often failing to represent them where they are to be expected, and again there are discrepancies between one author and another. The variation between two modes of pronunciation also accounts for the confusion that is evident in some descriptions of syllabic consonants. We have already seen how Smith hesitates to say whether or not there is a vowel present, and there are signs of the same thing in Hart's account. Hume says that 'the ear can hardlie judge quither their intervenes a voual or noe' before *l* and *n* in *little, mickle, mutton,* and *eaten. The English Schole-Master* (1646) says that *-ble* is pronounced *-bel*, but not with a clear *e*—rather as if the *e* were swallowed up, or as if it were possible to pronounce *-bl* without *e*; this clearly shows hesitation between [bəl] and [bl̩]. But perhaps the most striking case of this sort of confusion is Bullokar, who uses his 'half-vowel' symbols not only where syllabic consonants may be expected, but also to represent an [ə] glide before *r, l, m,* and *n* (see Vol. I, pp. 102 seq.). Other sources seem only or chiefly to have [ən] and [əl] in mind; such are Cheke (who shows [ɪl] < [əl] for ME *-le*), Salesbury (who shows [əl] for ME *-le*), Sherwood (who shows [əl]), Jonson (who shows [l̩] for ME *-le*, but [ɪn] < [ən] for ME *-en*), Howell (who shows [ɪl] but [ən]), Strong (who consistently avoids following Coles's 'phonetic spellings' when they represent syllabic consonants, though he plagiarizes Coles freely in other cases), and *WSC-RS* (which for once fails to follow Cooper and gives [əl], [ən] instead of [l̩], [n̩]).

It is important to remember this evidence of the co-existence of the [l̩], [n̩], and [əl], [ən] types and of the orthoepists' difficulty in distinguishing between them when we consider their evidence on syllabic [r̩]. This sound is not recognized by most orthoepists; even those who clearly describe syllabic [l̩] and [n̩] do not show syllabic [r̩], but instead give evidence of [ər] where [r̩] might be expected (so Smith, Robinson, Gil, Butler, Cooper, and Brown), and there are others who support them by providing unmistakable descriptions of [ər] (thus Palsgrave says that the English say *tenderment* for French *tendrement*, and the *Welsh Breviary* (1670) that *a* in *sugar* (ME *-re*) is pronounced like Welsh *y*, French 'feminine' *e*, i.e. as [ə]). But if evidence of syllabic [r̩] is less full, there is enough to prove its existence as a variant beside [ər]. The *Welsh Hymn* has *efr, efrlasting* 'ever', 'everlasting' beside *ffadyr* 'father' and *mwdyr* 'mother'. Salesbury says of *-re*, as of *-le*, that it is pronounced as if there were no *e* or as if the *e* were before the consonant. Hart, though he regularly writes *-er* in the *Orthographie*, commonly (though not always) writes *-r* in *Methode* (thus *dauhtr* 'daughter', *givr* 'giver', *lābr*, 'labour', &c.). Bullokar, though he normally has *-er*, has *sobR* 'sober'; but it must be remembered that he uses his symbol *R* to represent [ər] even when the [ə] is a glide. Waad shows syllabic [r̩] in *givr, mastr* (after Hart?), but has *-ur* (i.e. [ər]) in *Mr.* (see Vol. I, p. 130). Daines says of *acre* in one place that it is one syllable, and in another that the 'chief force of the syllable relies on the *r*'; these are his phrases for indicating a syllabic consonant. Hodges shows, and comments on, syllabic [r̩] in words conventionally spelt *-re* (in which the *e* is marked as silent), but not in those conventionally spelt *-er*; he does, however, show it in *anchor*, in which both *h* and *o* are marked as silent—with *anker* given as a variant spelling, so that variation between [r̩] and [ər] is made evident. Wallis says that *e* in *lucre* was formerly 'feminine' *e* but is now silent; we should write *luker*, &c.—again the variation shown by Hodges. Price says that *e* is 'obscure' (i.e. probably silent) in *-re* as in *-le*. Coles once shows syllabic [r̩] in his 'phonetic spellings'; see above. Lodwick twice transcribes *ever* as *evr*, but has *-er* in *deliver*. The shorthand-writers are the most consistent source of evidence; syllabic [r̩] is shown by such spellings as *datr* 'daughter', *labr* 'labour', *nebr* 'neighbour' by T. Shelton, Metcalfe, Farthing, Everardt, Bridges, Hopkins, Mason, Coles, Ridpath, and Nicholas. The reason why [r̩] is less regularly identified than [l̩] and [n̩] must be that it is still more difficult to distinguish between [r̩] and [ər] than between [l̩] and [əl], [n̩] and [ən], for ModE [r] is allied to the vowel [ə] and is similar to it in acoustic quality; if then the orthoepists found difficulty in distinguishing between the two easier pairs of sounds, it is not surprising that they often failed entirely to distinguish [r̩] from [ər].

§ 321. As the orthoepists were, in general, not very precise in their distinction between syllabic [l̩], [n̩], and [r̩] and the groups [əl], [ən], and [ər], it is hardly to be expected that they should give special treatment to the various phonetic combinations analysed in § 319; but certain tendencies may be observed in their evidence.

(1) *After consonants other than liquids or nasals*

It is in this position that syllabic consonants are most regularly shown—more often perhaps after stops, where alone Smith recognized that they occurred, but also after continuants (cf. the evidence of Gil and Hodges cited above, and many transcriptions in these and other authors). In PresE syllabic [n̩] is comparatively rare after the non-alveolar stops [p], [b], [g], and [k]; but the orthoepists show no sign of recognizing that this is a special case, and give evidence of syllabic [n̩] after these as after other stops (so Hart, Bullokar, Robinson, Gil, Hodges, Daines, Price, Coles, Richardson, Cooper, and Brown). The only possible exception is Brown, who says that *o* is pronounced in *dragon* though not in other words in *-on* (including *deacon*); but he is probably influenced by Latin *draconem* rather than by phonetic considerations.

(2) *After a group consisting of a nasal followed by a stop formed in the same position*

There are signs that several orthoepists recognized the difficulty of pronouncing syllabic [n̩] after the groups [nd] and [nt]. It is true that Smith gives syllabic [n̩] in *London* and that Hodges does so in *wantonness*, influenced perhaps by the apparently parallel cases of *Waldon* and *Norton*, in which they respectively give [n̩]; but Bullokar avoids syllabic [n̩] in *London* and *wanton*, Robinson and Gil in *wanton*, and Hodges, Coles, and Brown in *London*—despite their giving it in other words (such as *warden*) which seem, but are not, parallel.

(3) *After a liquid or nasal*

The evidence on words in which one liquid or nasal follows another is too slight to allow any definite conclusion. Hart has *-el* and not syllabic [l̩] in *camel* and *-er* in *hammer* (in the *Methode*, which in other cases does show syllabic [r̩]); but similar transcriptions occur after stops in other words, e.g. *candle*, *chapel*, and (in the *Methode*) *dagger*. Bullokar has *-el* in *camel* and Robinson in *spanel* 'spaniel'. There is extremely little evidence on the type in which syllabic [n̩] follows [l] or [r]; Robinson has *-en* in *woollen* and Gil *ĕ* in *villainous* and *ă* in *villain* (both probably for [ə]), but Hodges marks the *e* silent in *fallen*, &c. (in which, whether or not his [n] is syllabic, there is certainly no [ə]). Coles has *hern* 'heron' (in which, however, there may not be syllabic [n̩], since the form may represent the ME monosyllabic *hern*), but Cooper says that *baron* (in contrast to *bacon*) is two syllables, i.e. does not have syllabic [n̩]. That syllabic [n̩] did occur after [r] is, however, shown by the evidence on the *citron*, *iron* type of word discussed below (§ 328 seq.). After [r] syllabic [l̩] is not shown: Smith, Hart, Bullokar, Robinson, and Hodges have *-el* in *quarrel*, *squirrel*, and *laurel*, and Bullokar, Robinson, and Gil have *-el* in *apparel* (ME *-el* < OF *-ail*); but *-el* equally occurs in Smith, Hart, and Hodges in other words, and in any case it must be remembered that as no orthoepist except Hart and Bullokar had a sign for syllabic [l̩] different from that for [l], the representation of syllabic [l̩] after [r] was virtually impossible, since such spellings as *laurl* or *apparl* would suggest one syllable too few. Similarly syllabic [n̩] is not shown after [m] except by Bullokar and Gil in *condemn*; the failure of Hart, Bullokar, Robinson, Gil, and Hodges to show it in *woman*, *women*, *yeoman*, and *yeomen* is obviously to be explained on other than phonetic grounds, but it is also not shown by Robinson in *common* and *Damon*, by Gil in *common*, *cumin*, and *Wymondham*, and by Hodges in *colon* (which he gives with *ŏ*) and in *common* (which he gives with [ʌ], i.e. probably [ə]). But again we must allow for the difficulty created by the lack of a special sign for [n̩]; Robinson, for example, could hardly have transcribed *Damon* as *damn* even if he had used no vowel in the second syllable. Syllabic [n̩] is shown after [ŋ]; see § 324 (*b*) below. Insofar as one can generalize from such evidence, the orthoepists (especially perhaps Robinson) seem to show syllabic consonants less frequently after another liquid or nasal than after other consonants, which is what one might expect.

(4) *In non-final position*

In non-final position syllabic consonants are shown by the orthoepists in derivatives of words which have final syllabic consonants; thus by the *Welsh Hymn* in *everlasting*, by Hart in plurals such as *examples* and in *seventh* and *idly* (which he transcribes *eidLlei* [əidl̩ləi]), by Bullokar in *handled* [handl̩əd], *nimbleness*, and *reckoning*, by Robinson in *sickened* [sɪkn̩d], *heavenly*, and *oftentimes*, by Gil in *eleventh, seventeen*, &c., *heavenly*, and *oftentimes*, and by Hodges in *humbleness, drunkenness, opened* [oːpn̩d], and *openly*. It will be seen that in some of these words a syllabic consonant is shown before a following vowel; Gil, however, acutely observes the tendency of a syllabic consonant not to be used before a vowel when he explains that he writes *person* though the word is really pronounced *persn* because in the derivatives *personal* and *personality* the *o* 'does not yet vanish'. But if syllabic consonants are with some regularity shown in derivatives, they are with even greater regularity avoided in non-derivative words; thus retention of the vowel before *n* is shown by Hart in *parents, serpent, sentence, pleasant*, and *second*, by Bullokar in *parent*, by Robinson in *parent, serpents, thousand, servant*, and *warrant*, by Gil in *carpenter, present, pleasant, warrant*, and *thousand*, and by Hodges in *second, arrant*, and *servant*. But Gil shows syllabic [l̩] in *Wimbledon* (perhaps treated as a compound, though *wimble-* is not meaningful), Hodges [n̩] in *thousand* (nine times, against retention of *a* thrice; note that the final *d* is lost), and Coles [n̩] in *Wednesday* (transcribed *Wednsday*) and [r̩] in the second syllable of *froward* (see § 326 (*c*) below).

It should be remembered in assessing the orthoepists' evidence on syllabic consonants that the starting-point of their recognition of their existence was words conventionally spelt (in the sixteenth and seventeenth centuries) *-le, -re*, and *-ne* (e.g. *table, centre*, and *condigne*), in which it was easy to observe that the *-e* was 'silent'; this is shown by the facts that certain writers with no pretensions to phonetic understanding recognize (if sometimes confusedly) that in such words a consonant can constitute a syllable, and that even the better phoneticians are more consistent in transcribing such words with syllabic consonants than those spelt, for example, *-el*. But as *-le* and *-el, -re* and *-er, -ne* and *-en* were in many words interchangeable spellings, it was not difficult to proceed to the recognition that, for example, [n̩] existed in such words as *fasten*, and thence that it also occurred in such as *Drayton* and *treason*; but it is observable that syllabic consonants are much less often shown in words conventionally spelt, for example, *-an, -on*, and *-in* than in those spelt *-en* (see § 326 below). The next step, an obvious one, was to show syllabic consonants in derivatives; and it seems to us natural to proceed thence to show them in words like *presence*, but this final step the sixteenth- and seventeenth-century orthoepists do not take (with the rare exceptions noticed above). The reason was doubtless in part the influence of the traditional spelling and of etymology; most of our evidence on the words involved comes from the spelling reformers, who might well refrain from spellings such as *prezns* 'presence' (which would puzzle and repel an ordinary reader) even if they recognized that syllabic consonants were often used in such words. But the main reason is the influence of secondary stress, to which most of the words involved were obviously susceptible; it preserved pronunciations in which the vowel before the liquid or nasal was not reduced to [ə] and in which the substitution of a syllabic consonant was therefore impossible, and on these fuller pronunciations the orthoepists based their transcriptions.

Note 1: Milton, whose representation of syllabic consonants is in conformity with the practice of the best seventeenth-century orthoepists (notably of course Gil), agrees with them in showing syllabic consonants in derivatives, e.g. *rott'nness* (*Comus*, 598), *dark'n'd* (*P.L.*, i. 599), but not in words like *present* (cf. *P.L.*, i. 20).

Note 2: Secondary stress may be the cause of the preservation of the vowel in many of the words cited under (3) above, rather than the fact that the preceding consonant is itself a liquid or nasal. For further illustration of the effect of secondary stress in preventing the development of syllabic consonants, compare the discussion in § 326 of ME *ĕl* < OF stressed *el* and OF *ail*, of ME *ăl* < OF or Latin stressed *al*, and of ME *ĕn* < OF *ain*.

THE DEVELOPMENT OF SYLLABIC CONSONANTS IN LATE ME AND ModE

§ 322. From the foregoing discussion of the phonetic considerations involved it is clear that it is impossible to draw a rigid distinction between the processes of (*a*) the development of syllabic consonants and (*b*) that of a glide [ə] before liquids or nasals; for if a syllabic consonant ever develops (or occurs in a word adopted from a foreign language) in a difficult phonetic combination, the difficulty will automatically be eased in imprecise articulation by allowing a vowel-murmur, some member of the [ə] phoneme, to intervene before the consonant that should be syllabic. It is in precisely the same phonetic circumstances that syllabic consonants fail to develop or if developed are lost again; the development and the loss do not belong to different periods but are on the contrary concurrent processes which the evidence shows to have occurred at all periods from late ME up to the present time. The pairs [l̩] and [əl], [m̩] and [əm], [n̩] and [ən], and (in early ModE) [r̩] and [ər] are in fact best regarded as constituting each a single phoneme; the ordinary speaker of English is not conscious of the difference between the syllabic consonants and the groups of [ə] plus consonant, and even trained phoneticians, it may be suspected, often rely rather on an analysis of the movements of the organs of speech than on the evidence of their ears in distinguishing between them.

(1) *By the loss of final -e after liquids or nasals*

§ 323. The loss, in late ME, of final *-e* after liquids and nasals is in origin the same process as after other consonants, and proceeds at the same time (cf. Note 2 below); but its result was to produce syllabic consonants (cf. Luick, § 473 (3) and Anm. 2) in such words as *bladdre, kindle, herkne, botm(e)* and (from French) *centre, people, condigne, algorisme* (see further below). In most of the words involved the phonetic circumstances were such that the articulation of the newly developed syllabic consonants was easy; but in some there occurred circumstances of the sort which we have seen to be more or less difficult (e.g. [n̩] after [p], as in *deepen* and *happen*, or after [k], as in *hearken* and *liken*, or [m̩] after [t], as in *bottom*), and in these a glide [ə] before the [n] or [m] must have been an early development (in *bottom* syllabic [m̩], which is unknown in PresE, probably did not survive the late ME period—the latest spellings suggesting it which *OED* cites are from the *Promptorium Parvulorum*). ModE adoptions of words in *-ism*, and such words as *chasm, prism, enthusiasm*, have been modelled on ME adoptions in which OF, ME *-isme* [ızmə] developed into [ızm̩]; in these [əm] instead of [m̩] is now frequent, and though it is not shown by the orthoepists (see below) the glide probably developed early. In other cases the orthoepists show that pronunciations with the glide [ə] or with [ı] developed from it varied freely with those with syllabic consonants; and the position in the fifteenth century was probably the same.

Note 1: The development of syllabic consonants by this process may be deduced on general grounds, and is proved to have occurred by the interchange of the etymologically distinct endings *-le, -ne, -re* and *-el, -en, -er* in late ME. Luick, § 474 (3) and Anm. 2, takes these interchanged spellings as indicating in all cases syllabic [l̩], [n̩], and [r̩]; but they could as well, and often probably do, indicate [əl], [ən], and [ər], i.e. that a glide has developed.

Note 2: The date of the development is necessarily that of the loss of final *-e*, which began in the North in the thirteenth century and thence spread south, affecting London English in the last quarter of the fourteenth century and reaching fulfilment in the first few decades of the fifteenth century. The interchange of the spellings *-re*, &c. and *-er*, &c. begins at the same dates; early examples occur in the Northern *Cursor Mundi*, and southern examples are found in manuscripts of works written towards the end of the fourteenth century (e.g. Chaucer manuscripts have *-er* spellings in *(n)adder* and Trevisa, *De Prop. Rerum* (1398), has *idle, idleness*).

§ 324. The orthoepists show syllabic consonants developed by this process as follows.

(a) *Syllabic* [l̩]

Syllabic [l̩] < ME *-le* in *able, cribble, fable, handle*, &c. is shown by Smith, Hart, Baret, Robinson, Gil, Butler, Daines, Jonson, Hodges, Wallis, probably Price, Coles (followed by Young, Cocker, and Brown), and Cooper. But [əl], substituted for [l̩], is shown by Salesbury, who transcribes *-le* in *double* by Welsh *-yl*, i.e. [əl] (but elsewhere says that *-le* is pronounced as if there were no *e*, or as if the *e* were before the *l*); by Sherwood (1632), who says that *-ble*, &c. (as in *Bible*) is pronounced 'presque comme *bul*, &c.'; and by *WSC-RS*, which says *-le* is pronounced *-el*. Some authors hesitate: Bullokar writes *people*, &c. as *pe'pL*, &c., but says that the 'half-vowel' *L* is pronounced *ul* (see Vol. I, p. 102); and *The English Schole-Master* (1646) and Richardson say that *-ble* is pronounced *-bel*, but with no clear *e*—rather as if the *e* were swallowed up, or as if it were possible to pronounce *bl* without *e*. Some give [ɪl] developed from this [əl] which is substituted for syllabic [l̩]; so Cheke (who writes *abil, discipil*), Levins (regularly), Howell (who says that in *epistle* the *e* 'leaps before the *l*, and takes the half sound of *i*'), and Strong (who does not follow Coles in his representation of syllabic [l̩] and says that *able* is pronounced *abil*).

(*b*) *Syllabic* [n̩]

Syllabic [n̩] from *-ne* in such words as *happen, hearken* is shown by Hart, Gil, Hodges, Coles, and Young. Bullokar hesitates between syllabic [n̩] and [ən] (see Vol. I, p. 102). Strong's 'phonetic' spellings show both *en* (for [ən]), as in *thretten*, and *in* (for [ɪn] developed from [ən]), as in *harkin*. Bullokar and Gil have [n̩] in *condemn*. A special case is words from OF ending in *-igne*, &c. (e.g. *benigne, condigne, signe*); these seem to have been pronounced in ME not only with *n* for OF *gn* (in which case the syllable was open and the ME vowel long, whence the PresE pronunciation), but also (doubtless more rarely) with [gn] or [ŋn]. They thus ended in [gnə] or [ŋnə], which with the loss of the final [ə] became [gn̩] or [ŋn̩]; the vowel, being in a closed syllable, was of course short. The pronunciation with [gn̩] is shown by Gil in *benign* and *condign*; by Daines in *benign, condign*, and *oppugn* (he says that 'the chief force of the syllable relies upon' the *n* in words spelt *-gne*, and compares *benigne* to *spasme*, *benigne* and *oppugne* to *notable* and *fable*); by Richardson, who, apparently following Daines, says that *g* is silent before *n* as in *feign* but excepts *benigne, oppugne*, and *condigne*, in which he says *g* and *n* are equal and which are with difficulty so pronounced as not to be more than two syllables; and by Cooper, who says that *e* is silent in *shorten*, &c. and not written in *malign* and *catechism*, which shows that he regards *malign* as having syllabic [n̩] as *shorten* has, and as *catechism* has syllabic [m̩]. The variant [ŋn̩] is shown only by Gil (beside [gn̩]); he says that *benign* and *condign* can be pronounced *beningn, condingn*, and is supported by such ME spellings as *syngne* 'sign' (*Sir Gawain and the Green Knight*, l. 625, &c.). See further § 441 below.

(*c*) *Syllabic* [r̩]

Syllabic [r̩] from ME *-re* in such words as *tender, tiger*, and *centre* is shown most clearly by Hart in the *Methode*, where he has such spellings as *delivr* and *remembr*, and by Hodges, who shows it in words spelt *-re* (including *tigre*); Price seems to mean it when he says that in *-re* the *e* is 'obscure' (as also in *-le*). Others hesitate: Salesbury says that *-re* is pronounced as if there were no *e*, or as if the *e* were before the *r*; Bullokar usually writes *-er*, but has his 'half-vowel' *R* in *sobre* spelt *sōbR* (but this is inconclusive, since he also uses *R* for [ər] where the [ə] is a glide); and Wallis says that the *e* was formerly 'e feminine' but is now silent in such words as *lucre*—which is clear so far, but he adds that we should spell them *luker*, &c., which seems to imply [ər]. Otherwise [ər] substituted for syllabic [r̩] is shown; so by Palsgrave, Smith, Hart (*Orthographie*), Robinson, Gil, Butler (who says that in *-le* the *e* is silent, but that *-re* is pronounced *-er*), the *Welsh Breviary* (1670) (which says that in *sugar* (ME *-re*) the *a* is pronounced like Welsh *y*, French feminine *e*, i.e. [ə]), Coles (who gives *constur* < fifteenth-century *constre* as a 'phonetic' spelling of *construe*), Strong, Young, Lodwick, Cooper, *WSC-RS*, and Brown.

(d) Syllabic [m̩]

Syllabic [m̩] from ME *-me* in such words as *baptism, catechism, schism, chasm, rhythm*, and *logarithm* is shown by Daines, Hodges, and Cooper.

Note 1: Hart's spelling *repugned*, though it does not itself show syllabic [n̩], should mean that both *g* and *n* are pronounced; if so, his infinitive would have [gn̩].

Note 2: Bullokar would doubtless spell the words cited under (*d*) with his 'half-vowel' *M* (as he does *alarM* 'alarum'); but as he uses *M* for [əm] where the [ə] is a glide, there is here some sort of presumption that [əm] was substituted for syllabic [m̩] in the sixteenth century, though in fact it is not shown.

(2) By the so-called 'loss of vowels' before a liquid or nasal

§ 325. PresE exhibits syllabic [l̩] or [n̩], and early ModE had also syllabic [r̩], for a variety of ME and early ModE endings: *-el* (as in *saddle*), *-al* (*mortal*); *-en* (*ridden*), *-on* representing ME *-un* (*pardon*), *-an* (*republican*), and similarly in the endings *-ant* (*pleasant*), *-ent* (*student*), *-ence* (*prudence*); *-er* (*setter*), *-ar* (*pandar*), *-or* (*inventor*), *-our* (*creator* < *creatour*). Syllabic [l̩] occurs even in StE for *-il* in, for example, *civil, basil*; in other forms of PresE syllabic consonants are common both for *-il* and for *-in*. It is as a rule tacitly or openly assumed (but Luick is a notable exception; see Note 3 below) that the pronunciation which immediately preceded the development of syllabic [l̩], [n̩], and [r̩] was [əl], [ən], and [ər]; in other words, that reduction to [ə] of the unstressed vowels of the syllables involved is a prerequisite of the development of syllabic consonants. This assumption is certainly correct, but the case for it requires demonstration. Absolute proof is, in the nature of things, hardly possible; but the following considerations establish a presumption so strong that it cannot be doubted.

(i) ME *ŭ, ŏ*, and *ă* are regularly reduced to [ə] when fully unstressed (see

§§ 298-9, 302 above). The endings -*ur*, -*un*, -*al*, &c. consequently become [ər], [ən], [əl], &c. But in favourable phonetic circumstances there is evidence in eModE of, or there are observable in PresE, syllabic [r̩], [n̩], and [l̩] in place of these groups or as a variant beside them.

(ii) ME unstressed *ĕ*, after becoming [ə], shows a double development in late ME and ModE, either changing to [ɪ] or remaining [ə]. In PresE three developments of ME -*en* are observable, namely (*a*) [ɪn] in *chicken*, &c., (*b*) [ən] in *linden*, &c., and (*c*) [n̩] in *ridden*, &c. Luick would associate (*a*) and (*b*), deriving them from a common source, his ME *ĕn* (see Note 3 below); but in view of the variation between, for example, [ən] and [n̩] < ME -*on*, -*un*, -*an*, it is not to be doubted that it is rather (*b*) and (*c*) which are to be associated. We thus have two main types in ME -*en* words, the [ɪn] type and the [ən], [n̩] type (and similarly with -*el* words); these two main types obviously correspond to the double development of ME unstressed *e* to [ɪ] or [ə]. It follows that the process of development of ME -*en*, -*el* is either (*a*) ME unstressed *e* changes from [ə] to [ɪ], giving [ɪn], [ɪl], of which the former normally remains unchanged in PresE (see under (iii) below), or (*b*) ME unstressed *e* remains [ə], giving [ən], [əl], whence in favourable phonetic circumstances [n̩], [l̩]. Between the two types—[ɪn] on the one hand and [ən], [n̩] on the other—there has been a conflict in ModE; which prevails in any one word is, as usually in such cases, a matter largely of chance (though Jespersen, *ModE Gr*, § 9.52, has pointed out that, by a sort of vowel-harmony, [ɪn] seems to be preferred after syllables containing [ɪ]), and in some words, including *chicken* itself, there is variation between [ɪn] (dominant in this word), [ən], and [n̩]. But no double development of -*er* was possible, as [ə] < ME unstressed *e* seems not to have become [ɪ] before *r*, and if it had would again have become [ə]; late ME variation between -*er*, -*ir*, and -*yr* spellings seems to be of no significance, all of them representing [ər].

(iii) ME unstressed *ĭ* (including the *i* variant of ME unstressed *e*) is only exceptionally reduced to [ə] in present StE, and it is therefore very significant that syllabic [n̩] is rare in StE for ME -*in* (e.g. in *engine, resin, medicine, dolphin, feminine*). But one of the positions in which reduction of unstressed *i* to [ə] is likely even in StE is before *l*, for English final *l*, being 'dark', has strong retractive force (see § 219 above), and only retraction and a slight lowering of the tongue are needed to turn the English lax [ɪ] into the English [ə]; and it is significant that syllabic [l̩] for ME -*il* does occur— thus Daniel Jones gives [l̩] as more common than [ɪl] in *civil* and *basil*, though he records only [ɪl] in *chervil* and *beryl*. In forms of English in which reduction of unstressed *i* to [ə] is regular, syllabic [n̩] for ME -*in*, as well as syllabic [l̩] for ME -*il*, is common (beside [ən], [əl] variants). See further Note 1 below.

(iv) The eModE evidence makes it clear that there was a direct relationship between the loss of secondary stress and the development of syllabic consonants. But as the primary effect of the retention of secondary stress was to prevent the reduction to [ə] of the vowels on which it fell, there is a strong suggestion that reduction to [ə] and the development of syllabic consonants were associated processes.

In all cases, then, there is a correspondence between the regularity or irregularity of the reduction of the unstressed vowel in question to [ə] and the regularity or irregularity of the development of syllabic consonants; the two processes must therefore be inter-dependent, and it is clear that reduction to [ə] is the earlier. The process of change, once [ə] has developed, is not so much a syncope of the [ə] as the direct substitution of syllabic [l̩], [n̩], and [r̩] for the groups [əl], [ən], and [ər], of which (as we have seen) they may be regarded as phonematic variants.

As for the date of these developments, no *terminus ad quem* can be set for the process of substitution; if at the present day, in a word newly adopted or formed, the native unstressed [əl] (for example) be substituted for foreign *-al*, *-el*, &c. (as in the name *Goebbels*), then syllabic [l̩] can take its place provided the phonetic circumstances are favourable. For syllabic [r̩] there is of course a *terminus ad quem*, the date at which it was vocalized to [ə] in unstressed syllables. The *terminus a quo* is the date at which the unstressed vowel in question was reduced to [ə] (a change which had certainly occurred by the middle of the fifteenth century in the case of the ME back vowels, and was much earlier for ME unstressed *e*; see §§ 293 (*b*), 301–3 above); in the case of words originally subject to secondary stress the effective date is that of its loss in the word in question (unless this is earlier than the development of [ə] from the vowel involved). See further Note 2 below.

Note 1: In *gentle, cockle, purfle* ME *-il* (< OF) has so regularly > [əl] > [l̩] that the spelling has been affected. Syllabic [n̩] for ME *-in* is regular in *garden* and *basin*, but we have possibly to do with suffix-substitution; *garden* has *-en* forms from the fourteenth century. Similarly there may be suffix-substitution in *gentle*, which has *-el* from the fourteenth century. (See *OED*, s.vv.)

Note 2: The interchange of the spellings *-le, -ne, -re* and *-el, -en, -er* (see § 323, Notes 1 and 2 above), and the equivalence of, for example, *un, en, an, on,* and *yn* in spellings cited by Wyld (thus *Swithan* 'Swithun', *sesyn* 'season', *Devunshyre, y-writon* 'written'), probably depend, at least in part, on syllabic consonants, though they might depend on [ən], &c.; such spellings occur in the North at the beginning of the fourteenth century and in the South in the late fourteenth and early fifteenth centuries, and become more common in the later fifteenth century. Wyld cites from fifteenth-century texts spellings with simple *-r* for earlier *-er* which seem unmistakable evidence of syllabic [r̩] (*Coll. Eng.* (3rd edition), p. 407).

Note 3: Luick treats the development of syllabic consonants from ME *el, en,* and *er* as a process earlier than and distinct from their development from *on, an,* &c. (see § 472, Anm. 1, end). His theory may be summarized as follows.

(1) ME *el, en* (including *il, in* in words adopted from OF) were pronounced with a vowel *ė* (see § 293 above), which he identifies with PresE lax [ɪ], and ME *er* was pronounced with *ę*. This *ė* or *ę* was lost in late ME after a consonant other than a liquid or nasal; but

ẹ remained after [tʃ], [dʒ], *sp*, *nd*, and in *chicken*. After a liquid or nasal *ẹ* was lost before *r*, but *ẹ* remained as a rule before *l* and *n*; in the endings *-ren*, *-len* after a long vowel [he should add 'or diphthong'] there was a double development, thus *īren* or *īrn*, *fallen* or *faln* (§ 472). This position remained until the eighteenth century, and his definition of it is based on the evidence of later eighteenth-century pronouncing dictionaries (§ 472, Anm. 3). Subsequently there developed PresE [ə] (i) in the endings *-ence*, *-ent* from earlier unstressed *e* (not identified, by Luick, with his 'ME *ẹ*'), and (ii) from ME *ẹ* in the endings *-en*, *-el* regularly in some words, as a variant beside retained *ẹ* in others, and not at all in yet others (§ 592). The regularity with which [ə] appears in words now spelt *o* (e.g. *London*) is due to the spelling, which largely influences the operation of this sound-change (§ 472, Anm. 3). There has also been in recent times a tendency for syllabic [l̩] and [n̩], whether from ME *-el*, *-en* or *-le*, *-ne*, to become [əl], [ən], 'at least in Southern English in slow careful speech' (§ 593). On the other hand syllabic [l̩] and [n̩] sometimes occur nowadays where by rule there should only be [əl] and [ən]; this is 'probably a later phenomenon' (§ 472, Anm. 3, end).

(2) ME *on* was originally pronounced, Luick holds, with his vowel *ō̇*, which became [ə] *c.* 1500; the [ə] as a rule disappeared (giving syllabic [n̩]) after consonants other than liquids or nasals. But there was originally much variation between [ən] and [n̩], until *c.* 1800 a situation developed (largely owing to the influence of the preceding consonant) which can, he says, be simply defined: the [ə] was kept after liquids, nasals, *b*, *g*, [dʒ], [tʃ], [ʒ], and [ʃ], and also after a consonant plus [j]. But during the nineteenth century there was a tendency, clearly due to the spelling, to insert [ə] after [p] and [k], so that loss of the [ə] is [now] general only after dentals ([d], [t], [s], and [z]); on the other hand the loss of [ə] after [ʒ] and [ʃ], already not unknown *c.* 1800, has now become commoner (§ 589). He regards it as improbable that when in the early sixteenth century unstressed *or* became [ər] syllabic [r̩] developed, and does not consider the possibility of syllabic [m̩] < [əm] < ME *om* and *um* (which he does not distinguish). The rules given are again derived from later eighteenth-century pronouncing dictionaries (Anm. 1), and the subsequent developments described are assumed in order to account for the divergences between these dictionaries' evidence and PresE pronunciation.

(3) ME and eModE unstressed *a* became [ə], according to Luick, 'already' in the course of the sixteenth century; subsequently (probably first in the nineteenth century) a tendency developed in quick everyday speech to lose the [ə] before *l* and *n*, giving syllabic [l̩] and [n̩].

This theory is obviously far too complex to be true. Its complications are forced on Luick by (*a*) his views on the pronunciation of the ME unstressed vowels, and especially ME *e*, which we have already rejected, and (*b*) his uncritical acceptance of the evidence of certain later eighteenth-century authorities who, in a period of dogmatism, are on *a priori* grounds unlikely to have told the whole truth. The discrepancy between their evidence and the observable PresE position is itself a warning that they are not to be trusted; Luick has to invent inconsistent and contradictory sound-changes to explain how the PresE diversity develops from the assumed eighteenth-century regularity. He rejects (§ 472, Anm. 3; § 589, Anm. 1) the evidence of Buchanan (1769), which is inconsistent with his other authorities, with the unlikely explanation that Buchanan's book is probably erroneously printed; the truth is rather that Buchanan's evidence shows that the rules of the other writers are over-simplified. Earlier evidence, which also conflicts with Luick's rules, is not discussed, and the rules themselves seem to me most unlikely on phonetic grounds. Other weaknesses are (*a*) the explanation of PresE [əl], [ən] as a recent development partly from the assumed ME and ModE *ĕl*, *ĕn* (i.e. what is really [ɪl], [ɪn]) and partly from eModE [l̩], [n̩]—whereas in fact there is plentiful evidence of [əl] and [ən] in the sixteenth and seventeenth centuries; (*b*) the failure to realize that the lack of evidence, except in modern accounts written on strict phonetic principles, of syllabic [l̩] and [n̩] for *-al*, *-an*, &c. is not a sign of their very recent development in such cases but is due to an unwillingness, even in nineteenth-century works (and notably in *OED*), to admit their existence when the spelling does not suggest it. (E.g. *OED*'s notations of the pronunciation of *civil*, *special*, and *Titan* do not show that syllabic [l̩] or [n̩] may be used, though it has a convention—the use of small 'superior' letters to indicate elements that may be silent—which would make it easy to record them; in fact they are common in these words and are recorded as variants by Daniel Jones, *Eng. Pron. Dict.*)

It is of course not here denied that in certain of the classes of words discussed by Luick early evidence of the presence of syllabic consonants is lacking; but the reason is that these words retained secondary stress comparatively late, and the vowels that are shown in them are commonly not unstressed vowels at all.

§ 326. The orthoepists' evidence showing the development of syllabic consonants by the 'loss' of [ə] before liquids or nasals is set out below. (For their evidence on words in which special phonetic circumstances arise see § 321 above.)

(a) Syllabic [l̩]

Syllabic [l̩] for ME unstressed *-el* is shown in final position, and in derivatives of words with final *-el*, by Smith (only in words conventionally spelt *-le*, though he says that it is also spelt *-il* and *-ul*), Hart (chiefly in words spelt *-le*, but also in *evil*), Bullokar (in words spelt *-le* and *-el* and in *evil* and *devil*), Robinson (in *apple, evil, devil*), Gil (in words spelt *-le* and in *evil*), Hodges (in words spelt *-le, -el*, and *-il*), Wallis (in *candle*), Coles (e.g. in *evil, weasel*) followed by Young, Cocker, and Brown, Cooper (in *drivel, ravel, devil,* and *evil*), and by the shorthand-writers Farthing, Bridges, Hopkins, Mason, Coles, Ridpath, and Nicholas. The [əl] variant is shown by Smith's hesitation in the description of syllabic [l̩] (see § 320 above) and by Bullokar's confusion (see Vol. I, p. 102), and underlies certain transcriptions with *-el*, e.g. Smith's of *swaddle* and Strong's regularly where Coles has *-l* for [l̩]. Occasionally [ɪl] < [əl] is shown; Smith has *-il* in *devil* and *evil*, Jonson says that *e* sounds 'obscured, like the faint *i*' in *divel,* &c., and Howell says that *-le* is pronounced *-il* in *thistle* (and presumably in other such words). Cooper says that *swingil* (< MDu *swinghel*) and *hovel* are disyllables (unlike *drivel*, &c., which he counts as monosyllables), i.e. they have a vowel before the [l], perhaps [ɪ] in the one case and [ə] in the other.

The influence of secondary stress is often clear. Thus Hart has *-el* (not [l̩]) in *Mihel* 'Michael' (of dubious origin, but originally certainly end-stressed), *Michaelmas* (OF *Michel*), *chapel* (< OF), and *candle* (once, against [l̩] twice; the word is from OE *candel*, whence the form with [l̩], with some influence in ME from OF *chandelle*, which would account for the *-el* variant); and in purely native words only in *aphel* 'apple', a transcription in which his attention is concentrated on the representation of the English aspirated [p], and which is therefore abnormal. Similarly Smith has *-el* in *chapel*, Bullokar in *cattle* and *gravel*, Gil in *cattle*, and Hodges in *cattle, rebel* (sb.), and *revel*. For ME *-el* < OF *-ail* syllabic [l̩] is likewise rarely shown (cf. *-en* < OF *-ain* under (*b*) below); *-el* is retained by Bullokar in *battle* (beside a form with *-ail*) and *travel*, by Hodges in *battle*, and by the shorthand-writers T. Shelton and Mason in *victual* (ME *vitail* < OF). But the last word has syllabic [l̩] in Hodges, Wharton (followed by J. Smith), Coles (followed by Young), and the shorthand-writer Everardt; the 'homophone list' pairing of *vitals* and *victuals* (Hodges 'near', Fox and Hookes, Strong, and Cooper 'near') may depend on either [əl] or [l̩], and Strong's *vittils* shows [ɪl] < [əl] < ME unstressed -*el*. The reason for the avoidance of the representation of syllabic [l̩] in these words is doubtless the continued existence of forms with -*ail* retained under full secondary stress (see § 272 above); that [l̩] did occur in the sixteenth century (and probably earlier) is shown by the spellings *battle* and *vittle*, which *OED* records from that century. See further Note 1 below.

Syllabic [l̩] for ME -*al* is shown only in *metal* (by Robinson, Gil, Hodges, and Coles), in which the ME form *metel* shows that there was early loss of secondary stress, and possibly in *vitals* by the 'homophone list' pairing mentioned immediately above (which at least must show [əl], the precursor of [l̩]). It was, however, probably common in everyday, or at least in vulgar, speech; the failure to show it is due partly to the influence of the spelling and of Latin, but more to the existence in this case also of pronunciations in which the nature of the vowels used (see § 273 above) proves that secondary stress was still freely maintained up to the time of Hodges, after which the detailed evidence which extensive transcriptions afford is no longer available.

Syllabic [l̩] for ME -*il* may be shown by Smith in *scribble* (if the word is direct from MedLat *scribillare*) and in *niffles* (if it is from Lat *nichil*; but it is in any case influenced by *trifle*, which has ME -*le*); it is certainly shown by Bullokar in *gentle* (and in *council* and *counsellor*, but these have ME -*ĕl* < -*eil* beside ME -*il*) and by Hodges in *subtle*. The variant [əl] is shown by Bullokar's -*el* in *nostril* and Robinson's in *civil*. Unchanged [ɪl] is shown by Smith in *gentle* (glossed 'clemens, urbanus'), Bullokar in *cavil, civil*, and *lentil*, Robinson in *Virgil*, and Hodges in *civil*; retention of secondary stress is possible in all these cases.

(b) *Syllabic* [n̩]

Syllabic [n̩] for ME -*en* is shown in final position, and in derivatives of words with final -*en*, by the *Welsh Hymn*, Smith, Hart, Baret, Bullokar, Robinson, Gil, Hodges, Coles (followed by Young, Cocker, and Brown), and Cooper, probably also by Price. But Smith hesitates between [n̩] and [ən] (see § 320 above) and has a transcription *woxen* which fails to show syllabic [n̩] (Smith recognizes syllabic consonants only after stops); Bullokar is also confused (see Vol. I, p. 102). Gil has -*en* in *burthen, heaven* (once, beside syllabic [n̩] eight times), and *seventh* (once, beside [n̩] once); in *wagon*, influenced by the spelling, he gives *o* but must have used [ə], since the word is eModE *wagan, wagen* < Du *wagen*. Others show only [ən]; so probably Howell (who says that *e* 'passeth obscurely' in *spoken* and *broken*) and certainly Lye (who says that *e* is pronounced like short *u* in *beaten*, &c.), Strong (who does not adopt Coles's 'phonetic' spellings that show [n̩] and instead has such as *offen* 'often', *weppen* 'weapon'), and *WSC-RS* (which follows Lye). Others again have [ɪn] < [ən]; so Laneham (who has *heavins*), Gil (who has *aspin* 'aspen'), and Jonson (who says that *e* sounds 'obscured, like the faint *i*', in *written*, &c.).

For ME *-en* < OF *-ain* the orthoepists rarely show [n̩], probably because of the coexistence of forms with secondary stress in which *-ain* was preserved (see § 272 above) and the influence of the conventional spelling. Thus Hart has *serten* 'certain'; Bullokar *-en* in *foreign* and *sudden* and *-in* ([ɪn] < [ən]) in *sloven*; Robinson *-en* in *certain*; and Gil *-en* in *citizen*. But Bullokar, Gil, and Hodges have [n̩] in *dozen*. See further Note 2 below.

Syllabic [n̩] for ME *-in* is also rarely shown, but Bullokar has it in *cousin* and *garden*, Hodges in *cousin*, Coles in *medicine* and *raisin*, and *WSC-RS* in *basin* and *cousin*. The [ən] for which [n̩] is substituted is shown by Smith's *-en* in *lurdan* (< OF *lourdin*), Robinson's *-en* in *garden*, and Strong's *-un* in *medicine*. On the possibility of suffix-substitution (ME *-en* for *-in*) in *garden* see § 325, Note 1.

Syllabic [n̩] for ME back vowels followed by *n* is shown by Bullokar in *capon, button, reason(able), impersonal*, and *pardon* (but his *N* may mean [ən] as well as [n̩]); by Robinson in *pardon, person, prison, reason, treason*, and *Drayton*; by Hume in *mutton*; by Gil in *bacon, capon, lesson*, and *mutton* (and he admits it also to exist in *person*); by Jonson in *person* and *action*; by Hodges in *person, mason, bacon, pardon, mutton*, &c. and in *Weston, Preston, Wilson*, &c.; by Lloyd in *prison*; by Price in *bacon, capon*, &c.; by Coles in *Eton, reason*, and *venison* (followed by Young); by Cooper in *bacon* (followed by *WSC-RS*); and by Brown. But Hart has *on* in *reason(able)*, Bullokar *-en* in *caben* 'cabin' (ME *cabane*), Gil *-on* in *pardon*, Hodges [ʌ] (perhaps for [ə]) in *Overton*; all of these are words in which secondary stress is possible, but the *o* forms are probably due to the influence of the spelling (reinforced by that of Latin). In *venison*, pronounced as two syllables, Strong gives *-un* and Cocker *-en*, both of which must mean [ən]; Bullokar may also be taken as some sort of evidence for the [ən] variant which is the precursor of, and survives beside, syllabic [n̩].

(c) Syllabic r̩

Syllabic [r̩] for ME *-er* in final position, or in derivatives of words with final *-er*, is shown by the *Welsh Hymn*, Hart (*Methode*, not *Orthographie*), Waad, Daines, Hodges, Lodwick, and the shorthand-writers Metcalfe, Farthing, Bridges, Hopkins, Mason, Coles, Ridpath, and Nicholas; for details see § 320 above. The variant [ər] is alone shown by Smith, Bullokar, Robinson, Gil, Howell (who says that *e* 'passeth obscurely' in *coffer*), Strong, Young, Cooper (who distinguishes *acre*, &c., in which he says that *-re* is pronounced *-ur* or *-er*, from words in *-le, -en*, in which he says that the *e* is silent, *WSC-RS*, and Brown (as Cooper); it is also given as a more or less common variant by the *Welsh Hymn*, Waad, Hart (who has only -*er* in *O*. except in *ōvr-it* 'over it', where the hyphen shows elision, thus [oːvrɪt], and -*er* beside -*r* in *M*.), Daines (who shows [r̩] only in *acre*), and Hodges (who shows [r̩] only in words spelt -*re* and in *anchor*).

Syllabic [r̩] for ME -*ir* < OF [yr] is shown only by the shorthand-writer Bridges, who gives *kretrs* 'creatures', *ordr* 'ordure', *mesr* 'measure', and *fetr* 'feature'. Other orthoepists give only [ər]; for an outline of their evidence see § 282, under (*c*) and (*d*).

Syllabic [r̩] for ME -*ur* is shown by Hart, *Methode* (*labr* 'labour'); Coles, *Schoolmaster* (*ne-brr* 'neighbour', a 'phonetic' spelling clearly adopted from the shorthand books, of which Coles himself wrote one); and the shorthand-writers T. Shelton, Farthing, Everardt, Bridges, Hopkins, and Mason (who teach that *ou* is silent in *labour*, *neighbour*, and *favour*), and Bridges (who has also *tresr* 'treasure' < ME *tresur*). Otherwise -*ur* (which becomes [ər]) is shown.

Syllabic [r̩] for ME -*ar*- is shown only by Coles in his *Shorthand*, in which he gives *froward* as one of his examples showing how a vowel is 'drowned' by a following liquid. The instance is at first sight surprising, as one would hardly expect syllabic [r̩] to be used after [w], and it is indeed possible that Coles really used [ər] and failed to distinguish it from [r̩]; but his 'phonetic' spellings in the *Schoolmaster* show an exceptionally clear understanding of syllabic consonants, and the other examples given in the *Shorthand* are beyond question.

The rarity with which [r̩] is shown for unstressed -*ir*, -*ur*, and -*ar* is due to the fact that all the words involved had variant pronunciations with secondary stress.

(*d*) Syllabic [m̩]

Syllabic [m̩] in such words as *Adam*, *seldom*, *wisdom*, *accustom*, *blossom*, and *whilom* is shown by no orthoepist; Hodges has -*am* in *Adam*, and Hart, Bullokar, Robinson, Gil, and Hodges have -*um* in one or more of the other words cited (except that Gil has -*om* in *accustom*; see § 283 above). Bullokar has -*im* in *venom* (ME *venim* < OF). The failure to show syllabic [m̩] in these words (whereas it is shown in, for example, *schism* and *rhythm*) is due primarily to the influence of the spelling, perhaps aided in some cases by that of forms retaining some degree of secondary stress (e.g. in *Adam*, *accustom*, *venom*).

Note 1: Milton's spellings of the word do not normally suggest syllabic [l̩] in *battle*; see Wyld, *Coll. Eng.* (3rd edition), p. 407.

Note 2: On the retention of *e* in words like *presence* (where secondary stress is the main cause) see § 321 (4) above. Milton fails to show syllabic [n̩] in *sudden*; see Wyld, op. cit., p. 404, who cites a spelling dated 1644 to prove that it did however exist.

Note 3: For further confirmatory evidence on the development of syllabic consonants (including [r̩]) by 'loss' of [ə] see Wyld, op. cit., Appendix III, and (on Milton's spellings) Miss H. Darbishire, *The MS of Book I of Paradise Lost*.

METATHESIS OF *r* IN UNSTRESSED SYLLABLES

§ 327. In a number of words there occurs in unstressed syllables a metathesis of *r* which in many instances, if not in all, is to be attributed to the development of syllabic consonants. In some of these words an *r* which originally preceded the vowel of the unstressed syllable comes to follow it; in others the reverse process applies.

(1) *Pre-vocalic r becomes post-vocalic*

§ 328. In certain words ME *-ron*, *-ren* become [rən] and thence [rn̩] (with syllabic [n̩]); a shift of emphasis leads this group to become [r̩n] (with syllabic [r̩]) (see § 319, Note 1 above), from which develops the variant [ərn]. Both [r̩n] and [ərn] give PresE [ən]. (For further discussion of the process of change see Note 2 below.)

Examples are *apron*, *citron*, *saffron*, which were formerly pronounced with [ərn]; this pronunciation still occurs in *apron* in the dialects (Wright, § 263) and is recorded by *OED* as a variant. ME *patron* gives rise to two ModE forms, [pætrən] and [pætən]; the latter, and the appropriate spelling *pattern*, is now restricted to, and has always been more common in, one branch (the more 'popular') of the sense development. But *OED* records a fifteenth-century form *patorne* in the sense 'patron'; contrariwise I have heard [pætrən] in the sense 'pattern'. *Cathern* for *Catherine* develops similarly from the syncopated form *Cathrin*, in which *-rin* becomes [rən] > [rn̩] > [r̩n] > [ərn], whence PresE would have [ən]. Similarly the fifteenth- and sixteenth-century form *caudern* 'cauldron' develops by metathesis from the syncopated *caudren* (fourteenth century onwards) < ME *cauderon*. In the same way eModE *childern*, *brethern* must, at least in part, be developed from *children*, *brethren* (see Note 3 below). But in *iron* < ME *īren*, though the pronunciation [əiərn] is recorded by the same sources as give the [ərn] pronunciations of the foregoing words, there is the significant difference that the *r* is not preceded by a consonant, but by a vowel. The first stage of the phonetic process must have been the same, a change of [iːrən] to [əirn̩] (diphthongization of ME *ī* was probably later than the development of syllabic [n̩], but the order is immaterial), but thereafter loss of syllabic quality by the [n] cannot have been accompanied by its transference to the [r]. The word was simply reduced to a monosyllable (as Hodges plainly regards it), and the [ə] of [əiərn] > PresE [aiən] is the ordinary glide-vowel developed between a ModE diphthong and [r]. *Environ* was similarly [envəiərn] in the later seventeenth century. But forms without metathesis survive, in *environ* regularly in StE and in *iron* in dialects.

The orthoepists' evidence seems mostly to refer to the [ərn] stage; but Lloyd (who says that *o* is silent in *iron* and *prison* pronounced *irne* and *prisne*), Price (who, partly following Lloyd, says that *o* is silent in *iron*, *citron*, and *apron*), and Hawkins (who follows Price) seem to be trying to describe one of the syllabic consonant stages—probably [rn̩] in the case of Lloyd, and perhaps also in those of Price and Hawkins. Hart in the *Methode* transcribes *brethren* and *children* with *-rn* (and no unstressed vowel); it must be the [n] which is syllabic, for in the 1551 MS. he regards the forms *bretheren*, *childeren* as incorrect spellings of *brethren*, *children*. Hodges marks silent the *e* of *children* (twelve times; he omits to do so only once, perhaps by error) and the *o* of *iron*; the latter keeps company with monosyllables and is not included among the words of which 'the last syllable . . . is expressed without a vowel'. But *children* must have a syllabic consonant, and it may have been [r] (which, it will be remembered, Hodges is one of the few orthoepists to recognize). The rest of the evidence is as follows. *Apron* has [ərn] in Hunt and Coles (who give the 'phonetic' spelling *apurn*), followed by Strong, Young, and Cocker, and in Cooper, followed by *WSC-RS* and Brown. *Citron* has [ərn] in Cooper, followed by *WSC-RS* and Brown, and in the 'homophone lists' of Price, Coles (*Eng.-Lat. Dict.*), Young, Cooper 'near', Cocker, and Brown, which pair the word with *cittern* 'cithern'. *Saffron* has [ərn] in Coles (followed by Strong and Cocker) and in Cooper (followed by *WSC-RS* and Brown); Young's 1682 edition follows Coles, but that of 1722 has the 'phonetic' spelling *saf-run*. The PresE distinction of *patron* and *pattern* is known apparently to three sources (Robinson and Gil have *patron(ize)* in the PresE sense, and Hodges pairs *patterns* with *pattens*), but Brown in his 'homophone list' pairs the two forms together; whether he pronounced *patron* as [pætərn] or *pattern* as [pætrən] cannot of course be determined. For *Catherine* Hart preserves the form *Katerin*, but Coles gives as a 'phonetic' spelling *Cathern* and Strong and Young *Cattern*. Similarly for *cauldron* Hart has the old form *kauderon*, which in Bullokar becomes *caudorN* (with [n̩] or [ən]), and Cocker gives as a 'phonetic' spelling *caldrun*; but Bullokar also has the metathesized *cawdernz*. For *iron* and its derivatives Bullokar has *yrN* (with [n̩] or [ən]) and Robinson *eīrn* (presumably with syllabic [n̩]), and Fox and Hookes pair the word with *I ran*; but Gil has *jern* [əiərn], Hodges gives a monosyllable (see above), and Hunt, Coles (followed by Strong and Young), and Cooper (followed by *WSC-RS* and Brown) have [əiərn]. *Environ* has [ərn] in Coles (followed by Strong and Young) and Cooper (followed by Brown). For *children* Mulcaster gives *childern* or *children*, Gil *children* (five times), and Cooper *childern*; on Hart see above. For *brethren* Cheke gives *brethern*, Gil '*breðren* or *breðern*' once, *breðern* twice otherwise; on Hart see above.

The form *hunderd* (which Milton preferred to *hundred*, and which is the basis of Tennyson's rhyme *hundred : thundered : wondered*) is similar in appearance, but differently developed. With Jordan, § 290, Anm. 2, and in accordance with the evidence of Hodges (see below), I would assume that in *hundred* the *-re-* became syllabic [r̩]; the phonetic circumstances cannot be satisfactorily paralleled (since syllabic [r̩] in, for example, *wondred* 'wondered' may be developed from earlier *-re* not in the p.t. itself but in the infinitive and thence transferred to the p.t. by analogy), but in abstract phonetic theory it is an easy development from [ndrəd] to [ndr̩d], since omitting the [ə] permits the tongue to remain in contact with the palate throughout. The same change may have affected *kindred*, *hatred*, and (less probably) *sacred*, but evidence is lacking except for certain spellings of *sacred* (which may well not depend on syllabic [r̩] developed in the adj. itself, but on [r̩] in the infinitive of the verb *sacre*; see *OED*, s.v. *sacre*). Once syllabic [r̩] has developed there may be substituted for it the variant [ər], and the evidence shows that this did occur in *hundred*; the PresE development of both [r̩] and [ər] is [ə], which Wright, § 263, records in numerous and widespread dialects.

The orthoepists' evidence is as follows. *Hundred* preserves *-red* in Cheke (beside *-erd*), Levins (who rhymes the word with *red*, &c.), and Gil (ten times). But Hodges marks the *e* silent (five times; once he places a diacritic under the *e* which should show that it is pronounced as *a*, but this is certainly an error for the diacritic which is placed under a silent letter); he clearly means that the *r* is syllabic (cf. his marking of the *e* as silent in *hungred* 'hungered'). The spelling *-erd* (for [ərd]) is given by Cheke (beside *-red*; he also has *hunderder* 'centurion'), Bullokar, and Brown; Cooper says that *r* is pronounced after the *e* in *hundred*, but later says that *hundurd* is 'barbarous speaking' or (in the Latin text) 'facilitatis causa'. *Kindred* has *-red* in Bullokar and Gil, as has *hatred* in Gil; in both words secondary stress may have inhibited the development of syllabic [r̩]. *Sacred* has *-red* in Gil.

Note 1: *OED*'s lists of forms adequately illustrate the [ərn] stage, which is spelt *-ern(e)*, *-orn(e)*, even *-arn(e)* (which Brown uses in one place, though in his 'phonetic spellings' he follows Coles in using *-urn*), and once *-en* (sixteenth-century *patten*; cf. the 'homophone list' pairing cited above); the *-arn* spelling is doubtless due to the frequent interchange of *-er* and *-ar*, as in *pedlar*, and the *-en* spelling shows early loss of *r* in an unstressed syllable. (See *OED*, s.vv. *apron, cauldron, iron, patron, pattern, saffron*; also *child, brother*; no *-ern* spellings are recorded for *environ*.) Many of *OED*'s spellings may well be attempts to represent [rn̩] or [r̩n], thus fifteenth- and sixteenth-century *-eren, -eroun, -eron, -yron* forms of *saffron*.

Apart from *children* (which has *-ern* from the thirteenth century onwards; the earliest quotation with this form is from the *Life of Beket*, c. 1300) and *brethren* (which has *-ern* from the fourteenth century onwards), *OED*'s *-ern* forms are dated to the fifteenth and sixteenth centuries. But it is likely that the metathesis followed without much interval the development of syllabic consonants, in the North by the beginning of the fourteenth century and in the South in the later fourteenth century.

Wyld, *Coll. Eng.*, p. 301, cites *Kathern* from the Wentworth Papers (1712); see also op. cit. (3rd edition), p. 410.

Note 2: In certain cases an alternative explanation is put forward which on phonetic grounds is possible, but which in most should be rejected. This is that in the group *-ren* the *-en* was replaced by syllabic [n̥], which then became non-syllabic (in consequence of following the inherently more sonorous [r]). *OED* clearly sets out this view in regard to *iron*, tracing its development through [əi(ə)rn̥] (with syllabic [n̥] and a glide [ə] between ME *i* and [r]) to [əi(ə)rn] and thence [əiərn] and [əiən]. *Cathern* can be similarly explained from *Catherine* ([ərin] > [ərən] > [ərn̥] > [ərn]), *apern* 'apron' from *naperon* ([ərən] > [ərn̥] > [ərn]), and *caudern* from *cauderon*. This view is confusedly held by Ekwall, § 118, and Luick, § 472 (2), neither of whom realizes that a syllabic [n̥] stage must be allowed for; they speak simply of a loss of the unstressed vowel and (as a secondary consequence) the development in some words of a syllabic consonant, whereas the true process is that the whole group 'unstressed vowel (i.e. [ə]) plus liquid or nasal' is replaced by a syllabic consonant.

The chief objection to this view is that the process whereby syllabic [n̥] became non-syllabic seems always to have been limited in its operation in StE, and leaves no traces in PresE (unless a vowel follows). Thus in eModE non-syllabic [n] is unmistakably shown after [l] and [v] (*swol'n* for *swollen*, *heav'n* for *heaven*) only in verse, where there may be some artificiality; of the orthoepists only Hodges may show it (see § 330 below). *Born* [bɔːn], &c., which *OED* compares to *iron*, do not develop solely, or even perhaps primarily, from eModE forms with syllabic [n̥]; see further § 330 below.

The [ərn] pronunciation for *-ron* in *environ* proves that we cannot explain [əiərn] for *iron* from late ME *irne* < *irene* dative.

Only the process assumed in the text above will explain *saffern* < *saffron*, *citern* < *citron*, and *pattern* < *patron*, for in these words there is (*a*) no ME form with *-eron*, and (*b*) no possibility of a ModE glide [ə], which in StE develops only between certain vowels and diphthongs and [r]. The same process will explain *apron*, *caudern*, and *Cathern* and is therefore here assumed. But for *iron* and *environ*, in view of the different phonetic conditions, *OED*'s explanation is to be accepted.

Note 3: Early ME *breþren* becomes *breþeren* in the twelfth century by the development of a glide-vowel between the [ð] and the [r] after the long vowel of the preceding syllable (Luick, § 449; Jordan, § 147, Anm. 2). By analogy *children* may become *childeren*. From *breþeren*, *childeren* we can obviously explain the fourteenth-century *breþern* and the rather earlier *childern* (see Note 1 above), as Luick does (§ 470); but as the conditions for the process described in the text above are obviously present in *brethren* and *children*, late ME and ModE forms in *-ern* even in these words are probably mainly due to its operation.

Note 4: Luick, § 470, Anm. 4, explains *hunderd* beside *hundred* on the analogy of *breþern* beside *breþren* (see Note 3 above), but the analogy is far-fetched.

Note 5: *OED* records *hunderd*, &c. from the fourteenth century onwards; its earliest example is *hundird* from *Cursor Mundi*, which also shows syllabic consonants developed differently—a circumstance which supports the view taken above. The significance of the spelling *hundered*, which *OED* records from the thirteenth and later centuries, is not clear; it is susceptible of various explanations, as, for example, that it is on the analogy of *wondred* p.t. spelt *wondered* owing to the influence of the noun *wonder* on the verb. For other evidence see Wyld, op. cit., p. 410.

(2) *Post-vocalic* r *becomes pre-vocalic*

§ 329. In *southron* and the former *northren, eastren, westren* for *southern, northern, eastern, western,* and in *cistren* (which still survives in the dialects; see Wright, § 263) for *cistern,* the case is the reverse of that discussed above; an *r* which was post-vocalic has become pre-vocalic. The change is rarely shown by the orthoepists; Hart has *norðren,* and Coles (followed by Strong, Young, Cocker, and Brown) gives the 'phonetic' spelling *Suthrick* 'Southwark'. In the latter the development seems to be that OE *weorc* >

werk > (in this compound) *-erk*, pronounced [ərk], for which [r̩k] is substituted; then [suðr̩k] > [suðrək] > [sʌðrɪk]. In this instance, then, we find a glide [ə] developing after the syllabic [r̩], which becomes non-syllabic; and it is possible that this is the process in all the words cited. Alternatively in *northern*, &c. the process may be that [ərn] becomes [r̩n] (with syllabic [r̩]), whence [rn̩] (with syllabic [n̩]) in consequence of a shift of emphasis from the liquid to the nasal, and finally [rən].

Note 1: *OED* records *-ren*, *-rin* spellings from *Cursor Mundi* (*northrin*, *eastrin*) in the North at the beginning of the fourteenth century and from Chaucer (*southren*) and Trevisa, *De Prop. Rerum* (*westren*) in the South at its close. Such spellings are more common in the fifteenth century, when *-ren*, *-ron* spellings of *cistern* also occur. The parallel with the date of appearance of syllabic consonants in final position (see § 323, Note 2) is striking, and is evidence that the development of the *-ren* forms is connected with that of syllabic consonants. Spellings from the fourteenth and fifteenth centuries with *-eren*, *-erin* (thus *southeren*) may be attempts to represent one or other of the assumed syllabic consonant stages, [r̩n] or [rn̩].

Note 2: Luick, § 458, gives a somewhat different explanation; he regards the process as beginning in early ME with the loss by syncope of medial *e* in the trisyllabic *suðerne*; as the *r* in this event would have to be syllabic, his explanation in that respect resembles the one given above. Subsequently, he says, a glide develops after the *r*. He compares OE *laferce* > *laverke* > **lavrke* > (*larke* or) *lavrocke* > ModE *laverock*, and similarly *lord* < oblique *loverde(s)*. But it is difficult to accept that the *e* was regularly lost (as Luick assumes) in *suðerne* and that ModE [sʌðən] is consequently developed from ME [suðr̩n]. Moreover as the word *cistern* is first recorded in *Cursor Mundi*, it would be unlikely to be affected by Luick's presumed eME syncope; he is obliged to explain *cistren* for *cistern* on the analogy of *suthren* beside *suthern*; this is clearly less satisfactory than a phonetic explanation which covers all cases. And the chronology is against Luick's view: the date of appearance of the *suthren* forms accords with that of syllabic consonants (see Note 1), and *cistern* could be affected by a late thirteenth- and fourteenth-century change. Similarly the monosyllabic *lord* and *lark* forms do not appear until the fourteenth century, and are better explained as showing loss of intervocalic [v] (see § 400 below). The *laverock* form, or rather its precursor *lavrock*, shows the same development as the *Suthrick* discussed above—a glide [ə] (capable of becoming [ɪ]) after syllabic [r̩]; *lav(e)roc(k)* first appears in fifteenth-century manuscripts (including Chaucer manuscripts), in which the *o* may stand for [ə].

Note 3: The fourteenth- to seventeenth-century *-ren* forms of *western* are hardly to be connected with late OE forms in *-rene* (cited by *OED*), owing to the interval of time. Nor is it likely that the late ME *-ren* forms are due to ON influence. No such explanation is available for *cistern*.

REDUCTION OF SYLLABIC TO NON-SYLLABIC CONSONANTS

§ 330. A syllabic consonant is very apt to lose its syllabic quality if a vowel follows, since the greater sonority of the vowel makes it difficult for the consonant to retain the prominence necessary for it to be apprehended as syllabic. Similarly it may lose prominence if it is preceded by a comparably sonorous consonant; this as a rule means another liquid or nasal, but [v] commonly and others of the voiced continuants less often have power to deprive [n] of syllabic quality. If both conditions are present the loss of syllabic quality is the more likely. (Cf. Wyld, *Coll. Eng.* (3rd edition), p. 402.)

We must, however, be careful to distinguish cases in which syllabic quality is lost from those in which it has never developed. Thus from the point of view of descriptive phonetics it may be just to contrast, as Wyld does (loc. cit.), *opening* with *open*, *evening* with *even*, *prisoner* with *prison*; but from the historical point of view it is inaccurate. *Evening* and *prisoner* are not modern formations from *even* and *prison*; they antedate the late ME development of syllabic consonants, and instead show syncope of the medial vowel; in them syllabic [ṇ] never developed as it did in *even* and *prison*. Similarly the PresE pronunciation of *opening* is probably a direct development of the ME pronunciation, with the same syncope of the medial vowel instead of the development of syllabic [ṇ]; only if we regard the PresE verbal noun as a new formation from the infinitive and unconnected with the ME verbal noun are we entitled to speak of a loss of syllabic quality. *Suthrick* 'Southwark' and *lavrock* 'lark' seem clear cases of syllabic [ṛ] becoming non-syllabic before a vowel (actually a glide-vowel of comparatively late development); see above, § 329 and Note 2.

Loss of syllabic quality undoubtedly occurs in other cases discussed by Wyld, loc. cit.; thus in the p.ps. *fallen*, *swollen*, *stolen* and in such words as *even* and *prison*. In PresE syllabic quality is lost only when the following word begins with a vowel, and then only occasionally; but in sixteenth- and seventeenth-century English it is shown by the scansion of poets to have been much more common, even before a word beginning with a consonant (cf. Wyld, loc. cit.). Similar developments occur in the dialects; e.g. Wright, *EDG*, Index, records monosyllabic forms of *stolen* in which the [l] is now lost but the vowel has clearly been developed under *l*-influence, so that we must assume an earlier stage *stǭln* with non-syllabic [n]. But of the orthoepists only Hodges may record monosyllabic forms of *stolen*, &c., *heaven*, &c., *prison*, &c., and Wallis speaks of them as poetic; the failure to record them more generally may be due merely to inaccurate observation, but in view of the avoidance of such forms by present StE it seems more likely that even in the sixteenth and seventeenth centuries they were comparatively rare variants—in other words, that the orthoepists record the normal StE development, whereas the poets, with perhaps some artificiality, take advantage of a development which in StE is abnormal.

A case not discussed by Wyld is when syllabic [ṇ] follows [r]. It is sometimes assumed that the present monosyllabic pronunciation of such words as *born*, &c. is due to the loss of syllabic quality by [n] after [r] (see § 328, Note 2 above). The ModE pronunciation of *iron* must, as we have seen above (§ 328), be ascribed to this process, but it is doubtful whether it was sufficiently common to account fully for the regular ModE pronunciation of participles like *born*. Loss of syllabic quality after [l] is plainly not characteristic of the StE development, and there seems insufficient reason for us to assume that it would have occurred much more freely after [r] than after [l]. Indeed, the PresE pronunciation of such words as *barren* and *quarrel* is evidence that syllabic [n̩] and [l̩] do not become non-syllabic after [r] in StE, with subsequent loss of the [r], though they do in the dialects (cf. the monosyllabic pronunciations of *barrel, warrant*, and *currant* recorded by Wright, Index and § 262). I would therefore follow Jordan, § 142, in assuming that in ME the plurals *borene*, &c. became, by syncope of the medial vowel, *borne*, &c., whence by back-formation arose the singulars *born*, &c.; late ME would thus have a monosyllabic *born* and a disyllabic *boren*. From these would arise two ModE types, the monosyllabic [bɒ(:)rn] (> PresE [bɔ:n]) and the disyllabic [bɒ(:)rən] or [bɒ(:)rn̩]; the latter would occasionally, by loss of syllabic quality, become [bɒ(:)rn] and thus identical with the other type, but if it survived into PresE would normally still be disyllabic and would rhyme (in its short-vowel variant) with *warren*. The predominance in ModE of the monosyllabic form may be accounted for from the fact that it would be normal in the plural (after the loss of final *e*) and a variant in the singular, whereas the disyllabic form would be confined to the singular.

As the orthoepists considered words in isolation, they do not afford evidence of loss of syllabic quality before a word beginning with a vowel. An interesting case showing retention of syllabic [l̩] before a non-syllabic *l* is Hart's transcription *eidLlei* [əidl̩ləi], which shows, still fully preserved, the sense of the formation *idle* plus *-ly*. On the *heaven, fallen* type there is little clear evidence, as no orthoepist except Bullokar has separate signs for syllabic and non-syllabic [n]; but syllabic [n̩] seems always to be intended. There is one possible exception. Hodges appears to treat as monosyllables *fallen, swollen*, and *stolen*, which he spells *faln*, &c. and gives only in a list of syllables that end in two consonants (it includes also such as *elm, film, shelf, wolf*, and *health*); but he also has no special sign for syllabic [n̩], and it would not be altogether inconsistent with the context if he had [n̩] in these words. Wallis compares the practice of old (i.e. ME) poets with regard to final *e*, which he recognizes sometimes to count as a syllable and sometimes not, with that of poets in his own day in regard to words like *heaven* and *ever*, 'quæ promiscue vel pro monosyllabis vel pro dissyllabis apud Poetas occurrunt, ultimo scilicet *e* vel prolato vel quasi per Syncopen extrito prout carminis ratio postulaverit'; his terms do not suggest that in ordinary speech there was a common fluctuation between monosyllabic and disyllabic forms. With regard to the *born* type the same difficulty arises that the orthoepists do not have a distinctive symbol for syllabic [n̩], but Smith certainly means a monosyllable by his transcription *suorn* 'sworn', and so it seems do the others (Hart, for example, has *bŏrn*). Bullokar, however, gives *bŏrN* for *born(e)*, *worN* for *worn*, *tŏrN* for *torn*, spellings which show [n̩] or [ən]; but they need not represent the survival of the ME disyllabic forms, since Bullokar records a glide-vowel between [r] and a following consonant (see § 331 below), and in him therefore the ME monosyllabic forms *born*, &c. would themselves become disyllabic.

Note 1: Jordan, § 142, would apparently explain even the monosyllabic forms of *stolen*, &c. from ME *stoln* by back-formation from a syncopated plural *stolne*. This is possible, but (*a*) syncope between *l* and *n* is less well established than between *r* and *n*, (*b*) the distribution in ModE of the monosyllabic forms of *stol'n*, &c. is different from those of *born*, &c., and (*c*) the cases of *heav'n*, *ev'n*, &c. show that the process described in the text does occur, for they cannot well be explained otherwise.

Note 2: Luick, § 472, and Ekwall, § 118, believe that in these words, as in others (cf. § 325, Note 3 (1), § 328, Note 2), ME *e* is simply lost before a liquid or nasal, with the secondary consequence that syllabic consonants arise in some cases but not in such words as *iron*, *born*, *stol'n*, &c. Luick, to account for the contrast between *born*, &c. (which he derives from the ME disyllabic *boren*, &c.) and *warren*, &c., lays it down that the 'loss of *e*' does not occur after a short vowel in the preceding syllable; but *born* (*boren*), &c. often had a short *o* in late ME and eModE (see § 13 (2a)), and yet there is no satisfactory evidence of the survival of disyllabic forms after 1500. Syncope of *e* in phrasal groups, especially before a vowel (*boren in*, *boren of*), may have aided the adoption of the monosyllabic forms.

APPARENT CHANGE OF NON-SYLLABIC CONSONANTS TO SYLLABIC

§ 331. In many dialects (but not in StE) a non-syllabic consonant appears to have become syllabic, as in [elm̩] for *elm*, [film̩] for *film* (cf. Wright, § 265). It would be possible to regard this development as a direct change due to an increase in the sonority of the final consonant (so apparently Wright), but in fact the explanation appears to be different: in groups of two consonants of which the first is [r] or [l], a glide-vowel [ə] develops between the consonants. This development is widespread in the modern dialects (cf. Wright, § 234), and is found in ME after *r*, especially in East Midland texts (Jordan, § 146, Anm. 3). In cases in which the second consonant of the group is itself a liquid or nasal, there can be later substitution of a syllabic consonant for the group glide-vowel plus liquid or nasal (e.g. [n̩] for [ən], thus [kɒrn̩] for [kɒrən] < [kɒrn]; so [elm̩] for [eləm] < [elm]).

Evidence of this development is given by three orthoepists. On Bullokar's evidence see Vol. I, p. 104; he shows the change in, for example, *carl*, *storm*, *turn*, *helm* and even in unstressed syllables in *govern* and *quartern*. His transcriptions should show the syllabic consonant stage, but probably do not (e.g. his *storM* should mean [stɒrm̩], but probably means [stɒrəm]). Hayward says that the nature of *m* (he has been discussing whether it is *um*, as Bullokar suggested, or *em*) appears more clearly in *charm* and *realm* than in *name*; he is influenced by Bullokar and confused, but there can be little doubt that he means that *m* is pronounced [əm] in *charm* and *realm* but not in *name*. Cooper treats *m* in *whelm* on the same footing as in *catechism* and *schism*; he therefore has syllabic [m̩], or perhaps rather [əm].

Note 1: That the syllabic-consonant stage is preceded by a glide-vowel stage, and not vice versa, is shown by the following considerations. (*a*) ME spellings indicating a glide-vowel (e.g. *arum* 'arm'—cf. Jordan, loc. cit.) occur rather earlier than the date at which syllabic consonants appear. (b) The glide-vowel occurs in cases in which there is no possibility of a syllabic consonant, e.g. in *oref* < *orf* (Jordan, loc. cit.), *harp* scanned as two syllables in *Sir Orfeo*, [wɒrəd] 'word' (Wright, § 234). (c) Bullokar also shows a glide-vowel developed between a vowel and a liquid or nasal, e.g. in *shown, room,* &c., where no syllabic consonant stage is possible. (d) There is no parallel in English for the direct change of a non-syllabic consonant to a syllabic consonant.

Note 2: For further evidence see Wyld, *Coll. Eng.*, p. 299, and § 353, Note below.

Note 3: The orthoepistical sources indicate the dialectal status of the development in the sixteenth and seventeenth centuries (as in PresE). Bullokar was a native of Sussex; Hayward was born in New Sarum and educated at St. Julians by St. Albans; and Cooper was a native of Hertfordshire and taught at Bishop's Stortford. Both Bullokar and Cooper had other dialectal pronunciations; and Hayward and Cooper were liable to the influence of those East Midland dialects which also provide most of Jordan's ME evidence. But in the modern dialects the development is more widespread, as Wright shows.

THE VOCALIZATION OF *r* IN UNSTRESSED SYLLABLES

§ 332. During the ModE period [r], except before a vowel or syllabic consonant, is vocalized to [ə], to which the ModE [r] is closely allied. In unstressed syllables the result is to obliterate the distinction between syllabic [r̩] and [ər]; the former became directly [ə], and the latter, which in theory would become in the first stage [əː] (as in stressed syllables), was in fact immediately shortened, owing to the lack of stress, to [ə]. It is probable that this vocalization of [r] occurred earlier in unstressed syllables than stressed; only sources which reflect vulgar pronunciation give evidence of the change before 1700, and even they give little, but what they do give relates chiefly to unstressed syllables.

In the 'phonetically spelt' lists Coles gives *hang-ket-cher* 'handkerchief', *hah-puth* 'halfpennyworth', and *pennuth* 'pennyworth'; Strong follows with *pennuth* but has *hankercher*; Young 1682 has *pennuth* and *han-ke-cher*; Cocker has *pennith*; Brown, modifying Young, has *hankecher*, *pennoth*, and (an addition) *forrad* 'forward'. Cooper says that *hankecher* is 'barbarous speaking'; *WSC* follows, but inserts *r*, thus *hankercher*. If *WSC* correctly represents Cooper's meaning, we should have to conclude that only the *-cher* part was 'barbarous'; but Cooper probably means the loss of *r* in the second syllable as well (as Coles, Young, and Brown do), and *WSC*, careless as ever, fails to take this second point (cf. Strong, who similarly fails to follow Coles in this respect). The 'homophone lists' pair *patterns* with *pattens* (Hodges 'near'), *discomfort(ed)* with *discomfit(ed)* (Wharton, Strong), *pillars* with *pillows* (Fox and Hookes); Fox and Hookes also pair *winder* with *window*, but this probably rests on the analogical form *windoor*, &c. of *window*.

Note 1: Spellings showing loss of *r* in unstressed syllables are included among those cited by Wyld, *Coll. Eng.*, pp. 298–9 (where no distinction is made between several different cases of loss of *r*); they date from 1642 to the beginning of the eighteenth century (which agrees with the orthoepists' evidence) and are not very numerous. But he also cites *dryardes* 'dryads' from Laneham (1575), and *OED* cites *pattens* 'pàtterns' from Levins

(1570); these examples show that the loss in unstressed syllables was already known in the sixteenth century.

Note 2: ModE [ə] in *hammer*, &c. is not to be regarded (with Luick, § 472 (2)) as being developed solely from syllabic [r̩]; the sixteenth- and seventeenth-century evidence shows that [ər] was always in existence as a probably more common variant (see § 326 (*c*) above).

LATER CHANGES IN THE QUALITY OF UNSTRESSED VOWELS

THE CHANGE OF [ə] TO [ɪ]

§ 333. Both in later ME and in ModE there is a tendency for the unstressed vowel [ə] to become [ɪ]. The evidence for this change is in ME confined to words with ME *ĕ*, since only in these had [ə] at that time developed; but ModE evidence shows it affecting [ə] of any origin, and it is evident that we have to do with only a single tendency to change, and not with different and distinct ME and ModE processes (see § 293 (*b*) above). The tendency is one that in ME seems unaffected by the following consonant, but there are indications that in ModE certain following consonants aided the change, though it could occur independently. It is not always possible to determine at what date the change occurred in individual words; the change to [ɪ] of [ə] < ME back vowels cannot be earlier than the fifteenth century, during which these vowels first commonly became [ə]. But the change to [ɪ] of [ə] < ME *ĕ* may occur either in ME or in ModE. Normally it is a ME development, but sometimes we may be fairly sure that it has occurred in ModE; thus when Hodges shows [ɪ] in *kitchen* we may conclude that in his speech (whatever may be true of other people's) it is the result of a ModE change, since he has [ɪ] only before *n* and the words affected include the sixteenth-century adoption *wagon*.

The tendency for [ə] to become [ɪ] seems in the North to have had the character of a generalized sound-change, especially as regards the early [ə] from ME *ĕ*, but in the South ME *ĕ* is only rarely [ɪ] in the late fourteenth century, and in the sixteenth and seventeenth centuries the orthoepists provide less evidence of [ɪ] than of [ə] (though to some extent this may be due to the influence of the conventional spelling). The impression given by the southern evidence is of two conflicting modes of pronunciation, with [ɪ] and with [ə], of which the former was still the rarer even in those words in which it had developed earliest. In present StE this conflict has resulted in the [ɪ] type becoming almost invariable in words with ME *ĕ*; when [ə] was developed from other sources there is more variety, but in certain classes of words [ɪ] prevails (see further § 336 below). In general it appears that [ɪ] replaces [ə] (i) in those cases in which it was of early development and (ii) in those in which its development, though later, was aided by a following consonant.

(1) [ə] *from ME unstressed* ĕ *becomes* [ɪ]

§ 334. For ME unstressed ĕ the pronunciation [ɪ] is shown by Cheke in *written*; by Smith in *brewed* (second syllable), *leesest*, *devil*, *evil*, and *vinegar*, but otherwise he has ĕ (e.g. in *vowed* and *wooed*, pronounced as two syllables); and by Hart in *stayeth* and *stayed* (see Vol. I, pp. 78–79 above), but otherwise he has *e*. Laneham has *heavins*. Bullokar normally has ĕ, but he says that the inflexion *-es* of the genitive case might be better written *-iz*, 'our voice not disagreeing: e, and i, in those places being so shortly pronounced' (he is perhaps influenced by the popular view that this inflexion was derived from *his*); and he gives *i* in *enemy* (second syllable; once, against ĕ twice). Mulcaster (a Northerner) says that unstressed *e* as in *written*, *saieth* sounds like short *i*. Coote (1597) includes *-id* for *-ed* among the characteristics of 'the barbarous speech of your country people', and adds that it is Scottish (but cf. his own evidence on *prophet* cited below). Tonkis (1612) gives *Claudius'is* 'Claudius's' and *Plautus'is* 'Plautus's'; he is clearly influenced by the periphrases *Claudius his*, *Plautus his*, and otherwise says that the possessive singular is formed in *-us* (i.e. [əz]) when not syncopated. Robinson gives rather more evidence of [ɪ]; his regular *-ēz* for inflexional *-es* (whether in substantives or verbs) seems an attempt to indicate a lowered variety of [ɪ], and he has also ĭ once in *countenance* (against ĕ twice). Otherwise, however, he always has ĕ (e.g. in *wicked*). Gil has normally ĕ, but ĭ in *aspen*; he also says that *naked* is popularly spelt *nakid*, following the pronunciation, so his ĕ transcriptions may often conceal [ɪ]. Jonson, following Mulcaster, says that *e* is 'obscur'd, like the faint *i*' in *written*, &c., *saieth*, and *divel*; after *s*, he says, the genitive singular (but not the plural) adds *-is* (a statement clearly influenced by the supposed derivation from *his*). Hodges has ĕ except in *kitchen* (see § 333). Howell says that *e* 'leaps before the *l*, and takes the half sound of *i*' in *thistle*. Coles has the 'phonetic spellings' *parliment* 'parliament' (ME *parlement*) and *mung-gril* 'mongrel', Young *danil* 'Daniel' (*-iel* > *-el* > *-il*), and Hawkins *parliment*. Cooper spells *kitchin* thus, and pronounces it with [ɪŋ]. The 'homophone lists' have *causes* paired with *causeys* (Fox and Hookes, Coles (*Eng.–Lat. Dict.*), Strong, and Brown), *marred* with *married* (*WSC*), and *raven* with *raving* (Cocker).

Words originally end-stressed seem to show [ɪ] with comparable frequency. Bullokar and Robinson have ĭ in *hostess*. Coote, followed by Daines and Hunt, pairs *prophet* with *profit*. Gil has ĭ in *largesse*. Coles has the 'phonetic spellings' *damzil* 'damsel', *spannil* 'spaniel' (ME *spannel*), and *dublit* 'doublet'. ME ĕ < OF *ai* also appears as [ɪ], but in all but one case (Bullokar's ĭ in *sloven*) not until late in the seventeenth century: Coles gives ĭ in *Cologne* (ME *Cullen* < *Coleyne*) and in *carrion*, and Strong in *vittils* 'victuals'; *The Compendious School-Master* pairs *Calais* (ME unstressed ĕ < ai) with the family name *Callis* and with *challice* as homophones; *WSC* and Brown have ĭ in *forfeit, counterfeit, surfeit,* and *foreign*; and *WSC* has 'e or *i* short' in a list which contains *captain, villain, certain,* and *chamberlain* (these being apparently those that have ĭ, though he may mean that they vary). The late appearance of ĭ forms where ĕ is the unstressed development of OF *ai* is probably not because they were of later development here than elsewhere, but because of the influence exercised over the conventional spelling and over the orthoepists by forms in which secondary stress maintained ME *ai* (see § 272 above).

Note 1: Certain manuscripts of the *Welsh Hymn* use Welsh *y* for ME unstressed *e* in the endings *-en* and *-er*; but it must be in its 'obscure' value and represent [ə]. On ME ĭ in the ordinal numerals *twentith* 'twentieth', &c. see § 309, Note; it is not developed from ME unstressed *e*.

Note 2: For further evidence (from the fifteenth to the seventeenth century) see Wyld, *Coll. Eng.*, pp. 267-73, and Zachrisson, *Eng. Vowels*, p. 23 (where is cited Mauger on the pronunciation of the *e* of the superlative ending *-est*). On Newton's [ɪ] for pretonic *e* see § 344.

(2) *Late ME glide* [ə] *becomes* [ɪ]

§ 335. The [ə] of late ME [əl], [ən] for [l̩], [n̩] < ME *-le, -ne* becomes [ɪ] in the same way as [ə] < ME unstressed ĕ; [ɪl] < original *-le* is shown by Cheke, Howell, and Strong, and [ɪn] < original *-ne* by Strong (see § 324 (*b*) above). The Northerner Levins regularly has *-il* for original *-le*. Similarly [ɪ] from a glide [ə] is shown by Coles (followed by Strong and Young) in *Suthrick* 'Southwark' (see § 329 above). Present StE seems never to use [ɪ] in these words.

Note: *OED*'s spellings show *-il* for *-le* (as in *people*) and *-in* for *-ne* (as in *happen, hearken*) from the fourteenth century onwards, the fourteenth-century instances being Scottish and Northern. Wyld, op. cit., p. 272, cites spellings with *-il* for *-le* from the fifteenth century onwards.

(3) *ModE* [ə] *from ME back vowels becomes* [ɪ]

§ 336. The orthoepists show [ɪ] < [ə] developed from ME back vowels in two cases, before *n* and before [dʒ], and hardly at all elsewhere. Before *n* Hodges has [ɪ] in *pigeon* and *scutcheon*; so Coles in *dungeon* and *truncheon*, Strong and Young in *dungeon, crimson,* and *pigeon*, and Brown in *ruffin* 'ruffian' (ĭ < ă after syncope of the *i* in hiatus) but not in *scullion, scutcheon,* and *bullion*. Hunt and Coles, *Eng. Dict.*, pair *latten* (< OF *latun*) with *Latin* (cf. Shakespeare's reported pun). Before [dʒ] Gil has ĭ in *marriageable*, Coles in *carriage, courage,* and *marriage*, Strong and Young in *marriage* and *language* but not *courage*, Hawkins in *marriage* and other *-ia-* words, and Brown in *carriage, damage,* and *marriage*; Cooper (followed by *WSC-RS*) does not, however, have [ɪ] and says that he prefers the spelling *sausage* to *sausidge*. In other positions [ɪ] is shown by the Northerner Levins in *caril* 'carol' and by Strong and Young in the 'phonetic spellings' *idolitry* 'idolatry' and *cunstible* 'constable' (but in these two words [ɪ] might be by shortening of ME *ā*). Wilkins transcribes *kingdom* once with *-ym*, which in his system means [ʌm], and once with *-im*, which should mean [ɪm] but may well be a printer's error.

Present StE appears to preserve [ɪ] before [n] only in *pigeon*, but has it regularly in words in *-(i)age* and some in *-ace* and *-ate* (see Note 1). In others (e.g. *miracle* [mɪrɪkl], *philosopher* [fɪlɔsɪfə]) [ɪ] is a vulgarism.

> Note 1: It is here assumed that in *damage, carriage*, &c. the ModE [ɪ] is from [ə] < ME *ă* and not (as Luick, § 597 (6), takes it) by ModE shortening of ME *ā*, because the sixteenth- and seventeenth-century evidence shows that *ă* was very much more common than *ā* in the suffix *-age* (see § 271 above). Similarly the words in *-ace* (*palace, furnace, preface*) and *-ate* (*delicate, fortunate, desolate*) cited by Luick are shown to have late ME *ă* forms by *OED*'s spellings, and PresE [ɪ] should be explained from this *ă* through an [ə] stage.

> Note 2: Spellings confirm the orthoepists' evidence. *OED* records *-in*, *-yn* for *dungeon*, *pigeon*, *scutcheon*, and *truncheon* from the fifteenth to the seventeenth century; it attributes *-in* in *dungeon* to the fourteenth century, but has no quotation with this form. Wyld, *Coll. Eng.*, pp. 275–6, has *-yn* spellings for ME *-un*, &c. from the fifteenth to the seventeenth century; cf. also the seventeenth-century *compiny* cited by him on p. 274. For *-(i)age*, however, there seem to be few or no spellings with *i* before the sixteenth century; cf. Wyld, pp. 274–5. Wyld cites a few cases with *i* before a consonant other than [n] or [dʒ]; so the seventeenth-century *Donkister, stomichers, obsticle, carictor, tomis* 'Thomas', and *contry-dicting* and certain eighteenth-century examples (p. 274) and the seventeenth-century *Pigit* 'Piggot' (p. 276).

(4) *ModE* [ə] *becomes* [ɪ] *in recently adopted words*

§ 337. Hodges shows the change of [ə] to [ɪ] before [n] not only in words which had formed part of the ME vocabulary, but also in *wagon* (an adoption of Dutch *wagen*, first recorded in 1523); and Robinson has [ɪ] once beside *ĕ* once and *ē* once in the third syllable of *variety* (first recorded about 1533). In Hodges's case the [ɪ] seems to be due to a ModE change of [ə] to [ɪ]; in *variety*, however, the use of [ɪ] beside [ə] for Latin *ē* after it has become unstressed may be due simply to the analogy of similar variation in words of Latin origin which had formed part of the ME vocabulary.

ModE LOWERING OF UNSTRESSED [ɪ] TO [e]

§ 338. In PresE unstressed [ɪ] always tends to be laxer than stressed, and in consequence is often lowered to [e]; the more extreme varieties of the sound are indeed not very tense and are far removed from [ɪ], but are ordinarily to be regarded as members of the same phoneme. The lowered varieties are nevertheless easily recognized as phonetically distinct.

The lowering is certainly as early as the beginning of the seventeenth century, and may have occurred in the sixteenth. Robinson's regular *-ēz* for inflexional *-es* undoubtedly indicates tense [e], which must be developed by lowering of unstressed [ɪ] < [ə] < ME unstressed ĕ. Wallis says that -ey in *Marshalsey* 'Marshalsea' (which has final ME ĭ < OF) and in *Winchelsey* 'Winchelsea', *Langley*, and *Hendley* (which have late ME ĭ < ī < eME ẹi; see § 343, Note 2 below) is pronounced like ME ẹ̄, i.e. as [eː]; there must be lowering of [ɪ] to [e], with perhaps some subsequent lengthening. Price (*English Orthographie* (1688)), Young, Lye, Cooper, *The Compendious School-Master*, Hawkins, and Cocker say that *ey* is 'put for *e*' or 'has the sound of *e*', or that the *y* is silent, in *countrey* 'country', *attorney*, &c.; the illustrative lists contain words in which *ey* represents both ME *ei* and ME ĭ (on Price see further Note 2 below). The context in Price suggests that the *e* is short (since there is a separate list of words in which *ei* is said to be pronounced '*e* long'), and Lye marks the *e* short. It is probable that all these authors are describing [e] by lowering of [ɪ]. Similarly Richardson, explaining English pronunciation for Dutch readers, says that *ey* in *valley* is pronounced *ee* (by which he means the equivalent of ME ẹ̄, i.e. [eː]); final -*y*, on the other hand, he identifies with ME ĭ. But as he does not show ME *ai* to be identical with ME ẹ̄, his [e(ː)] in *valley* must be by lowering of [ɪ]; the influence of the spelling accounts for his giving it in this word and not those ending in -*y*. In fact all these authors after Wallis, with the exception of Cooper, are strongly influenced by the spelling and therefore show lowering only in words then spelt with -*ey*, which invites the comment that the *y* is silent; probably their pronunciation varied, so that it would be easy for them to persuade themselves that they used [ɪ] in words spelt -*y* and [e] in words spelt -*ey*. Cooper, however, is not so influenced; he not only makes the conventional comment on words spelt -*ey*, but also shows (see Vol. I, p. 300) that final -*y* is pronounced with a sound of the quality of ME ẹ̄, i.e. tense [e], which was probably short or half-long (he fluctuates in his descriptions of the quantity). A further indication of the lowering is the identification of unstressed *i* with French *ẹ*, shown by the 'phonetic spellings' *randyvooz* (Coles) and *randivooz* (Young) for *rendezvous*.

Note 1: On certain transcriptions with -*e* in Smith and Hart see § 275, Note 2. *WSC-RS*, though following Cooper's phrasing in discussing -*ey* and -*y*, certainly means [iː] not [e(ː)]. Brown also follows Cooper, and in addition says that *y* is silent in *chimney*, but seems to mean [iː]. He has the 'phonetic spellings' *hevve* 'heavy' but *atturnee* 'attorney', *autoritee* 'authority', &c. Strong and Young have 'phonetic spellings' with *e* for final -*y* (e.g. *furmite* 'frumenty'), but these have not been cited above as evidence of the lowering, since it is possible that in them *e* may be meant as a symbol for [iː].

Note 2: Price gives two lists, one of words in which *ey* is pronounced 'like *e*' and the other of words in which it is 'like *ee*'. The first contains sixteen words with unstressed -*ey*, of which six have ME -*ei* only, six have ME -*ei* as a variant, and four cannot have ME -*ei* (*attorney* with OF -*é*, *comfrey* and *pulley* with OF -*ie*, and *honey* with OE -*ig*). The second contains only one word (*valley*) which can but need not have ME -*ei*; of the rest, three words have OF -*ie*, one OE -*ie*, one (*barley*) ME -ī < OE -*īc*, and one (*monkey*) probably MLG -*e*. At first sight it may appear that Price intends a distinction between words with ME *ei* and words with ME ĭ, but (*a*) it could only be based on a continuously surviving distinction of pronunciation, of which there is no sufficient evidence so late, and which ought to result in a faultless distribution of the words between the lists (whereas one-quarter of the words in the apparent 'ME *ei*' list cannot have this sound); and (*b*) Lye and Young, who make use of Price's material, treat his distinction as arbitrary and ignore it; they say simply that -*ey* is pronounced -*e*, and Lye takes three and Young one of their examples from Price's '*ey* like *ee*' list. Evidently Price's pronunciation varied between [e] by lowering and [ɪ] (or [iː] by lengthening), and he thought he used (and in fact may have used) exclusively the one sound in the first list and the other in the second; individual speakers, in practice as well as in theory, do make such arbitrary distinctions between what are historically mere variants of the same sound.

Note 3: On ME (or ModE) *ĭ* as a variant beside ME unstressed *ei* see § 275, Note 2 above.

ROUNDING OF ME *ă*

§ 339. Robinson shows rounding to [ɒ] of ME *ă* in *was* (invariably) and *what* (except in one case), and Newton and Coles show it in *what* only (see § 194 above). It is evident that reduced stress has aided this rounding, since it is not shown in other words; on the other hand the reduction of stress must be partial, for otherwise ME *ă* would have become [ə]. Spellings show *ŏ* < ME *ă* in such weakly stressed words from the fifteenth century onwards (cf. Wyld, op. cit., p. 202).

Note: It is commonly assumed, as by Sweet, *New English Grammar*, § 1473, that ME *quod* and *quoth* are both weak-stressed forms with rounding of ME *ă*; but they should be distinguished. *Quod*, which occurs as early as *Ancrene Wisse* and its group, undoubtedly has ME *ŏ* < ME *ă* rounded under weak stress (though its final *d* is more simply explained from the OE plural stem than, with Sweet, as a special weak-stressed development of OE *þ*). *Quoth*, on the other hand, is not a blend-form with a ModE spelling-pronunciation, as Sweet thinks; the various ModE forms (see § 421 below) suggest strongly that the vowel descends from ME *ǭ*, which is to be explained from ON *á* in the p.t.pl. *kváðum*. Significantly the ME *quoþ* form first appears in the plural *quoðen* in the East Anglian *Genesis and Exodus* (c. 1250), and next in *Cursor Mundi*.

TENDENCY OF [ə] TO BECOME [ʌ]

§ 340. D. Jones, *Outline of English Phonetics*, §§ 361-2 and Luick, § 614, comment on a tendency of ModE [ə] to become, in final position, [ʌ]. This tendency may be old; in PresE the sounds [ə] and [ʌ] are not strictly to be accounted separate phonemes, and late seventeenth- and eighteenth-century observers do not regard them as distinct; it is therefore possible that they may have used the [ʌ] variant of this '[ə]-[ʌ] phoneme' in unstressed as well as in stressed position.

Note: Luick, it may be recalled, believes that at one time ME stressed *ŭ* was itself (stressed) [ə], his reason being the identification of the two sounds (ME *ŭ* and [ə]) by some orthoepists; but the reason is not that there was no difference between them, but that the difference was not significant (see Vol. I, pp. 241–3). The change of unstressed [ə] in some positions (i.e. final position) to unstressed [ʌ] is certainly no analogy to Luick's supposed change of stressed [ə] < ME *ŭ* to stressed [ʌ] in all positions (though he so takes it in § 614). Jones, op. cit., § 355 et seq., in fact distinguishes three main varieties of the PresE [ə]; how old these are it is pointless to inquire.

LATER CHANGES IN QUANTITY

§ 341. Changes in quantity in the ModE period are due either to loss of secondary stress (a natural and common process, which results in shortening) or to its reimposition (except in one case an artificial and rare process, which in open syllables causes lengthening).

SHORTENING DUE TO LOSS OF SECONDARY STRESS

(1) *ME ā becomes* [i]

§ 342. Shortening of ME *ā* could produce [i] if it occurred after ME *ā* had become [e:], and Luick, § 597 (6), would explain PresE [i] in certain words by this process. But ME *ā* did not become [e:] until the late sixteenth century in vulgar speech and after 1700 in good speech (see § 102 above), and the evidence is that the words involved had lost secondary stress before these dates; their pronunciation in PresE is to be otherwise explained (see § 336, Note 1 above).

(2) *ME* ai *becomes* [i]

§ 343. ME *ai* can similarly be shortened to [i] if the loss of secondary stress occurs after it has come to be pronounced [e:]; this might occur even in good speech in the seventeenth century in consequence of the rare development whereby ME *ai* was identified with ME *ẹ̄* (see § 228 above), but would normally (i.e. when it is identified with ME *ā*) occur in vulgar speech from the late sixteenth century and in good speech after 1700. The orthoepists normally show retention of ME *ai* (or a long vowel developed from it) under retained secondary stress; so Smith in the proper name *Yaxlei* (OE *geaces lēah*) and in *yesterday*, Bullokar in *Monday* and *yesterday*, and Gil in *Sunday*. But Brown, at the very end of the seventeenth century and in a 'phonetic spelling' list (based often on vulgar pronunciation), has '*Wensdee* or *Wensda*' for *Wednesday*. See further Notes 1–3 below.

Note 1: As the evidence on native words suggests that the shortening of ME *ai* is not to be expected before 1700 except in vulgar speech, it is highly probable that in the words of French origin discussed in § 275, Note 2 (*c*), ModE [i] is not developed by ModE shortening of ME *ai*.

Note 2: Wallis's [e(:)] in *Winchelsea* (< OE *ēg* 'island'), *Langley, Hendley* (< OE *lēah* 'wood') is to be explained from ME *ī* < *ī* < *ẹi*, not from late ME *ai*; see § 338 above.

Note 3: Wyld, *Coll. Eng.*, p. 280, cites *Mundy* 'Monday' from Gabriel Harvey (the son of a rope-maker of Saffron Walden), which confirms the deduction made above that in vulgar speech the shortening would be possible in the late sixteenth century; he also cites *Fridy* for 1642 and *Mundy* for 1647. Cf. also *shammee, shammy* 'chamois' (of which Wyld, p. 281, cites instances dated 1685 and 1686, earlier than any recorded by *OED*); the immediate precursor of this form is certainly *shammay, developed by loss of *w* (as in *forrard* 'forward', &c.) from the sixteenth- and seventeenth-century form *shamway* (which in turn is an anglicization of the contemporary French pronunciation of *chamois*).

(3) *ME ẹ̄ becomes* [ɪ]

§ 344. ME ẹ̄, if shortened after it had become [e:], would give [ɪ]. Of this development there is no reliable early evidence; Robinson's *ĭ* in the third syllable of *variety* is rather from [ə] < *ĕ*, and *ĭ* in the prefix *de-* in certain words is to be explained as in § 292 above. PresE [ɪ] in the prefixes *de-*, *e-*, and *pre-* and in other pretonic syllables is due to shortening; this pronunciation is shown by Newton in *desire*, *especially*, *recover*, and *reported*, but might (in view of *especially*) develop from [ə] < ME *ĕ*. The pronunciations with *ĕ* recorded in §§ 274 and 288 above could be due to ModE shortening while ME ẹ̄ was still pronounced [ɛ:], but are rather to be regarded as descending from ME.

(4) *ME ẹ̄ becomes* [ɪ]

§ 345. ModE shortening of [i:] < ME ẹ̄ to [ɪ] is the probable explanation of Gil's *ĭ* in *thirteen* (once, against [i:] four times) and in *thirteenth* (once); other orthoepists show [i:] in such words (e.g. Hodges in *eighteen*). But ME shortening of ME ẹ̄ could give the same result.

(5) *ME ọ̄ becomes* [ʊ]

§ 346. Whereas ME shortening of ME ọ̄ invariably produces *ŏ*, ModE shortening, if it acts after ME ọ̄ has become tense [o:], can produce [ʊ]; D. Jones, *Eng. Pron. Dict.*, shows [ʊ] as well as [o] in words with pretonic *pro-* (e.g. *protect*, *protract*). Of this development the orthoepists show no sign, whether in pretonic or post-tonic syllables, and it is probably comparatively recent. Their *ŏ* beside ọ̄ (see §§ 277 and 290 above) could be due to ModE shortening before ME ọ̄ had become [o:], but is rather to be regarded as descending from ME.

Note: PresE [ə] in such words may be recently developed from [ʊ] by ModE shortening of ME ọ̄, or a much earlier development from ME *ŏ*.

(6) *ME ọ̄ becomes* [ʊ] *and thence* [ə]

§ 347. ME ọ̄, if shortened in later ME or in ModE, becomes [ʊ]; if this change occurs early the resulting [ʊ] is identified with ME *ŭ* and (in unstressed position) becomes [ə]. But the [ʊ] recorded, though without distinction from ME *ŭ*, in *together* by Hart, Robinson, and Gil (once, against *ŏ* twice) and in *towards* by Hart is probably by more recent ModE shortening (see § 290 above). Much more doubt arises in the case of the suffix *-dom* (see § 278 above); shortening in ME would be as likely as in ModE. Later shortening (seventeenth century onwards in StE) gives [ʊ], which when not reduced to [ə] is kept apart from ME *ŭ*; Hodges may show this in the prefix *to-* (see § 290 above).

Whether the shortening is early or late, the vowel produced by it, being no longer protected by secondary stress, tends to become [ə]; when PresE shows only this development (as in the suffix *-dom*) the shortening is probably early.

Note: It is doubtful whether the shortening in the suffix *-hood* is due to loss of secondary stress; see § 278 above.

(7) *ME au becomes ŏ and thence* [ə]

§ 348. ME *au*, when shortened after *c.* 1450, becomes *ŏ*; if the shortening is the result of loss of secondary stress this *ŏ* tends to become [ə]. Robinson shows *ŏ* for ME *au* in the suffixes *-al* and *-an* (see Vol. I, p. 210); this shortening is apparently recent, for if there had been reduction to [ə] he would certainly not have replaced the conventional *-al* and *-an* by his symbols for *-ŏl* and *-ŏn*. Otherwise the shortening is shown only by the 'homophone lists', which pair *emeralds* (ME *emrauds*) with *emrods* 'hæmorrhoids' (so Hodges, Strong, Coles (*Eng.–Lat. Dict.*)), and *centaury* with *century* (so Strong, Coles (op. cit.), Young, Cooper 'alike', Cocker, Brown); of these pairings, the first may still depend on *ŏ*, but the latter shows the further reduction to [ə].

Note: The shortening need not be later than monophthongization of stressed ME *au* to [ɒː], as there is evidence of direct shortening of diphthongal *au* to *ŏ*; but in Robinson's case it probably is.

(8) *ModE* [juː] *becomes* [(j)ʊ] *and thence* [(j)ə]

§ 349. In words in which ME [iu] for OF [y] was protected by secondary stress and was therefore not reduced to *ĭ* in the ME period (see § 282) it becomes, by normal ModE development, [juː]; stressed [iu] had reached this stage by the end of the sixteenth century, and though [iu] seems still to have been preferred until the late seventeenth century, combinative developments depending on [juː] begin to be accepted from 1640 onwards (see § 185 above). Similarly pretonic ME *eu* in *rheumatic* becomes [iu] and then [juː] in the seventeenth century (see § 244 above). Subsequent loss of secondary stress causes [juː] to become [jʊ] by shortening, whence by further reduction there may arise [jə]. In post-tonic syllables after [s], [z], [t], and [d] the [j], even before the loss of secondary stress, often joins with the preceding consonant to give [ʃ], [ʒ], [tʃ], and [dʒ] (as in *pressure, measure, nature,* and *verdure*). In this case all that remains to represent OF [yr] is [ər], which becomes [ə] by vocalization of the [r]; but pronunciations so developed are differentiated from those which go back to ME *-ĭr* (by ME loss of secondary stress) by the combinative change of the consonants (contrast PresE [meʒə] 'measure' and [neitʃə] 'nature' with seventeenth-century [mezər] and [nɛːtər]). In pretonic syllables (i.e. after initial consonants) the combinative changes are avoided but the [j] often simply disappears (thus [su(:)] and [sə] beside [sju(:)] in *superior*); similar disappearance is common after initial *r* (thus [ru(:)] in *rheumatic*).

Of these changes there is no evidence in the seventeenth-century orthoepists, even in those who record vulgar pronunciations (e.g. in the 'phonetically spelt' lists); but there are rare seventeenth-century spellings which show them. Their extension into more general use probably occurred during the eighteenth century.

> Note 1: Wyld, *Coll. Eng.*, p. 294, records *pleshar*, *pleshur* (of date 1642); he cites other forms which show the combinative change of the consonants, but not the reduction of the vowel.
>
> Note 2: On Gil's transcription of *superior* see § 291 above.

LENGTHENING DUE TO REIMPOSITION OF SECONDARY STRESS

(1) [ɪ] becomes [iː]

(a) In post-tonic syllables

§ 350. ModE lengthening of unstressed [ɪ] to [iː] by reimposition of some degree of secondary stress is in post-tonic syllables relatively common and early; in some forms of English (e.g. Australian English) it is general. In syllables not immediately following the stress it is shown by Cheke (in *extremity* and *authority* spelt with *ee* against *narrowly*, &c. spelt with *i*), Laneham (in *Coventry*), Coote (who puts *unitee* for *unity* in his list of errors due to 'barbarous speaking'), Robinson (in *papistry*, beside [əi]), Gil (once in *chastity*, in accordance with Spenser's rhyme on *be*, once in *harmony* when in rhyme with *agree* (beside ĭ once elsewhere), and once (beside ĭ once) in *Faerie*), Hodges (in *difficulty*), *WSC-RS* (generally), and Brown (in *attorney*, *authority*, and *courtesy* 'phonetically spelt' with *ee*). But Hunt appears to regard *pietee* for *pietie* 'piety' as dialectal. In immediately post-tonic syllables it is shown by the *Welsh Hymn* (which uses Welsh *i*, normally used to transcribe ME ẹ̄, in *lady*, *pretty*, and *mighty*), Cheke (in *city*, *country* spelt with *ee* against *holy*, *city*, &c. spelt with *i*), Salesbury (who uses Welsh *i* (for [iː]) in *lady* and *lily* but Welsh *y* (for [ɪ]) in *holy*), Hart (in *uilī* if it is meant for 'wily' and not 'will ye'), Bullokar (who transcribes *truly* with ĭ but rhymes it with *be* transcribed [biː]), Waad in *Bodley's* (see Vol. I, p. 130), Gil (once beside ĭ once in *angry*, once beside ĭ once and [əi] twice in *greatly*, and once beside ĭ eight times and [əi] once in *lady*), Hodges (who gives *nautee* as a semi-popular transcription of *naughty*, and likewise in *alley*, *busy*, &c.), T. Jones (who uses Welsh *i* to transcribe *-y* in *thirty*), *WSC-RS* (generally), and Brown (in *body* and *honey* 'phonetically spelt' with *ee*, against *hevve* 'heavy').

The evidence shows that the lengthening occurred sporadically from as early as the beginning of the sixteenth century, and it may well have occurred in the late fifteenth century; the rhymes of poets support, and are supported by, the orthoepists' evidence.

(b) In pretonic syllables

§ 351. The reimposition of secondary stress is in pretonic syllables more artificial, and is due to recognition of the separate nature of prefixes and their consequent emphasis. Bullokar has [iː] < [ɪ] in *become, before, begin,* &c., and in *misbelief*, but ĭ in *because* (owing to a continuing association with *by*?) and in *enough*; Gil has [iː] five times against ĭ sixty-one times and ĕ twelve times in the prefix *be-*. See further § 294, Note 1.

(2) *Other apparent cases*

§ 352. Robinson gives ē in words with the prefix *be-* and in *enough* (against ĭ once in *before*, and ĕ once in *begot*). We could regard these transcriptions as showing a lengthening of [e] to [ɛː] if we accepted the *e* spelling of the prefix *be-* (ME bĭ-) and in *enough* (ME ĭnough) as showing a change of pretonic ME ĭ to [e]; but the probability is that it represents [ə], and that Robinson's transcriptions are entirely artificial (see § 294, Notes 2 and 3).

Robinson (occasionally), Gil (once), and Hodges (normally) give ME ā for pretonic *a*, where an artificial reimposition of secondary stress is possible; see § 285.

GLIDE-VOWELS

§ 353. On the development of a glide [ə] before syllabic [l̩], [m̩], [n̩], and [r̩] from ME *-le, -me, -ne,* and *-re* see §§ 323–4 above; cf. also § 328 on the development of [ə] before syllabic [r̩] followed by [n] and [d], and § 329 on its development between syllabic [r̩] and another consonant. On the dialectal and vulgar development of [ə] between [l] or [r] and a following consonant see § 331.

On the development of a glide [ə] before non-syllabic [r] see § 218. This [ə], though normally faint, can be so stressed as to become syllabic, e.g. *fire* [faiə(r)] can be pronounced either as a monosyllable or as a disyllable; in the latter case the unstressed syllable so developed is identified with ME *-ĕr*. The evidence cited in § 218 shows that the development had freely occurred in the sixteenth and seventeenth centuries in the cases there defined.

One other case remains to be considered here, the dialectal development of a glide [ə] between a back vowel, or an early ModE diphthong ending in a back vowel (i.e. [ʌu] < ME ū, ME *au*, and ME *ou*), and a nasal (especially [n]); it is shown, among the orthoepists, only by Bullokar and Sherwood.

Bullokar also shows, in rare instances, a glide [ə] between ME ī, ME *oi*, and [oː] < ME *ou*, and [l]. The evidence for both these developments is given in Vol. I, pp. 103–4. That they are primarily dialectal is suggested not only by the rarity with which they are shown and by their leaving no trace in PresE, but also by Bullokar's birth in Sussex and Sherwood's in Norfolk. But the developments were more widespread in the dialects; Wright gives only a little evidence, but see his §§ 41 and 86 on ME *ou* before *l*, § 156 on ME ī before *l*, and such words as *dawn*, *down*, and *oil* in his Index.

Note: Abbott, *Sh. Gram.*, § 485, shows that Shakespeare's pronunciation was affected by the development of a glide [ə] between [r] and a following consonant, thus [wŏrəd] 'word', [marək] 'mark'.

Shakespeare also shows a glide [ə] developed (i) between a long vowel or diphthong and [l], thus [auəl] 'all' (*Cymb.*, IV. ii. 373), [faiəl] 'fail' (*Coriol.*, IV. vii. 40), [fiːəl] 'feel' (*Macb.*, I. v. 58), [stiːəl] 'steel' (*Coriol.*, I. ix. 45), [kouəld] 'cold' (*Macb.*, IV. i. 6; *3 Hen. VI*, IV. iii. 14), [hoːəl] 'whole' (*Lear*, I. ii. 14), and so perhaps [hɛːəlp] 'health' (*A & C*, II. v. 38, *Ham.*, I. iii. 21); and (ii) between a long vowel or diphthong and [n], thus [kəiənd] 'kind' (*Coriol.*, I. ix. 83), [friːəndz] 'friends' (*M. for M.*, III. i. 28). See Abbott, § 484; his scansion of most of the lines he cites in this paragraph is faulty, but in the cases accepted above it does seem true that what are normally monosyllables are counted by Shakespeare as two syllables.

XI

CONSONANTS

VOICING AND UNVOICING

VARIATION BETWEEN VOICED AND VOICELESS CONSONANTS

(1) *Variation between* [z] *and* [s]

§ 354. Variation between [z] and [s], of which an excellent sketch is given by Ekwall, §§ 143 seq., occurs in native words and more frequently in those adopted from French and Latin.

(a) Native words

§ 355. In native words, in Anglian, *s* remained [s] in initial and final position but was voiced to [z] in medial position between voiced sounds (except at the beginning of the second element of a compound, as in *forsake, answer, handsome,* &c.); hence [s] in *house, horse,* &c. but [z] in *cleanse, choose,* &c. In many cases a differentiation arose between final [s] in a sb. or adj. and medial [z] in the derived verb; so *house* sb. with [s], *house* vb. with [z]. It is in accordance with this principle that *mouse* vb. has [z] in Willis and Wallis and *louse* vb. has [z] in Wallis and Price (against [s] in the corresponding sbs.). *WSC-RS* gives [s] in *loose* adj. but [z] in *loose* vb. (glossed 'unty'), which is a blend of *loose* [luːs] and OE *losian*; Bullokar similarly has [luːz] four times beside [loːz] twice as the verb corresponding to the adjective *loose* (which for him is [loːs], with vowel derived from *losian*), and Coles rhymes *loose* (presumably the verb, as in *WSC*) on [z]. Similar pairs were sometimes formed by analogy; thus Wallis has [z] in *fleece* vb. (in which [s], as in PresE, is to be expected, the vb. being a ModE formation from the sb.), in contrast to [s] in the sb. Contrariwise Hunt gives [s] in *rise* sb., which is formed from the verb.

In the normal development oblique forms such as *horses* gen. sing. would have [z] against [s] in the nominative; but analogy has commonly removed this variation, normally by extension of the [s] throughout (as in *horse, fleece*), sometimes by generalization of the [z], as in *furze* (see Ekwall, § 145). Bullokar gives [s] in *glazen, husband, houses* (beside [z]), and *lousy*; but as he is prone to give artificial transcriptions on 'etymological' grounds no reliance can be placed on this evidence. *Worse* probably owes its [s] to the fact that in OE *wursa* the *s* is derived from a geminate (cf. Luick, § 639.1); Laneham has [rz] < [rs], as also in wordsof French origin, e.g. *rehearse*.

Note: Gil records 'Saxon' [z] for initial OE *s* in his account of the 'Western' dialect. The Southern and SW Midland voicing of initial spirants is probably older than is commonly allowed (e.g. by Luick, § 703); the OE spelling-system did not distinguish [s], [f], [þ] from [z], [v], [ð] because in no dialect were they in free variation.

(b) Words from French and Latin

§ 356. (i) In OF, [z] became [s] in final position but remained in medial, so that a variation arose exactly similar to that in native English words discussed above. It is in accordance with this principle that *merchandise* has [z] but *paradise* [s] (as in Bullokar). Laneham's [z] in *base* sb. is regularly developed from OF *base*; PresE [s] (shown by Hodges) is due to the analogy of *base* adj. (so *OED*), probably aided by the influence of *basis* (from Latin). The adjective *base* (OF *bas*) and its derivatives normally have [s] (so Bullokar, Robinson, and Hodges), but Gil has [z] once (owing to the analogy of the sb., or to the OF feminine) beside [s] twice. The analogy of his variation in *base* adj. must account for Gil's [z] once beside [s] once in *face*.

OF shows the same distinction between (masculine) nouns in [s] and verbs in [z] as OE; so, for example, *use* sb. against *use* vb., *peace* against *appease*, *price* sb. against *prize* vb. (now differentiated in meaning and made the basis of a new verb *to price* and a sb. *prize*). These are regularly so recorded. On the model of such pairs others were analogically formed in English. *Sacrifice* has [z] in Daines, Lye, Cooper, and *WSC*; Cooper contrasts the verb with [z] with the sb. with [s]. Contrariwise *muse* sb. (OF *muse*) has [s] in Hume, Wharton, and J. Smith, apparently in contrast with *muse* vb. (OF *muser*), which has [z] in Salesbury; but it should be observed that Cooper (followed by *WSC*) glosses the word *muse* sb. which has [s] as 'a hole in a fence' (i.e. *meuse* < OF *muce*). Bullokar has [z] in *promise* vb., a fifteenth-century formation from the sb.; but [s] in *enterprise* sb. (OF *entreprise*), obviously on the model of *price*, and in *noise* (beside [z], which is to be expected from OF *noise*). Robinson thrice gives [s] (but sixteen times [z]) in *praise* sb., against [z] in *praise* vb., undoubtedly on the analogy of *price* against *prize*. Price gives [s] in *a lease*, [z] in *to lease* (presumably the verb meaning 'to let'); cf. Huloet–Higgins, who give [z] in an unglossed word *lease*. Coles rhymes *noose* on [z] (cf. the seventeenth- and eighteenth-century spelling *nooze*), and D. Jones, *Eng. Pron. Dict.*, records [z] as a PresE variant beside [s]; if the word be from OF *nos*, &c. (see *OED*), only [s] is to be expected, but [z] may have originated as an analogical pronunciation in the verb. *WSC-RS* give [s] in *premise* sb., [z] in *premise* vb. (as in PresE); the distinction must be analogical unless the verb is from OF *premise* fem. form of the p.p. of *premettre*.

But this distinction of sb. with [s] from vb. with [z] often breaks down owing to the influence of the one on the other; so PresE [s] in the verbs *practise* and *purpose*, which should have [z]. Contrariwise Hart and Bullokar have [z] in *purpose* sb. (OF *porpos*) as well as in the verb (OF *porposer*). Bullokar (perhaps on artificial 'etymological' grounds) gives [s] in *appease*. Willis has [s] in *souse* vb., but it is more probably formed from the sb.

(OF *sous*) than an adoption of an unrecorded OF *souser. See also Note 1 below.

(ii) In words from OF with a recognizable prefix the pronunciation of intervocalic *s* varies between [s] and [z] according as the word is treated as a combination or as a unit (cf. French *ressource*, English *resource* against *reserve*; see Ekwall, § 147). Most such words have [z] in PresE (in part owing to the seventeenth-century English change of [s] to [z] before the stress), but the orthoepists show some variation. Hart has [z] in *preserve*. Bullokar has [z] in *resist, resolve, resort*, and *reserve*. Robinson has [z] in *deserve, undeserved, resign*, and *resolved*. Gil has [z] in *resort* and twice (but [s] once) in *deserve*, and [s] in *resist, resound*, and *resemble* (OF *resembler*). Cooper has [z] in *preserve, resist, desire*, and *reside* (contrast the early seventeenth-century spelling *recide*), but [s] in *design* and *desist* (perhaps at this date owing to Latin influence).

(iii) OF intervocalic *s* < Latin *s*, as remarked above, is the voiced [z]; hence the [z] of English *persuasion, occasion, vision, delusion, measure, usual*, &c. The English pronunciation of Latin, which in late ME undoubtedly reflected French pronunciation in most of its features, must also have used [z] for Latin intervocalic *s*; cf. Bullokar's [z] in the names *Aesop, Naso, Thraso*, and *Ephesus*. But the 'reformed' pronunciation of the sixteenth century substituted [s] for [z] in the pronunciation of Latin *s*; admittedly this 'reform' appears to have been only partial, for the modern English pronunciation of Latin retains [z] in circumstances in which it is usual in comparable English words—e.g. in *Hercules* and *Thales*, presumably on the analogy of final [z] in *horses*, &c. (but Bullokar has [s] in these two names), and in the ending *-sionem* in, for example, *visionem, irrisionem*, &c. (which follow the earlier English pronunciation of *vision, derision*, &c.; but see further below) and in consequence for many other cases of *s* before *i*, e.g. in *ecclesia*. But in general Latin *s* was now pronounced [s], and in consequence words adopted from Latin (or believed to have been adopted from Latin) were given [s] (as in *asylum, desolate*, &c.; see Ekwall, § 148), whereas earlier adoptions from French or Latin had [z]. Thus [z] is given by Hart in *curiosity, because* and *cause* (normally), *comparison, parenthesis, usurp, usurpation, present(ly)* adj. and adv. (twice) and *present* vb. (once); by Bullokar in *parasite, comparison*, and *garrison*; by Robinson in *usurps, presently* (twice), *presence* (five times), *present* adj. and sb. (thrice) and vb. (once); by Hodges in *Jerusalem*; by Coles in *Dionysius* and *Elysian*; and by Cooper in *exquisite*. But [s], derived from the new pronunciation of Latin, is given by Hart in *because* (twice) and *caused* (once), *present(ly)* adj. and adv. (twice) and *present* vb. (twice), and *prepositions*; by Bullokar in *causeth* and *causes* sb. pl.; by Robinson in *presently* (once); by Coles in *Persia* and *ambrosia* (with [ʃ] < [sj]), *Mysia* (with [ʃj] < [sjɪ]), and *uncircumcision* (with [sj]); by Cooper in *hesitate* (first recorded 1623) and *proselyte* and (with [ʃ] < [sj]) in *allusion, circumcision*, and ten others in *-sion* (cf. Note 3 below); and by *RS* in *nauseous* (with [ʃ] < [sj]). It will be observed that Coles supports Cooper in giving [sj] > [ʃ] after vowels in the ending *-sion*, despite the PresE use of [ʒ] < [zj] in English words and [z] in their Latin etymons.

In the course of ModE the fluctuation in usage resulting from this cause has gradually been reduced, [z] being generalized in some endings (*-sible* and *-site*, as in *visible* and *opposite*), [s] in others (*-osity, -sory*, and *-sive*, as in *curiosity, illusory*, and *decisive*), though exceptions remain, e.g. [z] in *advisory* (see Ekwall, § 149). But in eModE there was clearly much uncertainty, and occasionally the variation between [s] and [z] in these words affected others by analogy; thus Hart has [s] once beside [z] twice in *reason*, Robinson [ʒ] < [zj] in *physician*, Gil [z] twice in *Cicero*, and Coles [zj] for *-ti-* in *transition* and [ʒ] < [zj] in *Diocletian*. See also below on confusion of suffixes.

Two special cases are the prefixes *dis-* and *trans-*; OF *des-* and *trans-* are pronounced with [z] before a following vowel, but the Latin prefixes, in the 'reformed' pronunciation, were given [s]. Hart has [s] in *disorder* and *disordering*, Bullokar in *diseases, dishonest*, and *disorder*, and Gil in *dishonour, dishonourable, dishonesty*, and *dishonestly*; but Hodges has [z] in *dishonour* and *dishonest* (which however is probably due to voicing before the stress). Bullokar has [s], but Coles [z], in *transition*, which varies in PresE.

(iv) Variation between [s] and [z] also results from confusion of suffixes in words of Romance origin (see Ekwall, § 149). Thus PresE [s] in *comparison* and *garrison* in place of the historical [z] shown by Hart and Bullokar is due to the analogy of, for example, *caparison* (Fr. *caparasson*), supported by the effect of the variation between [s] and [z] discussed under (iii) above. Similarly *courtesy* and *jealousy*, recorded with the historical [z] by Gil and Bullokar respectively, may owe their later pronunciations with [s] (recorded in *courtesy* by Bullokar, Robinson, and Hodges and in *jealousy* by Gil) to the influence of sbs. in *-cy* (e.g. *privacy*), as Ekwall suggests; but [s] in *courteous* and *jealous* is probably a more potent factor. A clearer case is the [z] shown in *suffice* by Robinson, Lye, and Cooper (and in *sufficient* by *WSC*, varying Cooper), and in *sacrifice* by Daines, Lye, Cooper, and *WSC*, which is due to confusion with the suffix *-ize* (aided in the case of *sacrifice* vb. by the analogy of pairs of words with [s] in the sb., [z] in the vb.; see above). Conversely Bullokar has [s] in *chastised*, perhaps owing to the analogy of *justice*; but the etymology is dubious (see *OED*).

Note 1: In *sacrifice* vb. [z] probably originates in confusion of suffixes; in *muse* sb. [s] may be due to the influence of a 'reformed' pronunciation of Latin *musa*. Smith, in his list of errata, gives [s] in *muse* vb. 'mirari meditando' (misprinted originally as *r*); unless this is a second error, it must be by analogy with [s] in *muse* sb. *OED* records the spelling *sacrifize* vb. (17th cent.); Chaucer rhymes *sacrifyse* sb. on [z] (e.g. *Pard. T.* 469).

Note 2: Bullokar's [s] in *citizen* is probably artificial.

Note 3: Cooper is not usually careful to distinguish words in which *-si-*, &c. are pronounced [ʒ] from those in which the pronunciation is [ʃ], perhaps because usage varied; but he seems certainly to intend [ʃ] in twelve words in *-sion* (see paragraph (iii) above), against [ʒ] in *derision, incision, provision,* and *inhesion*—obviously an artificial distinction. Perhaps he was merely careless.

Note 4: Ekwall, loc. cit., does not allow sufficiently for the influence of Latin, to which (and not to French pronunciation) the [s] of *unison* is due, nor for the tendency of [s] to become [z] between [n] and a vowel, as in OE *clænsian*, ModE *pansy* and *quinsy*. The conventional spelling also plays a part in securing the spread of [s] to words in which [z] should occur; Hayward (after 1625), admittedly a foolish man, says that the pronunciation [z] for intervocalic *s* is 'too much followed by the younger sort apt to embrace it' and is to be restrained by schoolmasters; he gives a list of words, native and adopted, in all of which ME had [z], and says 'we may easily sound the *s* if we bend our mindes and willes there-vnto' (f. 72ᵛ). Bullokar, he remarks, though he 'much favoured' [z] for intervocalic *s*, admitted that Latin may not have had [z].

(2) *Variation between* [v] *and* [f]

§ 357. In native words, in Anglian dialects, initial and final *f* was [f] but intervocalic *f* became [v]. Hence arose variation between nominative singulars with [f] and oblique forms with [v], e.g. *līf* 'life' with [f] but *līfes* gen. sing. with [v]. In the course of ModE the [f] of the nominative has been levelled throughout the singular but not usually to the plural (thus Gil has [f] in *lifes* gen. sing. but [v] in *lives*, as in PresE). Butler, however, gives [v] in the gen. sing. of *huswife* and *wife*, thus *huswives* and *wives* (though he contrasts *knifes* gen. sing. with *knives* pl.), and Cooper twice gives *wives* as the gen. sing. In some cases PresE also has analogical plurals, e.g. *staffs* beside *staves*, *wharfs* beside *wharves*. Robinson's [v] in *long-lived* (for which he has ME *ī*) is of course regular. Gil's [v] in *thyself* represents ME *-selve* < OE *selfum*; in *herself, himself,* and *myself* he has [f] < OE *self*. It is apparently on the model of *hoof, hooves* (for which Bullokar has [v]), and *hooved* that Hodges has [v] in *troves* plural of *trof* 'trough' and Cocker has *hoved* 'houghed'; these are then analogical formations.

Similar variation between final [f] and intervocalic [v] occurs in OF in, for example, *sauf* masc. beside *sauve* fem.; Robinson retains [v] in *safety*, Butler has [v] beside [f] in *safeguard*, and Bullokar, though showing [f] in *safeguard*, has a shortening of the vowel which seems to depend on [v] (see § 28 (*a*) above); otherwise analogical [f] is shown in *safety* (so Bullokar) and *safeguard* (so Gil).

In *Stephen* [v] (shown by Hodges and Coles) is from the OF form *Esteven*, [f] from the English pronunciation of Greek. For *prophecy* [v] is recorded by Coles, Strong, and Young, and would seem to point to a semi-popular OF form with [v]. The *ph* spelling of *nephew* (OF *neveu*) is modelled on *Stephen* and gives rise to a spelling-pronunciation with [f] recorded by Strong and Young and the shorthand-writer Hopkins; but Hodges has the historical [v].

Note: 'Saxon' [v] for initial OE *f*, which accounts for the StE pronunciation of *vat* and *vixen*, is recorded as a dialectalism by Salesbury and by Gil, who gives it for both 'Southern' and 'Western' dialects; the former dialect has also, Gil says, the reverse substitution of (analogical) [f] for etymological [v], as in *finegar* 'vinegar', *ficar* 'vicar'. Coote gives *feal* as a dialectal form of *veal*. Hunt follows Coote, and adds the converse case *vather* 'father'. On *fitch* 'vetch', recorded by Levins and (as his own form) by Gil, see § 77, Note 3. The Northerner Mulcaster has non-Saxon [f] in *fixen* 'vixen', and Fox and Hookes record *fate* 'vat'. On the date of the Southern and SW Midland voicing of initial *f* see § 355 Note.

(3) *Variation between* [ð] *and* [þ]

§ 358. OE *þ* was, in Anglian, pronounced as [þ] in initial and final position but became [ð] in medial position between voiced sounds, e.g. in *smiðas* 'smiths' and *eorðe* 'earth'. There thus arose a variation between [þ] in the nominative singular of sbs. and [ð] in the oblique forms which has largely been obliterated in the course of the later language by the operation of analogy. Extension of the [þ] of the nominative to the gen. sing. was early and complete, and there is no eModE evidence of the survival of genitives in [ð]. Analogical extension of [þ] from the singular to the plural was a more gradual and less regular process, of which an admirable discussion (here largely followed) is given by C. T. Onions in his paper 'The Plural of Nouns ending in *-th*' (*S.P.E.* Tract LXI (1943), 19–28). As Dr. Onions shows, four main cases have to be distinguished.

(*a*) In native words which in the singular have [þ] after a short vowel the formation of a new plural in [þs], and with the vowel of the singular, has been regularly carried through in PresE (e.g. in *breath*, *pith*, *smith*, &c.). But there is evidence that this situation did not apply so regularly in the sixteenth and seventeenth centuries. Hart gives, as the plural of *breath*, the forms *brēðz*, *brēðs*, and *brēðes* (on those with *s* see § 363 below); but it should be observed that words of the type of *breath* still often retained a long vowel in the singular in the sixteenth and seventeenth centuries. Present-day American English has the forms [bæðz] and [pæðz], which are undoubtedly survivals of seventeenth-century forms [baðz] and [paðz], with ME *ă* from the ME singular in place of ME *ā* but [ðz] from the ME plural. Butler actually records a form [swaðs] (on the final [s] see § 363) beside a fully analogical [swaþs] 'swaths'. From such forms develop, by lengthening of ME *ă* before the group [ðz], Hodges's [pɒːðz], Cooper's *paths* with [ðz] and apparently ME *ă* or its lengthened equivalent, and PresE [pɑːðz], [bɑːðz], and [swɑːðz] or [swɒːðz] (in contrast to [pɑːþs], [bɑːþs], and [swɒþs] and [swɒːþs], new analogical formations on the singular). Similarly [klɒːðz] 'clothes' shows lengthening of ME *ŏ* before [ðz] (in contrast to [klɒþs] and [klɒːþs] formed on the singular [klɒþ] or [klɒːþ]). In view of this evidence of forms with [ðz] after ME *ă* and *ŏ* at the date when lengthening occurred (i.e. in the seventeenth century in StE) it is not as surprising as it seemed to Onions that Hodges should retain [ðz] after ME *ĭ* in [smɪðz] 'Smiths'. Admittedly Hodges is inconsistent, giving [þs] (i.e. new analogical plurals) in *laths, baths, piths, moths*, and *broths* but [ðz] in *paths* and *Smiths*, but analogical processes are of their nature gradual and inconsistent in results.

If we seek a reason for the special susceptibility of words with a short vowel to the formation of analogical plurals in [þs], it is doubtless that in these words the traditional plural had come to differ from the singular not only in consonant, but also in vowel; original short vowels (as in *smith, path*, &c.) were liable to lengthening in the open syllable of the plurals, and original long vowels (as in *cloth, breath*) to shortening before the [þ] of the singular but not the [ð] of the plural (cf. Hart's long vowel in *breaths*). As the singulars and plurals thus came to differ too markedly, the tendency to the formation of new plurals was especially strong; sometimes only the short vowel of the singular was levelled into the plural, but more often a completely new plural was formed. The old plurals either disappeared (so ME *pāthes* 'paths', recorded by Cheke) or were assigned to new functions (so *clothes*, which Butler, Wallis, and Cooper, however, still treat as the plural of *cloth* (with shortened *ŏ*); whether Hodges's [klo:ðz] is sb. or vb. there is no sure means of telling). Similarly *swathes* is made the plural of *swathe* (< OE *swăðu*), as by Hodges (if the word he records is sb. and not vb.).

(*b*) In words with a long stem vowel there is less tendency to form new plurals in [þs]; *mouth* and *oath* always have [ðz] (so in Hodges). But *sheath, wreath, heath, youth*, and *truth* have new plurals in [þs] beside the old ones in [ðz]; *sheaths* has [ðz] in Hodges and Cooper, but [þs] occurs in *heaths* in Hodges, in *youths* in Gil and Hodges, and in *truths* in Bullokar and Hodges. It is to be observed that shortening of ME *ē* before [þ] was common (as in *breath* and *death*) and that *youth* had a variant pronunciation (recorded once by Gil and by others) with ME *ŭ*; the [þs] forms may therefore have belonged originally to the variants with the short vowel (cf. (*a*) above) and been extended to those with the long, and *truth* may subsequently have been influenced by the analogy of *youth*. PresE tends to treat on the same footing as words with ME long vowels those in which ModE lengthening occurs: thus *bath, path*, and *lath*, and *broth* and *cloth* when pronounced [brɒ:þ] and [klɒ:þ] (plurals [brɒ:ðz] and [klɒ:ðz]). But analogical plurals in [þs] are also common for these words with eModE short vowels.

(*c*) Words which, in the singular, have [þ] after a voiced consonant (so *breadth, length, month, fourth, hearth, birth*) would originally have [ð] in the plural (so too the re-formed *seventh, ninth, tenth*, &c.), but this in general has been replaced, the groups [dðz], [ŋðz], [nðz], [rðz] being more difficult to articulate than [dþs], &c.; [rðz] has, however, sometimes been retained, as in PresE [hɑ:ðz] < [ha:rðz] < [harðz], [bə:ðz] < [bərðz] < [berðz] 'berths'. Hodges has [þs] in *fourths* and *ninths*, and Cooper excepts *earth* (with eModE [rþ] < earlier [rð]) from his list of words in which [þ] in the singular changes to [ð] in the plural, saying that 'the sound of *r* does not easily pass over into *dh*' (which is of course the reason for the regular change of [ð] to [þ] in the singular itself), but it is evident that not all seventeenth-century speakers avoided the group [rðz]. From the PresE point of view [hɑːðz] and [bəːðz] of course belong to the class of word with [ðz] after a long vowel, but the loss of [r] is too late a change (and the consequent change of [ər] > [əː]) for the retention of [ðz] to owe much, if anything, to this fact.

(*d*) Words adopted from foreign languages (other than ON, which gives *birth*) or with [þ] after voiceless consonants (so *depth*) naturally do not have plurals with [ð]; in them such plurals could only be analogical.

Though the early evidence on these plurals is less full than might be desired, it is clear that the formation of analogical forms in [þs] is essentially a ModE process, being affected by ModE changes in vowel-quantity (the earlier shortening and the seventeenth-century lengthening), and that in the seventeenth century forms in [ðz] survived in words which now have only [þs].

With(e) sb. (OE *wiþþe*) should have [þ], as OE *þþ* remains voiceless even between vowels; Hodges and Willis record the historical [wɪþ], and Hodges gives the plural as [wɪþs]. In the eighteenth century variation is recorded between [þ] and [ð] (see the quotation from Walker given by Onions, op. cit., p. 25), and PresE has [wɪð] and [waɪð] beside [wɪþ]; the two former pronunciations are due to the analogy of *withy* (OE *wiðig*), which of course has [ð] and is capable of variation between original ME *ī* and ME *ĭ* by shortening. *Brothel* (OE *broðel*) should have [ð], as in Coote, Daines, and Wharton; PresE [þ] must be due to the purely formal analogy of *broth*.

Note: On originally prevocalic [ð] which becomes final in late ME by loss of final *e* and then shows a tendency to become unvoiced, see § 368 below.

(4) *Variation between* [gz] *and* [ks]

§ 359. In many words of Latin origin the consonant *x* is pronounced [gz]; as this occurs chiefly when the stress follows, the explanation has been advanced (Jespersen, *ModE Gr*, § 6.7; Horn, § 210) that [gz] develops from [ks] by voicing before the stress. But Ekwall, §§ 150–1, rightly rejecting this view, has drawn attention to the parallel that exists between the English and French pronunciations of the words in question. It is apparent, especially from the Modern French pronunciation, that the medieval French (and English) pronunciation of Latin must have used [gz] for Latin *x* between vowels (as in ModFr *exalter, exemple, examen, exécration*, &c.) and between a vowel and *h* (probably silent, as in ModFr *exhalaison, exhaustif, exhiber*, &c.), but [ks] for Latin *x* both before and after other consonants (as in ModFr *expérience*, &c. and *anxiété*). But at a later date (probably about 1500) the reform of the pronunciation of Latin led to the replacement of [gz] by [ks] for intervocalic *x*. By this change French pronunciation was little affected (but cf. [ks] in *Alexandre*), but English pronunciation was much altered, [ks] being introduced in many words. But the English tendency to use voiced consonants before the stress, which in the seventeenth century led to a voicing in this position of [s] to [z], influences the distribution of the old and new pronunciations: [gz] is retained in most words in which the stress follows (e.g. *example, exert, exalt, exult, exhibit, Alexander, luxurious*), but not in certain learned words (e.g. *proximity, doxology, luxation*), whereas [ks] has been substituted when the stress precedes (*exodus, execute, exercise,* &c.) except in derivatives which follow the simplex (*exaltation, exultation*); but there is some degree of variation, as usually when one pronunciation is replaced by another not phonetically developed from it.

Of the orthoepists, Hart shows [ks] not only when the stress precedes (*eksodus*) but also when it follows (*eksampl*), and uses *x* as a symbol for [ks] (so *exepting* 'excepting'; cf. *exerciz* 'exercise', *exampl*). Bullokar's retention of *x* (*example*, &c.; note *exort* 'exhort') can hardly be credited with phonetic significance. Mulcaster does not include *x* among his list of 'the dubled forced letters' (which does include *s*, pronounced [s] and [z], and *th*, pronounced [þ] and [ð]), and therefore presumably used [ks] in all words. Robinson has [ks] in *Alexander, exempt*, and *exile* vb., and Hodges's failure to supply a special diacritic to distinguish the value of *x* in *exalt, example, exhaust*, and *Exodus* from that in *expedition, extol*, &c. must, in so careful and exact a phonetician, mean that he used [ks] in all positions. But Gil, though he makes no comment on the pronunciation of *x* (which he seems to regard as a single letter), gives different treatment in his transcriptions to *eksel* 'excel', *exselensj* 'excellency', *eksept* 'except', *ekses* 'excess' on the one hand and *Alexander, exalted, example, exempt, exile* sb., and *exiled* (in which *x* is retained) on the other; it appears that intervocalic *x* must stand for some sound other than [ks], which must of course be [gz]. But before consonants he uses *x* to represent [ks] in *expect*, &c. Hunt says that *x* has the force of *cs*, 'or as some of *gs*' [*sic*].

PresE initial [z] in *Xerxes*, &c. is usually (and rightly) regarded as a reduction of [gz], but as French also has this pronunciation the reduction presumably occurred in the medieval pronunciation of Latin rather than in English itself. Cooper says that *x* in *Xenophon* is pronounced *z, gs* (for [gz]), or *ks*.

PresE [gz] in *anxiety* is a single case in which it seems likely that there may have been a ModE development of [ks] to [gz], since ModFr pronunciation suggests that the medieval pronunciation of the word had [ks]. This possibility is strongly supported by the evidence of Coles, whose 'phonetic' spelling shows [ŋkz]; the [s] of the group [ks] has been voiced to [z] before the stress by the common seventeenth-century change (see

§ 365), but the [k] remains. Subsequent voicing of [k] to [g] between [ŋ] and [z] would be very natural, and would be supported by the analogy of [gz] in other words.

> *Note* 1: A tendency of [ks] itself to become [kz], as shown by Coles, would obviously assist the survival (and possibly the re-entry into educated speech) of the older [gz], and would account for its marked predominance in words in which the stress follows.
>
> *Note* 2: PresE [gz] beside [ks] in *exile* is doubtless due to the earlier end-stressed form of the verb; cf. Ekwall, § 151.
>
> *Note* 3: That there was no general change in English of intervocalic [ks] before the stress to [gz] is conclusively shown by the fact that [gz] is found only for Latin *x*; there is no sign of [gz] < [ks] in *accept, accede, except, excel*, &c.
>
> *Note* 4: Salesbury says that English *x* is pronounced as [gz], but gives *axe* as his example; this seems incredible. He has probably chosen a bad example for a statement in itself generally true.

VOICING

(1) *In unstressed words and syllables in ME*

§ 360. In later ME (apparently, in all cases, in the fourteenth century) there was a voicing of initial [þ] to [ð] in unstressed words, and of final spirants and the affricative [tʃ] in unstressed words and syllables, which would seem to have been very regular in its operation; its failure is usually, though probably not always, to be attributed to the presence of secondary or primary stress.

(a) Initial [þ] > [ð] *in unstressed words*

§ 361. In the weak forms of the words *this, that, then,* &c. [þ] became [ð] in the fourteenth century (cf. Jordan, § 207). The change is regularly shown by the orthoepists, and the evidence for the survival of [þ], preserved in the stressed form, is slight: the *Welsh Hymn* has it (once in each case) in *the, thee,* and *this,* and the only later evidence is that of Robinson (once in each case) in *thee, this, those,* and *though.* Only [ð] is recorded in *their, there, these, they, thou,* and *thy.* It should be observed that [ð] spreads from the weak forms to those which, as far as the vowel-development is concerned, are strong. For further evidence see § 4 above.

(b) Final spirants in unstressed words

§ 362. The voicing of final spirants in unstressed words is of course the same phonetic process as in unstressed syllables, and appears to have occurred at various periods, though there may have been a special tendency to it in the fourteenth century; it is an example of the change which, in Primitive Germanic, is known as 'Verner's Law'. Forms with [z], [ð], and [v] are in ModE always to be regarded as developing in the late ME weak forms, even when associated with vowels developed under stress, and conversely the retention of [s] and [f] (and less certainly, perhaps, of [þ]; cf. Note 1 below) is characteristic of the ME strong forms, even when associated in ModE with vowels developed under weak stress; in other words, there has been much blending of the strong and weak forms. But *a priori* one would expect the ME voicing to fail in weak forms if the following word began with a voiceless consonant; and the important and careful evidence of Hart (cf. Jespersen, *Hart*, §§ 40–43) confirms this assumption, for he clearly attempts to distinguish the variant forms according to their phonetic context, giving forms without voicing not only in final position or before a pause (where the stressed forms would be expected) but also before voiceless consonants (so, for example, *his, is, was, with*), and forms with voicing before voiced sounds (so *as, this*).

The detailed evidence on most of the words involved is set out in § 4 above. In certain words failure of voicing is exceptional. *As* varies only in Hart, who in the *Orthographie* has [s] nearly forty times beside much more frequent [z], but in the *Methode* has only [z] (five times); in *whereas* he has [s] once, but otherwise [z]. *Has* is recorded only with [z] (e.g. by Gil, who regards it as a Northern form). *His* has a variant [s] in Higgins, Hart, Gil, Willis, Coles, and perhaps Fox and Hookes; for details see § 4. *Is* has [s] only in Smith, Hart, and Willis. *This* has a variant [z] in Hart, Laneham, Mulcaster, and Robinson. *These* and *those* have only [z]. *Was* has a variant [s] in Smith, Hart, Mulcaster, and Gil. In contrast to these words, *us* normally has [s] (e.g. in Smith, Robinson, Gil, and Hodges), but Hart has [z] five times (twice before a vowel, thrice before a voiced consonant) beside normal [s]. In *with* and its derivatives [þ] is the more frequent, but [ð] occurs as a variant in the *Welsh Hymn*, Hart, Bullokar, Robinson, and Gil and regularly in Price. *Doth* has [ð] beside [þ] in Hart, but otherwise only [þ]. *Hath* has [þ] except in Coles. Hart once has [ð] in *saith*, probably developed under weak stress. On *if, of, off, whereof*, &c. see § 4.

Note 1: The greater frequency of [þ] in *with*, which contrasts with the predominance of [z] in *was*, &c., is probably to be associated with the tendency of final [ð] to become [þ]; see § 368 below.

Note 2: It seems probable that [s] instead of [z] in [ɪst] 'is it' and [ɪts] 'it's, it is' is not due to ModE unvoicing (so Ekwall, § 152), but to the contractions having really developed in ME, before the voicing of [s] to [z] in *is*, and not in ModE, when they are first recorded. In *is't* we should in any case expect the stressed form of the verb.

(c) Final [s] *and* [tʃ] *in unstressed syllables*

§ 363. (i) The suffix *-es*. The most important case of the voicing of a final consonant in an unstressed syllable is in the inflexion *-es*, which becomes [əz]. The change is earlier than the fifteenth-century syncope of [ə], but on the other hand is later than ME syncope in, for example, *pence* (by back-formation from *twopence*, &c.), in which [s] is clearly from earlier [ɪs]; as *pans*, &c. 'pence' is recorded from *c.* 1300, the change of [əs] > [əz] may be set in the fourteenth century (cf. Jordan, § 160).

The consequences of this process do not seem usually to have been carefully worked out. Words in which early (ME) syncope occurred should, by phonetic process, have [s] even after voiced consonants (e.g. *lordings*; cf. [s] after [n] in *pence*); contrariwise words in which late syncope occurred should have [z] even after voiceless consonants (e.g. *hats*). Many of these combinations of voiced consonant plus [s], or of voiceless consonant plus [z], will seem impossible to a present-day Englishman, but probably only because of their unfamiliarity; they can be articulated. Obviously, however, there would be a tendency to assimilate the inflexion to the preceding consonant; and as by the fifteenth century there had developed two syncopated forms of the inflexion, the earlier [s] and the later [z], there took place a redistribution of the two forms (partly phonetic, partly analogical), [s] being applied to words ending in a voiceless consonant and [z] to those ending in a voiced consonant or a vowel. But in exceptional cases (e.g. *pence*, an abnormal plural form) the historical [s] is kept (thus providing, in this case, a distinction from *pens* with [z]).

That this redistribution of the two forms was not an automatic phonetic process is shown by the evidence of certain orthoepists, who show that in the sixteenth and early seventeenth centuries it was still incomplete. The main body of evidence comes from Hart, who was so good a phonetician and ordinarily so free from the influence of the conventional spelling that his testimony can hardly be doubted (especially as it is considerable in amount and largely self-consistent). He shows [s] in the plurals of some thirty words of French origin (mostly masculines) of the type of *autours* 'authors', *cavillations, compounds*, &c., i.e. words of two or more syllables in the singular which would in later ME be expected to have -*s* not -*es* in the plural; so too in a few ModE adoptions from Latin (*calumniators, semivocals*) which must follow the analogy of ME adoptions from OF (e.g. *progenitors*). Against these he has [z] in three similar words (*actives, governors*, and *matters*), and variation occurs in *inventors, pronouns*, and *vowels*. The [z] given in the monosyllabic *faults* must be due to fifteenth-century English syncope in ME *fautes* (< OF); but *pairs* varies, having normal [z] but [s] thrice, and *sounds, compares* and *verbs* have [s]. After vowels [z] occurs in *authorities, quantities*, and *virtues*, but *Hebrews* varies between [s] and [z] (once each).

In native words which can have early syncope, [s] occurs in *elders, forefathers, history-writers, nobleman's, others, players, sisters* (and in *seas*, monosyllabic from OE), but [z] in *neighbours, spellers*, and *thousands*; the suffix -*ing* is followed by [z] in *sayings* but [s] in *discouragings*. In words which should have late syncope [s] is found in *becomes, belongs, birds, men's, names, needs, things*, and *words*; *ours* and *selves* vary, the former having [s] twice beside [z] once and the latter [s] in the *Orthographie* and [z] in the *Methode*. *Breaths* is [brɛːðs] thrice and [brɛːðz] once, as well as [breðəs] once.

When -*es* is retained as a separate syllable (so in *ages*, *asses*, &c., and also in *contraries*, *copies*, *enemies*, *modes* 'moods', and *breaths* once) Hart usually has [əs] (so in thirteen words); but [əz] occurs in *exercises* and *premises*, and there is variation in *enemies*. The starting-point of the [əs] form must be failure of the ME voicing before a word beginning with a voiceless consonant (thus Hart gives [s] four times in the phrase *the Lord's Prayer* and similarly *enemies tu* against *enemiez of*; cf. also his evidence on failure of voicing in weakly stressed words, § 362 above); but there has clearly been a subsequent tendency, of which Hart is the only important representative among our sources, to regeneralize the forms in [əs] and [s], aided by the analogy of words which had [s] from a fourteenth-century inflexion -*s* instead of -*es*. His transcriptions *artikls* 'articles' (and similarly five other words in OF -*le*) and *leters* 'letters' and *mīters* 'metres' must represent new formations on the singulars (in which [l̩] < -*le* and [ər] < [r̩] < -*re* develop), and therefore show his regeneralization of [s]; and the latter's not infrequent occurrence instead of [z] in both native and foreign words in which only late syncope is to be expected shows either that the starting-point was [əs] not [əz], or analogical extension of [s] in place of [z].

There is a little evidence to support Hart's. Smith has [əs], as a separate syllable, in *Jews* (which is contrasted with the monosyllable *juice*). Laneham has [s] in *comes* (cf. Hart's [s] in *becomes*) but [z] in *beasts* and *nights* (cf. Hart's [z] in *faults*). Gil has [z] in *book's* gen. sing. in the phrase *the book's leaves* (i.e. before a voiced consonant), but elsewhere [s] in *books* plural. Gil also gives [s] in transcribing the Spenserian unsyncopated forms *wūndes* 'wounds' sb., *kloudes* 'clouds', and *handes* 'hands', but these may be imperfectly phonetic (despite their agreement with Hart's forms); elsewhere he has *kloudez* 'clouds' (again a Spenserian form). Butler gives a rule that the genitive and plural ending *s* is pronounced [z] except after certain voiceless consonants (including [ç] and [χ] in *thighs* and *howghs* 'hocks', though elsewhere it seems that Butler did not pronounce *gh* in *thighs* and he may not have done in *howghs*) and after [ð] in *boothes* and [swaðs] 'swaths', where it is [s] (cf. Hart's [s] in [brɛːðs] 'breaths').

We may sum up this part of the discussion by concluding that although in the seventeenth century the PresE situation normally obtained ([s] after voiceless consonants, [z] after voiced; so Robinson, Gil (cf. *Logonomia*, chap. X), and Hodges), nevertheless there is sixteenth-century evidence, and a little from the early seventeenth century, which shows (*a*) the survival after voiced consonants of [s] developed from ME [əs] by early syncope (or from the OF inflexion -*s*), (*b*) the survival after voiceless consonants of [z] developed from [əz] by fifteenth-century syncope, (*c*) an inflexion [əs] showing failure of ME voicing, apparently before a voiceless consonant, and [s] developed from it by fifteenth-century syncope, and some tendency (clearly marked in Hart) to generalize this inflexion [(ə)s] at the expense of [(ə)z].

In words which have become detached from the inflexional system the historical forms remain without disturbance by analogy. *Pence* has [s] in, for example, Robinson and Gil (who comments on it as an anomalous plural). Similarly [s] remains in PresE in *dice, bodice* (originally plural of *body*), and *truce* (< *trewes*); Bullokar has [dəiz] (now distinguished in meaning) but Levins and Smith have [dəis] and Gil [try:s]. An important class of words which belongs here is the adverbial forms *once, twice, thrice, else*, &c., which show early syncope under weak stress; such forms in [s] are the starting-point of *amongst, amidst, betwixt, whilst*, &c. But unsyncopated forms in *-es* remained in the fourteenth century, whence [əz] > [z] by fifteenth-century syncope, and in some words the orthoepists show variation. Thus Smith has [s] in *whiles* (see Vol. I, p. 54), but Hart has [z]. *Else* has [z] beside [s] in Laneham and in Gil (who has each form twice), but otherwise [s] (so Hart, Bullokar, Robinson, and Hodges). *Thrice* has [z] once beside [s] three times in Gil; but otherwise such words have [s].

(ii) Other suffixes. The voicing of the final consonant of an unstressed syllable affected other suffixes than *-es*. Final [tʃ] became [dʒ] in *knowledge, ostridge* 'ostrich', *cabbage, sausage, Greenwich, Harwich*, &c. (Jespersen, § 6.8; Jordan, § 180); [dʒ] is shown in *knowledge* by Hart, Gil, Hodges, Strong, and Brown. The suffix *-ous* is [ʊz] in Hart in *commodiously, curious, desirous* (twice), *jealous, notoriously, superfluous*, and *virtuous*; the only exceptions are that *desirous, commodious*, and *dangerous* are each once transcribed with *-ous* [ʌus], showing retention of [s] under the secondary stress that preserves ME *ū* unshortened. PresE [ʌs] for *-ous* represents an earlier *-ŭs* (recorded by Laneham, Bullokar, Robinson, Gil, and later sources), which is a blend-form with [s] preserved under secondary stress but ME *ŭ* by shortening; the use of [s] in Latin *-ōsus* has probably assisted the generalization of this form. In *treatise* (AF *tretiz*) Hart has [s] twice beside [z] five times; PresE also varies. In *witness* Hart has [z] (before a vowel) in the *Methode* (cf. PresE [mɪsɪz] < *mistress*); *Thomas* has [z] (before [b] of *Bodley*) in Waad. *Riches* (OF *richesse*) has [s] in Bullokar but [z] in Robinson, Gil, and Hodges.

Note 1: It is hardly an objection to the interpretation of Hart's evidence offered above under (i) that he himself attempts to distinguish the use of [s] and [z] entirely according to the initial sound of the following word. It is clear from what he says (see Vol. I, pp. 76–77) that usage varies, and that his rules are attempts, in part arbitrary, at rationalization; they should not be mistaken for an historical explanation.

Note 2: On Hodges's forms of the 2nd sing. pres. indic. see Vol. I, p. 183. They appear to show an inflexion *-es* pronounced [z] (by voicing and syncope) after vowels and voiced consonants and [s] after voiceless consonants, to which he adds a *t* which, though not marked silent, presumably was. He also has, without syncope, the StE *-est* [əst].

(2) *Voicing of* [s] *and* [þ] *in combination with voiced sounds*

§ 364. In the course of ModE [s] shows a tendency to become [z] in the neighbourhood of voiced sounds (cf. Ekwall, § 153); so in *muslin* and (beside retained [s]) in *Wesley* and *mistletoe*, in *prism, schism, enthusiasm*, &c. (contrast French [s]), *cosmic, dismal*, &c., and in *gooseberry, raspberry*, and (beside retained [s]) in *wristband*. The orthoepists give little evidence of the change, but Robinson has [z] in *dismal, disgrace*, and *disguise* (contrast [s] in *dispence*), Gil [z] in *sophisms*, and Hodges [z] in *schism* but [s] in *disguise* (as in PresE, doubtless owing to the analogy of [dɪs] before other consonants). Coles has [s], despite loss of [p], in *raspberry*, and so apparently Strong in *risban* 'wristband'; Bullokar has [s] in *Lesbos*. The prefix *trans-* has [s] in *translate* in Hart and Bullokar and in *transgress* in Robinson, Hodges, and Coles; sporadic voicing is shown by the PresE pronunciations of *transgress, transliterate, transmigrate*, &c., which have [z] beside [s] (in contrast to French [s]). In *pansy* and *quinsy* the change to [z] is regular.

A similar change affects [þ] before [m] in *rhythm* and *logarithm*, which in PresE vary between [þ] and [ð]; both words retain [þ] in Hodges.

Sporadic voicing of [s] to [z] also occurred in eModE after [r], and accounts for occasional PresE [ʒ] < [zj] beside normal [ʃ] < [sj] in *version*, &c. Hart has [z] in *discourse*, Laneham in *rehearse* and in *course* (beside [s]), and Robinson in *person*. Laneham's [z] in the native *worse* is to be similarly explained (cf. § 355 above). Otherwise [s] is shown; thus Hodges has [ʃ] < [sj] in *version* and *conversion*, as has Brown in the latter.

(3) *Voicing of medial* [s] *before a stressed vowel*

§ 365. During the seventeenth century in good speech, and earlier in vulgar speech, [s] became [z] before a stressed vowel. The change, though affecting less words than was supposed by Jespersen, *ModE Gr*, § 6.64 seq. (who did not allow sufficiently for OF [z], nor for [gz] for Latin *x*), nevertheless explains [z] in many words in PresE; so in *dessert, discern, dissolve, possess, resent, absolve, observe*, &c. (cf. Ekwall, § 153). But the change is a sporadic one, and [s] remains in *descend, decide, precise, assume, presage*, &c. and in *beside, research, resource*, &c. (which may be influenced by *side*, &c.). Some words vary, e.g. *absorb*.

The earlier orthoepists do not show the change; thus [s] is retained by Hart in *possessed, disorder, observe* (and *observation*), by Bullokar in *diseases, dishonest, disorder*, and *possessive*, by Robinson in *possesses* and *possession*, and by Gil in *dishonour, dishonest*, &c. But Hodges has [z] in *discern, dishonour*, and *dishonest*, Coles in *Thomasin* pronounced *Tom-ma-zeen* (Fr *Thomassine* with [s]) and *anxiety* (with [ŋkz]), and Cocker in *dezern* 'discern'. Cooper, followed by *WSC*, records *howzever* 'howsoever' as being used 'facilitatis causa'; the syncope of *o*, on which the change of [s] > [z] depends, is of course dialectal.

Note 1: In PresE *observation* has [z] owing to the analogy of *observe*. In *dishonest, disarm,* &c. [z] may be due to OF *des-* pronounced with [z] before a vowel, but note that the early orthoepists show [s] and that Hodges, who has [z], also shows it in *discern*. It seems more doubtful whether [z] in *transition* (shown by Coles, against [s] in Bullokar) is developed in English, as French *trans-* has [z] before a vowel.

Note 2: Thomas Pery in his letter (1539) has *z* twice in *recited*, which must show early voicing in his Cockney speech.

UNVOICING

(1) *Final* [ŋg] *becomes* [ŋk]

§ 366. The unvoicing of final [ŋg] to [ŋk] obviously precedes the reduction of [ŋg] to [ŋ], and occurs sporadically in late OE; it is regular in the North-west Midlands in ME and is a widespread vulgarism in ModE. The orthoepists, however, give no evidence of it. Wyld, *Coll. Eng.*, pp. 290–1, cites spellings from Wolsey and Queen Elizabeth, but the pronunciation was evidently almost unknown in StE; Elphinston (1787) remarks on it as an English vulgarism current in London. In medial position it occurs only in the inflexional forms of words with final [ŋg].

(2) *Final* [nd] *becomes* [nt]

§ 367. The unvoicing of final [nd] to [nt] is parallel to that discussed above. It is shown by Hart before a voiceless consonant in *feint faut* 'find fault', but apparently only as a hypothetical pronunciation; and in the word *errand* it is recorded by Hodges (who has the 'phonetic' spelling *arrant*) and by the 'homophone' list pairing with *errant* given by Hodges ('near alike'), Wharton, Price, Young, Coles (*Eng.–Lat. Dict.*), Cocker, and Brown. In the *Welsh Hymn* this unvoicing is a Western dialectalism.

Note: Wyld, op. cit., p. 313, cites *nt* spellings of *fiend* and *blind* from *St. Editha* (1420) and of *thousand* and *beckoned* from the *Verney Memoirs* (1641) and *Wentworth Papers* (1714) respectively. *OED* cites *nt* forms of *errand* from the sixteenth to the eighteenth century.

(3) *Final* [ð] *becomes* [þ]

§ 368. Though unvoicing of final consonants is a general tendency in English, the only case in which it has notable effects on StE is that of a [ð] which becomes final in late ME owing to the loss of final *-e*; unvoicing to [þ], which seems to proceed chiefly in the fifteenth century (earlier perhaps in Northern dialects in which final *-e* was lost early) is shown in many of the words involved (cf. Jespersen, *ModE Gr*, § 6.92; Ekwall, § 142). PresE regularly has [þ] after a consonant in *earth, fourth, birth, seventh, ninth, tenth,* &c. and after a short or unstressed vowel in *froth, pith, twentieth,* &c.

(eModE also *twentith*, &c.); after a long vowel it has [þ] in *wreath*, *beneath*, *underneath*, and *both*, but [ð] is normal (if not quite invariable) in *booth* and invariable in *lathe* 'a barn' (ON *hlaða*), *lathe* (the machine), *blithe*, *scythe*, *tythe*, and *smooth* (ME *smothe* by blending of OE *smōð* and *smēðe*). But verbs are largely unaffected by the change; the grammatical relationship between, for example, *bath* and *bathe*, *breath* and *breathe*, *cloth* and *clothe*, *sooth* and *soothe*, has been preserved (being supported by the analogy of, for example, *wife* and *wive*, *house* sb. and *house* vb.) and has formed the model for a new contrast between *wreath* (with [þ] < [ð] by unvoicing) and *wreathe*. But *bequeath*, not being supported by a contrasting sb., has (rarer) [þ] beside [ð]; on the other hand *betroth*, a ME formation on the sb., might be expected to have only or more usually [þ] (cf. Note 1 on the prevalence of [þ] in such sbs.) but in fact has [ð] as the more usual pronunciation, probably owing to the analogy of [ð] in *bathe*, &c.

After [r] the orthoepists normally show [þ] in *earth* and its derivatives *earthy* and *earthen* (so the *Welsh Hymn*, Bullokar, Gil, Butler, Hodges, Coles, and Cooper), in *fourth* (so Hart, Gil, Butler, and Hodges), and in *birth* (so Bullokar and Hodges). But Bullokar has [ð] in *fourth* and Robinson once each in *earth* and *earthly* (beside [þ] four times in *earth* and once each in *earthen* and *earth-worm*); these transcriptions might in both authors be errors owing to the omission of a diacritic, but they support each other and at this date [ð] is credible. After [n] in *seventh*, *ninth*, &c., only [þ] is shown (so Hart, Gil, and Hodges; cf. also Hart's [fəivþ] 'fifth'); similarly [þ] occurs in *froth* in Gil and Butler and in *frothy* in Hodges and in *pithy* in Bullokar, and in *twentieth*, &c. in Hart, Gil, and Butler. After ME long vowels there is more variation. *Wreath* sb. retains [ð] in Tonkis (a Midlander) and Willis; *wreathe* vb. has [ð] in Butler, Hodges, and Willis. *Beneath* has [ð] in Bullokar, Robinson (once), and Butler, but [þ] in Robinson (once) and Gil; *underneath* has [ð] in Tonkis and Butler but [þ] in Gil. *Both* has [ð] in Hart (often), Bullokar (ten times), Robinson (once), Gil (only in the Northern dialectal form *beað*), and Hodges (once), but [þ] in Bullokar (thrice), Robinson (eight times), Gil (ten times), Hodges (eight times), and Coles; Hodges's pairing of *both* with *booth* as 'near alike' probably depends on [ð] in each word. *Booth* has [ð] in Bullokar, Hodges, and Coles, but *lathe* 'barn' has [þ] in Bullokar (contrast PresE [ð]). *Blithe* has [ð] in Gil (so Hodges in *blither*) but [þ] in Cooper; *scythe* and *tythe* have [ð] in Hodges. *Smooth* has [ð] in Bullokar, Robinson, and Gil (as has *smoother* in Hodges), but Butler has [þ] beside [ð] in *smoothing*, which probably reflects [þ] in the adjective. *Breathe* vb. has [ð] in Bullokar, Robinson, Butler, Hodges, and Willis, but in Gil it has [þ] (in rhyme with *underneath*); Hunt appears to have [þ] in both *breathe* and *bathe*, but is perhaps confused. *Clothe* vb. has [ð] in Bullokar, Gil, and Hodges, but Hodges also once has [þ]. *Soothe* has [ð] in Bullokar, Hodges, and Coles, and *bathe* in Smith, Hart, Hodges, and Coles. *Sheathe* vb. has [ð] in Hodges and Willis; Tonkis records [ð] for *sheath* sb., which (if he is not in error) must owe it to the analogy of the verb or to OE oblique forms (see further Note 1); Willis has [þ] in the sb. *Bequeath* I do not find recorded. *Betroth* vb. has the historical [þ] in Price and Cooper.

The regular unvoicing of original [ð] after short and unstressed vowels accounts for the failure of voicing of original [þ] in the unstressed inflexional ending *-eth* (contrast the voicing of *-es* to [əz]), the extreme rarity of voicing in the weak forms of the monosyllabic verbs *hath*, *doth*, and *saith*, and the comparative rarity, in the sixteenth and seventeenth centuries, of [wɪð] 'with' preposition (beside which [wɪþ] still exists in PresE).

Note 1: OE feminines such as *health*, *length*, *wealth*, *youth*, *truth*, *troth*, and *sloth* are regarded by Jespersen, loc. cit., as owing their PresE [þ] to unvoicing of [ð]. But although the ME sing. forms ended in *-e* it is doubtful if the nom. regularly (or even usually) had [ð]. The OE nom. sing. would have [þ]; the ME nom. sing. might have [ð] if it represented the OE oblique forms, but [þ] if it was the OE nom. with final *-e* added in ME. Though the analogy of *glove* is in favour of the former assumption, it seems probable that ME usually had [þ] in these words, for the orthoepists regularly show [þ] (so Hart, Bullokar, Robinson, Gil, Butler, and Hodges) even in those which have a long vowel. The only exceptions are Robinson's [ð] (once, against [þ] four times) in *wealth*, which beyond reasonable doubt is an error; his [ð] (once, beside [þ] once) in *mirth*, also probably an error; and Tonkis's [ð] in *sheath* sb. (ME *shethe* < OE *scǣð* fem.), which may well derive from the OE oblique forms. In *Bath* (ME *Baþe*) and *Portsmouth* (OE *-mūða*) PresE [þ] is supported by or due to the analogy of [þ] in *bath* and *mouth*. See also Luick, § 639.2.

Note 2: Ekwall, loc. cit., suggests that the change of [ð] to [þ] was one that occurred after short vowels only, and that [bɪniːþ] and [bouþ] are mixed forms which owe their [þ] to eModE forms with short vowels. But though it is clear that the change was much more regular after short vowels, and probable that the existence of forms of *both* and *beneath* with shortening (and of *wreath* < OE *wrīða* without lengthening) influenced the development of these words, the orthoepists' evidence nevertheless shows that [ð] could and sporadically did become [þ] after long vowels. *Wreath* sb. retained [ð] in the eighteenth and even in the early nineteenth century (see Onions, op. cit., p. 25), but [þ] is shown beside [ð] by Walker, 1791, Jameson, 1828, 'and others' (Jespersen, loc. cit.). Ellis gives [þ] in *blithe*, which supports Cooper's evidence (see Jespersen, loc. cit.). PresE [þ] in the name *Latham* (probably from the dative plural of ON *hlaða*) is explained by, and supports, Bullokar's [þ] in the nom. sing. *lathe*.

Note 3: The numerals *seventh*, *ninth*, *tenth*, &c., though reformed in ME, must be reckoned to have had [ð], both because the OE forms *seofoða*, *nigoða*, *teoða*, &c. would have had it and because of [ð] in *fourth* (OE *feorða*). But *eighth* (OE *eahtoða*) and *fifth*, *sixth*, and *twelfth* (ME or eModE re-formations) must have had [þ] by assimilation to the preceding voiceless consonant. Gil preserves the forms *fift* (OE *fifta*), *sixt* (OE *sexta*), and *aiht* (ME *eiʒt*, &c., identical with the cardinal; see *OED*), but has *twelfþ*; *twelft* (OE *twelfta*) is recorded by P. G., and *sixt* by Coles in his 'homophone' list.

Note 4: Wyld, op. cit., p. 313, cites spellings which show sporadic unvoicing of other final consonants, and unvoicing of final [v] and [d] was of course characteristic of Northern dialects in late ME; but these changes do not affect StE. It is not clear to what extent Levins's rhyming together of words with final voiceless and voiced consonants (see Vol. I, pp. 20–21) is due to unvoicing of the latter or to a licence of rhyming. His confusion of *strive* with *strife* and of *devise* with *device* (see Vol. I, p. 30) suggests Northern unvoicing, and the rhymes could also depend on it; if so, he shows a general unvoicing of final [ð] (and of other consonants) which is, however, dialectal. The *Welsh Hymn* shows Welsh 'provection' in *kyt* 'kid' (= 'renowned'), *rwt-tri* 'rood-tree', &c. Hunt records Northern *-it* for *-ed*.

(4) *Initial* [hw] *becomes* [ʍ]

§ 369. Initial [hw], insofar as it escaped simplification to [w], tended to become by assimilation [ʍ]. The two sounds, [hw] and [ʍ], appear to have continued to exist side by side; D. Jones, *Outline of English Phonetics*, § 810, records [hw] as a variant to [ʍ] in present-day speech. The orthoepists' evidence is mostly in favour of [hw]; so Smith (see Vol. I, p. 52), Hart, Tonkis (who says *wh* is pronounced 'summa cum aspiratione', but he was a Midlander and may perhaps have used [χw]), Sherwood (who says that *wh* is 'presque comme *Hou*', i.e. [hu] or [hw]), Gataker (following Smith), Wallis (see Vol. I, p. 234), Newton (Vol. I, p. 252), Holder (Vol. I, p. 263), J. Smith (who equates English *wh* with Spanish *hu* in *huelgo*), Lodwick (Vol. I, p. 278), and Ray. But this analysis as [hw] may be due to the difficulty of distinguishing [ʍ] from [hw] (cf. D. Jones, loc. cit.). Robinson, though he treats *wh* as being [w] with initial aspiration, regards similarly all initial voiceless consonants and is thus debarred by his theory from distinguishing [hw] and [ʍ]; and Gil, though he says that in *wh* the aspiration precedes, also says that *wh*, like *w*, is a true and simple consonant and in the 1619 edition provided it with a separate letter (see Vol. I, p. 144). Clear evidence in favour of [ʍ] is given by Wilkins, who describes *wh* as the voiceless equivalent of [w], and by Cooper, who follows Wilkins but less clearly (see Vol. I, p. 296). Probably many of those who describe [hw] really used [ʍ], but both sounds must have been current as diaphonic variants.

Note: It is often assumed, as by Wyld, op. cit., p. 311, that the pronunciation [w] for *wh-* results from voicing, owing to the following vowel, of [ʍ] < [hw]; but though this process is theoretically not unlikely, the date of appearance of the [w] pronunciation and the analogy of other initial consonant-groups suggest that it results from a direct simplification of [hw] to [w] in certain dialects (see § 414 below), whereas in other dialects [hw] was retained and tended to become [ʍ]. Retention of [hw] or [ʍ] was clearly normal in good sixteenth- and seventeenth-century StE; the pronunciation [w] was a vulgarism until the eighteenth century (see further below, loc. cit.).

OTHER CHANGES OF ARTICULATION

ISOLATIVE CHANGES

(1) *Change in the nature of* r

§ 370. At some stage in the development of StE it is probable that there was a change in the nature of *r* from a point-trilled consonant to the PresE post-alveolar fricative, which in acoustic effect is closely allied to the vowel [ə]; but in intervocalic position it commonly remained either a trilled consonant or the PresE 'flap' [r]. When the change occurred it is impossible to determine, but the influence of *r* from the late fourteenth century onwards, and particularly its ModE influence on *ĭ*, *ĕ*, and [ʌ] < ME *ŭ*, suggest that it must have been closely similar to the PresE sound. The special treatment of intervocalic *r* must be assumed both from its PresE pronunciation and from its normal failure to produce lowering of a preceding vowel.

On the nature of *r* the orthoepists give us little reliable information; this is in part due to the difficulty of describing precisely the complex articulatory movements involved, in part to their adoption of traditional descriptions of *r* derived directly or indirectly from classical grammarians. To the latter cause must chiefly be ascribed the frequent descriptions which seem most naturally to refer to a trilled *r*, but we should also remember that intervocalic *r* was probably some variety of trilled *r* and would justify them. Such descriptions are given in Wallis, Newton, Wilkins, Holder, and Cooper—i.e. by most of the major seventeenth-century orthoepists. There are also identifications of English *r* with Italian *r* (so Florio) and with French *r* (so Tonkis; it is possible, but unlikely, that he may have used uvular *r*). Robinson's classification of *r* as a 'lesser obstrict', like [j], points to a fricative continuant like the PresE [r], and Wallis's description has a non-traditional feature (the turning-back of the tip of the tongue) which agrees with PresE articulation (see Vol. I, p. 230); Cooper follows Wallis (see Vol. I, p. 296).

The distinction between intervocalic and final *r* is made only by a minor source, Hayward (after 1625), who says that *r* is uttered 'with vehemency' in *carrier* but 'without vehemency' in *care*. On the other hand Hawkins (1692) says that '*r* is always sounded, but never variously wheresoever it is found; as *father, rather*, &c.'; but this remark, it seems, should be understood to assert only that *r* is never 'silent', and if it is intended to deny that intervocalic *r* is different from other *r*'s it must be less than the truth.

Note: The fact that Hayward is modifying a remark of the French grammarian Ramée (see Vol. I, p. 324) does not seem to lessen the value of his evidence much, if at all; but Ben Jonson, who merely plagiarizes Ramée (see Vol. I, p. 326), is worthless.

(2) *Change of* [χ] *to* [f]

§ 371. The late ME change of [χ] to [f] (see Jordan, §§ 196 Anm., 294) seems not to have occurred in educated StE, but in dialectal and vulgar speech from which StE gradually accepted pronunciations with [f]; insofar as the pronunciations native to StE survived, the [χ] remained pronounced as some sort of a spirant until the seventeenth century (see § 424).

In late ME [χ] stood after *au*, *ou*, and *ū*, and the change to [f] occurs after all three, of which shortening normally occurs as a consequence. The change affects final [χ] (as in *laugh*, *cough*, and *rough*) and final [χt] (commonly after ME *au*, as in *draught*, more rarely after ME *ou*, as in *brought*, and apparently only in Northern dialects after ME *ū* in *drought*); it also occasionally affects [χt] in medial position when the consonants are separated by the syllable-division (e.g. in *daughter*), but only in *laughter*, which is influenced by the analogy of *laugh*, is [f] at all common. StE has finally accepted [f] only in final position and in *draught* and *laughter*. In the sixteenth and early seventeenth centuries [χ] must be regarded as the normal pronunciation of good speech, but [f] was also used and from about 1625 onwards was normal in those words in which it is now accepted and occurred occasionally (probably chiefly as a vulgarism) in other cases.

The change also occurs after *r* in *dwarf* and dialectal *barf* < late OE *dweorh* and *beorh*; cf. *Brough* < *burh* (see *OED*, s.v. *dwarf*).

Note 1: For the detailed evidence of the orthoepists showing [f] < [χ] see §§ 28 (shortening of ME *au*), 34 (shortening of ME *ou*), and 39 (shortening of ME *ū*).

Note 2: It seems doubtful whether there was a parallel change of ME [ȝ] to [v], as Mr. Sisam has suggested; Hodges's [troːvz] 'troughs' and Cocker's *hoved* 'houghed' might be evidence of such a change, but can be otherwise explained (see Vol. I, pp. 182 and 366).

(3) *Dialectal change of* [χ] *and* [ç] *to* [þ]

§ 372. On a sporadic dialectal change of [χ] and [ç] to [þ], which sometimes affected the StE pronunciation of *sighs* (in which [þ] is shown by Hodges, *EP*), see Vol. I, pp. 181–2 above.

(4) *Dialectal and vulgar change of* [s] *to* [ʃ]

§ 373. In widespread dialects (mostly EMidl and Northern) there is a tendency for [s] to become [ʃ]; it affects chiefly final [s], but also medial, and even occasionally initial [s] (see Wright, § 321). In the seventeenth century the orthoepists' evidence of it is almost entirely restricted to 'homophone' lists, which marks it as a vulgarism; it is so described in the eighteenth century by Elphinston. Hodges in his 'near alike' list pairs *wist* with *wisht*; Wharton (followed by Brown) has *abase* : *abash*, and Brown (a Northerner) has *lace* : *lass* : *lash* and *kiss* : *Kish*. Hunt records *leash* 'lease' in his list of dialectalisms. Cooper, whose speech shows dialectal influence, evidently used [ʃ] himself in *liquorice*, for he says that he prefers the spelling *licorish* to *liquorish*, *licorice*, &c.

When the change occurred after *n*, the result was [n(t)ʃ], which was identified with older *-nch*. Thus Butler (followed by *WSC*, Cocker, and Brown) pairs *lance* with *launch* (but the words are etymological doublets) and Hawkins pairs *quince* with *quench*.

Note 1: The pairing *lease* : *leash*, given by Hunt and later writers, depends on the variant *lease* of *leash* (see *OED*).

Note 2: Wyld, *Coll. Eng.*, pp. 291–2, cites evidence from the beginning of the fourteenth century (Robert Mannyng) to the nineteenth (Dickens). See also Wright, §§ 321, 329.

Note 3: Such spellings as *wosse* 'wash' and *rysses* 'rushes' (Machyn), *arsbysshopes* 'archbishops' (Thomas Pery), and perhaps *pounysse* 'punish' (Pery), appear to be inverted spellings based on the pronunciation of *s* as [ʃ].

(5) *Other dialectal and vulgar changes*

§ 374. Bullokar describes a change of initial *th* (i.e. of Southern [ð]) to [d] in East Sussex and Kent in *that, thorn*, and *those*. Young's 'homophone list' pairing *thorn : torn* appears to rest on a similar change of initial [þ] to [t]; and Hunt gives *gurt* as a dialectal form of *girth*. Conversely Hunt also gives *cannoth* for *cannot*, and comments that 'sounding *th* for *t*' is 'the citizen's fault'. On *noting* 'nothing' see Vol. I, p. 390.

The orthoepists give no evidence of the changes of [þ] > [f], [ð] > [v], and [v] > [w], though these had currency in vulgar London English and (in the first two cases) apparently sometimes in the speech of educated persons; see Wyld, *Coll. Eng.*, pp. 291, 292–3. The use of *v* for [w], insofar as it is not merely an inverted spelling, is due to confusion in speech on the part of Cockneys endeavouring to use the StE [v]; the sound-change in the South-east was from [v] to [w] (see Jordan, § 300). In the North the reverse applied (see Jordan, § 163).

(6) *Alleged change of* [þ] *to* [s]

§ 375. It is sometimes suggested that the modern StE inflexion -(*e*)*s* in the 3rd sing. pres. indic. develops in StE itself from the earlier *-eth*. But there is no evidence of a tendency of [þ] to become [s], even in post-consonantal position (cf. the suffix *-th* in *length*, &c.), and it should be observed (*a*) that the inflexion *-s* in verbs shows regular syncope, whereas syncope is rare in *-eth* (see §§ 313–14 above), and (*b*) that whereas the *-s* inflexion is [z] after voiced sounds, -(*e*)*th* is almost without exception [þ], even after voiced sounds when syncope occurs (e.g. Hart's *servþ* 'serveth'). We should therefore have to put the change of [þ] to [s] back to a time before syncope and before the voicing of final *-s* in unstressed syllables, i.e. to the fourteenth century; but in this case the lack of fifteenth-century evidence of the verbal inflexion *-s* would be a still more serious difficulty than it is if we accept the much more probable hypothesis that the ModE inflexion is an adoption of the 'Northern' ME inflexion *-es* < ONhb *-es* (*-as*), which in fact is found in the south of Lincolnshire (Robert Manning) by the beginning of the fourteenth century and even in Chaucer in early poems for the sake of rhyme (*Boke of the Duchesse*, 73, 257; *Hous of Fame*, i. 426). On the other hand, if the alleged change is regarded as belonging to the sixteenth century, it is hard to see why it did not affect *breadth* (recorded by *OED* for 1523), in which there obtain the conditions ([þ] after a dental) which are held especially favourable to it.

Note: Bullokar and P. G., and to some extent Gil, regard *-s* as a feature of poetic language. Gil describes *hez* 'hath' as Northern (or Lincolnshire) dialect. Hodges shows that *-s* is the colloquial and *-eth* the literary inflexion; for his important statement (*Plain Directions*, pp. 60–61) on this point see Vol. I, p. 168. In his 'homophone' lists he has many pairings of the type *coats* : *quoteth*, *courses* : *courseth*. Hunt follows Hodges with only a slight difference (see Vol. I, pp. 338–9). Tonkis regards *lov's* as a 'contraction' of *loveth*; Butler gives the two forms as alternatives.

COMBINATIVE CHANGES

(1) *Palatalization of gutturals*

(a) *OE palatalization*

§ 376. The OE palatalization of WGmc *g* and *k* before original front vowels, and of *sk* in all positions, is a general change which affected all OE dialects, and ME forms with [g] and [k] in place of [j] and [tʃ] before original front vowels, and with *sk* in place of [ʃ], are always analogical or due to the influence of ON or some other Germanic language in which palatalization failed (cf. Jordan, §§ 179, 181–2, 189). In general the orthoepists show the same forms as those of PresE. But *gate* has [j] (from the OE singular) beside [g] (from the OE plural) in Butler, and [j] in Gataker; Smith once gives *yāt* as an example, but adds that 'we now pronounce and write' it *gāt*. Smith gives *iāv* or *iāf* 'gave' (once) beside *gāv* (once) and Butler has *yiven* beside *given*. *Guildhall* has [jiːld] as its first element in the 'homophone' lists of Butler, Hodges, Strong, Cooper ('near'), and *WSC*, and is 'phonetically' spelt *Yeeld-hall* by Coles; Butler says it is *yildhall* (beside giving the form with [g]). *Ache* sb. (OE *ǣce*) should have [tʃ], but *ache* vb. (OE *ăcan*) should have [k]. The sb. (or what is presumably the sb.) has [tʃ] in Hart, Gil, Butler, Wharton, J. Smith, Strong, and Young; Price says that the sb. has [tʃ] and the verb [k]. Levins puts both sb. and verb in his [atʃ] list (thus showing failure of lengthening of ME *ă* before [tʃ]); Poole, on the other hand, rhymes both sb. and vb. on -*ake*, and Brown gives the 'phonetic' spelling *ake* 'ache'. It may be observed that all three authors who show the analogical influence of the verb on the sb. or vice versa are Northerners. Smith gives [k] as a Northernism in *breach*, *breech*, *church*, and *bitch*; in the first case he has confused *break* sb. (from the verb) with *breach*, and in the others there is ON influence. He similarly records *brig* and *flig* as Northernisms for *bridge* and *flidge* 'fledge' adj. Gil also records the Northern [briːks] 'breeches', and Hunt a dialectal *belk* 'belch' and the Northern *kirk*.

Note: *The Compendious School-Master* records Norman [k] in place of Central French [tʃ] in *challice*, which it pairs with *Calais* and *Callis* (family name).

(b) *Changes of* [ŋ(g)]

§ 377. (i) The consonant-groups [ŋgþ] and [ŋkþ] in such words as *strengþ(u)*, *lengþ(u)*, and *pencþ* tended to be simplified, by omission of the stop, to [ŋþ], so that the guttural [ŋ] came to stand before the dental [þ]; by assimilation, [ŋ] became [n], exceptionally in OE (cf. Sievers–Brunner,

§ 184, Anm.) and more commonly in the fourteenth century (cf. Jordan, § 193, and *OED*, s.vv. *length* and *strength*). Cocker has the 'phonetic' spelling *lenthen* 'lengthen'; similarly the shorthand-writers Willis, T. Shelton, Bridges, Mason, S. Shelton, and Ridpath omit the *g* in *length* and/or *strength* (Ridpath marking this omission as a Scotticism). Wright, § 272, shows that [ŋ] has become [n] in these words in Scotland and Northern England, and observes that '[n] is also very common in other parts of England'. The shorthand-writer Willis also omits *g* in *yungling*, which shows the same assimilation before [l] (cf. the assimilation of [g] and [k] before [l] discussed in § 378 below).

(ii) It is commonly held (as by *OED* in its discussion of the *-ing* suffix of the present participle and by Jordan, § 174) that in ME *nd* became *ng* (which must mean that [nd] became [ŋg]) after ME *ĭ*. The main reason for this view is to explain the substitution of *-ing* for *-ind* as the ending of the pres. p., but it is altogether improbable that the alleged change occurred; we may observe (*a*) that the substitution of *-ing* can, and should, be explained by syntactic confusion of the verbal noun and the pres. p., (*b*) that to account for this general substitution of the suffix *-ing* for *-ind* a general sound-change would be required, of which there is no adequate evidence, and (*c*) that the sound-change postulated, from the dental group [nd] to the guttural group [ŋg], is highly unlikely to have occurred after the high-front vowel [ɪ]. D. Jones, *Outline of English Phonetics*, § 651, shows that a fronted variety of [ŋ] is used in PresE after [ɪ], and the vulgar [ɪn] for [ɪŋ] is due to an actual change of [ŋ] to [n] after [ɪ] (see below); it would therefore be more reasonable to suppose that in ME [ɪŋg] would become [ɪnd] than the reverse. Such a change may indeed have occurred sporadically, and would perhaps enable us to explain (as inverted spellings) rare forms such as *kinger* 'kinder', *gebung* 'gebund(en)' (cf. Jordan, § 174; but these may not always be due to phonetic causes). Similar spellings occur in the fifteenth century, e.g. *kynddome* 'kingdom' and conversely *manking*, *mankyng*, and even *mankyngde* 'mankind' (in unpublished manuscript sermons of East Midland provenance). But of such a change of [ŋg] to [nd] the orthoepists give no evidence, unless the vulgar [ɪn] for [ɪŋ] develops from [ɪnd] by loss of final [d] (a common process in vulgar speech) as [ɪŋ] develops from [ɪŋg] by loss of the [g].

(iii) If [ɪn] for [ɪŋ] in unstressed syllables is not to be explained as developing from ME [ɪnd] (see above), then it must develop directly from [ɪŋ] itself by later assimilation of [ŋ] to a dental articulation under the influence of the preceding high-front vowel. Only in sources which reflect advanced speech is [ɪn] shown by the orthoepists; Hart once has *ruš-šin* 'rushing', but this is perhaps an error. Newton has *-in* twice (in *loving* and *drinking*) beside more common [ɪŋ]. The 'homophone' lists have *beholding* : *beholden* (Hodges 'alike' and Strong; but the point may not be that the two forms are pronounced alike), *coughing* : *coffin* (Hodges 'near alike', Strong, Cooper 'alike', Aickin, *WSC*, and Brown), *coming* : *cumin* (Strong, Coles (*Eng.–Lat. Dict.*), Cooper 'alike', Aickin, *WSC*, and Brown), *jerking* : *jerkin* (Strong, Cooper 'alike', *WSC*, and Brown), and *raving* : *raven* (Cocker). Coles in the *Schoolmaster* has the isolated 'phonetic spelling' *hierlin* 'hireling', and Brown has *farthin* or *fard'n* 'farthing', *herrin* 'herring', *puddin* 'pudding', and *shillin* 'shilling'. The shorthand-writer Bridges has, for example, *defetin* 'defeating', *moin* 'mowing', and *wain* 'weighing'. In the sixteenth century the Northerner Levins has *puddin* 'pudding' (cf. Brown, another Northerner); the derivation of the word is unknown, but it has ME *-ing*. The nature of the evidence shows the vulgar and dialectal status of the pronunciation; there is some possibility that Cooper's own speech was affected, but if so it must be accounted one of his dialectalisms. In the eighteenth century the pronunciation became more general.

Note 1: OED, s.v. *-ing* suffix², refers to the thirteenth-century confusion of *-inde* and *-inge* by Anglo-Norman scribes, but it is doubtful how much reliance can be put on their aberrations as evidence of English pronunciation; the confusion may be non-phonetic. Fifteenth-century interchanges of *-ng* and *-nd* could be due to the development of [ŋg] through [ŋ] to [n] in the suffix *-ing* and loss of final *d* after *n*, so that *-ng* and *-nd* both become [n].

Note 2: Wyld, *Coll. Eng.*, pp. 289–90, cites spellings with *-in* for *-ing* from as early as the records of the Norfolk Guilds (1389); a still earlier instance is *haukin* 'hawking' in the Auchinleck MS of *Sir Orfeo*. Such spellings might easily be due to the mechanical omission of a letter, but they tend to suggest that in East Midland dialects [ɪn] for [ɪŋ] existed as early as the fourteenth century. Jordan, § 175, dates the change to the fourteenth century in the North and North Midlands but to the fifteenth in the South.

Note 3: The likely explanation of [ɪŋ] in words with original [ɪn] is that it is an analogical pronunciation modelled on the variation between [ɪn] and [ɪŋ] in words with original *-ing* (so Wyld, op. cit., p. 290, who cites spellings from *Palladius* onwards; but they may be inverted and not phonetic spellings). Cooper implies [ɪŋ] in *kitchen* and *Tomalin*; his editor J. D. Jones would take his 'homophone' list pairings as showing [ɪŋ] in *cumin*, *coffin*, and *jerkin*, as obviously they could, but they are more likely (in Cooper as in the earlier lists from which he derived his pairings) to show [ɪn] in *coming*, *coughing*, and *jerking*. *WSC*, following Cooper, shows [ɪŋ] in *kitchen* and *Machin*. The Northerner Levins has *frankling* 'franklin', but there may be confusion of suffixes. Note that evidence of [ɪŋ] for original [ɪn] comes only from sources that have [ɪn] for original [ɪŋ].

(c) Change of [g] *to* [d] *and* [k] *to* [t]

§ 378. Analogous to the assimilation of [ŋ(g)] to [n(d)] is that of [g] and [k] to [d] and [t] before the front palatal [l]; this change, which is widespread in modern dialects and affects the pronunciation of educated people (see Wright, §§ 335, 345), may well be old. Robinson shows [dl] for [gl] and [tl] for [kl] in the great majority of cases (so in *glad, glory, clad, decline*; cf. Vol. I, p. 211), and Daines records [dl] in *glory*. The pronunciation in the seventeenth century may perhaps have been vulgar or dialectal; Robinson represents London speech and Daines that of Suffolk.

Note: Wyld, op. cit., p. 294, cites *Bartly* 'Berkley' from Lady Wentworth (1711); cf. also

Jespersen, *ModE Gr*, § 12.75, who points out that *bantling* (first recorded 1593, from Drayton) is probably from German *bankling* (see *OED*). Kökeritz, *Mather Flint*, pp. 139-41, cites evidence of *dl* for *gl* and of *tl* for *kl* from Sewel, 1705, and Brommenhaer, 1738.

(d) Later palatalization of [k] *and* [g]

§ 379. The OE palatalization of [k] and [g] before front vowels has its counterpart in eModE, when they become [kj] and [gj] (or perhaps rather fronted [k] and [g]; cf. Sweet, *The Sounds of English*, § 135, who so regards 'the old-fashioned sounds in *sky, garden*'). The first evidence of this development seems to be Robinson's, who once gives [gj] in *guarded*; Hodges calls the letter *g*, when it expresses [g], *gyee* (which shows palatalization before [i:]) and gives *gates* as his example (but this seems to have no special significance; see Vol. I, pp. 170-1). Wallis shows palatalization of both [k] and [g] (transcribed as *ky* and *gy*) in *can, get,* and *begin*, and describes this as a Midland pronunciation not used by Scots and Northerners (see Vol. I, pp. 234-5). In the eighteenth century the pronunciation was more general, and was regarded as essential to good speech by Elphinston and Walker, though obviously unpalatalized [g] and [k] survived; it is shown before ME *ĭ, ī,* and *ă* by these later eighteenth-century sources (see Wyld, op. cit., p. 310; Lehnert, *Wallis*, § 186). Wright, § 249, shows a glide [j] between [g] and [k] and all the ModE front vowels and ME *ī*.

Note: In such words as *girl* and *girt* the palatalization may be assumed to have preceded the retraction of ME *ĭ* to [ə] before *r* (cf. the palatalization shown by Wallis in *begin* and by Wright in *kill*), especially as Robinson shows palatalization but no retraction and Wallis does not show retraction of ME *ĭ* (though he does of ME *ĕ*) before *r*. The best explanation of palatalization before ME *ī* would be that it occurred before diphthongization, or before diphthongization had proceeded beyond the stage [ɪi]; in this case palatalization must have been a protracted process, beginning in late ME and continuing until after ME *ă* had been fronted. Perhaps the palatalized pronunciations were originally vulgar or dialectal and had developed before the seventeenth century, but then forced their way for a time into StE, from which in the nineteenth century they were again expelled. Wyld's explanation of palatalization before ME *ī* is that it must have developed at 'some such stage as' [æi], but this rests on a false view of the development of ME *ī*, which in eModE was [əi] until it became [ai]. Palatalization before either [əi] or [ai] seems improbable, and we must therefore put back to late ME the date of palatalization before ME *ī*. The absence of early evidence may be accounted for by the fact that in a dialect in which the change was regular the palatalized consonants would be only contextual variants of the normal ones and would therefore not be observed or expressed in spelling; it is the choice possible between two modes of pronunciation, palatalized and unpalatalized, that causes them to be observed in the seventeenth and later centuries.

(2) *Assimilations of* [n]

(a) [n] *becomes* [ŋ]

§ 380. Before [g] or [k], at all periods of the language, [n] tends to become [ŋ]. The change is regular in stressed syllables (except in recognized prefixes) and occurs, for example, in *Lincoln* (OE *Lindcylene* < *Lindo-*

colina < *Lindum colonia*), *monk, anchor* (OE, from Latin), *anguish, language, languish, canker, rancour, blanket, blank, banquet* (ME or late ME adoptions from OF), *bankrupt* (a sixteenth-century adoption from French), *handkerchief* (a sixteenth-century formation, with early loss of [d]), and *monkey* (a sixteenth-century adoption, probably of MLG *moneke). The prefixes *in-* and *con-*, however, commonly retain [n] when stressed; the rule seems to be that they do so if the sense of their separate identity remains (cf. *un-* below), but that [ŋ] occurs alone or beside [n] in words in which the prefix is felt as inseparable (e.g. *income, conquer, concrete, congress, congregation,* &c.). There is also much analogical influence, to which it is hard to set limits, from related words in which the prefix is unstressed (e.g. of *incline* on *inclination, incongruous* on *incongruity, inquisitive* on *inquisition*, &c.), and this in many cases may be why [ŋ] appears as a variant where only [n] might be expected. In unstressed syllables followed by the main or a secondary stress [ŋ] varies with [n] (e.g. in *Anchises* and *melancholy*), and the prefixes *in-* and *con-* receive no special treatment but also vary (e.g. *incline*, &c. cited above, and *increase* vb., *ingratitude, conclude,* &c.). But the native prefix *un-*, though unstressed, has regular [n] because of the strong sense, among all speakers of the language, of its separate identity. In *anxious* and *anxiety*, in which the *n* and the [k] or [g] belong to the same syllable, [ŋ] is of course regular.

Only seventeenth-century orthoepists recognize the separate identity of [ŋ], and few of these give detailed evidence. But [ŋ] is shown in *Lincoln* by Coles, Strong, and Young, in *monk* by Hodges, in *anchor* by Hodges and Young, in *anguish* by Gil and Hodges, in *language* by Gil and Hodges, in *languish* by Gil, Hodges, Strong, and Young, in *canker* by Robinson, in *rancour* by Hodges, in *blanket* by Coles, Strong, and Young, in *banquet* by Hodges and Coles, in *bankrupt* by Hodges, in *handkerchief* by Coles (whose 'phonetic' spelling is *hang-ket-cher*), in *monkey, anxious,* and *anxiety* by Coles. For the prefixes [n] is normal, being shown by Robinson in *conquest* (contrast PresE), *increase,* and *incur* (and in *conclude, conclusions,* and *include*, but these have [tl] < [kl]), by Gil in *increase, incredible,* and *ingratitude,* and by Hodges in *increase* and *inquire*; but Wallis says that for Latin *inquam, tanquam,* and *nunquam* some use [nkw], others [ŋkw].

Note 1: Such spellings as *anker* (Strong), *banket* and *hanke(r)cher* (Strong, Young) are imperfectly phonetic and should not be taken as showing [n] as against [ŋ], even though they vary from Coles's (e.g. his *bang-quet* and *hang-ket-cher*) or from others used by Strong (e.g. *langgish* 'languish') and Young (e.g. *ang-cur* 'anchor') themselves.

Note 2: On [ŋ] in *kitchen*, &c. see § 377, Note 3.

Note 3: The nasal infix in *farthingale* (OF *verdugale*) seems from the beginning to have been [ŋ]; it is so given by Coles for the form *vardingale*. But in this word there appears to have been early contamination by *farthing* (which has a southern variant with [v] and an eModE form *farding*).

(b) [n] *becomes* [m]

§ 381. Assimilation of [n] to [m] in the neighbourhood of labials occurs sporadically in StE, e.g. in [kʌpm̩sɒ:sə] 'cup and saucer'. The only orthoepists to show such an assimilation are Newton (in *hapm* 'happen') and Coles, who has the 'phonetic' spellings *Bamberry* 'Banbury' (cf. D. Jones, *Eng. Pron. Dict.*, who records this as a variant), *cheapm* 'cheapen', *hapm* 'happen', *opm* 'open', and *weapm* 'weapon'. Strong declines to follow Coles, as does Young, except that the latter has *Bamberry*. The assimilation to [m] of final [n] after [p] must be a dialectalism in Newton and Coles; cf. Wright, § 269.

Note: Wyld, *Coll. Eng.*, p. 294, cites sixteenth- and seventeenth-century evidence showing assimilation of [n] to [m] before [f].

(3) *Changes of* [þ], [ð], *and* [d]

(a) [þ] *becomes* [t]

§ 382. In eME [þ] becomes [t] after spirants, by dissimilation, in such words as *theft*, and in the fourteenth century after [ç] and [χ] in *drought*, *height*, and *sleight* (Jordan, § 205). *Moth* (OE *mohðe* > *moȝte*) is [mo:t] in the 'homophone' lists of Wharton, Fox and Hookes, Cooper ('near alike'), Cocker, and Brown; but Levins has [mo:þ] < fourteenth-century *mouȝthe*. *Height* has [t] in Cheke, Gil, *WSC*, and Cocker, but [þ] in Laneham and Butler (cf. Milton's *highth*) and the blend [tþ] in Cooper. The change of [þ] > [t] may have been less regular after [ç] and [χ] than after other spirants, but blending of *mouȝte* and *moþþe* may account for *mouȝthe* 'moth' and analogy for the reintroduction of [þ] in *height*. Coles's 'homophone list' pairing *tilt* : *tilth*, which is supported by the seventeenth- to nineteenth-century spelling *tilt* 'tilth' cited by *OED*, may show that [þ] occasionally became [t] after other consonants than spirants (cf. Wright, § 316); but [t] in *tilth* might be due to the analogy of variation in *height*, &c. (especially as it is recorded late).

(b) [ð] *becomes* [d]

§ 383. In late OE and in ME [ð] became [d] before an immediately following non-syllabic [n], [m], and [r] (see Jordan, § 206; Sievers–Brunner, § 201, Anm. 7), with the result that in sbs. such as *fæðm* there arose variation between [ð], retained in the nom., and [d] developed in oblique forms (e.g. *fædme* dat. sing. < *fæðme*). Before [l] the change appears to have occurred even when the consonant was syllabic. Jordan would also explain, as further examples of this process, the [d] of *burden* and *murder*, which indeed may in both words be due in part to it; but it is evident from [d] beside [ð] in *farthing*, *further*, and *farther* that there was also a process whereby [rð] before a vowel (or syllabic consonant?) tended to become [rd], and *burthen* and *murther* would obviously be affected by this. The change is an assimilatory one, the tongue-position of [d] being closer than that of [ð] to the tongue-position of [r], and belongs to ME; *d*-forms are recorded by *OED* for *farthing* from the fourteenth century, *further* from the fourteenth, and *farther* (a ME variant of *further*) from the thirteenth. Another instance is the verb *afford* < *geforðian*, in which the change must occur in ME forms ending in *-en*, e.g. *aforthen; *OED* records the *d*-form only from the early sixteenth century.

Of the words involved, *fathom* is stated to vary by Butler and Daines (who gives [ð], but says that 'some' use [d]). *Feather* normally has [ð], but Salesbury says that *fedder* 'feather' has *dd* pronounced as in Welsh (i.e. as [ð]) only in 'some countries' of England, which implies that others use [d] (developed in oblique forms). *Burden* has [ð] in Gil and [d] in Bullokar and Brown; Daines gives [ð] but says that 'many' use [d]. *Murder* has [ð] in Hart and Robinson; Gil in one place gives [ð] and in another shows variation, Daines gives [ð] but says that 'many' use [d], and Butler and Hodges show variation; Brown shows [d]. *Farthing* is given as *farthin* or *fard'n* or *farding* in Brown's 'phonetically spelt' list; the first two forms show [ɪn] and [n̩] < [ɪŋ], but these developments are later than the change of [ð] to [d] and not the cause of it (as assumed by Horn, § 200, Anm. 2). *Further* has [ð] in Hart, Bullokar, and Robinson, but variation between [ð] and [d] is shown by Gil and Butler. *Farther* has [ð] in Gil, but [d] in Bullokar (who also gives it in *farther* vb.); Butler shows variation. *Afford* is recorded only with [d], in Bullokar, Mulcaster, and six seventeenth-century sources. It will be observed that evidence for the [d] form of the [rð] words increases with the passage of time, as though a vulgar or dialectal form was in process of entering StE. The final acceptance of [d] in *murder* and *burden*, but not in other instances, must be due in the one case to the influence of ME *murdre* (see Note 2 below) and in the other to confusion with *burden* 'an under-song' (which itself by analogy has *th* forms in Shakespeare). The predominance of [d] in *afford* must be associated with the corruption of the prefix, which suggests that the native origin and etymological connexions of the word had been forgotten.

Note 1: It would be possible to explain [d] in *murder* (with Jordan, loc. cit.) from the verb *morðrian*, assuming only the change of [ð] to [d] before non-syllabic [r]; similarly [d] in *farther* and *further* from the verbs *ferðren* and *forðren* < OE *fyrðr(i)an*. But no such explanation is possible for *farthing*, which is the test case establishing the [rð] > [rd] change.

Note 2: *OED* ascribes the change of [ð] to [d] in *murder* to the influence of AF *murdre* and Law Latin *murdrum*; but though ME certainly had forms in *-re* derived from the AF form it is much to be doubted whether these are the sole source of the ModE form, which rather represents both ME *murdre*, &c. and ME *murthir*, &c. (the latter being itself probably a blend of OE *morðor* and AF *murdre*; see § 92, Note 2).

(c) [d] *becomes* [ð]

§ 384. In contrast to the earlier change whereby [rð] became [rd] (see § 383), about 1400 post-vocalic [d] became [ð] before [r̩] or [ər] in *father, mother, together, weather, hither*, &c., perhaps through the intermediate stage [dð] preserved in Northern dialects (see Jordan, § 298, but contrast Wright, § 297). The change is shown almost without exception by the orthoepists, e.g. *father* has [ð] in Levins, Bullokar, Robinson, Gil, Hodges, and Coles and *mother* in Cheke, Hart, Bullokar, Mulcaster, Robinson, Gil, Butler, Hodges, and Wharton. But the alliteration of the *Welsh Hymn* requires [d] in both words. Hart's *Methode* has *d* twice in *father* (against [ð] four times, and twice in the *Orthographie*), but both are corrected to *ð* in the Folger Library copy. Wharton spells the dialect word *mother* 'puella' as *modder* but gives it as a homophone of *mother* 'mater', of which it may be a form (see § 97, Note 3). Other words have regularly [ð]. Hodges pairs with *either* a word *ether* 'stake in a fence', which is a form of *edder* (perhaps < OE *eodor*; see *OED*) and shows the change of [d] to [ð].

That the change could occur elsewhere than before syllabic [r̩] appears to be shown by Salesbury's statement that in 'some countries' of England *dd* in *addes* 'adze' (OE *adesa*) was pronounced as in Welsh; if so, it must have occurred in intervocalic position in the disyllabic form (still apparently preserved in eModE; cf. the sixteenth-century *adys* and the sixteenth- and seventeenth-century *addice, addis, addes* recorded by *OED*). But Wright records no comparable modern dialectal pronunciation.

Note: Farthingale owes its [ð] beside [d] (< OF *verdugale*) to the analogy of [ð] beside [d] in *farthing*; cf. § 380, Note 3. *Farthel* 'burden' for *fardel* (< OF *fardel*) is also an inverted spelling or analogical form, influenced partly by the variation between *farthing* and *farding*, but more directly by that between *farthel* and *fardel* 'fourth part' < OE *feorða dæl*, in which sometimes the *ð*, sometimes the *d*, survives. The sound-change [d] > [ð] is restricted to the case where a vowel precedes.

(4) *Intervocalic* [t] *becomes* [r]

§ 385. From early in the sixteenth century there appear the forms *porridge, porringer*, &c. for earlier *pottage, potager* (see *OED*, s.vv.), though the older forms also survived (thus Salesbury has *potanger* and Bullokar *potage*). Coles gives *porridg* and *porringer* as 'phonetic' spellings of *pottage* and *pottinger*, from which it appears that written forms with *t* may sometimes conceal spoken forms with [r].

(5) *Initial* [fn] *becomes* [sn]

§ 386. In the fifteenth century the initial group [fn] in *fneeze* became [sn], giving *sneeze* (see *OED*, s.vv. *fneeze* vb. and *sneeze* vb.); there is no record of the initial group [fn] after the fifteenth century. The form *neese* recorded by Fox and Hookes as a homophone of *knees* probably represents ON *hnjósa* (see *OED*, s.v. *neeze*).

(6) *Assimilations involving the absorption of a following* [j]

§ 387. Before [j] the spirants [s] and [z] are assimilated to [ʃ] and [ʒ] and the stops [t] and [d] to the affricatives [tʃ] and [dʒ]; the [j] is absorbed into the new preceding consonant. The [j] arises from four main sources: (i) ME [j] by reduction of unstressed ĭ in the endings *-ia, -ion, -ial, -ier*, &c. (the commonest source); (ii) ModE [j] by reduction of ModE [i(:)] in, for example, *Theseus* (a case often difficult to distinguish from the preceding); (iii) a glide [j] developed before retained [ɪ] in such endings as *-ia, -ion*, &c. (see § 433 below), in which case it is the glide [j] which is absorbed, the [ɪ] remaining or being itself subsequently reduced to a [j] which, at least temporarily, survives (see § 276 and Note); (iv) ModE (late sixteenth- and seventeenth-century) [juː] < [iu] for ME [yː], *iu*, and *ęu* and for ME *ęu* (see §§ 185 (iii) and 244 above).

(*a*) [sj] *becomes* [ʃ]

§ 388. The change of [sj] to [ʃ] occurs in such words as *profession, version, mansion, facial, position, sure, sugar*, &c. The original [sj] is shown unchanged by Salesbury, Smith, Hart, Bullokar (normally), Owen (1605), Gil (normally), Hayward, Daines, Jonson, Gataker, Wallis (see Vol. I, pp. 240–1), Wilkins, and T. Jones; so apparently in later spelling-books in which *ti* in *position* is said to be pronounced *si* (so Wharton, Lloyd, Price, Lye, *The Protestant Tutor*, and *The Compendious Schoolmaster*). This, however, does not necessarily mean [sj] rather than [ʃ]; the statement is a pedagogic commonplace, as Ray (1691) observes, without real significance. Robotham (1643) says that *lectio* is pronounced '*lecsio* (or *lecsho*)', and Wharton himself shows [ʃ] in his 'homophone' list. Hunt gives the 'phonetic' spelling *discreshon* 'discretion', and Newton has [ʃ] in *nation* and *especially*. Coles explicitly denies that *ti* in any English word is pronounced *si*; he means that it is [ʃ], as his 'phonetic' spellings show. He is attacked for this remark by Aickin, who stupidly understood him to mean that the pronunciation was [tɪ] and himself shows [ʃ]. Shorthand-writers, like the schoolmasters, write *si* for *ti*, but this does not prove that the pronunciation was not [ʃ].

Smith says that *si* [sj] is almost the same as [ʃ]; this might, but need not, imply a knowledge of [ʃ] as a variant beside [sj]. The change is certainly shown by Bullokar (only in *fashion*; see Note 2 below), Mulcaster (beside [sj]), Robinson (generally; note his [ʃ] in *Theseus*), Gil (in *fashion* only), Hodges (apparently beside [sj]; see Vol. I, pp. 170–1), Robotham, and Lodwick. Coles, in his 'phonetically spelt' list, gives much evidence (followed by Strong and Young); we may note [ʃ] in *axiom* (spelt *acshum*), *associate* (spelt *assoshate*), *conscientious* (spelt *conshenshus*), *omniscient*, *Cassia* (spelt *Casha*), *Lucian*, *ambrosia* (spelt *ambrosha*), *expatiate*, *pronunciation* (spelt *pronunshashun*), *satiate* (spelt *sashate*), *Byzantium* (spelt *By-zanshum*), and *Cappadocia*, in addition to more normal cases. Cooper also gives much evidence, showing [ʃ] in *nauseate, associate, ocean*, &c.; *WSC-RS* and Aickin give similar evidence, following Cooper, and the change is further shown by Cocker, Brown, the shorthand-writer Ridpath, and the 'homophone' lists of Wharton and Fox and Hookes, which pair *martial* with *marshal*.

For evidence of initial [ʃuː] < [sjuː] < [siu] see § 185 (iii) above; it is shown by Cooper, *RS*, and Brown and by 'homophone' list pairings from Hodges onwards.

Note 1: Wyld, *Coll. Eng.*, p. 293, cites spellings showing [ʃ] < [sj] from the mid-fifteenth century.

Note 2: *Fashion* (ME *facioun*) occurs as *faschyoun* in the fifteenth century (see *OED*) and exceptionally comes to be spelt with *sh*, which influences the orthoepists. A pronunciation [faʃɪʊn] or [faʃɪən], with [ʃ] from [s] plus glide [j] and [ɪ] retained, is shown by Bullokar (twice) and Gil, but [faʃən] by Bullokar (once), Robinson, Hodges, Lye, *The Compendious School-Master*, and *WSC*. Coles and Strong have 'phonetic spellings' which show [ʃj] < [ʃɪ] < [sjɪ], the [j] being a glide before [ɪ] (see § 276, Note). Cf. Margaret Paston's *sesschyonys* 'sessions' (1450), the first of Wyld's examples.

Note 3: Wyld, loc. cit., has, as would be expected, no *sh* spellings for *sure*, *suit*, &c. before the late sixteenth century, when [juː] < [iu] first developed.

(*b*) [zj] *becomes* [ʒ]

§ 389. The change of [zj] to [ʒ] occurs in such words as *usual, measure, persuasion, vision, osier*, &c. No change is shown by Salesbury, Hart, Bullokar, Percival, Gil, Wallis and Price; the sound [ʒ] is regarded as a foreign (French) sound by Hart, Howell, Wallis (see Vol. I, p. 234), Holder (see Vol. I, p. 263), and Lodwick (see Vol. I, p. 278; contrast his evidence of [ʃ] < [sj]). The analysis of the French sound given by Baret (as *izy*), Wallis (as *zy*), and Holder (who says that *zya* is like but not the same as it) may, but need not, imply that [ʒ] existed in English as a variant to [zj].

The change is certainly shown by Robinson (generally; note his [ʒ] in *physician*), Hodges (in *occasions*, but not in *measure* and *usual*, which have [z]), Newton (in *grazier*), and Wilkins (who recognizes [ʒ], apparently as an English sound). Coles gives much useful evidence in his 'phonetically spelt' list, where he uses the notation *zh*; [ʒ] occurs in *collusion, conclusion, confusion*, &c., *measure, treasure, osier, persuasion*, and *Diocletian* (spelt *Dioclezhan*), but [zj] is given for *circumcision, decision, Elysian, transition, derision, Dionysius, pleasure* (contrast *measure* and *treasure*), *subdivision*, and *vision*. Cooper's evidence is made less useful than it might be by his failure clearly to distinguish words with [ʒ] (which he too denotes *zh*) from words with [ʃ]; the former is certain or probable in *enthusiasm, ecclesiastical, usual* (which is also given with [z]), *derision, incision, provision,* and *inhesion,* and it must be assumed in other words (e.g. *allusion, circumcision, effusion*), though a literal interpretation of Cooper's terms would be that these had [ʃ] (he has been careless in his phrasing). But he shows [zj] in *brazier, crosier,* and *hosier. WSC-RS,* like Cooper, fails to distinguish clearly which words have [ʒ] and which [ʃ]; the former may be assumed for *transient.* But *osier* is said to have three syllables and must be [oːzɪər]. Coles's successors in the 'phonetically spelt' tradition (Strong, Young, Cocker, and Brown) decline to follow his *zh* notation (no doubt because in practice it was not used by persons who spelt falsely) and show [zj] in, for example, *measure, pleasure, treasure, misprision* (Strong; similarly Young), *osier* (Cocker), *decision, measure,* and *vision* (Brown). But Young 1682 has *confuzhun* and *evazhun,* and the spellings *decishun* 'decision', *vishun* 'vision', *devishun* 'division' (Strong), *osher* 'osier', *delushun* 'delusion' (Young) seem to show [ʒ], though by a less satisfactory means. Whether *Dionyshus* 'Dionysius' (Strong, Young) means the normal [ʃ] or Coles's [ʒ] it is impossible to say.

Note: Spellings can only show this change if *sh* is used for [ʒ] (since *zh* is not found in conventional English orthography and is a phonetician's invention, used, for example, by Wilkins, Coles, and Cooper). Wyld, op. cit., p. 294, cites *sh* spellings of *pleasure* from the *Verney Memoirs* (1642).

(c) [tj] *becomes* [tʃ]

§ 390. The change of [tj] to [tʃ], which occurs, for example, in *courteous, righteous, virtue,* and *tulip,* is not shown by any early orthoepist. Wallis analyses [tʃ] as *ty* (see Vol. I, p. 234), which may indicate that there was now variation between [tʃ] and [tj] for original [tj]; but he gives *ortyard* 'orchard' as his example, which, though it does indeed have original [tj], has also [tʃ] from late OE onwards (see Note 1 below). I do not think we can base any conclusions concerning the development of ModE [tj] on this mistaken analysis of Wallis's. Cooper shows [tj], not [tʃ], for original [tj]; so do minor late seventeenth-century writers, e.g. Lye, Strong, and Young in their 'phonetically spelt' lists, and *WSC.* But Coles in his 'phonetically spelt' list shows [tʃ] in *Christianity* and *righteous* (though [tj] in *courteous* and *courtier*), and Brown has [tʃ] in *courteous* (though [tj] in *Christian*). The change of initial [tjuː] < [tiu] to [tʃuː] is shown only by the Northerner Brown's 'homophone' list pairing *tulip : julep.*

Note 1: *Orchard* (OE *ortgeard*) has OE assimilation, shown by the forms *orcgeard* (Hatton MS of *Cura Pastoralis*) and *orceard* (Ælfric); see *OED,* s.v. The *ort-yard* spelling survives, however, as late as Evelyn (1693).

Note 2: Wyld, op. cit., p. 294, cites evidence only from Walker and Leigh Hunt.

(d) [dj] *becomes* [dʒ]

§ 391. The change of [dj] to [dʒ] in, for example, *soldier, guardian, due,* and *duel* is not shown by the majority of orthoepists. Even at the end of the seventeenth century [dj] is still shown in *soldier* by Cooper and *WSC*. The 'homophone' lists of Wharton, Price, and Cocker pair *soldier* with *solder*, showing syncope of *i* without change of [d]. But Coles (followed by Strong and Young) gives the 'phonetic' spelling *soger* 'soldier', and the Northerner Brown the 'homophone' list equations *due* : *dew* : *Jew* and *duel* : *jewel*.

> *Note*: Wyld, loc. cit., cites one sixteenth-century spelling (Machyn's *sawgears* 'soldiers'), *sogers* 'soldiers' and *teges* 'tedious' from the *Verney Memoirs* (1642 and 1647), and a few eighteenth-century examples.

(7) *Dialectal change of* [ʃr] *to* [sr]

§ 392. A change of [ʃr] to [sr] is shown by the Northerner Brown in *sril* 'shrill', *srimp* 'shrimp', and *srink* 'shrink'; cf. Wright, § 338, who gives evidence from Northern and many Midland dialects.

LOSS OF CONSONANTS

SIMPLIFICATION OF CONSONANT-GROUPS

(1) *Loss of final consonants*

§ 393. In certain final groups the second consonant is often lost, normally by assimilation to the first.

(*a*) *Loss of* [b] *after* [m]

§ 394. In the group [mb] the second consonant was assimilated to the first by 1300 (see Jordan, § 211). The change, which is shown, for example, by Hart (in *lamb*), Bullokar (in *dumb*), Robinson, Gil, Hodges, Willis, Wallis, Wharton, Hunt, J. Smith, *The English Schole-master*, and Cooper and by shorthand-writers from J. Willis (1602) onwards, is probably to be regarded as regular, notwithstanding occasional transcriptions with *b* (as by Smith in *thumb* and *womb*, Bullokar in *comb*, *lamb*, and *womb*) and the statement by Richardson that one can either pronounce or omit the *b* in *comb*, *dumb*, *lamb*, &c., which seem to be due to the influence of the traditional orthography.

(*b*) *Loss of* [n] *after* [m]

§ 395. Loss of [n] from the group [mn] in, for example, *damn*, *condemn*, and *hymn* must have occurred when the words were affected by loss of final *e*; [n] could be preserved only if it became syllabic or was preceded by a glide [ə]. Bullokar indeed records [n̩] or [ən] in *condemn*, and in the same word Gil has [n̩] (shown by his retaining the *n*; cf. his phonetic spelling *condign*, which has [gn̩]). But loss of [n] is shown by Hodges in *solemn* and by *The English Schole-master* (1646) and Hunt, who say that *n* is silent in the group *mn*. *Damn* has forms without *n* as early as the *York Plays* (*c.* 1400?) and *Ludus Coventriae* (*c.* 1460); see *OED*.

(*c*) *Loss of* [n] *after* [l]

§ 396. Assimilatory loss of [n] after [l] occurs in late OE in *mill*, and the orthoepists give no evidence of the survival of [n] (though spellings with *n* survive into the seventeenth century, and later dialectally; see *OED*). In *kiln* loss of [n] is first shown in the fifteenth century (see Jordan, § 173), and the form with [n] survives in present StE; the loss, however, is shown by Bullokar, Hunt, Lye (followed by *RS* and Cocker), and the 'homophone' list pairing *kill* : *kiln* (Hodges and ten later authors, including Coles and Cooper). *Ell* (< OE *eln*), in which also loss of [n] is first recorded in the fifteenth century, is *el* in Gil.

(*d*) *Loss of* [n] *after* [r]

§ 397. An analogous assimilatory loss of [n] after [r] occurred in vulgar speech in the seventeenth century, being shown by the 'homophone' list pairings *acorn* : *acre* : *Achor* (Wharton, Young, Cocker) and *eldern* : *elder* (Young, Coles (*Eng.–Lat. Dict.*)); it survives in *elder* (tree), of which Young and Coles's *eldern* is doubtless the old spelling. For this word *OED* records forms without *n* from the fourteenth century.

(*e*) *Loss of* [d] *and* [t] *after dentals and other consonants*

§ 398. From the late fourteenth century onward (see Wyld, *Coll. Eng.*, pp. 303–4) final [d] and [t] are lost after dentals, [k] (presumably palatalized), and [p]. The process is assimilatory: [d] (and more rarely [t]) is lost after [n], and [t] after voiceless consonants (especially [k] and [p]). It was apparently common in vulgar and dialectal speech but was resisted in careful educated speech; except for the evidence of Hodges, Coles, and Cooper cited below (and none of these is free of dialectal influence), it is shown only by sources that reflect vulgar speech. Hodges has [þʌuzn̩] 'thousand' (cf. his [hʌzbanz] 'husbands', but the latter occurs only in the plural); Cooper and *WSC* also show the loss in *thousand*. The 'phonetically spelt' lists show it in *almond* (Coles, followed by Strong, Young, Cocker, and Brown), *wristband* (spelt *risban* by Strong, followed by Young), *guest* (spelt *gess* by Strong), and *diamond* (Cocker followed by Brown). Levins, a Northerner, puts *Egypt* in his -*ip* list (cf. Machyn's *Egype*), and has other rhymes which seem to depend on loss of final *d* or *t* (but might depend on excrescent *d* or *t* in the other words involved); Bullokar has similar rhymes (see Vol. I, p. 112), but in his case excrescent consonants seem the more likely explanation. It should be observed that the evidence from the sources so far cited refers chiefly to unstressed syllables. But the shorthand-writers (who make use of any pronunciations, however vulgar, that shorten words) show loss freely in stressed syllables. Thus T. Shelton says that *t* is silent in *elect, reject, act, reflect*, and *object*, Everardt in *precept*, Mason in *act, elect*, and *object*, and Ridpath (who marks this as a Scotticism) in *ak* 'act'; Coles, in his *Shorthand*, says that *d* in *stand* and *t* in *act* and *kept* are 'not at all, or but little and seldom sounded' (so Nicholas, after Coles). Similar evidence is given by Jones (1701), probably after Coles; see Wyld, loc. cit. The equations of the 'homophone' lists are of course essentially ambiguous, as they may depend on excrescent *d* or *t* in the one word or their loss in the other; on the whole loss seems more probable. Hodges in his 'alike' list has *rind* : *rine* : *Rhine* (so Fox and Hookes). Strong pairs *wine* with *wind* (so *RS* and Brown), Young *leper* with *leopard* (so Coles, *WSC*, and Brown) and *mine* with *mind* (so Cocker and Brown). Cooper relegates such pairings to his 'near alike' list, but his imitator *RS* (followed in turn by Brown) gives *kine* : *kind*; Brown has also *patten* : *pattent* 'patent'. Young (followed by Cocker and Brown) has *mole* : *mould*, Cooper ('near alike') *wile* : *wild*, Brown *weal* : *wield*, and the anonymous manuscript list *foal* : *fold*. Price has *ease* : *east*, Fox and Hookes (followed by Strong and Young) *guess* : *guest*, and *WSC* (followed by Cocker) *less* : *least*: the pairing *ass* : *ask* (Young, Cocker) probably depends on [as] 'ask' (recorded by Wright for Northern dialects and that of Northamptonshire), which must develop, by loss of final [t], from the widespread [a(:)st], which shows assimilation of [k] to [t] after the dental [s]. For loss of [t] after [s] compare Wyld's spellings, especially *res* 'rest' (1651), and its loss in *thistle*, &c. (see § 406 below).

The loss is especially likely to occur if [t] follows a group of consonants (as in *nex* 'next', which recurs in Wyld's examples); cf. Shakespeare's use of *-s* instead of *-st* in the 2nd pers. sing., especially after *d* or *t* (but also after vowels, e.g. *thou goes*).

Note 1: Levins and Bullokar give *tuf* 'tuft', but this is the original form (ME *tuffe* < OF *touffe*?); similarly Bullokar's *graf* 'graft' sb. and vb. is the original form (see *OED*). *Tyran* (recorded by Bullokar) beside *tyrant* is due to variation in OF (see *OED*).

Note 2: On *an* 'and', where weak stress aids the loss, see § 4. On the loss in plurals (e.g. *acts*), which is to be regarded as a distinct process, see §§ 404–10 below.

Note 3: The vulgar [ɪn] for *-ing* may possibly develop, at least in part, from earlier [ɪnd] < [ɪŋg]; see § 377 above.

Note 4: The shorthand-writer West uses a special symbol for *-nd*; presumably he pronounced the [d].

Note 5: For modern dialectal evidence see Wright, §§ 295, 307. The form [as] 'ask' could be explained (as apparently by *OED*, s.v., though its note is not clear) as being by back-formation from the p.t. [ast], developed by loss of [k] from the group [skt]. But many dialects have [st] in the infinitive (see Wright, *Index*), which makes the explanation given above seem preferable.

Note 6: The loss of *t* after *s* in the 2nd sing. pres. indic., alluded to above, is widespread in the present dialects and appears to have been a feature of Hodges's speech; his transcriptions indicate that he used [z] after vowels and voiced consonants and [s] after voiceless (and also [əst] without syncope), but the influence of literary English causes him to add a *t* which he cannot really have pronounced (see Vol. I, p. 183). In this case the loss of *t* must occur before syncope and before the voicing of final consonants in unstressed syllables had ceased to operate—i.e. in the fourteenth century.

(*f*) *Loss of* [g] *after* [ŋ]

§ 399. The spelling-symbol *ng* was in OE pronounced [ŋg] in all positions, and this is also to be regarded as the normal ME pronunciation, even in final position (despite Jordan, § 193, who thinks that final -*ng* was probably [ŋ] except in those parts of the country where [ŋk] spelt -*nk* tends to occur); only so can we explain the eModE evidence. For sixteenth-century orthoepists, even the sound phoneticians Smith and Hart, do not recognize the separate existence of [ŋ], and the reason is clear if we suppose that in all positions *ng* was [ŋg]; so long as this pronunciation remains, [ŋ] is only a contextual variant of [n] used before [g] and [k], and will not be separately recognized or described. But if in any position [g] is lost after [ŋ] but the latter remains unchanged, there arises a separate phoneme [ŋ] which will alone distinguish, for example, *thing* from *thin* (whereas previously the final [g] had been the distinguishing feature) and will therefore be immediately recognized and described. Failure to recognize [ŋ] necessarily implies that [ŋg] is still regularly used, and we must therefore conclude that in educated StE of the sixteenth century [ŋg] was maintained in all positions. On the other hand, as Jordan points out, evidence of -*in* for -*ing* in unstressed syllables (if, as is probable, the process is [ɪŋg] > [ɪŋ] > [ɪn]) implies that final [g] has been lost (in unstressed syllables, if not in stressed); and there is evidence which suggests that [ɪn] occurred for [ɪŋ] from before 1350 in certain dialects (see § 377, Note 1 above). Moreover the loss of final [d] from the group [nd] is exactly parallel to that of final [g] from the group [ŋg], and occurs even in stressed syllables in Norfolk in the late fourteenth century (see Wyld, op. cit., p. 303). We have to do, then, with different modes of pronunciation in different dialects: in Eastern dialects (including no doubt vulgar London English) [g] is lost from final [ŋg] from as early as the fourteenth century, whereas StE maintained [ŋg] until the late sixteenth.

But recognition of [ŋ] as a distinct phoneme shows that the loss of [g] has occurred. Such recognition is found in P. G. (1594), Robinson, Gil, Hodges, Wallis, and later seventeenth-century phoneticians; informs the 'phonetic spellings' of Coles (and his successors Strong and Young); and occurs also in minor sources, e.g. Hexham, T. Jones, and the shorthand-writer West (who has a special symbol for *ng*; but so he has for -*nd*). It is clear that StE accepted pronunciations in which [g] was lost about 1600. The chief sources of detailed evidence are Robinson, Gil's 1619 edition, Hodges, and Coles's 'phonetic' spellings (which are imperfectly followed by Strong and

Young); these show regular [ŋ] < final [ŋg] both in stressed and unstressed syllables. Though [n] < final [nd] is exactly parallel, there is a significant difference in the treatment which StE accorded the two pronunciations; in the seventeenth century [ŋ] < [ŋg] is regular and is shown by the most careful sources, whereas [n] < [nd] is recorded chiefly in sources which reflect vulgar pronunciations (Coles being the only major source to speak of it as normal, except in unstressed syllables), and in PresE [ŋ] < [ŋg] alone survives, whereas [nd] has been fully maintained. The difference must be set down to the influence of the spelling; whereas the *d* of, for example, *wind* was a constant reminder that [d] should be pronounced, it was natural that *ng* should come to be regarded as the conventional spelling of the phoneme [ŋ] when this was first recognized, so that, for example, *wing* suggested merely [wɪŋ], the final *g* not being felt to have any special individual significance. Educated speakers therefore resisted the loss of [d], even though Coles's evidence suggests that it almost prevailed, but had no reason to resist that of [g] after [ŋ] in final position and therefore accepted it.

Medially between vowels [ŋg] remained in such words as *angular*, *singular* and *anger*, *hunger*, *finger*, &c. (if these be regarded as having had [ər] rather than syllabic [r̩]); so in P. G. (see Vol. I, p. 33), Robinson, Gil 1619 (see Jiriczek's edition, p. xlvii), Hodges (in *anger* and *finger*; but *hunger* varies—see § 412 below), Wharton, Coles (in *vardingale* as well as in *hunger*, &c.), Strong, and Young. But in derivatives of verbs with final *-ng* (e.g. *singer*, *ringer*, &c.) [ŋ] replaces [ŋg], in StE, by analogical substitution; so in Hodges in *singer*, *swinging*, *longeth*, and *stingeth*. But Robinson retains [ŋg] in *singing*, Gil in *belongeth*, *fanged*, *hanged*, *wranged* (*-ed* being a separate syllable), *hanging*, and *springing*, and Wharton apparently in *ringer* (which he does not distinguish from *conger*, *linger*, *hunger*, &c., which he says have 'hard g'), *longing*, *hanging*, *longeth*, &c. Evidently the analogical substitution, though shown by Hodges, was not regular in the seventeenth century. In comparative adjectives PresE lacks it (e.g. *longer*, *stronger*); in these two words [ŋg] is shown not only by Gil, but also by Hodges (whose pronunciations of *ng* words agree almost exactly with PresE), Wallis, and Coles.

Note 1: There is also reduction of [ŋg] to [ŋ], by phonetic change, in medial position before a consonant; see § 412 below. The view which I propounded in *Trans. Phil. Soc.* (1947), p. 55 and footnote 2, that [ŋg] > [ŋ] only in final position and that the change in medial position is always analogical, I now recognize to be false. The treatment in medial position (retention of [ŋg] before vowels, change to [ŋ] before consonants) suggests that there may well have been a stage (in StE, the sixteenth century and possibly even earlier) in which final *-ng* was pronounced [ŋ] before a word beginning with a consonant but [ŋg] before one beginning with a vowel, before a pause, or when the word was used in isolation; so long as [ŋg] and not [ŋ] was used before pauses and in isolated words, [ŋ] would not be recognized as a phoneme distinct from [n].

Note 2: There is no comparable loss of [k] from the group [ŋk]; cf. the usual retention of [t] after [n].

§ 399]   LOSS OF CONSONANTS   965

Note 3: On retention of final [ŋg] in stressed syllables in Northern and WMidl dialects see Wright, § 274; but in unstressed syllables it has become [ŋ] and thence [n]. In contrast *hunger, finger*, &c. have [ŋ] < [ŋg] in Scottish, Irish, Northern, NMidl, and some Southern dialects (§ 272); whether this represents a development before [ə] or before syllabic [r̩] it is impossible to determine, but in general theory the latter is much the more probable.

(2) *Loss of intervocalic consonants*

§ 400. Intervocalic [v] is frequently lost in ME; hence *pore* 'poor' < *povere*, *lark* < *laverke*, *lord* < *loverd*, *kerchief* < *keverchef*, *han* 'have', *hath*, *sennight*, *e'en* 'even', *dēl* 'devil', *hēd* 'head' < *heved*, *hussies* < *huswives* (whence the sing. *hussy*), &c. From this cause arise the forms *Densheer* 'Devonshire' (Coles) and *Lerpool* 'Liverpool' (Strong, Young). Gil records [gi:] 'give' as a pronunciation of the 'Mopsæ' (see Vol. I, p. 148), and the Northerner Levins has *ease* 'eaves'. The similar loss of intervocalic [k] in *tane* 'taken' is in ME Northern, but the use of *ta'en* by StE poets (as by Barnfield, whom Robinson transcribes) is due to its having also developed in Midland dialects (see Wright, § 339).

Note 1: For further evidence of the loss of intervocalic [v] see Jordan, §§ 216 and 263, and Wyld, *Coll. Eng.*, p. 304. Jordan believes that the loss occurs before consonants (e.g. before [n] in *sevne* pl., *evne* (oblique form) 'evening', &c.; but it is simpler to regard it as occurring between vowels, where the phonetic process (relaxation of the articulation until no friction occurs) is easier to explain; loss in *head* occurs in the nom. *heved*, in *poor* and *lady* in forms with svarabhakti *e*, thus *povere* and *lavedie*, &c. The pre-consonantal change is through [w] to [u], as in *haukes* < [hawkəs] < *havkes*, *aunter* < *avnture*, *laundre* < *lavndre*, as correctly explained by Jordan. Wyld, loc. cit., believes that there is also a process of loss of final *f*, but *kerchys* 'kerchiefs', *masties* 'mastiffs' rather show loss of [v] in the plurals *kerchives*, *mastives*, and the singular *masty* is by back-formation (cf. *hussy* commented on above). *Kerchers*, which Wyld seems to think a phonetic spelling of *kerchiefs* in which *er* stands for [ə], is not developed in English at all but represents an OF variant *couvrechier* (see *OED*); Hunt regards it as dialectal.

Note 2: For modern dialectal pronunciations showing loss of [v] see Wright, § 279.

Note 3: In present-day vulgar and dialectal speech intervocalic [t] has been entirely lost, as far as its dental articulation is concerned, though it is normally replaced by the glottal stop to preserve the separate identity of the preceding and following vowels. The process (which is similar to the ME loss of intervocalic [v]) is not mentioned by the orthoepists.

(3) *Assimilatory loss of medial consonants*

§ 401. In certain words a medial consonant is lost by being assimilated to a following consonant. The development is primarily characteristic of vulgar or dialectal speech, but in some words has affected StE; in general it dates from late ME.

(a) *Last consonant of syllable*

The loss of the last consonant of a syllable occurs in a number of cases. In *give me* the [v] is in vulgar speech assimilated to the following [m]; Cooper records *gimme* (or *gemme*) as 'barbarous speaking'. Tonkis has *ommee* 'of me'. Loss of [f] before [p] in *halfpenny*, shown already in Langland (*halpeny*, B-text, VI. 307), is recorded by Gil (whose pronunciation was [hɒːpenɪ]) and the 'phonetically spelt' lists of Coles (*hah-pen-y*; cf. *hah-puth* 'halfpennyworth'), Young, Cocker, and Brown (all of whom give *hapenny*); but Strong has *hafpenny*. Similarly the spelling *fip(p)ence* 'fivepence' is given by Coles, Strong, Young, and Brown. Loss of [p] before [b] is shown in *cupboard* by the shorthand-writer J. Willis (1602), Hodges, and Price, in *upbraid* by J. Willis, Price, and *WSC*, and in *raspberry* by Coles in his 'phonetically spelt' list. Loss of [s] before [n] occurs in *e'nt* 'isn't it', recorded by Cooper as 'barbarous speaking' (Latin text 'facilitatis causa'). Loss of [d] before [n] occurs in *Wednesday* in Price, Strong, Lye, *The Compendious School-Master*, *WSC-RS*, Aickin, Cocker, and Brown; but Coles, even in his 'phonetically spelt' list, retains [d] (thus *Wednsday*). Conversely [n] was occasionally lost in unstressed syllables before dentals. *Frumenty* (OF *frumentee*) has forms without [n] from the fifteenth century (see *OED*); so in the 'phonetically spelt' lists of Strong (*furmite*), Young (*furmete*), and Brown (*frummety* or *furmety*). Cooper condemns *firmity* (so English text; Latin text *furmity*) as 'barbarous speaking', and forms with retained [n] are given by Laneham, Gil, Wharton, and J. Smith. On loss of [n] before [s] in *Westminster* and before [l] in *son-in-law* see Wyld, op. cit., p. 303. Loss of [t] before [s] occurs in *Wis'ntide* 'Whitsuntide' in Brown. Loss of [ŋ] before [k] occasionally took place in the unstressed second syllable of *melancholy* (see Wyld, loc. cit.).

(*b*) *Initial consonant of syllable*

Loss of the initial consonant of a syllable occurs in the special phonetic conditions of *London*. In this word the [d] is normally articulated only by plosion before the [ən]; but if, because two [n]'s follow each other so closely, the first alveolar appulse is released too soon—simultaneously with the closure of the nasal passage instead of after it—the [d] disappears and the result is [lʊnən] > [lʌnən]. Gil records that Waad transcribed *London* as *Lunun*, which he comments (with some justice, though it cannot be the whole truth) is the pronunciation of 'tabellarii', postmen; and Brown gives the 'phonetic spelling' *Lonnon* (beside *Lundon*). Wyld, op. cit., p. 302, cites seventeenth- and eighteenth-century evidence; Gray in 1757 describes it as a vulgar pronunciation, but Wyld declares that it persisted among 'polite speakers' (!) far into the nineteenth century.

(*c*) *Consonant within syllable*

Loss of a consonant within the syllable occurs in *hundredth* pronounced [hʊndrəþ], recorded by Gil, and in *clothes* pronounced [kloːz], recorded by Brown. But the most important case is the early assimilatory loss of [r] before [s] and [ʃ] in *burst, curse, horse, harsh*, &c. and occasionally before other consonants. Loss before [s] is shown by Price (probably; see Vol. I, p. 344), Coles (see Vol. I, p. 441, note 2), and the Northerner Brown, who has the 'phonetic' spellings *hosler* glossed (falsely) 'horsler' and *sasenet* 'sarsenet' and the 'homophone' list pairings *hoarse* : *hose*, &c. Loss before [ʃ] in *harsh* is shown by Cooper, *WSC* (in his 'homophone' list), and Brown (in his 'phonetically spelt' list); even in Cooper it is a dialectalism or a vulgarism (see Vol. I, pp. 306–7). Brown shows this assimilatory loss of [r], without influence on the preceding vowel, before other consonants as well, e.g. in *hurl* and *order* (see Vol. I, p. 418). Bullokar's rhymes show loss, without influence on the vowel, before [s] (in *erst*, *worst*), [þ] (in *earth*), [t] (in *hurt*), and [m] (in *worm*), clearly a dialectalism (see Vol. I, p. 112). For *Worcester* the pronunciation [wustər] is recorded by Coles, Strong, Young, Cocker, and *WSC*; but the shorthand-writer Everardt gives *Worster*, which shows the syncopated form without the loss of [r].

Note 1: For spellings showing these and similar pronunciations from the fifteenth century onwards see Wyld, op. cit., pp. 301–2 (but he fails to distinguish these cases from others in which the middle consonant of a group of three is lost) and pp. 298–9 (loss of [r]; but he fails to distinguish the various processes of loss—see further § 427, Note). Jordan, § 166, shows that this assimilatory loss of [r] dates from c. 1300; see also his § 251, where he shows that it affects French words, in which the vowel often retains the length assigned to it when it stood before *r* plus consonant (so *dace* < *dars*, *souse* < *source*; cf. Brown's *sasenet* and his equation of *odour* with *order*) but is sometimes shortened (*fuss* < *force*). Modern dialectal evidence is to be found in Wright's Index.

Note 2: For loss of [r] in unstressed syllables, where it may sometimes be assimilatory, see § 332. On ModE loss of [r] by vocalization to [ə] in stressed syllables see below, § 427.

(4) *Loss of middle consonant of a group of three*

§ 402. From the fourteenth century onwards there is a marked tendency in English to simplify a group of three (or four) consonants by syncope of the middle one (or last but one); the consonants lost are those that are also lost in final position (see §§ 393–9 above) and the process is likewise assimilatory, but it occurs more frequently when another consonant follows. If the group of consonants is broken up by the syllable-division the second last is normally (but not always) retained if with the last it makes up a group capable, in English, of beginning a word; for this reason special attention has to be given to cases in which the last consonant is [l] or [r].

Note: Spellings showing the losses of consonants discussed in detail below are cited by Wyld, op. cit., pp. 301–3 (who, however, fails to distinguish this from other processes of loss); they occur from the early fifteenth century onwards.

(a) *Loss of* [b] *and* [p] *after* [m]

§ 403. (i) In *dumbness*, &c. the same loss occurs as in *dumb*, &c. But before [l] and [r], whether syllabic or non-syllabic (as in *bramble*, *mumble*, *assembled*, *resemblance*, *amber*, *embrace*, *encumbrance*), the [b] is normally kept; its loss is, however, shown by the shorthand-writer Farthing before syllabic [l] in *assembled* and *resembled*.

(ii) Loss of [p] in *empty, tempt, temptation, consumption, glimpse*, &c. is common (though far from invariable) in PresE. It is shown by Hart (in *temptation*), Robinson (in *consumption* and once in *tempt*), Hodges, Howell (in *consumption*), Lye, Hawkins, and *WSC-RS*; but the [p] is retained by Hart (in *attempted*), Bullokar (in *contempt* and *empty*), Robinson (four times in *tempt*), and Gil (in *empty*). Before [l] and [r] (in *ample, employ, (at)temper, whimper, comprise*, &c.) [p] is always kept.

Note: For loss of [b] in the modern dialects see Wright, § 276, who says that [b] 'hardly ever occurs' between [m] and syllabic [l] and [r]; cf. the spellings cited by Wyld, op. cit., p. 302, which show loss of [b] before non-syllabic [l] (*assemlyd, tremlyng, nimlest*—the last from Queen Elizabeth) and syllabic [r] (*Camerwell* and *Cammerell* 'Camberwell'). StE has perhaps been influenced by the conventional spelling.

(*b*) *Loss of* [t] *after* [p]

§ 404. Loss of [t] after [p] occurs in the plurals *attempts* and *precepts* (cf. the loss in the singular recorded by the shorthand-writer Everardt) but is not recorded by the orthoepists; it is not part of StE.

(*c*) *Loss of* [t] *after* [f]

§ 405. Loss of [t] after [f] is common only in *often*, where assimilation to the following [n] assists the loss, but occurs in other cases (see Wyld, p. 302, on *Toft's* and *Shaftesbury*). In *often* [t] is kept by Hart, Bullokar, Robinson, Gil, Hodges, and the shorthand-writer Hopkins (as often in PresE; Wyld, loc. cit., is surely wide of the mark in calling this 'a new-fangled innovation'), but shown as lost by the 'phonetically spelt' lists of Coles and his successors (Strong, Young, and Brown); despite its use by Queen Elizabeth, the pronunciation without [t] seems to have been avoided in careful speech in the seventeenth century, for record in these 'phonetically spelt' lists and nowhere else generally indicates a vulgarism.

(*d*) *Loss of* [t] *after* [s]

§ 406. Present StE shows regular loss of [t] in *Christmas, chestnut, listen, fasten*, &c. and *thistle, castle*, &c. In *Christmas* the loss is shown in the 'phonetically spelt' lists of Coles and Strong, and in *wristband* and *chestnut* in that of Strong. Before [n] the loss is shown by Hodges (in *Weston* and *Preston*), Coles, and Young (in *listen*), *RS* (who says that [t] 'can hardly be pronounced'), and Brown; but [t] is kept by Bullokar (in *chasten*), Hunt and Coles (in *fasten*), and Young (in *chasten* and *fasten*). In *beasts, priests, posts*, &c. loss of [t] is shown by Coles's rhymes in the *Schoolmaster* (e.g. *blasts* : *ass, priests* : *Greece*) and by *RS*, who says that in such words the *t* 'can hardly be pronounced'. Before [l] loss of [t] is shown by Hodges (regularly), Hunt (in *epistle*), Young (in *castle* and *wrestle*), *RS* (who comments as before), Cocker, Brown, and the shorthand-writers Everardt, Bridges, and Coles (who says that *t* is 'not at all, or but little and seldom sounded' in *castle*); but [t] is kept by Salesbury, Hart, Bullokar, Robinson, Gil, Coles himself (in *pestle* in the *Schoolmaster*), and Young (after Coles). Before non-syllabic [l] loss is shown by Strong in *wrestler* and by the shorthand-writer Farthing in *costly*; Jones (1701) shows loss in *costly, ghastly, lastly, beastly, mostly*, &c. (see Wyld, p. 302). PresE omits [t] in derivatives of words with syllabic [l] (e.g. *wrestler*) and shows variation in *mostly*, but otherwise keeps [t] in, for example, *beastly, costly*, and *ghastly*. Before [r], both non-syllabic and syllabic (e.g. in *blister, blistering*), [t] is regularly kept, [(s)tr] being an initial group.

Note 1: On dialectal pronunciation, which mostly agrees with StE, see Wright, §§ 289-90; loss of [t] in *ghastly* is recorded for scattered dialects.

Note 2: PresE retention of [t] in *pistol* must be due to eModE forms with secondary stress and therefore with retained vowel; but compare Mrs. Quickly's *Peesol*.

(e) Loss of [t] *after* [k]

§ 407. In the plurals *acts, effects*, &c. the orthoepists normally keep [t], as does PresE. But loss is shown by *RS* in the text; by the 'homophone' list pairings *acts : axe* (Hodges 'near alike', Wharton, Price, Fox and Hookes, Coles (*Eng. Dict.*), Young, Cooper 'near alike', and Cocker) and *sects : sex* (Price, Fox and Hookes, Coles in the normally careful *Schoolmaster*, Strong, and Cooper 'near alike'); and by the shorthand-writers J. Willis (1602), T. Shelton, Dix, Everardt, Hopkins, Mason, Steel, and Ridpath (who marks the pronunciation as a Scotticism). Before non-syllabic [l] loss of [t] is shown in *perfectly* by the shorthand-writer Farthing; so often in PresE (as also in *perfectness*). Before [r], as in *actress*, there is no loss, [tr] being a common initial group.

(f) Loss of dentals after [r]

§ 408. Loss of consonants after [r] is rare. Brown has the 'homophone' list pairing *hardness : harness* and Young has *morgage* 'mortgage' (so Margaret Paston, 1448) and the pairing *earthly : early* (cf. the spelling *erly* 'earthly' used by Thomas Pery, 1539). Loss of [n] in *government*, which is assisted by the following nasal and by lack of stress, is shown by the shorthand-writer J. Willis (1602), Robinson, and Hodges, but [n] is kept by Bullokar.

Note: Wright, § 301, shows loss of [d] in *garden* in Southern and South-western dialects and in Scotland.

(g) Loss of [d] *after* [l]

§ 409. Loss of [d] after [l] is also rare, but Hodges's 'near alike' list (followed, for example, by Strong) has *wilds : wiles*. Before non-syllabic [l] it occurs in *worldling* spelt *wurling* by Strong and *worling* by Young; cf. the forms *worl*, &c. (thirteenth to sixteenth century) and *warl'* (eighteenth century) recorded by *OED*, which show loss of final [d] in the simplex. Before [r] in *children*, &c. there is no evidence of loss.

Note: Wright, § 301, shows a loss of [d] in *childer* 'children' (i.e. before syllabic [r]) in Southern dialects and in [ɑːlər] 'older' in NE Scotland.

(h) Loss of [d] *and* [t] *after* [n]

§ 410. (i) Loss of [d] after [n] is a specially important case because it provides so close an analogue to that of [g] after [ŋ]; but it is less common, doubtless because of the influence of the conventional spelling, which suggests that [d] should be pronounced after [n] but not that [g] should be pronounced after [ŋ] (*ng* being taken as a digraph representing simply [ŋ]). PresE has lost [d] in, for example, *handsome* and *handkerchief*, varies in, for example, *handmaid, landscape, friendship, blindness, kindness*, and *thousands*, and has [d] regularly in, for example, *handshake, husbands, friends*, and *winds* (see D. Jones, *Eng. Pron. Dict.*, s.vv.). The orthoepists normally show retention of [d], doubtless themselves influenced by the conventional spelling. But in *handsome* Bullokar shows loss, Coles says that the *d* is 'not at all, or but little and seldom sounded', and *RS* shows loss. Loss in *handkerchief* is shown by Coles (with assimilation of [n] to [ŋ]), Strong, Young, *RS*, Cocker, and Brown. In *friendship, handmaid*, and *handsome* the *d* is said to be silent by Lye, who is directly or indirectly followed by *The Compendious School-Master, RS*, Aickin, Cocker, and Brown; so the shorthand-writer Ridpath. J. Willis (1602) says that in *landtschape* 'landscape' the *dt* is silent. The pronunciations [blǝinǝs] 'blindness' and [kǝinǝs] 'kindness' are shown by the shorthand-writers Farthing, Everardt, and Bridges. In *thousandth* (but not in *thousands*) Gil omits [d]; Hodges omits it in *thousands* and *husbands*. In such final groups loss in stressed syllables is shown only in the 'homophone' lists, which have *winds : wines* (Hodges 'near'), *fiends : fins* (Hodges 'near', Price), and *finds : fines* (Price).

Before non-syllabic [l] the [d] is normally kept, but it is lost in *friendly* in the shorthand-writer Farthing; so in *rundlet* and *kindled* (if the latter has not syllabic [l]) in the shorthand-writers J. Willis and Everardt. Before syllabic [l] it is normally kept in StE, but loss is shown in *bundle* and *kindle* by the shorthand-writer Bridges (compare also *kindled* above). It should be observed that loss before [l], whether syllabic or non-syllabic, is shown only by shorthand-writers, who depend on many vulgarisms to achieve their desired abbreviations. Before [r], whether syllabic or non-syllabic (e.g. in *wonder, thunder, hundred*), [d] is normally kept, [dr] being a common initial group.

(ii) Loss of [t] after [n] is not very common, but is shown by sources which reflect vulgar speech. Loss in unstressed syllables is shown by the 'homophone' list pairings *patents* : *pattens* (Hodges 'alike', Strong), *gallants* : *gallons* (Hodges 'near alike'), *assistants* : *assistance* (Price, Fox and Hookes, Strong, and Young), *accidents* : *accidence* (Fox and Hookes, Coles's *Eng.–Lat. Dict.*, Strong, Hawkins), *presents* : *presence* (Fox and Hookes, Coles's *Eng.–Lat. Dict.*), and *patients* : *patience* (Brown). In stressed syllables loss is shown by the shorthand-writer J. Willis, who says *t* is silent in *rents*, and the 'homophone' list pairings *tents* : *tens* (Hodges 'near alike'), *scents* : *sense* (Price), and *mints* : *mince* (Fox and Hookes).

The loss of [t] is most common, and affects StE, in the group [ntʃ], which in PresE is often reduced to [nʃ] in *branch*, &c. The pronunciation of *ch* after *n* is normally not distinguished by orthoepists from *ch* in other positions (i.e. it is [tʃ]); so even in Price (whose 'homophone' list shows loss of [t] in *scents*) and in Coles's 'phonetically spelt' list. But Gil has [nʃ] in *branches* once (against [ntʃ] twice) and in *inch* once (against [ntʃ] in *inches* once), and Brown has the 'phonetic' spellings *clensh* 'clinch' and *hansh* 'haunch'. Compare also the 'homophone' list pairings *launch* : *lance* and *quench* : *quince* discussed in § 373 above.

Note: Wright, §§ 300–1, records common loss of [d] after [n] and before syllabic [l̩] and [r̩] in the dialects; note that [hʌnər], [hʌnɪr] 'hundred' develops from a form [hʊndr̩] < [hʊndr̩d] with syllabic [r̩].

(*i*) *Loss of* [ʃ] *after* [t]

§ 411. Loss of [ʃ] between [t] and [s] in the special phonetic circumstances of *vouchsafe* is shown by spellings from the (late?) fourteenth century onwards (see *OED*); the form *voutsafe* is recorded by Gil (once, beside *vouchsafe* once), Strong, Young, Cocker, and Brown. It is of course Milton's form.

(*j*) *Loss of* [g] *after* [ŋ]

§ 412. When the ME group [ŋg] occurred before a third consonant, it was normally reduced to [ŋ] (cf. the reduction of final [ŋg] to [ŋ], discussed in § 399 above); the change, which is exactly analogous to the loss of [d] between [n] and a third consonant (see § 410), must have occurred in widespread dialects in the fourteenth century and sporadically in OE itself, in view of the occurrence of the assimilated forms *lenth* and *strenth* (see § 377), which cannot develop until [g] is lost. But the failure of sixteenth-century orthoepists, even Smith and Hart, to isolate [ŋ] as a separate phoneme implies that in StE [g] was still normally retained, for otherwise the distinction in meaning between, for example, *sings* and *sins* would have depended solely on the distinction between the sounds [ŋ] and [n] and the former would have had to receive separate description. Evidently there existed, beside the mode of pronunciation in which [g] was lost early, a conservative one in which it was retained; the latter gave place about 1600, and the evidence of Robinson shows that for a brief time there was some uncertainty in pronunciation.

The detailed evidence for the change comes chiefly from Robinson, Gil (1619 edition), Hodges, and Coles's 'phonetically spelt' list (followed imperfectly by Strong and Young). Before a consonant other than [l], [r], or [w] (on which see below) the change is regular. Loss of [g] is shown by Robinson in *length* and *amongst* (see also Note 1); by Gil in *amongst*, *Abington* 'Abingdon' (contrast *Sempringham*; see Note 1), *kingdom*, *length*, and *strength*; and by Hodges in *amongst*, *kingdom*, *length*, *lengthen*, *strength*, and *strengthen*. Similarly in the plurals of substantives (cf. loss of [t] in *acts*, &c. and of [d] in *winds*, &c.) [ŋ] in place of [ŋg] is shown by Robinson in *things* and *paintings*, by Gil in *songs*, *tongs*, *ratlings*, and *shillings*, and by Hodges in *pangs*, *songs*, *tongs*, *tongues*, *beginnings*, *doings*, *goslings*, &c. In the inflected forms of verbs Robinson varies: [ŋ] occurs in *singst*, *hangs*, and *smooth-tongued*, but [ŋg] in *belongs* and *belong'd* (disyllabic), probably because of the analogical influence of the forms *belongeth* and *belongèd* (trisyllabic) in which [ŋg], being intervocalic, was retained. Gil has only [ŋ] in, for example, *vang'd* and *wrong'd* (monosyllabic), but keeps intervocalic [ŋg] in *fangèd*, *wrangèd* (disyllabic), *springing*, and *belongeth* (cf. Robinson). Hodges has [ŋ] in *brings* and *swings* (presumably the verb) and even in *longeth* and *stingeth* (transcribed as disyllables); his pronunciation of the latter two, which agrees with that of PresE, is due to the analogy of [ŋ] in final position in the infinitive and before [z] in *longs* and *stings* (i.e. the reverse analogy to that which operates in Robinson's *belongs* and *belong'd*).

Before non-syllabic [l] and [r] in, for example, *England* and *angry* [ŋg] is normally retained, as in PresE, [gl] and [gr] being initial groups. *Angry* and *hungry*, in which retention of [ŋg] is aided by the analogy of (intervocalic?) [ŋg] in *anger* and *hunger* (see below), have [ŋg] in Robinson, Gil, Hodges, Wharton, and Coles; Coles also shows [ŋg] in *mung-gril* 'mongrel', a more decisive case because it is uninfluenced by analogy. In *England* and *English* retention of [ŋg] is normal in present StE, though [ŋ] is not at all uncommon (cf. D. Jones, *Eng. Pron. Dict.*, s.vv.); [ŋg] occurs in Robinson and Hodges, but [ŋ] in Gil and Coles (followed by Young). In *kingly*, *strongly*, and *exceedingly* the PresE [ŋ] is due in part at least to the analogy of final [ŋ] in the simplexes; Robinson has [ŋg] in *kingly* but [ŋ] in *strongly*, and Gil has [ŋ] in *exceedingly*; examples are lacking in Hodges and Coles.

Before syllabic [l̩] in, for example, *bangle*, *mingle*, *single*, and *singleness* present StE regularly retains [ŋg], doubtless because [l̩] can be and was commonly replaced by [əl], when [ŋg] became intervocalic; so Gil (in a passage added in the 1621 edition) in *spangle* and *entangle* and Hodges in *angle*, *bungle*, *mingle*, *single(ness)*, &c. Similarly before syllabic [r̩] (or perhaps rather before [ər], syllabic [r̩] having apparently been much rarer than syllabic [l]) in *hunger, finger, anger*, &c., [ŋg], as in present StE, occurs in Robinson, Gil, Hodges (in *anger* and *finger*), Wharton, and Coles (followed by Strong and Young). But Hodges has [ŋ] in *hunger* once (beside [ŋg] once), in which his transcription actually shows [ər] not [r̩], and in *hungered* once (beside [ŋg] once), in which he gives syllabic [r̩]; in *hungry* he has [ŋg]. These transcriptions of Hodges's are not errors, as assumed by Kauter; see Note 2 below.

Before [w] in *anguish, languish*, and *language* [ŋg] is regularly retained in StE, [gw] being an initial group (as in *Gwen*); so in Gil (who mistakenly gives *u*, which should mean [ʊ], and not *w*) and Hodges, and presumably in other sources which record these words but do not show clearly enough that [w] is pronounced.

Loss of [g] after [ŋ], it should be observed, is shown by sources (Robinson, Gil, and Hodges's *EP*) which do not show that of [d] after [n] except in unstressed syllables; the different treatment is due to the influence of the conventional spelling, as explained above. The analogy of [nd] would suggest that originally loss of [g] must have been commoner in unstressed than in stressed syllables (cf. § 399, Note 3), but of this state of affairs the seventeenth-century evidence, which is the earliest we have, gives no sign.

Note 1: For reasons explained in *Trans. Phil. Soc.* (1947), p. 54, Robinson's evidence before f. 122ʳ of MS Ashmole 1153 is excluded. He once gives a transcription of *amongst* which may show either retained [ŋg] or a glide [k] developed between [ŋ] and [s]; at this transitional date the former is more likely, and may be due to the analogy of the trisyllabic *amongest*, recorded by *OED* as late as 1586, in which [ŋg] is intervocalic. Gil in one passage uses expressions which Jiriczek, pp. xlvii–xlviii, interpreted as referring to a vulgar pronunciation [streŋgþs] or [streŋkþs]; but Gabrielson, *Studia Neophilologica*, xiv. 339, suggests, probably rightly, that the reading of the 1619 edition ('streŋþs, *& vulgo* strengths') refers not to a vulgar pronunciation but to the popular (i.e. unreformed) spelling; Gil is talking of how in English a syllable may contain as many as six consonants to one vowel, as in *streŋþs*, and then to rub it in gives the ordinary spelling *strengths* with its eight 'consonants'. In 1621, when he himself returned to the 'vulgar' use of *ng* for [ŋ] and *th* for [þ], he necessarily altered the passage. His pronunciation of *Sempringham* is due to retention of [ŋg] in intervocalic position, the [h] having been lost (as his transcription shows); our variant with [ŋ] develops in a form in which [h] is retained and the group [ŋgh] becomes [ŋh].

Note 2: Wright, § 272, shows [ŋ] < [ŋg] in *mingle, single, hunger, finger*, &c. in Scotland, Ireland, the North of England, the North Midlands, Kent, Sussex, and Somerset; so in *England* and *English*. He gives no information on *angry, hungry*, and *mongrel*, but presumably they also have, or can have, [ŋ] in place of [ŋg] in these dialects. Cf. Hodges's transcriptions of *hunger, hungered*, and *hungry* discussed above.

Note 3: On the change of final [ŋg] to [ŋ] and the retention of intervocalic [ŋg] except when it is replaced by analogy, see § 399 above. The view which I put forward in *Trans. Phil. Soc.* (1947), p. 55 and footnote 2, that medial [ŋ] for [ŋg], even before consonants, is to be explained from the analogy of final [ŋ], was incorrect and is now withdrawn.

Note 4: There is no evidence of a similar loss of [k] in *winks, thinks, winkle, tinkle*, &c.; cf. the normal retention of [t] after [n] in *hints*, &c.

(5) *Loss of first consonant of certain initial groups*

§ 413. Groups beginning with [h] were in ME commonly simplified by the loss of the [h]; thus in most dialects [hl], [hr], and [hn] became [l], [r], and [n], and similarly [hw] in many dialects became [w]. The group [wl] became [l] by about 1400. The groups [wr], [kn], and [gn] became [r] and [n] during eModE itself.

(a) *Groups with initial* [h]

§ 414. The loss of [h] in the groups [hl], [hn], and [hr] began in late OE and became normal during the twelfth century (cf. Jordan, § 195); StE shows invariable loss of [h]. Insofar as the original groups remained in ME (notably in Kent) there was probably assimilation to voiceless [l̥], [n̥], and [r̥].

The OE group *hw*, originally pronounced [χw] (which remained in the North), became [hw] and must still have had this value when in the thirteenth century *hǭ* 'who' developed from *hwǭ*. But in the South and the South-east Midlands, from the twelfth century onwards (see Jordan, § 195), there was simplification to [w] by loss of the initial [h], and this pronunciation had currency in vulgar London speech. In eModE, educated speech appears invariably to have retained [hw] (or [ʍ] < [hw]); but during the eighteenth century the previously vulgar [w] became increasingly current in good speech and was normal in the latter half of the century (see Wyld, *Coll. Eng.*, p. 312). To what extent [ʍ] and [hw] among Southern speakers at the present day represents a genuine survival of the traditional pronunciation is difficult to determine; probably in most cases it is an artificial pronunciation due to the spelling and the influence of non-Southern speakers in whose dialects [hw] or [ʍ] is retained.

The orthoepists normally retain [hw] or [ʍ]: so Smith, Hart, Bullokar (usually), the Northerner Tonkis, Robinson, Gil, Sherwood, Hodges, Gataker, Wallis, Wilkins, Holder, J. Smith, Lodwick, Cooper, and the shorthand-writer Rich (who has a special symbol for *wh*). Similar evidence is given by foreign observers, e.g. *Alphabet Anglois*, 1625 (see Wyld, loc. cit.). The pronunciation [w] is shown only by sources which are influenced by vulgar or dialectal speech. Laneham has it in *wear* 'where' and Bullokar in *weither* 'whether'; in both these cases weak stress may aid the development, as also in *wat* 'what', *wen* 'when', and *wo* 'who', recorded by the shorthand-writers Rich and Stringer. The 'homophone' lists have *whither : whether : weather* (Price, Fox and Hookes, Brown), *wheal : wheel : weal* (Young, Coles's *Eng.-Lat. Dict.*), *whey : way* (Strong, Cooper 'near alike'), *where : were* (*WSC*), *white : weight* (Cocker), *whey : weigh, wheat : whet : wet, while : wile, who : woo, whom : womb, whine : wine* (Brown), *which : witch, where : were, whet : wet* (anonymous manuscript list). Even this evidence comes chiefly in late lists, above all in Brown, who has many dialectalisms; there are no *wh* : *w* pairings in the majority of the lists, including the best (Hodges has none even in his 'near alike' list, Coles none in the *Schoolmaster* nor Cooper in his 'alike' list).

The change was capable of affecting the group [hw] developed in late ME by the insertion of a glide [w] between initial [h] and ME *ǭ* and *ǭ*; Brown pairs *whole* with *wool*, an undoubted dialectalism.

<small>Note 1: Wyld, loc. cit., cites spellings from the late fifteenth century onwards, but the evidence until 1700 is scanty. He is in error in supposing that the change is due to a voicing of [ʍ] to [w]; such a process would be natural enough, but the evidence shows that [w] develops when *wh-* was still [hw]. Ekwall, § 136, wrongly believes that *wh-* became identical with *w-* by an eighteenth-century change; what happened in the eighteenth century was that the long-existing vulgar pronunciation displaced the other.</small>

<small>Note 2: Wright, § 240, shows that [w] for *wh-* is normal in Southern and Midland dialects and occurs also in Northern; Machyn in the sixteenth century and Brown at the end of the seventeenth are evidence for the use of [w] for *wh-* by Northerners.</small>

<small>Note 3: The development of [hw] to [w] in *whole*, where the [w] is a glide, has as its parallel that of [hj] to [j] in [jə:(r)], &c. 'here' and similar pronunciations which must often arise from forms in which the [j] glide developed while the [h] was still pronounced.</small>

(b) Initial [wl] *becomes* [l]

§ 415. Though Chaucer still has *wlatsum*, *lisp* has *l*-forms from Chaucer onwards and no *wl*-forms after the fourteenth century (see *OED*); the change of [wl] to [l] was evidently completed about 1400 (cf. Jordan, § 162 (1)). The orthoepists give no evidence of the survival of [wl]; *lisp* has always [l] (as, for example, in Hodges).

(c) Initial [wr] *becomes* [r]

§ 416. The loss of [w] in *write*, *wrap*, &c. is due to the tongue being brought into position for [r] too soon; as [r] itself has lip-protrusion, the result is that from the start of the articulation there is produced simply a well-rounded [r] which is not a significantly different sound from any other variety of [r]. Spellings showing the change begin to appear about the middle of the fifteenth century and become common in the sixteenth, as *OED* points out in its valuable note on the group *wr-* (q.v.), but educated speech retained the older pronunciation until the seventeenth century. Retention of [w] is shown by the *Welsh Hymn*, Hart, Bullokar, Gil, Daines, and apparently Wallis (but he may be speaking only of the spelling). Variation between [wr] and [r] occurs in Robinson (who has [wr] nine times in all beside [r] seven times) and Hodges in *EP* (who has [wr] ten times beside [r] twenty-three times). The author of *WSC-RS*, who certainly did not himself use [wr], perhaps betrays a knowledge of a formal pronunciation in which it was still maintained, for he comments on the difficulty of pronouncing [w] before [r], which would seem pointless if no one in fact did so; thus *RS* says that '*w* is not sounded without difficulty' before *r* and that it is 'very little sounded without too much affectation and constraint', and refers to 'the forced sound' of [wr]. Otherwise seventeenth-century evidence shows the loss of [w]. On Robinson and Hodges, *EP*, who vary, see above; the loss alone is shown by Merriott, Strong (in his 'phonetically spelt' list), Young, Cooper, *The Compendious School-Master*, Hawkins, Aickin, *WSC-RS*, Cocker, and Brown, by the 'homophone' lists of Butler, Hodges in *SH-PD* ('alike'), and thirteen later authors, and by J. Willis and fourteen later shorthand-writers, including Ridpath (see Note 1 below). The change in pronunciation in educated speech evidently occurred between 1600 and 1650; after the latter date [wr], insofar as it survived, was abnormal.

Note 1: Wright, § 237, records the retention of [wr] among 'the older generation of dialect speakers' (i.e. in 1905) in Scotland, which explains why the Scot Ridpath marks the omission of *w* as an Anglicism.

Note 2: Brown, in giving 'phonetic spellings' of *wr-*, always gives *hr* as an alternative to *r* (thus *rap* or *hrap* 'wrap'), but this seems merely a stupid extension of Cooper's doctrine that *kn* was *hn*, there being no likelihood that *wr-* was ever voiceless [r̥]; see Vol. I, p. 368.

Note 3: See Jordan, § 162 (1), on the fourteenth-century loss of [w] in the combination [wrʊ].

(d) Initial [kn] *becomes* [n]

§ 417. In OE and ME [k] in the initial group *kn-* in, for example, *knife* had the same pronunciation as before other consonants (e.g. [l] in *cliff*), and is retained as [k] by all sixteenth- and most seventeenth-century orthoepists. The process of loss was that, in order to facilitate transition to the [n] (which is articulated with the point of the tongue, not the back as for [k]), the stop was imperfectly made, so that [k] became the fricative [χ], which in turn passed into [h]; the resulting group [hn] then, by assimilation, became voiceless [n̥], which was finally re-voiced under the influence of the following vowel.

Retention of [kn] is shown by the *Welsh Hymn*, Salesbury, Smith, Hart, Laneham, P. G., Tonkis, Gil, Jonson, Hodges, Coles's *Schoolmaster* (in which, for example, *Nell* and *knell*, *nit* and *knit* are given as rhymes but not as homophones), Strong's 'phonetically spelt' list of monosyllables (which is original), Hawkins, and even the shorthand-writers Dix, Metcalfe, Cartwright, Rich, Bridges, Hopkins, S. Shelton, and Ridpath (some of whom have a special symbol for *kn-*, others write *k* before *n*). Robinson's symbol (that for [n] with the mark for 'initial aspiration' added) may mean either [hn] (if literally interpreted) or [n̥] (compare, for example, [t], regarded as an 'aspirated' form of [d]). Cooper says *kn* is pronounced as '*hn* or *n* aspirated'. His phonetic theory on such combinations being somewhat confused, it is not in all places clear whether he means [hn] or [n̥] (or whether he could distinguish between them); but as in one place he says that *hn* and *hw* are 'simple sounds' we must decide in favour of [n̥] (see Vol. I, p. 296). Brown, following Cooper, says that *k* before *n* is 'but imperfectly pronounced' as *h*, and in his 'phonetically spelt' list gives two transcriptions of all *kn* words, thus *nack* or *hnack* 'knack'.

Simple [n] for *kn-* is shown by *WSC* (but *RS* says only that *k* 'almost loseth its sound' before *n*), Cocker's 'phonetically spelt' list, and Brown's similar list (the transcriptions with *n* probably representing his own pronunciation; see Vol. I, p. 368). The 'homophone' lists have the pairings *knead : need* (Price, Coles's *Eng.–Lat. Dict.*), *knees : neeze* (Fox and Hookes), *knave : nave* (Young, Coles, op. cit., Brown), *knight : night* (Young, Coles, op. cit., *WSC*, Cocker, Brown), *knot : not*, *knead : Ned*, *knew : new*, *known : none* (Brown), *know : no* (Brown, anon. manuscript), and *kneel : neal* (anon. manuscript). The loss of [k] is also shown by the shorthand-writers Everardt and Steel. It is important to observe that [n] for *kn-* is shown only in sources which normally reflect vulgar speech, and then only in a minority of such sources; the entry of this pronunciation into educated StE clearly belongs to the eighteenth century. The normal seventeenth-century pronunciation was still [kn], but the intermediate stages [hn] and/or [n̥] were also in (perhaps rare) use.

Note 1: The lateness of the development is shown by the extreme rarity of spellings with *n* for initial *kn-* (see the *kn-* words in *OED*); but sixteenth-century *n*-forms occur in *knack* sb.² (Surrey, 1540), *knop*, and *knuckle*; *knob* is *nob* as early as Trevisa, *De Prop. Rerum*, but this seems rather a distinct ME formation. Evidence from spellings (later sixteenth century onwards) and puns (e.g. in Shakespeare) is cited by Kökeritz (see Note 2).

Note 2: D. Abercrombie, *Trans. Phil. Soc.* (1948), 14–15, points out that G. W.'s *Magazine* (1703) shows *tn* for initial *kn*, which otherwise is recorded only by foreign sources (cf. H. Kökeritz, *Mather Flint*, pp. 136–52); this has been regarded as a stage in the StE development of *kn* to [n], but in fact represents a variant development, in which [k], instead of becoming a fricative, remains a stop, but is assimilated to [n] (cf. [tl] for initial [kl], § 378 above). This is shown (*a*) by the fact that the evidence of seventeenth-century English sources shows an intelligible phonetic process [kn] > [hn] > [n̥] > [n] in which [tn] has no place, and (*b*) by modern dialectal evidence, which shows [tn] only in the North; G. W. was certainly a Northerner (see Vol. I, p. 266, note 4), and the foreign grammarians, as Kökeritz shows, all derive their statement that *kn* is *tn* ultimately from Festeau, 1672, who seems to have picked up a dialectal pronunciation. Kökeritz himself would explain the phonetic process as being either (1) [kn] > [kŋ̊n] > [ŋ̊n] > [ŋn] (or [ŋn]) > [n] or (2) [kn] > [tn] > [tŋn] > [ŋn] > [n]. He is inclined to reject the second alternative because of the weak (and one might add late) evidence of the [tn] stage, and prefers the first, 'believing that it represents the normal development' (op. cit., p. 151), but in truth it accords even worse with the evidence than the second (despite his attempts to reconcile it with the statements of certain orthoepists) and is unduly complex. One may point out (*a*) that as [ŋ] was a recognized seventeenth-century phoneme, a stage [ŋn] could easily have been described, if it had existed, by saying that in the group *kn-* the *k* was pronounced as *ng*; (*b*) that the voiceless equivalent of [ŋ], assumed in Kökeritz's [ŋ̊n] stage, is treated by Wilkins (Vol. I, p. 255) and Cooper (Vol. I, p. 296) as a theoretical concept, which Cooper explicitly says we do not use. Neither of these alternatives represents the StE process. On the hypotheses of earlier phonologists, which are unsatisfactory, see Kökeritz.

(e) Initial [gn] *becomes* [n]

§ 418. Initial [gn] had two developments which affected educated speech in the sixteenth and seventeenth centuries. In the first the [g] was lost by a direct process of assimilation to [n]; too early opening of the nasal passage would tend to produce [ŋn], which would forthwith become [n]. In the second [gn] by dissimilation becomes [kn], the vibration of the vocal chords being delayed fractionally and coinciding, not with the making of the stop, but with the opening of the nasal passage; thereafter it develops with original *kn-* through [χn] and [hn] to [n̥] and [n].

(i) The former process, which results in early loss of [g], is proved to have occurred by the evidence of authors who give [n] for *gn-* but not for *kn-*. These are Robinson (in *Gnato('s)*), Hodges in *SH-PD* (who gives the 'homophone' list pairing *gnash* : *Nash* but no *kn* : *n* pairings), Coles (who also gives this pairing and in his *Shorthand* says that *g* in *gnat* is 'not at all, or but little and seldom sounded'), Strong (who in his list of monosyllables gives the 'phonetic' spellings *nash* 'gnash', *nat* 'gnat', and *naw* 'gnaw' and also has the *gnash* : *Nash* pairing), and Hawkins (who says that *g* is silent in *gnaw*). On retention of [kn] for *kn-* by these sources see § 417.

(ii) The evidence for the second process is as follows. *Gn* is identified with *kn* by Bullokar in *gnaw* (thrice transcribed with *kn*, against *gn* once); Coote describes *knaw* 'gnaw' and *knat* 'gnat' as the 'barbarous speech of your country people', and is followed by Hunt (in respect of *knat*). Butler varies between *kn* and *gn* in *gnaw*; Hodges in *EP* identifies *gn* with *kn* (which he would seem to have pronounced [kn], his name for the digraph being *knee*). In the 'homophone' lists there occur the pairings *gnat* : *knot* (Butler, Fox and Hookes; but the latter show [n] for *kn-*) and *gnaw(n)* : *know(n)* (Butler, Hodges 'alike'). The further development to [hn] or [n̥] is shown by Cooper followed by Brown (as for *kn-*, q.v.). Complete loss of both *g* and *k* before *n* is shown by *WSC*, Cocker, and Brown (beside *hn*, in his 'phonetically spelt' list; see § 417) and by the 'homophone' list pairings *gnash* : *Nash* (Cooper 'near', Brown), *gnat* : *not* (Brown), and *gnat* : *Nat* (anon. manuscript), to cite examples from lists which also have *kn* : *n* pairings.

(iii) Retention of *gn* as [gn] is shown only by Bullokar (in *gnat* once and in *gnaw* once beside *kn-* thrice), Coote (in *gnaw*), and Butler (in *gnaw*, beside *kn*); but it should be remembered that initial *gn-* was rare in eModE and that words containing it are seldom recorded.

Note 1: Smith's *nar* 'ringere more canum' probably does not show loss of [g] from *gnar*, but is a variant echoic word; see *OED*, s.v. *narr*. On Hayward's description of *gn* in *gnash*, &c., which seems an unintelligent adoption of a description of French *gn*, see Vol. I, p. 324.

Note 2: *OED* records *kn-* spellings of *gnat* from the fourteenth and of *gnaw* from the fifteenth century onwards.

Note 3: Evidence for a pronunciation [dn] for initial *gn-* is given by Sewel, 1705, followed by Brommenhaer, 1738, and Smith, 1758 (see Kökeritz, *Mather Flint*, pp. 139–41, 143), but is unconfirmed by modern dialectal evidence and is somewhat suspect (since it may be an alteration of the statement that *kn* is pronounced *dn*, given by Offelen, 1687, and later sources and itself probably an alteration of Festeau's statement that *kn* is pronounced *tn*). But a change of [gn] to [dn] would be parallel to that of [kn] to [tn] and analogous to that of

[gl] to [dl], and may well have occurred; it would, however, not have been a stage in the StE development, but a dialectal side-development (cf. § 417, Note 2). Kökeritz (op. cit., p. 151) proposes as alternative explanations of the development of *gn* either (1) [gn] > [gŋn] > [ŋn] > [n] or (2) [gn] > [dn] > [n], of which he prefers the first; it is essentially that given above to explain the process of immediate loss of the *g*, but we have also to account for the evidence identifying *gn* with *kn* given by sources which did not pronounce *kn* as [n] (let alone as [ŋn]; see § 417, Note 2) and for the evidence that *gn* could be pronounced [hn] or [n̥].

VOCALIZATION OF CONSONANTS

(1) *Loss of* [w]

§ 419. The consonant [w] is closely allied to the vowel [u(:)], and is only finely differentiated from it—partly by closer lip-rounding (especially if [u(:)] itself follows), partly by being a weakly stressed vowel-glide (cf. D. Jones, *Outline of English Phonetics*, § 800 seq.). It can therefore very easily become [u], and if it does (*a*) is absorbed by a preceding or following [u(:)], which it may lengthen, or (*b*) forms with a preceding vowel a falling diphthong, or (*c*) becomes a weakly stressed vowel, which in hiatus before another (which will necessarily be more strongly stressed) is liable to syncope or aphesis and will tend to be lost. Vocalization of [w] after *ŭ* and other vowels was a regular ME change, producing results that have already been discussed in Chapters VII and IX; vocalization in late ME after consonants produced an unstressed [u] which is discussed in Chapter X (§ 295). Here we are concerned with vocalization and loss of prevocalic [w] by processes (*a*) and (*c*) described above.

Note: ModE vocalization of post-consonantal [w], without loss, appears to be the explanation of the pronunciation [bʊʋi] recorded for *boy* by Gil and Cooper; it is a variant of the [bwʊi] recorded by Wallis, and seems likely to be developed from it. Cf. also Hodges's transcription of [wəi] < ME *ui* by symbols which should strictly mean [ʊəi] (see Vol. I, p. 174, footnote 3).

(*a*) *Loss before* [u(:)]

§ 420. (i) Loss in ME occurs in *such* and *suster* (see Jordan, § 162 (2)); the change is regularly carried through and is shown by the orthoepists in *such*. But in *swurd* 'sword' it commonly fails, probably because of the analogical influence of the *swerd* form; [w] is retained, despite its being followed by ME *ŭ*, by Levins (probably), Laneham (if his *oo* stands for [ʊ], as it commonly does, and not [uː]; he also has *sweards*), Gil, Butler (beside the [uː] form, which he has more often), Daines (probably; the [w] is certainly retained), Hodges, Price, and Poole (probably). The loss is not shown by any orthoepist who can be proved to have ME *ŭ*, but compare the fourteenth-century spelling *surd* (see *OED*). Loss before ME *ū* occurs in *swoon*, which derives ultimately from OE *geswōgen*, whence there develop a form with undiphthongized [uː], as if < ME *ǭ*, and another with [ʌu] from

ME *ū* which becomes ModE *s(w)oun(d)*(cf. *OED*, s.v. *swoon* vb.). The form *soun(d)* with loss of [w] before ME *ū* (and normally with excrescent [d]) occurs from the late fourteenth century (see *OED*, s.vv. *sound* sb.[4] and vb.[4]) and is recorded by Willis and Merriott, by the 'homophone' lists of Butler, Hodges 'alike' (probably for the vb., the sb. having [u:]; cf. Coles below), Wharton, Price, Ellis, Fox and Hookes, Coles (*Schoolmaster* and *Eng.–Lat. Dict.*, in the latter only in the vb., the sb. having [u:]—an artificial distinction), Strong (in the vb.), Young, Richardson, Cooper 'near alike' (in the p.t., spelt *swoond*; evidently he has no excrescent [d] and therefore cannot pair the infinitive, as he does the p.t., with *sound*), *The Compendious Schoolmaster*, *WSC*, Cocker, and Brown, and by the shorthand-writer Everardt. Similar loss of [w] before abnormal late ME *ū* < ME *ǭ* must be presumed to account for *WSC*'s [ʌu] in *owze* (unglossed, but apparently *ooze* 'sap' < OE *wōs*, which has the spelling *owze* from the sixteenth to the eighteenth century; see *OED*).

(ii) Loss in ModE before [u:] < ME *ǭ* may occur in *ooze* 'sap', *ooze* 'slime', *swore*, *sworn*, *sword*, and *swoon*, there being no ME evidence of loss of [w] in these forms; but there seems no sufficient reason to separate them from other analogous words in which the loss certainly occurred in ME itself before ME *ǭ* and ME *ǭ*, and they are therefore treated in § 421 below. In *swoon*, however, the loss is certainly later than 1400.

Note: Loss of initial [w] by vocalization before and absorption into a following [u(:)], as in [umən] 'woman', is not a normal StE change. Wyld, op. cit., p. 296, cites fifteenth-century evidence and the Welsh orthoepist Jones (1701). On the transcriptions of the *Welsh Hymn* and Salesbury see Vol. I, pp. 6 and 13. Hart's transcriptions should not be taken as showing this change; see Vol. I, pp. 86–87. Loss of initial [w] before [u(:)] is primarily a Scottish and Western development but is not confined to these dialects; see Wright, § 236. Dickens shows it in the Cockney speech of the Wellers.

(b) Loss before other vowels

§ 421. (i) In stressed syllables [w] is lost by vocalization and aphesis before ME *ǭ* in *ooze* 'sap' (OE *wōs*) and *ooze* 'slime' (ME *wǭse* < *wǭse* < OE *wāse*); Gil shows it in *ooze* vb. (ME *wǭsen* formed on OE *wōs*) and Hodges in an unglossed *ooze* which may be either word. Similar loss before unraised ME *ǭ* is shown by Gil's [oːz] 'slime' < ME *wǭse* (cf. the spellings *oase*, &c. cited by *OED*). In these cases evidence of the loss is not found before 1400, but loss by syncope between a preceding consonant and a following back vowel occurs in ME itself—most regularly when the consonant-group is one that is difficult to pronounce, as in *thwǭng* > *thǭng* 'thong' (cf. Jordan, § 162 (2)), but also in other cases. In *swoon(d)* 'swoon' the loss is first recorded in the sixteenth century (cf. the spelling *soond* recorded by *OED*, s.v. *sound* sb.[4]) and must be later than the diphthongization of ME *ū*, which the [w] inhibits. The form [suːn] is recorded by the 'homophone' lists of Hodges 'alike' (for the sb.), Coles (*Eng.–Lat. Dict.*, for the sb., not the vb.), and Young (beside [sʌund]); Brown's 'phonetically spelt' list has the spelling *soond* glossed 'swound'. *Sword* (when pronounced with [uː] < ME *ǭ*) has [w] in Butler but shows loss of it in Cooper followed by Aickin. *Sworn* (for which *OED* records the sixteenth-century spellings *soren* and *sorne*) is [suːrn] in Hodges (*EP*) and Cooper (followed by Aickin). In the 'homophone' lists *swore* is equated with *sore* and/or *soar* by Hodges ('alike'), Fox and Hookes, Coles, Strong, *WSC-RS*, and Brown; in Hodges the vowel is probably [uː], but in Coles it is certainly [oː] (which might, however, be by lowering before *r* of sixteenth-century [uː]). Cooper has the series *sour* : *swore* : *sower* : *sore*, which probably depends on [oːr] in all the words. *Swollen* is [soːln̩] in Hodges (cf. the sixteenth-century spelling *solne* recorded by *OED*); here loss has certainly occurred before ME *ǭ*, and there seems no reason, despite the late date of the evidence, not to assign the loss to ME itself. *Two* is recorded without [w] from Robert of Gloucester (1297) onwards; it is [tuː] in Salesbury (probably), Smith, and some twenty later sources; but Bullokar gives [twuː]. *Twopence* is *tuppence* in Coles's 'phonetically spelt' list (followed by Strong and Young). *Who* and its inflexional forms and derivatives are already recorded without *w* in the thirteenth and fourteenth centuries (see *OED*, svv.). Loss of [w] is shown by Daines (before [uː]), Hodges (thirty times, before [uː] in *who(se)* but [oː] in *whom*), Merriott (who has [hoːm] 'whom'), Cooper (before [uː]), *WSC*, Aickin, and the shorthand-writer Everardt; Coles, like Hodges, has [uː] in *who(se)* but [oː] in *whom* and shows loss of [w] in the latter, probably also in the former. But [w] is kept by Smith, Laneham, Hart, Bullokar, Robinson, Gil, Sherwood, Hodges (once only, perhaps an error), *The English Scholemaster* (1646), Wilkins, and the shorthand-writers T. Shelton and Rich (followed by Botley); the Northerner Brown's 'homophone' list has *who* : *woo* and *whom* : *womb* (beside pairings which show loss of [w]). Evidently StE normally kept pronunciations developed from the ME form which retained [w] until about 1650; [huː], &c. entered educated speech, it would seem, about 1640. *Quoth*, for which *OED* records the fourteenth-century forms *cope*, *coth*, and *cuth*, is [kɒþ] in Gil (once, beside [kwɒþ]), Butler, Daines, *The English Schole-master* (1646), and probably *WSC* (ME *ŏ* by shortening of ME *ǭ* or by blending with ME *quŏd*), and [kʌþ] in the Northerner Brown (ME *ŭ* by shortening of ME *ǭ* by raising of ME *ǭ*); but [kwɒþ] occurs in Gil (five times) and [kwoːþ] (ME *ǭ* without shortening) in Robinson and probably in Poole (who rhymes it with *oath*, &c.). *Quote* is [koːt] in Hodges's *EP* and in the 'homophone' lists of Hodges ('alike') and ten later authors, including Coles (*Schoolmaster*), and Cooper ('alike'); but in this case the explanation is probably OF *coter*, *cotter* (see *OED*). See further Notes 1–5 below.

(ii) In unstressed syllables [w] is lost, regardless of the nature of the following vowel, both when it is preceded by another consonant belonging to the same syllable and when it is itself initial in the syllable. It is to be observed that in all cases the following vowel is one that originally had secondary stress and would therefore have been more strongly stressed than the [u] developed from [w], which is in consequence syncopated. The loss begins in the twelfth century (see Jordan, § 162 (3)) in *Canterbury* (< *Cantwara-*) and *York* (< **3orwīk*), and is found in *upward* from *c.* 1200, both in the East and the West (*Trinity Homilies* and MS Bodley 17 of *St. Katherine*; see *OED*); in other cases evidence does not begin until after 1400, but in general the change is to be regarded as belonging to ME.

Answer retains [w] in Cheke, Hart, Gil, and Hunt (probably), but its loss is shown by Robinson, Hodges, Coles, Strong, Young, Cooper, *WSC-RS*, Aickin, and Brown and the shorthand-writers Bridges, Hopkins, and Nicholas. *Conquer* (which has ME [kw]; see *OED*) is unfortunately rarely recorded; retention of [w] is shown by Bullokar and Butler, but its loss must have occurred at much the same date as in the analogous *answer*. In *conquest* the retention of [w] (in Robinson as in PresE) is doubtless due to the longer survival of end-stressed forms of the sb. than of the vb.; cf. PresE [e] in *conquest*, [ə] in *conquer*. In *languish* lack of [w] is shown by Strong and Young, but the cause may be reduction of OF [yi], when unstressed, to [i] (cf. *circuit, conduit*). See also Note 7 below.

Loss of [w] when initial in the syllable is shown in (*un*)*toward* by Coles, Strong, Young, and Cooper, in *backward* by Merriott, in *forward* by Brown, in *bulwark* by the shorthand-writer J. Willis, in *Southwark* by Hodges, Coles, Strong, Young, Cocker, and Brown, in *Norwich* by J. Willis and Everardt, in *Ipswich* by Everardt, and in *huswives* by Hodges (once) and Brown (but Laneham and Hodges (once) retain [w]). The loss shown in *pennuth* 'pennyworth' (Coles, Strong, Young, and Cocker) and in *hah-puth* 'halfpennyworth' (Coles) differs only in that the process is absorption of [u] < [w] by the following ME *ŭ*.

Note 1: In *two, who*, &c., *quoth*, and perhaps *quote*, the greater frequency of the loss of [w] may be due to weak stress in the sentence; cf. its loss in weak forms of *would*, as in Hart (see Vol. I, p. 87, note 1). The starting-point of the various forms of *quoth* is here assumed to be ME *ǭ* < ON *á* in the p.t.pl. (see § 339, Note).

Note 2: For spellings showing loss of [w] in the words cited under (i) above see Wyld, op. cit., p. 296; *sor* 'swore' occurs in the *Paston Letters* (1451).

Note 3: *OED* regards *to* 'two' as occurring in the *Peterborough Chronicle*, anno 1137. But the phrase *& to munekes him namen* beyond all doubt means 'and the monks took him' (OE *þā*, with assimilation of *þ* to *t* after *and* and with *ǭ* < OE *ā*, a change shown in the last continuation of the *Chronicle* in unstressed words and syllables); cf. *& to other æuez men* (s.a. 1138), which, if the word-order is correct, means 'and the other loyal men'.

Note 4: Variation in AN between [gw] and [g] affects the English forms of *guerdon* (see *OED*); [gw] is recorded by Mulcaster, Butler, Jonson, Hodges, *The English Scholemaster*, and *RS*, but [g] apparently by *WSC*. For (the duke of) *Guise* the pronunciation [gwəiz] is recorded by Bullokar and Mulcaster, and represents a correct anglicization of the French form (see Vol. I, p. 115). But Baret does not distinguish *Guise* from the common noun *guise*; this pronunciation with [g] is probably a mere error, but is clearly old.

§ 421]   LOSS OF CONSONANTS   983

Note 5: Loss of initial [w] before vowels other than [u(:)], though rare, does occur in other words than those cited above; Jones (1701) records that *woad* may be pronounced *ode* and that *w* may be silent in *woven* (see Wyld, op. cit., p. 296). Wright, § 236, records its loss in western dialects in *want* (a mole); but in all his other instances it is lost before [u(:)] (e.g. *week*, *with*, &c. really show loss before [ʊ]; see his Index).

Note 6: For a few spellings illustrating the change discussed under (ii) above see Wyld, op. cit., pp. 296–7; see also *OED*, s.vv.

Note 7: *Language*, being an adoption of OF *langage*, normally lacks [w] in ME; so Hart and Bullokar (normally). But it is early affected, in spelling and pronunciation, by Latin *lingua* (cf. the fourteenth-century spelling *langwag* recorded by *OED*); hence [gw] in Bullokar (as a rarer variant), Mulcaster, Gil (who actually gives *u*), Butler, Hodges, *The English Schole-master*, Strong, Young, Cooper, and Brown. Similarly *banquet* (OF *banc*+*et*) should have [k], as in Levins, Laneham, Hodges, Strong, and Young; but Coles gives the 'phonetic' spelling *bang-quet* (contrast *blang-ket* 'blanket'), which shows the beginning of the PresE spelling-pronunciation. Cooper says that the word is *spelt* either *banquet* or *banket*.

(2) *Loss of* [j]

§ 422. The vocalization of [j], as a phonetic process, is exactly analogous to that of [w] (see § 419 above). Post-vocalic [j], when it becomes [i], is absorbed by a preceding [i(:)] or forms a diphthong with other vowels; the results of this process have been considered in previous chapters. Post-consonantal [j] in unstressed syllables varies with $\breve{\imath}$ in late ME, and this $\breve{\imath}$, when in hiatus before another vowel, is subject to syncope (see Chapter X above). But [j] differs from [w] in that, instead of being subject to vocalization and syncope after consonants in stressed and secondarily stressed syllables, it undergoes the assimilations described in §§ 387–91 above. Here we are concerned with the vocalization and loss of a [j] which is initial in the word or syllable. This is not a StE development and is recorded only by sources which reflect vulgar or dialectal speech (except in the special case of *yield*).

Loss by vocalization and aphesis before ME $\breve{e}$ occurs in *yard*, &c. (see Note 2 below). Loss before ME $\breve{\imath}$ (in all cases by raising of ME $\breve{e}$) occurs in *yet* in Price and the 'homophone' lists of Hodges ('near alike'), Price, Merriott, and *WSC*, in *yesterday* in the shorthand-writer Bridges (who uses the spelling *istrday*), and in *yeast* in *WSC* (who equates the word with *is't*); the loss in these cases may belong either to ME or to ModE. Loss before ME $\bar{e}$ occurs in *yield* in the *Welsh Hymn* and in Gil (once, in both editions, beside retained [j] four times); in this word it is aided by weakened stress in the phrase *God yield* (*you*). Loss before ME $\bar{ẹ}$ may also be shown by the 'homophone' list pairing *yeast : east* given by Hodges ('near alike'), Wharton, Price, Fox and Hookes, Coles (*Eng.-Lat. Dict.*), Strong, Young, *RS*, and Cocker; *yeast* occurs without [j] in modern dialects, but equally *east* shows 'parasitic' [j] and on the whole it seems more likely that the latter is intended. The evidence of the modern dialects, which have loss of [j] only before [iː] or [iə], suggests that it does not occur before ME $\bar{ẹ}$ and $\bar{ę}$ until they have changed to [iː]. In all these cases, then, the process is absorption of [i] < [j] by a following [i(ː)].

In *beyond* the loss shown by the shorthand-writers J. Willis and Everardt appears to involve absorption by the preceding [ɪ], since the modern dialects show retention of [j] in *yon* and *yonder* when ME *ŏ* follows, though they show loss in *beyond*. Loss before a back vowel is shown only by Price's 'homophone' list series *yolk* : *yoke* : *oak*, which is unsupported by modern dialect evidence but may be accepted as showing aphesis of [i] < [j]; cf. the spelling *oak* recorded by *OED* from a late fourteenth-century *Primer* for *yoke* vb. (under (7)).

Loss of initial [j] in a syllable with secondary stress is recorded in *churchyard* by the shorthand-writer Everardt; cf. *God yield* (*you*), discussed above.

Note 1: The 'homophone' list pairing *eat* : *yet* given by *WSC* under *e* seems intended to show 'parasitic' [j] in *eat* (thus [jet], recorded by Wright), in contrast to the pairing *yet* : *it* under *y*, which shows loss of [j] in *yet*. The *Welsh Hymn*'s *i* 'ye' is purely dialectal.

Note 2: For spellings showing loss of [j] in these words see *OED*; the earliest appears to be the fourteenth- and fifteenth-century *yt(t)* 'yet'. Kihlbom, pp. 78–79, records *elde* 'yield' (altered from *eve* 'yeve, give'), *erdys* 'yards', *eme* (< OE *gēme*), and *erthe* (< OE *gerd*), all from fifteenth-century texts, but misinterprets them as inverted spellings showing prosthetic [j]. With *erdys* compare Everardt's evidence on *churchyard*. Cf. also the verb *earn* 'desire, sorrow', which *OED* is undoubtedly correct in deriving from *yearn*.

Note 3: For modern dialectal evidence see Wright, § 248 and Index; loss of [j] occurs mainly in Western and South-western dialects but is not confined to them. There is no evidence of loss before back vowels, except in the special case of *beyond*; loss in *yonder* occurs only in the form *yender* or *yinder* (see Wright's Index)—perhaps primarily in *yinder*, with analogical extension to *yender*.

(3) *Vocalization of* [v] *and* [f] *to* [u]

§ 423. In ME, preconsonantal [v] becomes [w] by relaxation of the articulation, and is then vocalized to [u] in, for example, *hawk* < *havk-* (see § 400, Note); the change is analogous to the South-eastern dialectal change of intervocalic [v] to [w] but is more widespread and is regularly shown by the orthoepists, whereas the 'Cockney' [w] is not recorded.

It is of some importance to notice that a similar change, in dialectal and vulgar speech, affected [f] before [t]; the process, to argue from the analogy of [v], must have been that it first became voiceless [ʍ], was then voiced because of the influence of the preceding vowel, and so finally changed from [w] to [u]. The development is shown by the Scottish orthoepist Ridpath, who says that *f* may be omitted from *after* and *soft*, thus *ater* and *sot*, and marks these reductions as Anglicisms. As Ridpath (like other shorthand-writers but for phonetic and not conventional reasons) uses *a* for ME *au* and *o* for ME *ou*, his *ater* and *sot* may be taken as representing late ME or (less probably) eModE *auter and *sout. The form *auternoone* 'afternoon' does in fact occur in a text of *c.* 1578 (see § 43, Note 2), and from the sixteenth century onwards *after* rhymes on ME *au* or sounds which become identical with it (e.g. with *daughter* or *water*; cf. Note 2 below). In the modern dialects (see Wright, Index) *after* is [ɑ:tə(r)] in the Midlands and South, in dialects for which [ɑ:] is recorded in words which must have ME *au* (see Wright, §§ 38-40, 49), [æ:tə(r)] in Southern dialects for which [æ:] < ME *au* is recorded (except that [æ:] occurs in *after* in Kent, for which I can find no record of [æ:] < undoubted ME *au*), [ætə(r)] by shortening of [æ:tə(r)] in Wiltshire, and [ɒ:tə(r)] beside [ɑ:tə(r)] in Northamptonshire. Similarly *soft* is [sɑ:t] in Northamptonshire, Gloucestershire, Hampshire, Wiltshire, Dorset, and Somerset (cf. [krɑ:t] 'croft' Gloucestershire, [lɑ:t] 'loft' Somerset); here again we have [ɑ:] < ME *au*, developed by ME unrounding of *ŏ* to *ă* and the subsequent change of [f] to [u]. Wright records no dialectal pronunciations which have [o:] from ME *ou* < *ŏf*, as shown by Ridpath.

Note 1: All the dialects which have [ɑ:] < ME *au* in *soft*, &c. show the change of ME *ŏ* to *ă* before the labial [p]; see Wright, § 83.

Note 2: The views that *after* owes its [ɑ:], &c. to loss of [f] after lengthening of ME *ă*, or to the improbable process of 'compensatory lengthening' in consequence of the loss of [f], must be rejected, in view of (*a*) the sixteenth-century spelling *auter* 'after' referred to above, and (*b*) their failure to provide an adequate phonetic explanation of the process by which [f] was lost. Shakespeare's rhyme of *after* with *daughter, caught her, slaughter,* and *halter* must, because of the last word, depend on the reflex of ME *au* (with loss of [χ] in *daughter,* &c. and of [l] in *halter*).

Note 3: Miss A. H. Forester informs me of a spelling *haufeter* 'after' in the *Cely Papers*, which might show blending of *auter* and the normal orthography but is open to other explanations.

Note 4: On the 'homophone' list pairings *oft : ought* and *soft : sought* see § 34 (1): they seem likely to depend on [f] < [χ] in *ought* and *sought*.

(4) *Vocalization of* [ç] *and* [χ]

§ 424. The consonants [ç] and [χ] used in pronouncing the conventional digraph *gh* after front and back vowels respectively were vocalized (doubtless through the transient intermediate stages [j] and [ɜ] > [w]) to [i] and [u]. The change was capable of occurring either in ME or in ModE; if it occurred in ME, the groups [ıç] and [uχ], having become [i:] and [u:], were identified with ME *ī* and ME *ū* and shared their diphthongization, but if it occurred in ModE they remained as [i:] and [u:]. The present StE pronunciation of these two groups is obviously of the former type (ME vocalization), and the history of the sounds in the sixteenth and seventeenth centuries is simply a conflict between the unchanged pronunciations [ıç] and [uχ] (which seem originally to have been typical of educated StE) and the pronunciations [əi] and [ʌu] < late ME [i:] and [u:] entering StE from vulgar and dialectal speech (see §§ 140-3 and 177 above); there is no reason to doubt that the same is true of cases in which [ç] was preceded by ME *ai* (*ẹi*) and [χ] by ME *ou* and *au*. Indeed, it is demonstrable that vocalization of [ç] and [χ] after ME *ai*, *ou*, and *au* was earlier than monophthongization of these diphthongs, for otherwise it would have produced new diphthongs [ɛi], [ou], and [ɒu], of which there is no trace (unless we see a sign of such a development in Cooper's inclusion of *eight* among the four words in which alone, he says, the diphthong [æi] occurs—but this would be a false interpretation). ModE vocalization does however occur in Northern and NMidland dialects, giving [i:] < ME [iç] and [u:] < ME [uχ] (see Wright, § 77, and Index, s.v. *drought*).

In general the older StE mode of pronunciation in which [ç] and [χ] were retained is shown: thus—in addition to Welsh sources, i.e. the *Welsh Hymn*, Salesbury, and Owen—by Smith, Hart, Baret, Bullokar, Tonkis (a Midlander), Gil, Sherwood, Jonson, and Newton, and the shorthand-writer J. Willis (1602). But there is occasional loss in Smith, and Bullokar and Tonkis use [ç] in words which by etymology should not have it— probably owing to variation in those that should; on these three sources see § 141 (*a*). Cheke and Laneham normally retain the conventional digraph *gh*, but misuse it (see loc. cit.). The mode of pronunciation in which [ç] and [χ] were lost (or in which [χ] > [f]) is shown by Robinson (except that [χ] sometimes remains), Butler (but [χ] remains), the shorthand-writers T. Shelton, Dix, and Metcalfe, Hodges, and some twenty-five later sources, including the Scot Ridpath, who marks the omission of *gh* as an Anglicism.

The evidence of certain sources requires slightly more detailed consideration. Smith, who shows variation after ME *ī*, is a native of Essex. Bullokar is now known to be a native of Sussex. Coote, a Suffolk schoolmaster, says that *gh* is 'of most men but little sounded', that in final position (in *plough*, *slough*, and *bough*) 'some countries sound them fully, others not at all', but 'the truest is, both to write and pronounce them'; *dauter* 'daughter' is 'the barbarous speech of your country people'. He is somewhat inconsistent; see Vol. I, pp. 35–36 above. Robinson shows variation between retention and loss of [χ] between ME *au* and [t], and regular retention of final [χ] after ME *au* in *though*; when [χ] is retained so is the diphthongal pronunciation of ME *au*, an indication of the conservative nature of the pronunciation. Butler shows [χ], as a variant to [f], in *laugh*, *cough*, *tough*, *enough*, and *daughter*, but shows no sign of [ç]. Daines, another Suffolk schoolmaster, varies, but seems to know [ç] in *sigh* and [χ] in *tough* (see Vol. I, p. 334). Willis shows retention of [χ] after ME *ou* in *dough*, &c. (see Vol. I, p. 427), but not of ME [ç]. Wallis says that [χ] (by which he means also [ç]) was formerly used in English but is now almost completely omitted, except by Northerners and especially the Scots (see Vol. I, pp. 231–2). Newton retains [χ] in *nought*, *thought*, *though*, and *rough*, but gives no evidence on [ç]. Price, *VO*, shows [ç] or [χ] in *sigh*, *although*, and *almighty* and as a Westernism in words like *cough*, *tough*, *laugh*, and *daughter* which (he says) have [f]; in *Eng. O.* he adds *draught* and *trough* to the words like *sigh* in which *gh* is pronounced, as he says, like *h*. Here we have probably to do with Western dialectal pronunciation. Holder recognizes [χ] as an English sound in *through* (see Vol. I, p. 263). Richardson, a Northerner, insists on [χ] not [f] in *rough, enough, laugh, cough*, &c. (see Vol. I, p. 383). At the end of the century, in 1691, Ray still speaks of *gh* being pronounced as *h* as well as being 'double *f*' or silent (see Vol. I, p. 189).

It would appear from this evidence that the older mode of pronunciation in which [ç] and [χ] were kept was still normal in the sixteenth century among educated speakers, though the other is also shown, especially by those, like Smith and Coote, who have Eastern associations; but that the originally vulgar or dialectal pronunciation in which [ç] and [χ] were vocalized and absorbed by the preceding vowel (or in which [χ] became [f]) was normal in StE from early in the seventeenth century, though the other remained, apparently even after 1650 (though the late evidence is chiefly Western or Northern). It would seem that loss of [ç] was more common than that of [χ], and so affected StE rather more rapidly. Of special interest is the evidence of Sherwood, who in 1632 expresses a preference for [iç] in *light*, &c., but says that there is another pronunciation [əi], 'prononciation moderne, et fort usitée à Londres et ailleurs'; it is about this time that the balance, even in educated speech, shifts.

The sounds used by those who retained them were undoubtedly still [ç] and [χ]; the English pronunciation of *gh* is identified with Welsh *ch* by the *Welsh Hymn*, Salesbury, and Owen (1605), with Scottish *ch* by Salesbury and implicitly by Wallis, with German *ch* by Salesbury and Owen, and with Spanish *g* before *e* by Owen; Richardson says English *gh* is little different from Dutch *gh*. On Wallis's phonetic analysis of Welsh and German *ch* and the Northern pronunciation of English *gh* see Vol. I, pp. 231–2; though confused, it amounts to [χ]. Wilkins merely follows Wallis (see pp. 255–6). Lodwick correctly analyses Dutch *ch* in *dach* (presumably intended by Richardson's *gh*) as [χ]. But the traditional analysis of the English *gh* is that it is *h*, a 'simple aspiration': so in Smith, Hart, Baret, Bullokar, Daines, Jonson, Price, and Ray; Wallis and Richardson are both affected by this identification. It has been taken as showing a weakening of [ç] and [χ], but quite mistakenly; what it means is that [h], [ç], and [χ] were apprehended as contextual variants of the one phoneme, [h] being used before vowels, [ç] after front vowels, [χ] after back vowels—a correct enough view, especially as [ç] is in fact often used for [h] before [j] in, for example, *hue* or before [i(:)]. Wallis, who against his phonetic theory is driven to identify the Scottish pronunciation of *gh* with *h*, actually analyses *h* as the voiceless equivalent of [j], i.e. as [ç]. (Similarly in OE [ç] and [χ] were members of the [h] phoneme, as the spelling shows; but in eME they were commonly regarded as variants of [j] and [ʒ] respectively, and in consequence were spelt *ȝ* or in some texts *g*.) That the identification with

[h], though justified on phonemic grounds, was in fact inaccurate is shown by the evidence of the shorthand-writer J. Willis, of Gil, and of Holder. Willis (1602) describes *gh* in *though*, *night*, and *borough* as a 'thick aspiration'; so *h* in *ah* and *oh*, which, he says, are pronounced as if *agh* and *ogh*. Gil identifies English *gh* with Greek χ, *ch* (which, though of no direct evidential value, shows that he regarded *gh* as having a distinct sound), whereas *h* is identified with the 'rough breathing', and in his reformed spelling he provides a separate letter ħ for [ç] and [χ] (which of course he does not distinguish, as they are undoubtedly mere contextual variants). Holder distinguishes a glottal spirant, and says that 'our *gh* (as in *Through*) has something of it, being more than a bare Aspiration, if strongly pronounced' (see Vol. I, p. 263). There is in fact no reason to suppose that in modern StE there was any 'weakening' of [ç] and [χ] as part of a process of gradual evanescence; the pronunciations in which these sounds were used were simply displaced by others in which they had disappeared in ME.

Note 1: For early evidence of loss of [ç] and [χ] see Wyld, op. cit., pp. 305–6, and Jordan, § 295, Anm.; most of it is from Eastern texts (cf. § 140 above). No reliance is to be placed on *broute* 'brought' cited by Wyld from Laȝamon, as it is presumably an Anglo-Norman spelling, and *naut* 'naught' cited from *Hali Meiðhad* is a special case, developed from *nawit* (a thirteenth- and fourteenth-century form recorded by *OED*) which shows loss of [ç] in the unstressed syllable of *nawiht* (and not of [χ], as Wyld takes it). The true evidence begins in the late fourteenth and early fifteenth centuries.

Note 2: The apparent loss of final [ç] and [χ] in authors who normally retain them is a special case. Thus lack of [ç] is shown in *nigh* by the *Welsh Hymn* and Gil (once, beside [ç] four times), in *neigh* by Smith, in *high* by Gil (four times, beside [ç] fourteen times), and in *weighs* by Gil; but these forms show the normal ME vocalization of [j] < OE *g* (*hnǣgan* 'neigh', *wegan* 'weigh'; *nȳ-* < *nĕg-* and *hȳ-* < *hĕg-*, late OE oblique stems of *nēh* and *hēh*). Similarly the apparent loss of [χ] in *bough*, *plough*, and *rough* (as, for example, in Butler in *bough* and *plough*, despite his retention of [χ], and in Daines—see Vol. I, p. 334) is due to ME vocalization of ME [w] (OE oblique stems *bōg-*, *plōg-*, *rūw-*). On *higher* without [ç] see § 143 above.

(5) *Vocalization and loss of* [l]

§ 425. In the early fifteenth century [l] was vocalized to [u] after ME *ŭ* or after a diphthong ending in [u] (i.e. ME *au* and *ou*) and then absorbed by the preceding vowel or diphthong. The change was later than diphthongization of ME *ă* and *ŏ* to *au* and *ou* before *l*, and must therefore also be later than the development of ME *ŭ* to *ū* before *l* + consonant—changes which are due to the development of a [u] glide before back [l]. On the other hand it is earlier than fronting of ME *ā*, since the dialectal monophthongization of ME *au* to [a:] produced in *psalm*, *half*, &c. a sound which was identified with ME *ā* (see § 104 above); this development proves that even in cases in which loss of [l] is not recorded until ModE (notably in the group *-ălf*; see Jordan, § 292 A(II)), it must nevertheless have occurred at the beginning of the fifteenth century.

(a) *After late ME* au *and* ou

Loss after late ME *au* and *ou* and before [m] (as in *psalm, qualm,* and *holm*), [k] (as in *walk, talk, folk,* and *yolk*), [f] (as in *half, calf,* &c.), and [v] (as in *halves, calves,* &c.) is a regular feature of present StE and is normally shown in the seventeenth century. Gil says that *l* is more often silent in *folk, half, talk,* and *walk,* but that not all the educated drop the *l,* which he therefore retains in his spelling; some learned men, he says, read, and at times speak, thus. But in fact he gives transcriptions without *l* in *chalk* (once), *stalk* (once), *halfpenny,* and *walked* (so 1619 edition, Bodleian copy and that formerly belonging to Luick; 1621 retains [l]), in addition to those given where he discusses the variation of pronunciation. Daines in one place says 'some' omit the *l*, in another that it is 'often omitted'; the 'Orthoepie... is in a manner indifferent, equall in the ballance of custom'. Wallis, in observing that *l* is often lost, continues 'nec semper tamen nec ab omnibus'. Apart from these authors, retention of [l] is shown by Bullokar after late ME *au* in *alms, behalf, half, talk,* and *walk*; but there is apparently some degree of artificiality in his pronunciation. Robinson retains [l] in *walk, talk,* and *balk*. Otherwise loss is shown, by Gil (as above), Butler, Daines (as above), Hodges, Howell, Wallis (as above), and fifteen later authors, in addition to seven shorthand-writers (T. Shelton onwards) and seven 'homophone' lists (Hodges onwards). Evidence for the loss when it is succeeded by the change of *au* to *ā* will be found in § 104 (2) above.

Loss before [n] in *won't* 'will not' (see Note 4), *shan't* 'shall not', and *Lincoln* is assisted by weak stress. Coles and Cooper record *won't*, the latter as 'barbarous speaking'; loss in *Lincoln* is shown by Price, Young, Lye, *WSC*, and Cocker. Dialectally loss occurs before [n] in stressed syllables (Jordan, loc. cit.).

Loss before [t] is not normal in StE, and is shown only by Wallis in *malt* and *shalt*, the Northerner Poole (if this be the correct explanation of his rhymes of *halt* and *shalt* with *fault*; see Vol. I, pp. 436–7), Coles (who similarly rhymes *halt, malt, salt,* and *shalt* with *fault*), and the Northerner Brown (in *falter, halter, salt,* and *colt*). The shorthand-writer J. Willis (1602) also shows it in *shalt*, where it is probably assisted by weak stress.

Before [p] Daines shows variation between loss and retention of [l] in *scalp* (with late ME *au*); Hodges also shows loss in *scalp(s)* in *EP*, and in *holp* 'helped' in his 'alike' list in *SH-PD*. Similar loss before [b] occurs in *Holborn*, where it is shown by Price, Coles, Strong, Young, Lye, *WSC*, Cocker, and Brown; for loss before a consonant not belonging to the same syllable, cf. *Colman*, in which Daines says *l* is silent.

Dialectal loss before [s] in *bolster* is shown in the Northerner Brown's 'homophone' list.

(b) After late ME ū

Loss after late ME *ū* (normally < earlier *ŭ*) occurs in *scowk* 'skulk' in Barbour (see Jordan, § 292 A(1)) and in *Fowk(s)* 'Fulk(es)' in Hodges and Wallis (and in Jones 1701; see Lehnert, *Wallis*, § 101). The lengthening precedes the loss of [l] (see above), and diphthongization to [ʌu] may do also. Dialectal loss in [bʌud] 'bold' (late ME *ū* < earlier *ou*) is recorded by Salesbury.

(c) In final position

Loss of final *l* is recorded only as a dialectalism, for instance by Salesbury (see Vol. I, p. 17).

Note 1: Jordan's account of these developments is unsatisfactory; see § 104, Note 8.

Note 2: Loss of [l] does not occur if diphthongization of ME *ă* and ME *ŏ* fails (see §§ 60 and 88 above); so, for example, in Hart in *chalk* and *half*, which have [al]. Jordan, loc. cit., is entirely in error in saying that the loss occurs after all back vowels. Note especially that *alms* has [al] in Robinson and in Butler (beside *au*), but [ɒ:] < late ME *au* (with loss of [l]) in Butler (as a variant), Wharton, Young, and Brown and late ME *ā* < *au* (with loss of [l]) in Coles and the 'homophone' lists of Price, Hawkins, and Cocker.

Note 3: Shakespeare, *L.L.L.*, v. i. 24 seq., implies (as indeed Gil does also) that to say *calf* and *half* instead of *cauf* and *hauf* was pedantic, and on the same footing as to pronounce *b* in *debt*.

Note 4: The vocalism of PresE [wount] 'will not' is usually explained < ME *wŏlnt*, assumed to have ME *ŏ* because of the analogical influence of the p.t. *wŏlde*, and consequently Chaucer's *wol* pres. t. is often taken to have ME *ŏ*. But *wol* would more naturally have ME *ŭ* by rounding of ME *ĭ* between *w* and *l* in the normal pres. t. *will* (cf. eME *wulle*, &c.); and a late ME *wŭlnt* 'will not' would equally give *woulnt* > [wount] (cf. *shoulder* < ME *shŭlder*, &c.).

Note 5: *Balm, calm, palm, almond, falcon, salmon*, &c. should by etymology have no [l], being from OF *baume*, &c., and normally are recorded without [l]. But some of them had 'learned' OF forms, adopted directly from Latin, which retained [l] (see Jordan, § 252), and others came to be spelt with *l* partly on etymological grounds and partly on the model of *psalm*, &c., spelt with but pronounced without *l*; and from the OF 'learned' variants, and perhaps partly from the spelling in combination with the variation in pronunciation in *psalm*, &c., there arose pronunciations with ME *aul*, recorded by Salesbury in *calm*, Bullokar in *almond, balm*, and *calm*, Gil in *balm* (as a 'learned' variant), and Daines in *calm* (as a variant). In *malmsey*, recorded without [l] by Butler, Daines, Wharton, Coles, Strong, Lye, *The Protestant Tutor*, and Brown, the loss may occur in English, but OF *maumesye* would seem possible. *Cauldron* (OF *cauderon*) lacks [l] in Hart, Bullokar, *WSC*, and Brown; the latter two have the Latinistic spelling which has now affected the pronunciation. *Psalter* (ME *sauter* < OF) lacks [l] in Hodges and Brown but has it (owing to readoption from Latin *psalterium*) in Bullokar and as a variant in Brown; Hodges himself has [l] in *psaltery*. In *false* Hodges once shows lack of [l], but normally [l] is pronounced; so Bullokar, Robinson, Gil, and Hodges himself (thrice). The form without [l] is not an error, as assumed by Kauter, but represents OF *faus* beside *fals* (see *OED*).

Variation between pronunciations with and without *l* in such native words as *malt* and *salt* has clearly aided the establishment of the spelling-pronunciations with [l] in *fault* and *vault*, in which the orthoepists regularly show the *l* to be silent, with the following exceptions. Hart once retains *l* in *faults*, probably by error; Gil says that most omit the *l*, but some pronounce it, and twice gives transcriptions with *l* elsewhere (in Luick's copy of the 1619 edition a transcription *faut* is corrected by hand to *falt*); Tonkis fails to say that the *l* is silent, and the anonymous reviser (1684) of T. Shelton's *Tachygraphy* does not omit it (in contrast to his treatment of, for example, *balm*); and Hodges relegates to his 'near alike' list the pairing of *fault* and *fought*. Bullokar twice transcribes *vault* without *l*, but once retains it.

(6) *Loss of* [h] *before vowels*

§ 426. As English [h] before a vowel is simply a voiceless (or whispered) form of that vowel, the loss of pre-vocalic [h] is essentially a process of assimilation; it is vocalized and absorbed by the following vowel. In stressed syllables the dropping of [h] is essentially a mark of vulgar or dialectal speech, and what evidence there is in the sixteenth and seventeenth centuries relates exclusively to such speech. The alliteration of the *Welsh Hymn* shows that *h* is silent in two words metrically stressed (*hands* and *hight*) though pronounced in others. Lily (a Northerner) says that some pronounce *homo* as *omo*, and Brown, another Northerner, shows loss of [h] in *hard*, *heart*, and *his*, evidently as a feature of his own speech (see Vol. I, p. 369). The shorthand-writer Everardt says that *h* is silent in *harm* and *dehort* and *wh* in *whole*, *whom* and *whoredom* (see Vol. I, p. 389). Otherwise evidence of loss of initial [h] comes only from a minority of the 'homophone' lists. The series *heir* : *hear* : *air* : *hare* : *hair*, or forms of it, is given by Wharton, Ellis, Brown, and the anonymous MS list. *Earth* : *hearth* comes in Young, Cocker, and Brown, *arrows* : *arras* : *harass* in Young, *asp* : *hasp* and *airy* : *hairy* in Coles, *Eng.–Lat. Dict.* (his least careful list), *hour* : *hoar* : *whore* in Cocker, *awl* : *hall*, *and* : *hand*, *ark* : *hark*, *eight* : *height*, and *even* : *heaven* in Brown. Loss of post-consonantal [h] is shown by the shorthand-writers—in *inherit* and *inhabit* by T. Shelton and Farthing, in *abhor*, *inhance*, and *inhumane* by Everardt, and in *abhor* and *exhort* by Hopkins and Ridpath.

Loss in unstressed syllables and words is a more normal process and occurs in StE, but there is little evidence of it. The alliteration of the *Welsh Hymn* requires the forms *i* 'he', *ys* 'his', and *ath* 'hath', all metrically unstressed. Laneham has *inkorn* 'inkhorn' and Brown *forred* 'forehead' and *mannud* 'manhood'. The shorthand-writers from J. Willis (1602) onwards have *vement* 'vehement', in which loss of intervocalic [h] is especially likely, and Everardt also shows loss in *childhood*, *Godhead*, and *shepherd*; Ridpath writes *im* and *m* for 'him' after consonants.

Note 1: The 'homophone' list pairings could of course depend on the aspiration of initial vowels, but are less likely to do so than on loss of *h*.

Note 2: For spellings from the records of the Norfolk Guilds (1389) onwards which 'drop' *h* see Wyld, op. cit., pp. 295–6; they are not common. But many of the spellings in which *h* is inserted before an initial vowel (op. cit., pp. 310–11) may be inverted spellings showing loss of [h] rather than direct spellings showing aspiration, as Wyld takes them.

Note 3: Lack of [h] in words adopted through OF from Latin does not, of course, depend on an English sound-change, but on OF pronunciation (see Jordan, § 264). It is commonly shown from Salesbury onwards to Cooper (fifteen authors in all) in the following words: (i) *heir*, *honest*, *honour*, and *hour*; (ii) *habit*, *habitation*, *harmonious*, *herb*, *heritage*, *hospitable, host(ess), humble, humour, Humphrey,* and *hyssop*; (iii) *exhibition* and *prohibition*. But forms with [h] (due in part at least to re-adoption from Latin) also occur: thus Gil in *habitation* and *harmony*, Hodges in *historiographer*, &c. Hart even has *honor*, perhaps out of deference to the Latin form; Gil explicitly forbids *honor, honest,* and *houer* 'hour', saying that *h* neither is, nor ought to, nor can be heard.

(7) *Vocalization of* [r]

§ 427. In PresE [r] is maintained, in StE, only before vowels; it is lost before consonants and in final position (except in liaison before a word beginning with a vowel, where [r] is still used, though less often than formerly). The process is that [r] becomes an unstressed form of the vowel [ə], with which it is closely allied. This [ə] is identified with the glide-vowel [ə] developed in eModE between diphthongs and long vowels and [r]; or is assimilated to stressed [ə] < ME *ĭ, ĕ,* and *ŭ* before [r], with lengthening to [ə:]; or is absorbed by a preceding [ɑ:] or [ɒ:] < ME *ă* and *ŏ*; or remains. The change cannot have occurred in good speech much before the identification of ME *ǭr*, &c. with [ɒ:] < ME *ŏ* before *r* (see § 210 above), which is to be dated *c.* 1800; we should not therefore expect to find evidence of it in our sources, and in fact we do not.

Loss of [r] by assimilation to a following consonant, a distinct process, is dealt with in § 401 (c) above. Loss in unstressed syllables, either by vocalization (as is probable) or by assimilation to a following consonant, is earlier than loss in stressed syllables, but even so is seldom recorded before 1700 and then only in sources that reflect vulgar speech; the evidence is given in § 332 above. There remains only a loss associated with the dialectal and vulgar development of ME *ă* to [ɒ:] before [r] (see § 44 above); Fox and Hookes show [ɒ:] for ME *ăr* in *barm* by equating it, in their 'homophone' list, with *balm,* and Brown has the 'phonetic' spelling *chauter* 'charter'. The process in this development is different from the StE vocalization to [ə]; [r] is directly absorbed into the vowel [ɒ:], which is indeed a blend of the [a:] which would otherwise arise and the [r], the vowel taking lip-rounding from the consonant and the tongue-position of the consonant being assimilated to that of the vowel. The development is at least as old as 1527 (see § 43, Note 2 on the rhyme *carter : after*) and accounts for the StE pronunciation of *Marlborough*.

Note: The spellings collected by Wyld, op. cit., pp. 298–9, depend mostly on assimilatory loss of [r], especially before [s] and [ʃ]; omission of *r* in *father* 'farther' (1656), *Fottescue, Fotescue* (1635–6), *quater* 'quarter' (1642, 1665), and *Gath* 'Garth', *Dotchester* 'Dorchester', and *extrodinary* (early eighteenth century) equally depends on assimilatory loss of [r] without influence on the preceding vowel, as the spellings clearly show. Loss in *Albemal* 'Albemarle', *Author* 'Arthur', *Molbery* 'Marlborough' (early eighteenth century) is due to the dialectal change of *ăr* to [ɒ:] discussed above; so also the loss in *mart, parlour,* and *partridge* recorded by German writers of 1718 and 1748 and in *Marlborough* recorded by Bertram, 1753. The loss in *thirsty, harsh,* and *purse* recorded by these writers is assimilatory. The *Cely Papers'* alleged *farder* 'father' (Zachrisson, *Eng. Vowels*, p. 62) or *farther* (Wyld, loc. cit.) is a misreading of *faider*. Others of the spellings cited show loss of [r] in unstressed syllables. But there is no evidence at all of the StE vocalization and loss of [r] in stressed syllables in any of these fifteenth- to eighteenth-century sources which are alleged to show it.

GLIDE CONSONANTS

GLIDE [j] AND [w]

§ 428. In discussing the development of the glides [j] and [w] before vowels, it is necessary to distinguish an isolative development in which they occur before certain vowels in initial position and after [h] (which is not a significantly different position, since prevocalic [h] is merely a whispered vowel) and occasionally after other consonants, and a combinative development in which the glide is primarily due to the nature of the preceding consonant. But it is to be observed that the isolative development, when it occurs after consonants other than [h], does so chiefly after those consonants which cause the combinative development. There is thirdly a glide [j] which develops in unstressed syllables before ME ĭ.

(1) *Isolative development*

§ 429. Late ME and ModE evidence shows a widespread but sporadic tendency for a glide [j] to develop before the long front vowels ẹ̄ and ę̄ (and also ME ęu, the first element of which is identified with ME ę̄) and a glide [w] before the long back vowels ọ̄ and ǭ (and perhaps also rarely before ME ou < OE āw, āg). The process is that the first part of the front vowels is over-palatalized, and that of the back vowels is over-labialized, so that in each case this first part ceases to be vocalic and becomes a consonantal onglide. As part of the vowel is thus made into the consonant, the process is very commonly but not regularly accompanied by shortening. The failure of the process to affect ME ī and ū must be due to their incipient diphthongization, of which the first stage (which may long antedate 1400) was merely a laxing of the first part of the vowel—a process the reverse of that which produces the [j] and [w] glide.

ModE evidence shows that [je] had developed from ME ẹ̄ and ę̄ before the late ME change of ĕ before r to ă, so that the process of development of the [j] glide clearly begins before 1400; the parallel [w] glide must also do so, since in *whole* it develops before diphthongization of ŏ to ou (see § 431 below), and we may therefore connect the fifteenth-century (and later) evidence with evidence from spellings of before 1400. But there is no valid evidence earlier than the fourteenth century (see § 430, Note 3 below). On the other hand there is evidence from the later fifteenth century (see Kihlbom, p. 85) and from modern dialects (see Wright, § 248 and Index) that fifteenth-century [æ:] and [ɛ:] < ME ā became [jæ] (> Northern [ja]) and [je], so the process was still operating in the fifteenth century; and it is probably to this date that there belongs the development of [wʊ] (> [wʌ]) from [u:] < ME $\bar{u}$ undiphthongized before r in *scourge* (see below). The continuance of the process in the fifteenth century also enables us to account for the fact that ME $\bar{e}$ can give rise to [jɪ] as well as [je], ME $\bar{\varrho}$ to [wʊ] as well as [wɔ]; [jɪ] and [wʊ] are developed from fifteenth-century [i:] < ME $\bar{e}$ and [u:] < ME $\bar{\varrho}$.

The evidence of fifteenth- and sixteenth-century spellings, and of the early orthoepists, shows that the development of [j] and [w] was not only widespread throughout England, but also that it had some effect on educated speech. But from the last quarter of the sixteenth century there was a reaction against these pronunciations in StE (probably led by schoolmasters such as Coote) which caused them to be regarded as a mark of dialectal or vulgar speech, and as such they are described throughout the seventeenth century. They remained common, however, on the fringes of educated speech; thus the pronunciation [wɔn] 'one', which is probably what is represented by early *won* spellings, survives in widespread use in Midland dialects and among many Midland speakers of StE, and the originally vulgar and dialectal [wʊn] > [wʌn] (on which see further Note 2 below) forced its way into StE about 1700 and displaced the normally developed [o:n] (in *one* itself and *once*, but not in *only, alone, atone*). Similarly [j] was very common in *ear*, and D. Jones, *Eng. Pron. Dict.*, still records [jə:(r)] as a (rare) variant in StE itself.

Note 1: The glides are, in this isolative development, always to be regarded as developing before long vowels; in words in which the vowel varied in quantity in late ME the starting-point is the long variant, even though the resultant vowel in ModE is short. See further § 430, Note 5 and § 431, Note 5 below. The glide [j] in *eye* does not develop before ME $\bar{\imath}$, but only in the Northern form $\bar{e}$ > ModE [i:] (on which see Jordan, § 101 and Anm.); cf. the spellings *yeelid* 'eye-lid', *ȝen* 'eyes' (Digby *Mary Magdalene*), *ȝeȝen* 'eyes' (*Cursor Mundi*, Trinity MS)—the latter a blend-spelling showing apparent retention of intervocalic [ȝ]. (For these spellings see Kihlbom, pp. 79, 85; she misinterprets the last.)

Note 2: Wyld, *Rhymes*, p. 126, is scornful of *WSC*'s description of *wun* 'one' as a vulgar pronunciation, arguing that it was that of Henry VIII and Elizabeth; but if the evidence is correctly interpreted there is no discrepancy. The royal spellings on which Wyld relies (*Coll. Eng.*, p. 307) are of the *won* type and beyond real doubt represent the pronunciation [wɔn] (recorded by Hart, a man with Court associations), which was certainly used in educated pronunciation in the sixteenth century but was abandoned by it about 1600; [wʌn] < [wʊn], on the other hand, has as its starting-point fifteenth-century [u:n], which depends on the vulgar and dialectal raising of ME $\bar{\varrho}$ to ME $\bar{\varrho}$, and must therefore be itself originally vulgar and dialectal, as Cooper and *WSC* say; it cannot be shown to have had currency in educated speech before 1700 (the earliest rhyme cited by Wyld being from Pope). Its adoption was certainly aided by the usefulness of a distinction in pronunciation between *one* and *own*, since real ambiguity would otherwise result in such expressions as *my own idea, my one idea*; extension to *once* would naturally follow. But *alone, only*, &c., which are not liable to any confusion and are not so closely associated with *one* as *once* is, retained the normal educated pronunciation of the seventeenth century. On *none* see §§ 33 and 36 above. Expressions like *such an one* (*A. & C.*, I. ii. 118) depend on [o:n].

Note 3: Miss Kihlbom's explanation of the development of the glides [j] and [w] (that they arise to prevent hiatus in such groups as *the ear* and *the one*) is unsatisfactory, as it fails to account for their development after retained *h* and after other consonants; but their special prevalence before initial vowels may be aided by this factor. Her treatment (op. cit., pp. 77–87, 162–8) has the great merit of demonstrating that the development is widespread throughout England; she rightly rejects Luick's view (§ 435 and Anm.) that it is merely South-western and that similar pronunciations elsewhere in modern dialects are the result of a distinct later process (in itself phonetically improbable or even impossible), and points out that the early and modern forms cannot be thus distinguished.

(a) The evidence for [j]

§ 430. In many cases it is impossible to determine whether the starting-point of the development to [je] is ME ẹ̄ or ẹ̆ owing to ME variation between these vowels, especially when *r* follows; they are not therefore distinguished in what follows. In initial position the glide [j] is shown by Salesbury in *ease* (see Vol. I, p. 16), Coote in *yerb* 'herb' (which he condemns as 'barbarous'), Butler in *yer* 'ere' and *yerst* 'erst' (against which he warns his readers), Hodges (who himself uses the spelling *yer* 'ere' in *SH*), Hunt (who follows Coote), perhaps Newton in *eel* (see Vol. I, p. 251), and Cooper (followed by *WSC*) in *yerb* 'herb' and *yerth* 'earth', which he condemns as 'barbarous'; the *Welsh Hymn* has [jɪ] < [iː] < ME ẹ̄ in *earth*, and Lodwick has [jərþ], in which [ər] may represent sixteenth-century [ɪr] or [er] (see Vol. I, p. 279). The rest of the evidence given by the orthoepists of initial [j] comes from 'homophone' lists. The pairing *earn* : *yearn* is given by Butler, Hodges 'alike' (but *EP* shows no [j] in *earn*), Fox and Hookes, and Strong; in Hodges it depends on [e], the vowel given for *earn* in *EP*. But *earn* is paired with *yarn* in other lists, thus showing that ME ẹ̄ became [je] in time for the [e] to become [a] before [r]; some lists add *yearn*, perhaps because it also could have late ME ă, perhaps because *earn* varied between ĕ and ă. This *earn* : *yarn* pairing is given by Hodges 'near alike', Wharton, Price, Ellis, Young, and Hawkins. *East* : *yeast* is given by Hodges 'near alike', Wharton, Price, Fox and Hookes, Strong, Young, Coles (*Eng.–Lat. Dict.*), *WSC-RS*, and Cocker; in *RS* at least it depends on ME ĕ in *yeast*, which is spelt *yest*, and so perhaps in the other lists. *Early* : *yearly* (Hawkins, *WSC*, Cocker, and Brown) may also depend on ĕ, shortening being common in words with the *-ly* suffix; *WSC*'s *eat* : *yet* (which depends on [j] in *eat*; see § 422, Note 1 above) certainly rests on ĕ. On the other hand *ear(s)* : *year(s)* (Hodges 'near alike', Merriott, Price, Ellis, Fox and Hookes, Coles (*Schoolmaster* and *Eng. Dict.*), Young, Hawkins, and Cocker) probably depends on [iː] in both words (as it certainly does in Coles's *Schoolmaster*); cf., however, the ĕ shown by Gil in *shears* and *swear* (see § 30).

The glide [j] is shown in non-initial position after [h] by Hart in *heal* and *here* but not in *hear* (see Vol. I, p. 84) and by Hodges in *hear* and *hearse* but not in *here* (see Vol. I, p. 171), after [l] by Salesbury in *leave* (see Vol. I, p. 16), and after [m] by Hart in *mean*. On Newton's evidence on *shield* see Vol. I, p. 251. In Hart the following vowel is [ɛː] < ME ẹ̄, in

Hodges it is [iː] < ME ẹ̄; but Hart has also more frequent transcriptions of *here* as *hier*, with the *e* not marked long, which show [je] with the shortening that commonly accompanies the development of the glide.

Before ME *ęu* the glide is shown only by Hart, in initial position in *ieu* [jɛu] 'ewe', after [m] in *mieu* [mjɛu] 'mew', and after [f] in *fieu* [fjɛu] 'few' (once, beside *feu* once).

Note 1: Hart's *ie* (thrice, beside [iː] once) in *briefly* (*-ness*) may also represent [je], but as it is difficult to conceive of [j] being articulated after [br] it is better to ascribe the transcription to the influence of the traditional orthography. On Hart's [j] before ME *ęu* see also § 244, Note 5.

Note 2: It is difficult to decide whether the *Ayenbite*'s much-debated spellings *hyer(e)*, *hier(e)* 'here' and *hyere, yhyere* 'hear' and the still earlier spelling *hier* 'here' of the late thirteenth-century MS Arundel 248 (cf. Carleton Brown, *English Lyrics of the Thirteenth Century*, p. 79, l. 21) are due to the process described above. So to interpret them would make them at least comparable to the use of the digraphs *ie* and *ye* in other native words, and would enable them to be associated with later evidence of a [j] glide in these two words, notably Hart's of [je] and [jɛː] in *here* and Hodges's of [jiː] in *hear*; moreover it would be consistent with the *Ayenbite*'s evidence of a [w] glide before ME *ǭ* (cf. § 431, Note 2 below). On the other hand they might be taken as evidence of the development of ME *ẹ̄* to ME *ī*, which would be consistent with the probable explanation of the digraph *ie* in *clier* 'clear' and with other evidence of ME *ī* < ME *ẹ̄* in these two words *here* and *hear* (see § 136, Note 2 above). In either case the fact that the words *her* 'hair' and *here* 'haircloth' do not show the digraph *ie* is not a serious objection; both the raising of ME *ẹ̄* to *ī* and the development of the glide [j] before ME *ẹ̄* were sporadic processes and the inconsistency of the *Ayenbite*'s forms must be regarded as an example of dialectal mixture with the object of differentiating homophones. If the *Ayenbite*'s forms show the glide, then they do so only in phonetic contexts that seem especially to have encouraged it, namely before *r* and after *h*. Luick's view (§ 405 (1)) approximates to the explanation that the *ie*, *ye* in the *Ayenbite*'s forms represents a glide, but differs (*a*) in regarding the sound as a diphthong, first rising and then falling, and (*b*) in regarding the process as specifically Kentish; Wallenberg's explanation (*Vocabulary of the Ayenbite*, note to *hyer* and *hyere*), that the forms represent analogical pronunciations, is unconvincing.

Note 3: Wyld, op. cit., p. 308, cites fifteenth- to eighteenth-century evidence of [j] before ME *ẹ̄* and *ę̄*. Kihlbom, pp. 77–87, has a much fuller and more useful, but somewhat confused, collection of early evidence. She wrongly regards forms which omit etymological *y* as 'super-correct' (i.e. inverted) spellings, but they are phonetic (see § 422, Note 2 above). She fails to allow sufficiently for OE forms with the *ge-* prefix: thus *geuelic*, &c. (*Bestiary, Gen. and Exod.*) are from OE *ge-efenlic*, not (as she states) OE *efnelice* [sic], and *iefned* (*Trinity Homs.*) is from OE *ge-æfned*. *Geuelengŏhe* (*G. & E.*) is from ON *jǫfnlengd* (see *OED*, s.v. *even-length*), partially assimilated to English *even* and *length*; *Yerk* 'York' (*Havelok*) is a blend of *York* < **3orwīk* and ME *Euerwic* < OE *Eoforwic*); and *getenes*, &c. 'etens', &c. (*G. & E.*) is a blend of *eten* < OE *eoten* and ON *jǫtunn*, which is proved to have affected ME by the forms *yhoten* (*E. E. Psalter*, ed. Stevenson, Ps. xviii. 6) and *ʒoten* (*Wars of Alexander*). This accounts for all her alleged thirteenth-century instances. Her valid material begins from *c.* 1350 (*ʒer-while* 'erewhile', *Wm. of Palerne*).

Note 4: For modern dialectal evidence see Wright, § 248 and Index; he wrongly explains the pronunciation as being due to a falling becoming a rising diphthong. Cases in which [j] occurs before back vowels are of course to be distinguished. The WMidl and Southern [jɛnt] (glossed 'is not' by Wright) shows the development of [je] from eModE [ɛːnt] or [eːnt] 'ain't', which is to be derived (with *OED*, q.v.) from *ānt* < *ār(e)nt* < *āre not* (with assimilatory loss of *r* without influence on the preceding vowel). In other paragraphs Wright shows the development to [je] after consonants other than [h], e.g. in *beat*, *dead*, and *mean*. But [j] in *again*, *geese*, *keep*, &c. is due to palatalization of [k] and [g], and [jʌ] in *again*, *dead*, and *head* (§ 188, all in WMidl dialects) is due to shift of stress in the diphthong [iə] (the process assumed by Luick and by Wright himself to account also for [je]; but [iə] cannot become [je]).

Note 5: Kihlbom, loc. cit., states that the glide [j] develops before ME *ĕ* as well as ME *ę̄* and *ẹ̄*, but the evidence does not support this view. On *geuelic*, *getenes*, and *Yerk* see Note 3 above; their [j] is not developed as a glide. Words which appear to have a [j] glide developed before ME *ĕ* in fact have original ME *ę̄* or *ẹ̄* (as a variant to *ĕ*) which becomes [je]: so *yende* 'end', *yerst* 'erst', *yerth* 'earth'. In modern dialects, according to Wright, § 248, [j] occurs in *earn*, *earnest*, *earth*, *emmet*, *errand*, *head*, *health*, *heifer*, *heron*, *herring*, and *herb*; these words are all capable of a long vowel in ME (thus *emmet* is < OE *ǣmete*, *errand* < *ǣrende*, *herring* < *hǣring*, &c.; see §§ 8–9 on variation between ME *ĕ* and ME *ę̄*, *ẹ̄* in these and analogous words). The only exception is *hearth*, in which [j] occurs only in certain WMidl and South-western dialects; it probably owes its pronunciations with [j] to the analogy of *earth*, in which [j] is common and widespread and which still had a long variant in eModE. (Or *hearth* may itself have had ME *ę̄* < OE *ēo* by lengthening of *ĕo* before [rð] in oblique cases.) Of Kihlbom's own spellings, only one is of a word in which ME *ę̄* or *ẹ̄* is impossible, namely *yelles* 'ells' (*Cely Papers*, 1481); this can satisfactorily be explained as due to the analogy of the associated word *yard*, which varied in spelling and pronunciation between *yerd* [jerd] and *erd* [erd] (with loss of [j]; see § 422 and Note 2). Kihlbom herself cites *erdys* 'yards' from the *Stonor Papers* (1460). As initial ME *ĕ* is very common and occurs in such popular words as *edge*, *egg*, *elbow* (a compound of *ell*), *elder* (tree), *elder* (comp.), *eldest*, &c., one would expect much more evidence than is in fact available if [j] had really developed before it. It is against Kihlbom's assumption that [w] does not develop before initial ME *ŏ*. The glides are essentially connected with the ME and eModE long vowels.

(b) The evidence for [w]

§ 431. The evidence from early sources for the [w] glide before ME *ǭ* and *ō̧* (and fifteenth-century [uː] < ME *ū* before *r*) is rarer than that for the [j] glide; and there is a good deal more for [w] before ME *ǭ* than before ME *ō̧*, both in late ME and eModE and in the present-day dialects. In initial position the pronunciation [wɔ] (with shortening of the vowel) is shown by Hart in *uonli* 'only' (once) and by the Northerner Brown's 'phonetic' spelling *won* 'one'; Levins and Poole, both Northerners, rhyme *once* with *sconce*. There is little more evidence for fifteenth-century [wʊ] (> [wʌ]) from [uː] < ME *ǭ* by raising of ME *ǭ*; Lye says that *o* is pronounced *wu* in *one* and *once* (but also gives [oːn]), Cooper that *wun* 'one' and *wuts* 'oats' are 'barbarous speaking', and *WSC* (after Cooper) that *wun* is vulgar.

In non-initial position the glide is shown after [h] in *whole*, *whore*, and *hot*. Hart in his manuscript has *whoali* (which shows unshortened [oː]) beside *hoali*, and in the *Orthographie* has *huōl* [hwoːl] thrice beside *hōl* twice; in *huolei* 'wholly' there is shortening (cf. Lodge's rhymes of *wholly* with *jolly* and *folly*). Bullokar has regular [hwoː] in *whole* and *wholesome*, and Coote says *h* is silent in *whole*; Robinson has [hwoː] in both *whole* and *wholly*, and Gil [hwoː] in *whole* but [hoː] in (*un*)*wholesome*. Hunt says that *h* is silent in *whole*. The Northerner Brown shows the dialectal pronunciation [wʊl] 'whole' by his 'homophone' list pairing with *wool*; this develops from ME *ǭ* by raising of *ǭ* (cf. *one* and *oats* above), and is also recorded by Turner (1710) (see § 36 above). The Scot Ridpath gives *hol* (i.e. [hoːl]) as an 'Anglicism', and must therefore have himself used a form with [w]. A pronunciation with [w] may be assumed for *whole* in those sources which say *w* is silent in *wholesome* but are silent on *whole* (see below); this suggests the common survival of [(h)woːl] in the later seventeenth century (cf. Hunt above). But [hoːl] is shown by Cheke, Hart (as a variant), Laneham, Mulcaster, Gil (as a variant; see below), Daines, Hodges, and fourteen later sources. Butler draws a distinction between [hoːl] 'sanus' and [hwoːl] 'integer', in accordance with which he has [hwoː] in *wholly* and [hoː] in *wholesome* spelt *hol'soom* (beside *holsoom*, a variant of a spelling found from the fourteenth century (see *OED*) which shows ME ŏ by shortening in the compound). That this distinction, which in origin is not arbitrary (as assumed by Eichler, § 133), was not peculiar to himself is shown by Gil's evidence (which, Butler's warns us, must be deliberate in its distinction of *whole* and *(un)wholesome*) and by the choice of *wholesome* instead of *whole* as the example of 'silent *w*' by the shorthand-writer Bridges and by Cooper (in his text; *Eng. Teacher*, p. 73); similarly the 'phonetically spelt' lists of Strong, Young, and Cocker give *hole-sum* (or *holesome*) for *wholesome* but not **hole* 'whole'. For the explanation of this important evidence see below. *Whore* is [hwuːr] only in Bullokar, whose speech is vulgar or dialectal and who is much influenced by the spelling; [huːr] (or [hɔːr] by lowering) is recorded by Cheke, Smith, and seventeen seventeenth-century sources. Verstegen says 'some' write the word *hoor* as *whore*, 'I know not with what reason', and Butler that to *hoore* 'soom idly prefix *w*, it being neither in the sound, nor in the spelling'. For the rarity of [w] in this word see Wright, § 236, who says that no dialect has it. In *hot* the glide is shown by Cooper's *hwut* (with [wʌ] < [wʊ] < [uː] < ME ǭ by raising of ME ǫ), which he says is 'barbarous'. After other consonants the glide is shown by Salesbury in *evermore*; by Daines's *swut* 'soot' ([wʌ] < [wʊ] < [uː] < ME ǭ), which he regards as a less correct form; and by Cooper's *squrge* 'scourge' (cf. the sixteenth-century spelling *squorge* cited by *OED*; [wʌ] < [wʊ] < [uː] < undiphthongized ME ū), which in the Latin text he says is 'facilitatis causa' and in the English is 'barbarous speaking'.

The regular failure of the orthoepists to show short ŏ in *whole*, in contrast to the other words, proves that the process must have been completed in this word in the fourteenth century; for in that case, even when ME ǭ became *wǫ̆*, the ŏ, being before *l*, would undergo diphthongization c. 1400 to *ou*, whence late sixteenth-century [oː] (note that Hart, Bullokar, Robinson, and Gil all knew monophthongization of ME *ou*; see § 250 above). Hart's shortening in *wholly* is later and due to the secondary stress of the suffix. The special treatment of *wholesome* (see above) is due to the common ME shortening in the compound to ŏ (see *OED*, s.v.); the glide [w] does not develop before ME ŏ, so that *hŏl-* remains, to become late ME *houl-* > late sixteenth-century [hoːl], which would coalesce with the ME variant in ǭ insofar as the latter had avoided the change to wŏ or wǫ. Hence [w] would be much rarer in *wholesome* than in *whole*, and Gil's distinction between [(ʊn)hoːlsʊm] and [hwoːl] is a correct reflection of the fourteenth-century distinction between (*un*)*hǒlsum* and *hǫl*; Butler's distinction between [hoːl] 'sanus' and [hwoːl] 'integer' is a natural extension, a sort of back-formation, which apparently was known to Spenser (who generally has the spelling *whole* for the sense 'complete' and *hole* for 'cured', &c., though the distinction is not perfectly maintained; see Osgood, *Concordance to Spenser*, s.v. *whole*). It should be observed that the facts relating to *whole* and *wholesome* can be explained only by these assumptions (*a*) that the development of ǭ > wŏ is earlier than that of ŏ > ou before *l*, and (*b*) that no glide ever developed before ME ŏ; on the former point see further Note 4 below, and on the latter Note 5.

Before ME *ou* the orthoepists give no evidence of [w], but the glide may have developed there, though very rarely; Kihlbom, p. 163, cites *wowid* 'owed' from *Reg. Osney Abbey* (1460), but the starting-point may have been a fourteenth-century pronunciation in which ǭw < OE *āg* had not yet become the diphthong *ou*.

Note 1: *Whoop* is [hwuːp] in Bullokar but [huːp] in Hodges's 'homophone' list (followed by six later lists); but we have to do here not with a sound-change, but with two distinct interjectional formations, *hoop* and *whoop* (see *OED*, s.vv.). I do not feel justified in using Hexham's inclusion of *whole* and *whore* in a list of *wh-* words as evidence of pronunciation; see Vol. I, p. 380.

Note 2: As the [w] glide in *whole* is demonstrably of fourteenth-century origin and spelling evidence begins shortly after 1400, we may connect the widespread development discussed above with the *Ayenbite*'s forms of *bones, both, go, goi̯ng, good, goodhead, goodness*, and *goose* (thus *buones, guo*, &c.), which Wallenberg, op. cit., discusses s.v. *guo*. They show a consonantal [w] glide and not a 'rising diphthong', and certainly there was no development to a falling diphthong, as assumed by Luick, § 405 (2), without any reason. In *guodes* 'god's' we should probably not assume development of the glide before ME ŏ, as Wallenberg does (in which case it would have to be explained as a combinative glide due solely to the consonant; see § 432 below), but before ME ǭ by lengthening in the open syllable; note that *uo* occurs only in the genitive sing. (and there only once). In the *Ayenbite* the early development of the glide is obviously dependent on the preceding consonant, since it occurs only after [b] (which would favour rounding) and [g] (which would favour high tongue-position). Wallenberg is probably right in regarding *guod* 'good' in the Laud MS of the *South English Legendary* (c. 1280–90) as a still earlier instance, but it might be graphic, as he says; the word rhymes on ME ǭ, but the pronunciation of the author may have been [oː], that of the scribe [wɔ]. (Cf. § 430, Note 2 on the [j] glide in the *Ayenbite*.)

Note 3: On the development of [w] before ǭ and ǭ in words with initial *h* see *OED*, article on the digraph *wh*, which cites evidence from the early fifteenth century onwards and shows that [w] is recorded more frequently before ǭ than ǭ. Wyld, op. cit., pp. 307–8, also cites evidence from the early fifteenth century onwards, and a fuller collection of evidence is given by Kihlbom, pp. 162–8. On forms alleged to show [w] before ME ŏ, ŭ, and ū see Note 5 below. On *word* for OE *ord* see Onions, *Modern Language Review*, xxiv. 389–93; contamination by *word* 'verbum' has at least to be allowed for. The form *oon* for *woon* 'plenty' (*Guy of Warwick*) shows loss of initial [w] and is not an inverted spelling.

Note 4: Wright, *EDG*, deals with the development of the [w] glide in § 236, but there gives only part of the available evidence, which is scattered through some ten other sections on ME ǭ and ME ǭ of various origins. It accords well with the explanation here adopted of the process of development. (1) ME *ǭ* in *oak, oath, oats, one, once, only* and in *home* and *hope* appears as unshortened [woː], &c. and (with early shortening) as [wɒ], rarely [wɑ] and [wæ]. ME raising of *ǭ* to *ǭ* > fifteenth-century [uː] gives rise in these same words to unshortened [wuə] < [wuː] and (with shortening) as [wʊ], [wʌ], &c., also to [wəː] < *wŭr* in *oar*. The same developments occur after consonants other than *h* in some twenty words, e.g. *boat, coat, foam, goat, most, pony, road, brooch,* and *close*. (2) ME *ǭ* appears as [wuə] < [wuː] in *corn* and *good*, and (with shortening) as [wʌ] in *don't*; also as [wəː] < *wŭr* in *hoard*. Lowering of eModE [uː] < ME *ǭ* before *r* gives rise to [woə] < [wəː] in *board*. (3) But before *l* not only ME *ǭ* (in *old,* &c., *hole,* and *whole*) but also ME *ǭ* (in *cool* and *stool*) occurs as [woː] or its variant [woə], clearly < late ME *woul* < fourteenth-century *wǒl* (with shortening) < *ǒl* as well as *ōl*. Very occasionally in scattered dialects ME *ǭ* even before *l* appears with shortening as [wɒ], &c., which must arise from a sporadic development of [oː] > [wɔ] in the fifteenth century, too late for diphthongization to late ME *ou* before *l*; and fifteenth-century [uː] < late ME *ǭ* by raising of ME *ǭ* appears in *whole* (in widespread dialects) and in *old* and *told* (in Dorset and Somerset) as [wuə] or (with shortening) as [wʊ], [wʌ], &c.

Wright does not show [w] before final ME *ǭ* and *ǭ*, nor before ME *ou* (of whatever origin), ME *ū*, and ME *ŭ* and *ŏ*; *orchard* (OE *ort-geard*), stated to have initial [w] in Northern dialects (§ 236) but without details of the vowel(s), may safely be assumed to have been contaminated by *wort* 'plant, vegetable'.

Note 5: Kihlbom, loc. cit., asserts that the [w] glide develops before ME *ŏ, ŭ,* and *ū,* but there is no support for this view from early evidence. Spellings with *wh-* of *how,* which are common, occur continuously from *c.* 1200 and represent eME or late OE *hwū* (cf. *OED,* s.v. *how* and Stratmann–Bradley, s.v. *hwu*), a variant of *hū* < WGmc *hwō* which is undoubtedly due to the analogy of the etymologically related interrogative words in OE *hw-,* e.g. *hwȳ, hwæt,* &c. (cf. Tolkien, *Middle English Vocabulary,* s.v. *wou*). Margaret Paston's spelling *vus* 'us' certainly does not show initial [w]; *OED* records the same spelling from the fourteenth century, and it may be an example of doubled *u* to show length or mere dittography. *Wowl* is not a form of *howl* but a distinct echoic word (see *OED,* s.v. *wowl* and cf. *wow* sb. and vb. and *waul*). Otherwise *w* occurs before ME *ū* only when it precedes *r* and gives fifteenth-century [uː], and even in this case it is rare. If it had occurred before ME *ŭ* we should expect plentiful evidence, for initial *ŭ* is very common and occurs in many popular words, but apparent evidence of it comes only in obviously special cases. In *Ulster,* which is *Wolinster* in Capgrave and *Wolster* in *State Papers Hen. VIII* (1515), it is to be explained from late ME *ǭ* in **ǭli(n)ster* or **ǭlester* developed, by lengthening in the open syllable, from ME **ŭli(n)ster* or **ŭlester* (cf. modern Scottish *Ullister,* ON *Ulaztir,* &c., and Capgrave's own form). On *whort,* South-western form of *hurt,* and *whortle(berry),* South-western form of *hurtle(berry),* see *OED,* s.vv.; the etymology being unknown, these words cannot be used as proof of an otherwise unauthenticated sound-change, and indeed we are justified in requiring on phonological grounds that any proposed etymology should be such as to permit either ME *ǭ* or ME *ū* (> fifteenth-century [uː]) beside or as the source of eModE *ŭ* (unless there has been contamination by *wort*). There is likewise no early evidence of [w] before ME *ŏ*; *worder* 'order' and *wordeyniþ* 'ordaineth' have ME *ǭ* as their starting-point.

Miss Kihlbom, p. 166 footnote, refers to certain words given in *EDD* which she takes to show 'intrusive *w*' before (*inter alia*) ME *ŏ* and *ŭ*; but in fact they do not. *Horn* has ME *ǭ* beside *ŏ, hottle* (being derived from *hot*) has original ME *ǭ,* and *ort(ings)* may well have ME *ǭ* also (by lengthening in the open syllable of ME **ŏret*; see *OED*). The forms *wonder* 'under(n)' and *whumlick* for *humlock* 'hemlock' are probably analogical (based respectively on [ʊndə(r)] beside [wʊndə(r)] 'wonder' and [wʊm], &c. beside [(h)ʊm], &c. 'home', or more generally on the abandonment of dialectal forms without *w* in such words as *wonder* and *woman* for more 'correct' forms with *w*—a process of 'reformation' which, as parallels show, is often carried too far and applied to words in which it is historically inappropriate). But many forms supposedly derived from the simple *undern* are in fact < *over-undern* (see *OED,* s.v. *undern*), which became *ǭrunder(n)* > *ǭrnder(n)* > *ǭnder(n)* (assimilatory loss of preconsonantal *r*), from the last of which fifteenth-century [wəndər(n)] can develop, as *yeender* (see *OED,* s.v.) ultimately develops < *ǣrundern*. The remaining words in which *ŭ* follows are of no evidential value: *whossuck* for *hussock* 'dry cough', *(w)urgee* 'a cry to a horse', *(w)hulla-balloo*, and *(w)hoot* are echoic or interjectional words, in which parallel formations with and without *w* are common (cf. Note 1).

(2) *Combinative development*

§ 432. The glides [j] and [w] develop before other vowels than those discussed under (1) above, but more rarely, in consequence of the nature of the preceding consonant, which is the prime cause of the glide. Hart has [j] after [ʃ] in *show* (see Vol. I, p. 84); but similar spellings in manuscripts of the *Welsh Hymn* are not valid evidence for a glide. Wallis gives evidence for a glide [w] in *pwot* 'pot', *bwoy* 'boy' (cf. *Medium Ævum*, ix. 123, note 2), and *bwoil* 'boil' vb. (see Vol. I, p. 235). It should be observed that the nature of the preceding consonant influences the isolative development discussed under (1) above, which first appears (in the *Ayenbite*) only after certain consonants—[j] after [h], and [w] after [b] and [g].

Note: For evidence similar to Wallis's see Wright, Index, s.vv. *boil*, *boy*, *point*, and *poison*.

(3) *Glide* [j] *before unstressed* [ɪ]

§ 433. In unstressed syllables a glide [j] is shown before retained [ɪ] by Robinson in *Pecunia, oblivion*, &c. (see Vol. I, p. 210); this development underlies Bullokar's and Gil's transcription of *fashion* (see § 276 above) and the 'phonetic' spellings given by Coles in *Mysia, submission*, &c. and Strong in *tuition* and *tradition* (see § 276, Note above), which show [ʃ] from [s] plus the glide [j] and retention of the [ɪ] (or of [j] by ModE reduction of [ɪ]).

GLIDE AND 'EXCRESCENT' STOPS AFTER NASALS

§ 434. In late ME and ModE there is a tendency for 'inorganic' or 'excrescent' stops to develop after nasals; this is the result of a premature closing of the nasal passage, so that the release of the oral stop is a distinct articulatory process and is heard as a distinct sound.

(1) *Before another consonant*

§ 435. Glide stops are common, and in some cases become the regular StE pronunciation, between a nasal (especially one which ends a syllable) and a following consonant (especially syllabic [l̩] and [r̩]). A glide [b] after [m] and before [l] (cf. Jordan, § 212) is regularly developed in *bramble*, *thimble*, &c.; it is shown by Bullokar, Gil, and Butler in *bramble*, by Smith and Gil in *mumble*, by Bullokar, Gil, and Butler in *nimble*, by Bullokar and Gil in *shambles*, and by Hart in *thimble*. But before [r] in *hammer*, where it is shown by Capgrave's *hamber* (see Jordan, § 212), it is abnormal and is not shown by the orthoepists; Hart and Butler have the normal *hammer*. A glide [p] between [m] and a following voiceless consonant (cf. Jordan, § 210) is shown in *empty* by Bullokar, Gil, and Butler. A glide [d] between [n] and [l] or [r] (cf. Jordan, § 202) is a common development, and is shown in *spindle* by Hodges, in *thunder* by Smith, Gil, and Butler, and in *kindred* by Bullokar and Gil; but Hodges still has *kinred*.

In other cases the glide is a ModE development. A glide [t] is not uncommon in PresE between [n] and [ʃ], and is shown by Robinson (once) in *antšenter* 'ancienter' and by Strong in *anchent* 'ancient' (in contrast to Coles's 'phonetic spelling' *anshent*, which Strong modifies). Similarly a glide [k] develops (after [ŋg] has become [ŋ]) between [ŋ] and a following voiceless consonant; it is shown by Cooper in *lenkth* 'length' and in [streŋkþn̩] 'strengthen'. On Robinson's transcription of *amongst* see § 412, Note 1.

(2) *In final position*

§ 436. Excrescent stops develop after final nasals by exactly the same phonetic process as the glides discussed above, but may be either voiceless or voiced according as the vibration of the vocal chords ends with the closure of the nasal passage or continues until the release of the oral stop. The [t] of *tyrant*, *pheasant*, &c. is, however, to be explained by OF back-formation from *tirants*, &c. (see Jordan, § 262, Anm. 1). In *ancient*, *pageant*, and *parchment* the [t] is a fifteenth-century English development and is phonetic in origin, but was rapidly normalized because of confusion with the OF *-ant* of the present participle (cf. also forms in *-and*; see Jordan, loc. cit. and *OED*, s.v. *ancient*); the orthoepists regularly record [t] in these words. Bullokar has it also in *talants* (twice) beside *talanz* (once) 'talons', a word in which it was common in the fifteenth and sixteenth centuries (see *OED*, s.v.). Excrescent [d] in *sound* 'sonus' and 'sonare' is recorded from *c.* 1440 (see *OED*) and despite its condemnation by Stanyhurst (cited by *OED*) is normally recorded by the orthoepists (so Hart, Bullokar, Robinson, Gil, Butler, and Hodges). In *s(w)ound* and *s(w)oond* 'swoon' it also occurs from *c.* 1440 (see *OED*, s.vv. *swound* and *sound*) and is shown by Butler, Willis, Brown, and the shorthand-writer Everardt; in view of the evidence on *sound* 'sonus', excrescent [d] in *sound* 'swoon' must be the usual basis of the pairing of the two words as homophones by Hodges and fourteen later writers. But Young's pairing of *swoon* and *sound* with *sown* probably shows [sʌun] for all three.

Note 1: *Expound* beside *expoun* occurs from the thirteenth century and is due to OF variation (see *OED*, s.v.), and does not show fifteenth-century excrescent [d] as stated by Jordan, loc. cit.

Note 2: On excrescent [t] after [n] in *sermon*, *sudden*, and *vermin* see Wright, § 295; on [d] in *born*, *drown*, *gown*, &c. Wright, § 306.

GLIDE AND 'EXCRESCENT' STOPS AFTER OTHER CONSONANTS

§ 437. Excrescent [d] develops after [l] if the tongue is spread so as to close the lateral passage(s) before the tip is removed from the alveolar ridge; in this way the oral passage is closed, and the release of the stop is heard as a distinct sound. Before syllabic [r̩] a glide [d] is recorded in Chaucer MSS in *alder* < OE *ealra* and became regular in StE in the tree-names *alder* and *elder*, being shown in the former by Butler and in the latter by Coles and Young. Bullokar shows final excrescent [d] in *mole* (thrice). See further Note 1 below.

Excrescent [t] in *against, amidst, amongst, betwixt, whilst*, &c. is explained by *OED* as due to the analogy of the superlative ending *-est*, and by Jordan, § 199, as developing in phrasal groups when the prepositions were followed by *te* 'the'. But in view of the cases discussed in the preceding paragraph and in Note 1 and of the occurrence in modern dialects of [t] after [s] in words which do not have OE adverbial *-es* (see Note 3 below), we may explain [t] as developed by a phonetic process; at the end of the articulation of [s] the tip of the tongue is raised slightly so as to close the narrow passage left for [s], and the stop [t] is thus produced. But as this [t] is recorded earlier and more often, and in StE is confined to, prepositions and conjunctions, it is clear that a special factor is also operating, and that suggested by Jordan is altogether more likely than *OED*'s (for there seems no good reason why the superlative should exercise the influence alleged); [þ] becomes [t] after spirants, including [s] (see Jordan, § 205), and the tendency to develop excrescent [t] after [s] would therefore, in prepositions and conjunctions, be strongly aided by the fact that they were so commonly followed by the definite article in the form *te*. The development is shown sporadically from OE onwards in *betwixt* and in ME in *against* and *whilst* (see *OED* and Jordan, § 199), but is not commonly recorded until the fifteenth century; but as it presupposes final [s] it must either antedate the change of unstressed *-es* to [əz], which is to be dated to the fourteenth century (see § 363 above), or operate solely on forms with early syncope, and the paucity of evidence before 1400 must therefore be largely accidental.

The prepositions regularly have [t] in the orthoepists: so *against* in Hart, Bullokar, Robinson, Gil, Hodges, and Wallis, *amidst* in Robinson, *amongst* in Hart, Robinson, Gil, and Hodges, and *(be)twixt* in Hart, Bullokar, Robinson, and Hodges. The conjunction *whilst*, however, which would be less commonly followed by the definite article, occurs as [hwɪls] (showing early syncope) in Smith and as [hwəilz] in Hart (beside *-st*) and Gil (transcribing Spenser); but it has [st] in, for example, Hart, Bullokar, and Robinson. Bullokar also records excrescent [t] in *unless* (twice); in this case the occasional acceptance in the sixteenth century of the form with [t] is probably due to confusion with the superlative *least*, since *unless* is derived from the comparative *less* (see *OED*, s.vv. *unleast, unless,* and *unlest*).

Excrescent [t] after [f] occurs in StE in *graft* and *tuft* (see *OED*, s.vv., especially the note on the etymology of the latter), in which it is recorded from the early fifteenth century (*tuft* in Chaucer MSS), and dialectally and vulgarly in other words (cf. Wright, § 295, and *OED*, s.v. *tuft*). Levins and Bullokar have *tuf* 'tuft' and Bullokar has *graf* 'graft'; but [t] is shown in *tuft* by Butler and Hodges. The phonetic reason for the development is obscure. Hunt records *publict* as a Scottish form of *public* (cf. *OED*).

Note 1: Wright shows a glide [d] between [l] and [r] in *tailor, smaller*, &c. (§ 298) and final excrescent [d] after [l] in *feel, mile, school, soul*, &c. (§ 306). By a similar process [d] develops in certain dialects between [r] and [l] in *parlour, curls*, &c. (§ 298) and after final [r] in *miller* and *scholar* (§ 306).

Note 2: *Lest* conjunction does not have excrescent [t], but is from *les te* < (*þȳ*) *lǣs þē*.

Note 3: Wright, § 295, shows excrescent [t] in *once, twice* (adverbial genitives), *ice, nice,* and *hoarse* in widespread dialects.

Note 4: On 'homophone' list pairings which may (but probably do not) show excrescent [t] and [d] see § 398 above.

'INTRUSIVE' [n] AND [ŋ]

§ 438. The 'intrusive' [n] in *messenger, celandine*, &c. and [ŋ] in *nightingale* and *paringale* 'equal' (< *paregal*) is a species of consonantal glide easing the passage between the preceding vowel and the following [dʒ] or [g], and is found chiefly in adopted words; it is perhaps, as has been suggested, associated with a desire to make weightier the middle syllable so as to avoid syncope (cf. Luick, §§ 456, Anm. 4; 463, Anm. 4; and Jordan, §§ 176, 255). It appears to develop at various dates from the thirteenth century (*nightingale*) onwards. In words in which it is an established feature of StE, e.g. *nightingale* and *messenger*, it is regularly shown by the orthoepists. Salesbury has *potanger* 'potager' and *Portingal* (but the latter must represent an OF variant; see *OED*, s.v.); Coles says *pottinger* is pronounced *porringer*. On *farthingale* (OF *verdugale*), a sixteenth-century adoption, see § 380, Note 3.

Note: The reverse development (loss of [n] or [ŋ] by assimilation to a following dental or [k]) occurs occasionally in syllables which have become entirely unstressed, e.g. in *frumenty* and *melancholy*; see § 401 (*a*) above. In some cases a nasal infix is already found in OF; so in *Portingale*, as remarked above, and in *papenjay* (cf. Luick, § 740, Anm. 1).

MISCELLANEOUS NOTES ON THE CONSONANTS

METATHESIS

§ 439. The late ME metathesis of *rĭ* to *ĭr* or *ŭr* when preceded by a consonant and followed by a dental is regularly shown by the orthoepists in *bird* < *brid*, *dirt*, *third*, and *thirty*; so probably *burn* and *burst* (see § 84, Note 2). Analogous metathesis occasionally occurred in other words. Cooper says he prefers the spellings *grin* (without metathesis) to *girn* but *curd* (with metathesis) to *crud*. Brown has *shurl* or *sril* as 'phonetic' spellings of *shrill* (cf. Queen Elizabeth's *shirlest* 'shrillest'). Metathesis in different phonetic circumstances occurs in *frumenty*, which is *furmenty* in Laneham and in Wharton followed by J. Smith (beside *fru-*) and is 'phonetically' spelt *furmite* by Strong, *furmete* by Young, and *frummety* or *furmety* by Brown; *OED* cites similar forms from *c.* 1390. The Northerner Poole rhymes *rick* as if **irk*.

The OE metathesis of *sc* to *cs* accounts for *ax* 'ask', recorded by Smith and by the 'homophone' lists of Hodges ('near alike'), Price, Fox and Hookes, and *WSC* (which describes *ax* as vulgar); Smith gives *ask* as a variant form of *ax* 'securis', but probably there is a misprint and it was intended as a variant of *ax* 'quære'. The apparently similar *lax* beside *lask* 'profluvium ventris', also recorded by Smith, is to be differently explained: *lask* is from ONF *lasque* (see *OED*) and *lax* is due to the influence of Latin *laxus*, *laxāre*.

Note: Wyld, *Coll. Eng.*, p. 301, cites evidence showing metathesis not only of pre-vocalic *r* (as in the words cited above, and, for example, *grudge* and *Christmas*), but also of post-vocalic (in, for example, *durst*, *worthy*, and *curbed*); of the latter Cheke gives evidence in his *thrusty* 'thirsty'. On metathesis of *r* in unstressed syllables see §§ 327–9 above.

MISDIVISION OF ARTICLES, ETC. FROM A FOLLOWING WORD

§ 440. From ME onwards it has been common for final *n* in *pen* < OE *pæm* dat. sing., in *an*, and in *mine*, &c. to be added (by misdivision of the words) to a following noun beginning with a vowel, as in *for the nones*, *atte nale*, *a newt*, *my nuncle*, &c.; conversely an initial *n* may be added to a preceding indefinite article, as in *an adder* < *a nadder*, *an apron*, *an umpire* (cf. Jordan, § 171). StE has accepted the false forms only in a few cases, which it would seem had become established by the sixteenth century; the orthoepists give no indication that educated speech in the late sixteenth and seventeenth centuries differed from PresE. But certain sources show that in vulgar speech the incorrect addition of *n* to a following word was very much more prevalent. Laneham has *nyes* 'eyes' (see Vol. I, p. 93). Coote and Daines, both of whom were Suffolk schoolmasters, and Hunt (following Coote) condemn *a nasse* 'an ass', *a nox* 'an ox', &c. as 'barbarous speaking'. Hodges has such 'homophone list' pairings as *an arrow* : *a narrow*, *a notion* : *an ocean*, mostly in his 'near alike' list, but there are some in his 'alike' list (see Vol. I, p. 399). He is followed by Strong, Coles (only in his *Eng.–Lat. Dict.*), and Cooper, of whom the last admits such pairings even to his 'alike' list, an indication of dialectal influence on his own speech; but most of the 'homophone' lists do not give these equations, a clear indication of the vulgar or dialectal status of the development.

THE TREATMENT OF FRENCH [ɲ] AND LATIN gn

§ 441. English shows three treatments of the French consonant [ɲ], whatever its source: (*a*) the group [in], which forms a diphthong with the preceding vowel, as in *Spain, reign, feign, arraign*, &c.; (*b*) simple [n], as in *Spanish, sign, assign, benign, condign, oppugn*, and in the old pronunciation of *spaniel*; (*c*) the group [nj], in early use characteristic of Scotland but later employed also in the South, as in *Spaniard, onion*, and other more recent adoptions. In the distribution of these pronunciations the orthoepists agree in general with PresE; but we may note that *spaniel* is *spannel* (or *spannil*) in Robinson, Coles, Strong, Young, Cooper, Aickin, *WSC*, and Brown, and *spanyel* only in Bullokar.

But in addition to these pronunciations based on French there are two others, of words with Latin *gn*, which derive from the English pronunciation of Latin and reflect different treatments (both of which appear to have been in use from at latest the fourteenth century) of the Latin consonant-group. Of these the first, suggested by the Latin spelling, is [gn], and is used by PresE in *signify, significance, signet, signal, ignorant, repugnant, benignity*, &c. (ME adoptions, mostly in the fourteenth century) and other similar words adopted later. All these, as far as the English pronunciation of the consonant-group is concerned, are to be regarded as direct adoptions from Latin rather than from learned French. The orthoepists give the same pronunciations as in PresE (except for Bullokar; see below) and detailed illustration is unnecessary. The same pronunciation is occasionally used in other words recognized to derive from Latin words with *gn*, e.g. *benign, condign*, and *oppugn*, which are recorded with [gn̩] by Gil, Daines, Richardson, and Cooper (see § 324 (*b*) above). Similar Hart has *repugned* (in his phonetic spelling), Coles gives the syllable-division *lig-nal-o-es* (PresE [lainæloᴜz]), and *WSC* even says that *g* is other than silent in *reigning* as well as in *signally* (presumably meaning [gn] rather than the [ŋn] discussed below). By contrast Hodges has [n] not [gn] in *Agnes*. This pronunciation with [gn] in *condign*, &c. must be dated to at latest the fourteenth century; it is evidently earlier than the development of [n̩] < -*ne* by loss of final -*e*, and in any case there is no reason to doubt that it is of antiquity equal to [gn] in *signify*, &c.

The second pronunciation is [ŋ(g)n], which was evidently often used in the English pronunciation of Latin; Latin *gn* was [ŋn], by nasalization of the velar in the group [gn], in classical Latin itself, and this pronunciation must have been adopted in English schools in consequence of the study of Latin grammarians. Its existence in the fourteenth century is shown by the spelling-evidence referred to in Note 1 below. In the sixteenth century Salesbury says that Latin *agnus* is pronounced as *angnus*, *magnus* as *mangnus*, *ignis* as *ingnis*. In English the pronunciation was used, after 1500, only in words of more learned type (e.g. there is no evidence of it in *sign*, for which it is shown by fourteenth- and fifteenth-century spellings). Bullokar remarks that 'we vse (sauing a few of late, much resisted by old customaries) to sound *n* (vnwritten) before *g*', as in *The ingnorant mangnifie the ingnominious*; that he is not recording an unreal pedantic pronunciation is shown by his regarding this as incorrect, on the ground that 'the Latin hath no letter misplaced, nor left vnsounded, nor vnwritten if it be sounded' (*Booke at Large*, p. 17). Gil similarly records [ŋṇ] as a variant beside [gṇ] in *benign* and *condign*.

Note 1: Compare the spellings *dingnete* 'dignity', *dingneste* 'worthiest', *dingneliche* 'worthily' (*Ayenbite*), *syngne* 'sign' (*Sir Gawain*), *syngnetteʒ* 'signets', *rengne* 'reign' (*Pearl*), *benyngne* (Wyclif), and others cited by *OED*, s.vv. ME spellings with *gn* are uncertain evidence of [gn] in *sign*, &c., as they may be etymological and not phonetic.

Note 2: From the beginning of the fifteenth century the consonant-group [ŋ(g)n], become final in *sign*, &c. by loss of final -*e*, was simplified to [ŋ(g)] by loss of [n] (cf. loss of final [n] after [m] in *condemn*, &c.). This development, not recorded by the orthoepists, is shown by such spellings as *sing*(*e*) 'sign' (stated by *OED* to be fourteenth-century, but I find no example cited), *benyng* 'benign' (Chaucer MSS), *malyng* 'malign' (see *OED*, s.vv.); and by rhymes with words with original -*ng*, thus *assing* 'assign', *ryng* 'reign', *condyng* 'condign', and *malyng* 'malign' with vbl. sbs. in -*ing* (*Contemplacioun of Synnaris*, ll. 612, 626, 645, 647; ed. J. A. W. Bennett, *Devotional Verse and Prose*, pp. 107, 109). In the sixteenth and seventeenth centuries these forms appear to be distinctively Scottish.

Note 3: For the assumption that in late ME and eModE a glide [g] must often have interposed between [ŋ] and [n] in *syngne* 'sign', &c., cf. the glide [p] in *solempne* 'solemn', &c., and the fact that in native words *ng* was regularly [ŋg].

THE PRONUNCIATION OF CERTAIN WORDS

§ 442. The orthoepists often give interesting evidence of the pronunciation of the consonants in individual words, mostly such as have developed new pronunciations in ModE owing to classical influences or to the conventional spelling. A selection of such words is given below, in alphabetical order.

Architect has [tʃ] in Hodges (who says that it must not be pronounced with [k]), Wharton, Hunt, J. Smith (who says that in it *ch* is not [k], as usually in words from Greek and Hebrew), Strong, Young, and *The Compendious School-Master*. The PresE pronunciation is due to the English pronunciation of Greek, and there is a suggestion that it was beginning to come in already in the seventeenth century.

Arthur has [t], representing the OF pronunciation, in Gil.

Author and *authority* have [t] in Hart, Bullokar, Coote, Gil, Butler (to judge by his comment, not his spelling), Hodges, Wharton, Hunt (in *authority*), J. Smith, *The Compendious School-Master*, and Brown; but Robinson has [þ] in *authors* beside [t] in *authority*.

Bankrupt is *bankerout* (rhyming on ME *ū*) in Levins, Hodges gives a transcription equivalent to [baŋkrʌt], and Cooper prefers the spelling *bankrout*.

Baptism has silent *s* in Hart and the shorthand-writers J. Willis and T. Shelton (of whom the latter gives silent *s* in *paganism* also); Daines says that 'they may be said to do well who ... pronounce with omission of *s*, quasi *Baptim*', but elsewhere gives a pronunciation with syllabic [m̩], which implies [s]; Wallis clearly assumes regular pronunciation of [s].

Catherine has [t] in Hart, Strong, and Young, but [þ] in Coles.

Corpse is [kuːrs] in Hodges, [koːrs] in Bullokar and Gil, and probably [kɔrs] in Levins (who rhymes it with *horse*); the 'homophone list' pairing with *course* depends on [kuːrs] in Hodges, [koːrs] in Coles, and one or the other in Ellis. But Robinson has *korps* [kɔrps].

Debt always has silent *b*, despite Holofernes (*L.L.L.*, v. i); so *doubt*.

Diphthong, according to Lily, some pronounce *dipthong*; cf. Hart, in whose transcriptions *diphthong* and *diphpongz* the *ph* may stand for aspirated [p]. But Mulcaster seems to mean that *ph* is pronounced [f], and Hodges has [difþʊŋz]; so probably Butler. The *th* is [þ] except possibly in Hart, who may show aspirated [t] beside [þ] (see Vol. I, p. 72). Cf. the spellings cited by *OED*, which illustrate pronunciations [dɪptʊŋ(g)], [dɪftʊŋ(g)], and [dɪfþʊŋ(g)]. The form with [pt] represents the earlier French *dyptongue*, and the others varying degrees of assimilation to the English pronunciation of Greek.

Effect is *effet* (cf. French *effet*) in Levins.

Eunuch is said by Hodges to be pronounced 'by many like *ev-nuke*', and is 'phonetically spelt' *ev-nuch* by Coles and *evnuke* by Strong. Butler says it should be *eunukh* not *evnuk* and Cooper protests against the spelling *evnuch*; *WSC*, repeating this protest, adds 'as it is most usually and ignorantly pronounced'. This pronunciation with [v] is due to the old pronunciation of Greek. It is not shown by Young and Brown, whose 'phonetic' spelling is *eu-nuke*. ME [yː] or [iu] is shown in the second syllable by Hodges, Young, and Brown, but ME *ŭ* by Levins, Butler, and Coles. Levins rhymes the word with *much, such*, &c., and Coles's 'phonetic spelling' (and possibly *WSC*'s comment) also shows [tʃ] for the final *ch*— anglicization under the influence of the spelling.

Gyve has the historically developed pronunciation with [g] in Hodges; see *OED*, which cites late eighteenth-century pronouncing dictionaries. The PresE [dʒ] is erroneous.

Heterogeneous and *homogeneous* have [g] in Coles's *Schoolmaster*, evidently an artificial pronunciation (due to the reformed pronunciation of Greek?).

Hiccough has [f] in Lye, but Cooper prefers the spelling *hiccop* to *hicket* and *hiccough* and Brown's 'phonetic' spelling is *hikok*. On these variant forms see *OED*, s.vv. *hicket*, *hiccup*, and *hickock*.

Jaques is given as a homophone of *jakes* by Hodges followed by Strong.

Leopard is *libbard* (ME *libard*) in Bullokar.

Lethargy has [t] in Cocker (see Vol. I, p. 417).

Lieutenant has [f] in Gil, Hodges, Merriott, *WSC* (beside [v]), and Brown, and [v] in Butler, Wharton, Price, Coles, and *WSC*. Cooper says merely that he prefers the spelling *lieutenant* to *leeftenant*. The vowel is [iː], [ɪ], or [e]. Bullokar however has [liutenənt]. On the pronunciations of this word see *OED* and § 9 above.

Machine has [k] in *WSC* owing to classical influence.

Michael and *Michaelmas* are said by Salesbury to have *ch* pronounced as [ç] (i.e. as [h]), and Hart gives [h]; but otherwise [k] is shown (as by Coles, Strong, and Young). Hunt says of *Rachel* that 'some will pronounce [it] *Rahel*'. The forms with [h] go back to ME and OF, and are due to a mistaken treatment of *ch* in these names on the same footing as in the medieval spellings *michi* 'mihi' (which Salesbury actually compares) and *nichil* 'nihil', both of which Huloet ed. Higgins says were 'of late' actually pronounced with *ch*.

Obtain has [p] beside [b] in Bullokar; the form with *op-*, common from the fifteenth to the seventeenth century (see *OED*), is due to the Latin variant *op-* of the prefix *ob-* rather than to English unvoicing (as assumed by Wyld, *Coll. Eng.*, p. 313).

Orthography has [t] in Hart (perhaps beside [þ]), Bullokar, Mulcaster, and Hodges, but apparently [þ] in the shorthand-writers Bridges and Hopkins. Butler's use of his symbol for [þ] is not reliable evidence. The form with [t] represents OF *ortographie*.

Perfect appears in various forms. *Parfit* (OF *parfit* < *perfectum*) is regular in Hodges (so also for *perfectly* and *perfectness*), but Coote describes it as the 'barbarous speech of your country people' and Hunt lists it as dialectal. *Perfit* (which shows *parfit* modified in the first vowel by the influence of Latin *perfectum*) occurs in J. Willis and the shorthand-writer Everardt; cf. Hart's *perfitly*. *Perfite*, stressed on the second, occurs in Hart (once each in conventional and phonetic spelling); cf. Cheke's *unperfight*. *Perfet* (OF *parfet* < *per+factum*, but with latinized prefix) occurs in Hart (normally), Bullokar (thrice), and Robinson. The fully Latinized form [perfekt] occurs in Bullokar (seven times), Gil, and Hunt, and was doubtless used by Coote; it may well have been a schoolmaster's pronunciation in origin, and was probably helped to gain currency by the regular [k] in *perfection* (shown, for example, by Hart, Bullokar, and Hodges).

Piazzas, according to *WSC*, was vulgarly pronounced *piaches* in London.

Respect is *respet* in Levins, a blend of *respect* and *respite* (cf. *OED*, s.v. *respett*).

Schedule has [s] in Daines, Hodges, Hunt, J. Smith, Coles, Strong, Young, Lye, and Cocker. On this pronunciation, which represents OF *cedule* and survived to the time of Walker, see *OED*; the present U.S. [skedju:l] and the British [ʃedju:l] are both spelling-pronunciations. Strong, followed by Brown, similarly gives *scheme* as a homophone of *seam*; this must be due to the analogy of *sche-* pronounced [se:] in *schedule*, and of *schism*.

Schism (ME *sisme*, &c. < OF *cisme, scisme*) has only [s], in Daines, Hunt, J. Smith, Lye, Cooper, *WSC*, Cocker, and the shorthand-writers T. Shelton, Mason, and S. Shelton.

Sphere (ME *spere* < OF *(e)spere*) is given as a homophone of *spear* by Fox and Hookes, Young, Cocker, and Brown.

Thames has always [t], despite the latinized spelling (so Gil, Butler, Coles, Strong, Young, and Brown), except that Hart gives aspirated [t]. *Thame* has [t] in Gil. *Thanet* is *Tennet* (OE *Tenet*, &c.) in Coles, Strong, Young, and Cocker.

Throne (ME *trone* < OF) has [t] in the *Welsh Hymn* and Salesbury and aspirated [t] in Hart, but [þ] (owing to the English pronunciation of Latin and Greek) in, for example, Robinson, Gil, and Hodges.

Verdict (ME *verdit* < AF) has 'silent' *c* in Daines and *WSC-RS*, and is 'phonetically' spelt *vardet* by Strong and Cocker, *verdet* by Young, and *verdit* or *vardit* by Brown. The PresE form is from medieval Latin *verdictum* (see *OED*).

Victuals (OF *vitaille*) is [vɪtlz], &c. in J. Willis, T. Shelton, Daines, and later sources. But Cooper puts the 'homophone' pairing with *vitals* into his 'near alike' list, and in his text describes *vitles* as 'barbarous speaking' (so English text; Latin 'facilitatis causa'); evidently he hankered after a latinized pronunciation.

BIBLIOGRAPHY

THE Bibliography is in two parts: (A) a list of original sources used, with modern studies dealing with them, arranged in the order in which these sources are discussed in Vol. I and under the same chapter-headings; (B) a select list of general works consulted, in alphabetical order, with the abbreviations by which they are cited. Articles and monographs on special points of phonology are not here listed, but are cited as occasion requires in Vol. II. R. C. Alston, *A Bibliography of the English Language* (Leeds, 1965–; in progress), is of the highest importance.

(A) ORIGINAL SOURCES AND MODERN STUDIES

CHAPTER I: MINOR SIXTEENTH-CENTURY SOURCES

1. *The Hymn to the Virgin.* There are the following reprints of the manuscripts and modern studies:

   Transactions Phil. Soc. 1880–1, Appendix I (reprint of MSS Hengwrt 294 and 479, now Peniarth 111 and 98*b*, by Furnivall, with notes by Ellis).
   J. C. Morrice, *Gwaith barddonol Hywel Swrdwal a'i Fab Ieuan*, 1908 (includes text of hymn; unreliable).
   Anglia, xxxii (1909), 295–300 (reprint of MS British Museum Additional 14866, by O. T. Williams, from transcript by J. C. Morrice; unreliable).
   Anglia, xxxvi (1912), 116–26 (more correct reprint of MS Addit. 14866, by H. I. Bell; important metrical notes by J. G. Davies).
   Herrigs Archiv, cxl (1920), 33–42 (edition by F. Holthausen).
   Brandl-Festschrift (*Palaestra*, cxlviii; 1925), ii. 70–72 (English text by Holthausen, with further notes).
   Herrigs Archiv, cl (1926), 187–202 (important discussion, with reprint of MS Peniarth 96 (formerly Hengwrt 176), by Max Förster).
   Transactions of the Honourable Society of Cymmrodorion, Session 1954 (1955), pp. 70–124 (edition, with introduction and notes, based on all reported MSS, by E. J. Dobson).

2. Alexander Barcley, *Introductory to wryte and to pronounce Frenche*, 1521.
3. William Lily, *Short Introduction to Grammar*, of which I used the 1549 edition, also *An English Grammar* ... by R.R. (1641), a translation of Lily's grammar. The book is a posthumous conflation of two earlier works; Lily died in 1522.
4. John Palsgrave, *Lesclarcissement de la Langue Francoyse*, 1530.
5. William Salesbury, *Dictionary in Englyshe and Welshe*, 1547.
   —— *A briefe and a playne Introduction*, 1550; revised edition, 1567.
   (Both reprinted by Ellis, iii. 743–94, the latter from the 1567 edition, with a close translation of the Welsh text and with other material.)
6. Richard Huloet, *ABCedarium Anglico-Latinum*, 1552.
7. Anon., *Abc for chyldren*, 1551–8 (reprinted by E. Flügel in *Anglia*, xiii (1891), 461–7).
8. Peter Levins, *Manipulus Vocabulorum*, 1570 (edited for E.E.T.S. by Henry B. Wheatley (1867); reprint accurate, editorial apparatus now out of date).
9. John Baret, *Alvearie or Quadruple Dictionary*, 1574. (Studied by J. Sledd, 'Baret's *Alvearie*', *Studies in Philology*, xliii (1946), 147–63.)

10. John Florio, *Florio his firste Fruites*, 1578.
 —— *Queen Anna's New World of Words*, 1611.
 (The latter was revised by G. Torriano in 1659.)
11. John Thorius, *Spanish Grammar*, 1590.
12. Richard Percival, *Bibliotheca Hispanica*, 1591.
13. John Minsheu, *Spanish Grammar*, 1599.
 —— *Ductor in Linguas*, 1617.
14. P. Gr. (Greenwood or Greaves?), *Grammatica Anglicana*, 1594. (Studied in part by M. Rösler, *Englische Studien*, liii. 168–95, and reprinted, with introduction, by O. Funke, *Grammatica Anglicana von P. Gr. (1594)* (Wiener Beiträge zur englischen Philologie, lx, 1938).)
15. Edmund Coote, *English Schoole-Master*, 1596 (and some fifty later editions before 1704, of which I have used that of 1627. Studied by W. Horn, *Anglia*, xxviii. 479–87).

CHAPTER II: THE SIXTEENTH- AND SEVENTEENTH-CENTURY SPELLING REFORMERS

1. Joannis Cheki Angli, *De pronunciatione Graecae potissimum linguæ disputationes cum Stephano Vuintoniensi episcopo*, 1555.
 Thomas Hoby, *The Courtyer of count Baldessar Castillo*, 1561 (contains letter by Cheke to Hoby).
 Cheke, *The Gospel according to St. Matthew and part of the first chapter of the Gospel according to St. Mark*, published from the manuscript in 1843.
2. Thomas Smith, *De Recta et emendata linguæ graecæ pronuntiatione* and *De recta et emendata linguæ anglicæ scriptione, Dialogus*, 1568.
 (The latter is reprinted, with introduction and word-index, by O. Deibel, Neudrucke frühneuenglischer Grammatiken, Bd. 8 (1913); see also K. Luick, *Anglia*, xiv. 297.)
3. John Hart, *The opening of the unreasonable writing of our inglish toung*, 1551 (British Museum MS Reg. 17 C vii).
 —— *An Orthographie*, 1569.
 —— *A Methode or comfortable beginning for all vnlearned*, 1570.
 (*The Orthographie* was reprinted, largely in phonetic shorthand, by I. Pitman (1850). An important discussion was by O. Jespersen, *John Hart's Pronunciation of English* (*Anglistische Forschungen*, xxii (1907), cited in this study as Jespersen, *Hart*; see also A. Eichler, *Anglia Beiblatt*, xix. 169–75 and H. Kökeritz, 'John Hart and Early Standard English', *Philologica: The Malone Anniversary Studies*, 239–48. A complete edition of Hart's writings is in B. Danielsson, *John Hart's Works*, Parts I and II (Stockholm, 1955 and 1963).
4. Robert Laneham, *A Letter*, 1575 (edited by F. J. Furnivall as *Captain Cox, his ballads and books; or, Robert Laneham's Letter*, Ballad Society, 1871; also issued as *Robert Laneham's Letter*, New Shakspere Society, ser. 6, no. 14, 1890).
5. William Bullokar. For an account of his publications see Vol. I, pp. 94–96; the following survive:

 (a) A pamphlet (1580) possibly identical with that included at the end of the *Book at Large* after the table of contents.
 (b) *Book at Large*, 1581.
 (c) *A short Introduction or guiding*, 1580, second edition 1581.

(d) *Aesop's Fables and The Short Sentences of the wise Cato*, 1585.
(e) *Brief Grammar*, 1586.

(B. Danielsson and R. C. Alston, *The Works of Wm. Bullokar*, Vol. I (Leeds, 1966), give both texts of (c). Rest in M. Plessow, *Geschichte der Fabeldichtung in England bis zu Gay* (1726). *Nebst Neudruck von Bullokars 'Fables of Aesop' 1585* (&c.) (*Palaestra*, lii; 1906). Studies: E. Hauck, *William Bullokar* (Wiss. Beilage zum Jahresb. d. Oberrealschule zu Marburg, 1905, no. 499); E. Hauck, *Systematische Lautlehre Bullokars (Vokalismus)* . . ., Marburg, 1906; R. E. Zachrisson, *The English Pronunciation at Shakespeare's Time as taught by William Bullokar*, 1927 (with word-lists; cited as Zachrisson, *Bullokar*); O. Funke, 'William Bullokars Bref Grammar for English (1586)', *Anglia*, lxii (1938), 116–37.)

6. Richard Mulcaster, *The First Part of the Elementarie*, 1582. (Reprinted by E. T. Campagnac (1925). Studies: T. Klähr, *Leben und Werke Richard Mulcasters*, 1893; L.Wiener, 'Richard Mulcaster, an Elizabethan Philologist', *Modern Language Notes*, xii (1897), 129–39; and others from the point of view of pedagogy.)

7. Richard Stanyhurst's translation of the *Aeneid*, 1582. (Of no use for our purpose. Studied by K. Bernigau, *Orthographie und Aussprache in Richard Stanyhursts englischer Übersetzung der Äneide (1582)*.)

8. Waad or Wadus: see Vol. I, pp. 129–31.

9. Alexander Gil, *Logonomia Anglica*, 1619, 2nd edition 1621. (Reprinted from 2nd edition, with an excellent introduction which sets out all the interesting variants of the 1st edition, by O. L. Jiriczek, Quellen und Forschungen zur Sprach- und Culturgeschichte der Germanischen Völker, xc (1903). Studies: O. L. Jiriczek, 'Alexander Gill', *Studien zur vergleichenden Litteraturgeschichte*, Bd. ii, Heft 2 (Berlin, 1902); H. Kökeritz, 'Alexander Gil (1621) on the Dialects of South and East England', *Studia Neophilologica*, xi (1938–9), 277–88; A. Gabrielson, 'A Few Notes on Gil's *Logonomia Anglica*, 1619', *Studia Neophilologica*, xiv (1941–2), 331–9 (also published in *Phil. Misc. presented to Eilert Ekwall*).)

10. Charles Butler, *The English Grammar*, 1633, re-issued 1634.
    —— *The Feminine Monarchie*, 3rd edition, 1634.
    —— *The Principles of Musik*, 1636.
    (The first of these is reprinted by A. Eichler, Neudrucke frühneuenglischer Grammatiken, Bd. 4, 1. Study by A. Eichler, *Schriftbild und Lautwert in Charles Butler's English Grammar (1633, 1634) und Feminin' Monarchi' (1634)* (Neudrucke, Bd. 4, 2).)

11. Richard Hödges, *A Special Help to Orthographie*, 1643 (abbreviated *SH*).
    —— *The English Primrose*, 1644 (abbreviated *EP*).
    —— *The New Hornbook* (no date).
    —— *Most plain and familiar examples* (*taken out of the English Primrose*) (no date).
    —— *The Plainest Directions for the True-writing of English*, 1649 (abbreviated *PD*; revision of *SH*). Further edition as *Most plain directions . . .*, 1653.
    (*Special Help* was reprinted in facsimile in 1932, with an introductory note by C. C. F.; *The English Primrose* in facsimile, with a full word-list, by H. Kauter, Germanische Bibliothek, Abt. 2, Bd. 82, Heidelberg: Karl Winter, 1930. Study by H. Kauter, *Englische Lautlehre nach Richard Hodges' 'English Primrose', 1644* (Beiträge zur Erforschung der Sprache und Kultur Englands und Nordamerikas, Bd. vi, Heft 1, 1928).)

12. James Howell, *Epistolae Ho-Elianae*, 1645.
 —— *The New English Grammar*, 1662.
 (The latter is reprinted in *Pamphlet 6* (1909) of the Simplified Spelling Society, with introduction by Percy Simpson.)
13. John Ray, *A Collection of English Words not Generally Used*, 2nd edition 1691. (Studied by K. Luick, *Anglia Beiblatt*, xxxix. 323–4.)

CHAPTER III: THE SEVENTEENTH-CENTURY PHONETICIANS

M. Lehnert, 'Die Anfänge der wissenschaftlichen und praktischen Phonetik in England', *Archiv*, clxxiii. 163–80, clxxiv. 28–35.
J. R. Firth, 'The English School of Phonetics', *Trans. Phil. Soc.* (1946), 92–132.
D. Abercrombie, 'Forgotten Phoneticians', *Trans. Phil. Soc.* (1948), 1–34.

1. Robert Robinson, *The Art of Pronuntiation*, 1617.
 —— transcriptions in MSS Ashmole 826, ff. 110–11 and 113–14, and Ashmole 1153, ff. 117–38.
 (Studies: H. G. Fiedler, letter in *Times Lit. Sup.*, 16 Oct. 1919; H. G. Fiedler, *A Contemporary of Shakespeare on Phonetics and on the Pronunciation of English and Latin* (M.H.R.A., November 1936); E. J. Dobson, 'Robert Robinson and his Phonetic Transcripts of Early Seventeenth-Century Pronunciation', *Trans. Phil. Soc.* (1947), 25–63; D. Abercrombie, op. cit., p. 1.)
2. Thomae Gatakeri Londinatis *de Diphthongis . . . Dissertatio Philologica*, 1641.
3. John Wallis, *Grammatica Linguae Anglicanae*, 1653 (on the later editions see Vol. I, pp. 220–2). (Studies: Leo Morel, *De Johannis Wallisii Grammatica Linguae Anglicanae et Tractatu de Loquela* (1895); M. Lehnert, *Die Grammatik des englischen Sprachmeisters John Wallis (1616–1703)* (Sprache und Kultur der germanischen und romanischen Völker, Anglistische Reihe, Bd. xxi, 1936).)
4. Isaac Newton's phonetic notes, c. 1660–2 (printed by R. W. V. Elliott, *Modern Language Review*, xlix. 5–12).
5. John Wilkins, *Essay towards a Real Character and a Philosophical Language*, 1668. (Part iii, chs. x–xiv are reprinted by O. Funke, *Zum Weltsprachenproblem in England im 17. Jahrhundert* (Anglistische Forschungen lxix, 1929), pp. 107–44.)
6. William Holder, *Elements of Speech*, 1669.
7. Francis Lodwick, *Essay towards an Universal Alphabet* (in *Philosophical Transactions of the Royal Society*, vol. xvi, no. 182, June 1686). Also separately published, no date or place; c. 1685? (See Vol. I, p. 271 footnote, on the differences between the two editions.) Lodwick's manuscript notebooks are preserved in the British Museum (MSS Sloane 897 and 932). (Studies: Judica I. H. Mendels, 'Een Phoneticus uit de 17de. Eeuw', *Neophilologus*, Jaargang xxi (April 1936), 219–25; D. Abercrombie, op. cit., pp. 2–11.)
8. Christopher Cooper, *Grammatica Linguae Anglicanae*, 1685.
 —— *The English Teacher*, 1687 (apparently republished as *The Compleat English Teacher* by 'C. C.', 1698).
 (The *Grammatica* is reprinted by J. D. Jones in Neudrucke frühneuenglischer Grammatiken, Bd. 5 (1911 according to title-page, 1912 according to cover), with introduction and word-index; as appendixes Jones prints passages from the '*Welsh Breviary*' (1670) and from T. Jones, *Welsh–English Dictionary*

(1688). *The English Teacher* is reprinted, with introduction and notes, by B. Sundby (Lund Studies in English, xxii; 1953). See also E. Ekwall, 'The MS Collections of Prof. Anna Paues', *Studia Neophilologica*, xxi. 35.)

Chapter IV: Minor Seventeenth-Century Sources

Part 1: English Grammars and Spelling-Books

1. Thomas Tonkis (or Tomkis), *De analogia Anglicani Sermonis*, 1612 (MS British Museum Reg. F xviii).
2. Alexander Hume, *Of the Orthographie and Congruitie of the Britan Tongue*, c. 1617 (edited from the manuscript by Henry B. Wheatley, E.E.T.S. 1865).
3. Thomas Hayward, *The English Institutions*, after 1625 (MS British Museum Sloane 2609).
4. Ben Jonson, *English Grammar*, 1640–1 (first written before 1623). (Reprinted by Strickland Gibson (1927), with introductory note; edited by Herford and Simpson, *Ben Jonson*, viii. 455–553 (text, with introductory note) and xi. 165–210 (commentary); studies by Percy Simpson, op. cit., ii. 417–35, and O. Funke, *Anglia*, lxiv (1940), 117–34.)
5. Simon Daines, *Orthoepia Anglicana*, 1640. (Edited by Rösler and Brotanek, Neudrucke frühneuenglischer Grammatiken, Bd. 3 (1908).)
6. Jeremiah Wharton, *The English Grammar*, 1654.
7. Thomas Hunt, *Libellus Orthographicus: or The Diligent Schoolboy's Directory*, 1661.
8. Owen Price, *The Vocal Organ*, 1665 (cited as *VO*). (Study: A. Gabrielson, *Studia Neophilologica*, ii. 150–1.)
 —— *English Orthographie*, 1668, 2nd edition, 1670 (cited as *Eng.O.*).
9. John Hughes, *Allwyd neu Agoriad Paradwys i'r Cymry*, 1670 (cited as *Welsh Breviary*). (Reprinted by J. D. Jones as an appendix to his edition of Cooper's *Grammatica*, for which see above; edited by John Fisher, Cardiff, 1929.)
10. Elisha Coles, *The Compleat English Schoolmaster*, 1674.
 —— *The Newest, Plainest, and shortest Shorthand*, 1674.
 —— *An English Dictionary*, 1676.
 —— *Syncrisis*, 1677.
 —— *A Dictionary, English–Latin and Latin–English*, 2nd edition, 1679 (cited as *Eng.-Lat. Dict.*; the 1st edition of 1677 is of no use for our purposes). (Studies: Gerald Mander, 'The Identity of Elisha Coles', *The Library*, 3rd series, no. x (Jan. 1919); A. Gabrielson, 'Professor Kennedy's Bibliography ... A Review', *Studia Neophilologica*, ii (1929), 151–4; and 'Elisha Coles's "Syncrisis" (1675) ...', *Englische Studien*, lxx (1935–6), 149–52.)
11. Nathaniel Strong, *England's Perfect School-Master*, 2nd edition, 1676 (1st edition 1675–6). (Study: A. Gabrielson, *Studia Neophilologica*, ii. 138.)
12. E. Young, *The Compleat English Scholar*, 1676 (?); earliest surviving edition, 5th of 1682. (Study: A. Gabrielson, op. cit., pp. 155–6.)
13. Thomas Lye, *A New Spelling Book*, 1677. (Studied in K. L. Kern, *Die Englische Lautentwicklung nach Right Spelling (1704) und anderen Grammatiken um 1700*, 1913.) 2nd edition of *Reading and Spelling English made easie*, 1673.
14. Thomas Jones, *A Welsh–English Dictionary*, 1688. (Includes an account of 'How to read English', reprinted with English translation by J. D. Jones in his edition of Cooper's *Grammatica*, for which see above.)
15. Joseph Aickin, *The English Grammar*, 1693.

16. Anon. *The Writing Scholar's Companion*, 1695 (cited as *WSC*).
—— *Right Spelling very much Improved*, 1704 (cited as *RS*).
—— *The Expert Orthographist*, 1704.
 (These three books are by the same author; the third, known to Ellis but since lost, appears to have been identical, in all but titlepage, with the second, which in turn is a revised edition of the first. *WSC* is edited by E. Ekwall, Neudrucke frühneuenglischer Grammatiken, Bd. 6 (1911), with an introduction; see also Kemp Malone, 'Notes on *The Writing Scholar's Companion*', *Modern Language Notes*, xxxix. 502–4. *RS* is studied by K. L. Kern, op. cit. See also Ellis, i. 46–47 and ch. iii (*passim*).)
17. E. Cocker, *Cocker's Accomplished School-Master*, 1696; 18th edition, 1748.
18. R. Brown, *The English-School Reformed*, 1700. (Studies: K. L. Kern, op. cit.; A. Gabrielson, 'ME $\bar{e}$ in Brown 1700 = $\bar{\imath}$?', *Studia Neophilologica*, iii (1930), 11–16.)
19. *Lesser sources:*
 Richard Verstegan, *A Restitution of decayed Intelligence*, 1605.
 John Evelyn, *The English Grammar*, between 1641 and 1653 (MS British Museum Additional 15950, ff. 94–98).
 R. Lloyd, *The Schoole-Masters Auxiliaries*, 1654, 2nd edition, 1659.
 Jo. Brooksbank, *Plain, Brief, and pertinent Rvles for . . . Syllabification*, 1654.
 T. Merriott, *Grammaticall Miscellanies*, 1660.
 Ralph Johnson, *Ancilla Grammaticae*, 1662 (2nd edition, *The Scholars Guide*, 1665).
 George Fox and Ellis Hookes, *Instructions for Right Spelling*, 1673.
 J. Smith, *Grammatica Quadrilinguis*, 1674.
 Nathaniel Strong, op. cit.
 E. Young, op. cit.
 Anon., *A Treatise of Stops, Points, or Pauses*, 1680.
 Tobias Ellis, *The English School*, 2nd edition, 1670 (according to Kennedy's *Bibliography*; I have used the edition of 1680).
 —— *The True English School*, 1691 (abridged edition of the preceding).
 Moses Lane (?), *The Protestant Tutor*, 1681.
 Anon., *The Compendious School-Master*, 1687.
 T. Osborne, *A rational way of teaching*, 1688.
 —— *The grounds of reading*, 1694.
  (These two works were not used. On the former see Chr. Müller, *Englische Lautentwicklung nach Lediard* (&c.), 1915.)
 J. Hawkins, *The English School-Master Compleated*, 1692.
 E. Cocker, *op. cit.*
 A. Lane, *A Key to the Art of Letters*, 1700.

Part 2: Grammars of Foreign Languages and Interlingual Dictionaries

1. John Sanford, *Le Guichet François*, 1604.
 —— *A briefe extract*, 1605.
 —— *A Grammer or Introdvction to the Italian Tongue*, 1605.
 —— Προπύλαιον, *or an entrance to the Spanish Tongue*, 1611.
2. Lewis Owen, *The Key of the Spanish Tongue*, 1605.
3. Randle Cotgrave, *A Dictionarie of the French and English Tongves*, 1611.
 Robert Sherwood, *A Dictionarie English and French*, 1632.
 James Howell, *The French Grammar* (in his revision of Cotgrave and Sherwood), 1650.

4. William Colson, *The First Part of the French Grammar*, 1620.
5. I. W., *A Grammar Spanish and English*, 1622.
6. John Wodroephe, *The spared hovres of a sovldier*, 1623.
7. Joh. Robotham, *Preface* to 6th (1643) edition of Horn's translation of Comenius's *Janua Linguarum Reserata*.
8. Anon., *The English Schole-master*, 1646.
9. Henry Hexham, *An English Grammar* appended to *A Copious English and Netherduytch Dictionary*, 1647.
—— *Een Nederduytsche Grammatica* appended to *Het Groot Woordenboeck Gestelt in 't Neder-duytsch ende 't Engelsch*, 1648.
10. Edward Richardson, *Anglo-Belgica. The English and Netherdutch Academy*, 1677.

Part 3: Books on Shorthand Systems

Helge Kökeritz, 'English Pronunciation as described in Shorthand Systems of the 17th and 18th Centuries', *Studia Neophilologica*, vii (1935), 73–146.

W. Matthews, *English Pronunciation and Shorthand in the Early Modern Period* (University of California Publications in English, ix, 3; 1943).

1. John Willis, *The Art of Stenographie*, 1602 (I also used the 1628 edition).
2. William Folkingham, *Brachigraphy*, 1618.
3. E. Willis, *An Abbreviation of Writing by Character*, 1618.
4. Thomas Shelton, *Short-writing*, 1620 (2nd edition 1630, which I used).
—— *Tachygraphy*, 1641.
—— *A Tutor to Tachygraphy*, 1643.
—— *Zeiglographia*, 1650.
Anon., *The Art of Short-writing According to Tachygraphy*, 1684 (revision of Shelton's *Tachygraphy*).
5. Henry Dix, *The Art of Brachygraphy*, 1633 (I used the 1641 edition).
6. Theophilus Metcalf, *Radio-Stenography*, 1635 (I used the 1645 edition, which is entitled *Short-writing*).
7. William Cartwright, *Semography*, 1642.
8. Jeremiah Rich, *Characterie*, 1646 (not seen).
—— *Semigraphy or Arts Rarity*, 1654.
—— *The Pens Dexterity*, 1659.
Anon., *The Pens Dexterity compleated*, 1669 (revision of preceding, probably by Botley; see next entry).
9. Samuel Botley, *Maximo in Minimo, or Mr. Jeremiah Rich's Pens Dexterity Compleated*, 1674.
10. Simon West, *Arts Improvement*, 1647.
11. John Farthing, *Short-writing Shortened*, 1654 (I used the 1684 edition).
12. Job Everardt, *Epitome of Stenography*, 1658.
13. Noah Bridges, *Stenographie and Cryptographie*, 1659.
14. William Addy, *Stenographia*, 1664.
15. Thomas Heath, *Stenography*, 1664.
16. William Hopkins, *The Flying Pen-man*, 1670.
17. William Mason, *A Pen Pluck'd from an Eagles Wing*, 1672.
—— *Arts Advancement*, 1682.
—— *La Plume Volante*, 1707.
18. Lawrence Steel, *Short Writing*, 1672 (I used the 1678 edition).
19. S. Shelton, *Brachygraphy*, 1672.
20. Nathaniel Stringer, *Rich Redivivus*, 1680 (?).

21. Elisha Coles, *The Newest, Plainest, & shortest Shorthand*, 1674.
22. Abraham Nicholas, *Thoographia*, 1692.
23. George Ridpath, *Shorthand yet shorter*, 1687.

Part 4: Lists of 'Homophones'

Lists of 'homophones' are given in the following works:

Coote, op. cit., 1597.
Butler, op. cit., 1633 and 1634.
Daines, op. cit., 1640.
Hodges, *Special Help*, 1643.
—— *Plain Directions*, 1649.
Wharton, op. cit., 1654.
T. Merriott, op. cit., 1660.
Hunt, op. cit., 1661.
Price, *Vocal Organ*, 1665.
—— *English Orthographie*, 1668 and 1670.
Ellis, op. cit., 2nd edition, 1670.
Fox and Hookes, op. cit., 1670.
E. Coles, *Schoolmaster*, 1674.
—— *English Dictionary*, 1676.
—— *Eng.–Lat. Dictionary*, 2nd edition, 1679.
Strong, op. cit., 2nd edition, 1676 (and in 1st edition before 1675).
Young, op. cit., 1675.
Richardson, op. cit., 1677.
Cooper, *Grammatica*, 1685.
—— *English Teacher*, 1688.
Anon., *Compendious School-Master*, 1688.
T. Osborne, op. cit., 1688 (not seen).
J. Hawkins, op. cit., 1692.
Aickin, op. cit., 1693.
Writing Scholar's Companion, 1695, and *Right Spelling*, 1704.
Cocker, op. cit., 1696.
Brown, op. cit., 1700.
MS British Museum Sloane 719, ff. 110*b*–116*a* (after 1700).

Part 5: Rhyming Dictionaries

1. Thomas Willis, *Vestibulum Linguæ Latinæ*, 1651.
2. Josua Poole, *The English Parnassus*, 1657 (published posthumously).
3. Elisha Coles, *The Compleat English Schoolmaster*, 1674.

(B) SELECT LIST OF GENERAL WORKS

J. Bosworth and T. N. Toller, *An Anglo-Saxon Dictionary*, 1898, with Supplement by T. N. Toller, 1921 (cited as Bosworth–Toller).
K. D. Bülbring, *Altenglisches Elementarbuch*, 1902 (cited as Bülbring).
R. W. Chambers and Marjorie Daunt, *A Book of London English 1384–1425*, 1931.
Constance Davies, *English Pronunciation from the fifteenth to the eighteenth Century*, 1934.
The Dictionary of National Biography (*DNB*), 1882– .
E. Ekwall, *Historische neuenglische Laut- und Formenlehre*, 1922 (cited as Ekwall).
—— *The Oxford Dictionary of English Place-Names*, 1936.

A. J. Ellis, *On Early English Pronunciation*, 1869–89 (cited as Ellis).
The English Place-Name Society (E.P.-N.S.) county surveys 1925–
R. Girvan, *Angelsaksisch Handboek*, 1931.
W. Horn, *Historische neuenglische Grammatik*, 1908 (cited as Horn).
—— *Laut und Leben: Englische Lautgeschichte der neueren Zeit (1400–1950)*, bearbeitet von Martin Lehnert, 1954.
O. Jespersen, *A Modern English Grammar*, Part I, 1909 (cited as Jespersen, *ModE Gr*).
Daniel Jones, *An Outline of English Phonetics*, 1919, 5th edition 1936.
—— *An English Pronouncing Dictionary*, 1917, 4th edition 1937.
R. Jordan, *Handbuch der mittelenglischen Grammatik*, 1925, revised edition by H. Ch. Matthes 1934 (cited as Jordan).
A. G. Kennedy, *A Bibliography of Writings on the English Language . . . to the end of 1922*, 1927.
A. Kihlbom, *A Contribution to the Study of Fifteenth Century English*, 1926 (cited as Kihlbom).
H. Kökeritz, *Shakespeare's Pronunciation*, 1953.
K. Luick, *Untersuchungen zur englischen Lautgeschichte*, 1896.
—— *Historische Grammatik der englischen Sprache*, 1914–40 (cited as Luick).
L. Morsbach, *Mittelenglische Grammatik*, 1896.
G. G. Nicholson, *A Practical Introduction to French Phonetics*, 1909.
The Oxford English Dictionary, ed. Murray, Bradley, Craigie, and Onions, 1888–1933 (cited as *OED*).
M. K. Pope, *From Latin to Modern French with especial Consideration of Anglo-Norman*, 1934 (cited as Pope).
W. Ripman, *English Phonetics*, 1931.
E. Sievers, *Angelsächsische Grammatik*, 1882, &c., revised by K. Brunner as *Altenglische Grammatik*, 1942 (cited as Sievers–Brunner).
F. H. Stratmann and H. Bradley, *A Middle-English Dictionary*, 1891.
H. Sweet, *History of English Sounds*, 1888.
—— *A Primer of Phonetics*, 1890, 3rd edition 1906.
—— *A New English Grammar*, 1892.
—— *The Sounds of English*, 1908.
W. Viëtor, *Shakespeare's Pronunciation*, 1906 (cited as Viëtor).
J. Wright, *English Dialect Dictionary*, 1896–1905 (*EDD*).
—— *English Dialect Grammar*, 1905 (cited as Wright, *EDG*, or as Wright; 'Wright, Index' refers to the Index to this book).
—— and E. M. Wright, *An Elementary Historical New English Grammar*, 1924.
H. C. Wyld, *A Short History of English*, 1914, 3rd edition, 1927.
—— *A History of Modern Colloquial English*, 1920, 3rd edition 1936 (cited as Wyld, *Coll. Eng.*).
—— *Studies in English Rhymes from Surrey to Pope*, 1923 (cited as Wyld, *Rhymes*).
R. E. Zachrisson, *Pronunciation of English Vowels 1400–1700*, 1912 (cited as Zachrisson, *Eng. Vowels*).

APPENDIX I

CHRONOLOGICAL LIST OF ORTHOEPISTS

(For shorthand-books see the Bibliography above)

a. 1500 *Hymn to the Virgin* (Welsh Hymn).
1521 Barcley, *Introductory*.
c. 1521 Lily, *Short Introduction of Grammar* (published 1549).
1530 Palsgrave, *Lesclarcissement*.
1542 Cheke, *De pronunciatione Graecae . . . linguæ*.
1542 Smith, *De linguæ graecæ pronuntiatione* (published 1568).
1547 Salesbury, *Dictionary*.
1550 Salesbury, *Introduction*.
c. 1550 Cheke's translation of the Gospels.
1551 Hart MS.
1552 Huloet, *ABC*.
1551–8 *Abc for chyldren*.
1557 Cheke's letter to Sir T. Hoby.
1566 Smith, *De linguæ anglicæ scriptione* (originally drafted *c.* 1542, published 1568).
1569 Hart, *Orthographie*.
1570 Hart, *Methode*.
1570 Levins, *Manipulus*.
1574 Baret, *Alvearie*.
1575 Laneham, *Letter*.
1578 Florio, *First Fruites*.
1580 Bullokar's pamphlet included in *Book at Large*.
1580 Bullokar, *Short Introduction* (2nd edition, 1581).
1581 Bullokar, *Book at Large*.
1582 Mulcaster, *Elementarie*.
1582 Stanyhurst's translation of the *Aeneid*.
1585 Bullokar, *Fables*.
1586 Bullokar, *Brief Grammar*.
1590 Thorius, *Spanish Grammar*.
1591 Percival, *Bibliotheca Hispanica*.
1594 P.G. *Grammatica Anglicana*.
1596 Coote, *English Schoole-Master*.
1599 Minsheu, *Spanish Grammar*.
1602 Waad.
1604 Sanford, *Guichet François*.
1605 Sanford, *Briefe Extract*.
1605 Sanford, *Italian Grammar*.
1605 Verstegan, *Restitutions*.
1605 Owen, *Key to the Spanish Tongue*.
1611 Cotgrave, *Dictionarie*.
1611 Sanford, Προπύλαιον.
1611 Florio, *New World of Words*.
1612 Tonkis, *De Analogia*.
1617 Minsheu, *Ductor in Linguas*.
1617 Robinson, *Art of Pronuntiation*.
p. 1617 Robinson MSS.
c. 1617 Hume, *Orthographie*.
1619 Gil, *Logonomia*.
1620 Colson, *French Grammar*.
1621 Gil, *Logonomia* (2nd edition).
1622 I. W., *Grammar Spanish and English*.
1623 Wodroephe, *Spared Hours*.
p. 1625 Hayward, *English Institutions*.
1632 Sherwood, *Dictionary*.
1633 Butler, *English Grammar*.
1634 Butler, *Feminine Monarchie* (3rd edition).
1636 Butler, *Principles of Musik*.
1640 Daines, *Orthoepia*.
1640–1 Jonson, *English Grammar* (originally written before 1623).
1641 Gataker, *De diphthongis*.

APPENDIX I

1643 Robotham's preface to the 6th edition of Horn's translation of Comenius's *Janua Linguarum Reserata*.
1643 Hodges, *Special Help*.
1644 Hodges, *English Primrose*.
1645 Howell, *Epistolae Ho-Elianae*.
1646 Anon., *English Schole-master*.
1647 Hexham, *English Grammar*.
1648 Hexham, *Nederduytsche Grammatica*.
1649 Hodges, *Plainest Directions*.
1650 Howell, *French Grammar*.
1651 Willis, *Vestibulum*.
a. 1653 Evelyn, *English Grammar*.
1653 Wallis, *Grammatica*.
1654 Wharton, *English Grammar*.
1654 Brooksbank, *Plain Rules*.
1654 Lloyd, *Schoole-Masters Auxiliaries*.
1657 Poole, *English Parnassus* (written earlier; posthumous publication).
1659 Lloyd (2nd edition).
1660 Merriott, *Grammaticall Miscellanies*.
1661 Hunt, *Libellus Orthographicus*.
c. 1660–2 Newton's notebook.
1662 Howell, *New English Grammar*.
1662 Johnson, *Ancilla Grammaticae*.
1664 Wallis (2nd edition).
1665 Johnson, *Scholars Guide* (new edition of *Ancilla*).
1665 Price, *Vocal Organ*.
1668 Price, *English Orthographie*.
1668 Wilkins, *Essay towards a Real Character*.
1669 Holder, *Elements of Speech* (in MS before 1668).
1670 Price, *English Orthographie* (2nd edition).
1670 Hughes, 'Welsh Breviary'.
1670 Ellis, *English School* (2nd edition).
1672 Wallis (3rd edition).

1673 Fox and Hookes, *Instructions*.
1674 Wallis (4th edition).
1674 J. Smith, *Grammatica*.
1674 E. Coles, *Schoolmaster*.
1676 Strong, *England's perfect Schoolmaster* (2nd edition; probably originally published before Young's book).
?1676 Young, *Compleat English Scholar* (5th edition, 1682).
1676 E. Coles, *English Dictionary*.
1677 E. Coles, *Syncrisis*.
1677 Lye, *New Spelling Book*.
1677 Richardson, *Anglo-Belgica*.
1679 E. Coles, *English–Latin Dictionary* (2nd edition; the first edition of 1677 is of no value for our purposes).
1680 Anon., *Treatise of Stops*.
1680 Ellis, *English School* (further edition, which I have used, of book listed above under 1670).
1681 M. Lane (?), *Protestant Tutor*.
c. 1685 Lodwick, *Essay* (separate edition as pamphlet; draft referred to by Wilkins in 1668).
1685 Cooper, *Grammatica*.
1686 Lodwick, *Essay* (in *Philos. Trans. Royal Soc.*).
1687 Anon., *Compendious SchoolMaster*.
1687 Cooper, *English Teacher*.
1688 T. Jones, *Welsh–English Dictionary*.
1688 T. Osborne, *Rational Way of Teaching*.
1691 Ellis, *True English School* (abridged edition of his *English School*).
1691 Ray, *Collection of English Words* (2nd edition).
1692 Hawkins, *English SchoolMaster*.
1693 Aickin, *English Grammar*.
1695 Anon., *Writing Scholar's Companion*.

1696 Cocker, *Accomplished School-Master*.
1699 Wallis (5th and definitive edition).
1700 Brown, *English-School Reformed* (2nd edition of lost work published *c*. 1693).
1704 Anon., *Right Spelling* (by the author of *WSC* 1695, of which it is a revised edition).
1704 Anon., *Expert Orthographist* (known to Ellis but since lost; apparently identical, in all but title-page, with *RS*).

APPENDIX II

THE HART GENEALOGIES

IN my discussion of Hart's origins (Vol. I, pp. 64–65 above) I was unable to take into account the detailed and erudite genealogical information contained in Part I of Dr. B. Danielsson's edition of *John Hart's Works* (Stockholm, 1955), which appeared after my own account of Hart was already in proof. But I find great difficulty in accepting Danielsson's hypothesis, which he states (p. 13) as if it were a recorded fact, that John Hart the herald and orthoepist was the son of a Middlesex yeoman of the same name. This hypothesis rests on a conflation of the statements of a pedigree of 1634—originally brought to notice by H. Kökeritz—which gives the descent of the Harts of Northolt,[1] and information gathered by Danielsson from the records of the manors of Northolt and Down Barns and from the parish registers of Northolt.[2] Both the pedigree and the records show that the Harts of Northolt descend from one William Hart of Northolt (d. 1559), but beyond this point they begin to diverge. The records show that this William Hart was the son of Robert Hart of Northolt; the pedigree states that he was the son of a Robert Hart who is described as 'of London marcht. Lived in Cornhill'. The pedigree states that Robert Hart of Cornhill's brother was John Hart Chester Herald; the records have 'only cursory mentions' of a John Hart Junior, brother of Robert Hart of Northolt.[3] The pedigree states that the father of Robert Hart of Cornhill and John Hart Chester Herald was Thomas Hart 'of [blank] in Com. Devon'; the records show that the father of Robert Hart and John Hart Junior of Northolt was John Hart of Northolt. Danielsson, in an attempt to harmonize the two sources of evidence, assumes that Robert Hart of Northolt must be identical with Robert Hart of Cornhill, and consequently also identifies John Hart Junior of Northolt with John Hart Chester Herald; and he therefore concludes, on the evidence of the Northolt records, that the herald must have been the son of John Hart of Northolt. But this involves the deliberate rejection of the pedigree's statement that the herald was the son of Thomas Hart of Devon, for at this point the two sources of evidence clearly become incompatible; indeed there is no room at all for Thomas Hart of Devon in the descent of the Northolt family, which Danielsson has traced from the mid-fifteenth century to the beginning of the seventeenth.

Danielsson's process of reasoning may appear justifiable, but that it is in reality misleading is shown by a simple fact. John Hart of Northolt died in 1500 and must then have been at least sixty years old, since in 1461 he was a grown man holding the office of headborough.[4] Any son of his must therefore have been born in the first months of 1501 at latest (as Danielsson himself observes[5]) and probably a good while earlier; but Hart the orthoepist refers to himself, in the 1551 MS,

---

[1] Cf. Danielsson, op. cit., i. 17, 37; it comes from *The Visitation of Middlesex*, 1634.
[2] Danielsson, i. 13 and footnotes.   [3] Ibid., i. 15, 42.   [4] Ibid., i. 13, note 4.
[5] Ibid., i. 42.

as 'young', which no man of fifty or over could possibly do.[1] Similarly, if he had been born in or before 1501, it would be surprising that the earliest record of his official employments is dated 1563, when he would have been at least 62;[2] he would have been at least 60 when he was involved in the affray in 1561 which led to his killing a man in self-defence,[3] at least 68 when the *Orthographie* was published, and at least 72 when in 1573 his wife was assailed by York Herald, Garter's son, with personal violence and opprobrious epithets even more unsuitable to an ageing than to a young woman.[4] The suggestion throughout is of a much younger man. Moreover it seems unlikely that the accomplished Chester Herald, a man of some social rank, should have sprung from the Northolt family of tenant farmers.[5]

Danielsson, in Part II (1963) of his edition of Hart's works, has returned (pp. 269 ff.) to the question of Hart's identity and origins. Attempting to rebut the evidence that in 1551 Hart was a young man, he writes (p. 269):

> Unfortunately this passage (like numerous other passages in the 1551 MS) is a free translation from Meigret [Meigret 1545, f. 10a–11a] and does not seem to allow of any conclusions at all. On the contrary imputations of immaturity and youth are not infrequent in the contemporary discussions of orthographic reforms in France, especially in the exchange of pamphlets between Meigret and Guillaume des Autels . . .

The apparent intention is to suggest that the phrase 'vainglorious young fool' is taken, with the rest of the passage in which it comes, from Meigret; but this is untrue. It is true that Hart, from the foot of his p. 54 to the end of his p. 61, is following lines laid down by Meigret,[6] though only towards the end is he in any sense 'translating', even freely; but the critical phrase, so far from being taken from Meigret, is on the contrary part of his expansion of Meigret. The latter writes (f. Bii):

> Ie sçay bien toutesfois, qu'il s'en trouuera quelsques vngs qui courroucez demanderont en fureur, si ie pense plus sauoir que les autres. Aux quelz aussi ie demanderay en semblable . . .

To this there corresponds in Hart:

> Yet will not some of them be contented: but in their malice (when they see reason thus assaile theim) as men amazed, they will stand and skold, untill they be

---

[1] See Vol. I, p. 64. There is no evidence at all for supposing that the MS was not composed, as well as copied out fair, in 1551; in the *Orthographie* Hart refers to it as having been written 'about .xx. yeares passed' (ff. 5ᵛ–6ʳ), but this is quite consistent with the date 1551. Even if we ignored the 'about' it would still put the date of composition of the MS work no earlier than 1549, which does not at all remove the difficulty of his age.

[2] Danielsson, op. cit., i. 24.

[3] See note 5 below.   [4] Danielsson, op. cit., i. 77–78.

[5] It is true that the John Hart who in 1561 was pardoned for killing a man in London in self-defence (ibid., i. 24, 67–70) and who seems clearly to have been the orthoepist (since the handwriting and spelling of his letter to Cecil describing the incident are closely similar to those of the 1551 MS; cf. ibid., Figs. 7–9) is described in the pardon as 'John Harte of London yeoman'; but the term *yeoman* was often loosely used (cf. *OED*, s.v.). In other legal documents Hart is described as a gentleman or as 'generosus' (ibid., i. 72–73, 80).

[6] Louis Meigret, *Traité touchant le commun usage de l'escriture françoise* (2nd edition, Paris, 1545), ff. Bii–Biii (= ff. 10a–11a).

overcome: and say see the vainglorious young foole, which thinketh him self to kno more, and see further then other aunsient men: which have spent manie yeares in studie of letters, and yet find no souch faultes. To them I answere . . .'[1]

Hart has completely rewritten Meigret, and the expression 'vainglorious young fool', with the contrasted 'other aunsient men' (other men who are old) where Meigret has only 'les autres', is his own addition; there is nothing even to suggest it in this passage of Meigret, unless possibly the word *vainglorious* was derived from Meigret's remark a little later (f. Biii), 'Ie confesse bien qu'à bonne rayson on me iugera en ce traicté le plus impatient, le plus *oultrecuydé* [my italics], & finablement le plus damnable de tous.'

Danielsson, knowing that there is nothing about youth in the passage in Meigret which Hart was following, refers to the fact that in other controversial works of 1548 and 1549 Meigret alludes to the youth of his opponent Guillaume des Autels, and that the latter in a reply acknowledged that these accusations of youth had been levelled against him. It is possible, though unproved, that Hart may have known of these lesser controversial writings and may have deduced from them that Meigret regarded his opponent, the defender of the traditional orthography, as not only young but a fool; but the situation that Hart imagines is the reverse, the defenders of tradition referring to himself, the reformer, as a 'vainglorious young fool'. Writers do not make up phrases, and apply them in a new way, from bits and pieces in other men's works in a sort of automatic trance, without considering their appropriateness to the situation envisaged. That Hart did consider the appropriateness of his phrase is shown by the fact that eighteen years later, in the *Orthographie*, he varied it by dropping the adjective 'young'. Danielsson admits that this was for the obvious reason, that it was no longer appropriate; it follows in logic that when Hart made up the phrase (as he did) and imagined men applying it to himself (as he did), he must indeed have been young —or at least capable of being thought young in contrast to 'aunsient' men who had spent long years in study. It is a mere matter of fact that the phrase is Hart's, and that he represents it as being applied to himself. And in any case the other evidence cited above, that he was a much younger man than Danielsson would make him, remains unchallenged.

The pivot of Danielsson's attempt to reconcile the 1643 pedigree of the Harts of Northolt with the records is his identification of Robert Hart of Northolt, an innkeeper and tenant-farmer who had a house in Down and whose activities are pretty continuously chronicled in the Northolt manor records from 1490 to 1537,[2] with Robert Hart the London merchant who lived in Cornhill; but the occupations, residences, and implied social status are so different that it is incredible that the two men can really be one and the same. It is not simply a case of a London merchant owning property in Northolt. That each had a brother John[3] is merely

---

[1] Hart, *MS*, pp. 58–9 (ed. Danielsson, i. 124).

[2] Danielsson, op. cit., i. 41–42.

[3] Assuming that Robert Hart of Northolt did have a brother John. It does not appear to be well established from the Northolt records; Danielsson, i. 42, speaks vaguely of 'only passing mentions of a John Hart, Junior, in the Northolt Manor Court Rolls', but does not cite his evidence. He really assumes that Robert of Northolt had a brother John because he identifies Robert of Northolt with Robert the merchant of London, and then relies on the evidence of the 1634 pedigree that Robert the merchant had a brother, John the herald.

a coincidence such as can easily arise when both the Christian and surnames are common; there were only too many John Harts in the sixteenth century.[1] As John Hart the herald flourished between 1551 and 1574, any brother of his would be expected to have lived about the same time; but Robert Hart of Northolt had been sworn a tithingman in 1478,[2] and died at latest in the 1530s.[3] Moreover, the 1634 pedigree makes John Hart the herald, who was young in 1551 and died in 1574, the great-great-uncle of a Matthew Hart of Northolt who was baptised in 1581;[4] not even in a precocious family would there have been enough time for the necessary wedding and bedding. Everything is against the identification of Robert Hart of Cornhill with Robert Hart of Northolt; it is plain that there is an error in the pedigree. Danielsson recognizes that Thomas Hart of Devon has no place in it, but the same is true of Robert Hart of Cornhill and John Hart the herald; none of them fits. Information relating to the herald and his family has been grafted on to the top of the pedigree of the Harts of Northolt, by a false identification of the two Robert Harts; information concerning his forbears correctly supplied by Matthew Hart of Northolt to the heralds at the 1634 visitation of Middlesex has been conflated with knowledge which the College of Heralds must already have possessed concerning the kindred of the sixteenth-century Chester Herald. And the motive for the conflation (whether deliberately fraudulent, or made in the honest but naïve belief that men of the same name must be identifiable) is obvious—to connect the Harts of Northolt with a known armigerous family, and so give them a right to bear the arms of the Harts of Devon.

Other relevant information is contained in the pedigree, in the 1619 Visitation of Kent, of Sir Eustace Hart, then head of another family known as the Harts of

[1] It would be easy to make up a list of well over a dozen, most of them apparently unrelated. In addition to those mentioned in Danielsson's study, I list the following whose names are mentioned in City of London documents (mostly parish registers), none of whom can certainly be identified with another. (1) John Harte who served as juror on an inquisition post mortem on the estate of the Duke of Buckingham at the Guildhall on 16 Oct. 1525; perhaps identical with the next. (2) John Hart Goldsmith, mentioned several times in the registers of St. Mary Woolnoth between 1540 and 1544. T. F. Reddaway kindly informed me that he is identifiable as a man who was apprenticed to Robert Alee in 1511, contributed 20s. to a royal loan raised in the City in 1522, and had a son William who in 1545 was apprenticed to Thomas Pacy, a mercer of Bristol. There is nothing to connect him with the goldsmith Constantine Hart(e), on whom see below; if the latter's father John had been a goldsmith and citizen, one would expect the fact to be stated in the records. (3) John Harte of St. Botolph without Aldgate; letters of administration dated 1542 (Commissary Court; Guildhall Library MS 9171/11). (4) John Hart who married Annes Palmar on 3 Feb. 1548–9 in St. Dionis Backchurch. (5) John Harte, Skynner, mentioned in the parish registers of St. Mary Aldermanbury in 1559 and 1563. (6) John Hart who was buried in St. Botolph, Bishopsgate, on 22 June 1574, a month before the death of John Hart the herald; conceivably the son of (3) above. (7) John Hart who was married in St. Botolph, Bishopsgate, on 19 August 1576; probably the son of the preceding. (8) Sir John Hart, mentioned in the churchwarden's accounts of St. Michael, Cornhill, in 1594. In view of this array, I find it ingenuous to believe that people named Hart are necessarily related to each other, however remotely, even in cases in which the ingenuous seventeenth-century heralds allowed them the same arms.

[2] Danielsson, op. cit., i. 41.

[3] Danielsson, i. 42, suggests 'about 1536–8'. If this indeed was the same man as was sworn a tithingman in 1478, he must have been very old at his death.

[4] Danielsson, i. 38–39, 48.

Highgate.[1] The descent of this family is traced in the 1619 pedigree from Alice Eustace of Highgate and her husband, named as Thomas Hart and stated to have been 'borne in ye West Country and descended from ye family of y^t surname there'; of Thomas's son John it is said that he 'sould all these [*for* those] his lands in the West Country y^t came to him from his Auncestors'; and the whole pedigree is headed 'The descent aliance and marriages of Sir Eustace Hart and his auncestors since they came out of the West Country'. But Danielsson has now proved beyond doubt, from documentary evidence,[2] that Alice Eustace's husband was really one Richard Hart, also of Highgate; and he supposes that the pedigree's Thomas Hart was simply a conflation of Richard Hart and Alice's brother Thomas Eustace. But Thomas Hart cannot be got rid of so easily, for he is not a mere name; there is the whole story of a West Country origin, which is supported by the 1634 pedigree with its 'Thomas Hart of [blank] in Com. Devon'. There must be some source for this circumstantial tale, and the later pedigree is obviously not derived from the earlier, since it is more detailed. Again, in the 1619 pedigree, there has evidently been confusion of names; for Alice Eustace and her husband Richard really did have a son John Hart (d. 1565), but there is no reason at all why he should have inherited and sold ancestral lands in the West Country. John Hart of the West Country has been falsely identified with John Hart of Highgate, the son of Alice Eustace; and in consequence the former's father, Thomas Hart of the West Country, has supplanted Richard Hart of Highgate as Alice's husband. Once more the result, and probably the motive, of the false identification of two namesakes is clear—the Harts of Highgate were made out to be descendants of the arm-bearing Harts of Devon, and Sir Eustace Hart (who had married, as her second husband, the sister of Edward de Vere, 17th Earl of Oxford) was enabled proudly to quarter the arms of Eustace with those of Hart. A man married to a de Vere no doubt felt that he had to keep his end up as best he could.

It is convenient at this point to bring together the information that has been intruded into the two pedigrees. (1) At the head of the 1619 pedigree of the Highgate family is the name of Thomas Hart 'of the West Country'; at the head of the 1634 pedigree of the Northolt family is 'Thomas Hart of [blank] in Com. Devon'. (2) The 1619 pedigree says that Thomas Hart had a son John who sold all the lands in the West Country that he had inherited from his ancestors.[3] (3) The 1634 pedigree shows as Thomas Hart's sons John Hart Chester Herald and Robert Hart, a merchant who lived in Cornhill. Obviously the intruded material of the two pedigrees has a common source, and the probability is, as I have already assumed, that it was some memorandum possessed by the College of Heralds in the early seventeenth century, but since lost, concerning the immediate family connexions of John Hart the herald. It is also most likely that the source of the information was John Hart himself.

[1] *The Visitation of Kent, 1619*, ed. R. Hovenden, p. 198; cf. Danielsson, i. 50.
[2] Op. cit., ii. 270–3.
[3] Danielsson, i. 53 (who there conflates John Hart of Highgate and John Hart of the West Country, since he had not yet discovered the error in the 1619 pedigree), adds 'and settled in Kent', but there is no early evidence for this; it seems to be the guess of a nineteenth-century antiquary, and to be based merely on the fact that Sir Eustace Hart's pedigree is given in the Visitation of Kent.

APPENDIX II

Most of the registers of freemen of the City of London were destroyed by fire in 1786, but two fragments survive, of which one is British Museum MS Egerton 2408. On f. 28[r] it has a record of a Constantine Harte, of which a summarized translation runs:

Constantine Harte son of John Harte of [blank] com. Devon yeoman deceased, apprentice of Edward Gilberte citizen and Goldsmith. Served with same. Witness aforesaid wardens. Admitted on same day and year. Entry N. 1 October 36 Henry VIII. Fee 4s.[1]

The last part of this entry (which follows a standard form) means that Constantine Harte was admitted a freeman on the last date mentioned in the preceding entries, which in fact is 21 November of 6 Edward VI, i.e. 1552,[2] and that the record of his admission as an apprentice was in record-book N under the date 1 October 1544 (36 Henry VIII). He had served an apprenticeship of over eight years and was now presumably about 23 or 24 years old, i.e. he must have been born about 1528–9. His father was John Harte, a yeoman of Devon;[3] and his own name Constantine (or its reduced form Costin) was, according to Miss Withycombe, 'particularly common in Devon and Cornwall'.[4] But he was unable to say whereabouts in Devon his father had belonged to, presumably because his father was already dead and the connexion with Devon had been broken; for the space for the place-name has been blank from the beginning and is not the result of fire-damage.

Further information about Constantine Harte comes from the records of the Goldsmiths' Company. He completed his apprenticeship to Edward Gilbert (Edmund Gilberd) and was sworn a freeman of the company on 5 November 1552. He probably practised as a goldsmith and he certainly took two apprentices, Robert Warner in 1556 and Hiereme Monke in 1563. He was dead by May 1564, leaving a widow.[5]

His will is preserved in Register 3 of the Archdeaconry of London Court.[6] It rehearses that it is the will of Constantine Harte 'cetezen and Goldsmythe of London', made on 6 September 1563, he being then 'sicke and weeke in bodie'.

---

[1] Cf. Charles Welch, *Register of Freemen of the City of London in the reigns of Henry VIII and Edward VI* (London, 1908), p. 69. In 1908 the leaves of the MS were wrongly bound; what is now f. 28[r] was then f. 24[b] (the reference given by Welch). The MS. was rebound in 1916 in a corrected order suggested by Bower Marsh in an article 'A London Manuscript' in *The Genealogist*, n.s., xxxii (April 1916), 217–20.

[2] The day and month are given in an entry higher on f. 28[r] relating to one Fox, where the MS has clearly *vicesimo primo die Novembris* (misprinted by Welch as 1 Nov., for 21 Nov.).

[3] 'filius Johannis Harte de [blank] in com. Devon yoman defuncti.' Welch renders this 's. of John H. late of . . . co. Devon deceased', but he has inserted the 'late'.

[4] *Oxford Dict. of Eng. Christian Names*, s.n.

[5] Goldsmiths' Company, MS. court minutes and wardens' accounts, I pp. 163, 256; K pp. 222, 250. I owe this information to the kindness of T. F. Reddaway, of University College, London; it is published by permission of The Worshipful Company of Goldsmiths of London, to whom I am indebted. Reddaway added that Gilbert was a big man and able to pick and choose his apprentices, and that the West Country supplied a stream of apprentices to the London goldsmiths.

[6] Guildhall Library, London, MS 9051/3, f. 53[r–v]. I am grateful to the Librarian of the Guildhall Library, Mr. Godfrey Thompson, for his assistance.

He instructs that his body is to be buried in 'the parishe churche of St. Peter in Weste Chepe in London, where I am a parishioner, as nighe [as possible] vnto the place where my late wief Anne Harte lieth buried'. According to the practice of the City of London, he divides his property into three parts, one to go 'vnto Prudence my wief', the second 'vnto my children', and the third as he himself may will and bequeath; and he in fact directs that this third part shall also go 'vnto the said Prudence my wief and to my said children . . . to be equallie devided Betwene them'. He appoints as executors his wife Prudence and 'Anthony Harte my son' and requests his brother-in-law 'Anthony Bonde of London scrivener to have the ouersighte of this my presente Testament' and to assist the executors.[1] The transcript of the will ends:

In witnes whereof This my presente Testament and Last will I have put my hande and seale Their being witnesses of the same [John Harte *struck through*] by me Constantyn Harte.

The will was proved on 23 January 1563 (i.e. 1563–4) by the executrix Prudence Hart, the other executor nominated being a minor.

It will be seen that the clerk, after beginning in the usual way to write out the names of the witnesses, for some reason changed his mind and struck out the one name which he had written; but it remains clearly legible. This first witness was John Harte, obviously a close kinsman of the testator. When we find that in September 1563 a John Harte is the chief witness of the will of Constantine Harte, son of John Harte 'yoman' of '[blank] in com. Devon', and remember that John Hart the spelling-reformer was active in London at this time (he had become Hamiltue pursuivant in the previous year), that he was himself described as a yeoman in 1561, and that he was, according to the 1634 pedigree, the son of Thomas Hart 'of [blank] in Com. Devon', it is clear that we are dealing with something much more definite than a mere coincidence of names. John Hart the future Chester Herald and Constantine Harte the goldsmith were members of the same family.

The accuracy of the 1552 entry in the Register of Freemen, being a contemporary record, can hardly be questioned; much more doubt is possible in the case of the 1619 and 1634 pedigrees, which are not only much later but derive their 'intruded' information at second hand from some other source. Two hypotheses seem possible. (1) John Hart the herald and Constantine Hart the goldsmith were cousins, the sons respectively of Thomas Hart and of John Hart, both of [blank] in Devon. But in this case it is difficult to explain why neither cousin knew whereabouts in Devon his family came from; one would have to suppose that both their fathers had died before the sons had learned the name of the family's place of origin. Moreover, if we bring in the evidence of the 1619 pedigree, we should have to suppose that it was John the herald, the son of Thomas of the West Country, who sold ancestral lands there; but if he sold them he would of course know where they were, and the blank in the 1634 pedigree would be inexplicable —indeed, if one cousin knew, it would be hard enough to explain why Constantine, on being admitted to the freedom of the city, was unable to give the

[1] It seems likely that Anthony Bond was the brother of Constantine Hart's first wife Anne, and that his function was to keep an eye on the stepmother and protect the interests of his dead sister's children.

place-name. (2) John the herald and Constantine the goldsmith were brothers. But in that case we must accept the evidence of the 1552 register that their father's name was John, and reject that of the 1634 pedigree that John the herald was the son of Thomas Hart. The probability is that the 1634 pedigree has omitted a generation, and that Thomas Hart was the grandfather, not the father, of John the herald; the error would be easily explicable if John the herald had been the son of another John, as Constantine certainly was.

My reconstruction of the family history, from the scanty and in part conflicting evidence, is as follows. Thomas Hart was a yeoman, or perhaps a gentleman, of the West Country and descended from a West Country family of that surname (1619 pedigree); a little more specifically he was 'of [blank] in Com. Devon' (1634 pedigree). He may himself have migrated from Devon ('since they came out of the West Country', 1619 pedigree); his son John the elder, a 'yoman' of '[blank] in com. Devon' (Register of Freemen), must have done. The latter was probably married in London; and settled residence in London would explain why, when he inherited family lands in the West Country, he sold them (1619 pedigree). John the elder was dead by 1552 (Register of Freemen). He had three sons. (1) John Hart the younger, who was 'young' in 1551 and must have been born after 1520, perhaps about 1526–8; he entered the public service, became a dependant of Cecil's, a member of the College of Heralds and an official of the Court of Wards, and died in 1574. He is first known from his MS work on English spelling, dated 1551. (2) Constantine Hart, who was born about 1628–9, apprenticed in October 1544, admitted a freeman of the Goldsmiths' Company and of the City of London in November 1552, and died between 6 September 1563 and 23 January 1564. (3) Robert Hart the merchant of Cornhill (1634 pedigree), about whom I have been able to find nothing,[1] but who was presumably still living when the memorandum about the kindred of John the herald was drawn up (I assume by John himself) and may have survived his brother. All three made their careers in London, and must have lived there all their lives; as early as 1552 Constantine did not know where in Devon the family had come from. John the elder must have been born in Devon, since he is described as 'of Devon' in the 1552 record, but he had probably died while his sons were still young, so that they did not learn the name of the place from him. It would be wrong to reject the tradition that the family originated in Devon, especially as Lant's Roll (1595) gives to John Hart the herald the arms of the Harts of Devon; but it is obvious that a family which could not remember where in Devon it came from had long broken its connexion with the county. In theory it is conceivable that John Hart's speech may have contained vestigial traces of the dialect of Devon, picked up in childhood from his father, but I can find no evidence of it. I maintain my view, which Dr. Danielsson shares, that Hart is to be regarded as a Londoner and that his speech is that of London.

---

[1] An Agnes Harte was buried in St. Michael's, Cornhill, on 8 February 1548 (i.e. 1548–9), and a Margaret Harte was married there on 14 December 1579 (*Parish Registers of St. Michael, Cornhill*, ed. J. L. Chester (London, 1882; Harleian Registers, vol. vii), pp. 178 and 12). The latter could well be the daughter of a brother of John Hart, as far as dates go, but there is nothing to connect them beyond the common surname and the Cornhill location. There may have been more families named Hart than one in Cornhill.

APPENDIX II 1031

Danielsson has also suggested[1] that Hart may have been educated at one of the universities, probably Cambridge, but Hart's own words cited in Vol. I, p. 65 seem to rule this out. Certainly he cannot well be identical with the John Hart who between 1557 and 1572 was a Fellow of Trinity Hall, Cambridge, and was a civil lawyer; the ages of the two men do not tell against the identification, as Danielsson thinks, but I can see little else beyond the name to connect them. It is, I suppose, not impossible for a man to have remained a fellow of a Cambridge college, signing college documents, while also acting as one of Cecil's assistants in London, but it is highly improbable; and though Mary Hart is not heard of until about a year after the Cambridge Hart had vacated his fellowship,[2] her own words in her letter to Burleigh[3] in May 1573 show that she had been the herald's wife 'long sence'. It is through Cecil or the Court, not through the University of Cambridge, that we must trace Hart's knowledge of Cheke and Smith and his interest, before either of them had published, in the reform of Classical pronunciation and English spelling. For there is the clearest evidence of a continuing interest in these questions at Court. The originators were Cheke and Smith, the former Cecil's tutor and brother-in-law and the latter his associate in government; their earliest supporter was Hart, from 1561 at latest Cecil's dependant[4] and already by 1551 connected in some way with the Court; and

[1] Op. cit., i. 21, 65–67.
[2] Danielsson, i. 65–66, insists that we do not know when the Cambridge Hart vacated his fellowship. But a successor was elected on 1 June 1572 to the fellowship 'quam Jo. Hart prius habuit', from which Venn, *Alumni Cantabrigienses*, naturally assumed that Hart held his fellowship until 1572; and the presumption is so strong that it could be rebutted only by definite contrary evidence.
[3] Danielsson, i. 78.
[4] The earliest documents to connect Hart with Cecil belong to 1561; see Danielsson, op. cit., i. 68–71. But the third of the letters there printed is wrongly dated 8 May 1562 instead of 1561; it is written from Berwick, which Lord Grey left in 1561 (see *DNB*), and it is, moreover, clearly from this letter that Hart refers in his own to Cecil, written between April and October 1561. In Hart's letter the reference to 'my L. James' is not, as Danielsson states, to James Hamilton, already Earl of Arran, who never returned to France after he was got away thence in mid-1559, but to Lord James Stewart, who between January and June 1561 was in France negotiating the return to Scotland of Mary Queen of Scots.

These letters show that Hart had been employed in connexion with the return of Lord Grey of Wilton from France at the end of 1558; his services had not given full satisfaction and he had refused a post in Grey's household as insufficiently well paid, and in 1561 he was complaining of promises unfulfilled and of enemies and of the poverty to which the affair had allegedly reduced him, and asking that at least he might be paid what was due to him. The cause of the difficulty was probably, in part at least, Grey's impoverishment by the ransom he had had to pay the French. But even these letters show that Hart was Cecil's man, not Grey's; Grey asks Cecil 'to be good to Hart', and Hart himself speaks of having often begged Cecil to intercede with Grey, says that he has 'of long time . . . accompted your honour my especiall good master', and finally asks Cecil to grant two petitions which he forwards on behalf of other men, implying in the clearest fashion that he himself will be rewarded if they are successful. The request is so open that it suggests a confidential relationship between Hart and Cecil; and that the petitions had been presented through Hart must also mean that it was known that he had access to Cecil. Note further how Hart dates Hedley's letter to Tremayne by reference to an event which must have engrossed the minds of Cecil and his assistants—the Scottish negotiations for Mary's return.

If Hart had already been a member of Cecil's household by 1551, it would sufficiently

a successor was Waad, successively one of Cecil's foreign agents, an ambassador, clerk of the Privy Council, and (in James's reign) Lieutenant of the Tower. It may be coincidence that this group seems to centre on Cecil, since necessarily almost all the activities of Elizabeth's government did; but at least it is certain that the movement was active at Court—hence, no doubt, Mulcaster's reference to the reformers as men of 'great place' as well as of 'good learning'.

account for his knowledge of the reform of Greek pronunciation at Cambridge and for the curiously guarded and tactful terms in which he refers to Cheke, who was not only the King's tutor but also Cecil's brother-in-law (MS, pp. 97–98; Danielsson, op. cit., i. 133). Certainly Hart's dedication of his MS to Edward VI and his reference to his having 'lately' received the King's 'gracious liberality' (MS, p. 13; Danielsson, op. cit., i. 114) prove that he already had some connexion with the Court.

INDEX OF WORDS

The following Index includes all words cited in illustration either in Vol. I or in Vol. II; references in ordinary roman type (thus 123) are to the *pages* of Vol. I, and those in boldface type (thus **345**) are to the numbered *sections* of Vol. II. The abbreviation n. stands for Note: thus the entry '**100** n.' refers to the Note to § **100** of Vol. II, and '**213** & nn. 1, 2, 4, 7' refers to § **213** and Notes 1, 2, 4, and 7 thereto. Words are normally cited in the Index in the present English spelling. When words are cited from languages other than Modern English they are preceded by one of the following abbreviations: D. = Dutch, F. = French, G. = German, Gr. = Greek, I. = Italian, Ir. = Irish, L. = Latin, ME = Middle English, OE = Old English, Sp. = Spanish, W. = Welsh. Bracketed elements are ignored in determining the alphabetical order of the entries: thus *age(s)* precedes *-age* suffix and *aged*. Brief glosses or other aids to the identification of the words are given where necessary; Latin glosses are occasionally used when to do so ensures brevity and/or the words are so glossed by one or other of the orthoepists.

a, 77, 252, 397; **4.**
-a *suffix*, **271.**
abase(d), 156; **285, 373.**
abash, **373.**
abbey, 275 n. 2.
abbreviate, **308.**
abbreviation, 23.
abhor(red), 387, 389, 432; 47, 48 n. 1, 426.
abide, **433.**
ability, **269, 275,** 294 n. 3, **303.**
Abington 'Abingdon', **302, 412.**
L. abjicio, 215.
able, 61, 252; **6, 320, 324.**
-able (-ably) *suffix*, **1, 271.**
abode, 33 n. 3, **150** n. 1.
abound, **285.**
about, **264, 269, 285.**
above, 123–4, 314, 360, 433; **18,** 151 n. 2, **285.**
abraids, 92; **302.**
abroad, 287, 357, 362; **33,** 53 & n. 3, **115** n. 8, **216.**
absent *vb.*, 29; **2** n. 3.
absolve, 88, **365.**
absorb, **365.**
abundance, 90; **19.**
abuse *sb.* & *vb.*, **339; 2,** 183 n. 5, 185 n. 6, **285**
academy, 298, 300; **2.**
accede, **359** n. 2.
accent *sb.*, 161; *vb.*, 29, 161.
accept, **302, 359** n. 3.
acceptable, 161, **372; 2.**
accessory, 29; **2,** 59 n. 2.
accidence, **410.**
accidents, **410.**

accloy, **255** n. 1.
accole, 431.
accord, 432; **13** n. 2.
accoutred, accoutrements, 157.
accurst, **213** n. 4.
accustom, **283, 293, 302, 326.**
ace, 418; **6, 8.**
-ace *suffix*, **336** & n. 1.
ache, 44, 432; **115** n. 5, **376.**
Achor, **397.**
acknowledge, 44.
acorn(s), **53** n. 1, **297, 299, 397.**
acquaint, 54, **307, 433.**
acquaintance, 54.
acre, 184; **320, 326, 397.**
acrimony, **1.**
act(s), 387, 388, 392, 398; **59** n. 2, **398** & n. 2, **407, 412.**
action, 216, 325–6; **276, 302, 326.**
active(s), **275, 363.**
actors, 92; **281.**
actress, **407.**
Adam, **326.**
adder(s), **59** n. 2, **97** n. 7, **323** n. 2, **440.**
adieu, 217, 414; **183** n. 5, **185.**
adjacent, **2.**
adjourn, **19.**
admirable, **1.**
admiral, **273.**
admire, 353; **218.**
admit, **212.**
ado, 414; **185.**

adore, 48 n. 1.
adorn(ed), 91; **19, 165.**
adultery, **275, 285.**
adumbrate, 29; **2.**
advance, **239** & n. 2.
advantage, **62.**
adventure, **293, 400** n.
adventurous, **281.**
adversary, **374; 1, 2.**
advertised, **275.**
advice, 114, **404; 12.**
advise, advisedly, 114, **404; 12.**
advisory, **356.**
adze, 17; **384.**
Aeneas, **288.**
aery, 151.
Aesop, **356.**
afeared, 28.
affinity, 275 n. 2.
affirm, 104.
afford, 418, 432; **13** n. 2, **16** & n. 1, **18** n. 3, **46** n. 1, **92** & n. 2, **208** & n. 1, **209, 213** n. 4, **383.**
affright, 315.
Afric, 187.
after, 393–4; **43** n. 2, **44, 50** nn. 1, 2, **59** n. 2, **423** & nn. 2, 3, **427.**
afternoon, **43** n. 2, **423.**
again, **230; 26** & n., **226** n. 4, **302, 430** n. 4.
against, 27, 77, 274; **26** & n., **437.**
age(s), 21, 307, 430; **63** n. 2, **363.**
-age *suffix*, **271** & n., **308, 336** & nn. 1, 2.
aged, **6.**

INDEX OF WORDS

agestred, 106.
aggrieved, **116** n. 2, **124** n. 1.
agist, 106.
agister, 106.
Agnes, 335; **441**.
L. agnus, 13; **441**.
ago, **40**, **148** n.
agree(s, -d), **120** n., **132** n., **350**.
agrise, **12**.
ague, **6**, **282**.
ah, 386, 427; **103**, **424**.
ahha, **103**.
aid, 250.
ail(s), 432; **104**.
F. aille, 376.
aims, 406, 416; **104**.
ain't, 238, 430 n. 4.
air, 151, 388, 405, 413; **4**, **43** n. 3, **126** n. 5, **218**, **426**.
airy, 150, 151, 406; **100**, **218**, **229**, **231**, **426**.
-al *suffix*, **273**, **325**, **326**, **348**.
alarm, 324 n. 2.
alas, 112; **50**.
alb, **60**.
Albemarle, 427 n.
Albion, **60**.
alchemy, **60**.
alder (tree), **437**.
alder 'of all', **437**.
ale, 323, 347, 404; **42**, **53**, **104** & n. 4, **440**.
-ale *suffix*, **271**.
aleconner, **94**.
Alexander, **359**.
F. Alexandre, **359**.
Alfred, **60**.
algate, **60**, **229** n. 1, **271**.
algorism, **60**, **323**.
alias, **312** n. 3.
Alice, 432; **305**.
alien, **23**.
alienate, **23**.
alike, **138**.
L. aliquis, **93**, **101**.
L. alius, 7; **93**, **101**.
all, 103, 111, 314, 342, 347, 404; **23**, **42**, **44** n. 4, **53**, **104** & n. 4, **235**, **237** & n. 2, **273**, **353** n.
allay, 404, 407, 410, 421; **261** n. 2, **275** n. 2.
allegory, **1**, **60**.

alley(s), 169, 404, 407, 410, 421; **60**, **137** n. 2, **275** & nn. 1, 2, **350**.
alliance, 27.
allow(ed, -est), 110; **172** n. 1, **315**.
alloy, 410; **261** n. 2.
allusion, **356**, **389**.
ally, 404, 410; **275**.
Almain, **60**.
F. almanac, 287.
almighty, **60**, **424**.
almond, 304, 349, 366; **60**, **104** & n. 6, **238**, **398**, **425** n. 5.
almost, **60**.
alms, 369, 406, 416, 432, 439, 440, 442; **60** & n. 1, **104**, **425** & n. 2.
aloes, 348; **312** n. 3.
alone, 108; **429** & n. 2.
along, 438; **92** n. 1.
alpha, **60**.
alphabet, **60**.
Alps, **60**.
already, **8**.
altar, 19; **60**, **299**.
alter, **60**, **299**.
although, **89**, **424**.
altitude, **60**.
altogether, **290**.
always, 71, 90, 110; **60**, **261** n. 2, **272**.
L. amabant, 318.
L. amat, 31.
amaze, **399**.
amber, **403**.
amble, 406.
ambrosia, **356**, **388**.
ambulatory, **2**.
ambuscade, -o, **235** n.
amen, 274.
America, **212** n. 5.
amidst, **363**, **437**.
among(st), 23, 182; **7** n. 2, **13** & n. 3, **92** & n. 1, **191**, **302**, **363**, **412** & n. 1, **435**, **437**.
amorous, **281**.
ample, 406; **403**.
an, 37, 77, 399, 410, 415; **440**.
-an *suffix*, **273**, **325**, **348**.
ancestor, **239**.
Anchises, **380**.
anchor, 352; **320**, **326**, **380** & n. 1.

ancient, 147, 314, 325, 331; **6** n. 3, **59** n. 2, **62** & n. 1, **104**, **239**, **276**, **435**, **436**.
ancienter, **435**.
ancle, 406; **53** n. 2.
and, 6, 77–78, 238, 250, 252–3, 274; **4**, **398** n. 2, **426**.
andiron, **62**, **239**.
Andromache, **274**.
ane, 125.
angel, 162, 210, 404; **6** n. 3, **62**, **63**, **104** & n. 3.
angelical, **62**.
anger, 33, 104, 331, 351; **62** & n. 1, **239**, **399**, **412**.
angle, 404, 406; **412**.
anglophobe, **269** n. 2.
angry, 104; **350**, **412** & n. 2.
anguish, 115, 326; **380**, **412**.
angular, **399**.
F. animal, 286.
annal, **282**, **308**.
Anne, 378.
annihilate, 367.
annihilation, 348.
annoy(ed), 315, 437; **255** n. 1, **256** & nn. 1, 4, **272** n.
annual, **270**, **282**, **308**.
anoint, 121, 389; **255** & n. 3.
anon, 29; **33**, **148** n.
another, 361; **4**, **15**.
answer, 45, 85, 154, 314; **56** n., **62**, **213**, **237** n. 2, **238**, **239** n. 3, **355**, **421**.
ant, 27, 331, 401, 410, 424, 436, 442; **62** & n. 1, **238**, **239**.
-ant *suffix*, **325**.
a'n't 'am not', **238**.
antique, **269**.
F. anxiété, **359**.
anxiety, **359**, **365**, **380**.
anxious, **380**.
any, 77; **6**, **40**, **70** & n. 1.
Apollo('s), **277**.
apostrophe, **274**.
apparel, **272**, **321**.
apparent, **390**.
appeal, 25.
appear(ed), 44, 72, 156, 373; **8**, **126** & nn. 3, 4, **136** n. 2, **218**.
appearance, 390.
appease, **356**.

INDEX OF WORDS

apple, 76, 314, 325; **326**.
appliable, 114; **40**.
applied, **40**.
apply, 114; **40**, **285**.
appoint, 69, 437; **255**.
approve, 342, 360; **36**, **37**.
apron, 267; **53** n. 1, **328** & nn. 1, 2, **440**.
apt, 430.
aquiline, **269**.
-ar *suffix*, **325**.
arch, **87**.
archaism, **270**.
archbishops, **373** n. 3.
architect, **442**.
arduous, **209**.
are, 72, 153, 331, 333, 389, 413; **4**, **43** & n. 1, **129** n. 3, **130**.
aren't, **238**.
argal, 66.
argument, **282** n. 1.
ark, **426**.
Ariel, **2**.
arise, **137** n. 2.
arm, 347; **42**, **53**, **331** n. 1.
armada, **269**.
armful, 267.
armour, **281**.
army, **275** & n. 2.
arraign, **441**.
arrand, 44, **55** n. 2.
arrant, 398; **44**, **67** & n. 3, **321**.
arras, 403; **302**, **426**.
arrear(s), **44**, **55** n. 2, **126** & n. 4.
arrest, **44**.
arrow(s), 403; **55** n. 2, **302**, **426**, **440**.
arse, 431.
ārt *sb.*, 274, 279, 331–2, 389, 391; **6**, **42**.
art *vb.* (2 *sg. pres.*), **4**.
Arthur, **427** n., **442**.
article(s), 77; **362**.
-ary *suffix*, **1**, **266**, **271**.
as, 21, 76, 77, 90, 92, 274, 424, 444; **4**, **362**.
ascend, **285**.
ascent, **285**.
ash *sb.*, 17, 402; **53** n. 1, **63**.
ash *vb.* 'ask', **63**.
ask, 6, 402; **50** & n. 2, 398 & n. 4, **439**.
asp, **50**, **52**, **426**.
aspen, **326**, **334**.

ass(es), 304, 361, 418, 430, 443, 444; **6**, **50**, **56** n., **363**, **398**, **406**, **440**.
assays, **301**, **302**.
assembled, **403** & n.
assessing, 399.
assign, 114; **12**, **441** & n. 2.
assistance, **410**.
assistants, **410**.
assister, 397.
associate, **271**, **276**, **302**, **388**.
assoil, **255** & nn. 1, 3.
assume, **365**.
assure, 369; **178** n. 5, **185** & n. 1.
assuredly, **311**, **315**.
astonied, **315**.
asylum, **356**.
at, 76.
ate, 399.
-ate *suffix*, **271**, **336** & n. 1.
atheism, **308**.
atheist, **389**; 308.
-ation *suffix*, **271**.
-ative *suffix*, **271**.
atone, **429**.
-ator *suffix*, **270**.
attain, **229** n. 1.
attemper(ed), **306**, **403**.
attempted, **403**.
attempts, **404**.
atte nale 'at the ale', **440**.
attire, **218**.
attorney, **19**, **338** & nn. 1, 2, **350**.
attract, 397.
attributed, **282** n. 1.
F. au(x), 9.
F. aucun, 9.
audience, 393; **104**.
auditor, **292**.
augment, **286**.
august *adj.*, 389.
August, **29**, **104** n. 7, **237** n. 2.
Augustus, **286**.
aunt, 389, 401, 410, 425, 436, 442; **29**, **54** n. 3, **62**, **104** n. 2, **237** n. 2, **238**, **239**.
auricular, **299**.
F. aussi, 9.
austere, 406; **2** & n. 2, **29**, **256** n. 2.
F. auteur, 9.
author(s), **236**, **281**, **292**, **363**, **442**.

authority, -ies, 35; **338** n. 1, **350**, **363**, **442**.
F. autre, 9.
autumn, 104.
avail, 176, 186.
avarice, **275**, **302**.
avenger, **274** n. 3.
Avenon, **194** n. 3.
avisht 'a-fishing', 143.
avoid, **256** & n. 4.
avow, **173** n. 1.
away, **228** n. 5, **235** n.
awe, 12; **206**, **236**, **237**.
awful, **237** n. 2.
awl, 404; **104**, **235**, **426**.
awry, 406.
axe, 17, 54, 398, 402; **53** n. 2, **359** n. 4, **407**, **439**.
axiom, **388**.
ay 'ever', 256; **233**.
aye 'yes', 137, 141; **226**, **233**.

b (letter-name), **40**.
Baal, 328, 356, 409; **104**.
babble, 443; **6**.
babe, 236.
baby, 236; **275** & n. 1.
bachelor, **59** n. 2.
back, 417; **59** nn. 2, 3.
backbite, **2**.
backslide, **2**.
backward, **421**.
bacon, 416; **321**, **326**.
bad, 110; **53** n. 1.
badge, 430.
baff, **431**.
bag, **53** n. 2.
bails, **432**; **104**.
bait, 307, 424, 425; **226**.
bake, 417; **25**.
bakehouse, 92.
balance, **60**.
balcony, **2**.
bald, 103, 407; **60** n. 1.
bale, **104**.
balk, **425**.
ball(s), 20, 276, 409, 432; **104** & n. 4.
balm, 102, 331, 342, 343, 369, 408, 432, 436, 439, 440, 442; **44**, **104**, **238**, **425** n. 5, **427**.
ban, 443.
Banbury, 350, 351, 353; **381**.

INDEX OF WORDS

band, 6, 27; **7, 71**.
bangle, **412**.
Bangor, 352; **299**.
bank, **53** n. 2.
bankrupt, **380, 442**.
banner, 406; **308**.
banquet, 380 & n. 1, **421** n. 6.
bantling, **378** n.
baptism, 236; **310, 324, 442**.
bar(s), 236, 305, 318, 331–3, 431; **42, 43, 49**.
barb, **87**.
Barbara, **303**.
barbarian, **276**.
barbarity, 29; **2**.
barbarous, **2**.
Barbary, **303**.
F. barbu, 9.
bard, 431.
bare, 236, 291, 318, 355, 398; **6, 118, 130, 204, 226** n. 4.
barely, 402, 412; **6**.
barf 'barrow', **371**.
bargain, 308, 354; **272**.
barge, 305; **42**.
barley, 402, 412; **6, 44, 59** n. 2, 275 n. 1, 338 n. 2.
barm, 408; **42, 44, 427**.
barn, 331–3; **42, 43, 65**.
baron, **321**.
barrel, **55** n. 2, **319, 330**.
barren, **268, 272, 319, 330**.
barrow, 398; **55** n. 2.
Bartholomew, **307**.
Bartimeus, **274**.
Baruch, 394.
base *adj.*, 355, 429 (?); **356**.
base *sb.*, 90; **356**.
basil, **325**.
basin, **325** n. 1, **326**.
basis, **356**.
basket, 367.
bat, 226, 238, 361.
bate, 226, 238.
bath, 361, 399, 412, 431, 442; **6, 368** & n. 1.
Bath, 368 n. 1.
bathe, 399, 412, 439; **4, 6, 368**.
baths, **50** n. 3, **53, 55, 358**.
battery, **306**.
battle(s), **269, 272, 326** & n. 1.
bauble, 301.

bawd, **104** n. 4.
bawl, 409.
bawled (?), 407.
be, 60, 87, 109, 153, 211, 274, 279, 356; **4, 125** n., **228** n. 5, **350**.
be- *prefix*, 288 n. 3, **294** & nn. 1, 2, **351, 352**.
beacon, 416; **8**.
bead, 25, 426.
beadle, 371, 443; **10**.
beak, 25, 426; **116** n. 2.
beam, 25; **120** n.
bean(s), 25, 410, 433, 436; **4, 115** n. 4, **123**.
bear(s) *sb.*, 113, 425; **204**.
bear *vb.*, 16, 79, 146 (*forms of p.t.*), 187, 372, 397, 398, 425, 436, 440; **43** n. 3, **100** n., **109, 115** n. 8, **118, 122** & n. 1, **203, 204** & nn. 1, 3, **228** n. 5.
beard, 430; **8, 9** n. 1, **122** & n. 4, **126, 201** & n., **204** & n. 3, **218**.
bearish, **204**.
bearn 'bairn', **8**.
beast(s), 90, 112, 236, 354, 366, 425; **8, 310, 312, 362, 406**.
beastly, **406**.
beat, 25; **30, 116** n. 2, **430** n. 4.
beat(en) *p.p.*, 91; **326**.
F. beau, 57.
Beauchamp, **244**.
Beaumont, **244**.
beautifieth, 389; **314**.
beautify, 71; **244** n. 5, **275**.
beauty, 93, 239, 323, 387, 388, 389, 393; **244** & n. 4, **275**.
beaver, **8**.
Beawley 'Beaulieu?', **244**.
because, **294** & n. 1, **351, 356**.
beckon(ed), 416; **367** n.
become(s), **294** & n. 3, **351, 363**.
bed, 291.
bee, 23; **40, 107**.
been, 162, 169, 391, 404, 410; **4**.
been 'bees', 404; **4**.
beer, 16, 372, 426; **115, 126** n. 3, **218**.

beet, 60.
beetle, **10, 80**.
before, **13, 148** n., **294, 351, 352**.
began, **194**.
begin, 234; **293, 294, 351, 379** & n.
beginning(s), 355; **412**.
begot, 314; **294, 352**.
beguile, 124.
behalf, **29, 237** n. 2, **425**.
behave, **25, 115** n. 1.
behaviour, **25**.
beheld, **126** n. 4.
behind, 35; **12**.
behold, 90, 103, 104, 211; **169** n. 3.
beholden, -ing, 398; **377**.
behove, 342; **36, 37**.
belch, **376**.
belfry, **275** n. 2.
belie, 404; **275**.
belief, 326; **109, 115** n. 1, **120**.
believe, 189; **116** n. 2, **120, 124** n. 1, **132** n.
bell, 187.
bellicose, **269**.
I. bello, 32.
bellows, 416; **85** n. 3.
belly, -ies, 404, 416; **275**.
belong(ed, -eth, -s), 438; **363, 399, 412**.
beloved, **315**.
below, 162.
Belphoebe, **274**.
bemoan(ed), 430.
bench, 26; **77**.
I. bene, 32.
beneath, 20, 25, 315; **30, 309** n., **368** & n. 2.
benevolence, **288**.
benign, 380; **324, 441** & nn. 1, 2.
benignity, 380; **441**.
bequeath(ed), **116** n. 2, **368**.
bereave, **116** n. 2.
Bergavenny, **212** n. 2.
Berkley, 378 n.
berry, **212** n. 5, **218**.
berths, **358**.
beryl, **325**.
beseech(ed), **116** n. 2, **132** n.
beseeking, **132** n.
beside, **365**.

INDEX OF WORDS

besiege, **294** n. 2.
besmear, **120, 136** n. 2.
besom, **85** n. 3.
bestir, 162.
bestow(ed), 162, 434; **173** n. 2, 280, **315**.
bet, 300.
betake, **115** n. 7.
bethought, **170** n. 2, **177** n. 2, **251**.
betray, **228** n. 5.
betroth, **368**.
better, 79; **85** n. 3.
betwixt, **363, 437**.
beyond, 306, 359, 387, 389; **90, 422** & n. 3.
Bezaleel, **288**.
Bible, **324**.
bid(den), 318; **320**.
bide, 318.
bield, 25; **9**.
bier, 16, 372, 397; **118, 126** n. 4, **204** n. 3.
Sp. Bilbao, 32.
bile, 401.
bill, **85** n. 3.
Billingsgate, **80**.
Billingshurst, 105.
billow, 325–6; **295**.
bin, 404, 410; **4**.
bind, **12, 85** n. 3.
biology, **270**.
birch, 435; **213**.
bird(s), 162, 209, 343, 345, 419, 430, 435, 441; **84** & n. 1, **212** n. 3, **213** & nn. 1, 2, 4, 7, **214** n. 4, **363, 439**.
birth, 347, 442; **75, 212** n. 3, **213, 358, 368**.
bishop, **85** & nn. 2, 5, **293**.
bit, 300, 325.
bitch, **376**.
bite, 48, 59, 112, 251, 256, 325; **40**.
blackamore, 236.
blackberry, **265, 311**.
blackbird, **311**.
black bird(s), **3, 311**.
bladder, **323**.
blame, 110; **6, 229** n. 1.
blanch, 27, 425, 442; **62**.
blank, **380**.
blanket, **380, 421** n. 6.
blaspheme, 25.
blast(s), 361, 443; **50, 406**.

blaze, 430.
-ble *ending*, **1**.
bleach, 25; **116** n. 2.
bleak, **115** n. 6.
blear, 425; **122** & n. 2.
blear-eyed, **122**.
bleed, 18.
bless, 443; **9**.
blessed, blest, 91; **311, 315**.
blight, 112.
blind, 35; **12, 367** n.
blindness, **410**.
blister(ing), **406**.
blithe(r), **368** & n. 2.
bloach, 433.
blood, 22, 27, 55, 160, 189, 269, 298, 306, 314, 320, 345, 351, 361, 371, 391, 425; **4, 36, 37, 38, 158** n. 2, **185** n. 6.
bloody, 55; **275**.
bloom, 22.
blossom, **293, 326**.
blot, **53** nn. 1, 2.
blow(n), 44, 434.
blue, **40** n. 1.
boa, **210** & n. 2.
boar, 36, 306, 401, 415; **149** & n. 2, **208** n. 2, **210** & n. 2.
board, 414, 419, 429, 432; **16** & n. 2, **208** n. 1, **431** n. 4.
boast(er), 418, 431; **13**.
boat(s), 36, 338, 372, 402; **33, 124** n. 2, **150, 431** n. 4.
Bocking, **87** n. 3.
bode, 356–7.
bodice, **363**.
Bodley's, 129, 130; **350**.
body, -ies, **40, 265, 275, 350, 363**.
boil *sb.* 'ulcer', 428, 437, 441; **144, 259** & n. 2, **262**.
boil *vb.*, 235, 353, 401, 428, 437, 441; **255** & nn. 1, 3, **256** n. 3, **259** & nn. 2, 3, **262, 263, 432** & n.
boiling, 168.
F. bois, **114**.
boisterous, 341; **255**.
boistious, **20, 255** & n. 1, **281**.
bold(er), 17, 55, 90, 337,

371; **169** & n. 5, **249, 251**.
boldly, **264, 275**.
bole(s), 22, 344, 406, 416; **169** & n. 4.
Bolnhurst, **87** n. 3.
bolster, 343–4, 418; **169** & n. 5, **425**.
bolt, 22, 437.
bombast, **94**.
bond, 430; **7, 13, 53** n. 1, **71**.
bone(s), 58, 236, 237, 267; **431** n. 2.
book(s), 267, 287, 289–90, 342, 404, 440, 443; **35, 36, 37, 38, 362**.
boor, **149** n. 2, **208** & n. 2, **209**.
boot(s), 89, 287, 402, 425, 443; **37, 38, 150**.
Bootes, 159.
booth(s), 23, 114–15, 399, 402, 443; **150, 158, 362, 368**.
booze *see* bouse.
border(er), **16, 154, 282**.
bordure, **282**.
bore, 401, 409, 415; **149, 208** n. 2.
bored, 414, 432; **16, 165** n. 1.
Borham, **87** n. 3.
born, 110, 261, 442; **13, 16, 46, 47** n. 1, **97** n. 1, **148** n., **165** n. 1, **210** n. 3, **328** n. 2, **330** & nn. 1, 2, **436** n. 2.
borne, 44; **13, 16, 46, 149**.
borough, 386; **214** n. 5, **424**.
borrow(ed), 398; **55** n. 2, **218, 280, 295** & n. 1, **308**.
Bosham, 105.
bosom, **293, 302**.
both, 20, 146, 253, 399, 402, 424, 431; **33, 116** n. 2, **124** n. 2, **148** n., **150, 368** & n. 2; **431** n.
bother, **53** n. 1.
bottom(less), **92, 319, 323**.
bouge 'wallet', **167**.
bough(s), 23, 35, 98, 334, 363, 378, 397, 398, 427, 433; **160, 171** & n., **172, 313, 424** & n. 2.

INDEX OF WORDS

bought, 126, 163, 184, 244, 329, 353, 363, 370, 389, 433; **141, 170, 240** & n. 1.
boughtest, 183.
Boulogne, **272** n.
boulter, 364.
bound, **377**.
bourd, **165** n. 1.
bourn 'boundary', 16, **165** & n. 1, 208 & n. 3, **209**.
bouse vb., 424; **157**.
bow sb. 'arcus', 10, 12, 23, 90, 126, 320, 357, 398, 415, 416; **4, 171, 172** & n. 4, **173** n. 1.
bow vb. 'flectere', 320, 378, 415, 416; **39** n. 2, **172** n. 1.
bower(s), **158** n. 3, **173** n. 1, **218** n. 1, **281**.
boweth 'flectet', 397; **313**.
bowing 'flectens', **173** n. 1.
bowl(s) 'globus', 19, 22, 43, 49, 160, 233, 356, 377, 398, 406, 409, 412, 415, 416; **161, 169** n. 4.
bowl(s) 'poculum', 22, 43, 49, 90, 160, 233, 398, 406, 409, 412, 415, 416; **161, 169** n. 4, **249**.
box, **53** n. 2.
boy(s), 10, 59, 83, 85, 174–5, 215, 233, 235, 251, 256, 315, 334, 412, 416, 428; **252** n. 1, **256** & nn. 1, 3, 4, **261** n. 2, **263, 419** n., **432** & n.
Boyce, 412.
boyish, 168.
brace, 429.
brain, 125; **229** n. 1.
bramble, **403, 435**.
branch(es), 6, 27, 360, 365, 425, 442; **56** n., **62** & n. 1, **63, 238, 239, 410**.
brand, 19.
brand-iron, **71**.
brass, 167.
Sp. bravada, **101, 235** n.
bravado, **101**.
brazen, 6.
brazier, **389**.
breach(es), **8, 116** n. 2, **123, 376**.
bread, 25, 43, 274, 404, 405, 425, 426; **30, 123**.

breadth, 91; **8, 358, 375**.
break sb., 58; **376**.
break vb., 25, 58, 365, 426; **115** & nn. 3, 6–8, **217**.
breakfast, **8, 116** n. 2, **212**.
breaking, **116** n. 2.
breast(s), 425, 443; **8**.
breath(s), 71, 77, 112, 354, 399, 425; **30, 118, 312, 358, 363, 368**.
breathe, 182, 399, 424; **30, 116** n. 2, **368**.
bred, 404.
brede 'breadth', 19, 21, 25.
breech(es), **11, 123, 376**.
breed, 18, 112, 404, 405.
breeding, **132** n.
brethren, 70; **9, 77** n. 1, **328** & nn. 1, 3, 4.
brew(ed), 26, 49, 54; **40** n. 1, **246, 315, 334**.
brewis, 341, 398; **244, 246, 297**.
briar, 21, 410; **128, 136**.
bridge(s), 23, 37, 61; **75, 311, 376**.
bridle, 54, 154; **12, 320**.
briefly, 71; **430** n. 1.
briefness, **430** n. 1.
bright, 187; **141**.
bringeth, -s, 13; **412**.
Britain, **272**.
Britomart, **277**.
broad, 184, 189, 287, 357, 362, 443; **33, 53** & n. 3, **55, 56** n., **115** n. 2, **216, 240** n. 4.
broid(en, -ed), **188, 258** & n.
broider, **258**.
broil sb., **252** n. 1.
broil(ed) vb., 92, 428; **256** & n. 3, **262**.
broke(n), 102; **53** n. 3, **297, 326**.
Bromley, **97** n. 6.
brooch, 22; **431** n. 4.
brood, 314.
brook sb., 342, 443; **37, 38**.
brook vb., **39** n. 2.
broom, 126.
broth, 20, 29, 361–2, 431; **13, 358**.
brothel, 36; **358**.
brother, 54, 314, 361; **15, 18** & n. 2, **328** n. 1.
brotherhood, **15**.
Brough, **371**.

brought, 169, 353, 366, 371, 443; **34, 89, 160** n. 2, **170** & n. 3, **237** n. 2, **240, 371, 424** n. 1.
brow(s), **172** nn. 1, 4, **173** n. 1.
brown, 103, 107, 377.
Broxted, **87** n. 3.
bruise(d), 114–15, 398; **158, 185** n. 3, **189** n. 2.
bruit, 179.
brush, **96**.
bubble, 439.
buck, 404.
buckle, 356.
budge vb., **167**.
OE bufan, **270**.
bugle, 20.
build, 24, 26, 141, 174, 407–8, 432; **12, 75** & n., **135**.
building, 90.
bulb, **196**.
bulk, **196** & n. 2.
bull, 17, 49, 427, 428, 440; **196**.
Bullen, **272** n.
bullion, 369; **308, 336**.
bullock, **293**.
Bullokar, **293**.
bull's-eye, **311**.
bulwark, 387; **421**.
bunch, **19**.
bundle, **410**.
bungalow, **59** n. 6, **93** n. 3.
bungle, 21; **412**.
buoy, 83, 174, 416; **256, 262, 263**.
burden 'load', **383**.
burden 'undersong', **383**.
burgh, 125.
burial(s), **270**.
burn vb., 104; **84** n. 2, **439**.
burst, 344, 350, 441, 444; **84** n. 2, **401, 439**.
burthen, **326**.
bury, 14; **75, 80, 189, 212** & n. 5, **213** n. 6.
-bury suffix, **75**.
bush, 427, 440; **196**.
bushel, **96**.
busied, **315**.
business, 15, 45, 154; **75, 82, 306**.
bustard, **299**.
busy, 14, 169; **82, 350**.

INDEX OF WORDS

but, 76, 79, 241, 249, 268, 274, 315, 344, 427; **96**, **196**, **212**.
butcher('s), 148; **96** & n., **129** n. 3, **196**.
butter, **196**.
button, **326**.
buy, 110, 114, 174, 416; **40**, **256**.
buyer, **218**.
buying, 114; **40**.
buy it, 48, 55, 59; **40**.
by, 167, 416; **4**, **137** n. 2, **351**.
bye, **40**, **256**.
by me, **310** n.
bynempt, **289**.
by'r Lady, 18.
Byzantium, **388**.

c (letter-name), **40**.
cabbage, **363**.
cabin, **326**.
Caesar, **22** & n.
Caesarea, 372; **2**, **271**, **288**.
cage, 430; **6**.
caitiff (-ive), **226**, **275**.
Calais, 272, 334, 376 n.
calamity, 29; **2**.
calf, 300, 304, 353, 354, 365, 366, 369, 436, 440, 442; **28** & n. 3, **54** n. 3, **104** n. 9, **238**, **239**, **425** & n. 3.
California, **1**.
call(ed, -s), 17, 90, 167, 305, 392, 432; **47**, **104** & n. 4, **236**, **237**, **239**.
caller, **319**.
callet, **60**.
Callis (surname), **334**, **376** n.
callous, **60**.
calm, 90, 104, 342, 343, 432, 442; **60** & n. 1, **104** & n. 6, **238**, **425** n. 5.
calumniators, **363**.
calve(s), 343, 366; **238**, **425**.
Camberwell, **403** n.
cambric, 148.
came, **115** n. 4.
camel, **319**, **321**.
can, 234, 286, 292, 293, 297–8; **226**, **233**, **236**, **379**.
candle, **321**, **326**.

cane, 292, 293, 297–8, 307, 356, 357; **115** n. 5, **226**.
canker, **380**.
cannel, **399**.
cannot, **374**.
cant sb., **442**, **443**.
can't vb., **56** n., **238** & n. 1.
canteen, **269**.
Canterbury, **212**, **421**.
cap, **417**.
capacity, 29; **2**.
caparison, **356**.
cape, **417**.
capital, 349; **1**, **273**.
capon, 113, 145, 148; **102**, **110**, **302** & n. 1, **326**.
Cappadocia, **388**.
captain, 268, 272, 306 & n. 1, **334**.
captive, 19.
car(s), 305, 361, 431; **42**, **43**, **55** n. 1.
card, 177, 333, 415, 426, 431; **6**.
cardinal, 184.
care(s), 216, 250, 252–3, 324, 355; **42**, **43** n. 3, **204** n. 4, **213** n. 1, **370**.
cared, 333, 415; **6**.
carl, 104, 331–2; **42**, **331**.
carnal, 66.
carol, **273** n. 2, **336**.
carp, 305, 331–3; **42**.
carpenter, **321**.
Carr, **68** n. 2.
carriage, 308, **336** & n. 1.
carrier, **324**; **370**.
carrion, 272 & n., 308 n. 2, **334**.
carrot, **55** n. 2, **59** n. 2.
carry, **55** n. 2, **218**.
cart, 392; **44**, **86** n. 2.
carter, **43** n. 2, **44**, **50** n. 1, **427**.
L. carus, 161.
carve, 26, 435; **65** n. 2.
case, **355**.
Cassia, **388**.
cast, 137, 286, 288, 292, 293, 297–8; **50**; **226**, **233**, **236**, **311** n. 2.
castle, 92, 353; **51**, **406**.
casualty, **2**.
cat, **53** n. 1, **59** n. 2.
catalogue, **269**.
catastrophe, **269**.
catch, 371; **70**.

catechism, **324**, **331**.
L. caterva, 209; **212**.
Catherine, **275**, **328** & nn. 1, 2, **442**.
Cato, **22** & n., **23** n., **277**.
cattle, **272**, **326**.
caught, 315, 402, 433; **28**, **170**, **237** n. 2, **423** n. 2.
cauldron, **328** & nn. 1, 2, **425** n. 5.
cause(s), 443; **51**, **236**, **237** n. 2, **275** n. 2, **334**, **356**.
caused, -eth, **356**.
causey(s) 'causeway(s)', **275** n. 2, **334**.
cave, 343.
cavil, **326**.
cavillations, **363**.
cease, 414, 424; **8**.
ceasing, 399.
cedar, 167.
ceil(ing), 25, 366; **123**, **131**.
celandine, **438**.
cement, **2** & n. 2.
censer, **282**, **299**.
censor, **282**, **299**.
censure, **282**.
centaury, **282**, **306**, **348**.
centre, **321**, **323**, **324**.
century, **269**, **282**, **306**, **348**.
L. cerdo, 241.
Ceres, **22** & n.
certain, 37; **64** n. 3, **66** & n. 4, **213** n. 1, **264**, **272**, **326**, **334**.
ceruleous, **281**.
cess, 414.
F. ceux, 81.
chafe(d), 431; **28**.
chaff, 431.
chain, 26, 353; **108** n. 3, **131** & n. 1, **228** n. 3.
chair, 400, 405; **231**.
chaldron, **28** n. 2, **238** n. 3.
chalk, **60**, **425** & n. 2.
challenge, **6**, **60**.
challice, **334**, **376** n.
chamber, 45, 103, 343; **6** n. 3, **59** n. 3, **62**, **104**, **239**.
chambering, 184; **306**.
chamberlain, **6** n. 3, **62**, **272**, **334**.
chameleon, 210; **285**.
chamois, **254** n. 2, **343** n. 2.

INDEX OF WORDS

chance, 27, 331, 425; **62**, **104** n. 2.
chancellor, **62**, **281**, **306**.
change, 20, 27, 162, 164, 331, 425; **6** n. 3, **62**, **63** & n. 3, **104** & nn. 1, 3, **107**, **226**, **239**.
changeling, **306** n. 1.
channel, 399.
chant(er), 27, 425, 431, 442; **62**, **104** & n. 2, **238**.
chaos, **269**.
chaotic, **269**, **270**.
chap vb., **87** n. 4.
chapel, 19; **321**, **326**.
chaplain, **272**.
charact(er), 121; **336** n. 2.
chare, 398, 400; **204**, **231**.
charge, 6, 44 nn. 2, 3.
chariot, **308** n. 2.
Charissa, **271**.
charity, **59** n. 2, **275** n. 2.
chark, 435; **78**.
Charlbury, **44**.
Charles, 370; **44** & n. 2, **56** n.
charm, **6**, **331**.
charter, 369, 370; **43** n. 2, **44**, **427**.
chasm, **323**, **324**.
chaste(n), 321, 430; **6**, **406**.
chastise(d) (chastising), 114; **6**, **275**, **356**.
chastity, **6**, **350**.
chasuble, **59** n. 2.
chat, 121.
Chatham, 229.
cheap sb. & adj., 56; **120** n., **124** n. 1.
cheap vb., **119**.
cheapen, 350; **381**.
checks, **59** n. 3.
cheer, 398, 405, 409, 426, 439; **126** & nn. 3, 4, **204**, **218**, **231**, **274** n. 3.
cheese, 56; **118**, **132** n.
cheesecake, **11**.
cherish, **212** n. 3.
cherry, -ies, 55; **10**, **77**, **275**.
chervil, **325**.
chess, **60** n. 1.
chestnut, **406**.
che vore ye 'I warrant you', 143.
chews, **159**.

chicken, **325** & n. 3.
chicory, **275** n. 2.
chief, **132** n., **136** n. 2.
child(er), 15, 54, 109; **12**, **328** & n. 1.
childhood, **426**.
children, 70; **12**, **319** n. 1, **328** & nn. 1, 3, **409** & n.
chimney, 373; **338** n. 1.
chin, 417.
chine, 417; **12**.
chip vb., **87** n. 4.
chirk, 435; **78**.
chirp, 435; **78**, **213**.
chirurgeon, 284, 386.
chisel, **10**.
choice, 83, 121, 174, 428, 437, 440, 441; **254**.
choir, 21, 23; **128**, **136**.
choise vb., 28.
choler, **88**, **299**.
Chomley, **97** n. 6.
choose, 83; **159** & n. 2, **355**.
chop vb., **87** n. 4.
F. chose, **206**.
chough, 23, 391, 427; **34**, **39**, **171**.
Christ, 221, 425, 443; **12**.
Christian, **12**, **276**, **390**.
Christianity, 350, 351; **308**, **390**.
Christmas, **302**, **406**, **439** n.
church, 54, 435; **82**, **189**, **212** n. 2, **213** n. 1, **376**.
churchyard, **3**, **422** & n. 2.
churl, 104; **18** n. 3, **46** & n. 1, **74**, **208** n. 1, **212** n. 2.
churn, 435; **82**, **213**.
chute, **185**, **188**.
Cicero('s), **277**, **356**.
cider, **12**.
F. cieux, 81.
ciphering, **306**.
Circe, **269**.
circle, 441; **213**.
circuit, 184, 308; **213** & n. 1, **282** & n. 5, **421**.
circumcision, **356**, **389**.
cistern, 348; **329** & nn. 1–3.
cithern, **328**.
citizen, **264**, **272**, **326**, **356** n. 2.
citron, **321**, **328** & n. 2.
city, **293**, **350**.
civil, **303**, **325** & n. 3, **326**.
clad, 211; **378**.

clag, **433**.
claim, **211**.
Clapham, **229**.
Claudius's, **334**.
clause, 407; **104** n. 7.
claw, **239** n. 1.
clay, **211**.
cleam, **433**.
clean, 91; **115** n. 3, **116** n. 2, **123**.
cleanse, **8**, **355**, **356** n. 4.
clear, 91, 426; **126** & nn. 3–5, **136** n. 2, **204** n. 3, **228** n. 5, **430** n. 2.
cleave 'findere', 56, 406, 436; **119**, **120** & n., **136** n. 1.
cleave 'haerere', 56, 406, 436; **119**, **136** n. 1.
cleaver 'one who slits', 411; **31**.
cleft, 326; **120** n.
clerk, 26, 434–5; **65** & n. 2, **212** n. 3.
clever, 411; **80**.
cliff, **417**.
climb, 114; **12**.
clinch, **410**.
cloak, 418, 419; **13**, **250** n. 3.
clock, 418, 419.
clock vb. 'cluck', 419.
cloister, **254**.
Clopham, **87** n. 3.
Clophill, **87** n. 3.
close adj., **431** n. 4.
close vb., 407, 418.
closet, **51** n.
clot, **87** n. 2, **92**.
cloth(s), 29, 300, 361–2, 431; **33**, **358**, **368**.
clothe(d), 20; **315**, **368**.
clothes, 164, 236, 418; **310**, **312**, **358**, **401**.
clouds, **312**, **362**.
clown, 23, 126.
cloy(ed), 59, 83, 341, 428, 437; **255** & n. 1, **263**.
cluck vb., 418, 419.
clyster, 399.
coal, 22, 264, 265; **169** n. 5.
coarse, 418; **48** n. 1, **165** & n. 2, **207** n. 1, **208**.
coast, 408, 438.
coat(s), 402–3, 418; **34**, **263** n. 2, **375** n. 2, **431** n. 4.

INDEX OF WORDS

Cobham, 229.
cock, **53** n. 2.
cockle, **325** n. 1.
cockney, **275** n. 2.
coequal, **290**.
coeternal, **290**.
coff, 125.
coffer, **297**, **326**.
coffin, 398; **377** & n. 3.
cog, **53** n. 2.
Cogwell, 87 n. 3.
co-habit, **270**.
coif, 341; **255** & n. 2.
coil *sb*. 'tumult', 428, 437; **255** n. 1.
coil *vb*. 'cull', **260**.
coil *vb*. 'wind', 388, 437; **255** & nn. 1, 3.
coin(s, -ed), 28, 303, 428; **255** & n. 3, **263** nn. 1, 2.
coiners, 168, 303.
cold, 55, 343, 406; **4**, **169** n. 4, **353** n.
colf, 125.
coll, 430–1; **13**.
collar, **299**, **308**.
collection, 170.
collier, **276**, **299**, **308**.
collop, 406.
collusion, **389**.
Colman, **431** n. 4.
Cologne, **91**, **94**, **272** & n., **334**.
colon, **321**.
colonel, **91**.
colony, **91**.
colour, 89, 91, 92; **281**, **298**, **299**.
colt, 22, 54, 211, 337, 344, 418, 437; **88**, **169**, **425**.
columbaceous, **269**.
Colworth, 87 n. 3.
com- *prefix*, **292**.
comb, 22, 379, 408, 430, 440; **7** & n. 2, **13** & n. 3, **15** & n., **151**, **394**.
combustible, **2**.
come(s), 89, 226, 248, 249, 250, 274, 324, 430; **18**, **362**.
cometh, 70; **97** n. 6, **314**.
comfort, 183; **299**.
comfrey, **338** n. 2.
coming, 415; **154** n. 6, **377** & n. 3.
comma, **248** n. 2.

command(eth), 102, 236; **292**.
commandment, 16, 102, 184, 221, 222, 236; **237** n. 2, **306** & n. 1.
F. comme, **248** n. 2.
commendable, **2**.
commendations, 90.
commit, **292**.
commodious(ly), **23**, **281**, **363**.
commodity, -ies, **275**, **292**.
common(ly), 252; **275**, **283**, **302**, **319**, **321**.
commune, **283**.
communication, **292**.
communion, **276**, **292**.
companion, **91**, **276**, **292**.
company, 355; **275**.
comparable, 90.
comparative(ly), **6**.
compare(d, -s), 110, 145–6; **6**, **292**, **363**.
comparison, **6**, **356**.
compassion, **276**, **292**.
complain, **292**.
complaint, **292**.
complaisance, **2**.
complete, 25; **237** n. 2.
complexion, 170; **276**.
composedness, **311**.
composer, **292**.
compound(s) *sb*., **267**, **363**.
compounded, **292**.
comprehend, **308**.
comprise, **403**.
con, 432.
con- *prefix*, **292**, **380**.
conceit(ed), 167; **131**.
conceive, **116** n. 2, **131**, 226.
concern *vb*., 104.
conclude, **380**.
conclusion, **380**, **389**.
concordance, **2**.
concourse, **19**, **267**.
concrete, **380**.
condemn, 104; **321**, **324**, **395**, **441** n. 2.
condign, **380**; **319**, **321**, **323**, **324**, **395**, **441** & n. 2.
condition, 15; **276**.
conduit, 174, 184, 308; **282** & n. 5, **421**.
coney, 94, 97.
confederacy, **275**.
confessor, **2**.

confines, **267**.
confirm, 411; **213**.
confirmation, 181.
confiscate, **2**.
conform, 411; **19**, **213**.
confusion, 352; **389**.
conger, 337; **399**.
congregation, **380**.
congress, **380**.
conjure(r), **2**, **264**, **282**.
conner, **94**.
conquer, 125; **380**, **421**.
conqueror, **281**.
conquest, 125; **380**, **421**.
conscience, 394; **276**, **301**, **311** n. 2 (*gen. sg*.).
conscientious, 394; **388**.
conserve, 26; **65** n. 4.
considered, **306** & n. 2.
conspire, **218**.
constable, **336**.
constancy, **275**.
Constantinople, **22**.
conster *see* construe.
constraint, **433**.
construction, 105; **282** n. 2.
construe, 105; **282** n. 2, **324**.
consume, **369**.
consumption, 187; **403**.
contemplate, **2**.
contemplation, **277**.
contempt, **403**.
continual, **273**, **282**.
continue, **282**, **315**.
contract *sb*., 29; **2** n. 3.
contradict(ing), **265**, **271**, **336** n. 2.
contraries, **312**, **363**.
contrarily, **6**.
contribute, 372; **2**.
contrive, **136**.
control(led), 344, 430, 434, 436; **169** n. 3.
convenient, 29; **2**, **276**.
conventicle, 161; **2**.
converse, 435.
conversion, **364**.
convert, 26, 435; **2**, **65** n. 4.
convey, **115** n. 5.
convince, **292**.
cook, **37**, **38**.
cool(ed), 406; **4**, **431** n. 4.
coomb (a measure), 408; **19**, **164**.
coomb 'valley', **19**, **164**.
coop, 126; **164**.
Copford, **87** n. 3.

copious, 349; **1**.
coppice, 407.
copy, -ies, 407; **275, 312,** 363.
coral, **273** & n. 2.
cord, 177, 429; **13, 46**.
cork, **13**.
corn, 418; **46, 331, 431** n. 4.
corpse, **13, 16, 149, 165** n. 1, **208** n. 3, **442**.
correctors, **299**.
corruptible, **2**.
cosen, 325.
cosmic, **364**.
cost, 29, 361–2, 408, 431; **16**.
costly, **406**.
cot, 53 nn. 1, 2, **86** n. 1.
Cotswold, **13, 280** n.
couch(ed), 22, 109; **167** & n. 1.
cough(ed), 23, 126, 163, 170, 187, 326, 334, 366, 371, 383, 402–3, 418, 427, 432, 443; **4, 24** & n. 1, **28, 34, 39, 89** n., **104, 170, 240, 371**.
coughing, 398; **377** & n. 3.
could, 90, 221, 239, 251, 316, 344, 361, 362, 389, 406, 436, 440, 443; **4, 161, 166, 169** n. 4, **196** n. 3.
coulter, 364; **174**.
council, **326**.
counsellor, **326**.
count, **19**.
countenance, **19, 273, 334**.
counter, **19**.
counterfeit, **131, 272, 334**.
country, 90, 92, 226; **19, 275** & n. 2, **338, 350**.
couple(d), 23, 44, 89, 91; **19**.
courage(ous), 91; **6, 19, 165, 281, 336**.
courier(s), 92, 411; **299, 308** n. 2.
course(s), 90, 91, 239, 358, 362–3, 418; **13, 16, 19, 46** n. 1, **48** n. 1, **165** & nn. 1, 2, **207** n. 1, **208** & nn. 2, 3, **364, 375** n., **442**.
courseth, **375** n.
court, 90, 91, 432; **19,**
48 n. 1, **165** & n. 1, **208, 209**.
courteous(ly), 91, 92, 350; **19, 274, 281, 356, 390**.
courtesan, **19**.
courtesy, 91; **19, 275, 306, 350, 356**.
courtier, 349, 350, 391; **19, 165, 390**.
courtly, 90.
cousin, 124; **19, 326**.
covenant, **306**.
Coventry, 129; **92** & n. 2, **350**.
cover, 147, 148; **83, 96**.
coverture, **282**.
covetise, **275**.
covetous, 350; **97**.
cow, 22, 215, 383.
cowl, 126.
Cowper, **164**.
coy, 10, 28, 59, 168, 303, 428, 437, 440; **254** & n. 2.
cracks, 59 n. 3.
craft, 431; **28**.
Cranmer, 59 n. 2.
crave, **25, 115** n. 3.
creance, cranes (falconry term), **101, 104** n. 2.
create(d), **115** n. 3, **288**.
creation, **270**.
creator, **288, 325**.
creature(s), 390; **115** n. 3, **127, 282, 326**.
L. credere, 378.
creech, 433.
creek, 404; **31**.
creep, 162; **124** n. 1.
crept, **120** n.
crew, **184**.
crib, 21.
cribble, **324**.
crick, 404.
cricket (game), 242.
cricket (insect), 26; **80**.
criest, -eth, 183; **314**.
crimson, **336**.
cripple, 162, 409; **10**.
crocodile(s), **275, 306**.
croft, **51** n.
crone, 360.
crook(ed), 267, 342, 443; **37, 38**.
crop, 53 n. 2, 87 n. 2.
crosier, **389**.
cross(ed), 431; **59** n. 2, **87** n. 2.

crouch, **167** & n. 1.
croup 'rump', **164**.
crow, 10, 23, 107, 434; **241**.
crown, 126, 377; **172** n. 1, **173** n. 1.
Croydon, **188, 258** n.
crucified, 261; **275**.
cry(ing), 45; **40**.
cuckoo, **196**.
cucumber, **178**.
cud, **4**.
cuff, 418, 433.
L. cui, 79.
cuit, 54.
cull, 427, 428; **260**.
Cullen 'Cologne', **91, 94, 272** & n.
Cumae, **22**.
cumin, 415; **321, 377** & n. 3.
cup and saucer, **381**.
cupboard, 183; **401**.
cur, 417; **20**.
curbed, **439** n.
curd, **19, 439**.
cure, 103, 417; **20, 22, 185** n. 4, **218**.
curfew, **267**.
curiosity, 72; **275** n. 2, **356**.
curious, **363**.
curls, **437** n. 1.
currant, **330**.
current, **301**.
currier, 411.
curse, 418; **401**.
curst, 344, 441; **213** n. 4.
curtain, **268, 272, 303**.
curtsies, 91, 92; **165**.
cushion, **196, 276, 308** n. 2.
custard, **299**.
custom, **283, 293**.
cut, 293, 356; **93**.

d (letter-name), **40**.
dace, **401** n. 1.
D. dach, **275, 276**; **424**.
Daedalus, **22**.
dagger, **321**.
daily, **274, 279**; **264, 265, 275**.
dainty, 307.
dais, 25, 91; **131**.
daisy, **311**.
dalliance, **60**.
dally, **60, 275**.
dam, **6**.
damage, **336** & n. 1.

INDEX OF WORDS

dame, 6, **226** n. 4.
damn, **395**.
Damon, **321**.
dam(o)sel, **306**, **334**.
damson, **352**; **320**.
dance, 27, 147, 148, 154, 425; **44** n. 2, **54**, **62**, **104** n. 2, **235** n., **238** & n. 1, **239**.
danger, 162, 331, 380; **59** n. 3, **63**, **104** & nn. 1, 3, **238**, **239**, **281**.
dangerous, **363**.
Daniel, 369; **308**, **334**.
F. danse, 276.
dare(d, -s), 431; **43** n. 3.
dark(ness), 87, 236; **43** n. 1, **64** n. 1.
darkened, **321** n. 1.
darling, 161, 164; **126** n. 1.
darn, 435; **44**.
darnel, 66.
dart, **42**.
daub, **239** n. 1.
daughter(s), 36, 92, 329, 372, 390; **28** & nn. 1, 3, **87** & n., **170**, **238** n. 4, **240** & n. 2, **320**, **371**, **423** & n. 2, **424**.
daunt, 304, 425, 436, 442; **104** n. 2, **239**.
daw, 9.
day(s), 72, 77, 238, 274, 307; **40** & n. 2, **107**, **229**.
de- *prefix*, **288** & n. 1, **292** & n., **344**.
deacon, **321**.
dead, 25; **30**, **123**, **430** n. 4.
deadly, **275**.
deaf, 425; **30**, **36**.
deal, 25, 91, 436; **123** & n. 2.
dear, 84, 91, 161, 390, 397, 409, 426; **126** & nn. 1, 3-5, **132** n., **136** & n. 2, **204** nn. 3, 4, **218**.
dearth, 435; **8**.
death, 354, 425; **30**, **228** n. 3, **358**.
debar, **68** n. 3.
debt, 45, 157, 169, 386; **425** n. 3, **442**.
deceit(s), 79, 241, 382; **131**, **288**.
deceive(d), 290; **116** n. 2, **131**, **226** n. 4, **228** nn. 3, 4, **288**.
decent, **399**.

decide, **365**.
decision, 352; **389**.
decisive, **356**.
declare, **204** n. 4, **288**.
declension, 216.
declination, 216.
decline, **378**.
deed(s), 109; **31**, **118**, **132** n.
deemeth, deems, **110**, **132** n.
deep(en), **124** n. 1, **133**, **323**.
deer, 150, 397, 409, 426; **126** n. 3, **136**, **218**.
default(s), **237** n. 2.
defeat(ed, -ing), 25, 390; **115** n. 3, **377**.
defend, **288**.
defensory, **29**; **1**, **2**.
defer, 435; **68** n. 3
defile, **260** n. 2.
defoil *vb.*, **260** & n. 2.
deform, **47**.
defoul, **260** & n. 2.
degree, **228** n. 5.
dehort, **426**.
delectable, 29; **2**.
delicate, 92; **336** n. 1.
delight(ful), 144; **141**, **143**.
deliver(ed), 26, 77, 274, 279; **315**, **320**, **324**.
delusion, **356**, **389**.
demand, 27, 276, 279, 304; **101**, **210**, **238**, **239**.
F. demande, 286; **59**.
demean, 25.
demonstrated, **288**.
demurred, **218**.
denial, **273**.
denied, deny(eth, -ing), 34, 114; **40**.
depart, 26.
depeach, 25.
depth, **358**.
Derby, 66 n. 4.
Dereham, **132** n., **136** n. 2.
deride, 109–10.
derision, **356** & n. 3, **389**.
derivative, **2**, **271**.
derive(d), **12**.
des- *prefix*, **292**.
descend, **365**.
descension, **292**.
descent, **399**.
describe, **288**.
descry, **288**.

desert 'meritum', 137, 435; **65**.
desert 'solitudo', 137.
deserve(d), 435; **356**.
design, **356**.
desire, 252, 324; **288**, **344**, **356**.
desirous, **12**, **281**, **363**.
desist, **356**.
desolate, **336** n. 1, **356**.
despair(ed, -s), 431; **204** n. 4, **226** n. 4, **228** n. 3, **292**.
desperado, **235** n.
despise, 109, 210; **12**, **288**, **292**.
despoil, **255** n. 1.
dessert, **365**.
destiny, **275**, **303**.
destroy(ed), 334, 437; **255** & nn. 1, 3, **262** nn. 2, 3, **288**.
detail, **269**.
deter, 435.
determine(d), **275**, **303**.
L. deus, -m, 31, 79.
device, 20, 30, 114; **12**, **368** n. 4.
devil, 55, 162, 397; **9** & n. 2, **11**, **326**, **334**, **400**.
devise(r), 114; **12**, **292**, **368** n. 4.
devoid, **256**.
Devonshire, 351; **325** n. 2, **400**.
devour *sb.* 'devoir', **279**.
devour *vb.*, **218** n. 1.
dew, 9, 49, 168, 217, 314, 372, 380, 387, 406, 409, 418; **185**, **243**, **244** & n. 4, **391**.
di- *prefix*, **288** n. 1, **292** & n.
diadem, 25; **271**.
dialogue, **267**, **309**.
diamond, **23**, **302**, **309**, **398**.
Diana, **289**.
dice, 19, 106; **136**, **363**.
dictionary, **307**.
did, **82** n. 2.
die(s) *sb.*, 114; **40**, **136**, **363**.
die(d) *vb.*, 23, 24, 167; **40**.
Dieppe, **133**.
F. dieu, 9.
differ, **297**.
difficulty, **350**.

ME digneliche 'worthily', **441** n. 1.
ME dignest 'worthiest', **441** n. 1.
dignity, **441** n. 1.
digress, 112.
digression, **292** n.
dike, 108; **138** & n. 2.
diligent, **23**.
Diocletian, **356**, **389**.
Dionysius, **356**, **389**.
diphthong(s), 72; **442**.
dipped, **315**.
dire, **218**.
direction, **289**, **292** n.
dirge, **127**, **213** n. 3.
dirt(y), 37, 162, 163; **84**, 213 nn. 1, 4, **439**.
dis- *prefix*, **292**, **356**.
disarm, **365** n. 1.
discern(ed), 109, 435; **365** & n. 1.
disciple, 104; **324**.
discipline, 104, 105.
discomfit(ed), **299**, **303**, **332**.
discomfort(ed), **299**, **303**, **332**.
discommodity, **275** n. 2.
discouragings, **363**.
discourse, 362–3, 432; **19**, **165** n. 1, **364**.
discrete, **25**.
discretion, **388**.
diseases, **356**, **365**.
disfigure, **17**.
disgorge, **13** n. 2.
disgrace, **364**.
disguise, **364**.
dishonest(ly), **356**, **365** & n. 1.
dishonesty, **275**, **356**.
dishonour(able), **356**, **365**.
disloined, **255**, **256** n. 3.
disloyal, **254** n. 4.
dismal, **364**.
disorder(ing), **306**, **356**, **365**.
disown, **294**, **304**; **249**.
dispence, **364**.
displays, 91.
displease, **25**.
displeasure, **44**.
disregard, **2**.
disrespect, **2**.
dissension, **292**.
dissent, **399**.

dissolve, **88**, **365**.
distinction, **292** n.
distract *sb.*, **29**.
distribute, 29, 372; **1, 2**.
district(s), **392**.
ditch(es), **12**, **301**.
dive, 106, 430; **135**.
divers *adj.*, **12**, **59** n. 2, **289**.
diverse(ly), **12**, **289**.
divest, **354**; **8**.
divide, **289**, **292**.
divine(ly), 137, 210; **264**, **289**, **292** n.
divinity, **129**.
divisible, 29; **2**.
division, 351; **292** & n., **389**.
divisor, **292**.
divulgate, 29; **2**.
do, 18, 124, 240, 418, 431; **4**, **40**, **148** n., **152** n., **153** n., **155** & n., **183** n. 5, **308**.
docile, **275**.
doctrine, 45; **275**.
doe, 18, 22, 418, 427, 433–4; **4, 40**.
doer, 414; **155** n., **218**.
dog, 249, 253; **53** n. 2, **92**.
doing(s), 124; **40**, **412**.
doit, **257**.
dole, 22, 211, 344.
doll, 430.
dolphin, **325**.
dolt, 344; **88**, **169**.
-dom *suffix*, **278**, **347**.
domage, 17; **63**.
domain, **131**.
L. dominus, 62.
don, 23.
Doncaster, **336** n. 2.
done, 187, 274, 387, 397, 412; **4**.
Donne, 378.
don't, **431** n. 4.
doom, **148** n.
door, 36, 267, 414; **155** & n., **201** n., **208** n. 2, **209** n. 1, **213** n. 4, **218** & n. 1.
dor, 36, 432; **47**.
Dorchester, **427** n.
dorm, 432, 433.
dort, 433.
dost, 401; **4**, **310** n.
dote, 36.
doth, 71, 360, 401, 431; **4, 313, 314, 368**.

double, 382, 389; **19**, **301**, **324**.
doublet, 91; **334**.
doubt, 90, 157, 250; **442**.
dough, 353, 363, 370, 418, 427, 433, 434; **4**, **34**, **39** & n. 1, **160**, **170** & n. 4, **424**.
doughty, **177**.
dove, 123–4, 160, 360, 418, 424, 425, 433, 443; **18**, **39** & nn. 2–4.
Dover, **154** n. 1.
down, 107, 126, 391, 412; **4**.
dowry, **275**.
doxology, **359**.
dozen, 124; **19**, **272**, **326**.
dragon, **321**.
drain, **108** n. 3, **115** n. 9, **129** n. 5.
drake(s), 399, 412; **6**.
draught, 383, 418, 431; **28** & n. 1, **371**, **424**.
Drax, 399, 412.
Drayton, **321**, **326**.
dread, 426; **30**, **118**.
dream(s), 25, 366; **115** n. 3, **120** & n.
dreary, **126** & n. 4, **204**.
dregs, 26; **77**.
dressed, **8**.
drew, 406.
drinking, 15, 253; **377**.
drivel, **326**.
droil, 428.
droll, 364.
drone, 22.
droop, 126; **164**.
drop, **53** n. 2.
drought, 338, 370, 418; **97** & n. 5, **140** n. 3, **175**, **177**, **371**, **382**, **424**.
drove, 424; **151**.
drown, **436** n. 2.
drunk, 249.
drunkenness, **321**.
dry, 109; **40**.
dryads, **332** n. 1.
duality, **270**.
duck, 412, 417; **20**.
due, 372, 380, 409, 418; **40** n. 1, **185**, **244**, **391**.
duel, 418; **185** & n. 1, **391**.
duet, **270**.
duke, 412, 417; **20**, **188**.
dull, 226.
dumb(ness), **394**, **403**.

INDEX OF WORDS 1045

dun, 397, 412.
dunce, 432.
dungeon, **336** & n. 2.
F. dure, 276.
during, **218** n. 1.
durst, 441; **439** n.
dust, 401; **96**.
duty, **244** n. 4.
dwarf, 331–2, 442; **49, 371**.
dwelled, 430.
Dyamond, **23**.
dye(d), 167; **40, 315**.
dyer, **218**.

e- *prefix*, **127, 288, 344**.
each, 25; **8, 116** n. 2.
eager, **8**.
eagle, 102.
eam, 25.
ear(s) *sb.* 'auris', 6, 372, 398, 407, 409, 426; **122** & n. 2, **204** & n. 4, **218, 226** n. 4, **228** nn. 3, 5, **429** & n. 3, **430**.
ear *sb.* 'spica', 407; **122, 204**.
ear *vb.* 'arare', 113, 425; **204**.
earl, 150, 390, 435; **8, 65, 126** & n. 4, **218**.
early, 391; **8, 203** n., **204, 408, 430**.
earn, 398, 435; **8, 65** & n. 5, **203** n., **204, 430** & n. 5.
earn 'yearn', **422** n. 2.
earnest(ly), 252; **8, 126** & n. 4, **275, 430** n. 5.
earth(s), 5, 6, 16, 21, 112, 274, 279, 300, 338, 391, 435; **8, 65, 212** & n. 3, **358, 368, 401, 426, 430** & n. 5.
earthen, **368**.
earthly, **368, 408**.
earth-worm, **368**.
earthy, **368**.
ease, 16, 25, 424, 426; **115** n. 3, **398, 430**.
ease 'eaves', 25.
easel, **110** n.
east, 44, 398, 399, 412, 417; **8, 13, 398, 422, 430**.
Easter, 351, 399; **8**.
eastern, **329** & n. 1.
easy, **8, 275** & n. 2.
eat *infin.*, 25, 399; **422** n. 1, **430**.

eat *p.t.*, **30**.
eaten, 252; **320**.
eath 'facilis', 25.
eaves, **400**.
L. ecclesia, **356**.
ecclesiastical, **276, 389**.
eche *vb.*, 443.
echo, **277**.
eclogue, 351.
economic, **23**.
-ed (*inflexion & suffix*), 260–1, 316; **311, 312, 315** & n., **334, 368** n. 4.
edder, 401; **384**.
Eden, **127**.
edge, **430** n. 5.
edify, **23**.
educate, **269**.
eel, 251, 264, 320, 436; **430**.
-eer (-ier) *suffix*, **274** n. 3.
e'er, **122** & n. 5, **218**.
effect(s), 386; **407, 442**.
efficacy, 390.
effusion, **389**.
eftsoons, 22.
egg, **430** n. 5.
Egypt, 21; **23, 398**.
eight, 22, 169, 353, 382, 383, 418, 424, 425; **139** & n., **226, 424, 426**.
eighteen, 348; **1, 345**.
eighth, 78; **368** n. 3.
either, 113, 161–2, 382, 401; **4, 8, 115** n. 5, **129** & n. 2, **384**.
eke, 24, 25; **119, 138** n. 2.
-el *suffix*, **323** n. 1, **325** & nn. 2, 3, **326**.
elbow(s), 92; **250, 430** n. 5.
eld, 25; **9**.
elder *sb.* 'sambucus', 397, **430** n. 5, **437**.
elder(s) 'senior(es)', **363**, 397, **430** n. 5.
eldest, **430** n. 5.
Eleanor, 348; **308**.
elect, **288, 398**.
elephant, **301**.
eleven(th), 352; **301, 321**.
Eliza, **271**.
ell(s), 320; **395, 430** n. 5.
elm, 101, 434; **330, 331**.
else, 90, 432; **363**.
elsewhere, 348; **1**.
Elysian, **356, 389**.
em- *prefix*, **292**.
'em 'them', 238, 316, 394.

emaciate, **276**.
embalm, 342, 366.
embossed, **29** n. 1.
embrace, **403**.
embroider(y), **258**.
eme 'uncle', **228** n. 4.
emerald(s), **273** n. 3, **348**.
emmet, emot 'ant', **301, 430** n. 5.
emperor, **264, 281, 306**.
empire, 348; **1, 265, 267, 275**.
employ(ment), 175, 341; **254** & n. 3, **403**.
empty, **319, 403, 435**.
emroids, 341.
emulate, **23**.
en- *prefix*, **292**.
-en *suffix*, **323** n. 1, **325** & nn. 2, 3, **326, 334** n. 1.
enamoured, **281**.
-ence *suffix*, **325** & n. 3.
enchant, 27.
encouraged, **292**.
encumbrance, **403**.
end, 109, 112, 253; **9, 57, 77, 430** n. 5.
endeavour, 91; **8, 279, 281, 299**.
endited, **141**.
endive, 348.
endueth, 72.
endure, **165** n. 6, **185** n. 6.
enduring, 325.
enemy, -ies, **137** n. 2, **275, 306, 312, 334, 363**.
enervate, **2**.
enforce, **292**.
engine, 406; **325**.
England, 19, 159, 350, 351, 352; **57, 77, 412** & n. 2.
English, 350; **57, 77, 412** & n. 2.
engross, 364; **150**.
enhance, 27, 304, 331, 389; **426**.
enjoin, **255** n. 3, **292**.
enjoy(ed), 69, 437; **254** & n. 4.
enlarge, **43** n. 1.
enlightening, **306**.
enough, 91, 126, 210, 221, 334, 371, 383, 388, 402; **39, 171** n., **288** n. 3, **294** & nn. 2, 3, **351, 352, 424**.
enow, 401–2; **39**.

enquire, 103.
enquiry, 411.
enriched, **116** n. 2.
enroll(ed), 22; **169** n. 3.
enrolment, 29; **1, 2**.
ensign, 406.
-ent *suffix*, **325** & n. 3.
entangle, 143; **412**.
F. entendement, 238; **59**.
enter(ed), 104, 412; **306**.
enter- *prefix*, **292**.
enterprise *sb.*, **356**.
enthroned, 430; **13**.
enthusiasm, **276, 323, 364, 389**.
entire, 89, 412; **2, 218**.
entrails, 24; **267**.
entreat, 25.
entry, 104.
envied, **315**.
environ, **328** & nn. 1, 2.
envy *sb.*, 161; **2**.
envy *vb.*, 161; **2**.
Ephesians, **288**.
Ephesus, **356**.
Ephraim, **271**.
epistle, **324**, 406.
epitaph, **269**.
epitome, 21.
equal, 347; **23**.
equerry, 411.
equity, **23**.
-er *suffix*, **274** n. 3, **297, 299, 323** nn. 1, 2, **325** & nn. 2, 3, **326, 334** n. 1.
Erasmus, **288**.
ere, 398, 407; **122** & nn. 2, 5, **204** n. 3, **430**.
erect, **288**.
erelong, 286.
erewhile, **430** n. 3.
L. ergo, 7; **66**.
err(ed, -s), 26, 110, 332; **68** & n. 1, **212** & n. 3, **213, 315**.
errand, 398; **8, 67, 367** & n., **430** n. 5.
errant, **67, 367**.
error, **212** n. 3, **281**.
erst, 112, 163; **401, 430** & n. 5.
-ery *suffix*, **269**.
-es *sb. inflexion*, **288** n. 2, **311, 312, 334, 363**.
-es *vbl. inflexion*, **288** n. 2, **313** & nn. 1, 2, **314** & n. 1, **334, 363, 375** & n.

escape, **288**.
escheat, 25.
especial(ly), 252; **270, 273, 275, 288, 344, 388**.
espy, **288**.
esquire, 411.
essays, **301, 302**.
essoin, 441; **255, 262**.
-est *superlative inflexion*, **311, 317, 334** n. 2.
-est *vbl. inflexion*, 316; **311, 316** & n., **363** n. 2, **398**.
establish(ed), **288**.
esteem, 210; **288**.
Esther, 352.
estranged, 380.
etens 'giants', **430** nn. 3, 5.
eternal, **273, 288**.
eternity, **288**.
-eth *inflexion*, 316, 327, 338, 397; **311, 313** & nn. 1–2, **314** & n. 1, **368, 375** & n.
Eton, 326.
eucharist, 217; **244**.
eunuch, **282** n. 2, **442**.
F. eureux 'heureux', 9.
Eustace, **244**.
Eva, 22; Eve, **127**.
evasion, 352; **389**.
even-length, **430** n. 3.
even *adj.* & *adv.*, 72, 162, 347, 352, 419; **8, 10, 120, 330** & n. 1, **400, 426**.
even *sb.* 'evening', **330, 400** n.
evening, 9, **306, 330**.
evenly *adj.*, **430** nn. 3, 5.
ever, 79, 236, 253, 274, 279, 347; **8, 77, 109, 212, 320, 330**.
everlasting, **320, 321**.
evermore, 16; **431**.
every, **59** n. 2, **275** & n. 1, **306**.
evil, 55, 61, 72, 162, 169, 274, 279, 352; **10, 75, 132** n., **326, 334**.
ewe, 84, 215, 217, 251, 253, 341; **4, 178** n. 5, **183** n. 5, **185, 244** & n. 5, **245** n. 2, **430**.
ewer, 217, 302, 398, 406, 414; **185, 209, 244** & n. 5.
exalt(ed), **60, 359**.

exaltation, **359**.
F. exalter, **359**.
F. examen, **359**.
examine, **59** n. 2.
example(s), 387; **62** & n. 1, **239, 312, 321, 359**.
exceedingly, **412**.
excel, **359** & n. 3.
excellency, **359**.
excellent, **306**.
except(ing), **302, 359** & n. 3.
F. excès, 286.
excess, **359**.
exchange, 386.
exclamation, **271**.
excusable, 29; **2**.
excuse *sb.* & *vb.*, 339; **2**.
F. exécration, **359**.
execute, **359**.
executioner, **274** n. 3.
F. exemple, **359**.
exempt, **359**.
*exercary, **59** n. 2.
exerce, **59** n. 2.
exercise, -ing, 71, 72; **299, 359**.
exercises, **363**.
exert, **359**.
Exeter, **306**.
F. exhalaison, **359**.
exhaust, **29** n. 1, **359**.
F. exhaustif, **359**.
F. exhiber, **359**.
exhibit, **359**.
exhibition, 15; **276, 426** n. 3.
exhort, 390, 432; **359, 426**.
exile(d), **359** & n. 2.
exodus, **359**.
exonerate, **23**.
exorcise, **299**.
exorcist, **2**.
expatiate, **388**.
expect, **359**.
expectation, **271**.
expedition, **359**.
experience, **23**.
F. expérience, **359**.
explete, 25.
explicable, 29; **2**.
exploit, 341; **254**.
expound, **436** n. 1.
exquisite, 92; **356**.
extol, 22, 344; **88, 169** & n. 2, **359**.
extract *sb.*, 29.

INDEX OF WORDS

extraordinary, 1, 271, 427 n.
extreme(s), 25; 110.
extremity, 350.
exult, 359.
exultation, 359.
eye(s), 23, 24, 85, 93, 137, 141, 170, 320, 432; 137 n. 2, 139, 233, 429 n. 1, 440.
eye-lid, 429 n. 1.
eyer, 218.
eye-salve, 366.
Ezekiel, 127, 288, 308.

fable, 54; 6, 324.
face(s), 301, 356.
L. facere, 376; 301.
facial, 388.
facile, 275.
facts, 53 n. 2.
fade, 106.
Faerie (Queene), 218, 350.
fail, 111; 104, 131 n. 1, 353 n.
faint, 307, 433.
fair(s), 89, 103, 329, 400; 118, 126 n. 5, 137, 218, 226 & n. 4, 228 n. 5, 231.
fairly, 218.
fairy, 205, 218.
faith(ful), 326, 431; 4, 6, 226 n. 4, 228 n. 3.
falcon(er), 354; 306, 425 n. 5.
fall, 225, 264, 269, 347, 392; 53, 237 n. 2.
fallacy, 60.
fallen, 29, 237 n. 2, 319, 321, 325 n. 3, 330.
fallow, 162, 276, 370, 398; 60.
false, 86; 104, 425 n. 5.
falter, 425.
fame, 347; 53.
familiar, 353; 299.
famous(er), 6.
fancy, 284; 62.
fang(ed), 7 n. 1, 399, 412.
far, 410; 43 & nn. 1, 3, 44 n. 4, 55 n. 1, 68 & n. 3, 212 n. 2.
fardel, farthel 'burden', 384 n. 1.
fardel, farthel 'fourth part', 384 n. 1.
fare(d, -s), 400, 431; 43 n. 3, 118, 231.

farm(er), 398, 435; 65 & n. 2, 87 n. 1.
farrier, 67.
farther, 137; 66 & n. 4, 383 & n. 1, 427 n.
farthing, 369; 377, 380 n. 3, 383 & n. 1, 384 n. 1.
farthingale, 380 n. 3, 384 n. 1, 399, 438.
fashion, 53 n. 1, 276, 388 & n. 2, 433.
fast, 286; 86 n. 2, 210.
fasten, 350; 320, 321, 406.
fat, 264, 408; 53 n. 1.
fate, 264, 408.
father, 177, 178, 274, 279, 347, 374, 408; 6, 8, 42, 50 nn. 1, 3, 53 & nn. 1, 5, 55, 56 n., 195 & n. 2, 297, 320, 357 n., 370, 384, 427 n.
fathom, 53 n. 1, 59 n. 2, 383.
fatigue, 368; 116, 133.
fault(s), 45, 77, 244, 357, 401, 424, 436, 444; 363, 367, 425 & n. 5.
fautors, 104 n. 7.
favour, 6, 281, 298, 299, 326.
fawn, 103, 376, 406; 236.
fealty, 198 n.
fear(ed), 187, 251, 426, 430; 118, 122 & n. 6; 204 n. 4, 274 n. 3.
feast, 8.
feat adj., 90; 123.
feat sb., 25.
feather, 17, 408; 8, 383.
feature(d), 93, 390; 115 n. 3, 282, 326.
February, 307.
fee, 119 n. 1, 132 n.
feeble, 55, 167; 11.
feed, 44, 160.
feel, 251; 132 n., 353 n., 437 n. 1.
feet, 408; 31.
feign, 368, 382; 115 n. 5, 131, 324, 441.
fell p.t., 11.
fellow, 147, 162; 280, 295.
female, 286, 290; 271.
feminine, 275, 303, 325.
fence, 167.
Fenchurch, 213 n. 3.
ferk, 434; 212 n. 2.

fern, 435; 8, 212.
fertile, 275.
fervent, 66 n. 4.
fetch, 121.
feud, 244.
feverfew, 217.
few, 9, 49, 84, 90, 217, 239, 250, 341; 244 & nn. 4, 5, 430.
fewer, 209.
fewter, 93; 244.
fiction, 386.
fie interj., 40.
field, 109, 251, 328, 430; 9 & n. 2, 11.
fieldfare, 9.
fiend(s), 189, 400, 412; 9 & n. 2, 11, 77 n. 1, 367 n., 410.
fierce, 8 & n. 1, 9, 126, 201 & n., 204 n. 3, 218.
fiery, 103, 154; 218.
fifth, 72; 368 & n. 3.
fight, 22, 35, 306, 344, 424; 139 n., 141.
fight p.t. 'fought', 415.
figure(d), 282 & n. 1.
file sb. (tool), 262.
file(d) vb. 'defile(d)', 89; 260 n. 2.
fillest, 183.
film, 434; 80, 330, 331.
find(s), 35, 77, 109, 111, 112, 412–13; 12, 77, 262, 263, 367, 410.
fine(d, -s), 406, 412; 410.
finger, 27, 337, 350; 399 & n. 3, 412 & n. 2.
L. finis, 22.
finish, 348.
fins, 400; 410.
fir, 242, 400, 410; 82, 136 & n. 3, 213, 214 n. 4.
fire, 27, 89, 103, 147, 150, 154, 329, 410; 135, 136 n. 2, 137, 218, 226, 297, 353.
firing, 103.
firkin, 343; 212 n. 2.
firm, 212 n. 2.
firmament, 260; 212, 213.
first, 162, 209, 249, 252, 343, 435, 441; 82, 212 n. 3, 213 & nn. 1, 3, 4.
fish(er), 17; 293.
fit, 90, 306, 408, 415; 123.
fitch, 77 n. 3.

INDEX OF WORDS

five, 17, 114; **32**.
fivepence, **12**, **401**.
fixed, **315**.
flakes, 412.
flame, **104** & n. 6.
Flanders, 62.
flatwise, **275**.
flaunt, 304, 425, 436.
flax(en), 412; **320**.
flay(ed), 18, 19, 25; **40**, **115**, **129**, **315**.
flea, 410, 412; **115**, **116** n. 2, **125** & n.
fleak 'flake', 25.
fleam, 416.
fleck, 412.
fledge *adj.*, 61; **75**, **376**.
flee, 109, 410, 412; **40**, **125**.
fleece, 106, 115, 229; **136** (*sb.*), **355** (*vb.*).
fleer(ed), 430; **126** n. 3.
fleet *vb.*, 137.
flesh, 331.
fling, **77**.
float(ing), 89, 137.
flock, **53** n. 2.
flood, 22, 27, 189, 298, 314, 320, 361, 425; **36**, **37**, **38**.
floor(s), 408, 414; **158** nn. 2, 3, **165** n. 3, **207** n. 1, **208** & n. 2, **209**.
Florentine, **275**.
flour, 408, 414; **165** & n. 4, **218**.
flourish, **19**, **165**, **212** n. 3.
flow(ed), 434; **160** n. 2, **173** nn. 1, 2.
flower(s), **165**, **218**.
flown, 103, 434; **172** n. 4.
flute, **184**.
fly, **40**.
foal, 293, 294, 417; **150**, **398**.
foam, 22; **431** n. 4.
foe(s), 22; **40**, **155**, **206**.
foil *sb.* 'leaf, setting, &c.', 428; **256**, **262**.
foil *vb.* 'trample down' and *sb.* 'repulse', **260**, **262**.
foin *sb.* and *vb.* 'lunge', 28; **255**.
foist *sb.* 'cask', **20**, **260**.
foist *sb.* 'galley', 28, 437; **260**.
foist *vb.* 'cheat, palm off', **257**.
fold, 85, 251; **169** n. 3, **398**.

folk, 337; **88**, **104** n. 8, **169**, **250** n. 3, **425**.
folio, **22**, **277**.
follow(eth), 92, 398; **53** n. 2, **73** n., **88**, **250**, **265** & n. 2, **267**, **269**, **280** & n., **295**, **302**.
folly, 225, 264; **431**.
food, 248, 287, 289, 425; **36**, **37**, **185** n. 6.
fool, 239, 248, 261, 264, 265, 267, 268–9, 270, 417; **38**.
foot, 239–40, 261, 287, 289, 342, 440, 443; **36**, **37**, **38**.
for, 77, 236, 250, 274, 345; **47**, **55** n. 1, **210** n. 2.
forbid, **265**.
force(d), 236, 432, 443; **13** & nn. 1, 2, **16**, **46** n. 1, **97** n. 1, **154**, **165** n. 2, **208** n. 3, **210** n. 2, **401**.
ford, 418, 429; **16** & n. 2.
fore, 236, 409, 432; **13**, **47**, **48** n. 1.
-fore *suffix*, **277**.
forecastle, **206** n. 2.
forefathers, **363**.
forego(ing), **40**, **47**, **284**.
forehead, **13**, **426**.
foreign(s), **272**, **326**, **334**.
foreigner, **328**.
fore-oppressed, **315**.
forfeit, **131**, **334**.
forge, **13** & nn. 1, 2, **16**, **154**, **206**.
forgive, 77, 274, 279; **299**.
forgo, **40**, **47**.
forgrown, 92.
fork, **13**, **47**, **48** n. 2.
forlorn, **13**, **46**, **148** n., **208** n. 3.
form, 21, 398, 411, 432, 442; **13** & n. 1, **16** n. 4, **17** & n., **19**, **47** n. 1, **87** n. 1, **91**, **154** & n. 3, **165**, **208** & n. 3.
L. forma, **47** & n. 1.
former, **47**, **87** n. 1.
fornication, **91**.
forsake, **355**.
forsook, **37**.
forsooth, 342; **36**, **37**, **148** n., **150**.
forswear, **204**.
fort, **13**.
Fortescue, **427** n.

forth *adv.*, 89, 443; **16** & n. 1, **208**, **209**.
forth *vb.*, **16** n. 1, **92** & n. 2.
fortunate, **336** n. 1.
fortune, **282**.
forty, **14**, **47**, **173**.
forward, **212**, **332**, **343** n. 3, **421**.
fought, 126, 366, 401; **170** & n. 1, **425** n. 5.
foul *adj.*, 167; **169** n. 3, **172** n. 1.
foul *vb.* 'trample down', **260**.
found *infin.*, **19**.
found *p.t.*, 109, 392.
foundation, 90.
founder *sb.*, **19**.
fount, **19**.
fountain, **268**, **269**, **272**.
four, 17, 19, 45, 163, 294, 337, 362–3, 409; **14**, **16**, **165**, **173**, **208** n. 1, **210**.
F. fourchu, 9.
fourscore, 348.
fourteen, 45; **173**.
fourteenth, 348.
fourth(s), 362–3; **14** n. 1, **16**, **165**, **173**, **208** & n. 1, **209**, **358**, **368** & n. 3.
fowl, 22, 383.
fox, 17.
frail, 111; **104**.
France, 331, 425; **239**.
Francis, **59** n. 2.
frankincense, **85** & n. 2.
franklin, **377** n. 3.
fraud, **53** n. 3.
fraught *sb.*, 24; *p.p.*, 315, 371.
freckle, 29; **8**.
free(d), **132** n., **268**.
freight, 408; **139**.
French, 6.
frenzy, **275**.
fresh, 91.
fret *vb.*, 25; **30** n. 1.
friar, 21; **136**.
Friday, **343** n. 2.
friend(s), 189, 358; **9** & n. 2, **11**, **353** n., **410**.
friendly, friendship, **9**, **410**.
Friesland, 162.
fright, 408.
fringe, 26, 434; **80**.
fro, **427**.
frog, 249, 253; **92**.

INDEX OF WORDS

froise, 10, 28, 419; **254** & n. 2, **256** n. 1.
from, 77, 274, 430, 432.
front, **91**.
frontier, **2**.
frontlets, **91** & n.
frost, 361–2, 438; **51, 53** & n. 2.
froth(y), 425, 431; **32, 368**.
froward, 381; **172, 321, 326**.
fro ye, **310** n.
frozen, 124.
fruit, 44, 110, 179; **20, 282**.
fruition, **277, 291**.
frumenty, 353; **338** n. 1, **401, 438** n., **439**.
fry, fries *vb.*, 419; **254**.
fugitive, **275**.
L. fui(t), 79.
Fulk(es), **425**.
full, 17, 239, 249, 250, 261, 264, 265, 268–9, 270, 271, 289, 293, 294, 342, 417, 427; **196**.
fulminate, **196**.
fulsome, **196**.
fume, **185** n. 6.
fungoid, **269**.
fur, 242, 249, 400, 410; **82**.
furnace, **336** n. 1.
furniture, **282**.
furrow(s), 249; **97** n. 1, **214** n. 5.
further(ance), 79, 137, 411; **306, 383** & n. 1.
L. furtum, 241.
furze, **355**.
fuss, **401**.
fust 'cask', **20**.
fusty, **20, 260**.
F. fût, 79, 81.
-fy *suffix*, **275**.

g (letter-name), **40, 379**.
gad 'goad', 22.
D. gaen, 275, 276.
gage, 430; **6**.
gain, 353, 355.
gainsay, **261** n. 2.
gait, **226** n. 4.
Galathians, 351.
Galatians, 351.
Galilee, 160; **127**.
gallant(s), 398; **2, 60, 410**.
galleon, 308 & n. 2.
galleys, **295** n. 2.

gallon(s), 398; **59** n. 2, **308, 410**.
gallop, 406; **60**.
gallows, **295** n. 2, **302**.
ganch, 304; **239**.
gane 'yawn', 22.
garden, 6, 303, 308 n. 2, **325** n. 1, **326, 379, 408** n.
garrison, **356**.
Garth, **427** n.
gate(s), 62, 216, 326; **115** n. 4, **376, 379**.
gather(s), 178; **53** & nn. 1, 5, **319**.
gauge, 24; **104, 220**.
gaunt, 304, 425, 436.
gauntlet, 304.
gauze, **235** n., **237** n. 4.
gave, 62; **25, 376**.
gaze, 24.
gazette, **2** & n. 2.
gear, **109, 122** & n. 2, **204** n. 3, **212** n. 3.
geese, **430** n. 4.
general, 438; **273**.
genteel, **133**.
Gentile, **275**.
gentle, **325** n. 1, **326**.
gentleman, 90.
gentlewoman, 148.
geometry, **308**.
George, **308**.
German, 71; **272**.
Gervase, **66**.
gest, 29.
gesture, 400; **282**.
get, 26, 234; **77, 148** n. (*p.p.*), **228** n. 4, **379**.
ghastly, **406** & n. 1.
gherkin, **212** n. 2, **213** n. 3.
ghost, 159, 339, 361, 364, 382; **150**.
giant, **276**.
Gifford, **302**.
Gilbert, 15.
ginger, 15; **57, 301**.
gird, 441; **78**.
girdle, 124; **78, 213** n. 1.
girl(s), 435; **78** & n. 2, **204, 212** n. 3, **213** n. 1, **379** n.
girt, **379** n.
girth, 37, 435; **78** & n. 1, **212, 214, 374**.
give(n), 19, 20, 44, 77, 148, 167, 274, 352, 430; **10,** **116** n. 2, **124** n. 1, **376, 400**.
give me, **401**.
giver, 129, 130; **320**.
glad, **59** n. 2, **378**.
glance, 331; **239**.
glass, 211, 398.
glaze(n), 398; **355**.
glede, 25, 426; **119**.
glimpse, **403**.
glister, 399.
gloom, 22.
glorious, **13, 276, 281**.
glory, 211, 261, 274, 278, 279, 336; **13, 16, 47, 149, 275, 378**.
gloss, 398.
Gloucester, 184, 386; **306**.
glove, 123–4, 325, 342, 360, 424, 425, 443; **36, 37, 116** n. 2, **368** n. 1.
glow(ed), 22, 377, 434; **173** n. 2.
glue, 9.
gnar, **418** n. 1.
gnash, 324, 353, 399, 409; **418** & n. 1.
gnat(s), 36, 324, 335, 353, 368, 392, 397, 398; **418** & n. 2.
Gnato('s), **277, 418**.
gnaw(n), 36, 324, 335, 353, 398; **241, 418** & n. 2.
go(eth, -ing), 18, 113, 240; **40, 152** & n., **431** n. 2.
goad, 338.
goal, 22.
goat, 22; **431** n. 4.
W. goch, 376.
God(s), 23, 44, 110, 181, 188, 276, 357; **33** & n. 3, **53** & nn. 1, 2, **87** & n. 1, **431** n. 2.
God be with you, 18.
God give you good even, 378.
Godhead, 389; **426**.
God yield you, **422**.
Goebbels, **325**.
goes 'goest', **398**.
gold(en), 78, 85, 90, 211, 343, 366; **15, 146, 169** n. 3, **249**.
Goldhanger, **87** n. 3.
goll 'hand', 430-1.
gone, 40, 43, 48, 143, 431; **33, 40, 53** & n. 1, **56** n., **97** n. 1.

INDEX OF WORDS

gong 'forica', 21.
good, 14, 27, 55, 79, 81, 126, 160, 168, 181, 188, 239–40, 249, 250, 289, 314, 342, 371, 376, 379, 382, 391, 393, 425, 440; **36**, **37**, **38**, **158** n. 4, **159**, **184**, **431** nn. 2, 4.
goodhead, goodness, **431** n. 2.
go on, 48, 55.
goose, 69; **158** n. 2, **431** n. 2.
gooseberry, **364**.
gore, 409.
gorgeous, **276**.
goslings, **412**.
gossip, **303**.
Gothenburg, **319**.
gouge, **157**, **167**.
gourd, 391, 429, 432; **19**, **165** & n. 1, **208** & n. 3, **209** & n. 2.
gout, 356.
govern(ors), 104; **281**, **331**, **363**.
government, **408**.
go we, 49; **310** n.
gown, **172** n. 1, **436** n. 2.
grace(th), 168, 408; **6**.
gracious(ly), 15; **6**, **276**.
graduate *sb.*, **271**.
graft, **398** n. 1, **437**.
grain, 355; **108** n. 3, **229** n. 2.
grandeur, **269**.
grange, 27, 425; **104**.
grant, 27, 425, 436, 442; **104** n. 2, **239**.
grass, 408; **6**, **56** n.
grate, 365, 416; **115**.
grave(n) *vb.*, 72; **25**.
gravel, **194** n. 3, **326**.
gravity, 286, 290, 300.
graze, **6**.
grazier, 252; **389**.
grease, 25, 424; **136**.
great(ly), 25, 43, 189, 365, 416; **107**, **109**, **115** & nn. 3, 4, 8, **116** n. 2, **217** & n., **225** n. 2, **350**.
greater, 8, **115** n. 6.
great oaths, **311**.
greaves 'refuse of tallow', **104**, **110** n.
Greece, 443; **406**.
green(ish), 404; **11**, **31**.

Greenwich, **11**, **363**.
greve 'grove', **109**.
grew, 89, 314.
grey, **129**.
grieve, 189, 436.
grievous, 366; **132** n., **281**.
grin, 404; **439**.
grise *sb.*, **136**.
grisly, **12**.
grist, 443; **12**.
groan, **53** n. 3.
groat (coin), 184, 287, 357, 362, 384, 411, 412, 443; **33**, **53** & n. 3, **55**, **56** n., **115** n. 8, **216**.
groats (meal), **33**, **53** n. 3.
groin, 437, 441; **144**, **259** & n. 2.
grope, **53** n. 3.
grot, 411, 412; **33**.
ground, **19**.
groundsel, 28; **260**.
grove(s), 433; **53** n. 3, **151** & n. 2.
grovel(ling), 104–5; **94**.
grow(ing, -n), 357, 373, 377, 434; **160** n. 2, **173** nn. 1, 2, **248**, **250**.
growth, 434.
grudge, **439** n.
guard(ed), 210, 380, 426, 431; **6**, **378**.
guardian, 348; **303**, **308** n. 2, **391**.
gud, 181.
guerdon, 124, 171, 326; 66 n. 4, **421** n. 4.
guess, **398**.
guest(s), 124, 326; **50** n., **398**.
Guichiardine, 124.
guide, 115–16, 124, 326.
guild, 141, 414; **12**.
guildhall, 163; **135** n., **376**.
guile, 326.
Guin 'Gwynne?', 124, 326.
guise, 114, 115, 124, 326; **12**, **421** n. 4.
Guise (Duke of), 115–16, 124; **421** n. 4.
gulf, 432.
gun, 187.
gut, 249.

h (letter-name), **40**, **115** n. 5.

G. haar, 150; **101**, **235** n.
habit, **426** n. 3.
habitation, **426** n. 3.
had, **55**.
haemorrhoids, **279**, **348**.
Hague, 440.
hail *interject.*, 319.
hail *sb.*, 175, 319; **104**.
hair, 176–7, 186, 335, 405, 407, 413, 417; **115** n. 3, **126** & n. 5, **130**, **204** & n. 4, **226** n. 4, **231**, **426**, **430** n. 2.
haire *sb.*, **430** n. 2.
hairy, **426**.
hake, 416; **104**.
Hal 'Harry', **60**, **88**.
halberd, **60** & n. 2.
hale, 319; **104**.
half, 37, 304, 342, 343, 353, 366, 431, 432, 440, 442; **28** & n. 3, **54**, **60**, **104**, **238** & n. 1, **239**, **425** & nn. 2, 3.
halfpenny, 37, 343, 349; **28**, **104**, **239**, **401**, **425**.
halfpennyworth, 349; **239**, **332**, **421**.
hall, 152, 188, 319; **104**, **426**.
hallow(ed, -ing), 92, 274, 276, 279, 398, 410, 414; **60**.
Halse, 244.
halt, 424, 436, 444; **60**, **425**.
halter, **29**, **60**, **237** n. 2, **423** n. 2, **425**.
halve(s), **238**, **312**, **425**.
Hamden, **319**.
hammer, **319**, **321**, **332** n. 2, **435**.
Hamton, **319**.
hand(s), 70, 109, 250; **7** & n. 1, **53** n. 1, **71**, **238** n. 1, **312**, **362**, **426**.
handful, 267.
handkerchief, **332**, **380** & n. 1, **410**.
handle, 352; **321**, **324**.
handmaid, **410**.
handshake, **410**.
handsome, **355**, **410**.
hang(ed, -ing, -s), 337; **7**, **53** n. 2, **71**, **399**, **412**.
ha'n't 'has not', **238**.
hantle, 267.

INDEX OF WORDS

happen(eth), 253, 350, 353; 59 n. 2, **306**, **323**, **324**, **335** n., **381**.
happy, **275**.
harass, **426**.
harbour, **66** n. 4, **281**.
hard, 369, 404, 409, 410, 426, 431, 442; **43** n. 3, **44** n. 4, **54**, **55**, **65**, **426**.
Harding, **59** n. 2.
hardness, 418; **408**.
Hardy, **59** n. 2.
hardy 'harden', 350.
hare, 335, 407, 413, 417; **130**, **131**, **204**, **426**.
hark, 26, 434–5; **65** & n. 2, **426**.
harm, 104, 110, 389; **426**.
harmonious, **426** n. 3.
harmony, **262** n. 3, **275**, **350**, **426** n. 3.
harness, 418; **408**.
Harold, **273** n. 3.
harp, **43** n. 1, **331** n. 1.
harre 'hinge', **68** n. 2.
harrow(ing), 92; **55** n. 2.
Harry, **60**, **67** & n. 3.
harsh, 307, 370, 416; **401**, **427** n.
harvest, **59** n. 2, 66.
Harwich, **363**.
has, 142–3, 444; **313**, **362**, **375** n.
hash, 307, 416.
hasp, **50**, **426**.
hast, **177**; **4**, **6**.
haste, 430; **4**, **6**.
hastened, **306**.
hasty, **6**.
hat(s), 188, 325; **363**.
hate(s, -st, -th), 33, 188, 325; **313**.
hath, 177, 431, 439; **4**, **226** n. 4, **313**, **314**, **362**, **368**, **400**, **426**.
hatred, **328**.
L. haud, 216.
Haughton, **44** n. 2.
haughty, **28** n. 3.
haulm, 103, 111, 304, 357, 432; **104**, **238**.
haunch, 27, 425, 442; **62** & n. 1, **239** & n. 1, **410**.
haunt(eth), 27, 102, 304, 353, 425, 436, 442; **62** n. 1, **104** n. 2, **238**, **239** & n. 1.

have, having, 77, 153, 177, 236, 252, 316, 323, 439, 440; **4**, **59** n. 2, **226** n. 4, **400**.
haven, 405; **6**.
haw, 9, 182.
Hawes, 244.
hawk(s), 416; **43** n. 2, **104** & n. 7, **400** n., **423**.
hawking, **377** n. 2.
hawser, 244; **44** n. 2, **238** n. 3.
hazel, 26.
he, 92, 143, 376, 397; **4**, **120**, **301**, **426**.
head, 25, 91, 373, 425; **30**, **120** n., **124** n. 1, **400** & n., **430** nn. 4, 5.
-head *suffix*, 25.
heal, 16, 25, 84; **123**, **430**.
health, 253; **8**, **57**, **77**, **80**, **330**, **353** n., **368** n. 1, **430** n. 5.
heap, **115** n. 4, **120** n., **124** n. 1.
hear(s), 98, 99, 101, 106, 171, 335, 405, 409, 413, 417, 426; **65** n. 1, **126** & nn. 3, 4, **132** n., **136** & n. 2, **274** n. 3, **426**, **430** & n. 2.
heard, 98, 145–6, 404–5, 409, 410, 431, 435; **8**, **9**, **42**, **43** n. 3, **64** n. 3, **65**, **126** n. 4, **132** n., **204** n. 1.
hearken, 351; **65** & n. 1, **323**, **324**, **335** n.
hearsay, **132** n., **136** n. 2.
hearse, 435; **8** & n. 1, **9**, **122** & n. 4, **126**, **430**.
heart, 156, 357, 369, 373, 389, 390, 391, 435; **65** & n. 2, **426**.
hearth(s), 357, 435; **43** n. 3, **50** n. 1, **65**, **212** n. 2, **358**, **426**, **430** n. 5.
heat, 25.
heat *p.p.* 'heated', 28.
heath(s), 366, 424; **4**, **358**.
heathen, 79; **8**.
heaven(s), 92, 236, 274, 279, 379, 390, 405, 419; **8**, **320**, **326**, **328** n. 2, **330** & n. 1, **334**, **426**.
heavenly, **265**, **275**, **321**.
heavy, **8**, **338** n. 1, **350**.
Hebrews, **363**.

heed, 69; **132** n.
heel, 16, 55; **31**.
D. heer, 383, 384.
heifer, 107; **8**, **129**, **430** n. 5.
height, 22, 234, 418, 424, 432; **115** n. 3, **137** n. 2, **139** & n., **382**, **426**.
heinous, 368; **131**.
heir, 328, 369, 391, 405, 407, 413, 440; **4**, **115** n. 5, **128**, **131**, **426** & n. 3.
held, **11**, **77**.
hele 'cover', 106, 113; **123**.
hell, 19.
helm, 104, 432; **331**.
helve, 105, 112; **77**.
hemlock, **431** n. 5.
hempen, **319**.
hence, 325.
Hendley, **338**, **343** n. 2.
her, 26, 37, 93, 180, 181, 209, 316, 343, 345, 347, 391, 397, 413, 417, 435, 442; **4**, **10**, **68** & n. 1, **78**, **212** & n. 1, **214**, **218** n. 1, **226** n. 4, **228** n. 5, **282**, **423** n. 2.
herald, **67** n. 4, **273** n. 3.
herb, 37, 435; **426** n. 3, **430** & n. 5.
herbage, **66** n. 4.
Hercules, **356**.
herd(s), 343, 404, 405, 410, 430, 435; **8**, **65**, **126** & n. 4, **201**, **212** n. 3.
herd 'herdsman', 112.
here, 84, 89, 91, 99, 171, 242, 409, 413, 417, 426, 436; **126** & nn. 2–5, **132** n., **136** & n. 2, **160** n. 3, **204** n. 3, **218**, **414** n. 3, **430** & n. 2.
hereafter, **53** n. 6, **132** n.
hereby, **309**.
herein, **218** n. 1.
hereof, **4**.
heretofore, **290**.
Herford, **66** n. 4.
heritage, 17; **63**, **271**, **426** n. 3.
hern *sb.* 'corner', **214**.
hero(ism), **269**, **270**.
heron, **8**, **321**, **430** n. 5.
herring, 369; **67** n. 3, **377**, **430** n. 5.

INDEX OF WORDS

herself, **357**.
Hesione, **288**.
hesitate, **356**.
Hester, **399**.
heterogeneous, **442**.
hew(n), 90; **244**.
hey, 250.
Heywood, **228** n. 4.
hiccough, **442**.
hid, 109.
hideous, **274**.
hie, 412; **256**.
Hierome 'Jerome', 386.
high, 412; **136** n. 2, **139**, **142**, **256**, **424** n. 2.
higher, 413, 417; **136**, **142**, 218, **424** n. 2.
hight, **426**.
hill, 37; **75**.
him(self), 316, 394; **357**, **426**.
hind, **12**.
hinder(eth), **306**.
hinge, 77.
hints, **412** n. 4.
hire, 27, 103, 413; **218** & n. 1.
hireling, 350; **377**.
his, 21, 45, 76, 92, 369, 424, 444; **4**, **334**, **362**, **426**.
hiss, **4**.
historiographer, 183; **302**, **426** n. 3.
history, **275**.
history-writers, **363**.
hither, 161; **80**, **384**.
ho!, 71; **40**.
hoar, 181, 404, 409, 417; **48** n. 1, **149** & n. 1, **165** n. 4, **208** nn. 2, 4, **426**.
hoard, **16**, **207** n. 1, **208** & n. 1, **209**, **431** n. 4.
hoarse, 181, 432; **149**, **401**, **437** n. 3.
hocks, **362**.
hoist, 28, 71, 83, 172, 174, 303, 437, 441; **144**, **259** & n. 3.
Holborn, **425**.
hold, 71, 85, 90, 251; **146**, **169** n. 3, **251**.
hole, 398; **169** n. 4, **431** n. 4.
holiday, 372; **228** n. 5, **229**, **265**.
hollow, 398, 410, 414; **194** n. 3, **295** n. 2.

holly, **401**; **88**, **295** n. 2.
holm(e), 104; **151** n. 3, **425**.
holocaust, **29** n. 1.
holp(en) *p.p.*, 103; **88**, **425**.
holt, **22**.
holy, **401**; **13**, **265**, **275** n. 1, **293**, **350**.
home, 21, 22, 188, 403, 409, 440, 443; **33**, **36** & n. 1, **148** n., **151** nn. 3, 6, **431** nn. 4, 5.
homely, 403; **13**, **306**.
homily, 403; **306**.
L. homo, 7; **426**.
homogeneous, **442**.
hone, **28**.
honest, 112, 137; **301**, **426** n. 3.
honesty, **275**.
honey, **338** n. 2, **350**.
honour, 137, 187, 189; **264**, **297**, **299**.
hoo 'he', 143.
hoof, hooves, 440; **357**.
hood, 27, 55, 160, 188, 342, 425; **36**, **37**, **38**, **278**.
-hood *suffix*, **36**, **278**, **347** n.
hook, 443; **37**, **38**, **151** n. 4.
hoop *interject.*, **431** n. 1.
hoop *sb.*, **38**.
hoot, **431** n. 5.
hooved, **357**.
hope(d), 391; **13**, **431** n. 4.
Hope, **237** n. 2.
horde, 429; **13**, **16**, **18**, **91**.
horizon, 372; **1**, **2**.
horn, 418; **46**, **431** n. 5.
horror, **298**.
horse(d, -s), 307, 369, 432, 438; **47**, **48** nn. 1, 2, **50** n. 1, **59** n. 2, **206**, **311**, **355**, **356**, **401**, **442**.
hose(n), 124, 401; **145** n. 4, **401**.
hosier, **389**.
hospitable, **2**, **426** n. 3.
host(ess), **431**; **13**, **334**, **426** n. 3.
hostler, 369; **401**.
hostility, **269**.
hot, 29, 92; **33**, **431** & n. 5.
hots *sb.* 'panniers', **87**.
hotter, **150** n. 2.
hottle, **431** n. 5.
hough(ed), 366; **34** & n., **39**, **170**, **357**, **371** n. 2.

hound(ed), **19**, **311**.
hour, 137, 417; **149** n. 1, **165** & n. 4, **208** nn. 2, 4, **426** & n. 3.
house(s) *sb.*, 22, 69, 90, 229, 300, 424; **355**, **368**.
house *vb.*, 229; **355**, **368**.
householder, **265**.
housewife, **19**, **265**.
hove 'hover', 123–4; **36**, **92** n. 3.
hove *p.t.* 'raised', **36** n. 3.
hovel, **92** & n. 2, **326**.
hover, **92** n. 3.
how, 90, 250; **160** n. 3, **431** n. 5.
howbeit, **309**.
howl(ed), 126, 398; **169** nn. 3, 4, **172** n. 1, **431** n. 5.
howsoever, **365**.
hoy, 69, 83, 172, 174, 412; **256**, **257**, **263**.
Huberden, **14**.
hue *sb.*, 232; **178** n. 4, **183** n. 5, **424**.
hue *vb.*, 90.
Sp. huelgo, **369**.
huge, 93; **178**.
L. huic, 215.
F. huile, 269; **282** n. 5.
F. huit, 234.
hull, 418.
hulla-balloo, **431** n. 5.
human(e), **2**.
humanity, **291**.
humble(ness), 391; **321**, **426** n. 3.
humidity, **29**; **2**.
humour, **178** n. 5, **298**, **426** n. 3.
Humphrey, **426** n. 3.
hundred, 299; **328** & nn. 4, 5, **410** & n.
hundreder 'centurion', **328**.
hundredth, **401**.
hunger(ed), 337, 351; **328**, **399** & n. 3, **412** & n. 2.
hungry, 44; **412** & n. 2.
hunt(ed), **93** n. 1, **311**.
Hur, 180; **212**.
hurl, 104, 418; **401**.
hurricane, **235** n.
hurry, 243; **55**, **218**.
hurt *sb.* & *vb.*, 110, 112, 242; **213** nn. 3, 4, **311** n. 2, **401**.

INDEX OF WORDS

hurt, hurtle(berry), **431** n. 5.
husband(s), **19**, **265**, **311**, **355**, **398**, **410**.
hussock 'cough', **431** n. 5.
hussy, -ies, **96**, **400** & n.
huswife, -wives, **357**, **421**.
hut, 242.
hymn(s), 355; **395**.
hypocrite, 20, 355.
hyssop, 355; **302**, **426** n. 3.

I, 79, 85, 89, 137, 141, 251; **233**.
-ia *suffix*, **271**, **387**.
-ial *suffix*, **270**, **387**.
-ible *suffix*, **1**.
ice, **437** n. 3.
idle(ness), **323** n. 2, **330**.
idly, 72; **321**, **330**.
ido 'done', 143.
idol, **289**.
idolaters, idolatry, **289**, **336**.
ME i-efned 'performed', **430** n. 3.
-ier *suffix*, **387**.
-ieth numerals, **309** n.
if, 77; **4**, **362**.
ifrore 'frozen', 143.
L. ignis, **441**.
ignominious, **441**.
ignorant, **441**.
-il(e) *suffix*, **275**, **325** & n. 1, **326**.
ill, 15, 264.
I'll 'I will', 316.
illusory, **356**.
illustrate, **2**.
im- *prefix*, **292**.
image, **12**.
immoderately, **271**.
impeach, 25.
imperative(ly), **67**.
impersonal, **326**.
implacable, **23**.
impleach, **116** n. 2.
imply, **254** n. 3.
importunate, importunity, 314, 348.
impossible, **303**.
in, 76, 108, 129, 244, 274.
in- *prefix*, **292**, **325** & n. 1, **326**, **380**.
inch(es), 26, 434; **80**, **410**.
incision, **356** n. 3, **389**.
inclination, **380**.

incline, **292**, **380**.
include, **380**.
income, **380**.
incommunicability, **271**.
incomprehensible, -bility, **288**, **320**.
incongruity, incongruous, **380**.
inconvenient, 29; **2**.
incorruptible, **372**; **2**.
increase *sb.*, **265**, **267**; *vb.*, **292**, **380**.
incredible, **380**.
inculcate, 29; **2**.
incur, **213** n. 4, **380**.
-ind *inflexion (pres. p.)*, **377**, **398** n. 3.
indeed, **132** n.
India, **271**.
indifferently, **307**.
-ine *suffix*, **275**.
inexorable, **372**; **2**.
infer, **68** n. 3.
infinite(ly), **275**.
infirmity, 29; **2**.
influence, **209**.
-ing *inflexion*, 253; **377** & nn. 1–3, **398** n. 3, **399**, **441** n. 2.
ingenious, 403, 414; **23**, **282**.
ingenuity, 403.
ingenuous, 403, 414; **23**, **270**, **282**.
ingratitude, **380**.
inhabit, **387**, **391**; **426**.
inherit, **387**; **426**.
inhesion, **356** n. 3, **389**.
inhumane, **426**.
injury, **275**.
inkhorn, **426**.
inn, 244.
innocent, **277**.
L. inquam, **380**.
inquire, **380**.
inquisition, inquisitive, **380**.
inseparable, **302**.
insert, **435**.
inside, **3**.
inspires, **218**.
instruments, **282** n. 1.
inter *vb.*, **412**; **2**.
inter- *prefix*, **292**.
interchange, **292**.
interfere, **292**.
interference, **269**.

intermeddle, **292**.
into, 274.
intrigue, 347, 352, 368; **116**, **133**.
inure, 179, 414; **185**.
inveigh, **292**.
inveigle, 365; **131**.
inventor(s), **299**, **325**, **363**.
involve, **432**.
inward, 77.
-ion *suffix*, **270**, **276**, **277**, **281**, **292**, **387**.
-ious *suffix*, **270**.
L. ipsum, 79.
Ipswich, **421**.
ire, **218**.
Ireland, **218**.
irk(someness), 347, **441**; **213** & nn. 1, 3.
iron, 167, 267; **321**, **325** n. 3, **328** & n. 1, **328** n. 2, **330** & n. 2.
irrational, **213**.
L. irrisionem, **356**.
is, 76, 77, 109, 137, 143, 274, 424, 444; **4**, **362** & n. 2.
island, 103.
isle, 104, 114; **12**.
-ism *suffix*, **323**.
isn't it, **401**.
issue, 369; **185** n. 2.
is't 'is it', 416; **362** n. 2, **422**.
it, 274, 372, 394, 397, 398, 406; **4**, **77**, **422** n. 1.
Italy, 20.
Italian, **19**.
-ite *suffix*, **275**.
L. iter, 241.
it is, **309**.
its, 164.
it's, **362** n. 2.
itself, 109.
L. itur, 241.
-ive *suffix*, **275**.
ivory, **12**, **279**.
iwis, 59; **289**, **294**.
-ize *suffix*, **356**.

j (letter-name), **115** n. 9, **261** n. 2.
jakes, **103**.
James, 6.
January, **59** n. 2.
L. Janus, 215.
Jaques, **103**, **442**.

INDEX OF WORDS

jarred, 431.
jasper, **59** n. 2.
jaunt, 304; **239**.
jealous(y), 354; **8**, **281**, **356**, **363**.
jeer, 426; **126** n. 3.
Jehovah, 216; **271**, **288**.
F. je ne sais quoi, **195**.
L. jento, 215.
jeopard(y), 69; **8**, **74**.
Jeremiah, **271**.
jerk, 26, 434, 435; **65** n. 4.
jerkin, 398; **377** & n. 3.
jerking, 398; **377** & n. 3.
Jerome, **277**, **302**.
Jerusalem, **288**, **356**.
Jervis, **66**.
jest, 29, 425; **8**.
jester, 400; **282**.
Jesuit, **23**, **275**.
Jesus, 62, 215.
jet, **30**.
Jew(s), 418; **185**, **244**, **312**, **362**, **391**.
jewel, 418; **185** & n. 1, **391**.
Jezreel, **274**.
L. jocus, 215.
John, 129.
join(ed), 83, 111, 341, 389, 391, 392, 428, 441; **235** n., **255** & n. 3, **259** nn. 2, 3, **262**, **263**.
F. joindre, 10.
joiner, 341.
joint, 13, 341, 428; **255**.
jointer, **282**.
jointure, **255**, **282**.
joist, 28, 111, 115–16, 174, 414; **144**, **259** & nn. 1, 2, **263**.
jolly, **431**.
journal, **19**.
journey, 421; **19**, **272**, **275** nn. 1, 2.
joust, 83.
joy(s), 110, 111, 152, 174, 215, 251, 390, 428; **254** & nn. 2, 4, **256** n. 1, **261** n. 2.
Joyce, 174; **254**.
judge, **83** n., **96**.
judgement, **306** & n. 1.
juggle, 20.
juice, 111, 115–16, 174, 414; **189**, **259** & n. 1, **260** n. 3, **312**, **362**.
julep, 418; **185**, **390**.

July, 29; **2** & n. 2.
just, 44, 111; **83** n., **96**.
justice, 129; **356**.
justify, **265**.
L. justus, 215.
juvenile, **269**.

k (letter-name), **40**, **115** n. 9.
D. kaai, 383.
keel, 416; **31**.
keen, 416; **31**.
keep(eth), **116** n. 2, **124** n. 1, **132** n., **430** n. 4.
Keighley, 182.
ken, 292, 293, 297; **77**, **226**.
kennel, 399.
kept, **398**.
Ker(r), 68 n. 3.
kercher, 37; **400** n.
kerchief(s), **66**, **400** & n.
kernel, **66**.
ketch, 371.
key, 353, 373, 438; **108** n. 3, **115** nn. 5, 9, **129**, **225** n. 1, **228** n. 3.
kid 'renowned', **368** n. 4.
kidney, **275** n. 2.
kill, 15, 416; **379** n., **396**.
kiln, **396**.
kin, 416; **77**, **435**.
kind(er), 87; **12**, 353 n., **377**, **398**.
kindle(d), 386; **323**, **410**.
kindness, **410**.
kindred, **328**, **435**.
kine, 244, 326; **135**, **398**.
kingdom, 45, 274; **336**, **377**, **412**.
kingly, **412**.
kirk, **213** n. 4, **376**.
Kish, **373**.
kiss(es), 39, 41, 444; **311**, **373**.
kitchen, 183, 414–15; **333**, **334**, **377** n. 3, **380** n. 2.
kite, 112; **141**.
knack, **417** & n. 1.
knar, 68 n. 2.
knave, **417**.
knead, **123**, **417**.
knee(s), 18, 335, 366; **386**, **417**.
kneel, **417**.
knell, **417**.
knew, 89, 239, 335; **417**.
knife('s), 164; **34**, **357**, **417**.

knight, 353; **139**, **417**.
knit, 37, 335; **75**, **417**.
knives, 164, 182; **34**, **357**.
knob, **417** n. 1.
knocks, 389.
knop, **417** n. 1.
knot(s), 397, 398; **417**, **418**.
know(n), 85, 92, 103, 126, 294, 335, 338, 353, 357, 361, 377, 388, 398, 434; **4**, **160** n. 2, **172** n. 1, **173** n. 1, **175**, **241**, **248**, **249**, **250**, **417**, **418**.
knowest, 183.
knowledge, **14**, **34**, **363**.
knuckle, **417** n. 1.
Gr. κύσαι, 39.

labour(ing), 387; **6**, **281**, **306**, **320**, **326**.
labyrinths, **303**.
lace(d), 177, 418; **6**, **8**, **373**.
lack, 167.
lad, 167; **53** n. 1.
lady, **275** & n. 1, **350**, **400** n.
laid, 400, 402; **137** n. 2, **228**.
lair, **218**.
lamb, 7, **71**, **394**.
lament vb., **285**.
lamp(s), 45; **104**.
lamprey, **275** n. 2.
lance, 27, 397, 425; **62**, **239**, **373**, **410**.
landscape, **410**.
Langley, 338, 343 n. 2.
language, 17, 115, 124–5, 351; **63**, **336**, **380**, **412**, **421** n. 6.
languish, 115, 326; **380** & n. 1, **412**, **421**.
lard, 426, 431; **6**, **44** & nn. 2, 3, **59**.
large(ly), **6**.
largesse, **77**, **334**.
lark, **329** n. 2, **330**, **400**.
lascivious, **285**.
lash(es), **311**, **373**.
lask 'diarrhoea', **439**.
lass, 418; **6**, **373**.
last(ly), 110, 177; **50**, **52**, **406**.
latch vb., **70**.
late(ly), **115** n. 3.
Latham, **368** n. 2.

INDEX OF WORDS

lath(s), 431, 442; **6, 358**.
lathe 'barn', **368** & n. 2.
lathe (machine), **368**.
lather, 178; **53** & nn. 1, 5, **55**.
Latin, **336**.
latten, **336**.
lattice, 408.
laugh(ed, -ing), 353, 357, 366, 369, 383, 392, 418, 431; **24, 28** & nn. 1, 3, **50, 61, 87** n. 1, **104**, 238 n. 4, **315, 371, 424**.
laughter, 329, 366, 390; **28** & n. 3, **238** n. 4, **371**.
launch, 304, 397, 442; **44** n. 2, **62** & n. 1, **239** & n. 1, **373, 410**.
launder, **400** n.
laundress, 304.
laurel, 293; **29** n. 2, **236, 321**.
Laurence, **29** n. 2, **264, 302**.
law(s), 77, 305, 372; **51, 104**.
lawful, **237** n. 2.
lawn (linen), 111, 148; **104** & n. 2, **238** & n. 2.
lawyer, 372; **104**.
lax sb. 'diarrhoea', **439**.
lay(est) vb., **228** n. 5, **261** n. 2, **316**.
lay-figure, **110** n., **115**.
layman 'laicus', **110** n., **228** n. 3.
layman 'lay-figure', **110** n.
-le suffix, **323** n. 1, **324, 325** nn. 2, 3, **335** & n., **362**.
lea adj. & sb., **129**.
leach, 25.
lead sb. 'plumbum', 25, 402, 425; **30**.
lead(eth) vb. 'ducere', 25, 77, 111, 167, 168, 274, 400; **228**.
leaf(y), 369, 418; **8**.
leal, 25.
leam(s) (of lightning, &c.), 25, 91; **120** & n.
lean adj., 25; **228** n. 5.
lean vb., 25.
leap(t), **116** n. 2, **120** n.
leaper, 397; **8**.
learn(ing), 110, 355, 390, 435; **8, 64** n. 3, **65** & n. 5, **126** & n. 4.

learned adj., **311, 315**.
lease, 25, 55; **8, 356, 373** & n. 1.
leash, **8, 373** n. 1.
least, 108; **8, 398, 437**.
leather(n), **8, 319** n. 1.
leave sb., 16, 113, 148, 149; **109, 114, 115** n. 3, **120, 124** & n. 1, **132** n., **430**.
leave vb., 56.
leaven, **8**.
leaving, **8**.
lechery, **8**.
L. lectio, 379; **276, 388**.
lector, **282**.
lecture, **282**.
led p.p., **402**; **311** n. 2.
leech, 25, 56; **118**.
leer, **126** n. 3, **136** n. 2.
leese(st) 'lose(st)', **132** n., **334**.
left adj., 91; **9**.
left p.p., 326; **9, 213** n. 1.
legate, 29; **2**.
legible, **23**.
Leicester, **306**.
leisure, 125, 365, 414; **8, 131, 268, 282, 293** & n. 3, **299, 300**.
leman, 80.
lemon, 80.
length, 388, 392; **358, 368** n. 1, **375, 377, 412, 435**.
lengthen, 366; **376, 412**.
lentil, **326**.
leopard, **398, 442**.
leper, 397; **8, 398**.
Lesbos, **364**.
less, **60** n. 1, **398, 437**.
lessee, **8**.
lesser, 414; **282**.
lesson, **326**.
lessor, **8**.
lest, 112; **8, 437** n. 2.
let vb. 'lease', 61.
lethargy, 417; **442**.
letter(s), 221; **362**.
lettered, **306**.
Lettice, **282**.
lettuce, 408; **282**.
lever, **8**.
leveret, **8**.
lewd, 341; **243, 244**.
liar, **40**.
liberal, **212**.
libertine, **269**.

liberty, 343; **212**.
library, 129; **271**.
lice, 244; **135**.
lie sb. 'mendacium', **40**.
lie(st, -th), vb. 'jacere', 20, 109, 183; **40, 261** n. 2, **314, 316**.
lied, **315**.
lief(er), 93; **9**.
lieger, **9**.
lieu, 217.
F. lieu, 9.
lieutenant, 323, 358; **9, 11, 442**.
liever, **132** n.
life('s), lives sb., 109, 114; **32, 357**.
light, 159, 315, 321, 378, 383; **141, 424**.
lightens, -eth, **313**.
lignaloes, 348; **441**.
like adj., 54; **12, 138** & n. 2.
like(d, -th) vb., 107-8, 114; **10** n. 1, **138** & n. 2.
liken, **323**.
lily, 15; **275** n. 1, **350**.
Liman, **80**.
limpet, 80.
Lincoln, **302, 380, 425**.
linden, **325**.
linen, **319**.
linger, 337, 351, 352; **399**.
L. lingua, 125.
lion, 114; **12**.
liquor, 183; **299**.
liquorice, **373**.
lisp, **415**.
list vb. 'listen', 61; **75**.
listen, 350; **406**.
lite 'little', 110.
little, 20, 351-2; **10, 11, 320**.
liturgy, 417.
live(d) vb., 20, 44; **10, 275, 315**.
livelong, 93.
Liverpool, 351; **400**.
lo, 372; **40**.
load, 22; **33** n. 3.
loaf, loaves, 22, 443; **33, 34**.
loath, **33, 53** n. 3.
loch, 394.
loft, **87** n. 1.
logarithm, **324, 364**.
Ir. logh, 231.
logic, 167.

INDEX OF WORDS

F. loi, 10.
loin, 428, 441; **255** & n. 3, **261** n. 2, **262** & n. 2.
loiter, **257**, **260** n. 1.
loke 'pinfold', 106.
loll, 430.
London, 129, 130; **319**, **321**, **325** n. 3, **401**.
long(er) *adj.*, 132, 326; **13**, **71**, **399**.
longeth, -ing, -s, 337, 408; **92**, **399**, **412**.
long-lived, **357**.
look, 189, 248, 249, 250, 289, 443; **36**, **37**, **38**.
loom, 125–6.
loose *adj.*, 22, 89, 115, 188, 189, 240, 399, 433; **155**, **186**, **355**.
loose *vb.*, 115, 240, 439; **155**, **355**.
lord('s), 429, 442, 443; **13**, **46**, **329** n. 2, **363**, **400**.
lordings, **363**.
lore, **148** n., **218**.
lorry, **55** n. 2, **87** n. 2.
lose(s), losing, 115, 399, 439; **13**, **155**, **183** n. 5, **185** n. 6, **187**, **311**.
loss, 110, 287, 293, 305; **51**.
lost, 45, 250, 287, 293, 305, 361–2, 431; **51**.
lot, **13**.
loud, 373, 398, 412; **173**.
lough 'loch?', **34**.
iouk *vb.*, **39** n. 2.
lour *vb.*, 398; **172**.
louse *sb.* & *vb.*, 229, 357; **355**.
lousy, **355**.
lout *vb.*, **39** n. 2.
love(-d, -s, -st, -th), 123–4, 248, 250, 314, 325, 342, 360, 425, 443; **18**, **36** n. 3, **92** n. 2, **151** n. 2, **309** n., **311**, **313**, **315**, **316**, **375** n.
loving, 249, 253; **377**.
low(er) *adj.*, 372, 392, 434 (?); **124** n. 2, **172**, **218**.
low(ed) *vb.* 'mugire', 398, 412; **124** n. 2, **172**, **173**, **250** n. 1.
lowly, **92**.
loy(al), **254**.
lubber, **299**.

luce, 189; **186**.
L. lucet, 79.
Lucian, **388**.
luck, 248, 249.
lucre, 236; **320**, **324**.
Luke, 189.
lukewarm, 113; **244**.
L. lumen, -ine, 43, 79.
lunch, **93** n. 4.
lungs, 408; **92**.
lurch, 435.
lurdan, **326**.
lure, **209**, **218**.
lurk, 429, 441.
lust, 249.
lustre, 352.
lute, 376; **184**, **185**, **188**.
L. lux, 79.
luxation, **359**.
luxurious, **359**.
-ly *suffix*, **275**.
lying, **293**.
Lyons, 114; **12**.
Lysander, **289**.

ma'am 'madam', **238** n. 1.
mace, 399; **6**.
Machin, **377** n. 3.
machine, **442**.
made, 325; **115** n. 1, **229** n. 1.
magazine, **133**.
magistrate, **271**.
magnify, **441**.
L. magnus, **441**.
G. Mahl, 150; **101**, **235** n.
Mahumetry, 29; **2**.
maid(s), 148, 400; **115** n. 3, **228**.
maiden(s), **301**, **311**.
mail 'bag, packet of letters', 111, 414.
mail 'lorica', 125, 414.
main, 278, 307.
maintain, **287**.
majesty, **6**, **275**.
make(st, -th), 168, 183, 236; **115** nn. 3, 7.
maker, **213** n. 1.
Mal 'Mary', 60, 88.
malapert, 435.
male, 414.
malice, 19, 92; **285**.
maliciousness, **285**.
malign, **324**, **441** n. 2.
Mall, **60** n. 3.
mallet, **60**.

mallow, **60**.
malmsey, 349, 354; **425** n. 5.
malt, 221, 222, 244, 436–7; **60**, **425** & n. 5.
man, 12, 77, 276, 279, 319, 357; **59** n. 2, **239**.
mane, 307.
manger, 307, 360, 365; **104** & n. 1.
mangy, 307; **104** & n. 1, **239**.
manhood, **36**, **278**, **426**.
mankind, **377**.
G. mann, **59**, **86**.
manner, 414; **212**, **282**.
mansion, **388**.
man's wit, **311**.
manure, 414; **282** & n. 4.
manuscript, 184; **282** & n. 3.
many, 29; **6**, **8**, **59** n. 2, **70**, **275**.
maple, 28, 29; **6**.
mar, **64** n. 1.
Marchant, **66** n. 1.
mare, 250, 252–3; **42**, **218**.
mark, **353** n.
market, **66** n. 1.
marl, **6**.
Marlborough, **44**, **427** & n.
marred, 431 (?); **43** n. 3, **315**, **334**.
marriage(able), **271**, **308**, **336**.
married, **315**, **334**.
marrow, **55** n. 2, **265**, **295** n. 2.
marry, **295** n. 2.
marsh, 307; **331**–2, **42**.
marshal, **388**.
Marshalsea, **338**.
mart, **427** n.
martial, **388**.
marvel, **66** & n. 4, **272**.
Mary, **60**.
masculine, 367; **275**.
mason, **326**.
mass 'massa', **50**.
mass 'missa', **59** n. 2, **70**.
mast, 177–8, 250; **6**.
master, 111, 129, 130; **6**, **50** n. 1, **97**, **320**.
mastiff(s), **400** n.
mate, 415; **115**.
material, **23**.
matters, **363**.

INDEX OF WORDS

matron, **6**.
matter, 419; **282**.
mature, 419; **282** & n. 4.
maugre, 390.
maunder, 304; **239**.
maundy, **237** n. 2.
Maurice, **29** n. 2.
maw, **9**.
May, 129, 130.
may, 79; **40**, **228** n. 5.
mayor, **198** n.
me, 89, 155, 156, 187, 211, 356; **4**, **125** n., **228** n. 5.
mead(s), 19, 400, 426; **118**, **228**.
meadow, 22; **8**.
meal 'flour', 16, 25.
meal 'repast', 16; **118**.
mealman, **116** n. 2.
mean *sb*. 'medium', 110; **31**.
mean *vb*., 25, 84; **115** n. 4, **123**, **226** n. 4, **430** & n. 4.
meant, 91; **8**.
measles, 352.
measurable, **282**.
measure, 113, 179, 210, 350, 351, 352, 367, 390; **8**, **282**, **326**, **349**, **356**, **389**.
meat, 25, 43, 113, 146, 148, 149, 405, 415, 416; **115** & n. 4, **123**.
medal, **273** n. 2.
meddle, **273** n. 2.
medicinal, 360.
medicine, 92, 347, 351, 352, 360; **303**, **306**, **311**, **325**, **326**.
meekly, **132** n.
meet, 286, 325, 405, 415, 416; **109**, **124** n. 1, **132** n.
melancholy, **275**, **380**, **401**, **438** n.
melons, 77, **308**.
Melpomene, **274**.
memoir, **195**.
memorable, 184; **1**.
memory, **275**, **277**.
men('s), 90, 110, 356; **59** n. 2, **363**.
G. menschen, 286.
merchandise, **275**, **356**.
merchant, 343; **64** n. 1, **66** nn. 1, 2.

Mercury, **189**, **275**, **282**.
mercy, **66** n. 4, **275**.
merd (?), 431.
mere *adj*., 252, 426; **118**, **126** & n. 4, **127**, **204**.
merits, **212** n. 3.
mermaid, **8**, **204** & n. 3.
merrily, 355; **275**.
merry, 90, 243; **10**, **55**, **67** n. 3, **75**, **80**, **189**, **212** n. 5, **213** n. 6, **269**.
Merton, **66** n. 4.
mess, 25; **8**.
message, **59** n. 2, **282**, **308**.
messenger, **59** n. 2, **438**.
messuage, **282**, **308**.
met, 325; **213** n. 1.
metal, 184; **264**, **273** n. 1, **320**, **326**.
metaphysics, **265**.
mete, 28, 405, 415, 416; **109**, **110**, **115**, **123**.
meteor, **299**, **308**.
meter, **308**.
methinks, 139; **313**.
methought(s), 139; **170** n. 2, **177** n. 2, **251**.
metre(s), **8**, **123**, **362**.
mettle, 184.
L. meus, 31.
meuse *sb*., **356**.
meve 'move', **132** n.
mew (hawking term?), **9**.
mew (of a cat), 49, 57, 84; **244** & n. 5, **430**.
mice, 244, 359; **108** n. 3, **135**.
Michael, 14; **308**, **326**, **442**.
Michaelmas, 14; **302**, **326**, **442**.
miche(r), **138** & n. 1.
mickle, **320**.
miel (?), 320.
mien, **412**.
might, 35, 326, 392; **137** n. 4, **139**, **141**.
mighty, **275** n. 1, **350**.
L. mihi, 14, 59, 318; **442**.
mile, 104, 114; **32**, **437** n. 1.
milfoil, 28; **256**.
mill, 37; **75**, **396**.
miller, **437** n. 1.
millions, **77**, **308** & n. 2.
milt *sb*., **80**.
mince, **410**.
mind, 412; **12**, **398**.

mine (*pron*.), 37, 77, 144, 330, 412; **398**, **440**.
mingle, **412** & n. 2.
minnow, 22, 26; **80**.
mints, **410**.
minute *adj*., **2**.
minute *sb*., **2**, **282**.
miracle, **67** & nn. 1, 3, **80**, **213**, **336**.
mire, 27, 103; **218**.
mirror, 80, **212** n. 3, **213** & n. 3, **218**.
mirth, 442; **75**, **212** n. 3, **213**, **368** n. 1.
misbelief, **351**.
mischievous, **2**.
miser, 324.
misery, 152; **275**.
mislike, 107; **138**.
misplacing, **6**.
misprision, 351; **389**.
missed, **315**.
missive, **275**.
mistletoe, **364**.
mistress, **311**, **363**.
mixture, **282**.
mo 'more', **40**.
moan, 43.
moat, **14**.
modes, **312**, **363**.
F. moi, 10, 59, 315; **137** (Norman *my*).
moil, 428; **255** & n. 1, **262**.
moist, 341, 390; **255** & nn. 1, 2.
moisture, **255**, **282**.
moiety, **254**.
F. moitié, 10.
mole, 108, 419; **150**, **398**, **437**.
molest, **290**.
moll, 430.
molten, 22, 344; **169**.
momentary, 349; **1**.
monarchy, **268**.
Monday, **343** & n. 2.
money, **272**, **275** & n. 2.
monger, **92**.
mongrel, **92**, **334**, **412** & n. 2.
monk, **380**.
monkey, 373; **338** n. 2, **380**.
L. montes, 7.
month(s), **18** & n. 2, **196**, **358**.
monument, **282** n. 2.

INDEX OF WORDS

mooch, **167** & nn. 1, 2.
mood, 239, 314; **37**.
moon's, **312** n. 2.
moor(s), 404; **149** n. 2, **208** & n. 2, **209**.
Moor, 409; **208**, **209**.
moral, **273**.
more *adj.* & *adv.*, 181, 267, 401, 404, 409; **48** n. 1, **148** n. 1, **149** & n. 2, **208** & n. 2, **210** n. 2, **218**.
more *sb.* 'root', **148** n.
morion, **308**.
morn, 250; **16** & n. 2, **46** & n. 2, **209**.
morning, 400; **16** & n. 2, **46** n. 2, **165** n. 1.
morrow, 71; **47**, **55** n. 2, 280, 295.
mortal, **273**, **325**.
L. mortem, **47** & n. 1.
mortgage, **408**.
Moses, **22**.
most(ly), 337, 364, 431; **13**, **97**, **150**, **406**, **431** n. 4.
-most *suffix*, **277**.
mote, 414; **14**.
moth(s), 411, 414, 425, 431; **14** & n. 2, **50** n., **170**, **358**, **382**.
mother 'mater', 124; **4**, **18** & n. 2, **97** n. 3, **196**, **297**, **320**, **384**.
mother 'puella', 124; **97** n. 3, **384**.
mought 'might' *p.t.*, 126; **4**, **177**.
mould, 103, 364, 370, 377, 419; **174** nn. 1, 2, **249**, **251**, **398**.
moulder *vb.*, **174** n. 1.
moulding, 90; **174** n. 2, **251**.
moult, **174** n. 1.
moulter, 364, 370; **174** nn. 1, 2, **251**.
mountain, **272**.
mourn(ing), 239, 252, 400–1, 425; **16** n. 2, **19**, **46** n. 2, **97** n. 1, **165** & n. 1, **208** & n. 3, **209**.
mouse *sb.* & *vb.*, 54, 167, 229, 424; **355**.
mouth(s), 236, 411; **312**, **358**, **368** n. 1.
movable, 89.
move, 123–4, 240, 325, 360, 424, 425, 433, 443; **36** & n. 3, **37**, **154**.
mow *sb.* 'heap', 415.
mow(est, -ing, -n) *vb.*, 183, 415, 434; **172** n. 1, **377**.
mower, 401.
F. moyen, 10.
Mr., 129, 130; **297**.
Mrs., **363**.
much, 18, 45, 61, 249; **82**, **442**.
much good do it you, 18, 378; **82**.
D. muis, 276, 277.
mumble, **403**.
mule, 320.
multiply, -iable, **275**.
multitude, **282**.
mumble, 54; **435**.
murder, 92 & n. 2, 383 & nn. 1, 2.
murrain, **308**.
murmur, **282** n. 4.
muse, 320; **159**, **187**, **356** & n. 1.
musical, **273**.
muslin, **364**.
must, 110, 249, 344, 345.
mustard, **299**.
muster, **97**.
mutton(y), **319**, **320**, **326**.
mutual, **282**.
L. mutuatur, 215.
my, 77, 137, 144, 167; **4**.
myrrh, **213**.
myself, **4**, **357**.
Mysia, 349; **276** n., **356**, **433**.
mystery, **306**.

G. nacht, 376.
naked, **311**, **315**, **334**.
name(s), 77, 274, 307; **331**, **363**.
namely, **275**.
nard, 431; **6**.
narr, **418** n. 1.
narrow(ly), **295**, **350**, **440**.
Nash, 399, 409; **418**.
Naso, **22** & n., **23** n., **277**, **356**.
Nat, **418**.
Nathan, **319**.
nation, 153, 221, 240, 252, 386; **276**, **388**.
nativity, 137.
natural, **282** & n. 1.
nature, 308; **6**, **115** n. 3, **282**, **349**.
naught, 252, 315, 372, 376, 389, 410; **28**, **240**, **242**, **424** n. 1.
naughty, **28** n. 3, **242**, **350**.
nauseate, **276**, **388**.
nauseous, **276**, **356**.
nave, **417**.
nay, **115** n. 6.
-ne *suffix*, **323** n. 1, **324**, **325** nn. 2, 3, **335** & n.
neal 'anneal', **417**.
near(er), 24, 25, 91, 401, 426; **6**, **8** (*comp.*), **119**.
neat *adj.*, 25.
neat *sb.*, 411; **30**.
necessary, 184; **1**.
neck, **59** n. 3.
Ned, **417**.
need(s), 44, 109, 286; **363**, **417**.
needful, **132** n.
ne'er 'never', 406; **8**, **119**, **122** & n. 5.
neeze 'sneeze', **386**, **417**.
neigh, 24, 368, 432; **129**, **424** n. 2.
neighbour(s), 350, 351, 352, 387, 389; **115** n. 5, **129** & nn. 1, 2, **139**, **228** n. 3, **281**, **320**, **326**, **363**.
neither, 161–2, 401; **4**, **8**, **77**, **129**, **225** n. 1.
Nell, **417**.
neme 'take', **115** n. 4.
nephew, **267**, **357**.
Neptune, **282**.
nerve, **435**; **213**.
-ness *suffix*, **1**.
nest, 108, 399; **8**.
net, 411.
nether, 401; **8**.
neuter, 239, 341, 393; **244** & n. 5.
never, **8**, **109**.
new(s), 89, 239; **244**, **417**.
Newman, **244**.
newt, **244**, **440**.
Newton, **244**.
next, **398**.
nib, **77**.
nibble, 21.
nice, 114, 416, 419; **12**, **254**, **437** n. 3.
Nicholas, **302**, **306**.
niece, 416, 419.

niffles, 326.
nigh, 4, 15, 378, 383; **139, 140**, 142 & n., **424** n. 2.
night(s, 's), 88, 90, 98, 252, 284, 386; **139, 140, 141,** 312 n. 2, 362, **417, 424**.
nightingale, **438**.
L. nihil, **442**.
nimble(ness), 25, 29; **11, 321, 435**.
nimblest, **403** n.
nine, **433**.
ninth(s), **358, 368** & n. 3.
nipple, 29; **11**.
nit, **417**.
no, 4, **40** n. 3, 206, **417**.
Noah('s), **210** & n. 2, **309**.
nobility, **290**.
noble, **13**.
nobleman('s), **13, 363**.
noise, 303, 341, 419, 428, 440; **254** & n. 1, **261** n. 3, 262, 263, **356**.
noisome, **256**.
nonce, 440, 443; **33** & n. 2, **440**.
none, 417, 432, 440; **33** & n. 2, **36, 37, 150, 417, 429** n. 2.
nook, 342, 443; **37, 38**.
noon, **417**.
noose, **439**; **356**.
nor, 250, 432; **47, 48** n. 1.
Nore, **210** & n. 2.
north(wards), 361–2; **47, 311**.
northern, **329** & n. 1.
Norton, **321**.
Norwich, **421**.
nose, 419; **210, 261** n. 3, **309**.
nostril(s), 12, 361–2; **13, 326**.
not, 77, 79, 274, 279, 314, 325; 4, **417, 418**.
notable, **23, 271, 324**.
note(s), 325, 372; **240** n. 2, **242**.
nother 'neither', 4, **15**.
nothing, 355, 390; **374**.
notion, **440**.
Notley, **97** n. 4.
notoriously, **290, 363**.
nought(y), 366, 371, 372, 410; **89, 160** n. 2, **170** & n. 3, **240, 242, 424**.
noun, **126**.

nourish(ment), **19, 165,** **212** n. 3.
now, 22, 90, 427; **172** n. 1, **173** n. 1.
noyous, **256**.
numbered, **306, 315**.
L. nunc, 7, 43; **93**.
nuncle 'uncle', 330; **440**.
nurse, **19, 165** n. 1, **208** n. 3.
nurture, 351, 353; **282**.
nyes 'eyes', **440**.

O *interj.*, **40**.
oak, **422, 431** n. 4.
oar(s), 103, 409, 428; **154** n. 6, **155** n., **208** n. 2, **218, 250, 431** n. 4.
oat(s), 410; **150** n. 2, **431** & n. 4.
oath(s), 431; **358, 421, 431** n. 4.
oaths great, **311**.
obdurate, **2**.
obedient (-ce), **23, 290**.
obey, 388, 438; **137** n. 2, **265, 290**.
object, **398**.
oblige, **12** n. 1, **133, 138**.
oblique, **133** & n., **160** n. 1.
oblivion, **276, 433**.
obscene, **110**.
observance, 29; **2**.
observation, **365** & n. 1.
observe, **365**.
obstacle, **336** n. 2.
obtain, **442**.
occasion, **356, 389**.
occupation, **282**.
occupy, -ied, 72; **267**.
ocean, 19; **276, 388, 440**.
Ockendon, **87** n. 3.
odour, 418; **401** n. 1.
Oedipus, **22**.
of, 21, 36, 77, 85, 87, 129, 238, 316, 326, 424; **4, 362**.
off, 108, 305, 326, 361–2, 424; **4, 13, 51, 56** n., **362**.
offer(ed), **51** n., **237** n. 2, **315**.
of me, **401**.
oft, 402, 406; **34**.
often, 314, 350, 351, 352; 326, 405.
oftentimes, **321**.

oh, 386, 427; **89, 424**.
oil(s), 104, 174, 233, 428, 437; **256, 259** n. 3, **262** & n. 4.
F. oindre, **10**.
oint(ment), 342; **255**.
old(er), 5, 90, 125, 211, 345, 371; **169** & n. 3, **249** n., **409** n., **431** n. 4.
ominous, **23**.
omniscient, **388**.
on, 92, 108, 236, 394, 405; **13**.
once, 23, 432, 440, 443; **33** & n. 2, **363, 429** & n. 2, **431** & n. 4, **437** n. 3.
one(s), 236, 237, 299, 401, 405, 440, 443; **33** & n. 2, **36, 37** & n., **150** & nn. 1, 2, **429** & nn. 2, 3, **431** & n. 4.
onerate, **23**.
onion, 353; **276, 441**.
only, 84, 355, 380; **13, 33** & n. 2, **36** & n. 1, **37, 150, 237** n. 2, **275, 429** & n. 2, **431** & n. 4.
-ony *suffix*, **277**.
ooze *sb*. 'sap', **420, 421**.
ooze *sb*. 'slime', **153, 420, 421**.
ooze *vb*. 'flow', **153, 158** & n. 1, **421**.
open(ed, -est, -ing), 76, 350, 353; **13, 306, 315, 320, 321, 330, 381**.
openly, **13, 321**.
opportunity, **282** n. 1.
opposite, **356**.
oppugn, 380; **324, 441**.
or, 432; **47**.
-or *suffix*, **281, 292, 297, 299, 325**.
orange(s), 17; **63, 271** n., **301**.
oration, **314**.
orator, 374; **2**.
orb, 442; **47, 87**.
orchard, **390** & n. 1, **431** n. 4.
ordaineth, **431** n. 5.
order, 68, 390, 418;. **13, 282, 320, 401** & n. 1, **431** n. 5.
ordinary, **271, 307**.
ordure, 390; **282, 326**.

INDEX OF WORDS

ore, 409; **155** n., **208** n. 2, **218**.
Orestes, **290**.
orf 'cattle', **331** n. 1.
Orpheus, **274**.
ort(ings), **431** n. 5.
orthography, 390; **442**.
-ory *suffix*, **1, 269, 277**.
osier, 351, 352; **276, 389**.
-osity *suffix*, **356**.
ostler, 369; **401**.
ostrich, 17; **363**.
other(s), 314; **4, 15, 18, 363**.
otherwise, 114.
ought *vb.*, 36, 126, 337, 344, 371, 402, 406, 410, 433; **34, 89, 170, 240** & n. 4, **423** n. 4.
our(s), 77, 137, 274; **165** & nn. 4, 6, **281, 363**.
-our *suffix*, **281, 292, 297, 299, 325**.
-ous *suffix*, 354; **281, 292, 363**.
out, 36, 108, 250, 433; **4.**
outrage, **3** & n.
F. outrage, 381.
outrun, **3** & n.
ouzel, 381; **158**.
oven, 92.
over, **13, 212, 306, 326**.
overthrown, 90.
Overton, **326**.
overture, **23**.
over-undern, **431** n. 5.
owe(d, -st), 23, 126–7, 183, 357, 377, 427; **172** nn. 1, 3, **248, 431**.
ower, **218**.
owl, 233, 434; **172** n. 1.
own(ers), 5, 23, 71, 90, 92, 103, 107, 111, 112, 377, 401, 405, 414, 434; **104** & n. 2, **172** & n. 1, **237** n. 2, **241, 248, 250, 429** n. 2.
ox(en), 154; **320, 440**.
Oxford, 129, 130; **299**.
oyster, 71, 83, 406; **256** & nn. 2, 4, **259** n. 3.

p (letter-name), **40**.
paced, 333.
pack, **59** n. 2.
paganism, **442**.
page 'leaf in book', 430; **6.**
page 'servant', 55; **6.**
pageant(y), **276, 302, 312** & n. 1, **436**.
pail, 175, 397.
pain, 355, 417; **104** n. 2.
F. paine, 286.
paintings, **412**.
pair(s), 24, 103, 176, 405, 407; **103, 126** n. 3, **205, 231, 363**.
palace, 60, **271** n., **336** n. 1.
Paladine, **275**.
palate, 60, **271, 301, 302, 308**.
pale, 397.
palfrey, **275** n. 2.
pall, 419; **242**.
pallet, 60, **271, 301, 302, 308**.
palliate, **308**.
Pall Mall, 60 n. 3.
palm, **104, 425** n. 5.
pan, **53** n. 1.
pandar, **325**.
pane, 417; **104** n. 2.
pang(s), 417; **412**.
pannier, 406; **308**.
pansy, **356** n. 4, **364**.
pant, 424, 436, 442.
pantheism, **270**.
F. paon, 376; **236**.
papal, **23**.
papenjay, **438** n.
paper, **297, 301**.
papistry, **275, 350**.
paradise, **137** n. 2, **275, 356**.
paramour, **281**.
paraphrase, **115** n. 3.
parasite, **275, 356**.
parboiled, 66.
parchment, **436**.
pardon, **44** n. 4, **195, 325, 326**.
pare, 405, 407; **103, 204, 205, 231**.
parent(s), **23, 321**.
parentage, 430; **23**.
parenthesis, **356**.
paringale 'equal', **438**.
F. Paris, 314; **59**.
parity, **23**.
park, **44**.
parliament, **301, 334**.
parlour, **427** n., **437** n. 1.
parlous, **67** n. 3.
parse, 401; **6, 65**.

parson, 397, 414; **44** n. 4, 66, **195**.
part, 361; **6, 42, 43** n. 1, **44, 50, 65, 86** n. 2.
particular, 72; **66, 282, 299**.
partridge, **427** n.
F. pas, 314.
pass(ed), 110, 286, 304; **50, 315**.
past, 112, 286, 333, 400, 418; **6, 50** & n. 1, **53, 238**.
paste, 400, 418; **6.**
pastor, 367; **282**.
pasture(s), **282**.
patches, **311**.
patent(s), 398; **23, 398, 410**.
patentee, **23**.
path, 178, 300, 304; **6, 43** n. 3, **50** & n. 1, **53**.
paths, 178–9, 442; **6, 50** n. 3, **53** & n. 4, **55, 195** & n. 2, **358**.
patience, **410**.
patients, **410**.
patron(ize), **328** & n. 1, **328** n. 2.
patten(s), 398, 401; **328, 332, 398, 410**.
pattern(s), **401**; **328** & nn. 1, 2, **332** & n. 1.
Paul('s), 401, 419; **88, 145, 242, 250**.
paunch, 27, 304, 425, 442; **62**.
paw, **239** n. 1.
pawn, 417; **104** n. 2.
pay, 49; **40** n. 2, **226** n. 3.
payer, **198** n., **204**.
pea, 286, 442.
peace, 25, 407; **123, 356**.
peach, 25.
peak, **116** n. 2.
peal, 25.
pear, 16, 405, 425; **109, 122** nn. 1, 3, **204** & n. 3.
pearl(s), 435; **8** & n. 1, 9, **122** & n. 4, **126, 212** & n. 3.
peasant, 367; **8.**
pease, 25, 426; **119.**
peat, 25.
pebble, **11, 77**.
peculiar, **288**.
L. pecunia, **1, 288, 433**.

INDEX OF WORDS

pedant, **2**.
pedlar, **328** n. 1.
pee, 433.
peek *vb.*, 25.
peel, 107.
peer(s), 16, 401, 404, 405; **126** & nn. 3, 4, **204** & n. 3.
peerless, **218**.
peevishly, **132** n.
peise 'weight', **137** n. 2.
pelican, **229** n. 1.
pence, **293**, **363**.
Penelope, **226** n. 4, **228** n. 5.
penny, 76.
pennyfather, **59** n. 3.
pennyworth, **332**, **421**.
pens, **363**.
people, 69, 216; **323**, **324**, **335** n.
L. perago, **67**.
perboiled, 66.
perceive, **126** n. 4, **131**.
perch, 435; **8** & n. 1, 9, **122**, **126**.
F. père, **114**.
peremptory, 161; **2**.
perfect(ed), 36, 71; **66** n. 3, **272**, **275**, **442**.
perfection, **66** n. 3, **442**.
perfectly, **272**, **407**, **442**.
perfectness, **407**, **442**.
perform, 104; **13** & n. 1, **16** n. 4, **17** & n., **19**, **154** & n. 3, **165**, **208** & n. 3, **209**.
peril, **67** nn. 2, 3.
F. perle, 286.
pernicious, 66.
perpetual, **273**.
perquisite, **275**.
persecute, 44.
persevere, 26; **77**.
Persia, **356**.
person(s), 137, 157, 325–6, 397, 414; **66** & n. 4, **302** & n. 1, **321**, **326**, **364**.
personal(ity), 137; **302**, **306**, **321**.
persuade, 328.
persuasion, **356**, **389**.
pert, 21; **65**.
pertain, **212**.
Perth, 435.
perturbate, 29; **2**.
pestle, **406**.

Peter, 347; **127**.
petition, **288**.
petty, **8**.
pewter, **244**.
G. pfeiff, 76.
Phalaris, **22**.
phantasy, 284.
Pharaoh, 347; **308**.
pharisee, 160; **127**.
pheasant, 8, **436**.
phenomenon, **269**.
L. philosophia, 53.
philosopher, **336**.
phlegm, 416, 425; **8**.
Phoebus, **22**.
photograph, **269**.
photostat, **269** n. 2.
phrase, **254** n. 2.
Phrygian, **273**.
physician, 210; **273**, **356**, **389**.
physiognomy, 92; **307**.
piazzas, **442**.
pick-axe, **80**.
picked, **282**.
picture, picturing, 325; **282**.
piece, 407; **123**.
pier, **136** n. 2, **204** & n. 3.
pierce *vb.* 401, 404, 435; **8** & n. 1, 9, **13**, **65**, **122** & n. 4, **126**, **201** & n., **204** & n. 3, **218**.
Pierce, 404; **65**.
F. piété, 286.
piety, **350**.
pigeon, 183; **336** & n. 2.
Piggot, **336** n. 2.
Pilate, **271**.
pilgrimage, 430.
pillar(s), 408; **299**, **302**, **332**.
pillow(s), 408; **302**, **332**.
pin, 187.
pink(le) *vb.*, pinkle-pankle, **125**.
pipe, 76.
pique, **133**.
pistol, **406** n. 2.
pith(s, -y), **358**, **368**.
L. pituita, 215.
pity, **275**.
place(th), 338–9, 400; **228**.
plague, 21, 440.
plaice, 400; **228**.
plaid, **233**.
plain, 388.

plait, **233** & n. 1.
plaster, **6**.
plant, 27, 424, 442; **62** & n. 1, **104** n. 2.
plat, **87**, **233**.
plate, 24; **233**.
Plato, **22**, **23** n.
Plautus's, **334**.
play(ed, -s), 91, 148, 400, 405; **228** & nn. 2, 5.
players, 79; **363**.
plea, 286, 353, 405; **228** n. 2.
plead, 25, 400, 426; **228**.
pleasant, **8**, **321**, **325**.
please(r), 252, 400; **123**, **228**, **282**.
pleasure(s), 90, 92, 187, 350, 351, 352, 400; **8**, **218**, **268**, **282**, 300 n., **349** n. 1, **389** & n.
pleat, 30, **233**.
pleurisy, 341; **244**.
plight, 20.
plot, **87**, **233**.
plough, 23, 35, 126–7, 189, 334, 427; **424** & n. 2.
pluck, 89.
plum, 76.
plumb, 430, 432.
poesy, 92.
poet, **23**.
poetic, **270**.
poetry, **274**.
F. poindre, 10.
point(s), 83, 92, 428; **255**, **262**, **432** n.
poise, 303, 341, 428, 437, 440; **254**.
poison, 69, 341; **255** & n. 3, **262**, **432** n.
poisonous, **306**.
poke(d) *vb.*, 105, 113; **151**.
pole(s), 90, 344, 401, 419; **150**, **242**.
pole-ax, 90.
polish, **91**.
politician, **273**.
poll, 22, 90, 103, 419, 430–1, 434; **169** n. 2, **251**.
Poll, 431.
pollute, 29; **2** & n. 2.
pomegranate, **13**.
poniard, **94**.
pool, 239, 261, 419.
poop, **164**.
poor, 391, 401, 404, 409;

INDEX OF WORDS

154 & nn. 1, 4, **165** n. 4, 207 n. 1, 208 n. 2, **209** n. 1, **218**, **400** & n.
popple, 23.
porch, **13** & n. 1, **16**, **47** n. 1.
porcupine, **275**, **282** n. 2.
pore(d), 409, 432; **154** n. 4.
pork, **13**, **154**.
porpoise, **279**.
porridge, porringer, **385**, **438**.
port, 443; **13**, 86 n. 2, **154**, **248** n. 2.
F. port, **248** n. 2.
Portingale 'Portugal', **438**.
portion, **13**, **154**.
portraiture, 24; **282**.
Portsmouth, 368 n. 1.
posh, 125.
position, **276**, **308** n. 3, **388**.
possess(ed, -es), 211; **290**, **365**.
possession, -ive, **290**, **365**.
possible, 308; **303**.
post(s), 364; **150**, **406**.
pot, 235; **432**.
pota(n)ger, **385**, **438**.
pottage, pottinger, **385**.
pouch, **167** & n. 1.
poultice, 370; **95**, **174** & n. 2, **251**.
poultry, 364, 370, 437; **174** & n. 2, **251**.
pound, **19**.
pour, 401, 404; **158** n. 2, **162**, **165** & nn. 4, 5, **208** & n. 4, **209** & n. 2.
poverty, **92** n. 4.
power, 274, 402; **165** n. 4, **218** n. 1, **309**.
practice, **356**.
Prague, 440.
praise, **137** n. 2, **356**.
prance, 27.
pray, 148, 368; **131**, **228** n. 3.
prayer 'petition' **388**; **126** n. 5, **130**, **198** n.
pre- *prefix*, **127**, **288**, **344**.
preach, 25; **116** n. 2.
precedent, **303**.
precept(s), **23**, **398**, **404**.
precious, 45; **281**.
precipitate, 29; **2**.
precise, **365**.

predecessor(s), 71; **23**, **281**.
preeminence, 159, 160; **270**.
preen 'pin', **272** n.
preen 'trim feathers', **272** n.
preface, **336** n. 1.
prefer, **68** n. 3, **212**.
preferment, 29; **1**, **2**.
prehensile, **270**.
pre-joiningly, **288**.
prelate, 29; **2**.
premise(s), **356**, **363**.
prepared, 145–6; **43** n. 3.
prepositions, **356**.
presage, **365**.
presence, **321**, **326** n. 2, **356**, **410**.
present(s) *adj. & sb.*, 90; **8**, **321** & n. 1, **356**, **410**.
present *vb.*, **356**.
presently, **1**, **264**, **356**.
preserve, **356**.
president, **303**.
press(ed), 25, 408; **8**, **123**.
pressure, **282**, **349**.
Preston, **326**, **406**.
presumption, 90.
pretty, **8**, **11**, **275** n. 1, **350**.
preve 'proof', **124** n. 1, **132** n.
prevent, **288**.
prey, 215, 368, 382, 391, 393, 444; **131**.
price, 114; **12**, **356**.
pride, **251**.
priest(s), 408, 443; **77** n. 1, **132** n., **406**.
L. prima facie, 193.
primitive, **275**.
principal, **273**.
principle, **273**.
prism, **323**, **364**.
prison(er), 154; **306**, **326**, **328**, **330**.
pristine, **275**.
privacy, **356**.
private, 72; **23**.
privily, **275**.
prize, **137** n. 2, **356**.
pro- *prefix*, **290**, **346**.
probity, **23**.
proceed(eth), 71, 216.
process *sb.*, **267**.
prodigal, **23**.
profession, **388**.
profit, 37; **334**.
progenitors, **363**.

progress, **23**.
prohibit(ion), 15; **270**, **276**, **426** n. 3.
prolixity, **267**.
prologue, **23**.
prolong, **438**.
Prometheus, **290**.
promise, 20; **356**.
promulgate, **2**.
prong, 23, **438**.
pronoun(s), **23**, **363**.
pronunciation, **388**.
prophecy, **357**.
prophesyings, **275**.
prophet, 37; **334**.
propitiation, **276** n.
propitiatory, 29; **1**, **2**.
propriety, 29; **2**.
prorogation, prorogue, **268** n.
prose, 89, 403; **176**, **309**.
proselyte, **356**.
prosperity, 29; **2**.
prostrate *adj.*, **271**.
protect, 240; **346**.
F. proteste, 286.
Protheus, **22**.
protomartyr, **23**, **284**.
protoplast, **23**.
prototype, **23**.
protract, **346**.
proud, 22, 27.
provide, **23**, **265**.
provision, **356** n. 3, **389**.
prove(d), 325, 342, 345, 360, 424, 425, 433, 440; **36** & n. 3, **37**.
prow *adj.*, **176**.
prowess, 403; **176**, **309**.
prowl, **169** n. 1.
proximity, **359**.
prudence, **325**.
prune 'preen, trim feathers', **272** n.
psalm, 304, 366, 369, 390, 416; **60** n. 1, **104** & n. 9, **425** & n. 5.
psalter(y), **60**, **425** n. 5.
public, **437**.
pudding, 27, 369; **377**.
puff, **196**.
pule, **325**.
pull(s), 239, 261, 268, 287, 289, 325, 342, 401, 414, 427; **196**.
pulley, **338** n. 2.
pulp, **196**.

INDEX OF WORDS

pulse, 401, 414; **196**.
pun, **196**.
pundit, **59** n. 6, **93** n. 3.
punish, **196** & n. 2, **373** n. 3.
punkah, **59** n. 6, **93** n. 3.
pure, 103, 377; **209, 218**.
purl, **212**.
purchase *vb*., **271**.
purfle, **325** n. 1.
purloin, 334; **255** & n. 3, **256** n. 3.
purple, 352.
purpose, 180, 183; **277, 302, 356**.
purse, **427** n.
push, 427; **156, 196**.
puss, **196**.
put, 121, 315, 427; **93, 196** & n. 2, **311** n. 2.
putt, **196**.

q (letter-name), **40** n. 1.
quadrant, **53, 55, 195**.
quadrate, 29; **2, 53, 195**.
quaff, **52, 53, 56** n.
quail, 23, 24.
quaint, 328.
quake, 23.
quality, 305; **194**.
qualm, 299, 304, 442; **104, 195, 425**.
quantity, -ies, 71; **363**.
quarrel, 252, 407; **55** n. 2, **67** & n. 3, **194, 321, 330**.
quarry, 407, 411.
quart, 301, 331, 443; **49** & n. 1, **194**.
quarter, 301; **49** n. 1, **427** n.
quartern, 104; **49, 331**.
Sp. quatro, 211; **53, 101, 195, 235** n.
quean, 25, 405, 414; **123**.
queasy, 393, 394.
queen, 394, 405, 414; **123, 132** n.
quell, 250.
quench, **77, 373, 410**.
querk, 435.
quern, **43, 49, 55, 65**.
querp, 435.
query, 411.
question, 308.
quick, 23.
L. quies, quiesco, 318.
quiescent, **270**.
quiet, **302, 309** n.
quiff, quift, 433.

quill, 250.
quince, **77, 373, 410**.
quinsy, **356** n. 4, **364**.
quire, 23; **136**.
quirk, quirp, 435; **78**.
L. quis, 216.
quit, 137; **12, 309** n.
quite, 250, 251; **12, 309** n.
quod 'said', **339** n., **421**.
quoin, **255**.
quoit, **254** & n. 1.
quote(th), **375** n., **421** & n. 1.
quoth, 431; **339** n., **421** & n. 1.

r (letter-name), 68, **115** n. 5.
race, 399.
Rachel, **442**.
radish, 399.
Rafe *see* Ralph.
rage, raging, 24, 236, 323; **6**.
rail, **268**.
rain, 355, 433.
raise, 400; **228**.
raisin, **131, 326**.
raising, 151; **100, 231**.
Ralph, 86, 343, 431; **28, 104**.
ran, **93** n. 2.
rancorous, **302**.
rancour, **297, 380**.
range(d), 27, 162, 425; **62, 63** & n. 1, **104**.
rank *sb*., 143; **59** n. 2.
ranker, **212, 297**.
ransom, 92.
rant, **442**.
rare, 250.
rarify, rarity, **23**.
raspberry, **364, 401**.
rathe, 400, 402; **6**.
rather, 177, 178, 374; **6, 50** n. 3, **53** & nn. 1, 5, **55, 56** n., **115** n. 4, **370**.
ratlings, **412**.
raught, 315.
ravel, **326**.
raven *sb*., **334, 377**.
raven(ing) *vb*., **6, 306**.
raving, **334, 377**.
ravish, **59** n. 2.
raze, 399, 400; **228**.
razor, 24; **282**.
re- *prefix*, **127, 288**.

-re *suffix*, **323** nn. 1, 2, **324, 325** nn. 2, 3, **362**.
reach, 25; **8, 116** n. 2.
reachless 'reckless', **8**.
read *infin*., 19, 30, 91, 167, 373, 401, 404, 409, 426; **30, 39** n. 2, **118**.
read *p.t*., 373; **8, 30, 311** n. 2.
reading, 85, 86, 373.
Reading, **8**.
ready, 91, 379; **8**.
real, 354; **198** n.
realm, 36; **8, 115** n. 4, **331**.
ream 'cream', **120** n.
ream (of paper), 25.
reap, 387.
rear *adj*. & *sb*., 409; **126** & n. 4, **204, 218**.
rear *vb*., 409, 425; **109, 122, 204**.
rearward, **126**.
reason(able), 314; **8, 302, 326, 356**.
rebel *sb*., **326**.
recalcitrant, **60**.
recant, 27, 436.
recapitulate, **271**.
receipt, **131**.
receive, 241, 244, 328, 391; **115** n. 4, **124** n. 1, **131, 226**.
receptacle, 161; **1, 2**.
recite(d, -th), 72; **23, 365** n. 2.
reck, 55; **77**.
reckoning, **306, 321**.
recoil *vb*., 437; **260**.
recompense *sb*. & *vb*., 161; **2**.
reconciliation, **284**.
record(s), 432; **13** n. 2, **97** n. 1.
recourse, 432; **165** n. 1.
recover, 252; **344**.
recreation, 90.
recusant, **2**.
red, 25, 29, 404, 425; **30** n. 1, **213** n. 1.
reddish, 399.
reed, 401, 404, 409.
reek *sb*. & *vb*., 426; **120, 124**.
reeves, **132** n.
refer, **212**.
L. refertum, 241.
reflect, **398**.

reform, 47.
refractory, 2.
refute, 315.
regard, 6 n. 2.
regiment, 306.
region, 23.
rehabilitate, 270.
rehearsal, 8.
rehearse, 90; 8, 122, 126, 204, 355, 364.
reign(ing), 383; 441 & nn. 1, 2.
rein, 107, 111, 444; 108 n. 3, 131.
F. reine, 10; 227.
reising 'travelling', 228 n. 4.
reject, 398.
rejoice(d), 437; 254 & n. 4.
relapse, 161; 2 & n. 2.
relieve(th), 116 n. 2, 136 n. 1.
remain, 226 n. 4.
remediless, remedy, 348; 2.
remember(ed), 59 n. 3, 306, 324.
remonstrate, 2.
remorse, 432; 13 n. 2.
remove, 123-4; 36.
renate, 29; 2.
rendezvous, 59, 157, 338.
renown, 22; 172 n. 1, 173 n. 1.
rents, 410.
repair, 226 n. 4, 228 n. 5.
repeal, 25.
repeat, 25.
repent, 252.
repine, 10 n. 1, 138.
replete, 25.
report(ed), 252; 13, 154, 344.
reprieve, 136 n. 1.
reproach, 13.
republican, 325.
repugnant, 441.
repugn(ed), 324 n. 1, 441.
repute, 315.
require, 103, 114; 12.
requisite, 275.
rescue, 267.
research, 365.
resemblance, 403.
resemble(d), 356, 403.
resent, 365.
reserve, 356.
reside, 356.

resign, 267, 356.
re-sign, 267.
resin, 325.
resist, 356.
resolve(d), 88, 356.
resort, 13, 356.
resound, 356.
resource, 356, 365.
respect, 442.
respite, 442.
rest, 110, 111; 77, 398.
restorative, 2.
restraint, 433.
resurrection, 261.
retinue, 2.
retract *sb.*, 29.
retreat, 115 n. 3, 131.
retrieve, 31, 136 n. 1.
retro- *prefix*, 269 n. 1.
retroact, 269 n. 1.
retrogression, 269 n. 1.
return, 97 n. 1.
reveal, 25.
revel, 326.
revenge, 434; 77.
revenue, 2.
reversed, 212 n. 3.
revolt, 88.
revolve, 432.
reward, 431; 6.
rey (probably 'ray, striped cloth'), 444; 131.
rheubarb, 244.
rheum, 404; 185, 188.
rheumatic, 349.
rhine 'hemp', 400; 398.
Rhine, 398.
rhyme, 110; 12.
rhythm, 324, 326, 364.
rice, 399.
rich, 12, 96 n.
riches, 60 n. 1, 363.
rick, 162, 434; 31, 77 n. 1, 116 n. 2, 439.
ridden, 325.
riddle(s), 77 n. 1, 319.
ride, 30.
ridge, 23, 61; 75.
rife, 114; 32.
right, 11, 112, 378, 392, 397; 139, 142.
righteous(ness), 350, 351, 387, 390; 274 & n. 1, 293, 308 n. 2, 390.
rind, 400; 398.
ringer, 337; 399.
riot, 302.

rise, 111, 399; 254, 262, 263, 355.
rite, 378, 397.
rivet, 26; 80.
road, 53, 104 n. 4, 431 n. 4.
roam(ing), 407, 415; 154 & n. 6, 250.
roast, 362, 364, 438 (?); 150.
rod, 399; 33 & n. 3, 53 n. 1, 86 n. 1.
rode, 399; 33, 115 n. 3.
Roding, 87 n. 3.
roe, 18, 22; 40.
F. roi, 10.
roil *sb.* 'clumsy woman', 28; 257.
roil *vb.* 'wander', 28; 255 & n. 1.
roister, 260.
roll(ed), 103, 329, 344, 356, 430, 434; 169 n. 3, 249.
L. Roma(m), 211; 154.
Roman, 23, 272.
Rome, 103, 211, 407, 415; 154 & n. 6, 164.
Romford, 97 n. 6.
rood, 18, 314; 185.
rood-tree, 368 n. 4.
roof, 114-15, 412; 36, 158.
rook, 443; 38.
room, 92, 103, 126, 404, 407; 24, 38, 154 n. 6, 158 n. 2, 164, 185, 331 n. 1.
root, 240, 443; 37, 38.
F. rose, 145 n. 3.
rot, 399.
rote, 401.
rottenness, 321 n. 1.
rouge(s), 157, 160 n. 1, 167, 311.
rough(ly), 23, 91, 126, 163, 252, 253, 334, 383, 387, 388, 391, 412, 427, 432; 28 n. 1, 34, 39, 371, 424 & n. 2.
row *adj.* & *vb.* 'rough(en)', 160 n. 2, 173 n. 1.
row *sb.* (?), 434.
row(est) *vb.* 'remigare', 71, 183, 434 (?); 40.
rowan, 198 n.
rowen, 294, 302, 304; 176, 244 n. 3, 245, 246, 249.
rower, 198 n.
roy, 28; 254.

INDEX OF WORDS

royal(ly, -ty), 175; **254** & n. 3, **273**.
rude, **185**, **188**.
rue, 9; **183** n. 5.
ruff, 412.
ruffian, 369; **308**, **336**.
ruffle, 21.
Rugwood, **97** n. 6.
ruin, 20, 302; **275**.
rule, 109, 264, 265, 266.
rumour, **244**.
run(neth), 112; **93** n. 2, **314**.
rundlet, **410**.
rung, **92**.
runnel, **319**.
rush(es) *sb.*, 26, 434; **80**, 373 n. 3.
rush(ing) *vb.*, 115, 427; **377**.
ruth, 429; **178** & n. 4.
Ruth, **178** n. 3.

-s *sb. inflexion*, 316, 357; **311**, **312**, **363**.
-s *vbl. inflexion*, **311**, **313** & nn. 1, 2, **314** & n. 1, **363**, **375** & n.
sack 'bag', **59** nn. 2, 4.
sack (wine), **59** n. 4.
sackful, 267.
sacrament, **23**.
sacre *vb.*, **328**.
sacred, 6, **328**.
sacrifice, 23; **275**, **356** & n. 1.
sacrilege, 6, **23**.
saddle, 167; **320**, **325**.
sadness, **59** n. 2.
safe(r), 343, 418, 431; **28**, **104** & n. 6, **238**, **275**, **357**.
safeguard, **28**, **357**.
safety, **28**, **125** n., **357**.
saffron, **328** & nn. 1, 2.
said, 76, 77, 390; **26** & n., **123**.
saith, 431; **26**, **313**, **314**, **362**, **368**; *see also* sayest, -eth.
sake, **115** n. 7, **311** n. 2.
salary, **23**, **59** n. 2, **60**.
Salisbury, **307**.
salmon, 351, 352, 354; **59** n. 2, **62**, **104**, **302**, **425** n. 5.
salt, 54, 76, 418, 437; **29**, **44** n. 4, **60**, **237** n. 2, **425** & n. 5.

Salter, **29**, **237** n. 2.
Salton, **29**, **237** n. 2.
salutation, **282** n. 1.
salvation, **60**.
salve, 304, 342, 343, 408, 416; **104** & n. 9, **238**, **239**.
same, 416.
sample, 36.
sanctuary, **275**, **282** n. 1.
F. saoul, 376.
saphire, **275**.
Sarah, **271**.
sarce, 6, **8** n. 2.
sardine, **133** & n.
sardonic, **269**.
sarsenet, 369; **50** n. 1, **401**.
Satan, 76.
satiate, **388**.
satiety, 167; **302**.
satisfactory, 29; **1**, **23**.
satisfy, **59** n. 2, **275**.
Saturday, 92, 367; **23**, **298**.
Saturn, 367; **23**.
satyr, **275**, **300**.
sauce, **28** n. 2, **238** n. 3.
saucer, 244; **28** n. 2, **238** n. 3.
sausage, **28** n. 2, **29**, **238** n. 3, **336**, **363**.
save *vb.*, 408, 416; **28**, **104** & n. 6.
saver, **212**, **297**, **308**.
saviour, **281**, **297**, **308**.
savour(y), **6**, **292**, **302**.
say, 147, 329, 388, 400; **226** n. 4, **228** & nn. 2, 5, **229** & n. 1.
sayest, -eth, 371; **26**, **316**, **334**; *see also* saith.
saying(s), 34, 45; **363**.
says, 26 & n., **313**.
scaffold, 344; **169**.
scalp(s), **60**, **425**.
scant, 27, 424, 442; **238** n. 1.
scaped, 430.
scarce(ly), 415, 431; **6**, **25**, **205**, **218**.
scarcity, **6**.
scarf, 332.
scathe, **6**.
scents, **410**.
Sceva, 167.
schedule, 352, 412; **8**, **442**.
scheme, 412; **110**, **442**.
schism, 252; **324**, **326**, **331**, **364**, **442**.

G. schlagen, 230.
scholar(s), 110, 137, 148; **87**, **264**, **299**, **437** n. 1.
school(s), 129, 371; **437** n. 1.
scissors, **298**.
scold, 22.
sconce, 23, 432; **431**.
scorn, **13** & n. 2, **46**, **97** n. 1, **208** n. 3.
scoundrel, **19**.
scourge, 249; **19**, **165** n. 1, **208** n. 3, **429**, **431**.
scowl, 126.
scraped, 430.
scratch, **59** n. 3.
screak, 25.
scream, 291; **115** n. 5, **217**.
screech, scritch, **138** & n. 1.
scribble, **326**.
scrine, 20.
scripture(s), **282** & n. 1.
scrivener, **306**.
scroll, 344, 430, 434; **169** n. 3.
scruple, **282**.
scrupulous, 308, 354; **269**, **282**, **303**, **306**.
scullion, 369, 376; **276**, **308**, **336**.
scum, **185** n. 6.
scurf, 332.
scutcheon, 183; **276**, **302**, **336** & n. 2.
scythe, **368**.
L. se, **40**.
sea(s), 35, 286, 393, 400; **40**, **115** nn. 3, 4, **116** n. 2, **119**, **125** & n., **228** & nn. 2, 5, **363**.
seal (mammal), 25.
seal 'signet', 25, 264, 269, 414; **115** n. 4, **123**.
seam, 25, 412; **442**.
seamstress, **8**.
sear, 425; **122** & n. 2.
searce, **8** & n. 2, **204** n. 2.
search, 435; **8** & n. 2, **65** n. 5, **204**, **212**.
season(able), **302**, **307**, **325** n. 2.
seated, -s, 167; **8**, **115** n. 3.
sea-wall, **3**.
second, **302**, **321**.
secret, **23**.
secrete *vb.*, 25.
sects, 409, 414; **407**.
secure, **288**.

INDEX OF WORDS

sedness 'sowing', **59** n. 2.
see(ing, -n), 60, 89, 244, 276, 277; **110**, **116** n. 2, **125**, **132** n.
seed(s), 167, 216, 390.
seed-lip, **115** n. 4.
seel, 414.
seek, **116** n. 2, **132** n., **138**.
seem(eth, -s), 31, **110**, **116** n. 2, **120** n., **132** n.
seer, 409.
seest, **316**.
seeth 'sees', **314**.
seethe, 399; **314**.
seine 'net', **130**.
Seine, **115** n. 3.
seize, 241, 252, 444; **131**.
selah, **271**.
seld(om), 430; **9**, **293**, **302** n. 2, **326**.
self, selves, **357**.
sell, 264, 269.
semivocals, **363**.
Sempringham, **412** & n. 1.
senate, **23**.
sennight, **400**.
sense, **410**.
sentence, **321**.
sentry, **306**.
separate(d) *vb.*, **269**, **271**, **302**.
sepulture, **282**.
sere 'individual', **126** n. 4.
sere 'withered', 409; **119** n. 2.
serge, 435; **65**.
sergeant, 169; **66**, **276**.
series, **312** n. 2.
sermon, **64** n. 1, **212** n. 2, **436** n. 2.
serpent(ine), 66, **269**, **321**.
servant, 27; **66** & n. 4, **321**.
serve(th), 26, 435; **65** & nn. 4, 5, **213**, **314**, **375**.
service, **66** & n. 4, **275**.
F. serviteur, 226.
servitude, **185** n. 6.
L. servus, 41.
sessions, **388** n. 2.
set, 110.
setter, **325**.
seven, **8**, **400** n.
seventeen, **321**.
seventh, **8**, **321**, **326**, **358**, **368** & n. 3.
several, 210; **273**, **306**.
Severus, **288**.

sew, 377, 415; **172**, **244**, **245**.
sewer 'conduit', **188**, **243**, **244**.
sewer 'one who sews', **165** n. 4.
sex, 414; **407**.
shade, **115** n. 3.
shaft, 431.
Shaftesbury, **405**.
Shakespeare, **274**.
shall, 153, 316; **4**, **60**.
shallow, **60**.
shalm, 304, 442; **104**.
shalt, 221, 222, 244, 436, 444; **4**, **425**.
shalt thou, 238.
shambles, **435**.
shame, **115** n. 3.
shamefaced, shamefast, 76, 177–8; **6**.
shan't, 394; **56** n., **238**, **425**.
shape(d), 28, 430; **6**.
shard, 426, 430, 435; **8**, **65**, **204**.
share(s) *sb.*, 405; **122**, **204** n. 4.
share *vb.* 'shear', 146; **204** n. 3.
sharp, 331–2, 361; **42**.
shawm, 103; **104**.
she, 187; **4**.
shear(s) *sb.*, 91; **30**, **122** & n. 2, **136** n. 2, **204** n. 3, **430**.
shear *vb.*, 146 (*forms of p.t.*), 405, 426; **109**, **122** & nn. 1, 2, **204** & n. 3.
sheath(s), 300, 315, 366, 424; **358**, **368** & n. 1.
sheathe, 424; **368**.
shed, 25; **30** n. 1.
sheep, 37, 402; **31**, **132** n.
sheer, 405, 409, 440; **122** n. 1.
shelf, **330**.
shepherd, 45; **426**.
sheriff, 19, 386, 390; **80**.
shew(ed) 'show(ed)', 84, 90, 113, 302, 398, 412, 414; **244** & nn. 3, 5, **245**.
shield, 251; **430**.
shilling(s), 369; **377**, **412**.
ship, 402.
shire, 27, 347, 405, 409, 440; **122** & n. 1.

shirt, 75, 82, **213** & nn. 1, 3, **214** n. 4.
shiver, 26; **80**.
shoe, 302, 391, 398, 412, 414, 434; **159**, **185** n. 2, **244** & n. 4.
shone, 430, 431, 440; **33**, **53**.
shoo, **185**.
shook, 443; **37**, **38**, **159**, **185** n. 2.
shoon 'shoes', **37** n., **150** n. 1.
shoot(er), 160, 179, 239, 413, 417, 443; **36**, **37**, **38**, **159** & n. 3, **185** & nn. 1, 2.
ME shop *p.t.* 'created', **151** n. 4.
shore(s), 76; **165** n. 6.
shorn, **13**, **16**, **46**, **149**.
short(en), 361–2, 442; **47**, **48** nn. 1, 2, **210**, **324**.
should, 221, 239, 248, 249, 250, 251, 316, 342, 344, 361, 362, 371, 436, 443; **4**, **169** n. 3, **174**, **196** n. 3.
shoulder, 92, 113, 364, 370; **4**, **95**, **97**, **174** & n. 2, **251**, **425** n. 4.
shout, 413.
shove, 123–4, 425, 443; **39** & nn. 2, 4, **92** n. 2.
shovel, 342; **92** & n. 2.
show(ed, -n), 84, 434; **40**, **172** n. 1, **245** & n. 1, **331** n. 1, **432**.
shower(s), **165** n. 5, **218**.
shream 'scream', 291; **217**.
shred, 25; **30** & n. 1.
shrew, 9, 23, 434; **243**, **244**, **245**.
shrewd, **14** n. 2, **244**, **245**.
shriek, **138** & n. 2.
shrieve, 386.
shrike, **138**.
shrill(est), 370; **392**, **439**.
shrimp, 370; **392**.
shrink, 370; **392**.
shritch, **138**.
shudder, **97** n. 7.
shut, 45, 61, 413, 417; **82**.
Shute, 179; **185** & n. 1.
shuttle, 61; **82**.
-sible *ending*, **356**.
sick(ness), **31**, **77** n. 1, **116** n. 2, **136** n. 2.

INDEX OF WORDS

sickened, **321**.
sickle, 187.
side, **137** n. 2, **365**.
sieve, 20; **10**.
sigh(ed, -s), 30, 52, 181–2, 184, 334, 370; **141, 142, 143, 372, 424**.
sight, 181–2, 344, 392; **141, 143**.
sign, 380; **324, 441** & nn. 1, 3.
signal(ly), **441**.
signet(s), **441** & n. 1.
significance, **441**.
signify, **275, 441**.
silence, 167.
silly, **11**.
simony, **23**.
sin(s), 15, 244, 276, 277, 356; **412**.
since, 80.
sincere, **110**.
sinews, 90.
sing(est, -eth, -ing, -s), 13, 167, 170, 380, 415; **316, 399, 412**.
singe, 13; **77**.
singer, 27, 380; **399**.
single(ness), **412** & n. 2.
singular(ly), **269, 282** & n. 1, **399**.
-sion *ending*, **356** & n. 3.
sir, 37, 180, 260, 343, 441; **67** n. 1, **212** n. 4, **213** & n. 1, **214**.
sire, **136** n. 2.
sirloin, **212** n. 2, **213** n. 3.
sirrah, 403; **67** & n. 1, **213, 303**.
siss, 433.
sister(s), 37, 397; **82** n. 2, **363, 420**.
sitch, **138** & n. 1.
-site *ending*, **356**.
sithe 'sigh', 182.
sitteth, **314**.
-sive *ending*, **356**.
six(th), **139, 368** n. 3.
skein, 409, 436; **131**.
skeleton, 352.
skene (dagger), 409.
skill, 221.
skirt, 442; **75** & n.
skulk, **104** n. 8, **425**.
sky, skies, 323; **379**.
slant, 425.

slaughter, 331; **28** & n. 3, **61, 423** n. 2.
slay, 18, 19, 230; **40, 125** n., **129**.
sleave, **119, 124** & n. 2.
sleep, **124** n. 1.
sleeve(s), **124, 132** n.
sleight, 22, 424; **139** & n., **382**.
slew, 250.
slight, 22, 424; **139** & n.
slitch, **138** & n. 1.
sloe(s), **34, 171**.
sloth(ful), 23, 431; **14, 34, 368** n. 1.
slough 'cast skin', **34, 39** n. 1.
slough 'quagmire', 23, 35; **34, 39, 171, 172, 424**.
slough [unglossed], 126; **171**.
sloven, **272, 326, 334**.
slow, 393, 434; **34, 171, 172, 241**.
slyly, **40**.
small(er), 111, 392; **104, 437** n. 1.
smart, 110, 331; **42**.
smear(ed), 425; **120, 136** n. 2.
smith(s), 54; **358**.
smoke(s), 22; **151** & n. 1, **313**.
smooth(er, -ing), **368**.
smooth-tongued, **412**.
snake, 24.
snare, 24.
snarl, 331–2.
sneeze, **386**.
snew *p.t.* 'snowed', 239.
snirl *vb.*, **214**.
snored, **208** n. 2.
snow, 10, 434.
so, 4, **40** n. 3, **153** n.
soap, 54.
soar, 409, 428; **421**.
sober(ly), 252; **13, 275, 320, 324**.
sobriety, **290**.
society, **302**.
sod, 33, **53** n. 2.
-soever *suffix*, **277**.
soft, 393–4, 406; **34, 51** n., **237** n. 2, **423** & nn. 1, 4.
soil *sb.* 'earth', 28, 428; **256**.
soil *sb.* 'filth', 152, 428; **252** n. 1, **255, 256**.

soil *vb.* 'defile, stain', 28, 428; **255** & n. 1, **260**.
soil [unglossed], 353.
sojourn, **19**.
L. sol, **169**.
sold, 5, 103, 244, 414; **250**.
solder, **13, 308** n. 2, **391**.
soldier, 308, 344, 350, 351; **169, 276, 299, 308** n. 2, **391** & n.
soled, **250**.
solemn, **395, 441** n. 3.
solute, 29; **2**.
some, 187, 248; **18**.
Somerset, 97 n. 6.
somewhat, 71, 89; **194**.
son, 23, 89.
song(s), 23; **92** n. 1, **412**.
son-in-law, **401**.
soon, 22, 413; **37** n., **150** n. 1, **163**.
soot, 336, 342, 425, 443; **37, 38, 431**.
sooth, 429, 443; **36, 37, 38, 152** n., **178** & nn. 2, 4, **368**.
soothe, 443; **368**.
soothsayer, 351.
sop, **53** n. 2.
Soper Lane, 97 n. 6.
sophisms, **364**.
sore, 267, 409, 414; **165** n. 4, **244, 421**.
sorrow(s), sorrowful, **55** n. 2, 97 n. 1, **280**.
sorry, 47, **55** n. 2, **269**.
sort, 443; **13, 16, 48** n. 1, **149**.
-sory *ending*, **356**.
sought, 126, 163, 244, 387, 406, 418; **34, 89, 170, 239** n. 1, **240** & n. 2, **423** n. 4.
soul(s), 5, 22, 71, 90, 108, 211, 233, 337, 345, 357, 377, 434; **169** n. 3, **172** & n. 1, **249** & n., **250, 437** n. 1.
soun(d) 'swoon' *see* swoon.
sound *sb.* 'sonus' *and vb.* 'sonare', 71, 76, 388, 413; **163, 172, 363, 436**.
sour, 413, 414, 415; **165** nn. 4–6, **172, 185** n. 6, **244, 421**.
source, 239, 432; **19, 165** & n. 1, **208** & n. 3, **209**.

souse, 356, 401 n. 1.
south, 90, 163, 429; 178.
southern, southron, 163; 329 & n. 2.
Southwark, 329 & n. 2, 330, 335, 421.
sovereign(ize), 91 & n., 97, 272, 301, 306, 307.
sow *sb.* 'sus', 416; 172.
sow(ed, -n), 44, 103, 108, 126, 357, 377, 413, 415–16, 434; 17, 172 & n. 1, 249, 250, 436.
sower, 413, 414, 415; 165 n. 4, 172, 421.
Spa, 235 n., 237 n. 4.
Spain, 272 n., 441.
spake, 111, 112; 104, 115 n. 3.
spangle, 143; 412.
Spaniard, 276, 441.
spaniel, 321, 334, 441.
Spanish, 441.
spar *vb.*, 136 n. 2.
spare(d, -s), 417, 431 (?); 204 n. 4.
sparred (?), 431.
sparrow, 265, 295.
spasm, 324.
speak(eth, -ing, -s), 25; 115 nn. 3, 4, 7, 116 n. 2, 313.
spear *sb.*, 417, 426; 122 & n. 2, 136, 204 n. 3, 218, 442.
spear *vb.* 'shut', 136 n. 2.
special, 273, 325 n. 3.
spectacle, 90.
speech, 25; 118.
speed(y), 132 n.
spellers, 363.
spent, 433.
sperm, 435.
L. sperma, 66.
spew, 26, 356.
sphere, 417; 126 & n. 4, 136 & n. 2, 204, 442.
spiest, 183.
spindle, 93; 80, 435.
spire, 323, 417.
spirit(s), 185; 40, 80 & nn. 1, 3, 212 n. 3, 213 n. 6.
spiritual, 20; 282.
spirituality, 1.
spit, 26; 80.
spite, 112.

spleen, 18, 436.
spleet *sb.*, 110 n.
spoil *sb.* & *vb.*, 353, 428; 255 & nn. 1, 3.
spoke(n), 111, 112; 104, 297, 326.
spoon, 107.
sport, 443; 13, 154.
spread, 91, 425; 30.
springing, 399, 412.
springtime, 265.
sprite, 315; 141.
spur, 213 n. 4.
spurn, 435.
spy, 114; 40.
squabble, 443.
squadron, 53, 195, 238 n. 3.
square, 100 n.
squeak, 436.
squeeze, 426.
squire, 27.
squirrel, 213 & nn. 3, 6, 321.
-st *vbl. inflexion: see* -est.
staff(s), 178, 333, 431; 6, 50, 53, 357.
stain, 318–19.
stake, 416; 115.
stalk, 357; 425.
stallion, 60.
stamp, 37; 62, 71.
stand, 71, 238 n. 1, 398.
staple, 28, 29; 6.
star(red), 26, 431; 43 n. 3, 68.
stare(d), 19, 405; 43 n. 3.
starve, 26.
state(s), 115 n. 3.
station, 276.
stature, 267, 282.
staunch, 20, 27, 425, 442; 62, 104.
stave(s), 164, 178, 333, 440; 6, 53, 357.
stay(ed, -eth), 78; 261 n. 2, 314, 334.
stead, 25, 91, 162, 401, 425; 10, 30, 115 n. 1, 120.
steady, 8.
steak, 414, 416, 426: 109, 115 & nn. 5, 6.
steal, 123.
stealth, 26; 77, 80.
steam, 120.
steed, 401.
steel, 132 n., 353 n.

steep, 116 n. 2, 124 n. 1.
steeple, 26; 132 n.
steer *sb.* 'juvencus', 426; 136 n. 2.
steer *vb.*, 405, 426; 126 nn. 3, 4, 136 nn. 2, 3, 204 n. 3, 218.
stench, 26, 434; 77.
Stephen, 357.
sterile, 275.
stern *sb.*, 435.
steven 'voice', 90.
steward, 209.
stick *vb.*, 55.
stingeth, -s, 399, 412.
stir, 162, 164, 260, 435, 441; 18 n. 1, 82, 93 n. 1, 136 n. 3, 212 n. 3, 213 n. 4.
stirrup, 213 & nn. 3, 6.
stole(n), 419; 150, 330 & nn. 1, 2.
stomach, 91 & n., 97.
stomachers, 336 n. 2.
stone, 58, 236, 237, 267, 318–19, 440; 33 n. 2, 36 & n. 1.
stone wall, 3.
stood, 239–40, 306, 342, 415, 430; 36, 37, 38, 150 n. 1.
stool, 419; 431 n. 4.
stoop *vb.*, 126; 164.
stopple, 23.
store(s), 428; 165 n. 6.
stork, 47.
storm, 104; 47, 48 n. 2, 331.
story, 47.
stow, 434.
straight(er), 22, 72, 424, 425; 115 n. 3, 139 n.
straits, 112.
straitened, 306 n. 2.
strake *p.t.*, 36.
strand, 430; 71.
strange, 27, 162, 307–8, 323, 331, 393, 425; 6 n. 3, 62, 63 & n. 2, 104 & nn. 1, 3, 6.
stranger, 162, 365; 6 n. 3, 62, 63, 104 & n. 1, 212, 239.
strap, strop, 87.
strea 'straw', 125 n.
streak *sb.*, 442–3.
streak *vb.* 'stroke', 442–3.

INDEX OF WORDS

stream(s), 25; **116** n. 2, **120** & n.
strength(s), 386, 388, 392; 377, **412** & n. 1.
strengthen(eth), 306, **412**, 435.
stretch, 25, 29; **8**.
strew(ed), 90; **243**, **244**, **245** n. 2.
strick(en), 36, **151**.
strife, 19, 30; **368** n. 4.
strive, 19, 20, 30, 114; **12**, **368** n. 4.
stroke *p.t.*, 36, **151**.
stroke *sb.*, 113; **151**.
strong(er), 7, **13** & n. 3, **71**, 399.
strongly, **412**.
strook(en), 36, 37, **151** & n. 4.
strove, 433; **151** n. 2.
strow 'strew', 434; **172** n. 4.
struck(en), 182; **36**, **116** n. 2, **151**.
Stuart, 209.
stubborn, **299**.
stud, 415.
stufled 'stifled', 105.
stumps, 54.
Sturmer, 97 n. 6.
L. suadeo, 216.
subdivision, **389**.
submission, 349; **433**.
subtile, **275**.
subtle, 154; **326**.
successor, 2.
such, 45, 61; **82**, **420**, **442**.
suck *vb.*, **39** n. 2.
sudden, **272**, **326** & n. 2, **436** n. 2.
sue(r), 35; **185** & n. 2, **218**.
suffer(ed, -ing), 306 & n. 2, 315.
suffice, **356**.
sufficient, **356**.
sugar, 305, 345, 350, 359, 369, 377, 392; **185** & n. 1, **186**, **320**, **324**, **388**.
suing, **183** n. 5, **185** n. 6.
suit(or), 179, 369, 372; **159** n. 3, **185** & nn. 1, 2, 6, **388** & n. 3.
suitably, 89.
sullen, **319**.
sum, 187, 249.
summertime, **265**.
summoner, 306.

sun, **97** n. 1.
Sunday, **275** n. 2, **343**.
sunken, **319**.
L. sunt, 41, 79.
supererogatory, -oriously, **277**, **285**.
superfluity, **275** n. 2, **282** n. 1.
superfluous, **363**.
superior, **23**, **291**, **349** & n. 2.
supernatural, **23**.
supine, **275**.
supped, 70; **315**.
supply, 28; **254** & n. 1.
supreme, **110**.
Sur, **213**.
surcoat, **212** n. 2, **213** n. 3.
L. surdo, 241.
sure(ly), 16, 27, 44, 103, 299, 305, 369; **178** n. 5, **185**, **186**, **188**, **209**, **218**, **388** & n. 3.
surfeit, **131**, **272**, **334**.
surge, 91; **19**, **165**.
surgeon, 284, 386; **292**.
surname, **213** n. 3.
surpcloth, surplice, **212** n. 2, **213** n. 3.
Surrey, 403; **213**, **303**.
survey(ance), 368; **131**.
sute, 179.
swaddle, **326**.
swain, 23; **228** n. 5.
swallow *sb.* 'hirundo', **194** n. 3.
swallow *sb.* 'throat', **194** n. 3.
swallow(ed) *vb.*, **53** n. 2, **194** n. 3, **265**.
swam, **194**.
swank, **194**.
sward, **49** n. 1.
sware, **204**.
swarm, 331, 443; **49**, **55**, **194**.
swart, 331; **49**.
swath(s), **52** & n., **53**, **195**, **358**, **362**.
swathe(s), **6**, **358**.
swear *vb.*, 146 (*forms of p.t.*), 328, 390, 440; **30**, **105**, **136** n. 2, **204** & nn. 1, 3, **430**.
sweat, 58, 405; **30**, **123**.
sweet(ened), 405; **306**.
swerve, 331; **49**, **65** & n. 5.

swine, 9.
swinge, 325.
swinging, swings, **399**, **412**.
swingle, **326**.
swipple, 26, 29; **11**.
Swithun, **325** n. 2.
ME swok 'betrayed', **151** n. 4.
swollen, 103; **328** n. 2, **330**, **421**.
swoon, 413; **163**, **420**, **421**, **436**.
sword, 328, 342, 429; **8**, **16** & nn. 2, 3, **18**, **74**, **165** n. 3, **208** & n. 1, **209**, **420**, **421**.
swore, sworn, 409, 414, 443; **13**, **16**, **149**, **153**, **165** n. 4, **330**, **420**, **421** & n. 2.
swound *see* swoon.
sycophant, **277**.
syllabe 'syllable', 326.
synagogue, 45.
syncope, **274**.
syrup, 80, 213 & nn. 3, 6.
system, 371.

t (letter-name), 40, **115** n. 5.
tabernacle, **270**.
table, 323; **321**.
tach, tack, 416.
taffrail, 268.
tail, 319, 413.
tailor, **437** n. 1.
take(n, -st, -th), 77, 183, 236, 394; **115** n. 4, **314**, **400**.
tale, 24, 150, 276, 277, 319, 404, 405, 413; **104** & n. 4.
talk, 111, 354; **60**, **104**, **425**.
tall, 150, 276, 319, 404, 413; **104**.
tallage, **60**.
tallow, 150, 276; **60**.
tally, **60**.
talon(s), 108; **60**, **436**.
L. tanquam, 380.
tar, 43.
tare, 60, 405.
tart, **6**, **42**.
tassel, 301.
taste, 400, 430; **6**.
taught, 315, 431, 433; **28**, **170**, **237** n. 2, **240** n. 2.
taunt, 27, 304, 353, 389,

INDEX OF WORDS

425, 442; **62** n. 1, **104** n. 2, **239** n. 1.
taut, **86** n. 2.
tax, 416.
ME te 'the', **437**.
L. te, **40**.
tea, 196; **110** n.
teach(er), 25; **115** n. 5, **116** n. 2.
teal, 276, 277, 405, 413.
team, 25, 410; **120, 124**.
tear(s) *sb*. 'lacrima', 368, 405, 415, 426; **116, 122** & nn. 2, 6, **136** n. 2, **203** & n., **204** & n. 4.
tear *sb*. 'rent' and *vb*. 'rend', 60, 113, 368, 405, 415, 425; **105, 115** n. 7, **116** & n. 1, **122** & n. 1, 203 n., **204** & nn. 1, 3.
teat, 25, 425; **30**.
tedious, **391**.
teem, 410; **124**.
G. teil, 76.
tell(est), 70, 276, 277; **316**.
temper, **403**.
temperament, **1**.
tempestuous, **282** n. 2.
temporary, **265**.
tempt, temptation, 261, 274, 278; **403**.
tender, **324**.
F. tendrement, **320**.
tenor, **282**.
tens, 398; **410**.
tenth, **358**, 368 & n. 3.
tents, 398; **410**.
tenure, **282**.
L. ter, 241.
term, 104, 435; **8**.
L. ternus, 241.
terrace, 92; **271, 302**.
terrible, 308; **303**.
L. terris, 241; **212**.
testimony, **277**.
tew 'taw', 26; **244**.
texture, **282**.
Thales, **22** & n., **23** n., **356**.
Thame, **442**.
Thames, 76; **72** n., **103, 115** n. 3, **442**.
than, **70**.
Thanet, **70, 442**.
thank(ing), **53** n. 2, **59** n. 2.
that, 274; **361, 374**.
thaw, **242**.
the, 6 (*th'east*), 55, 77, 129, 252, 274, 279, 316, 345, 387, 391, 399; 4, **110, 120**, 270, 306, 308, 361.
theatre, **271**.
thee *pron.*, 6; **4, 361**.
thee *vb*. 'thrive', **40**.
theft, 26; **77, 382**.
their(s), 79, 359, 382, 407, 409; **4, 204, 226** & n. 4, **228, 231, 361**.
them, 274.
theme, **115** n. 3.
then, **70, 361**.
ME þen (*dat. sg.*) 'the', **440**.
OE þencþ, **377**.
Theophrastus, **288**.
there, 89, 242, 359, 407, 409, 426; **4, 100** n., **105, 118, 122** & n. 5, **132** n., **204** & n. 4, **228** n. 5, **288, 361**.
thereby, **4**.
therein, **288**.
thereof, **4**.
thereto, **183** n. 5.
these, 394; **4, 115, 116** n. 2, **120** & n., **361, 362**.
Theseus, **387**.
they, 151, 316, 382, 391; **4, 226, 229, 361**.
they're, **4**.
thief, 55; **31**.
thigh(s), **142, 362**.
thimble, **435**.
thin, 61, 188, 216; **75, 399**.
thine, 37, 188, 216, 274.
thing(s), 143; **363, 399, 412**.
think(s), **77** n. 2, **412** n. 4.
third, 162–3, 260; **84** & n. 1, **213** nn. 1, 3, **439**.
thirst(y), 45, 162, 164, 441; **82, 427** n., **439** n.
thirteen(th), **345**.
thirty, 355; **84, 275** & n. 1, **350, 439**.
this, 6, 76, 77, 87, 274; **4, 361, 362**.
thistle, **326, 334, 398, 406**.
thither, 161.
tho 'then', 60; **40**.
tho 'those, the', **421** n. 3.
thole, 22; **169** n. 1.
Thomas, 76, 129, 130; **302, 336** n. 2, **363**.
Thomasin, **365**.
thong, **421**.
thorn, 413; **16, 374**.
thorough(ly), **4**.
those, 394; **4, 33, 150, 361, 362, 374**.
th'other, 270.
thou, 167, 337, 398; **4, 170, 175, 361**.
though, 60, 92, 163, 251, 252, 345, 386, 387, 389, 398, 427; **4, 34, 89, 170, 237** n. 5, **240** & n. 3, **248** n. 1, **249, 250, 361, 424**.
thought(s), 163, 244, 252, 443; **89, 170, 177** n. 2, **240** & n. 2, **424**.
ME thoughte 'seemed', **177** & n. 2.
thousand(s, -th), **19, 321, 363, 367** n., **398, 410**.
thrall, **60** n. 2.
Thrasimene, **110**.
Thraso, **22** & n., **23** n., **277, 356**.
thread, 91, 425; **77, 118**.
threap, **116** n. 2.
threat(en), 25, 425; **8, 30, 233, 324**.
threepence, **9** & n. 2, **11, 265**.
threw, 353.
thrice, 114; **32, 363**.
thrid 'third' (?), **77**.
throat, **397**.
throne, 430; **150, 277, 442**.
thropple, 125.
through, 23, 36, 163, 263, 267, 334, 353, 366, 373, 392, 427, 433; **4, 34, 97, 166, 175, 177**.
throughout, 182.
throw(n), 397, 414, 434; **250**.
thumb, 54; **394**.
thunder(ed, -ing), **306, 328, 410, 435**.
thundery, **319**.
thus, 249.
thwart, 331, 336, 443; **49, 194**.
thy, 251, 274, 391; **4, 361**.
thyself, **357**.
L. tibi, 318.
tie(d), **40, 315**.
tierce, **9**.
tiger, **324**.
tile, 276.

INDEX OF WORDS

till, 276.
tilt, 409; **382**.
tilth, 409, 434; **77, 80, 382**.
time, **137** n. 4, **310** n.
tinder, **82** n. 2.
tinkle, **412** n. 4.
Titan, **23** & n., **325** n. 3.
Tithon, **23**.
title, 20; **320**.
to, 124, 129, 148, 249, 316, 335, 378, 394, 405, 434; **4, 40, 152** n., **153** n., **155, 208, 218** n. 1, **290, 293, 308**.
to- *prefix*, **290, 347**.
toast, 361–2, 411; **13**.
toe(s), 323, 335, 336, 361, 405, 418; **4, 40, 145** n. 4, **152, 172** n. 4.
Toft's, 405.
together, **4, 8, 59** n. 3, **77, 290, 293, 347, 384**.
toil, 28, 152, 233, 390, 428; **252** n. 1, **255** & nn. 1, 3, **256, 262** nn. 3, 4, **263** n. 1.
told, 90, 276, 277; **251, 431** n. 4.
toll, 55, 103, 104, 335, 430, 434; **169** n. 2.
Toll (surname), 335.
Tolleshunt, **87** n. 3.
Tollington, **87** n. 3.
Tomalin, 415; **377** n. 3.
tomb, 379, 407; **164**.
tome, 407; **154**.
Tomson, 314.
tone, 22, 276.
tong(s), 402, 409, 414; **53** n. 2, **92, 412**.
tongue(s), 23, 370, 390, 402, 409, 414, 438; **92, 97** & nn. 1, 2, **412**.
too, 113, 248, 378, 405, 434, 440; **4, 152, 244**.
took, 443; **36, 37, 38**.
tool, 28, 276, 278; **158** n. 4.
toom, 125.
tooth, 429, 443; **37, 38, 178** & n. 2.
top, **53** n. 2, **97** n. 1.
torch, 87.
torn, 413; **13, 16, 46, 149, 330, 374**.
tortoise, **255**.
F. tortu, 9.
torture, 351, 353; **282**.

tossed, 411; **51** n.
to 't 'to it', 335, 336.
touch(ing), 91, 163, 373; **19, 96** & n., **167** n. 3.
tough, 23, 163, 334, 388, 392, 418; **39, 171** n., **172** n. 4, **424**.
tour, **165** & n. 5.
tow *vb.*, 405, 418, 434 (?); **4, 172** n. 4.
toward *adj.*, **2, 173**.
toward(s) *prep.*, 87; **2, 208, 290, 347, 421**.
tower(s), **158** n. 3, **218** & n. 1.
town, **172** n. 1.
toy(s), 59, 152, 233, 315, 428; **252** n. 1, **256** & nn. 1, 3.
tracked *p.t.*, 397.
tradition, 433.
tragedy, **59** n. 2, **275**.
trance, 425.
trans- *prefix*, **356, 364**.
transform, 47.
transgress(ion), 208; **364**.
transient, **276, 389**.
transition, 348; **356, 365** n. 1, **389**.
transitory, **62**.
translate, -ing, **62, 364**.
transliterate, **364**.
transmigrate, **364**.
trash, 331.
travail, 267, 268.
travel(ler), 268, 272, 299, 326.
treachery, 8.
tread, 25, 425; **30, 115** n. 3.
treason, 321, 326.
treasure, treasury, 350, 351, 367, 390; **8, 282, 326, 389**.
treated, 71.
treatise, 71; **363**.
treaty, 8.
tree(s), 16; **40, 132** n., **301, 312**.
trefoil, 28.
trembling, **403** n.
trespass(es), 274, 279.
trial, 114; **40, 254** n. 4.
tried, trier, 114; **40**.
trieth, 314.
trifle, 68, 76; **326**.
trifoil, **256**.
tripartite, **275**.

tripod, **269**.
triumph(ing), **23**.
trivet, **77**.
trod, 23; **33** n. 3.
Gr. τροίη ἐν εὐρείη, 59.
Trojan(s), **23, 273**.
trot, **194**.
troth, 22; **34, 368** n. 1.
trouble, 382; **19**.
trough(s), 23, 170, 182, 184, 326, 338, 366, 372, 418, 427, 432, 443; **4, 34, 104, 124** n. 2, **357, 371** n. 2, **424**.
trow, 418, 434; **4, 34, 173** nn. 1, 2.
Troy, 428; **255, 310** n.
truce, 363.
true, 9, 81, 109, 187, 252, 380; **173** n. 1, **178** n. 4, **183** n. 5, **185, 244** n. 4.
truly, 252, 355; **275, 350**.
trumpetors, 92; **281**.
truncheon, **336** & n. 2.
trust, 14; **82** n. 1.
truth(s), 429; **173** n. 2, **178** & n. 4, **358, 368** n. 1.
try(ing), 114; **40**.
try-out, 112.
Tuesday, 41, 90; **188, 312**.
tuft, 21; **398** n. 1, **437**.
tuilyie, 125.
tuition, 276 n., **433**.
tulip, 418; **185, 390**.
tumultuous, **291**.
G. tün, 76.
tun, 276.
L. tunc, **93**.
tune, **188**.
Turk, 441.
turmoil, 54; **255** & n. 1, **279**.
turn, 104, 110, 112, 226, 249, 413; **19, 331**.
L. Turnus, 241.
L. turris, 241; **212**.
L. turtur, 241.
twain, 24.
twang, **194**.
twattle, 215.
twelfth, **368** n. 3.
twentieth, **309** n., **334** n. 1, **368**.
twenty, **309** n.
twice, **363, 437** n. 3.
twine(d), 52, 59; **263** n. 1.
twins, 215.

INDEX OF WORDS

'twixt, **437**.
two, 124, 264, 265, 269, 306, 378, 405; **40**, **153** & n., **421** & nn. 1, 3.
twopence, **18**, **153**, **293**, **363**, **421**.
-ty *suffix*, **275**.
tympany, **275**.
tyrant, 114, 326; **12**, **398** n. 1, **436**.
tythe, 399; **368**.

u (letter-name), 179, 218, 386; **4**.
-ual *suffix*, **270**.
Ulster, **431** n. 5.
umbragious, 92; **281**.
umpire, **136**, **440**.
F. un, 276.
un- *prefix*, **380**.
unawed, **53**.
unbarred, **43** n. 3.
uncertain, **272**.
uncircumcision, **356**.
uncle, 330; **440**.
uncourteous, 91, 92; **281**, **308** n. 2.
uncouth, 92, 163; **161**, **166**.
under(n) *sb.*, **431** n. 5.
undermost, **277**.
underneath, 315; **368**.
understand(est), 183; **265**.
undeserved, **288**, **356**.
undo(ne), 124, 355, 378; **196** n. 1.
F. une, 276.
uneath 'difficilis', 25.
unexpert, 71.
unfitty, 105.
unison, **356** n. 4.
unity, 36; **244**, **350**.
universal, **66** n. 4.
university, **275**.
unless, 108; **8**, **437**.
unperfect, **141**.
unprevented, **288**.
until, 355; **196** n. 1.
unto, 79.
untoward, **421**.
unwary, **6**.
unwholesome, **431**.
unwise, 355; **196** n. 1.
-uous *suffix*, **270**.
up, 108; **97** n. 1.
upbraid, 111; **401**.
upheaveth, **116** n. 2.
uphold, 104.

upon, 108, 432; **97** n. 6.
upstairs, **3**.
upward, **421**.
urchin, **213** n. 3.
ure, 179, 302, 398; **4**, **185**, **244**.
-ure *suffix*, **282**, **300**, **326**.
urge, **206**.
urgee *interj.*, **431** n. 5.
us, 77, 125, 188, 274, 316; **96**, **362**, **431** n. 5.
use *sb.*, 20, 188; **356**.
use(d) *vb.*, 20, 72, 85, 144–5, 325; **159**, **185**, **315**.
useful, **178** n. 5.
useless, 293, 305; **185**.
usual, **185**, **270**, **356**, **389**.
usurer, **282**.
usurp(s), usurpation, **291**, **356**.
usury, 305; **185**, **282**, **303**.
utensil, **275**.
utter(most), **185** n. 6, **302** n. 3.

vain, 221.
vale, 176, 186, 405.
valley, 403, 421; **60**, **137** n. 2, **272**, **275** nn. 1, 2, **282**, **338** & n. 2.
value, 403, 414; **60**, **282**.
vanged 'fanged', **412**.
vanity, **275**.
variance, **6**.
variety, **274** n. 2, **285**, **337**, **344**.
varlet, **66** n. 2.
varnish, **66**.
'Varsity, **66** n. 4.
vary, 28; **6**, **205**, **218**.
vase, **60**, **235** n., **237** n. 4.
vat, 408; **6**, **357** n.
vault, 169, 357, 408, 424; **242**, **425** n. 5.
vaunt, 27, 304, 353, 425, 436, 442; **44** n. 2, **62** n. 1, **104** n. 2, **238**, **239** n. 1.
veal, 25, 37, 405; **357** n.
vehement(ly), 386; **309**, **426**.
veil, 25; **115** n. 5, **131** & n. 1.
vein, 368, 393, 444; **131**.
velvet, **301**.
venison, **306**, **326**.
venom, **326**.
venture(d), 184; **282**, **306**.

Venus, **22** & n.
verb(s), **435**; **363**.
L. verbum, 79.
verdict, **66**, **303**, **442**.
verdure, **282**, **349**.
verge, **435**.
verily, 380; **275**, **303** n. 1.
verjuice, 184; **66**, **282**, **303**.
vermin, **436** n. 2.
verse, 9, **122**, **126**.
version, **364**, **388**.
very, 252; **59** n. 2, **67** n. 3, **275** n. 2.
vetch, 24; **77** n. 3, **357** n.
viage 'voyage', 114; **12**.
vial, **273** n. 2.
vicar, **357** n.
vice, 109; **12**.
vicious, **276** n.
victory, **275**, **277**.
victual(s), 299, 351, 401, 414; **12**, **23**, **326**, **334**, **442**.
Sp. viergen, 376.
view(er), 26, 341; **178** n. 4, **183** n. 5, **218**.
vigilancy, **275**.
villa, **212**.
villain(ous), 19; **272**, **301**, **321**, **334**.
vinegar, **334**, **357** n.
vineyard, 45.
viol, **273** n. 2.
violate, violence, 114; **23**, **277**.
Virgil, **326**.
virgin, **212**.
Virginia, **115** n. 3.
virtue(s), 81, 226; **185**, **212** & n. 2, **213** n. 1, **282**, **363**, **390**.
virtuous, **213** n. 1, **282** & n. 1, **363**.
visard, *see* vizard.
visible, **356**.
vision, 171, 208, 351, 352; **308** n. 3, **356**, **389**.
L. visionem, **356**.
visitation, **115** n. 4.
visitest, 183.
visor, 114; **12**.
vital(s), 401, 414; **12**, **23**, **326**, **442**.
vitiate, **276** & n.
vitrifiable, **275**.
vixen, **357** n.
vizard, 114; **12**.

INDEX OF WORDS

voice(d), 83, 428, 437, 440; **255** & nn. 2, 3, **260** n. 3.
void, 334, 342, 437, 440; **256** & n. 4.
volley, 414; **282**.
F. volonté, **114**.
volume, **283**.
vote, 408; **242**.
vouch, **167** & n. 1.
vouchsafe, **411**.
vow(ed, -s), **4**, **172** n. 1, **315**, **334**.
vowel(s), **176**, **363**.
voyage, 353; **137** n. 4, **254** & n. 3, **261** n. 2; see also viage.
F. vu, **182** n. 2.
vulgar, **299**.

w (letter-name), **137**.
wad, 398; **33** n. 1, **194** n. 1.
Wade, 129.
Wadham, 229.
waft, **52**, **53** & n. 7.
wag, **53** n. 2, **194**.
wage, 24.
wagon, 183; **301**, **326**, **333**, **337**.
wail, 413.
wainscot, 354; **26** & n.
waist, 178, 409, 410; **6**, **226** n. 4, **233** n. 2.
waistcoat, **26** n.
wait, **229** n. 1.
wake(n), 252; **229** n. 1.
Waldon, **321**.
wale, 54.
walk(ed, -est), 90, 183, 210, 354; **60**, **315**, **425**.
wall, **60** n. 2.
wallop, **60**.
wallow, **60**.
Walsh, **60**.
Walsingham, **237** n. 2.
Walter, 399; **53** & n. 6.
waltz, **60**.
wan, 305, 443; **194**, **210**.
wander(ed), **53** n. 1, **306**.
wane, 19, 307.
wangle, **194**.
want 'lack', 210, 425, 436, 442, 443; **53** n. 1, **54** n. 1, **59**, **194**.
want 'mole', **421** n. 5.
wanton(ness), **319**, **321**.
war(s), 187, 301, 331, 333, 361, 362, 417, 443; **42**, 43 & n. 3, **49** & n. 1, **55** n. 1, **56** n., **68**, **195**.
warble, 443; **49**.
ward, 301, 331, 426, 431, 442, 443; **6**, **49** & n. 1, **195**.
warden, 301; **49**, **321**.
ware(s) *sb.*, 333, 417; **204**.
ware *vb.* 'defend', **204** n. 3.
ware 'wast', **43** n. 2.
warling, 164.
warm, 104, 301, 331, 442, 443; **49**, **54** n. 1, **194**.
warn(er), 301, 331-3, 442, 443; **42**, **49** & n. 1, **55**, **194**.
warp, 331-2, 443; **49**.
warrant, 210; **55** n. 2, **194**, **321**, **330**.
warren, 301-2, 305, 360; **49** & n. 1, **55** n. 2, **330**.
wart, 301, 331, 414, 442, 443; **49**, **194**.
wary, **6**.
was, 21, 71, 92, 209, 252, 260, 301-2, 430, 443; **4**, **52** n., **53** & n. 4, **194** & n. 3, **195**, **339**, **362** & n. 1.
wash(eth), 17, 301-2, 331, 333, 338-9; **53** & nn. 1, 4, **59** n. 2, **195**, **373** n. 3.
wasp, 178, 305, 306; **6**, **52**, **53**, **194**.
wast, 31, 400, 410, 415; **6**, **52**, **194**.
waste, 24, 31, 215, 400, 409, 410, 415, 430; **6**, **50** n. 1.
Wat, **53** n. 6.
watch(eth), 17, 301-2, 305, 338-9; **53** & nn. 1, 4, **63**, **194**, **195**, **229** n. 1.
water(y), 191, 211, 301, 305, 336, 399; **6**, **53** & n. 6, **54** & n. 2, **55**, **56** n., **59**, **195**, **226**, **235** n., **306**, **423**.
waterest, 183; **306** n. 2.
wattle, 301-2, 305; **53** & n. 4, **195**.
Watts, **53** n. 6.
waul, 269; **431** n. 5.
wave, 24.
wawe 'wave', 12.
wax(en), 54; **194**, **320**.
way(s), 52, 76, 215, 221, 250, 256, 328, 414; **40** n. 2, **137** n. 2, **228** n. 5, **275** n. 2, **414**.
we, 85, 250, 256, 274, 279, 292, 294, 295, 368, 419; **4**, **132** n.
weak, 26, 404, 405, 426; **10**, **115** n. 6, **124**.
weal, 293, 297-8, 413, 418; **123**, **398**, **414**.
weald, 404.
wealth, 338; **8**, **77**, **80**, **368** n. 1.
wean(ed), 25, 26, 250, 251, 286, 290, 298, 366; **123**.
weapon, 350, 351; **8**, **326**, **381**.
wear(ing) *vb.*, 113, 251, 417, 425; **109**, **122**, **204** & n. 3.
weariness, **8**.
weary, 401; **8**, **9**, **11**, **74**, **85** & nn. 2, 4, **126** & nn. 3, 4, **132** n., **136** n. 2, **218**.
weasand, **8**.
weasel, 26, 162, 349; **77**, **123**, **320**, **326**.
weather, 406; **8**, **80**, **85** n. 3, **384**, **414**.
weaved, **124** n. 1.
wedding, 348.
wedlock, **293**.
Wednesday, 350; **306**, **321**, **343**, **401**.
wee (?), 286.
week, 402, 404, 405; **10**, **124**, **421** n. 5.
ween, 18, 286.
weep(ing), **120** n., **124** n. 1, **132** n.
weevil, 162; **10**.
weigh(ed, -ing, -s), 250, 252, 353, 368, 389, 419, 432, 433, 438, 444; **129**, **139**, **313**, **377**, **414**, **424** n. 2.
weight, 22, 250, 252, 353, 382, 417; **139** & n., **414**.
weir, 426; **122** & n. 2, **129** n. 5, **204** & n. 3.
weird, 24; **213** n. 1.
well, 76, 77, 418; **4**, **85** n. 3, **123** n. 2.
well-beloved, **315**.
we'll do it, 387.
wench, **85** n. 3.
wend, **6**.

1074 INDEX OF WORDS

were, 92, 347, 391, 417, 436; **4**, **100** n., **122** & n. 5, **204**, **414**.
wert, 414; **4**.
Wesley, **364**.
western, **329** & nn. 1, 3.
Westminster, **401**.
Weston, **326**, **406**.
West Thurrock, **97** n. 6.
wet, 29, 250, 418, 425; **30** & n. 1, **85** n. 3, **213** n. 1, **414**.
wether, **85** n. 3.
wharf, wharves, 23, 331–2, 442; **49** & n. 1, **357**.
what, 209–10, 252, 263, 301, 388, 443; **4**, **53** n. 1, **194**, **339**, **414**.
whatsoever, **277**.
wheal 'mark of blow', 413.
wheal 'pustula', 25, 405; **123**, **414**.
wheat, 25, 408, 418; **30**, **115** n. 4, **414**.
wheel, 405, 413; **414**.
wheeze, wheezle, 443.
whelm, **8**, **331**.
when, 388; **414**.
whence, 91.
where, 426, 436; **100** n., **118**, **122** & n. 5, **132** n., **204**, **288**, **414**.
whereas, **362**.
whereat, **288**.
whereby, 89.
wherefore, **277**.
whereof, 77; **4**, **362**.
whereunto, 89.
wherewith, 77; **4**.
wherry, **10**, **80**, **213** & n. 3.
whet, 408, 418; **414**.
whether, 113, 161–2, 401; **80**, **85** & n. 2, **414**.
whew, 250, 252.
whey, 368, 414, 419, 438, 444; **129**, **414**.
which, 48, 62, 274; **85** n. 3, **414**.
whiff(ed), 433.
while(s), 54; **12**, **262** n. 3, **263** n. 1, **363**, **414**, **437**.
whilom, **277** n., **293**, **302** n. 2, **326**.
whilst, **363**, **437**.
whimper, **403**.
whine, **414**.

whip, 23.
whirl *sb.* & *vb.*, 441; **78**, **85** n. 2, **213** & n. 1.
whirling-wind, **85**, **213**, **214**.
whirlpool, 22; **78**.
whirr, whirry *vb.*, **10**, **213** & n. 3.
whistle, 325; **398**.
whit, 234.
white(r), 54, 114, 417; **12**, **414**.
whither, 161, 401, 406; **80**, **414**.
Whitsuntide, **401**.
who, 306, 321, 380, 388, 434; **4**, **33**, **153**, **414**, **421** & n. 1.
whole, 35, 84, 380, 382, 389, 394, 419; **13**, **36** & n. 1, **150** n. 2, **353** n., **414** & n. 3, **426**, **429**, **431** & nn. 1, 2, 4.
wholesome, **431**.
wholly, 84; **13**, **36**, **275**, **431**.
whom, 344, 388, 389, 409, 430, 440; **4**, **33** & n. 2, **36**, **37**, **151** n. 3, **153**, **414**, **421**, **426**.
whoop, **164**, **431** n. 1.
whoot 'hoot', **431** n. 5.
whore(d), 267, 380, 382, 404, 409, 417, 428; **149** n. 1, **165** n. 4, **201** n., **207** n. 1, **208** & nn. 2, 4, **209**, **426**, **431** & n. 1.
whoredom, 389; **426**.
whort, whortle(berry), **431** n. 5.
whose, 401, 439, 440; **4**, **33** & n. 2, **153**, **421**.
whrine, 433.
whulla-balloo, **431** n. 5.
why, 48, 52, 215, 251, 252; **40**.
wick, 25, 29, 45, 402, 404; **10**, **31**.
wicked(ly, -ness), **311**, **315**, **334**.
G. wider, 290.
widow, 354.
wield, 404, 418; **398**.
wife, **357**, **368**; *see also* wives.
wild(s), 15, 400, 404, 414; **12**, **398**, **409**.

wile(s), 236, 256, 320, 347, 400, 414; **398**, **409**, **414**.
will, 215, 236, 250, 274, 293, 297, 298, 316, 320, 347; **85** & n. 2, **425** n. 4.
willow, 325–6; **295**.
Wilson, 326.
wilt thou, **310** n.
wily, **12** n. 1, **350**.
Wimbledon, **321**.
win, 290, 298.
Winchelsea, **338**, **343** n. 2.
wind(s) *sb.*, 400; **12**, **85** n. 3, **398**, **399**, **410**, **412**.
wind *vb.*, **85** n. 3.
winder(s), 408; **12**, **302**, **332**.
window, 408; **12**, **85** n. 3, **302**, **332**.
wine(s), 400; **398**, **410**, **414**.
wing, 15, 355; **77**, **399**.
winking, winks, 15; **412** n. 4.
winkle, **412** n. 4.
Wirral, **55**.
wisdom, 72; **326**.
wise *adj.*, 324.
wise *sb.* 'manner', 114; **275**.
-wise *suffix*, 114; **275**.
wish(ed), 402; **85** n. 3, **124** n. 2, **315**, **373**.
wist, 402; **373**.
wit, 187.
witch, **85** n. 3, **414**.
with, 6, 77, 85, 316, 424; **4**, **85** & nn. 2, 3, **362** & n. 1, **368**, **421** n. 5.
withal, **4**.
withdraw, **4**.
withe(s), 424; **12**, **358**.
wither, 406; **85**.
within, 77; **4**.
without, **4**.
withy, **12**, **358**.
witness(ed), **315**, **363**.
wive *vb.*, **368**.
wives *gen. sg.*, **300**; **357**.
ME wlatsum, **415**.
wo *interj.*, **40**.
woad(ed), 22, 28, 29, 55, 338, 372, 398; **25**, **33** & n. 1, **144** n. 4, **194** n. 1, **421** n. 5.
woe(s), 215, 250, 267, 306, 412, 415; **40**, **153** & n., **312** n. 3.

INDEX OF WORDS

ME wol 'will', **425** n. 4.
wolf, wolves, 249, 250, 287, 289, 298, 342, 360, 432; **93**, **196**, **330**.
woman, 87, 148, 342, 360; **85** & n. 1, **196**, **302**, **321**, **420** n., **431** n. 5.
womb, 54, 306, 379, 440; **7** & n. 2, **13** & n. 3, **15** & n., **36**, **153**, **394**, **414**, **421**.
women, 90–91, 148, 149; **10**, **80**, **85** & n. 1, **321**.
won, 342, 432; **196**.
wonder(ed, -ing), 13, 86, 87, 289, 298, 306, 342, 360; **196**, **328** & n. 5, **410**, **431** n. 5.
wonderment, 319.
wone 'dwell', 6.
wone 'plenty', **431** n. 3.
wont, 235, 359; **94**, **97**, **194**, **196** & n. 2.
won't, 394; **95** n., **174**, **425** & n. 4.
woo(ed, -er, -ing), 12, 13, 18, 22, 239, 256, 306, 412, 415, 430, 434; **40**, **153** & n., **163**, **165** n. 4, **183** n. 5, **185** n. 6, **315**, **334**, **414**, **421**.
wood, 18, 23, 239, 248, 250, 287, 342, 361, 382, 430; **18**, **36** n. 2, **93**, **196**.
wool(len), 215, 248, 249, 250, 342, 361, 382, 387, 419, 427; **36** n. 2, **93**, **196**, **321**, **414**, **431**.
Worcester, 352; **196**, **306**, **401**.
word 'beginning', **431** n. 3.
word(s) 'verbum', 249, 250, 298, 342, 360, 425, 429; **16** & n. 2, **18**, **92**, **97** n. 1, **196**, **208**, **353** n., **363**, **431** n. 3.
work, 71, 87, 112, 298, 360, 429, 432, 441; **90** n. 2, **196**, **212** n. 3, **213** n. 4.
world, 87, 112, 298, 360; **90**, **409**.
worldling, 352; **90**, **409**.
worm, 21, 112, 298, 360, 432; **82**, **401**.
worn, 443; **13**, **16**, **46**, **149**, **153**, **330**.

worry, 298, 360, 401; **74**, **75** n., **82**, **85** & n. 4, **196**.
worse, 90, 425; **90** & n. 2, **97** n. 6, **355**, **364**.
worship(per), 298, 360; **196**, **274** n. 3.
worst, 112, 298, 441; **97** n. 1, **213** n. 4, **401**.
worsted, 298; **196**.
wort(s), 298, 432; **97**, **196**, **431** nn. 4, 5.
worth(y), 77, 89, 112, 298, 425; **90** & n. 1, **439** n.
worthily, **265**.
wot, 29, 443; **33**, **194**.
would(est), 5, 6, 87, 221, 239, 249, 316, 342, 344, 361, 362, 436, 443; **4**, **146**, **174**, **196** n. 3, **421** n. 1.
wound(s) *sb.*, 373; **158** n. 2, **162**, **163**, **312**, **362**.
wound *p.t.*, 250; **163**.
woven, **421** n. 5.
wow, wowl, **431** n. 5.
woxen, **326**.
wranged 'wronged', **399**, **412**.
wrap, **416** & n. 2.
wrath(ful), 177, 235, 301, 305, 353, 373, 398, 400, 402, 425, 431, 442; **6**, **53** & n. 7, **55**, **194**, **195**, **200**.
wreak, 25, 352, 386; **116**, **124**.
wreath(s), 315, 424; **358**, **368** & n. 2.
wreathe, **368**.
wrest, **77**.
wrestle(r), 351, 352; **194**, **406**.
wretch, 26, 373; **59** n. 3, **77**.
wright, 397.
wring, 80.
wrist, 93; **77**, **80**.
wristband, **364**, **398**, **406**.
write, writing, 87, 235, 368, 373, 378, 397; **137** n. 4, **416**.
written, **325** n. 2, **326**, **334**.
wrong(ed), 388; **53** n. 2, **92**, **412**.
wrote, 399, 414; **33**.
wroth, 29, 361–2, 398, 402; **33**, **53** n. 7, **194**.

wrought, 126, 163, 244, 353, 366, 401, 414, 443; **170**, **237** n. 2, **240** & n. 2.
wrung, 92.
ME wruxled *p.p.*, **195** n. 1.
wry, 40.
wurgee *interj.*, **431** n. 5.
wych-elm, **138** & n. 1.
Wymondham, **321**.

Xenophon, **359**.
Sp. Xeres, 241.
Xerxes, **359**.

y (letter-name), **136**.
-y *suffix*, **1**, **275**.
yacht, 371.
yard(s), 26, 44, 250, 426, 431; **8**, **44** nn. 2, 3, **65**, **422** & n. 2, **430** n. 5.
yarn, **42**, **44** nn. 2, 3, **65**, **430**.
yarrow, **295** n. 1.
yate 'gate', 62, 215.
yaud, 433.
yave 'gave', 62.
yaw, **236**.
yawn, 250.
Yaxley, **343**.
ye, 6, 89, 153, 256, 292, 316 (*objective*), 409; **4**, **119** n. 1, **422** n. 1.
yea, 250, 252, 409; **4**, **40**, **115** & n. 6, **119** & n. 1.
year(s), 91, 372, 398, 407, 409, 426, 439; **119**, **122** n. 6, **203**, **204** n. 4, **218**, **430**.
yearly, 366; **275**, **430**.
yearn, 398; **9**, **65**, **422** n. 2, **430**.
yeast, 55, 398, 412, 416, 417, 425; **8**, **77**, **422**, **430**.
yeender, **431** n. 5.
yeld *p.t.* 'yielded', **9**, **77**, **315** n. 2.
yelled, 91.
yellow, **73** n., **87**, **295** & n. 1.
yeme 'care', **120** n., **422** n. 2.
yen 'yon', 45.
yeoman, -men, **8**, **77**, **302**, **321**.

yerk, 434, 435; **65**.
yes, 250, 253, 347, 391; **77**.
yesterday, 390; **59** n. 2, **77**, **275** n. 2, **343**, **422**.
yet, 215, 250, 253, 372, 398, 406; **30**, **77**, **422** & nn. 1, 2, **430**.
yeve 'give', **422** n. 2.
yew, 179, 217, 250, 253, 256; **4**, **178** n. 5, **182** n. 1, **183** n. 5, **185**, **244**.
yield, 414; **135** n., **422** & n. 2.
yoke, **422**.
yolk, 36; **73**, **422**, **425**.
yon(d), **73**, **422**.

yonder, 250; **73**, **422** & n. 3.
yore, 406; **165** n. 4, **208**, **244**.
York, 250, 429, 432; **47**, **421**, **430** nn. 3, 5.
you, 6, 18, 80, 81, 85, 148, 149, 163, 179, 208, 251, 256, 295, 386, 389, 390, 407; **4**, **165**, **166**, **173** n. 1, **178** & n. 4, **183** & n. 5, **185**, **209**.
young, 23, 74, 215, 370; **19**.
youngling(s), 386; **376**.
your(s), 6, 148, 179, 208, 251, 390, 406, 414; **4**, **165** & n. 4, **178** & n. 4, **185**, **208**, **209**, **218** n. 1, **244**.
youth(s), 80, 81, 145, 163, 208, 251, 334, 337, 341, 386, 389, 429, 443; **38**, **39**, **178** & nn. 2–4, **183** n. 5, **185** & n. 1, **358**, **368** n. 1.
yowl, 250.

Zacheus 'Zacchaeus', 354.
zeal, 25, 372.
zealot, zealous(ly), **8**.
Zebedee, 160.
Zenobia, **288**.
zodiac, **23** & n.
'zounds, 328.

SUBJECT-INDEX TO VOLUME II

The references are to the numbered sections of Vol. II. Prefixed abbreviations (ME, OF, &c.) are ignored in determining the order of entries, and phonetic symbols are entered under the alphabetic letters of which they are modifications or forms (thus [ə] under *e*, [ʒ] under *z*, and [χ] under *x*) or which they normally replace (thus [þ] and [ð] in the order of *th*, and [ŋ] after *ng*). There are separate entries for stressed and weak-stressed vowels; the latter term comprises both secondarily stressed and unstressed vowels. In the order of entries, stressed vowels precede weak-stressed, short vowels long, and close vowels open.

ME *ă* (stressed): free development, 59; dialectal development to ME *ai*, 63; development after *w*, 194–5; before [χ], 61; before *l*, 60; before *r*, 211: lengthening before *r*, 42–44; before voiceless spirants, 50; between *w* and *r*, 49; between *w* and voiceless spirant, 52; in other cases, 53; phonetic process involved in lengthening, 54–56: variation with ME *ā*, 6; with ME *au* before nasals, 62; with ME *ĕ*, 64–70; with ME *ŏ*, 71; with ME *ǭ*, 7.

ME *ă* (weak-stressed): quality in ME, 293; reduction to [ə], 299 (before *r*), 302 (free); rounding to [ɒ], 339; in pretonic syllables, 285–6: possible lengthening by reimposition of secondary stress, 352: variation in post-tonic syllables with ME *ā*, 271; with ME *au*, 273.

ME *ā* (stressed): free development, 98–102; in special words, 103; before *r*, 205; developed from, and varying with, ME *au*, 104: shortening, 25: variation with ME *ă*, 7; with ME *ē̜*, 105.

ME *ā* (weak-stressed): in pretonic syllables, 285; ModE shortening to [ɪ], 342; variation in post-tonic syllables with ME *ă*, 271.

ME *ai* (*ęi*) (stressed): free development, 225–30, 232; in special words, 233; before *r*, 205, 231: dialectal ME *ai* from ME *ă*, 63: shortening, 26: variation with ME *ē̜*, 129–31; with ME *ī*, 139.

ME *ai* (*ęi*) (weak-stressed): ModE shortening for [ɪ], 343: variation with ME *i* in pretonic syllables, 287; in post-tonic syllables, 272.

ME *au* (stressed): free development to [ɒ:], 234–7; development to late ME *ā*, 104; combinative development to [ɑ:], 238–9: shortening, 27–29: variation with ME *ă* before nasals, 62; with ME *ā*, 104; with ME *ou*, 240–2 (before [χ], 240; OE *āw*, *āg*, 241; in special words, 242).

ME *au* (weak-stressed): in pretonic syllables, 286; ModE shortening to *ŏ* > [ə], 348; variation in post-tonic syllables with ME *ă*, 273.

[b]: loss after [m] in final position, 394; in medial position, 403: glide between [m] and [l] or [r], 435.

[ç]: *see under* gh.
Classical influence on pronunciation of certain words, 442.

[d]: development to [t] in final position after [n], 367; to [ð] between preceding vowel and following [r̩] or [ər], 384: development from [ð] (i) before non-syllabic [n], [m], and [r], (ii) between preceding [r] and following vowel or syllabic consonant, 383: assimilation to following [j] to give [dʒ], 387, 391: loss in final position after dentals, &c., 398: loss by assimilation to following [n], 401 (*a*); to preceding [n], 401 (*b*); to following [þ], 401 (*c*): loss in medial position after [r], 408; after [l], 409; after [n], 410 (i): glide between [n] and [l] or [r], 435; between [l] and [r], 437: 'excrescent' [d] in final position after [n], 436; after [l], 437.

Dentals: influence on development of vowels, 220.

[dʒ]: development from [tj], 387, 391.

ME *ĕ* (stressed): free development, 72; late ME development to, and variation with, ME *ă* before *r*, 64–69, 201; ModE development to [ə] before *r*, 212, 215: dialectal lengthening, 57: raising of ME *ĕ* to ME *ĭ*, 76–77: variation with ME *ă*, 64–70; with ME *ē̜*, 9; with ME *ē̜*, 8; with ME *ĭ*, 75–78 (ME *ĕ* < OE *ў*, 75); with ME *ŏ*, 73; with ME *ŭ*, 74.

ME *ĕ* (weak-stressed): quality in ME, 293;

development from, and variation with, pretonic ĭ, 294; evidence of reduction to [ə], 297 (before r), 301 (free): possible lengthening to ME ē̜ by reimposition of secondary stress, 352: loss in final position, 310, 323–4; by syncope in medial position, 306–7; before consonants in inflexional endings, 311–17; before liquids and nasals, 325–6: variation with ME ĭ in prefixes, 292; with ME ai (e̜i), 287 (pretonic syllables), 272 (post-tonic syllables); with ME ē̜, 288 (pretonic syllables), 274 (post-tonic syllables).

ME ē̜ (stressed): free development, 132; in adopted words, 133; lowering to late ME ḗ before r, 126, 201; raising to ME ī, 136: shortening, 31: variation with ME ĕ, 9; with ME ē, 117–27; with ME ĭ, 10–11; with ME ī, 134–6 (ME ē̜ < OE ȳ, 135).

ME ē̜ (weak-stressed): ModE shortening to [ɪ], 345.

ME ē (stressed): free development, 106–16 (general discussion, 106–11; development as distinct sound, 112–14; identity with ME ā, 115; substitution of [i:], 116); in ModE adoptions, 110, 127: development after r, 217; before r, 203–4: raising to ME ē̜, 121–5: shortening, 30: variation with ME ā, 105; with ME ai (e̜i), 129–31; with ME ĕ, 8; with ME ē̜, 117–27; with ME ĭ, 128.

ME ē (weak-stressed): ModE shortening to [ɪ], 344: variation with ME ĕ in pretonic syllables, 288; in post-tonic syllables, 274.

OF -é: treatment in ME in final position, 275.

[ə] (stressed): development in ModE from ME ĕ, ĭ, and ŭ before r, 212–15.

[ə] (unstressed): development in ME from unstressed ĕ, 293; from pretonic ĭ, 294; evidence of [ə] from unstressed vowels generally, 296–303; development of [ə] to unstressed [ɪ], 293, 333–7; tendency of [ə] to become [ʌ], 340. See also Glide-vowels.

ME e̜i: see ME ai.

ME e̜u: identification with ME iu, 188; see further ME iu.

ME e̜u (stressed): development, 243–4: variation with ME ou, 245; with ME ū, 246.

ME e̜u (weak-stressed), 349.

[f]: variation with [v], 357: development to [v] in final position in unstressed words, 362; to [s] in initial position before [n], 386: loss by assimilation to following [p], 401 (a); by vocalization to [u] before [t], 423.

Final vowels, stressed: shortening of, 40.

[g]: unvoicing to [k] in final position after [ŋ], 367; in initial position before [n] in group gn-, 418: ON g, 376: development of [g] to [d] before [l], 378; palatalization to [gj] in ModE before front vowels, 379; early loss from group [ŋgþ], 377; loss from group [ŋg] in final position, 399; in medial position before consonants, 412: loss in initial position before [n], 418: [gn] for Latin gn in adopted words, 441.

gh (ME [ç] and [χ]): survival of [ç], beside variant pronunciations, 140–3, 424; development to [þ], 372; loss by vocalization to [i], 140–3, 424: survival of [χ], beside variant pronunciations, 177, 424; development to [f], 371; to [þ], 372; loss by vocalization to [u], 177, 424.

Glide-consonants, 428–37: isolative development of [j] and [w], 429–31; combinative development, 432; [j] before unstressed [ɪ], 433: glide and 'excrescent' stops after nasals, 434–6; after other consonants, 437; 'intrusive' [n] and [ŋ], 438.

Glide-vowels: [ə] after l and r, 331; after syllabic r, 329; before nasal, especially n, 353; before r, 218, 353; before syllabic consonants, 323–4, 328; ŏ before w in late ME, 295.

gn- (initial group): pronunciation and development, 418.

F. gn [ɲ]: treatment in English in adopted words, 441.

L. gn: pronunciation in English in adopted words, 441.

Gutturals: influence on development of vowels, 221; palatalization of gutturals, 376–9.

[gz]: variation with [ks] in pronunciation of x in words adopted from Latin, 359.

[h]: loss in initial position before [l], [n], [r], and [w] (i.e. from the OE initial groups hl, hn, hr, and hw), 414; loss before vowels, 426.

Hiatus, vowels in, 270.

OE hw- (initial group): development to [ʍ], 369; to [w] by loss of [h], 414.

ME ĭ (stressed): free development, 79;

SUBJECT-INDEX TO VOLUME II

lowering to ME *ĕ*, 80; development to [ə] before *r*, 213, 215: dialectal lengthening, 57: variation with ME *ē̜*, 10–11; with ME *ī*, 12; with ME *ŭ*, 81–85 (OE *ȳ*, 82; OF [y], 83; ME *rĭ*, 84; rounding of *ĭ*, 85).

ME *ĭ* (weak-stressed): quality in ME, 293; development to and variation with unstressed *ĕ* [ə] in pretonic syllables, 294; reduction to [ə], 300 (before *r*), 303 (free); ModE lowering to tense [e], 338: ModE lengthening to [i:] by reimposition of secondary stress, 350–1: variation with ME *ĕ* in prefixes, 292; with ME *ī* in pretonic syllables, 289; with ME *ī* in post-tonic syllables, 275; with the consonant [j] in post-tonic syllables, 276; with ME [y:] in post-tonic syllables, 282.

ME *ī* (stressed): free development, 137; alleged failure of diphthongization, 138; replacement by analogical [ʊi] and [ɔi], 144: shortening, 32: development from, and variation with, ME *ē̜*, 136; variation with ME *ai* (*ęi*), 139; with ME *ē̜*, 128; with ME *ĭ*, 12; with ME [iç], 140–3 (ME *igh*, 140–1; ME *īgh*, 142).

ME *ī* (weak-stressed): variation with ME *ĭ* in pretonic syllables, 289; in post-tonic syllables, 275.

OF *-ie*: treatment in ME in final position, 275.

ME *īgh*: development to and variation with ME *ī*, 140–3.

-ing: development to [ɪn], 399.

ME *iu* (stressed): free development, 179–88 (theories of development, 180; evidence, 181–6; review of evidence, 187; explanation of development, 188); combinative changes resulting from development to [ju:], 185 (iii).

ME *iu* (weak-stressed): *see* ME [y:] (weak-stressed).

[j]: development from and variation with ME *ĭ* in hiatus with following vowel in post-tonic syllables, 276; in OF *-ie*, 275; from OE *g*, 376: assimilations involving [j], 387–91 ([ʃ] < [sj], 388; [ʒ] < [zj], 389; [tʃ] < [tj], 390; [dʒ] < [dj], 391): loss of [j] by vocalization before vowels, 422: glide [j] by isolative development before ME *ē̜*, *ę̄*, and *ęu* and fifteenth-century [æ:] and [ɛ:] < ME *ā*, 429–30; by combinative development after [ʃ], 432; before unstressed [ɪ], 433.

[k]: representing ON *k*, 376; Norman *k*, 376 n. 1: development to [t] before [l], 378; palatalization to [kj] in ModE before front vowels, 379: early loss from group [ŋkþ], 377; loss in initial position before [n], 417: glide between [ŋ] and [þ] or [s], 435.

kn- (initial group): pronunciation and development, 417; development from earlier *gn-*, 418.

[ks]: variation with [gz] in pronunciation of *x* in words adopted from Latin, 359.

[l]: influence on development of vowels, 219: syllabic [l̩], 319–26, 330: loss of [l] by vocalization to [u] in various contexts, 425.

Labials: influence on development of vowels, 222.

Lengthening of vowels in stressed syllables, 41–57: ME *ă* and *ŏ* (i) before *r* 42–49, (ii) before voiceless spirants, 50–52, (iii) in other cases, 53; phonetic process of lengthening of ME *ă* and *ŏ*, 54–56: dialectal lengthening of ME *ĭ* and *ĕ*, 57: lengthening in weak-stressed syllables by reimposition of secondary stress, 350–2.

Loss of consonants: assimilations of [j], 387–91: loss of consonants in final position, 393–9; in intervocalic position, 400: assimilatory loss of medial consonants, 401: loss of middle consonant of group of three, 402–12; of first consonant of certain initial groups, 414–18: loss by vocalization, 419–27.

[m]: syllabic consonant, 319–26, 330–1.

Metathesis of consonants, especially [r], in stressed syllables, 439; of [r] in unstressed syllables, 327–9.

[n]: syllabic consonant, 319–26, 330–1: development to [ŋ] before [g] and [k], 380; to [m] in neighbourhood of labials, 381: loss in final position after [m], 395; after [l], 396; after [r], 397: assimilatory loss before dentals, 401 (*a*): loss medially after [r], 408: 'intrusive' [n], 438; prosthetic [n], 440.

Nasals: influence on development of vowels, 223.

ng (final and medial group): pronunciation of, 377, 399, 412. *See also next entry*.

[ŋ]: development from [n] before [g] and [k], 380; reversion to [n] before [þ] after loss of intervening [g] or [k], 377 (i); reduction of group [ŋg] to [ŋ], and recognition of [ŋ] as distinct phoneme,

399, 412; development of [ŋ] to [n] in suffix -*ing*, 377 (ii)–(iii), 399; analogical [ɪŋ] for original final [ɪn], 377 n. 3: use of [ŋn], later [ŋ] (especially in Scottish), for Latin *gn* in adopted words, 441: 'intrusive' [ŋ], 438.

ME *ŏ* (stressed): free development, 86; identification with ME *ă*, 87; development before *l*, 88, 169; before [χ], 89, 170; raising to ME *ŭ*, 92: lengthening before *r*, 45–48; before voiceless spirants, 51; in other cases, 53; phonetic process involved in lengthening, 54–56: variation with ME *ă*, 71; with ME *ĕ*, 73; with ME *ǭ*, 15–16; with ME *ǭ*, 13; with ME *ou*, 14; with ME *ŭ*, 90–92; with ME *ū*, 17.

ME *ŏ* (weak-stressed): quality in ME, 293; reduction to [ə], 299 (before *r*), 302 (free): variation with ME *ŭ* and ModE [oː] in certain prefixes and suffixes, 277, 292; with ME *ǭ* in pretonic syllables, 290; allegedly with ME *oi* in post-tonic syllables, 279; with ME *ou* in post-tonic syllables, 280.

ME *ǭ* (stressed): free development, 156; in adopted words, 157; after palatals, 159; before [χ], 171; before *r*, 207–10; before *w*, 173: shortening, 35–38: variation with ME *ŏ*, 15–16; with ME *ǭ*, 147–55; with ME *ŭ*, 18; with ME *ū*, 158; with ME [yː], 159.

ME *ǭ* (weak-stressed): shortening in ModE to [ʊ] > [ə], 347: variation in post-tonic syllables with ME *ŭ*, 278.

ME *ǭ* (stressed): free development, 145; raising to ME *ǭ*, 148–53 (isolative, 148–52; after *w*, 153); development after *r*, 216; before [χ], 170; before *l*(*d*), 146, 169; before *r*, 206, 210; before *w*, 172; shortening, 33: variation with ME *ă*, 7; with ME *ŏ*, 13; with ME *ǭ*, 147–55.

ME *ǭ* (weak-stressed): shortening in ModE to [ʊ], 346: variation with ME *ŏ* in pretonic syllables, 290; with ME *ŏ* in post-tonic syllables, 277; with ME *ŭ* in the suffix -*ion*, 277; in the suffix -*ous*, 292.

OF *o* in labial contexts, 154.

ME *oi* (stressed): development, 261; distribution of ME *oi* and ME *ui*, 251–60.

ME *oi* (weak-stressed): alleged variation with ME *ŏ*, 279.

OF *ǫi* (stressed in English), 20, 252, 254–6.

OF *ǭi* (stressed in English), 252–6.

ME *ou* (stressed): free development, 248–50; before [χ], 251; before *l*, 251; before *r*, 210: shortening, 34: variation with ME *ęu*, 245; with ME *ŏ*, 14.

ME *ou* (weak-stressed): variation in post-tonic syllables with ME *ŏ*, 280; with ME *ŭ* for earlier -*we*, 295.

[p]: loss by assimilation to following [b], 401 (*a*); loss medially after [m], 403: glide between [m] and [t], 435.

Quantity variations in stressed syllables descended from ME, 5–20; in learned adoptions, 21–23; in pretonic syllables, 284–91; in post-tonic syllables, 271–83.

[r]: nature of English consonant, 370; influence on development of vowels and diphthongs, 198–217 (rounding, 199–200; lowering, inhibition of raising, and centralization, 201–17); glide [ə] before [r], 218; syllabic consonant, 319–26, 330: metathesis in unstressed syllables, 327–9; in stressed syllables, 439: assimilatory loss in ME before [s], [ʃ], and other consonants, 401 (*c*); assimilatory development of ME *ăr* to [ɒː], with loss of [r], 44, 427: loss by vocalization to [ə] in unstressed syllables, 332; in stressed syllables, 427.

Raising of vowels before *ng*, 191; before dentals and other consonants, 192.

Rounding of vowels under labial influence, 193–7.

[s]: variation with [z], 354–6; voicing to [z] in final position in unstressed words, 362; in unstressed syllables, 363; in combination with voiced sounds, 364; medially before a stressed vowel, 365: dialectal development to [ʃ], 373; assimilation to following [j] to give [ʃ], 387–8: loss by assimilation to following [n], 401 (*a*).

-*s* inflexion of verbs, 375.

[ʃ]: development from [sj], 387–8; dialectal change of [ʃr] to [sr], 392: loss medially after [t], 411.

Shortening of stressed vowels in late ME and ModE, 24–39; of stressed final vowels, 40; of weak-stressed vowels in ModE in consequence of loss of secondary stress, 342–9.

Spelling-pronunciations of certain words, 442.

Stress: variation in position of primary stress, 2; 'fluctuating' stress, 3: secondary stress, 1, 265–8; in late ME and

SUBJECT-INDEX TO VOLUME II

ModE adoptions, 269–70: effects in ME of presence or absence of secondary stress on vowel-quality and vowel-quantity, 264, 267, 271–91: ModE shortening due to loss of secondary stress, 342–9; ModE lengthening due to reimposition of secondary stress, 350–2.

Strong forms, 4.

Syllabic consonants: general phonetic considerations, 319; review of evidence, 320–1; development of syllabic consonants, 322–6; metathesis of *r* in unstressed syllables, 327–9; syllabic consonants becoming non-syllabic, 330; apparent development of non-syllabic to syllabic consonants, 331.

Syncope: of vowels before consonants, 305–7; of vowels in hiatus, 308–9; of unstressed *ĕ* in inflexional endings, 311–17.

[t]: development to [r] between vowels, 385; assimilation to following [j] to give [tʃ], 387, 390; dialectal development to [þ], 374: loss in final position after dentals, &c., 398: assimilatory loss before [s], 401 (*a*): loss in medial position after [p], 404; after [f], 405; after [s], 406; after [k], 407; after [r], 408; after [n], 410 (ii): glide between [n] and [ʃ], 435: 'excrescent' [t] in final position after [n], 436; after [s], [f], and [k], 437.

[þ]: variation with [ð], 358: voicing to [ð] in initial position in unstressed words, 361; in final position in unstressed words, 362; in combination with voiced sounds, 364: ME development to [t] after spirants and perhaps [l], 382; dialectal developments to [t] and [f], 374; alleged development to [s], 375: loss medially after [r], 408.

[ð]: variation with [þ], 358; unvoicing to [þ] in final position, 368: development to [d] in late OE and ME before non-syllabic [n], [m], and [r], 383; in ME between preceding [r] and following vowel or syllabic consonant, 383: development from [d] between preceding vowel and following [r̩] or [ər], 384: dialectal developments to [d] and [v], 374: loss by assimilation to following [z], 401 (*c*).

[tʃ]: developed from OE *c*, 376; from Central French, 376 n. 1; by assimilation from [tj], 387, 390: voicing to [dʒ] in unstressed syllables, 363 (ii).

ME *ŭ* (stressed): free development, 93; in special words, 94; retention of [ʊ] after labials, 196; development to [ɪ] or [e], 96; lowering in ME dialects and identification with ME *ŏ* and ME *ă*, 97; development before [χ], 95, 175, 177; before *ld* and *lt*, 95, 174; before *r* (development to [ə]), 214–15: variation with ME *ĕ*, 74; with ME *ĭ*, 81–85; with ME *ŏ*, 90–92; with ME *ǭ*, 18; with ME *ū*, 19.

ME *ŭ* (weak-stressed): quality in ME, 293; reduction to [ə], 298 (before *r*), 302 (free): variation with ME *ŏ* in certain prefixes and suffixes, 277, 292; with ME *ǭ* in post-tonic syllables, 278; with ME *ou* < *-we*, 295; with ME *ū* in post-tonic syllables, 281; with ME [y:] in post-tonic syllables, 283.

ME *ū* (stressed): free development, 160; development to ME [y:] after palatals, 178; in special words, 161; failure of diphthongization, 162–6 (after *w*, 163; before *m* and *p*, 164; before *r*, 165); alleged failure of diphthongization, 167; development before *r*, 165, 207–10: shortening, 39: variation with ME *ęu*, 246; with ME *ŏ*, 17; with ME *ǭ*, 158, 167; with ME *ou*, 168–76; with ME *ŭ*, 19; with [ʊχ] for ME *ūgh*, 177; with ME [y:], 178.

ME *ū* (weak-stressed): variation in post-tonic syllables with ME *ŭ*, 281.

ME *ūgh*: development to and variation with ME *ū*, 177.

ME *ui* (stressed): development, 262–3; distribution of ME *ui* and ME *oi*, 251–60.

Unvoicing, 366–9.

[v]: variation with [f], 357; dialectal development to [w], 374: loss between vowels in ME, 400; by assimilation to following [m], 401 (*a*); by vocalization to [u] before consonants, 423.

Voicing, 360–5.

[w]: dialectal development from [v], 374: loss in initial position before *l*, 415; before *r*, 416: loss by vocalization before vowels, 419–21: glide [w] by isolative development before ME *ǭ*, *ǭ*, and perhaps *ou* and before fifteenth-century [u:] < ME *ū* before *r*, 429, 431; by combinative development after [p] and [b], 432.

ME *-we*: development to *ou* and *ŭ*, 295.

Weak forms, 4.

wh- (initial group): development to [w] by loss of [h] from OE *hw*, 414; survival of [hw] and development to [ʍ], 369, 414.

wr- (initial group): development to [r], 416.

x in 'learned' words adopted from French and Latin: variation between [ks] and [gz], 359.

[χ]: *see under* gh.

ME [yː] (stressed): development, 179–88 (theories of development, 180; evidence, 181–6; review of evidence, 187; explanation of development, 188); combinative changes resulting from development to [juː], 185 (iii); ME [yː] in special words, 189; before *r*, 209–10: variation with ME ō, 159; with ME ū, 178.

ME [yː] (weak stressed): in pretonic syllables, 291; development of [juː] to [(j)ʊ] and [(j)ə], 349: variation in posttonic syllables with ME ĭ, 282; with ME ŭ, 283.

OF [y], stressed in English, 20, 260; *see also* ME [yː].

OF [yi], stressed in English, 20, 256; weak-stressed in English, 282 (*e*). See *also* ME [yː].

[z]: variation with [s], 354–6; development from [s] by voicing, 362–5; assimilation to following [j] to give [ʒ], 387, 389.

[ʒ]: development from [zj], 387, 389.

REPRINTED LITHOGRAPHICALLY IN GREAT BRITAIN
AT THE UNIVERSITY PRESS, OXFORD
BY VIVIAN RIDLER
PRINTER TO THE UNIVERSITY